Uncle Anthony's UNABRIDGED ANALOGIES

QUOTES AND PROVERBS FOR LAWYERS AND LECTURERS

THOMAS J. VESPER

Mat #40762313

Material in this book is for educational purposes only. This book is sold with the understanding that neither any of the authors or the publisher is engaged in rendering legal, accounting, investment, or any other professional service. Neither the publisher nor the authors assume any liability for any errors or omissions or for how this book or its contents are used or interpreted or for any consequences resulting directly or indirectly from the use of this book. For legal advice or any other, please consult your personal lawyer or the appropriate professional.

The views expressed by the individuals in this book (or the individuals on the cover) do not necessarily reflect the views shared by the companies they are employed by (or the companies mentioned in this book). The employment status and affiliations of authors with the companies referenced are subject to change.

Aspatore books may be purchased for educational, business, or sales promotional use. For information, please e-mail West.customer.service@thomson.com.

ISBN 978-0-314-19548-7

For corrections, updates, comments or any other inquiries please e-mail TLR.AspatoreEditorial@thomson.com.

First Printing, 2008
10 9 8 7 6 5 4 3 2 1

DEDICATION (2-4-08)

This book is dedicated to my Uncle Anthony (whom I always called "Ant'ny"), the last living member of my mother Carmella Nicolella Vesper's immediate family. My only uncle born in the USA, he was my mother's "little brother" whom she showered with love and pasta-chichi soup. My mother was one of nine brothers and sisters born of Guisepe and Leonildia Nicolella, from Esernia, Italy:

Mary Carlo (from "The Holy Borough" of Brooklyn, NY)
Angelo Nicolella
Frank
Carmella (my mother)
Alfredo, aka "Al" (or as my mother pronounced it "Hal")
Michael, aka "Dean"
Mario, aka "Matt"
Conchetta, aka "Connie" Borelli
Anthony, aka Tony (when he wore number 44 and starred on Overbrook High School's football team), Ant'ny

Of all my uncles and aunts, Uncle Anthony always offered the funniest story or one liner to end any and all our family "discussions." He was "THE Last Word." My mother's family (as well as my father Rocco Vesper's family—consisting of Rocco, Anna, Antoinette, Marie, Frederico, Alice, Joseph) called themselves "Greenhorns," but were typically Italian and peerless when it came to family debates or discussions. At any gathering or meal—I should say at every meal—there was always a healthy, vocal, and high-volume discussion on everything from the best biscottis or gnochis, to whether Eisenhower was a better general than MacArthur, to whether the Yankees Joe DiMaggio was as good as the Brooklyn Dodgers' "Reading Rifle" Carl Furillo. Whether discussing food, politics, religion, sports, wine, history, or again the ever popular food topic, my Uncle Anthony was usually the loudest as well as the most effective at making his points.

In the movie *"My Cousin Vinny"* one of the college boys, Bill (played by Ralph Macchio) charged with murder and armed robbery says to his co-defendant: "Aw' right, Stan, listen t'me, ya haveta see the Gambini's in action; I mean these people, THEY LOVE TO ARGUE, I mean THEY LIVE TO ARGUE." Stan says: My parents argue too—but that doesn't make them good lawyers. Bill: "Stan, I've seen your parents argue … trust me, they're amateurs." That remark could easily have been made about my Uncle Anthony. He was born, loves and lives to argue. He is the best in our family—and as far as I can remember most of West Philadelphia—at arguing and making his pointed remarks. A close second was my aunt Mary Carlo from Brooklyn, who took me to Ebbetts Field, and whose quotes/comments on everything in life I also cherish.

I love my Italian heritage and family. I love all the help, advice and understanding my family has given me. I especially love "Uncle Ant'ny," an 18-year-old volunteer who (despite the fact that he could NOT swim) served in United States Navy during WW II, and was a seaman on board the June 6, 1944 D-Day cruiser and flagship, *USS Augusta.* He gave me the best advice for life or law: "Tommy, remember three things: one, always take care of your family, two, do what's right, and three, fight like hell against anybody who tries to mess with the first two!"

William Wordsworth in a poem To The Planet Venus (aka The Vesper Star. the Morning Star and the Evening Star) wrote: "What strong allurement draws, what spirit guides thee Vesper?" My spirit sherpa is my family.

Thank you, and I love you, Uncle Anthony!

Uncle Anthony: Quotations found in books of that stuff are like bullpens for lawyers—when you find yourself in a jam you can go to your best quote like a good closer or middle relief pitcher.

Peter Anderson: Stealing someone else's words frequently spares the embarrassment of eating your own.

Sir Winston Churchill: Apt analogies are among the most formidable weapons of the rhetorician.

ACKNOWLEDGEMENT

I thank my three unnamed co-authors and family: Mary Alice, Maggie and Catie for their constant and enthusiastic help, and daily words of wisdom; my father-in-law Fran Trzuskowski, Esq. for his regular exchange of audio books and ideas for proverbs; and my mother-in-law Anne for her many maxims, pronouncements, "pointers" (inside joke) and family traditions.

I must thank my partners and friends, Rudy Westmoreland, Dara Quattrone and Dave Sinderbrand, for their steadfast, patient and loyal support for my book; as well as our office manager and my personal "IT" person, my teenage daughter Maggie for their technological support and rescues of my computer disk.

I will remain forever grateful to my dear friends and tireless paralegal assistants, Nancy Cattie, Carmen Ventura, and Linda Vitucci, for their daily support, constructive criticism and creative input.

My gratitude is expressed to the following clients, trial lawyers and jury consultants who generously gave their time and resources to review and proof my drafts, suggest additions, and inspire me to finish:

Gerald Baker, Esquire of Hoboken, NJ;
David Ball, Jury Watch, Inc., Durham, NC;
Alan Blumenfeld, ACT of Communication of Culver City, CA;
Gordon Cowan, Esquire, of Reno, NEV;
Greg Cusimano, Esquire of Gadsden, AL;
Richard Hailey, Esquire of Indianapolis, IND;
"Gentleman Jim" Kitchens, Esquire of Jackson, MISS;
Katherine James, ACT of Communication of Culver City, CA;
Rodney Jew, Jury Consultant of Palo Alto, CA;
Joshua Karton, Trial Consultant of Santa Monica, CA;
Phil Miller, Esquire of Nashville, TN;
Howard L. Nations, Esquire of Houston, TX;
Eric Oliver, Metasystems Consultants of Detroit, MI;
Jim Perdue, Esquire of Houston, TX;
Lance Sears, Esquire of Denver, COL;
Marcus Z. Shar, Esquire of Baltimore, MD;
Janabeth Taylor, RN, RNC of Attorneys Medical Services Inc. of Corpus Christi, TX;

I also salute all the great trial lawyers, jury consultants, communication experts, men and women who thought and taught the great thoughts; sharing them with the world for our use.

Special thanks and recognition goes to my "North American" friends Elizabeth Ann "Libby" Kinghorne, Executive Director of APTLA, Tom Harding, Esquire (BC), and Ed Montague (BC) who single handedly led and illustrated for me an untapped source of wisdom and wit from Canada's 10 Provinces and 3 Territories.

Finally, my deepest gratitude to the entire Margate City Library Staff for their inspirations, insights, and indulgences to me. Without their kind permission to "borrow" reference materials, and stay late in my "sound proof booth" this project would have taken many lifetimes for me to complete:

James Cahill, Librarian
Terri Lee Tabasso, Reference Librarian
Charles Featherer, Supervising Librarian Assistant
Gwen Meade, Senior Librarian Assistant
Joy Smith, Librarian Assistant

AN INTRODUCTION TO PAREMIOLOGY

PAREMIOLOGY = the systematic study of proverbs.

Analogies - adages, admonitions, advices, anecdotes, aphorisms, apothegms, axioms, *bon mots*, brocards, bumper stickers, bywords, catchphrases, caveats, cites, clichés, common sense, concepts, counsel, credos, creeds, cyres, dictums, dogmas, doxies, drollery, epitomes, euphemisms, expressions, features, fundamentals, gags, gibe, gists, gnomes, gospels, guidance, highlights, highlightings, hints, horse sense, ideas, insights, instructions, *italics*, japes, jests, jokes, kabbala, keys, keynotes, laws, logia, lore, maxims, messages, metaphors, monitions, morals, *mots*, mottos, nail, nail head (as in hitting the nail/nail head), nub, nutshell, *obiter*, observations, oddities, offerings, one-liners, oners, old sayings, pearls, pearls of wisdom, pet phrases, piths, platitudes, precepts, prescripts, principles, principiums, proverbs, quintessences, quips, quotations, quotes, rules, rules of thumb, sagacity, sally, sapience, saws, sayings, similes, slogans, sound bites, suggestions, teachings, tenets, theorem, tips, truisms, truths, underlines, underlings, underscores, universals, universal truths, upshots, usages, ventings, verities, waggery, warnings, wisdom, wise cracks, words of wisdom, witticism, xeniums, yard sticks, yarns, yolk, zingers—whatever you wish to call them—I have been addicted to reading/ rereading, collecting such wise writings and things of beauty since I was a high school freshman (Camden Catholic High School) in Camden, NJ. For this life-long obsession with words I must thank my NFL (National Forensic League) coaches: Sister Mary James ("mon petite etouille"), who was my Oratory Coach and also my French teacher for four years, and my debate coach, Sister Doris (The "Knute Rockne" of our "Fighting Irish" debate team), also my physics teacher. Both of these tireless and dedicated ladies introduced me to and inspired me with the value of doing research for the facts, and also having a "good quote" on hand. Sister Doris prepared me for both debate and extemporaneous speaking by having me and my fellow debate team members cull through newspapers, used magazines, and old and new books for facts, statistics, and quotes that could be copied onto index cards or cut out and saved. We each had our own little index boxes of sagacity which we carried with us to and from our debate tournaments. Whether the subject was economics, education, civil rights, the space program. or Vietnam we had under each possible current event "heading" our quotes and statistics written down or pasted onto color-coded index cards—either the "affirmative" (color-coded green) or "negative" (color-coded red)—for instant "authoritative" data on both "sides" of an issue.

My fascination with quotations continued through college and law school; and for the past 30 years my high school index box has become a foot locker filled with quotes I have collected over many years that I find useful for writing or speaking on various topics. About three years ago, thanks to my friend Richard Halpern introducing me to "The Dragon" voice recognition system I began to dictate and save my "Famous Sayings" on my computer. Then, a year or so ago my good friend Gerald Baker asked if I had any quotes or (as he put it in his North Jersey accent) "some good stuff" about trial lawyers because he was going to make a speech and wanted something positive to say about our profession. That inspired me to gather up all the random clippings, index cards, and books of quotes with my under-linings, post-it notes and folded page corners and put them in one usable place—this book.

Since ancient Egypt, every civilization has collected proverbs. In the English language, *The Proverbs of Alfred* (1150-80) is one of the earliest known collections of proverbs. In North America, *Poor Richard's* (1732-57) by Benjamin Franklin http://www.britannica.com/ebc/article?eu=390159 is probably the most celebrated collection of proverbs.

As you may have already noticed proverbs often contradict one another. You can easily find one maxim that cancels another. The wisdom that advises us to look before we leap also warns us that if we hesitate all is lost; that absence makes the heart grow fonder, but out of sight, out of mind. So what can we learn from that? Simply that life is full of contradictions, and that proverbs and maxims, etc., reflect and express these disagreements, and that many apothegms are more witty than true.

All of us, not just trial lawyers, recite famous quotes and proverbs to better express ourselves. Adages are the wit of the inarticulate. Proverbs are the gospel of the poor. Folk sayings are the college of the masses. More important: Proverbs are what a people—any people—believe, cherish, and teach their young. They are those harvested crops of knowledge and experience with which the dead dower each generation of the living.

Shakespeare has a phrase that runs: "We patch grief with proverbs." I think I have tried to do more than that. I think I have patched my ignorance and verbal impotence with them. The Proverb is often reason laid bare, arguments stripped of fat, complexity clarified beyond this interpretation.

Proverbs, said Emerson, are "the sanctuary of our institutions." But for me they are more: they are the precious distillation of what many great men have learned from centuries of experience. Aristotle considered apothegms the product of intellectual maturity and, recognizing their enormous power, declared it "unbecoming" for the young to utter maxims!

Whether writing a letter, drafting a brief, or giving an opening statement, we all like to refer to someone wiser and more well known to support our position. What I hope you will find is that on many subjects that affect us on a daily basis there are some good nuggets of knowledge to help make our point.

As my Uncle Anthony used to say: Quotations found in books of that stuff are like bullpens for lawyers—when you find yourself in a jam you can go to your best quote like a good closer or middle relief pitcher.

Peter Anderson says: Stealing someone else's words frequently spares the embarrassment of eating your own.

Sir Winston Churchill: It is a good thing for an uneducated man to read books of quotations. *Bartlett's Familiar Quotations* is an admirable work, and I studied it intently. The quotations when engraved upon the memory give you good thoughts. They also make you anxious to read the authors and look for more.

Joseph Roux: A fine quotation is a diamond on the finger of a man of wit, and a pebble in the hand of a fool.

What I have done, as a personal preference, is to include my personal favorites for each category; that is, for almost every topic in this book I have found an extract from the Bible, Ambrose Bierce, Winston Churchill, Will Rogers, William Shakespeare and Mark Twain; and on legal topics I have added two of my all-time heroic wordsmiths: former U.S. Supreme Court Justice Oliver Wendell Holmes, Jr., and former Pennsylvania Supreme Court Justice Michael A. Musmanno.

You will note that popular catchphrases and their origins are indicated by **bold letters.** EDITOR'S comments or NOTES are within [ ], as are my suggested paraphrasing or commentary. And, if you chance to wonder what the difference is between national "proverbs" and "sayings," all I can say is that I tried to record exactly how well-respected collectors of such phrases characterize them. I personally believe that a "proverb" is synonymous with a "saying" but, perhaps a "saying" needs a more famous ancestry or more patina before it becomes an official "proverb."

The great thing about a reference book of quotations (whether they are proverbs or sayings) is that if you don't have an Uncle Anthony from Philly or an Aunt Mary from Brooklyn, you can "borrow" any of the sayings in this book and "loan" them to one of your own aunts and uncles. Another good thing abut a good quote is that you don't even have to be correct when you cite the source in everyday conversation (as opposed to a writing, such as this book). My Uncle Anthony used to say "Shakespeare said that … I think … and if he didn't HE SHOULDA! Like a bag of peanuts at a ballgame, I challenge you to try to read just one of the many quotations I have "salted away" for your use.

Italian Proverb: A country can be judged by the quality of its proverbs.

[Contents Finding Aids: Materials in this publication are arranged by Topics, and then by sources within each Topic in alphabetical order. To find start pages for Topics, use the headers on odd-number pages or go to the Topic in the Index at the back of the book; each major topic includes that topic's start page.]

TABLE OF CONTENTS OF TOPICS

ACCUSATIONS (See ALLEGATIONS)

ACCIDENT (See also NEGLIGENCE; CONSISTENCY/MISTAKE)

Uncle Anthony: Y'know an "accident" is sometin ya can't avoid—'dis was NO ACCIDENTAL injury/death!
Uncle Anthony: That waddn't no "accident waitin' ta happen"—it happemed before it happened!
Uncle Anthony: Yeah, he/she did 'dat "accidentally … on purpose."
Uncle Anthony: "Pure Accidents" got nobody's fingerprints on 'em—nobody started da dominoes fallin'.
Aunt Mary Carlo: Y'know, a few good peoples and accidents can change history.
Aunt Mary Carlo: Nobody gits drunk "accidentally!"
Henry Adams: Accident counts for much in companionship as in marriage.
Aristotle (Greek philosopher, 384-322 BC): Life is full of chances and changes, and the most prosperous of men may in the evening of his days meet with great misfortunes.
Richard Bentley (1692): Epicureans, that ascribed the origin and frame of the world not to the power of God, but to the fortuitous concourse of atoms.
Richard Bentley (1692): That ordinary cant of illiterate atheists, the fortuitous or casual concourse of atoms.
Georges Bernanos: What is the use of working out chances? There are no chances against God.
Ugo Betti: We cannot bear to regard ourselves simply as playthings of blind chance; we cannot admit to feeling ourselves abandoned.
Bible: Ecclesiastes, 9:11: The race is not to the swift, not the battle to the strong, neither yet bread to the wise, nor yet riches to men of understanding, nor yet favour to men of skill; but time and chance happeneth to them all.
Bible: Proverbs, 16:33: The lot is cast into the lap; but the whole disposing thereof is of the Lord.
Ambrose Bierce (American journalist, satirist, 1842-1914?): ABRUPT, adj. Sudden, without ceremony, like the arrival of a cannon-shot and the departure of the soldier whose interests are most affected by it. Dr. Samuel Johnson beautifully said of another author's ideas that they were "concatenated without abruption."
Ambrose Bierce: ACCIDENT, n. An inevitable occurrence due to the action of immutable natural laws.
Ambrose Bierce: CALAMITY, n. A more than commonly plain and unmistakable reminder that the affairs of this life are not of our own ordering. Calamities are of two kinds: misfortune to ourselves, and good fortune to others.
Ambrose Bierce: DISTRESS, n. A disease incurred by exposure to the prosperity of a friend.
Ambrose Bierce: MISFORTUNE, n. The kind of fortune that never misses.
Ambrose Bierce: PLAN, v.t. To bother about the best method of accomplishing an accidental result.
Bulgarian Proverb: Your own calamity is more useful to you than another's triumph.
John Cage: Chance, to be precise, is a leap, provides a leap out of reach of one's own grasp of oneself.
W. B. Carpenter: He was led to the discovery by a series of happy accidents.
Cervantes: They who lose today may win tomorrow.
Cervantes: I think it a very happy accident.
S. G. Champion: There is no ladle which never strikes the edge of the pot.
Philip Dormer Stanhope, Earl of Chesterfield (about the book *The Doctor*): The chapter of accidents is the longest chapter in the book.
Chinese Proverb: Even genii sometimes drop their swords.
Chinese Proverb: Misfortune is not that which can be avoided, but that which cannot.
Agatha Christie: "Look here," I said, "people like to collect disasters."
Agatha Christie: Accidents happen in the best-regulated households.
Sir Winston Churchill: All men make mistakes, but only wise men learn from their mistakes.
Marcus Tullius Cicero (Roman lawyer, statesman, philosopher, 106-43 BC): By some fortuitous concourse of atoms.
George Colman, Sr. (1763): Accidents, accidents will happen.

Joseph Conrad: It is not Justice the servant of men, but accident, hazard, Fortune—the ally of patient Time—that holds an even and scrupulous balance.

Alan Coren: The Act of God designation on all insurance policies; which means, roughly, that you cannot be insured for the accidents that are most likely to happen to you.

Edward Dahlberg: We are ruled by chance but never have enough patience to accept its despotism.

Charles Dickens (English novelist, 1812-1870, *David Copperfield*, 1850): "Copperfield," said Mr. Micawber, "Accidents will occur in the best-regulated families; and in families not regulated by … the influence of Woman, in their lofty character of Wife, they may be expected with confidence, and must pay be borne with philosophy."

Charles Dickens: Fortuitous combination of circumstances.

John Sloan Dickey: The American male at the peak of his physical powers and appetites, driving 160 big white horses across the scenes of an increasingly open society, with weekend money in his pocket and with little prior exposure to trouble and tragedy, personifies "and accident going to happen."

King Edward VII (1840-1910, King of United Kingdom, rebuking a footman who had spilt cream on him): "My good man, I am not a strawberry!"

Albert Einstein: The unleashed power of the atom has changed everything save our modes of thinking and we thus drift toward unparalleled catastrophe.

George Eliot (pseud. of Mary Ann Evans Cross, English novelist, 1819-1880): What quarrel, what harshness, what unbelief in each other can subsist in the presence of a great calamity, when all the artificial vesture of our life is gone, and we are all one with each other in primitive mortal needs?

Ralph Waldo Emerson (Massachusetts essayist, poet, 1803-1882): You may regret calamities if you can thereby help the sufferer, but if you cannot, mind your own business.

Euripides: Enjoy yourself, drink, call the life you live today / your own, but only that, the rest belongs to chance.

Thomas Fuller (English clergyman and author, 1608-1661): The best Cloth may have a Moth in it.

Thomas Fuller: A wise man turns chance into good fortune.

Nikki Giovanni: Mistakes are a fact of life.

Nikki Giovanni: It is the response to error that counts.

Oliver Goldsmith (English poet, essayist, dramatist, 1728-1774): To what a fortuitous concurrence do we not owe every pleasure and convenience of our lives.

Oliver Goldsmith: To what happy accident is it that we owe so unexpected a visit?

Hafiz: There is an ambush everywhere from the army of accidents; therefore the rider of life runs with loosened reins.

Oliver Hardy (1890- 1957, to his partner Stan Laurel): Well, here's another fine mess you've got me into!

Robertson Hare: Oh, calamity!

Gabriel Harvey (1590): That may happen to many / Which doth happen to any.

Jacquetta Hawkes: We live in a world made seemingly secure by the four walls of our houses, the artificiality of our cities, and by the four walls of habit. Volcanoes [EDITOR: and accidents] speak of insecurity, of our participation in process. They are openings not any longer into a properly appointed hell, but into an equally alarming abysm of thought.

John Heywood: Well (quoth his man) the best cart maie overthrowe.

Al Hillale: Let me say three things which shall become proverbs after my death: the best of horses may stumble, the best sword rebound without cutting, the best man commit a fault.

Thomas H. Huxley (1880): It will … trust to the chapter of accidents.

Thomas Jefferson (Virginia lawyer, US President, 1743-1826, in 1807 said): As for Buonaparte, … let us trust to the chapter of accidents.

James Joyce: A man of genius makes no mistakes. His errors are volitional and are the portals of discovery.

Charles Kingsley: Our wanton accidents take root, and grow / To vaunt themselves God's laws.

Fiorello La Guardia (on appointing Herbert O'Brien as a judge in 1936): When I make a mistake, it's a beaut!

Charles Lindbergh (May 13, 1932, 73 days after his baby son "Charles, Jr.," was kidnapped, one day after the body was found on Mt. Rose Road., 2 miles from Hopewell, in Hunterdon County, near Mercer County, NJ): You can guard against the high percentage of chance, but not chance itself.

John Locke (English philosopher, 1632-1704): A blind, fortuitous concourse of atoms.

Henry Wadsworth Longfellow: At first laying down, as a fact fundamental, / That nothing with God can be accidental.

Henry Wadsworth Longfellow: Nothing is or can be accidental with God.

Thomas B. Macaulay (English lawyer, historian, Baron, 1800-1859): We must judge a form of government by its general tendency, not by happy accidents.

Don Marquis: Now and then / there is a person born / who is so unlucky / that he runs into accidents / which start to happen / to somebody else.

William McFee: People don't ever seem to realize that doing what's right is no guarantee against misfortune.

Thomas Middleton: By many a happy accident.

Wayne Lyman Morse (American Democratic politician, in a Senate debate on the Tonkin Gulf Resolution, which committed the US to intervene in Viet Nam; Morse was the only Senator to vote against the resolution): I believe history will record that we made a great mistake.

Palladas (400 AD): There is many of slip 'twixt the cup and the lip.

M.P. "Pappy" Papadakis: The aircraft nicknamed "Ensign Eater," "Widow Maker," "All 3 Dead," and the "Lawn Dart" were earned at accident scenes just like this one.

Sir Robert Peel (1835): That fortuitous concourse of atoms.

Cole Porter (1935 song title): Just one of those things.

Duc De La Rochefoucauld: Fortune and humor govern the world.

Duc De La Rochefoucauld: No accidents are so unlucky but that the wise may draw some advantage from them; nor are there any so lucky but that the foolish may turn them to their own prejudice.

De La Rochefoucauld: Accidents sometimes occur in life, from which only a touch of madness can extricate us.

Will Rogers (American humorist, 1879-1935): People who fly into a rage always make a bad landing.

Will Rogers: It looks like the only way you can get any publicity on your death is to be killed in a plane. It's no novelty to be killed in an auto anymore.

Rowan and Martin (*Rowan and Martin's Laugh-In*, 1967-73 TV show): "The Flying Fickle Finger of Fate Award."[EDITOR: a take-off of a U.S. Marine expression used by other services in the 1930's: "F-d by the fickle finger of fate."]

David Rowan (*A Glossary for the Nineties*, 1998 book): ACCIDENT n. A word which no longer exists, according to America's National Highway Safety Administration. "Continuation of the use of this word, in lieu of 'crash', works against a public perception of the preventability of injuries and fatalities in the highway environment," according to a memo from its boss. So, very deliberately, accidents will officially no longer happen.

Dorothy L. Sayers (English writer of detective novels, 1893-1957; her 1940 book *In the Teeth of the Evidence*, Mr. Egg quotes *The Salesman's Handbook*): If accidents happen and you are to blame. / Take steps to avoid repetition of same.

Publius Syrus (Latin writer of mimes, 1st century BC): Whatever can happen to one man can happen to every man.

Friedrich Von Schiller: What reason, like the careful ant, laboriously drags together into a heap, the wind of accident will collect in one breath.

Schopenhauer: Every possession and every happiness is but lent by chance for an uncertain time, and may therefore be demanded back the next hour.

Sir Walter Scott (Scottish lawyer, novelist, 1771-1832): The happy combination of fortuitous circumstances.

Seneca (Roman philosopher, dramatist, 8 BC-65 AD): Chance makes a football of man's life.

William Shakespeare (English dramatist, 1564-1616, *Antony and Cleopatra*, Act III, ix): Fortune knows, / We scorn her most, when most she offers blows.

William Shakespeare (*Antony and Cleopatra*, Act V, ii): I shall show the cinders of my spirits / Through the ashes of my chance.

William Shakespeare (*The Comedy of Errors*, Act IV, iii): "On purpose shut the doors against his way."

William Shakespeare (*Hamlet*, Act V, ii): Hamlet: Sir, in this audience, / Let my disclaiming from a purpos'd evil / Free me so far in your most generous thoughts, / As that I have shot my arrow o'er the house, / And hurt my brother.

Shakespeare (*Othello*, Act I, iii): Wherein I spake of most disastrous chances, / Of moving accidents by flood and field.

William Shakespeare (*Winter's Tale*, Act IV, iii): Florizel: As the unthought-on accident is guilty / Of what we wildly do, so we profess / Ourselves to be the slaves of chance, and flies / Of every wind that blows.

Sophocles (Greek dramatist and poet, 495-406 BC): Why should men fear since chance is all in all / for him, and he can clearly foreknow nothing? / Best to live lightly, as one can, unthinkingly.

John Lancaster Spalding: We are more disturbed by a calamity which threatens us than by one which has befallen us.

Ruth Suckow: To most people, it (World War I) [EDITOR: or a serious accident] had seemed far away, something that could never come close. Some resented it, others seized upon it now to help break up the long monotony of everyday living – more terribly thrilling than a fire in the business district, a drowning in the river, or the discovery that the cashier of the Farmers' Bank had been embezzling. Something had come, it seemed, to shake up that placid, solid, comfortable life of home, changing things around, shifting values that had seemed to be fixed.

Edward, First Baron Lord Thurlow (Lord Chancellor of Great Britain, 1731-1806): The accident of an accident.

Margaret Turnbull: When a man confronts catastrophe [EDITOR: an accident] on the road, he looks in his purse – but a woman looks in her mirror.

UA (a phrase known by 1760; see best version, Charles Dickens, above): "Accidents will happen."

UA (a phrase often used by US Marines): Shit happens!

UA (inscription on the Hiroshima cenotaph): Rest in peace. The mistake shall not be repeated.

UA (phrase used by comedians from dance hall/vaudeville days; and 1966 film and musical comedy *A Funny Thing Happened to Me On the Way to the Forum*): A funny thing happened to me on the way to the theatre (tonight)...

Daniel Webster (New Hampshire & Massachusetts lawyer, statesman, 1782-1852): Fearful concatenation of circumstances.

H.G. Wells (English author, 1866-1946): Human history becomes more and more a race between education and catastrophe.

Rebecca West: All the world over, the most good-natured find enjoyment in those who miss trains or sit down on frozen pavements.

Wordsworth: The moving accident is not my trade.

ACCURACY (See HONESTY)

ACHIEVEMENT (See FAILURE; SUCCESS)

ACT OF GOD (See NEGLIGENCE)

ACTION (See AGGRESSIVE)

ACTOR (See ORATORY)

ADVERSARY (See also ARGUMENT)

Uncle Anthony: Don't think you won the argument just because the other guy stopped talking.

Uncle Anthony: When arguing with a stupid person be sure he ain't doing the same thing.

Uncle Anthony: I think they started arguing right after the wedding—even the two little figures on top of their wedding cake were arguing with each other.

Aunt Mary Carlo: Yer uncle Anthony loves to argue so much he talks back to bumper stickers!

African Proverb: When there is no enemy within, the enemies outside cannot hurt you.

Fisher Ames: The gentleman puts me in mind of an old hen which persists in setting after her eggs taken away.

Mary Jo Antone: There are people who complain about everything, they even complain about the noise when opportunity knocks.

Oren Arnold: Speak well of your enemies, sir, you made them.

Bible: Exodus, 1:12: The more they afflicted them, the more they multiplied and grew.

Bible: 2 Corinthians 4:8: We are perplexed, but not in despair; Persecuted, but not forsaken; cast down but not destroyed.

Bible: Isaiah 30:20: And though the Lord give you the bread of adversity, and the water of affliction, yet shall not thy teachers be removed into a corner any more, but thine eyes shall see thy teachers.

Bible: James 3:16: Where envying and strife is, there is confusion and every evil work.

Bible: Luke 9:50 (spoken by Jesus Christ): He that is not with me is against me.

Bible: Matthew 5:39: Whosoever shall smite thee on thy right cheek, turn to him the other also.

Bible: Matthew 5:44: Love your enemies.

Bible: 1 Peter 5:8: Be sober, be vigilant; because your adversary the devil, as a roaring lion, walketh about, seeking whom he may devour.

Bible: Proverbs 13:10: Only by pride cometh contention: but with the well advised is wisdom.

Bible: Proverbs 18:6: A fool's lips enter into contention, and his mouth calleth for strokes.

Bible: Proverbs 25:21: If thine enemy be hungry, give him bread to eat.

Ambrose Bierce: AGITATOR, n. A statesman who shakes the fruit trees of his neighbors – to dislodge the worms.

Ambrose Bierce: CONTEMPT, n. The feeling of a prudent man for an enemy who is too formidable safely to be opposed.

Ambrose Bierce: DISABUSE, v.t. To present your neighbor with another and better error than the one which he has deemed it advantageous to embrace.

Ambrose Bierce: ENEMY, n. A designing scoundrel who has done you some service which it is inconvenient to repay. In military affairs, a body of men actuated by the barest motives and pursuing the most iniquitous aim.

Ambrose Bierce: HARANGUE, n. A speech by an opponent, who is known as an harangue-outang.

Ambrose Bierce: MACHINATION, n. The method employed by one's opponents in baffling one's open and honorable efforts to do the right thing.

Ambrose Bierce: OBSTINATE, adj. Inaccessible to the truth as it is manifest in the splendor and stress of our advocacy. The popular type and exponent of obstinacy is the mule, a most intelligent animal.

Ambrose Bierce: OPPOSE, v. To assist with obstructions and objections.

Ambrose Bierce: PITIFUL, adj. The state of an enemy or opponent after an imaginary encounter with oneself.

Ambrose Bierce: REBEL, n. A proponent of a new misrule who has failed to establish it.

Robert Benchley: Most of the arguments to which I am a party fall somewhat short of being impressive, owing to the fact that neither I nor my opponent knows what we are talking about.

Giosue Borsi: Men are conquered only by love and kindness, by quiet, discreet example, which does not humiliate them and does not constrain them to give in. They dislike to be attacked by the man who has no other desire but to overcome them.

Coach Paul "Bear" Bryant (legendary U. of Alabama college football coach): It's not the size of the dog in the fight that matters, it's the size of the fight in the dog that counts.

William F. Buckley, Jr.: Liberals claim to want to give a hearing to other views, but then are shocked and offended to discover that there are other views.

Edmund Burke: He that wrestles with us strengthens our nerves, and sharpens our skill. Our antagonist is our helper.

George Burns and Gracie Allen: As soon as my wife starts to quarrel, she gets historical. You mean hysterical? No, historical. She always rakes up the past.

George Burns and Gracie Allen: He has a very even temper. Yes he does, he is very even tempered – always angry!

Samuel Butler (English satirical poet, 1612-1680): A man convinced against his will is of the same opinion still.

Wilt Chamberlain: Nobody roots for Goliath.

Cyrus Ching: I learned long ago never to wrestle with a pig. You get dirty, and besides, the pig likes it.

Gilbert Keith Chesterton (English critic, writer, 1874-1936): The thing I hate about an argument is that it always interrupts a discussion.

G.K. Chesterton: People generally quarrel because they cannot argue.

Sir Winston Churchill: When the eagles are silent, the parrots begin to jabber.

Sir Winston Churchill: The worst quarrels only arise when both sides are equally in the right and equally in the wrong.

Sir Winston Churchill: You have enemies? Good. That means you've stood up for something, sometime in your life.

Cicero: We must make a personal attack when there is no argumentative basis for our speech.

Marcus Tillius Cicero: If you have no basis for an argument, abuse the plaintiff.

Clarence Darrow: To think is to differ.

Benjamin Disraeli (Earl of Beaconsfield, English writer, statesman, 1804-1881): Nothing ever perplexes an adversary so much as an appeal to his honour.

Elaine Goodale Eastman (teacher at Fort Maion, Florida and Carlsile Indian Industrial School, and biographer of Gen. William Henry Platt, the founder of Carlisle, speaking about him): "A man who had to square every corner of an idea or argument (tolerating no ambiguities whatsoever)"

Albert Einstein (to his friend about his 1913 "Antwerp Outline"): I enjoy controversies, in the manner of Figero: "Would my noble Lord venture a little dance? He should tell me. I will strike up the tune for him."

Ralph Waldo Emerson: Let me never fall into the vulgar mistake of dreaming that I am persecuted whenever I am contradicted.

Ralph Waldo Emerson: One lesson we learn early,—that in spite of seeming different, men are all of one pattern.... In fact, the only sin which we never forgive each other is difference of opinion.

Euripides: There is nothing like the site of an old enemy down on his luck.

Sam Ewing: Nothing is so frustrating as arguing with someone who knows what he's talking about.

Gene Fowler: Everyone needs a warm personal enemy or two to keep him free from rust in the movable parts of his mind.

H.W. Fowler: The obvious is better than obvious avoidance of it.

Benjamin Franklin (American philosopher and statesman, 1706-1790): Love your enemies, for they tell you your faults.

Benjamin Franklin: It is ill manners to silence a fool, and cruelty to let him go on.

Benjamin Franklin: He that blows the coals in quarrels that he has nothing to do with has no right to complain if the sparks fly in his face.

Thomas Fuller: He that has the worst cause makes the most noise.

W.L. George: Wars teach us not to love our enemies, but to hate our allies.

Oliver Goldsmith (*Life of Johnson*, 1769): There is no arguing with Johnson; for when his pistol misses fire, he knocks you down with the butt end of it.

Frederick Goodyear: I am sorry you found my last note so cross-grained. It is my fate that, somebody having made a statement, I contradict it, thinking that the argument is just beginning, while my correspondent or interlocutor is apt to take the line that "if that's the way you answer me it's no good talking to you."

Baltasar Gracian: A wise man gets more use from his enemies than a fool from his friends.
Baltasar Gracian: Never contend with a man who has nothing to lose.
Greek Proverb: Even from a foe a man may learn wisdom.
Alexander Hamilton (New York lawyer, statesman, 1753?-1804; Referring to his opponent Theophilis Parsons): I have known gentlemen to split a hair, and I may have tried to do it myself. But I never before saw any one decimate a hair and count the pieces before the court.
Jascha Heifetz: No matter what side of the argument you are on, you always find people on your side that you wish were on the other.
Robert Heinlein: Never appeal to a man's better nature. He may not have one. Invoking his self interest gives you more leverage.
Eric Hoffer: You can discover what your enemy fears most by observing the means he uses to frighten you.
Oliver Wendell Holmes, Jr.: You cannot argue with your neighbor, except on the admission for the moment that he is as wise as you, although you may by no means believe it.
Elbert Hubbard: If you can not answer a man's argument, all is not lost. You can still call him vile names.
Victor Hugo: Friend is sometimes a word devoid of meaning; enemy, never.
Thomas Henry Huxley: No mistake is so commonly made by clever people as that of assuming a cause to be bad because the arguments of its supporters are, to a great extent, nonsensical.
Italian Proverb: Have you fifty friends? – it is not enough. Have you one enemy? – it is too much.
Jewish Saying: Be sure you have the support of your equals before you challenge your superiors.
Samuel Johnson (English lexicographer, critic, conversationalist, 1709-1784): Treating your adversary with respect is striking soft in battle.
Samuel Johnson: It is unjust, Sir, to censure lawyers for multiplying words when they argue; it is often necessary for them to multiply words.
Abraham Lincoln (Illinois lawyer, US President, 1809-1865): The moment my learned adversary begins to talk, his mental processes cease, He is like a little steamboat which I once saw on the Saugamon River. The little steamer had a five-foot boiler and a seven-foot whistle, and every time it whistled the engine stopped – like my opponent's mind.
Phyllis McGinley (American poet): When blithe to argument I come, / Though armed with facts and merry, / May Providence protect me from / The fool as adversary, / Whose mind to him a kingdom is / Where reason lacks dominion, / Who calls conviction prejudice / And prejudice opinion.
John Stuart Mill: If all mankind minus one were of one opinion and only one person were of the contrary opinion, mankind would be no more justified in silencing that person than he, if he had the power, would be justified in silencing mankind... if the opinion is right, they are deprived of the opportunity of exchanging error for truth; if wrong, they lose, what is almost as great a benefit, the clearer perception and livelier impression of truth, produced by its collision with error.
Christopher Morley: When someone tries to argue with you, say, "You are nothing if not accurate, and you are not accurate." Then escape from the room.
Ogden Nash: In real life it takes only one to make a quarrel.
Frederich Nietzsche: At times one remains faithful to a cause only because its opponents do not cease to be insipid.
Daniel O'Connell (Irish lawyer and statesman, 1775-1847): He was a bad lawyer, said O'Connell, but he was the most sensible looking man talking nonsense he ever saw.
Austin O'Malley: In dealing with a foolish or stubborn adversary remember your own mood constitutes half the force opposing you.
Thomas Paine (English political writer, emigrated to the American colonies in 1774, 1737-1809): To argue with a person who has renounced the use of reason is like administering medicine to the dead.
William Penn (Quaker, founder of Pennsylvania, 1644-1718): Truth often suffers more by the heat of its defenders, than from the arguments of its opposers.
John Cowper Powys: What renders the least flicker of an argument so profitless, so sterilizing, is that the minds of both the disputants are turned towards something quite different from either's authentic inner truth.
Robert Quillen: Discussion is an exchange of knowledge; argument is an exchange of ignorance.

John W. Raper: There is no sense in having an argument with a man so stupid he doesn't know you have the better of him.

Isaac Samuel Reggio: He who seeks the truth must listen to his opponent.

Christiane Rochefort: Julia: Never argue with them. You're always forgetting you're a woman. They never listen to what you're saying, they just want to listen to the music of your voice.

Roy Rogers: There's two theories to arguing with a woman. Neither one works.

Will Rogers: There is nothing as easy as denouncing..... It don't take much to see that something is wrong, but it does take some eyesight to see what will put it right again.

Leo Rosten: Extremists think "communication" means agreeing with them.

Joseph Roux: The same arguments which we deem forcible as applied to others, seem feeble to us when turned against ourselves.

Russian Proverb: An enemy will agree, but a friend will argue.

William Shakespeare (*Love's Labour's Lost*, Act V, i): He draweth out the thread of his verbosity finer than the staple of his argument.

William Shakespeare (*Measure for Measure,* Act I, iii): She hath prosperous art / When she will play with reason and discourse, / And well she can persuade.

William Shakespeare (*Merchant of Venice*, Act I, i): His reasons are two grains of wheat hid in two bushels of chaff; / you shall seek all day ere you find them; / and, when you have them, they are not worth the search.

William Shakespeare (*Sonnets*, 35): Thy adverse party is thy advocate.

William Shakespeare (*The Taming of the Shrew*, Act I, ii): And do as adversaries do in the law—Strive mightily, but eat and drink as friends.

William Shakespeare (*Venus and Adonis*, St. 148): Finding their enemy to be so curst, / They all strain curt'sy who shall cope him first.

George Bernard Shaw (British dramatist, novelist, 1856-1950): A man never tells you anything until you contradict him.

Walter Parker Stacey: It would be almost unbelievable, if history did not record the tragic fact that men have gone to war and cut each others throat because they could not agree as to what was to become of them after their throats were cut.

Joseph Stalin: He who is not with us is against us.

Talmud: A legal decision depends not on the teacher's age, but on the force of his argument.

Talmud: When two men quarrel, the one who yields first displays the nobler nature.

Alfred Lord Tennyson (English poet, 1809-1892): He makes no friend who never made a foe.

Mao Tse-tung: Despise the enemy strategically, but take him seriously tactically.

Mark Twain (pseud. of Samuel Langhorn Clemens, Missouri humorist, writer, lecturer, 1835-1910): You can't reason someone out of something they weren't reasoned into.

Mark Twain: There is nothing so annoying as to have two people go right on talking when you are interrupting.

UA: The world is divided into people who think they are right.

U.S. Marine Corps Saying: He/she is a "PENNY WHISTLE" – meaning a person who makes a lot of noise.

Carmella Vesper (my mother): There are two sides to a pitselle (a very thin Italian waffle).

Rocco Vesper (my father): The only horses rear bigger than the guy who knows all is the guy who argues with him.

George Washington (American general, 1st President of US, 1732-1799): No nation (or man) is to trusted farther than it is bound by its (his) interests.

Oscar Wilde (Irish poet, wit, dramatist, 1856-1900): Always forgive your enemies—nothing annoys them so much.

Oscar Wilde: A man can't be too careful in the choice of his enemies.

Oscar Wilde: I choose my friends for their good looks, my acquaintances for their good characters, and my enemies for their intellects. A man cannot be too careful in the choice of his enemies.

James McNeill Whistler (*The Gentle Art of Making Enemies*, 1890): I am not arguing with you – I am telling you.

Virginia Woolf: When an arguer argues dispassionately he thinks only of the argument.

Yiddish Proverb: When your enemy falls, don't rejoice—but don't pick him up either.

ADVERSITY (See TROUBLE)

ADVERTISING (See CORPORATE THINKING)

ADVICE

Uncle Anthony: Only two times you should ever give advice – first, only if someone requests it, and second, only if someone's life is threatened.

Uncle Anthony: If it works, keep doing the same thing. If it ain't working, stop doin' it. And, if you got no idea what to do, do nothing.

Uncle Anthony: Ya ever notice that when advice is most needed it's least listened to.

Uncle Anthony: Don't ever believe all ya hear, spend all ya have or sleep all ya want.

Aunt Mary Carlo: Most people really don't like good advice – it's like an insult to their "intelligence."

Aunt Mary Carlo: When ya say, "I'm sorry," look da person in da eye.

Aunt Mary Carlo: Marry a man ya love t'talk to. 'Cause when ya get older, dere conversational skills are gonna be as important as any udder.

Aunt Mary Carlo: Talk slow, but think quick!

Scott Adams (Author of Dilbert): Ten Rules of Management:

1. You're always right, even when you're stupid.
2. The physical laws of time and space were meant to be broken.
3. The problem is not a lack of response, it's a lack of meetings.
4. When in doubt, ask for status reports.
5. If you're talking, you're communicating.
6. Low morale is caused by character flaws in your employees.
7. If 10 people can complete a project in 10 days, than one person can complete the project in one day.
8. Teamwork is when the other people do your work for you.
9. Employee illness is a manifestation of laziness.
10. Abuse is a form of recognition. And recognition is what every employee wants.

Aeschylus: It is easy when we are in prosperity to give advice to the afflicted.

Aesop (Greek fabulist, circa 560 BC): Never trust the advice of a man in difficulties.

African Proverb: Advice is a stranger; if welcome he stays for the night; if not welcome he returns home the same day.

African Proverb: The egg shows the hen the place where to hatch.

African Proverb: Do not look where you fell, but where you slipped.

African Proverb: Every morning a lion wakes up and knows it must out run the slowest gazelle; every morning a gazelle wakes up and knows it must outrun the fastest lion. Whether you are a gazelle or a lion, when you wake up, you better start running!

Louisa May Alcott: "... when women are the advisers, the lords of creation don't take the advice till they have persuaded themselves that it is just what they intended to do; then they act upon it, and if it succeeds, they give the weaker vessel half the credit of it; if it fails, they generously give her the whole.

William Rounseville Alger: We give advice by the bucket, but take it by the grain.

Arabian Proverb: Never give advice in a crowd.

Arabian Proverb: Seek counsel of him who makes you weep, and not of him who makes you laugh.

Francis Bacon (Baron Verulam and Viscount St. Albans, philosopher, writer, Lord Chancellor of England, 1561-1626): He that gives good advice, builds with one hand; he that gives good counsel and example, builds with both; but he that gives good admonition and bad example. Builds with one hand and pulls down with the other.

Francis Bacon: Ask counsel of both times: of the ancient time what is best; and of the latter time what is fittest.

Jacques Barzun: Do not talk yourself out of good ideas by trying to expound them at haphazard meetings.

Louise Beal: Love thy neighbor as yourself, but choose your neighborhood.

St. Bernard of Clairvaux: Whenever my advice is followed I confess that I always feel oppressed with a great burden of responsibility, and I can never be confident, and always await the outcome with anxiety.

Bible: 2 Chronicles 10:8: But he forsook the counsel which the old men gave him.

Bible: Ecclesiastes, 4:13: Better is a poor and a wise child than an old and foolish king, who will no more be admonished.

Bible: Judges 19:30: Consider of it, take advice, and speak your minds.

Bible: Proverbs, 1:5: A wise man will hear, and will increase learning; and a man of understanding shall attain unto wise counsels.

Bible: Proverbs, 10:21: The lips of the righteous feed many.

Bible: Proverbs, 11:14: Where no counsel is, the people fall: but in the multitude of counselors there is safety.

Bible: Proverbs, 12:5: The thoughts of the righteous are right; but the counsels of the wicked are deceit.

Bible: Proverbs, 12:15: The way of a fool is right in his own eyes: but he that harkeneth unto counsel is wise.

Bible: Proverbs, 15:23: A word spoken in due season, how good it is!

Bible: Proverbs 16:18: Pride goeth before destruction, and an haughty spirit before a fall.

Bible: Proverbs, 19:20: Hear counsel, and receive instruction; that thou mayest be wise in thy latter end.

Bible: Proverbs, 23:9: Speak not in the ears of a fool: for he will despise the wisdom of thy words.

Bible: Proverbs, 26:28: A flattering mouth worketh ruin.

Ambrose Bierce: ADVICE, n. The smallest current coin.

Ambrose Bierce: CONSULT, v. To seek another's approval of a course already decided on.

Josh Billings: I never had a man come to me for advice yet, but what I soon discovered that he thought more of his own opinion than he did of mine.

William Blake (*Proverbs of Hell,* 1790): He whose face gives no light, shall never become a star.

William Blake (*Proverbs of Hell,*" 1790): Think in the morning. Act in the noon. Eat in the evening. Sleep in the night.

Erma Bombeck: Never go to a doctor whose office plants are dead.

Erma Bombeck: Never lend your car to anyone to whom you have given birth.

Jimmy Braddock, (aka *"The Cinderella Man,"* Jersey James, The Bear of North Bergen, The Bergen Battler): Keep your left hand high and your keester off the canvas!

David Brown: Don't worry about growing older or pleasing others. Please yourself.

Frank Broyles (legendary U. of Arkansas "Razorbacks" football coach from 1957-1976): Have a big front door, and a little back door. [EDITOR: meaning you should take in and listen and learn more than you throw away as bad advice].

Alexis Carrel: All of us, at certain moments of our lives, need to take advice and to receive help from other people.

Lewis Carroll: If you don't know where you are going, any road will take you there.

Chinese Proverb: What you can not avoid, welcome.

Chinese Proverb: Do not use a hatchet to remove a fly from your friend's forehead.

Chinese Proverb: The pine stays green in winter...Wisdom in hardship.

Chinese Proverb: When you lose, don't lose the lesson.

Chinese Proverb: If you are patient in one moment of anger, you will escape a hundred days of sorrow.

Chocktaw Native American Proverb: The nail that stands up gets hammered down [EDITOR: so keep a low profile].

Sir Winston Churchill: The greatest lesson in life is to know that even fools are right sometimes.

Samuel Taylor Coleridge: Advice is like snow; the softer it falls, the longer it dwells upon, and the deeper it sinks into the mind.

John Churton Collins: Never claim as a right what you can ask as a favor.

Davy Crockett: I leave this rule for others when I'm dead, Be always sure you're right—then go ahead.

James G. Cozzens: "When you can, always advise people to do what you see they really want to do, so long as what they want isn't dangerously unlawful, stupidly unsociable or obviously impossible. Doing what they want to do, they may succeed; doing what they don't want to do, they won't."

Danish Proverb: He who builds to every man's advice will have a crooked house.

Danish Proverb: The best advice is found on the pillow.
Phyllis Diller: Never go to bed mad. Stay up and fight.
Benjamin Disraeli: Be frank and explicit. That is the right line to take when you wish to conceal your own mind and to confuse the minds of others.
Queen Elizabeth I (in letter to her cousin, Mary, Queen of Scots): Remember, those who add with two strings (that is, adding an ally) to their bow, may shoot stronger, but rarely shoot strait.
Werner Erhard: Ride the horse in the direction that it's going.
Ralph Waldo Emerson: Trust men, and they will be true to you; treat them greatly, and they will show themselves great.
Ralph Waldo Emerson: Go put your creed into the deed, Nor speak with double tongue.
English Proverb: Advice when most needed is least heeded.
English Proverb: Every cloud has a silver lining.
English Proverb: Every dog hath its day.
English Proverb: Every garden may have some weeds.
English Proverb: Honesty is the best policy.
English Proverb: Let sleeping dogs lie.
English Proverb: Make hay while the sun shines.
English Proverb: Never love with all your heart, it only ends in breaking.
English Proverb: Never put off till tomorrow what may be done today.
English Proverb: No time like the present.
English Proverb: One of these day is none of these days.
W. C. Fields: Never give a sucker an even break.
Edward Fitzgerald: Leave well – even "pretty well" – alone. That is what I learn as I get old.
Minnie Fisk: Among the most disheartening and dangerous ... advisors, you will often find those closest to you, your dearest friends, members of your own family, perhaps, loving, anxious, and knowing nothing whatsoever....
Benjamin Franklin: Thus, like a whetstone, many men are wont / To sharpen others while themselves are blunt.
Benjamin Franklin: Wise men don't need advice. Fools won't take it.
Benjamin Franklin: Beware of the young Doctor and the old Barber.
Benjamin Franklin: Keep your mouth wet, feet dry.
Benjamin Franklin: Teach your child to hold his tongue, he'll learn fast enough to speak.
Benjamin Franklin: Eat to please thyself, but dress to please others.
Benjamin Franklin: If you would keep your Secret from an enemy, tell it not to a friend.
Benjamin Franklin: Be civil to all; sociable too many; familiar with few; Friend to one; Enemy to none.
Benjamin Franklin: Fools need Advice most, but wise Men only are the better for it.
Benjamin Franklin: Early to Bed, and early to rise, Makes a Man healthy, wealthy, and wise.
French Proverb: Nothing is given so freely as advice.
French Proverb: Don't imitate the fly before you have wings.
French Proverb: Good advice is often annoying, bad advice never.
Robert Fulghum: Flush.
Buckminster Fuller: Don't fight forces; use them.
Michael J. Gelb (*How to Think Like Leonardo da Vinci: Seven Steps to Genius Every Day*): The Seven Da Vincian Principles:

1. *Curiosita* - An insatiably curious approach to life and an unrelenting quest for continuous learning.
2. *Dimostrazione* - A commitment to test knowledge through experience, persistence, and a willingness to learn from mistakes.
3. *Sensazione* - The continual refinement of the senses, especially site, as the means to enliven experience.
4. *Sfumato* - (meaning "Going up in Smoke)—A willingness to embrace ambiguity, paradox, uncertainty.

5. *Arte/Scienza* - The development of the balance between science and art, logic and imagination. "Whole-brain" thinking. (Right hemisphere = logical; (the Left hemisphere = artistic).
6. *Cororalita* - Cultivation of grace, ambidexterity, fitness, and poise.
7. *Connessione* - A recognition of and appreciation for the interconnectedness of all things and phenomena. Systems thinking.

German Proverb: Think with the wise but walk with the vulgar.

Lefty Gomez (NY Yankee Hall of Fame pitcher): If you don't throw it, they can't hit it.

Horace Greeley (repeated John Babsone Lane Soule's headline from the Terre Haute, Indiana, *Express* in *his* New York newspaper, the *Tribune*, in 1851): Go west, young man, and grow with the country.

Walter Hagen: Don't hurry, don't worry. You're only here for a short visit. So be sure to stop and smell the flowers.

Hebrew Proverb: Do not speak of secrets in a field that is full of little hills.

George Herbert: Go not for every grief to the physician, nor for every quarrel to the lawyer, not for every thirst to the pot.

John Heywood "The Proverbs of John Heywood" (1546): All is well that ends well.

John Heywood "The Proverbs of John Heywood" (1546): Better late than never.

John Heywood "The Proverbs of John Heywood" (1546): When the iron is hot, strike.

John Heywood "The Proverbs of John Heywood" (1546): When the sun shineth, make hay.

John Heywood "The Proverbs of John Heywood" (1546): No man ought to look a gift horse in the mouth.

John Heywood "The Proverbs of John Heywood" (1546): Look before you leap.

Oliver Wendell Holmes, Jr.: The advice of the elders to young men is very apt to be as unreal as a list of the hundred best books.

Horace (Quintus Horatius Flaccus, Latin poet, 65-8 BC): Whatever advice you give, be brief.

Edgar Watson Howe: A good scare is worth more to a man than good advice.

Indian Proverb: Call on God, but row away from the rocks.

Irish Proverb: Listen to the sound of the river and you will get a trout.

Italian Proverb: Teeth placed before the tongue give good advice.

Italian Proverb: Give neither counsel nor salt till you are asked for it.

Italian Proverb: It is often necessary to disguise a bad game with a good face.

Italian Saying: *Quando feste, e festa!* = When it's a feast, feast!

Rev. Jesse Jackson: Never look down on anybody unless you're helping them up.

William James: The art of being wise is the art of knowing what to overlook.

Thomas Jefferson: A Decalogue of Cannons for observation in practical life:

1. Never put off till tomorrow what you can do today.
2. Never trouble another for what you can do yourself.
3. Never spend your money before you have it.
4. Never buy what you do not want, because it is cheap; it will be dear to you.
5. Pride costs us more than hunger, thirst, and cold.
6. We never repent of having eaten too little.
7. Nothing is troublesome that we do willingly.
8. How much pain have cost us the evils which have never happened.
9. Take things always by their smooth handle.
10. When angry, count ten, before you speak; if very angry, an hundred.

Jewish Saying: Caution at first is better than tears at last.

Erica Jong: Advice is what we ask for when we already know the answer but wish we didn't.

Elizabeth "Libby" Kinghorne (Exec. Director of Atlantic Provinces Trial Lawyers Assoc.; advice given to both my daughter Maggie and me in PEI, Canada): The guy who is nice to you, but not nice to the waiter - is not a nice guy!

Mary Lamb: It is well enough, when one is talking to a friend, to hedge in an odd word by way of counsel now and then; but there is something mighty irksome in its staring upon one in a letter, where one ought to see only kind words and friendly remembrances.

Ann Landers: If you want to catch a trout, don't fish in a herring barrel.

Latin Proverb (also called *Verb. Sap.*, an abbreviation of *Verbum sapienti sat est*): A word to the wise is enough.

Abraham Lincoln: A lawyer's advice is his stock in trade.

Abraham Lincoln: When you have got an elephant by the hind leg, and he is trying to run away, is best to let him run.

Abraham Lincoln (about the bragging of his Union General Joseph "Fighting Joe" Hooker, before the 1863 Battle of Chancellorsville – and Hooker's retreat): The hen is the wisest of all animal creation because she never cackles until after the egg is laid.

Henry Wadsworth Longfellow: Consult the dead upon the things that were, / But the living only on things that are.

W. Somerset Maugham: People ask you for criticism, but they only want praise.

Robert McKee: Never sleep with anybody who has more problems than you do.

Phyllis McGinley (American poet, 1905-1978, *A Garland of Precepts*): Though a seeker since my birth, / Here is all I've learned on earth, / This the gist of what I know: / Give advice and buy a foe. / Random truths are all I find / Stuck like burs about my mind. / Salve a blister. Burn a letter. / Do not wash a cashmere sweater. / Tell a tale but seldom twice. / Give a stone before advice....

Henry Louis Mencken (American writer and satirist, 1880-1856): Never let your inferiors do you a favor. It will be extremely costly.

Midrash: Ecclesiastes Rabbah, 11:9: If you don't run so far, the way back will be shorter.

Robin Morgan: Don't accept rides from strange man, and remember that all men are strange.

Muslim Proverb: Trust in Allah, but tie your camel.

Oriental Proverb: Do not talk Arabic in the house of a Moor.

Sir William Osler: Shut out the past except that which will help you weather your tomorrows.

Persian Proverb: Epigrams succeed where epics fail.

Miss Piggy: Never eat more than you can lift.

Portuguese Proverb: Never cut what can be untied.

Col. William Prescott (June 17, 1775 at the Battle of Bunker Hill): Men, you are all marksmen – don't one of you fire until you see the whites of their eyes."

Joan Rivers: Never floss a stranger.

Joan Rivers: Never buy a fur from a vegetarian.

Will Rogers: Believe in something for another World, but don't be too set on what it is, and then you won't start out that life with a disappointment.

Will Rogers: If you want to be successful, it's just this simple. Know what you are doing. Love what you are doing. And believe in what you are doing.

Will Rogers: Don't let yesterday use up too much of today.

Will Rogers: Live in such a way that you would not be ashamed to sell your parrot to the town gossip.

Will Rogers: So live that you wouldn't be ashamed to sell the family parrot to the town gossip.

Will Rogers: Never let yesterday use up too much of today.

Will Rogers: We are all here for a spell, get all the good laughs you can.

Will Rogers: You've got to go out on a limb sometimes because that's where the fruit is.

Will Rogers: Do the best you can, and don't take life too serious.

Will Rogers: The best way out of a difficulty is through it.

Will Rogers: The worst thing that happens to you may be the best thing for you if you don't let it get the best of you.

Will Rogers: Buy land. They ain't making any more of the stuff.

Eleanor Roosevelt: The thing always to remember is that you must do the thing you think you cannot do

Franklin Delano Roosevelt: When you get to the end of your rope, tie a knot and hang on!

Russian Proverb: Sit a beggar at your table and he will soon put his feet on it.

Russian Proverb: Take thy thoughts to bed with thee, for the morning is wiser than the evening. & THINK
Edna St. Vincent Millay: Please give me some good advice in your next letter. I promise not to follow it.
Sears Repairman: If it's not working, plug it in.
Ted Shackelford: If you don't like something about yourself, change it. If you can't change it, accept it.
William Shakespeare (*Epistulae ad Lucilium,* Epis. Xciv, 11): Share the advice betwixt you: if both gain, all / The gift doth stretch itself as 'tis receiv'd, / And is enough for both.
William Shakespeare (*I Henry IV*, Act III, i): Friendly counsel cuts off many foes.
William Shakespeare (*Henry VIII*, Act I, i): Bosom up my counsel, / You'll find it wholesome.
William Shakespeare (*King Lear*, Act II, iv): When a wise man gives thee better counsel, give me mine again.
William Shakespeare (*A Lover's Complaint*, l. 159): Counsel may stop awhile what will not stay; / For when we rage, advice is often seen / By blunting us to make our wits more keen.
William Shakespeare (*Measure for Measure*, Act IV, i): Here comes a man of comfort, whose advice / Hath often still'd my brawling discontent.
William Shakespeare (*Much Ado About Nothing*, Act V, i): I pray thee, cease thy counsel, / Which falls into mine ears as profitless / As water in a sieve.
William Shakespeare (*Richard II*, Act II, i): Direct not him whose way himself will choose: / 'Tis breath thou lack'st, and that breath wilt thou lose.
Hannah Whitall Smith: The true secret of giving advice is, after you have honestly given it, to be perfectly indifferent whether it is taken or not and never persist in trying to set people right.
Horace Smith: *Good advice* is one of those injuries which a good man ought, if possible, to forgive, but at all events to forget at once.
Solon (Greek lawgiver, statesman, 638?-559?): In giving advice, seek to help, not to please, your friend.
Warren Spahn (Hall of Fame pitcher): Hitting is timing; pitching is upsetting timing.
Spanish Proverb: Live with wolves, and you learn to howl.
Spanish Proverb: Since we cannot get what we like, let us like what we can get.
Spanish Proverb: Visit your aunt, but not every day of the year.
Walt Stark: Start slow and taper off.
Gertrude Stein: Silent gratitude isn't very much use to anyone.
John Steinbeck: Keep your eyes open and your mouth shut.
John Steinbeck: No one wants advice – only corroboration.
Adlai Stevenson: We should be careful and discriminating in all the advice we give. We should be especially careful in giving advice that we would not think of following ourselves. Most of all, we ought to avoid giving counsel which we don't follow when it damages those who take us at our word.
Annie Sullivan: It's queer how ready people always are with advice in any real or imaginary emergency, and no matter how many times experience has shown them to be wrong, they continue to set forth their opinions, as if they had recieved them from the Almighty!
Swedish Proverb: Advice should be viewed from behind.
Swedish Proverb: One should go invited to a friend in good fortune, and uninvited in misfortune.
Jonathan Swift: How is it possible to expect that mankind will take advice, when they will not so much as take warning?
Publilius Syrus: Many receive advice, only the wise profit by it.
Talmud, Berakoth, 4a: Teach your tongue to say "I do not know," lest you invent something.
Talmud, Niddah, 3b: Set a fence around your words.
Talmud, Sanhedrin, 14a: Be obscure, that you may endure.
Talmud, Ta'anith, 20b: Be pliable – like a reed, not rigid – like a cedar.
Sir Henry Taylor: A secret may be sometimes best kept by keeping the secret of its being a secret.
Alice B. Toklas: She quoted a friend who used to say any advice is good as long as it is strong enough.
Henry David Thoreau (Massachusetts writer, naturalist, 1817-1862): Aim above morality. Be not simply good; be good for something.
Henry David Thoreau: I have lived some thirty years on this planet, and I have yet to hear the first syllable of valuable or even earnest advice from my seniors.

Harry S. Truman (US President): Study men, not historians.
Harry S. Truman: I have found the best way to give advice to children is to find out what they want and then advise them to do it.
Sophie Tucker: Keep breathing.
Mark Twain: Have a place for everything and keep the thing somewhere else. This is not advice, it is merely custom.
Mark Twain: Put all your eggs in one basket—and watch that basket.
Mark Twain: He had only one vanity: he thought he could give advice better than any other person.
Mark Twain: Always do right—this will gratify some and astonished the rest.
Mark Twain: It is easier to stay out than to get out.
Mark Twain: Few things are harder to put up with than the annoyance of a good example.
UA: If wisdom's ways you would early seek, / Five things observe with care, / To whom you speak, of whom you speak, / And how, and when, and where.
UA: Do not offer advice which has not been seasoned by your own performance.
UA: When a man asks you for advice, you can figure he isn't married.
UA: Both medicine and advice are easy to prescribe but hard to take.
UA: The best time to give advice to your children is while they're still young enough to believe you know what you're talking about.
UA: Good advice is one of those insults that ought to be forgiven.
UA: Sweet words won't warm you, but sweet thoughts will.
UA: A good saying at the right moment is like a piece of bread during a famine.
UA: When you're hungry, sing; when you're hurt, laugh.
UA: If you're going to do something wrong, at least enjoy it.
UA: Never consult a woman about her rival, a coward about a war, or a merchant about a bargain.
UA: Words should be weighed, not counted.
UA: If you can't bite, don't show your teeth.
UA: In a restaurant, choose a table near a waiter.
UA: If things aren't the way you like, like them the way they are.
UA: It is better to be embarassed than ashamed.
UA: It is better to be ridiculed than shamed.
UA: Don't pat your stomach while the fish is still in the pond.
UA: What you can do, do; what you have, hold; what you know, keep to yourself.
UA: If you know, tell; if you can, do; if you have, hold on to it.
UA: For a long, happy life, breathe through your nose and keep your mouth shut.
UA: Don't offer pearls to men who deal in onions.
UA: Better ask ten times than get lost once.
UA: Treat him like a rabbi, and watch him like a thief.
UA: Because of the thorns, don't uproot the garden.
UA: Don't throw the baby out with the bath water.
UA: Anybody can give advice—the trouble is finding someone interested in using it.
UA: When we ask advice, we are usually looking for an accomplice.
Abigail Van Buren: People who fight fire with fire usually end up with ashes.
Maggie & Catie Vesper Words of "T-Shirt Wisdom":

Never judge a day by the weather.
The best things in life are not things.
Always tell the truth – there's less to remember.
Speak softly and wear a loud shirt.
Goals are deceptive—the unaimed arrow never misses.
He who dies with the most toys... still dies.
Age is relative—when you're over the hill, you pick up speed.
There are two ways to be rich—make more or desire less.
Beauty is eternal—looks mean nothing.

No rain—no rainbows.

Remember: Life is like a piece of toast – sometimes you get buttered and sometimes you just get burnt!

George Washington: Associate yourself with men of good-quality if you esteem your own reputation; for 'tis better to be alone than in bad company.

George Washington (from his 110 Precepts, based upon the 1595 Rules of the Jesuit Scholars): Rule 9: "Spit not into the fire ... Rule 19: Every action should show respect for those present."

Chris Watson (AC Press article "That's Not All, Floks! Lessons Learned From Cartoons Over Into Adult Situations"): ... Foghorn Leghorn, that pompous rooster-about-town, taught me how to spot vanity and pretentiousness. Because he had a valuable diploma from Chicken Tech (I kid you not!), I listened when he spoke. Like the time he gave a math lesson to Little Henery Hawk. "Two nuthins is nuthin," Foghorn said. "Two half nuthins is a whole nuthin." This sage advice is held me in good stead when I've felt the compulsion to buy something worthless off a sale table.... And Tweety (Bird) taught me that anyone with brains, guts and willpower can upset the status quo.... Rocky and Bullwinkle taught that it never mattered who was shot from the cannon, tied to a burning stake or going down on a sinking ship. Moose was always there for Squirrel and Squirrel for Moose....The Flintstones and Rubbles taught me that marriage, friendship and work could be ticklish affairs...Gumby taught me that home is never far away, even when it seems you're totally lost.... Dudley DoRight showed me the two faces courage, the brave one and a stupid one....Even Woody Woodpecker, one my least favorite cartoon characters, taught me something—that you should always be who you are, not what others want you to be.... And Daffy Duck, my favorite of them all (don't laugh unless you tell me yours) showed me there is always more than one way to look at the situation. Daffy's illogical universe had its own logic. That crazy duck taught me to value my idiosyncrasies even when others frowned on them.

Oscar Wilde: It is always a silly thing to give advice, but to give good advice is absolutely fatal.

Oscar Wilde: The only thing to do with good advice is to pass it on. It is never of any use to oneself.

Earl Wilson: One way to get high blood pressure is to go mountain climbing over molehills.

Zeno: He is the best of all men who follows good advice.

AFFLICTION (See TROUBLE)

AGE/AGING (See also LIFE)

Uncle Anthony: People are like cars: some a great going uphill, others are only good coasting downhill, and the one you hear knocking all the time whether going up or down, they got something wrong under their hoods.

Uncle Anthony: It used to be you "homesteaded," then it was "suburban living," then it was "cocooning," now they're talkin' about "hiving" ... what da hell is HIVING? (See J. Walker Smith, below)

Uncle Anthony: The older ya get, the tougher it is to lose weight, 'cause by then your body and your fat have gotten to be really good friends.

Aunt Mary Carlo: Y'know what's fun when you get old? Looking back at the people you didn't marry.

Aunt Mary Carlo: Our momma always said: " The older you get, the better you get... unless you're a banana."

Aunt Mary Carlo: Didja ever notice: The Roman Numerals for forty (40) are XL.

Aunt Mary Carlo: Dere's always a lot to be thankful for if ya take time to look for it. For example I'm sittin' here thinking how nice it is that wrinkles don't hurt.

Franklin P. Adams: There must be a day or two in a man's life when he is the precise age for something important.

Joey Adams: Don't worry about avoiding temptation. As you grow older, it will avoid you.

Doug Adams: I may not have gone where I intended to go, but I think I have ended up where I intended to be.

A. Bronson Alcott: The surest sign of age is loneliness.

Gracie Allen (Comedian 1906-1964): When I was born I was so surpriesed I didn't talk for a year and a half.

Woody Allen: You can live to be a hundred if you give up all the things that make you want to be a hundred.

Woody Allen: In short, the best thing to do is behave in a manner befitting one's age. If you are 16 or under, try not to go bald.

Woody Allen: The true test of maturity is not how old a person is but how he reacts to awakening in the mid-town area in his shorts.

Woody Allen: Is old age really so terrible? Not if you've brushed your teeth faithfully.

Henri Frederic Amiel: To know how to grow old is the masterwork of wisdom, and one of the most difficult chapters in the great art of living.

Margaret Anderson: My greatest enemy is reality. I have fought it successfully for thirty years.

Aristophanes: Everyone knows that old men are twice boys.

Margaret Atwood: Another belief of mine: that everyone else my age is an adult, whereas I am merely in disguise.

Francis Bacon: Men of age object too much, consult too long, adventure too little, repent too soon, and seldom drive business home to the full period, but content themselves with a mediocrity of success.

Lucille Ball: The secret of staying young is to live honestly, eat slowly, and lie about your age.

Tallulah Bankhead: The only thing I regret about my life is the length of it. If I had to live my life again, I would make all the same mistakes only sooner.

P.T. Barnum: I've lived so long on excitement, pepper and mustard, that plain milk and bread don't agree with me.

John Barrymore: A man is not old until regrets take the place of dreams.

Bruce Barton: When you're through changing, your through!

Bernard Baruch: To me, old age is always fifteen years older than I am.

The Beatles: When I get older losing my hair / Many years from now / Will you still be sending me a valentine / Birthday greetings, bottle of wine? / If I'd been out till quarter to three / Would you lock the door? / Will you still need me, will you still feed me / When I'm sixty-four?

Henry Ward Beecher: A man in old age is like a sword in a shop window.

Jack Benny: Age is strictly a case of mind over matter – if you don't mind, it don't matter.

Ingmar Bergman: Old age is like climbing a mountain. You climb from ledge to ledge. The higher you get, the more tired and breathless you become, but your views become more extensive.

Yogi Berra: I looked like this when I was young, and I still do.

Ludwig van Beethoven: Recommend to your children virtue; that alone can make them happy, not gold.

Bible: I Chronicles, 29:28: And he died in a good old age, full of days, riches, and honour.

Bible: 1 Corinthians 13:11: When I was a child, I spake as a child, I understood as a child, I thought as a child: but when I became a man, I put away childish things.

Bible: Ecclesiastes 3:1: To everything there is a season, and a time to every purpose under heaven / A time to be born, and a time to die; a time to plant, and a time to pluck up that which is planted; / A time to kill, and a time to heal; a time to break down, and a time to build up; / A time to weep, and a time to laugh; a time to mourn, and a time to dance; / A time to cast away stones, and a time to gather stones together; a time to embrace, and a time to refrain from embracing; / A time to get, and a time to lose; a time to keep, and a time to cast away; / A time to rend, and a time to sew; a time to keep silence, and a time to speak; / A time to love, and a time to hate; a time of war, and a time of peace.

Bible: Genesis, 15:15: Thou shalt be buried in a good old age.

Bible: Hebrews 5:14: Strong meat belongeth to them that are of full age.

Bible: Job 8:9: We are but of yesterday, and know nothing, because our days upon the earth are a shadow.

Bible: Job: 12:12: With the ancient is wisdom; and in length of days understanding.

Bible: Job, 32:9: Great men are not always wise: neither do the aged understand.

Bible: Leviticus, 19:32: Thou shalt rise up before the hoary head, and honour the face of the old man.

Bible: Proverbs, 10:27: The fear of the Lord prolongeth days.

Bible: Proverbs, 16:31: The hoary head is a crown of glory, if it be found in the way of righteousness.

Bible: Proverbs, 23:22: Despise not thy mother when she is old.

Bible: Psalms, 71:9: Cast me not off in the time of old age; forsake me not when my strength faileth.

Bible: Psalms 103:15: As for man, his days are as grass: as a flower in the field, so he flourisheth.

Bible: 1 Timothy, 5:1: Rebuke not an elder, but entreat him as a father.

Bible: Titus, 2:2: Aged men be sober, grave, temperate, sound in faith, in charity, in patience.

Ambrose Bierce: AGE, n. That period of life in which we compound for the vices that we still cherish by reviling those that we have no longer the enterprise to commit.

Ambrose Bierce: OLD, adj. In that stage of usefulness which is not inconsistent with general inefficiency, as an *old man*. Discredited by lapse of time and offensive to the popular taste, as an *old* book.

Ambrose Bierce: YESTERDAY, n. The infancy of youth, the youth of manhood, the entire past of age.

Ambrose Bierce: YOUTH, n. The Period of Possibility, when Archimedes finds a fulcrum, Cassandra has a following and seven cities compete for the honor of endowing a living Homer. Youth is the true Saturnian Reign, the Golden Age on earth again, when figs are grown on thistles, and pigs betailed with whistles and, wearing silken bristles, live in clover, and cows fly over, delivering milk at every door, and Justice is never heard to snore, and every assassin is made a ghost and, howling, is cast into Baltimost!—Polydore Smith.

William Blake: The child's toys and the old man's reasons / Are the fruits of the two seasons.

Lew Brown (song in the 1931 musical *Scandals*): Life is just a bowl of cherries.

Elizabeth Barrett Browning: A woman's always younger than a man of equal years.

Pearl S. Buck: Perhaps one has to be very old before one learns how to be amused rather than shocked.

Pearl S. Buck: Ah well, perhaps one has to be very old before one learns how to be amused rather than shocked.

Lois McMaster Bujold: If you can't do what you want, do what you can.

George Burns: How can I die? I'm booked.

George Burns: I don't worry about getting old. I'm old already. Only young people worry about getting old.... I don't believe in dying. It's been done. I'm working on new exit. Besides, I can't dying now—I'm booked.

George Burns: You can't help getting older but you don't have to get old.

James Branch Cabal (The Silver Stallion): The optimist proclaims that we live in the best of all possible worlds; and the pessimist fears this is true.

Joseph Campbell: "FOLLOW YOUR BLISS."

Emily Carr: It is not all bad, this getting old, ripening. After the fruit has got its growth it should juice up and mellow. God forbid I should live long enough to ferment and rot and fall to the ground in a squash.

Pablo Casals: To retire is to begin to die.

Willa Cather: What was any art but a mould in which to imprison – like hurrying past us and running away, too strong to stop, too sweet to lose.

G. W. Carver: I love to think of Nature as an unlimited broadcasting station, through which God speaks to us every hour, if we only will tune in.

Chinese Proverb: The woman who tells her age is either too young to have anything to lose our too old to have anything to gain.

Sir Winston Churchill: We are happier in many ways when we are old than when we were young. The young sow wild oats. The old grow sage.

Cicero: No one is so old as to think he cannot live one more year.

Cicero: Rashness is a quality of the budding-time of youth, prudence of the harvest-time of old age.

Alice Corbin: Then welcome Age and fear not sorrow; / Today's no better than tomorrow.

Bill Cosby: You can teach an old dog new tricks, you just don't want to watch the dog doing them.

Quentin Crisp: The young always have the same problem – how to rebel and conform at the same time. They have solved this by defying their parents and copying one another.

Madam Marie Curie: Nothing in life is to be feared, it is only to be understood. Now is the time to understand more, so that we may fear less.

Greg Cusimano: Some say I'm in a rut, but I think I'm in a groove.

Greg Cusimano: We often spend too much time making a living, and not enough time making a life.

Clarence Darrow: This is life and all there is of life; to play the game, to play the cards we get; play them uncomplainingly and play them to the end. The game may not be worth a while. Mistakes may not be worth the winning. But the playing of the game is the forgetting of self, and we should be game sports and play bravely to the end.

Clarence Darrow: At twenty a man is full of fight and hope. He wants to reform the world. When he's seventy he still wants to reform the world, but he knows he can't.

Robertson Davies: The world is full of people whose notion of a satisfactory future is, in fact, a return to the idealized past.

Leonardo da Vinci: As a day well spent brings a blessed sleep, so a life well lived brings a blessed death.

Leonardo da Vinci: The average human looks without seeing, listens without hearing, touches without feeling, eats without tasting, moves without physical awareness, inhales without awareness of odor or fragrance, and talks without thinking.

Emily Dickinson: We turn not older with years, but newer every day.

Charles Dickens: I may not be Meethosalem, but I am not a child in arms.

Diogenes (when told he should rest since he was an old man): If I were running in the stadium, ought I to slacken my pace when approaching the goal? Ought I not rather to put on speed?

Benjamin Disraeli: Youth is a blunder; Manhood a struggle; Old Age a regret.

Benjamin Disraeli: The blunders of youth are preferable to the triumphs of manhood, or the success of old age.

Benjamin Disraeli: The disappointment of Manhood succeeds to the delusion of Youth; let us hope that the heritage of Old Age is not despair.

Norman Douglas: Nothing ages a man like living always with the same woman.

Marie Dressler: By the time we hit fifty, we have learned our hardest lessons. We have found out that only a few things are really important. We have learned to take life seriously, but never ourselves.

Umberto Eco: The real hero is always a hero by mistake; he dreams of being an honest coward like everybody else.

Irwin Edman: Life is always at some turning point.

Tony Edwards: Age does not depnd upon years, but upon temperment and health. Some men are born old, and some never grow so.

Albert Einstein (about his famous habit of not wearing socks, which he only "wheeled out on special occasions as a curiosity"): I have reached an age when if someone tells me to wear socks I DON'T HAVE TO!

George Eliot: Few women, I fear, have had such reason as I have to think the long sad years of youth were worth living for the sake of middle age.

Mercer Ellington and Ted Parsons (1939 song): Things Ain't What They Used To Be.

Ralph Waldo Emerson: We do what we must, and call it by the best names.

Ralph Waldo Emerson: It is time to be old, To take in sail.

Ralph Waldo Emerson: Nature is full of freaks, and now puts an old head on young shoulders, and then a young heart beating under fourscore winters.

Ralph Waldo Emerson: Within I do not find wrinkles and used heart, but unspent youth.

Ralph Waldo Emerson: Youth is everywhere in place. Age, like woman, requires fit surroundings.

Ralph Waldo Emerson: In youth, we clothe ourselves with rainbows, and go as brave as the zodiac. In age, we put out another sort of perspiration —gout, fever, rheumatism, caprice, doubt, fretting, avarice.

Erasmus (Dutch philosopher, writer, 1466?-1536): An angelic boyhood becomes a satanic old age.

Marie Ebner von Eschenbach: In youth we learn; in age we understand.

William Feather: Setting a good example for your children takes all the fun out of middle age.

Edward Fitzgerald: Leave well – even "pretty well" – alone. That is what I learn as I get old.

Ian Fleming: I shall not waste my days in trying to prolong them.

Ben Franklin: All would live long, but none would be old.

Ben Franklin: Old boys have their playthings as well as young ones; the difference is only in the price.

Ben Franklin: The Consitution only gives people the right to pursue happiness. You have to catch it yourself.

French Proverb: Forty is the old age of youth; fifty is the youth of old age.

French Proverb: And old rat is a brave rat.

R. Buckminster Fuller: Now there is one outstandingly important fact regarding Spaceship Earth, and that is that no instruction book came with it.

John Galsworthy (English novelist and playwright, 1867-1933): I shall pass through this world but once; any good things, therefore, that I can do, or any kindness that I can show to ay human being, or dumb animal, let me do it now. Let me not deter it or neglect it, for I shall not pass this way again.

James A. Garfield: If wrinkles must be written upon our brows, let them not be written upon the heart. The spirit should never grow old.

Andre Gibe: It is better to the hated for what you are then to be loved for what you are not.

Johann Wolfgang von Goethe (German lawyer, poet, 1749-1832): To grow older is a new venture in itself.

Ruth Gordon: How old would you be if you didn't know how old you were?

Greek Proverb: Gray hair is a sign of age, not of wisdom.

Greek Proverb: A society grows great when old men plant trees whose shade they know they shall never sit in.

Senator Theodore F. Green (at age 87): Most people say that as you get old, you have to give up things. I think you get old because you give up things.

Tom Hanks (as the hero of the 1994 film *Forrest Gump*): My momma always said life is like a box of chocolates ... you never know what you're gonna get.

Janet Harris: "... with the beginnings of middle years, we face an identity crisis for which nothing in our past has prepared us."

Helen Hayes: The hardest years in life are those between 10 and 70.

John Heywood (1546): There is no fool to the old fool.

William Ernest Hocking: I find that a man is as old as his work. If his work keeps him moving forward, he will look forward with the work.

John Andrew Holmes: At middle age the soul should be opening up like a rose, not closing up like a cabbage.

Oliver Wendell Holmes, Jr.: To be 70 years young is sometimes far more cheerful and hopeful then to be 40 years old.

Oliver Wendell Holmes, Jr. (at age 92 after seeing a pretty young girl): What I wouldn't give to be 70 again!

Oliver Wendell Holmes, Jr.: You make me chuckle when you say that you are no longer young, that you have turned 24. A man is or may be young to after 60, and not old before 80.

Oliver Wendell Holmes, Jr. (on his 90th birthday): The riders in a race do not stop short when they reach the goal. There is a little finishing canter before coming to a standstill. There is time to hear the kind voice of friends and to say to one's self: "The work is done."

Bob Hope (1903-2003): ON TURNING 70: You still chase women, but only downhill.

Bob Hope: ON TURNING 80: That's the time of your life when even your birthday suit needs pressing.

Bob Hope: ON TURNING 90: You know you're getting old when the candles cost more than the cake.

Bob Hope: ON TURNING 100: I don't feel old. In fact I don't feel anything until noon. Then it's time for my nap.

Maureen Howard: Acceptance is the word we must substitute for dependence in dealing with the aged. Their acceptance of help, ours of their need.

E.W. Howe: No one thinks he looks as old as he is.

Italian Proverb: Years and sins are always more than owned.

Samuel Johnson: The conversation of the old and the young ends generally with contempt or pity on either side.

Carl Jung: The nearer we approach to the middle of life, and the better we have succeeded in entrenching ourselves in our personal standpoints and social positions, the more it appears as if we had discovered the right course and the right ideals and principles of behavior.... We wholly overlook the essential fact that the achievements which society rewards are won at the cost of diminution of personality. Many – far too many – aspects of life which should also have been experienced lie in the lumberroom among dusty memories. Sometimes, even, they are glowing coals under grey ashes.

Danny Kaye: Life is a great big canvas; throw all the paint on it you can.

Elizabeth "Libby" Kinghorne (Exec. Director of Atlantic Provinces Trial Lawyers Assoc.: advice given to both my daughter Maggie and me in PEI, Canada): The guy who is nice to you, but not nice to the waiter - is not a nice guy!

Charles Kingsley: We act as if comfort and luxury are the chief requirements of life, when all that we need to make as happy is something to be enthusiastic about.

Soren Kierkegaard: My life is absolutely meaningless. When I consider the different periods into which it falls, it seems like the word *Schnur* in the dictionary, which means in the first place a string, in the second a daughter-in-law. The only thing lacking is that the word *Schnur* should mean in the third place a camel, in the fourth, a dust-brush.

Michael Landon: Somebody should tell us, right at the start of our lives, that we are dying. Then we might live life to the limit, every minute of every day.

Sir Edwin Landseer (1838 painting entitled): The Life's in the Old Dog Yet.

Lily Langtry: The sentimentalist ages far more quickly than the person who loves his work and enjoys new challenges.

Latin Saying: *vita non est vivere sed valere vita est*: life is more than merely staying alive.

David Herbert Lawrence (English poet and novelist, 1885-1930): I believe that one has to be seventy before one is full of courage. The young are always half-hearted.

Madeleine L'Engle: The great thing about getting older is that you don't lose all the other ages you've been.

Max Lerner (American writer): The real sadness of fifty is not that you change so much but that you change so little.... My only birthday resolution is to change some of my habits every year, even if for the worse.

Doris Lessing: Growing up is after all only the understanding that one's unique and incredible experience is what everyone shares.

Anne Morrow Lindbergh (*Gift from the Sea*, 1955): Perhaps middle-age is, or should be, a period of shedding shells; the shell of ambition, the shell of material accumulations and possessions, the shell of ego.

Anne Morrow Lindbergh: People "died" all the time in their lives. Parts of them died when they made the wrong kinds of decisions – decisions against life. Sometimes they died bit by bit until finally they were just living corpses walking around. If you were perceptive you could see it in their eyes; the fire had gone out.... But you always knew when you made a decision against life. When you denied life you were warned. The cock crowed, always, somewhere inside of you. The door clicked and you were safe inside – safe and dead.

John Lithgow: Time sneaks up on you like a windshield on a bug.

Henry Wadsworth Longfellow: Whatever poet, orator, or sage / May say of it, old age is still old age. / It is the waning, not the crescent moon; The dusk of evening, not the blaze of noon; It is not strength, but weakness; not desire, / But its surcease; not the fierce heat of fire, / The burning and consuming element, / But that of ashes and of embers spent.

John Lyly (1592): There is no fool like an old fool.

Earl Mac Rauch: Remember, no matter where you go, there you are.

Merrit Malloy: What we are is our parents' children; what we become is our children's parents.

W. Somerset Maugham: Old age has its pleasures, which, though different, are not less than the pleasures of youth.

Golda Meir: Old-age is like a plane flying through a storm. Once you're aboard, there's nothing you can do.

Golda Meir: Being seventy is not a sin.

H.L. Mencken: The older I grow the more I distrust the familiar doctrine that age brings wisdom.

Michel Eyquem de Montaigne (French philosopher and essayist, 1533-1592): The is no man so decrepit, whilst he has Methuselah before him, who does not think he has still twenty years of life in his body.

Christopher Morley: There is only one success – to be able to spend your life in your own way.

Michael A. Musmanno (Justice of Pa. Supreme Court, 1959): Seventy-five is Not the End of Productivity: It is a mistaken assumption that because one is eligible to Social Security benefits at 65, this age represents the end of the line for productive work on the part of the average person. Longevity is not so rare in modern life that it must be dismissed as bizarre. The advances made in medical science, the widely publicized rules of health and better living have all contributed to a constantly increasing lifespan which one has the right to enjoy free of pain and suffering caused by tortious happenings. Therefore, it is error to say that at 65 one can no longer work remuneratively and therefore must be cast on the economic ash heap. There is no reason dogmatically to assume that, given reasonable health, one can not for some years continue as efficiently after the 65th milestone has been reached as for the few years which preceded that heretofore awesome marker. The ripened experience, the matured intellect, the self-control, the storehouse of knowledge gathered through the years also contribute to the efficiency of the human mechanism that it may continue to produce after 65 years with an effectiveness that no employer or society at large should want unthinkingly to discard. (Cuneo v. Philadelphia Transportation Co., 405 Pa. 532).

Ogden Nash (American poet, 1902-1971, *Crossing the Border*): Senescence begins / And middle age ends / The day your descendants / Outnumber your friends.

Ogden Nash: Middle age is when you've met so many people that every new person you meet reminds you of someone else.

Bill Naughton (1966 song, stage show, radio play and film *Alfie*): What's it (EDITOR: life) all about, Alfie?

Kathleen Norris: In spite of the cost of living, it's still popular.

Sean O'Casey: All the world's a stage and most of us are desperately unrehearsed.

Sean O'Casey: When one has reached 81 one likes to sit back and let the world turn by itself, without trying to push it.

Robert Orben: Old people should not eat health foods. They need all the preservatives they can get.

Satchel Paige: How old would you be if you didn't know how old you was?

Eddie Rickenbacker: If a thing is old, it is a sign that it was fit to live. The guarantee of continuity is quality.

Francois de La Rochefoucauld: Why is it that our memory is good enough to retain the least triviality that happens to us, and yet not good enough to recollect how often we have told it to the same person?

Carlos Pena Romulo: Age does not matter if the matter does not age.

Carlos Pena Romulo: I always wake up in the morning a young man.

Pete Rose (famous major league baseball player): If people start letting me know how old I am, and I start listening, I might start playing like an old man. So, I don't listen.

Helen Rowland: At twenty, a man feels awfully aged and blase; at thirty, almost senile; at forty, "not so old"; and at fifty, positively skittish.

Helena Rubenstein: I have always felt that a woman has the right to treat the subject of her age with ambiguity until, perhaps, she passes into the realm of over ninety. Then it is better she be candid with herself and the world.

John Ruskin: Every increased possession loads us with new weariness.

Johnny Sain (famous major league baseball player): The older we get, the better we were when we were younger.

Edna St. Vincent Millay: I dread no more the first white in my hair, / Or even age itself, the easy show, / The cane, the wrinkled hands, the special chair: / Time, doing this to me, may alter too / My anguish, into something I can bear.

Carl Sandburg: I am an idealist. I don't know where I'm going, but I'm on my way!

George Santayana: I agree that the last years of life are the best, if one is a philosopher.

George Santayana: There is no cure for birth and death save to enjoy the interval.

Arthur Schopenhauer: The first forty years of life give you the text; the next thirty supply the commentary on it.

Charles Schultz: Just remember, once you're over the hill you begin to pick up speed.

Florida Scott-Maxwell: No matter how old a mother is she watches her middle-aged children for signs of improvement.

Dr. Martin Seligman, et als (a scientific study shows): THE determinant ... THE critical determining element in life and business success is resilience in the face of adversity.

William Shakespeare (*All's Well That Ends Well,* Act I, ii): "Let me not live," quoth he, / "After my flame lacks oil, to be the snuff / Of younger spirits."

William Shakespeare (*All's Well That Ends Well,* Act IV, iii): The web of our life is of a mingled yarn, good and ill together.

William Shakespeare (*All's Well That Ends Well,* Act V, iii): For we are old, and on our quick'st decrees / The inaudible and noiseless foot of Time / Steals ere we can effect them.

William Shakespeare (*As You Like It,* Act II, iii): Though I look old, yet I am strong and lusty; / For in my youth I never did apply / Hot and rebellious liquors in my blood; / Nor did not with unbashful forehead woo / The means of weakness and debility; / Therefore my age is as a lusty winter, / Frosty, but kindly.

William Shakespeare (*As You Like It,* Act II, vii): And his big manly voice, / Turning again towards childish treble, Pipes / And whistles in his sound.

William Shakespeare (*As You Like It,* Act II, vii): And so, from hour to hour, we ripe and ripe, / And then, from hour to hour, we rot and rot.

William Shakespeare (*As You Like It,* Act II, vii): All the world's a stage, / And all the men and women merely players.

William Shakespeare (*As You Like It,* Act II, vii): Last scene of all, / That ends this strange, eventful history, / Is second childishness and mere oblivion, / Sans teeth, sans eyes, sans taste, sans everything.

William Shakespeare (*Comedy of Errors,* Act V, i): Though now this grained face of mine be hid / In sap-consuming winter's drizzle snow, / And all the conduits of my blood froze up, / Yet hath my night of life some memory.

William Shakespeare (*Cymbeline,* Act III, ii): What should we speak of / When we are as old as you? When we shall hear / The rain and wind beat dark December.

William Shakespeare (*Hamlet,* Act II, ii): An old man is twice a child.

William Shakespeare (*Hamlet,* Act III, iv): At your age, / The hey-day in the blood is tame, it's humble, / And waits upon the judgement.

William Shakespeare (*Hamlet,* Act IV, vii): A very riband in the cap of youth, / Yet needful too; for youth no less becomes / The light and careless livery that it wears / Than settled age his sables and his weeds, / Importing health and graveness.

William Shakespeare (*II Henry IV,* Act II, iv): Begin to patch up thine body for heaven.

William Shakespeare (*Julius Caesar,* Act II, i): His silver hairs / Will purchase us a good opinion, / And buy men's voices to commend our deeds.

William Shakespeare (*King Lear,* Act I, iv): As you are old and reverend, you should be wise.

William Shakespeare (*King Lear,* Act II, iv): I confess that I am old; Age is unnecessary.

William Shakespeare (*King Lear,* Act II, iv): You are old; / Nature in you stands on the very verge / Of her confine.

William Shakespeare (*King Lear,* Act III, ii): A poor, infirm, weak, and despised old man.

William Shakespeare (*Macbeth,* Act V, v): Life's but a walking shadow, a poor player, / That struts and frets his hour upon the stage / And then is heard no more. It is a tale / Told by an idiot, full of sound and fury, / Signifying nothing.

William Shakespeare (*Measure for Measure,* Act III, i): When thou art old and rich, / Thou hast neither heat, affection, limb, nor beauty, / To make thy riches pleasant.

William Shakespeare (*The Merchant of Venice,* Act I, ii): Superfluity comes sooner by white hairs, but competency lives longer

William Shakespeare (*The Merchant of Venice,* Act II, vii): Young in limbs, in judgement old.

William Shakespeare (*The Merchant of Venice,* Act IV, i): I never knew so young a body with so old a head.

William Shakespeare (*Much Ado About Nothing,* Act III, v): When the age is in, the wit is out.

William Shakespeare (*Othello,* Act III, iii): I am declined Into the vale of years.

William Shakespeare (*Richard II,* Act I, iii): The dantiest last, to make the end most sweet.

William Shakespeare (*Richard II,* Act V, v): I wasted time, and now doth time waste me.

William Shakespeare (*Timon of Athens,* Act I, ii): Men shut their doors against a setting sun.

William Shakespeare (*Titus Andronicus,* Act I, i): Give me a staff of honour for mine age, / But not a sceptre to control the world.

William Shakespeare (*Winter's Tale,* Act I, i): They that went on crutches ere he was born, desire yet their life to see him a man.

George Bernard Shaw: A life spent making mistakes is not only more honorable but more useful than a life spent doing nothing.

George Bernard Shaw: This is the true joy of life, the being used for a purpose recognized by yourself as a mighty one; the being thoroughly worn out before you are thrown on the scrap heap; the being a force of Nature instead of a feverish little clod of ailment and grieving, complaining that the world will not devote itself to making you happy.

Susan Sontag: How does an inexpressive face age? More slowly, one would suppose.

Muriel Sparks: Be on the alert to recognize your prime at whatever time of your life it may occur.

J.A. Spender: Hostility to youth is the worst vice of the middle-aged.

Ben Stein: The indispensible first step to getting the things you want out of life is this: decide what you want.

Casey Stengel: The trick is growing up without growing old.

Robert Louis Stevenson: Age may have one side, but assuredly Youth has the other. There is nothing more certain than that both are right, except perhaps that both are wrong.

Robert Louis Stevenson: All sorts of allowances are made for the illusions of youth; and none, or almost none, for the disenchantments of age.

Robert Louis Stevenson: When an old gentleman waggles his head and says: "Ah, so I thought when I was your age," it is not thought an answer at all if the young man retorts: "My venerable sir, so shall I most probably think when I am yours." And yet the one is as good as the other.

Harriet Beecher Stowe: The bitterest tears shed over graves are for words left unsaid and deeds left undone.

Roland "Cooks Books" Suarez (slogan and emblem painted on his taxi, "Atlantic City's Goodwill Amabassador," popular entertaier and taxi driver in Atlantic City, NJ, stabbed to death March 31, 1985): Every day is a miracle.

Kathleen Sutton: When you can't get what you want, it's time to start wanting what you have.

Jonathan Swift: Old men and comets have been reverenced for the same reason: their long beards, and pretences to foretell events.

Jonathan Swift: No wise man ever wished to be younger.

Jonathan Swift: Old men view best at a distance, with the eyes of understanding, as well as with those of nature.

Publilius Syrus: To love is natural in a young man, a crime in an old one.

Alfred Lord Tennyson: A young man will be wiser by and by; / An old man's wit may wander ere he die.

Marguerite Thatcher: Look at a day when you are supremely satisfied at the end. It's not a day when you lounge around doing nothing; it's when you had everything to do, and you've done it.

Mark Twain: We can't reach old age by another man's road. My habits protect my life, but they would assassinate you.

Mark Twain: Why is it that we rejoice at a birth and grieve at a funeral? It is because we are not the person involved.

Mark Twain: A man cannot be comfortable without his own approval.

Mark Twain: All say, "How hard it is to die" – a strange complaint from people who have had to live. Pity is for the living, envy for the dead.

Mark Twain: When I was younger I could remember anything, whether it happened or not; but my faculties are decaying, now, and soon I shall be so I cannot remember any but the latter. It is sad to go to pieces like this, but we all have to do it.

Mark Twain: Fame is a vapor, popularity an accident; the only earthly certainty is oblivion.

Mark Twain: Life should begin with age and its privileges and accumulations, and end with youth and its capacity to splendidly enjoy such advantages.

Mark Twain: Consider well the proportions of things. It is better to be a young June-bug than an old bird of paradise.

Mark Twain: A human being has a natural desire to have more of a good thing than he needs.
UA (US Idiom): Act your age.
UA (British Idiom): Act your age, not your shoe size (in UK normal shoe sizes range 4 to 12)
UA: Youth is a gift of Nature, Age is a WORK OF ART.
UA: The trouble with life is there's no background music.
UA: Every old person is really inside a young person who is very surprised.
UA: Everyone wants to live on the top of the mountain, but all the happiness and growth occurs while you're climbing it.
UA: You're only young once... ONCE!
UA: It's never too late to have happy childhood.
UA: I used to have a handle on life, but it broke.
UA: Don't take life too seriously; no one gets out alive.
Abigail Van Buren: Wisdom doesn't automatically come with old age. Nothing does – except wrinkles. It's true, some wines improve with age. But, only if the grapes were good in the first place.
Dominic (my grandfather) and Rocco (my father) Vesper: If you find a job you love to do, you will never work a day in your life.
Jane Wagner: The ability to delude yourself may be an important survival tool.
Bob Wells: Your true value depends entirely on what you are compared with.
Herbert George Wells: It is good to be a part of life. Just as the sundial counts only the sunny hours, so does life know only that it is living.
Rudy Westmoreland: Living well is the best revenge.
John A. Wheeler: If you haven't found something strange during the day, it hasn't been much of a day.
E.B. White: I get up every morning determined to both change the world and have one hell of a good time. Sometimes this makes planning my day difficult.
Walt Whitman: Youth, large, lusty, loving – youth full of grace, force, fascination. / Do you know that Old Age may come after you with equal grace, force, fascination?
Ella Wheeler Wilcox: The days grow shorter, the nights grow longer; / The headstones thicken along the way; / And life grows sadder, but love grows stronger / For those who walk with us day by day.
Oscar Wilde: The tragedy of old-age is not that one is old, but that one is young.
Oscar Wilde: The old believe everything, the middle-aged suspect everything, the young know everything.
Margery Williams (*"The Velveteen Rabbit"*): "What is real?" asked the Rabbit one day, ... "Real isn't how you are made," said the Skin Horse. "it's a thing that happens to you. When a child loves you for a long, long time, not just to play with, but really loves you, then you become real." "Does it hurt?" asked the Rabbit. "Sometimes," said the Skin Horse, for he was always truthful. "When you are Real you don't mind being hurt."
Shelley Winters: Now that I'm over 60, I'm veering towards respectability.
Thomas Wolfe: A young man of twenty-five is the Lord of life. The very age itself is, for him, the symbol of his mastery.... Like an ignorant fighter, for he has never been beaten, he is exultant in the assurance of his knowledge and his power.
Virginia Wolfe: How little one counts, I think: how little anyone counts; how fast and furious and masterly life is; and how all these thousands are swimming for dear life.
William Wordsworth: A happy youth, and their old age / Is beautiful and free.
Yiddish Proverb: A young tree bends, an old tree breaks.

AGREEMENT (See COMPROMISE)

AGGRESSIVE/AGGRESSIVENESS/AGGRESSOR (See also ATTITUDE)

Uncle Anthony: If you're gonna climb into the ring to fight, don't look for a place to lay down – FIGHT!
Uncle Anthony: Actions speak louder than words – but not too often with most people.
Aunt Mary Carlo: Whenever ya gets a chance to hit away (like in baseball) – be sure ya takes yer full swing!

Alfred Adler: The truth is often a terrible weapon of aggression. It is possible to lie, and even to murder, with the truth.
Aeschylus: Push on, pursue, in no wise faint of foot.
Aeschylus: Not for laggards doth a contest wait.
African Proverb: When two elephants fight, it is the grass underneath that suffers.
William Rounseville Alger: Men often make up in wrath what they want in reason.
Dr. Robert Anthony: The angry people are those people who are most afraid.
Isaac Asimov: Violence is the last refuge of the incompetent.
Athenogoras of Syracuse (415 B.C.): If a man does not strike first, he will be the first struck.
James Baldwin: To act is to be committed, and to be committed is to be in danger.
Hilaire Belloc: All men have in them an instinct for conflict: at least, all healthy men.
Bible: Ecclesiastes 9:10: Whatsoever thy hand findeth to do, do it with thy might.
Bible: Ephesians, 4:6: Be ye angry, and sin not: let not the sun go down upon your wrath.
Bible: Isaiah, 5:29: They shall roar like young lions: yea, they shall roar, and lay hold of the prey.
Bible: James, 1:19: Let every man be swift to hear, slow to speak, slow to wrath: For the wrath of man worketh not the righteousness of God.
Bible: Job, 5:2: Wrath killeth the foolish man and envy slayeth the silly one.
Bible: Matthew 5:39: Whosoever shall smite thee on thy right cheek, turn to him the other also.
Bible: Proverbs, 15:1: A soft answer turneth away wrath.
Bible: Proverbs, 16:32: He that is slow to anger is better than the mighty; and he that ruleth his spirit than he that taketh a city.
Bible: Proverbs, 22:24: Make no friendship with an angry man, and with a furious man thou shalt not go: Lest thou learn his ways, and get a snare to thy soul.
Bible: Proverbs 26:20: Where no wood is, there the fire goeth out; so where there is no tale-bearer, the strife ceaseth.
Bible: Psalms, 104:21: The young lions roar after their prey, and seek their meat from God.
Ambrose Bierce: AGITATOR, n. A statesman who shakes the fruit trees of his neighbors—to dislodge the worms.
Ambrose Bierce: DEFENCELESS, adj. Unable to attack.
Ambrose Bierce: MEEKNESS, n. Uncommon patience in planning a revenge that is worth while.
Ambrose Bierce: OFFENSIVE, adj. Generating disagreeable emotions or sensations, as the advance of an army against its enemy.
Ambrose Bierce: WAR, n. A by-product of the arts of peace. The most menacing political condition is a period of international amity. The student of history who has not been taught to expect the unexpected may justly boast himself inaccessible to the light. "In time of peace prepare for war" has a deeper meaning that is commonly discerned; it means, not merely that all things earthly have an end—that change is the one immutable and eternal law—but that the soil of peace is thickly sown with seeds of war and singularly suited to their germination and growth. It was when Kubla Khan had decreed his "stately pleasure dome"—when, that is to say, there were peace and fasting in Xanadu—that he "heard from far / Ancestral voices prophesying war." One of the greatest poets, Coleridge was one of the wisest of men, and it was not for nothing that he read us this parable. Let us have little less of "hands across the sea," and a little more of that elemental distrust that is the security of nations. War loves to come like a thief in the night; professions of eternal amity provide the night.
Ambrose Bierce: WRATH, n. Anger of a superior quality and degree, appropriate to exalted characters and momentous occassions; as, "the wrath of God," "the day of wrath," etc. ....
J. H. Boetcher: The individual activity of one man with backbone will do more than 1000 men with a mere wishbone.
Boston-Irish saying (especially used by Joseph Kennedy): When the going get tough, the tough get going.
Pearl S. Buck: Fate proceeds inexorably ... only upon the passive individual, the passive people.
Pearl S. Buck: "Men of action," whose minds are too busy with the day's work to see beyond it .... are essential men, we cannot do without them, and yet we must not allow all our vision to be bound by the limitations of "men of action."

Arleigh A. Burke: There is never a convenient place to fight a war when the other man starts it.

Willa Cather: We all like people who do things, even if we only see their faces on a cigar-box lid.

Cato the Elder: An angry man opens his mouth and closes his eyes.

Chinese Proverb: The fire you kindle for your enemy often burns yourself more than him.

Sir Winston Churchill: The nose of the bulldog has been slanted backwards so that he can breathe without letting go.

Sir Winston Churchill: Dictators ride to and fro upon tigers which they dare not dismount.

Sir Winston Churchill: I was not the lion, but it fell to me to give the lion's roar.

Clausewitz (*On War*, 1832): Offensive war, that is, taking advantage of the present moment, is always imperative when the future holds out a better prospect, not for ourselves, but to our adversary.

Basil Collier: The Boers broke off negotiations (in 1899) and made the familiar complaint of aggressors that they were about to be attacked.

Charles Horton Cooley: When one ceases from conflict, whether because he has won, because he has lost, or because he cares no more for the game, the virtue passes out of him.

Oliver Cromwell (English Lord Protector, 1599-1658): Not only strike while the iron is hot, but make it hot by striking.

Bernard DeVoto: The trouble with Reason is that it becomes meaningless at the exact point where it refuses to act.

Frederick Douglas (asked by a young man "what should be done with my life?"): Agitate, agitate, agitate!

Robert Duvall (in Francis Ford Coppola's 1979 film *Apocolypse Now*): I love the smell of napalm in the morning. It smells like victory.

Clint Eastwood (playing a police detective, "Dirty Harry," to a gunman he is holding at bay in beginning and end of the 1983 film *Sudden Impact*): Go ahead, make my day!

Abba Eban: You can't achieve anything without getting in someone's way.

Esso (now Exxon) gasoline slogan (1960's): Put a tiger in your tank!

Bob Fitzsimmons (British-born boxer, 1900): The bigger they come, the harder they fall.

Sigmund Freud (1932 Letter to Albert Einstein): You surmise that Man has in him an active instinct for hatred and destruction. I entirely agree. Psychoanalysts have come to the conclusion that two types of human instincts were woven together: those that conserve and unify which we call "erotic" and secondly the instincts to destroy and kill which we assimilate as the "aggressive" or "destructive" instincts. Each of these instincts is every wit as indeispensible as its opposite, and all of the phenomena of life derive from their activity, whether they work in concert or opposition ... The upshot of these observations is that there is no likelihood of our being able to suppress humanity's aggressive tendencies..."

Thomas Fuller: Boldness in business is the first, second, and third thing.

Johann Wolfgang von Goethe: There is nothing worse than aggressive stupidity.

Ernest Hemingway (*The Old Man and the Sea*, 1952): Man is not made for defeat.

Hindu Proverb: Anger has no eyes.

Adolph Hitler (1939): Today Germany belongs to us – tomorrow the whole world.

Eric Hoffer: To dispose a soul to action we must upset its equilibrium.

Anthony Hopkins (playing Hannibal "The Cannibal" Lecter, in the 1991 film *The Silence of the Lambs*): I ate his liver with some fava beans and a nice chianti.

Herbert Hoover: Words are not of any great importance in times of economic disturbance. It is action that counts.

Icelandic Proverb: Wrath often consumes what goodness husbands.

Lyndon B. Johnson (US President; statement after North Vietnamese torpedo attacks on US warships in the Gulf of Tonkin 1964): Aggression unchallenged is aggression unleashed.

Carl Jung: The stirring up of conflict is a Luciferian quality in the true sense of the word. Conflict creates the fire of affects and emotions, and like every fire it has two aspects: that of burning and that of giving light.

Helen Keller: Sick or well, blind or seeing, bound or free, we are here for a purpose and however we are situated, we please God better with useful deeds than with many prayers or pious resignation

Florence R. Kennedy: The biggest sin is sitting on your ass.

Ursula LeGuin: When action grows unprofitable, gather information; when information grows unprofitable, sleep.

Frederick W. Lewis: The time to win a fight is before it starts.

Joe Louis (June 1946 World Heavyweight Championship fight with Billy Conn who was a fast moveing fighter): He can run, but he can't hide.

George Lucas (1980 sequel to his 1977 movie *Star Wars*): The Empire Strikes Back.

George Lucas (1977 film *Star Wars*): Man your ships, and may The Force be with you.

Malabar Proverb: Anger is as a stone cast into a wasp's nest.

Malcom X: Usually when people are sad, they don't do anything. They just cry over their condition. But when they get angry, they bring about a change.

Henry Miller: Any genuine philosophy leads to action and from action back to wonder, to the enduring fact of mystery.

Montaigne: It is dangerous to attack a man from whom you have taken away all other means of escape except his arms.

Baron de Montesquieu (Charles Louis de Secondat, French lawyer & philosopher, 1689-1755): Self-defense sometimes dictates aggression. If one people take advantage of peace to put itself in a position to destroy another, immediate attack on the first is the only means of preventing such disruption.

Jawaharlal Nehru: It is the habit of every aggressor nation to claim that it is acting on the defensive.

Friedrich Nietzsche: Courage is the best slayer, - courage which *attacketh:* for in every attack there is the sound of triumph.

General Thomas S. Power: It is invariably the weak, not the strong, who court aggression and war.

Rough Riders (1st US Volunteer Cavalry and route to Cuba, 1898): Rough-tough, we're the stuff! We want to fight and we can't get enough!

Will Rogers: We can get hot and bothered quicker over nothing, and cool off faster than any nation in the world.

Will Rogers: Chaotic action is preferable to orderly inaction.

Will Rogers: Even though you are on the right track - you will get run over if you just sit there.

Eleanor Roosevelt: You must do things you think you cannot do.

Franklin D. Roosevelt (Fireside Chat September 11, 1941): When you see a rattlesnake poised to strike, you do not wait until he has struck before you crush him.

Theodore Roosevelt (New York lawyer, US President, 1858-1919): Rhetoric is a poor substitute for action, and we have trusted only to rhetoric. If we are really to be a great nation, we must not merely talk, we must act big.

Theodore Roosevelt: Don't hit at all if it is honorably possible to avoid hitting; but never hit soft.

Leo Rosten: CHUTSPA: Hebrew: "insolence." Gall, brazen effrontery, indescribable presumption-plus-arrogance. The classic definition of *chutspa* is this: *Chutspa* is that quality enshrined in the man who, having killed his mother and father, throws himself on the mercy of the court because he is an orphan.

Arnold Schwarzenegger (in his 1984 film *The Terminator*): I'll be back.

William Shakespeare (*As You Like It,* Act I, ii): If I had a thunderbolt in mine eye, / I can tell who should down.

William Shakespeare (*Coriolanus,* Act IV, ii): Anger's my meat; I sup upon myself, / And so shall starve with feeding.

William Shakespeare (*Cymbeline,* Act I, vi): Boldness be my friend! / Arm me, audacity, from head to foot!

William Shakespeare (*Hamlet,* Act I, i): Some enterprise That hath a stomach in 't.

William Shakespeare (*I Henry IV,* Act I, i): What, drunk with choler?

William Shakespeare (*II Henry IV,* Act I, ii): Better to be eaten to death with a rust than to be scoured to nothing with perpetual motion.

William Shakespeare (*II Henry IV,* Act II, i): You call honourable boldness impudent sauciness.

William Shakespeare (*III Henry VI,* Act IV, iv): Fearless minds climb soonest unto crowns.

William Shakespeare (*III Henry VI,* Act III, iii): Yield not thy neck / To fortune's yoke, but let thy dauntless mind / Still ride in triumph over all mischance.

William Shakespeare (*Henry VIII,* Act I, i): Anger is like / A full-hot horse; who being allow'd his way, / Self-mettle tires him.

William Shakespeare (*King John,* Act V, i): Be stirring as the time; be fire with fire; / Threaten the threat'ner and outface the brow / Of bragging horror: so shall inferior eyes, / That borrow their behaviours from the great, / Grow great by your example and put on / The dauntless spirit of resolution.

William Shakespeare (*King John,* Act V, i): Show boldness and aspiring confidence.

William Shakespeare (*King Lear,* Act II, iv): Touch me with noble anger! / And let not women's weapon, water drops / Stain my man's cheeks.

William Shakespeare (*Macbeth,* Act I, vii): I dare do all that may become a man; / Who dares do more is none.

William Shakespeare (*Macbeth,* Act V, viii): Lay on, Macduff; / And damn'd be he that first cries, "Hold, enough!"Popularly phrased as "Lead on Macduff!"

William Shakespeare (*Measure for Measure,* Act II, ii): That in the captain's but a choleric word, / Which in the soldier is flat blasphemy.

William Shakespeare (*Richard II,* Act I, i): In rage deaf as the sea, hasty as fire.

William Shakespeare (*Richard II,* Act I, ii): A jewel in a ten-times-barr'd-up chest / Is a bold spirit in a loyal breast.

George Bernard Shaw: You don't hold your own in the world by standing on guard, but by attacking and getting well hammered yourself.

Isaac Bashevis Singer: We know what a person thinks not when he tells us what he thinks, but by his actions.

Margaret Chase Smith: One of the basic causes for all the troubles in the world today is that people talk too much and think too little. They act impulsively without thinking. I always try to think before I talk,

Benjamin Spock: Man is distinctly more aggressive, cruel, and relentless than any of the other apes.

Oliver Stone (1987 film *Wall Street*): Lunch is for wimps.

Henry David Thoreau: The civilized man is a more experienced and wiser savage.

Melvin Tolson: The question is: Who will get to heaven first – the man who talks or the man who acts?

Harry S. Truman: Carry the battle to them. Don't let them bring it to you. Put them on the defensive. And don't ever apologize for anything.

Mark Twain ("The War Prayer," 1905): O lord our God, help us to tear their soldiers to bloody shreds with our shells; help us to cover their smiling fields with the pale forms of their patriot dead; help us to drown the thunder of the guns with the shrieks of their wounded, writhing in pain.... For our sakes who adore Thee, Lord, blast their hopes, blight their lives, protract their bitter pilgrimage, make heavy their steps, water their way with tears, stain the white snow with the blood of their wounded feet!

John J. Wade: What makes Christ's teachings difficult is that they obligate us to do something about them.

Woodrow Wilson (New Jersey lawyer, NJ Governor, US President, 1856-1924, in 1909): Caution is the confidential agent of selfishness.

Woodrow Wilson (May 1915): There is such a thing as a nation being so right that it does not need to convince others by force that it is right.

Woodrow Wilson (April 6, 1918; first anniversary of US entry into World War I): There is... but one response possible from us: force, force to the utmost, force without stint or limit, the righteous and triumphant force which shall make right the law of the world and cast every selfish dominion down in the dust.

Owen Wister (1902 novel; and in the 1929 film *The Virginian,* Gary Cooper says): When you call me that, smile!

Isoroku Yamamoto (Japanese Admiral/Commander-in-Chief responsible for plan of December 4, 1941 Japanese attack on Pearl Harbor): I fear all we have done is awaken a sleeping giant and fill him with a terrible resolve.

ALLEGATIONS (See also CRITICS)

Uncle Anthony: A big mouth and a bunch of bad names ain't proof of nuthin'!
Uncle Anthony: Pointin' a finger at somebody don't make 'em a crook.
Uncle Anthony: He's an expert at HINT-timidation.
Uncle Anthony: He always gives you "the benefit of the DIRT."
Uncle Anthony: He's the kinda guy that loves to be "THE FIRST WITH THE WORST."
Aunt Mary Carlo: Wit 'im, a rumor goes inta one ear and out his mouth.
Aunt Mary Carlo: She slings da dirt faster den a steamshovel!
Aunt Mary Carlo: Dat lady's got a sword for a tongue, and she keeps it from gettin' rusty.
Aunt Mary Carlo: She never repeats any gossip – at least not the way she heard it.
Aunt Mary Carlo: She always listens to both sides of an argument – especially if her neighbors are talkin' on a party (telephone) line.
Aunt Mary Carlo: She's like a vacuum cleaner – she just sucks up all the dirt!
Zoe Akins (*Declasse*, Act I): Lady Helen: To accuse is so easy that it is infamous to do so where proof is impossible!
American Indian Proverb: Don't judge any man until you have walked two moons in his mocaassins.
John Anstey (English lawyer, poet, *Pleader's Guide*, 1796): John Doe and Richard Roe his crony, / Good men, and true, who never fail / The needy and distress'd to bail / Direct unseen the dire dispute. / And pledge their names in ev'ry suit.
Arabic Proverb: The dogs bark, but the caravan moves on.
Arabic Proverb: The camel never sees its own hump, but that of its brother is always before its eyes.
Arnold Bennett: There can be no doubt that the average man blames much more than he praises.
Robert Hugh Benson: I think that the insane desire one has sometimes to bang and kick grumblers and peevish persons, is a Divine instinct.
Bernard de Fontenelle (French writer, 1757): To despise theory is to have the excessively vain pretension to do without knowing what one does, and to speak without knowing what one says.
Bible: Exodus, 23:1: Thou shalt not raise a false report: put not thine hand with the wicked to be an unrighteous witness.
Bible: Matthew, 5:11: Blessed are ye, when men shall revile you, and persecute you, and shall say all manner of evil against you falsely, for my sake.
Bible: Matthew 7:1: Judge not, that ye be not judged.
Bible: John 8:7: He that is without sin among you, let him first cast a stone.
Bible: John 8:10: Woman, where are those thine accusers?
Ambrose Bierce: ACCUSE, v.t. To affirm another's guilt or unworth; most commonly as a justification of ourselves for having wronged him.
Ambrose Bierce: ASPERSE, v.t. Maliciously to ascribe to another vicious actions which one has not had the temptation and opportunity to commit.
Ambrose Bierce: BACKBITE, v.t. To speak of a man as you find him when he can't find you.
Ambrose Bierce: FOREFINGER, n. The finger commonly used in pointing out two malefactors.
Edmund Burke: It is a general popular error to imagine the loudest complainers for the public to be the most anxious for its welfare.
Robert Burns (Scottish poet, 1759-1796): I have always despised the whining yelp of complaint, and the cowardly feeble resolve.
Benjamin Cardozo: Justice, though due to the accused, is due to the accuser also. The concept of fairness must not be strained till it is narrowed to a filament. We are to keep the balance true.
Lewis Carroll (pseud. of Charles Lutwidge Dodgson, English mathematician, writer, 1832-1898): "The time has come," the Walrus said, "To talk of many things: Of shoes—and ships—and sealing wax—Of cabbages—and Kings—And why the Sea is boiling hot—And whether pigs have wings."
Lewis Carroll: What I tell you three times is true.

Sir Winston Churchill: If you have an important point to make, don't try to be subtle or clever. Use the pile driver. Hit the point once. Then come back and hit it again. Then hit it a third time; a tremendous whack.

Sir Winston Churchill: Say what you have to say and first time you come to a sentence with a grammatical ending; sit down.

Sir Winston Churchill: The reserve of modern assertions is sometimes pushed to extremes, in which the fear of being contradicted leads the writer to strip himself of almost all sense and meaning.

Sir Winston Churchill: Everyone threw the blame on me. I have noticed that they nearly always do. I suppose it is because they think I shall be able to bear it best.

Cicero: When you have no basis for an argument, abuse the plaintiff.

John H. Clarke (Ohio lawyer, Assoc Justice US Supreme Court, 1857-1945): It is not uncommon for grand and corrupt men to falsely charge others with doing what they imagine that they themselves, in their narrow minds and experience, would have done under the circumstances....

Sir Edward Coke (Lord Chief Justice of England, 1552-1634, *First Institute: Preface*): Good pleading – the heart-string of the common law.

Charles Caleb Colton: Murmur at nothing: if our ills are irreparable, it is ungrateful; if remediless, it is vain.

Lewis Carroll (pseudoname of Charles Lutwidge Dodgson, English mathematician & writer, 1832-1898, *Huntingof the Snark: The Barrister's Dream*): The indictment had never been clearly expressed, / And it seemed that the Snark had begun / And had spoken three hours before anyone guessed / What the pig was supposed to have done.

Ernest Dimnet: Prejudices subsist in people's imagination long after they have been destroyed by their experience.

John Dryden (English poet and dramatist, 1631-1700): But far more numerous was the herd of such, Who think too little and who talk too much.

Finley Peter Dunne (Illinois humorist, 1867-1936): It's a good thing to have people size ye up wrong; whin they've got ye'er measure ye'er in danger.

Amelia Earhart: There are two kinds of stones, as everyone knows, one of which rolls.

Ralph Waldo Emerson: Every man is entitled to be valued (judged) by his best moment.

Erik H. Erikson: Such is the historical importance of "griping" in this country that a man, to stand on his own feet in a powerfully changing world, must keep himself up by his own gripes.

Frederick W. Faber: To ourselves it is always good to make the best of a bad case; but in persuading others it is good to admit the worst in that which is the subject of their complaints.

Thomas Fuller (1732): Even doubtful accusations leave a stain behind them

Thomas Fuller (1732): Accusing is proving, where Malice and Force sit judges.

German Proverb: He who wants to blame sometimes finds the sugar sour.

Andre Gide: Obtain from yourself all that makes complaining useless. No longer implore from others what you yourself can obtain.

Johann Wolfgang von Goethe: I will not be as those who spend the day in complaining of headache, and the night in drinking the wine that gives it.

Emma Goldman: Those who sit in a glass house do wrong to throw stones about them; besides, the American glass house is rather thin, it will break easily, and the interior is anything but a gainly sight.

Baltasar Gracian: Complaint always brings discredit in its train: it serves rather to stimulate the audacity of the hostile than to prompt the compassionate to console you.

Greek Proverb: Don't hear one and judge two.

Judge Learned Hand (New York lawyer, Judge US District & Circuit Court, 1872-1961): I believe that the community is already in process of dissolution where each man begins to eye his neighbor as a possible enemy, where non-conformity with the accepted creed, political as well as religious, is a mark of disaffection; where denunciation, without specification or backing, takes the place of evidence, where orthodoxy chokes freedom of dissent; where faith in the eventual supremacy of reason has become so timid that we dare not enter our convictions in the open lists, to win or lose.

Lillian Hellman (Letter to the House Committee on Un-American Activities, 1952): I am not willing, now or in the future, to bring bad trouble to people who, in my past association with them, were completely innocent of any talk or any action that was disloyal or subversive .... I cannot and will not cut my conscience to fit this year's fashions, even though I long ago came to the conclusion that I was not a political person and could have no comfortable place in any political group.

Marrietta Holley: We are blind creeters, the fun-seein'est of us; weak creeter, when we think we are the strong-mindedest. Now, when we hear of a crime, it is easy to say that the one who committed that wrong stepped flat off from goodness into sin, and should be hung. It is so awful easy and sort of satisfactory to condemn other folk'es faults that we don't stop to think that it may be that evil was fell into through the weakness and blindness of a mistake.

Edgar Watson Howe: What people say behind your back is your standing in the community in which you live.

Elbert Hubbard: Gossip is only the lack of a worthy theme.

Joseph W. Huston (Assoc. Justice Supreme Court, Idaho, 1833-1905): The wisdom of Solomon, accentuated by the legal lore of Coke and Mansfield, could not devise a judgment which this complaint would support. _Wilson v. Thompson_, 4 Idaho 678, 680 (1896).

Ben Jonson: Conjecture as to things useful, is good; but conjecture as to what it would be useless to know, is very idle.

Ben Jonson: It is much easier to design than to perform. A man proposes his schemes of life in a state of abstraction and disengagement, exempt from the enticements of hope, the solicitations of affection, the importunities of appetite, or the depressions of fear, and is in the same state with him that teaches upon land the art of navigation, to whom the sea is always smooth, and the wind always prosperous.

Samuel Johnson: The usual fortune of complaint is to excite contempt more than pity.

Erica Jong: Gossip is the opiate of the oppressed.

Junius: Assertion, unsupported by fact, is nugatory. Surmise and general abuse, in however elegant language, ought not to pass for truth.

Junius: It is an impudent kind of sorcery to attempt to blind us with the smoke, without convincing us that the fire has existed.

Michael Korda: Gossip, unlike river water, flows both ways.

Latin Proverb: It is honorable to be accused by those who deserve to be accused.

Abraham Lincoln: In law it is good policy to never plead what you need not, lest you oblige yourself to prove what you can not.

Alice Roosevelt Longworth: If you haven't got anything nice to say about anybody, come sit next to me.

Malay Proverb: Do not measure another's coat on your own body.

Merrit Malloy: Everything we say about other people is really about ourselves.

John Marshall (Virginia lawyer, Chief Justice US Supreme Court, 1755-1835): The law does not expect a man to be prepared to defend every act of his life which may be suddenly and without notice alleged against him.

W. Somerset Maugham: When we come to judge others it is not by ourselves as we really are that we judge them, but by an image that we have formed of ourselves from which we have left out everything that offends our vanity or would discredit us in the eyes of the world.

W. Somerset Maugham: Our natural egoism leads us to judge people by their relations to ourselves. We want them to be certain things to us, and for us that is what they are; because the rest of them is no good to us, we ignore it.

Gabriel Meurier: He who excuses himself accuses himself.

John Milton: The best apology against false accusers is silence and sufferance, and honest deeds set against dishonest words.

Lance Morrow: From the morning of the first individual folly of the race, gossip has been the normal nattering background noise of civilization: Molly Goldberg at her kitchen window, Voltaire at the water cooler. To say that gossip has been much condemned is like saying that sex has sometimes been held in low esteem. It is true, but it misses some of the fun of the thing.

J. Middleton Murry: We like to know where we are, and that depends upon our knowing where everybody else is.... A prejudice that we can allowfor is much more dependable than a suspension of judgment that we cannot.

Michael A. Musmanno (Justice of Pennsylavaia Supreme Court, 1959): Declaring a horse to be a cow will never draw milk from the udderless beast.

Michael A. Musmanno (Justice of Pennsylvania Supreme Court, 1959): Anyone who sews the seeds of a whirlwind in his allegata (allegations in a complaint) must prove it in his probata (evidence in court). Anyone who asserts a cyclone must be prepared to prove a cyclone.

Napoleon I: When people cease to complain, they cease to think.

Louis Nizer: When a man points a finger at someone else, he should remember that four of his fingers are pointing at himself.

Sir William Osler: Learn to accept in silence the minor aggravations, cultivate the gift of taciturnity, and consume your own smoke with an extra draft of hard work, so that those about you may not be annoyed with the dust and soot of your complaints.

Polybius (circa 200 B.C.): There is no witness so dreadful, no accuser so terrible as the conscience that dwells in the heart of every man.

Claude Rains (in the 1942 film *Casablanca*): Major Strasser has been shot. Round up the usual suspects.

Will Rogers: There is nothing as easy as denouncing..... It don't take much to see that something is wrong, but it does take some eyesight to see what will put it right again.

Will Rogers: The only time people dislike gossip is when you gossip about them.

Will Rogers: Lettin' the cat outta the bag is a whole lot easier 'n puttin' it back in.

Will Rogers: It isn't what we don't know that gives us trouble, it's what we know that ain't so.

Will Rogers: A remark generally hurts in proportion to its truth.

Jean Jacques Rousseau (French philosopher, writer, 1712-1778): Do not judge, and you will never be mistaken.

William Shakespeare (*As You Like It,* Act III, ii): I will chide no breather in the world, but myself; against whom I know most faults.

William Shakespeare (*II Henry IV*, Act II, ii): Let the end try the man.

William Shakespeare (*Lucrece*, 353): Thoughts are but dreams till their effects be tried.

William Shakespeare (*Macbeth*, Act III, iv): Thou can'st not say I did it; / never shake / Thy gory locks at me.

Willaim Shakespeare (*Measure for Measure*): Angelo: Who will believe thee, Isabel? / My unsoil'd name, the austereness of my life, / My vouch against you, and my place i' the state, / Will so your accusation overweigh, That you shall stifle in your own report, / And smell of calumny.

Willaim Shakespeare (*Othello*, Act I, iii): Duke: To vouch this is no proof. / Without more certain and more overt test, / Than these thin habits, and poor likelihoods / Of modern seeming do prefer against him.

William Shakespeare (*Winter's Tale*, Act III, ii): Innocence shall make / False accusation blush, and tyranny / Tremble at patience.

Percy Bysshe Shelley: The breath of accusation kills an innocent name, / And leaves for lame acquittal the poor life, / Which is a mask without it.

Thomas Sherlock: Most men take least notice of what is plain, as if that were of no use; but puzzle their thoughts, and lose themselves in those vast depths and abysses which no human understanding can fathom.

Sir Phillip Sidney: Weigh not so much what men assert, as what they prove. - Truth is simple and naked, and needs not invention to apparel her comeliness.

Liz Smith: Gossip is news running ahead of itself in a red satin dress.

Patricia Meyer Spacks: Gossip, even when it avoids the sexual, bears around it a faint flavor of the erotic.

John Lancaster Spalding: Our prejudices are like physical infirmities – we cannot do what they prevent us from doing.

Spanish Proverb: To deny all, is to confess all.

Thoreau: I do not judge men by anything they can do. Their greatest deed is the impression they make on me.
Turkish Proverb: He that falls by himself never cries.
Mark Twain: By the argument of counsel it was shown that at half past ten in the morning on the day of the murder,... (the defendant) became insane, and remained so for eleven hours and a half exactly.
Mark Twain (*The Gilded Age*, v. 2, ch. 23): The clerk then read the indictment, which was in the usual form. It charged Laura Hawkins, in effect, with the premeditated murder of George Selby, by shooting him with a pistol, with a revolver, shotgun, rifle, repeater, breech-loader, cannon, six-shooter, with a gun, or some other weapon; with killing him with a slung-shot, a bludgeon, carving knife, bowie-knife, pen-knife, rolling-pin, car-hook, dagger, hairpin, with a hammer, with a screwdriver, with a nail, and with all other weapons and utensils whatsoever, at the Southern Hotel and in all other hotels and places whatsoever, on the thirteeth day of March and all others days of the Christian era whensoever.
UA: A murderer is one who is presumed to be innocent until he is proved insane.
UA: When a man points a finger at someone else, he should remember that three of his fingers are pointing at himself.
Carmen Ventura (my friend & legal assistant): We need to brainstorm NOT "**BLAMESTORM**!" [EDITOR: most in our office repeat this mantra to keep meetings and debriefings from turning into fingerpointing and negative critiques]
John Weiss: The theory that can absorb the greatest number of facts, and persist in doing so, generation after generation, through all changes of opinion and detail, is the one that must rule all observation.
John Weiss: Theory is the guide to practice, and practice the ratification and life of theory.
Elinor Wylie: I love smooth words, like gold-enameled fish / Which circle slowly with a silken swish ....
Yugoslav Proverb: Complain to one who can help you.

AMBITION (See MOTIVE)

ANCESTRY

Uncle Anthony: Never forget where we came from (Italy), 'cause if you do you become a weed and if you don't you will be an oak. You either got roots or you don't.
Aunt Mary Carlo: You can't look ahead if you not gonna look where you (and your family) come from.
A. Bronson Alcott: Blood is a destiny. One's genius descends in the stream from long lines of ancestry.
Shana Alexander: Evolution is fascinating to watch. To me it is most interesting when one can observe the evolution of a single man.
Aristotle: Honorable descent is, in all nations, greatly esteemed. It is to be expected that the children of men of worth will be like the progenitors; for nobility is the virtue of the family.
Vicki Baum: To be a Jew is a destiny.
Bible: Ecclesiastes 7:8: Better is the end of a thing than the beginning thereof.
Bible: Ezekiel, 16:44: As is the mother, so is her daughter.
Bible: Ezekiel, 18:2: The fathers have eaten sour grapes, and the children's teeth are set on edge.
Bible: Proverbs 22:6: Train up a child in the way he should go: and when he is old, he will not depart from it.
Bible: Romans, 11:16: If the root be holy, so are the branches.
Bible: 1 Timothy 6:7: We brought nothing into this world, and it is certain we can carry nothing out.
Ambrose Bierce: BOTTLE-NOSED, adj. Having a nose created in tthe image of its maker.
Ambrose Bierce: DEGENERATE, adj.Less conspicuously admirable than one's ancestors. ...
Ambrose Bierce: GENEALOGY, n. An account of one's descent from an ancestor who did not particularly care to trace his own.
Ambrose Bierce: LEGACY, n. A gift from one who is legging it out of this vale of tears.
Ambrose Bierce: MONKEY, n. An arboreal animal which makes itself at home in genealogical trees.
Ambrose Bierce: PEDIGREE, n. The known part of the route from an arboreal ancestor with a swim bladder to an urban descendant with a cigarette.
Ambrose Bierce: POSTERITY, n. An appellate court which reverses the judgment of a popular author's contemporaries, the appellant being his obscure competitor.

Ambrose Bierce: A man is the sum of his ancestors; to reform him you must begin with a dead ape and work downward through a million graves. He is like the lower end of a suspended chain; you can sway him slightly to the right or the left, but remove your hand and he falls into line with the other links.

Franz Boas: The behavior of an individual is determined not by his racial affiliation, but by the character of his ancestry and his cultural environment.

Kenneth Boulding: One of the odd things about evolution is why it has gone on so long, because you would have thought that any decent world would have stopped with the amoeba. It's an extraordinarily satisfying organism and we've been going into what you might call pathological complexity ever since, ending up, of course, with the Federal Reserve System.

Louis Brandeis: There are no shortcuts in evolution.

Heywood Broun: Posterity is as likely to be wrong as anybody else.

William Jennings Bryan (Illinois lawyer, American political leader, newspaper editor, orator, 1860-1925): There is no more reason to believe that man descended from some inferior animal than there is to believe that a stately mansion has descended from a small cottage.

William Jennings Bryan: All the ills from which America suffers can be traced back to the teaching of evolution. It would be better to destroy every other book ever written, and save just the first three verses of Genesis.

William Jennings Bryan: Evolution theory is a program of infidelity masquerading under the name of science.

Edmund Burke: People will not look forward to posterity, who never look backward to their ancestors.

Sir Winston Churchill: Do not let spacious plans for a new world divert your energies from saving what is left of the old.

Sir Winston Churchill: Those who forget history are bound to repeat it.

Clarence Day: As to modesty and decency, if we are simians we have done well, considering: but if we are something else—fallen angels—we have indeed fallen far.

Emily Dickinson: The pedigree of honey / Does not concern the bee; / A clover, any time, to him / Is aristocracy.

Alexander Dumas (interviewed by a reporter): "Is it true that you are a quadroon, M. Dumas?" "I am, Sir." "So your father—?" "Was a mulatto." "And your grandfather—?" "Was a Negro." "May I inquire who your great-grandfather was?" "A baboon, Sir! A baboon! My ancestry begins where yours ends!"

Albert Einstein: Exploration of my ancestors leads nowhere.

Loren Eiseley: It was the failures who had always won, but by the time they won they had come to be called successes. This is the final paradox, which man call evolution.

Ralph Waldo Emerson: Men resemble their contemporaries even more than their progenitors.

Ralph Waldo Emerson: Every book is a quotation, and every house is a quotation out of all forests and mines and stonequarries, and every man is a quotation from all his ancestors.

English Proverb: Clogs to clogs in three generations.

William Faulkner: The past is never dead, it's not even past.

Sir Humphrey Gilbert: I can trace my ancestry back to a protoplasmal primordial atomic globule. Consequently, my family pride is something inconceivable. I can't help it. I was born sneering.

Greek Proverb: A society grows great when old men plant trees whose shade they know they shall never sit in.

Oliver Wendell Holmes, Jr.: People often speak of correcting the judgment of the time by that of posterity. I think it is quite as true to say that we must correct the judgment of posterity by that of the time.

Oliver Wendell Holmes, Sr. (Massachusetts poet and essayist, 1809-1894): There is something frightful in the way in which not only characteristic qualities, but particular manifestations of them, are repeated from generation to generation.

Oliver Wendell Holmes, Sr.: This body in which we journey across the isthmus between the two oceans is not a private carriage, but an omnibus.

Horace: It is of no consequence of what parents a man is born, so he be a man of merit.

Horace: Nor do fierce eagles produce the peaceful dove.

Irish Proverb: The raggy colt often made a powerful horse.

Hugo Keim: If you believe in evolution... you can trace all of our lower back problems to the time when the first hominid stood erect.

Helen Keller: There is no king who has not had a slave among his ancestors, and no slave who has not had a king among his.

Sam Levenson: The reason grandparents and grandchildren get along so well is that they have a common enemy.

Abraham Lincoln: I don't know who my grandfather was, but I am much more concerned to know what his grandson will be.

Robert Lynd: One of the odd things about ancestors, even if they are no older than grandfathers, is that we can scarcely help feeling that, compared to them, we are degenerate.

John P. Marquand: It is worthwhile for anyone to have behind him a few generations of honest, hard-working ancestry.

Edna St. Vincent Malay: With him for a sire and her for a dam, What should I be but just what I am?

Phyllis McGinley: Though doubless now our shrewd machines / Can blow the world to smithereens / More tidily and so on, / Let's give our ancestors their due. / Their ways were coarse, their weapons few. / But ah! How wondrously they slew / with what they had to go on.

Ogden Nash (American poet, 1902-1971, *What, No Sleep?*): WHAT, NO SLEEP? These are a few of the 600 products sold in the "sleep shop" of a New York department store. – From an advertisement of the Consolidated Edison Company in the TIMES. / I don't need no sleepin' medicine – I seen a ad by ole Con Edison. Now when I lay me in my mattress / You kin hear me snore from hell to Hatteras, / With muh Sleep Record, / Muh Vaporizer, / Muh Electric Slippers, / Muh Yawn Plaque, / Muh Slumber Buzzer, / Muh miniature Electric Organ, / An' muh wonderful Electric Blanket. // .... // I pity muh pioneer an-cestors. / They rode the wilderness wide and high, / But how did they ever go sleepy-bye / Without their Eye Shade, / Their Clock-Radio, / Their Sleep Record, / Their Vaporizer, / Their Sinus Mask, / Their Electric Slippers, / Their Yawn Plaque, / Their Slumber Buzzer, / Their Massagin' Pillow, / Their Snore Bell, / Their miniature Electric Organ, / An' their wonderful Electric Blanket?

Ogden Nash: Children aren't happy with nothing to ignore, And that's why parents were created for.

Thomas Paine: When we are planning for posterity, we ought to remember that virtue is not hereditary.

Plato (Greek philosopher and writer, 427?-347 BC): Every king springs from a race of slaves, and every slave has had kings among his ancestors.

Plato: Nothing is more disgraceful than for a man who is nothing, to hold himself honored on account of his forefathers; and yet hereditary honors are a noble and splendid treasure to descendants.

John O'Connor Power: The mules of politics: without pride of ancestry, or hope of posterity.

Will Rogers: My forefathers didn't come over on the *Mayflower*, but they met the boat.

Will Rogers: Don't let yesterday use up too much of today.

Will Rogers: Things ain't what they used to be and never were.

Russian Proverb: Do not be born good or handsome, but be born lucky.

George Santayana: The family is one of nature's masterpieces.

William Shakespeare (*Much Ado About Nothing,* Act V, iv): Bull Jove, sir, had an amiable low; / And some such strange bull leap'd your father's cow, / And got a calf in that same noble feat / Much like to you, for you have just his bleat.

William Shakespeare (*Titus Andronicus,* Act V, i): But where the bull and cow are both milk-white, / They never do beget a coal-black calf.

William Shakespeare (*Twelfth Night,* Act II, ii): Alas, our family is the cause, not we! / For such as we are made of, such we be.

Cornelia Otis Skinner: It is disturbing to discover in oneself these curious revelations of the validity of the Darwinian theory. If it is true that we have sprung from the ape, there are occasions when my own spring appears not to have been very far.

Mark Twain: We are always too busy for our children; we never give them the time or interest they deserve. We lavish gifts upon them; but the most precious gift—our personal association, which means so much to them—we give grudgingly.

Jane Wagner: If evolution was worth its salt, by now it should've evolved something better than survival of the fittest. Yeah, I told 'em I think a better idea would be survival of the wittiest. At least, that way, the creatures that didn't survive could've died *laughing.*

ANGER (See AGGRESSIVE)

APOTHEGMS (See ADVICE; MAXIMS, and CHARLEY CHAN)

APPEAL

Uncle Anthony: If there's a rule against frivolous lawsuits, shouldn't there be some rule against frivolous appeals?

Uncle Anthony: Y'know, deez guys are always droppin' da ball, an' den dey complain about da way it bounces!

Uncle Anthony: They waited (for the appeal) for their ship to come in, but it took so long their pier collapsed.

Aunt Mary Carlo: Somad'em appeals (and cases) don't seem to go up or down, jes' seem to go 'round in circles.

Justice Richard S. Arnold, *The Future of the Federal Courts*, 60 Mo. L. Rev. 533, 536 (1995): The third duty of the court is to write an opinion which is intelligible, which explains the result, and which we hope, is acceptable to the losing side. I think about the losing litigants a lot. Those are the people who need to understand that they have been heard - that a reasoning creature of some kind has evaluated their argument and comes to some sort of conclusion about it. They won't like it; they won't enjoy losing, but I hope that they will have a sense that they have been heard.

Francis Bacon: Philip, Alexander's father, gave sentence against a prisoner, what time he was drowsy, and seemed to give small attention. The prisoner, after sentence was pronounced, said: *I Appeal.* The king somewhat stirred, said; *To whom do you appeal?* The prisoner answered; *From Philip when he gave no ear, to Philip when he shall give ear.*

Chief Judge Edward Becker, discussing the decision of the Third Circuit to drastically reduce the number of cases resolved without comment (from 52.9% in 1997 to 12.6% in 1999, later to 2.8% in 2002): "We realized that this [the large number of cases without comment] was a mistake, that we owed the bar more."

Bible: Acts, 25:10: But Paul said, "I am standing at the tribunal of Caesar; there I ought to be tried. To Jews I have done no wrong, as thou thyself very well knowest. For if I ahve done any wrong or committed a crime deserving of death, I do not refuse to die. But if there is no ground to their charges against me, no one can give me up to them; I appeal to Caesar." Then Festus, after conferring with the council, answered, "Thou hast appealed to Caesar; to Caesar thou shalt go."

Bible: Amos, 5:24: Let judgment run down as waters, and righteousness as a mighty stream.

Bible: Habakkuk, 2:3 and Hebrews, 10:37: Though it tarry, wait for it; because it will surely come.

Bible: Job, 31:35: Oh that one would hear me!

Bible: Paul, Acts, 22:1: Men, brethren, and fathers, hear ye my defence.

Ambrose Bierce: APPEAL: In law, to put the dice into the box for another throw.

Logan E. Bleckley (Chief Justice of Georgia Supreme Court, 1827-1907): The court erred in some of the legal propositions announced to the jury, but all the errors were harmless. Wrong directions which do not put the traveler out of his way, furnish no reasons for repeating the journey. Cherry v. Davis, 59 Ga. 454 (1877)

Paul D. Carrington, Daniel J. Meador & Maurice Rosenburg, *Justice on Appeal* 10 (West 1976): "When reasons are announced and can be weighed, the public can have assurance that the correcting process is working. Announcing reasons can also provide public understanding of how the numerous decisions of the system are integrated. In a busy court, the reasons are an essential demonstration that the court did in fact fix its mind on the case at hand. An unreasoned decision has very little claim to acceptance by the defeated party, and is difficult or impossible to accept as an act reflecting systematic application of legal principles. Moreover, the necessity of stating reasons not infrequently changes the results by forcing the judges to come to grips with nettlesome facts or issues which their normal instincts would otherwise cause them to avoid." (emphasis added)

Marcus Tullius Cicero (106-43 B.C.): The solidity of a state is very largely bound up with its judicial decisions.

Justice Frank M. Coffin (*The Ways of a Judge: Reflections From the Federal Appellate Bench*, Houghton Mifflin, 1980, p. 57; Chief Judge on First Circuit from 1972-1983.): "[A] remarkably effective device for detecting fissures in accuracy and logic is the reduction to writing of the results of one's thought processes . . . . Somehow, a decision mulled over in one's head or talked about in conference looks different when dressed up in written words and sent out into the sunlight . . . . [W]e may be in the very middle of an opinion, struggling to reflect the reasoning all judges have agreed on, only to realize that it simply "won't write." The act of writing tells us what was wrong with the act of thinking."

Hon. William Cranch (U.S. Circ. Ct of D.C.; in 1804 explained why he took it upon himself, while a sitting Circuit Judge, to report US Supreme Ct cases, even though he had no appointment to do so. He did it because no one else was, and he saw the need): In a government which is emphatically stiled a government of laws, the least possible range ought to be left for the discretion of the judge. Whatever tends to render the laws certain, equally tends to limit that discretion; and perhaps nothing conduces more to that object than the publication of reports. Every case decided is a check upon the judge. He can not decide a similar case differently, without strong reasons, which, for his own justification, he will wish to make public. The avenues to corruption are thus obstructed, and the sources of litigation closed.

Finley Peter Dunne: An appeal is where ye ask wan coort to show its contempt f'r another coort.

Finley Peter Dunne: No matter whether th' constitution follows th' flag or not, th' supreme coort follows th' iliction returns.

Finley Peter Dunne (*Mr. Dooley on Making a Will: On Criminal Trials*, 1963): Th' lawyer f'r th' defense objicts to all th' questions an' whin th' coort overrules him he takes an exciption. That is as much as to say to th' judge: "I'll make a jack iv ye in th' supreem coort."

English Saying: Trial courts search for the truth and appellate courts search for error.

Jerome Frank (*Law and the Modern Mind*, 1930): The United States Supreme Court has wittily been called the "court of ultimate conjecture."

Felix Frankfurter: In this Court dissents have gradually become majority opinions.

Harvard Law School (Old Harvard Law School Class Song, sung to the WWI tune *It's A Long Way to Tipparerey"*): It's a long way to certiorari / It's a long way to go / It's a long way to certiorari / And the highest court I know.

Arthur D. Hellman (Witness testimony to House Judicary Subcommittee on Courts, the Internet, and Intellectual Property in *Oversight Hearings on Unpublished Judicial Opinions*, June 27, 2002. Hellman is a Professor of Law and Distinguished Faculty Scholar at the U. of Pittsburgh Law School. Professor Hellman also participated in the Hruska Commission): " I believe that deciding cases by judgment orders is an unacceptable practice that should not be considered among the alternatives available to the courts of appeals. More than a quarter of a century ago, the Hruska Commission endorsed the "basic proposition" that in every appellate case the court should provide "some record, however brief, and whatever the form, of the reasoning which impelled the decision." Although time has out-distanced some of the Hruska Commission's recommendations, this one remains as cogent and compelling as it was in 1975. The reason is simple. We pride ourselves in having a government of laws, not of men. When an appellate court decides a case, the court's explanation – a "record [of the court's] reasoning" – provides tangible evidence that the decision is the product of the law, not simply the preferences of the judges who happened to sit on the panel." . . . "The Federal Rules of Appellate Procedure should be amended, as the Hruska Commission recommended, to require that in every appellate case the court should provide "some record, however brief, and whatever the form, of the reasoning which impelled the decision."

Chief Justice William J. Holloway, Jr., dissenting in *In re Rules of the United States Court of Appeals for the Tenth Circuit, Adopted Nov. 18, 1986*, 955 F.2d 36, 38 (10th Cir. 1992): "[T]he basic purpose for stating reasons within an opinion or order must never be forgotten—that the decision must be able to withstand the scrutiny of analysis, against the record evidence, as to soundness under the Constitution and the statutory and decisional law we must follow, as to its consistency with our precedents. Our orders and judgments, like our published opinions, should never be shielded from searching examination."

Marshall Houts & Hon. Walter Rogosheske (Former Senior Justice, Minnesota Supreme Court), *The Art of Advocacy*, Appeals (1983): Chief Justice Sheran of the Minnesota Supreme Court says, "at some point after losing in the trial court, the lawyer must step back from his case and try to give it an objective appraisal." This is one of his toughest tasks: Emotions during and immediately after trial run high. The client is angry at the unfairness and the injustice of it all. The lawyer is personally and professionally embarrassed. Both look for someone to blame; and it can only be the jury and trial judge: Together, they become the common enemies against whom client and lawyer can join forces to vent their frustrations. The knee-jerk reaction is automatic, "Of course, we'll appeal!" As Chief Justice Sheran continues, "only 50% of the cases that are appealed should be." This does not mean that the "unwinnable" appeals are frivolous in the worse sense of that word; but it does mean that many are "hopeless" in that the appellant doesn't stand any realistic chance of showing reversible error.

Charles Evans Hughes (New York lawyer, Governor, Assoc Justice US Supreme Court, 1862-1948): Dissents are appeals to the brooding spirit of the law, to the intelligence of another day.

Charles Evans Hughes, *The Supreme Court of the United States,* 1928, p. 64. Sourced from Bryan A. Garner, *Style of Opinions, The Oxford Companion to the Supreme Court of the United States,* ed. by Kermit L. Hall (1992), p. 608; Hughes was Supreme Court Chief Justice from 1930 to 1941 and Supreme Court Justice from 1910 to 1916: "[T]here is no better precaution against judicial mistakes than setting out accurately and adequately the material facts as well as the points to be decided."

Justice Robert Houghwout Jackson: We are not final because we are infallible, but we are infallible only because we are final. *Brown v. Allen,* 344 US 443, 97 L ed 469, 73 S Ct 397 (1953)

Justice Robert Houghwout Jackson: We granted certiorari, and in this Court the parties changed positions as nimbly as if dancing a quadrille. *Orloff v. Willoughby*, 345 US 83, 87, 97 L. ed. 842, 846, 73 S. Ct. 534 (1953).

Justice Edith Jones, dissenting in *United States of America v. Mcfarland*, 00-10569 (5th Cir. 2002); joined by Justices Jolly, Smith, DeMoss, and Clement: "This court is an institution defined by the reasoned exercise of power. It [silence] signals disregard for the public—the federal prosecutors and defense attorneys—who remain unenlightened over how to avert, or precipitate, serious discussion of the limits now imposed by the commerce clause on federalization of local crime. Silence exhibits a unique unconcern for appellant McFarland ... [who was] entitled to know how the power of the federal government consitutionally bore down on [him]."

Justice Edith Jones, dissenting in *United States of America v. Mcfarland*, 00-10569 (5th Cir. 2002). Joined by Justices Jolly, Smith, DeMoss, and Clement: "The benefits of issuing reasoned opinions—fostering public understanding of the law, accountability and transparancy, and imposing self-discipline on the judges—are not limited to majority opinions."

Justice Carolyn D. King (reported by Nathan Koppel, "Counsel Claims Significant 5th Circuit Cases Get Short Shrift," *Texas Lawyer* April 27, 1998. Carolyn King is currently Chief Justice of the Fifth Circuit, serving on that Court since 1979): "I personally favor giving reasons for what we do, because we have an accountability issue. I am troubled by the fact that we are using summary dispositions."

Latin Proverb: Appeal from Philip drunk to Philip sober.

Abraham Lincoln: There can be no successful appeal from the ballot to the bullet.

Judith A. Livingston & Thomas A. Moore (*ATLA's Litigating Tort Cases*, Vol. 4, chap. 47, Appeals, West Group, 2003): The success of an appeal at any time during litigation depends upon one cardinal factor—preparation. The trial lawyer must be vigilant during all of the prior phases of litigation, as well as while drafting briefs and outlining oral argument.

Judith A. Livingston and Thomas A. Moore (*ATLA's Litigating Tort Cases*, West Group, 2003): In general, there are two broad types of pretrial appeals. One category of pretrial appeal is interlocutory appeals, which raise issues during the pendency of an action but do not finally dispose of the action. In some jurisdictions, interlocutory orders regarding discovery and orders pretaining to motions in limine are not appealable as of right and an appeal may lie only with leave of court or it may not be available at all.... The other broad category of pretrial appeals involve those which are not, interlocutory, but are final, at least as to a cause of action, a single issue, or a party. They include orders granting summary judgment and motions to dismiss on grounds such as failure to state a cause of action, violation of statutes of limitations, lack of jurisdiction, or res judicata.

Judith A. Livingston and Thomas A. Moore (*ATLA's Litigating Tort Cases*, West Group, 2003): The decision to appeal is specific to each case. Obviously, not every adverse decision and verdict should be appealed. At a minimum, there should be an appeal only if the result which would be appealed is prejudicial to the client's case and if the grounds for appeal have sufficient merit that there is a reasonable likelihood of success. An additional, more global consideration is whether the facts of a given case provide an opportunity to make "good law."

Judith A. Livingston & Thomas A. Moore (*ATLA's Litigating Tort Cases*, West Group, 2003), Oral Argument of Appeals: For several reasons, a party should always orally argue an appeal where there is an option to do so. First, an appearance for oral argument lets the court know that you take the appeal seriously; a failure to seek oral argument could give the opposite impression. Second, after reading the briefs, members of the court may have questions which they plan to ask counsel during oral argument, and waving oral argument could deprive the court of important answers. Third, statements made by the opposing party at the oral argument may require a response or clarification, which can only be accomplished if you are present at the argument.

Judith A. Livingston and Thomas A. Moore (*ATLA's Litigating Tort Cases*, West Group, 2003) Summary and Practice Pointers Checklist: "... The salient points with regard to appellate litigation pertain to ...: 1) Thorough Preparation...Establish Credibility... Logical and Cohesive Presentation."

James Macintosh (Scottish Enlightment philosopher): There is not, in my opinion, in the whole compass of human affairs, so noble a spectacle as that which is displayed in the progress of jurisprudence. Where we may contemplate the cautious and unwearied exertions of wise men through a long course of ages, withdrawing every case as it arises from the dangerous power of discretion and subjecting it to inflexible rule, extending the dominion of justice and reason, and gradually contacting within the narrowest possible limits, the domain of brutal force and arbitrary will.

Michael A. Musmanno (Justice of Pennsylvania Supreme Court, 1959): The ordering of a new trial in this case represents superfluity at its zenith, utility at its nadir and expenditure of time and money at its climactic futility.

Michael A. Musmanno (Justice of Pa. Supreme Court, 1959): Ordering a new trial over an issue already decided is like having a dress rehearsal of a play which has closed.

Michael A. Musmanno (Justice of Pennsylvania Supreme Court, 1959): To say that a new trial should not be granted, if a major error has been committed, only because the lawyer failed to do what he should have done, is like saying that a sick person should not be given additional treatment and should be allowed to die if the doctor erred in his original diagnosis and prescribed the wrong medicine.

Michael A. Musmanno (Justice of Pennsylvania Supreme Court, 1959): Law is Not a Merry-Go-Round: The law is intended to be, and is in fact, a highway for litigants to travel until the destination of justice is reached. It is not a carousel on which litigants are to ride in never-ending circular journeying. The issues involved in this case have been litigated, adjudicated and definitively decided. The end of the highway has been reached, and the appellant here should not attempt to board again a legal merry-go-round. (*Helmig v. Rockwell Mfg. Co.*, 414 Pa. 518).

Michael A. Musmanno (Justice of Pennsylvania Supreme Court, 1959): The error in the Majority's arithmetic here, following the figuring done by the Court below, is that it has taken the highest minuend figures from the Commonwealth's evidence, and the highest subtrahend figures from the plaintiffs evidence. The mathematical mixture of that character is not apt to add up to justice, but confusion. (*Braughler v. Commonwealth*, 388 PA. 581).

Michael A. Musmanno (Justice of Pa. Supreme Court, 1959): Remittitur: The jury awarded plaintiff a verdict of $40,000 which the Majority of this Court has reduced to $30,000.... we have frequently said that a verdict is to be reduced only when it shocks our sense of justice. I feel no shock.... the Majority Opinion calls into review cases of the past where reductions were made in verdicts, but this court should not prepare a Procrustean bed on which to place verdicts for lopping, so that they may fit artificial standards. Procrustes, of Greek legend, used also to stretch his victims if they were too short for his bed, but this Court never augments verdicts. (Kite V. Jones, 389 PA. 353).

Michael A. Musmanno (Justice of Pa. Supreme Court, 1959): Why Not Be Shocked by a Desiccated Crust? Our Supreme and Superior Court reports abound with decisions to the effect that where a verdict is so grossly excessive as the shock our sense of justice, the verdict must be reduced or a new trial ordered. If we can be shocked by an excessive verdict, why can we not be shocked by an obviously inadequate verdict? If too much causes a revulsion, why shouldn't too little underlying too little awaken an equal abhorrence? If we recoil from a verdict which is bloated, why should we be indifferent to a verdict which is gaunt? Why should an overflow larder shock our conscience more than an empty or half-full one? Why should an extra loaf of bread be more disturbing than a desiccated crust?... if an appellate court may, and it does, substitute its judgment for the jury's judgment when the jury overfills the well, why should it decline to intervene when the jury empties the well? If a jury can be corrected when it overstocks the pantry, why should the correcting measure be withheld when the jury strips the pantry bare? (*Takac v. Bamford*, 370 Pa. 389).

Robert M. Parker ("Speech before the Commission on Structural Alternatives for the Federal Courts of Appeals," March 25, 1998; Robert Parker was Fifth Circuit Justice from 1994-2002 and District Judge of the Eastern District of Texas from 1979-1994): "LOCAL RULE 47.6 This rule permits a case to be decided by a simple "Affirmed." The statistics regarding the utilization of Local Rule 47.6 are *deceiving* however. Most judges think that it is more politic to prepare a per curiam opinion of one-half to one and one-half pages saying in effect no more than "finding no error, the judgment is Affirmed." The difference is one of form instead of substance," and "What is more likely is that the Fifth Circuit with 10,000 filings will not operate as it does today. Instead we will witness an *incremental corruption* of case management techniques. *Discretionary review* will take the form of *one word or one paragraph dispositions* on the summary calendar. The conference calendar will dispose of more cases with less conference. It is a small step for the jurisdictional defect calendar to be expanded to encompass cases that have merit defects (as determined by central staff attorneys); and all the while, we will be holding ourselves out as providing plenary review for all appeals. *With good intentions driven by the need to dispose of our docket, we will compromise the integrity of the court by providing a level of review that is in fact not plenary.* It matters not that we may not realize it or that we may have no other choice, the result will be the same. The difference between what we say we are doing and what we will actually be doing will not go unnoticed by pundits, the academy, and the bar. *We will erode confidence of the public in the federal courts.* Discretionary review in the guise of case management techniques will not play in Peoria or New Orleans or anywhere else." (emphasis added)

William Reynolds & William Richman, *The Non-Precedential Precedent—Limited Publication and No-Citation Rules in the United States Courts of Appeals*, 78 Columbia Law Rev. 1167, 1203 (1978): "[T]he real accountability of the courts of appeals is to the bench, the bar, the scholars, and the public. Unpublished opinions, especially ones that cannot be cited, will generally not receive critical commentary from those groups for the obvious reason that they will go unnoticed."

Will Rogers: If Stupidity got us into this mess [Editor: a bad verdict/judgment], then why can't it get us out?

Will Rogers: A difference of opinion is what makes horse racing and missionaries (Editor: and appellate decisions).

Alvin Rubin (*Bureaucratization of the Federal Courts: The Tension Between Justice and Efficiency*, 55 Notre Dame Law. 648, 655, 1980): "Every judge should be required to give his reasons for a decision, and those reasons should be sufficient to explain the result to the litigants but also to enable other litigants to comprehend its precedential value and limits to its authority."

William Shakespeare (*Cymberline*, Act V, iv): Help, Jupiter; or we appeal, / And from thy justice fly

William Shakespeare (*II Henry IV*, Act IV, i): When ever yet was your appeal denied?

William Shakespeare (*Henry VIII*, Act II, iv): Appeal unto the pope, / To bring my whole case 'fore his holiness.

William Shakespeare (*Measure for Measure*, Act V, i): The duke's unjust, / Thus to retort your manifest appeal

William Shakespeare (*Sonnet* 117, 13): Since my appeal says I did strive to prove

William Shakespeare (*Winter's Tale*, Act III, ii): I appeal / To your own conscience, sir

Justice John Paul Stevens, dissenting in *Connecticut Board of Pardons v. Dumschat*, 452 U.S. 458, 472 (1981): The judges [in former times] were guided by few written laws, but developed a meaningful set of rules by the process of case-by-case adjudication. Their explanations of why they decided cases as they did provided guideposts for future decisions and an assurance to litigants that like cases were being decided in a similar way. Many of us believe that those statements of reasons provided a better guarantee of justice than could possibly have been described in a code written in sufficient detail to be fit for Napoleon."

Alexis de Tocqueville (French political writer, 1805-1859, writing about the US Supreme Court in *Democracy in America*): Their power (the US Supreme Court) is enormous, but it is the power of public opinion.

Mark Twain: Are you going to hang him *anyhow* – and try him afterward?

Patricia Wald (Chief Justice of D. C. Circuit Court of Appeals from 1986-1991, Justice on that Court from 1979-1986; retired from the bench in 1999 to serve as judge on the International Criminal Tribunal for the former Yugoslavia; *The Problem with the Courts: Black-Robed Bureaucracy or Collegiality Under Challenge,* 42 MD. L. Rev. 766, 782 (1983): My own guiding principle is that virtually every appellate decision requires some statement of reasons. The discipline of writing even a few sentences or paragraphs explaining the basis for the judgment insures a level of thought and scrutiny by the court that a bare signal of affirmance, dismissal, or reversal does not.

Rudy Westmoreland: Their appeal was a Rube Goldberg contraption that metastacized regularly with each novel issue they invented and briefed.

George Will (hypothesizing the Democrats' last resort if they passed legislation which restricted the President, but the President ignored their restrictions): What would the Democrats do? Cross First Street NE and ask the Supreme Court to compel the president to acquiesce in congressional micromanagement ..."

APPELLATE COURT (See APPEALS; and COURTS)

APPEARANCE(S)

Uncle Anthony: Every goat is not a rabbi just because of its beard.

Uncle Anthony: Everybody looks/seems normal, until you get to know them

Uncle Anthony: Y'now that old sayin' "ya can't judge a book by its cover" ... well, most of da time ya get a pretty good idea of da book from the library it came outta ... so, just check out da guy's street or neighborhood.

Aunt Mary Carlo: Ya wanna know how's my lasagna? The proof of da pasta is ta eat it, not look at it.

Aunt Mary Carlo: You don't get no chance to make a good "second impression."

Aunt Mary Carlo: We don't see t'ings as they are, we see t'ings AS WE ARE!

Aesop: Outside show is a poor substitute for inner worth.

Aesop: We should look to the mind, and not to the outward appearance.

Henri Frederic Amiel: As always the appearance is precisely the opposit of the reality; my ostensible life is the reverse of my fundamental aspiration.

Minna Antrim: Illusion is the dust the devil throws in the eyes of the foolish.

Aristotle: Personal beauty is a greater recommendation than any letter of introduction.

Elias Root Beadle: Half the work that is done in this world is to make things appear what they are not.

Eric Bentley: Ours is the age of substitutes: instead of language, we have jargon; instead of principles, slogans; and, instead of genuine ideas, bright ideas.

Bible: John, 7:24: Judge not according to the appearance, but judge righteous judgement.

Bible: Matthew 10:16: Be ye therefore wise as serpents, and harmless as doves.

Bible: Matthew 23:27: Ye are like unto whited sepulchres, which indeed appear beautiful outward.

Bible: Matthew 23:28: Ye also outwardly appear righteous unto men, but within ye are full of hypocrisy and iniquity.

Bible: 1 Samuel 16:7: The Lord seeth not as man seeth; for man looketh on the outward appearance, but the Lord looketh on the heart.

Bible: 1 Samuel 17:33 (Saul to David about the giant Goliath): Thou art but a youth, and he a man of war.

Ambrose Bierce: IMPOSTOR, n. A rival aspirant to public honors.

Ambrose Bierce: LOOKING-GLASS, n. A vitreous plane upon which to display a fleeting show for man's disillusion given.

Lady Marguerite Blessington: To appear rich, we become poor.

Daniel Boorstin: The making of illusions which flood our experience has become the business in America, some of its most honest and most necessary and most respectable business. I am thinking not only of advertising and public relations and political rhetoric, but of all the activities which purport to inform and comfort and improve and educate and elevate us: the work of our best journalists, our most enterprising book publishers, our most energetic manufacturers and merchandisers, our most successful entertainers, our best guides to world travel, and our most influential leaders in foreign relations. Our every effort to satisfy our extravagant expectations simply makes them more extravagant and makes our illusions more attractive.

Daniel Boorstin: Demanding more than the world can give us, we require that something be fabricated to make up for the world's deficiency. This is only one example of our demand for illusions.

William Cullen Bryant: Features – the great soul's apparent seat.

Miguel de Cervantes: All that glitters is not gold.

Edwin Hubble Chapin: The bosom can ache beneath diamond brooches; and many a blithe heart dances under coarse wool.

Geoffrey Chaucer (English poet, 1340-1400): Habit maketh no monk, ne wearing of gilt spurs maleth no knight.

Chinese Proverb: Not the cry, but the flight of the wild duck, leads the flock to fly and follow.

Sir Winston Churchill: If this is a blessing, it is certainly very well disguised.

Sir Winston Churchill: We shape our dwellings, and afterwards our dwellings shape us.

Sir Winston Churchill: A communist is like a crocodile: when it opens its mouth you cannot tell whether it is trying to smile or preparing to eat you up.

Confucius: Fine words and an insinuating appearance are seldom associated with true virtue.

Congolese Proverb: The teeth are smiling, but is the heart?

James Fenimore Cooper: We can all perceive the difference between ourselves and our inferiors, but when it comes to a question of the difference between us and our superiors we fail to appreciate merits of which we have no proper conceptions.

Greg Cusimano: Some say I'm in a rut, but I think I'm in a groove.

John Dryden: What brutal mischief sits upon his brow! / He may be honest, but he looks damnation.

Paul Lawrence Dunbar (1872-1906; a descendent of slaves, he published four novels and short stories and poetry, including this poem: "We Wear the Mask"): "We wear the mask that grins and lies, / It hides our cheeks and shades our eyes—/ This debt we pay to human guile; / With torn and bleeding hearts we smile, / And mouth with myriad subtleties. // Why should the world be otherwise, / In counting all our tears and sighs? / Nay, let them only see us, while / We wear the mask. // We smile, but, O great Christ, our cries / To thee from tortured souls arise. / We sing, but oh the clay is vile / Beneath our feet, and long the mile; / But let the world dream otherwise, / We wear the mask."

English Proverb: They are not all saints who use holy water.

Jean de la Fontaine: Beware, as long as you live, of judging people of appearances.

French Proverb: A throne is only a bench covered with velvet.

Thomas Fuller: A good presence is letters of recommendation

Thomas Fuller: By the husk you may guess at the nut.

Thomas Fuller: 'Tis not the habit that makes the monk.

Charles Dickens: Take nothing on its looks; take everything on evidence. There's no better rule.

Charles Dickens: To be plain with you, friend, you don't carry in your countenance a letter of recomendation.

Robert C. Edwards: You are only what you are when no one is looking.

Albert Einstein (used this BLIND BEETLE ANALOGY to describe his great insight that Gravity was the curving of the fabric of Space-Time, when his youngest son Edward asked him why he was so

famous?): When a blind beetle crawls over the surface of a curved branch, it doesn't notice that the track it has covered is indeed curved. I was lucky enough to notice what the beetle didn't notice.

Dwight D. Eisenhower: Decency—generosity—cooperation,—assistance in trouble—devotion to duty; these are the things that are of greater value than surface appearances and customs.

T.S. Eliot (American-British poet & essayist, *The Hollow Men*, 1925): We are the hollow men/ We are the stuffed men / Leaning together.

Ralph Waldo Emerson: The world is his who can see through its pretension.

Ralph Waldo Emerson: Good and bad are but names very readily transferable to this or that.

Ralph Waldo Emerson: What is a weed? A plant whose virtues have not yet been discovered.

Michael Ferrara: Light travels faster than sound. This is why some people appear bright until you hear them speak.

Benjamin Franklin: Patch on your Coat, and Money in your Pocket, is better and more creditable then a Writ on your Back, and no Money to take it off.

French Proverb: Appearances are very deceitful.

German Proverb: With nice appearance people want to be deceived.

William S. Gilbert (English playwright, 1836-1911, *H.M.S. Pinafore*, 1878): Things are seldom what they seem, / Skim milk masquerades as cream; / Highlows pass as patent leathers; / Jackdaws strut in peacock's feathers.

Ellen Glasgow: After all, you can't expect men not to judge by appearances.

Baltasar Gracian (1647): What is not seen is as if it was not. Even the Right does not receive proper consideration if it does not seem right.

Baltasar Gracian: Things do not pass for what they are, but for what they seem. Most things are judged by their jackets.

Horace Greeley: The illusion that times that were are better than those that are, has probably pervaded all ages.

John Heywood (*The Proverbs of John Heywood*, 1546): One swallow maketh not a summer.

Oliver Wendell Holmes Sr: The outward forms the inward man reveal,—We guess the pulp before we cut the peel.

Horace: We are decieved by the appearance of right.

Hubert H. Humphrey: In real life, unlike Shakespeare, the sweetness of the rose depends upon the name it bears. Things (and people) are not only what they are. They are, in very important respects, what they seem to be.

Hungarian Proverb: An ox remains an ox, even if driven to Vienna.

Italian Proverb: Appearance oft decieves.

William James: Whenever two people meet there are really six people present. There is each man as he sees himself, each man as the other sees him, and each man as he really is.

Jewish Saying: Look at the contents, not at the bottle.

Jewish Proverb: The man who lives in a house did not necessarily build it.

Jewish Proverb: Don't look at the pitcher, but at its contents: for a new pitcher may be full of old wine, and an old pitcher may be empty.

R. D. Laing: We live in a moment of history where change is so speeded up that we begin to see the present only when it is almost disappearing.

Georg Christoph Lichtenberg: There are people who think that everything one does with a serious face is sensible.

Vachel Lindsay: Life is a loom, weaving illusion.

Anita Loos ("*Gentlemen Prefer Blondes*," 1925): "... I always say that a girl never really looks as well as she does on board a steamship, or even a yacht."

Edward G. Bulwer-Lytton (Baron Lytton): A good face is a letter of recommendation, as a good heart is a letter of credit.

Malay Proverb: An ox with long horns, even if he does not butt, will be accused of butting.

W. Somerset Maugham: Sometimes people carry to such perfection the mask they have assumed that in due course they actually become the person they seem.

Mary McCarthy: The happy ending is our national belief.

Margaret Mitchell (*Gone With the Wind*, 1936): You kin polish a mule's feet an' shine his hide an' put brass all over his harness an' hitch him ter a fine cah'ige. But he a mule jes' de same. He doan fool nobody.

Ethel Watts Mumford (*The Limmerick Up-t- Date Book*, "Appearances Deceitful," 1903): There was a young lady from Skye, / With a shape like a capital I; / She said, "It's too bad! / But then I can pad," / Which shows you that figures can lie.

Michael A. Musmanno (Justice of Pa. Supreme Court, 1959): What is trivial is strictly a matter of comparison. Even an earthquake of sizable proportions is trivial against an atomic blast which lays waste half a continent.

Nietzsche (1886): Anyone who has looked deeply into the world may guess how much wisdom lies in the superficiality of men. The instinct that preserves them teaches them to be flighty, light, and false.

Frank O'Hara: It is easy to be beautiful; it is difficult to appear so.

Ovid (Roman poet, 43-18 BC): How in looks does conscious guilt appear.

Grace Paley: Rosiness is not a worse windowpane than gloomy gray when viewing the world.

Joan Patterson: Fantasy discourages reality, particularly in that reality is, in itself, discouraging.

Phaedrus: Things are not always what they seem.

Edgar Allan Poe (*"A Dream Within a Dream,"* 1827): All that we see or seem Is but a dream within a dream.

Thomas Brackett Reed: Everything we do not know anything about always looks big. The human creature is imaginative. If he sees a tail disappearing over a fence, he imagines the whole beast and usually imagines the wrong beast....Whenever we take a trip into the realms of fancy, we see a good many things that never were.

Will Rogers: If we ever pass out as a great nation we ought to put on our tombstone "America died from a delusion that she had moral leadership."

Will Rogers: One Ad is worth more to a paper than forty Editorials.

Will Rogers: One-third of the people in the United States promote, while the other two-thirds provide.

Will Rogers: If advertisers spent the same amount of money on improving their products as they do on advertising then they wouldn't have to advertise them.

Will Rogers: Advertising is the art of convincing people to spend money they don't have for something they don't need.

Will Rogers: Liberty doesn't work as well in practice as it does in speeches.

Russian Proverb: Long whiskers cannot take the place of brains.

Margaret Sanster: Not always the fanciest cake that's there / Is the best to eat!

Seneca: There are no greater wretches in the world than many of those whom people in general take to be happy.

Seneca: *Fallaces sunt rerum species.* ~ The appearances of things are deceptive.

William Shakespeare (*Hamlet,* Act I, ii): Seems, madam! Nay, it is; I know not "seems."

William Shakespeare (*Hamlet,* Act I, iii): The apparel oft proclaims the man.

William Shakespeare (*I Henry IV,* Act V, ii): Look how we can, or sad or merrily, / Interpretation will misquote our looks.

William Shakespeare (*The Merchant of Venice,* Act I, iii): O what a goodly outside falsehood hath!

William Shakespeare (*The Merchant of Venice,* Act II, vii): All that glistens is not gold; / Often have you heard that told.

William Shakespeare (*The Merchant of Venice,* Act III, ii): So may the outward shows be least themselves: / The world is still deceived with ornament .... / Thus ornament is but the guiled shore / To a most dangerous sea; the beauteous scarf / Veiling an Indian beauty; in a word, / The seeming truth which cunning time puts on / To entrap the wisest.

William Shakespeare (*A Midsummer Night's Dream,* Act V, i): Such tricks hath strong imagination, / That, if it would but apprehend some joy; / Or in the night, imagining some fear, / How easy is a bush supposed a bear!

William Shakespeare (*The Rape of Lucrece,* 1.29): Beauty itself doth of itself persuade / The eyes of men without an orator.

William Shakespeare (*Richard II,* Act I, iii): Things sweet to taste prove in digestion sour.

William Shakespeare (*Richard III,* Act II, ii): Oh, that deceit should steal such gentle shapes, / And with a virtuous vizard hide foul guile!

William Shakespeare (*Richard III,* Act III, iii): Nor more can you distinguish of a man / Than of his outward show; which, God he knows, / Seldom or never jumpeth with the heart.

William Shakespeare (*Romeo and Juliet,* Act II, ii): What's in a name? That which we call a rose by any other name would smell as sweet.

William Shakespeare (*Romeo and Juliet,* Act III, ii): O serpent heart, hid with a flowering face! / Did ever a dragon keep so fair a cave?

William Shakespeare (*Romeo and Juliet,* Act III, ii): Was ever book containing such vile matter / So fairly bound? O, that deceit should dwell / In such a gorgeous palace!

William Shakespeare (*Troilus and Cressida,* Act II, iii): Light boats sail swift, though greater hulks draw deep.

Gail Sheehy: The best way to attract money, she had discovered, was to give the appearance of having it.

Robert Southey: How little do they see what really is, who frame their hasty judgment upon that which seems.

Elizabeth Cady Stanton: The more complete the despotism, the more smoothly all things move on the surface.

Harriet Beecher Stowe: One wants to the very something, very great, very heroic; or if not that, then at least very stylish and very fashionable.

Dorothy Thompson: Dissolution comes only to the illusioned. One cannot be disillusioned of what one never put faith in.

Henry David Thoreau: No man ever stood the lower in my estimation for having a patch in his clothes; yet I am sure that there is great anxiety, commonly, to have fashionable, or at least clean and unpatched clothes, than to have a sound conscience.

Henry David Thoreau: It is an interesting question how far men would retain their relative rank if they were divested of their clothes.

Henry David Thoreau: The perception of beauty is a moral test.

Henry David Thoreau: Beware of all enterprises that require new clothes.

John Ronald Reuel Tolkien: All that is gold does not glitter; not all those who wander are lost.

Leo Tolstoy: I am sure that nothing has such a decisive influence upon a man's course as his personal appearance, and not so much his appearance as his belief in its attractiveness or unattractiveness.

Barbara Tuchman: Honor wears different coats to different eyes.

Agnes Sligh Turnbull: There is still vitality under the winter snow, even though to the casual eye it seems to be dead.

Mark Twain: A round man cannot be expected to fit a square hole right away. He must have time to modify his shape.

Mark Twain: Noise proves nothing. Often a hen who has laid an egg cackles as if she had laid an asteroid.

Mark Twain: Clothes make the man. Naked people have little or no influence in society.

Mark Twain: Every one is a moon, and has a dark side which he never shows to anybody.

Mark Twain: At bottom he was probably fond of them, but he was always able to conceal it.

Mark Twain: News is history in its first and best form, its vivid and fascinating form... history is the pale and tranquil reflection of it.

Mark Twain: There are no grades of vanity, there are only grades of ability in concealing it.

Mark Twain: Emperors, kings, artisans, peasants, big people, little people – at bottom we are all alike and all the same; all just alike on the inside, and when our clothes are off, nobody can tell which of us is which.

Mark Twain: Even the clearest and most perfect circumstantial evidence is likely to be at fault, after all, and therefore ought to be received with great caution. Take the case of any pencil, sharpened by any woman: if you have witnesses, you will find she did it with a knife; but if you take simply the aspect of the pencil, you will say she did it with her teeth.

UA: At night, all cows look black.

UA: No fine clothes can hide the clown.

UA: Not everyone at whom dogs bark is a thief.

UA: A homely patch is prettier than a beautiful hole.
UA: The proof of the pudding is in the eating, not in its looks.
UA: It is the worm that lures the fish, not the fisherman and not the rod.
UA: A man looks to you the way you look to him.
UA: An optimist sees opportunity in every calamity. A pessimist sees calamity in every opportunity.
UA: The drunkard smells of whiskey—but so does the bartender.
UA: Where there's a flame there must be fire; and there is no smoke except from fire.
Roger von Oech: Take advantage of the ambiguity in the world. Look at something and think about what else it might be.
Charles Dudley Warner (1873): A cynic might suggest as the motto of modern life this simple legend – "Just as good as the real."
Daniel Webster: The world is governed more by appearances than realities, so that it is fully as necessary to seem to know something as to know it.
Orson Welles (as Charles Foster Kane, the William Randolph Hurst-like owner of "The New York Inquirer," he asks his editor why the Inquirer did not have a big headline on its front page in *Citizen Kane*): Mr. CARTER: Because the news was not big enough. Mr. KANE: Mr. Carter, if the headline is big enough it makes the news big enough."
Jessamyn West: The tragedy of our time is that we are so eye centered, so appearance besotted.
R. C. Westmoreland: A bad idea (or person) that looks good will have the real result (or real person) revealed as ignominiously as a shapeless snail without its shapely shell.
Walt Whitman (*Leaves of Grass*, 1855): Nothing out of its place is good and nothing in its place is bad.
Walt Whitman (*Miracles*, 1881): Every cubic inch of space is a miracle.
Oscar Wilde: Only the shallow know themselves.
Oscar Wilde (*The Picture of Dorian Gray*, 1891): It is only shallow people who do not judge by appearances. The true mystery of the world is the visible, not the invisible.
Oscar Wilde: The first duty in life is to be as artificial as possible. What the second duty is no one has yet discovered.
Yiddish Proverb: Your neighbor's apples are the sweetest.

APPEASEMENT (See COMPROMISE; NEGOTIATION)

ARGUMENT (See also ADVERSARY)

Uncle Anthony: I think they started arguing right after the wedding—even the two little figures on top of their wedding cake were arguing with each other.
Aunt Mary Carlo: Yer uncle Anthony loves to argue so much he talks back to bumper stickers!
Aunt Mary Carlo: Y'know yer mowt (mouth) is da most dangerous part of yer whole body.
John Barrymore: My wife was too beautiful for words – but not for arguments.
Bible: Mark 3:25: If a house be divided against itself, that house cannot stand.
Bible: Proverbs: 26:20: Where no wood is, there the fire goeth out; so where there is no tale-bearer, the strife ceaseth.
Ambrose Bierce: BATTLE, n. A method of untying with the teeth a political knot that would not yield to the tongue.
Ambrose Bierce: CONTROVERSY, n. A battle in which spittle or ink replaces the injurious cannonball and the inconsiderate bayonet....
Ambrose Bierce: DISCUSSION, n. A method of confirming others in their errors.
Ambrose Bierce: DUEL, n. A formal ceremony preliminary to the reconciliation of two enemies. Great skill is necessary to its satisfactory observance; if awkwardly performed the most unexpected and deplorable consequences sometimes ensue. A long time ago a man lost his life in a duel....
Ambrose Bierce: GRAPESHOT, n. An argument which the future is preparing in answer to the demands of American Socialism.
Ambrose Bierce: GUNPOWDER, n. An agency employed by civilized nations for the settlement of disputes which might become troublesome if left unadjusted. By most writers the invention of gunpowder is

ascribed to the Chinese, but not upon very convincing evidence. Milton says it was invented by the devil to dispel angels with, ...

Ambrose Bierce: HARANGUE, n. A speech by an opponent, who is known as an harangue-outang.

Ambrose Bierce: LOGOMACHY, n. A war in which the weapons are words and the wounds punctures in the swim-bladder of self-esteem – a kind of contest in which, the vanquished being unconcious of defeat, the victor is denied the reward of success....

Ambrose Bierce: MACHINATION, n. The method employed by one's opponents in baffling one's open and honorable efforts to do the right thing.

Ambrose Bierce: OBSTINATE, adj. Inaccessible to the truth as it is manifest in the splendor and stress of our advocacy. The popular type and exponent of obstinacy is the mule, a most intelligent animal.

Ambrose Bierce: OPPOSE, v. To assist with obstructions and objections.

Ambrose Bierce: REPARTEE, n. Prudent insult in retort. Practiced by gentlemen with a constitutional aversion to violence, but a strong disposition to offend. In a war of words, the tactics of the North American Indian.

Ambrose Bierce: RIDICULE, n. Words designed to show that the person of whom they are uttered is devoid of the dignity of character distinguishing him who utters them. It may be graphic, mimetic or merely rident....

Ambrose Bierce: SOPHISTRY, n. The controversial method of an opponent, distinguished from one's own by superior insincerity and fooling. This method is that of the later Sophists, a Grecian sect of philosophers who began by teaching wisdom, prudence, science, art and, in brief, whatever men ought to know, but lost themselves in a maze of quibbles and a fog of words.

Ambrose Bierce: VITUPERATION, n. Satire, as understood by dunces and all such as suffer from an impediment in their wit.

Josh Billings (pseud. of Henry Wheeler Shaw, American humorist, 1818-1885): Silence is one of the hardest things to refute.

Pierre Agustin de Beaumarchais: It is not necessary to understand things in order to argue about them.

Robert Benchley: Most of the arguments to which I am a party fall somewhat short of being impressive, owing to the fact that neither I nor my opponent knows what we are talking about.

Giosue Borsi: Men are conquered only by love and kindness, by quiet, discreet example, which does not humiliate them and does not constrain them to give in. They dislike to be attacked by the man who has no other desire but to overcome them.

Louis Dembitz Brandeis (Massachusetts lawyer, Assoc Justice US Supreme Court, 1856-1941): In the case at bar, also, the logic of words should yield to the logic of realities.

Louis Brandeis: If there be time to expose through discussion of falsehood and fallacies, to avert the evil by the process of education, the remedy to be applied is more speech, not enforced silence.

Sir William Browne: The King to Oxford sent a troop of horse, For Tories own no argument but force: Wit equal skill to Cambridge books he sent, For Whigs admit no force but argument.

Coach Paul "Bear" Bryant: It's not the size of the dog in the fight that matters, it's the size of the fight in the dog that counts.

William F. Buckley, Jr.: Liberals claim to want to give a hearing to other views, but then are shocked and offended to discover that there are other views.

George Burns and Gracie Allen: As soon as my wife starts to quarrel, she gets historical. You mean hysterical? No, historical. She always rakes up the past.

Samuel Butler (English satirical poet, 1612-1680): A man convinced against his will is of the same opinion still.

Benjamin N. Cardozo (Assoc Judge & Chief Judge, NY Court of Appeals, Assoc Justice US Supreme Court, 1870-1938): Metaphors in law are to be narrowly watched, for starting as devices to liberate thought, they end often by enslaving it. Berkey v. Third Ave. Ry Co., 244 N.Y. 84 (1926)

Benjamin Cardozo: Expediency may tip the scales when arguments are nicely balanced.

Benjamin Cardozo: A picture cannot be painted if the significant and the insignificant are given equal prominence. One must know how to select.

Lewis Carrol (*Alice in Wonderland*): "In my youth," said his father, "I took to the law, / And argued each case with my wife; / And the muscular strength which it gave to my jaw / Has lasted the rest of my life."

Dale Carnegie: The only way to get the best of an argument is to avoid it.

Gilbert Keith Chesterton (Engliush critic, writer, 1874-1936): The thing I hate about an argument is that it always interrupts a discussion.

Gilbert Keith Chesterton: People generally quarrel because they can not argue.

Sir Winston Churchill: Don't argue about difficulties. The difficulties will argue for themselves.

Sir Winston Churchill: When the eagles are silent, the parrots begin to jabber.

Sir Winston Churchill: The worst quarrels only arise when both sides are equally in the right and equally in the wrong.

Sir Winston Churchill: If we opened a quarrel between the past and the present, we shall find that we have lost the future.

Sir Winston Churchill: If you try to set forth in a catalogue what will be the exact settlement of an affair you will find that the moment you leave the area of pious platitude you will descend into the arena of heated controversy.

Sir Winston Churchill: If you have an important point to make, don't try to be subtle or clever. Use the pile driver. Hit the point once. Then come back and hit it again. Then hit it a third time; a tremendous whack.

Cicero: We must make a personal attack when there is no argumentative basis for our speech.

Marcus Tillius Cicero: If you have no basis for an argument, abuse the plaintiff.

Samuel Taylor Coleridge (English poet, 1772-1834): The juggle of sophistry consists, for the most part, in using a word in one sense in the premise, and in another sense in the conclusion.

Emily Collins: People are more willing to be convinced by the calm perusal of an argument than in a personal discussion.

Leonardo Da Vinci: Anyone who conducts an argument by appealing to authority is not using his intelligence just his memory.

Clarence Darrow: To think is to differ.

Benjamin DeMott (*"Seduced by Civility"*): When you are in an argument with a thug, there are things much more important than civility....Civility is what slaveholders called for when abolitionists marched.

Benjamin Disraeli (Earl of Beaconsfield, English writer, statesman, 1804-1881): Nothing ever perplexes an adversary so much as an appeal to his honour.

Elaine Goodale Eastman (teacher at Fort Maion, Florida and Carlsile Indian Industrial School, and biographer of Gen. William Henry Platt, the founder of Carlisle, speaking about him): "A man who had to square every corner of an idea or argument (tolerating no ambiguities whatsoever)"

Albert Einstein (to his friend about his 1913 Antwerth Outline): I enjoy controversies, in the manner of Figero: "Would my noble Lord venture a little dance? He should tell me. I will strike up the tune for him."

Ralph Waldo Emerson: Let me never fall into the vulgar mistake of dreaming that I am persecuted whenever I am contradicted.

Ralph Waldo Emerson: When we quarrel, O then we wish we had always kept out appetites in rein, that we might speak so coolly and majestically from the unquestionable heights of character.

Joshua Evans (English lawyer): Necessity is always a suspicious argument and never wanting to support the worst of measures. <u>Home v. Bentinck</u>, 2 Brod. & B. 130 (1820), *arguendo*.

Sam Ewing: Nothing is so frustrating as arguing with someone who knows what he's talking about.

William Feather: Nothing will ruin an interesting intelligent argument more quickly than the arrival of a pretty girl.

E. M. Forster: Most quarrels are inevitable at the time; incredible afterwards.

Gene Fowler: Everyone needs a warm personal enemy or two to keep him free from rust in the movable parts of his mind.

Felix Frankfurter (Massachusetts lawyer, Assoc Justice US Supreme Court, 1882-1965): Answers are not obtained by putting the wrong question and thereby begging the real one.

Benjamin Franklin: He that blows the coals in quarrels that he has nothing to do with has no right to complain if the sparks fly in his face.

Thomas Fuller: He that has the worst cause makes the most noise.

Peter Gail: History is an argument without an end.

W.L. George: Wars teach us not to love our enemies, but to hate our allies.

German Proverb: A bad cause requires many words.

Jascha Heifetz: No matter what side of the argument you are on, you always find people on your side that you wish were on the other.

Robert Heinlein: Never appeal to a man's better nature. He may not have one. Invoking his self interest gives you more leverage.

George Herbert: Be calm in arguing; for fierceness makes error a fault, and truth discourtesy.

Eric Hoffer: You can discover what your enemy fears most by observing the means he uses to frighten you.

Billie Holiday: Sometimes it's worse to win a fight than to lose.

Oliver Wendell Holmes, Jr. (Massachusetts lawyer, Assoc Justice and Chief Justice Supreme Court of Massachusetts, Assoc Justice US Supreme Court, 1841-1935): But to generalize is to omit.

Oliver Wendell Holmes, Jr.: You cannot argue with your neighbor, except on the admission for the moment that he is as wise as you, although you may by no means believe it.

Oliver Wendell Holmes, Jr.: The elaborate argument does not need an elaborate answer.

Earl Hoover (Ohio, Common Pleas Judge): We need not consider all the reasons advanced by defendant in support of its motion. One arrow, if fatal, is fatal enough. Inland Properties Co. v. Union Properties, Inc., 60 Ohio L. Abs. 150 (1951)

Elbert Hubbard: If you can not answer a man's argument, all is not lost. You can still call him vile names.

Victor Hugo: Friend is sometimes a word devoid of meaning; enemy, never.

Thomas Henry Huxley: No mistake is so commonly made by clever people as that of assuming a cause to be bad because the arguments of its supporters are, to a great extent, nonsensical.

Thomas Henry Huxley: There is no greater mistake than the hasty conclusion that opinions are worthless because they are badly argued.

Italian Proverb: Have you fifty friends? – it is not enough. Have you one enemy? – it is too much.

Robert H. Jackson: The price of freedom of religion, or of speech, or of the press, is that we must put up with a good deal of rubbish.

Robert H. Jackson: The petitioner's problem is to avoid Scylla without being drawn into Charybdis.

Thomas Jefferson: An association of man that will not quarrel with one another is a thing which never yet existed, from the greatest confederacy of nations down to a town meeting or a vestry.

Thomas Jefferson: And, finally, that truth is great and will prevail if left to herself; that she is the proper and sufficient antagonist to error, and has nothing to fear from the conflict unless by human interposition disarmed of her natural weapons, free argument and debate; errors ceasing to be dangerous when it is permitted freely to contradict them.

Jewish Saying: Be sure you have the support of your equals before you challenge your superiors.

Jewish Saying: A quarrel is like an itch: the more you scratch, the more it itches.

Jewish Saying: When you quarrel, quarrel in such a way that you can make up.

Samuel Johnson (Englih lexicographer, critic, conversationalist, 1709-1784): Treating your adversary with respect is striking soft in battle.

Samuel Johnson: It is unjust, Sir, to censure lawyers for multiplying words when they argue; it is often necessary for them to multiply words.

Samuel Johnson: Nay, Sir, argument is argument. You cannot help paying regard to their arguments if they are good

Samuel Johnson: Some men weave their sophistry till their own reason is entangled.

Walter Kidde: Judicious omission is preferable to correct superfluity.

John F. Kennedy (US Senator, 35th US President, 1917-1963): Don't explain and don't complain.

Elizabeth Kenny: He who angers you, conquers you.

Latin Saying: *ab absurdo*: From the absurd (establishing the validity of your argument by pointing out the absurdity of your opponent's position).

Latin Saying: *adversus solem ne loquitor:* Don't speak against the sun (don't waste your time arguing the obvious)

Latin Saying: *argumentum ad hominem:* An argument against the man. (Directing an argument against an opponent's character rather than the subject at hand).

Abraham Lincoln (Illinois lawyer, US President, 1809-1865): The moment my learned adversary begins to talk, his mental processes cease, He is like a little steamboat which I once saw on the Saugamon River. The little steamer had a five-foot boiler and a seven-foot whistle, and every time it whistled the engine stopped – like my opponent's mind.

Emil Ludwig: Debate is the death of conversation.

Bob Mandel: The only way to win a power struggle is to give it up.

Don Marquis: If you make people think they're thinking, they will love you; but if you really make them think, they will hate you.

Phyllis McGinley (American poet, *Note to My Neighbor*): We might as well give up the fiction / That we can argue any view. / For what in me is pure Conviction / Is simple Prejudice in you.

Phyllis McGinley (American poet): When blithe to argument I come, / Though armed with facts and merry, / May Providence protect me from / The fool as adversary, / Whose mind to him a kingdom is / Where reason lacks dominion, / Who calls conviction prejudice / And prejudice opinion.

John Stuart Mill: If all mankind minus one were of one opinion and only one person were of the contrary opinion, mankind would be no more justified in silencing that person than he, if he had the power, would be justified in silencing mankind... if the opinion is right, they are deprived of the opportunity of exchanging error for truth; if wrong, they lose, what is almost as great a benefit, the clearer perception and livelier impression of truth, produced by its collision with error.

John Milton (English poet and writer, 1608-1674): Give me the liberty to know, two other, and to argue freely according to conscience, above all liberties.

Christopher Morley: When someone tries to argue with you, say, "You are nothing if not accurate, and you are not accurate." Then escape from the room.

Myson of Chen (600B.C.): We should not investigate facts by the light of arguments, but arguments by the light of facts.

Ogden Nash: In real life it takes only one to make a quarrel.

Cardinal Newman (1831 sermon): It is absurd to argue men, as to torture them, into believing.

Frederich Nietzsche: At times one remains faithful to a cause only because its opponents do not cease to be insipid.

Daniel O'Connell (Irish lawyer and statesman, 1775-1847): He was a bad lawyer, said O'Connell, but he was the most sensible looking man talking nonsense he ever saw.

Austin O'Malley: In dealing with a foolish or stubborn adversary remember your own mood constitutes half the force opposing you.

Robert Owen: Never argue; repeat your assertion.

Thomas Paine (English political writer, emigrated to the American colonies in 1774, 1737-1809): To argue with a person who has renounced the use of reason is like administering medicine to the dead.

Vernon Louis Parrington: Casuistry is useful for purposes of defense, and a skillful apologist can explain away much.

William Penn (Quaker, founder of Pennsylvania, 1644-1718): Truth often suffers more by the heat of its defenders, than from the arguments of its opposers.

Wendell Phillips: Men always lose half of what is gained by violence. What is gained by argument, is gained forever.

Matthew Prior: In argument, similes are like songs in love; they describe much, but prove nothing.

John Cowper Powys: What renders the least flicker of an argument so profitless, so sterilizing, is that the minds of both the disputants are turned towards something quite different from either's authentic inner truth.

Robert Quillen: Discussion is an exchange of knowledge; argument is an exchange of ignorance.

John W. Raper: There is no sense in having an argument with a man so stupid he doesn't know you have the better of him.

Isaac Samuel Reggio: He who seeks the truth must listen to his opponent.

Christiane Rochefort: Julia: Never argue with them. You're always forgetting you're a woman. They never listen to what you're saying, they just want to listen to the music of your voice.

Roy Rogers: There's two theories to arguing with a woman. Neither one works.

Will Rogers: People's minds are changed through observation and not through argument.

Will Rogers: Even if you're on the right track you'll get run over if you just sit there.

Will Rogers: There is nothing as easy as denouncing..... It don't take much to see that something is wrong, but it does take some eyesight to see what will put it right again.

Franklin Delano Roosevelt (New York lawyer, New York Governor, US President, 1882-1945): Repetition does not transform a lie into a truth.

Leo Rosten: Extremists think "communication" means agreeing with them.

Joseph Roux: The same arguments which we deem forcible as applied to others, seem feeble to us when turned against ourselves.

Jill Ruckelshaus: The best way to win an argument is to begin by being right.

John Ruskin: He who has truth in his heart need never fear the want of persuasion on his tongue.

Bertrand Russell: The most savage controversies are those about matters as to which there is no good evidence either way.

Russian Proverb: An enemy will agree, but a friend will argue.

Robert Louis Stevenson (Scottish lawyer and novelist, 1850-1894): To state one argument is not necessarily to be deaf to all others.

Joseph Story (Massachusetts lawyer, Assoc Justice US Supreme Court, legal writer, 1779-1845): Spare me quotations, which though learn'd are long, / On points remote at best, and rarely strong.

Jonathan Swift (English satirist, 1667-1745): Argument, as usually managed, is the worst sort of conversation, as in books it is generally the worst sort of reading.

Publilius Syrus: In a heated argument we lose sight of the truth.

William Shakespeare (*Henry V*, Act II, iv): In cases of defence 'tis best to weigh / The enemy more mighty than he seems.

William Shakespeare (*Henry V*, Act III, i): And sheath'd their swords for lack of argument.

William Shakespeare (*Julius Caesar*, Act III, ii): Romans, countrymen, and lovers! Hear me for my cause; and be silent, that you may hear.

William Shakespeare (*Love's Labour's Lost*, Act V, i): He draweth out the thread of his verbosity finer than the staple of his argument.

William Shakespeare (*Measure for Measure*, Act I, iii): She hath prosperous art / When she will play with reason and discourse, / And well she can persuade.

William Shakespeare (*Merchant of Venice*, Act I, i): His reasons are two grains of wheat hid in two bushels of chaff; / you shall seek all day ere you find them; / and, when you have them, they are not worth the search.

William Shakespeare (*The Taming of the Shrew*, Act I, ii): And do as adversaries do in the law—Strive mightily, but eat and drink as friends.

William Shakespeare (*Venus and Adonis*, St. 148): Finding their enemy to be so curst, / They all strain curt'sy who shall cope him first.

Walter Parker Stacey: It would be almost unbelievable, if history did not record the tragic fact that men have gone to war and cut each others throat because they could not agree as to what was to become of them after their throats were cut.

Talmud: A legal decision depends not on the teacher's age, but on the force of his argument.

Talmud: Theere are seven times seven ways to argue any side of any issue.

Talmud: When two men quarrel, the one who yields first displays the nobler nature.

Talmud: A quarrel is like a stream of water: once it opens a way, it becomes a wide path.

Alfred Lord Tennyson (English poet, 1809-1892): He makes no friend who never made a foe.

James Thurber: There are two kinds of light—the glow that illumines, and the glare that obscures.

Mao Tse-tung: Despise the enemy strategically, but take him seriously tactically.

Mark Twain (pseud. of Samuel Langhorn Clemens, Missouri humorist, writer, lecturer, 1835-1910): You can't reason someone out of something they weren't reasoned into.

Mark Twain: There is nothing so annoying as to have two people go right on talking when you are interrupting.

Mark Twain: The more you explain it, the more I don't understand it.

Mark Twain: It were not best that we should all think alike; it is the difference of opinion that makes horse races.

UA: The world is divided into people who think they are right.
UA: If you protest long enough that you're right, you're wrong.
U.S. Marine Corps Saying: He/she is a "PENNY WHISTLE" – meaning a person who makes a lot of noise.
Voltaire (Francois Marie Arouet, French writer, 1694-1778): A long dispute means both parties are wrong.
Carmella Vesper (my mother): There are two sides to a pitselle (a very thin Italian waffle).
Rocco Vesper (my father): The only horse's rear bigger than the guy who knows all is the guy who argues with him.
George Washington (American general, 1st President of US, 1732-1799): No nation (or man) is to trusted farther than it is bound by its (his) interests.
Joseph Weintraub, (Chief Justice, New Jersey Supreme Court, 1973): More automobile accidents in New Jersey occur on yellow legal pad's (used by lawyers) than on the highways in New Jersey.
Wendy's hamburger ad campaign slogan (1984 TVcommercial, with the elderly lady saying): Where's the beef?
Oscar Wilde (Irish poet, wit, dramatist, 1856-1900): Always forgive your enemies—nothing annoys them so much.
Oscar Wilde: A man can't be too careful in the choice of his enemies.
Oscar Wilde: I choose my friends for their good looks, my acquaintances for their good characters, and my enemies for their intellects. A man cannot be too careful in the choice of his enemies.
James McNeill Whistler (*The Gentle Art of Making Enemies*, 1890): I am not arguing with you – I am telling you.
Walt Whitman: How beggarly arguments appear before a defiant deed!
George F. Will: Invariably, it is this for which I write: the joy, than which there is nothing pure, of an argument firmly made, like a nail straightly driven, its head flush to the plank.
Virginia Woolf: When an arguer argues dispassionately he thinks only of the argument.
Yiddish Proverb: When your enemy falls, don't rejoice—but don't pick him up either.

ARMY (See MILITARY)

ASSIDUITY (See WORK)

ATTITUDE (See also AGING; AGGRESSIVE)

Uncle Anthony: He sticks out his hand like he wants you to kiss it, not shake it.
Uncle Anthony: His voice is waterproof – nobody can drown it out.
Uncle Anthony: Success don't go to his head – just his mouth.
Uncle Anthony: Yer attitude about (X) today will pretty much set yer attitude about (X) for tomorrow.
Aunt Mary Carlo: He's got such an attitude'dat he brags about somethin' he knows more 'den anybody, and 'den if he don't know anythin' he brags about not knowin' it.
Aunt Mary Carlo: Attitude don't prove nuthin! ... and it don't get nuthin' dine neither!
Aunt Mary Carlo: He's gotta real high-hattitude.
Aunt Mary Carlo: An eye for an eye leaves two people blind!
Herm Albright: A positive attitude may not solve all your problems, but it will annoy enough people to make it worth the effort.
Erna Asp: Instead of crying over spilt milk, go milk another cow.
Bible: Psalms 119:105: Thy word is a lamp unto my feet, and a light unto my path.
Bible: Romans, 7:6: We should serve in newness of spirit, and not in the oldness of the letter.
Bible: Romans, 8:6: To be carnally minded is death; but to be spiritually minded is life and peace.
Bible: Romans, 14:14: There is nothing unclean of itself; but to him that esteemeth any thing to be unclean, to him it is unclean.
Bible: Tutus, 1:15: Unto the pure all things are pure.
Bible: Titus, 1:15: Unto them that are defiled and unbelieving is nothing pure; but even their mind and conscience is defiled.

Ambrose Bierce: MIND, n. A mysterious form of matter secreted by the brain. Its chief activity consists in the endeavor to ascertain its own nature, the futility of the attempt being due to the fact that it has nothing but itself to know itself with. From the Latin *mens*, a fact unknown to that honest shoe-seller, who, observing that his learned competitor over the way had displayed the motto "*Mens conscia recti*," emblazoned his own shop front with the words "Men's, women's and children's conscia recti."

Ambrose Bierce: OPTIMISM, n. The doctrine, or belief that everything is beautiful, including what is ugly, everything good, especially the bad, and everything right that is wrong. It is held with greatest tenacity by those most accustomed to the mischance of falling into adversity, and is most acceptably expounded with the grin that apes smile. Being a blind faith, it is inaccessible to the light of disproof – an intellectual disorder, yielding to no treatment but death, It is hereditary, but fortunately not contagious.

Ambrose Bierce: OPTIMIST, n. A proponent of the doctrine that black is white....

Ambrose Bierce: PESSIMISM, n. A philosophy forced upon the convictions of the observer by the disheartening prevalence of the optimist with his scarecrow hope and his unsightly smile.

Ambrose Bierce: PHILOSOPHY, n. A route of many roads leading from nowhere to nothing.

Ambrose Bierce: POSITIVISM, n, A philosophy that denies our knowledge of the Real and affirms our ignorance of the Apparent. Its longest exponent is Compte, its broadest Mill and its thickest Pencer.

Elizabeth Bowen: If you look at life one way, there is always cause for alarm.

Jacob M. Braude: Life is a grindstone; whether it grinds you down our polishes you up depends on what you're made of.

Art Buchwald: Whether it's the best of times or the worst of times, it's the only time we've got.

Chinese Proverb: The pine stays green in winter...Wisdom in hardship.

Sir Winston Churchill: I like a man who grins when he fights.

Sir Winston Churchill: A pessimist sees the difficulty in every opportunity; an optimist sees the opportunity in every difficulty.

Sir Winston Churchill: A hopeful disposition is not the sole qualification to be a prophet.

Sir Winston Churchill: Attitude is a little thing that makes a big difference.

Sir Winston Churchill: Never give in, never give in, never; never; never; never - in nothing, great or small, large or petty - never give in except to convictions of honor and good sense.

Clarence Darrow: The world is made up for the most part of morons and natural tyrants, sure of themselves, strong in their own opinions, never doubting anything.

Dostoyevsky: There is no object on earth which cannot be looked at from a comic point of view.

Adriana Doyle: The only difference between stumbling blocks and stepping stones is the way in which we use them.

Ralph Waldo Emerson: poverty consists in feeling poor.

F. Scott Fitzgerald: Optimism is the content of small men in high places.

Will Foley: The world is full of cactus, but we don't have to sit on it.

Benjamin Franklin: There are no ugly loves nor handsome prisons.

Mohandas Karamchand (Mahatma) Gandhi: I am an irrepressible optimist. No scientist starts his experiment with a faint heart. I belong to the tribe of Columbus and Stevenson, who hoped against hope in the face of heaviest odds. The days of miracles are not gone. They will abide so long as God abides.

Whoopi Goldberg: I don't have pet peeves, I have whole kennels of irritation!

Elbert Hubbard: We awaken in others the same attitude of mind we hold toward them.

Victor Hugo: Certain thoughts are prayers. There are moments when; whatever be the attitude of the body, the soul is on its knees.

William James: The greatest discovery of my generation is that human beings can alter their lives by altering their attitudes of mind.

William James: Human beings, by changing the inner attitudes of their minds, can change the outer aspects of their lives.

James Jeans: To travel hopefully is better than to arrive.

Susan Jeffers: We have been taught to believe that negative equals realistic and positive equals unrealistic.

Sir George Jessel (English judge, 1824-1883; Reply to Attorney General Coleridge when asked if he had any doubts regarding a recent issue, Jessel admitted that the story was true but rebuked the AG's misquotation of what Jessel had said by adding): "Coleridge, with his constitutional inaccuracy has told it wrong. I can never have said 'Often wrong.' **I may be wrong, and often am, but never in doubt.**

Carl Jung: It all depends on how we look at things, and not on how they are in themselves.

Harry Kalas (Philadelphia Phillies' Hall of Fame broadcaster, immediately after the Phillies 6-1 win over the Washington Nationals, at Citizens' Bank Ballpark, Philadelphia, PA to come from 7 games behind with 17 games to play and beat out the NY Metropolitans or Mets for The Greatest Comeback in Major League Baseball history, clinch the NL East Division Championship on the last day of the season, September 30, 2007, sang the song *"High Hopes"*): Once there was a little ole ant, thought he'd move a rubber tree plant; everyone knows an ant can't move a rubber tree plant, BUT HE HAD HIGH HOPES, HE HAD HIGH HOPES, HE HAD HIGH APPLE PIE IN THE SKY HOPES! So anytime you're feelin' low, 'stead of lettin' go, just remember that ant ... whoops there goes another rubber tree plant!

Charles Kettering: Where there is an open mind, there will always be a frontier.

Ann Landers: There are really only three types of people: those who make things happen, those who watch things happen, and those who say, What happened?

Sherman Langer: "Hostility" was his default mode.

John Lyly: It is the disposition of the foot that altereth the nature of the thing.

H.L. Mencken: An idealist [EDITOR: and some optimistic manufacturers, employers, and trial lawyers] is one who, on noticing that a rose smells better than a cabbage, concludes that it will also make better soup.

George Meredith: Always imitate the behavior of the winners when you lose.

John Homer Miller: You're living is determined not so much by what life brings to you as by the attitude you bring to life.

Minnesota Saying: Your mental attitude often depends upon your gastronomic attitude.

Alexander Pope (English poet, 1688-1744): All seems infected that the infected spy, / As all looks yellow to the jaundiced eye.

John Cowper Powys: What we steadily, consciously, habitually think we are, that we tend to become.

Will Rogers: Worrying is like paying on a debt that may never come due.

Will Rogers: What the country needs is dirtier fingernails and cleaner minds.

Will Rogers: Do the best you can, and don't take life too serious.

Will Rogers: The best way out of a difficulty is through it.

Will Rogers: The worst thing that happens to you may be the best thing for you if you don't let it get the best of you.

Will Rogers: The farmer has to be an optimist or he wouldn't still be a farmer.

Theodore Roosevelt: Whenever you are asked if you can do a job, tell him, Certainly, I can!—and get busy and find out how to do it.

Leo Rosten: CHUTSPA: Hebrew: "insolence." Gall, brazen effrontery, indescribable presumption-plus-arrogance. The classic definition of *chutspa* is this: *Chutspa* is that quality enshrined in the man who, having killed his mother and father, throws himself on the mercy of the court because he is an orphan.

Antoine de Saint-Exupery: The meaning of things lies not in the things themselves, but in our attitude towards them.

Carl Sandburg: In these times you have to be an optimist to open your eyes when you awake in the morning.

David Joseph Schwartz: How we think shows through in how we act. Attitudes are mirrors of the mind. They reflect thinking.

William Shakespeare (*Antony and Cleopatra,* Act II, iii): Keep yourself within yourself.

William Shakespeare (*The Rape of Lucrece,* 1.158): Then where is truth, if there be no self-trust?

George Bernard Shaw: The people who get on in this world are the people who get up and look for the circumstances they want and, if they can't find them, make them.

George Bernard Shaw: Do you know what a pessimist is? A man who thinks everybody as nasty as himself, and hates them for it.

Spanish Proverb: The eye of the master flattens the speed.

Benedict Spinoza: As long as a man imagines that he cannot do a certain thing, it is impossible for him to do it.

Lawrence Sterne: Every man will speak of the fair as his own market has gone in it.

Clement Stone: There is little difference in people... the little difference is attitude. The big difference is whether it is positive or negative.

Roland "Cooks Books" Suarez (slogan and emblem painted on his taxi, "Atlantic City's Goodwill Amabassador," popular entertaier and taxi driver in Atlantic City, NJ, stabbed to death March 31, 1985): Every day is a miracle.

Charles R. Swindoll: Words can never adequately convey the incredible impact of our attitude toward life. The longer I live the more convinced I become that life is 10% what happens to us and 90% how we respond to it.

Charles R. Swindoll: This may shock you, but I believe the single most significant decision I can make on a day-to-day basis is my choice of attitude. It is more important than my past, my education, my bankroll, my successes or failures, fame or pain, what other people think of me or say about me, my circumstances, or my position. Attitude is that "single string" that keeps me going our cripples my progress. It alone fuels my fire or assaults my hope. When my attitudes are right, there's no barrier too high, no valley too deep, no dream too extreme, no challenge too great for me.

James Thurber: You might as well fall flat on your face as lean over too far backward.

Leo Tolstoy: We lost because we told ourselves we lost.

Dale E. Turner: In all the work we do, our most valuable asset can be the attitude of self-examination. It is forgivable to make mistakes, but to stand fast behind a wall of self-righteousness and make the same mistake twice is not forgivable.

Mark Twain: The man who is a pessimist before 48 knows too much; if he is an optimistic after it, he knows too little.

UA: Growl all day and you'll feel dog tired at night.

John Updike: Any activity becomes creative when the doer cares about doing it right, or better.

Jimmy Valvanno (aka "Jimmy V," legendary college basketball coach): "Never give up! Don't ever give up!"

J. Donald Walters: Happiness is an attitude of mind, born of the simple determination to be happy under all outward circumstances.

Peter Weiss: The important thing/ is to pull yourself up by your own hair / to turn yourself inside out / and see the whole world with fresh eyes.

Oscar Wilde: Things are in their essence what we choose to make them. A thing is, according to the mode in which one looks at it. "Where others," says Blake, "see but the dawn coming over the hill, I see the sons of God shouting for joy."

Oscar Wilde: Selfishness is not living as one wishes to live; it is asking others to live as one wishes to live.

ATTORNEY FEES (See FEES)

AVARICE (See CHEAP; MONEY)

AVERAGE(S) (See STATISTICS)

BABY (See CHILDREN)

BAD/BADNESS (See EVIL)

BASEBALL (See GAME; GOLF)

BATTLE (See MILITARY)

BELIEFS (See ADVICE; CHARLEY CHAN; MAXIMS; TRUTH)

BIAS (See also CIVIL RIGHTS)

Uncle Anthony: You know, it's very tough to erase a first impression.

Uncle Anthony: Y'now there are bigots in every country – in Italy some people think they're better than others jes because they come from a "better" hill-town than the other people's hill-town.

Uncle Anthony: I ain't biased against nobody. Why, soma my best friends are ....

Aunt Mary Carlo: When somebody's thinkin' is weak, their prejudice is usually strong.

Aunt Mary Carlo: She sucha blue-blooded-snob-of-a-bitch dat when she sneezes she blows 'er damn hat off!

American Proverb: Acquaintances soften prejudices.

Simone de Beauvoir: Justice can never be done in the midst of injustice.

Simone de Beauvoir: But it is doubtless impossible to approach any human problem with a mind free from bias.

Henry Ward Beecher: Nothing dies so hard, or rallies so often as intolerance.

Ben American Horse (graduate of Carlisle Indian Industrial School, said to US Senator Albin Barkley, formerly Harry Truman's Vice President, in 1954): Young man (Senator Barkley), let me give you a little advice: be careful with your immigration laws; we were careless with ours.

Bible: Ecclesiastes, 3:20: All are of the dust, and all turn to dust again.

Bible: Ecclesiastes 9:16: The poor man's wisdom is despised, and his words are not heard.

Bible: Genesis, 43:32: The Egyptians might not eat bread with the Hebrews; for that is an abomination unto the Egyptians.

Bible: Jeremiah 13:23: Can the Ethiopian change his skin, or the leopard his spots?

Bible: Job, 19:25: They shall lie down alike in the dust, and the worms shall cover them.

Bible: John, 4:9: The Jews have no dealings with the Samaritans.

Bible: John 8:7: He that is without sin among you, let him first cast a stone.

Bible: John 13:16, and 15:20, and Matthew 10:24: The servant is not greater than his lord; neither is he that is sent greater than he that sent him.

Bible: Mark, 2:16: How is it that he eateth and drinketh with publicans and sinners?

Bible: Mark 10:31 and Matthew 19:30, and 20:16: The last shall be first, and the first last.

Bible: Proverbs, 22:2: The rich and poor meet together: the Lord is maker of them all.

Bible: Psalms 127:1: Except the Lord build the house, they labour in vain that build it.

Ambrose Bierce: A prejudice is a vagrant opinion without visible means of support.

Ambrose Bierce: BIGOT, n. One who is obstinately and zealously attached to an opinion that you do not share.

Ambrose Bierce: DISCRIMINATE, v. To note the particulars in which one person or thing is, if possible, more objectionable than another.

Ambrose Bierce: PREFERENCE, n. A sentiment or frame of mind, induced by the erroneous belief that one thing is better than another. An ancient philosopher, expounding his conviction that life is no better than death, was asked by a disciple why, then he did not die. "Because," he replied, "death is no better than life." It is longer.

Ambrose Bierce: PREJUDICE, n. A vagrant opinion without visible means of support.

Ambrose Bierce: REASON, n. Propensitate of prejudice.

Christian Nestell Bovee: Even when we fancy we have grown wiser, it is only, it may be, that new prejudices have displaced old ones.

Louis Brandeis: We must be ever on our guard, lest we erect our prejudices into legal principles.

Charlotte Bronte: Prejudices, it is well known, are most difficult to eradicate from the heart whose soil has never been loosened or fertilized by education; they grow there, firm as weeds among stones.

Archie Bunker (*"All in the Family"* TV show): Jesus was a Jew, yes, but only on his mother's side.

Archie Bunker: I got nothin' against mankind. It's people I can't stand.

Robert Byrne: Prejudices save time.

Lyman Lloyd Bryson: In totalitarian governments the bigots rule.

Albert B. "Happy" Chandler (MLB Commissioner and former US Senator from Kentucky, said in 1982 about integration of baseball by Jackie Robinson of the Brooklyn Dodgers in 1947): For 24 years my predecessor (MLB Comm. Mountain Keneshaw Landis) did not let the black man play. If you were black you did not qualify. It wasn't entirely his fault. It was what the (16 at the time) club owners wanted. But I didn't think it was right for these fellows to fight at Okinowa and Iwo Jima and then come home and not be allowed to play.

Carrie Chapman Catt: What is prejudice? An opinion, which is not based upon reason; a judgment, without having heard the argument; a feeling, without being able to trace from whence it came.

Lord Chesterfield (1752): Our prejudices are our mistresses; reason is at best our wife, very often heard indeed, but seldom minded.

Shirley Chisholm: Laws will not eliminate prejudice from the hearts of human beings. But that is no reason to allow prejudice to continue to be enshrined in our laws to perpetuate injustice through inaction.

Sir Winston Churchill: If the human race wishes to have a prolonged and indefinite period of material prosperity, they have only got to behave in a peaceful and helpful way toward one another.

Sir Winston Churchill: No folly is more costly than the folly of intolerant idealism.

Sir Winston Churchill: I cannot pretend to feel impartial about colors. I rejoice with the brilliant ones and am genuinely sorry for the poor browns.

Charles Caleb Colton: We hate some persons because we do not know them; and we will not know them because we hate them.

Charles Curtis (Massachusetts lawyer, 1891-1959, *Commonplace Book*, 1957): There are only two ways to be quite unprejudiced and impartial. One is to be completely ignorant. The other is to be completely indifferent. Bias and prejudice are attitudes to be kept in hand, not attitudes to be avoided.

Ernest Dimnet: Prejudices subsist in people's imagination long after they have been destroyed by their experience.

Frederick Douglass (invited to have tea with President Lincoln at the White House): Lincoln is the first white man I ever spent an hour with who did not reminded me that I am a Negro.

Sir William Drummond: He who will not reason is a bigot; he who cannot is a fool; and he who dares not is a slave.

W. E. B. DuBois: Any discrimination based simply on race or color is barbarous, we care not how hallowed it be by custom, experience or prejudice.

Ralph Waldo Emerson: We do what we must, and call it by the best names.

Ralph Waldo Emerson: We are born believing. A man bears beliefs as a tree bears apples.

W.C. Fields: I am free of all prejudice. I hate everyone equally.

Al Frankin: It's (unfair media accusations of bias/prejudice) like accusing the local library of having a murder-mystery-bias – when you only go to the "Murder-Mystery" aisle!

Frederick The Great (letter to Voltaire, 1771): Drive out prejudices by the door, they will come back by the window.

James M. Gilis: Whom the gods would make bigots, they first deprive of humor.

Goethe (German lawyer, poet, 1749-1832): I can promise to be upright but not to be unprejudiced.

Horace Greeley: There is no bigotry like that of "free thought" run to seed.

Dick Gregory: If the man calls me a nigger, he is calling the something I am not. The nigger exists only in his own mind; therefore his mind is the nigger. I must feel sorry for such a man.

William Hazlitt (English essayist, 1778-1830): Prejudice is the child of ignorance.

William Hazlitt: There is no prejudice so strong as that which arises from a fancied exemption from all prejudice.

William Hazlitt: Prejudice is never easy unless it can pass itself off for reason.

Lillian Hellman: Nobody outside of a baby carriage or a judge's chamber believes in an unprejudiced point of view

Heraclitus (c. 500 B.C.): Dogs bark at a person whom they do not know.

Eric Hoffer: Absolute faith corrupts as absolutely as absolute power.

Oliver Wendell Holmes, Jr.: Any man who says he is impartial about any subject on which he speaks is either ignorant or a liar.

Oliver Wendell Holmes, Jr.: Deep-seated preferences cannot be argued about – you cannot argue a man into liking a glass of beer – and therefore, when differences are sufficiently far-reaching, we try to kill the other man rather than let him have his way. But that is perfectly consistent with admitting that, so far as appears, his grounds are just as good as ours.

Oliver Wendell Holmes Sr.: The mind of the bigot is like the pupil of the eye. The more light you shine on it, the more it will contract.

William James: A great many people think they are thinking when they are merely rearranging their prejudices.

Jewish Saying: Prejudice joins hate to fear.

Jewish Saying: Prejudice is a sickness in the brain.

Jewish Saying: Prejudice is reason's enemy.

Juan Ramon Jimenez: The world is like a map of antipathies, almost of hates, in which everyone picks the symbolic color of his difference.

Samuel Johnson: To be prejudiced is always to be weak.

Junius: When once a man is determined to believe, the very absurdity of the doctrine does but confirm him in his faith.

Florynce R. Kennedy: Every form of bigotry can be found in ample supply in the legal system of our country. It would seem that Justice (usually depicted as a woman) is indeed blind to racism, sexism, war and poverty.

Walter Lippman: The tendency of the casual mind is to pick out or stumble upon a sample which supports or defies its prejudices, and then to make it the representative of a whole class

Walter Lippman: In the blood of the Martyrs to intolerance are the seeds of unbelief.

Clare Booth Luce (American playwright, congresswoman, US Ambassador to Italy): What generally passes for "thought" among the majority of mankind is the time one takes out to rearrange one's prejudices.

Joseph McCarthy: I cannot tolerate bogots. They are all so obstinate, so opinionated.

H.L. Mencken: Criticism is prejudice made plausible.

H.L. Mencken: One may no more live in the world without picking up the moral prejudices of the world than one will be able to go to hell without perspiring.

Edward R. Murrow: Everyone is a prisoner of his own experiences. No one can eliminate prejudices—just recognize them.

J. Middleton Murry: We like to know where we are, and that depends upon our knowing where everybody else is.... A prejudice that we can allow for is much more dependable than a suspension of judgment that we cannot.

Michael A. Musmanno (Justice of Pennsylvania Supreme Court, 1959): A prejudiced person may have the right to hurt himself through the indulgence of his prejudices, but he has no right to affect the liberty of others.

Michael A. Musmanno (Justice of Pennsylvania Supreme Court, 1959): No juror has the right to enter the jury box with a personal ax to grind, a blade to sharpen, or a row to hoe. Every juror must be as neutral as the rays of the sun which light up hill and dale with equal impartiality, he must be as unprejudiced as the falling snow, he must be as unbiased as the angel of truth. A juror should have only one obligation, only one duty, and only one objective, and that is to look always to the Truth, as the needle of the compass points always to the North. And as the compass can not be affected by the elements, the mind of the juror should not be influenced by thoughts of reward or the infliction of revenge, or, as in this case, by the possible motivation of brandishing red or menace.

Caliph Omar (regarding the disruption of 700,000 manuscripts of the Alexandria Library): Either these books conform to the Koran or they do not. If they do, they are not needed; if they do not, they are positively harmful. Therefore, let them be destroyed.

Thomas Paine: No man is prejudiced in favor of a thing knowing it to be wrong. He is attached to it on the belief of its being right.

William Penn: It were better to be of no church than to be bitter for any.

James Harvey Robinson: Most of our so-called reasoning consists in finding arguments for going on believing as we already do.

Will Rogers: You know everybody is ignorant, only on different subjects.

Will Rogers: People's minds are changed through observation and not through argument.

Will Rogers: We will never have true civilization until we have learned to recognize the rights of others.

Will Rogers: An ignorant person is one who doesn't know what you have just found out.

Charles Victor Roman: The ignorant are always prejudiced and the prejudiced are always ignorant.

Eleanor Roosevelt: I believe it is essential to our leadership in the world and to the development of true democracy in our country to have no discrimination in our country whatsoever. This is most important in the schools of our country.

J.K. Rowling: Indifference and neglect often do much more damage then outright dislike.

Bertrand Russell: A stupid man's report of what a clever man says can never be accurate, because he unconsciously translates what he hears into something he can understand.

Bertrand Russell: Every man, wherever he goes, is encompassed by a cloud of comforting convictions, which move with him like flies on a summer day.

Antoine de Saint-Exupery: The meaning of things lies not in the things themselves, but in our attitude towards them.

William H. Seward (New York lawyer, NY Governor, statesman, 1801-1872, speaking to Stephen Douglas on the U.S. Senate floor): Douglas, no man will ever be president of United States who spells Negro with two g's.

Diane B. Schulder: "... prejudice (the mythology of class oppression) is enshrined in laws. Laws lead to enforcement of practices. Practices reinforce and lead to prejudice. The cycle continues ...."

William Shakespeare (*Hamlet*, Act II, ii): All which, sir, I most powerfully and potently believe, yet I hold it not honestly to have it thus set down.

William Shakespeare (*The Merchant of Venice*, Act I, iii): I will buy with you, sell with you, talk with you, walk with you, and so following; but I will not eat with you, drink with you, nor pray with you.

Lillian Smith: Knowing that bitterness (and prejudice, slavery and racism) is a poor bend key to use to unlock the old rusty door of human failure, I wanted her to begin her search for these answers with sympathy for those who had not found them.

John Lancaster Spalding: Our prejudices are like physical infirmities – we cannot do what thay prevent us from doing.

Gerry Spence: I would rather have a mind opened by wonder than one closed by belief.

Jonathan Swift: Some men, under the notion of weeding out prejudices, eradicate virtue, honesty, and religion.

Glenn Terrell (Chief Justice Florida Supreme Court, 1876-1964): It is doubtful if the sinister influence of the remarks ... made to the jury ... could be erased by withdrawal or any abmonition the Court could give. In fact, this thing of softening prejudices and erasing sinister influences once created is extremely tenuous and of doubtful consummation and if it is in the nature of a prejudice, it is more difficult to get rid of.... It clings to the mind like a tatoo on the epidermis. Carlile v. State, 129 Fla 860, 865 (1937)

Bess Truman: I deplore any action which denies artistic talent and opportunity to express itself because of prejudice against race origin.

Mark Twain (in *Concerning the Jews*, 1899): I have no race prejudices, and I think I have no color prejudices nor creed prejudices. Indeed, I know it. I can stand any society. All I care to know is that a man is a human being – that is enough for me; he can't be any worse.

Mark Twain: We are chameleons, and our partialities and prejudices change places with an easy and blessed facility.

Mark Twain: In religion and politics people's beliefs and convictions are in almost every case gotten at second-hand, and without examination.

Mark Twain: The very ink with which all history is written is merely fluid prejudice.

Voltaire: Prejudices, friend, are the kings of the vulgar herd.

Booker T. Washington: You can't hold a man down without staying down with him

George Washington: No nation (or man) is to trusted farther than it is bound by its (his) interests.

Naomi Weisstein: The problem with insight, sensitivity and intuition is that they tend to confirm our biases. At one time people were convinced of their ability to identify witches. All it required was sensitivity to the workings of the devil. Clinical experience is not the same thing as empirical evidence.

BIG BUSINESS (See CORPORATE THINKING)

BIGOTRY (See BIAS)

BLAME (See ALLEGATION)

BOLD/BOLDNESS (See AGGRESSIVE)

BOOKS (See also WORDS)

Uncle Anthony: You keep crackin' those books like your father says and you'll make yourself and him proud.

Uncle Anthony: Don't forget to read the best book your mom used read to me when I was a kid – the Bible.

Aunt Mary Carlo: If you love books, you'll never go to bed alone.

Aunt Mary Carlo: If ya look at yer mom's bookshelf you'll see her childhood.

A. Bronson Alcott: One must be a wise reader to quote wisely and well.

A. Bronson Alcott: That is a good book which is opened with expectation, and closed with profit.

A. Bronson Alcott: Books are the most mannerly of companions, accessible in all times, in all moods, frankly declaring the author's mind, without offence.

Arab Proverb: A book is like a garden carried in the pocket.

Francis Bacon: Books are ships which pass through vast seas of time.

Francis Bacon: Some books are to be tasted, others to be swallowed, and some few to be chewed and digested.

James Baldwin: It was books that taught me that the things that tormented me were the very things that connected me with all the people who were alive, or who have ever been alive.

Henry Ward Beecher: A library is but the soul's burial ground. It is the land of shadows.

Henry Ward Beecher: Where is human nature so weak as in the bookstore?

Bible: Ecclesiastes 12:12: Of making many books there is no end; and much study is a weariness of the flesh.

Bible: Job, 19:23: Oh that my words were now written! Oh that they were printed in a book.

Bible: John, 5:39: Search the scriptures; for in them ye think ye have eternal life: and they are they which testify of me.

Bible: John, 21:25: If they should be written every one, I suppose that even the world itself could not contain the books that should be written.

Bible: Psalms, 119:105: Thy word is a lamp unto my feet, and a light unto my feet.

Ambrose Bierce: The covers of this book are too far apart.

Ambrose Bierce: DIARY, n. A daily record of that part of one's life, which he can relate to himself without blushing.

Ambrose Bierce: DICTIONARY, n. A malevolent literary device for cramping the growth of a language and making it hard and inelastic. The dictionary, however, is a most useful work.

Ambrose Bierce: ELEGY, n. A composition in verse, in which, without employing any of the methods of humor, the writer aims to produce in the reader's mind the dampest kind of objection....

Ambrose Bierce: HISTORIAN, n. A broad-guage gossip.

Ambrose Bierce: HISTORY, n. An account mostly false, of events mostly unimportant, which are brought about by rulers mostly knaves, and soldiers mostly fools.

Ambrose Bierce: MYTHOLOGY, n. The body of a primitive people's beliefs concerning its origin, early history, heroes, deities and so forth, as distinguished from the true accounts which it invents later.

Ambrose Bierce: NOVEL, n. A short story padded. A species of composition bearing the same relation to literature that the panorama bears to art. As it is too long to be read at a sitting the impressions made by its successive parts are successively effaced, as in the panorama. Unity, totality of effect, is impossible; for besides the few pages last read all that is carried in mind is the mere plot of what has gone before. To the romance the novel is what photography is to painting. Its distinguishing principle, probability, corresponds to the literal actuality of the photograph and puts it distinctly into the category of reporting;

whereas the free wing of the romancer enables him to mount to such altitudes of imagination as he may be fitted to attain; and the first three essentials of the literary art are imagination, imagination and imagination. The art of writing novels, such as it was, is long dead everywhere except in Russia, where it is new. Peace to its ashes – some of which have a large sale.

Ambrose Bierce: PLAGIARISM, n. A literary coincidence compunded of a discreditable priority and an honorable subsequence.

Ambrose Bierce: PLAGIARIZE, v. To take the thought or style of another writer whom one has never, never read.

Ambrose Bierce: POETRY, n. A form of expression peculiar to the Land beyond the Magazines.

Ambrose Bierce: PUBLISH, v. In literary affairs, to become the fundamental element in a cone of critics.

Ambrose Bierce: QUILL, n. An implement of torture yielded by a goose and commonly wielded by an ass. This use of the quill is now obsolete, but its modern equivalent, the steel pen, is wielded by the same everlasting Presence.

Ambrose Bierce: READING, n. The general body of what one reads. In our country it consists, as a rule, of Indiana novels, short stories in "dialect" and humor in slang.

Ambrose Bierce: REVELATION, n. A famous book in which St. John the Divine concealed all that he knew. The revealing is done by the commentators, who know nothing.

Ambrose Bierce: RIME, n. Agreeing sounds in the terminals of verse, mostly bad. The verses themselves, as distinguished from prose, mostly dull. Usually (and wickedly) spelled "rhyme."

Ambrose Bierce: RIMER, n. A poet regarded with indifference or disesteem.

Ambrose Bierce: ROMANCE, n. Fiction that owes no allegiance to the God of Things as They Are. In the novel the writer's thought is tethered to probability, as a domestic horse to the hitching-post, but in romance it ranges at will over the entire region of the imagination – free, lawless, immune to bit and rein. ...

Ambrose Bierce: SALACITY, n. A certain literary quality frequently observed in popular novels, especially in those written by women and young girls, who give it another name and think that in introducing it they are occupying a neglected field of letters and reaping an overlooked harvest. If they have the misfortune to live long enough they are tormented with a desire to burn their sheaves.

Ambrose Bierce: SATIRE, n. An obsolete kind of literary composition in which the vices and follies of the author's enemies were expounded with imperfect tenderness....

Ambrose Bierce: SCRAP-BOOK, n. A book that is commonly edited by a fool. Many persons of some small distinction compile scrap-books containing whatever they happen to read about themselves or employ others to collect.

Ambrose Bierce: SCRIPTURES, n. The sacred books of our holy religion, as distinguished from the false and profane writings on which all other faiths are based.

Ambrose Bierce: SERIAL, n. A literary work, usually a story that is not true, creeping through several issues of a newspaper or magazine. Frequently appended to each instalment is a "synopsis of preceding chapters" for those who have not read them, but a direr need is a synopsis of succeeding chapters for those who do not intend to read *them*. A synopsis of the entire work would be still better.

Ambrose Bierce: SPOOKER, n. A writer whose imagination concerns itself with supernatural phenomena, especially the doings of spooks....

Ambrose Bierce: STORY, n. A narrative, commonly untrue....

Horace Binney (Pennsylvania lawyer, 1780-1875, *Letter to S. Austin Allibone*, 1866): One may recollect generally that certain thoughts or facts are to be found in a certain book; but without a good Index such a recollection may hardly be more available than that of the cabin-boy, who knew where the ship's tea-kettle was, because he saw it fall overboard. In truth, a very large part of every man's reading falls overboard, and unless he has good Indexes he will never find it again.

Alice Williams Brotherton (Ballade of Poor Bookworms" 1930): Books we must have though we lack bread.

Pearl S. Buck: There are persons who honestly do not see the use of books in the home, either for information – have they not radio and even television? – or for decoration – is there not the wallpaper?

Lord Byron: A drop of ink may make a million think.

Lord John Campbell (Chief Justice, Queen's Bench, and Lord Chancellor of Great Britain, 1779-1861, 3 *Lives of the Chief Justices: Preface*): So essential did I consider an Index to be to every book, that I proposed to bring a Bill into parliament to deprive an author who publishes a book without an Index of the privilege of copyright; and moreover, to subject him, for his offence, to a pecuniary penalty.

Raymoond Chandler: A good title is the title of a successful book.

Chinese Proverb: A book is like a garden carried in the pocket.

Sir Winston Churchill: There is a good saying to the effect that when a new book appears one should read an old one. As an author I would not recommend too strict an adherence to this saying.

Sir Winston Churchill (September 1944 Incription on his gift to FDR of his 1944 book of WWII War Speeches, *"ON TO VICTORY"*at The Second Quebec Conference): A fresh egg from the faithful hen. Quebec 1944.

Sir Winston Churchill: Please be good enough to put your conclusions and recommendations on one sheet of paper in the very beginning of your report, so I can even consider reading it.

Sir Winston Churchill: History will be kind to me for I intend to write it.

Sir Winston Churchill: Writing is an adventure. To begin with, it is a toy and an amusement. Then it becomes a mistress, then it becomes a master, then it becomes a tyrant. The last phase is that just as you are about to be reconciled to your servitude, you kill the monster and fling him to the public.

Cicero: A room without a book is like a body without a soul.

Adelaide Crapsey ("The Immortal Residue," 1914): Wouldst thou find my ashes? Look / In the pages of my book; / And, as this thy hands doth turn, / Know here is my funeral urn.

R. D. Cumming: A good book has no ending.

George W. Dalzell (Washington, D.C. lawyer, *Benefit of Clergy: Preface*, 1955): I anticipate slippered readers rather than academicians.

George W. Dalzell (*Benefit of Clergy: Preface*, 1955): The function of the preface is to ingratiate the author with the reader in a naive effort to forestall criticism by a show of modesty.

Robertson Davis: A truly great book should be read in youth, again in maturity and once more in old age, as a fine building should be seen by morning light, at noon and by moonlight.

Benjamin Disraeli: A book may be as great a thing as a battle.

William Orville Douglas (Connecticut lawyer, Assoc Justice US Supreme Court): Book burning is as old as books.

Albert Einstein (asked if he knew the speed of sound in Boston, 1921): I did not carry such information in my mind because it is readily available in books.

Dwight D. Eisenhower: Don't join the book-burners. Don't think you're going to conceal faults by concealing evidence that they ever existed.

Charles W. Eliot: Books are the quietest and most constant of friends... and the most patient of teachers.

T.S. Eliot (American born, British poet, dramatist and literary critic; 1888-1965): Most editors are failed writers, but so are most writers.

Ralph Waldo Emerson: What's a book? Everything or nothing. The eye that sees it all.

Ralph Waldo Emerson: A man is known by the books he reads.

Ralph Waldo Emerson: Some books leave us free and some books make us free.

Ralph Waldo Emerson: If we encountered a man of rare intellect, we should ask him what books he read.

Ralph Waldo Emerson: Men over forty are no judges of a book written in a new spirit.

Ralph Waldo Emerson: There are books ... which take rank in our life with parents and lovers and passionate experiences.

Ralph Waldo Emersen: The book that alarms one man, threatening the disorganization of society, is heard by one of higher principle with no more emotion than the cheeping of a mouse in the wall.

English Church saying (An medievil form of excommunication closed with these words): "Do to the book, quench the candle, ring the bell!" Hence the expression: Bell, book and candle.

English Saying: The three proverbial roads to success at the bar – influence, a book, or a miracle.

Clifton Fadiman: When you reread a classic you do not see more in the book than you did before; you see more in *you* than was there before.

Professor J. Rufus Fears (Professor of Classics, University of Oklahoma; *Books That Have Made History: Books That Can Change Your Life,* The Teaching Company, 2005): "What do we mean by a great book? Can we even speak of great books? // The answer is yes. *Great book* is an unfathionable, even controversial term today, because it implies value judgments. As a society, we do not wish to make value judgments. *Judgmental* is an expression of reproach. However, great books are great precisely because they challenge us to make value judgments. // A great book has the following three essential qualities:

1. Great theme. A great book is concerned with themes and issues of enduring importance.
2. Noble language ..., language that elevates the soul and ennobles the mind. It is not the specific language, say Latin or English, that is noble. Any language can be used in such a way that it conveys ideas and emotions powerfully and memorably.
3. Universality. A great book is "a possession for all time" (Thucydides). It speaks across the ages, reaching the hearts and minds of men and women far removed in time and space from the era and circumstances in which it was composed. Thus, a great book summarizes the enduring values and ideas of a great age and gives them as a legacy to generations to come.

William Feather: Finishing a good book is like leaving a good friend.

E.M. Forster: One always tends to overpraise a long book, because one has got through it.

Benjamin Franklin: Read much, but not many Books.

Joseph Goerbels, German Propoganda Minister (May 10, 1933, "THE BOOK BURNING" in Berlin, outside the Berlin Opera House, to 40,000 Germans): Jewish Intellectualism is dead! ... the German soul can again express itself!

Oliver Goldsmith: The first time I read an excellent book, it is to me as if I had gained a new friend. When I read over a book I have perused before, it resembles the meeting with an old one.

Sam Goldwyn: I read part of it all the way through.

Alfred Whitney Griswold: Books won't stay banned. They won't burn. Ideas won't go to jail.

Ernest Hemingway: All good books are alike in that they are truer than if they really happened and after you are finished reading one you will feel that all that happened to you and afterwards it all belongs to you.

Lenore Hershey: Do give books – religious or otherwise – for Christmas. They're never fattening, seldom sinful, and permanently personal.

Oliver Wendell Holmes, Sr.: The foolishest book is a kind of leaky boat on a sea of wisdom; some of the wisdom will get in anyhow.

Oliver Wendell Holmes, Sr.: The first thing naturally when one enters a scholar's study or library, is to look at his books. One gets a notion very speedily of his tastes and the range of his pursuits by a glance around his bookshelves.

Victor Hugo: It is from books that wise men derive consolation in the troubles of life.

Irish Proverb: Time is a great story teller.

Italian Proverb: There is no worse robber than a bad book.

Japanese Proverb: If you believe everything you read, better not read.

Thomas Jefferson: I cannot live without books.

Carolina Maria de Jesus: The book is man's best invention so far.

Charles E. Jones: You are the same today as you will be five years from now except for two things ... the people you meet and the books you read.

Benjamin Jowett: One man is as good as another until he has written a book.

Amy Lowell: All books are either dreams or swords, / You can cut, or you can drug, with words.

Martin Luther: Every great book is an action, and every great action is a book.

Martin Luther (in 1545, Martin Luther wanted to refute Islam by publishing the Koran in several languages for all to read): To honor Christ, to do good for Christians, to harm the Turks, to vex the Devil, SET THIS BOOK [the Koran] FREE, and do not withhold it.

Groucho Marx: From the moment I picked up your book until I laid it down, I was convulsed with laughter. Some day I intend reading it.

Herman Melville (New York lawyer, sailor, novelist, 1819-1891): Those whom books will hurt will not be proof against events. If some books are deemed most baneful and their sale forbid, how, then, with deadlier facts, not dreams of doting men? Events, not books, should be forbid.

H.L. Mencken: There are some people who read too much: bibliobibuli. I know some who are constantly drunk on books, as other men are drunk on whiskey or religion. They wander through this most diverting and stimulating of worlds in a haze, seeing nothing and hearing nothing.
Henry Miller: Until it is kindled by a spirit as flaminbgly alive as the one which gave it birth a book is dead to us.
Henry Miller: A book is a part of life, a manifestation of life, just as much as a tree or a horse or a star. It obeys its own rhythms, it own laws, whether it be a novel, a play, or a diary.
Milton: A wise man like a good refiner, can gather gold out of the drossiest volume.
Michel de Montaigne: There are more books upon books than upon any other subject.
Christopher Morley: The real purpose of books is to trap the mind into doing its own thinking.
Christopher Morley: There is no mistaking a real book when one meets it. It is like falling in love.
Kathleen Norris: Just the knowledge that a good book is awaiting one at the end of a long day makes the day happier.
Austin Phelps: Wear the old coat and buy the new book.
Emile Poulsson: Books are keys to wisdom's treasure; / Books are gates to lands of pleasure; / Books are paths that upward lead; / Books are friends. Come, let us read.
Ezra Pound: Literature is news that stays news.
Roscoe Pound (American lawyer, dean Harvard Law School, legal writer, 1870-1964, *Book Review*, 60 Yale L.J. 200, 1951): Sir Frederick Pollock [EDITOR: an English lawyer, writer, legal historian, 1847-1937] used to say that a man who would publish a book without an index ought to be banished ten miles beyond Hell where the Devil himself could not go because of the stinging nettles.
Royal Air Force saying (referring to the officer of the day's log, something remarkable was): One for the book.
Will Rogers: When you put down the good things you ought to have done, and leave out the bad ones you did do – well, that's Memoirs.
Will Rogers: There aint nothing that breaks up homes, country, and nations like somebody publishing their memoirs.
Will Rogers: I read about eight newspapers in a day. When I'm in a town with only one newspaper, I read it eight times.
Will Rogers: All I know is just what I read in the papers, and that's an alibi for my ignorance.
Franklin D. Roosevelt: We all know that books burn—yet we have the greater knowledge that books cannot be killed by fire. People die, but books never die. No man and no force can abolish memory.
Bertrand Russell: There are two motives for reading a book: one, that you enjoy it; the other, that you can boast about it.
George Santayana: People compare books with other books, not with experience.
William Shakespeare *(As You Like It*, Act V, iv): O, sir, we quarrel in print, by the book; as you have books for good manners.
William Shakespeare (*Cymbeline*, Act V, iv): A book? O rare one! / Be not, as in our fangled world, a garment / Nobler than it covers.
William Shakespeare (*Love's Labour's Lost*, Act IV, ii): You two are book-men.
William Shakespeare (*Love's Labour's Lost*, Act IV, ii): Sir, he hath never fed of the dainties that are bred in a book.
William Shakespeare (*The Merchant of Venice*, Act IV, i): We turn'd o'er many books together.
William Shakespeare (*Othello*, Act I, i): The bookish theoric.
William Shakespeare (*Romeo and Juliet*, Act I, iii): That book in many's eyes doth share the glory, / That in gold clasps locks in the golden story.
William Shakespeare (*The Tempest*, Act I, ii): Knowing I loved my books, he furnish'd me / From mine own library with volumes that / I prize above my dukedom.
William Shakespeare (*The Tempest*, Act I, i): Deeper than did ever plummet sound, / I'll drown my book.
George Bernard Shaw: This unseemly wretch should be seized and put out, bell, book, candle and all, until he learns to behave himself.
Thomas Sheridan: While you converse with lords and dukes, I have their betters here – my books.
Roy L. Smith: A good book contains more real wealth than a good bank.

Roy L. Smith: Some good book is usually responsible for the success of every really great man.
Sydney Smith (English clergyman, writer, wit, 1771-1845): No furniture is so charming as books.
Gerttrude Stein: The central theme of the novel is that they were glad to see each other.
Jonathan Swift: When I am reading a book, whether wise or silly, it seems to me to be alive and talking to me.
Henry David Thoreau: Books must be read as deliberately and reservedly as they are written
Henry David Thoreau: How many a man has dated a new era in his life from the reading of a book.
Henry David Thoreau: Books are the treasured wealth of the world, the fit inheritance of generations and nations.
Henry David Thoreau: Read the best books first, or you may not have a chance to read them at all.
Mark Twain: It takes a heap of sense to write good nonsense.
Mark Twain: A successful book is not made of what is *in* it, but of what is left *out* of it.
Mark Twain: The man who doesn't read good books has no advantage over the man who can't read them.
Mark Twain: Good friends, good books and a sleepy conscience: this is the ideal life.
Mark Twain: The very ink with which all history is written is merely fluid prejudice.
Mark Twain: Write without pay until somebody offers pay. If nobody offers within three years the candidate may look upon his circumstances with the most implicit confidence as the sign that sawing wood is what he was intended for.
Mark Twain: There ain't nothing more to write about, and I am rotten glad of it, because if I'd knowed what a trouble it was to make a book I wouldn't a tackled it, and ain't agoing to no more.
Mark Twain (On reading statutes) (*Roughing It*, while on his way to Nevada to be secretary to his brother, Governor of the Teritory, Twain read the U.S. Rev. Statutes): I had many an exciting day ... reading the statutes and the dictionary and wondering how the characters would turn out.
Mark Twain (on the Bible): It is full of interest. It has noble poetry in it; and some clever fables; and some blood-drenched history; and some good morals; and a wealth of obscenities; and upwards of a thousand lies.
Mark Twain: The Christian's Bible is a drug store. Its contents remain the same, but the medicine practice changes.
Mark Twain: "*Classic.*" A book which people praise and don't read.
Mark Twain: Biographies are but the clothes and buttons of the man—the biography of the man himself cannot be written.
Gore Vidal: Today's public figures can no longer write their own speeches or books, and there is some evidence that they can't read them either.
James J. Walker (mayor of New York City): No girl was ever ruined by a book.
Carolyn Wells: The books we think we ought to read are poky, dull, and dry; / The books that we would like to read we are ashamed to buy; / The books that people talk about we never can recall; / And the books that people give us, oh, they're the worst of all.
Woodrow Wilson: I would never read a book if it were possible for me to talk half an hour with the man who wrote it.
Francis Yeats-Brown: To me the charm of an encyclopedia is that it knows – and I needn't.

BORE (See ORATORY)

BOYS (See CHILDREN)

BRAINS (See IGNORANCE; TRUTH; WISDOM)

BRAVE/BRAVERY (See COURAGE)

BREVITY (See ORATORY)

BROMIDES (See ADVICE; CHARLEY CHAN)

BURDEN OF PROOF (See EVIDENCE)

BUREAUCRACY (See GOVERNMENT)

BUSINESS (See CORPORATE THINKING)

BUSY (See Work)

CALAMITY (See TROUBLE)

CANADA (See STATES of U.S. & CANADA)

CARE (See NEGLIGENCE; RISK)

CARELESS/CARELESSNESS (See NEGLIGENCE)

CAUSATION

Uncle Anthony: Don't go confusing coincidence with cause and effect. Just because I dim the lights when the sun sets, don't mean I caused the night to fall.

Uncle Anthony: It ain't that he causes accidents, it's just that he starts things he can't finish, and then sometimes he even starts things he can't even begin to start.

Aunt Mary Carlo: I tink he ran inta an accident dat started out ta happen to somebody else.

Aunt Mary Carlo: Yer Uncle picked a horse he was sure would win ina walk – problem was da udder horses ran.

African Proverb: Do not look where you fell, but where you slipped.

St. Thomas Aquinas (Italian philosopher, 1225-1274, *Summa Theologicae*, 1265): What ever moves is moved by another.

Henri Frederic Amiel: How true it is that our destinies are decided by nothings and that a small imprudence helped by some insignificant accident, as an acorn is fertilized by a drop of rain, may raise the trees on which perhaps we and others shall be crucified.

Aristotle: Wisdom is the knowledge of causes

Aristotle: There are 4 Causes according to Aristotle:

1. Efficient cause = circumstances that produce it/something/someone
2. Material cause = material of which it was composed
3. Formal cause = its structural or developmental principles
4. Final cause = its purpose or place in the natural scheme

Bahya Ben Asher: The man who ascribes things to accident sees a bird's nest and thinks it has no special purpose.

Bible: James 3:5: How great a matter a little fire kindleth!

Bible: Luke 6:28 and Mark 4:24: With what measure ye mete, it shall be measured to you.

Bible: Psalms, 7:16: His mischief shall return upon his own head.

Bible: Romans, 5:19: By one man's disobedience many were made sinners.

Francis Bacon: To know truly is to know by causes.

Ambrose Bierce: DESTINY, n. A tyrant's authority for crime and a fool's excuse for failure.

Ambrose Bierce: EFFECT, n. The second of two phenomena which always occur together in the same order. The first, called a Cause, is said to generate the other – which is no more sensible than it would be for one who has never seen a dog except in pursuit of a rabbit to declare the rabbit the cause of the dog.

Ambrose Bierce: INTENTION, n. The mind's sense of the prevalence of one set of influences over another set; an effect whose cause is the imminence, immediate or remote, of the performance of an involuntary act.

Ambrose Bierce: PREDESTINATION, n. The doctrine that all things occur according to programme. This doctrine should not be confused with that of foreordination, which means that all things are programmed, but does not affirm their occurrence, that being only by implication from other doctrines by which it is entailed. The difference is great enough to have deluged Christendom with ink, to say nothing of the gore. With the distinction of the two doctrines kept well in mind, and a reverent belief in both, one may hope to escape perdition if spared.

Cervantes (*Don Quixote*, 1605): Take away the cause, and the effect ceases; what the eye ne'er sees, the heart ne'er rues.

Cervantes: Do away with the cause, you do away with a sin.

G.K. Chesterton: There is something strange in the modern mind, by which a material cause always seems more like a real cause. (See Aristotle, above)

Sir Winston Churchill: It is a mistake to look too far ahead. Only one link of the chain of destiny can be handled at a time.

Sir Winston Churchill: I pass with relief from the tossing sea of Cause and Theory to the firm ground of Result and Fact.

Chinese Proverb: Not the cry, but the flight of the wild duck, leads the flock to fly and follow.

Cicero: The causes of events are evermore interesting than the events themselves.

Sir Edward Coke (1628): The cause having ceased, the effect ceases also.

Dante Alighieri (Italian epic poet, 1265-1321): A mighty flame followeth a tiny spark

Dante: If thou follow thy star, thou canst not fail of glorious heaven.

Ralph Waldo Emerson: The sower may mistake and sow his peas crookedly; the peas make no mistake, but come up and show his line.

Ralph Waldo Emerson: The secret of the world is the tie between person and event. Person makes event and event person.

Ralph Waldo Emerson: Shallow men believe in luck .... Strong men believe in cause and effect.

Ralph Waldo Emerson: What we seek we shall find; what we flee from flees from us.

Ralph Waldo Emerson: As we are, so we do; and as we do, so is it done to us; we are the builders of our fortunes.

Ralph Waldo Emerson: Behind the course of that is a fine cause.... Cause and effect are two sides of one fact.

Ralph Waldo Emerson: Cause and effect, means and ends, seed and fruit, cannot be served; for the effect already blooms in the cause, the end preexists in the means, the fruit in the seed.

Ralph Waldo Emerson: Do not clutch at sensual sweetness until it is ripe on the slow tree of cause and effect.

Ralph Waldo Emerson: Cause and effect are two sides of one fact.

Ralph Waldo Emerson: Cause and effect, the chancellors of God.

Ralph Waldo Emerson: Everything is the cause of itself.

English Proverb: Take away the cause and the effect must cease.

Euripides (c. 423 B.C.): A bad beginning makes a bad ending.

Jean Giraudoux: Destiny is simply the relentless logic of each day we live.

Goethe: Everything we do has a result. But that which is right and prudent does not always lead to good, nor the contrary to what is bad.

Goethe: Destiny grants us our wishes, but in its own way, in order to give us something beyond our wishes.

Dag Hammarskjold: We are not permitted to choose the frame of our destiny. But what we put into it is ours.

George Herbert: The effect speaks, the tongue needs not.

Russ Herman: A " substantial cause" for any catastrophe ("accident," incident, or traumatic event) need not be a matter of a large percentage or majority or more than 50% of the overall input into the happening of the event ("accident," incident, collision, etc): a substantial cause can be just 1% or one drop in the overall factual situation. [DEMONSTATE with a glass of water and a drop of dye] When you drop one little drop of poison (or negligence, or fault) into a big glass of pure water, it only constitutes a small % of the glass of water, BUT IT DOES MAKE A SUBTANTIAL DIFFERENCE doesn't it? That is because a little bit of negligence (or fault or wrongful conduct) in the overall scheme of the factual events of this case, can be, were, and will forever be "A SUBSTANTIAL CAUSE" of the bad result (or the serious injury or wrongful death) to this plaintiff Mr./Mrs./Miss/Ms. (X).

Homer (c. 850 B.C.): In seeing the stubble one may judge what the grain was.

Thomas Henry Huxley: Logical consequences are the scarecrows of fools and the beacons of wise men.

Irish Proverb: Even a small thorn causes festering.

William James: As in the night all cats are gray, so in the darkness of metaphysical criticism all causes are obscure.

William James: The word CAUSE is an altar to an unknown god.

Sir William Rann Kennedy (English judge, 1846-1915): The classic quotation in **"EGGSHELL" SKULL CASES**; that is, a tortfeasor must take his victim as he finds him): If a man is negligently run over or otherwise negligently injured in his body, it is no answer to the sufferer's claim for damages that he would have suffered less injury, or no injury at all, if he had an unusually thin skull or an unusually weak heart. *Dulieu v. White & Sons*, 2 K.B. 669 (1901)

Henri De Lubac: The man who does not go down to underlying causes will never get at the heart of evil.

Lucan: The parent of the universe... fixed for eternity the causes whereby he keeps all things in order.

Lucan: Even from the beginnings of the world the descends a chain of causes.

Lucretius (1st century B.C.): Nothing comes from nothing.

Malay Proverb: It is the fate of the coconut husk to float, for the stone to sink.

Marcus Aurelius (Meditations, 2nd century): Love nothing but that which comes to you woven in the pattern of your destiny. For what could more aptly fit your needs?

Marcus Aurelius (c. A.D. 174): That which follows ever conforms to that which went before.

Owen Meredith: To all facts there are laws, / The effect has its cause, and I mount to the cause.

Michael A. Musmanno (Justice of the Sup. Ct. of Pennsylvania, 1959): (Joseph Dugan, a fireman, descended into the hold of a steamship to extinguish a fire, and 18 months later died from the effects of the burns he had received. The Philadelphia Fireman's Pension Fund refused to pay any pension to his widow and children because their bylaws provided that death must follow within 60 days after injuries were sustained.): This bylaw is not only unreasonable, but it challenges the working of the undeviating law of cause and effect. Hospitals, military and civil, contain innumerable case histories of patients who succumbed to the invader Death months and years after he first crossed the threshold. It is common knowledge that the poison gas which entered the lungs of many soldiers in World War I did not finish its lethal work until years after it had started its grim, mordant process of destroying the lung cells. That the lifeline of survival should be kept operating a year or two after the shipwreck is not so extraordinary a phenomenon as to be adjudicated uninhappenble. The injuries Joseph Dugan incurred on March 8, 1942, never healed; the lowering into the hold of a burning ship never ceased until Joseph Dugan was lowered into his grave. (Dugan v. Fireman's Pension Fund of Philadelphia, 372 Pa. 29).

Friedrich Nietzsche: The consequences of our actions take hold of us quite indifferent to our claim that meanwhile we have "improved."

Friedrich Nietzsche: Our destiny rules over us, even when we are not yet aware of it; it is the future that makes laws for our today.

Omar Khayyam: 'Tis all a Chequer-board of Nights and Days / Where Destiny with Men for Pieces plays: / Hither and thither moves, and mates, and slays, / And one by one back in the Closet lays.

Ovid: Their cause is hidden, but our woes are clear.

Ovid: The cause is hidden, but the result is known.

Ovid: Everything come gradually and at its appointed hour.

George Pettie (1576): The cause taken away, the effect vanisheth.

George Pettie: Such as the cause of every thing is, such will be the effect.

George Pettie: How is it possible that of an il cause, can come a good effect?

Alexander Pope: The Universal Cause Acts to one end, but acts by various laws.

Alexander Pope: The Universal Cause Acts not by partial but by general laws.

Alexander Pope: Thou Great First Cause, least understood.

Blaise Pascal: In each action we must look beyond the action at our past, present, and future state, and at others whom it affects, and see the relations of all those things. And then we shall be very cautious.

Will Rogers: Ancient Rome declined because it had a Senate, now what's going to happen to us with both a House and a Senate?

Pulilius Syrus: Where destiny blunders, human prudence will not avail.

Sir Walter Raleigh (1614) (quoting Aristotle): A sufficient and effectual cause being granted, an answerable effect thereof is also granted.

Will Rogers: If I could kick the person in the tail that causes me the most problems I could not sit down for a week.

Will Rogers (to his niece on seeing the *Venus de Milo*): See what will happen if you don't stop biting your fingernails?

Francis Rouse: To produce effects beyond the cause; which is indeed to make something out of nothing.

Russian Proverb: It is not the horse that draws the cart, but the oats.

William Shakespeare (*All's Well That Ends Well,* Act II, i): Great floods have flown / From simple sources.

William Shakespeare (*The Comedy of Errors*, Act II, ii): ANTIPHOLUS OF SYRACUSE: Shall I tell you why? DROMO OF SYRACUSE: Ay, sir, and wherefore; for they say every why hath a wherefore.

William Shakespeare (*Cymbeline*, Act IV, iii): Fortune brings in some boats that are not steered.

William Shakespeare (*Hamlet*, Act II, ii): And now remains / That we find out the cause of this effect; / Or, rather say, the cause of this defect, / For this effect defective comes by cause.

William Shakespeare (*Hamlet*, Act V, ii): There's a divinity that shapes our ends, /

William Shakespeare (*I Henry IV*, Act II, iv): Give you a reason on compulsion! If reasons were as plenty as blackberries, I would give no man a reason upon compulsion.

William Shakespeare (*Henry V*, Act V, i): There is occasions and causes why and wherefore in all things.

William Shakespeare (*Macbeth,* Act III, ii): Things bad begun make strong themselves by ill.

William Shakespeare (*Othello,* Act II, i): O most lame and impotent conclusion!

William Shakespeare (*Othello*, Act V, ii): It is the cause, it is the cause, my soul,—/ Let me not name it to you, you chaste stars!—/ It is the cause.

William Shakespeare (*Richard III*, Act I, ii): Thou art the cause, and most accursed effect.

William Shakespeare (*Romeo and Juliet,* Act II, vi): These violent delights have violent ends, / And in their triumph die, like fire and powder.

Baruch (Benedict) Spinoza: God is the free cause of all things.

Talmud, Gittin, 45a: The hole, not the mouse, is the thief.

Henry David Thoreau: Our least deed, like the young of the land crab, wends its way to the sea of cause and effect as soon as born, and makes a drop there to eternity.

Henrik Tikkanen: Because we don't think about future generations, they will never forget us.

Mark Twain: Half of the results of a good intention are evil; half the results of an evil intention are good.

UA: If you don't eat garlic, you won't smell.

Virgil (Roman poet, 70-19 BC): Happy the man who has been able to understand the causes of things.

Richard Whately (*Elements of Logic*, 1826): After this, therefore on account of this. False argument from cause to effect from mere precedence of circumstance.

E. B. White: There's no limit to how complicated things can get, on account of one thing always leading to another.

Alfred North Whitehead: The causes I am inclined to think are there all along, and the events which we see, and which look like freaks of chance, are only the last steps in long lines of causation.

CAUTION (See RISK)

CERTAINTY (See FACT)

CHANCE (See ACCIDENT)

CHANGE (See CONSISTENCY)

CHARACTER

Uncle Anthony: Character is like a brick wall—you can't strengthen or fix it with whitewash.
Uncle Anthony: Life ain't about a how long you can reach, or how far you can run, or how high you can touch the back board, but how often you can bounce back.
Uncle Anthony: He's the type that not only wants somethin' for nuthin' – he wants it gift wrapped.
Uncle Anthony: He's so two-faced, he stands up in both the top and bottom halves of the seventh inning.
Uncle Anthony (an artist and a painter): Some people don't change they're like black paint. Black don't take no other colors.
Uncle Anthony: What did ya expect from a pig except a grunt?
Aunt Mary Carlo: He had "Quizonart Ideals" that turned to mush very quick.
Aunt Mary Carlo: He's one of dem professional reformers dat takes da pie (money) otta the piety.
Aunt Mary Carlo: He's da kinda guy dat not only wants his cake t'eat – but your and your cookies too.
Aunt Mary Carlo: When he slaps ya on yer back, it's soz ta make sure ya swallow what he told ya.
A. Bronson Alcott: One's outlook is a part of his virtue.
A. Bronson Alcott: Temperament is a fate from whose jurisdiction its victims hardly escape, but do its bidding herein, be it murder or martyrdom.
Louisa May Alcott: "My lady"... had yet to learn that money cannot buy refinement of nature, that rank does not always confer nobility, and that true breeding makes itself felt in spite of external drawbacks.
Joseph Allegretti (book *The Lawyer's Calling*): The lesson of Thomas More's life is not that he refused to sign the Kings oath, but that he was willing to draw a line somewhere. He was not willing to surrender his whole self to anyone or anything.
American Proverb: Cut off a dog's tail and he will still be a dog.
Maya Angelou: The quality of strength lined with tenderness is an unbeatable combination, as are intelligence and necessity when unblunted by formal education.
Thomas Antrim: Three failures denote uncommon strength. A weakling has not enough grit to fail thrice.
Aristotle: Our characters are the result of our conduct.
Aristotle: We are what we repeatedly do.
Aristotle: Day-to-day does not consist in possessing the honours, but in deserving them.
Aristotle: Men acquire a particular quality by constantly acting in a particular way ... you become just by performing just actions, temperate by performing temperate actions, brave by performing brave actions.
Ashanti Proverb: Rain beats a leopard's skin, but it does not wash off the spots.
Walter Bagehot: Only this much is certain, - all men and all nations have a character, and that character, when once taken, is, I do not say unchangeable ... but the least changeable thing in this ever-varying and changeful world.
Enid Bagnold (*"The Chalk Garden,"* 1953): MRS. ST. MAUGHAM: You can't fit false teeth to a woman of character. As one gets older and older, the appearance becomes such a bore.
Faith Baldwin: Character builds slowly, but it can be torn down with incredible swiftness.
Tallulah Bankhead: No one can be exactly like me. Sometimes even I have trouble doing it.
Tallulah Bankhead: I am the foe of moderation, the champion of excess. If I may lift a line from a diehard whose identity is lost in the shuffle, "I'd rather be strongly wrong than weakly right."
Bruce Barton: When you're through changing, you're through!
Margaret Ayer Barnes: "Character comes before scholarship ...."
Bernard Baruch: During my eighty-seven years I have witnessed a whole succession of technological revolutions. But none of them has done away with the need for character in the individual or the ability to think.
Henry Ward Beecher: Happiness is not the end of life: character is.
Henry Ward Beecher: The prouder a man is, the more he thinks he deserves; and the more he thinks he deserves, the less he really does deserve.
Henry Ward Beecher: The cynic is one who never sees a good quality in a man, and never fails to see a bad one. He is the human owl, vigilant in darkness, and blind to light, mousing for vermin, and never seen noble game.

Bible: Apocrypha, Ecclesiasticus 13:1: Whoever touches pitch will be defiled.
Bible: Judges, 8:21: As the man is, so is his strength.
Bible: Luke 6:43 and Matthew 7:17: Every good tree bringeth forth good fruit; but a corrupt tree bringeth forth evil fruit.
Bible: Luke 6:44 and Matthew 12:33: The tree is known by his fruit.
Bible: Luke, 16:10: He that is faithful in that which is least is faithful also in much; and he that is unjust in the least is unjust also in much.
Bible: Matthew, 5:13: Ye are the salt of the earth.
Bible: Matthew 7:16: Of a thorn springs not a fig.
Bible: Proverbs 6:27: Can a man take fire in his bosom, and his clothes not be burned?
Bible: Proverbs 22:1: A good name is rather to be chosen than great riches.
Bible: Proverbs 23:7: As he thinketh in his heart, so is he.
Bible: Proverbs: 27:17: Iron sharpeneth iron; so a man sharpeneth the countenance of his friend.
Ambrose Bierce: "The human heart has four animals living there: a tiger, a pig, an ass, and a nightingale. The character of a person depends on the strength of one of the four."
Ambrose Bierce: DISSEMBLE, v.i. To put a clean shirt upon the character. "Let us dissemble." – Adam.
Ambrose Bierce: HONORABLE, adj. Afflicted with an impediment in one's reach. In legislative bodies it is customary to mention all members as honorable; as, "the honorable gentleman is a scurvy cur."
Ambrose Bierce: PHYSIOGNOMY, n. The art of determining the character of another by the resemblances and differences between his face and our own, which is the standard of excellence. "There is no art," says Shakespeare, foolish man, / "To read the mind's construction in the face." / The physiognomists his portrait scan, / And say: "How little wisdom here we trace! / He knew his face disclosed his mind and heart, / So, in his own defence, denied our art." Lavatar Shunk.
Ambrose Bierce: RUMOR, n. A favorite weapon of the assassins of character.
Josh Billings: Every man has his follies—and often they are the most interesting things he has got.
Jacqueline Bisset: Character contributes to beauty. It fortifies a woman as her youth fades. A mode of conduct, a standard of courage, discipline, fortitude and integrity can do a great deal to make a woman beautiful.
Jacob Braude: Always behave like a duck - keep calm and unruffled on the surface, but paddle like the devil underneath.
David Brin: It is said that power corrupts, but actually it's more true that power attracts the corruptible. The sane are usually attracted by other things than power.
Haywood Hale Broun: Sports do not build character. They reveal it.
Pearl Buck: The secret of joy in work is contained in one work—excellence. To know how to do something well is to enjoy it.
Eric Byrne: We are born princes and the civilizing process makes us frogs.
Walter Camp (legendary Yale football coach): There is no substitute for hard work and effort beyond the call of mere duty. That is what strengthens the soul and ennobles one's character.
Thomas Carlyle: Instead of saying that man is the creature of circumstance, it would be nearer the mark to say that man is the architect of circumstance. It is character which builds an existence out of circumstance. From the saying the materials one-man builds palaces, another hovels; one warehouses, another villas; bricks and mortar are mortar and bricks until the architect can make them something else.
Dale Carnegie: You can make more friends in two months by becoming interested in other people then you can in two years by trying to get other people interested in you.
Dick Cavett: It's a rare person who wants to hear what he doesn't want to hear.
Nicholas Chamfort: In great affairs men show themselves as they wish to be seen; in small things they show themselves as they are.
G.K. Chesterton: To have a right to do a thing is not at all the same as to be right in doing it.
Chinese Proverb: The diamond cannot be polished without friction, nor the man perfected without trials.
Sir Winston Churchill: You can measure a man's character by the choices he makes under pressure.
Sir Winston Churchill: It is not enough that we do our best; sometimes we have to do what is required.
Sir Winston Churchill: Success is the ability to go from one failure to another with no loss of enthusiasm.
Sir Winston Churchill: Character may be manifested in the great moments, but it is made in the small ones.

Ivy Compton-Burnett: Life makes great demands on people's characters, and gives them great opportunities to serve their own ends by the sacrifice of other people. Such ill doing may meet with little retribution, may indeed be hardly recognized, and I feel so surprised if people yield to it.

Calvin Coolidge (Vermont lawyer, US President, 1872-1933): Nothing takes the place of persistence. Talent will not; nothing is more common than unsuccessful men with talent. Genius will not; unrewarded genius is almost a proverb. Education will not; the world is full of educated derelicts. Persistence and determination alone are omnipotent.

Cyrus H. Curtis: There are two kinds of men who never amount to much: those who cannot do what they are told and those who can do nothing else.

Greg Cusimano: The true test of character is how we behave when no one is looking.

Joan Didion: Character—the willingness to accept responsibility for one's own life—is the source for which self-respect springs.

Joan Didion: The dismal fact is that self-respect has nothing to do with the approval of others—who are, after all, deceived easily enough; has nothing to do with reputation, which, as Rhett Butler told Scarlett O'Hara, is something people with courage can do without.

Everett Dirksen: Life is not a static thing. The only people who do not change their minds are incompetents in asylums, who can't, and those in cemeteries.

Benjamin Disraeli: Nurture your mind with great thoughts; to believe in the heroic makes heroes.

Benjamin Disraeli: Characters do not change. Opinions alter, but characters are only developed.

Helen Gahagan Douglas: Character isn't inherited. One builds it daily by the way one thinks and acts, thought by thought, action by action. If one lets fear or hate or anger take possession of the mind, they become self-forged chains.

Norman Douglas: You can tell the ideals of a nation by its advertisements.

Dutch Proverb: You can't hatch chickens from fried eggs.

Umberto Eco: The real hero is always a hero by mistake; he dreams of being an honest coward like everybody else.

Dwight D. Eisenhower: Decency—generosity—cooperation—assistance in trouble—devotion to duty; these are the things that are of greater value than surface appearances and customs.

George Eliot: Our deeds determine us, as much as we determine our deeds.

Ralph Waldo Emerson: A little integrity is better than any career.

Ralph Waldo Emerson: A character is like an acrostic – read it forward, backward, or across, it still spells the same thing.

Ralph Waldo Emerson: No change in circumstances can repair a defect of character.

Raplph Waldo Emerson: Every man is entitled to be valued (judged) by his best moment.

Ralph Waldo Emerson: Some men appear to feel that they belong to a Pariah caste. They fear to offend, they bend and apologize, and walk through life with a timid step.

Ralph Waldo Emerson: The louder he talked of his honor, the faster we counted our spoons.

Ralph Waldo Emerson: Character is that which can do without success.

Ralph Waldo Emerson: Character is higher than intellect.... A great soul will be strong to live, as well as to think.

Ralph Waldo Emerson: Character, that sublime health which values one moment as another, and makes us great in all conditions.

Ralph Waldo Emerson: Don't say things. What you are stands over you the while, and thunders so that I cannot hear what you say to the contrary.

Ralph Waldo Emerson: There is no end to the sufficiency of character. It can afford to wait; it can do without what is called success.

Ralph Waldo Emerson: Do what you know and perception is converted into charcter.

Ralph Waldo Emerson: Character is centrality, the impossibility of being displaced or overset.

Ralph Waldo Emerson: The most fugitive word or deed, the mere air of doing a thing, the intimated purpose, expresses character, and the remote results of character are civil history and events that shake or settle the world. If you act, you show character; if you sit still, you show it; if you sleep.

Ralph Waldo Emerson: What lies behind us and what lies before us are tiny matters compared to what lies within us.

English Proverb: A smooth sea never made a skillful mariner.

English Proverb: Fine feathers make fine birds.

Epictetus: It is difficulties which show what men are.

Sam Ervin: (Confederate General Robert E.) Lee took the blame. "It was all my fault," he said to Pickett's troops. That's quite different from some people I know.

Joseph Farrell: When a man thinks he is reading the character of another, he is often unconsciously betraying his own; and this is especially the case with those persons whose knowledge of the world is of such sort that it results in extreme distrust of men.

Edna Ferber (*So Big*, 1924): "Any piece of furniture, I don't care how beautiful it is, has got to be lived with, kicked about, and rubbed down, and mistreated by servants, and repolished, and knocked around and dusted and sat on or slept in or eaten off of before it developes its real character," Salina said. "A good deal like human beings."

W.C. Fields: You can't cheat an honest man.

F. Scott Fitzgerald: He believed in character, he wanted to jump back a whole generation and trust in character again as the eternally valuable element. Everything else wore out.

Henry Ford: It is all one to me if a man comes from Sing Sing or Harvard. We hire a man, not his history.

Henry Ford: You can't build a reputation on what you are going to do.

Malcolm Forbes: You can judge the character of others by how they treat those who can do nothing to them or for them.

Ann Frank (*The Diary of a Young Girl*, July 15, 1944): "Parents can only give good advice or put them on the right paths, but the final forming of a person's character lies in their own hands ...."

Felix Frankfurter: Old age and sickness bring out the essential characteristics of a man.

Sigmund Freud: There are people who are good because nothing evil occurs to them, and others who are good because they conquer their evil thoughts. I had reckoned you to the former class. No doubt it is my fault that you have lost your guilelessness. It doesn't matter greatly; whoever has much contact with life must lose it, and in place of it build up a character.

Robert Frost: The world is full of willing people, some willing to work, the rest willing to let them.

James A. Froude: You cannot dream yourself into a character; you must hammer and forge yourself one.

John W. Gardner: Some people strengthen the society just by being the kind of people they are.

José Ortega y Gasset: We distinguish the excellent man from the common man by saying that the former is the one who makes great demands upon himself, and the latter who makes no demands on himself.

German Proverb: A man shows his character by what he laughs at.

Andre Gibe: It is better to the hated for what you are then to be loved for what you are not.

Ellen Glasgow: We have refused to acknowledge that the disintegration of character is the beginning, not the end, of defeat, or that this weakening moral fibre is first revealed in the quick or slow decline of human relationships, and in the abrupt conversion to a triumphant materialism.

Johann Goethe: Talents are best nurtured in solitude: character is best formed in the stormy billows of the world.

Johann Goethe: If you would create something, you must be something.

Greek Proverb: Character is habit long continued.

Marguerite Halsey: Humility is not my forte, and whenever I dwell for any length of time on my own shortcomings, they gradually begin to seem mild, harmless, rather engaging little things, not at all like the staring defects in other people's characters.

Joseph Heller: Some men are born mediocre, some men achieved mediocrity, and some men have mediocrity thrust upon them.

Don Herold: Many people have character who have nothing else.

Hindustani Proverb: True nobility is in being superior to your previous self.

Eric Hoffer: Woe to him inside a nonconformist clique who does not conform to nonconformity.

Oliver Wendell Holmes, Jr.: The great thing in this world is not so much where you stand, as in what direction you are moving.

Oliver Wendell Holmes, Jr.: But the character of every act depends upon the the circumstances in which it is done.

Elbert Hubbard: God will not look you over for medals, degrees or diplomas, but for scars.

Victor Hugo: Adversity makes men, and prosperity makes monsters.

Irish Proverb: Put silk on a goat, and it's still a goat.

Irish Proverb: You cannot make a silk purse out of a sow's ear.

Italian Proverb: We cannot direct the wind, but we can adjust the sails.

William James: I have often thought that the best way to define a man's character would be to seek out the particular mental or moral attitude in which, when it came upon him, he felt himself most deeply and intensely active and alive. At such moments there is a voice inside which speaks and says: "*This* is the real me!"

Thomas Jefferson: In matters of style, swim with the current; in matters of principal, stand like a rock.

Thomas Jefferson: I have a great believer in luck, and I find the harder I work the more I have of it.

Jesse Jackson: If in my high moments, I have done some good, offered some service, shed some light, healed some wounds, rekindled some hope, or stirred someone from apathy and indifference, or in any way along the way helped somebody, then this campaign has not been in vain.... if in my low moments, in word, deed or attitude, through some error of temper, taste or tone, I have caused anyone discomfort, created pain or revived someone's fears, that was not my truest self.... I am not a perfect servant. I am a public servant doing my best against the odds. As I develop and serve, be patient. God is not finished with me yet.

Jewish Proverb: There are three types of "doers": If a man says, "I shall do it soon," his character is poor; if he says, "I am ready to do it," his character is average; if he says, "I am doing it," is character is praiseworthy.

Jewish Saying: A saloon cannot corrupt a good man, and a synagogue cannot reform a bad one.

Lyndon B. Johnson: The good Lord endowed me with a wonderful constitution, twenty hours a day; I was plenty sturdy and tough, and I had reasonable perception and astuteness, I was not a temple of wisdom or fountain of justice, but I could comprehend things. No one ever said I was a goddamn boob, no one from Bobby (Kennedy) up or down ever said that.

Carl Jung: The little world of childhood with its familiar surroundings is a model of the greater world. The more intensively the family has shaped its character upon the child, the more it will tend to feel and see its earlier miniature world again in the bigger world of adult life.

Helen Keller: Character cannot be developed in ease and quiet. Only through experience of trial and suffering can the soul be strengthened, vision cleared, ambition inspired, and success achieved.

Edward M. Kennedy: Where is the moral strength within us? The qualities of character that we attribute in stories to our children of the American heroes that have gone before us?

Franz Kafka: There art two cardinal sins from which to all others spring: impatience and laziness.

Martin Luther King Jr.: Our lives begin to end the day we become silent about things that matter.

General Charles Krulak (former Commandant of US Marine Corps; 1998 poem *"The Eagle and The Wolf"*): There is a great battle that rages inside me: / One side is a soaring eagle. / Everything the eagle stands for is good and true and beautiful. / It soars above the clouds. / Even though it dips down into the valleys, it lays its eggs on the mountain tops. / The other side of me is a howling wolf; / And that raging, howling wolf represents the worst that is in me. / He eats upon my downfalls and justifies himself by his presence in the pack. / Who wins this great battle? / The one I feed.

And Landers: Keep in mind that the true meaning of an individual is how he treats a person who can do him absolutely no good.

Tom Landry (legendary Dallas Cowboys football coach): A team that has character doesn't need stimulation.

Latin Proverb: Who lies with dogs shall rise up with fleas.

Gerald Stanley Lee: Turning the other cheek is a kind of moral jiujitsu.

Oscar Levant: Underneath his flabby exterior is an enormous lack of character.

Abraham Lincoln: Character is like a tree and reputation like its shadow. The shadow is what we think of, the tree is the real thing.

Abraham Lincoln: Ability may get you to the top, but it is character that will keep you there.

Abraham Lincoln: Nearly all men can stand adversity, but if you want to test a man's character, give him power.

F.L. Lucas: Character is not only a compound of extremely various qualities, but the qualities themselves vary from year to year, even from hour to hour. The Spaniard will wisely say of a man, "He was brave *that* day." We are all at war with ourselves; if an "individual" meant one literally "undivided," no such creature would exist.

Clare Booth Luce: I don't have one personal enemy left. They all died off. I miss them terribly because they helped define me.

John Luther: Good character is more to be praised than outstanding talent. Most talents are, to some extent, a gift. Good character, by contrast, is not given to us. We have to build it piece by piece—I thought, choice, courage and determination.

Lord Macauley: The measure of a man's real character is what he would do if he knew he would never be found out.

Norman Mailer (speaking about political activist Abbie Hoffman): He had a charisma that must have come out of an Immaculate Conception between Fidel Castro and Groucho Marx. They went into his soul and he came out looking like an ethnic milkshake—Jewish revolutionary, Puerto Rican Lord, Italian street kid, Black Panther with the old Afro haircut, even a glint of Irish gunman in his mad, green eyes.

Horace Mann: Character is what God and the angels know of us; reputation is what men and women think of us.

Andre Maurois: If you create an act, you create a habit. If you create a habit, you create a character. If you create a character, you create a destiny.

Mencius: Listen to a man's words and look at the pupil of his eye. How can a man conceal his character?

James Michener: Character consists of what you do on the third and fourth tries.

Olin Miller: You probably wouldn't worry about what people think of you if you could know how seldom they do.

Mohammedan Proverb: If you hear that a mountain has moved, believe; but if you hear that a man has changed his character, believe it not.

Molière: Men are all alike in their promises. It is only in the our deeds that they differ.

Dwight L. Moody: If I take care of my character, my reputation will take care of itself.

Dwight L. Moody: Character is what you are in the dark.

Michael A. Musmanno (Justice of Pennsylvania Supreme Court, 1959): A man's good name is as much his possession as his personal property. It is more than property, it is his guardian angel of safety and security; it is his lifesaver in a sea of adversity; it is his parachute when he falls out of the sky of good fortune; it is his plank of rescue in the quicksands of personal disaster.

Constantine Nash: A human being has no discernible character until he acts.

Abot de Rabbi Nathan: Character is tested through three things: business, wine, and conversation.

Derek Neitzel: I am the most antisocial person I know. But of course, I don't know anyone because I'm so antisocial.

Friedrich Nietzsche: If a man has character, he also has his typical experience, which always recurs.

Thomas Paine: Character is much easier kept than recovered.

Bahya Ibn Paquda: Watching for other people's blemishes prevents me from investigating my own—which task is more urgent.

Hesketh Pearson: A man's character never changes radically from youth to old age. What happens is that circumstances bring out characteristics which had not been obvious to the superficial observer.

Phaedrus: Everyone ought to bear patiently the results of his own conduct.

Plutarch (Greek biographer, 46?-120? AD): Character is habit long continued.

Jean-Paul Richter: A man never discloses his own character so clearly as when he describes another's.

Edward Rickenbacker: The four cornerstones of character on which the structure of this nation was built are: Initiative, Imagination, Individuality and Independence.

La Rochefoucauld: Moderation is an ostentatious proof of our strength of character.

Will Rogers: Too many people spend money they haven't earned to buy things they don't want to impress people they don't like.

Will Rogers: I bet you if I had met him [Trotsky] and had a chat with him, I would have found him a very interesting and human fellow, for I never yet met a man that I didn't like.

Will Rogers: Get someone else to blow your horn and the sound will carry twice as far.

Eleanor Roosevelt: Character building begins in our infancy, and continues until death.

Eleanor Roosevelt (Meet The Press, 1956, speaking about Richard Nixon's smear campaign against Helen Gahagan Douglas): I have always felt that anyone who wanted an election so much that they would use those (smear) methods did not have the character that I really admired in public life.

Leo Rosten: MITZVAH: (plural *mitzvot*): Hebrew: "commandment." (1) Commandment; divine commandment. (2) A meritorious act, a "good work," a truly virtuous, kind, ethical deed. *Mitzvah* is second only to *Torah* in the vocabulary of Judaism. *Mitzvot* are of various kinds: those of positive performance (e.g., caring for the widow and orphan), and those of negative resolve (e.g., not accepting a bribe); and those between man and God (fasting on *Yom Kippur*) and those between man and man (paying a servant promptly). *Mitzvot* are regarded as profound obligations, but must be performed not from a sense of duty but with "a joyous heart." There are 613 separate *mitzvot* listed in the *Sefer Mitzvot Gadol*, of which 248 are positive and 365 negative. Maimonides listed all the *mitzvot* in his *Book of the Mitzvot*; he remarked that the man who performed only one of the 613 deserved salvation – *if* he did so not to win credit, but entirely for its own sake. The potential number of *mitzvot* is endless. Israel Zangwell called *mitzvot* the Jews' "sacred sociology."

Joseph Roux: With character both proud and timid, one never amounts to anything.

William Saroyan: Every man in the world is better than someone else. And not as good as someone else.

Arthur Schopenhauer: Talent hits a target no one else can hit; genius hits a target no one else can see.

Sir Walter Scott: I begin to find that too good a character is inconvenient.

William Shakespeare (*All's Well That Ends Well*, Act I, i): I know him a notorious liar, / Think him a great way fool, solely a coward; / Yet these fix'd evils sit so fit in him, / That they take place, when virtue's steely bones / Look bleak in the cold wind.

William Shakespeare (*Hamlet*, Act II, ii): Come, give us a taste of your quality.

William Shakespeare (*III Henry VI*, Act III, i): Look, as I blow this feather from my face, / And as the air blows it to me again, / Obeying with my wind when I do blow, / And yielding to another when it blows, / Commanded always by the greater gust; / Such is the lightness of you common men.

William Shakespeare (*Henry VIII*, Act IV, ii): Men's evil manners live in brass; their virtues we write in water.

William Shakespeare (*Julius Caesar*, Act I, iii): O, he sits high in all the people's hearts: / And that which would appear offence in us. / His countenance, like richest alchymy, / Will change to virtue and to worthiness.

William Shakespeare (*King Lear*, Act I, i): Thou art, most rich, being poor; / Most choice, forsaken; and most lov'd, Despis'd. / Thee and thy virtues here I seize upon.

William Shakespeare (*Love's Labour's Lost*, Act II, i): A man of sovereign parts he is esteem'd; / Well fitted in arts, glorious in arms: / Nothing becomes him ill that he would well.

William Shakespeare (*Measure for Measure*, Act I, i): There is a kind of character in thy life, / That to the observer doth thy history / Fully unfold.

William Shakespeare (*Measure for Measure*, Act III, i): Be absolute for death; either death, or life, shall thereby be the sweeter.

William Shakespeare (*Measure for Measure,* Act V, i): They say, best men are moulded out of faults, / And, for the most, become much more the better, / For being a little bad.

William Shakespeare (*Merchant of Venice*, Act I, i): Nature hath fram'd strange fellows in her time: / Some that will evermore peep through their eyes, / And laugh, like parrots, at a bagpiper: / And other of such vinegar aspect, / That they'll not show their teeth in way of smile, / Though Nestor swear the jest be laughable.

William Shakespeare (*Othello*, Act II, iii): Reputation is an idle and most false imposition; oft got without merit and lost without deserving.

William Shakespeare (*Othello*, Act III, iii): Good name in man and woman, dear my lord, / Is the immediate jewel of their souls: / Who steals my purse steals trash; 'tis something, nothing; .... But he that filches from me my good name, / Robs me of that which enriches him, / And makes me poor indeed.

William Shakespeare (*Othello*, Act V, i): He hath a beauty in his life / That makes me ugly.

William Shakespeare (*Richard II*, Act I, i): The purest treasure mortal times afford / Is spotless reputation.

William Shakespeare (*Troilus and Cressida*, Act I, ii): Manhood, learning, gentleness, virtue, youth, liberality, and such like, the spice and salt that season a man.

William Shakespeare (*Twelfth Night*, Act II, v): Put thyself into the thick of singularity.

William Shakespeare (*Two Gentlemen of Verona*, Act II, vi): He wants wit that wants resolved will.

William Shakespeare (*Two Gentlemen of Verona*, Act II, vii): His words are bonds, his oaths are oracles; / His love sincere, his thoughts immaculate; / .... His heart as far from fraud as heaven from earth.

General William Tecumseh Sherman (speaking of President Abraham Lincoln, whom he met with Gen. U. S. Grant, and Adm. Porter aboard Grant's floating HQ, *The River Queen*, in early March 1865 to plan one last campaign and the surrender of the Confederacy): I never saw him again. Of all the men I ever met he seemed to me to possess more of the elements of greatness combined with goodness than any other.

Logan Pearsall Smith: The Saints see men through the golden haze of their own goodness; and too nice a discrimination of the characters of others is a sign that you are not too nice a character yourself.

Ralph W. Sockmann: A man has no more character then he can command in a time of crisis.

Spanish Proverb: No revenge is more honorable than the one not taken.

Spanish Proverb: The wolf loses his teeth, but not his inclinations.

Gertrude Stein (1903): You are so afraid of losing your moral sense that you are not willing to take it through anything more dangerous than a mud-puddle.

Gloria Steinem: We can tell our values by looking at our checkbook stubs.

Stendhal: One can acquire everything in solitude except character.

Charles Swindoll: "Sincerity" is considered the international credit card of acceptance.... no matter how deeply in debt the user may be or how the card is misused, "sincerity" will erase all suspicion and validate all actions.

Sandra Swinney: It is amazing how much people can get done if they do not worry about who gets the credit.

Thomas Szasz: The stupid never forgive nor forget; the naïve forgive and forget; the wise forgive but do not forget.

Talmud: Man's advocates are repentance and good deeds.

Talmud: Nidda, 16b: God decides what shall befall a man, but not whether he shall be righteous or wicked.

Talmud: You can know a man by three signs: his tips, his tippling, and his temper.

Talmud: Like garden, like gardener.

Marguerite Thatcher: Look at a day when you are supremely satisfied at the end. It's not a day when you lounge around doing nothing; it's when you had everything to do, and you've done it.

J. Arthur Thomson: The most powerful factors in the world are clear ideas in the minds of energetic men of goodwill.

Henry David Thoreau: How often must one feel as he looks back on his past life that he has gained a talent but lost a character.... Society does nominally estimate men by their talents—but really feels and knows them by their characters.

Henry David Thoreau: I do not judge men by anything they can do. Their greatest deed is the impression they make on me. Some serene, inactive men can do everything. Talent only indicates a depth of character in some direction.

Leo Tolstoy: Everyone thinks of changing the world, but no one thinks of changing himself.

Harry S. Truman: Three things ruin a man. Power, money, and women. I never wanted power. I never had any money, and the only woman in my life is up at the house right now.

Orhot Tsadikim: Remember the virtues you lack and the faults you have; forget the good you did and the wrong you received.

Mark Twain: It is noble to be good; it is still nobler to teach others to be good—and less trouble.

Mark Twain: Everyone is a moon and has a dark side which he never shows to anybody.

Mark Twain: It is better to deserve owners and not have them than to have them and not deserve them.

Mark Twain: There is no character, howsoever good and fine, but it can be destroyed by ridicule, howsoever poor and witless.

Mark Twain: Praise is well, compliment is well, but affection – that is the last and final and most precious reward that any man can win, by character or achievement.

Mark Twain: A human being has a natural desire to have more of a good thing than he needs.

UA: You cannot make a crab walk straight.

UA: What can you expect from a hog but a grunt.

UA: Character is much easier kept than recovered.

UA: Saloons can't corrupt good men, and synagogues can't reform and ones.

UA: It is better to have nobility of character than nobility of birth.

UA: Every innkeeper praises his beer.

UA: To drunkards, no liquor is bad; to merchants, no money is tainted; to lechers, no woman is ugly.

UA: You can't make an arrow out of a pig's tail.

UA: An eagle does not catch flies.

Abigail Van Buren: The best index to a person's character is (a) how he treats people who can't do him any good, and (b) how he treats people who can't fight back.

Kurt Vonnegut, Jr.: We are what we pretend to be.

Kurt Vonnegut: Another flaw in human character is that everybody wants to build and nobody wants to do maintenance.

George Washington: Few men have virtue to withstand the highest bidder.

George Washington: I hope I shall always possess firmness and virtue enough to maintain (what I consider the most enviable of all titles) the character of an "honest man."

Evelyn Waugh: Punctuality is the virtue of the bored.

Bob Wells: Your true value depends entirely on what you are compared with.

Walt Whitman: Nothing endures but personal qualities.

Oscar Wilde: I forgot that every little action of the common day makes or unmakes character, and that therefore what one has donein the secret chamber one has some day to cry aloud on the house-tops.

George F. Will: There is something awfully small about someone who can not admit that anyone else is exceptionally large.

Woodrow Wilson: If you think about what you ought to do for other people, your character will take care of itself.

John Wooden (legendary UCLA basketball coach): Be more concerned with your character than with your reputation, because your character is what you really are, while your reputation is merely what others think you are.

John Wooden (legendary UCLA basketball coach): Ability may get you to the top, but it takes character to keep you there.

Yiddish Proverb: If you want your dreams to come true, don't sleep!

Yiddish Proverb: Everyone is kneaded out of the same dough but not baked in the same oven.

CHARITY (See COMPASSION)

CHARLEY CHAN WORDS OF WISDOM & PROVERBS (See also ADVICE; MAXIMS)

Uncle Anthony: Y'now, that little guy (Charlie Chan) has got a lotta smarts under that Panama hat

Uncle Anthony: I always liked that little guy – he dressed good, acted good to women, and said some good stuff.

Aunt Mary: Y'know sum'tin? I tink alotta deez provoibs come from Italy not China. [EDITOR: To my Aunt Mary – and most of my mother's family – almost everything ever invented came from Italy or an Italian-American]

Park Benjamin: Another phrase, which often glides in music from the lip, / Is one of fine significance and beauty, "Let her rip!"

Bible: Ecclesiastes, 1:18: In much wisdom is much grief.

Bible: Ecclesiastes, 8:1: A man's wisdom maketh his face to shine.

Bible: Job, 28:18: The price of wisdom is above rubies.

Bible: Job, 32:9: Great men are not always wise.

Bible: Matthew 7:24: A wise man, which built his house upon a rock.

Bible: Matthew, 10:16: Be ye therefore wise as serpents, and harmless as doves.

Bible: Psalms, 90:12: So teach us to number our days, that we may apply our hearts unto wisdom.

Ambrose Bierce: EPIGRAM, n. A short, sharp saying in prose or verse, frequently characterized by acidity or acerbity and sometimes by wisdom. Following are some of the more notable epigrams of the learned and ingenious Dr. Jamrach Holobom: "We know better the needs of ourselves than of others. To serve oneself is economy of administration. / In each human heart are a tiger, a pig, an ass and a nightingale. Diversity of character is due to their unequal activity. / There are three sexes; males, females and girls. / Beauty in women and distinction in men are alike in this: they seem to the unthinking a kind of credibility. / Women in love are less ashamed than men. They have less to be ashamed of. / While your friend holds you affectionately by both your hands you are safe, for you can watch both his."

Ambrose Bierce: PHILISTINE, n. One whose mind is the creature of its environment, following the fashion in thought, feeling and sentiment. He is sometimes learned, frequently prosperous, commonly clean and always solemn.

Ambrose Bierce: WITTICISM, n. A sharp and clever remark, usually quoted, and seldom noted; what the Philistine is pleased to call a "joke."

Gelett Burgess: Bromides and sulfites (Two words coined in 1907. Bromide = the majority of mankind who think and talk alike; sulfites = the select minority who "eliminate the obvious from their conversation.")

Cervantes: Many a one goes for wool and comes back shorn.

Charles Chan: Advice like snow: the softer it falls, the longer it dwells upon, and the deeper it sinks into the mind.

Charlie Chan: *(to Number 3 son, Tommy)* (Your) Assistance is welcome like water in sinking ship.

Charlie Chan: Cannot see contents of nut until shell is cracked.

Charles Chan: (Mr./Mrs./Ms. X) is like toothpaste – will not go backwards.

Charles Chan: Even a broken clock tells truth twice each day.

Charlie Chan: Grain of sand in eye may hide mountain.

Charlie Chan: Hasty conclusion like gunpowder. Easy to explode

Charles Chan: He who keeps face to sunshine can not see the shadows.

Charlie Chan: Holiday mood like fickle girl - privileged to change mind.

Charles Chan: Humble postage stamp achieves success through its ability to stick to one thing until it gets there.

Charles Chan: Ideas are like great arrows, but they must have a bow.

Charles Chan: If strength were all that mattered, the tiger would not fear the scorpion.

Charlie Chan: Joy in heart more desirable than bullet.

Charles Chan: Man like tea bag – only know how strong with hot water.

Charles Chan: Men like nails, lose their effectiveness when they lose direction and begin to bend.

Charles Chan: Mind is like parachute – work better when open.

Charles Chan: Never fear winds of adversity. Remember, a humble kite rises against the wind, not with it.

Charlie Chan: Perfect case, like perfect doughnut, has hole. Inspector Renard: Ha, I see. Same old pessimist, aren't you?

Charlie Chan: Optimist only sees doughnut. Pessimist sees hole.

Charles Chan: Reputation like soap bubble – it bursts if one self inflates.

Charles Chan: Rooster today may become feather duster tomorrow.

Charlie Chan: Some heads like hard nuts - much better if well cracked.

Charles Chan: Tree does not withdraw its shadow, even from the woodcutter. Hospitality is commanded to be exercised even toward an enemy when he comes to thy house.

Charles Chan: Truth, like oil, will in time rise to surface.

Charles Chan: Whale that spouts gets harpoon!

Charles Chan: Wise man sees storm before clouds appear.

Charles Chan: Words do not make rice.

Charlie Chan: You talk like rooster, who thinks sun come up just to hear him crow.

Charlie Chan: You should marry and raise large family. Once have large family, all other troubles mean nothing.

Yvette Lamartine: Too bad you don't dance, Mr. Chan. Charlie Chan: Mud turtle in pond more safe than man on horseback.

Tommy Chan: Gosh, Pop, are you a mind reader? Charlie Chan: If mind not too small.

Chinese Proverb: One cannot manage too many affairs; like pumpkins in water, one pops up while you try to hold down the other.

Sir Winston Churchill: It is a good thing for an uneducated man to read a book of quotations.

Sir Winston Churchill: It's no use saying, ''We are doing our best.'' You have got to succeed in doing what is necessary.

Sir Winston Churchill: In those days he was wiser than he is now—he used frequently to take my advice.

Sir Winston Churchill: Never hold discussions with the monkey when the organ grinder is in the room.

David H. Comins: People will accept your ideas much more readily if you tell them Benjamin Franklin said it first.

Greek Anthology (UA): I will tell you in verse the cities, names, and sayings of the seven sages:
Cleobulus of Lindus said, "Moderation is best."
Chilon in hollow Lacedaemon said, "Know thyself."
Periander, who dwelt in Corinth, said, "Master anger."
Pittacus, who was from Mytilene, said, "Nothing in excess."
And Solon, in holy Athens, "Look at the end of life."
Bias of Priene declared that "Most men are bad."
And Thales of Miletus said, "Shun suretyship."

John Heywood (Proverbs, 1546): Set the cart before the horse.

David Starr Jordan: Wisdom is knowing what to do next; virtue is doing it.

Kane O'Hara (1761): There's catch as catch can, hit or miss, luck is all.

Persian Proverb: Use your enemy's hand to catch a snake.

Francois Rabelais (French satirist, 1494?-1553): It is folly to put the plough in front of the oxen.

Will Rogers: If you find yourself in a hole, stop digging.

Will Rogers: Spinnin' a rope is fun if your neck ain't in it.

Theodore Roosevelt: Nine-tenths of wisdom consists in being wise in time.

Theodore Roosevelt: The large mollycoddle vote – ("Mollycoddle") the people who are soft physically and morally. (TR cited Herodotus – *History*, Book ii, sec. 35 – describing the soft habits of the Egyptians).

William Shakespeare (*All's Well That Ends Well*, Act I, i): Full oft we see / Cold wisdom waiting on superfluous folly.

William Shakespeare (*All's Well That Ends Well*, Act II, i): Share the advice betwixt you: if both gain, all / The gift doth stretch itself as 'tis receiv'd, / And is enough for both.

William Shakespeare (*I Henry VI*, Act III, i): Friendly advice cuts off many foes.

William Shakespeare (*III Henry VI*, Act V, iv): Wise men ne'er sit and bewail their loss, / But cheerly seek how to redress their harms.

William Shakespeare (*Henry VIII*, Act I, i): Bosom up my counsel, / You'll find it wholesome.

William Shakespeare (*King Lear*, Act II, iv): When a wise man gives thee better counsel, give me mine again.

William Shakespeare (*A Lover's Complaint*, l.159): Counsel may stop awhile what will not stay; / For when we rage, advice is often seen / By blunting us to make our wits more keen.

William Shakespeare (*Measure for Measure*, Act IV, i): Here comes a man of comfort, whose advice / Hath often still'd my brawling discontent.

William Shakespeare (*Much Ado About Nothing*, Act V, i): I pray thee, cease thy counsel, / Which falls into mine ears as profitless / As water in a sieve.

William Shakespeare (*Richard II*, Act II, i): Direct not him whose way himself will choose: / 'Tis breath thou lack'st, and that breath wilt thou lose.

Mark Twain: The staements was interesting, but tough.

Mark Twain: I don't see no p'ints about that frog that's any better'n any other frog.

CHEAP/CHEAPNESS (See also INSULTS; MONEY) (AVARICE)

Uncle Anthony: Ever notice how he/she gets those little "alligator arms" whenever the check comes?
Uncle Anthony: Y'now the way it is these days a miser is probably just a guy who lives within his income.
Uncle Anthony: They wouldn't even offer us (my brothers and I working as painters) a glass a water!
Uncle Anthony: When he's buyin' he nurses his drink like it was an hourglass.
Uncle Anthony: Notice how he always sits wit his back to the check.
Uncle Anthony: The closest that guy ever got to buying his wife jewelry was buying her onion rings!
Aunt Mary Carlo: His pockets always outlast the rest of his suits
Aunt Mary Carlo: He's so cheap he could skin a flint!
Aunt Mary Carlo: He's so cheap when guys give three cheers – he gives only two.
Aunt Mary Carlo: He's so small and cheap, if he ever sat his ass down on a dollar, ninety cents'd show!
Aunt Mary Carlo: Yeah, he took me ona whattchamacallit "Dutch treat" date, an we danced check to check!
Aunt Mary Carlo (See also Mary Alice Vesper): Ya don't need more tchotchke (cheap stuff) in yer life!
Agesilaus: By sowing frugality we reap liberty, a golden harvest.
Ali Ibn-Aba-Talib (7th century): A covetous man's penny is a stone.
Fred Allen (about Jack Benny): He is so cheap he wouldn't give you the parsley off his fish.
Vincent Astor: Each dollar is a soldier that does your bidding.
George Bancroft: Avarice is the vice of declining years.
Washington Barrow: There is not in nature anything so remotely distant from God, or so extremely opposite to Him, as a greedy and griping miser.
H. W. Beecher: I have great hope of a wicked man; slender hope of a mean one. A wicked man may be converted and become a prominent saint. A mean man ought to be converted six or seven times, one right after the other, to give him a fair start and put him on an equality with a bold, wicked man.
Bible: Ecclesiastes 5:10: He that loveth silver shall not be satisfied with silver; nor he that loveth abundance with increase.
Bible: Galatians 6:9: Let us not be weary in well doing: for in due season we shall reap, if we faint not.
Bible: Luke, 12:15: Take heed, and beware of covetousness: for a man's life consisteth not in the abundance of the things which he possesseth.
Bible: Matthew 6:21: Where your treasure is, there will your heart be also.
Bible: Matthew 25:42: I was hungry, and ye gave me no meat: I was thirsty, and ye gave me no drink.
Bible: Psalms, 10:3: The wicked boasteth of his heart's desire, and blesseth the covetous, whom the Lord abhorreth.
Bible: Psalms, 119:36: Incline my heart unto thy testimonies, and not to covetousness.
Bible: Proverbs 11:26: He that withholdeth corn, the people shall curse him: but blessing shall be upon the head of him that selleth it.
Bible: Proverbs 21:13: Whoso stoppeth his ears at the poor, he also shall cry himself, but shall not be heard.
Bible: Proverbs 25:17: Withdraw thy foot from thy neighbor's house; lest he be weary of thee, and so hate thee.
Bible: Proverbs 28:20: He that maketh haste to be rich shall not be innocent.
Bible: 1 Timothy, 6:9: They that will be rich fall into temptation and a snare, and into many foolish and hurtful lusts, which drown men in destruction and perdition.
Ambrose Bierce: CLOSE-FISTED, adj. Unduly desirous of keeping that which many meritorious persons wish to obtain....
Ambrose Bierce: ENVY, n. Emulation adapted to the meanest capacity.
Ambrose Bierce: GENEROUS, adj. Originally this word meant noble by birth and was rightly applied to a great multitude of persons. It now means noble by nature and is taking a bit of a rest.
Ambrose Bierce: HOG, n. A bird remarkable for the catholicity of its appetite and serving to illustrate that of ours....
Ambrose Bierce: JEALOUS, adj. Unduly concerned about the preservation of that which can be lost only if not worth keeping.
Ambrose Bierce: SELFISH, adj. Devoid of consideration for the selfishness of others.

Matthew Broderick: He is so tight, if you stuck a piece of coal up his ass, in two weeks you would have a diamond.

Edmund Burke: Frugality is founded on the principle that all riches have limits.

George Burns (about Jack Benny): When he has a party, you not only bring your own Scotch, you bring your own rocks.

G. K. Chesterton: The miser is the man who starves himself, and everybody else, in order to worship wealth in its dead form, as distinct from its living form.

Chinese Proverb: Cheap things are not good, good things are not cheap.

Sir Winston Churchill: Nothing is more costly, nothing is more sterile, than vengeance.

Sir Winston Churchill: We are stripped bare by the curse of plenty.

Charles Caleb Colton: If the prodigal quits life in debt to others, the miser quits it still deeper in debt to himself.

Charles Caleb Colton: To cure us of our immoderate love of gain, we should seriously consider how many goods there are that money will not purchase, and these the best; and how many evils there are that money will not remedy, and these the worst.

Confucius: Superior men, and you not always virtuous, there have been; but there never has been a mean man, and at the same time virtuous.

Abraham Cowley: Poverty wants some things, luxury many, avarice all things.

William Cowper (English poet, 1731-1800): To dally much with subjects mean and low, proves that the mind is weak or makes it so.

Edward Dahlberg: Man hoards himself when he has nothing to give away.

Pen Densham and John Watson (their 1991 film *Robin Hood, Prince of Thieves*): Cancel the kitchen scraps for lepers and orphans. No more merciful beheadings. And call of Christmas!

Mike Ditka (all-pro end in 1976 roasting "Papa" George Halas, Chicago Bears owner): He throws nickels around like manhole covers.

Tryon Edwards: The word "miser," so often used as expressive of one who is grossly covetous and saving, in its origin signifies one that is miserable, the very etymology of the word thus indicating the necessary unhappiness of the miser spirit.

Benjamin Franklin: He does not possess wealth; it possesses him.

Benjamin Franklin: Wealth is not his that has it, but his that enjoys it.

Benjamin Franklin: Frugality is fair fortune; and habits of industry a good estate.

Benjamin Franklin: The way to wealth is as plain as the way to market. – It depends chiefly on two words, industry and frugality; that is, waste neither time nor money, but make the best use of both. – Without industry and frugality nothing will do; with them, everything.

French Proverb: The miser and the pig are of no use until dead.

Thomas Fuller: The prodigal robs his heir, the miser himself.

Thomas Fuller: He is not poor that hath not much, but he that craves much.

Thomas Fuller: If your desires be endless, your cares and fears will be so too.

Henry George: Nature lasts at a miser. He is like the squirrel who buries his nuts and refrains from digging them up again.

German Proverb: Who will not feed the cats, must feed the mice and rats.

Oliver Goldsmith: If frugality were established in the state, if our expenses were laid out rather in the necessaries than the superfluities of life, there might be fewer wants, and even fewer pleasures, but infinitely more happiness.

Charles Montagu Halifax (1715): He that spareth in everything is an inexcusable niggard. He that spareth in nothing is an inexcusable madman. The mean is to spare in what is least necessary, and to lay out more liberally in what is most required.

Rowland Hill: There is a perpetual frost in the pockets of some rich people; as soon as they put their hands into them, they are frozen so they cannot draw out their purses. – Had I my way, I would hang all misers; but reversing the common mode, I would hang them up by the heels, that their money might run out of their pockets.

Homer (9th century B.C.): Nothing in the world is so incontinent as a man's accursed appetite.

Elbert Hubbard: Meanness is more in half-doing than in omitting acts of generosity.

Robert G. Ingersoll: Few rich men own their own property. The property owns them.
Italian Proverb: Big mouthfuls often choke.
Jewish Saying: Some people are like new shoes: the cheaper they are, the louder they squeak.
Samuel Johnson: The lust of gold, unfeeling and remorseless, the last corruption of degenerate man.
Anne Morrow Lindbergh: One cannot collect all the beautiful shells on the beach.
Henry Wadsworth Longfellow: We often excuse our own want of philanthropy by giving the name of fanaticism to the more ardent zeal of others.
Malay Proverb: Water will not slip through the miser's grasp.
Ogden Nash: Bankers are just like anybody else, except richer.
Friedrich Nietzsche: He who cannot give anything away cannot feel anything either.
Thomas Paine (*The American Crisis*, December 23, 1776): These are the times that try men's souls.... What we obtain to cheap, we esteem to lightly; it is dearness only that gives everything its value. Heaven knows how to put a proper price upon its goods; and it would be strange indeed, if so celestial an article as *Freedom* should not be highly rated.
Jim M. Perdue (*Who Will Speak For The Victim? A Practical Treatise on Plaintiff's Jury Argument*, State Bar of Texas, 2002): Isn't it strange that the only place where pain becomes cheap is in the courthouse? We spend billions of dollars a year in this country in quest for cures for diseases, in quest of means to alleviate pain.... When corporations fight among themselves, there is never any quarrel about the fact that the loss of profits, loss of business, or loss of property is worth millions of dollars. Yet when we talk about the individual and the pain and agony that irresponsible conduct can bring, it is only then – in the courtroom – that pain becomes cheap.
Lawrence J. Peter: Every man serves a useful purpose: a miser, for example, makes a wonderful ancestor.
Will Rogers: Ten men in our country could buy the whole world and ten million can't buy enough to eat.
Will Rogers: There is not a man in the country that can't make a living for himself and family. But he can't make a living for them and his government, too, the way his government is living. What the government has got to do is live as cheap as the people.
Will Rogers: I see a good deal of talk from Washington about lowering taxes. I hope they do get 'em lowered enough so people can afford to pay 'em.
Will Rogers: If the other fellow sells cheaper than you, it is called dumping. 'Course, if you sell cheaper than him, that's mass production.
Will Rogers: "I am a great believer in high-priced people. If a thing cost a lot it may not be any better, but it adds a certain amount of class that the cheap thing can never approach; in the long run it's the higher-priced things that are the cheapest." (Letters of a Self-Made Diplomat to his President, May 20, 1926)
Will Rogers: "What's the matter with the world? Why, there ain't nothing but one word wrong with everyone of us, and that's selfishness."
John Ruskin: There is no such thing as cheapness in the universe. Everything costs its own cost, and one of our best virtues is a just desire to pay it.
Seneca: For greed all nature is too little.
Seneca: Greed's worst point is its ingratitude.
Seneca: With parsimony a little is sufficient; without it nothing is sufficient; but frugality makes a poor man rich.
William Shakespeare (*II Henry V*, Act II, iv): Doth, like a miser, spoil his coat with scanting / A little cloth.
William Shakespeare (*I Henry VI*, Act V, iv): Decrepit miser; base, ignoble wretch; / I am descended of a gentler blood.
William Shakespeare (*III Henry VI*, Act II, ii): Happy always was it for that son / Whose father for his hoarding went to hell.
William Shakespeare (*Julius Caesar*, Act IV, iii): When Marcus Brutus grows so covetous, / To lock such rascal counters from his friends, / Be ready, gods, with all your thunderbolts: / Dash him to pieces!
William Shakespeare (*Macbeth*, Act IV, iii): This avarice / Sticks deeper, grows with more pernicious root.
William Shakespeare (*Romeo and Juliet*, Act V, i): There is thy gold; worse poison to men's souls.
Margaret Chase Smith (1964): In today's growing, but tragic, emphasis on materialism, we find perversion of the values of things in life as we once knew them. For example, the creed once taught children as

they grew up was that the most important thing was not whether you won or lost the game but rather "how you played the game." That high level attitude that stresses the moral side no longer predominates in this age of pragmatic materialism that increasingly worships the opposite creed that "the end justifies the means" or the attitude of get what you can in any way, manner, or means that you can.

Baruch (Benedict) Spinoza: Avarice, ambition, lust, etc. are species of madness.

Lawrence Sterne (English humorist, 1768): I have so great a contempt and detestation for meanness, that I could sooner make a friend of one who had committed murder, then of a person could be capable, in any instance, of the former vice. Under meanness, I comprehend dishonesty; under dishonesty, ingratitude; under ingratitude, irreligion; and under this laughter, every species of vice and immorality.

Norman Thomas: The doctrine of thrift for the poor is dumb and cruel, like advising them to try to lift themselves by their bootstraps.

Henry David Thoreau: A man is rich in proportion to the number of things which he can afford to let alone.

Henry David Thoreau: That man is the richest whose pleasures are the cheapest.

Turkish Proverb: To beg of the miser is to dig a trench in the sea.

Mark Twain: In order to make a man or boy want a thing, it is only necessary to make the thing difficult to attain.

Mark Twain: Prosperity is the surest breeder of insolence I know.

Thorstein Veblen (American author, educator, 1857-1929): Conspicuous consumption of valuable goods is a means of reputability to the gentlemen of leisure.

Mary Alice Vesper (my wonderful and wise wife): NO MORE TCHOTCHKES!!

Ronnie Wood (about Rod Stewart): He's tighter than two coats of paint.

Zeno: The avaricious man is like the barren sandy ground of the desert which sucks in all the rain and dew with greediness, but yields no fruitful herbs or plants for the benefit of others.

CHEATING (See EVIL; FRAUD; LIES)

CHILDREN

Uncle Anthony: Y'know, little kids nowadays seem to know all the questions, and then by the time they're sixteen they think they know all the answers too.

Uncle Anthony: Our father always told us there's four things that kids need: lots of love, good food, sleep, and plenty of soap and water. After that, just give 'em some time to be alone.

Uncle Anthony: My kid sister was sent from heaven—they mustta liked it quiet up there.

Uncle Anthony: The only purpose for a child's middle name is so he can tell when he's really in trouble.

Aunt Mary Carlo: Didja ever notice - kids never go 'round showin' off snapshots of der grandparents?

Aunt Mary Carlo: She's got two wonderful kids—and two out of five ain't too bad.

Aunt Mary Carlo: A son is a son till he gets him a wife, / But a daughter's a daughter the rest of your life.

Henry Adams: Young men have a passion for regarding their elders as senile.

Henry Adams: Want one knows is, in youth, of little moment; they know enough who know how to learn.

Alfred Adler: Whenever a child lies you will always find a severe parent. A lie would have no sense unless the truth were felt to be dangerous.

James Agee: In every child who is born, under no matter what circumstances, and of no matter what parents, the potentiality of the human race is born again.

Robert C. Alberts: The young have no depth perception in time. Ten years back or ten years forward is an eternity.

Gordon W. Allport: Is ominous for the future of a child when the discipline he receives is based on the emotional needs of the disciplinarian rather than on any consideration of the child's own needs.

Henri Frederic Amiel: Blessed be childhood, which brings down something of heaven into the midst of our rough earthliness.

Maya Angelou: Children's talent to endorse stems from their ignorance of alternatives.

Maya Angelou: At fifteen life had taught me undeniably that surrender, in its place, was as honorable as resistance, especially if one had no choice.

Maya Angelou: To be left alone on the tightrope of youthful unknowing is to experience the excruciating beauty of full freedom and the threat of eternal indecision.
Arab Proverb: The discontented child cries for toasted snow.
Arab Proverb: The fine pullet shows its excellence from the egg.
Aristotle: The life of children, as much as that of intemperate men, is wholly governed by their desires.
Fred Astaire: The hardest job kids face today is learning good manners without seeing any.
Pearl Bailey: When you're young, the silliest notions seem the greatest achievements.
Russell Baker: As I vaguely recalled from my own experience, adolescence was a time when you firmly believed that sex had not been invented until the year you started high school, when the very idea that anything interesting might have happened during your parents' lifetime was unthinkable.
James Baldwin: Children have never been good at listening to their elders, but they have never failed to imitate them.
James Baldwin: It seems to be typical of life in America, where opportunities, real and fancy, are thicker than anywhere else on the globe, that the second generation has no time to talk to the first.
Tallulah Bankhead: I am serious about wishing I had children, beautiful children. I wouldn't care for the other variety.
Henry Ward Beecher: That energy which makes a child hard to manage is the energy which afterward makes him a manager of life.
Stephen Vincent Benet (American poet and novelist, 1886-1943): Young blood! Youth will be served!
Nicolas Bentley: He followed in his father's footsteps, but his gait was somewhat erratic.
Bible: 1 Corinthians 13:11: When I was a child, I spake as a child, I understood as a child, I thought as a child: but when I became a man, I put away childish things.
Bible: Genesis 27:27: The smell of my son is as the smell of a field which the Lord hath blessed.
Bible: Genesis 43:14: If I be bereaved of my children, I am bereaved.
Bible: Hebrews 12:7: What son is he whom the father chasteneth not?
Bible: Isaiah 11:6: A little child shall lead them.
Bible: Luke 17:2; Mark 9:42; Matthew 18:6: Whosoever shall offend one of these little ones that believe in me, it is better for him that a millstone were hanged about his neck, and he were cast into the sea.
Bible: Luke, 18:16; Mark, 10:14; Matthew 19:14: Suffer the little children to come unto me, and forbid them not; for of such is the kingdom of God.
Bible: Luke 18:17; Mark 10:15: Whosoever shall not receive the kingdom of God as a little child, he shall not enter therein.
Bible: Matthew, 18:3: Except ye be converted, and become as little children, ye shall not enter into the kingdom of heaven.
Bible: Matthew, 18:4: Whosoever therefore shall humble himself as this little child, the same is greatest in the kingdom of heaven.
Bible: Matthew, 19:14: Suffer little children, and forbid them not, to come unto me; for of such is the kingdom of heaven.
Bible: Matthew 21:16: Out of the mouth of babes and sucklings / Thou hast perfected praise.
Bible: Psalms, 127:4: As arrows are in the hand of a mighty man; so are children of the youth. Happy is the man that hath his quiver full of them.
Bible: Proverbs, 10:1: A wise son maketh a glad father: but a foolish son is the heaviness of his mother.
Bible: Proverbs 15:5: A fool despiseth his father's instruction.
Bible: Proverbs, 20:11: Even a child is known by his doings.
Bible: Proverbs, 22:6: Train up a child in the way he should go: and when he is old, he will not depart from it.
Bible: Proverbs 23:13: Withhold not correction from the child: for if thou beatest him with the rod, he shall not die. Thou shalt beat him with the rod, and shalt deliver his soul from hell.
Bible: Proverbs 24: 21: He that spareth his rod hateth his son.
Ambrose Bierce: BABE or BABY, n. A misshapen creature of no particular age, sex, or condition, chiefly remarkable for the violence of the sympathies and antipathies it excites in others, itself without sentiment or emotion.

Ambrose Bierce: CHILDHOOD, n. The period of human life intermediate between the idiocy of infancy and the folly of youth—two removes from the sin of manhood and three from the remorse of age.

Ambrose Bierce: ENTHUSIASM, n. A distemper of youth, curable by small doses of repentance in connection with outward applications of experience.

Ambrose Bierce: INFANCY, n. The period of our lives when, according to Wordsworth, "Heaven lies about us." The world begins lying about us pretty soon afterward.

Ambrose Bierce: MAIDEN, n. A young person of the unfair sex addicted to clewless conduct and views that madden to crime. The genus has a wide geographical distribution, being found wherever sought and deplored wherever found. The maiden is not altogether unpleasing to the eye, nor (without her piano and her views) insupportable to the ear, though in respect to comeliness distinctly inferior to the rainbow, and, with regard to the part of her that is audible, beaten out of the field by the canary – which, also, is more portable.

Ambrose Bierce: ORPHAN, n. A living person whom death has deprived of the power of filial ingratitude – a privation appealing with a particular eloquence to all that is sympathetic in human nature....

Ambrose Bierce: YOUTH, n. The Period of Possibility, when Archimedes finds a fulcrum, Cassandra has a following and seven cities compete for the honor of endowing a living Homer. Youth is the true Saturnian Reign, the Golden Age on earth again, when figs are grown on thistles, and pigs betailed with whistles and, wearing silken bristles, live in clover, and cows fly over, delivering milk at every door, and Justice is never heard to snore, and every assassin is made a ghost and, howling, is cast into Baltimost!—Polydore Smith.

Josh Billings: Never teach your child to be cunning for you may be certain that you will be one of the first victims of his shrewdness.

Dr. Smiley Blanton: I have seen infants who, at the age of only two months, had already developed real neuroses because of the way they had been handled by their mothers and fathers. The infants had absorbed their parents' anxieties like a blotter.

Dr. Smiley Blanton: No one who has ever brought up a child can doubt for a moment that love is literally the life-giving fluid of human existence.

Erma Bombeck: In general my children refused to eat anything that had not danced on TV.

Randolph Bourne: It is one of the surprising things about youth that it can so easily be the most conservative of all ages.

Heywood Broun: The average child is an almost nonexistent myth. To be normal one must be peculiar in some way or another.

Elizabeth Bowen: There is no end to the violations committed by children on children, quietly talking alone.

Elizabeth Bowen: Childish fantasy, like the sheath over the bud, not only protects but curbs the terrible bubbing spirit, protects not only innocence from the world, but the world from the power of innocence.

Pearl S. Buck: The young do not know enough to be prudent, and therefore they attempt the impossible—and achieve it, generation after generation.

Pearl S. Buck: I do not believe in a child world. It is a child world. It is a fantasy world. I believe the child should be taught from the very first that the whole world is his world, that adult and child share one world, that all generations are needed.

Carol Burnett: Adolescence is just one big walking pimple.

Robert F. Capon: Children can stand vast amounts of sternness. They rather expect to be wrong and are quite used to be punished. It is injustice, in equity and inconsistency that kill them.

Rachel Carson: If a child is to keep alive his inborn sense of wonder, he needs the companionship of at least one adult who can share it, rediscovering with him the joy, excitement and mystery of the world we live in.

George Washington Carver: People murder a child when they tell it to keep out of the dirt. Dirt is life.

G.K. Chesterton: Boys like romantic tale; but babies like realistic tales—because they find them romantic.

Children's Defense Fund poster (about teenage pregnancies, 1986): Will Your Child Learn to Multiply Before She Learns to Subtract?

Sir Winston Churchill: Solitary trees, if they grow at all, grow strong.

Sir Winston Churchill: Any 20 year-old who isn't a liberal doesn't have a heart, and any 40 year-old who isn't a conservative doesn't have a brain

Ramsey Clark: Young people should remain idealistic all their lives. If you have to choose between being Don Quixote and Sancho Panza, for heaven's sake, be the Don.

Eldridge Cleaver: The sins of the fathers are visited upon the heads of the children—but only at the children continue in the evil deeds of others.

Richard Henry Dana: Better to be driven out from among men than to be disliked of children.

Bette Davis: If you have never been hated by your child, you have never been a parent.

Midge Decter: The hatred of the youth culture for adult society is not a disinterested judgment but a terror-ridden refusal to be hooked into the... ecological chain of birthing, growing, and dying. It is the demand, in other words, to remain children.

Midge Decter: From one end of this country to another in each of the comfortable suburbs and fashionable neighborhoods that have been settled by members of the "new class," are to be found people my age huddling together from time to time... asking one another (what) has gone wrong with the children?

Charles Dickens: In the little world in which children have their existence, whosoever brings them up, there is nothing so finely perceived and so finely felt, as injustice.

John Sloan Dickey: The college undergraduate is lots of things—many of them as familiar, predictable, and responsible as the bounce of a basketball, and others as startling (and occasionally as disastrous) as the bounce of a football.

Isadora Duncan: The finest inheritance you can give to a child is to allow it to make its own way, completely on its own feet.

Marion Wright Edelman: Our children are growing up now in an ethically polluted nation where substance is being sacrificed daily for shadow.

Albert Einstein: Oh Youth: Do you know that yours is not the first generation to yearn for a life full of beauty and freedom? Do you know that all your ancestors felt as you do—and fell victim to trouble and hatred? Do you know, also, that your fervent wishes can only find fulfillment if you succeed in attaining love and understanding of men, and animals, and plants, and stars, so that every joy becomes your joy and every pain your pain? Open your eyes, your heart, your hands, and avoid the poison your forebears so greedily sucked in from History. Then will all the earth be your fatherland, and all your work and effort spread forth blessings.

Edward Einstein (youngest son of Albert Einstein): It is at times difficult to have such an important father because one feels so unimportant.

Dwight D. Eisenhower: Fortunately for us and our world, youth is not easily discouraged. Youth with its clear vista and boundless faith and optimism is uninhibited by the thousands of considerations that always bedevil man in his progress. The hopes of the world rest on the flexibility, vigor, capacity for new thought, the fresh outlook of the young.

T.S. Eliot: "And youth is cruel, and has no remorse / And smiles at situations which it cannot see." / I smile, of course, / And go on drinking tea.

Ralph Waldo Emerson: Children are all foreigners.

Ralph Waldo Emerson: Respect the child. Be not too much his parent. Trespass not on his solitude.

Ralph Waldo Emerson: As soon as a child has left the room his strewn toys become affecting.

Ralph Waldo Emerson: There never was a child so lovely but his mother was glad to get him asleep.

Ralph Waldo Emerson: We find a delight in the beauty and happiness of children that makes the heart too big for the body.

Ralph Waldo Emerson: (Boys) know truth from counterfeit as quick as the chemist does. They detect weakness in your eye and behavior a week before you open your mouth, and have given you the benefit of their opinion quick as a wink.

Ralph Waldo Emerson: What art can paint or guild any object in the afterlife with the glow which nature gives to the first baubles of childhood! St. Peter's cannot have the magical power over us that the red and gold covers of our first picture book possessed.

Ralph Waldo Emerson: The child with his sweet pranks the fool of his senses, commanded by every sight and sound, without any power to compare and rank his sensations, abandoned to a whistle or a painted chip, to a lead dragoon or a gingerbread-dog, individualizing everything, generalizing nothing, delighted with every new thing, lies down at night overpowered by the fatigue which this day of continual pretty madness has incurred. But nature has answered her purpose with the curley, dimpled lunatic.

English Proverb: Children suck the mother when they are young and the father when they are old.
English Proverb: Children are poor men's riches.
English Proverb: Children and fools must not play with edged tools.
English Proverb: Children (drunkards) and fools cannot lie (or slaternatively: Children and fools cannot speak truth).
English Proverb: He that has no children knows not what love is.
English Proverb: Young men may die, old men must.
Henry Ford: Youth has one great element in its favor—it can live in the future.
Edgar Z. Friedenberg: In a world as empirical as ours, a youngster who does not know what he is good *at* will not be sure what he is good *for*.
Edgar Z. Friedenberg: Juvenile appraisals of other juveniles make up in clarity what they lack in charity.
Sigmund Freud: Children are completely egoistic; they feel their needs intensely and strive ruthlessly to satisfy them.
Erich Fromm: The scars left from the child's defeat in the fight against irrational authority are to be found at the bottom of every neurosis.
Erich Fromm: The "good" child may be frightened, and insecure, wanting only to please his parents by submitting to their will, while the "bad" child may have a will of his own and genuine interests but ones which do not please the parents.
Thomas Fuller: What children hear at home soon flies abroad.
Theodore Geisel (Dr. Seuss): Adults are obsolete children and the hell with them.
German Proverb: You can do anything with children if you only play with them.
Kahlil Gibran: Your children are not your children. / They are the sons and daughters of Life's longing for itself.
Charlotte Perkins Gilman: Noticed, study, commented on, and incessantly interfered with; forced into miserable self-consciousness by this unremitting glare; our little ones grow up permanently injured in character by this lack of one of humanity's most precious rights—privacy.
Johann Wolfgang von Goethe: If children grew up according to early indications, we should have nothing but geniuses.
Goethe: One must ask children and birds how cherries and strawberries taste.
Ellen Goodman: Think about how hard it is for kids to shock the sort of elders who once played in college productions of *Hair*. Imagine rebelling against today's parents who accept rebellion is a normal stage of life. Try being outrageous in front of a teacher who refuses to notice that you have waxed your eyebrows off and are wearing black lipstick on the upper lip and light on the lower.
Paul Goodman: Their intolerance is breath-taking. Do your thing means do their thing.
David Grayson: As for boys and girls, it is one of the sorriest mistakes to talk down to them: almost always your lad of fifteen thinks more simply, more fundamentally then you do; and what he accepts as good coin is not facts or precepts, but feelings and convictions.
David Grayson: Never be surprised when you shake a cherry tree if a boy drops out of it; never be disturbed when you think yourself in complete solitude if you discover a boy peering out at you from a fence corner.
Greek Proverb: Young wood makes a hot fire.
Dick Gregory: The number-one thing young people in America—indeed, young people around the world—have going for them is their sense of honesty, morality, and ethics. Young people refuse to accept the lies and rationalizations of the established order.
Billie Holiday: Mom and Pop were just a couple of kids when they got married. He was eighteen, she was sixteen, and I was three.
Oliver Wendell Holmes Sr.: There is no time like the old-time, when you and I were young.
Oliver Wendell Holmes Sr.: One of the greatest pleasures of childhood is found in the mysteries which it hides from the skepticism of the elders, and works up into small mythologies of its own.
Oliver Wendell Holmes, Sr.: There are no graves that grow so green as the graves of children.... If no pang is sharper than parting with a beloved child, no recollection clears itself so naturally and perhaps I might say so early, of all but what is lovely to dwell upon.

Sir John Holt (Chief Justice, King's Bench, England, 1642-1710): For we like children who are a little afraid of us, docile, deferential children, though not, of course, if they are so obviously afraid that they threaten our image of ourselves as kind, lovable people whom there is no reason to fear.

Herbert Hoover: Blessed are the younger, for they shall inherit the national debt.

Joe Houldsworth: The only thing worth stealing is a kiss from a sleeping child.

Victor Hugo: A little girl without a doll is almost as unfortunate and quite as impossible as a woman without children.

Harold S. Hulbert: Children need love, especially when they do not deserve it.

Aldus Huxley: Children are remarkable for their intelligence and ardor, for their curiosity, their intolerance of shams, the clarity and ruthlessness of their vision.

Eugen Ionesco: Childhood is the world of miracle and wonder: as if creation rose, bathed in light, out of darkness, utterly new and fresh and astonishing. The end of childhood is when things cease to astonish us. When the world seems familiar, when one has got used to existence, one has become an adult.

Irish Proverb: As the big hound is, so will the pup be.

Irish Proverb: Praise the young and they will blossom

Irish Proverb: Walk straight, my son - as the old crab said to the young crab.

Irish Proverb: The raggy colt often made a powerful horse.

Irish Proverb: Youth does not mind where it sets its foot.

Irish Proverb: Youth sheds many a skin. The steed (horse) does not retain its speed forever.

William James: Our Gilded Youths should be packed off to coal and iron mines, to freight trains, to fishing fleets in December, to dishwashing and clothes-washing, to road building and tunnel making, according to their choice, to get the childishness knocked out of them, and to come back into society with healthier sympathies and soberer ideas.

Anna Jameson: Childhood sometimes does pay a second visit to man; youth never.

Jewish Saying: Do not threaten a child: either punish or forgive him.

Jewish Saying: The rich have heirs, not children.

Joseph Joubert: Children need models rather than critics.

Carl Jung: The little world of childhood with its familiar surroundings is a model of the greater world. The more intensively the family has shaped its character upon the child, the more it will tend to feel and see its earlier miniature world again in the bigger world of adult life.

Carl Jung: If there is anything that we wish to change in a child, we should first examine it and see whether it is not something that could better be changed in ourselves.

Franz Kafka: Parents who expect gratitude from their children (there are even some who insist on it) are like usurers who gladly risk their capital if only they receive interest.

Franz Kafka: The bringing up of children as a conspiracy on the part of adults: We lure them from their unconstrained rompings into our narrow dwellings by pretenses in which we perhaps believe, but not in the sense we pretend.

Bel Kaufman: Children are the true connoisseurs. What's precious to them has no price—only value.

Sally Kempton: All children are potential victims, dependent upon the world's goodwill.

Edward M. Kennedy: If I can leave a single message with the younger generation, it is to lash yourself to the mast, like Ulysses, if you must come to escape the siren calls of complacency and indifference.

Joan Kiser: The sins of the fathers are often visited upon the sons-in-law."

Charles Lamb (English essayist, critic, 1775-1834): A sweet child is the sweetest thing in nature.

Charles Lamb: A child's nature is too serious a thing to admit of its being regarded as a mere appendage to another being.

Mary Lamb: Thou, straggler into loving arms, / Young climber up of knees, / When I forget thy thousand ways, / Then life and all shall cease.

Ann Landers: What the vast majority of American children need is to stop being pampered, stop being indulged, stop being chauffeured, stop being catered to. In the final analysis it is not what you do for your children but what you have taught them to do for themselves that will make them successful human beings.

Louis H. Lapham: I have begun to suspect that American society has little liking for its children, that more often than not children find themselves cast in the role of expensive enemies.

Fran Lebowitz: Ask your child what he wants for dinner only if he is buying.

Eda J. Le Shan: We have kept our children so busy with "useful" and "improving" activities that we are in danger of raising a generation of young people who are terrified of silence, of being alone with their own thoughts.

Meridel Le Sueur: Every generation must go further than the last or what's the use in it?

Sam Levenson: The high IQ has become the American equivalent of a Legion of Honor, positive proof of the child's intellectual aristocracy.... It has become more important to be smart kid than a good kid or even a healthy kid.

Ben B. Lindsey: We still put a blight on the "illegitimate" child, though we have never defined how he differs from ordinary children.

Ben B. Lindsey: I am for children first, because I am for Society first, and the children of today are the Society of tomorrow. I insist, therefore, on the right of the child to be born, and that there be no "illegitimate" children.

Art Linkletter: Children have an unerring instinct for knowing when they are being patronized. They go immediately on the defensive against head-patting adults who treat them like strange beings.

Henry Wadsworth Longfellow: Youth comes but once in a lifetime.

Henry Wadsworth Longfellow: Oh, thou child of many prayers! / Life hath quicksands—life hath snares! / Care and age come unawares!

Henry Wadsworth Longfellow: Childhood is the bough, where slumbered / Birds and blossoms many-numbered.

Henry Wadsworth Longfellow: Between the dark and the daylight, / When the night is beginning to lower, / Comes a pause in the day's occupations / That is known as the children's hour.

Henry Wadsworth Longfellow: There was a little girl, she had a little curl / Right in the middle of her forehead; / And when she was good, she was very, very, good, / And when she was bad, she was horrid.

Henry Wadsworth Longfellow: How beautiful is youth! How bright it gleams / With its illusions, aspirations, dreams! / A book of Beginnings, Story without End, / Each maid a heroine, and each man a friend!

Henry Wadsworth Longfellow: And my youth comes back to me. / And a verse of a Lapland song space / Is haunting my memory still: / "A boy's will is the wind's will, / And the thoughts of youth are long, long thoughts."

Henry Wadsworth Longfellow: A torn jacket is soon mended; but hard words bruise the heart of a child.

Amy Lowell: Youth condemns; maturity condones.

James Russell Lowell (law school graduate and American poet, 1819-1897): If youth be a defect, it is one that we outgrow only too soon.

James Russell Lowell: Children are God's apostles, day by day / Sent forth to preach a love, and hope, and peace.

Jackie "Moms" Mabley: The teenagers ain't all bad. I love 'em if nobody else does. There ain't nothin' wrong with young people. Jus' quit lyin' to 'em.

Archibald MacLeish: Children know the grace of God / Better than most of us. They see the world / The way the morning brings it back to them, / New and a born and fresh and wonderful.

Don Marquis: If a child shows himself incorrigible, he should be decently and quietly beheaded at the age of twelve, lest he grow to maturity, marry, and perpetuate his kind.

Don Marquis: In order not to influence a child, one must be careful not to be that child's parent or grandparent.

Judith Martin: In point of fact, we are all born rude. No it has ever appeared yet with the grace to understand how inconsiderate it is to disturb others in the middle of the night.

Groucho Marx: My mother loves children—she would have given anything if I had been one.

Ann McGovern: In those days, people did not think it was important for girls to read. Some people thought much reading gave girls brain fever.

Margaret Mead: Even very recently, the elders could say: "You know I have been young, and *you* can never have been old." But today's young people can reply: "You have never been young in the world I am young in, and you never can be...." this break between generations is wholly new: it is planetary and universal.

Margaret Mead: The adult on the verge of death may be permitted a return to childhood, as is the Japanese *kamikase* flier who is given toys to play with.

Karl A. Menninger: To cease to be loved is for the child practically synonymous with ceasing to live.

Karl Menninger: What's done to children, they will do to society.

Agnes Meyer: The children are always the chief victims of social chaos.

Edna St. Vincent Millay: This be our solace: that it was not said / When we were young and warm and in our prime, / Upon our couch we lay as lie the dead, / Sleeping away the unreturning time.

Edna St. Vincent Millay: Childhood is the Kingdom Where Nobody Dies.

Robert Morley: Show me the man who has enjoyed his school-days and I'll show you a bully and a bore.

Clark Moustakas: Viewing the child as an immature person is a way of escaping confronting him.

Daniel Moynihan: We have become the first society in history in which children are the poorest group in the population.

Lewis Mumford: The commonest axiom of history is that every generation revolts against its fathers and makes friends with its grandfathers.

Ogden Nash (American poet, 1902-1971, *Song to Be Sung by the Father of Infant Female Children*): ....Oh, somewhere he bubbles bubbles of milk, / And quietly sucks his thumbs. / His cheeks are roses painted on silk, / And his teeth are tucked in his gums. / But alas, the teeth will begin to grow, / And the bubbles will cease to bubble; / Given a score of years or so, / The roses will turn to stubble. / He'll sell a bound, or he'll write a book, / And his eyes will get that acquisitive look, / And raging and ravenous for the kill, / He'll boldly ask for the hand of Jill. / This infant whose middle / Is diapered still / Will want to marry / My daughter Jill. / Oh sweet be his slumber and moist his middle! / My dreams, I fear, are infanticiddle. / A fig for embryo Lohengrins! / I'll open all of his safety pins, / I'll pepper his powder, and salt his bottle, / And give him readings from Aristotle. / Sand for his spinach I'll gladly bring, / And Tabasco sauce for his teething ring. / Then perhaps he'll struggle through fire and water / To marry somebody else's daughter.

Friedrich Nietzsche: Innocence is the child, and forgetfulness, a new beginning, a game, a self-rolling wheel, a first movement, a holy Yea.

Dorothy Law Nolte: If a child lives with approval, he learns to live with himself.

Kathleen Norris: To children childhood holds no particular advantage.

Oriental Saying: Parents who are afraid to put their foot down usually have children who step on their toes.

George Orwell (pseud. of Eric Arthur Blair, British author and satirist, 1903-1950): Not to expose your true feelings to an adult seems to be instinctive from the age of seven or eight onwards.

George Orwell: The child thinks of growing old as an almost obscene calamity, which for some mysterious reason will never happen to itself. All who have passed the age of thirty are joyless grotesques, endlessly fussing about things of no importance and staying alive without, so far as the child can see, having anything to live for. Only child life is real life.

George Orwell: One can love a child, perhaps, more deeply than one can love another adult, but it is rash to assume that the child feels any love in return. Looking back on my own childhood ... I do not believe that I ever felt love for any mature person except my mother, and even her I did not trust, in the sense that shyness made me conceal most of my real feelings from her. Love, the spontaneous, unqualified emotion of love was something I could only feel for people who were young.

George Orwell: A child may be a mass of egoism and rebelliousness, but it has not accumulated experience to give it confidence in its own judgments. On the whole it will accept what it is told, and it will believe in the most fantastic way in the knowledge and power of the adults surrounding it.

Dorothy Parker: The best way to keep children home is to make the home a pleasant atmosphere—and let the air out of the (car's) tires.

Joe Paterno: It's time we let kids grow up naturally. Suppose they don't grow up to be athletic superstars. That isn't so terrible. Let them find their own interests and their own levels. Let them be kids instead of forcing them to play being adults.

Jim M. Perdue (*Who Will Speak For The Victim? A Practical Treatise on Plaintiff's Jury Argument*, State Bar of Texas, 2002): Childhood is that wonderful time when all you have to do to lose weight is take a bath. The only thing that children wear out faster than shoes are parents and teachers. It seems that the thing most children save for a rainy day is lots of energy. And while healthy children may tear up a house, they will never break up a home. A child's ear is a delicate instrument that cannot hear a parent's shout from the next room, but picks up the faintest tinkle of the ice cream vendor's bell .... The best Christmas gift of all is the presence of a happy family all wrapped up with one another.

Jim M. Perdue (*Who Will Speak For The Victim? A Practical Treatise on Plaintiff's Jury Argument*, State Bar of Texas, 2002): We all know that fear magnifies pain and mental anguish in a person of any age. But a child cannot build the same bridge over troubled waters as can an adult. Children lack the armor of maturity – an aquired stoic attitude that what cannot be endured must somehow be tolerated. They have been taught that pain means punishment or discipline; in a child, needless and accidental pain may plague the conscience as well as the soul.... Pain and anguish do not come to children in reduced doses like baby aspirin. The torture of broken bones and ravaged flesh may be the same for a child as an adult, but it is magnified many times by the child's fear, which lies beyond the reach of any remedy – any pill, treatment or therapy.

Jim M. Perdue (*Who Will Speak For The Victim? A Practical Treatise on Plaintiff's Jury Argument*, State Bar of Texas, 2002): It is said that God laughs every time he makes a boy. The Greek philosopher Plato noted that "[o]f all the animals, the boy is the most unmanageable." Boys are found everywhere but seldom standing still. They may be climbing a tree, digging a hole, crawling under a bush, or building something that they haven't quite figured out yet what it will be when it is finished. A boy is truth with freckles on his face, beauty with a frog in his pocket, the wonders of a mind that can master the multiplication tables, and the hope of the future with a poster in his room that says, "He who dies with the most toys wins!" To a father, being with a son is like being subjected to an inquisition. "Why does it work?" "Why is the sky blue?" .... To mothers, boys can sometimes be an aggravation. They can clutter up a room faster than three adults can clean it. But simply ask any mother about her son and watch the pride appear on her face as she reaches into her purse for those photographs that she loves so much to share with other people.... The argument tthat the victim was less than perfect and that, therefore, damages ought to be less is specious on its face. There are no perfect boys.

Jim M. Perdue (*Who Will Speak For The Victim? A Practical Treatise on Plaintiff's Jury Argument*, State Bar of Texas, 2002): Little girls are the nicest things that can happen to people. Somewhere between the blossoms of spring and the laughter of summer resides the spirit of a daughter. Little girls are freedom in pigtails, innocence sitting next to a puddle while making mud pies, and independence with a pout on her face. Little girls like playing in mommy's makeup, having tea parties in their playhouse, and dressing up with bows and ribbons. They always seem to smell of lilacs and springtime. To men, one of life's unresolved mysteries is what young girls giggle about. But to everyone, they are, without doubt, the sweetest of God's creatures.

William Lyon Phelps: Nature makes boys and girls lovely to look upon so they can be tolerated until they acquire some sense.

Edgar Allan Poe: Childhood knows the human heart.

Alexander Pope: Just as the twig is bent, the tree's inclined.

Dan Pursuit: All children wear the sign: "I want to be important NOW." Many of our juvenile delinquent problems arise because nobody reads the sign.

John Ray: Children pick up words as pigeons peas / And utter them again as God shall please.

John Ray: Children, when they are little, they make parents fools; when great [EDITOR: when *they think* they have grown up], mad.

Malvina Reynolds: Where are you going, my little one, little one, / Where are you going, my baby, my own? / Turn around and you're two, / Turn around and you're four, / Turn around and you're a young girl going out of my door.

James Whitcomb Riley: Oh! The old swimming hole! when I last saw the place, / The scenes was all changed, like the change in my face.

Edwin Arlington Robinson: Youth sees too far to see how near it is / To seeing farther.

Will Rogers: We changed with the times, so we cant blame the children for just joining the times, without even having to change.

Will Rogers: I was not a child prodigy, because a child prodigy is a child who knows as much when it is a child as it does when it grows up.

Franklin D. Roosevelt: I confess to pride in this coming generation. You are working out your own salvation; you are more in love with life; you play with fire openly, where we did in secret, and few of you are burned!

John Ruskin: Give a little love to a child, and you get a great deal back.

Bertrand Russell: Children, after being limbs of Satan in traditional theology and mystically illuminated angels in the minds of educational reformers, have reverted to being little devils—not theological demons inspired by the Evil One, but scientific Freudian abomination's inspired by the Unconscious.

Bertrand Russell: The pleasures of childhood should in the main be such as the child extracts from his environment by means of some effort and inventiveness.

Russian Proverb: If you live without being a father you will die without being a human being.

Russian Proverb: Small children give you headache; big children heartache.

Saint-Exupery: A child is not frightened at the thought of being patiently transmuted into an old man.

Carl Sandberg: A baby is God's opinion that the world should go on.

George Santayana: Children are natural mythologists: they beg to be told tales, and love not only to invent but to enact falsehoods.

George Santayana: Our youth is like a rustic at the play / That cries aloud in simple-hearted fear, / Curses the villain, shudders at the fray, / And weeps before the maiden's wreathed bier.

George Santayana: Children are on a different plane, belong to a generation and way of feeling properly their own; there is seldom complete understanding between them and their parents, so that affection here suffers from some strain and uncertainty, all the more painful the greater the affection is.

Milton Sapirstein: Making terms with reality, with things as they are, is a full-time business for the child.

Olive Schreiner: The barb in the arrow of childhood's suffering is this – its intense loneliness, its intense ignorance.

William Shakespeare (*Cymbeline,* Act V, v): Briefly die their joys / That place them on the truth of girls and boys.

William Shakespeare (*III Henry VI*, Act V, v): How sweet a plant have you untimely cropp'd! / You have no children, butchers! / If you had, / The thoughts of them would have stirr'd up remorse.

William Shakespeare (*King Lear*, Act I, iv): How sharper than a serpent's tooth it is / To have a thankless child!

William Shakespeare (*Macbeth*, Act II, ii): 'Tis the eye of childhood / That fears a painted devil.

William Shakespeare (*The Merry Wives of Windsor*, Act V, iii): Better a little chiding than a great deal of heart-break.

William Shakespeare (*Much Ado About Nothing*, Act IV, i): Grieved I, I had but one? / Chid I for that at frugal nature's frame? / O, one too much by thee! Why had I one?

William Shakespeare (*Othello*, Act IV, ii): Those that do teach young babes / Do it with gentle means and easy tasks

William Shakespeare (*Richard II*, Act IV, iv): Unruly children make their sire Stoop.

William Shakespeare (*Richard III*, Act IV, iv): Your children were vexation to your youth, / But mine shall be a comfort to your age.

William Shakespeare (*Romeo and Juliet*, Act III, v): Wife, we scarce thought us blest / That God had lent us but this only child; / But now I see this one is one too much.

William Shakespeare (*Twelfth Night*, Act II, iv): I am all the daughters of my father's house, / And all the brothers too.

George Bernard Shaw: Youth is such a wonderful thing. What a crime to waste it on children.

George Bernard Shaw: A child hasn't a grown-up person's appetite for affection. A little of it goes a long way with them; and they like a good imitation of it better than the real thing, as every nurse knows.

Isaac Bashevis Singer (on receiving the Nobel Prize for Literature, 1978): Children don't read to find their density, to free themselves from guilt, to quench the thirst for rebellion or to get rid of alienation. They have no use for psychology. They detest sociology too. They still believe in God, the family, angels, devils, witches, goblins, logic, clarity, punctuation, and other such obsolete stuff.... When a book is boring, they yawn openly. They don't expect their writer to redeem humanity, but to leave to adults such childish illusions.

Slogan for free speech, 1964: I am a student. Please do not fold, spindle, or mutilate me.

Logan Pearsall Smith: The denunciation of the young is a necessary part of the hygiene of older people, and greatly assists in the circulation of their blood.

Sophocles: Children are the anchors that hold a mother to life.

Dr. Benjamin Spock: Perhaps a child who is fussed over gets a feeling of destiny, he thinks he is in the world for something important and it gives him drive and confidence.

Dr. Benjamin Spock: Every child senses, with all the horse sense that's in him, that any parent is angry inside when children misbehave, and they dread more the anger that is rarely or never expressed openly, wondering how awful it might be.

Dr. Wilhelm Stekhel: Child desires are eternal and seldom yield to the lapse of time.

Dr. Wilhelm Stekhel: The child is surrounded by so much authority, so much school, so much dinity, so much law, that it would have to break down under the weight of all these restraints if it were not saved from such a fate by meeting with a friend.

Robert Louis Stevenson: A child should always say what's true, / And speak when he is spoken to, / And behave mannerly at table: / At least as far as he is able.

Thomas Szasz: A child becomes an adult when he realizes that he has a right not only to be right but also to be wrong.

Thomas Szasz: Childhood is a prison sentence of twenty-one years.

Rabindranath Tagore: Life's aspirations come / in the guise of children.

Janabeth Fleming Taylor: Raising kids is like being pecked to death by a duck!

Dorothy Thompson: Healthy children are, among other things, little animals, who only slowly evolve (if they ever do) into civilized human beings.... Children are not naturally "good," according to any standards ever set by a civilized society. They are natural barbarians.

Mark Twain: Familiarity breeds contempt—and children.

Mark Twain: Life should begin with age and its privileges and accumulations, and end with youth and its capacity to splendidly enjoy such advantages.

Mark Twain: Consider well the proportions of things. It is better to be a young June-bug than an old bird of paradise.

UA: Adolescence is the agent which children stop asking questions because they know all the answers.

UA: One thing a child outgrows in a hurry is your pocketbook.

UA: A boy is an appetite with the skin pulled over it.

UA: A spoilt child never loves its mother.

UA: Children pick up words as pigeons peas.

UA: Bachelor's wives and maid's children are well taught.

UA: If anything makes a child thirstier than going to bed, it's knowing that his parents have gone to bed too.

UA: One of the mysteries of life is how the incompetent boy who was not good enough to marry the daughter can be the father of the smartest grandchild in the world.

UA: A little boy handed his father a poor report card. He asked: " Father, what do you think is my trouble—heredity or environment?"

UA: First you teach a child to talk; then you have to teach it to be quiet.

UA: The more you love your children, the more care you should take to neglect them occasionally. The web of affection can be drawn too tight.

UA: When I was younger, my parents told me what to do; now that I am old, my children tell me what to do. I wonder where I'll be able to do what I want to do.

John Updike: The difference between a childhood and a boyhood must be this: our childhood is what we alone have had; our boyhood is what any boy in our environment would have had.

John Updike: If men do not keep on speaking terms with children, they cease to be men, and become merely machines for eating and earning money.

Gore Vidal: Never have children, only grandchildren.

Gore Vidal: Until the rise of American advertising, it never occurred to anyone anywhere in the world that the teenager was a captive in a hostile world of adults.

Charles Dudley Warner: It is true that a child is always hungry all over; but he is also curious all over, and his curiosity is excited about as early as his hunger.

David Weinberger (slogan of the 1970's attributed to him): "Don't trust anyone over 30."

John Greenleaf Whittier (Amrican poet, 1807-1892): Blessings on thee, little man, / Barefoot boy, with cheek of tan!... / From my heart I give thee joy—/ I was once a barefoot boy!

John Greenleaf Whittier: Oh, for boyhood's painless play, / Sleep that wakes in laughing day, / Health that mocks the doctors rules, / Knowledge never learned of schools.

John Greenleaf Whittier: I mourn no more my vanished years: / Beneath a tender rain, / And April rain of smiles and tears, / My heart is young again.

Doctor Who: There's no point in being grown up if you can't be childish sometimes.

Oscar Wilde: In America the young are always ready to give to those who are older than themselves the full benefits of their inexperience.

Oscar Wilde: Children begin by loving their parents. After a time they judge them. Rarely, if ever, do they forgive them.

George Will: Americans are predisposed to believe too much in environmental determinism. They are inclined to regard infants as malleable uncles of "potential"—clay on which determined parents, handbooks in hand, can work wonders. In the "nature versus nurture" argument, Americans are can-do optimists who believe that skilled nurturing is all-important in shaping individuals. The United States is a manufacturing nation that sometimes seems to regard to children as raw material from which ever-better products can be manufactured as know-how increases.

George Will: I have been slow to understand that the contrariness of the "terrible twos" is the bloody-mindedness of little people trying to get a grip on their partially formed selves. I used to think that a two-year-old's father needs only what a Washington columnist needs, the ability to look perfectly grave no matter what nonsense is being spoken to him. But I no longer think that what two-year-olds say is nonsense.

Margery Williams (*"The Velveteen Rabbit"*): "What is real?" asked the Rabbit one day, ... "Real isn't how you are made," said the Skin Horse. "it's a thing that happens to you. When a child loves you for a long, long time, not just to play with, but really loves you, then you become real." "Does it hurt?" asked the Rabbit. "Sometimes," said the Skin Horse, for he was always truthful. "When you are Real you don't mind being hurt."

Woodrow Wilson: The most conservative persons I ever met are college undergraduates.

William Wordsworth: A simple Child, / That lightly draws its breath, / And feels its life in every limb, / What should it know of death?

Frank Lloyd Wright: To me, young has no meaning. It's something you can do nothing about. Nothing at all. But youth is a quality. And if you have youth you never lose it.

CHOICE

Uncle Anthony: The Navy made life simple – there were no choices for us – we just followed orders.

Uncle Anthony: Sometimes some guys suffer from "Analysis Paralysis" – they spend too much time thinking about all the possible choices they got, and they don't make one.

Aunt Mary Carlo: Y'know what da poet (Robert Frost) said about "da path not taken" – well, dat's life – lots and lots of choices and T intersections we gotta make decisions and then live wit' 'em.

American Saying: You pays your money and you takes your choice (or chances).

Maya Angelo: At fifteen life had taught me undeniably that surrender, in its place, was as honorable as resistance, especially of one had no choice.

W.H. Auden: Choice of attention – to pay attention to *this* or ignore *that* – is to the inner life what choice of action is to the outer. In both cases, a man is responsible for his choice and must accept the consequences, whatever they may be.

Saul Bellow: Alternatives, and particularly desirable alternatives, grow only on imaginary trees.

Bible: Acts 20:35: It is more blessed to give than to recieve.

Bible: Deuteronomy, 30:19: I have set before you life and death, blessing and cursing: therefore choose life, that both thou and thy seed may live.

Bible: Job, 34:3: Let us choose to use judgment: let us know among ourselves what is good.

Bible: John 15:16: Ye have not chosen me, but I have chosen you, and ordained you, that ye should go and bring forth fruit.

Bible: 3 John 11: Follow not that which is evil, but that which is good.

Bible: Joshua, 24:15: Choose you this day whom ye will serve.

Bible: Mark 12:17: Render to Caesar the things that are Caesar's, and to God the things that are God's.

Ambrose Bierce: DECIDE, v. To succumb to the preponderance of one set of influences over another set.

Ambrose Bierce: PREFERENCE, n. A sentiment, or frame of mind, induced by the erroneous belief that one thing is better than another.

Ambrose Bierce: "There's no free will," says the philosopher; "to hang is most unjust." / "There is no free will," assents the officer; "we hang because we must."

Louise Bogan: The good novelist is distinguished from the bad one chiefly by a gift of choice. Choice, itself a talent, as taste is a talent, is not, however, enough. Only extreme sanity and balance of selection can give to prose fiction the dignity and excitement inherent in more rigid forms of writing: drama, poetry, and the expositions of ideas.

Phillips Brooks: As you emphasize your life, you must localize and define it. The more truly and earnestly you come to do anything, the more clearly you will see that you cannot do everything. He who is truly good must be good for something. To be good for everything is to be good for nothing.

Robert Browning: Life's business.

Ken Burke: If decisions were a choice between alternatives, decisions would come easy. Decision is the selection and formulation of alternatives.

Sir Winston Churchill: Some men change their party for the sake of their principles; others their principles for the sake of their party.

Sir Wnston Churchill: They are decided only to be undecided, resolved to be irresolute, adamant for drift, solid for fluidity, all-powerful to be impotent.

Dinah Mulock Craik: It seemed as if she had given these treasures and left him alone – to use them, or lose them, apply them, or misapply them, according to his own choice. That is all we can do with children, when they grow into big children, old enough to distinguish between right and wrong, and too old to be forced to do either.

John Dewey: Mankind likes to think in terms of extreme opposites. It is given to formulating its beliefs in terms of *Either-Ors,* between which it recognizes no intermediate possibilities. When forced to recognize that the extremes cannot be acted upon, it is still inclined to hold that they are all right in theory but that when it comes to practical matters circumstances compel us to compromise.

Dostoevsky: What man wants is simply *independent* choice, whatever that independence may cost and wherever it may lead.

Marie Dressler: Fate cast me to play the role of an ugly duckling with no promise of swanning. Therefore, I sat down when a mere child – fully realizing just how *utterly* "mere" I was – and figured out my life early. Most people do it, but they do it too late. At any rate, from the beginning I have played my life as a comedy rather than the tragedy many would have made of it.

Dutch Proverb: Trouble.

Max Eastman: In practical life, when confronted with one of its diverging grand highways, I was incapable of any decision whatever. I wanted to go both ways; I wanted to go all ways. I never could find the reason for a choice, and I rarely made one.

Jonathan Edwards: The Will (without any metaphysical refining) is plainly, that by which the mind chooses any thing. The faculty of the Will is that faculty or power or principal of mind by which it is capable of choosing.

George Eliot: The strongest principle of growth lies in human choice.

T.S. Eliot: In a minute there is time / For decisions and revisions which in a minute will reverse.

Ralph Waldo Emerson: To hazard the contradiction—freedom is necessary.

Ralph Waldo Emerson: As a man thinketh so is he, and as a man chooseth so is he.

Epictetus: It is your own conviction which compels you; that is, choice compels choice.

Edna Ferber: Don't you believe 'em when they say that what you don't know won't hurt you. Biggest lie ever was. See it all and go your own way and nothing'll hurt you. If what you see ain't pretty, what's the odds! See it anyway. Then next time you don't have to look.

Annie Johnson Flint: Have you come to the Red Sea place in your life / Where, in spite of all you can do, / There is no way out, there is no way back, / There is no other way but through?

Henry Ford (1909 Model T debut): "People can have it **an**y colour – so long as it's black."

Robert Frost ("The Road Not Taken," 1916): Two roads diverged in a wood, and I—/ I took the one less traveled by, / And that has made all the difference.

Kahlil Gibran: We choose our joys and sorrows long before we experience them.

Robert Grant: The demands of modern living are so exacting that men and women everywhere must exercise deliberate selection to live wisely.

Judge Learned Hand: We accept the verdict of the past until the need for change cries out loudly enough to force upon us a choice between the comforts of further inertia and the irksomeness of action.

Japanese Proverb: He who hunts two hares leaves one and loses the other.

William James: When you have to make a choice and don't make it, that is in itself a choice.

William James: The question of free will is insoluble on strictly psychologic grounds.

John Jay New York Governor, first Chief Justice of US, 1745-1829): It is not a new observation that the people in the country [EDITOR: meaning farmers in the country side] (if, like the Americans, intelligent and well-informed) seldom adopt and steadily preserve for many years an erroneous opinion respecting their interests.

Jewish Proverb: No choice is also a choice.

Jeane Kirkpatrick: All of us confront limits of body, talent, temperament. But that is not all. We are, all of us, also constrained by our time, our place, our civilization. We are bound by the culture we have in common, that culture which distinguishes us from other people in other times and places. Cultural constraints condition and limit our choices, shaping our characters with their imperatives.

Henry Kissinger: The public life of every political figure is a continual struggle to rescue an element of choice from the pressure of circumstance.

Marie Leneru: I will never abdicate. I shall always want everything. To accept my life I must prefer it.

Thomas Mann: Some of necessity go astray, because for them there is no such thing as a right path.

Margaret Mead: A society which is clamoring for choice, which is filled with many articulate groups, each urging its own brand of salvation, its own variety of economic philosophy, will give each new generation no peace until all have chosen or gone under, unable to bear the conditions of choice.

Margaret Mead: Chief among our gains must be reckoned this possibility of choice, the recognition of many possible ways of life, where other civilizations have recognized only one. Where other civilizations give a satisfactory outlet to only one temperamental type, be he mystic or soldier, businessman or artist, a civilization in which there are many standards offers a possibility of satisfactory adjustment to individuals of many different temperamental types, of diverse gifts and varying interests.

Thomas Merton: A superficial freedom to wander aimlessly here or there, to taste this or that, to make a choice of distractions (in Pascal's sense) is simply a sham. It claims to be a freedom of "choice" when it has evaded the basic task of discovering who it is that chooses.

Lucy Montgomery: When a man is alone he's mighty apt to be with the devil – if he ain't with God. He has to choose which company he'll keep, I reckon.

George Moore: The difficulty in life is the choice.

Toni Morrison: Which you want? A whipping and no turnips or turnips and no whipping?

Napolean I (French Emperor, 1769-1821): Nothing is more difficult, and therefore more precious, than to be able to decide.

Republican campaign slogan (Goldwater, 1964): A Choice Not an Echo.

Will Rogers: I don't care how poor and inefficient a little country is; they like to run their own business. I know men that would make my wife a better husband than I am; but, darn it, I'm not going to give her to 'em.

Will Rogers: A difference of opinion is what makes horse racing and missionaries.

Alvin E. Rolland: You cannot walk the middle of the road holding hands with tradition on one side and modernism on the other. You have to make a choice.

Eleanor Roosevelt: ... we do not always like what is good for us in this world.

Joseph Roux: We often experience more regret over the part we have left, then pleasure over the part we have preferred.

Muriel Rukeyser: The strength, the grossness, spirit and gall of choice.

Herbert L. Samuel: The power of choice must involve the possibility of error—that is the essence of choosing.

Jean Paul Sartre: What is not possible is not to choose.

William Shakespeare (*Hamlet*, Act I, iii): On his choice depends / The safety and health of this whole state.

William Shakespeare (*I Henry VI,* Act V, i): I shall be well content with any choice / Tends to God's glory.

William Shakespeare (*Julius Caesar,* Act IV, iii): There is a tide in the affairs of men / Which, taken at the flood, leads on to fortune; / Omitted. All the voyage of their life / Is bound in shallows and in miseries.

William Shakespeare (*The Merchant of Venice*, Act II, i): In terms of choice, I am not solely led / By nice direction of a maiden's eyes; / Besides, the lottery of my destiny / Bars me.

William Shakespeare (*The Merchant of Venice*, Act II, ix): I will not choose what many men desire, / Because I will not jump with common spirits, / And rank me with the barbarous multitude.

William Shakespeare (*The Merchant of Venice*, Act III, ii): Let music sound while he doth make his choice

William Shakespeare (*A Midsummer Night's Dream*, Act I, i): If there were a sympathy in choice, / War, death, or sickness did lay seige to it

William Shakespeare (*Othello*, Act I, i): Perferment goes by letter, and affection.

William Shakespeare (*Pericles*, Act II, v): Your choice agrees with mine; I like that well.

William Shakespeare (*Taming of the Shrew*, Act I, i): There's small choice in rotten apples.

William Shakespeare (*Troilus and Cressida*, Act I, iii): And choice, being mutual act of all our souls, / Makes merit her election.

Gertrude Stein: One must either accept some theory or else believe one's instinct or follow the world's opinion.

John Steinbeck: When a man is finally boxed and he has no choice, he begins to decorate his box.

George Sutherland (Utah lawyer, US Senator, Assoc Justice US Supreme Court, 1862-1942): In reality, the carrier is given no choice, except a choice between the rock and the whirlpool, - an option to forego a privilege which may be vital to his livelihood or submit to a requirement which may constitute an intolerable burden. *Frost & F. Trucking Co. v. Railroad Com,* 271 US 583, 70 L. ed. 1101, 76 S.Ct. 605, (1926).

Mark Twain: Life does not consist mainly—or even largely—of facts and happenings. It consists mainly of the storm of thoughts that is forever blowing through one's head.

Mark Twain: Well, then, says I, what's the use you learning to do right, when it's troublesome to do right and ain't no trouble to do wrong, and the wages is just the same?

CIGARS/SMOKING (TOBACCO)

Uncle Anthony: Just because you got a big cigar to smoke don't mean you're a big shot.

Aunt Mary Carlo: Some of these guys struttin' around with those great BIG Havanas act like they're manhood is really that big.

Aunt Mary Carlo: I callsim Mr. SNUFF, 'cause he's always puttin' his cigar smoke in udder people's noses.

Steve Allen: Asthma doesn't seem to bother me any more unless I'm around cigars or dogs. The thing that would bother me most would be a dog smoking a cigar.

Old American Indian Saying: Follow cigar smoke, fat men there.

John Bain: There are two things a man never forgets—his first love and his first cigar.

R. H. Barham: For this you've my word, and I never yet broke it. / So put that in your pipe, my Lord Otto, and smoke it.

J.M. Barrie: The Elizabethan age might be better named the beginning of the smoking era.

Dave Barry: Cigarette sales would drop to zero overnight if the warning said "CIGARETTES CONTAIN FAT."

Bible: Proverbs 30:15: There are three things that are never satisfied, yea, four things say not, It is enough: The grave; and the barren womb; the earth that is not filled with water; and the fire that saith not, It is enough.

Ambrose Bierce: MEERSCHAUM, n. (Literally, seaform, and by many erroneously supposed to be made of it.) A fine white clay, which for convenience in colouring it brown is made into tobacco pipes and smoked by the workmen engaged in that industry. The purpose of coloring it has not been disclosed by the manufacturers.

Ambrose Bierce: SALAMANDER, n. Originally a reptile inhabiting fire; later, an anthropomorphous immortal, but still a pyrophile. Salamanders are now believed to be extinct, the last one of which we have an account having been seen in Carcassonne by the Abbe Belloc, who exorcised it with a bucket of holy water.

Brazilian Proverb: Every cigar goes up in smoke.

Robert Williams Buchanan: The post-prandial [EDITOR: after mealtime] cigar.

E. G. Bulwer-Lytton: A good cigar is as great a comfort to a man as a good cry to a woman.

George Burns: I smoke ten to fifteen cigars a day. At my age I have to hold on to something.

George Burns: If I paid ten dollars for a cigar, first I'd make love to it, then I'd smoke it.

Lord Byron (*The Island*, Canto II): Sublime tobacco! / Divine in hookas [EDITOR: water pipes], glorious in a pipe, / When tipp'd with amber, mellow, rich, and ripe; / Like other charmers, wooding the caress / More dazzlingly when daring in full dress. /Yet thy true lovers more admire, by far, / Thy naked beauties—give me a cigar!

Richard Carleton: I am sure there are many things better than a good cigar, but right now, I can't think of what they might be.

Joyce Cary: The cigar, which is, in caricatures, the symbol of the ruthless plutocrat, the oppressor of the poor, in Churchill's mouth expresses a hundred admirable and popular qualities, such as vitality, love of life, defiance of popular opinion, independence of mind, together with all sorts of fine shades in allusion, according to the personal idea.

Alexander Chase: To the average cigarette smoker the world is his ashtray.

Sir Winston Churchill: I must point out that my rule of life prescribed as an absolutely sacred rite smoking cigars and also the drinking of alcohol before, after, and if need be during all meals and in the intervals between them.

Sidonie Gabriella Colette: Smokers, male and female, inject and excuse idleness in their lives every time they light a cigarette.

Sidonie Gabriellaq Colette: If a woman knows a man's preferences, including his preference in cigars, and if a man knows what a woman likes, they will be suitably armed to face one another.

William Cowper: Pernicious weed! whose scent the fair annoys, / Unfriendly to society's chief joys, / Thy worst effect is banishing for hours / The sex whose presence civilizes ours.

Cuban Saying: Where there's a good smoke there's a cigar smoker.

Cuban Saying: As you approach thirty, you have a thirty ring gauge; as you approach fifty, you have a fifty ring gauge.

Zino Davidoff: The cigar...is something that commands respect. It is made for all the senses, for all the pleasures, for the nose, the palate, the fingers, the eyes... A good cigar contains the promise of a totally pleasurable experience.

Zino Davidoff: To know how to smoke is to recover certain forgotten rhythms, to re-establish communication with the self.

Zino Davidoff: The best cigar in the world is the one you prefer to smoke on special occasions, enabling you to relax and enjoy that which gives you maximum pleasure.

Zino Davidoff: If your wife doesn't like the aroma of your cigar, change your wife.

Benjamin Disraeli: Tobacco is the tomb of love.

Arthur Conan Doyle: It is quite a three-pipe problem.

King Edward VII of England (after assuming the throne. His mother, Queen Victoria, had previously banned smoking in court): "Gentlemen, you may smoke."

Albert Einstein (when he gave up smoking at the request of his second wife Elza): You see I am no longer a slave to my pipe, but I am a slave to that woman.

T.S. Eliot: Let us take the air, in a tobacco trance, / Admire the monuments, / Discuss the late events, / Correct our watches by the public clocks, / Then sit for half an hour and drink our bocks.

Queen Elizabeth I of England (1553-1603) (Speaking to Sir Walter Raleigh): I have seen many a man turn his gold into smoke, but you are the first who has turned smoke into gold.

Ralph Waldo Emerson: The believing we do something when we do nothing is the first illusion of tobacco.

Ralph Waldo Emerson: The scatterbrain, Tobacco. Yet a man of no conversation should smoke.

Estonian Proverb: It is better to be without a wife for a bit than without tobacco for an hour.

Eugene Field: What smells so? Has somebody been burning a Rag, or is there a Dead Mule in the Back yard? No, the Man is Smoking a Five-Cent Cigar.

Philip Freneau: Tobacco surely was designed / To poison, and destroy mankind.

Sigmund Freud: Sometimes a cigar is just a cigar

Sigmund Freud: Smoking is indispensable if one has nothing to kiss.

Sigmund Freud: My boy! Smoking is one of the greatest and cheapest enjoyments in life, and if you decide in advance not to smoke, I can only feel sorry for you.

Robert Frost: The difference between a man and his valet: they both smoke the same cigars, but only one pays for them.

John Galsworthy: By the cigars they smoke, and the composers they love, ye shall know the texture of men's souls.

Lou Gehrig: The enjoyment of a cigar after a hard week gives me a feeling of well-being and relaxation that a Valium could not match. While there may be a more ideal form of stress reduction, I haven't yet discovered anything else as effective and easy.

W. S. Gilbert: I smoke like a furnace.

Horace Greely: A cigar has "...a fire at one end and a fool at the other."

Sydney J. Harris: Nobody can be so revolutingly smug as the man who has just given up smoking.

Ernest Hemingway: Cigarettes smell so awful to you when you have a nose that can truly smell.

Graham Lee Hemminger: Tobacco is a dirty weed. I like it. / It satisfies no normal need. I like it. / It makes you thin, it makes you lean, / It takes the hair right off your bean. / It's the worst darn stuff I've ever seen. / I like it.

Russell Hoban: But when I don't smoke I scarcely feel as if I'm living. I don't feel as if I'm living unless I'm killing myself.

Oliver Wendell Holmes, Sr: Certain things are good for nothing until they have been kept a long while; and some are good for nothing until the have been long kept and *used.* Of the first, wine is the illustrious and immortal example. Of those which must be kept and used I will name three,—meershaum pipes, violins, and poems. The meershaum is but a poor affair until it has burned a thousand offerings to the cloud-compelling deities.... The fire is lighted in its central shrine, and gradually the juices which the broad leaves of the Great Vegetable had sucked up from an acre and curdled into a drachm are diffused through its thirsting pores.

Betty Hutton (as Annie Oakley in 1935 movie *Annie Oakley*): Close, Colonel, but no cigar!

Robert G. Ingersoll: For my part I had rather smoke one cigar than hear two sermons.

Irish Proverb: Smoke your pipe and be silent; there's only wind and smoke in the world.

King James I of England (1573-1625): A custom loathsome to the eye, hateful to the nose, harmful to the brain, dangerous to the lungs, and in the black, stinking fume thereof, nearest resembling the horrible Stygian smoke of the pit that is bottomless.

King James I of England: Herein is not only a great vanity, but a great contempt of God's good gifts, that the sweetness of man's breath, being a good gift of God, should be willfully corrupted by this stinking smoke.

King James I of England: A branch of the sin of drunkenness, which is the root of all sins.

Ben Jonson (English playwright, poet, 1573?-1637): Neither do thou lust after that tawney weed tobacco.

Ben Jonson: Ods me, I marvel what pleasure or felicity they have in taking their roguish tobacco. It is good for nothing but to choke a man, and fill him full of smoke and embers.

Samuel Johnson: Smoking ... is a shocking thing, blowing smoke out of our mouths into other people's mouths, eyes and noses, and having the same thing done to us.

Dr. John Harvey Kellogg: The tobacco business is a conspiracy against womanhood and manhood. It owes its origin to that scoundrel Sir Walter Raleigh, who was likewise the founder of American slavery.

Rudyard Kipling (English writer, poet, 1865-1936): A woman is only a woman, but a good cigar is a smoke.

Rudyard Kipling: A million surplus Maggies are willing to bear the yoke; / And a woman is only a woman, but a good Cigar is a Smoke.

Rudyard Kipling: For Maggie has written a letter to give me my choice between / The wee little whimpering Love and the great god Nick o' Teen.

Fletcher Knebel: It is now proved beyond doubt that smoking is one of the leading causes of statistics.

Charles Lamb: For thy sake, Tobacco, I / Would do anything but die.

Charles Lamb: This very night I am going to leave off tobacco! Surely there must be some other world in which this unconquerable purpose shall be realized.

Charles Lamb: Tobacco has been my evening comfort and my morning curse for these five years.

Charles Lamb: Thou through such a mist dost show us, / That our best friends do not know us.

Abraham Lincoln: Hold on with a bulldog grip, and chew and smoke as much as possible.

Thomas R. Marshall (US politician, 1875): What this country really needs is a good five cent cigar.

Thomas R. Marshall (US Vice President, 1920): The chief need of the country... is a really good 5-cent cigar.

Groucho Marx (Responding to a woman contestant who, explaining why she had twenty-two children, said "because I love children, and I think that's our purpose here on earth, and I love my husband"): I love my cigar too, but I take it out of my mouth once in awhile.

Groucho Marx: Given the choice between a woman and a cigar, I will always choose the cigar.

Groucho Marx: A thing that has always baffled me about women is that they will saturate themselves with a pint of perfume, a pound of sachet powder, an evil-smelling lip rouge, a peculiar-smelling hair ointment and a half-dozen varieties of body oils, and then thay have the effrontery to complain of the aroma of a fine dollar (EDITOR:$5) cigar.

Somerset Maugham: I promised myself that if ever I had some money that I would savor a cigar each day after lunch and dinner. This is the only resolution of my youth that I have kept, and the only realized ambition which has not brought disillusion.

Napolean III (1808-1873): This vice brings in one hundred million francs in taxes every year. I will certainly forbid it at once – as soon as you can name a virtue that brings in as much revenue.

Ogden Nash: There was a young man of Herne Bay / who was making some fireworks one day: / but he dropped his cigar / in the gunpowder jar. / There was a young man of Herne Bay.

Carry Nation (after snatching lit cigars from smokers' mouths): I want all hellions to quit puffing that hell fume in God's clean air!

Mary S. Ott: Cigarettes are killers that travel in packs.

Malcolm Potts, M.D.: It would be a service to mankind if the pill were available in slot machines and the cigarette were placed on prescription.

George Dennison Prentice: Some things are better eschewed than chewed; tobacco is one of them.

Branch Wesley Rickey (lawyer and legendary baseball executive, because of the clouds of cigar smoke, called his Office): "THE CAVE OF THE WINDS"

Will Rogers: Never slap a man who's chewing tobacco.

Will Rogers: My father was one eighth Cherokee and my mother one fourth Cherokee, which I figure makes me about an eighth cigar-store Injun.

George Sand: The cigar is the perfect complement to an elegant lifestyle.

William Shakespear (*Much Ado About Nothing*, Act I, iii): I was smoking a musty room....

William Shakespeare (*Ttus Andronicus*, Act I, i): And entrails feed the sacrificing fire, / Whose smoke, like incense, doth perfume the sky.

George Sand: The cigar numbs sorrow and fills the solitary hours with a million gracious images.

Brad Shaw: After a truly good meal, an outstanding cigar is still the most satisfying after-dinner activity that doesn't involve two human beings.

Frank Sinatra: Fresh air makes me throw up. I can't handle it. I'd rather be around three Denobili cigars blowing in my face all night

Spanish Proverb: He who has money smokes cigars / But who has no money smokes paper.

Robert Louis Stevenson, *Virginibus Puerisque:* Lastly (and this is, perhaps the golden rule), no woman should marry a man who does not smoke.

Henry G. Strauss: I have every sympathy with the American who was so horrified by what he had read of the effects of smoking that he gave up reading.

Robert Sylvester: I asked a coughing friend of mine why he doesn't stop smoking. "In this town it wouldn't do any good," he explained. "I happen to be a chain breather."

William Thackery: I vow and believe that the cigar has been one of the greatest creature comforts of my life—a kind companion, a gentle stimulant, an amiable anodyne, a cementer of friendship.

William Thackery: Women are really jealous of cigars...they regard them as a strong rival.

Henry David Thoreau: I have a faint recollection of pleasure derived from smoking dried lily-stems, before I was a man. I have never smoked anything more noxious.

Mark Twain: I made it (a) rule never to smoke more than one cigar at a time.

Mark Twain: As an example to others, and not that I care for moderation myself, it has always been my rule never to smoke when asleep, and never to refrain from smoking when awake.

Mark Twain: If I cannot smoke cigars in Heaven, I shall not go.

Mark Twain: To cease smoking is the easiest thing I ever did. I ought to know because I've done it a thousand times.

Mark Twain: There are people who strictly deprive themselves of each and every eatable, drinkable and smokable which has in any way acquired a shady reputation. They pay this price for health. And health is all they get for it.

Mark Twain: Eating and sleeping are the only activities that should be allowed to interrupt a man's enjoyment of his cigar.

Mark Twain: No one can tell me what is a good cigar—for me. I am the only judge... There are no standards—no *real* standards. Each man's preference is the only standard for him, the only one which he can accept, the only one which can command him.

UA (Statement required by law to appear on cigarette packaging and advertisements since 1965): Warning: The Surgeon General Has Determined Cigarettes Smoking Is Dangerous to Your Health.

UA: To smoke a cigar through a mouthpiece is equivalent to kissing a lady through a respirator.

UA: Cigar smoking knows no politics. It's about the pursuit of pleasure, taste, and aroma.

UA: A good cigar is like tasting a good wine: you smell it, you taste it, you look at it, you feel it—you can even hear it. It satisfies all the senses.

Tobias Venner: (1577-1660, in his 1621 book, *An Accurate Treatise on Taking the Fume of Tobacco*): Tobacco drieth the brain, dimmeth the sight, vitiateth the smell, hurteth the stomach, destroyeth the concoction, disturbeth the humors and spirits, corrupteth the breath, induceth a trembling of the limbs, exsiccateth the windpipe, lungs, and liver, annoyth the milt, scorcheth the heart, and causeth the blood to be adjusted.

Vermont Proverb: You can't make a cigar out of a pig's tail.

Evelyn Waugh: The most futile and disastrous day seems well spent when it is reviewed through the blue, fragrant smoke of a Havana cigar.

Katherine Whitehorn: There are some circles in America where it seems to be more socially acceptable to carry a hand-gun than a packet of cigarettes.

Oscar Wilde: A cigarette is the perfect type of the perfect pleasure. It is exquisite, and it leaves one unsatisfied. What more can one want?

Oscar Wilde (*The Importance of Being Earnest*): "Lady Bracknell: Do you smoke? / Earnest: Well, yes, I must admit I smoke. / Lady Bracknell: I am glad to hear it. A man should always have an occupation of some kind."

ZenWarrior: The end of a good smoke is a little saddening. In some regard, it's a bit like losing a best friend who had time to sit and listen.

CIRCUMSTANTIAL EVIDENCE (See EVIDENCE)

CIVIL RIGHTS (See also BIAS)

Uncle Anthony: Y'know what's great about America? It's the way me and any other Dago (Italian) kid can go to court and have the same rights as some Rockerfeller.

Uncle Anthony: If we was all equal, and all of us rich, and all of us sittin' at the table ... who'd be servin' us da food?

Uncle Anthony: Put a poor man's penny and a rich man's penny in yer pocket, they come out lookin' pretty much alike.

Aunt Mary Carlo: Y'know, we were all discriminated against – your mom and dad ... your dad's grandfather, Domenico Vespe, couldn't get a job because in America the big bosses wouldn't hire "greasy dagos" (Italians) – so he put the "R" on the end of his name and pretended he was French. Then the big boss gave him a shovel to build the Pennsylvania Railroard. Almost two hundred yeards after Jefferson wrote the Declaration of Independence, and a hundred years after Lincoln signed the Emancipation Proclamation no American should have to march or sit-in or demonstrate to get into a hotel or eat at a lunch counter or go to a moving picture show.

Aristotle: The only stable state is the one in which all men are equal before the law.

Samuel Adams: Among the natural rights of the colonists are these: first, a right to life; secondly, to liberty; thirdly, to property; together with the right to support and defend them in the best manner they can.

Samuel Adams: Political right and public happiness are different words for the same idea. They who wander into metaphysical labyrinths, or have recourse to original contracts, to determine the rights of men, either in impose on themselves or mean to delude others. Public utility is the only certain criteria.

African Proverb: The rain falls on every roof.

Bernard Baruch: How can you have states' rights when you keep running to Washington for money?

Henry Becque: The defect of the equality is that we only desire it with our superiors.

Ruth Benedict: Racism is the new Calvinism which asserts that one group has the stigmata of superiority and the other has those of inferiority.

Bible: Deuteronomy 10:19: Love ye therefore the stranger: for ye were strangers in the land of Egypt.

Bible: Ecclesiastes 7:7: surely oppression maketh a wise man mad.

Bible: Exodus 22:21: Thou shalt never vex a stranger, nor oppress him: for ye were strangers in the land of Egypt.

Bible: Genesis 4:9: Cain: Am I my brother's keeper?

Bible: Isaiah 58:6: Is not this the fast that I have chosen? To loose the bands of wickedness, to undo the heavy burdens, and to let the oppressed go free.

Bible: 1 John 2:9: He that saith he is in the light, and hateth his brother, is in darkness even until now.

Bible: Leviticus 19:18; Matthew 19:19: Thou shalt love thy neighbor as thyself.

Bible: Leviticus 25:14: Ye shall not oppress one another.

Bible: Luke 2:14: On earth peace, good will toward men.

Bible: Luke 6:31; Matthew 7:12: As ye would that men should do to you, do ye also to them likewise.

Bible: Matthew 25:40: Inasmuch as ye have done it unto one of the least of these my brethren, ye have done it unto me.

Bible: Zechariah 7:9: Execute true judgment, and show mercy and compassions every man to his brother.

Ambrose Bierce: DISOBEDIENCE, n.. The silver lining to the clout of servitude.

Ambrose Bierce: RIGHT, n. Legitimate authority to be, to do or to have; as the right to be a king, the right to do one's neighbor, the right to have measles, and the like.The first of these rights was once universally believed to be derived directly from the will of God; and this is still sometimes affirmed *in partibus infidelium* outside the enlightened realms of Democracy;...

Ambrose Bierce: RIGHTEOUSNESS, n. A sturdy virtue that was once found among the Pantidoodles inhabiting the lower part of the peninsula of Oque. Some feeble attempts were made by returned missionaries to introduce it into several European countries, but it appears to have been imperfectly expounded....

Hugo Black (Alabama lawyer, Assoc. Justice US Supreme Court): Freedom of speech means that you shall not do something to people either for the views they have, or the views they express, or the words they speak or write.

Hugo Black: For racial discrimination to result in the exclusion from jury service of otherwise qualified groups not only violates our Constitution and laws enacted under it but is at war with our basic concepts of a democratic society and a representative government.

Sir William Blackstone (English lawyer, author of *Commentaries*, 1723-1780; *Commentaries*, bk 1, 125): Civil liberty, which is that of a member of society, is no other than natural liberty, so far restrained by human laws, and no farther, as is necessary and expedient for the general advantage of the public.

Humphrey Bogart: They'll (House Un-American Activities Committee) nail anyone who ever scratched his ass during the National Anthem.

Louis D. Brandeis: They (the makers of the Constitution) conferred, as against the government, the right to be let alone—the most comprehensive of rights and the right most valued by civilized men.

Heywood Broun: Free speech is about as good a cause as the world has ever known. But, like the poor, it is always with us and gets shoved aside in favor of things which seem at some given moment more vital.

Heywood Broun: Almost nobody means precisely what he says when he makes the declaration, "I'm in favor of free speech."

William Jennings Bryan: Anglo-Saxon civilization has taught the individual to protect his own rights; American civilization will teach him to respect the rights of others.

Jimmy Carter: The 1964 Civil Rights Act was the best thing that ever happened to the South in my lifetime.

Albert B. "Happy" Chandler (MLB Commissioner and former US Senator from Kentucky, said in 1982 about integration of baseball by Jackie Robinson of the Brooklyn Dodgers in 1947): For 24 years my predecessor (MLB Comm. Mountain Keneshaw Landis) did not let the black man play. If you were black you did not qualify. It wasn't entirely his fault. It was what the (16 at the time) club owners wanted. But I didn't think it was right for these fellows to fight at Okinowa and Iwo Jima and then come home and not be allowed to play.

Sir Winston Churchill: Everyone is in favor of free speech. Hardly a day passes without its being extolled, but some people's idea of it is that they are free to say what they like, but if anyone says anything back, that is an outrage.

Sir Winston Churchill: There is no finer investment for any community than putting milk into babies.

Sir Winton Churchill: Nothing can be more abhorrent to democracy than to imprison a person or keep him in prison because he is unpopular. This is really the test of civilization.

Ramsey Clark: Behind the phrase "law and order" many conceal their opposition to civil rights enforcements and to dissent.

Calvin Coolidge: Men speak of natural rights, but I challenge anyone to show where in nature any rights existed or were recognized until there was established for their declaration and protection a duly promulgated body of corresponding laws.

George S. Counts: Where the press is under strict and efficient control, literacy can become a weapon for the support of a universal tyrant.

Clarence Day: It is fair to judge peoples by the rights they will sacrifice most for.

William O. Douglas: Literature should not be suppressed merely because it offends the moral code of the censor.

William O. Douglas: The prohibition of the Equal Protection Clause goes no further than the invidious discrimination. Williamson v. Lee Optical of Okla., Inc., 348 US 483, 99 L ed 563, 75 S Ct 461 (1955)

William O. Douglas: Exact equality is no prerequisite of equal protection of the laws within the meaning of the Fourteenth Amendment. Norvell v. Illinois, 373 US 420, 10 L ed 2d 456, 83 S Ct 1366 (1963)

Frederick Douglass: No man can put a chain about the ankle of his fellow man without at last finding the other end fastened about his own neck.

Hansell B. Duckett: What this country needs is more free speech worth listening to.

W. E. B. DuBois: The problem of the 20th century is the problem of the color line.

Albert Einstein (1921 letter to friend about why he was going to America to help raise money for the Jewish University in Jerusalem): Despite my emphatic Internationalist beliefs I have always felt an obligation to stand up for my persecuted and morally oppressed tribal companions. The prospect of establishing a Jewish University (in Jerusalem) fills me with particular joy having recently seen countless instances of perfidious and uncharitable treatment of splendid young Jews with attempts to deny their chances of education.

Ralph Waldo Emerson: Wherever snow falls there is usually civil freedom.

Ralph Waldo Emerson: The Spartan principle of "calling that which is just, equal; not that which is equal, just."

Ralph Waldo Emerson: Be as beneficent as the sun or the sea, but if your rights as a rational being are trenched on, die on the first inch of your territory.

Ralph Waldo Emerson: There is a little formula, couched in pure Saxon, which you may hear in the corners of streets and in the yard of the dame's school, from very little republicans: "I'm as good as you be," which contains the essence of the Massachusetts Bill of Rights and of the American Declaration of Independence.

English Proverb: Sauce for the goose is sauce for the gander.

Thomas Erskine: Thus I have maintained by English history, that in proportion as the Press has been free, English Government has been secure.

Brendan Francis: Rights are something other people grant you after you've fought tooth-and-nail for them.

Justice Frankfurter: The history of liberty has largely been the history of observance of proceedural safeguards. McNabb v. United States, 318 US 332, 347, 87 L ed 819, 827, 63 S. Ct. 608 (1943)

Justice Frankfurter: It is a fair summary of history to say that the safeguards of liberty have frequently been forged in controversies involving not very nice people. Dissenting opinion, U.S. v. Rabinowitz, 339 US 56, 69, 94 L ed 653, 662, 70 S Ct 430 (1950).

Paul A. Freund (American law professor, legal writer): The hope is that the sanctions of law will not be forever required to curb discrimination; that in due course after civil rights will come civility.

Muhandas Gandhi: Rights that do not flow from duty well performed are not worth having.

William Lloyd Garrison: Wherever there is a human being, I see God-given rights inherent in that being, whatever may be the sex or complexion.

Horace Greeley: I am the inferior of any man whose rights I trample underfoot.

Frank Hague (Jersey City Chamber of Commerce dinner, 1938): We hear about constitutional rights, free speech and the free press. Every time I hear those words I say to myself, "That man is Red!"... you never hear a *real* American talk like that.

Garrett Hardin: Beyond the limits of his confining skin, no man can own any *thing*. "Property" refers not to things owned but to the rights granted by society; they must periodically be re-examined in the light of social justice.

John Marshall Harlan (Kentucky lawyer, Assoc. Justice US Supreme Court, 1833-1911): Our constitution is color-blind. (dissenting opinion) Plessy v. Ferguson, 163 US 537, 41 L ed 256, 16 S Ct 1138 (1896)

John Marshall Harlan (Assoc. Justice US Supreme Court): By the Louisiana statute, the validity of which is here involved, all railway companies (other than street railroad companies) carrying passengers in that State are required to have **separate but equal** accomodations for white and colored persons. (dissenting opinion) Plessy v. Ferguson, 163 US 537, 41 L ed 256, 16 S Ct 1138 (1896) (EDITOR: The US Supreme Court in Plessy v. Ferguson held that the Louisiana statute did not violate the US Constitution. Mr. Justice Harlan was the lone dissenter. In his dissenting opinion he turned the words of the statute "equal but separate" into **"separate but equal"** and it is his terminology that has since prevailed]

John Marshall Harlan: In respect of civil rights, all citizens are equal before the law. The humblest is the peer of the most powerful.

Wilma Scott Heide: To date, we have taught men to be brave and women to care. Now we must enlarge our concepts of bravery and caring. Men must be *brave enough to care* sensitively, compassionately and contrary to the masculine mystique about the quality and equality of our society. Women must *care enough* about their families and all families to *bravely assert* their voices and intellects to every aspect of every institution, whatever the feminine mystique. Every social trait labelled masculine or feminine is in truth a human trait. It is our human right to develop and contribute our talents whatever our race, sex, religion, ancestry, age. Human rights are indivisible!

Thomas Hobbes (English philosopher, 1588-1679): The question who is the better man has no place in the condition of mere nature, where... all men are equal. The inequality that now is has been introduced by the laws civil.

Oliver Wendell Holmes Jr.: The best test of truth is the power of the thought to get itself accepted in the competition of the market.... We should be eternally vigilant against attempts to check the expression that we loathe.

Oliver Wendell Holmes Jr.: The liberty of the citizen to do as he likes so long as he does not interfere with the liberty of others to do the same, which has been a shibboleth from some well-known writers, is interfered with by school laws, by the Post Office, by every state or municipal institution which takes his money for purposes thought desirable, whether he likes it or not.

Oliver Wendell Holmes Jr.: If there is any principal of the Constitution that more imperatively calls for attachment more than any other, it is the principal of free thought—not free thought for those who agree with us but freedom for the thought that we hate.

Oliver Wendell Holmes Sr.: The very aim and end of our institutions is just this: that we may think what we like and say what we think.

Hubert H. Humphrey: The right to be heard does not automatically include the right to be taken seriously.

Hubert H. Humphrey: Order is the first responsibility of government; without it there can be no justice and no progress. Those who imply that continued rioting and disruption will lead to social progress are very wrong; such behavior leads instead to hardening resistance to progress, and to repression.

Robert C. Ingersoll: I am the inferior of any man whose rights I trample underfoot.

Italian Proverb: At the end of the game the king and the pawn go into the same bag (or box).

Italian Proverb: The balance distinguishes not between gold and lead.

Robert H. Jackson: The price of freedom of religion or of speech or of press is that we must put up with, and even pay for, a good deal of rubbish.

Robert H. Jackson: No official, high or petty, can prescribe what shall be orthodox in politics, nationalism, religion, or other matters of opinion, or force citizens to confess by word or act their faith therein.

Thomas Jefferson: If we cannot secure all our rights, let us secure what we can.

Thomas Jefferson: A bill of rights is what the people are entitled to against every government on earth, general or particular; and what no just government should refuse, or rest on inference.

Thomas Jefferson: Bear in mind this sacred principle, that though the will of the majority is in all cases to prevail, that will to be rightful must be reasonable; that the minority possess their equal rights, which equal law must protect, and to violate would be oppression.

Thomas Jefferson: No man has a natural right to commit aggression on the equal rights of another, and this is all from which the laws ought to restrain him; every man is under the natural duty of contributing to the necessities of the society, and this is all the laws should enforce on him; and no man having a natural right to be the judge between himself and another, it is his natural duty to submit to the umpirage of an impartial third.

Thomas Jefferson: We hold these truths to be self evident—that all men are created equal; that they are endowed by their Creator with certain inalienable rights; that among these are life, liberty and the pursuit of happiness.

Thomas Jefferson: All, too, will bear in mind this sacred principle, that though the will of the majority is in all cases to prevail, that will to be rightful must be reasonable; that the minority possess their equal rights, which equal law must protect, and to violate would be oppression.

Thomas Jefferson: Our liberty depends on freedom of the press, and that cannot be limited without being lost.

Rudolph Von Jhering (German legal scholar and writer, 1818-1892, *Law as a Means to an End*, ch 8, sec 11): Equality may be as much as anything else equality of misery.

Lyndon B. Johnson: Democracy will never solve its problems at the end of a billy club.

Lyndon B. Johnson: Let no one ever think for a moment that national debate means national division.

Lyndon B. Johnson: Let us be very clear on this matter: if we condemn people to inequality in our society we also condemn them to inequality in our economy.

Lyndon B. Johnson: A rioter with a Molotov cocktail in his hands is not fighting for civil rights any more than a Klansmen wearing a sheet and a mask.

Lyndon B. Johnson (Address, *Howard University Commencement Exercises*, 1965): We seek not just freedom but opportunity. We seek not just legal equality, but human equality. Not just equality as a right and a theory but equality as a fact and equality as a result.

Barbara Jordan: "We, the people." It is a very eloquent beginning. But when that document was completed on the seventh of September in 1787, I was not included in that "We, the people." I felt somehow for many years the George Washington and Alexander Hamilton just left me out by mistake. But through the process of amendment, interpretation, and court decision I have finally been included in "We, the people."

John F. Kennedy: I am not so much concerned with the right of every one to say anything he pleases as I am about our need as a self-governing people to hear everything relevant.

John F. Kennedy (message on 100th anniversary of Emancipation Proclamation, September 22, 1962): In giving rights to others which belong to them, we give rights to ourselves and to our country.

John F. Kennedy: I do not say that all men are equal in their ability, character and motivation. I do say that every American should be given a fair chance to develop all the talents they may have.

John F. Kennedy: This nation was founded by men of many nations and backgrounds. It was founded on the principle of all men were created equal, and that the rights of every man are diminished when the rights of one man are threatened.

John F. Kennedy: No one has been barred on account of his race from fighting or dying for America—there are no "white" or "colored" signs on the foxholes or graveyards of battle.

John F. Kennedy: Let the word go forth from this time and place, to friend and foe alike, that the torch has been passed to a new generation of Americans – born in this century, tempered by war, disciplined by a hard and bitter peace, proud of our ancient heritage – and unwilling to witness or permit the slow undoing of those human rights to which this nation has always been committed, and to which we are committed today at home and around the world.

Martin Luther King Jr.: It may be true that the law cannot make a man loved me, but it can keep him from lynching me, and I think that's pretty important.

Martin Luther King Jr.: In any nonviolent campaign there are four basic steps: collection of the facts to determine whether injustices exist, negotiation, self purification, and direct action.

Martin Luther King Jr.: Nonviolent action, the Negro saw, was the way to supplement, not replace, the process of change. It was the way to divest himself of passivity without parading himself in vindictive force.

Martin Luther King Jr.: I am aware that there are many who wince at a distinction between property and persons – who hold both sacrosanct. My views are not so rigid. A life is sacred. Property is intended to serve life, and no matter how much we surrounded with rights and respect, it has no personal being. It is part of the earth man walks on; it is not man.

Martin Luther King Jr.: We shall overcome.

Rudyard Kipling: Ancient Right unnoticed as the breath we draw - / Leave to live by no man's leave underneath the law.

Henry Kissinger: A nation riven by factions, in which the minority has no hope of ever becoming a majority, or in which some group knows it is perpetually outcast, will seem oppressors to its members, whatever the legal pretensions.

Harold J. Laski: The only real security for social well-being is the free exercise of men's minds.

Pope Leo XIII: There is an inequality of right and authority which emanates from God himself.

G. C. Lichtenberg: The equality we want is the most tolerable degree of inequality.

Abraham Lincoln: Let us have faith that right makes might, and in that faith let us to the end do our duty as we understand it.

Abraham Lincoln: No man is good enough to govern another man without that other's consent.

Abraham Lincoln: The fight must go one. The cause of civil liberty must not be surrendered at the end of one or even one hundred defeats.

James Russell Lowell: They have rights who dare maintain them.

Lester Maddox: That's part of American greatness, is discrimination. Yes, sir. Inequality, I think, breeds freedom and gives a man opportunity.

James Madison (US President, 1751-1836): As a man is said to have rights to his property, he may be equally said to have property in his rights.

James Madison (*The Federalist*, 1788: In a free government the security for civil rights must be the same as for religious rights. It consists in the one case in the multiplicity of interest, and in the other in the multiplicity of sects.

Malcolm X.: I think that the black man in America wants to be recognized as a human being and it's almost impossible for one who has enslaved another to bring himself to accept the person who used to pull his plow, who used to be an animal, subhuman, who used to be considered as such by him—it's almost impossible for that person in his right mind to accept that person as his equal.

Malcolm X.: We are not fighting for integration, nor are we fighting for separation. We are fighting for recognition as human beings.

Malcolm X.: I for one believe that if you give people a thorough understanding of what confronts them and the basic causes that produce it, they'll create their own program, and when the people create a program, you get action.

Marya Mannes: The suppression of civil liberties is to many less a matter for horror than the curtailment of the freedom to profit.

H. L. Mencken: What men value in this world is not rights but privileges.

John Stuart Mill: If all mankind, minus one, were one opinion, and only one person were of the contrary opinion, mankind would be no more justified in silencing that one person, then he, if he had the power, would be justified in silencing mankind.

Montaigne: Equality is the chief groundwork of equity.

Frank Murphy (Michigan lawyer, Governor of Michigan, Assoc. Justice US Supreme Court, 1890-1949): The law knows no finer hour than when it cuts through formal concepts and transitory emotions to protect unpopular citizens against discrimination and persecution. (dissenting opinion) Falbo v. US, 320 US 549, 88 L ed 305, 64 S Ct 346 (1944)

Edward R. Murrow: It is well to remember that freedom through the press is the thing that comes first. Most of us probably feel we couldn't be free without newspapers, and that is the real reason we want the newspapers to be free.

Napoleon I: A people which is able to say everything becomes able to do everything.

Friedrich Nietzsche: Nobody talks more passionately of his rights then he who, in the depths of his soul, is doubtful about them.

Friedrich Nietzsche: The rights which a man arrogates to himself are relative to the duties which he sets himself, and to the tasks which he feels capable of performing.

William Cardinal O'Connell: Anyone who possesses a natural right may make use of all legitimate means to protect it, and to safeguard it from violation.

George Orwell (*Animal Farm*, ch 10): All animals are equal, but some animals are more equal than others.

Francis Parkman: It is in the concrete, and not in the abstract, that rights prevail in every sound and wholesome society.

Wendell Phillips: Freedom of the press is the staff of life for any vital democracy.

Will Rogers: I don't care how poor and inefficient a little country is; they like to run their own business. I know men that would make my wife a better husband than I am; but, darn it, I'm not going to give her to 'em.

Will Rogers: I see where we are starting to pay some attention to our neighbors to the south. We could never understand why Mexico wasn't just crazy about us; for we have always had their good will, and oil and minerals, at heart.

Will Rogers: We will never have true civilization until we have learned to recognize the rights of others.

Franklin D. Roosevelt: The moment a mere numerical superiority by either states or voters in this country proceeds to ignore the needs and desires of the minority, and for their own selfish purpose or advancement, hamper or oppress that minority, or debar them in any way from equal privileges and equal rights—that moment will mark the failure of our constitutional system.

Jean Jacques Rousseau: To reign by opinion, begin by trampling it under your feet.

Bertrand Russell: The fundamental argument for freedom of opinion is the doubtfulness of all our beliefs.

Bertrand Russell: Freedom of opinion can only exist when the government thinks itself secure.

Edward Terry Sanford: Freedom of speech and press... does not protect disturbances to the public peace or the attempt to subvert the government. It does not protect publications or teachings which tend to subvert or imperil the government, or to impede or hinder it in the performance of its governmental duties.

Scottish Proverb: Right is right, and right wrongs no man.

William Shakespeare (*Antony and Cleopatra*, Act I, iii): Equality of two domestic powers / Breeds scrupulous faction.

William Shakespeare (*I Henry IV*, Act I, ii): He will give the devil his due.

William Shakespeare (*II Henry IV*, Act V, iv): O God, that right should thus overcome might!

William Shakespeare (*King John*, Act I, ii): Heralds, from off our towers we might behold, / From first to last, the onset and retire / Of both your armies; whose equality / By our best eyes cannot be censured: / Blood hath bought blood, and blows have answer'd blows; / Strength match'd with strength, and power confronted power; / Both are alike, and both alike we like.

William Shakespeare (*King John*, Act II, ii): She in beauty, education, blood, / Holds hand with any princess of the world.

William Shakespeare (*The Winter's Tale* Act V, i): The odds for high and low's alike.

Adam Smith: Whenever there is great property, there is great in equality.... For one very rich man, there must be at least five hundred poor.

Margaret Chase Smith: The key to security is public information.

Sydney Smith (English clergyman and writer, 1771-1845, *Assize Sermon at York, 1824*): Equal rights to unequal possessions, equal justice to the rich and poor; this is what men come out to fight for and to defend.

J.A. Spender: When men say they have rights, they generally mean that they are suffering wrongs.

J.A. Spender: Man first becomes formidable in action when he conceives his ideals as rights.

Adlai Stevenson: The sound of tireless voices is the price we pay for the right to hear the music of our own opinions.

Ralph W. Stockman: Government laws are needed to give us civil rights, and God is needed to make us civil.

C. S. Tallentyre: I disapprove of what you say, but I will defend to the death your right to say it.

Henry David Thoreau: Voting for the right is doing nothing for it.

James Tobin: Despite legendary examples of spectacular social mobility, the unequal outcomes of one generation are generally the unequal opportunities of the next.

Alexis de. Tocqueville: The passion for equality produces uniformity which produces mediocrity.

Alexis de Tocqueville: Americans are so enamored of equality that they would rather be equal in slavery than unequal in freedom.

Harry S. Truman: In the cause of freedom, we have to battle for the rights of people with whom we do not agree; and whom, in many cases, we may not like. These people test the strength of the freedoms which protect all of us. If we do not defend their rights, we endanger our own.

Mark Twain: It is by the goodness of God than in our country we have those three unspeakably precious things: freedom of speech, freedom of conscience, and the prudence never to practice either of them.

Booker T. Washington: You can't hold a man down without staying down with him.

Booker T. Washington: There are two ways of exerting one's strength: one is pushing down, the other is pulling up.

Colonel Gerald Wellman (ROTC Instrutor): We don't necessarily discriminate. We simply exclude certain types of people.

Frederick Wertham: The greatest achievement of the civil rights movement is that it has restored the dignity of indignation.

E. B. White: There is nothing much to be "taught" about equality—you either believe it or you don't. But there is much that can be taught about rights and about liberty, including the basic stuff: that a right derives from a responsibleness, and that men become free as they become willing to except restrictions on their acts. These are elementary concepts, of course, but an awful lot of youngsters seem to emerge from high school and even from college without acquiring them. Until they are acquired, the more subtle, intricate, and delicate problems of civil rights and freedom of speech are largely incomprehensible to.

Woodrow Wilson: A right is worth fighting for only when it can be put into operation.

Yiddish Proverb: At the baths, all are equal.

Yiddish Proverb: Everyone is kneaded out of the same dough but not baked in the same oven.

Whitney M. Young Jr.: The core of the civil rights problem is the matter of achieving equal opportunity for Negroes in the labor market. For it stands to reason that all our other civil rights depend on that for fulfillment. We cannot afford better education for our children, better housing or medical care unless we have jobs.

COMEDY

Uncle Anthony: When you stop laughing at yourself, it's time for us/others to start.

Uncle Anthony: You can tell a lot about a guy by what he thinks is funny or not.

Uncle Anthony: Ya can spread smiles a lot easier than tears.

Aunt Mary Carlo: Didjaever notice –if ya agree on what's funny, ya can agree on alotta udder stuff too.

Joseph Addison: A man should always consider how much he has more than he wants, and how much more unhappy he might be than he really is.

Aesop: Clumsy jesting is no joke.

Fred Allen: All that the comedian has to show for his years of work and aggravation is the echo of forgotten laughter.

Woody Allen: Humorists always sit at the children's table.

Dr. Robert Anthony: He who laughs, lasts.

Aristotle: Wit is educated insolence.

Aristotle: Humor is the only test of gravity, and gravity of humor; for a subject which will not bear raillery is suspicious, and a jest which will not bear serious examination is false wit.

Lee Beck (Associate Director at Center for Neuroimmunology at Loma Linda School of Medicine, in *Parenting* magazine, November 2000): Children laugh an average of 400 times a day, adults 15.... laughter keeps life in balance and is a key part to a helthy lifestyle .... laughter helps produce NK cells, which fight infections, including pneumonia and bronchitis. Laughter also suppresses the release of cortisol, a hormone that weakens the immune system. It functions as a natural analgesic, which raises the body's pain threshold, and acts as a muscle relaxer. And laughter increases circulatory capacity and strengthens organs, helping the body to become more resistant to infection while boosting energy levels. (EDITOR: We all need to laugh more to stay and become more healthy).

Henry Ward Beecher: Good humor makes all things tolerable.

Henry Ward Beecher: Men will let you will use them if only you will make them laugh.

Henry Ward Beecher: The mere wit is only a human bauble. He is to life what bells are to horses—not expected to draw the load, but only to jingle while the horses draw.

Henry Ward Beecher: A person without a sense of humor is like a wagon without springs. It's jolted by every pebble on the road.

Hilaire Belloc: Genuine laughter is the physical effect produced in the rational being by what suddenly strikes his immortal soul as being damned funny.

Henri Bergson: You would hardly appreciate the comic if you felt yourself isolated from others. Laughter appears to stand in need of an echo.

Henri Bergson: To produce the whole of its effect ... the comic demands something like a momentary anesthesia of the heart. Its appeal is to the intelligence, pure and simple.

Jimmy Buffett: If we couldn't laugh, we would all go insane.

Bible: Ecclesiastes 3:4: A time to weep, and a time to laugh.

Bible: Ecclesiastes: Give not over thy soul to sorrow; and afflict not thyself in thy own counsel. Gladness of heart is the life of man and the joyfulness of man is length of days.

Bible: Matthew, 14:27: Be of good cheer, it is I; be not afraid.

Bible: Proverbs 14:13: Even in laughter the heart is sorrowful; and the end of mirth is heaviness.

Bible: Proverbs, 15:13: A merry heart maketh a cheerful countenance.

Bible: Proverbs 17:22: He that is of a merry heart hath a continual feast.

Bible: Proverbs 17:22: A merry heart doeth good like a medicine.

Ambrose Bierce: HAPPINESS, n. An agreeable sensation arising from contemplating the misery of another.

Ambrose Bierce: HUMORIST, n. A plague that would have softened down the hoar austerity of the Pharaoh's heart and persuaded him to dismiss Israel with his best wishes, cat-quick.

Ambrose Bierce: JESTER, n. An officer formerly attached to a king's household, whose business it was to amuse the court by ludicrous action and utterances, the absurdity being attested by his motley costume. The king himself being attired with dignity it took the world some centuries to discover that his own conduct and decrees were sufficiently ridiculous for the amusement not only of his court but of all mankind. The jester was commonly called a fool, but the poets and romancers have ever delighted to represent him as a singularly wise and witty person. In the circus of to-day the melancholy ghost of the court fool effects the dejection of humbler audiences with the same jests wherewith in life he gloomed the marble hall, panged the patrician sense of humor and tapped the tank of royal tears....

Ambrose Bierce: LAUGHTER, n. An interior convulsion, producing a distortion of the features and accompanied by inarticulate noises. It is infectious and, though intermittent, incurable. Liability to attacks of laughter is one of the characteristics distinguishing man from the animals.

Ambrose Bierce: WIT, n. The salt with which the American humorist spoils his intellectual cookery by leaving it out.

Ambrose Bierce: WITTICISM, n. A sharp and clever remark, usually quoted and seldom noted; what the Philistine is pleased to call a "joke."

Ambrose Bierce: ZANY, n. A popular character in old Italian plays, who imitated with ludicrous incompetence the *buffone*, or clown, and was therefore the ape of an ape; for the clown himself imitated the serious characters of the play. The zany was progenitor to the specialist in humor, as we to-day have the unhappiness to know him.In the zany we see an example of creation; in the humorist, of transmission. Another excellent specimen of the modern zany is the curate, who apes the rector, who apes the bishop, who apes the archbishop, who apes the devil.

Geoffrey Bocca: Wit is a treacherous dart. It is perhaps the only weapon with which it is possible to stab one self in one's own back.

Victor Borge: Laughter is the shortest distance between two people.

Victor Borge: Humor is the shortest distance between two people.

Fanny Brice: Being a funny person does an awful lot of things to you. You feel that you mustn't get serious with people. They don't expect it from you, and they don't want to see it. You're not entitled to be serious, you're a clown, and they only want you to make them laugh.

Jacob Braude: Always behave like a duck - keep calm and unruffled on the surface, but paddle like the devil underneath.

Charles S. Brooks: Humorous persons have pleasant mouths turned up at the corners.... But the mouth of a merely witty man is hard and sour until the moment of its discharge.

Mel Brooks: Tragedy is if I cut my finger. Comedy is if I walk into an open sewer and die.

Lenny Bruce: Sometimes I look at life in the fund mirror at the carnival. I see myself as a profound, incisive wit, concerned with man's inhumanity to man. Then I stroll to the next mirror and I see a pompous, subjective ass whose humor is hardly spiritual.

Lenny Bruce: Comedy equals tragedy plus distance.

Abe Burrows: You can teach taste, editorial sense, but the ability to say something funny is something I've never been able to teach anyone.

Samuel Butler: A sense of humor keen enough to show a man his own absurdities will keep him from the commission of all sins, or nearly all, save those worth committing.

Lord Byron: All tragedies are finished by a death, All comedies are ended by a marriage.

Lord Byron: All tragedies are finished by a death, / All comedies are ended by a marriage.

Albert Camus: To be happy, we must not be too concerned with others.

Thomas Carlyle: Wondrous is the strength of cheerfulness, and its power of endurance—the cheerful man will do more in the same time, will do it better, will preserve it longer, then the sad or sullen.

Dick Cavett: There's so much comedy on television. Does that cause comedy in the streets?

Allen K. Chalmers: The grand essentials of happiness are: something to do, something to love, and something to hope for.

Charles Chaplin: If you've got something funny to do, you don't have to be funny doing it.

Lord Chesterfield: A man must have a good share of wit himself to endure a great share in another.

Lord Chesterfield: Wit is so shining a quality that everybody admires it; most people aim at it, all people fear it, and few love it unless in themselves.

G.K. Chesterton: When once you have got hold of a vulgar joke, you may be certain that you have got hold of a subtle and spiritual idea.

Chinese Proverb: Keep a green tree in your heart and perhaps a singing bird will come.

Sir Winston Churchill: A joke is a very serious thing.

Sir Winston Churchill: In my belief: you cannot deal with the most serious things in the world unless you also understand the most amusing.

Frank Colby: Men will confess to treason, murder, arson, false teeth, or a wig. How many of them will own up to a lack of humor?

Joseph Conrad: It is very difficult to be wholly joyous or wholly sad on this earth. The comic, when it is human, soon takes upon itself the face of pain.

George William Curtis: Happiness lies, first of all, in health.

Czech Proverb: Many a friend was lost through a joke, but none was ever gained so.

Phyllis Diller: Comedy is tragedy revisted.

John Donne: Who are a little wise, the best fools be.

Finley Peter Dunne: Th' las' man that makes a joke owns it.

Ecclesiasticus: One day's happiness makes a me and forget his misfortune; and one day's misfortune makes him forget his past happiness.

Charles Leroy Edson: We love a joke that hands us a pat on the back while it kicks the other fellow down stairs.

Albert Einstein: A good joke should not be repeated too often.

George Eliot: A difference of taste in jokes is a great strain on the affections.

Ralph Waldo Emerson: Wit makes its own welcome and levels all distinctions. No dignity, no learning, no force of character, can make any stand against good wit.

English Proverb: Many a true word is spoken in jest.

Epictetus: There is only one way to happiness and that is to cease worrying about things which are beyond the power of our will.

Sam Ervin: Humor is one of God's most marvelous gifts. Humor gives us smiles, laughter, and gaiety. Humor reveals the roses and hides the thorns. Humor makes our heavy burdens light and smooths the rough spots in our pathways. Humor endows us with the capacity to clarify the obscure, to simplify the complex, to deflate the pompous, to chastise the arrogant, to point a moral, and to adorn a tale.

W.C. Fields: I never saw anything funny that wasn't terrible. If it causes pain, it's funny; if it doesn't, it isn't. I try to hide the pain with embarrassment, and the more I do that, the better they like it. But that doesn't mean they are unsympathetic. Oh no, they laugh often with tears in their eyes.

W.C. Fields: For reasons I have never understood, Alexandria, Virginia, is screamingly funny to Washingtonians, while the great city of Oakland never fails to get a chuckle out of San Franciscans. And Bismarck, North Dakota, is funny anywhere in the United States.

Benjamin Franklin: Thou canst not joke an enemy into a friend, but thou may'st a friend into an enemy.

French Proverb: The sign of wisdom is a continual cheerfulness.

Christopher Fry: Comedy is an escape, not from the truth but from despair; a narrow escape into faith.

Thomas Fuller: Better lose a jest than a friend.

Thomas Fuller: A joke never gains over an enemy, but often loses a friend.

Thomas Fuller: Men never think their fortune too great, nor their wit too little.

John Kenneth Galbraith: Where humor is concerned, there are no standards—no one can say what is good or bad, although you can be sure that everyone will. Only a very foolish man will use a form of language that is wholly uncertain in its effect. And that is the very nature of humor.

Mohandas Karamchand (Mahatma) Gandhi: If I had no sense of humor, I would long ago have committed suicide.

Romain Gary: Humor is an affirmation of dignity, a declaration to man's superiority to all that befalls him

Larry Gelbart: One doesn't have a sense of humor. It has you.

Brendan Gill: In black comedy, you murder your grandmother by shoving her off a high cliff in a wheelchair; in sick comedy, you do precisely the same thing, but she is already dying of cancer, and you know it.

James M. Gilis: Whom the gods would make bigots, they first deprive of humor.

Johann Wolfgang von Goethe: Man show their characters in nothing more clearly than in what they think laughable.

David Grayson: I wonder sometimes if any one learns to laugh – *really* laugh – much before he is forty.

Sacha Guitry: You can pretend to be serious; you can't pretend to be witty.

William Hazlitt: Wit is the salt of conversation, not the food.

William Hazlitt: Comedy naturally wears itself out—destroys the very food on which it lives; and by constantly and successfully exposing the follies and weaknesses of mankind to ridicule, in the end leaves itself nothing worth laughing at.

Ernest Hemingway: They say the seeds of what we will do are in all of us, but it always seemed to me that in those who make jokes in life the seeds are covered with better soil and with a higher grade of night soil.

George Herbert: Wit's an unruly engine, wildly striking / Sometimes a friend, sometimes the engineer.

Oliver Wendell Holmes Sr.: The wit knows that his place is at the tail of a procession.

Bob Hope: ON WHY HE CHOSE SHOWBIZ/COMEDY FOR HIS CAREER: When I was born, the doctor said to my mother, "Congratulations. You have an eight-pound ham."

Horace: A jest often decides matters of importance more effectually and happily than seriousness.

Edgar Watson Howe: Wit that is kindly is not very witty.

Elbert Hubbard: The free mind must have one policeman, Irony.

Langston Hughes: Humor is laughing at what you haven't got when you want to have it.

Langston Hughes: Humor is when a joke is on you but hits the other fellow first—before it boomerangs.

Eugene Ionesco: To become conscious of what is horrifying and to laugh at it is to become master of that which is horrifying.... Laughter alone does not respect any taboo, laughter alone inhibits the creation of new anti-taboos; the comic alone is capable of giving us strength to bear the tragedy of existence.

Washington Irving: Wit and coin are always doubted with a threadbare coat.

Italian Proverb: He that jokes confesses.

Italian Proverb: He who has the courage to laugh is almost as much master of the world as he who is ready to die.

Molly Ivins: Satire is traditionally the weapon of the powerless against the powerful.

Bede Jarrett: Only the solemn things are ever comic.

Jewish Saying: Think Yiddish, but speak British (EDITOR: meaning think crazy, but speak intelligently/articulately)

Philander Johnson: Wit, at its best, consists in the terse intrusion into an atmosphere of serene mental habit of some uncompromising truth.

Samuel Johnson: Of all the griefs that harass the distressed, / Sure the most bitter is a scornful jest.

Samuel Johnson: That frolic which shakes one man with laughter will convulse another with indignation.

Junius: Be not affronted at a jest; if one throw ever so much salt at thee thou wilt receive no harm unless thou art raw and ulcerous.

Helen Keller: When one door of happiness closes, another opens; but often we look so long at the closed-door that we do not see the one which has been opened for us.

Lewis Kronenberger: Humor simultaneously wounds and heals, indicts and pardons, diminishes and enlarges; it constitutes inner growth at the expense of outer gain, and those who possess and honestly practice it make themselves more through a willingness to make themselves less.

La Bruyere: Impertinent wits are a kind of insect which are in everybody's way and plentiful in all countries.

La Rochefoucauld: A wit would often be embarrassed without the company of fools.

La Rochefoucauld: The greatest fault of a penetrating wit is to go beyond the mark.

Charles Lamb: The teller of a mirthful tale has latitude allowed him. We are content with less than absolute truth.

Walter Savage Landor (English essayist and poet, 1775-1864): What is perfectly true is imperfectly witty

Walter Savage Landor: True wit, to every man, is that which falls on another.

D.H. Lawrence: So long as there's a bit of a laugh going, things are all right. As soon as this infernal seriousness, like a greasy sea, heaves up, everything is lost.

Gershon Legman: Ultimately, all jokes, parables, lies, and in fact all fictions and fables of whatever sort are simply the decorative showcases of their tellers' anxieties, their impressions, and generally of their neuroses.

Jay Leno (comedian and *The Tonight Show* TV host): Some comedians are like Democrat Presidents – they think they can handle everytthing themselves without any help

Abraham Lincoln: With the fearful strain that is on me night and day, if I did not laugh I should die.

William Lloyd: Judge of a jest when you have done laughing.

Lucretius: In the midst of the fountain of wit there arises something bitter, which stings in the very flowers.

Marya Mannes: Wit has a deadly aim and it is possible to prick a large pretense with a small pin.

Tom Masson: Think of what would happen to us in America if there were no humorists; life would be one long Congressional Record.

William Somerset Maugham: Impropriety is the soul of wit.

William Somerset Maugham: The humorist has a good eye for the humbug; he does not always recognize the saint.

William Somerset Maugham: Comedy appeals to the collective mind of the audience and this grows fatigued; while farce appeals to a more robust organ, their collective belly.

William Somerset Maugham: You are not angry with people when you laugh at them. Humor teaches them tolerance.

Elsa Maxwell: Laugh at yourself first, before anyone else can.

John T. McCutcheon: The political cartoon is a sort of pictorial breakfast food. It has the cardinal asset of making the beginning of the day sunnier.

Margate Mead: Laughter is man's most distinctive emotional expression. Man shares the capacity for love and hate, anger and fear, loyalty and grief, with other living creatures. But humor, which has an intellectual as well as an emotional element, belongs to man.

Herman Melville: A good laugh is a mighty good thing, and rather too scarce a good thing; the more's the pity.

H.L. Mencken: It (humor) always withers in the presence of messianic delusion, like justice and truth in front of patriotic passion.

Dr. Karl Menninger: Anything which can be made funny must have at its heart some tragic implication.

Marianne Moore: Among animals, one has a sense of humor. Humor saves a few steps, it saves years.

Christopher Morley: Nothing disturbs, or surprises, man so much as the discrepancy between his professions and his actual behavior; in that discrepancy lies the mother lode of intellectual comedy.

Malcolm Muggeridge: Good taste and humor are a contradiction in terms, like a chaste whore.

George Jean Nathan: The test of a real comedian is whether you laugh at him before he opens his mouth.

Bob Newhart: Comedy defuses tensions in many areas. It gives you distance so you can stand back and laugh at things.

Friedrich Nietzsche: Wit is the epitaph of an emotion.

Friedrich Nietzsche: Not by wrath, but by laughter, do we slay.

Bill Nye: The more you find out about the world, the more opportunities there are to laugh.

George Orwell: The aim of a joke is not to degrade the human being but to remind him that he is already degraded.

Dorothy Parker: Wit has truth in it; wisecracking is simply calisthenics with words.

Mary Pettibone Poole: He who laughs, lasts.

Alexander Pope: Gentle Dulness ever loves a joke.

Alexander Pope: The greatest advantage I know of being thought a wit by the world is, that it gives one the greater freedom of playing the fool.

Alexander Pope: True wit is Nature to advantage dressed, / What oft was thought, but never so well expressed.

Michael Pritchard: You don't stop laughing because you grow old; you grow old because you stop laughing.

V. S. Pritchett: The profoundly humorous writers are humorous because they are responsive to the hopeless, uncouth concatenations of life.

John Ray: There's many a true word spoken in jest.

Carl Reiner: Improvisation is just writing in front of an audience.

Carl Reiner: The absolute truth is the thing that makes people laugh.

Agnes Repplier: Humor distorts nothing, and only false gods are laughed off their earthly pedestals.

Agnes Repplier: People who cannot recognize a palpable absurdity are very much in the way of civilization.

Agnes Repplier: Humour brings to insight and tolerance. Irony brings a deeper and less friendly understanding

Agnes Repplier: The preservation of the Comic Spirit depends in some measure the ultimate triumph of civilization. Science may carry us to Mars, but it will leave the earth peopled as ever by the inept.

Agnes Repplier: The essence of humour is that it should be unexpected, that it should embody an element of surprise, that it should startle us out of that reasonable gravity which, after all, must be our habitual frame of mind.

Agnes Repplier: It has been wisely said that we cannot really love anybody at whom we never laugh.

Agnes Repplier: There is always a secret irritation about a laugh in which we cannot join.

Mordecai Richler: If you don't count some of Jehovah's instructions, there are no humorists I can recall in the Bible.

Joan Rivers: There is not one female comic who was beautiful as a little girl.

Constance Roarke: An emotional man may possess no humor, but a humorous man usually has deep pockets of emotion, sometimes tucked away or forgotten.

Will Rogers: I joked about every prominent man of my time, but I never met a man I didn't like.

Will Rogers: I have always noticed that people will never laugh at anything that is not based on truth.

Will Rogers: I don't make jokes. I just watch the government and report the facts.

Will Rogers: Everything is funny as long as it is happening to Somebody Else.

Will Rogers: If I studied all my life, I couldn't think up half the number of funny things passed in one session of Congress.

Will Rogers (1949): The banker, the lawyer, and the politician are still our best bets for a laugh. Audiences haven't changed at all, and neither has the three above professions.

Will Rogers: You have to have a serious streak in you or you can't see the funny side in the other fellow.

Will Rogers: A comedian can only last till he either takes himself serious or his audience takes him serious.

Will Rogers: An onion can make people cry but there's never been a vegetable that can make people laugh.

Will Rogers: There's no trick to being a humorist when you have the whole government working for you.

Will Rogers: And the thing about my jokes is, they don't hurt anybody. You can take 'em or leave 'em - you can say they're funny or they're terrible or they're good, or whatever, but you can just pass 'em by. But with Congress, every time they make a joke, it's a law! And every time they make a law, it's a joke!

Eleanor Roosevelt (Letter to Harry Truman, May 14, 1945): "... when you know to laugh and when to look upon things as too absurd to take seriously, the other person is ashamed to carry through even if he was serious about it."

Anna Russell: The reason that there are so few women comics is that so few women can bear being laughed at.

Russian Proverb: When we sing everybody hears us, when we sigh nobody hears us.

George Santayana: The quality of wit inspires more admiration than confidence.

Johann Christoph Friedrich von Schiller: The jest loses its point when he who makes it is the first to laugh.

Scottish Proverb: Be happy while you're living, for you're a long time dead.

William Shakespeare (*All's Well That Ends Well*, Act III, vi): For the love of laughter, hinder not the humor of his design.

William Shakespeare (*As You Like It*, Act V, ii): How bitter a thing it is to look into happiness through another man's eyes!

William Shakespeare (*Hamlet*, Act II, scene ii): Brevity is the soul of wit.

William Shakespeare (*Hamlet*, Act V, i): Alas, poor Yorick! I knew him, Horatio: a fellow of infinite jest, of most excellent fancy.... Here hung those lips that I have kissed I know not how oft. Where be your gibes now? Your gambols? Your songs? Your flashes of merriment, that were wont to set the table on a roar? Not one now, to mock your own grinning? Quite chap-fallen?

William Shakespeare (*I Henry IV*, Act I, ii): Thy quips and thy quiddities.
William Shakespeare (*I Henry IV*, Act II, ii): It would be argument for a week, laughter for a month, and a good jest for ever.
William Shakespeare (*I Henry IV*, Act III, i): Now, I percieve the devil understands Welsh; / And 'tis no marvel, he's so humorous.
William Shakespeare (*King Lear*, Act V, iii): Jesters do oft prove prophets.
William Shakespeare (*Love's Laborer's Lost*, Act V, ii): A jest's prosperity lies in the ear / Of him that hears it, never in the tongue / Of him that makes it.
William Shakespeare (*Measure for Measure*, Act I, iv): 'Tis my familiar sin / With maids to seem the lapwing and to jest.
William Shakespeare (*The Merchant of Venice*, Act I, i): Though Nestor swear the jest be laughable.
William Shakespeare (*The Merry Wives of Windsor*, Act II, i): I love not the humour of bread and cheese, / and there's the humour of it.
William Shakespeare (*Much Ado About Nothing*, Act II, i): Silence is the perfectest herald of joy. I were but little happy if I could say how much.
William Shakespeare (*Othello*, Act II, i): These are old fond paradoxes to make fools laugh i' the alehouse.
William Shakespeare (*Othello*, Act IV, i): They laugh who win.
William Shakespeare (*Twelfth Night*, Act I, iii): A dry jest, sir .... I have them at my fingers' end.
William Shakespeare (*Two Gentlemen of Verona*, Act II, i): O jest unseen, inscrutable, invisible, / As a nose on a man's face, or a weather-cock on a steeple.
William Shakespeare (*The Winter's Tale*, Act IV, iii): A merry heart goes all the day, / Your sad tires in a mile-a.
George Bernard Shaw: We have no more right to consume happiness without producing it than to consume wealth without producing it.
George Bernard Shaw: My method is to take the utmost trouble to find the right thing to say, and then to say it with the utmost levity.
R.B. Sheridan: From the silence which prevails I concluded that Lauderdale has been making a joke.
Alfred E. Smith: If you can make a man laugh, you can make him think and make him like and believe you.
Susan Sontag: If tragedy is an experience of hyperinvolvement, comedy is an experience of underinvolvement, of detachment.
Sir Richard Steele (British essayist, dramatist, 1672-1729): There is hardly that person to be found who is not more concerned for the reputation of wit and sense, than honesty and a virtue.
Laurence Sterne: For every ten jokes, thou hast got an hundred enemies.
Andre Suares: The art of the clown is more profound than we think; it is neither tragic nor comic. It is the comic mirror of tragedy and the tragic mirror of comedy.
R. H. Tawney: If a man has important work, and enough leisure and income to enable him to do it properly, he is in possession of as much happiness as is good for any of the children of Adam.
Mother Teresa: Everytime you smile at someone, it is an action of love, a gift to that person, a beautiful thing.
Mother Teresa: Peace begins with a smile.
Mother Teresa: Let us always meet each other with a smile, for the smile is the beginning of love.
Mother Teresa: We shall never know all the good that a simple smile can do.
William Makepeace Thackeray (English novelist, 1811-1863): Good humor is one of the best articles of dress one can wear in society.
James Thurber: Humor is the other side of tragedy. Humor is a serious thing. I like to think of it as one of our greatest and earliest national resources which must be preserved at all costs. It came over on the Mayflower and we should have it, all of it.
James Thurber: Humor is emotional chaos remembered in tranquility.
James Thurber: As brevity is the soul of wit, form, it seems to me, is the heart of humor and the salvation of comedy.
James Thurber: We (America) are a nation that has always gone in for a loud laugh, the wow, the belly laugh and the dozen other labels for the roll-'em-in-the-aisle gagerissimo.
James Thurber: The perfect tribute to perfection in comedy is not immediate laughter, but a curious and instantaneous tendency of the eyes to fill.

James Thurber: Comedy has ceased to be a challenge to the mental processes. It has become a therapy of relaxation, a kind of tranquilizing drug.

James Thurber: The only rules comedy can tolerate are those of taste, and the only limitations those of libel.

James Thurber: Humor is a serious thing. I like to think of it as one of our greatest earliest natural resources, which must be preserved at all cost.

Mark Twain: The best way to cheer yourself up is to try to cheer somebody else up.

Mark Twain: Grief can take care of itself, but to get the full value from joy you must have somebody to divide it with.

Mark Twain: The secret source of humor is not joy but sorrow. There is no humor in heaven.

Mark Twain: Wit is the sudden marriage of ideas which before their union were not perceived to have any relation.

Mark Twain: Power, Money, Persuasion, Supplication, Persecution—these can lift at a colossal humbug—push it a little—crown it a little – weaken it a little, century by century: blood only Laughter can blow it to rags and atoms at a blast. Against the assault of Laughter nothing can stand.

Mark Twain: Everything human is pathetic. The secret source of Humor itself is not joy but sorrow. There is no humor in heaven.

Mark Twain: There is no character, howsoever good and fine, but it can be destroyed by ridicule, howsoever poor and witless.

Mark Twain: There are several kinds of stories, but only one difficult kind – the humorous.

Mark Twain: Guides cannot master the subtleties of the American joke.

UA: A comedian is someone who knows a good joke when he steals one.

UA: Humor is a universal language.

Peter Ustinov: Comedy is simply a funny way of being serious.

Mark Van Doren: Wit is the only wall Between the us and the dark.

Agnes Varda: Humor is such a strong weapon, such a strong answer. Women have to make jokes about themselves, laugh about themselves, because they have nothing to lose.

Bill Veeck: I wish you the WD40 of life – laughter. We don't laugh nearly enough.

Gore Vidal: Although every American has a sense of humor—it is his birthright and encoded somewhere in the Constitution—few Americans have ever been able to cope with wit or irony, and even the simplest jokes often cause unease, especially today when every phrase must be examined for covert sexism, racism, agism.

Voltaire: He who cannot shine by thought, seeks to bring himself into notice by a witticism.

Voltaire: Pleasantry is never good on serious points, because it always regards subjects in that point of view in which it is not the purpose to consider them.

Peter deVries: The satirist shoots to kill, while the humorists brings his prey back alive and eventually releases him again for another chance.

Naomi Weisstein: Humor as a weapon in the social arsenal constructed to maintain caste, class, race, and sex inequalities is a very common thing.

Mae West: It's hard to be funny when you have to be clean.

E.B. White: Your can't be dissected, as a frog can, but the thing dies in the process.

E.B. White: Whatever else an American believes or disbelieves about himself, he is absolutely sure he has a sense of humor.

E.B. White: The world likes humor, but it treats it patronizingly. It decorates its artists with laurel, and its wags with Brussels sprouts.

E.B. White: I think the stature of humor must vary some with the times. The court fool in Shakespeare's day had no social standing and was no better than a lackey, but he did have some artistic standing and was listened to with considerable attention, there being a well-founded belief that he had the truth hidden somewhere about his person. Artistically he stood probably higher than the humorist of today, who has gained social position but not the ear of the mighty.

Ella Wheeler Wilcox ("Solitude," 1883): Laugh and the world laughs with you; / Weep and you weep alone ...

Oscar Wilde: Seriousness is the only refuge of the shallow.

P.G. Wodehouse (*Laughing Gas*, 1936): " 'Anything for a laugh' is your motto."
Virginia Woolf: Humor is the first of the gifts to perish in a foreign tongue.
Henny Youngman (Walter Winchell named him "THE KING OF THE ONE-LINER;" a very few of them are):
If I had blood I'd blush
Gimme $10 'till payday. When's payday? You should know – you're the one that's working.
I haven't eaten in 2 days – I said Y'should force yourself.
I have't tasted food in a week – don't worry – it tastes the same.
My wife and I hold hands all the time – if I let go SHE SHOPS!

COMMON SENSE (See also TRUTH/UNDERSTANDING)

Uncle Anthony: Common sense ain't so common a thing.
Uncle Anthony: Y'know, common sense is rare gift from God; most people I know only have a high school, technical or trade school education.
Uncle Anthony: An intelligent idea dies quick in his head – it can't stand solitary confinement!
Aunt Mary DiCaro: She must have a sixth sense – I don't see dat she's got de udder five woikin (working).
Aunt Mary Carlo: He keeps loinin (learning) more and more about less and less, pretty soon he'll know everythin' about nuttin'!
Aunt Mary Carlo: I tink he's recoverin' from an accident – a thought just struck 'em!
James Adams: It may be that without a vision men shall die. It is no less true that, without hard practical sense, they shall also die. Without Jefferson the new nation might have lost its soul. Without Hamilton it would assuredly have been killed in body.
Ashanti Proverb: No one tests the depth of a river with both feet.
Nancy Astor: The most practical thing in the world is common sense and common humanity.
William Barrett: Common sense, however logical and sound, is after all only one human attitude among many others; and like everything human it may have its limitations – or *negative* side.
Beaumarchais: I would rather worry without need than live without heed.
Bible: Ecclesiastes 1:18: He that increseth knowledge increseth sorrow.
Bible: Matthew 15:14: If the blind lead the blind, both shall fall into the ditch.
Bible: Proverbs, 14:15: The simple believeth every word: but the prudent man looketh well to his going.
Bible: Psalms 32:9: Be ye not as the horse, or as the mule, which have no understanding.
Ambrose Bierce: BRAIN, n. An apparatus with which we think that we think. That which distinguishes the man who is content to *be* something from the man who wishes to *do* something. A man of great wealth, or one who has been pitchforked into high station, has commonly such a headful of brain that his neighbors cannot keep their hats on. In our civilization, and under our republican form of government, brain is so highly honored that it is rewarded by exemption from the cares of office.
Ambrose Bierce: CUNNING, n. The faculty that distinguishes a weak animal or person from a strong one. It brings its possessor much mental satisfaction and great material adversity. An Italian proverb says: "The furrier gets the skins of more foxes than asses."
Ambrose Bierce: INNATE, adj. Natural, inherent – as innate ideas, that is to say, ideas that we are born with, having had them previously imparted to us.
Ambrose Bierce: LORE, n. Learning – particularly that sort which is not derived from a regular course of instruction but comes of the reading of occult books, or by nature. This later is commonly designated as folk-lore and embraces popularly myths and superstitions....
Burmese Proverb: Though you would like to beat the dog, you must consider its master's face as well.
Sir William Draper Best (British judge, 1767-1845, in 1820): Presumption means nothing more than, as stated by Lord Mansfield, the weighing of probablilities, and deciding, by the powers of common sense, on which side the truth is.
William Blake: Prudence is a rich, ugly old maid courted by Incapacity.
Oliver Braston: Philosophy is common sense in a dress suit.
Daniel Callahan: There's no guarantee that high IQ people produce better people or a better society. It is not the retarded kids of the world who produce the wars and destruction.

Cervantes: 'Tis the part of a wise man to keep himself today for tomorrow, and not venture all his eggs in one basket.

William Ellery Channing: They who have read about everything are thought to understand everything, too, but it is not always so; reading furnishes the mind only with materials of knowledge; it is thinking that makes what we read ours. We are of the ruminating kind, and it is not enough to cram ourselves with a great load of collections – we must chew them over again.

Lord Chesterfield: Common sense (which, in truth, is very uncommon) is the best sense I know of.

Lord Chesterfield: Judgment is not upon all occasions required, but discretion always is.

Sir Winston Churchill: True genius resides in the capacity for evaluation of uncertain, hazardous, and conflicting information.

Sir Winson Churchill: Out of intense complexities intense simplicities emerge.

Charles C. Colton: In order to try whether a vessel be leakey, we first prove it with water before we trust it with wine.

Charles Caleb Colton: Pedantry prides herself on being wrong by rules; while common sense is contented to be right without them.

Congreve: Who would die a martyr to sense in a country where the religion is folly?

Danish Proverb: Act so in the valley that you need not fear those who stand on the hill.

Rene Descrates: Good sense is, of all things among men, the most equally distributed; for every one thinks himself so abundantly provided with it, that those even who are the most difficult to satisfy in everything else, do not usually desire a larger measure of this quality then they already possess.

Rene Descartes: Common sense is the most fairly distributed thing in the world, for each one thinks he is so well-endowed with it that even those who are hardest to satisfy in all other matters are not in the habit of desiring more of it than they already have.

Sir Arthur Conan Doyle (The Sherlock Holmes phrase that suggests the answer is obvious to anyone with the smallest amount of intelligence): Doctor John H. Watson: "Amazing, Holmes!" Sherlock Holmes: "Elementary, my dear Watson, elementary."

Dutch Proverb: One cannot shoe a running horse.

Albert Einstein: Common sense is the collection of prejudices acquired by the age of 18.

T.S. Eliot: Intellectual ability without the more human attributes is admirable only in the same was as the brilliance of a child chess prodigy.

Ralph Waldo Emerson: Common sense is as rare as genius.

Ralph Waldo Emerson: Common sense is the wick of the candle.

Ralph Aldo Emerson: Common Sense, which, one would say, means the shortest line between two points.

Ralph Waldo Emerson: Nothing astonishes men so much as common sense and plain dealing.

Ralph Waldo Emerson: The eye of prudence may never shot.

Ralph Waldo Emerson: Poverty, Frost, Famine, Rain, Disease, are the beadles and guardsmen that hold us to Common Sense.

English Proverb: If thou canst not see the bottom, wade not.

Euripides: Talk sense to a fool to and he calls you foolish.

Euripides (412 B.C.): The best prophet is common sense, our native wit.

French Proverb: Don't try to fly before you have wings.

Thomas Fuller: If thy heart fails in the, climb not at all.

Thomas Fuller: A mariner must have his eyes upon rocks and sands, as well upon the North Star.

German Proverb: A dram of discretion is worth a pound of wisdom.

Andre Gide: When you have nothing to say, or to hide, there is no need to be prudent.

Baltasar Gracian: There is no greater panacea for every kind of folly than common sense.

Baltasar Gracian: Attend easy tasks as if they were difficult, and difficult as if they were easy; in the one case that confidence may not fall asleep, in the other that it may not be dismayed.

Matthew Green: Preferring sense, from chin that's bare, / To nonsense throned in whiskered hair.

Lord Halifax (Sir George Savile, Marquis of Halifax, English member of Parliament and political pamphleteer, 1633-1695): Where Sense is wanting, everything is wanting.

Sir William Hamilton: Be sober, and to doubt pretense,/These are the sinews of good sense.

George Herbert: I had rather ride on an ass that carries me than a horse that throws me.

Thomas Hobbes: Prudence is but experience, which equal time equally disposed on all men, in those things they equally apply themselves unto.

Oliver Wendell Holmes: Science is a first-rate piece of furniture for man's upper chamber, if he has common sense on the ground floor.

Elbert Hubbard: Logic is one thing and common sense another.

Hungarian Proverb: A prudent man does not make the goat his gardener.

Thomas Huxely: Science is nothing but trained and organized common sense.

Irish Proverb: The world would not make a racehorse of a donkey

Irish Proverb: When the drop (drink) is inside, the sense is outside.

Italian Proverb: Tell not all you know, believe not all you hear, do not all you are able.

William James: Common sense is NOT sense common to everyone, but sense in common things.

Jami (15th century Persian poet): Good intentions are useless in the absence of common sense.

Japanese Proverb: Without oars you cannot cross in a boat.

Thomas Jefferson: We Americans sip our hot soup. The French gulp it. (Speaking of the violent French Revolution)

Jewish Proverb: On black earth, the best corn grows. (Simple folk often have the best hearts/heads).

Jewish Saying: You can live with someone else's seykhl (good sense or brains).

John F. Kennedy: We cannot expect that everyone, to use the phrase of the decade ago, will "talk sense to the American people" but we can hope that fewer people will listen to nonsense. And the notion that this Nation is headed for defeat through deficit, or that strength is but a matter of slogans, is nothing but just plain nonsense.

Korean Proverb: Even a fish would not get into trouble if it kept its mouth shut.

Ann Landers: If you want to catch a trout, don't fish in a herring barrel.

La Bruyere: Between good sense and good taste there is the difference between cause and effect.

La Bruyere: If poverty is the mother of crimes, want of sense is the father.

Pierre Simon de Laplace: The theory of probabilities is at bottom nothing but common sense reduced to calculus.

Abraham Lincoln: God must love the common man, he made so many of them.

Walter Lichtman: The final test of a leader is that he leaves behind him in other men the conviction and the will to carry on... The genius of a good leader is to leave behind him a situation which common sense, without the grace of genius, can deal with successfully.

Walter Lippmann: A rational man acting in the real world may be defined as one who decides where he will strike a balance between what he desires and what can be done.

Alice Roosevelt Longworth (said it of Thomas E. Dewey's nomination as the Republican challenger in 1948 after Dewey had previously run against and lost to FDR in 1944): You can't make a souffle rise twice!

Allard Lowenstein: The question should be, is it worth trying to do, not can it be done.

Marcel Proust: "SENTILLIGENCE" = is a combination of common sense + intelligence

Maylay Proverb: Although it rain, cast not away the watering pot.

Maylay Proverb: Don't borrow from a *nouveau riche*; don't visit the newly wed.

Sir Thomas More (Lord Chancellor of England, 1478-1535, canonized 1935: Plato by a goodly similitude declareth, why wise men refrain to meddle in the commonwealth. For when they see the people swarm into the streets, and daily wet to the skin with rain, and yet cannot persuade them to go out of the rain, they do keep themselves within their houses, seeing they cannot remedy the folly of the people. (The modern phrase = "Not sense enough to come in out of the rain.").

John Mortimer (English lawyer): My father told me that all you need to succeed in the law is a certain amount of common sense and clean fingernails.

Michael A. Musmanno (Justice of the Supreme Court of Pennsylvania, 1959): Common sense is the mountain peak of reason which projects above the ever-rising flood of legal formulae, complicated terminology, dicta, syllabi, clauses, and phrases pouring from the reservoirs of formal law.

Michael A. Musmanno (Justice of the Supreme Court of Pennsylvania): Common sense at one time was supposed to designate an untutored knowledge combined with a rough homely application of practical measures two given situations. The phrase, over the years, has taken on a rather discriminating connotation so that, from the category of simple, uneducated thought, it has graduated into the advance class of select wisdom. To ascribe common sense these days to anyone is to bestow on him almost the attributes of Solomonic judgment.

Michael A. Musmanno (Justice of the Supreme Court of Pennsylvania, 1959): In the present case the Trial Judge called upon the jury several times to use "horse sense." It is suggested, in the absence of any showing that an equine evaluation of real estate values is of particular merit, that in the future such phrase be omitted from instructions to juries because the birth rate of horses is declining so steadily there is definite danger that within the foreseeable future, juries will not know what a horse is.

Friedrich Nietzsche: He who is not a bird should not build his nest over abysses.

Onondaga Saying: There are no secrets. There is no mystery. There is only common sense.

William Penn: If thou thinkest twice before thou speakest once, thou wilt speak twice the better for it.

Periander: Be moderate in prosperity, prudent in adversity.

Persian Proverb: He who once a rose must respect the thorn.

Persian Proverb: One pound of learning requires ten pounds of common sense to apply it.

Petronius: A bit of sound sense is what makes men; the rest is all rubbish.

Titus Maccius Plautus (Roman dramatist, 254?-184 BC): Consider the little mouse, how sagacious an animal it is which never entrusts its life to one hole only.

Alexander Pope: Fine sense and exalted sense are not half so useful as common sense.

Alexander Pope: Good Sense, which only is the gift of Heav'n, /And tho' no science, fairly worth the seven.

Alexander Pope: And splendor borrows all her rays from sense.

Alexander Pope: Fool! 'tis in vain from wit to wit to roam: Know, Sense, like Charity, "begins at home."

James Robinson: Most of our so-called (common sense) reasoning consists of finding agreements for going on believing as we already do.

François, Duc de La Rochefoucauld: We rarely find that people have good sense unless they agree with us.

Duc de La Rochefoucauld: We seldom attribute common sense except to those who agree with us.

Will Rogers: There are three kinds of men. The one that learns by reading. The few who learn by observation. The rest of them have to pee on the electric fence for themselves.

Will Rogers: There is not a better day in the world to be spent than with a lot of wise old cowmen around barbecued beef, black coffee and good "free holy" beans.

Will Rogers: It don't take a genius to spot a goat in a flock of sheep.

Bertrand Russell: A stupid man's report of what a clever man says can never be accurate, because he unconsciously translates what he hears into something he can understand.

Carl Sagan: Skeptical scrutiny is the means, in both science and religion, by which deep insight can be winnowed from deep nonsense.

Saint-Exupery: We are prudent people. We are afraid to let go of our petty reality in order to grasp at a great shadow.

Scottish Proverb: Better eat gray bread in your youth than in your age.

William Shakespeare (*I Henry IV*, Act V, scene iv): The better part of valor is discretion.

William Shakespeare (*Henry V*, Act V, Chorus): Now behold, / In the quick forge and working-house of thought, / How London doth pour out her citizens!

William Shakespeare (*Love's Labour's Lost*, Act I, i): At Christmas I no more desire a rose / Than wish a snow in May's new fangled mirth; / But like of each thing in season grows.

George Bernard Shaw: A man of great common sense and good taste – meaning thereby a man without originality or moral courage.

Sophocles: If you are out of trouble, watch for danger. /And when you live well, then consider the most / your life, lest ruin take it unawares.

John Lancaster Spalding: The mere intellect is perverse; it takes all side, maintains all paradoxes, and comes to understanding only when it listens to the whisperings of common sense.

Gertrude Stein: Everybody gets so much information all day long that they lose their common sense.

Adlai Stevenson: Let's face it. Let's talk sense to the American people. Let's tell them the truth, that there are no gains without pains, and we are now on the eve of great decisions, not easy decisions, like resistance when you are attacked, but a long, patient, costly struggle which alone can assure triumph over the great enemies of man—war, poverty and tyranny—and the assaults upon human dignity which are the most grievous consequences of each.

Robert Louis Stevenson: So soon as prudence has begun to grow up in the brain, like a dismal fungus, it finds its first expression in a paralysis of generous acts.

Calvin Ellis Stowe: Common sense is the knack of seeing things as they are, and doing things as they ought to be done.

Publilus Syrus: It is well to moor your bark with two anchors.

Tehyi Hsieh: Prudence is sometimes stretched too far, until it blocks the road of progress.

Terence: No wise man stands behind an ass when he kicks.

Henry David Thoreau: A true account of the actual is the rarest poetry, for common sense always takes a hasty and superficial view.

Henry David Thoreau: Why level downward to our dullest perception always, and praise that as common sense? The commonest sense is the sense of men asleep, which they express by snoring.

Mark Twain: The fact that a man knows right from wrong proves his *intellectual* superiority to the other creatures; but the fact that he can *do* wrong proves his *moral* inferiority to any creatures that *cannot.*

Mark Twain: In the matter of intellect the ant must be a strangely overrated bird. During many summers, now, I have watched him, when I ought to have been in better business, and I have not yet come across a living ant that seemed to have any more sense than a dead one. I refer to the ordinary ant, of course; I have had no experience of those wonderful Swiss and African ones which vote, keep drilled armies, hold slaves, and dispute about religion.

Anne Tyler: People always call it luck when you've acted more sensibly than they have.

Voltaire: Common sense is not so common.

Kurt Vonnegut: Another flaw in human character is that everybody wants to build and nobody wants to do maintenance.

Horace Walpole, Fourth Earl of Oxford (1776): This world is a comedy to those that think, a tragedy to those that feel.

Barbara Walters: A great many people think that polysyllables are a sign of intelligence.

Alfred North Whitehead: Common sense is genius in homespun.

Oscar Wilde: Most people die of a sort of creeping common sense, and discover when it is too late that the only things one never regrets are one's mistakes.

Edward Young: Plain sense but rarely leads us far astray.

Edward Young: Sense is our helmet, wit is but the plume; / The plume exposes, 'tis our helmet saves. / Sense is the diamond, weighty, solid, sound; / When cut by wit, it casts a brighter beam; / Yet, wit apart, it is a diamond still.

COMMUNICATION (See ADVERSARY; WORDS)

COMPASSION

Uncle Anthony: Sympathy is what you get when you ask your friends or relatives for a loan.

Uncle Anthony: People don't care unless they share.

Uncle Anthony: Der's a big difference between (SYMPATHY) feelin' sorry for somebody without thinkin' about how dey got to where dey got, and (EMPATHY) thinkin' about somebody's trouble by puttin' yer feet in their shoes.

Aunt Mary Carlo: Ya can't cry for everybody in the world, you gotta choose.

Aunt Mary Carlo: Ya can't ask 'em to be human beans an be fair about it 'cause dey can't do imitations.

Aunt Mary Carlo: An eye for an eye leaves two people blind!

Jean Anoulh: (French playwright, dramatist and screenwriter; 1910-1987, : One cannot weep for the entire world, it is beyond the human strength. One must choose.

Minna Antrim: Sympatica is the touchstone that leads to talent's highest altitude.

Diane Arbus: It's important to get out of your skin into someone else's ... that somebody else's tragedy is not the same as your own.

Nancy Astor: The most practical thing in the world is common sense and common humanity.

Enid Bagnold: She keeps 'er brains in 'er 'eart. An' that's where they ought ter be. An' a man or woman who does that's one in a million an' 'as got my backing.

David Ball (jury consultant): When the plaintiff is an abstraction you lose the jury's interest and understanding. The jury cannot imagine an abstraction, the jury cannot imagine the plaintiff's problem or problems.

Balzac: The response man has the greatest difficulty in tolerating is pity, especially when he warrants it. Hatred is a tonic, it makes one live, it in spires vengeance, but pity kills, it makes our weakness weaker.

Catherine Esther Beecher: The delicate and infirm go for sympathy, not to the well and buoyant, but to those who have suffered like themselves.

Henry Ward Beecher: It takes longer for man to find out man than any other creature that is made.

Saint Bernard of Clairvaux: Justice seeks out the merits of the case, but pity only regards the need.

Bible: Acts, 4:32-35 (St. Luke, called "the Gentile Physician): "… and distribution was made unto every man according as he had need."

Bible: Colossians, 3:12: Put on ... bowels of mercies, kindness, humbleness of mind, meekness, longsuffering.

Bible: Colossians, 3:14: Put on charity, which is the bond of perfection.

Bible: 1 Corinthians, 13:1: Though I speak with the tongues of men and of angels, and have not charity, I am become as sounding brass, or a tinkling cymbal. And though I have the gift of prophesy, and understand all mysteries, and all knowledge; and though I have all faith, so that I could remove mountains, and have not charity, I am nothing. And though, I bestow all my goods to feed the poor, and though I give my body to be burned, and have not charity, it profiteth me nothing.

Bible: 1 Corinthians, 13:13: Now abideth faith, hope, charity, these three; but the greatest of these is charity.

Bible: Deuteronomy 15:7: Thou shalt not harden thine heart, nor shut thine hand from thy poor brother.

Bible: Deuteronomy 15:11: Thou shalt open thine hand wide unto thy brother, to thy poor, and to thy needy, in thy land.

Bible: Genesis, 21:23: According to the kindness that I have done unto thee, thou shalt do unto me.

Bible: Hebrews 13:3: Remember them that are in bonds, as bound with them; and them which suffer adversity, as being yourselves also in the body.

Bible: Isaiah, 54:8: With everlasting kindness will I have mercy on thee.

Bible: Job 16:2: (Job to his friends): Miserable comforters are ye all.

Bible: Job 29:15: I was eyes to the blind, and feet was I to the lame.

Bible: Matthew, 5:7: Blessed are the merciful: for they shall obtain mercy.

Bible: Micah, 6:8: What doth the Lord require of thee, but to do justly, and to love mercy, and to walk humbly with thy God?

Bible: Peter, 4:8: Charity shall cover the multitude of sins

Bible: 2 Peter, 3:8: Add to ... godliness brotherly kindness; and to brotherly kindness charity.

Bible: Proverbs, 3:3: Let not mercy and truth forsake thee: bind them about thy neck; write them upon the table of thine heart.

Bible: Proverbs, 11:17: The merciful man doeth good to his own soul.

Bible: Proverbs, 14:21: He that hath mercy on the poor, happy is he.

Bible: Psalms 37: 21: The wicked borroweth, and prayeth not again: but the righteous sheweth mercy, and giveth.

Bible: Romans, 12:10: Be kindly affectioned one to another with brotherly love; in honour preferring one another.

Bible: Romans, 12:15: Rejoice with them that do rejoice, and we with them that weep.

Ambrose Bierce: MERCY, n. An attribute beloved of detected offenders.

Ambrose Bierce: PITY, n. A failing sense of exemption, inspired by contrast.

William Blake: Pity would be no more / If we did not make somebody Poor; / And Mercy no more could be / If all were as happy as we.

Elizabeth Bowen: There is no consoler, no confidant that half the instinct does not want to reject. The spilling over, the burst of tears and words, the ejaculation of the private personal grief accomplishes itself, like a convulsion, in circumstances that one would never choose.

Bertolt Brecht: There are a few things that'll move people to pity, a few, but the trouble is, when they've been used several times, they no longer work.

Sir Thomas Browne: By compassion we make others' misery our own, and so, by relieving them, we relieve ourselves also.

Carlisle Indian Industrial School Motto: God helps those who help themselves

Alexander Chase: To understand is to forgive, even oneself.

G.K. Chesterton: If you do not understand a man you cannot crush him. And if you do not understand him, very probably you will not.

Sir Winston Churchill: We shall draw from the heart of suffering itself the means of inspiration and survival.

Sir Winston Churchill: We have a lot of anxieties, and one cancels out another very often.

Cicero: A tear dries quickly, especially when it is shed for the troubles of others.

Charles Caleb Colton: Most of our misfortunes are more supportable than the comments of our friends upon them.

Confucius: Grieve not that men do not know you; grieve will that you do not know men.

Joseph Conrad: There is a kind way of assisting our fellow-creatures which is enough to break their hearts while it saves their outer envelope.

Danish Proverb: No man limps because another is hurt.

Mary Carolyn Davies (poem "If I Had Known"): If I had known what trouble you were bearing; / What griefs were in the silence of your face; / I would have been more gentle, and more caring, / And tried to give you gladness for a space.

Emily Dickinson: Endow the Living—with the Tears—/ You squander on the Dead.

Emily Dickinson: On to a broken heart / No other one may go / Without the high prerogative / Its self hath suffered too.

Norman Douglas: The bowels of compassion: a wonderful old phrase. They ought to be kept open.

John Dryden: Pity melts the mind to love.

W.E.B. DuBois: Herein lies the tragedy of the age: not that men are poor, - all men know something of poverty; not that men are wicked, - who is good? not that men are ignorant, - what is truth? Nay, but that men know so little of men.

George Eliot: We hand folks over to God's mercy, and show none ourselves.

Ralph Waldo Emerson: You may regret calamities if you can thereby help the sufferer, but if you cannot, mind your own business.

Ralph Waldo Emerson: Sympathy is a supporting atmosphere, and in it we unfold easily and well.

Ralph Waldo Emerson: A sympathetic person is placed in the dilemma of a swimmer among drowning man, who all catch at him, and if he gives so much as a leg or a finger, they will drown him.

Ralph Waldo Emerson: All persons are puzzles until at last we find in some word or act the key to the man, to the woman; straightway all their past words and actions lie in light before us.

Ralph Waldo Emerson: Man's conclusions are reached by toil. Woman arrives at the same by sympathy.

Ralph Waldo Emerson: The best service one person can render to another is to help him to help himself.

English Proverb: The rough net is not the best catcher of birds.

English Proverb: Honey catches more flies than vinegar.

Charles J. Fox: True humanity consists not in a squeamish ear; it consists not in starting or shrinking at tales of misery, but in a disposition of heart to relieve it.

Anne Frank: If you think of your fellow creatures, then you only want to cry, you could really cry the whole day long. The only thing to do is to pray that God will perform a miracle and save some of them. And I hope that I am doing enough!

Thomas Fuller: Search not a wound too deep lest thou make a new one.

Thomas Fuller: Sacrifice not thy heart upon every altar.

Thomas Fuller: Pour not water on a drowning mouse.

Thomas Fuller: God grant me to contend with those that understand me.

German Proverb: Charity looks at the need and not at the cause.

Edward Gibbon: Our sympathy is cold to the relation of distant misery.

Andre Gide: Each of us really understands in others only those feelings he is capable of producing himself.

Andre Gide: True kindness presupposes the faculty of imagining as one's own the sufferings and joy of others. Without imagination, there can be weakness, theoretical or practical philanthropy, but not true kindness.

Baltasar Gracian: It is profound philosophy to sound the depths of feeling and distinguish traits of character. Men must be studied as deeply as books.

Hasdai: If one is cruel to himself, how can we expect him to be compassionate with others?

Wilma Scott Heide: To date, we have taught men to be brave and women to care. Now we must enlarge our concepts of bravery and caring. Men must be *brave enough to care* sensitively, compassionately and contrary to the masculine mystique about the quality and equality of our society. Women must *care enough* about their families and all families to *bravely assert* their voices and intellects to every aspect of every institution, whatever the feminine mystique. Every social trait labelled masculine or feminine is in truth a human trait. It is our human right to develop and contribute our talents whatever our race, sex, religion, ancestry, age. Human rights are indivisible!

Eric Hoffer: We can see through others only when we see through ourselves.

Edgar Watson Howe: When you are in trouble, people who call to sympathize are really looking for the particulars.

Elbert Hubbard: Wisdom must go with Sympathy, else the emotions will become maudlin and pity may be wasted on a poodle instead of a child—on a field-mouse instead of a human soul.

Irish Proverb: Patience is poultice for all wounds.

Italian Proverb: The comforter's head never aches.

Jewish Proverb: On black earth, the best corn grows. (Simple folk often have the best hearts).

Jewish Saying: I felt sorry for myself because I had no shoes—until I met a man who had no feet.

Jewish Saying: A man devoid of sympathy is not a man but a monster.

Jewish Saying: Some men can't even spare a sigh.

Jewish Saying: When you pour your heart out (in tears) it feels lighter.

Jewish Saying: What good is a golden urn that is full of tears?

Lady Bird Johnson: It's odd that you can get so anesthetized by your own pain or your own problem that you don't quite fully share the hell of someone close to you.

Samuel Johnson: We may have uneasy feelings for seeing a creature in distress without pity; for we have not pity unless we wish to relieve them.

Samuel Johnson: The applause of a single human being is of great consequence.

Martin Luther King Jr.: Pity may represent little more than the impersonal concern which prompts the mailing of a check, but true sympathy is the personal concern which demands the giving of one's soul.

Walter Savage Landor: Of all cruelties those are the most intolerable that come under the name of condolence and consolation.

La Rochefoucauld: It is easier to know (and understand) men in general than one man in particular.

La Rochefoucauld: We all have enough strength to bear the misfortunes of others.

La Rochefoucauld: We like to read others but we do not like to be read.

Latin Proverb: Nothing dries sooner than tears.

Haniel Long (letter to St. Augustine): When individual fear or apathy passes by the unfortunate, life is of no account.

Henry Wadsworth Longfellow: No one is so accursed by fate, / No one so utterly desolate, / But some heart, though unknown, / Responds unto his own.

Catherine Marshall: So once I shut down my privilege of disliking anyone I chose and holding myself aloof if I could manage it, greater understanding, growing compassion came to me....

Sommerset Maugham: The world is quickly bored by recital of misfortunes, and willingly avoids the sight of distress.

Maylayan Proverb: The deep sea can be fathomed, but who knows the hearts of men?

Maylayan Proverb: One can pay back the loan of gold, but one dies forever in debt to those who are kind.

Alice Neel: You can't leave humanity out. If you didn't have humanity, you wouldn't have anything.

Nietzsche: Compassion for the friend should conceal itself under a hard shell.

Nietzsche: Verily, I do not like them, the merciful who feel blessed in their pity: they are lacking too much in shame. If I must pity, at least I do not want it known; and if I do pity, it is preferably from a distance.

Arch Obler (WWII radio play *"I Have No Prayer"*): "Life and let live … no, live and HELP LIVE!"
Ojibway Saying: Sometimes I go about pitying myself, and all the time I am being carried on great wings across the sky.
Margaret Oliphant: She was not clever; you might have said she had no mind at all; but so wise and right and tender at heart, that it was as good as genius.
Joel Oppenheimer: Who cries for another's / pain hasn't enough of his own.
Persian Proverb: By a sweet tongue and kindness, you can drag an elephant with a hair.
Harry Philo: You can tell the philosophy of a judge by whether or not he/she likes (has compassion for) people.
Plato: Be kind, for everyone you meet is fighting a hard battle.
Alexander Pope: Teach me to feel another's woe, / To hide the fault I see; / That mercy eye to others show, / That mercy show to make.
Mary Roberts Rinehart: The great God endows His children variously. To some He gives intellect – and they move the earth. To some He allots heart – and the beating pulse of humanity is theirs. But to some He gives only a soul, without intelligence – and these, who never grow up, but remain always His children, are God's fools, kindly, elemental, simple, as if from His palette the Artist of all has taken one colour instead of many.
Will Rogers: Liberty (Editor: and compassion/empathy) doesn't work as well in practice as it does in speeches.
Will Rogers: "What's the matter with the world? Why, there ain't nothing but one word wrong with everyone of us, and that's selfishness."
Will Rogers: People love high ideals, but they got to be about 33-percent plausible.
Will Rogers: It's great to be great, but it's greater to be human
Will Rogers: I can remember way back when a liberal was generous with his own money
Theodore Roosevelt: I don't know the way people do feel, I only know the way they ought to feel.
Russian Proverb: A kind word is like a Spring day.
Russian Proverb: Clemency is the support of justice.
Russian Proverb: When you live next to the cemetery, you cannot weep for everyone.
Russian Proverb: When we sing everybody hears us, when we sigh nobody hears us.
Saint-Exupery: What value has compassion that does not take its object in its arms?
Saint-Exupery: Pathos is the sense of distance.
George Santayana: There is nothing sweeter than to be sympathized with.
George Santayana: Piety to mankind must be three-fourths pity.
George Santayana: The milk of human kindness is less apt to turn sour if the vessel that holds it stands steady, cool, and separate, and is not too often uncorked.
Arthur Schopenhauer: Compassion is the basis of all morality.
Franz Schubert: No one really understands the grief or joy of another.
Seneca The Elder: The entire world would perish, if pity were not to limit anger.
William Shakespeare (*Coriolanus*, Act III, iii): Pent to linger / But with a grain a day, I would not buy / Their mercy at the price of one fair word.
William Shakespeare (*Hamlet*, Act III, iii): Whereto serves mercy / But to confront the visage of offence?
William Shakespeare (*Henry V*, Act II, ii): You must not dare, for shame, to talk of mercy; / For your own reasons turn into your bosoms, / As dogs upon their masters, worrying you.
William Shakespeare (*I Henry VI*, Act V, iii): I cry you, mercy, 'tis but Quid for Quo.
William Shakespeare (*III Henry VI*, Act I, iv): Open the gate of mercy, gracious God! / My soul flies through these wounds to seek out thee.
William Shakespeare (*III Henry VI*, Act IV, viii): My pity hath been balm to heal their wounds, / My mildness hath allay'd their swelling griefs.
William Shakespeare (*Measure for Measure*, Act II, i): Mercy is not itself, that oft looks so; / Pardon is still the nurse of second woe.
William Shakespeare (*Measure for Measure*, Act II, ii): How would you be, / If He, who is the top of Judgment should / But judge you as you are? O think on that; / And mercy then will breathe within your lips, / Like man new made.

William Shakespeare (*Measure for Measure*, Act II, ii): Well believe this, / No ceremony that to great ones 'longs, / Not the king's crown, nor the deputed sword, The marshal's truncheon, nor the judge's robe, / Become them with one half so good a grace, / As mercy does.

William Shakespeare (*Measure for Measure*, Act II, iv): Lawful mercy / Is nothing kin to foul redemption.

William Shakespeare (*The Merchant of Venice*, Act IV, i): The quality of mercy is not strained; / It droppeth as the gentle rain from heaven / Upon the place beneath. It is twice blessed—/ It blesseth him that gives, and him that takes: / 'Tis mightiest in the mightiest: it becomes / The throned monarch better than his crown; His sceptre shows the force of temporal power, / The attribute to awe and majesty, / Wherein doth sit the dread and fear of kings, / It is an attribute to God himself; / And earthly power doth then show likest God's / When mercy seasons justice.

William Shakespeare (*The Merchant of Venice*, Act IV, i): Though justice be thy plea, consider this - / That in the course of justice, none of us / Should see salvation; we do pray for mercy; / And that some prayer doth teach us all to render / The deeds of mercy.

William Shakespeare (*The Merchant of Venice*, Act IV, i): We do pray for mercy; / And that same prayer doth teach us all to render / The deeds of mercy.

William Shakespeare (*Richard III*, Act I, ii): Charity, / Which renders good for bad, blessings for curses.

William Shakespeare (*Richard III*, Act I, iv): Which, of you, if you were a prince's son, / Being pent from liberty, as I am now, - / If two such murderers as yourself came to you, - / Would not retreat for life? / My friend, I spy some pity in thy looks; / O, if thine eye be not a flatterer, / Come thou on my side, and entreat for me, / As you would beg, were you in my distress. / A begging prince what beggar pities not?

William Shakespeare (*Richard III*, Act IV, ii): Tear-falling pity dwells not in this eye.

William Shakespeare (*Romeo and Juliet*, Act III, i): Mercy but murders, pardoning those that kill.

William Shakespeare (*Romeo and Juliet*, Act III, v): Is there no pity sitting in the clouds, / That sees into the bottom of my grief?

William Shakespeare (*Sonnet CXLVi*): Straight in her heart did mercy come.

William Shakespeare (*Timon of Athens*, Act I, ii): We are born to do benefits.... O, what a precious comfort 'tis to have so many, like brothers, commanding one another's fortunes!

William Shakespeare (*Timon of Athens*, Act III, ii): But, I percieve, / Men must learn now with pity to dispense; / For policy sits above conscience.

William Shakespeare (*Timon of Athens*, Act III, v): Pity is the virtue of the law, / And none but tyrants use it cruelly.

William Shakespeare (*Timon of Athens*, Act III, v): Nothing emboldens sin so much as mercy.

William Shakespeare (*Titus Andronicus*, Act I, i): Sweet mercy is nobility's true badge.

William Shakespeare (*Titus Andronicus*, Act I, i): Wilt thou draw near the nature of the gods? / Draw near them then in being merciful: / Sweet mercy is nobility's true badge.

William Shakespeare (*Titus Andronicus*, Act IV, i): O heavens! Can you hear a good man groan, / And not relent, or not compassion him?

William Shakespeare (*Troilus and Cressida*, Act V, iii): Brother, you have a vice of mercy in you, / Which better fits a lion than a man.

William Shakespeare (*Twelfth Night*, Act III, i): VIOLA: I pity you. OLIVIA: That's a degree of love.

Bishop Fulton J. Sheen (Roman Catholic Bishop of New York, and Rochester, writer, orator, *Sermon at Red Mass*, 1965): A sign of the loss of freedom is the new compassion which extends pity not to the raped but to the rapist.

Percy Bysshe Shelley: A man, to be greatly good, must imagine intensely and comprehensively; he must put himself in the place of another and of many others; the pains and pleasures of his species must become his own.

Elizabeth Cady Stanton (Seneca falls Convention): "... they had souls large enough to feel the wrongs of others...."

Laurence Sterne: Before an affliction is digested, consolation ever comes too soon; and after it is digested, it comes too late.

Talmud: When a man has compassion for others, God has compassion for him.

Talmud: When the Egyptians were drowning in the Red Sea, the Angels in Heaven began to break forth in songs of jubilation, but the Holy One, blessed be He, silenced them: "My creatures are perishing—and ye are ready to sing!"

Mark Twain: One learns peoples through the heart, not the eyes or the intellect.

Mark Twain: By trying we can easily learn to endure adversity. Another man's, I mean.

Mark Twain: We all do no end of feeling, and we mistake it for thinking.

Mark Twain: Praise is well, compliment is well, but affection – that is the last and final and most precious reward that any man can win, by character or achievement.

Mark Twain: The vast majority of the race, whether savage or civilized, are secretly kind-hearted and shrink from inflicting pain, but in the presence of the aggressive and pitiless minority they don't dare to assert themselves.

UA: People in distress never think that you feel enough.

UA: A childhood milestone is when another's tears are more unbearable than your own.

Peter Weiss: Compassion is the property of the privileged classes / When the pitier lowers himself / to give to a beggar / he throbs with contempt.

Ross Wetzsteon: Compassionate understanding too often buys a long-range peace with a small-change gesture – like giving a quarter to a beggar.

Walt Whitman: And whoever walks a furlong without sympathy walks to his own funeral drest in his shroud.

Tennessee Williams: I don't ask for your pity, but just your understanding—not even that—no. Just for your recognition of me in you, and the enemy, time, in us all.

William Wordsworth: Worse than idle is compassion / If it ends in tears and sighs.

W.B. Yeats: But pity is not love .... Pity is only pity.

W.B. Yeats: Why does the struggle to come at truth take away our pity, and the struggle to overcome our passions restore it again?

Yiddish Proverb: Ten lands are sooner known than one man.

Robert Zend: There are too many people, and too few human beings.

COMPENSATION (See DAMAGES)

COMPLAINT (See ALLEGATION)

COMPROMISE (See also NEGOTIATION/SETTLEMENT)

Uncle Anthony: The bigger the bully the less your share of any split will be.

Aunt Mary Carlo: Wouldn't it be jes' great if all our elementary schools got all the money 'dey needed and the Air Force had to go have a bake sale to buy a new bomber?

Aesop: Yield to all and you will soon have nothing to yield.

Dean Atchison: Negotiation today means war carried on by other means and does not mean our getting between parties both wanting to reach agreement.

Athenian Ambassador to the Lacadaemonians (433 B.C.): Men begin with blows, and when a reverse comes upon them, then have recourse to words.

Jane Austen: I do not want people to be very agreeable, as it saves me the trouble of liking them a great deal.

Bible: Apocrypha, Ecclesiasticus 34:23: When one builds and another tears down, what do they gain but toil?

Bible: Galatians 3:20: A mediator is not a mediator of one.

Bible: Isaiah 1:18: Come now, and let us reason together, saith the Lord.

Bible: Isaiah, 9:6: His name shall be called ... The Prince of Peace.

Bible: Isaiah 52:8: They shall see eye to eye.

Bible: James 1:19: Be swift to hear, slow to speak, slow to wrath.

Bible: Jeremiah 6:14: They have healed also the hurt of the daughter of my people slightly, saying, Peace, peace, when there is no peace.

Bible: John 14:27: Peace I leave with you, my peace I give unto you.

Bible: 1 Kings 3:25: Divide the living child in two, and give half to the one, and half to the other.

Bible: Luke 2:14: Glory to God in the highest, and on earth peace, good will toward men.

Bible: Luke 10:5: Peace be to this house.

Bible: Matthew 5:9: Blessed are the peacemakers: for they shall be called the children of God.

Bible: Matthew 10:34: Think not that I am come to send peace on earth: I came not to send peace, but a sword.

Bible: Proverbs 15:1: A soft answer turneth away wrath.

Bible: Proverbs, 17:7: When a man's ways please the Lord, he maketh even his enemies to be at peace with him.

Bible: Proverbs 20:14: It is naught, it is naught, saith the buyer: but when he is gone his way, then he boasteth.

Bible: Psalms, 37:37: Mark the perfect man, and behold the upright: for the end of that man is peace.

Bible: Psalms, 122:7: Peace be within thy walls, and prosperity within thy palaces.

Bible: Romans 8:6: To be spiritually minded is life and peace.

Bible: Romans 12:18: If it be possible, as much as lieth in you, live peaceably with all men.

Bible: Zechariah 11:12: If ye think good, give me my price; and if not, forbear.

Ambrose Bierce: ACCORD, n. Harmony.

Ambrose Bierce: COMPROMISE, n. Such an adjustment of conflicting interests as gives each adversary the satisfaction of thinking he has got what he ought not to have, and is deprived of nothing except what was justly his due in.

Ambrose Bierce: GUNPOWDER, n. An agency employed by civilized nations for the settlement of disputes which might become troublesome if left unadjusted.

Ambrose Bierce: PEACE, n. In international affairs, a period of cheating between two periods of fighting.

Heywood Broun: Appeasers believe that if you keep on throwing steaks to a tiger, the tiger will turn vegetarian.

McGeorge Bundy (National Security Adviser, talking about foreign policy goals in Eutrope in 1966): Settlement is the name of the game.

Warren Burger (ABA speech 1984): Trials by the adversarial contest must in time go the way of the ancient trial by battle and blood.

Edmund Burke: All government – indeed, every human benefit and enjoyment, every virtue and every prudent act, – is founded on compromise and barter.

Samuel Butler: He that complies against his will / Is of his own opinion still.

Benjamin Cardozo: The judicial process is one of compromise, a compromise between paradoxes, between certainty and uncertainty, between the liberalism that is the exaltation of the written word and the nihilism that is destructive of regularity and order.

Neville Chamberlain (British Prime Minister, September 30, 1938, the day after returning from Munich, after conferring with Hitler and Mussolini): My good friends, this is the second time in our history that there has come back from Germany to Downing Street peace with honor. **I believe it is peace for our time.** We thank you from the bottom of our hearts. And now I recommend you to go home and sleep quietly in your beds.

G.K. Chesterton (1910): Compromise used to mean that half a loaf was better than no bread. Among modern statesmen it really seems to mean that half a loaf is better than a whole loaf.

Chinese Proverb: He who cannot agree with his enemies is controlled by them.

Sir Winston Churchill: An appeaser is one who feeds the crocodile hoping it will eat him last.

Sir Winston Churchill: If you will not fight for the right when you can easily win without bloodshed, if you will not fight when your victory will be sure, you may come to the moment when you will have to fight with all the odds against you and only a precarious chance of survival.

Sir Winston Churchill (June 27, 1954): Better to jaw-jaw than to war-war.

Charles Horton Cooley: Prudence and compromise are necessary means, but every man should have an impudent end which he will not compromise.

Richard Cortese: Whatever you think it's gonna take, double it. That applies to money, time, stress. It's gonna be harder than you think and take longer than you think.

Robert Coulson (ABA President in 1976): In most cases, both sides have much to gain by accommodating and very much to lose by litigating. But in many situations, the lawyers, following their professional attachment to strict adversary loyalties, find themselves obstructing the way toward mutual compromise.

Dante: Blessed are the peacemakers, / For they have freed themselves from sinful wrath.

Charles de Gaulle: Treaties are like roses and young girls. They last while they last.

Benjamin Disraeli: If you are not very clever, you should be conciliatory.

Benjamin Disraeli: "My idea of an agreeable person," said Hugo Bohun, "is a person who agrees with me."

John Foster Dulles: You have to take chances for peace, just as you take chances in war. The ability to get to the verge without getting into the war is the necessary art. If you try to run away from it, if you are scared to go to the brink, you are lost.

John Gregory Dunne: The eleventh commandment of a motion picture negotiation: Thou shalt not take less than thy last deal.

Anthony Robert Eden: The essence of all successful international negotiation is compromise.

Tyron Edwards: Compromise is but the sacrifice of one right or good in the hope of retaining another, too often ending in the loss of both.

Dwight D. Eisenhower: I think that people want peace so much that one of these days governments had better get out of the way and let them have it.

Queen Elizabeth I (in letter to her cousin, Mary, Queen of Scots): "Remember, those who add with two strings (that is, adding an ally) to their bow, may shoot stronger, but rarely shoot strait."

Ralph Waldo Emerson: We do what we must, and call it by the best names.

Ralph Waldo Emerson: Peace has its victories, but it takes a brave man to win them.

Ludwig Erhard: A compromise is the art of dividing a cake in such a way that everyone believes he has the biggest piece.

Gerald Ford (1973): I believe in friendly compromise. I said over in the Senate hearings (on my nomination for Vice President of the United States) that truth is the glue that holds government together. Compromise is the oil that makes governments go.

Benjamin Franklin: Even peace may be purchased at too high a price.

Benjamin Franklin: May we never see another war! For in my opinion, there never was a good war or a bad peace.

Benjamin Franklin: I have never known a peace made, even the most advantageous, that was not censured as inadequate, and the makers condemned as injudicious or corrupt. "Blessed are the peacemakers" is, I suppose, to be understood in the other world; for in this they are frequently cursed.

Indira Gandhi: You cannot shake hands with a clenched fist.

Andre Gide: If one could recover the uncompromising spirit of one's youth, one's greatest indignation would be for what one has become.

Samuel Goldwyn (in a dispute with Jack Warner of Warner Brothers, 1945): "How can we sit together and deal with this industry if you're going to do things like this to me? If this is the way you do it, gentlemen, **include me out!**"

Learned Hand: We believe that when the men who met in 1787 to make a Constitution made the best political document ever made, they did it very largely because they were great compromisers.

Ernest Hemingway (A Farewell to Arms, 1929): I did not want to read about the war. I was going to forget war. I had made a separate peace.

Ernest Hemingway: There are worse things than war. Cowardice,... treachery,... and simply selfishness.

George Herbert: A lean compromise is better than a fat lawsuit.

John Heywood (*The Proverbs of John Heywood*, 1546): Half a loaf is better than none.

Thomas Hughes: There isn't such a reasonable fellow in the world, to hear him talk. He (Tom Brown) never wants anything but what's right and fair; only when you come to settle what's right and fair, it's everything he wants, and nothing that you want. And that's his idea of a compromise.

Italian Proverb: It is better to lose the saddle than the horse.

Italian Proverb: He who divides honey with the bear gets the lesser share.

Lyndon B. Johnson (speech to the UN General Assembly, 1973): Peace is a journey of a thousand miles and it must be taken one step at a time.

John F. Kennedy (Inaugural Address, Jan. 20, 1961): Let us never negotiate out of fear. But let us never fear to negotiate.

Joseph Kennedy (US ambassador to England in a cable to President FDR on May 26, 1940 during the start of the "Miracle of Dunkirk; "when 338,226 Allied British, French and Belgium troops, surrounded by Nazi troops with their backs to the English Channel, were finally evacuated by 693 boats of all sizes from Dunkirk on June 4, 1940): Only a miracle can save the B.E.F. (the British Expeditionary Force) from being wiped out or as I said yesterday surrender. The English people, while they suspect a terrible situation, really do not realize how bad it is. When they do, I don't know what group they will follow – the "Do or Die" or the group that wants a settlement.

Nikita Khrushchev (1958): If you cannot catch a bird of paradise, better take a wet hen.

Rudyard Kipling: Once you have paid him the Danegeld / You never get rid of the Dane.

Henry Cabot Lodge, Jr.: It is never right to compromise with dishonesty.

Andrea de Loo (Spanish Ambassador to England, speaking to Queen Elizabeth I, 1588): Your Majesty will not hear words, so we must come to the cannon.

James Russell Lowell: Compromise makes a good umbrella but a poor roof.

Allard Lowenstein: The question should be, is it worth trying to do, not can it be done.

General Douglas MacArthur: It is fatal to enter any war without the will to win it.

Christopher Marlowe: Our swords shall play the orators for us.

James Ramsey McDonald (British Prime Minister 1929-1935): A government official discussing Prime Minister McDonald's point of view on peace: "The desire for peace does not necessarily ensure peace." McDonald replied: "Quite true. Neither does the desire for food satisfy hunger. But at least it gets you started toward a restaurant." '

Phyllis McGinley: Compromise, if not the spice of life, is its solidity.

Edna St. Vincent Millay: My candle burns at both ends; / It will not last the night; / But, ah, my foes, and, oh, my friends – / It gives a lovely light.

John Milton: Untwisting all the chains that tie / The hidden soul of harmony.

Nachman of Bratslav: Arbitration is justice blended with charity.

Jawaharlal Nehru: Life is always forcing us to compromise.

Lord Nelson: A fleet of British ships of war are the best negotiators in Europe.

Lord Nelson: While the negotiation is going on, the Dane should see our flag waving every moment he lifted his head.

Frederick Nietzsche: At times one remains faithful to a cause only because its opponents do not cease to be insipid.

North American Proverb: Necessity never made a good bargain.

Gerard J. O'Brien: The advantage of a settlement is that the defense can never appeal.

O. Henry: It's a bad bargain that can't run both ways. Or: It's a bad rule that won't work both ways.

Lord Palmerston, Henry Temple, 3rd Viscount Palmerston, and Prime Minister of England (demanding the release of two Confederate diplomats John Slidell and James Murray Mason, sailing to England on a British ship, the *Trent*, were stopped by the Union ship *San Jacinto*, commanded by Captain Charles Wilkes, who, acting without authority arrested the two and took them prisoners – hence: "The Trent Affair" – President Lincoln acceded; in his 1861 speech to Parliament he roared): You may stand for this, but damned if I will!

General George Patton (attributed to him during WWII, prior to the Normandy landing June 6, 1944): There is no end to the shit being swallowed thanks to Ike's steady drum beat of "in the interests of inter-Allied unity."

Laurence J. Peter: The man who say he is willing to meet you halfway is usually a poor judge of distance.

Harry Philo: Whatever you think the case is worth and the costs will be to litigate, cut the case value in half and then multiply the out-of-pocket costs by three.

Charles Pinckney (one of President John Adams' ambassadors to France in 1797, when asked by French agents XYZ – in "the XYZ Affair" – for a bribe): "No, no, not a sixpence!" Later this became immortalized into the popular slogan "MILLIONS FOR DEFENSE, NOT ONE CENT FOR TRIBUTE."

Lester J. Pourciau: There is no monument dedicated to the memory of a committee.

Jeannette Rankin: You can no more win a war than you can win an earthquake.

Will Rogers: Diplomacy (Editor: and compromising) is the art of saying "Nice doggie" until you can find a rock.

Will Rogers: Diplomats are just as essential to starting a war as soldiers are for finishing it... You take diplomacy out of war, and the thing would fall flat in a week.

Will Rogers: I have always noticed at any time a man can't come in and settle with you without bringing his lawyer, why, look out for him.

Eleanor Roosevelt: It isn't enough to talk about peace. One must believe in it. And it isn't enough to believe in it. One must work at it.

Franklin D. Roosevelt (Fireside Chat, Dec. 29. 1940): No man can tame a tiger into a kitten by stroking it. There can be no appeasement with ruthlessness. There can be no reasoning with an incendiary bomb.

Theodore Roosevelt: A really great people, proud and highspirited, would face all the disasters of war rather than purchase that base prosperity which is bought at the price of national honor.

Carl Sandburg: Sometime they'll give a war and nobody will come.

Scottish Proverb: Better bend than break.

William Shakespeare (*As You Like It*, Act V, iv): Your If is the only peacemaker. Much virtue in If.

William Shakespeare (*II Henry IV*, Act IV, ii): A peace is of the nature of a conquest; / For then both parties nobly are subdued, / And neither party loser.

William Shakespeare (*Henry V*, Act III, i): In peace, there's nothing so becomes a man / As modest stillness and humility.

William Shakespeare (*II Henry VI*, Act II, i): Blessed are the peace-makers on earth.

William Shakespeare (*II Henry VI*, Act II, ii): Peace, / Dear muse of arts, plenties, and joyful births.

William Shakespeare (*Henry VIII*, Act III, ii): Still in thy right hand carry gentle peace, / To silence envious tongues.

William Shakespeare (*Richard II*, Act II, ii): Basely yielded upon compromise / That which his noble ancestors achieved with blows.

Jonathan Swift: Supposing the War to have commenced upon a just Motive; the next Thing to be considered is when a Prince ought in Prudence to receive the Overtures of Peace: Which I take to be, either when the Enemy is ready to yield the Point originally contended for, or when that Point is found impossible to be ever attained.

James Thurber: You might as well fall flat on your face as try to lean over too far backward.

Harry S. Truman: I want peace and I'm willing to fight for it.

Mark Twain: The timid man yearns for full value and demands a tenth. The bold man strikes for double value and compromises on par.

Louis Untermeyer: From compromise and things half done, / Keep me with stern and stubborn pride; / And when at last the fight is won, / God keep me still unsatisfied.

Henry Van Dyke: A peace which depends upon fear is nothing but a suppressed war.

Lord St. Vincent: You are now placed in the most happy and enviable situation: no negotiations to retard your operation, and a scene of glory immortal before you.

Senator James E. Watson (1932): If you can't lick 'em, jine 'em.

Walt Whitman: Peace is always beautiful.

Oscar Wilde: When people agree with me I always feel that I must be wrong.

Woodrow Wilson: There is a price which is too great to pay for peace, and that price can be put in one word. One cannot pay the price of self-respect.

Woodrow Wilson: No man can sit down and withhold his hands from the warfare against wrong and get peace from his acquiescence.

Woodrow Wilson: settlements may be temporary, but the action of the nations in the interest of peace and justice must be permanent. We can set no permanent processes. We may not be able to set up permanent decisions.

William Wrigley Jr.: When two men in business always agree, one of them is unnecessary.

COMPUTERS (See also SCIENCE & TECHNOLOGY)

Uncle Anthony: To err is human, but to really foul things up ya need a computer!

Uncle Anthony: Y'know how they always say "one picture is worth a thousand words?" Well, that's true but it uses up three thousand times the memory (in your computer)!

Uncle Anthony: I useta hear "WHOOPS" – now I hear 'dis "w00t, w00t, **w00t!**" comin' from people in da stands. [EDITOR: 'W00t" is a hybrid word of letters and numbers used by online gamers as an exclamation of happiness].

Aunt Mary Carlo: Y'now what computers done? Dey turned every office worker into a computer Solitaire player!

Aunt Mary Carlo: I got no time for "133t speak!" [EDITOR: Meaning "elite" speak]

Douglas Adams: Macintosh - we might not get everything right, but at least we knew the century was going to end.

Scott Adams ("Dogbert"): As network administrator I can take down the network with one keystroke. It's just like being a doctor but without getting gooky stuff on my paws.

Scott Adams: If you have any trouble sounding condescending, find a Unix user to show you how it's done.

Guy Almes: There are three kinds of death in this world. There's heart death, there's brain death, and there's being off the network.

American Library Association (statement on Univac computer exhibited at New York World's Fair, 1964): The computer is only a fast idiot, it has no imagination; it cannot originate action. It is, and will remain, only a tool to man.

Jeremy S. Anderson: There are two major products that came out of Berkeley: LSD and UNIX. We do not believe this to be a coincidence.

David Ansel: Stay the patient course / Of little worth is your ire / The network is down

Isaac Asimov: If arithmetical skill is the measure of intelligence, then computers have been more intelligent than all human beings all along. If the ability to play chess is the measure, then there are computers now in existence that are more intelligent than any but a very few human beings. However, if insight, intuition, creativity, the ability to view a problem as a whole and guess the answer by the "feel" of the situation, is a measure of intelligence, computers are very unintelligent indeed. Nor can we see right now how this deficiency in computers can be easily remedied, since human beings cannot program a computer to be intuitive or creative for the very good reason that we do not know what we ourselves do when we exercise these qualities.

Norman Augustine: One of the most feared expressions in modern times is "The computer is down."

Dave Barry: Database: the information you lose when your memory crashes.

Dave Barry: User, n. The word computer professionals use when they mean "idiot."

Dave Barry: Hardware: Where the people in your company's software section will tell you the problem is. Software: where the people in your company's hardware section will tell you the problem is.

Dave Barry: SPREADSHEET: a kind of program that lets you sit at your desk and ask all kinds of neat "what if?" questions and generate thousands of numbers instead of actually working.

Jacques Barzun: The technology of so-called mass communication seemingly extended the reach of ideas, but actually dulled public attention by excess and abolished the capacity of quick, common response. In short, the gains produced by the ideal of diffusion proved, as might have been expected, diffuse.

Bible: Galatians 6:5: Every man shall bear his own burden. (EDITOR: ... and his own computer virus)

Bible: Isaiah 47:13: Let now the astologers, the stargazers, the monthly prognosticators, stand up, and save thee from these things (EDITOR: like computer problems).

Bible: Matthew 16:3: Can ye not discern the signs of the times? (EDITOR: a word to the computer-challenged like me)

Ambrose Bierce: INVENTOR, n. A person who makes an ingenious arrangement of wheels, levers and springs, and believes it civilization.

Ambrose Bierce: TELEPHONE, n. An invention of the devil which abrogates some of the advantages of making a disagreeable person keep his distance.

Ambrose Bierce: TELESCOPE, n. A device having a relation to the eye similar to the telephone to the ear, enabling distant objects to plague us with a multitude of needless details. Luckily it is unprovided with a bell summoning us to the sacrifice.

David J. Bolter: The computer is in some ways a grand machine in the Western mechanical-dynamic tradition and in other ways a tool-in-hand from the ancient craft tradition. A machine is characterized by sustained, autonomous action. A tool, unlike a machine, is not self-sufficient or autonomous in action. It requires the skill of a craftsman and, when handled with ski up, permits him to reshape the world in his way.... However, the computer is not really a tool-in-hand; it is designed to extend the human brain rather than the hand, to allow the manipulation of mathematical and logical symbols at high speed. Yet it can be used with a kind of mental dexterity and reminds us of the craftsman's hand.

Kenneth Boulding: The computer... has given us continuously compounded interest at banks, easier airplane reservations, and a large quantity of unread Ph.D. theses.

Joseph Campbell: Computers are like Old Testament gods; lots of rules and no mercy.

Sir Winston Churchill: The empires of the future are empires of the mind.

Sir Winston Churchill: The latest refinements of science are linked with the cruelties of the Stone Age.

Edsger W. Dijkstra: Computer Science is no more about computers than astronomy is about telescopes.

Edsger W. Dijkstra: The question of whether computers can think is just like the question of whether submarines can swim.

Marcus Dolengo: The best way to accelerate a Macintosh is at 9.8m/sec/sec.

William O. Douglas: Man is about to bcome an automaton; he is identifiable only in the computer. As a person of worth and creativity, as a being with an infinite potential, he retreats and battles the forces that make him inhuman. The dissent we witness is a reaffirmation of faith in man; it is protest against living under rules and prejudices and attitudes that produce the extremes of wealth and poverty and that make us dedicated to the disruption of people through arms, bombs, and gases, and that prepare us to think alike and be submissive objects for the régime of the computer.

Peter Drucker: The main impact of the computer has been the provision of unlimited jobs for clerks.

***Farmer's Almanac*, 1978:** To err is human, but to really foul things up requires a computer.

Richard P. Feynman: There is a computer disease that anybody who works with computers knows about. It's a very serious disease and it interferes completely with the work. The trouble with computers is that you 'play' with them!

Richard Feynman: The inside of a computer is as dumb as hell but it goes like mad!

Bill Gates: Information technology and business are becoming inextricably interwoven. I don't think anybody can talk meaningfully about one without the talking about the other.

Bill Gates: I feel certain that the personal computer is as revolutionary in terms of the way it will change the way we work, learn, and entertain ourselves as any of these previous advances.

J.H. Goldfuss: There is only one satisfying way to boot a computer.

Doug Gwyn: Unix was not designed to stop you from doing stupid things, because that would also stop you from doing clever things.

Sydney J. Harris: The real danger is not that computers will begin to think like men, but that men will begin to think like computers.

Garrett Hazel, "Help Desk Blues," 2002: Rebooting is a wonder drug - it fixes almost everything.

Robert A. Heinlein: Don't explain computers to laymen. Simpler to explain sex to a virgin.

John F. Kennedy: Man is still the most extraordinary computer of all.

Louis H. Lapham (1984): No businessman these days dares to embark upon the journey of incorporation without first acquiring a computer so huge and so omniscient as to strike terror into the software of its enemies.

Doug Larson: Home computers are being called upon to perform many new functions, including the consumption of homework formerly eaten by the dog.

David J. Liszewski, 1998: A file that big? / It might be very useful. / But now it is gone.

Staunton Lynd (1970): Automized and computerized industry requires more and more young men and women who have white-collar skills but behave with the docility expected of blue-collar workers.

James Magary: Computers can figure out all kinds of problems, except the things in the world that just don't add up.

Warren S. McCulloch (1956): A computer with as many vacuum tubes as a man has neurons in his head would require the Pentagon to house it, Niagara's power to run it, and Niagara's waters to cool it.

Marshall McLuhan: The computer is the most extraordinary of man's technological clothing; it's an extension of our central nervous system. Beside it, the wheel is a mere hula-hoop.

David Moschella: Industry executives and analysts often mistakenly talk about strategy as if it were some kind of chess match. But in chess, you have just two opponents, each with identical resources, and with luck playing a minimal role. The real world is much more like a poker game, with multiple players trying to make the best of whatever hand fortune has dealt them. In our industry, Bill Gates owns the table until someone proves otherwise.

Lewis Mumford: The life-efficiency and adaptability of the computer must be questioned. It's judicious use depends upon the ability of its human employers quite literally to keep their own heads, not merely to scrutinize the programming but to reserve for themselves the right of ultimate decision. No automatic system can be intelligently run by automatons – or by people who dare not assert human intuition, human autonomy, human purpose.

Lewis Mumford: If anything could testify to the magical powers of the priesthood of science and their technical acolytes, or declare onto mankind the supreme qualifications for absolute rulership held by the Divine Computer, this new invention alone should suffice. So the final purpose of life in terms of the megamachine at least becomes clear: it is to furnish and process an endless quantity of data, in order to expand the role and ensure that domination of the power system.

Murphy: If builders built buildings the way programmers wrote programs, then the first woodpecker that came along would destroy civilization. ~One of Murphy's Laws of Technology

Nicholas Negroponte: Computing is not about computers any more. It is about living.

Nicholas Negroponte: It's not computer literacy that we should be working on, but sort of human-literacy. Computers have to become human-literate.

Ken Olson (Convention of the World Future Society, 1977): There is no reason for any individual to have computer in their home.

Pablo Picasso (about computers): But they are useless. They can only give you answers.

Jeff Pesis: Hardware: the parts of a computer that can be kicked.

John Pierce: After growing wildly for years, the field of computing appears to be reaching its infancy.

Brian M. Porter (1998): To have no errors / Would be life without meaning / No struggle, no joy

Eric Porterfield: The most overlooked advantage to owning a computer is that if they foul up, there's no law against whacking them around a little.

Richard Power: In the old days, people robbed stagecoaches and knocked off armored trucks. Now they're knocking off servers.

Rob Pike: Unix never says "please."

Mitch Ratcliffe: A computer lets you make more mistakes faster than any invention in human history - with the possible exceptions of handguns and tequila.

Dennis Ritchie: Unix is simple. It just takes a genius to understand its simplicity.

Will Rogers: Nothing you can't spell will ever work.

Will Rogers: America is a nation that conceives many odd inventions for getting somewhere but it can think of nothing to do once it gets there.

Andy Rooney: Computers make it easier to do a lot of things, but most of the things they make it easier to do don't need to be done.

Peter Rothman, 1998: Windows NT crashed. / I am the Blue Screen of Death. / No one hears your screams.

Margaret Segall (1998): Yesterday it worked / Today it is not working / Windows is like that

William Shakespeare (*All'sWell That Ends Well,* Act V, iii): Plutus himself, / That knows the tinct and multiplying medicine, / Hath not in nature's mystery more science / Than I have in this ring.

William Shakespeare (*Henry V*, Act V, ii): (We) do not learn for want of time / The sciences which should become our country.

William Shakespeare (*Love's Labour's Lost,* Act I, i): Small have continual plodders ever won / Save base authority from others' books. / These earthly godfathers of heaven's lights / That give a name to every fixed star / Have no more profit of their shining nights / Than those that walk and wot not what they are. / Too much to know is to know naught but fame; / And every godfather can give a name.

William Shakespeare (*Measure for Measure,* Act I, i): I am put to know that your own science / Exceeds, in that, the lists of all advice.

William Shakespeare (*Taming of The Shrew,* Act II, i): Instruct her fully in those sciences

B.F. Skinner (1969): The real problem is not whether machines think but whether men do.

Rahul Sonnad: There is a chasm / of carbon and silicon / the software can't bridge

Gertrude Stein: Everybody gets so much information all day long that they lose their common sense.

Clifford Stoll: Treat your password like your toothbrush. Don't let anybody else use it, and get a new one every six months.

Lewis Thomas: I do not worry much about the computers that are wired to help me find a friend among fifty thousand. If errors are made, I can always take a day off with a headache. But what of the vaster machines that will be giving instructions to cities, to nations? If they are programmed to regulate human behavior according to today's view of nature, we are surely in for apocalypse.

Alan Turing: Unless in communicating with it (a computer) one says exactly what one means, trouble is bound to result.

Mark Twain: When I'm playful I use the meridians of longitude and parallels of latitude for a seine, and drag the Atlantic Ocean (Editor: or "surf the net") for whales! I scratch my head with the lightning and purr myself to sleep with the thunder!

UA (1960's computer term): Garbage in, garbage out. Or **GIGO.**

UA (1980's computer expression meaning what the operator sees on the computer screen is exactly how the material will appear when printed out): What you see is what you get. Or WYSIWYG

UA: OTHER COMPUTER TEXT LINGO:

133t = "leet" when spoken, short for "elite."
? = I have a question or don't understand
@TEOTD = At the end of the day
.02 = My (or your) two cents worth
2G2BT = Too good to be true
2MI = Too much information
411 = "Information"
4COL = For crying out loud
AYTMTB = And you're telling me this because ...?
ROTFLBO = Rolling on the floor, laughing my butt off
BF or GF = Boyfriend or girlfriend
BFF = Best friend forever
CUL8R = See you later alligator
GIAR = Give it a rest
GIGO = Garbage in, garbage out
GOI = Get over it
H2CUS = Hope to see you soon
He should GIAR and GOI = He should give it a rest and get over it
HRU? = How are you?
JMO = Just my opinion
LTNS = Long time, no see
MUSM = Miss you so much
NW! = No way!
OMG = Oh my God
PRW or POS = Parents are watching or parent over shoulder
RUOK? = Are you OK?
SIG2R = Sorry, I got to run
TTFN = Ta ta for now
TTYL = Talk to you later
UGTBK = You got to be kidding
WDYT? = What do you think?
w00t = Exclamation of happiness
WYSIWYG = What you see is what you get

UA: If it draws blood, it's hardware.

UA: The original point and click interface was a Colt or Smith and Wesson revolver.

UA: In God we trust, all others we virus scan.

UA: Jesus saves! The rest of us better make backups.

UA: RAM disk is not an installation procedure.

UA: The attention span of a computer is only as long as its power cord.

UA: Computers have lots of memory but no imagination.

UA: The Unix philosophy basically involves giving you just enough rope to hang yourself. And then a couple of feet more, just to be sure.

UA: Microsoft, where quality is job 1.1.

UA (referring to CEOs of Intel and Microsoft): Software is slowing faster than hardware is accelerating. ~Martin Reiser, quoted by Nicklaus Wirth, 1995, which spawned "Grove giveth, and Gates taketh away,"

UA: Some people can hack it, others can't.

UA: I wish life had an Undo function.

UA: In a few minutes a computer can make a mistake so great that it would have taken many men many months to equal it.

UA: Mac users swear by their computers. PC users swear at their computers.

UA: DOS computers manufactured by companies such as IBM, Compaq, Tandy, and millions of others are by far the most popular, with about 70 million machines in use worldwide. Macintosh fans, on the other hand, may note that cockroaches are far more numerous than humans, and that numbers alone do not denote a higher life form.

UA: Home is where you hang your @.

UA: A user and his leisure time are soon parted.

UA: Apathy Error: Don't bother striking any key.

UA: At least my pencil never crashes!

UA: Those parts of the system that you can hit with a hammer (not advised) are called hardware; those program instructions that you can only curse at are called software.

UA: There are 10 types of people in this world: those who understand binary and those who don't.

UA: What boots up must come down.

UA: Windows is just DOS in drag.

UA: Computers must be female. No one but the creator understands their internal logic. The native language they use to communicate with other computers is incomprehensible to everyone else. The message "Bad command or file name" is about as informative as, "If you don't know why I'm mad at you, then I'm certainly not going to tell you." Even the smallest mistakes are stored in long term memory for later retrieval. As soon as you make a commitment to one, you find yourself spending half your paycheck on accessories for it.

UA: Computers must be male. As soon as you commit to one you realize that if you had waited a little longer, you could have obtained a better model. In order to get their attention, you have to turn them on. Big power surges knock them out for the rest of the day.

UA: If computers get too powerful, we can organize them into committees. That'll do them in.

UA: The problem with troubleshooting is that trouble shoots back.

UA: Never let a computer know you're in a hurry.

UA: Back up my hard drive? How do I put it in reverse?

UA: Don't anthropomorphize computers - they hate it. ~Author Unknown

UA: I haven't lost my mind; I have a tape back-up somewhere.

UA: I just wish my mouth had a backspace key.

Werner von Braun: Man is the best computer we can put aboard a spacecraft... and the only one that can be mass produced with unskilled labor.

Suzie Wagner, 1998: Chaos reigns within. / Reflect, repent, and reboot. / Order shall return.

Joseph Weizenbaum: Humans, if they are machines at all, are vastly general-purpose machines and... they understand communications couched in natural languages (e.g., English) that lack, by very far, the precision and unambiguousness of ordinary programming languages.

Joseph Weizenbaum (1983): Right now, the children of the well-to-do are given liberal access to computers. People may very well attribute the success of these children to their computer experience. In reality, these children will have had many other important advantages right from the start. If you want to reduce inequality, the solution is to give the poor money, not computers.

Joseph Weizenbaum: There is a myth that computers are today making important decisions of the kind that were earlier made by people. Perhaps there are isolated examples of that here and there in our society. But the widely believed picture of managers typing questions of the form "What shall we do now?" into their computers and then waiting for their computers to "decide" is largely wrong. What is happening instead is that people have turned the processing of information on which decisions must be based over to enormously complex computer systems. They have, with few exceptions, reserve for themselves the right to make decisions based on the outcome of such computing processes.

Norbert Wiener: Render unto man the things which are man's and unto the computer the things which are the computer's. This would seem the intelligent policy to adopt when we employ men and computers together in common undertakings. It is a policy as far removed from that of the gadget worshiper as it is from the man who sees only blasphemy and the degradation of man in the use of any mechanical adjuvants whatever to thoughts. What we need now is an independent study of systems involving both human and mechanical elements. This system should not be prejudiced either by a mechanical or antimechanical bias.

CONFLICT(S) (See ISSUES/PROBLEMS)

CONFORM/CONFORMITY (See NORM)

CONSCIENCE (See ETHICS; HYPOCRICY)

CONSEQUENCES (See CAUSATION)

CONSISTENCY/MISTAKES (See also NEGLIGENCE)

Uncle Anthony: Show me a good loser, and I'll show you a loser.

Uncle Anthony (and my father Rocco Vesper): You can't win 'em all, but with very little effort you can lose 'em all.

Uncle Anthony: They ain't resting, they're RUSTING on their past glory (laurels).

Uncle Anthony: For those guys, every morning is "the dawn of a new error."

Aunt Mary Carlo: I tink when he left da job his fellow woikers got togehter to give em'a little momentum.

Aunt Mary Carlo: When dere's nuttin' more to be said, he's still sayin it!?

St. Ambrose: Even brute beasts and wandering birds do not fall into the same traps or net twice.

St. Augustine: Habit, if not resisted, soon becomes necessity.

Bernard Berenson: Consistency requires you to be as ignorant today as you were a year ago.

Yogi Berra: We made too many wrong mistakes.

Yogi Berra: Little things are big.

Bible: Acts 7:51: As your fathers did, so do ye.

Bible: Hebrews 13:9: Be not carried about with divers and strange doctrines.

Bible: Jeremiah 6:16: Ask for the old paths, where is the good way, and walk therein, and ye shall find rest for your souls.

Bible: 2 Kings 17:41: As did their fathers, so do they unto this day.

Bible: Proverbs 22:28: Remove not the ancient landmark, which the fathers have set.

Bible: Romans 12:2: Be not conformed to this world.

Bible: Titus 3:10: A man that is a heretic after the first and second admonition reject.

Ambrose Bierce: HABIT, n. A shackle for the free.

Ambrose Bierce: PREDICAMENT, n. The wage of consistency.

Edmund Burke: No one could make a greater mistake than he who did nothing because he could do only a little.

Sir Winston Churchill: It is a mistake to try to look too far ahead. The chain of destiny can only be grasped one link at a time.

Sir Winston Churchill: If you simply take up the attitude of defending a mistake, there will no hope of improvement.

Dr. Frank Crane: Habits are safer than rules; you don't have to watch them. And you don't have to keep them either. They keep you.

Bill Cosby: I don't know the key to success, but the key to failure is trying to please everybody.

Cyrus H. Curtis: There are two kinds of men who never amount to much: those who cannot do what they are told and those of who can do nothing else.

Leonardo da Vinci: He who fixes his course to a star changes not. (EDITOR: therefore, be flexible).

John Dewey: A laxity due to decadence of old habits cannot be corrected by exhortations to restore old habits in their former rigidity. Even though it were abstractly desirable it is impossible. And it is not desirable because the inflexibility of old habits is precisely the chief cause of their decay and disintegration.

Charles Dickens: It's over, and can't be helped, and that's one consolation, as they always say in Turkey, when they cut the wrong man's head off.

Fyodor Dostoevsky: It seems, in fact, as though the second half of a man's life is made up of nothing but the habits he accumulated during the first half.

Leo Durocher: Show me a good loser and I'll show you an idiot.

Tyron Edage: He that never changes his opinions, never corrects his mistakes, and will never be wiser on the morrow than he is today.

Ralph Waldo Emerson: a foolish consistency is the hobgoblin of little minds, adored by little statesmen and philosophers and divines.

Ralph Waldo Emerson: I wish to say what I think and feel today, with the proviso that tomorrow perhaps I shall contradict it all.

Ralph Waldo Emerson: We do what we must, and call it by the best names.

Ralph Waldo Emerson: Speak what you think today in words as hard as cannon balls, and tomorrow speak what tomorrow thinks in hard words again, though it contradict everything you said today.

Michael Ferrara: History repeats itself because human nature changes with geological leisureliness or glacier speed.

Henry Ford: Failure is the only opportunity to begin again more intelligently.

Errol Flynn: Any man who has $10,000 left when he dies is a failure.

Ellen Glasgow: The only difference between a rut and a grave is their dimensions.

Georges Gurdjieff: Every grown-up man consists wholly of habits, although he is often unaware of it and even denies having any habits at all.

Eric Hoffer: Absolute faith corrupts as absolutely as absolute power.

Eric Hoffer: When people are free to do as they please, they usually imitate each other.

Oliver Wendell Holmes, Sr.: People who honestly mean to be true really contradict themselves much more rarely than those who try to be "consistent."

Elbert Hubbard: The greatest mistake you can make in life is to be continually fearing you will make one.

Aldous Huxley: The only completely consistent people are dead.

Aldous Huxley: Too much consistency is as bad for the mind as for the body. Consistency is contrary to nature, contrary to life. The only completely consistent people are dead.

Aldous Huxley: Consistency is a verbal criterion, which cannot be applied to the phenomena of life. Taken together, the various activities of a single individual may "make no sense," and yet be perfectly compatible with biological survival, social success and personal happiness.

Aldous Huxley: The consistent thinker, the consistently moral man, is either a walking mummy or else, if he has not succeeded in stifling all his vitality, a fanatical monomaniac.

Italian Proverb: Any man may make a mistake; none but a fool will persist in it.

Holbrook Jackson: Beware of your habits. The better they are the more surely will they be your undoing.

J. Jenkins: To err is human, but when the eraser wears out ahead of the pencil, you're overdoing it.

Jewish Saying: When a habit begins to cost money, it's called a hobby.

Jewish Saying: If you always drink vinegar, you don't know there's anything sweeter.

Jewish Saying: The most common habit is gossip—and it causes the most trouble.

Lynden B. Johnson: If two men agree on everything, you may be sure that one of them is doing the thinking.

Samuel Johnson: The chains of habit are too weak to be felt until they are too strong to be broken.

Elizabeth "Libby" Kinghorne: Some people always have their heads up their butts, but he is so single minded and biased that his head is always up his butt and always facing the same direction!

Latin Proverb: A nail is driven out by another nail; habit is overcome by habit.

Abraham Lincoln 1864): It is not best to swap horses while crossing the river.

James Russel Lowell: The foolish and the dead alone never change their opinions.

Henri de Lubac: Habit and routine have an unbelievable power to waste and destroy.

E.V. Lucas: One must expect inconsistency. Every moment conditions are different, and therefore we are; every moment we are older, and there is less of life to live, and the thought can lead to odd impulses.

Maimonides: Men cling to the opinions of habit.

Nelson Mandela: There is nothing like returning to a place that remains unchanged to find the ways in which you yourself have altered.

Horace Mann: Habit is a cable; we weave a thread of it every day, and at last we cannot break it.

Margaret Mead: Never doubt that a small group of thoughtful, committed citizens can change the world. Indeed, it is the only thing that ever has.

Montaigne: I will believe in anything rather than in any man's consistency.

Jim Morrison: Some of the worst mistakes of my life have been haircuts.

Judah Aryeh Moscato: Those who live near a waterfall are not disturbed by its roar.

Michael A. Musmanno (Justice of Pennsylvania Supreme Court, 1959): Habit is stronger than memory and, unless memory is reinforced by concentration and resolution, habit will usually carry the day. Repetitive routine will smother any momentary spark of fleeting recollection, unless it is kept burning with mental resolution unaffected by other distractions.

Abraham Myerson: Great men have been characterized by the greatness of their mistakes as well as by the greatness of their achievements.

Frederick Nietzsche: At times one remains faithful to a cause only because its opponents do not cease to be insipid.

Robert Orben: There are days when it takes all you've got just to keep up with the losers.

E.J. Phelps: The man who makes no mistakes does not usually make anything.

Marcel Proust: The one thing more difficult than following a regimen is not imposing it on others.

The Riziner Rabbi: It is harder to break evil habits than to split rocks.

Francois de La Rochefoucauld: Why is it that our memory is good enough to retain the least triviality that happens to us, and yet not good enough to recollect how often we have told it to the same person?

Will Rogers: People who fly into a rage always make a bad landing.

Will Rogers: If Stupidity got us into this mess, then why can't it get us out?

Will Rogers: An ignorant person is one who doesn't know what you have just found out.

George Santayana: Habit is stronger than reason.

George Santayana: These who cannot remember the past are condemned to repeat it.

George Santayana: Consistency is a jewel; and, as in the case of other jewels, we may marvel at the price that some people will pay for it.

Shakespeare (*Antony and Cleopatra*, Act I, ii): What our contempt doth often hurl from us, / We wish it ours again.

William Shakespeare (*Antony and Cleopatra*, Act V, ii): Now from head to foot / I am marble-constant: now the fleeting moon / No planet is of mine.

William Shakespeare (*Coriolanus*, Act II, iii): Custom calls me to 't: - / What custom wills, in all things should we do 't? / The dust on antique time would lie unswept, / And mountainous error be too highly heap'd / For truth to overpeer.

William Shakespeare (*Hamlet*, Act I, iv): And to my mind, though I am a native here, / And to the manner born, it is custom / More honor'd in the breach than the observance.

William Shakespeare (*Hamlet*, Act III, iv): That monster, custom,... is angel yet in this, / That to the use of actions fair and good / He likewise gives a frock, or livery, / That aptly is put on.

William Shakespeare (*Hamlet*, Act III, iv): Use can almost change the stamp of nature, / And master the devil, or throw him out / With wonderous potency..

William Shakespeare (*Hamlet*, Act V, ii): Purposes mistook / Fall'n on the inventor's heads.

William Shakespeare (*Henry VIII*, Act I, iii): New customs, / Though they be never so ridiculous, / Nay, let 'em be unmanly, yet are followed.

William Shakespeare (*Julius Caesar*, Act III, i): I am constant as the northern star, / Of whose true-fix'd and resting quality / There is no fellow in the firmament.

William Shakespeare (*King Lear*, Act I, iv): How far your eyes may pierce, I cannot tell; / Striving to better, oft we mar what's well.

William Shakespeare (*Measure for Measure*, Act V, i): It may be right; but you are in the wrong / To speak before your time.

William Shakespeare (*Othello*, Act I, iii): The tyrant custom, most grave senators, / Hath made the flinty and steel couch of war / My thrise driven bed of down.

William Shakespeare (*Romeo and Juliet*, Act II, ii): O swear not by the moon, the inconstant moon, / That monthly changes in her circled orb, / Lest that thy love prove likewise variable.

William Shakespeare (*The Two Gentlemen of Verona*, Act IV, ii): I would always have one play but one thing.

William Shakespeare (*The Two Gentlemen of Verona*, Act V, iv): O heaven, were man / But constant he were perfect!

William Shakespeare (*The Two gentlemen of Verona*, Act V, iv): How use doth breed a habit in a man! / This shadowy desert, unfrequented woods, / I better brook than flourishing peopled towns.

William Shakespeare (*Troilus and Cressida*, Act III, iii): Omission to do what is necessary / Seals a commission to a blank of danger.

William Shakespeare (*Troilus and Cressida*, Act V, ii): The error of our eye directs our mind. / What error leads must err.

Logan Pearsall Smith: Uncultivated minds are not full of wild flowers; [EDITOR: And, some tort reformers are] like uncultivated fields villinous weeds grow in them and they are full of toads.

John Lancaster Spalding: What we have grown accustomed to seems good enough, and they who fall into ways and ruts find it natural to walk therein to the end.

Robert Louis Stevenson: To hold the same views at forty as we held at twenty is to have been stupefied for a score of years and to take rank, not as a prophet, but as an unteachable brat, well birched and none the wiser.

Talmud, *Shabbat*: Do not use the conduct of a fool as a precedent.

Talmud: Sins repeated seem permitted.

Henry David Thoreau: All change is a miracle to contemplate; but it is a miracle which is taking place every instant.

Leo Tolstoy: Everyone thinks of changing the world, but no one thinks of changing himself.

Mark Twain: There are those who would misteach us that to stick in a rut is consistency – and a virtue, and that to climb out of the rut is inconsistency – and a vice.

Mark Twain: Habit is a habit and not to be thrown out of the window by any man but coaxed downstairs a step at a time.

Mark Twain: It used to be a good hotel, but that proves nothing—I used to be a good boy, for that matter.

Mark Twain: Loyalty to petrified opinions never yet broke a chain or freed a human soul in *this* world - and never *will*.

Mark Twain: I have no respect for any man who can spell a word only one way.

Mark Twain: Nothing so needs reforming as other people's habits.

Mark Twain: Have a place for everything and keep the thing somewhere else. This is not advice, it is merely custom.

Mark Twain: The altar cloth of one nation is the doormat of the next.

UA: If you never change your opinions, and never correct your mistakes, you will never be any wiser tomorrow that you are today.

Daniel Webster: An individual is more apt to change, perhaps, than all the world around him.

Edward Wescott: The only man who can change his mind is a man that's got one.

Walt Whitman: Do I contradict myself? / Very well then I contradict myself, / (I am large, I contain multitudes).

Oscar Wilde: Anybody can sympathize with the sufferings of a friend, but it requires a very fine nature to sympathize with a friend's success.

Oscar Wilde: Consistency is the last refuge of the unimaginative.

William Wrigley Jr.: When two men in business always agree, one of them is unnecessary.

CONTENTION (See ALLEGATION)

CONTINGENT FEE (See FEES)

CORPORATE THINKING (See also THOUGHT/THINKING)

Uncle Anthony: If you tell everybody about your business, pretty soon they'll be doing it instead of you.

Uncle Anthony: You don't know anything about a guy's business until you have to meet that guy's payroll.

Uncle Anthony: Businessmen invest money for one reason – to make more money – they call it profit. Governments and charities invest for political or charitable reasons. Private corporations do it for lots of profit dollars. So, you gotta expect a certain amount of greed since profit is the prime motive.

Aunt Mary Carlo: He made money "the old fashioned way" – (unlike the Smith Barney ad) he borrowed it.

Scott Adams: There's a reason that executives lie – the alternative is worse!

Fred Allen: Advertising is 85% confusion and 15% commission.

St. Augustine: The playthings of our elders are called business.

Russell Baker: Usually, terrible things that are done with the excuse that progress requires them are not really progress at all, but just terrible things

Richard Barnet and Ronald Muller: The men who run the global corporations are the first in history with the organization, technology, money, and ideology to make a credible try at managing the world as an integrated unit.

P.T. Barnum (also attributed to Edward Francis Albee; most associated with W.C. Fields who ad-libbed it in 1923 musical and 1936 film *Poppy*; repeated in 1941 film entitled): Never Give A Sucker an Even Break.

Bernhard Baruch: I have never believed in abandoning our economy to the ruthless workings of the marketplace regardless of the human suffering that might be ceased.

Milton Berle: A committee is a group that keeps the minutes and loses hours.

Bible: Deuteronomy 25:13: Thou shalt not have in thy bag divers weights, a great and a small.

Bible: Hosea 12:7: He is a merchant, the balances of deceit are in his hand: he loveth to oppress.

Bible: John 2:16: Make not my Father's house an house of merchandise.

Bible: Matthew 16:26: What is a man profited, if he shall gain the whole world, and lose his own soul?

Bible: Matthew 19:24: It is easier for a camel to go through the eye of a needle, than for a rich man to enter into the kingdom of God.

Bible: Matthew 25:16: He that had recieved the five talents went and traded with the same, and made them other five talents.

Bible: Proverbs 11:1: A false balance is abomination to the Lord: but a just weight is His delight.

Bible: Proverbs 11:26: He that withholdeth corn, the people shall curse him: but blessing shall be upon the head of him that selleth it.

Bible: Proverbs 20:10; 20:23: Divers weights, and divers measures, both of them are alike abomination to the Lord.

Bible: Proverbs 22:29: Seest thou a man diligent in his business? He shall stand before kings.

Bible: Psalms 39:6: He heapeth up riches, and knoweth not who shall gather them.

Bible: 1 Timothy 6:10: The love of money is the root of all evil.

Bible: Titus 1:11: Teaching things which they ought not, for filthy lucre's sake.

Ambrose Bierce: AUCTIONEER, n. The man who proclaims with a hammer that he has picked a pocket with his tongue.

Ambrose Bierce: COMMERCE, n. A kind of transaction in which A plunders from B the goods of C, and for compensation B picks the pocket of D of money belonging to E.

Ambrose Bierce: CORPORATION, n. An ingenious device for obtaining individual profit without individual responsibility.

Ambrose Bierce: MERCHANT, n. One engaged in a commercial pursuit. A commercial pursuit is one in which the thing pursued is a dollar.

Ambrose Bierce: PIRACY, n. Commerce without its folly-swaddles, just as God made it.

Ambrose Bierce: PLUNDER, v. To take the property of another without observing the decent and customary reticences of theft. To effect a change of ownership with the candid concomitance of a brass band. To wrest the wealth of A from B and leave C lamenting a vanished opportunity.

Ambrose Bierce: TRUST, n. In American politics, a large corporation composed in greater part of thrifty working men, widows of small means, orphans in the care of guardians and the courts, with many similar malefactors and public enemies.

Ambrose Bierce: The gambling known as business looks with austere disfavor upon the business known as gambling.

Ambrose Bierce: A man is known by the company he organizes.

Louis Brandeis: Strong responsible unions are essential to industrial fair play. Without them the labor bargain is wholly one-sided.

Louis Brandeis: When ... you increase your business to a very great extent ... the man at the head has a diminishing knowledge of the facts, and ... a diminishing opportunity of exercising a careful judgment upon them.

Louis D. Brandeis: The real fight today is against inhuman, relentless exercise of capitalistic power.... The present struggle in which we are engaged is for social and industrial justice.

Norman O. Brown: The dynamics of capitalism is postponement of enjoyment to the constantly postponed future.

James Bryce: No invention of modern times, not even that of negotiable paper, has so changed the face of commerce and delighted lawyers with a variety of new and intricate problems as the creation of incorporated joint stock companies.

Harold Burns (New York City Building Commissioner, on the confusion of housing and building law, 1963): One might risk establishing the following mathematical formula for bribery, namely OG = PLR x AEB: The opportunity for graft equals the plethora of legal requirements multiplied by the number of architects, engineers and builders.

Nolan Bushnell (Atari founder): Business is a good game – lots of competition and a minimum of rules. You keep score with money.

Thomas Carlyle: Laissez-faire, supply-and-demand,—one begins to be weary of all that. Leave it all to egoism, to ravenous greed of money, of pleasure, of applause;—it is the gospel of despair.

Andrew Carnegie: Mr. Morgan buys his partner; I grow my own.

Andrew Carnegie: The amassing of wealth is one of the worst species of idolatry, no idol more debasing.

Nancy Cattie: Procrastination is actually good time management for some people – because, if some people didn't procrastinate they would never prioritize their work.

G.K. Chesterton: Capitalism is it itself a crime.

Shirley Chisholm: When morality comes up against profit, it is seldom that profit loses.

Sir Winston Churchill: The substance of the eminent Socialist gentleman's speech is that making a profit is a sin. It is my belief that the real sin is taking a loss.

Sir Winston Churchill (November 1914 speech): "The maxim of the British people is 'Business as usual.'"

Sir Winston Churchill: Some people regard private enterprise as a predatory tiger to be shot. Others look on it as a cow they can milk. Not enough people see it as a healthy horse, pulling a sturdy wagon.

Sir Winston Churchill: The inherent vice of capitalism is the unequal sharing of blessings; the inherent vice of socialism is the equal sharing of miseries.

John Bates Clark: Strife is increasing in our times because true competition is diminishing.

Edward Coke: Corporations can not commit treason, nor be outlawed, or excommunicated, for they have no souls.

Alistair Cooke: Andrew Carnegie exemplifies to me a truth about American money men that many earnest people fail to grasp—which is that the chase and the kill are as much fun as the prize, which you then proceed to give away.

Calvin Coolidge: The business of America is business.

Calvin Coolidge: Civilization and profits go hand-in-hand.

James Fenimore Cooper: Commerce is entitled to a complete and efficient protection in all its legal rights, but the moment it presumes to control a country, or to substitute its fluctuating expedients for the high principles of natural justice that ought to lie at the root of every political system, it should be frowned on and rebuked.

Norman Cousins: Government in the US today is a senior partner in every business in the country.

Clarence Darrow: The employer puts his money into... business and the workman his life. The one has as much right as the other to regulate that business.

Charles Dickens: "A bargain," said the son. "Here's the rule for bargains—"Do other men for they would do you." That's the true business precept. All others are counterfeits."

Michael Douglas (in movie Wall Street): Greed is good! Greed is right! Greed works! Greed will save the USA!

Norman Douglas: You can tell the ideals of a nation by its advertisements.

Peter Drucker: Ethics stays in the preface of the average business science book.

Peter Drucker: The modern Corporation is a political institution; its purpose is the creation of legitimate power in the industrial sphere.

David Dunham: Efficiency is intelligent laziness.

Finley Peter Dunne: I niver knew a politician to go wrong ontil he's been contaminated by contact with a businessman.

Dwight D. Eisenhower: Your business is to put me out of business.

Alice Embree: Humans must breathe, but corporations must make money.

Ralph Waldo Emerson: Commerce is of trivial import; love, faith, truth of character, the aspiration of man, these are sacred.

Ralph Waldo Emerson: We rail at trade, but the historian of the world will see that it was the principle of liberty; that it settled America, and destroyed feudalism, and made peace and keeps peace; that it will abolish slavery.

Ralph Waldo Emerson: The greatest meliorator of the world is selfish, huckstering trade.

Ralph Waldo Emerson: The Americans have little faith. They rely on the power of the dollar.

Ralph Waldo Emerson: The craft of the merchant is bringing a thing from where it abounds to where it is costly.

Frederich Engels: Competition is the most extreme expression of that war of all against all which dominates modern middle-class society.

Michael Ferrara: A committee is a cul-de-sac down which ideas are lured and then quickly strangled.

F. Scott Fitzgerald: No grand idea was ever born in a conference, but a lot of foolish ideas have died there.

F. Scott Fitzgerald: Advertising is a racket... Its constructive contribution to you may be exactly minus zero.

Benjamin Franklin: Drive thy business; let it not drive thee.

Benjamin Franklin: Let all your things have their places; let each part of your business have its time.

John Kenneth Galbraith: Meetings are indispensable when you don't want to do anything.

John Kenneth Galbraith: Few people at the beginning of the 19th-century needed an adman to tell them what they wanted.

John Kenneth Galbraith: Men have been swindled by the other men on many occasions. The autumn of 1929 was, perhaps, the first occasion when men succeeded on a large scale in swindling themselves.

J. Paul Getty: Some people find oil. Others don't.

General Motors ad: Putting you first made us #1.

Johann Wolfgang von Goethe: Divide and rule, a sound motto. Unite and lead, a better one.

Justice Arthur J. Goldberg (Illinois lawyer, Assoc Justice US Supreme Court, US Ambassador to United Nations): If Columbus had an advisory committee he would probably still be at the dock.

Samuel Goldwyn: I don't want any yes man around me. I want everybody to tell me the truth even if it costs them their jobs.

Tim Gould: I've been promoted to middle management. I never thought I'd sink so low.

Richard Harkness: What is a committee? A group of the unwilling, picked from the unfit, to do the unnecessary.

Benjamin Harrison: Earnest attention should be given to those combinations of capital commodity commonly called Trusts.

Michael Harrington: One of the things capitalism brought into the world was democracy, though I do not think the two are inseparable.

Robert L. Heilbroner: The cure for capitalism's failing would require that a government would have to rise above the interests of one class alone.

Verne E. Henderson: The survival of business is not only a matter of profits but of prophets, of anticipating ethical consequences.

Eric Hoffer: Absolute faith corrupts as absolutely as absolute power.

Oliver Wendell Holmes: "... the notion that a business is clothed with a public interest and has been devoted to the public use is little more than a fiction intended to beautify what is disagreeable to the sufferers."

Herbert Hoover: You know, the only trouble with capitalism is capitalists; they're too damn greedy.

Kin Hubbard: If government was as afraid of disturbing the consumer as it is of disturbing business, this would be some democracy.

Kin Hubbard: If capital an' the labor ever do git t'gether it's good night fer the rest of us.

James Hulbert: Any company is judged by the president it keeps.

David Hume: Avarice, the spur of industry.

Aldous Huxley: What is capital? It is what is left over when the primary needs of a society have been satisfied.

Lee Iacocca: In the end, all business operations can be reduced to three words: people, product, and profits. People come first.

Italian Proverb: The buyer needs a hundred eyes, the seller not one.

Thomas Jefferson: Money, and not morality, is the principle of commercial nations.

Thomas Jefferson: Ministers and merchants love nobody.

Thomas Jefferson: The selfish spirit of commerce, which knows no country, and feels no passion or principle but that of gain.

Thomas Jefferson: Banking establishments are more dangerous than standing armies.

Lynden B. Johnson: If two men agree on everything, you may be sure that one of them is doing the thinking.

Nicholas Johnson: If all I'm offered is a choice between monopolistic privilege with regulation and monopolistic privilege without regulation, I'm afraid I have to opt for the former.

Nicholas Johnson: It used to be that people needed products to survive. Now products need people to survive.

Samuel Johnson: Promise, large promise, is the soul of an advertisement.

Helen Keller: The few who profit by the labor of the masses want to organize the workers into an army which will protect the interests of the capitalists.

Edward M. Kennedy (1978): The legal system is in part responsible for the very size and growth (of big business and big government). And too often when the individual finds himself in conflict with these forces, the legal system sides with the giant institution, not the small businessman or private citizen.

John F. Kennedy: Private enterprise... makes OK private action which would be considered dishonest in public action.

James J. Kilpatrick: If business leaders had channeled one tenth of the energy they devoted to fighting this bill (consumer protection) into improving their products and services they would not to find themselves in this fix.

Steve Kravitz: Ford used to have a better idea; now they don't even have a clue.

Nikita Khrushchev: When you are skinning your customers you should leave some skin on to grow again so that you can skin them again.

Nikita Khrushchev: "Freedom" in capitalist countries exists only for those who possess money and who consequently hold power.

Ray Kroc: It is ridiculous to call this an industry. This is not. This is a rat eat rat, dog eat dog. I'll kill them before they kill me. You're talking about the American way of survival of the fittest.

Stephen Leacock: Advertising may be described as the science of arresting the human intelligence long enough to get money from it.

Sinclair Lewis: Advertising is a valuable economic factor because it is the cheapest way of selling goods, particularly if the goods are worthless.

Abraham Lincoln: These capitalists generally act harmoniously and in concert, to fleece the people.

Art Linkletter: Committees are to get everybody together and homogenize their thinking.

Walter Lippman: The simple opposition between the people and big business has disappeared because the people themselves have become so deeply involved in big business.

Walter Lippmann: Where all men think alike, no one thinks very much.

Sir Richard Livingstone: The aim of commerce is not to sell what is best for people or even what they really need, but simply to sell: its final standard is successful sale.

Gerald Lee: Business today consists in persuading crowds.

Sinclair Lewis: People will buy anything that is one to a customer.

Henry Demarest Lloyd: Corporations have no souls, but they can love each other.

Henry Demarest Lloyd: Monopoly is business at the end of its journey.

Henry Cabot Lodge: The businessman dealing with a large political question is really a painful sight. It does seem to me that businessmen, with few exceptions, are worse when they come to deal with politics then men of any other class.

Karl Marx: In the pre-capitalist stages of society, commerce rules industry. The reverse is true of modern society.

Karl Marx: Capitalism is not merely the production of commodities; it is essentially the production of surplus value.

Karl Marx: Accumulation of wealth at one pole is... at the same time accumulation of misery, agony of toil, slavery, ignorance, brutality, mental degradation at the opposite pole.

W. Somerset Maugham: You can't learn too soon that the most useful thing about a principle is that it can always be sacrificed to expediency.

H.L. Mencken: When I hear artists and authors making fun of business men I think of a regiment in which the band makes fun of the cooks.

H.L. Mencken: Perhaps the most revolting character that the United States ever produced was the Christian businessman.

H.L. Mencken: He (the businessman) is the only one who always seeks to make it appear, when he attains the object of his labors, i.e., the making of a great deal of money, that it was not the object of his labors.

J. Irwin Miller: A great deal of the so-called government encroachment on the area of business, labor and the professions has been asked for by the people misusing their freedom.

C. Wright Mills: Nobody talks more of free enterprise and competition and of the best man winning than the man who inherited his father's store or farm.

de Montaigne: No man profiteth but by the loss of others.

Daniel Patrick Moynihan: Years ago William Jennings Bryan once described big business as "nothing but a collection of organized appetites."

Ralph Nader: I am responsible for my actions, but who is responsible for those of General Motors?

Jawarhalal Nehru: The forces of a capitalist society, if left unchecked, tend to make the rich richer and the poor poorer.

Frank Norris (title of his 1901 novel concerning the railroad monopoly in the West): The Octopus.

Aristotle Onassis: The secret of business is to know something that nobody else knows.

Lester J. Pourciau: There is no monument dedicated to the memory of a committee.

François Quesnay: Laissez-faire, laissez passer I think (No interference, and complete freedom of movement).

Ayn Rand: Capitalism and altruism are incompatible; they are philosophical opposites; they cannot co-exist in the same man or in the same society.

Ronald Reagan: We cannot play innocents abroad in a world that is not innocent.

Ronald Reagan: The system has never failed us once. But we have failed the system every time we lose faith in the magic of the market place.

Jack E. Reichert (President & CEO of Brunswick Corp.): I would rather have a first-class manager running a second-rate business than a second-class manager running a first-rate business.

Charles Revson: I don't meet competition, I crush it.

Joseph Rickaby: All real government (EDITOR: and a corporate board and/or committee) is what may be called a Pentegerontamphitrapezy, i.e. five (more or less) old (more or less) gentlemen (more or less) sitting around a table.

Tom Robbins: Disbelief in magic can force a poor soul into believing in government and business.

John D. Rockefeller: Do you know the only thing that gives me pleasure? It's to see my dividends coming in.

John D. Rockefeller: The growth of a large business is merely a survival of the fittest.

Will Rogers: A Holding Company is a thing where you hand an accomplice the goods while the policeman searches you.

Will Rogers: If you can build a business up big enough, it's respectable.

Will Rogers: One third of the people in United States promote, while the other two thirds provide.

Will Rogers: Let Wall Street have a nightmare and the whole country has to help get them back in bed again.

Will Rogers: When should a college athlete turn pro? Not until he has earned all he can in college as an amateur.

Andy Rooney: I think Bill Gates has every right to keep every penny he made and continue to make more. If it ticks you off, go and invent the next operating system that's better, and put your name on the building.

Franklin D. Roosevelt: We have always known that heedless self interest was bad morals; we know now that it is bad economics.

Franklin D. Roosevelt: No business which depends for existence on paying less than living wages to its workers has any right to continue in this country. By business I mean the whole of commerce as well as the whole of industry; by workers I mean all workers—the white-collar class as well as the man in overalls; and by living wages I mean more than a bare subsistence level—I mean the wages of decent living.

Theodore Roosevelt: Where a trust becomes a monopoly, the state has an immediate right to intervene.

Theodore Roosevelt: The biggest corpoation, like the humblest private citizen, must be held to strict compliance with the will of the people.

Theodore Roosevelt: We demand that big business give people a square deal; in return we must insist that when anyone engaged in big business honestly endeavors to do right, he shall himself be given a square deal.

Theodore Roosevelt: The best executive is one who has sense enough to pick good men to do what he wants done, and self-restraint enough to keep from meddling with them while they do it.

J.K. Rowling: Indifference and neglect often do much more damage then outright dislike.

Bertrand Russell: A stupid man's report of what a clever man says can never be accurate, because he unconsciously translates what he hears into something he can understand.

William Shakespeare (*Hamlet*, Act I, v): Every man has business and desire, / Such as it is.

William Shakespeare (*Hamlet*, Act V, i): Has this fellow no feeling of his business?

William Shakespeare (*II Henry VI*, Act I, i): This weighty business will not brook delay.

William Shakespeare (*King Lear*, Act IV, i): Bad is the trade that must play fool to sorrow.

William Shakespeare (*King Lear*, Act IV, vi): Half way down / Hangs one that gathers samphire, dreadful trade!

William Shakespeare (*Love's Labour's Lost*, Act IV, iii): To things of sale a seller's praise belongs.

William Shakespeare (*Merchant of Venice*, Act IV, i): Losses, / That have of late so huddled on his back, / Enough to press a royal merchant down, / And pluck commiseration of his state / From brassy bosoms, and rough hearts of flint.

William Shakespeare (*Taming of the Shrew*, Act I, i): A merchant of great traffic through the world.

William Shakespeare (*Taming of the Shrew*, Act IV, ii): I have bills for money by exchange / From Florence, and must here deliver them

William Shakespeare (*Timon of Athens*, Act I, i): Traffic's thy god, and thy god confound thee!

George Bernard Shaw: Capitalism has destroyed our belief in any of effective power but that of self interest backed by force.

Smith Barney ad: We make money the old fashioned way—we earn it.

Adam Smith: Monopoly... is a great enemy to good management which can never be universally established but in consequence of that free and universal competition which forces everybody to have recourse to it for the sake of self-defense.

Roy L. Smith (Uncle of Jim Kitchens, 1909-1974): Nervous as a whore in church.

E. Ralph Stewart: Of course there's a different law for the rich and the poor; otherwise who would go into business?

Talmud, Pesahim, 113a: Better a small profit at home than a large one from abroad.

Richard H. Tawney: The interests of men who own property used in industry is that their capital should be dear and human beings cheap.

Richard H. Tawney: No one can argue that a monopolist is impelled by "an invisible hand" to serve the public interest.

Norman Thomas: After I asked him what he meant (by "Free Enterprise"), he replied that freedom consisted of the unimpeded right to get rich, to use his ability, no matter what the cost to others, to win advancement.

Henry David Thoreau: Men have become the tools of their tools.

Edward Thurlow (English judge 1775): Did you expect a corporation to have a conscience, when it has no soul to be damned and no body to be kicked?

Lily Tomlin: The trouble with the rat race is that even if you win you're still a rat.

Benjamin R. Tucker: Is not competition, but monopoly, that deprives labor of its product.

Mark Twain: October. This is one of the peculiarly dangerous months to speculate in stocks in. The others are July, January, September, April, November, May, March, June, December, August, and February.

Mark Twain: All saints can do miracles, but few of them can keep a hotel.

Mark Twain: The political and commercial morals of the United States are not merely food for laughter, they are an entire banquet.

U.A: Both business and love require the temperament of a vampire combined with the discretion of an anemone.

UA: Business is not a brotherhood.

UA: Better a steady dime than a rare dollar.

UA: He doesn't want the truth. He wants something he can tell Congress.

UA (early expression by street-tradesmen): Never mind the quality, feel the width!

UA: The only business that makes money without advertising is the United States mint.

UA: It is not what you know that counts, is what you think of in time for an excuse.

UA (popular American corporate/advertizing catchphrases): Let's run it up the flagpole (and see who salutes it)! Or ... Let's put it on the porch and see if the cat will eat it ... or ... Let's put it on the train and see if it gets off at Westchester (or wherever) ... or... Let's leave it in the water overnight and see if it springs any leaks ... or ... Let's pull something out of the hat here and see if it hops for us.

Cornelius Vanderbilt (1854): Gentlemen: you have undertaken to ruin in me. I will not sue you, for law takes too long. I will ruin you.

William H. Vanderbilt: The public be damned.

William H. Vanderbilt: The railroads are not run for the benefit of the dear public. That cry is all nonsense. They are built for men who invest their money and expect to get a fair percentage on the same.

Gore Vidal: The genius of our ruling class is that it has kept a majority of the people from ever questioning the inequity of a system where most people drudge along, paying heavy taxes for which they get nothing in return.

Gore Vidal: Free enterprise ended in United States a good many years ago. Big oil, big steel, big agriculture avoid the open marketplace.

Tom Waitts: The big print giveth and the small print taketh away.

The Wall Street Journal: Opportunity can't knock unless it's on your doorstep.

Howell Walsh (Irish lawyer, circa 1825): A corporation cannot blush. It was a body it was true; had certainly a head – a new one every year – an annual acquisition of intelligence in every new lord mayor. Arms he supposed it had, and long ones too, for it could reach at any thing. Legs, of course, when it made such long strides. A throat to swallow the rights of a community, and a stomach to digest them! But whoever yet discovered, in the anatomy of any corporation, either bowels, or a heart?

Evelyn Waugh: Punctuality is the virtue of the bored.

H. G. Wells: Advertising is legalized lying.

E. B. White: The trouble with a profit system has always been that it was highly unprofitable to most people.

Oscar Wilde: Industry is the root of all ugliness.

Wendell Wilkie: The glory of United States is business.

George Will: The short, unhappy life of that automobile (named for Henry Ford's late son Edsel, and launched in September 1957) is rich in lessons, and not only for America's beleaguered automobile industry. The principal lesson is: Most Americans are not as silly as a few Americans suppose.... No industry boomed more in the 1950's than the manufacturing of social criticism excoriating Americans for their bovine "conformity," crass "materialism" and mindless manipulability at the hands of advertising's "hidden persuaders." Vance Packard's "*The Hidden Persuaders*" was atop The New York Times best-seller list as Edsels arrived in showrooms.... S.I. Hayakawa, a professor of semantics (and later a Republican U.S. senator from California), ascribed the Edsel's failure to the Ford executives' excessive confidence in the power of motivational research to enable them to predict and modify Americans' behavior. In their attempt to design a car that would cater to customers' sexual fantasies, status anxieties and the like, Ford's deep thinkers neglected to supply good transportation.... the real lesson of 1957: Americans are more discerning and less herdable than their cultured despisers suppose, so what matters most is simple. Good products.

Harold Wilson: One man's wage rise is another man's price increase.

Charles Erwin Wilson (industrialist, testifying before the Senate Armed Forces committee, 1952): What is good for the country is good for General Motors, and what's good for General Motors is good for the country.

Woodrow Wilson: The masters of the government of United States are the combined capitalists and manufacturers of the United States.

Woodrow Wilson: We have witnessed in modern times the submergence of the individual within the organization, and yet the increase to an extraordinary degree of the power of the individual, of the individual who happens to control the organization. Most men are individuals no longer so far as their business, its activities, or its moralities are concerned. They are not units but fractions.

Woodrow Wilson: Business underlies everything in our national life, including our spiritual life. Witness the fact that in the Lord's Prayer, the first petition is for daily bread. No one can worship God or love his neighbor on an empty stomach.

Woodrow Wilson: Is there any man here or any woman – let me say, is there any child here – who does not know that the seed of war is commercial and industrial rivalry?

John David Wright: The business is like riding a bicycle. Either you keep moving or you fall down.

William Wrigley Jr.: When two men in business always agree, one of them is unnecessary.

Andrew Young: Nothing is illegal if a hundred businessmen decide to do it.

COUNTRY-WESTERN EXPRESSIONS

Uncle Anthony: Y'know, some damn smart things have been said by people who didn't sound smart.

Aunt Mary Carlo: I tink dey call her "Winnie" 'cause she's got a laugh lika horse.

Bible: Psalms 149:4: The Lord taketh pleasure in His people.

Sherwood Anderson: Perhaps at bottom I'm ... a country man. The warm earth feeling gets me hardest. It's land love, ground love.

Sherwood Anderson: There is such a lack of conversational opportunities here (in the country vs. the city). It is the real limitation to country town life.

Joe Arnold (Friend of Jim Kitchens, 1926-2007): Old *Can't* died way back before the war!" (EDITOR: Jim Kitchens remembers: "When I was a kid and would tell him "I can't," this is what he'd always say to me).

Joe Arnold: I'm so hungry I could eat a wet mule.

Bible: Psalms 133:1: Behold, how good and how pleasant it is for brethern to dwell together in unity!

Bible: 1 samuel 22:27: With the pure thou wilt show thyself pure.

Bible: Titus 1:15: Unto the pure all things are pure.

Ambrose Bierce: WITTICISM, n. A sharp and clever remark, usually quoted, and seldom noted; what the Philistine is pleased to call a "joke."

Henry Ward Beecher: Nothing marks the change from the city to the country so much as the absence of grinding noises. The country is never silent. But its sounds are separate, distinct, and, as it were, articulate.

Frank Broyles (legendary U. of Arkansas "Razorbacks" football coach from 1957-1976): Have a big front door, and a little back door. [EDITOR: meaning you should take in and listen and learn more than you throw away as bad advice].

Jane Welsh Carlyle: The solitude is not so irksome as one might think – if we are cut off from good society, we are also delivered from bad.

Sir Winston Churchill: When I am abroad, I always make it a rule to never criticize or attack the government of my own country. I make up for lost time when I come home.

Sir Winston Churchill: If the Almighty were to rebuild the world and asked me for advice, I would have English Channels round every country. And the atmosphere would be such that anything which attempted to fly would be set on fire.

English Proverb: Corn and horn go together. (referring to market prices of corn and cattle rising and falling together).

English Proverb: A famine in England begins at the horse-manger (referring to the fact that a shortage of oats is generally followed by a shortage of other crops).

English Proverb: One for the mouse, one for the crow, one to rot and one to grow (referring to the mishaps that commonly befall a crop of beans and the suggestion of only a 25% crop yield to be expected).

English Proverb: A leap year is never a good sheep year.

English Proverb: Pigs see the wind (referring to the restlessness of pigs whenever storms and winds approach).

English Proverb: A red cow gives good milk.

English Proverb: Butter is once a year in the cow's horn (referring to the time of year the cow gives no milk).

English Proverb: Butter is mad twice a year (referring to summer when butter is too soft and winter when too hard).

English Proverb: Sow in the slop, 'twill be heavy at top (meaning to sow wheat in wet ground for maximum yield).

English Proverb: Turnips like a dry bed but a wet head.

Harry Herman, Esq., (father of Russ and Maury): The higher a monkey climbs up a pole, the more he shows his ass.

Italian Proverb: Cheese and money should always sleep together one night (referring to the custom of farmers to insist that payment for the cheese be recieved in advance).

Jim Kitchens, Esq (a great trial lawyer from Mississipi): Uncle Roy and my Daddy's cousin, the hilarious Eddie Anderson, has a saying about easiness: "That's as easy as shitting in a well, and not half as dangerous."

Jim Kitchens, Esq (a great trial lawyer from Mississipi; has coined a phrase that is a take off on being way down in the pecking order, or totem pole, or behind on just about anything): Y'know the phrase "He's really sucking hind titty?" Well, I'm worse off than *that,* I'd say: "If the cow had a big wart on her bag, back behind hind titty, that's what I'd be sucking."

Jim Kitchens: When one wishes to express loathing and contempt for another person, about the nastiest saying I know is: "I wouldn't piss in his ass if his guts were on fire." I don't know where I got that one, and should probably try and forget it.

Jim Kitchens: I'm so broke I can't pay attention.
Jim Kitchens: I'm trying to work UP to being broke.
Jim Kitchens: He didn't know whether to shit or go blind, so he shut one eye and farted.
Jim Kitchens (ordering a rare steak): I want there to be a chance the calf will get well.
Jim Kitchens: That's as futile as farting in a whirlwind.
Jim Kitchens: My Uncle Roy L. Smith had a quote about futility that's right up there with the old whirlwind quote: "You'd just as well be pootin' in a jug," Uncle Roy would say. Now think about that. If you were trying to capture and save some self-made methane gas, how the hell would you do it? Back in the old days, when Uncle Roy grew up, jugs were really important. Of greatest importance, country folks made whiskey and put it in whatever kinds of jugs they could find. It's fairly easy to put whiskey into a jug. But a FART? You'd have to be real fast to fart into a jug, then put a stopper (whether a fancy cork stopper or a more conventional corn cob stopper) in the top of the jug before the gas escaped!
Lloyd W. Kitchens (Father of Jim, 1916-1976): Pore folks got pore ways.
Lloyd W. Kitchens (Father of Jim, 1916-1976): Every tub's gotta sit on its own bottom.
Dr. Lloyd Kitchens, Jr. (Brother of Jim, 1946-2001): I've been working like a grown person.
Agnes Repplier: There is a vast deal of make-believe in the carefully nurtured sentiment for country life, and the barefoot boy, and the mountain girl.
Agnes Repplier: Our first parents (EDITOR: Adam & Eve) lived in the country, and they promptly committed the only sin they were given a chance to commit.
Judge J. Gordon Roach (McComb, Mississippi, 1903-1979): That ground is richer than six foot up a bull's ass.
Judge J. Gordon Roach: He ran like a cat shot in the ass with a dish rag.
Judge J. Gordon Roach: He denied him like Peter denied Christ.
Will Rogers: He/she was so ugly he/she could make a mule back away from an oat bin.
Never slap a man who's chewing tobacco.
Always drink upstream from the herd.
There's two theories to arguing with a woman. Neither one works.
Never miss a good chance to shut up.
We can't all be heroes because someone has to sit on the curb and clap as they go by.
Never kick a cow chip on a hot day.
If you find yourself in a hole, stop digging.
I never expected to see the day when girls would get sunburned in the places they now do.
The best way out of a difficulty is through it.
There are three kinds of men: The ones that learn by reading. The few who learn by observation. The rest of them have to pee on the electric fence.
What the country needs is dirtier fingernails and cleaner minds.
Diplomacy is the art of saying "Nice doggie" until you can find a rock.
An onion can make people cry but there's never been a vegetable that can make people laugh.
If you're riding' ahead of the herd, take a look back every now and then to make sure it's still there.
Lettin' the cat outta the bag is a whole lot easier'n puttin' it back.
Nothing you can't spell will ever work
Will Rogers: There is not a better day in the world to be spent than with a lot of wise old cowmen around barbecued beef, black coffee and good "free holy" beans.
Will Rogers: I am just an old country boy in a big town trying to get along. I have been eating pretty regular and the reason I have been is because I have stayed an old country boy.
Will Rogers: They may call me a rube and a hick, but I'd a lot rather be the man who bought the Brooklyn Bridge than the man who sold it.
William Shakespeare (*King John*, Act I, i): Our country manners give our betters way
William Shakespeare (*Pericles*, Act II, iii): Sure, he's a gallant gentleman, - / He's but a country gentleman.
William Shakespeare (*Winter's Tale*, Act III, ii): Innocence shall make / False accusation blush, and tyranny / Tremble at patience.
Harry S. Truman: Never kick a fresh turd around before breakfast.

Mark Twain: This poor little one-horse town.

UA:

Always take a good look at what you're about to eat. It's not so important to know what it is, but it's sure crucial to know what it was.

Always look at the whole herd before chosing a horse to ride.

Always fish where the fish are, and drill where the oil is.

Behind every successful rancher is a wife who works in town.

Don't squat with your spurs on.

Don't worry about bitin' off more'n you can chew; your mouth is probably a whole lot bigger'n you think.

Don't interfere with something that ain't botherin' you none.

Don't judge people by their relatives.

Generally, you ain't learnin' nothing when your mouth's a-jawin'.

Good judgment comes from experience, and a lotta that comes from bad judgment

He/she is "all hat and no horse" = someone who is all show and no substance

He/she's so skinny he could stand under a clothes line to get out of the rain.

His breath was so bad he could knock a buzzard off a sh-t wagon!

I don't know whether to kill myself or go bowling. (Song lyric)

I wouldn't take you to a dogfight, even if I thought you could win. (Song lyric)

I'm sick and tired of waking up so sick and tired. (Song lyric)

If you want to keep the beer real cold, put it next to my ex-wife's heart. (Song lyric)

If brains was lard Mr/Mrs/Miss(X) couldn't grease a pan!

If you get the feeling I don't love you, feel again. (Song lyric)

If today was a fish, I'd throw it back in. (Song lyric)

If you get to thinkin' you're a person of some influence, try orderin' somebody else's dog around.

If you're ridin' ahead of the herd, take a look back every now and then to make sure it's still there with ya.

Iffin yer too busy to go fishin" – yer too busy

If it don't seem like it's worth the effort, it probably ain't.

If lawyers are disbarred and clergymen are defrocked, shouldn't it follow that cowboys would be deranged?

If a frog had wings, he wouldn't bump his ass on the ground.

If [so and so; whatever], then my ass is a Chinese typewriter.

It was so quiet you can hear a cat piss on a ball of cotton

It don't take a genius to spot a goat in a flock of sheep.

Lettin' the cat outta the bag is a whole lot easier than puttin' it back

Live a good, honorable life. Then when you get older and think back, you'll enjoy it a second time.

"My wife ran off with my best friend, and I miss him." (Song lyric)

Never approach a bull from the front, a horse from the rear, or a fool from any direction.

Never miss a good chance to shut up

Never ask a barber if you need a haircut.

Remember that silence is sometimes the best answer.

She stepped on my heart and stomped the sucker flat. (Song luric)

Sometimes you get and sometimes you get got.

Talk slowly, think quickly.

Tellin' a man to git lost and makin' him do it are two entirely different propositions.

That dog won't hunt (EDITOR: that argument/person/thing won't work)

The only thing I can count on now is my fingers. (Song lyric)

The biggest troublemaker you'll probably ever have to deal with watches you shave his face in the mirror every morning.

The easiest way to eat crow is while it's still warm. The colder it gets, the harder it is to swaller.

The quickest way to double your money is to fold it over and put it back into your pocket.

Timing has a lot to do with the outcome of a rain dance.

Useless as tits on a boar hog.

We (Country folk/Westerners/Southerners/etc) speak the same as any other place like (New York/Boston/etc) ... it just takes us a little longer.

When the phone don't ring, you'll know it's me. (Song lyric)

When you give a personal lesson in meanness to a critter or to a person, don't be surprised if they learn their lesson.

When you lose, don't lose the lesson.

When you're throwin' your weight around, be ready to have it thrown around by somebody else.

You got more trouble than a squirrel on an eight lane highway!

You can't tell how good a man or a watermelon is 'til they get thumped. (Character shows up best when tested.)

Ronnie Whittington, Esq. (Trial lawyer in McComb, Mississippi): He's scratchin' a worried man's ass.

COURAGE

Uncle Anthony: Sometimes courage is just being ignorant of the facts.

Uncle Anthony: Sometimes silence is not golden, it's just yellow!

Aunt Mary Carlo: What's 'da saying? Cowards die a hundred deaths, brave men only once – ain't once enough?

Aesop: It is easy to be brave from a safe distance.

Robert Altman: to play it safe is not to play.

Maya Angelou: I see in the acorn the oak tree. I see growth, rebuilding and restoring the American psche ... the developement of courage. Because without courage, you can't practice any of the other virtues consistently.

Dr. Robert Anthony: We fear the thing we want the most.

Dr. Robert Anthony: The thing we run from is the thing we run to.

Dr. Robert Anthony: Feelings of inferiority and superiority are the same. They both come from fear.

Minna Thomas Antrim: Three failures denote uncommon strength. A weakling has not enough grit to fail thrice.

Margaret Atwood: Fear has a smell, as love does.

Marilyn C. Barrick: For the most part, fear is nothing but an illusion. When you share it with someone else, it tends to disappear.

Bible: Ezekiel 2:6: Be not afraid of them, neither be afraid of their words.

Bible: Hebrews 13:6: The Lord is my helper, and I will not fear what man shall do unto me.

Bible: Isaiah 35:3: Strengthen ye the weak hands, and confirm the feeble knees.

Bible: Isaiah 40:3; John 1:23; Luke 3:4; Maqrk 1:3; Matthew 3:3: The voice of one crying in the wilderness.

Bible: 1 John 4:18: There is no fear in love; but perfect love casteth out fear.

Bible: John 15:13: Greater love hath no man than this, that a man lay down his life for his friends.

Bible: Leviticus 26:17: Ye shall flee when none pursueth you.

Bible: Phillippians 4:13: I can do all things through Christ that stentheneth me.

Bible: Psalm 23:4: Yea, though I walk through the valley of the shadow death, I will fear no evil: for Thou art with me.

Bible: Psalm 27:1: The Lord is the strength of my life; of whom shall I be afraid?

Bible: Psalms 31:24: Be of good courage, and he shall strengthen your heart, all ye that hope in the Lord.

Bible: 1 Samuel 4:9: Be strong, and quit yourselves like men.

Ambrose Bierce: COWARD, n. One who in a perilous emergency thinks with his legs.

Ambrose Bierce: DARING, n. One of the most conspicuous qualities of a man in security.

Ambrose Bierce: GHOST, n. The outward and visible sign of an inward fear.

Ambrose Bierce: VALOR, n. A soldierly compund of vanity, duty and the gambler's hope....

Napoleon Bonaparte: The first virtue in the soldier is endurance of fatigue; courage is only the second virtue.

General Omar Bradley: Bravery is the capacity to perform properly even when scared half to death.

Louis Brandeis: Those who won our independence believed that the final end of the State was to make men free to develop their faculties; and that in its government the deliberative forces should prevail over the arbitrary. They valued liberty both as an end and as a means. They believed liberty to be the secret of happiness and courage to be the secret of liberty.

Benjamin Cardozo: The heroic hours of life do not announce their presence by drum and trumpet, challenging us to be true to ourselves by appeals to the martial spirit that keeps the blood at heat. Some little, unassuming, unobtrusive choice presents itself before us slyly and craftily, glib and insinuating, in the modest garb of innocence. To yield to its blandishments is so easy. The wrong, it seems, is venial.... Then it is that you will be summoned to show the courage of adventurous youth.

Art Carney as Norton (in TV show "The Homeymooners"): As we say in the sewer: if you're not prepared to go all the way, don't put your boots on in the first place.

G.K. Chesterton: Brave men are all vertebrates: they have their softness on the surface and a thin toughness in the middle.

Chinese Proverb: He who rides a tiger is afraid to dismount.

Sir Winston Churchill: Success is the ability to go from one failure to another with no loss of enthusiasm.

Sir Winston Churchill: Courage is rightly esteemed the first of human qualities because it is the quality which guarantees all others.

Sir Winston Churchill: This is no time for ease and comfort. It is the time to dare and endure.

Sir Winston Churchill: Courage is what it takes to stand up and speak; courage is also what it takes to sit down and listen.

Sir Winston Churchill: Courage is going from failure to failure without losing enthusiasm.

Confucius: To see what is right and not to do it, is want of courage.

Howard Cosell: Courage takes many forms. There is physical courage, there's moral courage. Then there is a still higher type of courage – the courage to brave pain, to live with it, to never let others know of it and to still find joy in life; to wake up in the morning with enthusiasm for the day ahead.

William O. Douglas: We need to be bold and adventuresome in our thinking to survive.

John Dryden: Courage from hearts and not from numbers grows.

Amelia Earhart: Courage is the price that life exacts for granting peace.

Albert Einstein: Never do anything against conscience, even if the state demands it.

Ralph Waldo Emerson: They conquer who believe they can. He has not learned the first lesson of life who does not every day surmount a fear.

Ralph Waldo Emerson: Heroism feels and never reasons and therefore is always right.

Ralph Waldo Emerson: The courage of the tiger is one, and of the horse another.

Ralph Waldo Emerson: A great part of courage is the courage of having done the thing before.

Ralph Waldo Emerson: The charm of the best courages is that they are inventions, inspirations, flashes of genius.

English saying (during "The Battle of Britain" of WWII Joseph Kennedy fled London): I thought my daffodils were yellow before I met Joe Kennedy. (Joseph Kennedy was US Ambassador to England in 1940).

F. Scott Fitzgerald: Never confuse a single defeat with a final defeat.

F. Scott Fitzgerald: Show me a hero and I will write you a tragedy.

Percy Foreman: Courage in the courtroom is more important than brains. If I were hiring a lawyer and had to choose between one that was all brains and one that was all guts, I would take the guts.

French Proverb: Courage is often caused by fear.

French Proverb: And old rat is a brave rat.

Thomas Fuller: Some have been thought brave because they were afraid to run away.

German Proverb: Great things are done more through courage than through wisdom.

Dr. Rob Gilbert: It's all right to have butterflies in your stomach. Just get them to fly in formation.

Winifred Gordon: Many women miss their greatest chance of happiness through a want of courage in the decisive moments of their lives.

Graham Greene: Courage can be a very difficult neurosis.

Wayne Gretzky: You miss 100% of the shots you never take.

Sir Douglas Haig (British Commander-in-Chief on the Western Front during WWI, in April 1918 issued an order for his troops to stand firm): "With **our backs to the wall**, and believing in the justice of our cause, each one of us must fight on to the end."

Judge Learned Hand: Of those qualities on which civilization depends, next after courage, it seems to me, comes an open mind, and, indeed, the highest courage is, as Holmes used to say, to stake your all upon a conclusion which you are aware tomorrow may prove false.

Heinrich Heine: When the heroes go offstage, the clowns come on.

Ernest Hemingway: Grace under pressure.

Indian Proverb: To a real hero life is a mere straw.

Robert G. Ingersoll: Courage without conscience is a wild beast.

Irish Proverb: Two-thirds of help is to give courage.

Irish Proverb: Fear is a fine spur, so is rage.

Italian Proverb: All are brave when the enemy flies.

Andrew Jackson (US President, 1767-1845): One man with courage is a majority.

George Jackson: Patience has its limits. Take it too far, and it's cowardice.

Henry James: My dear thing, it all comes back, as everything always does, simply to personal pluck. It's only a question, no matter when or where, of having enough.

Erica Jong: Everyone has talent. What is rare is the courage to follow the talent to the dark place where it leads.

Joshua Karton: Let your fears be your counselors, not your jailors. Don't let others' insecurities be your bars. Don't let what you can't do interfere with what you can.

John F. Kennedy (asked how he became a hero in WW II): It was involuntary. They sank my boat.

Sister Elizabeth Kenny: It is better to be a lion for a day than a sheep all your life.

Soren Kierkegaard: It requires moral courage to grieve; it requires religious courage to rejoice.

D.H. Lawrence: The great virtue in life is real courage, that knows how to face facts and live beyond them.

C.S. Lewis: Courage is not merely *one* of the virtues but the form of every virtue at the testing point, which means at the point of highest reality.

James Russell Lowell: They are slaves who fear to speak, / For the fallen and the weak.

Robert Lynd: One of the great disadvantages of being a coward is that one is constantly having to eat things that one does not wish to eat.

General Douglas MacArthur: Last, but by no means least, courage—moral courage, the courage of one's convictions, the courage to see things through. The world is in a constant conspiracy against the brave. It's the age-old struggle – the roar of the crowd on one side and the voice of your conscience on the other.

Rollo May: To say a person is a coward has no more meaning than to say he is lazy: it simply tells us that some vital potentiality is unrealized or blocked.

Herman Melville: Familiarity with danger makes a brave man braver, but less daring. Thus with seamen: he who goes the oftenest round Cape Horn goes the most circumspectly.

Herman Melville: Few men's courage is proof against protracted meditation unrelieved by action.

Moorish Proverb: He who fears something gives it power over him.

Friedrich Nietzsche: Courage is the best slayer, - courage which *attacketh:* for in every attack there is the sound of triumph.

Friedrich Nietzsche: In their hearts they want simply one thing most of all: that no one hurt them. Thus do they anticipate every one's wishes and do well unto every one. That, however, is *cowardice*, though it be called "virtue."

Cardinal John Henry Newman: Courage does not consist in calculation, but in fighting against chances.

Nigerian Proverb: When the mouse laughs at the cat, there is a hole nearby.

Louis Nizer: Still, I know of no higher fortitude than stubbornness in the face of overwhelming odds.

North American Proverb: Without justice, courage is weak.

George Orwell: When it comes to the pinch, human beings are heroic.

General George S. Patton: Courage is fear holding on a minute longer.

Joseph Persico: Courage is like a bank balance, after enough withdrawals you go bankrupt b/c you're overdrawn.

Edgar Allan Poe: That man is not truly brave who is afraid either to seem or to be, when it suits him, a coward.

Plautus: Courage in danger is half the battle.

Plutarch: Courage consists not in hazarding without fear, but being resolutely minded in a just cause.

Jean Paul Richter: A timid person is frightened before a danger, a coward during the time, and a courageous person afterward.

Eddie Rickenbacker: Courage is doing what you are afraid to do. There can be no courage unless you're scared.

Ronald Reagan: Above all, we must realize that no arsenal, or no weapon in the arsenals of the world, is so formidable as the will and moral courage of free men and women. It is a weapon our adversaries in today's world do not have.

Renoir: One must from time to time attempt something beyond one's capacity.

Kenny Rogers: Don't be afraid to give up the good and go for the great.

Will Rogers: Being a hero is about the shortest-lived profession on earth.

Will Rogers: The main thing about being a hero is to know when to die.

Will Rogers: This thing of being a hero, about the main thing to do is to know when to die. Prolonged life has ruined more men than it ever made.

Field Marshal Erwin Rommel (WWII Nazi General known as "The Desert Fox"): But courage which goes against military expediency is stupidity, or, if it is insisted upon by a commander, irresponsibility.

Eleanor Roosevelt: You must do the thing you think you cannot do.

Franklin D. Roosevelt: We cannot afford to accumulate a deficit in the books of human fortitude.

Theodore Roosevelt: It is not the critic, who counts, not the man who points out how the strong man stumbled or where the doer of deeds could have done them better. / The credit belongs to the man who is actually in the arena, whose face is marred by dust and sweat and blood, whose strives valiantly, who errs and comes short again and again...; / Who knows the great enthusiasms, the great devotions, and spends himself in a worthy cause; / Who, at the best, knows in the end the triumph of high achievement; / And who, at the worse, if he fails at least fails while daring greatly, so that his place shall never be with those cold and timid souls who know neither victory nor defeat.

Judith Rossner: It takes far less courage to kill yourself than it takes to make yourself wake up one more time. It's harder to stay where you are than to get out.

John Ruskin: He who has truth in his heart need never fear the want of persuasion on his tongue.

Bertrand Russell: A woman who is courageous has to conceal the fact if she wishes conventional men to like her. The man who is courageous in any manner except physical danger is also thought ill of.

General Winfield Scott (address to the 11th Infantry Regiment before its victory over British forces at Chippawa, Canada, July 5, 1814): The enemy say that Americans are good at a long shot, but cannot stand the cold iron. I call upon you instantly to give a lie to the slander. Charge!

Frank Scully: Why not go out on a limb? Isn't that where the fruit is?

Seneca: Gold is tried by fire, brave men by adversity.

Seneca: The bravest sight in the world is to see a great man struggling against adversity.

A.G. Sertillanges: Courage is sustained ... by calling up anew the vision of the goal.

William Shakespeare (*All's Well That Ends Well*, Act I, ii): He did not look far / Into the service of time, and was / Discipled of the bravest; he hasted long, / But on us both did haggish age steal on, / And wore us out of act.

William Shakespeare (*Antony and Cleopatra*, Act III, ii): When valour preys on reason, / It eats the sword it fights with.

William Shakespeare (*Antony and Cleopatra*, Act IV, xv): What's brave, what's noble, / Let's do it after the high Roman fashion, / And make death proud to take us.

William Shakespeare (*Coriolanus*, Act I, iv): You souls of geese, / That bear the shapes of men, how have you run / From slaves that apes would beat!

William Shakespeare (*Coriolanus*, Act II, ii): In that day's feats .... / He prov'd the best man i' the field; and for his meed / Was brow-bound with the oak.

William Shakespeare (*Hamlet*, Act III, i): To be, or not to be, that is the question: - / Whether 'tis nobler in the mind, to suffer / The slings and arrows of outrageous fortune; / Or, to take arms against a sea of troubles, / And, by opposing, end them?

William Shakespeare (*I Henry IV*, Act I, ii): I know them to be a true-bred cowards as ever turned back.

William Shakespeare (*I Henry IV*, Act I, iii): O, the blood more stirs / To rouse a lion than to start a hare!

William Shakespeare (*I Henry IV*, Act II, iv): A plague of all cowards, I say, and a vengeance, too!

William Shakespeare (*I Henry IV*, Act II, iv): What a slave art thou, to hack thy sword as thou hast done, and say it was in fight!

William Shakespeare (*I Henry IV*, Act II, iv): I was now a coward on instinct.

William Shakespeare (*I Henry IV*, Act IV, i): Come let us take a muster speedily: / Doomsday is near; die all, die merrily.

William Shakespeare (*I Henry VI,* Act I, v): So bees with smoke and doves with noisome stench / Are from their hives and houses driven away. / They call'd us for our fierceness English dogs; / Now, like whelps, we crying run away.

William Shakespeare (*II Henry IV*, Act II, iii): By his light / Did all the chivalry of England move / To do brave acts.

William Shakespeare (*III Henry VI*, Act II, i): Methought, he bore him in the thickest troop / As doth a lion in a head of neat: / Or as a bear, encompass'd round with dogs; / Who, having pinch'd a few, and make them cry, / The rest stand all aloof, and bark at him.

William Shakespeare (*III Henry VI*, Act IV, vii): Fearless minds climb soonest unto crowns.

William Shakespeare (*III Henry VI*, Act V, iv): Why, courage, then! What cannot be avoided, / 'Twere childish weakness to lament, or fear.

William Shakespeare (*Henry V*, Act IV, i): Gloucester, 'tis true that we are in great danger; / The greater therefore should our courage be.

William Shakespeare (*Henry V*, Act IV, iii; The English Camp, on St. Crispin's Day, Oct 25, 1415 at Battle of Agincourt: The Agincourt Speech or "St Crispin's Day Speech"): HENRY V: We few, we happy few, we band of brothers; / For he today that sheds his blood with me / Shall be my brother; be he ne'er so base, / This day shall gentle his condition: / And gentlemen in England, now a-bed, / Shall think themselves accurs'd they were not here: / And hold their manhoods cheap, while any speaks / That fought with us upon Saint Crispin's day.

William Shakespeare (*III Henry VI*, Act V, iv): Why, courage then! What cannot be avoided / 'Twere childish weakness to lament or fear.

William Shakespeare (*Julius Caesar*, Act II, ii): Cowards die many times before their deaths; / The valiant never taste of death but once.

William Shakespeare (*King John*, Act II, i): But how much unexpected, by so much, / We must awake endeavor for defense; / For courage mounteth with occasion.

William Shakespeare (*King John*, Act III, i): Thou slave, thou wretch, thou coward! / Thou little valiant, great in villainy! / Thou ever strong upon the stronger side! / Thou Fortune's champion, that dost never fight / But when her humourous ladyship is by / To teach thee safety!

William Shakespeare (*King John*, Act IV, iii): Out, dunghill! Dar'st thou brave a nobleman?

William Shakespeare (*King Lear*, Act II, ii): A lily-livered, action-taking knave.

William Shakespeare (*Love's Labour's Lost*, Act V, ii): Muster your wits: stand in your own defence; / Or hide your heads like cowards, and fly hence.

William Shakespeare (*Macbeth*, Act I, vii): But screw your courage to the sticking-place, / And we'll not fail.

William Shakespeare (*Macbeth*, Act I, vii): Art thou afraid / To be the same in thine own act and valour / As thou art in desire? Wouldst thou have that / Which thou esteem'st the ornament of life, / And live a coward in thine own esteem?

William Shakespeare (*Macbeth*, Act I, vii): I dare do all that may become a man: / Who dares do more, is none.

William Shakespeare (*Macbeth*, Act III, i): 'Tis much he dares; / And, to that dauntless temper of his mind, / He hath a wisdom that doth guide his valour / To act in safety,

William Shakespeare (*Macbeth*, Act III, iv): You can behold such sights, / And keep the natural ruby of your cheeks, / When mine is blanch'd with fear.

William Shakespeare (*Macbeth*, Act III, iv): What man dare, I dare: / Approach thou like the rugged Russian bear, / The arm'd rhinoceros, or the Hycean tiger, / Take any shape but that, and my firm nerves / Shall never tremble.

William Shakespeare (*Much Ado About Nothing*, Act I, i): He hath borne himself beyond the promise of his age; / doing in the figure of a lamb, the feats of a lion.

William Shakespeare (*Richard II*, Act III, ii): Wise men ne'er wail their present woes, / But presently prevent the ways to wail.

William Shakespeare (*Richard III*, Act V, iv): I have set my life upon a cast, / And I will stand the hazard of the die.

William Shakespeare (*Taming of the Shrew*, Act I, ii): Think you, a little din can daunt mine ears? / Have I not in my time heard lions roar? .... Have I not heard great ordinance in the field, / And heaven's artillery thunder in the skies? / .... And do you tell me of a woman's tongue, / That gives not half so great a blow to hear, / As will a chestnut in a farmer's fire?

William Shakespeare (*Tempest*, Act V, i): O brave new world, That has such people in't!

William Shakespeare (*Timon of Athens*, Act III, v): He's truly valiant, that can wisely suffer / The worst that man can breathe; and make his wrongs / His outsides; wear them like his raiment, carelessly: / And ne'er prefer his injuries to his heart, / To bring it into danger.

William Shakespeare (*Troilus and Cressida*, Act I, iii): The thing of courage, / As rous'd with rage, with rage doth sympathise, / And, with an accent tun'd in self-same key, / Returns to chiding fortune.

William Shakespeare (*Twelfth Night*, Act III, iv): A coward, a most devout coward, religious in it.

George Bernard Shaw: It is courage, courage, courage, that raises the blood of life to crimson splendor.

George Bernard Shaw: Hatred is the coward's revenge for being intimidated.

William Tecumseh Sherman: I would define true courage to be a perfect sensibility of the measure of danger, and a mental willingness to endure it.

Logan Pearsall Smith: What is more mortifying than to feel that you missed the plum for want of courage to shake the tree?

Spanish Proverb: In a calm sea every man is a pilot.

Robert Louis Stevenson: Courage, the footstool of the Virtues, upon which they stand.

Joe Sutton: If you're scared, just holler and you'll find it ain't so lonesome out there.

Henry David Thoreau: I am less affected by their heroism who stood up for half an hour in the front line at Buena Vista, than by the steady and cheerful valor of the men who inhabit the snowplow for their winter quarters; who have not merely the three-o'clock-in-the-morning courage, which Bonaparte thought was the rarest, but whose courage does not go to rest so early, who go to sleep only when the storm sleeps or the sinews of their iron steed are frozen.

Mark Twain: Courage is resistance to fear, mastery of fear—not absence of fear.

Mark Twain: Courage is resistance to fear, mastery of fear—not absence of fear. Except a creature be part coward it is not a compliment to say it is brave; it is merely a loose misapplication of the word. Consider the flea!—incomparably the bravest of all the creatures of God, if ignorance of fear were courage. Whether you are asleep or awake he will attack you, caring nothing for the fact that in bulk and strength you are to him as are the massed armies of the earth to a sucking child; he lives both day and night and all days and nights in the very lap of peril and the immediate presence of death, and yet is no more afraid than is the man who walks the streets of the city that was threatened by an earthquake ten centuries before. When we speak of Clive, Nelson, and Putnam as men who "didn't know what fear was," we ought always to add the flea—and put him at the head of the procession.

Mark Twain: The human race is a race of cowards: and I am not only marching in that procession but carrying a banner.

Mark Twain: There are several good protections against temptations, but the surest is cowardice.

Vincent Van Gogh: What would life be if we had no courage to attempt anything?

Rocco Vesper: When you get into the ring (to box) or the court room (to try a case) don't look around for a place to fall down.

John Wainwright: There is no such thing as bravery; only degrees of fear.

Chris Watson (AC Press article "That's Not All, Folks! Lessons Learned From Cartoons Over Into Adult Situations"): And Tweety (Bird) taught me that anyone with brains, guts and willpower can upset the status quo.... Dudley DoRight showed me the two faces of courage, the brave one and a stupid one.

John Wayne (born Marion Morrison, legendary film actor in over 200 films, 1926-1979): Courage is being scared to death, but saddling up anyway.

Jessamyn West: It is very easy to forgive others their mistakes. It takes more guts and gumption to forgive them for having witnessed your own.

Chuck Yeager: You do what you can for as long as you can, and when you finally can't you do the next best thing. You back up but you don't give up.

COURT(S) (See JUDGES; JUSTICE; LAW; LAWYERS)

CREATIVITY (See THINKING)

CREDIBILITY (See HONESTY)

CRIME (See EVIL)

CRITICS/CRITICISM (See also ALLEGATION)

Uncle Anthony: It's easy to throw a bomb (or hand grenade) at someone; it's a lot tougher to be the catcher.

Uncle Anthony: I wouldn't mind the criticism so much if it wasn't right so often.

Uncle Anthony: Put the spot light on what's under the rock, not on who's trying to roll it over.

Aunt Mary Carlo: Never criticize anybody until and unless they are first convinced of your unconditional confidence in their abilities.

Edward Abbey: Literary critics, like a herd of cows or a school fish, always face in the same direction, obeying that love for unity that every critic requires.

Joseph Addison: It is ridiculous for any man to criticize the works of another if he has not distinguished himself by his own performances.

Joseph Aebo: The Torah does not tell us to believe what is absurd.

John Aiken: He, whose first emotion on the view of an excellent production is to undervalue it, will never have one of his own to show.

Sherwood Anderson: Again and again I have been attacked for looseness, lack of beauty in my prose, and the one attacking me used, as the vehicle of attack, prose I would have been ashamed to write.

Brenden Behan: Critics are like eunuchs in a harem. There are there every night, they see a gun every night, they see how it should be done every night, but they can't do it themselves.

Bible: Apocrypha, Ecclesiasticus 28:17: The blow of the whip raises a welt, but a blow of the tongue crushes bones.

Bible: Ecclesiastes 7:5: It is better to hear the rebuke of the wise, than for a man to hear the song of fools.

Bible: James 4:12: Who art thou that judgest another?

Bible: John 6:43: Murmur not among yourselves.

Bible: John 8:7: He that is without sin among you, let him first cast a stone.

Bible: Lamentations 3:39: Wherefore doth a living man complain, a man for the punishment of his sins?

Bible: Luke 2:26: Woe unto you, when all men shall speak well of you!

Bible: Luke 6:37: Judge not, and ye shall not be judged: condemn not, and ye shall not be condemned.

Bible: Matthew 7:1: Judge not, that ye be not judged.

Bible: Proverbs 9:8: Reprove not a scorner, lest he hate thee; rebuke a wise man, and he will love thee.

Bible: Proverbs 10:17: He that refuseth reproof erreth.

Bible: Proverbs 17:10: A reproof entereth more into a wise man than an hundred stripes into a fool.

Bible: Psalms 74:22: the foolish man reproacheth Thee daily.

Bible: Romans 2:1: Wherein thou hudgest another, thou condemnest thyself.

Bible: Romans 9:20: Who are thou that repliest against God? Shall the thing formed say to him that formed it, Why hast thou made me thus?

Ambrose Bierce: CAVILER, n. A critic of our own work. [EDITOR: from the word cavil = to find fault unnecessarily; to quibble; to carp; to detect petty flaws].

Ambrose Bierce: CRITIC, n. A person who boasts himself hard to please because nobody tries to please him....

Ambrose Bierce: CYNIC, n. A blackguard whose faulty vision sees things as they are, not as they ought to be. Hence the custom among the Scythians of plucking out a cynic's eyes to improve his vision.

Ambrose Bierce: PAINTING, n. The art of protecting flat surfaces from the weather and exposing them to the critic.

Ambrose Bierce: PROOF-READER, n. A malefactor who atones for making your writing nonsense by permitting the compositor to make it unintelligible.

Richard Bentley: It is a maxim with me, that no man was ever written out of a reputation but by himself.

Jim Bishop: A good writer is not, per se, a good book critic. No more so than a good drunk is automatically a good bartender.

Harry A. Blackman: It is easier to be cynical than to be correct. I know that from the judging business. It is easier to write a stinging dissent than a persuasive majority opinion.

Christian Nestell Bovee: The legitimate aim of criticism is to direct attention to the excellent.—The bad will dig its own grave, and the imperfect may safely be left to that final neglect from which no amount of present undeserved popularity can rescue it.

Sir Thomas Browne: He who is discommendeth others obliquely commendeth himself.

Jean de la Bruyere: Criticism is as often a trade as a science; requiring more health than with, more labor than capacity, more practice than genius.

Jean de la Bruyere: The pleasure of criticism takes from us that of being deeply moved by very beautiful things.

Edmund Burke: Is it in destroying and pulling down that skill is displayed?—The shallowest understanding, the rudest hand, is more than equal to that task.

Charles Buxton: Silence is sometimes the severest criticism.

Dale Carnegie: Criticism is dangerous, because it wounds a man's precious pride, hurts his sense of importance, and arouses his resentment.

Chinese Proverb: Deal with the faults of others as gently as with your own.

Chinese Proverb: Everyone pushes a falling fence.

Sir Winston Churchill: It is better to be making the news than taking it; to be an actor rather than a critic.

Sir Winston Churchill: Criticism may not be agreeable, but it is necessary. It fulfills the same function as pain in the human body. It calls attention to an unhealthy state of things.

Sir Winston Churchill: When the eagles are silent, the parrots begin to jabber.

Sir Winston Churchill: I do not resent criticism, even when, for the sake of emphasis, it parts for the time with reality.

Sir Winston Churchill: I have adhered to my rule of never criticizing any measure of war or policy after the event unless I had before expressed publicly or formally my opinion or warning about it. Indeed in the after-light I have softened many of the severities of contemporary controversy.

Henry Steele Commager: Men in authority will always think that criticism of their policies is dangerous. They will always equate their policies with patriotism, and find criticism subversive.

Charles Horton Cooley: One should never criticize his own work except in a fresh and hopeful mood. The self-criticism of a tired mind is suicide.

Greg Cusimanno: Any jackass can kick down a beautiful structure that took years to build.

Tyne Daly: A critic is someone who never actually goes to the battle yet he afterwards comes out shooting the wounded.

Benjamin Disraeli: The most notable criticism is that in which the critic is not the antagonist so much as the rival of the author.

Benjamin Disraeli: It is much easier to be critical than to be correct.

Benjamin Disraeli: He wreathed the rod of criticism with roses.

Albert Einstein: To see with one's own eyes, to feel and judge without succumbing to the suggestive power of the fashion of the day, to be able to express what one has seen and felt in a trim sentence or even in a cunningly wrought word – is that not glorious?
T. S. Eliot: Honest criticism and sensitive appreciation are directed not upon the poet but upon the poetry.
Ralph Waldo Emerson: Criticism should not be querulous and wasting, all knife and root-puler, but guiding, instructive, inspiring, a south wind, not an east wind.
Ralph Waldo Emerson: Let none presume to measure the irregularities of Michelangelo or Socrates by village scales.
Ralph Waldo Emerson: We resent all criticism which denies us anything that lies in our line of advance.
Ralph Waldo Emerson: Blame is safer than praise.
Malcolm Forbes: If you have no critics you likely have no successes.
Dr. Emmet Fox: Criticism is an indirect form of self-boasting.
Anatole France: The good critic is he who relates the adventures of his soul among masterpieces.
Benjamin Franklin: Blame-all and praise-all are two blockheads.
Benjamin Franklin: The sting of a reproach is the Truth of it.
French Proverb: Men count up the faults of those who keep them waiting.
German Proverb: Even the lion has to defend himself against flies.
J. M. Gibson: Only God can form and paint a flower, but any foolish child can pull it to pieces.
Arnold Glasow: Criticism is most effective when it sounds like praise.
R.W. Griswold: It is a barren kind of criticism which tells you what a thing is not.
Arthur Guiterman: The Stones that Critics hurl with Harsh Intent / A Man may use to build his Monument.
William Hazlitt: The only impeccable writers are those that never wrote.
William Hazlitt: The severest critics are always those who have either never attempted, or who have failed in the original composition.
Robert Heinlein: A critic is a man who creates nothing and thereby feels qualified to judge the work of creative men. There is logic in this; he is unbiased—he hates all creative people equally.
Lillian Hellman: Cynicism is an unpleasant way of saying the truth.
Marrietta Holley: We are blind creeters, the fun-seein'est of us; weak creeter, when we think we are the strong mindedest. Now, when we hear of a crime, it is easy to say that the one who committed that wrong stepped flat off from goodness into sin, and should be hung. It is so awful easy and sort of satisfactory to condemn other folk'es faults that we don't stop to think that it may be that evil was fell into through the weakness and blindness of a mistake.
Oliver Wendall Holmes, Sr.: What a blessed thing it is that Nature, when she invented, manufactured, and patented her authors, contrived to make critics out of the chips that were left!
Gerard Manley Hopkins: I hate being asked to criticize what what I cannot praise.
Horace: I'll play a whetstone's part, which makes iron sharp, though unable itself to cut.
E.W. Howe: When a man tells you what people are saying about you, tell him what people are saying about him; that will immediately take his mind off your troubles.
James Huneker: A critic is a man who expects miracles.
Irish Proverb: If you want to be criticized, marry.
Washington Irving: Critics are a kind of freebooters in the republic of letters, who, like deer, goats, and diverse other graminivorous animals, gained subsistence by gorging upon buds and leaves of the young shrubs of the forest, thereby robbing them of their verdure and retarding their progress to maturity.
Thomas Jefferson: I find the pain of a little censure, even when it is unfounded, is more acute than the pleasure of much praise.
Jewish Proverb: Reprove not a scorner, lest he hate you; reprove a wise man, and he will love you.
Jewish Proverb: A rebuke stings deeper into a man of intelligence than a hundred lashes into a fool.
Jewish Saying: The reddest apple can contain a worm.
Jewish Saying: What was written and is believed is not thereby proved true.
Jewish Saying: Rather a skeptic than a fool.
Jewish Saying: Some people are like new shoes: the cheaper they are, the louder they squeak.
Robert Jackson: The price of freedom of religion, or of speech, or of the press, is that we must put up with a good deal of rubbish.

Ben Jonson: Criticism, as it was first instituted by Aristotle, was meant as a standard of judging well.

Lynden B. Johnson: If one morning I walked on top of the water across the Potomac River, the headline that afternoon would read, "President Can't Swim."

Samuel Johnson: Criticism, as it was first instituted by Aristotle, was meant as a standard of judging well.

Franklin P. Jones: Honest criticism is hard to take, particularly from a relative, a friend, an acquaintance, or a stranger.

Junius: It behooves the minor critic, who hunts for blemishes, to be a little distrustful of his own sagacity

Walter Savage Landor: The eyes of critics, whether in commending our carping, are both on one side, like those of a turbot. [EDITOR: a large European flatfish with both eyes on left side of the head]

Latin Proverb: Censure pardons the ravens but rebukes the doves.

D.H. Lawrence: The proper function of a critic is to save the tale from the artist who created it.

Abraham Lincoln: He has a right to criticize who has a heart to help.

Listerine mouthwash ad (1920's): Even your closest (best) friends won't tell you.

Henry Wadsworth Longfellow: The strength of criticism lies only in the weakness of the thing criticized.

Henry Wadsworth Longfellow: Doubtless criticism was originally benigna, pointing out the beauties of a work rather than its defects.—The passions of men have made it malignant, as the bad heart of Procrustes turned the bed, the symbol of repose, into an instrument of torture.

Henry Wadsworth Longfellow: Critics are sentinels in the grand army of letters, stationed at corners of newspapers and reviews, to challenge every new author.

Henry Wadsworth Longfellow: Some critics are like chimney-sweepers; they put out the fire below, and frighten the swallows from their nests above; they scrape a long time in the chimney, cover themselves with soot, and bring nothing away but a bag of cinders, and then sing out from the top of the house, as if they had built it.

Janes Russell Lowell: A wise skepticism is the first attribute of a good critic.

Thomas Macaulay: The opinion of the great body of the reading public, is very materially influenced even by the unsupported assertions of those who assume a right to criticize.

Malay Proverb: He can see a louse as far away as China but is unconscious of an elephant on his nose.

Norman Mailer: I can imagine nothing more distressing to a critic than to have a writer see accurately into his own work.

Joseph Mankiewicz: I am a critic – as essential to the theater as ants to a picnic.

Henry Cardinal Manning: Cricism is asserted superiority.

Henry Cardinal Manning: A critic knows more than the author he criticises, or just as much, or al least somewhat less.

W. Somerset Maugham: It is salutary to train oneself to be no more affected by censure than by praise.

H.L. Mencken: Criticism is prejudice made plausible.

H.L. Mencken: It is impossible to think of a man of any actual force and originality... who spent his whole life of appraising and describing the work of other men.

Montaigne: Since we cannot equal it, let us avenge ourselves by abusing it.

George Moore: The lot of critics is to be remembered by what they failed to understand.

Thomas Moore (Irish poet, 1852): Is quite cruel that a poet cannot wander through his regions of enchantment without having a critic, forever, like the old man of the sea, upon his back.

Christopher Morley: There are some literary critics... who remind me of a gong at a grade crossing clanging loudly and vainly as the train roars by.

Ogden Nash: I don't care how unkind the things people say about me so / long as they don't say them to my face.

G.J. Nathan: Criticism is the art wherewith a critic tries to guess himself into a share of the artist's fame.

G.J. Nathan: There are two kinds of dramatic critics: destructive and constructive. I am destructive. There are two kinds of guns: Krupp and pop.

Louis Nizer: We are likely to believe the worst about another because the capacity for evil is so pronounced in ourselves.

Peggy Noonan: Cynicism is not realistic and often it is unrealistic and kind of cowardly because it means you don't have to try.

John O'Hara: Book reviewers are little old ladies of both sexes.

Dr. Norman Vincent Peale: The trouble with most of us is that we would rather be ruined by praise than saved by criticism.

William Penn: They have a right to censure that have a heart to help.

William Penn: We are apt to be very pert at censuring others, where we will not endure advice ourselves.

Plautus: I much prefer a compliment, insincere or not, to sincere criticism.

Plutarch: To find a fault is easy; to do better may be difficult.

Alexander Pope: Get your enemies to read your works in order to mend them; for your friend is so much your second self that he will judge too much like you.

Quintlian: They damn what they do not understand.

Ronald Reagan (speaking about his critics): They sort of remind me of the fellow who was asked which was worse, ignorance or apathy, and he said, "I don't know and I don't care."

Jean Paul Richter: Criticism often takes from the tree caterpillars and blossoms together.

Will Rogers: An ignorant person is one who doesn't know what you have just found out.

Will Rogers: A remark (Editor: critical remark) generally hurts in proportion to its truth.

Will Rogers: In Hollywood the woods are full of people that learned to write but evidently can't read. If they could read their stuff, they'd stop writing.

Will Rogers: There is nothing as easy as denouncing..... It don't take much to see that something is wrong, but it does take some eyesight to see what will put it right again.

Theodore Roosevelt: It is not the critic, who counts, not the man who points out how the strong man stumbled or where the doer of deeds could have done them better. / The credit belongs to the man who is actually in the arena, whose face is marred by dust and sweat and blood, whose strives valiantly, who errs and comes short again and again...; / Who knows the great enthusiasms, the great devotions, and spends himself in a worthy cause; / Who, at the best, knows in the end the triumph of high achievement; / And who, at the worse, if he fails at least fails while daring greatly, so that his place shall never be with those cold and timid souls who know neither victory nor defeat.

Jean Rostand: Take heed of critics even when they are not fair; resist them even when they are.

Josiah Royce: The critic creates nothing, he only points out. But his pointing may show you powers that were indeed always there, and that were even effective, but that, once afresh seen, suggest to active passion a thousand devices whereby the world is revolutionized.

Bertrand Russell: A stupid man's report of what a clever man says can never be accurate, because he unconsciously translates what he hears into something he can understand.

Sainte-Beuve: The critic is only the secretary of the public, but a secretary who does not wait to take dictation, and who divines, who decides, who expresses every morning what everybody is thinking.

George Santayana: Skepticism is the chastity of the intellect, and it is shameful to surrender it too soon or to the first-come or; there is nobility in preserving it coolly and proudly through a long youth, until at last, in the ripeness of instinct and discretion, it can be safely exchanged for fidelity and happiness.

Sir Walter Scott: O ye critics, will nothing melt ye?

Sir Walter Scott: Court not the critic's smile, nor dread his frown.

Mendele Mocher Seforim: A man can detect a speck in another's hair, but can't see the flies on his own nose.

William Shakespeare (*Hamlet*, Act I, iii): Take each man's censure, but reserve thy judgment.

William Shakespeare (*Julius Caesar*, III, ii): The most unkindest cut of all.

William Shakespeare (*Julius Caesar*, Act IV, iii): In such a time as this it is not meet / That every nice offence should bear its comment.

William Shakespeare (*Measure for Measure*, Act IV, vi): 'Tis a physic / That's bitter to sweet end.

William Shakespeare (*The Merry Wives of Windsor*, Act V, iii): Better a little chiding than a great deal of heartbreak.

William Shakespeare (*Othello*, Act II, scene i): For I am nothing, if not critical.

William Shakespeare (*Richard III*, Act III, scene v): The carping censures of the world.

George Bernard Shaw: A drama critic is a man who leaves no turn unstoned.

George Bernard Shaw: The power of accurate observation is commonly called cynicism by those who have not got it.

George Bernard Shaw: You don't expect me to know what to say about a play when I don't know who the author is, do you? ... If it's by a good author, it's a good play, naturally. That stands to reason.

Irwin Shaw: Critics in New York are made by their dislikes, not by their enthusiasms.

William Shenstone: Critics must excuse me if I compare them to certain animals called asses, who, by gnawing vines, originally taught the great advantage of pruning them.

Jean Sibelius: No statute has ever been put up to a critic.

William Gilmore Simms: Neither praise nor blame is the object of true criticism.—Justly to discriminate, firmly to establish, wisely to prescribe, and honestly to award—these are the true aims and duties of criticism.

Logan Pearsall Smith: Uncultivated minds are not full of wild flowers, like uncultivated fields. Villainous weeds grow in them, and they are full of toads.

Spanish Proverb: Do not rejoice at my grief, for when mine is old, yours will be new.

Sir Richard Steele: Of all mortals a critic is the silliest; for, inuring himself to examine all things, whether they are of consequence or not, he never looks upon anything but with a design of passing sentence upon it; by which means he is never a companion, but always a censor.

Lawrence Sterne: Of all the cants in this canting world, deliver me from the cant of criticism.

Jonathan Swift: Censure is the tax a man pays to the public for being eminent.

Talmud: Wheat needs grinding, and men need correction.

Mother Teresa: I think I'm more difficult than critical.

Mark Twain: I like criticism, but it must be my way.

Mark Twain: The trade of critic, in literature, music, and the drama, is the most degraded of all trades.

Mark Twain: It is easy to find fault, if one has that disposition. There was once a man who, not being able to find any other fault with his coal, complained that there were too many prehistoric toads in it.

Mark Twain: We can secure other people's approval, if we do right and try hard; but our own is worth a hundred of it, and no way has been found out of securing that.

Mark Twain: Each man is afraid of his neighbor's disapproval – a thing which, to the general run of the race, is more dreaded than wounds and death.

Kenneth Tynan: A critic is a man who knows the way but can't drive the car.

UA: When you hark to the voice of the Knocker, / As you listen to his hammer fall, / Remember the fact that the knocking act / Requires no brains at all.

John Updike: Critics are like pigs at the pastry cart.

Luc de Clapiers Vauvenargues (French philosopher, 1747): It is easy to criticize an author, but difficult to appreciate him.

Bill Veeck: The best remedy for a batting slump is two wads of cotton – one for each ear.

Bill Veeck: If U.S. Grant had been leading an army of baseball players (or critics), they'd have second guessed him all the way to the doorknob of the Appomattox Courthouse.

Voltaire: Really to stop criticism they say one must die.

Kurt Vonnegut: Any reviewer who expresses rage and loathing for a novel is preposterous. He or she is like a person who has put on full armor and attacked a hot fudge sundae.

Jane Wagner: I worry no matter how cynical you become, it's never enough to keep up.

John Wanamaker (American businessman): I learned thirty years ago that it is foolish to scold. I have enough trouble overcoming my own limitations without fretting over the fact that God has not seen fit to distribute evenly the gift of intelligence.

George Washington (referring to his critics): Hyperbolic prejudices conjured up by designing men to work their own purposes upon terrified imaginations.

J. McNeill Whistler: You should not say it is not good. You should say you do not like it; and then, you know, you're perfectly safe.

R.G. White: Criticism is the child and handmaiden of reflection.—It works by censure, and censure implies a standard.

Oscar Wilde: What is a cynic? A man who knows the price of everything and the value of nothing.

Oscar Wilde: When critics disagree, the artist is in accord with himself.

Sir Henry Wotton: Critics are like rushers of noble men's clothes.

J.B. Yeats: To criticise is to neither praise or denounce, but to *get nearer your subject.*

Yiddish Proverb: If you're out to beat a dog, you're sure to find a stick.
Yiddish Proverb: The girl who can't dance says the band can't play.
Zeuxis: Criticism comes easier than craftsmanship.

CURSE/CURSING (See PROFANITY)

CUSTOM (See CONSISTENCY)

CYNIC/CYNICISM (See CRITIC)

DAMAGES

Uncle Anthony: Y'know why pain and life's enjoyments (the non-economic or "human" losses of pain, suffering, embarrassment, depression, anxiety, fear, disability, impairment, and lost enjoyments of life) is worth more than your "out of pockets?" (the economic losses of medical bills, wages, earning capacity)? Because, when you go see a friend in the hospital y'don't ask 'em "how's yer specials or bills?" do ya? No, ya ask 'em "how do you feel?" and "how soon are you gonna be back doin' what you liked to do before?"
Uncle Anthony: Priceless don't mean worthless. Just 'cause ya can't find a price tag or a stock market quote for pain and suffering (or any intangible "non-economic" damages such as life's lost pleasures) don't mean their worthless.
Aunt Mary Carlo: Love, not time, heals all wounds.
Aesop: The injuries we do and those injuries we suffer are seldom weighed on the same scale.
Aesop: Injuries may be forgiven, but not forgotten.
Aristotle: It makes no difference whether a good man has defrauded a bad men or a bad men defrauded a good man, or whether a good or bad men has committed adultery: the law can look only to the amount of damage done.
Francis Bacon: Wounds cannot be cured without searching.
Francis Bacon: Injuries come from them that hath the upper hand.
Francis Bacon: He that injures one threatens an hundred.
Francis Beaumont: If men wound you with injuries, meet them with patience: hasty words rankle the wound, soft language dresses it, forgiveness cures it, and oblivion takes away the scar. It is more noble by silence to avoid an injury than by argument to overcome it.
Melvin Belli: (referring to the itemization of damages as) "The Grisly Audit."
Bernard of Clairvaux: Nothing can work me damage except myself. The harm that I sustain I carry about with me, and am never a real sufferer but by my own fault.
Bible: Exodus 21:23-25: And if any mischief follow, then thou shalt give life for life, / Eye for eye, tooth for tooth, hand for hand, foot for foot, / Burning for burning, wound for wound, stripe for stripe.
Bible: Exodus 22:7: If the thief be found, let him pay double.
Bible: Exodus 22:9: Whom the judges shall condemn, he shall pay double unto his neighbour.
Bible: Galatians 6:7: Whatsoever a man soweth, that shall he also reap.
Bible: Isaiah 59:18: According to their deeds, accordingly he will repay, fury to his adversaries, recompense to his enemies.
Bible: Leviticus 5:16: He shall make amends for the harm that he hath done.
Bible: Leviticus 6:4: He shall restore that which he took violently away.
Bible: Leviticus 24:18: He that killeth a beast shall make it good; beast for beast.
Ambrose Bierce: LOSS, n. Privation of that which we had, or had not....
Ambrose Bierce: RECONCILIATION, n. A suspension of hostilities. An armed truce for the purpose of digging up the dead.
Ambrose Bierce: REDRESS, n. Reparation without satisfaction. Among the Anglo-Saxons a subject conceiving himself wronged by the king was permitted, on proving his injury, to beat a brazen image of the royal offender with a switch that was afterward applied to his own naked back. The latter rite was performed by the public hangman, and it assured moderation in the plaintiff's choice of a switch.

Ambrose Bierce: REPARATION, n. Satisfaction that is made for a wrong and deducted from the satisfaction felt in committing it.

Ambrose Bierce: RESPOND, v.i. To make answer, or disclose otherwise a consciousness of having inspired an interest in what Herbert Spencer calls "external coexistences," as Satan "squat like a toad" at the ear of Eve, responded to the touch of the angel's spear. To respond in damages is to contribute to the maintenance of the plaintiff's attorney and, incidentally, to the gratification of the plaintiff.

Ambrose Bierce: RETRIBUTION, n. The founding or endowing of universities and public libraries by gift or bequest.

Lord Chesterfield: An injury is much sooner forgotten than an insult.

Sir Winston Churchill: Criticism may not be agreeable, but it is necessary. It fulfills the same function as pain in the human body. It calls attention to an unhealthy state of things.

Cicero: Injury may be done by two methods, by fraud or by force.

Cicero: It is better to receive than to do an injury.

Charles Caleb Colton: I will not be revenged, and this I owe to my enemy; but I will remember, and this I owe to myself.

Charles Horton Cooley: There is no mathematical law of compensation....Much depends upon your attitude, as confident or otherwise, and upon what energy you have to assimilate or transform the hurt.

Diogenes: No man is hurt but by himself.

Thomas Fuller: Forgetting of a wrong is a mild revenge.

Thomas Fuller: 'Tis better to suffer wrong and than to do it.

Thomas Fuller: Slight small injuries, and they will become none at all.

Kahlil Gibran: If the other person injures you, you may forget the injury; but if you injure him you will always remember.

Sir John Holt (Chief Justice, King's Bench, England, 1642-1710): It is a vain thing to imagine a right without a remedy, for want of right and want of remedy are reciprocal. Ashby v. White, 2 Ld. Raym. 938, 953 (1703)

Edgar Watson Howe: Everyone suffers wrongs for which there is no remedy.

Langston Hughes: Hold fast to dreams / For if dreams die / Life is a broken-winged bird / That cannot fly. / Hold fast to dreams / For when dreams go / Life is a barren field / Frozen with snow.

Italian Proverb: Who offends writes on sand, who is offended on marble.

Alice James: All loss is gain. Since I have become so near-sighted I see no dust or squalor, and therefore conceive of myself as living in splendor.

Thomas Jefferson (when considering damages): The hole and the patch should be commensurate. The patch should fit the hole.

Ben Jonson: He threatens many that hath injured one.

Sir William Rann Kennedy (English judge, 1846-1915): This is the classic quotation in "EGGSHELL" SKULL CASES; that is, the tortfeasor must take his victim as he finds him): If a man is negligently run over or otherwise negligently injured in his body, it is no answer to the sufferer's claim for damages that he would have suffered less injury, or no injury at all, if he had an unusually thin skull or an unusually weak heart. *Dulieu v. White & Sons*, 2 K.B. 669, 679 (1901)

Professor Tom Lambert: I have heard men beg for death, but never beg for more pain.

Stanislaw Lec: Wounds heal and become scars. But scars grow with us.

Max Lerner: To deaden yourself against any hurt is to deaden yourself also against the hurt of others.

Moe Levine (NYC trial lawyer): No one loses "just a leg." The "whole man (or woman)" are lost.

William Wadsworth Longfellow: "Of all sad words of tongue or pen, the saddest are these... 'It might have been.' "

Alan Medvin (referring to Langston Hughes' poem): Members of the jury, let your verdict restore (the Plaintiff) to flight. Let your verdict thaw the barren fields of his/her life and plant for him/her the seeds of new hopes and new dreams.

William McFee: There are some men whom a staggering emotional shock, so far from making them mental invalids for life, seems, on the other hand, to awaken, to galvanize, to arouse into an almost incredible activity of soul.

Marcus Aurelius: Reject your sense of injury and the injury itself disappears.

Cotton Mather: The injuries of life, if rightly improved, will be to us as the strokes of the statuary on his marble, forming us to a more beautiful shape, and making us fitter to adorn the heavenly temple.

Sir William Henry Maule (English judge, Common Pleas, 1788-1858): Nominal damages are a mere peg on which to hang costs. *Beaumont v. Greathead,* 2 C.B. 494 (1846)

Richard Miller: The "Emotional Skid Marks" of a trauma are often left on faces and foreheads.

Michael A. Musmanno (Justice of Pennsylvania Supreme Court, 1959): My judicial spectacles are not equipped with such microscopic and diagnostic lenses as will show me that $8,422 is so grossly excessive as to shock my conscience and that $6,422 is, by every rule of law, medicine and logic, just right. The swing of a knee hinge cannot be measured with such precise monetary calipers that one can say with mathematical certitude where the free arc ends which makes $8,422 shockable and $6,422 just right. (Logue v. Potts Manufacturing Co., 381 PA. 144).

Michael A. Musmanno (Justice, Sup. Ct. of Pennsylvania, 1959): Loss of the Ability to Play a Violin: Whether it be a singer, sculptor, painter, poet or actor, there is a personal joy in an artist's work which rises above and beyond that which he receives in legal tender for the objective productions emanating from the exercise of his talents. The enjoyment of music particularly falls into that domain of personal happiness, the distortion of which is a loss that cannot be ignored in law. The plaintiff was not a musician only because of the money put into his pocket. He derives pleasure from giving lessons on the violin to destitute children.... The defendant City of Pittsburgh is not to be exempted from responsibility for damages sustained by Nossokoff because he happens to be a generous man. No one, without legal liability, may deprive another of his inalienable right to donate his time or money gratuitously. When the City of Pittsburgh allowed a street condition to exist which so injured Nossokoff that he may no longer work artistic magic with his violin, it robbed him not only of the joy of playing but it deprive him also of the wealth of charitable donation to others. In doing so it became monetarily liable for the worth of that treasure now destroyed forever. If the law allows recovery, as it does for the happiness torn from athletes who, because of physical injury, may no longer perform at tennis courts, golf links, baseball diamonds, football fields and swimming pools, it certainly must take cognizance of the fact that the creation with one's hands or voice of that ineffable substance known as music constitutes a felicity of the highest order in the appraisement of all phenomena which bring contentment to man. And the destruction of that felicity is compensable. (Nossokoff v. Pittsburgh, 380 Pa. 422).

Michael A. Musmanno (Justice of Pennsylvania Supreme Court, 1959): Remittitur: The jury awarded plaintiff a verdict of $40,000 which the Majority of this Court has reduced to $30,000.... we have frequently said that a verdict is to be reduced only when it shocks our sense of Justice. I feel no shock.... the Majority Opinion calls into review cases of the past where reductions were made in verdicts, but this court should not prepare a Procrustean bed on which to place verdicts for lopping, so that they may fit artificial standards. Procrustes, of Greek legend, used also to stretch his victims if they were too short for his bed, but this Court never augments verdicts. (Kite V. Jones, 389 PA. 353).

Michael A. Musmanno (Justice of Pennsylvania Supreme Court, 1959): Brain Damage: Once the delicate membranes of the brain have been lacerated, one can no more be certain that they will heal and the scars vanish than that scratches on fine Venetian glass will disappear with the passage of time. (Kite v. Jones, 389 PA. 353).

Michael A. Musmanno (Justice of the Sup. Ct. of Pennsylvania, 1959): Loss of Consortium: Thus, down through the corridors of time, and particularly during the last century or two, the law has so developed that what at one time was regarded as incapable of legal evaluation, is now the accepted subject of monetary compensation. For instance, in the early stages of personal-injury law, no recovery was allowed for disfigurement because damage had to be predicated only on economic loss. Since a bricklayer, by way of illustration, could lay just as many bricks with a scar illuminating his cheek as one with an unblemished countenance, it was assumed that he suffered no ascertainable loss on account of his disfigurement. Courts, however, now recognize that a disfigured person carries a mental burden of humiliation which seriously affects his enjoyment of life, and the tortfeasor responsible for reducing that enjoyment is legally responsible to make compensation in money.... It is generally supposed that love, affection, and devotion are abstract terms which have no palpable reality and therefore cannot be translated into money. In the spiritual world this undoubtedly is true, but where a trespass action for a demonstrated wrongful act is involved, these terms, because of the inexorable law of necessity, must find practical transmutation. The music produced by a symphony orchestra and the fragrances which emanate from a flower garden also fall into the world of the incorporeal, but they are nonetheless very real and can be the subject of material compensation if they cease to exist because of the disruption of the means which bring them into existence. The mere presence of a mother who cooks and serves a meal adds an enjoyment which is something beyond what one tastes in the food prepared by a hired housekeeper, no matter how conscientious and able that housekeeper may be. The extinguishment of that enjoyment is something which goes into the accounting of the person who extinguished it. The affectionate greeting, the tender solace, the never-failing inspiration are all part of a wife's companionship and a mother's care, which disappear with the intervention of death, and there is no reason why the person responsible for the death should not be required to pay for those lost treasures, as much as he is required to pay the wages of the strange housekeeper, the employed seamstress, the new cook or the hired tutor. Who is to compute the financial counterpart of these cherished resources which have been laid in ruins? The answer is, the jury. Who is to appraise the hurt and the haunting emptiness of a home when the mother has permanently departed, even though all the curtains are in place and every piece of furniture is still in use? The answer is again, the jury, who, from the testimony, may visualize the decedent and re-create in their minds what she brought to the household which was dependant upon her. (dissenting opinon, Neuberg v. Bobowiez, 401Pa. 146).

Michael A. Musmanno (Justice of the Sup. Ct. of Pennsylvania, 1959): A Permanent Cripple: A permanent cripple is an object of constant pity and a subject for repeated discard. He awakens sympathy but not assistance; he arouses compassion but not employment. In the economic world he is the last one to be employed and the first one to be discharged. In the race of life for the awards of comfort, promotion and happiness, he always arrives last. In the words of John Davidson:

In anguish we uplift
A new on the unhallowed song;
The race is to the swift;
The battle to the strong.

The Majority has decided that $35,000 is an excessive verdict, but, after deduction for medical expenses it will be none too much as the plaintiff limps across the span of life left to him in the arduous years of this fast-moving 20th century which has little or no time for cripples. (Shields v. Larry Construction Co., 370 Pa. 582).

Friedrich Nietzsche: Is far pleasanter to injure and afterwards beg forgiveness than to be injured and grant forgiveness. He who does the former gives evidence of power and afterwards of kindness of character.

Jim M. Perdue (*Who Will Speak For The Victim? A Practical Treatise on Plaintiff's Jury Argument*, State Bar of Texas, 2002): With the gravely injured, the single word that hurts the most is *permanent*. All of us have been ill from time to time. Some of us have suffered serious injury. Most of us have labored through those illnesses, diseases, or injuries with the knowledge that one day we would recover. The word *permanent* breaks the soul. // A wise teacher once asked his students what was the saddest thing they had ever seen. One of his pupils answered that the saddest thing was a bird that could not fly. Another suggested a young deer that could not walk or run. Finally, after hearing all responses from his students, the teacher answered that the saddest thing in the world was a person without hope.

Jim M. Perdue (*Who Will Speak For The Victim? A Practical Treatise on Plaintiff's Jury Argument*, State Bar of Texas, 2002): What is life without pleasure? It is biological existence – nothing more and nothing less. It is as sad as a flower that will never bloom or a bird that will never fly. It is a simple recipe for torturing a soul. A Hemingway who could not write, a Remington who could not paint the West, a Ginger Rogers who could not dance, a Jesse Jackson who could not preach or speak, a Van Cliburn who could not play piano, a Mark Spitz who could not swim, an Amelia Earhart who could not fly. They would all exist, but would they truly live?

Jim M. Perdue (*Who Will Speak For The Victim? A Practical Treatise on Plaintiff's Jury Argument*, State Bar of Texas, 2002): The question of future damages is always troublesome to juries....// It is not the first few chapetrs that are so significant in Ms. Thomas' case. The defense reads those chapters and says to her, "You don't have anything to worry about." It is the chapters that are yet to be written that are so significant to her. According to the stattstics and the Good Book, she has thirty chapters left to be written. 10, 950 days or pages. It is the pain, the disability, the frustration, the worry, and the torture of those pages that you must concern yourselves about with your verdict.

M. R. Plumer (1842): The very definition of a good award is, that it gives dissatisfaction to both parties.

Will Rogers: We will never have true civilization until we have learned to recognize the rights of others.

Will Rogers: Last year we said, 'Things can't go on like this', and they didn't, they got worse.

Theodore Roosevelt: To submit tamely and meekly to theft or any other injury is to invite almost certain repetition of the offense.

Publilius Syrus: It is the mark of a good man not to know how to do an injury.

Seneca: It is more wretched to commit than to suffer an injury.

Seneca: Whom they have injured they also hate.

William Shakespeare (*All's Well That Ends Well*, Act I, i): Our remedies oft in ourselves do lie, / Which we ascribe to heaven.

William Shakespeare (*Antony and Cleopatra*, Act II, v): Thou shalt be whipp'd with wire, and stewed in brine, / Smarting in the ling'ring pickle.

William Shakespeare (*Hamlet*, Act IV, iii): Diseases desperate grown / By desperate appliances are relieved.

William Shakespeare (*I Henry VI*, Act IV, i): He hath done me wrong.

William Shakespeare (*Henry VIII*, Act IV, ii): Men's evil manners live in brass; their virtues / We write in water.

William Shakespeare (*King Lear*, Act II, iv): The injuries that they themselves procure / Must be their schoolmasters.

William Shakespeare (*King Lear*, Act III, i): His heart-struck injuries.

William Shakespeare (*Much Ado About Nothing*, Act V, ii): Some of us will smart for it.

William Shakespeare (*Timon of Athens*, Act I, i): "Tis not enough to help the feeble up, / But to support him after.

William Shakespeare (*Titus Andronicus*, Act V, iii): Wrongs, unspeakable, past patience, / Or more than any living man could bear.

Charles Simmons: The injuries we do, and those we suffer, are seldom weighed in the same balance.

Spanish Proverb: Since I wrong to you, I have never liked you.

Stuart M. Speiser (<u>Lawyers and the American Dream,</u> 1993): "... the states are far from uniform on pecuniary loss (in wrongful death cases). New York (EDITOR: and New Jesey), the leader in development of many other branches of law, is still mired in 19th-century wrongful death restrictions. It adheres strictly to the outmoded pecuniary loss rule, a position that lessens respect for the law in the eyes of jurors as well as claimants. How would you like to tell the parents of the teenager killed in an accident that according to New York (EDITOR: and New Jersey) law, their child's life is worthless, except to the extent that the jurors are allowed to guess at what the child might have contributed to the parents' support in later life? Because Lord Ellenborough severed wrongful death cases from the common law in 1808, Anglo-American wrongful death law is an outcast among civilized nations. Most other countries have adopted the *Code Napoleon* (derived from Roman law) as the cornerstone of civil law. Under the French construction of that code, followed in most other code nations, both "material" and "moral" damages must be paid in all tort cases that are that won by the claimants. No distinction is made between personal-injury cases and fatal accidents. Moral damages include grief and loss of society. While the amounts paid for moral damages in wrongful death cases are low by American standards, they are consistent with the foreign awards in personal-injury cases. Even at nominal levels, they reaffirm the dignity of life and create a sense of justice being done. This is missing from the American courts that are reduced to invoking fictional notions of young children supporting their parents.

Stuart M. Speiser (quoting the Texas Supreme Court, <u>Sanchez v. Schindler</u>, 651 S.W. 2d 249 (Tex. 1983): "The jurisdictions that do not limit recovery to pecuniary loss realize that damages for loss of companionship and society of a child are not too uncertain to be measured in pecuniary terms in an attempt to address the actual loss which a parent suppers. These elements of damage are not too speculative to be given the monetary value. Recovery is allowed in other tort areas for injuries which are equally intangible: e.g., pain and suffering. The fear of excessive verdict is not a sufficient justification for denying recovery for loss of companionship. The judicial system has adequate safeguards to prevent recovery of damages based on sympathy or prejudice rather than fair and just compensation for plaintiffs' injuries.

Stuart M. Speiser: Among the authorities cited by the Supreme Court. of Texas (Sanchez v. Schindler, supra.) was my book *Recovery for Wrongful Death*, as well as a 1976 article I had written for the *Tulane Law Review*. In the *Tulane* article, I had called attention to the ultimate absurdity in wrongful death law: New York, which would not permit a daughter to sue for the mental anguish caused by her mother's death, in a 1975 case allowed a daughter to sue for mental anguish caused by a telegram erroneously informing her that her mother had died in a state hospital. In other words, mental anguish damages could be awarded in New York because of a false report of death, but not for the actual killing of a human being! The sole reason for this mindless distinction was that the action for the false death report came under the common law, whereas the action for a real death had to be brought under the wrongful death statute that carries its own 19th-century pecuniary loss stricture.

Swedish Proverb: What breaks in a moment may take years to mend.

Tacitus: It belongs to human nature to hate those you have injured.

Mark Twain: The cross of the Legion of Honour has been conferred upon me. However, few escape that distinction.

DANGER (See RISK)

DEATH

American Proverb: if your time any come, not even a doctor can kill you.

Uncle Anthony: It's not Death, but dying that is terrible.

Uncle Anthony: The best way to get good press and lots of praise is to die

Uncle Anthony: I wish I said "I love you" one more time to my dad before he died.

Aunt Mary Carlo: When we left Riccia, Italy for the United States our liitle village had what the Irish people call an **"American Wake"** [EDITOR: The Irish, and I suppose many other nationalities held formal mournings for those who were emmigrating to America because they believed they would never see their townsfolk and loved ones again.

Aunt Mary Carlo: We each take 23,000 breaths take every day ... even our last day, and on our last day our last breaths gotta be our most precious.

Aunt Mary Carlo: You only really understand death when it comes and takes away someone you love.

Abd-El-Kader: Death is a black Camel, which kneels at the gates of hell.

Joseph Addison: The end of a man's life is often compared to the winding up of a well-written play, where the principal persons still act in character, whatever the fate is which they undergo.

Aeschylus: Pain lays not its touch / Upon a corpse.

Aeschylus: Death ever loves to pluck the fairest flower of an armed host.

African Proverb: Death does not recognize strength.

Agathias (c. 575): Death cometh but once to mortals, and no man ever saw it come twice.

Woody Allen: Death is an acquired trait.

Woody Allen: I do not believe in an afterlife, although I am bringing a change of underwear.

Woody Allen: It's not that I am afraid to die, I just don't want to be there when it happens.

Woody Allen: Death is one of the few things that can be done as easily lying down.

Woody Allen: Death is a wonderful way of cutting down on your expenses.

Anaxagoras: The descent to Hades is much the same from whatever place we start.

Jean Anouilh: Death has to be waiting at the end of the ride before you truly see the earth, and feel your heart, and love the world.

Aristophanes (422 B.C.): To die a dog's death. (This phrase had a worse significance to the Greeks than merely to die as a dumb brute; it refers to the dread of being left unburied after death).

Matthew Arnold: Truth sits upon the lips of dying men.

W.H. Auden (1907-1973)(The poem "Funeral Blues" expresses the grief of losing a lover): "Stop all the clocks, cut off the telephone, / Prevent the dog from barking with a juicy bone, / Silence the pianos and with muffled drum / Bring out the coffin, let the mourners come. // Let aeroplanes circle moaning overhead / Scribbling on the sky the message He is Dead, / Put crepe bows round the white necks of the public doves, / Let the traffic policemen wear black cotton gloves. // He was my North, my South, my East and West, / My working week and my Sunday rest, / My noon, my midnight, my talk, my song; / I thought that love would last forever: I was wrong. // The stars are not wanted now: put out everyone; / Pack away the moon and dismantle the sun; / Pour away the ocean and sweep up the wood. / For nothing now can ever come to any good.

Jane Austen: Only think of Mrs. Holder's being dead! Poor woman, she has done the only thing in the world she could possibly do to make one cease to abuse her.

Bacchylides (5th century B.C.): Hardest of deaths to a mortal / Is the death he sees ahead.

Bacchylides (468 B.C.): Death foreseen is the hatefullest death to man.

Francis Bacon: It is as natural to die as to be born; and to a little infant, perhaps, the one is as painful as the other.

Francis Bacon: Men fear death, as children fear to go in the dark; and as that natural fear in children is increased with tales, so is the other.

Henry Ward Beecher: It is a man dying with his harness on that angels love to escort upward.

Yogi Berra: Always go to other people's funerals, otherwise they won't come to yours.

Ugo Betti: Every tiny part of us cries out against the idea of dying, and hopes to live forever.

Bible: Acts 8:32; Isaiah 53:7; Jeremiah 11:19: He is brought as a lamb to the slaughter.

Bible: 1 Corinthians 15:26: The last enemy that shall be destroyed is death.

Bible: 1 Corinthians 15:55: O death, where is thy sting. O grave, where is thy victory.

Bible: Genesis 3:19: Dust thou art, and unto dust shalt thou return.

Bible: Genesis 15:8: Then Abraham gave up the ghost... and was gathered to his people.

Bible: Isaiah 22:13: Let us eat and drink; for tomorrow we shall die.

Bible: Isaiah 28:15: We have made a covenant with death.

Bible: Job, 7:10: He shall return no more to his house, neither shall his place know him anymore.

Bible: Job, 10:21: The land of darkness and the shadow of death.

Bible: Job, 18:14: The king of terrors.

Bible: John 5:24: Passed from death unto life.

Bible: John 19:30: It is finished.

Bible: Matthew, 5:4: Blessed are they that mourn: for they shall be comforted.

Bible: Matthew, 8:22; Luke, 9:60: Let the dead bury their dead.

Bible: Numbers 23:10: Let me die the death of the righteous, and let my last end be like his!

Bible: Proverbs 14:32: The righteous hath hope in his death.

Bible: Psalms 18:4: The sorrows of death compassed me.

Bible: Psalms, 23:4: Yea, though I walk through the valley of the shadow of death, I will fear no evil.

Bible: Psalms 82:6: I have said, Ye are gods; ... But ye shall die like men.

Bible: Revelation, 6:8: And I looked, and behold a pale horse: and his name that sat on him was Death, and Hell followed with him.

Bible: Romans 6:7: He that is dead is freed from sin.

Bible: Romans 7:24: Who shall deliver me from the body of this death?

Bible: 1 Samuel 14:14: We must needs die, and are as water spilt on the ground, which cannot be gathered up again.

Bible: 2 Samuel 3:31: Rend your clothes, and gird you with sackcloth, and mourn.

Bible: 1 Timothy 6:7: We brought nothing into this world, and it is certain we can carry nothing out.

Ambrose Bierce: Death is not the end; there remains the litigation.

Ambrose Bierce: CEMETARY, n. An isolated suburban spot where mourners match lies, poets write at a target and stone-cutters spell for a wager. ....

Ambrose Bierce: DEAD, adj. Done with the work of breathing; done / With all the world; the mad race run / Through to the end; the golden goal / Attained and found to be a hole!

Ambrose Bierce: EPITAPH, n. An inscription on a tomb, showing that virtues acquired by death have a retroactive effect.

Ambrose Bierce: FUNERAL, n. A pageant whereby we attest our respect for the dead by enriching the undertaker, and strengthen our grief by an expenditure that deepens our groans and doubles our tears.

Ambrose Bierce: GRAVE, n. A place in which the dead are laid to await the coming of the medical student.

Ambrose Bierce: HEARSE, n. Death's baby-carriage.

Ambrose Bierce: HOMICIDE, n. The slaying of one human being by another. There are four kinds of homicide: felonious, excusable, justifiable and praiseworthy, but it makes no great difference to the person slain whether he fell by one kind or another – the classification is for the advantage of the lawyers.

Ambrose Bierce: LONGEVITY, n. Uncommon extension of the fear of death.

Ambrose Bierce: MARTYR, n. One who moves along the line of least reluctance to a desired death.

Ambrose Bierce: MAUSOLEUM, n. The final and funniest folly of the rich.

Ambrose Bierce: REQUIEM, n. A mass for the dead which the minor poets assure us the winds sing o'er the graves of their favorites. Sometimes, by way of providing a varied entertainment, they sing a dirge.

Ambrose Bierce: R.I.P. A careless abbreviation of *requiescat in pace*, attesting an indolent goodwill to the dead. According to the learned Dr. Drigge, however, the letters originally meant nothing more than *reductus in pulvis.*

Ambrose Bierce: SAINT, n. A dead sinner revised and edited....

Ambrose Bierce: SARCOPHAGUS, n. Among the Greeks a coffin which being made of a certain kind of carnivorous stone, had the peculiar property of devouring the body placed in it. The sarcophagus known to modern obsequiographers is commonly a product of the carpenter's art.

William Blake (*Proverbs of Hell*, 1808): A dead body revenges not injuries.

John Bright (Speech Against the Crimean war, House of Commons, 1855): The Angel of Death has been abroad throughout the land: you may almost hear the beating of his wings

Robert Browning: You never know what life means till you die; / Even throughout life, 'tis death that makes life live, / Gives it whatever the significance.

William Cullen Bryant (1794-1878) (This poem entitled "Thanatopsis" - which means "View of Death" - was written when Bryant was 17 years old, and is a great poem of consolation and meditation on humankind's relationship with the rest of Nature and Death): "To him who, in the love of Nature, holds / Communion with her visible forms, she speaks / A various language: for his gayer hours / She has a voice of gladness, and a smile / And eloquence of beauty; and she glides / Into his darker musings, with a mild / And healing sympathy, that steals away / Their sharpness, ere he is aware. When thoughts / Of the bitter hour come like a blight / Over thy spirit, and sad images / Of the stern agony, and shroud, and pall, / And breathless darkness, and the narrow house / Make thee to shudder; and grow sick at heart, - .... So live that when thy summons comes to join / The innumerable caravan that moves / To that mysterious realm, where each shall take / His chamber in the silent halls of death, / Thou go not, like the quarry slave at night, / Scourged to his dungeon, but, sustained and soothed / By an unfaltering trust, approach thy grave / Like one who wraps the drapery oh his couch / About him, and lies down to pleasant dreams.'

Ken Burns (speaking about his latest PBS documentary, "The War," about how more than 1,000 WWII veterans and "The Greatest Generation" are dying every day and taking with them invaluable shards of history): When a man dies, it's like a library burning down.

Samuel Butler: To die completely, a person must not only forget but be forgotten, and he who is not forgotten is not dead.

William Camden: The end makes all equal.

Thomas Campbell: To live in hearts we leave behind Is not to die.

Albert Camus: It is death which gives gambling and heroism their true meaning.

Albert Camus: Men are convinced of your arguments, your sincerety, and the seriousness of your efforts only by your death.

Albert Camus: What is called a reason for living is also an excellent reason for dying.

Thomas Carlyle: The crash of the whole solar and stellar systems could only kill you once.

Johnny Carson: For three days after death, hair and fingernails continue to grow but phone calls taper off.

Cervantes: Death eats up all things, both the young lamb and old sheep.
Lord Chesterfield: All I desire for my own burial is not to be buried alive.
Chinese Proverb: Look upon death as a going home.
Chinese Proverb: Heaven lent you a soul; Earth will lend a grave.
Sir Winston Churchill: I am ready to meet my maker. Whether my maker is prepared for the great ordeal of meeting me is another matter.
Sir Winston Churchill: Although prepared for martyrdom, I prefer that it be postponed.
Sir Winston Churchill: Death came very easily to her. She had lived such an innocent and loving life of service to others and held such a simple faith, that she had no fears at all and did not seem to mind very much.
Sir Winston Churchill: Broadly speaking, human beings may be divided into 3 classes: those who are billed to death, those who are worried to death and those who are bored to death.
Sir Winston Churchill: Death and sorrow will be the companions of our journey; hardship our garment; constancy and valor our only shield.
Sir Winston Churchill: Never abandon life. There is a way out of everything except death.
Claudian (c. A.D. 395): Death levels all things.
Walter Colman: Death levels master and slave, the scepter and the spade.
Joseph Conrad: The dead can live only with the exact intensity and quality imparted to them by the living.
Randall Cotgrave: The dead haue no friends, the sicke but faint ones.
Danish Proverb: Death does not blow a trumpet.
English Proverb: Death always comes too early or too late
English Proverb: Death closes all doors.
English Proverb: Death pays all debts.
English Proverb: Gray hairs are death's blossoms.
Leonardo da Vinci: As a day well spent brings a blessed sleep, so a life well lived brings a blessed death.
Emily Dickinson (1830-1886) ("Because I Could Not Stop for Death"): Because I could not Stop for Death—/ He kindly stopped for me—/ The Carriage held but just Ourselves—/ And Immortality. // We slowly drove—He knew no haste / And I had put away / My labor and my leisure too, / For His Civility—// We passed the School, where Children strove / At Recess—in the Ring—/ We passed the Fields of Gazing Grain—/ We passed the Setting Sun – // Or rather—He passed Us—/ The Dews drew quivering and chill—/ For only Gossamer, my Gown—/ My Tippet – only Tulle—// We pause before a House that seemed / A Swelling of the Ground—/ The Roof was scarcely visible – / The Cornice—in the Ground—// Since then – 'tis Centuries—and yet / Feels shorter than the Day / I first surmised the Horses' Heads / Were toward Eternity.
Charles Dickens: Dead men never bring awkward stories to light.
John Donne: Any man's death diminishes me, because I am involved in mankind; and therefore never send to know for whom the bell tolls; it tolls for thee.
John Dryden: Dead men tell no tales.
John Dryden: Death in itself is nothing; but we fear / To be we know not what, we know not where.
Paul Lawrence Dunbar (1872-1906) (A descendent of slaves, Paul Laurence Dunbar published four novels and short stories and poetry, including this poem: "We Wear the Mask"): "We wear the mask that grins and lies, / It hides our cheeks and shades our eyes—/ This debt we pay to human guile; / With torn and bleeding hearts we smile, / And mouth with myriad subtleties. // Why should the world be otherwise, / In counting all our tears and sighs? / Nay, let them only see us, while / We wear the mask. // We smile, but, O great Christ, our cries / To thee from tortured souls arise. / We sing, but oh the clay is vile / Beneath our feet, and long the mile; / But let the world dream otherwise, / We wear the mask."
Leo Durocher: I don't want to achieve immortality by being inducted into baseball's Hall of Fame. I want to achieve immortality by not dying.
Tryon Edwards: This world is the land of the dying; the next is the land of the living.
Ebenezer Elliott (1831): The best die first.
T.S. Eliot: I have seen the eternal Footman hold my coat, and snicker.

Ralph Waldo Emerson: The event of death is always astounding; our philosophy never reaches, never possesses it; we are always at the beginning of our catechism; always the definition is yet to be made. What is death?

Ralph Waldo Emerson: Our fear of death is like our fear that summer will be short, but when we have had our swing of pleasure, our fill off fruit, and our swelter of heat, we say we have had our day.

English Proverb: Death always comes too early or too late.

English Proverb: Death closes all doors.

English Proverb: Death pays all debts.

English Proverb: Gray hairs are death's blossoms.

Epictetus: Let death be daily before your eyes, and you will never entertain any abject thought, nor too eagerly covet anything.

Epicurus: Death, the most dreaded of evils, is therefore of no concern to us; for while we exist death is not present, and when death is present we no longer exist.

Epicurus: It is possible to provide security against other ills, but as far as death is concerned, we men all live in a city without walls.

Erasmus: Death takes the best, and leaves the worst.

Euripides: Death is a debt we all must pay.

Euripides: Death is what men want when the anguish of living / is more than they can bear.

Euripides: It is better that we live ever so / Miserably than die in glory.

Euripides: To die with glory, if one has to die at all, / is still, I think, pain for the dier.

Euripides: What greater pain could mortals have been this: / To see their children dead before their eyes?

Euripides: What good can come from meeting death with tears?... If a man / Is sorry for himself, he doubles death.

Euphemisms (from Wikipedia: www.wikipedia.org):

The English language contains numerous euphemisms related to dying, death, burial, and the people and places which deal with death. The practice of using euphemisms for death likely originated with the "magical belief that to speak the word "death" was to invite death; where to "draw Death's attention" is the ultimate bad fortune—a common theory holds that death is a taboo subject in most English-speaking cultures for precisely this reason. It may be said that one is not dying, but *fading quickly* because *the end is near*. People who have died are referred to as having *passed away* or *passed* or *departed. Deceased* is a euphemism for "dead," and sometimes the *deceased* is said to have *gone to a better place*, but this is used primarily among the religious with a concept of Heaven. Christians often use phrases such as *gone to be with the Lord* or ***called to higher service*** (this latter expression being particularly prevalent in the Salvation Army) to express their belief that physical death is not the end.

There are many euphemisms for the dead body or corpse, some polite and some profane, as well as dysphemisms such as *worm food*, or *dead meat*. The corpse was once referred to as *the shroud (or house or tenement) of clay*, and modern funerary workers use terms such as ***the loved one*** (title of a novel about Hollywood undertakers by Evelyn Waugh) or *the dear departed*. (They themselves have given up the euphemism *funeral director* for ***grief therapist***, and hold ***arrangement conferences*** rather than *viewings* with the relatives of the deceased.) Among themselves, mortuary technicians often refer to the corpse as *"the client."* A recently dead person may be referred to as "the late John Doe." The terms *cemetery* for "graveyard" and *undertaking* for "burial" are so well-established in our culture that most people do not even recognize them as euphemisms. In fact, undertaking has taken on a negative connotation.

Contemporary euphemisms, dysphemisms, and cacophemisms for death tend to be quite colorful, and someone who has died is said to have *passed away*, *passed on*, *checked out*, *bit the big one*, *kicked the bucket*, *bitten the dust*, *popped their clogs*, *bought the farm*, *cashed in their chips*, *croaked*, ***given up the ghost*** (originally a more respectful term, cf. the death of Jesus as translated in the King James Version of the Bible Mark 15:37), *gone south*, ***shuffled off this mortal coil*** (from William Shakespeare's *Hamlet*), or *assumed room temperature*. When buried, they may be said to be *pushing up daisies* or *sleeping the big sleep* or *taking a dirt nap* or *six feet under*. There are hundreds of such expressions in use. (For example: Old Burma-Shave jingle: **"If daisies are your favorite flower, keep pushin' up those miles per hour!"**)

Henry Fielding (Eng1ish novelist, playwright, 1707-1754; 1751): It have often been said, that it is not death, but dying, which is terrible.

Benjamin Franklin: When death puts out the flame, the snuff will tell / If we are wax or tallow, by the smell.

Benjamin Franklin: Take Courage, Mortal; Death can't banish thee out of the Universe.

French Proverb: The dead are always wrong.

Eric Fromm: Death is never sweet, not even if it is suffered for the highest ideal.

Robert Frost (1874-1963): (Once considered a regional poet, who thematically focused on New England landscapes, Frost's work, especially this poem "Stopping by Woods on a Snowy Evening," reveals a transcendent sense of the human condition): "Whose woods are these I think I know. / His house is in the village though; / He will not see me stopping here / To watch his woods fill up with snow //.... The woods are lovely, dark and deep. / But I have promises to keep, / And miles to go before I sleep, / And miles to go before I sleep.

Thomas Fuller: No man should be afraid to die, who hath understood what it is to live.

Thomas Fuller: He is miserable, that dyeth not before he desires to die.

Thomas Fuller: He that dies half a year ago is as dead as Adam.

German Proverb: The absent are always wrong.

Jackie Gleason as Ralph Kramden (The Honeymooners): Well, Norton, I guess they'll be no bus rides for me. I've come to the end of the line. I'm going to that big bus depot in the sky. It's a one-way trip with no transfers.

Greek Proverb: Charon waits for all (referring to the Greek myth of Charon, the ferryman, who conveys the souls of the dead across the River Styx to Hades).

Joseph Hall: Death did not first strike Adam, the first sinful man, nor Cain, the first hypocrite, but Abel, the innocent and righteous.—The first soul that met death overcame death; the first soul parted from earth went to heaven. – Death argues not displeasure, because he whom God loved best dies first, and the murderer is punished with living.

Nathaniel Hawthorne: We sometimes congratulate ourselves at the moment of waking from a troubled dream; it may be so the moment after death.

John Hay: At my door the Pale Horse stands.

George Herbert: He pulls with a long rope, that waits for another's death.

Eric Hoffer: There is need for some kind of make-believe in order to face death unflinchingly. To our real, naked selves there is not a thing on earth or in heaven worth dying for.

Eric Hoffer: Death has but one terror, that it has no tomorrow.

Hal Holbrook: Death ends a life. But it doesn't end a relationship.

Oliver Wendell Holmes, Jr.: You may have heard before this of the death of my wife, which only takes away a half of my life but gives me notice. She was of the same age as I and at 88 the end is due. I may work on for a year or two, but I cannot hope to add much to what I have done. I am too sceptical to think that it matters much, but too conscious of the mystery of the universe to say that it or anything else does not. I bow my head, I think serenely, and say as I told someone the other day, O Cosmos – Now lettest thou thy ganglion dissolve in peace.

Oliver Wendell Holmes, Sr.: There are no graves that grow so green as the graves of children.... If no pang is sharper than parting with a beloved child, no recollection clears itself so naturally and perhaps I might say so early, of all but what is lovely to dwell upon.

Bob Hope: He was so crooked there when he died they screwed him into the ground.

Bob Hope: ON GOING TO HEAVEN: I've done benefits for ALL religions. I'd hate to blow the hereafter on a technicality.

Elbert Hubbard: Whom the gods love die young no matter how long they live.

Elbert Hubbard: Men do not live any longer than they wish to.

Elbert Hubbard: One thing you sure, there are just two respectable ways to die. One is of old age, and the other is by accident.

Irish Proverb: Both your friend and your enemy think you will never die.

Irish Proverb: There is hope from the sea, but none from the grave.

Italian Proverb: At the end of the game, the king and the pawn go back into the same box.

Italian Proverb: Our last garment is made without pockets.

General Thomas "Stonewall" Jackson (on his deathbed with pneumonia from "friendly fire" wounds suffered during the 1863 Battle of Chancellorsville, speaking to his surgeon): Doctor Maguire, my wife tells me I'm going to die today. Is that true? (Doctor Maguire said): Yes it is (Jackson replied): Good, Very good. I always wanted to die on a Sunday.

General Thomas "Stonewall" Jackson (his last words to his wife, as he died of pneumonia from "friendly fire" wounds suffered during the 1863 Battle of Chancellorsville): Let us cross over the river and rest under the shade of the trees.

Dr. Donald Jason (Forensic Pathologist): In traumatic events there is no "instantaneous death"—except for a violent trauma to the brain, especially to the back of the head, or a "hangman's fracture" (C1-C2 fracture).

Dr. Donald Jason: Often when there is a fatal accident, well-meaning emergency medical or police on the scene, tell the survivors and family of deceased victims that "he/she did not suffer" or "there was no pain." They may say this to spare the survivors from added grief and pain. They may even believe it to be true themselves. But, upon careful examination that is often, sadly, not true.

Thomas Jefferson: The dead have no rights. They are nothing; and nothing can not own something.

John Jensen: The trouble with life in the fast lane is that you get to the other end in an awful hurry.

Jewish Saying: It is better not to have had children than to bury them.

Jewish Saying: It is the Angel of Death who nurtures our synagogues, for if not for the *Kaddish* (prayer for the dead) how many men would attend them?

Richard Johnson: Death's pale flag advanced in his cheeks.

Samuel Johnson: Death, kind Nature's signal of retreat.

Samuel Johnson: when a man knows he is to be hanged in a fortnight, it concentrates his mind wonderfully.

George S. Kaufman and Moss Hart (1936 play and 1938 film): You Can't Take It With You.

Garrison Keillor: They say such nice things about people at their funerals that it makes me sad to realize that I'm going to miss mine by just a few days.

Kurdish Proverb: It is better to be a male for one day than a female for ten.

Charles Lamb: Men die but once, and the opportunity / Of a noble death is not an everyday fortune: / It is a gift which noble spirits pray for.

Ring Lardner (American short story writer, humorist, 1885-1933; in 1926): When you're dead, you stay a long time dead.

Latin Saying: *si post fata venit gloria non propero:* if glory comes after death, I'm not in a hurry (If one must die to be recognised, I can wait)

D.H. Lawrence: The dead don't die. They look on and help.

Leonardo da Vinci: Our life is made by the death of others.

Charles Lindbergh (before he died on Aug 26, 1973, in his book*"Autobiography of Values"*): After my death the molecules of my being will return to the earth; they came from the stars, I am of the stars.

Sir Oliver Lodge: Death is not a foe, but an inevitable adventure.

Henry Wadsworth Longfellow: Such was the wreck of the Hesperus, / In the midnight and the snow! / Christ save us from a death like this, / On the reef of a Norman's Woe!

Martin Luther (in 1522 after his trial, and hearing of threats to his life): The summons of death comes to us all, and no one can die for another. Everyone must fight his own battle with death by himself.

Thomas Mann: A man's dying is more the survivors affair than his own.

Marcus Aurelius: Death, like birth, is a secret of Nature.

Marcus Aurelius: The act of dying is also one of the acts of life.

Groucho Marx (1937 film *A Day at the Races*): Either he's dead, or my watch stopped.

Herman Melville: Even death may prove unreal at the last, and stoics be astounded into heaven.

Menage: A slight touch of apoplexy may be called a retaining the fee on the part of death.

Menander of Athens (291 B.C.): He whom the gods love, dies young.

Menander of Athens: Not death is dreadful, but a shameful death.

Michelangelo (Buonarroti): Death and love are the two wings that bear the good man to heaven.

Edna St. Vincent Millay: Heap not on this mound / Roses that she loved so well; / Why bewilder her with roses, / That she cannot see or smell?

Henry Milman: It matters not at what hour the righteous fall asleep.—Death cannot come untimely to him who is fit to die.—The less of this cold world the more of heaven, the briefer life, the earlier immortality.

John Milton: The grieslie terror.

John Milton: Death is the golden key that opens the palace of eternity.

Molière: Even Rome cannot grant us a dispensation from death.

Montaigne: Is not death, it is dying that alarms me.

Montaigne: She (Nature) have appointed but one entrance into life, but a hundred thousand ways out.

Montaigne: God is favorable to those whom he makes to die by degrees; 'tis the only benefit of old age. The last death will be so much the less painful: it will kill but a quarter of a man or but half a one at most.

Sir Thomas More (at the steps of the scaffold): I pray you, Master Lieutenant, see me safe up; and for my coming down let me shift for myself.

Sir Thomas More (to the executioner before placing his head on block): Stay friend, until I put aside my beard, for that never committed treason.

Mother Jones: Pray for the dead and fight like hell for the living!

Michael A. Musmanno (Justice of Pennsylvania Supreme Court, 1959): Presumption of Due Care to Avoid Death: There is a presumption in law that a person killed in an accident exercised due care to avoid being killed. This is a sensible rule because although it is inevitable that everyone must eventually turn in his bat and glove, no one actually wants to hasten the end of the ballgame.

Michael A. Musmanno (Justice of Pennsylvania Supreme Cour, 1959): Even if the jury would find that the blows inflicted by the first car had mortally wounded Sciandra, this finding would not absolve Swingle from responsibility for Sciandra's death if the blows negligently inflicted by Swingle accelerated Sciandra's death even by an hour, minutes or seconds. The burning candle of life is so precious a light in anyone's existence that no one has the right to extinguish it before it flickers out into perpetual darkness and oblivion.

Michael A. Musmanno (Justice of Pennsylvania Supreme Court, 1959): A Married Woman's Worth: The decedent Mrs. Spangler, who, at the time of her death, had a life expectancy of 32.59 years, was survived by her husband and three children, aged respectively 14 years, 13 years, and five months. The only question on this appeal must be stated in terms which might seem materialistic, namely: what did Mrs. Spangler mean to these people in terms of money? Naturally, no husband and no children see in the person dearest to them a money equivalent, and, during life, such an evaluation would be unqualifiedly brutal and offensive. However, with death, problems arise which must be solved, harsh and heartrending as they may be. Thus, as Mr. Spangler and his children now face a future with the main pillar of their family structure missing, the question inescapably follows: how much do they need to supplant that pillar? To begin with, there was very definite physical work performed by Mrs. Spangler, for which no sums were drawn from the family budget. Money is now needed to pay for those services. Mrs. Spangler did the household work; she washed, ironed, cooked, and sewed. She did all the housecleaning, made some of the children's clothing, helped her husband paint the house, she put together draperies and rugs. All these services can be translated into pecuniary values because one can presumably go into the labor market and find a housekeeper to perform those labors. But the amount paid to such a housekeeper would not compensate for Mrs. Spangler's displacement. There are services which no housekeeper can supply. The evidence reveals that Mrs. Spangler was unstintingly devoted to her family. The record shows that her loyalty was expressed in an incessant activity, tireless energy and never-flagging concern. She took the children to church regularly, she added to their religious instructions, she prayed with them and she accompanied them to baseball games and on fishing trips. All these things—such as companionship, comfort, society, guidance, solace and protection which go into the vase of family happiness—are the things for which a wrongdoer must pay when he shatters the vase. (*Spangler v. Helm's,* 396 Pa. 482).

Anais Nin: I postpone death by living, by suffering, by error, by risking, by giving, by losing.

Friedrich Nietzsche: One should part from life as Odysseus parted from Nausicca—blessing it rather than in love with it.

Friedrich Nietzsche: One should died proudly when it is no longer possible to live proudly.

William of Orange: I will die in the last ditch.

Dorothy Parker: It costs me never a stab or squirm / To tread by chance upon a worm. / "Aha, my little dear," I say, / "Your clan and will pay me back one day."

Jim M. Perdue (*Who Will Speak For The Victim? A Practical Treatise on Plaintiff's Jury Argument*, State Bar of Texas, 2002): It is said that God laughs every time he makes a boy. The Greek philosopher Plato noted that "[o]f all the animals, the boy is the most unmanageable." Boys are found everywhere but seldom standing still. They may be climbing a tree, digging a hole, crawling under a bush, or building something that they haven't quite figured out yet what it will be when it is finished. A boy is truth with freckles on his face, beauty with a frog in his pocket, the wonders of a mind that can master the multiplication tables, and the hope of the future with a poster in his room that says, "He who dies with the most toys wins!" To a father, being with a son is like being subjected to an inquisition. "Why does it work?" "Why is the sky blue?" .... To mothers, boys can sometimes be an aggravation. They can clutter up a room faster than three adults can clean it. But simply ask any mother about her son and watch the pride appear on her face as she reaches into her purse for those photographs that she loves so much to share with other people.... The argument tthat the victim was less than perfect and that, therefore, damages ought to be less is specious on its face. There are no perfect boys.

Jim M. Perdue (*Who Will Speak For The Victim? A Practical Treatise on Plaintiff's Jury Argument*, State Bar of Texas, 2002): Death of a Son: ... When someone suggests that the passage of time will somehow quiet these parents' hurt, I cannot help but be reminded of a poem about the loss of a son. It goes like this: I shall see his toys and his empty chair. / And the horse he used to ride, / And they will speak with a silent speech / Of the little boy that died."

Jim M. Perdue (*Who Will Speak For The Victim? A Practical Treatise on Plaintiff's Jury Argument*, State Bar of Texas, 2002): Death of a Daughter: .... When I contemplate this type of tragedy, I cannot help but recall the words of one of America's most beloved poets, Edgar A. Guest: "Little girl, just half-past three, / Thius is what you mean to me, / More than all that money buys, / More than any selfish prize, / More than fortune, more than fame, / And I learned this when you came. / Other fathers know it, too. / Nothing matters more than you."

Jim M. Perdue (*Who Will Speak For The Victim? A Practical Treatise on Plaintiff's Jury Argument*, State Bar of Texas, 2002): Death of a Husband: .... The phrase "building a life together" may be hackneyed and worn, but it applies so well to these people. Where is this lady to find her happiness? She will be alone. Yes, she will take pride and satisfaction in her children, their families, and their accomplishments. But, in contemplating what the future holds for this lady, I could not help but feel it appropriate to share with you a short portion of a poem by Edgar A. Guest: "Thery're all away / And the house is still, / And the dust lies thick / On the window sill, / And the stairway creaks / In a solemn tone / This taunting phrase: / 'You are all alone.'"

Jim M. Perdue (*Who Will Speak For The Victim? A Practical Treatise on Plaintiff's Jury Argument*, State Bar of Texas, 2002): Death of a Wife: .... A good wife and good health are a man's best wealth. Of all the home remedies, a good wife is the best. // We should think about these things as we ponder the value of the life that has been lost. Do you think this man misses his wife most when he finds himself making supper for the family or when he finds himself lying silently in bed – alone – at night.... Or maybe – just maybe – he misses her most when he comes in from work every day and stands for a moment in the living room of their little house waiting to hear those familiar words, "Welcome home, darling, how did your day go?"

Jim M. Perdue (*Who Will Speak For The Victim? A Practical Treatise on Plaintiff's Jury Argument*, State Bar of Texas, 2002): Death of a Father: .... How much does the loss of a father mean to a young child, adolescent, or young person? Simply ask someone of middle age who enjoyed the full lifetime of a father's fraternity, companionship, and love. Such a man (Edgar.A. Guest) wrote the following poem (*Father*): Used to wonder just why father / Never had much time for play, / Used to wonder why he'd rather / Work each minute of the day. / Used to wonder why he never / Loafed along the road an' shirked; / Can't recall a time whenever / Father played while others worked. / Father didn't dress in fashion, / Sort of hated clothing new; / Style with him was not a passion; / He had other things in view. / Boys are blind to much that's going / On about 'em day by day, / And I had no way of knowing / What became of father's pay. // All I knew was when I needed / Shoes I got 'em on the spot; / Everything for which I pleaded, / Somehow, father always got. / Wondered, season after season, / Why he never took a rest, / And that I might be the reason / Then I never even guessed.

Jim M. Perdue (*Who Will Speak For The Victim? A Practical Treatise on Plaintiff's Jury Argument*, State Bar of Texas, 2002): Death of a Mother: .... While many poems have been written about the loss one feels on the death of a mother, perhaps the one most appropriate to these fine children, who must now await your verdict, is this by Edgar A. Guest: "Never a sigh for the cares that she bore for me, / Never a thought of the joys that flew by; / Her one regret that she couldn't do more for me, / Thoughtless and selfish, her Master was I. // Oh, the long nights that she came at my call to me! / Oh, the soft touch of her hands on my brow! / Oh, the long years that she gave up her all to me! / Oh, how I yearn for her gentleness now! // Slave to her baby! Yes, that was the way of her, / Counting her greatest of services small; / Words cannot tell what this old heart would say of her, / Mother – the sweetest and fairest of all."

Persian Proverb: Death is a camel that lies down at every door.

Plato (c. 375 B.C.): Death is the separation of the soul from the body.

Paula Poundstone: The wages of sin are death, but by the time taxes are taken out, it's just sort of a tired feeling.

Rabelais: Last Will and Testament: I owe much, I have nothing, the rest I leave to the poor.

Saint-Exupery: Man imagines that it is death he fears; but what he fears is the unforeseen, the explosion. What man fears is himself, not death.

Sir Walter Raleigh: On death and judgment, heaven and hell, who oft doth think, must needs die well.

Jean Paul Richter: The darkness of death is like the evening twilight; it makes all objects appear more lovely to the dying.

Will Rogers: This thing of being a hero, about the main thing to do is to know when to die. Prolonged life has ruined more men than it ever made.

Will Rogers: Being a hero is about the shortest-lived profession on earth.

Will Rogers: If the world comes to an end, I want to be in Cincinnati. Everything comes there ten years later.

Will Rogers: The only way you can beat the lawyers is to die with nothing.

Will Rogers: Lord, let me live until I die.

Will Rogers: If you live right, death is a joke to you as far as fear is concerned.

Will Rogers: If there are no dogs in Heaven, then when I die I want to go where they went.

Will Rogers: It looks like the only way you can get any publicity on your death is to be killed in a plane. It's no novelty to be killed in an auto anymore.

Will Rogers: I don't see why a man shouldn't pay an inheritance tax. If a Country is good enough to pay taxes to while you are living, it's good enough to pay in after you die. By the time you die you should be so used to paying taxes that it would just be almost second nature to you.

Andy Rooney: Death is just a distant rumor to the young.

Russian Proverb: Death carries a fat tsar on his shoulders as easily as a lean beggar.

Russian Proverb: When you live next to the cemetery you cannot weep for everyone.

Babe Ruth (to Connie Mack the day before Babe died of cancer): The termites have got me.

Carl Sandburg: Death is stronger than all the governments because the governments are men and men die and then death laughs: now you see 'em, now you don't.

George Santayana: The dark background which death supplies brings out the tender colors of life in all their purity.

Jean-Paul Sartre: One always dies too soon – or too late. And yet one's whole life is complete at that moment, with a line drawn neatly under it, ready for the summing up.

Walter Scott: Is death the last sleep? No, it is the last and final awakening.

Seneca: Death takes us piecemeal, not at a gulp.

Seneca (c. A.D. 60): Death is sometimes a punishment, often a gift; to many it has been a favor.

William Shakespeare (*Coriolanus*, Act V, vi): Bea from hence his body, / And mourn you for him: let him be regarded / As the most noble corse that ever herald / Did follow to his urn.

William Shakespeare (*Cymbeline*, Act V, v): Golden lads and girls all must, / As chimney-sweepers, come to dust.

William Shakespeare (*Cymbeline*, Act V, v): By medicine life may be prolonged, yet death / Will seize the doctor too.

William Shakespeare (*Hamlet*, Act I, ii): All that live must die, / Passing through nature to eternity.

William Shakespeare (*Hamlet*, Act I, ii): He was a man, take him for all in all, / I shall not look upon his like again.

William Shakespeare (*Hamlet*, Act I, v): Cut off even in the blossoms of my sin, / Unhous'd, disappointed, unanel'd; / No reckoning made, but sent to my account / With all my imperfections on my head.

William Shakespeare (*Hamlet*, Act II, ii): After your death you were better have a bad epitaph, than their ill report while you lived.

William Shakespeare (*Hamlet*, Act III, i): When we have shuffled off this mortal coil.

William Shakespeare (*Hamlet*, Act III, i): In that sleep of death what dreams may come.

William Shakespeare (*Hamlet*, Act III, i): To die, - to sleep; / No more; and by a sleep to say we end / The heart-ache and the thousand natural shocks / That flesh is heir to, 'tis a consummation / Devoutly to be wish'd. To die, to sleep; / To sleep: perchance to dream: ay, there's the rub; / For in that sleep of death what dreams may come / When we have shuffled off this mortal coil, / Must give us pause: there's the respect / That makes calamity of so long life.

William Shakespeare (*Hamlet*, Act IV, iii): A man may fish with the worm that hath eat of a king, and eat of the fish that hath fed of that worm.

William Shakespeare (*Hamlet*, Act IV, v): They bore him barefac'd on the bier; / .... / And on his grave rains many a tear.

William Shakespeare (*Hamlet*, Act V, i): We shall profane the service of the dead, / To sing sage requiem, and such rest to her, / As to peace-parted souls.

William Shakespeare (*Hamlet*, Act V, i): To what base uses we may return, Horatio! / Why may not imagination trace the noble dust of Alexander, till we find it stopping a bung-hole?

William Shakespeare (*Hamlet*, Act V, i): Lay her i' the earth; / And from her fair and unpolluted flesh, / May violets spring!

William Shakespeare (*Hamlet*, Act V, ii): O proud death! / What feast is toward in thine eternal cell, / That thou so many princes, at a shoot, / So bloodily hast struck?

William Shakespeare (*Hamlet*, Act V, ii): This fell sergeant, Death, / Is strict in his arrest.

William Shakespeare (*Hamlet*, Act V, ii): Death, / The undiscover'd country, from whose bourne / No traveller returns.

William Shakespeare (*I Henry IV*, Act V, ii): And we shall feed like oxen at a stall, / The better cherish'd still the nearer death.

William Shakespeare (*II Henry IV*, Act III, ii): A man can die but once; we owe God a death.

William Shakespeare (*II Henry IV*, Act III, ii): Certain, 'tis certain; very sure, very sure: death, as the Psalmist saith, is certain to all; all shall die.

William Shakespeare (*II Henry IV*, Act III, ii): He that dies this year is quit for the next.

William Shakespeare (*II Henry IV*, Act III, ii): A man can die but once: we owe God a death.

William Shakespeare (*II Henry IV*, Act V, iii): FALSTAFF: What, is the old King dead? PISTOL: As nail in door.

William Shakespeare (*Henry V*, Act I, ii): Either our history shall, with full mouth / Speak freely of our acts, or else our grave, / Like Turkish mute, shall have a tongueless mouth, / Not worshipp'd with a waxen epitaph.

William Shakespeare (*Henry V*, Act II, iii): As cold as any stone.

William Shakespeare (*Henry V*, Act II, iii): 'A made a finer end and went away, an it had been any christom child; 'a parted even just between twelve and one, e'en at the turning o' th' tide: for after I saw him fumble with the sheets, and play with the flowers, and smile upon his fingers' ends, I knew there was but one way; for his nose was as sharp as a pen, and 'a babbled of green fields. How now, sir John? Quoth I: what, man! Be of good cheer, So 'a cried out – God, God, God! Three or four times; now I, to comfort him, bid him 'a should not think of God; I hoped there was no need to trouble himself with any such thoughts yet.

William Shakespeare (*II Henry VI*, Act III, iii): He dies, and makes no sign.

William Shakespeare (*II Henry VI*, Act IV, x): As dead as doornail.

William Shakespeare (*III Henry VI*, Act II, vi): Here burns my candle out; ay, here it dies, / Which, whiles it lasted, gave King Henry light.

William Shakespeare (*III Henry VI*, Act V, ii): Why, what is pomp, rule, reign, but earth and dust? / And, live we how we can, yet die we must.

William Shakespeare (*III Henry VI*, Act V, ii): My sick heart shows, / That I must yield my body to the earth, / And, by my fall, the conquest to my foe. / Thus yields the cedar to the axe's edge, / Whose arms gave shelter to the princely eagle; / Under whose shade the ramping lion slept; / Whose top-branch overpeer'd Jove's spreading tree, / And kept low shrubs from winter's powerful wind.

William Shakespeare (*Henry VIII*, Act I, iii): Death! My lord / Their clothes are after such a pagan cut too.

William Shakespeare (*Henry VII*, Act IV, ii): He gave his honours to the world again, / His blessed part to Heaven, and slept in peace.

William Shakespeare (*Julius Caesar*, Act II, ii): Cowards die many times before their deaths.

William Shakespeare (*Julius Caesar*, Act II, ii): It seems to me most strange that men should fear; / Seeing that death, a necessary end, / Will come when it will come.

William Shakespeare (*Julius Caesar*, Act II, ii): When beggars die, there are no comets seen; / The heavens themselves blaze forth the death of princes.

William Shakespeare (*Julius Caesar*, Act III, i): That we shall die we know; 'tis but the time / The drawing days out, that men stand upon.

William Shakespeare (*Julius Caesar*, Act III, i): That we shall die we know; 'tis but the time, / And drawing days out, that men stand upon.

William Shakespeare (*Julius Caesar*, Act III, i): He that cuts off twenty years of life / Cuts off so many years of fearing death.

William Shakespeare (*Julius Caesar*, Act IV, iii): We must die, Messala: / With meditating that she must die once, / I have the patience to endure it now.

William Shakespeare (*King John*, Act III, iv): Death, death! Oh, amiable, lovely death, ... / Come grin on me, and I will think thou smil'st.

William Shakespeare (*King John*, Act IV, ii): We cannot hold mortalitie's stong hand.

William Shakespeare (*King Lear*, Act V, ii): Men must endure / They're going hence, even as their coming hither.

William Shakespeare (*King lear*, Act V, iii): O, our lives' sweetness! / That we the pain of death would hourly die, / Rather than die at once!

William Shakespeare (*King John*, Act V, iv): Have I not hideous death within my view, / Retaining but a quantity of life / Which bleeds away, even as a form of wax / Resolveth from its figure 'gainst the fire?

William Shakespeare (*Macbeth*, Act I, iv): Nothing in his life / Became him like the leaving it; he died / As one that had been studied in his death / To throw away the dearest thing he owed, / As 't were a careless trifle.

William Shakespeare (*Macbeth*, Act II, i): It is a knell / That summons thee to heaven or to hell.

William Shakespeare (*Macbeth*, Act III, ii): After life's fitful fever, he sleeps well; / Treason has done his worst: nor steel, nor poison, / Malice domestic, foreign levy, nothing, / Can touch him further.

William Shakespeare (*Macbeth*, Act III, iv): Safe in a ditch he bides, / With twenty trenched gashes on his head; / The least a death to nature.

William Shakespeare (*Macbeth*, Act V, v): At least we'll die with harness on our back.

William Shakespeare (*Macbeth*, Act V, viii): Your son, my lord, has paid a soldier's debt.

William Shakespeare (*Measure for Measure*, Act III, i): Dar'st thou die? The sense of death is most in apprehension, / And the poor beetle that we tread upon, / In corporal sufferance finds a pang as great / As when a giant dies.

William Shakespeare (*Measure for Measure*, Act III, i): The weariest and most loathed worldly life / That age, ache, penury, and imprisonment / Can lay on nature is a paradise / To what we fear of death.

William Shakespeare (*Measure for Measure*, Act III, i): The weariest and most loathed worldly life, / That age, ache, penury, and imprisonment / Can lay on nature, is a paradisre / To what we fear of death.

William Shakespeare (*Measure for Measure*, Act III, i): If I must die, / I will encounter darkness as a bride, / And hug it in mine arms.

William Shakespeare (*Measure for Measure,* Act III, i): To be imprison'd in the viewless winds, / And blown with restless volence round about / The pendant world; or to be worse than worst / Of those, that lawless and incertain thoughts / Imagine howlings! – 'tis too terrible!

William Shakespeare (*Measure for Measure*, Act III, ii): What's yet in this, / That bears the name of life? Yet in this life / Lie hid more thouseand deaths: yet death we fear, / That makes these odds all even.

William Shakespeare (*The Merchant of Venice*, Act II, vii): Gilded tombs do worms infold.

William Shakespeare (*Othello,* Act V, ii): Here is my journey's end, here is my butt, / And very sea-mark of my utmost sail.

William Shakespeare (*Pericles*, Act V, ii): Now our sands are almost run.

William Shakespeare (*Richard II*, Act II, i): The tongues of dying men / Enforce attention like deep harmony.

William Shakespeare (*Richard II*, Act II, i): The ripest fruit first falls, and so doth he; / His time is spent.

William Shakespeare (*Richard II*, Act III, ii): Let's choose executors, and talk of wills: / And yet not so, - for what can we bequeath, / Save our deposed bodies to the ground?

William Shakespeare (*Richard II*, Act III, ii): Nothing can we call our own but death; / And that small model of the barren earth, / Which serves as paste and cover to our bones.

William Shakespeare (*Richard II*, Act III, ii): Within the hollow crown, / That rounds the mortal temples of a king, / Keeps death his court; and there the antic sits, / Scoffing his state, and grinning at his pomp.

William Shakespeare (*Richard II*, Act IV, i): And there, at Venice, gave / His body to that pleasant country's earth, / And his pure soul unto his captain Christ, / Under whose colours he had fought so long.

William Shakespeare (*Richard II,* Act V, v): Go thou, and fill another room in hell. / That hand shall burn in never-quenching fire, / That staggers thus my person. – Exton, thy fierce hand / Hath, with thy king's blood, stain'd the king's own land. / Mount, mount my soul! Thy seat is up on high; / Whilst my gross flesh sinks downward, here to die.

William Shakespeare (*Richard III,* Act I, iv): I pass'd, methought, the melancholy flood / With that sour ferryman which poets write of, / Unto the kingdom of perpetual night.

William Shakespeare (*Richard III*, Act III, ii): 'Tis a vile thing to die, my gracious lord, / When men are unprepared and look not for it.

William Shakespeare (*Richard III*, Act III, ii): Woe, destruction, ruin, loss, decay; / The worst is – death, and death will have his day.

William Shakespeare (*Romeo and Juliet*, Act III, iii): Taking the measure of an unmade grave.

William Shakespeare (*Romeo and Juliet*, Act IV, v): Death lies on her like an untimely frost / Upon the seetest flower of all the field.

William Shakespeare (*Romeo and Juliet*, Act V, iii): Death, that hath suck'd the honey of thy breath, / Hath had no power yet upon thy beauty: Thou art not conquer'd; beauty's ensign yet / Is crimson in thy lips, and in thy cheeks, / And death's pale flag is not advanced.

William Shakespeare (*Romeo and Juliet*, Act V, iii): Eyes, look your last! / Arms, take your last embrace! And lips, O you, / The doors of braeth, seal with a rightreous kiss /

William Shakespeare (*Romeo and Juliet*, Act V, iii): How oft, when man are at a point of death, / Have they been merry! which their keepers call / A lightning before death.

William Shakespeare (*The Tempest*, Act I, i): The wills above be done! But I wouldfain die a dry death.

William Shakespeare (*The Tempest*, Act III, ii): He that dies pays all debts.

William Shakespeare (*The Tempest,* Act IV, i): We are such stuff / As dreams are made on, and our little life / Is rounded with a sleep.

William Shakespeare (*Twelfth Night*, Act III, iv): Snatched... out of the jaws of death.

William Shakespeare (*Venus and Adonis*, St. 170): For he being dead, with him is beauty slain, / And, beauty dead, black chaos comes again.

George Bernard Shaw: Life levels all men: death reveals the eminent.

George Bernard Shaw: Death is for many of us the gate of hell; but we are inside on the way out, not outside on the way in.

George Bernard Shaw: Life does not cease to be funny when people die any more than it ceases to be serious when people laugh.

John A. Shedd: Yes, all men are dust, but some are gold-dust.

Brooke Shields (Actress, in an interview to become spokesperson for federal anti- smoking campaign): Smoking kills. If you're killed, you've lost a very important part of your life.

Simonides (c. 475 B.C.): Though they died, they are not dead, for their valor brings them back in glory from the world below.

Red Smith (Nov. 30, 1974 at age 69 former Heavyweight Champion, James J. Braddock aka "The Cinderella Man" died): If death came easily (to James Braddock in his sleep), it was the only thing in his life that did.

Socrates (Greek philosopher, 469-399 BC): Be of good cheer about death, and know this of a truth, that no evil can happen to a good man, either in life or after death.

Socrates: Nobody knows, in fact, what death is, nor whether to man it is not perchance the greatest of all blessings; yet people fear it as if they surely knew it to be the worst of evils

Sophocles: Even the bold will fly when they see Death / drawing in close enough to end their life.

South Carolina (Department of Social Services, Greenville, South Carolina notice to food stamp recipient): Your food stamps will be stopped effective March 1992 because we received notice that you passed away. May God bless you. You may reapply if there is a change in your circumstances.

Spanish Proverb: A dog that's dead will never bite.

Joseph Stalin: A single death is a tragedy, one million deaths is a statistic.

Secretary of War Edwin Stanton (Saturday, April 15, 1865 at 0722 AM, in the rooming house across 10th Street from Ford's Theater, Washington, DC, when Abraham Lincoln died of the fatal gunshot wound): Now he belongs to the ages.

Harriet Beecher Stowe: The bitterest tears shed over graves are for words left unsaid and deeds left undone.

Bishop William Stubbs (1875): Like most medieval workers they all died in harness.

Jonathan Swift: It is impossible that anything so natural, so necessary, and so universal as death, should ever have been designed by Providence as an evil to mankind.

Publilius Syrus: To know the hour of doom is continual death.

Publilius Syrus: A man dies as often as he loses his loved ones.

Publilius Syrus: Lucky to die before you implore death to come.

Publilius Syrus: Nobody dies prematurely who dies in misery.

Publilius Syrus: How wretched to long for death yet fail to die.

Tacitus: An honorable death is better than a dishonorable life.

Rabindranath Tagore: Death's stamp gives value to the coin of life; making it possible to buy with life what is truly precious.

Babylonian Talmud: *Baba Bathra*, (c. 450): No man deceives while in his death agony.

Talmud: The death of a woman is felt by no one so keenly as by her husband.

Alfred Lord Tennyson: Let us have a quiet hour,/Let us hob-and-nob with Death.

Alfred Lord Tennyson: Deaths truer name / Is "Onward," no discordance in the roll / And march of that Eternal Harmony / Whereto the world beats time.

Alfred Lord Tennyson (*The Charge of the Light Brigade*, 1854): Into the jaws of death Rode the six hundred.

Alfred Lord Tennyson: Every minute dies a man, every minute one is born.

Theodotus: Dead men bite not.

Dylan Thomas (1914-1953) (Poem "Do Not Go Gentle into that Good Night," dedicated to Dylan Thomas's father, terminally ill at the time): Do not go gentle into that good night, / Old age should burn and rave at close of day; / Rage, rage against the dying of the light. // Though wise men at their end know dark is right, / Because their words had forked no lightning they / Do not go gentle into that good night. // Good men, the last wave by, crying how bright / Their frail deeds might have danced in a green bay, / Rage, rage against the dying light. // Wild men who caught in saying the sun in flight, / And learn, too late, they grieved it on its way, / Do not go gentle into that good night. // Grave men, near death, who see with blinding sight / Blind eyes could blaze like meteors and be gay, / Rage, rage against the dying of the light. // And you, my father, there on the sad height, space/ Curse, bless, me now with your fierce tears, I pray. / Do not go gentle into that good night. / Rage, rage against the dying of the light.

Paul Tillich: In the depth of the anxiety of having to die is the anxiety of being eternally forgotten.

R.C. Trench (1853): Death is a black camel, which kneels at every man's gate.

Ivan Turgenev: Death is like a fisherman who catches fish in his net and leaves them for a while in the water; the fish is still swimming but the net is around him, and the fisherman will draw him up—when he thinks fit.

Mark Twain: Each person is born to one possession which outvalues all the others—his last breath.

Mark Twain: Let us endeavour so to live that when we come to die even the undertaker will be sorry.

Mark Twain: Why is it that we rejoice at birth and grieve at a funeral? It is because we are not the person involved.

Mark Twain: Pity is for the living, and envy is for the dead.

Mark Twain: Oh Death where it is by staying! It has none. But life has.

Mark Twain: Alexander the Great, seeing Diogenes looking attentively at a parcel of human bones, asked the philosopher what he was looking for. "That which I cannot find," was the reply; "the difference between your father's bones and those of his slaves."

Mark Twain (quoted in the New York Journal, June to 1897): James Ross Clemens, of St. Louis, a cousin of mine, was seriously ill two or three weeks ago in London, but is well now. The report of my illness grew out of his illness. The report of my death was an exaggeration.

Mark Twain: Reports of my death have been greatly exaggerated.

Mark Twain: There was no truth in the rumor of my death.

Mark Twain: To go abroad has something of the same sense that death brings. I am no longer of ye – what ye say of me is of no consequence.

Mark Twain: If you've got a nice *fresh* corpse, fetch him out!

Tseng Tzu (disciple of Confucius, c. 500 B.C.): When a man's dying his words are worth listening to.

UA: Better ten times sick than once dead.

UA (Epitaph at Mount Zion Baptist Church in MISS to the three Civil Rights Workers brutally urdered by the Klu Klux Klan on Father's Day, June 21, 1964, "Freedom Summer" Michael Schwarner, James Earl Chaney and Andrew Goodman): "Out of one blood God hath made all men. This plaque is dedicated to the memory of Michael Schwermer, James Chaney, Michael Goodman, whose concern for others, and more particularly those of this community, led to their early martyrdom. Their deaths quickened men's consciences and more firmly established justice, liberty and brotherhood in our land."

Henry Van Dyke: Some people are so afraid to die that they never begin to live.

Guiseppe Verdi (as he almost put his piano stool on his dog): In the midst of Life...We are so near Death!

Voltaire: It is in defying it (death) that the brave escapes it.

Jane Wagner: There will be sex after death, we just won't be able to feel it.

Daniel Webster: One may live as a conqueror, a king, or a magistrate; but he must die a man. The bed of death brings every human being to his pure individuality, to the intense contemplation of that deepest and most solemn of all relations—the relation between the creature and his Creator.

Gus Welch (Carlisle Indian School Quarterback, team mate and roomate of Jim Thorpe, 1912, and WWI hero): An Indian never dies, he just dries up and blows away.

Edith Wharton (about Theodore Roosevelt after his death on January 6., 1919 at Sagamore Hill, NY): He was so alive at all points, and so gifted with the rare faculty of living intensely and entirely in every moment as it passed.

Marguerite Widdemer: I am the Dark Cavalier; I am the Last Lover: My arms shall welcome you when other arms are tired.

Oscar Wilde: Death and vulgarity are the only two facts in the Nineteenth Century that one cannot explain away.

Oscar Wilde (When a huge fee was demanded for an operation during his last illness, he said in 1905): Ah, well, then, I suppose I shall have then died beyond my means.

Tennessee Williams: Death is one moment, and life is so many of them.

William Wordsworth: The good die first; and they whose hearts are dry as summer dust burn to the socket.

Frank Lloyd Wright (Answering two questions by Mike Wallace, *Biography*, 1959, "Are you afraid of death?" & "Do you believe you are immortal?"): No at all. Death is a great friend.... (Am I immortal?) Yes, insofar as I am immortal, I will be immortal. To me, young has no meaning. It's something you can do nothing about. Nothing at all. But youth is a quality. And if you have youth you never lose it. And when they put you into the box, that's your immortality.

Yiddish Proverb: Better a noble death than a wretched life.

Yiddish Proverb: Death does not knock on the door.

Yiddish Proverb: There's no bad mother, and no good death.

DEBT (See MONEY)

DECEIT (See FRAUD; LIES; PRINCIPLE)

DECISION/DECISION MAKING (See ISSUES/PROBLEM; JUDGMENT)

DEFAMATION (See LIES)

DEFENSES (See EXCUSES)

DELIBERATIONS (See ISSUES; JURY)

DEMOCRACY (See GOVERNMENT)

DEMOCRAT PARTY (See POLITICS)

DENIAL (See EXCUSES)

DEPRESSION (See EMOTIONAL DISTRESS)

DICTUM (See OPINION)

DIFFICULTY (See ISSUES; TROUBLE)

DIFFICULT PEOPLE (See ISSUES; TROUBLE)

DIPLOMACY (See POLITICS/POLITICIANS)

DISCOVERY

Uncle Anthony: The things that come to those who wait will be the things left by those who got there first.

Uncle Anthony: They give you what the law (or the Court Rule) requires as if they expect a receipt.

Uncle Anthony: Seems t'me dat the hardest thing for them to give is in.

Uncle Anthony: He's got a very even disposition – he's always crab-like, cross, cranky, crusty and crappy.

Uncle Anthony: They're always given ya a piece of their mind – an they can least afford it.

Aunt Mary Carlo: I tink dez guys are da kinda poisons who'd go tada library an tear out da last page of a mystery.

Aunt Mary Carlo: Seems tame dat they keep stickin' dere "NO'S" inta dis discovery stuff yer doin.

Aunt Mary Carlo: Ya can't ask 'em to be human beans an be fair about it 'cause dey can't do imitations.

Linda Miller Atkinson, *ATLA's Litigating Tort Cases*, 2002, Volume 2, Chapter 18, Depositions: A deposition has several advantages over discovery devices such as written interrogatories and requests for production. The most spontaneous form of discovery, depositions present the best opportunity for candor. Unlike interrogatories or admissions, a deposition provides no delay between question-and-answer, no delay that would allow the respondent to construct evidence or evade the question.... Because of their spontaneity, flexability, depth and power to compel answers, depositions are the most affected discovery tool.

Linda Miller Atkinson, *ATLA's Litigating Tort Cases*, 2002, Volume 2, Chapter 18, Depositions: Depositions are also the most expensive discovery cool, so counsel will want to prepare thoroughly and maximize the opportunities presented in order to justify the additional expense of the client's money. Technology provides additional flexibility through video, telephone, and teleconferencing depositions.

Linda Miller Atkinson, *ATLA's Litigating Tort Cases*, 2002, Volume 2, Chapter 18, Depositions: It is not always advisable to depose the opposing expert, nor is it always advantageous to cross-examine the opposing expert at deposition when one will meet the same witness at trial. The decision requires judgment and discipline. In a medical negligence case, for example, counsel deposing the defense expert confronted the witness with an article written by the witness in which the witness mentioned with approval the particular maneuver plaintiff asserted was required by the standard of care, and which the expert witness had opposed. In the deposition, the witness, who had obviously forgotten the article or the views expressed, visibly reacted with surprise, hesitating and looking to defense counsel for guidance.... at trial, ..., when confronted with the particular journal in which the article appeared and asked foundational questions (as to its "authoritativeness"), of course, the witness smiled and answered... "no journal by itself is reliable or authoritative, even the ones I write for."

Linda Miller Atkinson, *ATLA's Litigating Tort Cases*, 2002, Volume 2, Chapter 18, Depositions: Some writers recommend opposing every opposing expert aggressively to force the opponent to reassess their position. A defense attorney, Walter Lancaster of Kirkland and Ellis, has offered a colorful exposition of this approach. Lancaster generally summarizes the "depose and destroy them all" approach and seems to assume that there is no question but to depose all opposing expert's. The approach is best summed up as follows: "you're now ready for the deposition. During the deposition you want to get all the expert's opinions and the basis for those opinions, and you also want to close the expert out, but above all, you want to leave the expert in a pool of blood."

A.C. Benson: It is curious how long the childish delight of *finding* something, quite apart from its value, survives in one – but it does survive.

Ronald J. Berke and Andrew L. Berke, *ATLA's Litigating Tort Cases*, Volume 2, Chapter 16, Interrogatories, 2002: "... Interrogatories are an essential part of the discovery stage in litigation. Although many practitioners use interrogatories on a daily basis, often attorneys respond and propound the interrogatories by rote, without examining the strategy or law in the case.

Ronald J. Berke and Andrew L. Berke, *ATLA's Litigating Tort Cases*, Volume 2, Chapter 16, Interrogatories, 2002: Interrogatories can be divided into two general categories. The first category includes questions designed to uncover facts in the other party's possession.... the second category of of interrogatories, contention interrogatories, are used to discover the factual basis behind a party's contentions.

Ronald J. Berke and Andrew L. Berke, *ATLA's Litigating Tort Cases*, Volume 2, Chapter 16, Interrogatories, 2002: Before using interrogatories, review the practical objectives for the particular case being considered. Interrogatories are often used to discover facts that constitute the basis of the defendant's case.... another consideration for practitioners in comparative fault states is the discovery of information regarding accusations of comparative negligence. In its answer, defendant may place blame for an incident on another individual or corporation....you may also wish to consider whether other discovery devices should be utilized instead of (or in addition) to interrogatories. An effective alternative to interrogatories is a request for admission.... consider the use of Federal Rules of Civil Procedure 36.

Ronald J. Berke and Andrew L. Berke, *ATLA's Litigating Tort Cases*, Volume 2, Chapter 16, Interrogatories, 2002: Just as the practitioner should take time and care for propounding interrogatories, he should view the answering of interrogatories as a serious affair. This step, often the first in the discovery process, can be neglected because of its routine nature and relative lack of appeal. Nevertheless, it is a key step in building the plaintiff's case. The defendant is always searching for lies or misleading statements by plaintiffs, for which the defendant and then impeach them.... Be wary of allowing misleading statements to be incorporated into your interrogatory responses because of inadvertence or inattention.

Bible: Ecclesiasticus 8:19: Do not reveal your thoughts to everyone, lest you drive away your good luck.

Bible: Ephesians 5:13: All things that are reproved are made manifest by the light.

Bible: Job 11:7: Canst thou by searching find out God?
Bible: Joshua 2:20: If thou utter this our business, then we will be quit of thine oath.
Ambrose Bierce: LITIGATION, n. A machine which you go into as a pig and come out of as a sausage.
Ambrose Bierce: OPPOSE, v. To assist with obstructions and objections.
Ambrose Bierce: RESPOND, v.i. To make answer, or disclose otherwise a consciousness of having inspired an interest in what Herbert Spencer calls "external coexistences," as Satan "squat like a toad" at the ear of Eve, responded to the touch of the angel's spear. To respond in damages is to contribute to the maintenance of the plaintiff's attorney and, incidentally, to the gratification of the plaintiff.
David Borsten (Historian): The idea of the search is what holds us together (in America). The quest is the enduring American experiment, The meaning is in the seeking.
Cicero: It is a shameful thing to be weary of inquiry when what we search for is excellent.
Frank A. Clark: If you can find a path with no obstacles, it probably doesn't lead anywhere.
Arthur C. Clarke: If we have learned one thing from the history of invention and discovery, it is that, in the long run – and often the in the short one – the most daring prophecies seem laughably conservative.
Bud Collyer (MC for the TV game show *To Tell The Truth*, shown 1956-1966; the panel had to decide which of three contestants, all claiming to be a certain person, was telling the truth): Will the real ___, please stand up?
Walt Disney: Around here, however, we don't look backwards for very long. We keep moving forward, opening up new doors and doing new things, because we're curious ... and curiosity keeps leading us down new paths.
William O. Douglas: The whole, though larger than any of its parts, does not necessarily obscure their separate identities.
Sir Arthur Conan Doyle (Sherlock Holmes' saying to start an investigation): Come Watson, the game's afoot!
English Proverb: Many things are lost for want of asking.
French Proverb: Feather by feather the goose can be plucked.
Francis H. Hare, Jr., James L. Gilbert, and Stuart A. Ollanik, *Full Disclosure: Combating Stonewalling and Other Discovery Abuses*, (ATLA Press, 1995): "INTRODUCTION: THE WHOLE TRUTH: A great deal of legal literature in recent years has been devoted to the topic of discovery abuse. The overwhelming majority of these articles focus on the misuse or overuse of discovery *requests* and ignore the flip side of the coin: "stonewalling" or responses that evade or suppress the disclosure of relevant information.... stonewalling is simply the failure or refusal to provide discoverable information properly requested by the opposing party. It occurs in many forms, ranging from groundless objections to the actual destruction of evidence. Unfortunately, this type of abuse has reached epidemic proportions in complex tort cases.... as in many kinds of tort cases, products liability presents a tremendous temptation to defendants to conceal information. The product manufacturer alone possesses evidence that can be used against it. In discovery, the manufacturer is asked to hand that evidence voluntarily to its litigation adversary. It is a lot to ask a corporate employee or counsel to turn over the "smoking gun" memo or the testing results proving that the defect was recognized before or during manufacture. Our justice system, of necessity, asks and demands no less. Unfortunately for trial lawyers and their clients, in an alarming (if not surprising) number of instances, a manufacturer's defensive instinct prevails over its legal and ethical duties. While it would be unfair to assert that every manufacturer cheats in litigation, the list of discovery abusers includes leading manufacturers whose behavior by example shapes American corporate culture. Ford Motor Company, General Motors, International Harvester, Honda Motor Company, and other giants of commerce in the United States and abroad have been taken to task by courts for stonewalling discovery.
Francis H. Hare, Jr., James L. Gilbert, and Stuart A. Ollanik, *Full Disclosure:* *Combating Stonewalling and Other Discovery Abuses*, (ATLA Press, 1995): Stonewalling (failing or refusing to disclose relevant information) affects not only individual litigants, but the consuming public at large as well. In an opinion ordering disclosure of cigarette manufacturing industry documents, Judge H. Lee Sarokin decried the practice of protecting profits by hiding product dangers. While Judge Sarokin was ultimately removed from the case because of his frank words, and his order reversed, his sentiments remain valid: "In light of the current controversy surrounding breast implants, one wonders when all industries will

recognize their obligation to voluntarily disclose risks from the use of their products. All too often in the choice between the physical health of consumers and the financial well-being of business concealment is chosen over disclosure, sales over safety, and money over morality. Who are these persons who knowingly and secretly decide to put the buying public at risk solely for the purpose of making profits and who believe that illness and death of consumers is an appropriate cost of their own prosperity. (Citing Haines v. Liggett Group, Inc., 140 F. R. D. 681, 683 (D.N. J., 1992), rev'd 975 F. 2d 81, (3d Cir. 1992), later proceedings 814 F. Supp. 414 (D. N. J., 1993).

Italian Proverb: Silence was never written down.

Justice Robert H. Jackson: A common-law trial is and always should be an adversary proceeding. Discovery was hardly intended to enable a learned profession to perform its functions either without wits or on wits borrowed from the adversary. *Hickman v. Taylor*, 329 US 495, 516, 91 L ed 451, 465, 67 S. Ct 385 (1947).

Justice Robert H. Jackson (dissenting opinion in *Ashcraft v. Tennessee*, 322 US 143, 88 L ed 1192, 64 S Ct 921, 1944): Questioning is an indispensable instrumentality of justice.

Justice Robert H. Jackson: He who must search a haystack for a needle is likely to end up with the attitude that the needle is not worth the search.

Randy James: "Albert Einstein is dumber than the stupidest lawyer in the world if that lawyer is preparing him for or taking his deposition."

J. Michael Jordan: (R.J.Reynolds Tobacco Company's lawyer on how the Company he had defended won dismissal of 9 cases in California; he credited an aggressive legal posture that made the cases burdensome and expensive): "To paraphrase General Patton, the way we won these cases was not by spending R. J. Reynolds' money, but by making sure that that other son of a bitch spent all of his!"

Lord Langdale (English Judge, 1783-1851): All interrogatories must, to some extent, make a suggestion to the witness. It would be perfectly nugatory to ask a witness, if he knew anything about something. *Lincoln v. Wright*, 4 Beav. 166 (1841)

John Leighton: I call depositions with no pre-planning **PINATA DEPOSITIONS!**

Joe Louis (Heavyweight boxing champ, before his first fight with Billy Conn, May 1941): He can run, but he can't hide.

Phillip Miller (a take-off on "If the truth were self-evident, eloquence would be unnecessary" by Cicero): "If the truth were self-evident, depositions would not be necessary"

A.A. Milne: One of the advantages of being disorderly is that one is constantly making exciting discoveries.

Michael A. Musmanno (Justice of the Sup. Ct. of Pennsylvania, 1959): Truth is a ripe fruit which must be timely plucked: Undue passage of time nearly always works adversely in the ascertainment of truth. Where there is controversy, truth is a ripe fruit which must be timely plucked. After maturity passes, disintegration sets in. Memory fades, and what is worse, it often enters into the shadowland of guesswork, loss of focus and even unconscious distortion. In addition, deaths, translocations and other mutations also make holes in the fabric intended to reproduce in testimony what has occurred in fact.

Michael A. Musmanno (Justice of Pa. Supreme Court, 1959): The history of the rigors of overzestful inquisitors – the excesses of inquests having no limit in time and scope, the injustices which can result from searches that are not confined to a particular subject—is etched too deeply into the conscience of the American people for a free country to allow a resumption of a practice so fraught with tyrannical threat, and emancipation from which a bloody war was fought to attain. The fact that no such usurpation of the rights of the people was intended does not guarantee that abuses could not result. Good intentions in releasing a juggernaut will not heal the wounds of those crushed beneath its remorseless wheels.

Michael A. Musmanno (Justice of Pa. Supreme Court, 1959): It is simply unthinkable that in a government of the people, the government should withhold from one of the people evidence which could prove him innocent of a crime against all the people.

Sir Isaac Newton: If I have ever made any valuable discoveries, it has been owing more to patient attention, than to any other talent.

Thomas Paine: It is error only, and not truth, that shrinks from inquiry.

Anthony Robbins: If you want to change our reality, change your focus. If you want to change our focus, change your questions.

Larry R. Rogers, Jr., *ATLA's Litigating Tort Cases*, 2002, Volume 2, Chapter 17, Requests for Admission: Federal Rule of Civil Procedure 36 permits litigants to serve requests for admission on opposing parties. Because admissions obtained under Rule 36 conclusively establish the matter admitted, requests for admission have the potential to bring the lawsuit to an early conclusion or to significantly limit the issues in the suit. They therefore are arguably the most effective, but least employed, procedural mechanisms available to a litigator. Attorneys routinely use interrogatories, document production requests, and depositions in civil litigation, but it has been reported that as few as 10% of attorneys avail themselves of requests for admission.... if properly used, requests for admission can be a potent tool in the trial attorneys arsenal.

Larry R. Rogers, Jr., *ATLA's Litigating Tort Cases*, 2002, Volume 2, Chapter 17, Requests for Admission: Unless the responding party timely answers (within 30 days of service) the request, it is deemed admitted. The Rule is thus considered self executing; and unanswered requests for admissions are automatically deemed judicially admitted under Rule 36 (a).

Will Rogers: An ignorant person is one who doesn't know what you have just found out.

Will Rogers: It isn't what we don't know that gives us trouble, it's what we know that ain't so.

Will Rogers: Lettin' the cat outta the bag is a whole lot easier 'n puttin' it back in.

Will Rogers: Lawyers make a living out of trying to figure out what other lawyers have written.

Will Rogers: Our investigations have always contributed more to our amusement than they have to knowledge.

Will Rogers: One revolution (EDITOR: deposition) is just like one cocktail, it just gets you organized for the next.

Will Rogers: The minute you read something and you can't understand it, you can be sure it was written by a lawyer. Then, if you give it to another lawyer to read and he don't know just what it means, then you can be sure it was drawn up by a lawyer. If its in a few words and is plain, and understandable only one way, it was written by a non-lawyer. Every time a lawyer writes something, he is not writing for posterity. He is writing so endless others of his craft can make a living out of trying to figure out what he said. Course perhaps he hadn't really said anything, that's what makes it hard to explain.

John Romano, *The Deposition Field Manual*, 2002: "... Rule 26 (a)(5) specifically permits a party to obtain discovery by deposition. The scope of discovery is quite broad and the rules state that they are to be liberally construed in favor of complete disclosure prior to trial. This represents a complete departure from the traditional approach in which there was no (or severely limited) discovery and every trial was a trial by surprise. Under the modern rules, a party may obtain discovery regarding any matter, unless privileged, that is relevant to the issues in the case. The information sought need not be admissible at trial as long as it is reasonably calculated to lead to the discovery of admissible evidence. Accordingly, there are a few limits to the questions that can be asked of a witness during a deposition. "Mutual knowledge of all the relevant facts gathered by both parties is essential to proper litigation." Hickman v. Taylor, 329 US 495, 507 (1947). The intent of the rules pertaining to discovery in general, and to depositions in particular, is to permit the parties to learn all relevant information, so that they can effectively investigate the case and prepare for trial. Sadly, many attorneys use the civil procedure rules at shields to avoid disclosing relevant information. They make groundless objections and motions for protective orders. In doing so, they violate the spirit of the rules, causing unnecessary frustration, inconvenience, and higher costs to litigants, attorneys, witnesses, and the court."

Hon. H. Lee Sarokin, U.S. District Court, New Jersey (Cipollone v. Liggett Group, et als): "All too often in the choice between the physical health of consumers and the financial well-being of business, concealment is chosen over disclosure, sales over safety, and money over morality ... despite some rising pretenders, the tobacco industry may be the king of concealment and disinformation."

Nicole Schultheis, *ATLA's Litigating Tort Cases*, 2002, Volume 2, Chapter 15, Document Discovery: It is pointless to draft document requests without having a clear understanding of how the documents are going to be used or could be used. Yet lawyers often delegate this task to associates who lack the experience to do the job properly.

Nicole Schultheis, *ATLA's Litigating Tort Cases*, 2002, Volume 2, Chapter 15, Document Discovery: The World Wide Web and its resources are increasingly effective tools for locating information that may be helpful, perhaps even critical, to building and defending a tort plaintiff's case. (The author provides "a taste of what is available and provides a methodology for obtaining it").

Nicole Schultheis, *ATLA's Litigating Tort Cases*, 2002, Volume 2, Chapter 15, Document Discovery: The term "document" is defined in Federal Rule of Civil Procedure 34 to include "writings, drawings, grants, charts, photographs, phono records, and other data compilations from which information can be obtained, translated, if necessary, by the respondent through detection devices into reasonably usable form." Because the term "document" is not exhaustively defined by Rule 34, it should be thoroughly defined in the request to be as broad as permissible under the Federal Rules of Civil Procedure.

Nicole Schultheis, *ATLA's Litigating Tort Cases*, 2002, Volume 2, Chapter 15, Document Discovery: ... most importantly, the term" "document" is becoming increasingly synonymous with the term "computerized data.".... Today, the clear majority of all business records are stored in electronic form, and nearly a third of it is *never* printed on paper.... Many databases have no paper counter part because a printed version cannot capture the formulas which produce the numbers that appear on screen. This type of data requires the services of a specialist, if one desires to create a meaningful document on paper.

Nicole Schultheis, *ATLA's Litigating Tort Cases*, 2002, Volume 2, Chapter 15, Document Discovery: Thus in framing the document requests, the definition of the term "document" should expressly state that it encompasses any media by which information is recorded, stored, communicated, or utilized, including paper (of any kind, type or character, including post-its, handwritten phone message pads, etc.) and any other method or media by which information may be manipulated, communicated, recorded, analyzed, or retrieved, including but not limited to computer and computerized devices, such as personal information managers, cell phones, and the like. The definition should also expressly list the following categories of documents are being requested: photographs, photostats, x-rays, motion pictures, audiotapes, videotape recordings, transparencies or photograph negatives, computer-generated material, computer disks, CD-ROMs, computer tapes, and any other form or type of computer- stored or computer-retrievable data, microfilm and microfiche and any other process by which information is reduced for storage or use.

Nicole Schultheis, *ATLA's Litigating Tort Cases*, 2002, Volume 2, Chapter 15, Document Discovery: The term "document" also should be defined broadly to include any "document" which relates to the principal document or the subject matter of the principal document, including, for example, material which was used or referenced to in the preparation of the principal document, attachments to the principal document, documents referred to in the principal document; and all drafts and versions of the principal document, including those with handwritten annotations or Post-it notes attached. Post-it notes themselves are also documents, and they can be important.

Nicole Schultheis, *ATLA's Litigating Tort Cases*, 2002, Volume 2, Chapter 15, Document Discovery: Start with the notion that the documents are not being sought for their own sake: they are being sought because the information is needed to develop evidence supporting the cause of action and the theme of the case. For example, a Post-it recovered from one of the defendant manufactures in the national Breast Implant litigation was directly probative of this of several potential causes of action (as well is giving rise to the potential for punitive damages in some states), as it demonstrated at the company's highest levels an intentional disregard for product safety as well as the motive for that disregard – corporate profits. If the plaintiffs had not thought to request notes and minutes relating to meetings which concerned product safety, or if they had not requested the files maintained in the offices of key management personnel, the Post-it note would not have been obtained.

William Shakespeare (*As You Like It*, Avt IV, iii): This is man's invention and his hand.

William Shakespeare (*II Henry VI*, Act I, ii): Seal up your lips, and give no words but mum: / The business asketh silent secrecy.

William Shakespeare (*Love's Labour's Lost*, Act IV, iii): Learning is but an adjunct to ourself, / And where we are, our learning likewise is.

William Shakespeare (*The Merry Wives of Windsor*, Act I, i): Persuade me not; I will make a Star-chamber matter of it.

William Shakespeare (*Othello*, Act IV, ii): I pray you, turn the key and keep our counsel.

William Shakespeare (*The Taming of the Shrew*, Act III, i): I am not so nice / To change true rules for old inventions.

William Shakespeare (*Twelfth Night,* Act I, iii): Wherefore are these things hid?

A. Russell Smith, *ATLA's Litigating Tort Cases,* 2002, Volume 2, Chapter 14, Discovery Strategy and Privileges: It is often said that opening statement and closing arguments should be thought of at case's inception. And that is true. But timing is key. Discovery should begin when the attorney first receives the case. Talking with and getting statements from witnesses, obtaining and examining the tangible evidence, laying out what discovery is needed, how it can be obtained, and starting to get what you can should be undertaken at the earliest stages of the case. Discovery—formal and informal—should then continue until the case is finally concluded. / Martin Luther King led us with "I Have a Dream." Ignace Jan Paderewski humbly stated, "Before I was a genius I was a drudge." / George Washington, Abraham Lincoln, and Ulysses S. Grant exemplified the quote that: "A quitter never wins—and a winner never quits." / There have been many magnificent leaders who have provided us with much to draw upon. The above messages of having a dream, working hard, and refusing to quit are good guides for life, including the discovery process. When you are working hard to get through stonewalls and you are being pushed by the court, it helps to have some sources of inspiration. / Think ("cerebrate") (Thank you to ATLA's beloved Ted Koskoff). Establish goals. Plan. Remain determined (yet flexible). Be resilient. Achieve your goals..... In war, the side that best knows the terrain and their opponent has a tremendous advantage. Patton read Rommel's book on strategy prior to confronting him in Africa.... Many great football coaches such as Paul Brown won games they should not have won because of their ability to discover their opponents' strengths and weaknesses and plan accordingly. Tiger Woods and Jack Nicklaus always study (discover) the golf course before they play it.... a trial lawyer faces the same requirements. Discovery is a major challenge and opportunity for a trial lawyer.

Dennis R. Suplee and Diana S. Donaldson, *The Deposition Handbook,* 3rd Edition, 1999: The most important preliminary question is whether to take a deposition: "Doctors order tests. Lawyers take depositions. It's the same thing. Half the time we don't really know exactly why we take depositions, but there seems to be some primordial need to do so. "Hmm," we say to our client, "this looks serious. Better take some depositions."

Dennis R. Suplee and Diana S. Donaldson, *The Deposition Handbook,* 3rd Edition, 1999: The deposition is a powerful discovery device, but one that is particularly subject to abuse. A witness is compelled to appear and testify in response to questions that may be posed in an aggressive, cross examination style, but no judge is present to maintain order. Thus, a deposition can degenerate into something that akin to a gang of ill-mannered children in a sandbox. An equally apt analogy—to the demeanor of a pit bull—was made in an article on deposition abuse published by the American Bar Association. (Referring to McElhaney, *The Pit Bull,* ABA Journal, July 1989). The views of the judiciary about abuse of deposition conduct are reflected in the following wishful observation of one federal judge: "If there is a hell to which disputatious, uncivil, vituperative lawyers go, let it be one in which the damned are eternally locked in discovery disputes with other lawyers of equally repugnant attributes."

Mark Twain: To succeed in other trades, capacity must be shown; in the law, concealment of it will do.

Mark Twain: There ain't no way to find out why a snorer can't hear himself snore.

Tom Vesper: Defending and preparing your own plaintiff personal injury clients for their discovery depositions starts with the preparation for the "first *de facto* deposition" [EDITOR: the defense medical examination is in fact another deposition conducted *ex parte* with the plaintiff unrepresented and the doctor asking questions and recording answers without a court reporter or independent witness present] – the defense medical examination, where the defense doctor [EDITOR: NEVER EVER let anyone try to refer to such paid experts as "IME's" or "Independent" – they are NOT in any way "independent"] will try to get your client to write out answers to interrogatories [EDITOR:the DME's own form questionnaires] and then cross-examine the plaintiff about how exactly the "accident" occurred.

Tom Vesper: Going into a deposition without any prior planning is like following the literal words of the theme song from the musical *"Paint Your Wagon"*: **"Where are we goin', I don't know, when will we get there, I ain't certain, all that I know is we are on our way!"**

Tom Vesper: Preparing our clients for depositions should be as thorough as if we were preparing them for trial.

Tom Vesper: "Day-of-dep-prep" will almost always result in a crappy dep!

Rudy Westmoreland: The defense (law firm with hundreds of lawyers) sent us A TSUNAMI OF DISCOVERY requests!

DISCRIMINATION (See BIAS; CIVIL RIGHTS)

DISCRETION (See COMMON SENSE; JUDGMENT)

DISCUSSION (See ADVERSARY; ORATORY; WORDS)

DISHONESTY (See LIES/LIAR)

DISPAIR (See EMOTIONAL DISTRESS)

DIVORCE

Uncle Anthony: I think they divorced for religious reasons: he thought he was God and she didn't!

Uncle Anthony (as told to him by Uncle "Flamingo Jim" Trusk): A man and his wife were getting a divorce in a local court, with child custody in issue. The mother jumped up and protested to the judge that since she had brought the children into this world, she should retain custody of them. The judge asked for the father's side ... after a long moment of silence, the father rose from his chair and replied: "Judge, when I put a dollar into a vending machine and a Pepsi comes out, does the Pepsi belong to me or to the machine?" (EDITOR: Don't laugh, I am told he won!)

Aunt Mary Carlo: Y'know, payin' alimony must be like keepin' up 'da payments on a car wit' four flat tires.

Polly Adler: The women who take husbands not out of love but out of greed, to get their bills paid, to get a fine house and clothes and jewels; the women who marry to get out of a tiresome job, or to get away from disagreeable relatives, or to avoid being called an old maid—these are whores in everything but name. The only difference between them and my girls is that my girls gave a man his money's worth.

Shana Alexander: When two people marry they become in the eyes of the law one person, and that one person is the husband!

Nancy Astor: I marry beneath me. All women do.

Lauren Bacall: Hollywood is the only place in the world where an amicable divorce means each one getting fifty percent of the publicity.

John Barrymore (as Gene Fowler, in Good Night, Sweet Prince): Alimony is the most exorbitant of all stud fees, and the worst feature of it is that you pay it retroactively.

John Barrymore: Paper napkins never return from a laundry, nor love from a trip to the law courts.

Vicki Baum: Marriage always demands the greatest understanding of the art of insincerity possible between two human beings.

Bible: Amos 3:3: Can two walk together, except they be agreed?

Bible: 1 Corinthians 7:27: Art thou bound unto a wife? Seek not to be loosed.

Bible: Mark 10:11; Matthew 19:9: Whosoever shall put away his wife, except it be for fornication, and shall marry another, committeth adultery.

Bible: Matthew 19:6: What therefore God hath joined together, let not man put assunder.

Bible: Proverbs 18:22: Whoso findeth a wife findeth a good thing.

Bible: Proverbs 21:9 and 25:24: It is better to dwell in a corner of the housetop, than with a brawling woman in a wide house.

Ambrose Bierce: DIVORCE, n. A resumption of diplomatic relations and rectification of boundaries.

Ambrose Bierce: DIVORCE, n. A bugle blast that separates the combatants and makes them fight at long-range.

George Burns: They make a business out of (marriage). When you work too hard at a business you get tired; and when you get tired you get grouchy; and when you get grouchy you start fighting; and when you start fighting you're out of business.

James Branch Cabell: People marry through a variety of other reasons, and with varying results; but to marry for love is to invite inevitable tragedy.

Richard E. Brennan (from "Reflections on Matrimonial Motion Day," poem, 1996): I wonder if they ever think of their wedding days, / The bright dresses, the tender words, the promises and dreams. / As they witness the end of their marriages / And engage in settlement talks and schemes.... /"Sell the house"; "Split the stuff we acquired through the years"; / "Start anew, move again, forget the former ways." / But I wonder as I watched them with their lawyers, / Do they ever think about their wedding days?

Will Carleton: Draw up the papers, lawyer, and make 'em good and stout, For things are running crossways, and Betsey and I are out.

Judge Karen Cassidy (New Jersey Superior Court Judge, Union County, speaking to BOTH parties and their lawyers in a court hearing over whether or not there could/should be joint custody at the birthday party of their 6-year-old daughter, Jacqueline McGreevey, of New Jersey's former gay governor Jim McGreevey and his estranged wife Dina Matos McGreevey): The hatred these two (Mr. and Mrs. McGreevey) have for each other seems to override the love for the child ... because it's so out of control ... sad ... that poor kid – I feel as if I'm the only one protecting her."

Cervantes: The worst reconciliation is better than the best divorce.

Lord Chesterfield: The only solid and lasting peace between a man and his wife is, doubtless, a separation.

Sir Winston Churchill: If I was your wife Sir, I'd poison you! Madam, if you were my wife, I'd let you!

Dorothy Dix: So many persons who think divorce a panacea for every ill find out when they try it, that the remedy is worse than the disease.

Isadora Duncan: Any intelligent woman who reads the marriage contract, and then goes into it, deserves all the consequences.

Isadora Duncan: I believe, as a wage-earning woman, that if I make a great sacrifice of strength and health and even risk my life, to have a child, I should certainly not do so if, on some future occasion, the man can say that the child belongs to him by law and he will take it from me and I shall see it only three times a year!

English Proverb: Needles and pins, needles and pins: when a man marries his troubles begin.

English Proverb: Marriage halves our griefs, doubles our joys, and quadruples our expenses.

Euripides: When cheated, wife or husband feels the same.

Benjamin Franklin: Where there's a marriage without love, / there will be love without marriage.

Betty Friedan: If divorce has increased by 1000%, don't blame the women's movement. Blame the obsolete sex roles on which our marriages were based.

Thomas Fuller: Better a tooth out than always aching.

Zsa Zsa Gabor: Husbands are like fires. They go out when unattended.

Malcolm Gladwell: "The 4 Horsemen" of Divorce: 1. Defensiveness, 2. Stonewalling, 3. Criticism, and 4. CONTEMPT

Herbert Gold: Don't tell me marriage is still a safe haven any place in America. Well, maybe among the Amish.

Nat Goodwin: It's a toss-up between marriage and divorce. They're both right and wrong now and then, but mostly right.

Cary Grant: Divorce is a game played by lawyers.

Haggadah (Palestinian Talmud, 4th century): There are four minds in the bed of a divorced man who marries a divorced woman.

Helen Hayes: Marriage is like a war. There are moments of chivalry and gallantry that attend the victorious advances and strategic retreats, the birth or death of children, the momentary conquest of loneliness, the sacrifice that ennobles him who makes it. But mostly there are the long dull sieges, the waiting, the terror and boredom. Women understand this better than men; they are better able to survive attrition.

O. Henry: If men knew how women passed the time when they are alone, they'd never marry.

Edward Hoagland: The great leveler nowadays is divorce; almost everybody thinks about it, whether because we expect to be happy all the time—daily, weekly—or because we want the smell of brimstone in lives made too affluent and easy.

Billie Holiday: Sometimes it's worse to win a fight than to lose.

David Hopkinson: I believe that we all should wise up and recognize that a marriage is a small business and that married couples are business partners.

Edgar Watson Howe: A man should be taller, older, heavier, uglier, and hoarser than his wife.

Edgar Watson Howe: A honeymoon is a good deal like a man laying off to take an expensive vacation, and coming back to a different job.

Elbert Hubbard: There are three sides to every question—where a divorce is involved.

Elbert Hubbard: The married man who wants a change of venue is probably headed for the divorce court.

Elbert Hubbard: The trouble with many married people is that they are trying to get more out of marriage than there is in it.

Elbert Hubbard: Marriage: A legal or religious ceremony by which two persons of the opposite sex solemnly agree to harass and spy on each other for ninety-nine years, or until death do them join.

Erica Jong: Bigamy is having one husband too many. Monogamy is the same.

Jean Kerr: Marrying a man is like buying something you've been admiring for a long time in a shop window. You may love it when you get it home, but it doesn't always go with everything else in the house.

Jean Kerr: Being divorced is like being hit by a Mack truck—if you survive you start looking very carefully to the right and left.

Ellen Key: Love is moral even without legal marriage, but marriage is immoral without love.

Suzanne LaFollette (1926): When one hear's the argument that marriage should be insoluble for the sake of children, one cannot help wondering whether the protagonist is really such a firm friend of childhood, or whether his concern for the welfare of children is merely so much protective coloration for a constitutional and superstitious fear of change.

Suzanne LaFollette: For man, marriage is regarded as a station; for women, as a vocation.

Ann Landers: All married couples should learn the art of battle as they should learn the art of making love. Good battle is objective and honest—never vicious or cruel; good battle is healthy and constructive, and brings to a marriage the principle of equal partnership.

Paul H. Landis: College women in general have greater difficulty in marrying period... Men still want wives will bolster their egos rather than detract from them.

Pope Leo XIII: The ancient Romans are said to have shrunk with horror from the first examples of divorce, but before long all sense of decency was blunted in their soul; the meager restraint of passion died out, and the marriage vow was so often broken that what some writers have affirmed would seem to be true – namely, women used to count years not by the change of consuls, but by their husbands.

George Levinger: What counts in making a happy marriage is not so much how compatible you are, but how you deal with incompatibility.

Sinclair Lewis: She had become so dully habituated to married life that in her full matronliness she was as sexless as an anemic nun.

Anne Morrow Lindbergh: Marriage is tough, because it is woven of all these various elements, the weak and the strong. "In loveness" is fragile for it is woven only with the gossamer threads of beauty. It seems to me absurd to talk about "happy" and "unhappy" marriages.

Norman Mailer: You don't know anything about a woman until you meet her in court.

Merrit Malloy: Relationships that do not end peacefully, do not end at all.

Judith Martin: I have always believed that the key to a happy marriage was the ability to say with a straight face, "Why, I don't know what you're worrying about. I though you were very funny last night, and I'm sure everybody else did, too." Perhaps the greatest rudenesses of our time come not from the callousness of strangers, but from the solicitousness of intimates who believe that their frank criticisms are always welcome, and who feel free to "be themselves" with those they love, which turns out to mean being their worst selves, while saving their best behavior for strangers.

H.L. Mencken: Alimony—The ransom that the happy pay to the devil.

H.L. Mencken: Adultery is the application of democracy to love.

H.L. Mencken: Who are happy in marriage? Those with so little imagination that they cannot picture a better state, and those so shrewd that they prefer quiet slavery to hopeless rebellion.

H.L. Mencken: For one American husband who maintains a chorus line in Leventine luxury around the corner, there are hundreds who are as true to their oaths, year in and year out, as so many convicts in the deathhouse.

Jawaharlal Nehru: Many people seem to imagine that by bringing in divorce you break up the system of $marriage. I am absolutely convinced that by bringing in divorce you make for happier marriages, normally.

Nancy S. Palmer (*American Bar Association Journal*, February 1977): Litigated divorce is like giving a judge a blank pad of paper that you sign your name to and that will decide how your family is going to operate.

Nancy Reagan: Love means giving one's self to another person fully, not just physically. When two people really love each other, this helps them to stay alive and grow. One must really be loved to grow. Love's such a precious and fragile thing that when it comes we have to hold on tightly. And when it comes, we're very lucky because for some it never comes at all. If you have love, you're wealthy in a way that can never be measured. Cherish it.

Will Rogers: I guess the only way to stop divorce is to stop marriage.

Will Rogers: I'm not a real movie star. I've still got the same wife I started out with twenty-eight years ago.

Will Rogers: Money and women are the most sought after and the least known about of any two things we have.

Helen Rowland: When you see what some girls marry, you realize how they must hate to work for a living.

Helen Rowland: A husband is what is left of the lover after the nerve has been extracted.

Helen Rowland: Marriage is the only thing that affords a woman the pleasure of company and the perfect sensation of solitude at the same time.

Edgar Saltus: Divorce is like matrimony: a fellow has got to go through it three or four times before he knows how.

Phyllis Schlafly: Marriage is like pantyhose. It all depends on what you put into it.

William Shakespeare (*Hamlet*, Act III, ii): In second husband let me be accurst! / None wed the second but who killed the first.

William Shakespeare (*Henry VIII*, Act II, ii): Duke of Suffolk: No; his conscience / Has crept too near another lady.

William Shakespeare (*Othello*, Act III, iii): O curse of marriage, / That we can call these delicate creatures ours, / And not their appetites! I had rather be a toad, / And live upon the vapour of a dungeon, / Than keep a corner in the thing I love / For others' uses.

William Shakespeare (*Romeo and Juliet*, Act IV, v): She's not well married that lives married long: / But she's best married that dies married young.

Benjamin Spock: Successful marriage is an art that can only be learned with difficulty. But it takes pride and satisfaction, like any other expertness that is hard won.... I would say that the surest measure of a man's or woman's maturity is the harmony, style, joy, dignity he creates in his marriage, and the pleasure and inspiration he provides for his spouse. An immature person may achieve great success in a career but never in marriage.

Talmud: A henpecked husband cannot get relief in a court.

Elizabeth Taylor (Who's Afraid of Virginia Woolf?): I swear, if you existed, I'd divorce you!

Melvin B. Tolson: A nagging woman is a bird beating her wings against the cage of matrimony.

Claire Trevor: What a holler would ensue if people had to pay the minister as much to marry them as they have to pay a lawyer to get them a divorce.

Calvin Trillin: In recent years it has become common to hear people all over the country speak of long-term marriage in a tone of voice that assumes it to be inextricably intertwined with the music of Lawrence Welk.

Mark Twain: Separately, foreign marriages and whiskey are bad; mixed, they are fatal.

Voltaire: Divorce is probably of nearly the same date as marriage. I believe, however, that marriage is some weeks more ancient.

Thornton Wilder: The best part of married life is the fights. The rest is merely so-so.

P.G. Wodehouse: Judges, as a class, display, in the matter of arranging alimony, that reckless generosity which is found only in men who are giving away someone else's cash.

DOCTORS/MEDICINE/HEALTH

Uncle Anthony: Some people you never want to ask "Howya doin'?" Because they'll tell you ... boy, will they tell you!
Uncle Anthony: Health is your most important asset.
Uncle Anthony: Y'now, ya gotta tell him/her that shakin' yer head ain't exerciing.
Uncle Anthony: Y'know what, I can say one thing fer him bein' fat – a lotta him is havin' a lotta fun.
Aunt Mary Carlo: Dat cheese cake will toin to "pounds cake" in no time.
Aunt Mary Carlo: Yeah, he went ona diet – all he lost was his temper.
Aunt Mary Carlo: I tink she weighs a hundred and plenty!
Aunt Mary Carlo: Deez IME's ("Independent" or Defense Medical Exams) are like Medical Blind Dates!
Aunt Mary Carlo (about IME exams): I had longer "visits" with the guy at the Garden State toll booth!
Arabian Proverb: He who has health, has hope; and he who has hope, has everything.
Francis Bacon: The poets did well to conjoin music and medicine, because the office of medicine is but to tune the curious harp of man's body.
Dr. John Baker: If you listen carefully, your patient will give you the correct diagnosis.
Jack Benny: I don't deserve this award, but I have arthritis and I don't deserve that either.
Yogi Berra: You saw Dr. Zhivago? Why? Aren't you feeling well?
Bible: Acts 14:9: He hath faith to be healed.
Bible: 1 Corinthians 9:24: Run, that ye may obtain.
Bible: II Chron. 16:12: In his disease he sought not to the Lord, but to the physicians.
Bible: Ecclesiasticus 38:1: Honour a physician with the honour due unto him for the uses which ye may have of him: for the Lord hath created him. For of the most High cometh healing, and he shall receive honour of the king. The skill of the physician shall lift up his head: and in the sight of great men he shall be in admiration.
Bible: Isaiah 53:5: With his stripes are we healed.
Bible: James 5:15: The prayer of faith shall save the sick, and the Lord shall raise him up.
Bible: Jeremiah 30:17: For I will restore health unto thee, and I will heal thee of thy wounds, saith the Lord.
Bible: Luke 4:23: Physician, heal thyself.
Bible: Luke 11:34; Matthew 6:22: The light of the body is the eye.
Bible: Malachi 4:2: But unto you that fear my name shall the Sun of righteousness arise with healing in his wings.
Bible: Mark 16:18: They shall lay hands on the sick, and they shall recover.
Bible: Matthew 9:12: They that be whole need not a physician, but they that are sick.
Bible: Matthew 9:22: Thy faith hath made thee whole.
Bible: Matthew 10:8: Heal the sick, cleanse the lepers, raise the dead, cast out devils.
Bible: Psalms 103:3: Who forgiveth all thine iniquities; who healeth all their wounds.
Bible: Psalms 147:3: He healeth the broken heart, and bindeth up their wounds.
Bible: Revelation 22:2: And the leaves of the tree were for the healing of the nations.
Bible: 1 Timothy 4:8: Bodily exercise profiteth little; but godliness is profitable unto all things.
Bible: 2 Timothy 4:7: I have fought a good fight, I have finished my course, I have kept the faith.
Ambrose Bierce: APOTHECARY, n. The physician's accomplice, undertaker's benefactor and grave worm's provider....
Ambrose Bierce: DIAGNOSIS, n. A physician's forecast of disease by the patient's pulse and purse.
Ambrose Bierce: DIAPHRAGM, n. A muscular partition separating disorders of the chest from disorders of the bowels.
Ambrose Bierce: GOUT, n. A physician's name for the rheumatism of a rich patient.
Ambrose Bierce: HOMOEOPATHIST, n. The humorist of the medical profession.
Ambrose Bierce: HOMOEOPATHY, n. A school of medicine midway between Allopathy and Christian Science. To the last both the others are distinctly inferior, for Christian Science will cure imaginary diseases, and they can not.
Ambrose Bierce: MEDICINE, n. A stone flung down the Bowery to kill a dog in Broadway.
Ambrose Bierce: PHYSICIAN, n. One upon whom we set our hopes when ill and our dogs when well.

Ambrose Bierce: PERSCRIPTION, n. A physician's guess at what will best prolong the situation with least harm to the patient.
Bob & Ray: Never argue with a doctor; he has inside information
Emma Bombeck: Never go to a doctor whose office plants have died.
James H. Boren: I got the bill for my surgery. Now I know why those doctors were wearing masks.
Fanny Brice: He cut you if you had dandruff.
Archie Bunker (TV show "All in the Family"): All them surgeons – they're highway robbers. Why do you think they wear them masks when they work on you?
William Camden: Few physicians live well.
Dorothy Canfield: Some people think that doctors and nurses can put scrambled eggs back into the shell.
Thomas Carlyle: Heroes have gone out, quacks have come in; the reign of quacks has not ended with the nineteenth century. The scepter is held with a firm grasp; the empire has a wider boundary. We are all the slaves of quackery in one shape or another. One portion of our being is always playing the successful quack to the other.
Anton Chekhov: Doctors are just the same as lawyers; the only difference is that lawyers merely rob you, whereas doctors rob you and kill you, too.
Chinese Proverb: An ignorant doctor is no better than a murderer.
Brock Chisholm: You can only cure retail but you can prevent wholesale.
Sir Winston Churchill: The surest road to health, say what they will, Is never to suppose we shall be ill; Most of those evils we poor mortals know, From doctors and imagination flow.
Caleb C. Colton: There is difference between the two temporal blessings—health and money; money is the most envied, but the least enjoyed; health is the most enjoyed, but the least envied; and this superiority of the latter is still more obvious when we reflect that the poorest man would not part with health for money, but that the richest would gladly part with all his money for health.
Caleb C. Colton: Anguish of mind has driven thousands to suicide; anguish of body, none. This proves that the health of the mind is of far more consequence to our happiness than the health of the body, although both are deserving of much more attention than either receives.
Adelle Davis: Thousands upon thousands of persons have studied disease. Almost no one has studied health.
Diodorus Siculus: Over the door of a library in Thebes is the inscription "Medicine for the soul."
Benjamin Disraeli: The health of the people is really the foundation upon which all their happiness and all their powers as the state depend.
George Du Maurier (1884): What sort of a doctor is he? Well, I don't know much about his ability, but he has a good bedside manner.
Finley Peter Dunne: A patient in th hands iv a doctor is like a hero in th hands iv a story writer. He's goin to suffer a good dale, but he's goin' to come out all right in th' end.
Finley Peter Dunne: If th' Christyan Scientists had some science an th' doctors more Christyanity, it wudden''t make anny diff'rence which ye called in—if ye had a good nurse.
Tryon Edwards: A sound mind in a sound body; if the former be the glory of the latter, the latter is indispensable to the former.
Ralph Waldo Emerson: The first wealth is health. Sickness is poor-spirited, and cannot serve anyone; it must husband its resources to live. But health answers its own ends, and has to spare; runs over, and inundates the neighborhoods and creeks of other men's necessities.
English Proverb: The best surgeon is he that hath been hacked himself.
English Proverb: While the doctors consult, the patient dies.
Dr. Oscar Fasker: Doctors are the guardians of our bodies, as priests, ministers, rabbis are the guardians of our souls. Doctors try to keep us from the heaven or hell that priests, ministers and rabbis promise.
Eugene Field: When one's all right, he's prone to spite / The doctor's peaceful mission; / But when he's sick, it's loud and quick / He bawls for a physician.
Henry Fielding: Every physician almost hath his favorite disease.
John Florio: Patience is the best medicine.
John Florio: From the physician and lawyer keep not the truth hidden.
Benjamin Franklin: God heals and the doctor takes the fee.
Benjamin Franklin: Beware of the young doctor and the old barber.

Benjamin Franklin: Be sober and temperate, and you will be healthy.
Benjamin Franklin: The best of all medicines are rest and fasting.
Benjamin Franklin: Many dishes, many diseases. Many medicines, few cures.
French Proverb: The doctor is more to be feared than the disease.
French Proverb: There are more old drunkards than old doctors.
French Proverb: God heals, and the physician takes the fee.
Sigmund Freud (after he met Albert Einstein, 1927): Einstein understands as much about psychology as I do about physics.
Thomas Fuller (English clergyman and author, 1608-1661, *The Holy State: The Good Advocate*, 1642): Commonly, physicians, like beer, are best when they are old; and lawyers, like bread, are best when they are young and new.
Thomas Fuller: Study sickness while you are well.
Sam Goldwyn: Anybody who goes to a psychologist ought to have his head examined!
Arthur S. Hardy: A wise physician is a John Baptist, who recognizes that his only mission is to prepare the way for a force greater than himself—Nature.
Don Harold: Doctors know only what you tell them.
Sir John Harrington: From your confessor, lawyer and physician, Hide not your case on no condition.
Heraclitus: Doctors cut, burn, and torture the sick, and then demand of them an undeserved fee for such services.
Herodotus (Greek historian, 484-424? BC): The practice of medicine is so specialized today that each doctor is a healer of one disease and no more. The country is full of physicians, some for the eye, some for the teeth, some for the stomach, some for the hidden diseases.
Joe Hickman: An apple a day keeps the doctor away. So does not having health insurance.
Marty Indik: Half of analysis is anal.
Hippocrates: Whenever a doctor cannot do good, he must be kept from doing harm.
Hippocrates: The physician must have at his command a certain ready wit, as dourness is repulsive both to the healthy and the sick.
Hippocrates: Keep a watch also on the faults of the patients, which often make them lie about the taking of things prescribed.
Oliver Wendell Holmes Sr.: Talk of your science! after all is said / There's nothing like a bare and shiny head; / Age lends the graces that are sure to please; / Folks want their doctors mouldy, like their cheese.
Oliver Wendell Holmes, Sr. (*Poet at the Breakfast Table*): The lawyers are the cleverest men, the ministers are the Most Learned, and the doctors are the most sensible.
Kin Hubbard: There's another advantage to being poor—a doctor will cure you faster.
Italian Proverb: A young doctor means a new graveyard.
Ben Jonson: Health is certainly more valuable than money, because it is by health that money is procured; but thousands and millions are of small avail to alleviate the tortures of the gout, to repair the broken organs of sense, or resuscitate the powers of digestion. Poverty is, indeed, an evil from which we naturally fly; but let us not run from one enemy to another, nor take shelter in the arms of sickness.
Sara Murray Jordan: In medicine, as in statecraft and propaganda, words are sometimes the most powerful drugs we can use.
Marjorie Karmel: Whoever said that doctors are truthful or even intelligent? You're getting a lot if they know their profession.
Sister Elizabeth Kenny ("Sister" is a term for an Australian WWI "Bush Nurse," creator of "The Kenny Method" of treating Infantile Paralysis): It's much easier to criticize a doctor than to try to be one.
La Bruyere: As long as men are liable to die and are desirous to live, a physician will be made fun of, but he will be well-paid.
Latin Proverb: There is more danger from the doctor than from the disease.
John Lavater (Swiss theologian, 1801): He who attempts to make others believe in means which he himself despises, is a puffer; he who makes use of more means than he knows to be necessary, is a quack; and he who ascribes to those means a greater efficacy than his own experience warrants, is an impostor.
Jerry Lester: What do you give a man who has everything? Penicillin.

Wilhelm von Leibnitz: I often say a great doctor kills more people than a great general.

Henry Wadsworth Longfellow: If the mind, that rules the body, ever so far forgets itself as to trample on its slave, the slave is never generous enough to forgive the injury, but will rise and smite the oppressors.

Henry Wadsworth Longfellow: Joy, temperance, and repose, slam the door on the doctor's nose.

Thomas Mann: All interest in disease and death is only another expression of interest in life.

Groucho Marx: A hospital bed is a parked taxi with the meter running.

Groucho Marx: If you're not feeling very well and you need a doctor immediately, ring the nearest golf course.

Philip Massinger: Out, you impostors; quack-salving, cheating mountebanks; your skill is to make sound men sick, and sick men to kill.

Midrash: Pay hommage to the physician before you need him.

Molière: There's a sort of decency among the dead, a remarkable discretion: you never find them making any complaint against the doctor who killed them!

Montaigne: Whoever saw one physician approve of another's prescription, without taking something away, or adding something to it?

Montaigne: The great order of things that takes care of fleas and moles also takes care of men, if they will have the same patience that fleas and moles have come to lead it to itself.

Napoleon Bonaparte: A physician and a priest ought not to belong to any particular nation and should be divested of all political opinions.

Laurence Olivier (as DR. CHRISTIAN SZELL in 1976 movie *Marathon Man*): **"Is it safe?"**

P.J. O'Rourke: If you think health care is expensive now, wait until you see what it costs when it's free.

Sir William Osler: There are only two sorts of doctors: those who practice with their brains, and those who practice with their tongues.

Hester Lynch Piozzi: A physician can sometimes parry the scythe of death, but has no power over the sand in the hourglass.

Polish Proverb: Better no doctor at all than three.

Marcel Proust: Medicine being a compendium of the successive and contradictory mistakes of medical practitioners, when we summon the wisest of them to our aid, the chances are that we may be relying on a scientific truth the error of which will be recognized in a few years' time.

Seneca: It is medicine, not scenery, for which a sick man must go searching.

William Shakespeare (*Coriolanus,* Act III, i): O, he's a limb, that has but a disease; / Mortal, to cut it off; to cure it easy.

William Shakespeare (*Hamlet,* Act IV, ii): Diseases, desperate grown, / By desperate appliances are reliev'd / Or not at all.

William Shakespeare (*Hamlet,* Act IV, vii): I bought an unction of a mountebank, / So mortal, that but dip a knife in it, / Where it draws blood, no cataplasm so rare, Collected from all simples that have virtue / Under the moon, can save the thing from death, / That is but scratch'd withal.

William Shakespeare (*I Henry IV,* Act IV, i): This sickness doth infect / The very life-blood of our enterprise.

William Shakespeare (*II Henry IV,* Act I, i): In poison there is physic; and these news, / Having been well, that would have made me sick; / Being sick, have in some measure made me well.

William Shakespeare (*II Henry IV,* Act I, ii): This apoplexy is, as I take it, a kind of lethargy, an't please your lordship; a kind of sleeping in the blood, a whoreson tingling.

William Shakespeare (*Henry VIII,* Act I, iii): "Tis time to give them phsic, their diseases / Are grown so catching.

William Shakespeare (*Henry VIII,* Act III, ii): In this point / All his tricks founder; and he brings his physic / After his patient's death.

William Shakespeare (*King John,* Act III, iv): Before the curing of a strong disease, / Even in the instant of repair and health, / The fit is stongest; evils that take leave, / On their departure most of all show evil.

William Shakespeare (*King Lear,* Act I, i): Kill thy physician, and the fee bestow / Upon thy foul disease.

William Shakespeare (*King Lear,* Act II, iv): Maybe he is not well: / Infirmity doth still neglecy all office, / Whereto our health is bound.

William Shakespeare (*King Lear,* Act III, iv): Take physic, pomp; / Expose thyself to feel what wretches feel.

William Shakespeare (*Macbeth,* Act III, iv): Now, good digestion wait on appetite, / And health on both!

William Shakespeare (*Macbeth,* Act V, iii): If thou couldst, doctor, cast / The water of my land, find her disease, / And purge it to a sound and pristine health, / I would applaud thee to the very echo, / That should applaud again.

William Shakespeare (*Macbeth,* Act V, iii): MACBETH: How does your patient doctor? / DOCTOR: Not so sick, my lord, / As she is troubled with sickening fancies.

William Shakespeare (*Macbeth,* Act V, iii): MACBETH: Canst thou not minister to a mind diseas'd; / Pluck from the memory a rooted sorrow: / Raze out the written trouble of the brain; And, with some sweet oblivious antidote, / Cleanse the stuff'd bosom of that perilous stuff, / Which weighs upon the heart? / DOCTOR: Therein the patient / Must minister to himself. / MACBETH: Throw physic to the dogs; I'll none of it.

William Shakespeare (*Merchant of Venice,* Act V, i): In such a night, / Medea gather'd the enchanted herbs / That did renew old Aeson.

William Shakespeare (*Merry Wives of Windsor,* Act II, ii): Methinks you prescribe to yourself very preposterously.

William Shakespeare (*Romeo and Juliet,* Act V, i): I do remember an apothecary, - / And hereabouts he dwells, - whom late I noted / In tatter'd weeds, with overwhelming brows, / Culling of simples; meagre were his looks, / Sharp misery had worn him to the bones: / And in his needy shop a tortoise hung, / An alligator stuff'd, and other skins / Of ill-shap'd fishes; and about his shelves / A beggarly account of empty boxes, / Green earthen pots, bladders and musty seeds, / Remnants of packthread, and old cakes of roses, / Were thinly scatter'd to make up a show.

William Shakespeare (*Sonnet,* CXL): Testy sick men, when their deaths be near, / No news but health from their physicians know.

William Shakespeare (*Tempest,* Act II, i): You rub the sore / When you should bring the plaster.

William Shakespeare (*Timon of Athens*, Act IV, iii): Trust not the physician; / His antidotes are poison, and he slays / More than you rob.

William Shakespeare (*Two Gentlemen of Verona,* Act II, iii): When I was sick you gave me bitter pills.

George Bernard Shaw (British dramatist and novelist, 1856-1950, *The Doctor's Dilemma*, Act I): All professions are conspiracies against the laity.

Publilius Syrus: There are some remedies worse than the disease.

Rabelais: Without health life is not life; it is only a state of languor and suffering, an image of death.

Joe Restivo: Never ask old people how they are if you have anything else to do that day.

Will Rogers: The best doctor in the world is the Veterinarian. He can't ask his patients what is the matter—he's got to just know.

Jerry Rubin: Medical doctors strike me as ignorant as to how a *healthy* body works. They know how to control or repair some disease bodies, but their medicine is often worse than the disease. And what about the pressure and competitiveness of the pharmaceutical industry and the make-profits-quick motives of the food corporations? Medical doctors put little or no emphasis on nutrition, exercise, and energy balance. They are paid when we are sick, not when we are well.

Russian Proverb: Only a fool will make a doctor his heir.

Jonas Salk (discoverer of polio vaccine, 1965): You must remember that nothing happens quite by chance. It's a question of accretion of information and experience... it's just chance that I happened to be here at this particular time when there was available and at my disposal a great experience of all the investigate worse who plotted along for a number of years.

Richard Selzer: Surgery is the red flower that blooms are among the leaves and thorns that are the rest of medicine.

George Bernard Shaw: Let no one suppose that the words Dr. and patient can disguise from the parties the fact that they are employer and employee.

Sir Philip Sidney: The ingredients of health and long life, are great temperance, open air, easy labor, and little care.

Milton Sills: We are beginning to recognize that amusement... is a commodity as essential to the physical and mental health and well-being of a human animal as lumber, wheat, oil, steel, or textiles.

Charles Simmons: Quackery has no such a friend as credulity.

Carrie Snow: A male gynecologist is like an auto mechanic who has never owned a car

Robert South (English preacher, 1716): Seldom shall we see in cities, courts, and rich families, where men live plentifully, and eat and drink freely, that perfect health and athletic soundness and vigor of constitution which are commonly seen in the country, where nature is the cook, and necessity the caterer, and where they have no other doctor but the sun and fresh air.

Spanish Proverb: There is no better surgeon than one with many scars.

Jack Starr: There are more doctors in a single North Shore medical building than in one entire West Side ghetto.

Peter Steinchrohn: Curiosity may have killed the cat, but it has never been detrimental to the doctor.

Laurence Sterne: There are worse occupations in this world then feeling a woman's pulse.

Jonathan Swift: The best doctors in the world are Doctor Diet, Doctor Quiet, and Doctor Merryman.

Talmud: A physician who takes no fee is worth no fee.

Jeremy Taylor: To preserve a man alive in the midst of so many chances and hostilities, is as great a miracle as to create him

Sir William Temple: Health is the soil that animates all the enjoyments of life, which fade and are tasteless without it.

Sir William Temple: The only way for a rich man to be healthy is by exercise and abstinence, to live as if he were poor.

Benjamin Thatcher: That science is worse than useless which does not point to the grade end of our being. – Therefore literary, scientific, and theological quacks have done immense mischief in human society.

Henry David Thoreau: Nothing more strikingly betrays the credulity of mankind than medicine. Quackery is a thing universal, and universally successful. In this case it is literally true that no imposition is too great for the credulity of men.

Alvin Toffler (1988): The next major explosion is going to the when genetics and computers come together. I'm talking about an organic computer—about biological substances that can function like semiconductors.

Roul Turley: Financial ruin from medical bills is almost exclusively an American disease.

Mark Twain: He had had much experience of physicians, and said, "The only way to keep your health is to eat what you don't want, drink what you don't like, and do what you'd druther not."

UA: Virus is a Latin word translated by doctors to mean: "your guess is as good as mine."

UA: Don't ask the doctor; ask the patient.

UA: The greatest doctor is time.

UA: A great doctor works with an angel at his side.

UA: No physician can cure a prejudice, which is a blindness in the mind.

Voltaire: The art of medicine consists in amusing the patient while nature cures the disease.

Voltaire: The art of medicine, like that of war, is murderous and conjectural.

Voltaire: I doubt not that in due time, when the arts are brought to perfection, some means will be found to give a sound head to a man who has none at all.

Voltaire: Men who are occupied in the restoration of health to other men, by the joint exertion of skill and humanity, are above all the great of the earth. They even partake of divinity, since to preserve and renew is almost as noble as to create.

Daniel Webster: Gold that buys health can never be ill spent; nor hours laid out in harmless merriment.

Daniel Webster: Physicians are like kings—They brook no contradiction.

James McNeill Whistler: The world is divided into two classes – invalids and nurses.

Rabbi Steven S. Wise: It is the superstition of medicine that is responsible for all the health cults of modern times. You have elevated the desire for health, youth and longevity to the position of a religion.

Steven Wright: I was walking down the street wearing glasses when the prescription ran out.

Ernst Wunder: Clearly, if disease is man-made, it can also be man-prevented. It should be the function of medicine to help people die young as late in life as possible.

Henny Youngman & Joey Bishop: My doctor is wonderful. Once when I could not afford an operation, he touched up my x-rays.

ECONOMICS/ECONOMY (See MONEY)

ECONOMIC LOSS (See also DAMAGES)

Uncle Anthony: It's easy to buy a $50,000 car—just buy $10,000 car on time.
Uncle Anthony: It seems like these days you need to have credit card to pay cash.
Aunt Mary Carlo: I tink dez guys got funny tailors – dere trousers only got "one way" pockets.
Aunt Mary Carlo: His pockets always outlast the rest of his suits.
Franklyn P. Adams: There are plenty of good five-ent cigars in the country. The trouble is they cost a quarter. What this country really needs is a good five-ent nickel.
Marty Allen: A study of economics usually reveals that the best time to buy anything is last year.
Yogi Berra: The future ain't what it used to be.
Bible: Daniel 5:27: Thou are weighed in the balances, and art found wanting.
Bible: Deuteronomy 5:6; Exodus 20:2: (The 7th Commandment) Thou shalt not steal ... (The 10th Commandement) ... Thou shalt not covet thy neighbor's house, ... nor his ox, nor his ass, nor any thing that is thy neighbour's.
Bible: Exodus 22:7: If the thief be found, let him pay double.
Bible: Leviticus 6:4: He shall restore that which he took violently away.
Bible: Matthew 25:29: Unto every one that hath shall be given, and he shall have abundance: but from him that hath not shall be taken away even that which he hath.
Bible: Psalms 19:9: The judgments of the Lord are true and righteous altogether. More to be desired are they than gold, yea than much fine gold: sweeter also than honey and the honeycomb.
Ambrose Bierce: ECONOMY, n. Purchasing the barrel of whiskey that you do not need for the price of the cow that you cannot afford.
Ambrose Bierce: LOSS, n. Privation of that which we had, or had not....
Josh Billings: Always live within your income, even if you have to borrow to do so.
Everett Dirksen (Illinois Senator 1968): A billion here, a billion there – pretty soon it adds up to real money.
Ben Franklin: Beware of little expenses: a small leak will sink a great ship.
Milton Friedman: Inflation is the one form of taxation that can be imposed without legislation.
John Kenneth Galbraith: One can relish the varied idiocy of human action during a panic to the full, for, while it is a time of great tragedy, nothing is being lost but money.
Molly Ivins: One function of the income gap is that the people at the top of the heap have a hard time even seeing those at the bottom. They practically need a telescope. The pharaohs of ancient Egypt probably didn't waste a lot of time thinking about the people who built their pyramids, either. OK, so it's not that bad yet—but it's getting that bad.
Jim Lees, Esq.: THE PLAINTIFF IN A "HARM HOLE" ILLUSTRATION: If you ask the jury to imagine or show them a drawing of a stick figure in a hole or a glass to illustrate the long term "harm" caused to plaintiff, you can analogize the plaintiff's disabling and costly injury(s) as putting plaintiff literally in a financial "hole" or "glass test tube." Use this image of the plaintiff in a "harm hole" as a depiction of how the payment of economic damages (past and future medical bills, past and future lost income, past and future lost income earning capacity, past and future economic value of lost services, etc.) does NOT lift the plaintiff out of his/her hole; indeed, payment of past and future economic damages only moves the plaintiff up but not out of this hole. The plaintiff's physical/emotional health, stamina, and the enjoyments of life which have been taken away are not compensated or replaced by the payment of economic damages only. Non-economic or "human" damages or "long term harm" for pain, suffering, emotional distress, disability, impairment, and lost enjoyments of life are very important elements of damage, which if not addressed by the jury will unfairly keep the plaintiff permanently in the hole. A plaintiff is not restored in any way to the prior pre-trauma situation, and plaintiff's "harm" is unfairly

ignored unless both economic and non-economic or "human" damages are addressed and allowed by the jury.

Jackie Mason: I have enough money to last me the rest of my life, unless I buy something.

Bill Maher: We survived the 1980s. Back then, the economic program was called "trickle down." That actually meant they were pissing on you. How the whole theory goes was this: "We have all the money. If we drop some, it's yours. Go for it."

Michael A. Musmanno (Justice of Pennsylvania Supreme Court, 1959): The Loss of a Strong Back: The plaintiff is a longshoreman by trade. This is an occupation which requires more muscular exertion than any other occupation except possibly the strongman at a circus who lifts staggeringly weighted dumbbells above his head. But whereas the circus man performs his feats two or three times a day, the longshoreman must accomplish it continuously. His job is to load and unload ships with cargoes ranging from baby carriages to pianos, steel bars, and iron safes. While mechanical devices and cranes assist in the loading and unloading process of oceangoing liners, basically what carries most of the cargo to and from decks is the longshoreman's back. And if his back is weak he becomes as useless as a blacksmith with scrawny biceps or the proverbial one-armed paper hanger. A longshoreman with a weak back is of no more use on a busy pier than a wheelbarrow without the wheel.... a longshoreman's back is to him what a gangplank is to a ship. As passengers and freight pass over the gangplank to fill the ship, so do all things, which a longshoreman needs to live, pass over his back. A longshoreman's back holds up his whole economic world as Atlas's shoulders sustained the earth. In considering damages in a personal injuries lawsuit, the monetary award must be based on the utilitarian value of the affected area of the body according to the importance that that area bears to the whole map of economic effort. To a sedentary professional, a weak back might mean only the loss of his golf game, but to a long-horeman a weak back could mean the collapse of the ramp over which his wife and children climb to reach the plateau of wholesome living to which they are entitled. (Rice v. Philadelphia Transportation Co., 394 PA. 454).

Michael A. Musmanno (Justice, Pennsylvania Supreme Court, 1959): Everyone knows that obtaining a return of 6% on one's money today is like growing watermelons in the Sahara. It is possible but highly unlikely, without the aid of experts whose cost could drain away the profit, making the venture a wholly desiccated investment. // When this Court said in 1922 that 6% was the lawful rate of interest, it did not say that 6% was and would for all time remain the routine, usual interest. Twenty years after the Windlel v. Davis, (275 Pa. 23) decision this Court held that a 6% yield on investment was not only not usual but that to depend on 6% constituted shaky financing .... To compel the plaintiff here to look for investments bringing a 6% return on what the jury awards him for loss of future wages is to ask him to attach skates to his disabled feet and, on wobbly legs, strikeout over thin ice to seek a solid island of guaranteed returns while moving over a constantly cracking surface beneath him. The tortfeasor in this case has already caused him to fall once; the Court should not force him into a situation where he may fall again—this time into a hole in the ice where he may lose all that an appreciative and fair-minded jury gave him for the necessities and slight comforts of a life which must from now on be clouded with unhappiness, at its best. // The lawful rate of 6% interest in Pennsylvania was established to protect people inexperienced in the ways of the world from the wolves of finance who might inveigle the unwary into the jaws of usurious destruction. The law never proclaimed that once money was put to work, it would of itself automatically augment yearly by 6%. Courts have no way of controlling markets, exchange, buying and selling anymore then they can by decrees guarantee rain and abundance of harvest to the farmer. (Richette v. Pennsylvania Railroad, 410 Pa. 6).

Michael A. Musmanno (Justice, Pennsylvania Supreme Court, 1959): Total Disability: All words and phrases must be accepted in the light of conditions prevailing at the time of their employment and not what they may have meant when they were first coined in the mint of lexicography. To be totally disabled no longer means that the victim must be a living cadaver. An intellectual who lives prostrate from disease or injury is indeed totally disabled, even though his brain may still be capable of creating railroads, books and cities. The giant with an unhinged mind is totally disabled but he can still lifts stones for a pyramid. (Schuchman v. Metropolitan Life, 374 PA. 48).

Kathleen Norris: In spite of the cost of living, it's still popular.

Robert Orben: Inflation is bringing us true democracy. For the first time in history, luxuries and necessities are selling at the same price.
Will Rogers: An economist's guess is liable to be as good as anybody else's.
Will Rogers: Invest in inflation. It's the only thing going up.
Will Rogers: I see a good deal of talk from Washington about lowering taxes. I hope they do get 'em lowered enough so people can afford to pay 'em.
Will Rogers: Government spending? I don't know what it's all about. I don't know any more about this thing than an economist does, and, God knows, he doesn't know much.
Will Rogers: The time to save is now. When a dog gets a bone, he doesn't go out and make a down payment on a bigger bone. He buries the one he's got.
Will Rogers: Money and women are the most sought after and the least known about of any two things we have.
Will Rogers: Don't gamble; take all your savings and buy some good stock and hold it till it goes up, then sell it. If it don't go up, don't buy it.
William Shakespeare (*Othello*, Act IV, ii): Who steals my purse steals trash.
William Shakespeare (*Othello*, Act IV, ii): I see thy glory like a shooting star / Fall to the base earth from the firmament. / Thy sun sets weeping in the lowly west.
William Shakespeare (*Timon of Athens*, Act IV, ii): So noble a master fallen! All gone! And not / One friend to take his fortune by the arm, / And go along with him.
Mark Twain: They inwardly resolved that so long as they remained in the business, their piracies should not again be sullied with the crime of stealing.
Voltaire: When it is a question of money, everybody is said to be of the same religion.

EDUCATION (See TEACHING)

ELDERLY (See AGE/AGING)

ELOQUENCE (See ORATORY)

EMPATHY (See COMPASSION)

EMPLOYMENT (See WORK)

EMOTIONAL DISTRESS

Uncle Anthony: When your emotional health gets wrecked or your mental stability gets overturned or your spirit just gets smashed and broken, there ain't no splints or bandages that can help.
Aunt Mary Carlo: It's easier to get over a leg that's broke than when it's your spirit.
Thomas Bailey Aldrich: Here is woe's self, and not the mask of woe.
Aristotle: Melancholy man of all others are most witty.
Bible: 2 Corinthians 4:8: We are perplexed, but not in despair.
Bible: 2 Corinthians 7:10: Godly sorrow worketh repentance to salvation not to be repented of.
Bible: Ecclesiastes 3:4: A time to weep, and a time to laugh; a time to mourn, and a time to dance.
Bible: Ecclesiastes 7:3: Sorrow is better than laughter; for by the sadness of the countenance the heart is made better.
Bible: Isaiah 53:4: Surely he hath bourne our griefs, and carried our sorrows.
Bible: John 16:20: Ye shall weep and lament, but the world will rejoice; and ye shall be sorrowful, but your sorrow shall be turned into joy.
Bible: Lamentations 1:12: Is it nothing to you, all ye that pass by? Behold, and see if there be any sorrow like unto my sorrow.
Bible: Proverbs 13:12: Hope deferred maketh the heart sick.
Bible: Proverbs 15:13: By sorrow of the heart the spirit is broken.
Bible: Proverbs 17:22: A merry heart doeth good like a medicine: but a broken spirit drieth the bones.

Bible: Proverbs 18:14: A wounded spirit who can bear?

Bible: Psalms 46:1: God is our refuge and strength, a very present help in trouble.

Bible: Psalms 102:11: My days are like a shadow that declineth; and I am withered like grass.

Ambrose Bierce: AFFLICTION, n. An acclimatizing process preparing the soul for another and bitter world.

Ambrose Bierce: CALAMITY, n. A more than commonly plain and unmistakable reminder that the affairs of this life are not of our ordering. Calamities are of two kinds: misfortune to ourselves, and good fortune to others.

Ambrose Bierce: DISTRESS, n. A disease incurred by exposure to the prosperity of a friend.

Ambrose Bierce: EMOTION, n. A prostrating disease caused by a determination of the heart to the head. It is sometimes accompanied by a copious discharge of hydrated chloride of sodium from the eyes.

Ambrose Bierce: HYPOCHONDRIASIS, n. Depression of one's own spirits....

Ambrose Bierce: PATIENCE, n. A minor form of despair, disguised as a virtue.

Sir Thomas Browne: It is the heaviest stone that melancholy can throw at a man, to tell him he is at the end of his nature; or that there is no further state to come.

Robert Browning: Let me not know that all is lost, / Though lost it be—leave me not tied / To this despair, this corpse-like bride.

John Bunyan (from *The Pilgrim' Progress*): Now there was a castle, called Doubting Castle, the owner whereof was Giant Despair.

Robert Burton: If there be a hell on earth it is to be found in a melancholy man's heart.

Robert Burton: That feral melancholy which crucifies the soul.

Lord George Gordon Byron: There are some feelings time cannot benumb.

Albert Camus: If you are convinced of your despair, you must either act as if you did hope after all – or kill yourself. Suffering gives no rights.

Dale Carnegie: When dealing with people remember you are not dealing with creatures of logic, but with creatures of emotion, creatures bristling with prejudice, and motivated by pride and vanity.

Cervantes: The beginning of health is to know the disease.

Cervantes: Melancholy was made, not for beasts, but for men; but if men give way to it overmuch they turn to beasts.

Geoffrey Chaucer: Men say, "To a wretch is consolation To have another fellow in his pain."

Lord Chesterfield: Physical ills are the taxes laid upon this wretched life; some are taxed higher, and some lower, but all pay something.

Chinese Proverb: You cannot prevent the birds of sadness from flying over your head, but you can prevent them from nesting in your hair.

Charles Churchill (English poet and satirist, 1731-1764): But, spite of all the criticizing elves, / Those who would make us feel, must feel themselves.

Sir Winston Churchill: Before you can inspire with emotion, you must be swamped with it yourself. Before you can move their tears, your own must flow. To convince them, you must yourself believe.

Cicero: Physicians consider that when the cause of a disease is discovered, the cure is discovered.

Cicero: Slight is the pleasure derived from the misery of others.

Cicero: So great an Iliad of woes threatens us.

Samuel Taylor Coleridge: I stood in unimaginable trance / And agony that cannot be remembered.

Joseph Collins: By starving emotions we become humorless, rigid and stereotyped; by repressing them we become literal, reformatory and holier-than-thou; encouraged, they perfume life; discouraged, they poison it.

Joseph Conrad: I can't tell if a straw ever saved a drowning man, but I know that a mere glance is enough to make despair pause. For in truth we who are creatures of impulse are not creatures of despair.

Christopher Pearse Cranch: Thought is deeper than all speech, / Feeling deeper than all thought.

John Dryden: Sure there's a lethargy in mighty woe, / Tears stand congeal'd and it cannot flow,... / Like Niobe we marble grow / and petrify with grief.

Egyptian Proverb: The worst things: / To be in bed and sleep not, / To want for one who comes not, / To try to please and please not.

George Eliot: There is no despair so absolute as that which comes with the first moments of our first great sorrow, when we have not yet known what it is to have suffered and be healed, to have despaired and have recovered hope.

Ralph Waldo Emerson: It is dainty to be sick, if you have leisure and convenience for it.

Erasmus: It is a step toward health to know the disease.

Euripides: There is no mortal whom sorrow and disease do not touch.

Benjamin Franklin: Despair ruins some, Presumption many.

Oliver Goldsmith: I have that within for which there are no plasters.

George Granville: There is no vulture like despair.

Nathaniel Hawthorne: In moods of heavy despondency, one feels as if it would be delightful to sink down in some quiet spot, and lie there forever, letting the soil gradually accumulate and form a little hillock over us, and the grass and perhaps flowers gather over it. At such times, death is too much of an event to be wished for; - we have not the spirits to encounter it; but choose to pass out of existence in this sluggish way.

W. C. Hazlitt: Sickness comes on horseback, but it goes away on foot.

Oliver Wendell Holmes, Jr.: We are all very near despair. The sheathing that floats us over its waves is compounded of hope, faith in the unexplainable worth and sure issue of its effort, and the deep, subconscious content which comes from the exercise of our powers.

Oliver Wendell Holmes, Sr.: There are a good many real miseries in life that we cannot help smiling at, but they are the smiles that make wrinkles and not dimples.

Homer: This, this is misery! the last, the worst, / That man can feel.

Homer: Have in the years in pity's hapless men like me, / Far sacred even to gods is misery.

Homer: Grief tears his heart, and drives him to and fro, / In all the raging impotence of woe.

Horace: If you wish me to weep, you must first feel grief.

Edgar Watson Howe: Most people have seen worse things in private than they pretend to be shocked at in public.

Victor Hugo: Melancholy is the pleasure of being sad.

William James: Despair lames most people, but it wakes others fully up.

Jewish Saying: No medicines heal sick souls.

Samuel Johnson: Employment, sir, and hardships, prevent melancholy.

Franz Kafka: Utter despair, impossible to pull myself together; only when I have become satisfied with my sufferings can I stop.

John Keble: Some are more strongly affected by the facts of human life; others by the beauty of earth and sky.

D.H. Lawrence: I have been fighting the powers of darkness lately. Still they prevail with me. But I have more or less got my head out of the inferno, my body will follow later. How one has to struggle, really, to overcome this accursed blackness. It would do me so much good if I could kill a few people.

Henry Wadsworth Longfellow: There are moments in life, when the heart is so full of emotion, / That if by chance it be shaken, or into its depths like a pebble / Drops some careless word, it overflows, and its secret, / Spilt on the ground like water, can never be gathered together.

Henry Wadsworth Longfellow: A feeling of sadness and longing / That is not akin to pain, / And resembles sorrow only / As the mist resembles the rain.

Charles R. Maturin: Preys on my heart that med'cine cannot reach.

John Milton: Moping melancholy, And moon-struck madness.

Austin O'Malley: Despair is vinegar from the wine of hope.

Pindar: Over woes long wept Oblivion softly lays / Her shadowy veil.

Plautus: It is easy to mock the miserable.

Alexander Pope: So perish all whose breast ne'er learned to glow / For others' good, or melt at others' woe.

Publilius Syrus: It is a consolation to the wretched to have companions in misery.

John Ray: Feeling hath no fellow.

John Ray: Misery loves company.

Will Rogers: Last year we said, 'Things can't go on like this', and they didn't, they got worse.

Will Rogers (writing in the First Hundred Days of FDR's Administration in 1934): [Franklin D. Roosevelt] swallowed our depression. He has inhaled fear and exhaled confidence.

Will Rogers: Do the best you can, and don't take life too serious.

Will Rogers: The worst thing that happens to you may be the best thing for you if you don't let it get the best of you.

Sir Walter Scott: Some feelings are to mortals given / With less of earth in them than heaven.

Seneca: A crowd of fellow sufferers is a miserable kind of comfort.

Seneca: 'Tis sweet to mingle tears with tears; / Griefs, where they wound in solitude, / wound more deeply.

William Shakespeare (*As You Like It*, Act II, v): I can suck melancholy out of a song.

William Shakespeare (*Antony and Cleopatra*, Act V, ii): My desolation does begin to make / A better life.

William Shakespeare (*Cymbeline*, Act IV, ii): O, melancholy! / Who ever yet could sound thy bottom? Find / The ooze, to show what coast thy sluggish crare / Might easiliest harbour in?

William Shakespeare (*Hamlet*, Act I, ii): O! that this too too solid flesh would melt, / Thaw, and resolve itself into a dew.

William Shakespeare (*Hamlet*, Act I, ii): 'Tis not alone my inky cloak, good mother, / Nor customary suits of solemn black, / Nor windy suspiration of forced breath, / No, nor the fruitful river in the eye, / Nor the dejected 'havior of the visage, / Together with all forms, moods, shapes of grief, / That can denote me truly; these indeed seem, / For they are actions that a man might play, / But I have that within which passeth show; / These but the trappings and the suits of woe.

William Shakespeare (*Hamlet*, Act IV, vii): One woe doth tread upon another's heel, / So fast they follow.

William Shakespeare (*I Henry IV*, Act II, iii): Tell me, sweet lord, what it's that takes from thee / Thy stomach, pleasure, and thy golden sleep? / Why dost thou bend thy eyes upon the earth; / And start so often when thou sitt'st alone? / Why hast thou lost the fresh blood in thy cheeks; / And given my treasures, and my tights of thee, / To thick-ey'd musing and curs'd melancholy?

William Shakespeare (*III Henry VI*, Act II, v): Would I were dead! If God's good will were so: / For what is in this world, but grief and woe?

William Shakespeare (*King John*, Act iv, i): Methinks no body should be sad but I.

William Shakespeare (*King Lear*, Act II, ii): Nothing almost sees miracles But misery.

William Shakespeare (*King Lear*, Act III, vi): Who alone suffers suffers most i' the mind, / Leaving free things and happy shows behind: / But then the mind much sufferance doth o'er-skip, / When grief hath mates, and bearing fellowship.

William Shakespeare (*Macbeth*, Act V, iii): Canst thou not minister to a mind diseased, / Pluck from the memory a rooted sorrow, / Raze out the written troubles of the brain, / And with some sweet oblivious antidote / Cleanse the stuffed bosom of that perilous stuff / Which weighs upon the heart?

William Shakespeare (*Much Ado About Nothing*, Act II, i): He is of a very melancholy disposition.

William Shakespeare (*Much Ado About Nothing*, Act III, ii): The greatest note of it is his melancholy.

William Shakespeare (*Richard II*, Act IV, i): My grief lies all within; / And these external manners of laments / Are merely shadows to the unseen grief / That swells with silence in the tortured soul.

William Shakespeare (*Romeo and Juliet*, Act V, i): Sharp misery had worn him to the bone.

William Shakespeare (*Taming of the Shrew*, Introduction, ii): Melancholy is the nurse of frenzy.

William Shakespeare (*The Tempest*, Act II, ii): Misery acquaints a man with strange bedfellows.

William Shakespeare (*Titus Andronicus*, Act III, i): O, what a sympathy of woe is this, / As far from help as Limbo is from bliss.

William Shakespeare (*Romeo and Juliet*, Act III, v): All these woes shall serve / For sweet discourses in our time to come.

William Shakespeare (*Venus and Adonis*, St. 170): For he being dead, with him is beauty slain, / And, beauty dead, black chaos comes again.

Jonathan Swift: We are so fond of each other, because our ailments are the same.

Henry David Thoreau: The mass of men lead lives of quiet desperation. What is called resignation is confirmed desperation.... A stereotyped but unconscious despair is concealed even under what are called the games and amusements of mankind.

Henry David Thoreau: If misery loves company, misery has company enough.

Mark Twain: It is easier to manufacture seven facts out a whole cloth than one emotion.

Marquis Luc de Clapiers Vauvenargues: Despair not only aggravates our misery, but our weakness.
Vergil: Night was our friend, our leader was Despair.

EMPATHY (See COMPASSION)

ENEMY(IES) (See ADVERSARY/ARGUMENTS)

ENJOYMENTS OF LIFE (See AGING)

EPIGRAMS (See ADVICE; CHARLEY CHAN; MAXIMS)

EPITAPH (See DEATH)

EQUALITY (See JUSTICE)

EQUITY (See JUSTICE; LAW)

ERROR (See also CONSISTENCY/MISTAKES; IGNORANCE)

Uncle Anthony: For those guys, every morning is "the dawn of a new error."
Uncle Anthony: Y'know the saying "A chain is only as strong as its weakest link"? Well, meet "THE WEAK LINK."
Uncle Anthony: The trouble with using your experience to teach you is that the final exam comes first and then the lesson follows.
Uncle Anthony: He's never gonna be too old to invent new ways to screw up.
Aunt Mary Carlo: He got a difficulty for every solution
Aunt Mary Carlo: He's dakinda guy dat goes tru life pushin' doors marked "Pull."
Aeschylus: The wisest of the wise may err.
Sholem Aleichem: Men make mistakes not because they think they know when they do not know, but because they think others do not know.
Henri Frederic Amiel: An error is more dangerous in proportion to the degree of truth which it contains.
Arabic Proverb: When a learned man errs, he errs with a learned error.
Matthew Arnold: Lack of recent information ... is responsible for more mistakes in judgment than erroneous reasoning.
St. Augustine: It is human to err; it is devilish to remain willfully in error.
Francis Bacon: He who errs quickly, is quick in correcting the error.
Francis Bacon: No man prospers so suddenly as by others' errors.
P. J. Bailey: Error is worse than ignorance.
P. J. Bailey: A double error sometimes sets us right.
Orlando A. Battista: An error doesn't become a mistake until you refuse to correct it.
Bible: Matthew, 27:64: So the last error shall be worse than the first.
Bible: Proverbs 22:3: A prudent man forseeth the evil, and hideth himself: but the simple pass on, and are punished.
Bible: Proverbs 29:20: Seest thou a man that is hasty in his words? There is more hope of a fool than of him.
Bible: 1 Samuel 26:21: Behold, I have played the fool, and have erred exceedingly.
Ambrose Bierce: MISCREANT, n. A person of the highest degree of unworth. Etymologically, the word means unbeliever, and its present signification may be regarded as theology's noblest contribution to the development of our language.
Ambrose Bierce: MISDEMEANOR, n. An infraction of the law having less dignity than a felony and constituting no claim to admittance into the best criminal society.
William Blake: The Errors of a Wise Man make your Rule / Rather than the Perfections of a Fool.
Logan E. Bleckley (Chief Justice of Georgia Supreme Court, 1827-1907): Some courts live by correcting the errors of others and adhering to their own. On these terms courts of final review hold their existence,

or those of them which are strictly and exclusively courts of review, without any original jurisdiction, and with no direct function but to find fault or see that none can be found. With these exalted tribunals, who live only to judge the judges, the rule of *stare decisis* is not only a canon of the public good, but a law of self-preservation. At the peril of their lives they must discover error abroad and be discreetly blind to its commission at home. Ellison v. Georgia R.R., 87 Ga. 691 (1891)

Logan E. Bleckley (Chief Justice of Georgia Supreme Court, 1827-1907): The court erred in some of the legal propositions announced to the jury, but all the errors were harmless. Wrong directions which do not put the traveler out of his way, furnish no reasons for repeating the journey. Cherry v. Davis, 59 Ga. 454 (1877)

Bertolt Brecht: Intelligence is not to make no mistakes / But quickly to see how to make them good.

Sir Thomas Browne: Many... have too rashly charged the troops of Error, and remain as trophies unto the enemies of Truth.

Robert Browning: Error has no end.

William Cullen Bryant: Truth, crushed to earth, shall rise again; / The eternal years of God are hers; / But Error, wounded, writhes in pain, / And dies among his worshipers.

Pearl S. Buck: Every great mistake has a halfway moment, a split second when it can be recalled and perhaps remedied.

Robert Burns (poem *To a Mouse*): The best-laid schemes of mice and men gang aft agley (or often go astray)

Edmund Burke: They defend their errors as if they were defending their inheritance.

Samuel Butler: Error and mistake are infinite, / But truth has but one way to be i' th' right.

Samuel Butler: There is no such source of error as the pursuit of absolute truth.

Samuel Butler: I do not mind lying, but I hate inaccuracy.

John Cage: An error is simply a failure to adjust immediately from a preconception to an actuality.

William Ellery Channing: Error is the discipline through which we advance.

Lord Chesterfield: Honest error is to be pitied, not ridiculed.

G.K. Chesterton: There is something to be said for every error, but whatever may be said for it, the most important thing to be said about it is that it is erroneous.

Chinese Proverb: The error of one moment becomes the sorrow of a whole life.

Sir Winston Churchill: All men make mistakes, but only wise men learn from their mistakes.

Cicero: I would rather err with Plato than perceive the truth with others.

Cicero: Any man can make mistakes, but only an idiot persists in his error

Cicero: It is the nature of every man to err, but only the fool perseveres in error.

Cicero: More is lost by indecision than by wrong decision.

Sir Edward Coke (Lord Chief Justice of England, 1552-1634, 5 Rep.: *Preface*): Error (Ignorance being her inseparable twin) doth in her proceeding so infinitly multiply herself, produceth such monstrous and strange chimaeras, floateth in such and so many uncertainties and sucketh down the poison from the contagious breath of Ignorance, as all such into whom she infuseth any of her poisoned breath, she dangerously infects or intoxicates.

Samuel Taylor Coleridge: Truth is a good dog; but beware of barking too close to the heels of an error, lest you get your brains kicked out

***Collier's* magazine (1932 cartoon of two trains about to collide, a signalman says):** What a way to run a railroad!

John Churton Collins: Half our mistakes in life arise from feeling where we ought to think, and thinking where we ought to feel.

Charles Caleb Colton: Ignorance is a blank sheet, on which we may write; but error is a scribbled one, one which we must first erase.

Confucius: The cautious seldom err.

Congreve: Error lives ere reason can be born.

e. e. cummings: may i be wrong / for whenever man are right they are not young.

Cyrus H. Curtis: There are two kinds of men who never amount to much: those who cannot do what they are told and those who can do nothing else.

Edward Dahlberg: Who has enough credit in this world to pay for his mistakes?

Clarence Day: This is a hard and precarious world, where every mistake and infirmity must be paid for in full.

Georges Duhamel: No doubt about it: error is the rule, truth is the accident of error.

Egyptian Proverb: He who is half wrong fights against himself.

English Proverb: Error is always in a hurry.

English Proverb: He who is shipwrecked the second time cannot lay the blame on Neptune.

English Proverb: Bernard did not see everything (referring to the theologian St. Bernard of Clairvaux, 1091-1153)

English Proverb (18th century): It is an equal failing to trust everybody, and to trust nobody.

Ilya Ehrenburg: People seldom learn from the mistakes of others—not because they deny the value of the past, but because they are faced with new problems.

Joseph Fouche: It is worse than a crime: it is a blunder.

Thomas Fuller: Error is always in haste.

Thomas Fuller: A stumble may prevent a fall.

Galileo Galilei (1564-1642; his admission of guilt after his trial by The Holy Office of the Inquisition in 1633): "My error has been, and I confess it, one of vainglorious ambition and of pure ignorance and inadvertence."

Mohandas Karamchand (Mahatma) Gandhi: Error ceases to be error when it is corrected.

Gandhi: Relaxation of an error, which amounts to a fixed resolve never to repeat it, is enough penance.

Gandhi: There is no defeat in the confession of one's error. The confession itself is victory.

Goethe: Man must strive, and in striving he must err.

Goethe: Error belongs to libraries, truth to the human mind.

Goethe: Truth belongs to the man, error to his age.

Goethe: Is much easier to recognize error than to find truth; error is superficial and may be corrected; truth lies hidden in the depths.

Goethe: I hate all bungling like sin, but most of all bungling in state affairs, which produces nothing but mischief to thousands and millions.

Greek Proverb: Homer sometimes nods (referring to the great Greek poet Homer – even the great have their limitations).

Learned Hand: One utterance of Oliver Cromwell has always hung in my mind. It was just before the Battle of Dunbar; he beat the Scots in the end, as you know, after a very tough fight; but he wrote them before the battle, trying to get them to accept a reasonable composition. These were his words: "I beseech ye in the bowels of Christ, think that ye may be mistaken." I should like to have that written over the portals of every church, every school, and every court house, and, may I say, of every legislative body in the United States.

Jimmy Hoffa: I may have my faults, but being wrong ain't one of them.

Eric Hoffer: Absolute faith corrupts as absolutely as absolute power.

Oliver Wendell Holmes (1 *Holmes-Pollock Letters* 219, 1914): One thinks that an error exposed is dead, but exposure amounts to nothing when people want to believe.

Elbert Hubbard: The greatest mistake you can make in life is to be continually fearing you will make one.

Victor Hugo: Dark Error's other hidden side is truth.

Victor Hugo: Great blunders are often made, like large ropes, of a multitude of fibers.

Thomas Henry Huxley: Irrationally held truths may be more harmful than reasoned errors.

Thomas H. Huxley: The most considerable difference I note among men is not in their readiness to fall into error, but in their readiness to acknowledge these inevitable lapses.

William Ralph Inge: A nation is a society united by delusions about its ancestry and by common hatred of its neighbors.

R.G. Ingersoll: An error cannot be believed sincerely enough to make it a truth.

Italian/**German Proverb:** An old error is always more popular than a new truth.

Thomas Jefferson: Delay is preferable to error.

Thomas Jefferson: Ignorance is preferable to error; and he is less remote from the truth who believes nothing, than he who believes what is wrong.

Thomas Jefferson: Ignorance of the law is not excsue in any country. If it were, the laws would lose their effect, because it can always be pretended.

Thomas Jefferson: Error of opinion may be tolerated where reason is left free to combat it.

Thomas Jefferson: (Washington) errs as other men do, but errs with integrity.

John Jewel: Error cannot be defended but by error. Untruth cannot be shielded but by untruth.

Jewish Proverb: It is better to measure ten times and cut once, than measure once and cut ten times.

Jewish Proverb: Error that comes from lack of study is a sin.

Samuel Johnson: He that has much to do will do something wrong.

Carl Jung: Error is just as important a condition of life as truth.

Pierre-Claude Nivelle de LaChaussee: When everyone is wrong, everyone is right.

La Rochefoucauld: Truth does not do so much good in the world, as the appearance of it does evil.

Barry LePatner: Good judgment comes from experience, and experience comes from bad judgment.

Abraham Lincoln: I shall try to correct errors where shown to be errors, and I shall adopt the new views as fast as they shall appear to be true views.

John Locke: It is one thing to show a man that he is in error, and another to put him in possession of the truth.

John Locke: All men are liable to error; and most men are, in many points, by passion or interest, under temptation to it.

John Locke: The strength of our persuasions is no evidence at all of their own rectitude; crooked things may be as stiff and inflexible as straight; and men may be as positive and peremptory in error as in truth.

John Locke: Knowledge being to be had only of visible and certain truth, error is not a fault of our knowledge, but a mistake of our judgment, giving assent to that which is not true.

Henry Wadsworth Longfellow: Sometimes we may learn more from a man's errors than from his virtues.

Henry Wadsworth Longfellow: Were half the power that fills the world with terror, / Were half the wealth bestowed on camps and courts, / Given to redeem the human mind from error, / There were no need of arsenals or forts.

William Connor Magee: The man who makes no mistakes does not usually make anything.

Malay Proverb: The body pays for a slip of the foot and gold pays for a slip of the tongue.

H. L. Mencken: Nine times out of ten, in the arts as in life, there is actually no truth to be discovered; there is only error to be exposed.

H.L. Mencken: The world always makes the assumption that the exposure of an error is identical with the discovery of the truth—that error and truth are simply opposite. They are nothing of the sort. What the world turns to, when it has been cured of one error, is. usually simply another error and may be one worse than the first one.

John Stuart Mill: The fatal tendency of mankind to leave off thinking about a thing, when it is no longer doubtful, is the cause of half their errors

Molière: The shortest errors are always the best.

Friedrich Nietzsche: The errors of great men are venerable because they are more fruitful than the truths of little men.

Richard Nixon: While technically I did not commit a crime, an impeachable offense... these are legalisms, as far as the handling of this matter is concerned; it was so botched up, I made so many bad judgments. The worst ones, mistakes of the heart, rather than the head. But let me say, a man in that top job - he's got to have a heart, but his head must always rule his heart."

Ovid: If it was an error, its causes were honorable.

Dorothy Parker: It's not the tragedies that kill us, it's the messes.

Blaise Pascal (1623-1662; French mathematician, physicist, and religious philosopher): The most powerful cause of error is the war existing between the senses and reason.

S.J. Perelman: To err is human, to forgive supine.

Plutarch: For to err in opinion, though it be not the part of wise men, is at least human.

Alexander Pope: Good nature and good sense must ever join; / To err is human, to forgive divine.

Hans Reichenbach: If error is corrected whenever it is recognized as such, the path of error is the path of truth.

Cardinal De Retz: The man who can own up to his error is greater than he who merely knows how to avoid making it.

Will Rogers: It's not what we don't know that hurts, it's what we know that ain't so.

Will Rogers: When ignorance (EDITOR: or mistake) gets started it knows no bounds.

Will Rogers: There is nothing so stupid as the educated man if you get him off the thing he was educated in.

Will Rogers: If Stupidity got us into this mess, then why can't it get us out?

Will Rogers: There are three kinds of men. The one that learns by reading. The few who learn by observation. The rest of them have to pee on the electric fence for themselves.

Will Rogers: An ignorant person is one who doesn't know what you have just found out.

Will Rogers: America is becoming so educated that ignorance will be a novelty. I will belong to the select few.

Will Rogers: Everybody is ignorant, only on different subjects.

Theodore Roosevelt: If I have erred, I err in company with Abraham Lincoln.

Joseph Roux: We are more conscious that a person is in the wrong when the wrong concerns ourselves.

J.K. Rowling: Indifference and neglect often do much more damage then outright dislike.

Bertrand Russell: A stupid man's report of what a clever man says can never be accurate, because he unconsciously translates what he hears into something he can understand.

Henry St. John: Truth lies within a little and certain compass, but error is immense.

Henry St. John: Plain truth will influence half a score men at most in a nation, or an age, while mystery will lead millions by the nose.

Seneca: To err is human.

Seneca: An error is not counted as a crime.

William Shakespeare (*Coriolanus*, Act II, iii): The dust on antique time would lie unswept, / And mountainous error be too highly heapt / For truth to o'er-peer.

William Shakespeare (*Hamlet,* Act I, iv): More honour'd in the breach than the observance.

William Shakespeare (*Hamlet*, Act V, ii): Purposes mistook / Fall'n on the inventor's heads.

William Shakespeare (*Julius Caesar*, Act V, iii): O hateful error, melancholy's child! / Why dost thou shew to the apt flaws of men / The things that are not? O error, soon conceiv'd, / Thou never com'st unto a happy birth, / But kill'st the mother that engender'd thee.

William Shakespeare (*King Lear*, Act III, ii): How far your eyes may pierce, I cannot tell; / Striving to better, oft we mar what's well.

William Shakespeare (*Macbeth*, Act III, i): Leave no rubs nor botches in the work.

William Shakespeare (*Troilus and Cressida*, Act III, iii): Omission to do what is necessary / Seals a commission to a blank of danger.

William Shakespeare (*Troilus and Cressida*, Act V, ii): The error of our eye directs our mind: / What error leads must err.

William Shakespeare (*Sonnets*, Number cxvi): If this be error, and upon me proved, / I never writ, nor no man ever loved.

George Bernard Shaw: A life spent in making mistakes is not only more honorable but more useful than a life spent doing nothing.

Red Skelton: All men make mistakes, but married men find out about them sooner.

Sophocles: To err is common to all men, but the man who, having erred, hugs not his errors, but repents and seeks the cure, is not a wastrel.

John Lancaster Spalding: The error which we hold inquiringly, striving to find what element of fact there be in it, is worth more to us than the truth which we accept mechanically and retain with indifference.

Spanish Proverb: Who errs and mends, to God himself commends.

Robert Louis Stevenson: All error, not merely verbal, is a strong way of stating that the current truth is incomplete.

Irving Stone (writing about Clarence Darrow): If someone made a mistake he (Darrow) would drawl, "Hell, that's why they make erasers."

Jonathan Swift: A man should never be ashamed to own he has been in the wrong, which is but saying, in other words, that he is wiser today than he was yesterday.

Jonathan Swift: Who can deny that all men are violent lovers of truth, when we see them so positive in their errors, which they will maintain out of their zeal to truth, although they contradict themselves every day of their lives?

Rabindranath Tagore: If you shut your door to all errors truth will be shut out.

Rabindranath Tagore: Mistakes live in the neighborhood of truth / and therefore delude us.

Rabindranath Tagore: Life's errors cry for the merciful beauty / that can modulate their isolation / into a harmony with the whole.

Talmud: Once error creeps in, it stays.

Jeremy Taylor: Men are apt to prefer a prosperous error to an afflicted truth.

Alfred Lord Tennyson: Shall Error in the round of time / Still father Truth?

Leo Tolstoy: Error is the force that welds men together; truth is communicated to men only by deeds of truth.

Martin F. Tupper: Error is a hardy plant; it flourisheth in every soil.

Mark Twain: They spell it Vinci and pronounce it Vinchy; foreigners always spell better than they pronounce.

Mark Twain: News is history in its first and best form, its vivid and fascinating form... history is the pale and tranquil reflection of it.

UA: The man who answers speedily errs speedily.

UA: Experience is our name for accumulated errors.

UA: Error that comes from lack of study is a sin.

Vauvenargues: All erroneous ideas would perish of their own accord if given clear expression.

Voltaire: The progress of rivers to the ocean is not so rapid as that of man to error.

Voltaire: Believe me, error also has its merit.

Voltaire: Love the truth, but pardon error.

Voltaire: Error flies from mouth to mouth, from pen to pen, and to destroy it takes ages.

William Wrigley Jr.: When two men in business always agree, one of them is unnecessary.

William Butler Yeats: The pain others give passes away in their later kindness, but that of our own blunders, especially when they hurt our vanity, never passes away.

Zeno of Citium (300 B.C.): Better to trip with the feet than with the tongue.

ESTIMATES (See STATISTICS)

ETHICS (See also PRINCIPLE/HYPOCRACY)

Uncle Anthony: Sometimes, the morally right or whaddyacallit the ethical thing to do is just to have the guts to make a decision.

Uncle Anthony: What's the difference between lying to somebody (like a jury) and pulling the wool over their eyes?

Aunt Mary Carlo: I think ethics is all about what's right, not who's right!

St. Augustine: Conscience and reputation are two things. Conscience is due to yourself, reputation to your neighbor.

Fred Astaire: The hardest job kids face today is learning good manners without seeing any.

Melvyn Belli: I'm not an ambulance chaser. I'm usually there before the ambulance.

Bible: Acts 24:16: Herein do I exercise myself, to have always a conscience void of offence toward God, and toward men.

Bible: Apocrypha, Ecclesiasticus 20:19: An ungracious man is like a story told at the wrong time.

Bible: Corinthians 15:33: Evil communications corrupt good manners.

Bible: Isaiah 1:17: Learn to do well.

Bible: Job 6:25: How forcible are right words.

Bible: Leviticus 19:11: Ye shall not steal, neither deal falsely, neither lie to one to another.

Bible: Matthew 7:12: All things whatsoever ye would that men should do to you, do ye even so to them: for this is the law and the prophets.

Bible: Proverbs 6:16: These six things doth the Lord hate: yea, seven are an abomination unto Him: a proud look, a lying tongue, and hands that shed innocent blood, An heart that deviseth wicked imaginations, feet that be swift in running to mischief, A false witness that speaketh lies, and he that soweth discord among brethren.

Bible: Proverbs 28:1: The wicked flee when no man pursueth: the righteous are bold as a lion.

Bible: 1 Thessalonians 5:22: Abstain from all appearance of evil.

Bible: 1 Timothy 1:5: The end of the commandment is charity out of a pure heart, and of a good conscience, and of faith unfeigned.

Ambrose Bierce: BEHAVIOR, n. Conduct, as determined, not by principle, but by breeding.

Ambrose Bierce: DECALOGUE, n. A series of commandments, ten in number – just enough to permit an intelligent selection for observance, but not enough to embarass the choice.

Ambrose Bierce: MORAL, adj. Conforming to a local and mutable standard of right. Having the quality of general expediency.

Ambrose Bierce: POLITENESS, n. The most acceptable hyprocrisy.

Ambrose Bierce: RITUALISM, n. A Dutch Garden of God where He may walk in rectilinear freedom, keeping off the grass.

Josh Billings: One of the gretaest victories you can gain over someone is to beat him at politeness.

James Boswell (Scottish lawyer and biographer of Samuel Johnson, 1740-1795, *Life of Samuel Johnson: 1768*): BOSWELL: I asked him whether, as a moralist, he did not think that the practice of the law, in some degree, hurt the nice feeling of honesty. JOHNSON: Why no, Sir, if you act properly. You are not to deceive your clients with false representations of your opinion: you are not to tell lies to a judge.

James Boswell (*Life of Samuel Johnson: 1768*): BOSWELL: But what do you think of supporting a cause which you know to be bad? JOHNSON: Sir, you do not know it to be good or bad until the Judge determines it. I have said that you are to state facts fairly; so that your thinking, or what you call knowing, a cause to be bad, must come from reasoning, must be from supposing your arguments to be weak and inconclusive. But, Sir, that is not enough. An argument which does not convince yourself, may convince the Judge, to whom you urge it: and if it does convince him, why, then, Sir, you are wrong, and he is right. It is his business to judge; and you are not to be confident in your own opinion that a cause is bad, but to say all you can for your client, and then hear the Judge's opinion. BOSWELL: But, Sir, does not affecting a warmth when you have no warmth, and appearing to be clearly of one opinion when you are in reality of another opinion, does not such dissimulation impair one's honesty? Is there not some danger that a lawyer may put on the same mask, in common life, in the intercourse with his friends? JOHNSON: Why no, Sir. Everybody knows you are paid for affecting warmth for your client; and it is, therefore, properly no dissimulation; the moment you come from the bar you resume your usual behaviour. Sir, a man will no more carry the artifice of the bar into the common intercourse of society, than a man who is paid for tumbling upon his hands will continue to tumble upon his hands when he should walk on his feet.

David R. Brink: Lawyers know that no other group or profession sets higher ethical standards, disciplines itself so rigorously, and contributes so much unpaid service to the public.

Piero Calamandrei (Italian lawyer and professor, 1889-1956, *Eulogy of Judges*, 1942): The difference between the true lawyer and those men who consider the law merely a trade is that the latter seek to find ways to permit their clients to violate the moral standards of society without overstepping the letter of the law, while the former look for principles which will persuade their clients to keep within the limits of the spirit of the law in common moral standards.

Benjamin Cardozo: There are many forms of professional misconduct that do not amount to crimes.

G.K. Chesterton: To have a right to do a thing is not at all the same as to be right in doing it.

Chinese Proverb: Laws control the lesser man. Right conduct controls the greater one.

Sir Winston Churchill: It is not enough that we do our best; sometimes we have to do what is required.

James Gould Cozzens: You just had to take the practical view that a man always lied on his own behalf, and paid his lawyer, who was an expert, a professional liar, to show him new and better ways of lying.

Charles P. Curtis: I don't see why we should not come out roundly and say that one of the functions of a lawyer is to lie for his client; and on rare occasions, as I think I have shown, I believe it is.

Danish Proverb: Act in the valley so that you need not fear those who stand on the hill.

John Dean (1983): How in God's name could so many lawyers get involved in something like Watergate.

Denis Diderot: There is no moral precept that does not have something inconvenient about it.

John F, Dillon (Judge, Iowa Supreme Court, US Circ. Ct, 1831-1914, *Laws and Jurisprudence of England and America*, Lecture I, 1894): Ethical considerations can no more be excluded from the administration of justice, which is the end and purpose of all civil laws, than one can exclude the vital air from his room and live.

Peter Drucker: Ethics stays in the preface of the average business science book.

Albert Einstein: Never do anything against conscience, even if the state demands it.

Albert Einstein: The ideals which have always shone before me and filled me with the joy of living are goodness, beauty, and truth. To make a goal of comfort or happiness has never appealed to me; a system of ethics built on this basis would be sufficient only for a herd of cattle.

Albert Einstein: I do not believe in immortality of the individual, and I consider ethics to be an exclusively human concern with no superhuman authority behind it.

Ralph Waldo Emerson: Friendship should be surrounded with ceremonies and respects, and not crushed into corners.

English Proverb: Honesty is the best policy.

Marvin Frankel (Federal Judge in 1978): We (lawyers) must alter our prime axiom – that we are combat mercenaries available indifferently for any cause or purpose a client is ready to finance ... We should all be what I would term "ministers of justice." As such, we would have to reconsider and revise a system of loyalty to clients that results too often in coverups, frauds, and injury to innocent people. A favorite quotation in the legal profession ... is Lord Brougham's declaration that an advocate "knows but one person in all the world, and that person is his client ...." For him Lord Brougham said, the advocate would stand against the world ... Lord Brougham was wrong; we should be less willing to fight the world and ... more concerned to save our souls. As ministers of justice, we should find ourselves more positively concerned than we now are with the pursuit of truth.

Monroe Freedman (*Understanding Lawyers' Ethics*, Matthew Bender; "Brandeis' Lawyer for the Situation" article): At every conference on lawyer's ethics and professionalism, someone is bound to say that lawyers should abandon adversary zeal and adopt instead Justice Louis Brandeis' ideal of "lawyer for the situation." We are rarely told just what it means to be a lawyer for situation—only that it is somehow superior to being the lawyer for a client.... Consider, first, the following case. Lennox is in financial trouble and has several creditors. Lawyer A., of the firm of A & B represents Creditor No. 1. Lawyer B, of the same firm, then becomes attorney for Creditor No. 2. Neither Creditor gives its informed consent for this conflict of interest. Lawyer B. than meets up with his client (Creditor No. 2) and with Lennox (the debtor), who is unrepresented. B questions Lennox, obtaining information from him that is both confidential and damaging. B then suggests that he "act for Mr. Lennox in this matter." Lennox asks whether that means that B would be "acting as my council." B replies ambiguously, "Not altogether as your council, but as a trustee of your property." Both Lennox and Creditor No. 2 understand that B has become Lennox's lawyer. Pursuant to B's advice, Lennox signs documents transferring all of his assets—his personal property as well as the company's to an assignee for the benefit of creditors. The assignee is none other than B's partner, Lawyer A. B does not tell Lennox that making the assignment gives his creditors the right to throw him into bankruptcy. The firm of A&B then institute involuntary bankruptcy proceedings against Lennox, citing the assignment as their grounds. Lennox retains a new lawyer, who confronts B with his conduct. B tells the new lawyer, "I did not intend to act personally for Mr. Lennox, nor did I agree to." The new lawyer replies, "Yes, but you advised him to make the assignment. For whom were you council when you advised him to do that, if not for (Lennox)?" B answers, "I should say I was council for the situation."... The facts of the case, including the quotations, are based directly on Louis Brandeis' representation of Jim Lennox in 1907.... Brandeis was an admirable person, lawyer, and judge. The Lennox episode was a rare lapse. Those who promote the phrase "lawyer for the situation" as an ideal for the profession cannot be aware of the unfortunate case that originally gave rise to it. In fatuously repeating the phrase, however, they do no service either to Brandeis or to lawyers' ethics.

Ann Gerber: I don't really mean that all lawyers are dishonest. Just that the honest ones are all poor.

German Proverb: A clear conscience is a soft pillow.

Jean Giraudoux: No poet ever interpreted nature as freely as a lawyer interprets truth.

Verne E. Henderson: The survival of business is not only a matter of profits but of prophets, of anticipating ethical consequences.

Italian Saying: THE PARAGONAE was an Italian contest between artists about how best to depict the moral qualities of their patron. Hence, the expression "PARAGON OF VIRTUE."

Immanuel Kant: In law a man is guilty when he violates the rights of others. In ethics he is guilty if he only thinks of doing so.

Joseph Wood Krutch: Custom has furnished the only basis which ethics have ever had.

Robert H. Jackson: As to ethics, the parties seem to me as much on a parity as the pot and the kettle.

Walter Savage Landor: A man's vanity tells him what is honour, a man's conscience what is justice.

Harper Lee: The one thing that doesn't abide by majority rule is a person's conscience.

Abraham Lincoln (*Notes for a Law Lecture*, 1850): There is a vague popular belief that lawyers are necessarily dishonest.... Let no young man choosing the law for a calling for a moment yield to the popular belief – resolve to be honest at all events; and if in your own judgment you cannot be an honest lawyer, resolve to be honest without being a lawyer. Choose some other occupation, rather than one in the choosing of which you do, in advance, consent to be a knave.

Lord Hugh Pattison MacMillan (Scottish judge, Baron, 1873-1952, *Law and Other Things, 1937*): The ultimate justification of the law is to be found, and can only be found, in moral considerations.

Groucho Marx: Those are my principles, if you don't like them ... I have others.

H.L. Mencken: Time is a great legalizer, even in the field of morals.

Merrit Malloy (American Poet, 1950-): What we might consider is how we are good rather than how good we are.

Ronald Reagan (answering high school reporters at White House, 1985): All you can do is try to do the best of your ability, and with all the input and knowledge you get, then hope that the decisions you make are based on what is morally right.

Will Rogers: Liberty doesn't work as well in practice as it does in speeches.

Will Rogers: People love high ideals, but they got to be about 33-percent plausible.

Will Rogers: If you want to be successful, it's just this simple. Know what you are doing. Love what you are doing. And believe in what you are doing.

Will Rogers: In Hollywood you can see things at night that are fast enough to be in the Olympics in the day time.

Will Rogers: What the country needs is dirtier fingernails and cleaner minds.

Will Rogers: Live in such a way that you would not be ashamed to sell your parrot to the town gossip.

Will Rogers: "Whoever wrote the Ten Commandments made 'em short. They may not always be kept but they can be understood. They are the same for everyone."

Will Rogers: "Ability is all right but if it is not backed up by honesty and public confidence you will never be a (successful person). The best a man can do is to arrive at the top in his chosen profession. I have always maintained that one profession is deserving of as much honor as another provided it is honorable."

Will Rogers: Personally I don't think you can make a lawyer honest by an act of the Legislature. You've got to work on his conscience. And his lack of conscience is what makes him a lawyer.

Will Rogers: Of course people are getting smarter nowadays; they are letting lawyers instead of their conscience be their guidance.

Romain Rolland: France fell because there was corruption without indignation.

Leo Rosten: MITZVAH: (plural *mitzvot*): Hebrew: "commandment." (1) Commandment; divine commandment. (2) A meritorious act, a "good work," a truly virtuous, kind, ethical deed. *Mitzvah* is second only to *Torah* in the vocabulary of Judaism. *Mitzvot* are of various kinds: those of positive performance (e.g., caring for the widow and orphan), and those of negative resolve (e.g., not accepting a bribe); and those between man and God (fasting on *Yom Kippur*) and those between man and man (paying a servant promptly). *Mitzvot* are regarded as profound obligations, but must be performed not from a sense of duty but with "a joyous heart." There are 613 separate *mitzvot* listed in the *Sefer Mitzvot Gadol*, of which 248 are positive and 365 negative. Maimonides listed all the *mitzvot* in his *Book of the*

Mitzvot; he remarked that the man who performed only one of the 613 deserved salvation – *if* he did so not to win credit, but entirely for its own sake. The potential number of *mitzvot* is endless. Israel Zangwell called *mitzvot* the Jews' "sacred sociology."

Eleanor Roosevelt: What we need in the world is manners ... I think that if, instead of preaching brotherly love, we preached good manners we might get a little further. It sounds less righteous and more practical.

Bernard Joseph Saurin: The law often permits what honor forbids.

Albert Schweitzer: The first step in the evolution of ethics is a sense of solidarity with other human beings.

William Shakespeare (*Coriolanus*, Act IV, vii): Our virtues / Lie in th' interpretation of the time.

William Shakespeare (*Hamlet*, Act III, iv): Assume a virtue, if you have it not.

William Shakespeare (*Hamlet*, Act III, iv): For in the fatness of these pursy times, / Virtue itself of vice must pardon beg.

William Shakespeare (*II Henry VI*, Act III, i): Virtue is chok'd with foul ambition.

William Shakespeare (*Henry VIII*, Act III, i): Virtue finds no friends.

William Shakespeare (*Henry VIII*, Act III, ii): My robe / And my integrity to heaven, is all / I dare now call mine own.

William Shakespeare (*Julius Caesar*, Act II, iii): My heart laments that virtue cannot live / Out of the teeth of emulation.

William Shakespeare (*Measure for Measure*, Act II, vi): Go to your bosom; / Knock there; and ask your heart, what it doth know.

William Shakespeare (*Othello*, Act II, iii): Come, you are too severe a moraler.

William Shakespeare (*Timon of Athens*, Act I, ii): Ceremony was but devised at first / To set a gloss on faint deeds, hollow welcomes, / recanting goodness, sorry ere 'tis shown; / But where there is true friendship, there needs none.

George Bernard Shaw (*Pygmalion*): I have to live for others and not myself, that is middle-class morality.

Sophocles: Nobody has a more sacred obligation to obey the law than those who make the law.

Mark Twain: Be virtuous and you will be lonesome.

Mark Twain: Good breeding consists in concealing how much we think of ourselves and how little we think of other people.

Mark Twain: The Moral Sense teaches us what is right, and how to avoid it – when unpopular.

Mark Twain: Few things are harder to put up with than the annoyance of a good example.

Mark Twain: There is no such thing as morality; it is not immoral for the tiger to eat the wolf, or the wolf the cat, or the cat the bird, and so on down; that is their business.... It is not immoral to create the human species – with or without ceremony; nature intended exactly these things.

UA: Ethics is not definable, is not implementable, because it is not conscious; it involves not only our thinking, but also our feeling.

Earl Warren California lawyer, Governor, Chief Justice US Supreme Court): In civilized life, law floats in a sea of ethics. Each is indispensable to civilization. Without law, we should be at the mercy of the least scrupulous; without ethics, law could not exist.

George Washington: Labor to keep alive in your breast that little spark of celestial fire, called Conscience.

John Wayne: There's right and there's wrong. You get to do one or the other. You do the one, and you're living. You do the other, and you may be walking around but you're as dead as a beaver hat.

Daniel Webster (*Speech, Charleston, S.C. Bar, 1847*): An eminent lawyer cannot be a dishonest man. Tell me a man is dishonest, and I will answer he is no lawyer. He cannot be, because he is careless and reckless of justice; the law is not in his heart and... is not the standard and rule of his conduct.

Oscar Wilde: Modern morality consists in accepting the standard of one's age.

Oscar Wilde: Morality is simply the attitude we adopt towards people we personally dislike.

Robin Williams: What's right is what's left if you do everything wrong.

EVIDENCE (See also FACTS/LIES)

Uncle Anthony: Every goat is not a rabbi just because of the beard

Uncle Anthony: The facts stuck out like lettuce from (one your mom's Italian hoagies) or an over packed BLT!

Aunt Mary Carlo: Direct evidence is me seein' Duke Snider hit the ball over the right field wall onto Bedford Avenue with two men on for a three run homer; circumstantial evidence is when I see 'Da Bums (Dodgers') scoreboard add three runs to the total and I see Duke crossin' the plate with two of 'Da Bums shaking his hand – I can figure from 'dat circumstantial evidence that Duke hit a three run homer

John Adams (Massachusetts lawyer, President of US; 1735-1826): Facts are stubborn things; and whatever may be our wishes, our inclinations, or the dictates of our passions, they cannot alter the state of facts and evidence.

Bible: Hebrews, 7:1: Compassed about with so great a cloud of witnesses.

Bible: Hebrews 11:1: Faith is the substance of things hoped for, the evidence of things not seen.

Bible: Joshua 24:27: Behold, this stone shall be a witness unto us.

Bible: Proverbs 14:15: A man should be able to classify everything he believes, so that he can say: "This I believe because it is handed down from the Prophets; this I believe from the evidence of my senses; and this I believe from reason." Whoever believes anything that does not fall within the three categories, to him apply the Saying: "The thoughtless believeth every word."

Bible: Proverbs 28:1: The wicked flee when no man pursueth.

Ambrose Bierce: INADMISSIBLE, adj. Not competent to be considered. Said of certain kinds of testimony which juries are supposed to be unfit to be entrusted with, and which judges, therefore, rule out, even of proceedings before themselves alone. Hearsay evidence is inadmissable because the person quoted was unsworn and is not before the court for examination; yet most momentous actions, military, political, commercial and of every other kind, are daily undertaken on hearsay evidence. Revelation is hearsay evidence; that the Scriptures are the word of God we have only the testimony of men long dead whose identity is not clearly established and who are not known to have been sworn in any sense. Under the rules of evidence as they now exist in this country, no single assertion in the Bible has in its support any evidence admissible in a court of law. It cannot be proved that the battle of Blenheim ever was fought, that there was such a person as Julius Caesar, such an empire as Assyria. / But as records of courts of justice are admissible, it can easily be proved that powerful and malevolent magicians once existed and were a scourge to mankind. The evidence (including confession) upon which certain women were convicted of witchcraft and executed was without a flaw; it is still unimpeachable. The judges' decisions based on it were sound in logic and in law. Nothing in any existing court was ever more thoroughly proved than the charges of witchcraft and sorcery for which so many suffered death. If there were no witches, human testimony and human reason are alike destitute of value.

Ambrose Bierce: PROOF, n.Evidence having a shade more of plausibility than of unlikelihood. The testimony of two credible witnesses as opposed to that of only one.

Ambrose Bierce: SELF-EVIDENT, adj. Evident to one's self and to nobody else.

Ambrose Bierce: TECHNICALITY, n. In an English court a man named Home was tried for slander in having accused a neighbor of murder. His exact words were: "Sir Thomas Holt hath taken a cleaver and stricken his cook upon the head, so that one side of the head fell upon one shoulder and the other side upon the other shoulder." The defendant was acquitted by instruction of the court, the learned judges holding that the words did not charge murder, for they did not affirm the death of the cook, that being only an inference.

Josh Billings: I have lived in this world just long enough to look carefully the second time into things that I am most certain of the first time.

William Blake: What is now proved was once only unimagin'd.

Logan E. Bleckley (Chief Justice of Georgia, 1827-1907): It is always probable that something improbable will happen. Warren v. Purtell, 63 Ga. 428, 430 (1979)

Curtis Bok (Judge, Supreme Court of Pennsylvania, 1897-1962, 1 *Too, Nicodemus* 322, 1946): Irrelevance can be highly enlightening. The witness who starts with what she had for breakfast and remembers it was Thursday because her husband's sister had come down with the measles when she shouldn't have if she had only gone to the other doctor, the one with glasses – should be a delight to the judge's heart and make the jury feel at home. Behind this leisurely swep of incident they can follow her as they please, and it will give them at least her barometric pressure at the time when she signed the note at the bank without reading it. After listening to enough of it, any idiot would know that she was an accomodation endorser who had done it to help her husband and had got nothing out of it herself.

Henry de Bracton (English Judge, died 1268, in a 1222 marginal notation): *Ea que manifesta sunt, non indigent probacione*: That which is obvious need not be proved.

Edward George Bulwer (English novelist, 1873): Upon any given point, contradictory evidence seldom puzzles the man who has mastered the laws of evidence, but he knows little of the laws of evidence who has not studied the unwritten law of the human heart; and without this last knowledge a man of action will not attain to the practical, nor will a poet achieve the ideal.

Edmund Burke (*Report on the Lords' Journal*, 1794): To refuse evidence is to refuse to hear the cause.

George Gordon Byron: There should always be some foundation of fact for the most airy fabric; pure invention is but the talent of a deceiver.

Benjamin N. Cardozo: The presumption does not consecrate as truth the extravagantly improbable. Matter of Findlay, 253 N.Y. 1, 8 (1930).

Benjamin N. Cardozo: There are breaths of human nature at which presumptions shrink and wither. Matter of Findlay, 253 N.Y. 1, 8 (1930).

Benjamin N. Cardozo: It is for ordinary minds, and not for psychoanalysts, that our rules of evidence are framed. They have their source very often in considerations of administrative convenience, of practical expediency, and not in rules of logic. Shepard v. US, 290 US 96, 104 L ed 196, 54 S Ct 22 (1933)

Cervantes: The proof of the pudding is the eating.

Nicholas Chamfort: In great affairs men show themselves as they wish to be seen; in small things they show themselves as they are.

Reuben A. Chapman (Chief Justice, Supreme Court, Massachusetts): Experience is not sufficiently uniform to raise a presumption that one who has the means of paying a debt will actually pay it. Atwood v. Scott, 99 Mass. 177, 178 (1868)

Canadian Prime Minister Jean Chrétien (on finding no Iraqi "WMD's" or weapons of mass destruction): A proof is a proof. What kind of a proof? It's a proof. A proof is a proof. And when you have a good proof, it's because it's proven.

Sir Winston Churchill: Dead birds don't fall out of their nests.

Leonard C. Crouch (Judge, Court of Appeals, New York, 1866-1953): Inference is never certainty, but it may be plain enough to justify a finding of fact. Tartora v. State, 269 N.Y. 167 (1935)

Lord Charles John Baron Darling (Justice, King's Bench, England, 1849-1936; *Scintillae Juris: Of Evidence*): If a man stays away from his wife for seven years, the law presumes the separation to have killed him; yet, according to our daily experience, it might well prolong his life.

John Dewey: Love of certainty is a demand for guarantees in advance of action.

Albert Einstein (in 1930 the Nazis Party in Germany and America published *"100 Authorities Against Einstein"* to disprove his theory of relativity, to which Einstein quipped): It would not take 100 authorities to prove relativity wrong, one single fact would do the trick."

Albert Einstein (to his friend Zenger in 1914 letter about his theory and circumstantial evidence): Nature shows us only the tail of the lion, but I have no doubt that the lion belongs to it, even if he cannot reveal himself all at once. We see him only the way a louse that sits upon him would.

Albert Einstein (June 1933 lecture at Oxford "On the Method of Theoretcal Physics"): To truly understand the methods and philosophies of physicists, don't listen to their words, fix your attention on their deeds.

Dwight D. Eisenhower: Don't join the book-burners. Don't think you are going to conceal faults by concealing evidence that they ever existed.

Ralph Waldo Emerson: I do not know what arguments mean in reference to any expression of a thought. I delight in telling what I think; but if you ask me how I dare say so, or why it is so, I am the most helpless of men.

Nathaniel Emmons: Any fact is better established by two or three good testimonies than by a thousand arguments.

English Legal Saying: Possession in Scotland – evidence of stealing in England. Or another version: Possession of trousers in Scotland – evidence of larceny in England.

Thomas Erskine (Lord Chancellor of Great Britain, 1750-1823, argument in *Trial of Thomas Hardy*, 24 How. St. Tr. 966, 1784): They (rules of evidence) are founded in the charities of religion, in the philosophy of nature, in the truths of history, and in the experience of common life.

Oscar W. Firkins: Certainty is a good even when it confirms a fear. When it relieves one it is trebly welcome.

Jerome Frank (New York, Judge, U.S. Circuit Court, 1889-1957): The improbable – by definition being not impossible – sometimes does occur. *Old Colony Bondholders v. N.Y.N.H. & H. R. Co.*, 161 F 2d 413 (1947) (dissenting opinion).

Galileo Galilei (1564-1642, born in Pisa): Reasoning (EDITOR: and jury verdicts?) is not the same as hauling; that is, the more horses you have means the more weight you can pull; but finding the truth does NOT depend on the number of horses you have, it depends on the fast steed. Nose counts do not equate with finding the truth.

Alex Haley: If you see a turtle on a fence post, you can be sure he had some help.

Thomas Chandler Haliburton (Canadian judge, Nova Scotian humorist, 1796-1865; in 1865): Hear one side and you will be in the dark; hear both sides, and all will be clear.

George Herbert: If you walk on snow you cannot hide your footprints.

Oliver Wendell Holmes, Jr.: Certitude is not the test of certainty. We have been cock-sure of many things that were not so.

Oliver Wendell Holmes, Jr.: If ... enough can be squeezed from these poor and puny anonymities to turn the color of legal litmus paper. *Abrams v. U.S.*, 250 US 616, 63 L. ed 1173, 40 S Ct 17 (1919).

David Hume: A wise man proportions his belief to the evidence.

Robert H. Jackson (Assoc. Justice US Supreme Court, 1892-1954): It is not required that testimony be so minute as to exclude every fantastic hypothesis that can be suggested. *Haupt v US,* 330 US 631, 640 L ed 1145, 67 S Ct 874 (1947).

Jewish Proverb: Half an answer also tells you something.

Jewish Proverb: No answer is a type of answer.

Jewish Saying: "For instance" is not proof.

Jewish Saying: To give an example only gives an example.

Ben Jonson: A good life is a main argument.

Samuel Johnson: To revenge reasonable incredulity by refusing evidence, is a degree of insolence with which the world is not yet acquainted; and stubborn audacity is the last refuge of guilt.

Henry Lamm (Associate and Chief Justice of Supreme Court of Missouri, 1846-1927): "Presumptions," as happily stated by a scholarly counselor, ore tenus, in another case, "may be looked on as the bats of the law, flitting in the twilight but disappearing in the sunshine of actual facts." *Mockowith v. Kansas City, St. J. & C.B. R.R.*, 196 Mo. 550, 571 (1906)

George Henry Lewes: We must never assume that which is incapable of proof.

George Henry Lewes: It is not true that a man can believe or disbelieve what he will. But it is certain that an active desire to find any proposition true will unconsciously tend to that result by dismissing importunate suggestions which run counter to the belief, and welcoming those which favor it. The psychological law, that we only see what interests us, and only assimilate what is adapted to our condition, causes the mind to select its evidence.

Abraham Lincoln: In law it is good policy never to plead what you need not, lest you oblige yourself to prove what you cannot.

Abraham Lincoln: We better know there is a fire whence we see much smoke rising than we could know it by one or two witnesses swearing to it. The witnesses may commit perjury, but the smoke cannot.

Abraham Lincoln (EDITOR: in 1858, Presidential candidate Abe Lincoln spoke about the "The Slave Power Conspiracy" in general and in particular the circumstantial evidence of 4 individual co-conspirators he criticized for being pro-slavers or "Dough Faces": Sen. Stephen Douglas aka "The Little Giant," ex-President Franklin Pierce, Chief Justice Roger Tawney – who in 1857 penned the Dred Scott decision - and President James Buchanan): When we see a lot of framed timbers, different portions of which we know have been gotten out at different times and places, and by different workmen – Steven (Douglas), Franklin (Pierce), Roger (Tawney) and James (Buchanan) – for instance. And we see these timbers joined together and see they exactly make the frame of a house or a mill; all the links and proportions of the different pieces exactly adapted to their respective places, and not a piece too many or too few, not omitting even scaffolding, or if a single piece be lacking we can see the place in the frame exactly fitted and prepared yet to bring such a piece in. In such a case we find it impossible to not believe that Steven and Franklin and Roger and James all understood one another from the beginning, and all worked upon a common plan or draft drawn up before the first lick was struck.

John Locke: The actions of men are the best interpreters of their thoughts.

Edward G. Bulwer-Lytton (Baron Lytton): Upon any given point, contradictory evidence seldom puzzles the man who has mastered the laws of evidence, but he knows little of the laws of evidence who has not studied the unwritten law of the human heart; and without this last knowledge a man of action will not attain to the practical, nor will a poet achieve the ideal.

Horace Mann: Never underestimate the human faculty for rejecting information.

Matthew 7:20: By their fruits ye shall know them.

Midrash: Genesis Rabbah, 45:10: If one man says, "your donkey," don't mind; if two say so, be worried; if three say so, get a saddle.

John Morley: You cannot demonstrate an emotion or prove an aspiration.

Richard Mounteney (Irish judge): Witnesses may lie, either be mistaken themselves, or wickedly intend to deceive others ... but ... circumstances cannot lie.

Michael A. Musmanno (Justice of the Sup. Ct. of Pennsylvania): To say that "counsel for the Authority" had a "very heavy burden" was wrong. Whatever burden counsel for the Authority carried was not a subject for judicial sympathy. They were counsel of ability and experience, as the trial record shows, and it was not sagacious to intimate that their backs might be broken by a heavy verdict and, therefore, the jury should spare them that spinal disaster. *Taylor v. Urban Redevelopment Auth. of Pittsburgh*, 419 Pa 430 (1965).

Michael A. Musmanno (Justice of the Sup. Ct. of Pennsylvania, 1959): There is no excuse for groping in the darkness of conjecture when a simple lifting of the blind will reveal the circumstances of reality.

Michael A. Musmanno (Justice of the Sup. Ct. of Pennsylvania, 1959): An auto vehicle which plows into another, often leaves behind identifying marks of aggression no less incriminating than the fingerprints on the dagger with which an assassin slays his victim.

Michael A. Musmanno (Justice of the Sup. Ct. of Pennsylvania, 1959): It has been demonstrated in myriads of cases that circumstantial evidence can be as revealing, under certain conditions, as the testimony of on-the-spot witnesses, especially when the concrete realities are not disputed. Irrefutable circumstances are like bricks, and, when they join, one with another, to form a solid wall, inseparably wedded by the mortar of nature's laws and inevitable cause and effect, the resulting barrier excludes fanciful hypotheses, airy guesses and uncontrolled imaginings as to how a given event occurred. And that wall becomes fact.

Michael A. Musmanno (Justice of the Sup. Ct. of Pennsylvania, 1959): Hearsay is merely a legal term for unconfirmed rumor. Pouring rumors and scandal into the bent ear of blabbering busybody's in a pool room or gambling house is no more disreputable then pronouncing it with clipped accent in a courtroom. Hearsay is not dross in one proceeding and gold in another. It is a deceptive commodity which should not he excepted in any market of freedom except under the unusual circumstances which certainly are not present here.

Michael A. Musmanno (Justice of the Sup. Ct. of Pennsylvania, 1959): It is a reassuring fact, in the phenomena of life, that most mishaps, which are not witnessed by human beings, leave behind them physical writings which clearly spell out the reason for the untoward event, and when those writings conclude with a precise, unerring explanation of the event, it would be a defiance of the law of cause and effect to ignore the explanation. It is one of the oddities in human affairs that there still exists the notion that circumstantial evidence cannot be as convincing as oral testimony. But a broken wheel with splintered spokes can tell its story of a weekend structure as clearly as it can be told by one who saw the wheel failing and disintegrating. A buckled fender, a pulverized curb, a fragmentized window glass can speak of violence as eloquently as any gifted narrator or writer.

Michael A. Musmanno (Justice of the Sup. Ct. of Pennsylvania, 1959): Events do not discourse only through the tongue of man. The twisted fragments of wrecked cars, the heavy, strained tire marks in the dust and dirt of the road, and the position of lifeless bodies on the highway frequently tell the story of a tragic accident with more convincing realism than witnesses whose memory may have been affected by the shock and excitement of the violent event as well as by human frailties which often chip at the edge of faithful recollection and leave something less than impeccable truth.

Michael A. Musmanno (Justice of the Sup. Ct. of Pennsylvania, 1959): It is not only in Omar Khayyam's poem that the moving finger writes an ineradicable tale. The wheels of every moving vehicle tell the account of its travels on the road, and here the streetcar chiseled its story in stone for the rest of the world to read.

Ovid: The event proves the act.

Elisha R. Potter (Assoc Justce of Rhode Island Supreme Court, died 1882): Human nature constitutes a part of the evidence in every case. Greene v. Harris, 11 R.I. 5 (1875)

Matthew Prior: For when one's proofs are aptly chosen, / four are as valid as four dozen.

Will Rogers: It don't take a genius to spot a goat in a flock of sheep.

Will Rogers: There are three kinds of men. The one that learns by reading. The few who learn by observation. The rest of them have to pee on the electric fence for themselves.

Will Rogers: Things ain't what they used to be and never were.

Will Rogers: In the early days of the Indian Territory, there were no such things as birth certificates. You being there was certificate enough.

Will Rogers: An ignorant person is one who doesn't know what you have just found out.

Will Rogers: All I know is just what I read in the papers, and that's an alibi for my ignorance.

Bertrand Russell: The most savage controversies are those about matters as to which there is no good evidence either way.

Mark Rutherford: The demand for certainty is a sign of weakness, and if we persist in it, it induces paralysis. The successful man is he who when he sees that no further certainty is attainable, promptly decides on the most probable side, as if he were completely sure it was right.

Carl Sagan: Extraordinary claims require extraordinary evidence.

John Seldon (English lawyer and writer, 1584-1654, *Table Talk: Reason*): The reason of a thing is not to be inquired after, till you are sure the thing itself be so. We commonly are at "What's the reason of it?" before we are sure of the thing. It was an excellent question of my Lady Cotton, when Sir Robert Cotton was magnifying of a shoe which was Moses' or Noah's, and wondering at the strange shape and fashion of it; "but Mr. Cotton," says she, "are you sure it is a shoe?"

Seneca: He who furnishes a voucher for his statements argues himself unknown.

William Shakespeare (*II Henry VI*, Act III, ii): QUEEN MARGARET: Then you, belike, suspect these noble noblemen / As guilty of Duke Humphrey's timeless death. // EARL OF WARWICK: Who finds the heifer dead and bleeding fresh, / And sees fast by a butcher with an axe, / But will suspect 'twas he that made the slaughter? / Who finds the partridge in the puttock's nest, / But may imagine how the bird was dead, / Although the kite soar with unbloodied beak? / Even so suspicious is this tragedy.

William Shakespeare (*II Henry VI,* Act IV, ii): Sir, he made a chimney in my father's house, and the bricks are alive at this day to testify it; therefore deny it not.

William Shakespeare (*Macbeth*, Act II, ii): LADY MACBETH: Why did you bring these daggers from the place? / They must lie there: go carry them, and smear / The sleepy grooms with blood. // MACBETH: I'll go no more.... // LADY MACBETH: Give me the daggers.... / I'll gild the faces of the grooms withal; / For it must seem their guilt.

William Shakespeare (*Othello*, Act I, iii): To vouch this, is no proof, / Without more wider and more overt test / Than these thin habits and poor likelihoods / Of modern seeming do prefer against him.

William Shakespeare (*Othello*, Act III, iii): Be sure of it; give me the ocular proof.

William Shakespeare (*Othello*, Act III, iii): IAGO: I will in Cassio's lodging lose this napkin, / And let him find it; trifles light as air / Are to the jealous confirmations strong / As proofs of holy writ.

William Shakespeare (*Othello*, Act V, ii): OTHELLO: That handkerchief which I so lov'd and gave thee / Thou gav'st to Cassio.

William Shakespeare (*Richard III*, Act I, iv): Where are the evidence that do accuse me?

Tobias George Smollett (English novelist, 1721-1771): Facts are stubborn things.

Gerry Spence: What is "reasonable doubt?" When I turn off the lights to go to bed, I sometimes wonder if I set the alarm clock. I probably did so. But, if I have to get up to see if I DID set it, that's "reasonable doubt."

Publilius Syrus (Latin writer, 43 B.C.): A man confesses guilt by avoiding trial.

Talmud: Judge a man only by his own deeds and words; the opinions of others can be false.

Talmud: An oath (in court) is worthless if it affirms the impossible: for instance, that you saw a camel fly.

Talmud: Silence (in a court) may be equivalent to confession.

Alfred Lord Tennyson: For nothing worthy proving can be proven, / Nor yet disproven.

Texas Saying (about likelihood): When you hear approaching hoof beats you don't think zebra, you gotta think horses.

James Bradley Thayer (Massahusetts lawyer, Dean of Harvard Law School, legal writer, 1831-1902): *Preliminary Treatise on Evidence* 314, 1898): The law has no mandamus to the logical faculty; it orders nobody to draw inferences.

Henry David Thoreau: Some circumstantial evidence is very strong, as when you find a trout in the milk.

Mark Twain: Even the clearest and most perfect circumstantial evidence is likely to be at fault, after all, and therefore ought to be received with great caution. Take the case of any pencil, sharpened by any woman: if you have witnesses, you will find she did it with a knife; but if you take simply the aspect of the pencil, you will say she did it with her teeth.

UA (attributed to an Unidentified English judge, referring to the weight to be given to a presumption): Weigh a bushel of horsefeathers against next Thursday.

UA: No answer is a type of answer.

UA: To assume is to fool one's self.

UA: The drunkard smells of whiskey—but so does the bartender.

UA: Where there's a flame there must be fire; and there is no smoke except from fire.

UA: Half an answer also tells you something.

UA: You don't have to see the lion if you see his lair.

UA: A man's deathtrap may be between his fellow cheeks (his words or testimony).

Willard D. Vandiver (Missouri Congressman, inspecting the Philadelphia Navy Yard, 1899): "I come from a state that raises corn and cotton and cockleburs and Democrats, and frothy eloquence neither convinces nor satisfies me. **I am from Missouri. You have got to show me.**"

Mary Augusta Ward: Every man is bound to leave a story better than he found it.

EVIL/CRIME/SIN

Uncle Anthony: There's an old Southern Spiritual that goes: There ain't no right way to do wrong"

Uncle Anthony: Evil is a lack of empathy. That is what one of the U.S. Army prosecutors said in the movie about the Nuremberg Trials. And, it's true.

Aunt Mary Carlo: She/he'd never go to bed angry ... she/he'd stay up all night and plot her revenge!

Woody Allen: I did not know Hitler was a Nazi. The truth was for years I thought he worked for the pnone company.

Aristotle: The greatest crimes are caused by surfeit, not by want. Men do not become tyrants in order that they may not suffer cold.

Bahya Ibn Paquda: A silk thread begins as the weakest of things, the mucus of a worm; yet how strong it becomes when entwined many times!... So it is with transgressions: they grow strong with repetition.

Thomas Bailey: The possession of unlimited power will make a despot of almost any man. There is a possible Nero in the gentlest human creature that walks.

Russell Baker: Usually, terrible things that are done with the excuse that progress requires them are not really progress at all, but just terrible things

Marion Barry (Mayor of DC): Outside of the killings, Washington has one of the lowest crime rates in the country.

Saint Basil: Just as a very little fresh water is blown away by a storm of wind and dust, in like manner the good deeds, that we think we do in this life, are overwhelmed by the multitude of evils.

Saint Bernard of Clairvaux: Were I to cry out against what is evil and say nothing about what is good, I would prove myself a mere backbiter and not a reformer, one who would rather carp at evil than remedy it.

Bible: 1 Corinthians 15:33: Evil communications corrupt good manners.

Bible: Genesis 8:21: The imagination of man's heart is evil from his youth.

Bible: Hosea 8:7: They have sown the wind, and they shall reap the whirlwind.

Bible: Isaiah 48:22; 57:21: There is no peace, sayeth the Lord, unto the wicked. No peace/rest for the wicked!

Bible: Job 28:28: And unto man he said, Behold, the fear of the Lord, that is wisdom; and to depart from evil is understanding.

Bible: John 3:19: Men loved darkness rather than light, because they're deeds were evil.

Bible: Matthew 6:34: Sufficient unto the day is the evil thereof.

Bible: Matthew 12:35: A good man out of the good treasure of the heart bringeth forth good things: and an evil man out of the evil treasure bringeth forth evil things.

Bible: Numbers 32:23: Be sure your sin will find you out.

Bible: Proverbs 8:13: The fear of the Lord is to hate evil.

Bible: Proverbs 9:17: Stolen waters are sweet, and bread eaten in secret is pleasant.

Bible: Proverbs 26:27: Whoso diggeth a pit shall fall therein.

Bible: Proverbs 28:1: The wicked flee when no man pursueth: but the righteous are as bold as a lion.

Bible: Psalms 37:1: Fret not thyself because of evildoers, neither be thou envious against the workers of iniquity. For they shall soon be cut down like the grass, and wither as the green herb.

Bible: Romans 6:23: The wages of sin is death; ...

Bible: Romans 7:19: For that which I do I allow not: for what I would, that do I not: but what I hate, that do I ...For the good that I would I do not; but the evil which I would not, that I do.

Bible: Romans 12:17: Recompense to no man evil for evil.

Bible: Romans 12:21: Be not overcome of evil, but overcome evil with good.

Bible: 1 Thessalonians 5:22: Abstain from all appearance of evil.

Bible: 1 Timothy 6:10: The love of money is the root of all evil.

Ambrose Bierce: ALONE, adj. In bad company....

Ambrose Bierce: DEBAUCHEE, n. One who has so earnestly pursued pleasure that he has had the misfortune to overtake it.

Ambrose Bierce: IMMORAL, adj. Inexpedient. Whatever in the long run and with regard to the greater number of instances men find to be generally inexpedient comes to be considered wrong, wicked, immoral. If man's notions of right and wrong have any other basis than this of expediency; if they originated, or could have originated, in any other way; if actions have in themselves a moral character apart from and nowise dependent on, their consequences – then all philosophy is a lie and reason a disorder of the mind.

Ambrose Bierce: MALEFACTOR, n. The chief factor in the progress of the human race.

Ambrose Bierce: OBSESSED, pp. Vexed by an evil spirit, like the Gadarene swine and other critics. Obsession was once more common than it is now....

Ambrose Bierce: PANDEMONIUM, n. Literally, the Place of All the Demons. Most of them have escaped into politics and finance, and the place is now used as a lecture hall by the Audible Reformer. When disturbed by his voice the ancient echoes clamor appropriate responses most gratifying to his pride of distinction.

Ambrose Bierce: SATAN, n. One of the Creator's lamentable mistakes, repented in sashcloth and axes....

Ambrose Bierce: WITCH, n. (1) An ugly and repulsive old woman, in a wicked league with the devil. (2) A beautiful and attractive young woman, in wickedness a league beyond the devil.

David Brin: It is said that power corrupts, but actually it is more true that power attracts the corruptible. The sane are usually attracted by other things than power.

Phillips Brooks: Never let yourselves do evil that good may come. If you do, you hinder the coming of the real, the perfect good in its due time.

Brendan Byrne (Former New Jersey Governor, speaking about the 1978 advent of casino gambling in Atlantic City, New Jersey): A year after I signed the Casino Control Act (1978), people said it was responsible for crime rising in Atlantic City. I said that's obvious. A year ago there wasn't anything to steal."

Brendan Byrne (Former New Jersey Governor, speaking of the fact that prior to legalization of casino gambling in Atlantic City, New Jersey, in 1978, there was a long standing "public secret" that Atlantic City clubs hosted a plethora of illegal, but seldom busted, backroom casinos): Some of you remember the old Atlantic City. When I first proposed casino gambling they thought it was a validating act.

Roger Caras: There are only three sins – causing pain, causing fear, and causing anguish. The rest is window dressing.

Alexis Carrel: It is tempting to deny the existence of evil since denying it obviates the need to fight it.

Chinese Proverb: Mankind fears an evil man but heaven does not.

Chinese Proverb: Not wine...men intoxicate themselves; Not vice...men entice themselves.

Sir Winston Churchill: We will have no truce or parlay with you [Hitler], or the grisly gang who work your wicked will. You do your worst—and we will do our best.

Sir Winston Churchill: From the days of Sparticus, Weishophf, Karl Marx, Trotski, Belacoon, Rosa Luxenburg, and Ema Goldman, this world conspiracy has been steadily growing. This conspiracy played a definite recognizable role in the tragedy of the French revolution. It has been the mainspring of every subversive movement during the 19th Century. And now at last this band of extraordinary personalities from the underworld of the great cities of Europe and America have gripped the Russian people by the hair of their head and have become the undisputed masters of that enormous empire.

Cicero: Crime and intention of crime are equal in their nature.

Czech Proverb: The big thieves hang the little ones.

Clarence Darrow: I may hate the sin but never the sinner.

Rene Descartes: The greatest minds are capable of the greatest vices as well as of the greatest virtues.

John Dewey: Non-resistence to evil which takes the form of paying no attention to it is a way of promoting it.

Ralph Waldo Emerson: The first lesson of history is the good of evil.

Ralph Waldo Emerson: Every reform was once a private opinion, and when it shall be private opinion again, it will solve the problem of the age.

English Proverb: Better the devil you know than the devil you don't know.

English Proverb: There is honor even among thieves.

Ethiopian Proverb: Evil enters like a needle and spreads like an oak tree.

Henry Ford: What we call evil is simply ignorance bumping its head in the dark.

H. E. Fosdick: Hating people is like burning down your own house to get rid of a rat.

Brendan Francis: One man's despicable evil is another man's delightful good.

Saint Francis de Sales: The greater part of our evils are not real but imaginary.

Benjamin Franklin: He that carries a small Crime easily, will carry it on when it comes to be an ox.

French Proverb: Hatred watches while friendship sleeps.

French Proverb: Rats desert a sinking ship.

Jerry Garcia: Constantly choosing the lesser of two evils is still choosing evil.

German Proverb: He who holds the ladder is as bad as the thief.

German Proverb: Virtue and vice divide the world; but vice has got the greater share.

German Proverb: One does evil enough when one does nothing good.

Rev. Billy Graham: Everybody has a little bit of Watergate in him.

John Heywood (*The Proverbs of John Heywood,* 1546): It's an ill wind that blows no good.

Eric Hoffer: Absolute faith corrupts as absolutely as absolute power.

Homer: Evil deeds never prosper.

Bede Jarrett: The world needs more anger. The world often continues to allow evil because it isn't angry enough.

Jewish Saying: Commit a sin twice and it will not seem a crime.

Jewish Saying: The knowledge of Scripture is no obstacle to sin.

Jewish Saying: He is so clever that he repents *before* he sins.

Jewish Saying: Trees are cut down by their own kind. (Ax handles are made of wood).

Decimus Junius Juvenal (Roman satirical poet. 40-125 AD): What man was ever content with one crime?

Franz Kafka: There art two cardinal sins from which to all others spring: impatience and laziness.

Franz Kafka: Evil does not exist; once you have crossed the threshold, all is good. Once in another world, you must hold your tongue.

Thomas Kempis: Of two evils we should always choose the less.

Martin Luther King, Jr.: Darkness can not drive out darkness; only light can do that. Hate can not drive out hate; only love can do that. Hate multiplies hate, violence multiplies violence, and toughness multiplies toughness in a descending spiral of destruction... The chain reaction of evil—hate begetting hate, wars producing more wars – must be broken, or we shall be plunged into the darkness of annihilation.

Latin Proverb: We hate whom we have injured.

Latin Proverb: Whom men fear they hate, and whom they hate they wish dead.

Legal Proverb: The law grows of sin, and chastises it.

John Lehman: Power corrupts. Absolute power is kind of neat.

Sergio Leone, Age Scarpelli and Luciano Vincenzoni (Clint Eastwood "Spaghetti Western" movie title, 1966): The good, the bad, and the ugly.

Abraham Lincoln: When I do good, I feel good; when I do bad, I feel bad, and that's my religion.

Livy: The evil best known is most tolerable.

Livy: No crime is founded upon reason.

Martin Luther: Every good work is a sin. [EDITOR: meaning good works done and designed to attract God's favors and rewards are not "good," but since done for selfish purposes are rather evil]

Margaret Mead: It may be necessary temporarily to accept a lesser evil, but one must never label a necessary evil as good.

Herman Melville (*Moby Dick,* 1851): All that most maddens and torments; all that stirs up the lees of things; all truth with malice in it; all that cracks the sinews and cakes the brain; although some old demonism of life and thought; all evil, to crazy Ahab, were visibly personified, and made practically assailable in Moby Dick. He piled upon the whale's white hump the sum of all the general rage and hate felt by his whole race from Adam down; and then, as if his chest had been a mortar, he burst his hot heart's shell upon it.

H.L. Mencken: It is a sin to believe evil of others, but it is seldom a mistake.

John Stuart Mill: A person may cause evil to others not only by his actions but by his inaction, and in either case he is justly accountable to them for the injury.

John Milton: Law can discover sin, but not remove it.

Mishrah: It is better to be called a fool all of one's days than to sin for one hour.

Midrash: At first, sin is like a spider's web; but in the end, it is like the cable of a ship.

Phyllis McGinley: Sin... has been made not only ugly but passe. People are no longer sinful, they are only in the two or our underprivileged or frightened or, more particularly, sick.

John Mortimer (spoken by Rumpole of The Bailey): "I believe in good and evil ... but sometimes they come mixed together like a cocktail"

Jawaharial Nehru: Evil unchecked grows, evil tolerated poisons the whole system.

Friedrich Neitzche: The Christian resolution to fibd the world ugly and bad has made the world ugly and bad.

Reinhold Niebuhr: In the collective life of man, at least, most evil arises because finite men involved in the flux of time pretend that they are not so involved. They make claims of virtue, of wisdom, and of power which are beyond their competence as creatures. These pretensions are the source of evil, whether they are expressed by kings and emperors or by, commissars and revolutionary statesmen.

Richard Nixon: While technically I did not commit a crime, an impeachable offense... these are legalisms, as far as the handling of this matter is concerned; it was so botched up, I made so many bad judgments. The worst ones, mistakes of the heart, rather than the head. But let me say, a man in that top job - he's got to have a heart, but his head must always rule his heart."

Austin O'Malley: When there is a choice of two evils, most men take both.

Roundell Palmer (British judge 1875): There is in many, if not all, men, a constant inward struggle between the principles of good and evil; and because a man has grossly fallen, and at the time of his fall added the guilt of hyprocrisy to another sort of immorality, it is not necessary, therefore, to believe that his whole life has been false, or that all the good which he ever professed was insincere or unreal.

Plato: It is not noble to return evil for evil; at no time ought we do an injury to our neighbors.

Plato: To a good man nothing that happens is evil.

Psalm 84:10: I had rather be a doorkeeper in the house of my God, then to dwell in the tents of wickedness.

La Rochefoucauld: There are men of whom we can never believe evil without having seen it. Yet there are few in whom we should be surprised to see it.

Will Rogers: Fanatical religion driven to a certain point is almost as bad as none at all, but not quite.

Will Rogers: American People like to have you repent; then they are generous.

Will Rogers: We don't seem to be able to check crime, so why not legalize it and then tax it out of business?

Will Rogers: It's one of the most progressive cities in the world. Shooting is only a sideline.

Romans 12:21: Be not overcome of evil, but overcome evil with good.

Romans 6:23: For the wages of sin is death.

Theodore Roosevelt: No man is justified in doing evil on the ground of expediency.

Joseph Roux: Evil often triumphs, but never conquers.

J.K. Rowling: Indifference and neglect often do much more damage then outright dislike.

Rumpole of The Bailey: "I believe in good and evil ... but sometimes they come mixed together like a cocktail."

Seneca: It is not goodness to be better than the worst.

Seneca: Let wickedness escape as it may at the bar, it never fails of doing justice upon itself; for every guilty person is his own hangman.

William Shakespeare (*Hamlet*, Act I, iv): Something is rotten in the state of Denmark.

William Shakespeare (*Hamlet*, Act I, v): One may smile and smile and be a villain still.

William Shakespeare (*Hamlet*, Act II, ii): There is nothing either good or bad, but thinking makes it so.

William Shakespeare (*II Henry IV*, Act IV, iv): Commit / The oldest sins the newest kind of ways.

William Shakespeare (*Henry V*, Act IV, i): There is some soul of goodness in things evil, / Would men observingly distil it out.

William Shakespeare (*II Henry VI*, Act V, i): It is a great sin, to swear unto a sin; / But greater sin, to keep a sinful oath.

William Shakespeare (*Henry VIII*, Act III, ii): Corruption wins not more than honesty.

William Shakespeare (*Henry VIII*, Act IV, ii): Men's evil manners live in brass; their virtues / We write in water.

William Shakespeare (*Julius Caesar*, Act II, i): Between the acting of a dreadful thing / And the first motion, all the interim is / Like a phantasma or a hideous dream. / The genius and the mortal instruments / Are then in council, and the state of man, / Like to a little kingdom, suffers then / The nature of an insurrection.

William Shakespeare (*Julius Caesar*, Act III, ii): The evil that men do lives after them; / The good is oft interred with their bones.

William Shakespeare (*King John*, Act I, i): Some sins do bear their privilege on earth.

William Shakespeare (*King Lear*, Act III, ii): I am a man / More sinn'd against than sinning.

William Shakespeare (*King Lear*, Act IV, vi): Robes and furr'd gowns hide all. Plate sin with gold. / And the strong lance of justice hurtless breaks; / Arm it in rags, a pigmy's straw doth pierce it.

William Shakespeare (*Measure for Measure*, Act III, i): O fie, fie, fie! Thy sin's not accidental, but a trade.

William Shakespeare (*Much Ado About Nothing*, Act IV, i): O, what authority and show of truth / Can cunning sin cover itself withal!

William Shakespeare (*Othello*, Act III, iii): Their best conscience / Is not to leave 't undone, but keep 't unknown.

William Shakespeare (*Pericles*, Act I, i): Few love to hear the sins they love to act.

William Shakespeare (*The Rape of Lucrece*, St. 51): The blackest sin is clear'd with absolution.

William Shakespeare (*Richard II*, Act I, iii): The apprehension of the good / Gives but the greater feeling to the worse.

William Shakespeare (*Richard II*, Act IV, i): Though some of you with Pilate wash your hands / Showing an outward pity; yet you Pilates / Have here deliver'd me to my sour cross, / And water cannot wash away your sin.

William Shakespeare (*Richard III*, Act I, iii): The world is grown so bad / That wrens make prey where eagles dare not perch.

William Shakespeare (*Richard III*, Act I, iii): But then I sigh, and, with a piece of Scripture, / Tell them, that God bids us do good for evil.

William Shakespeare (*Sonnets*, 94.14): Lilies that fester smell far worse than weeds.

William Shakespeare (*The Taming of the Shrew*, Act I, i): There's small choice in rotten apples.

Ben Sirach: Pride is the reservoir of sin.

Logan Pearsall Smith: Uncultivated minds are not full of wild flowers, like uncultivated fields. Villainous weeds grow in them, and they are full of toads.

John Lancaster Spalding: The darkened mind, the callous heart, the paralytic will – these are the root evils.

Spanish Proverb: Let your heart guide your head in evil matters.

Adlai Stevenson: Those who corrupt the public mind are just as evil as those who steal from the public purse.

Jonathan Swift: I never wonder to see men wicked, but I often wonder to see them not ashamed.

Publilius Syrus: He who is bent on evil can never want occasion.

Talmud: A sin repeated seems permitted.

Talmud: It is better to sin out of good intentions than to conform with evil (greedy) intent.

Talmud: Three things sat a man's strength: worry, travel, and sin.

Talmud: Wives save us from sin.

Talmud: Leave them alone: let men sin unwittingly rather than willfully.

Talmud: A sinner is like a man who sees open manacles—and puts his hands in them.

Talmud: Sin is sweet in the beginning, but bitter in the end.

Elizabeth Taylor: People who have no vices are pretty sure to have some annoying virtues.

Henry David Thoreau: There are a thousand hacking at the branches of evil to one who is striking at the root.

Mark Twain: Every one is a moon, and has a dark side which he never shows to anybody.

Mark Twain: I believe that our Heavenly Father invented man because he was disapointed in the monkey.

Mark Twain: Half of the results of a good intention are evil; half the results of an evil intention are good.

Mark Twain: We may not pay him (Satan) reverence, for that would be indiscreet, but we can at least respect his talents. A person who has for untold centuries maintained the imposing position of spiritual head of four fifths of the human race, and political head of the whole of it, must be granted the possession of executive abilities of the loftiest order. In his large presence the other popes and politicians shrink to midges for the microscope. I would like to see him. I would rather see him and shake him by the tail than any other member of the European Concept

Mark Twain: The vast majority of the race, whether savage or civilized, are secretly kind-hearted and shrink from inflicting pain, but in the presence of the aggressive and pitiless minority they don't dare to assert themselves.

Mark Twain: The kingly office is entitled to no respect. It was originally procured by the highwayman's methods; it remains a perpetuated crime, can never be anything but the symbol of a crime. It is no more entitled to respect than is the flag of a pirate.

Mark Twain: There is a charm about the forbidden that makes it unspeakably desirable.

UA: There is so much good in the worst of us, And so much bad in the best of us, That it hardly becomes any of us, To talk about the rest of us.

Ibn Verga: We are like mice: one man needs the cheese and all men are blamed.

Voltaire: Every man is guilty of all the good he did not do.

Simone Weil: Evil becomes an operative motive far more easily than good.

Otto Weininger: Everything evil is revenge.

Otto Weininger: All that is evil in man is the result of a lack of consciousness.

EVOLUTION (See ANCESTRY)

EXCUSES

Uncle Anthony: In the Navy we'd call these guys who always copped an excuse an "Alibi Ike."

Uncle Anthony (and many others): Excuses are like a-holes, everybody's got one.

Uncle Anthony: I think the reason he's "studied both side of the issue" is soz he can get around the issue.

Uncle Anthony: He can change subjects faster than a dictionary!

Uncle Anthony: I think they use the "Swiss Cheese Stack Defense" – they like to layer their protection by laying down a pile of arguments, each with a lot of holes in 'em, but they figure even if you don't cut through all of them excuses like the swiss cheese they are, then at least a jury will have trouble seeing through their whole big stack of defenses.

Aunt Mary Carlo: Yeah, he says he's standin' on his/dis "record" – 'cause he don't want nobody ta look at it!

Aunt Mary Carlo: He'll leave pussyfoot prints on whatever he done.

Aunt Mary Carlo: Y'know he's gotta try to save both his faces.

Aunt Mary Carlo: he's stuck – he can't decide whether he's handin' out too much baloney er not enough!

Dean Acheson: How vulnerable are those who explain

Russell Baker: Usually, terrible things that are done with the excuse that progress requires them are not really progress at all, but just terrible things.

Richard Barthelmess (an actor in the 1931 film The Last Flight, about a group of American airmen who stay in Europe after WWI; one is gored to death by a bull; journalists ask why the man jumped into the arena during a bullfight; his friend answers): Because it seemed like a good idea at the time.

Bible: Genesis 3:10: I was afraid, because I was naked.

Bible: Genesis: EVE: "The serpent beguiled me, and I did eat."

Bible: Luke 18:13: God be merciful to me a sinner.

Bible: Numbers 5:7: They shall confess their sin which they have done.

Bible: Proverbs 22:13; 26:13: The slothful man saith, There is a lion without, I shall be slain in the streets.

Bible: Proverbs 28:13: He that covereth his sins shall not prosper: but who confesseth and forsaketh them shall have mercy.

Bible: I Samuel 15:24: I feared the people, and obeyed their voice.

Ambrose Bierce: DESTINY, n. A tyrant's authority for crime and a fool's excuse for failure.

Ambrose Bierce: RESPONSIBILITY, n. A detachable burden easily shifted to the shoulders of God, Fate, Fortune, Luck or one's neighbor. In the days of astrology it was customary to unload it upon a star.

Lois McMaster Bujold: if you can't do what you want, do what you can.

George Washington Carver: 99% of failures come from people who have a habit of making excuses.

King Charles I: Never make a defense or apology before you be accused.

Sir Winston Churchill: "No comment" is a splendid expression. I am using it again and again.

Gregory S. Cusimano: To err is human. To blame it on somebody else is more human.

Peter DeVries: Confession is good for the soul only in the sense that a tweed coat is good for dandruff – it is palliative rather than a remedy.

Benjamin Disraeli (1903): Never complain and never explain.

Ralph Waldo Emerson: We do what we must, and call it by the best names.

British Admiral Lord Fisher (1919): Never contradict. Never explain. Never apologize. (Those are the secrets of a happy life!).

Benjamin Franklin: He that is good for making excuses is seldom good for anything else.

French Proverb: He who makes excuses, accuses himself.

French Proverb: Rats desert a sinking ship.

Thomas Fuller: All things are difficult before they are easy.

Gaelic Proverb: A bad reaper never gets a good sickle.

Sidney J. Harris: A person who is going to commit an inhuman act invariably excuses himself by saying, "I'm only human, after all."

Rex Harrison (in the 1940 film *Night Train to Munich*): "Captain Marsen was only obeying orders."

Herbert Hoover: About the time we think we can make ends meet, somebody moves the ends.

Italian Proverb: We cannot direct the wind, but we can adjust the sails.

Joe Jacobs (American manager of Max Schmeling, believing his fighter was cheated of the heavy-weight title in a 1932 fight with Jack Sharkey): We was robbed!

Franklin P. Jones: The trouble with being punctual is that nobody's there to appreciate it.

Oscar LeVan: I and the people who drink—at least they know what to blame everything on.

Martin Luther (evening of April 18, 1521, in candlelight, after being asked to recant his writings): Since then Your Serene Majesty and your lordships seek a simple answer I will give it in this manner – neither horned nor toothed – unless I am convinced by the testimony of the Scriptures or by clear reason, for I do not trust either in the Pope (Leo X) or in the Councils alone, since it is well known that they have often erred and contradicted themselves, I am bound by the Scriptures I have quoted, and my conscience is captive to the Word of God. I can not and I will not retract anything, since it is neither safe nor right to go against conscience. I can not do otherwise. Here I stand. May God help me. Amen. I AM FINISHED.

Phil Miller: "Some people would rather climb a tree to yell a lie than stand on the ground and say the truth"

Newton Minow: We've gotten to the point where everybody's got a right and nobody's got a responsibility.

Michael A. Musmanno (Justice of Pennsylvania Supreme Court, 1959): A Worker Working Near Hazards: This is like saying that a hole into which a pedestrian walks caused the pedestrian no harm, since it was the fall not the hole which broke his neck. No one in this case has advanced the droll proposition that the platform, in its inert, isolated and unused state, hurt or even could hurt anybody. Even a tiger will not harm anybody who stays away from him. An unguarded elevator shift will not injure anyone unless he steps into the shaft. // The purpose of the Health and Safety Act (OSHA) is something far more intelligent than that ascribed to it by the defendant. The drafters of that Act well knew that workers who were engaged in a task which takes them to perilous heights may easily overlook, in the preoccupation over discharging their tasks, the absence of a railing at the spot where they may be immediately engaged. Thus, the workers must be protected, not against foolhardiness, but against the most natural and human reaction, namely, that of concentration on the instant details of their job to the exclusion of a constant overall survey of the locale in which they are working. In addition, it cannot be doubted that a worker's efficiency will be lowered and the productiveness of his labors considerably diminished if he must continuously have an eye on the distance intervening between him and the brink of the surface his pressing chore requires him to occupy. // The defendant maintains that the ledge in question could not be a platform until the railing was installed. This argument completely misses the objective of the Safety Act, which is to protect the workmen while they <u>work.</u> If the railing is not to be added until the construction job has been completed an uncounted workmen have fallen to their injury or death in the meanwhile, the Act, whose very intendment is aimed at protecting workmen, becomes a mockery. The Act specifically refers to "building construction," and it says that platforms shall have railings "so as to avoid accident hazards to <u>workers</u> or the public." (Emphasis supplied.) (<u>*Windusch v. Babcock and Wilcox Co.,*</u> 412 Pa. 558)

Michael A. Musmanno (Justice of Pennsylvania Supreme Court, 1959): The Economic or Feasibility Excuse: Enigmatic as is the basic element of electricity, no one with the slightest mental equipment is ignorant of its vast potentialities for destruction. The degree of care required to protect people from this devastating element is no less than that required to prevent poisonous reptiles from breaking loose from their restraining enclosures. As the proprietor of ferocious beasts may not, by pleading excessive cost for confining them, escape liability for the loss of life occasioned by his savage wards, so also the owner of high-voltage machinery may not avoid responsibility, on the excuse of expense, for the devastation caused through his failure to adequately contain the fiery dragon of electricity. (<u>*Cooper v. Heintz Manufacturing Co.,*</u> 385 Pa. 298).

Michael A. Musmanno (Justice of Pennsylvania Supreme Court, 1959): Feasibility Defense by Power Company: If the wires or the towers supporting them had been painted or illuinated, they would have been visible to the pilot and he would have avoided them. This Court has said that "when human life is at stake, the rule of due care and diligence requires everything that gives reasonable promise of its preservation to be done, regardless of difficulties or expense." In comparison to the benefit of saving human life, the cost of a few cans of pain and a few electric bulbs would be negligible. And since the defendant company is engaged in the very manufacture and creation of electric current, the cost of the current needed to supply the desired illumination would be as insignificant as the cost of a few biscuits at a bakery. (Yoffee v. Pennsylvania Power Co., 385 Pa. 520).

Michael A. Musmanno (Justice of Pennsylvania Supreme Court, 1959): Feasibility/Economic Defense by Railroad: What are the ordinary and natural things to be expected of children? The obvious answer is that they will act like children. The playful instincts of boys of tender age are as much a part of the demonstrated forces of nature as the snows of January, the winds of March and the roses of June. To speak, in this afternoon of the universe, of these elementary and fundamental concepts, which were already accepted fact in the dawn of creation, would be sheer superfluity. And yet it would seem that this truism can at times be overlooked by sages of the law who would attribute to infants the reflection of graybeards, while at the same time excusing the neglect of adults who act with the irresponsibility of children.... The Majority, however, in discussing this phase of the case refuses to restrict the locus" to 67th Street where the accident occurred and where the Jungle was located, but speaks of fencing in vast distances and immeasurable areas over the 275 miles of electrified main tracks. There is no argument in logic so wearisome as that which seeks to prove a point by an irrelevant comparison or one so exaggerated in scope as to make it wholly foreign to the discussion. It is like equating an ant hill with Mount Everest because they are both protuberances from the earth's surface, or comparing a flea with an eagle because they both fly, or a monkey with an elephant because they both eat peanuts. It is absurd to say that because the railroad would be required to fence away the Jungle (20 to 30 ft. long) from the tracks, it would be compelled to fence the whole length of its 275 miles of electrified main tracks or even to fence areas where children have been seen playing beside the right-of-way or climbing on cars. Liability only arises where there is a known dangerous practice which a railroad company can avoid.... The argument that the railroad's treasury takes precedence over the value of human life runs counter to everything that has been advocated and done in America in the way of social and economic progress. In every progressive step of the laws of safety, there have been those who protested because of the cost involved in installing and maintaining the innovation. But we have seen how safety and greater appreciation of the precious commodity of existence advanced, notwithstanding. When a dangerous curve wrecks a train, railroad architects and civil engineers consider at once ways of straightening out the track so as to avoid future wrecks. When a hillside caves in, burying a train and its passengers beneath an avalanche of death and crippling injuries, the mountain is trussed up with bands of steel and fortified with masonry. When a flood washes a train into a swollen river the tracks are raised and future indentations balked. Tunnels are bored through mountain sides, interlocking systems are developed, bridges are thrown across chasms and ravines, all at huge expenditures of money, and all for safety, all for progress, and eventually for greater profit to the railroads too, because no railroad can hope to become successful if it's tracks are strewn with the skeletons and limbs of victims of brutal indifference to humanity. (Dugan v. Pennsylvania Railroad, 37 PA. 39).

Michael A. Musmanno (Justice of Pennsylvania Supreme Court, 1959): None of Our Other Patrons Were Injured: The Majority Opinion states that 1,297,802 "human bodies" had ridden the course "and absorbed the abruptness of this curve without injury." There was not a word or syllable in the testimony to support this statement; 1,297,802 persons did not testify that they had not been injured. This volunteered conclusion of the Majority is founded on the statement of the defendant's witness that there was no record of accident during the period in question. This is far from stating that no accident occurred or that no one had been injured. Many people could have sustained substantial jolts which did not seriously disable them. Others may not have developed symptoms until later and then they did not connect them with the roller coaster ride. Others may have known they were injured by the roller coaster ride but preferred not to litigate. In addition, it does not matter how many rode without injury. The question is: Was there anything wrong with the Blue Streak on the day, hour and minute that the plaintiff was injured?... Moreover, before the fact of the multitudinous rides can be compared to the single ride involved in this case, there must be proof that the conditions in the million rides were exactly similar to the one's present in the instant case, as, for instance that there were three passengers in the front seat as in this case,... that the weight of the passengers in the front seat, in all the million rides was the same as that on the Wood ride, that the heights of the persons in the front seat in all the other rides tallied with the heights of the persons of this ride. There would have to be a determination also as to whether the passengers all the other rides were aware that they were coming to an abrupt bend. Also, did the passengers of the other rides brace themselves when they came to the bend or did they all slide over and crush the person on the outside seat, as happened in this case? There are innumerable variables which have to be considered before one can base a conclusion on a multiplicity of events as against the one which is in focus. A million pedestrians may pass over a defect in the sidewalk and not been injured, but the 1,000,001st traveler may fall into the hole or trip over the defect and, if the facts reveal that the hole was caused by the negligence of the municipality, the injured person is entitled to a recovery, regardless of the army which had good luck to pass unscathed over the danger which reached up and pulled down that 1,000,001st traveler to his doom. If cases of this kind are to be decided on mere numbers instead of cause-and-effect, and logic and reason, there can be no need for a judicial inquiry. A computer will suffice, an IBM machine can dictate the verdict, a unifax can displace the jury and eventually the judge himself, all of which, of course, is absurd. (dissenting opinion, George Wood v. Conneaut Lake Park Inc., 417 Pa. 58).

Michael A. Musmanno (Justice of Pennsylvania Supreme Court, 1959): Charitable Immunity – A Charity is Not a Charity When it is Paid For: The hospital has not denied its negligence... It merely announces it is an eleemosynary institution, and therefore, owed no duty of care to its patient. It declares in effect that it can do wrong and still not be liable in damages to the person it has wronged. It thus urges a momentous exception to the generic proposition that in law there is no wrong without a remedy. From the earliest days of organized society it became apparent to man that society could never become a success unless the collectivity of mankind guaranteed to every member of society a remedy for a palpable wrong inflicted on him by another member of that society. In 1844 Justice Storrs of the Supreme Court of Connecticut crystallized into epigrammatic language that wise concept, as follows: "An injury is a wrong; and for the redress of every wrong there is a remedy: a wrong is a violation of one's right; and for the vindication of every right there is a remedy." The defendant hospital here does not dispute, as it indeed cannot, this fundamental rule of law, but it says that if the plaintiffs are allowed to invoke a remedy for the wrong done them, the enactment of that remedy will impose a financial burden on the hospital. Is that an adequate defense in law? // The owner of a hotel may not plead non-liability in a trespass action because, if it has to make payment, the hotel will be thrown into debt. A transit company cannot avoid payment of damages by explaining that it might be put out of business if it had to pay all the verdicts rendered against it as a result of negligence on the part of its employees. On what basis then, may a hospital, which expects and receives compensation for services, demand of the law that it be excused from responding in damages for injuries tortiously inflicted by its employees on paying patients? There is not a person or establishment in all civilization that is not required to meet his or its financial obligations, there is not a person or establishment that is not called upon by the law to render an accounting for harm visited by him or it on innocent victims. By what line of reasoning, then, can any institution, operating commercially, expect the law to insulate it from its debts?... Thus as a matter of integrity in nomenclature it must be stated that, although the hospitals here under discussion are known as charitable hospitals, it does not follow that they offer their services through the operation of charity. While in no way detracting from the contribution which these estimable institutions do make toward the alleviation and cure of the ills of mankind, a proper appraisement of the issue on appeal impels the candid statement that the hospital do receive payment for that contribution, and, where a hospital is compensated for services rendered, it cannot, if language to mirror reality, truly be called a charity hospital. To say that a person who pays for what is what he receives is still the object of charity is a self-contradiction in terms. (Flagiello v. Pennsylvania Hospital, 417 Pa. 486).

Michael A. Musmanno (Justice of the Sup. Ct. of Pennsylvania, 1959): The Plaintiff Returned to Work: ... Thedefendant contends further that the Trial Judge failed to explain to the jury "the difference between permanent, chronic and recurrent disability." In the first place, the words explain themselves. In second place, the issue was not only the impairment of earning power but the continuity of disabling pain. Even no one could with gritting teeth and aching body apply himself to remunerative employment, he would still be entitled to compensation for the physical anguish inflicted upon him by a tortfeasor. There is something more to life than earning one's bread and eating it salted with the agony of ceaseless pain. (Laurelli v. William Shapiro, 416 Pa. 308).

Michael A. Musmanno (Justice of the Sup. Ct. of Pennsylvania, 1959): Statute of Limitations: When the accusing sword of unpaid debts hangs over the head of the man for a long time without falling, justice requires and humanity demands that it be cut down. That is why we have statutes of limitations in contract, tort and criminal law. If one exposes himself to the fire of his potential adversaries in the open plain of answerability for more than enough time for those adversaries to set their sights and trigger their rifles, he should not be compelled thereafter to avoid every cluster of bushes for fear of belated attack and destruction. (Weizenbaum Estate, 414 Pennsylvania 462).

Alexander Pope: And excuse is worse and more terrible than a lie; for the excuse is a lie guarded.

Will Rogers: All I know is just what I read in the papers, and that's an alibi for my ignorance.

Royal Navy maxim (early 1900's): Never explain and never apologize.

Erich Segal (1970 novel and film Love Story): Love (or whatever) means never having to say you're sorry.

William Shakespeare *(Hamlet,* Act III, iv): And reason panders will.

William Shakespeare (*Hamlet*, Act III, iv): Confess yourself to heaven; / Repent what's past; avoid what is to come.

William Shakespeare (*Julius Caesar*, Act I, ii): The fault, dear Brutus, is not in our stars, / But in ourselves.

William Shakespeare (*King John*, Act IV, ii): And, often times, excusing of a fault / Doth make the fault the worse by the excuse.

William Shakespeare (*Measure for Measure*, Act II, ii): Under your good correction, I have seen, / When, after execution, judgment hath / Repented o'er his doom.

William Shakespeare (*Othello*, Act V, ii): Confess thee freely of thy sin; / For to deny each article with oath / Cannot remove, or choke, the strong conception / That I do groan withal.

William Shakespeare (*Venus and Adonis*, l. 791): O strange excuse, / When reason is the bawd to lust's abuse!

Spanish Proverb: To deny all, is to confess all.

Thomas Szasz: Two wrongs don't make a right, but they make a good excuse.

Harry S. Truman (U.S. President 1945-53): "The buck stops here."

Mark Twain (deleted dedication of Mark Twain's book "Roughing It"): To the Late Cain, This Book is Dedicated, Not on account of respect for his memory, for it merits little respect; not on account of sympathy with him, for his bloody deed placed him without the pale of sympathy, strictly speaking; but out of a mere human commiseration for him in that it was his misfortune to live in a dark age that knew not the beneficent Insanity Plea.

UA: It is not what you know that counts, is what you think of in time for an excuse.

UA: People who are always making allowances for themselves soon go bankrupt.

UA: Gluttons find ample excuses for gorging.

UA: Girls who can't dance say the musicians can't keep time.

UA: Ten excuses are less persuasive than one.

UA: Fools always find an excuse for their folly.

UA: If you measure before you cut, you'll avoid the need for excuses.

UA: The guilty make excuses before they are accused.

UA (1920, the question asked in disbelief by a small boy to "Shoeless Joe" Jackson as he came out of a grand jury session about the Chicago White Sox (aka "The Black Sox") accussed of deliberately losing the 1919 World Series): Say it ain't so, Joe.

Evelyn Waugh: Punctuality is the virtue of the bored.

Flip Wilson (as Geraldine): The devil made me do it!

EXPERIENCE

Uncle Anthony: Experience teaches you to see your mistakes when you make them again.

Uncle Anthony: Once you know what the hell your doin' – you can be more gutsy and try a lot more risky stuff.

Uncle Anthony: It's a whole lot safer to unlearn something, than to have to learn something brand new.

Aunt Mary Carlo: I stopped being scared of makin' mistakes when I figured out that when I made a mistake the world didn't come to an end, and the Lord didn't throw my ass into hell.

Henry Adams: All experience is an arch, to build upon.

F. L. Allen: It takes longer to hard boil a man or woman than an egg.
American Proverb: You have to kiss a lot of toads before you find a handsome prince.
Arabic Proverb: The tongue of experience has most truth.
Roger Ascham: Is costly wisdom that is bought by experience.
Roger Ascham: He hazardeth sore that waxeth wise by experience.
Roger Ascham: By experience we find out a shorter way by a long wandering. Learning teacheth more in one year than experience in twenty.
Shalom Aleichem: No dog is smarter than one who has been bitten.
Roger Ascham: He hazardeth much who depends for his learning on experience.—An unhappy master is he who is made wise only by many shipwrecks; a miserable merchant, who is neither rich nor wise till he has been bankrupt. – By experience we find out a short way by long wandering.
Roger Aacham: By experience we find out a shorter way by a long wandering. Learning teacheth more in one year than experience in twenty.
Sir Edwin Arnold: Experience—making all futures, fruits of all the pasts.
Sir Francis Bacon: By far the best proof is experience.
James Baldwin: Experience, which destroys innocence, also leads one back to it.
James Beattie (Scottish poet, 1803): In all instances where our experience of the past has been extensive and uniform, our judgment as to the future amounts to moral certainty.
St. Bernard of Clairvaux: Believe an expert; believe one who has had experience. (*Experto credite*).
Yogi Berra: He's learning me his experience.
Bible: Deuteronomy 32:7: Remember the days of old, consider the years of many generations: ask thy father, and he will show thee; thy elders, and they will tell thee.
Bible: Ecclesiastes 9:4: A living dog is better than a dead lion.
Bible: Hosea 4:9: Like people, like priest.
Bible: Isaiah 22:13: Let us eat and drink; for tomorrow we shall die.
Bible: Isaiah 38:19: The father to the children shall make known thy truth.
Bible: Isaiah 40:6: All flesh is grass, and all the goodliness thereof is as the flower of the field.
Bible: James 5:10: Take, my brethren, the prophets, who have spoken in the name of the Lord, for an example of suffering affliction, and of patience.
Bible: Job 12:12: With the ancient is wisdom; and in length of days understanding.
Bible: John 13:15: I have given you an example, that ye should do as I have done to you.
Bible: Proverbs 4:13: Take fast hold of instruction; let her not go: keep her; for she is thy life.
Bible: Proverbs 20:29: The glory of young men is their strength: and the beauty of old men is the grey head.
Bible: Romans 5:3: Tribulation worketh patience; And patience, experience; and experience, hope.
Bible: 1 Timothy 4:12: Be thou an example of the believers, in word, in conversation, in charity, in spirit, in faith, in purity.
Ambrose Bierce: Experience is a revelation in the light of which we renounce our errors of youth for those of age.
Ambrose Bierce: EXPERIENCE, n. The wisdom that enables us to recognize as an undesirable old acquaintance the folly that we have already embraced.
Earl Blank (Army football coach 1941-1858): You don't develop good teeth by eating mush.
Nicholas Breton: Experience is the mother of knowledge.
Lyman Lloyd Bryson: Youth thinks intelligence a good substitute for experience, and his elders think experience a substitute for intelligence.
Edward George Bulwer: Life consists in the alternate process of learning and unlearning, but it is often wiser to unlearn than to learn.
Byron: Experience, that chill touchstone whose sad proof reduces all things from their false hue.
Byron: Adversity is the first path to truth. He who hath proved war, storm, or woman's rage, whether his winters be eighteen or eighty, have won the experience which is deemed so weighty.
Joseph Campbell: I don't have to have faith, I have experience.
Albert Camus: You cannot acquire experience by making experiments. You cannot create experience. You must undergo it.

Benjamin Cardozo: Often a liberal antidote of experience supplies a sovereign cure for a paralyzing abstraction built upon a theory.

Thomas Carlyle: Experience takes dreadfully high school-wages, but he teaches like no other.

Thomas Carlyle: Experience is the best of school masters, only the school fees are heavy.

Miguel de Cervantes: There's only one thing more painful than learning from experience, and that is not learning from experience.

Reuben A. Chapman (Chief Justice, Supreme Court, Massachusetts): Experience is not sufficiently uniform to raise a presumption that one who has the means of paying a debt will actually pay it. Atwood v. Scott, 99 Mass. 177, 178 (1868)

Sir Winston Churchill: The farther back you can look, the farther forward you are likely to see.

Sir Winston Churchill: It is better to be frightened now than killed hereafter.

Samuel Taylor Coleridge: A sadder and a wiser man, / He rose the morrow morn.

Samuel Coleridge: This is one of the sad conditions of life, that experience is not transmissible. No man will learn from the suffering of another; he must suffer himself.

Samuel Coleridge: To most men experience is like the stern lights of the ship, which illumen only the track it has passed.

Dr. Joseph Collins: A prudent person profits from personal experience, a wise one from the experience of others.

Henry Steele Commager: Theory may mislead us; experience must be our guide.

Dante: Thou shalt know by experience how salt the savor is of other's bread, and how sad a path is to climb and descend another's stairs.

Walter De La Mare: Experience seems to be like the shining of a bright lantern. It suddenly makes clear in the mind what was already there, perhaps, but dim.

John Dewey: Experience cannot deliver to us necessary truths; truths completely demonstrated by reason. Its conclusions are particular, not universal.

Charles Dickens: Experientia does it—as papa used to say.

Charles Dickens (*Oliver Twist, ch. 51*): "That is no excuse," replied Mr. Brownlow. "You were present on the occassion of the destruction of these trinkets, and, indeed, are the more guilty of the two, in the eye of the law; for the law supposes that your wife acts under your direction." / "If the law supposes that," said Mr. Bumble, ... **"the law is a ass – a idiot.** If that's the eye of the law, the law's a bachelor; and the worst I wish the law is, that his eye may be opened by experience – by experience."

Emily Dickinson: This gave me that precious gate / Some call experience.

Benjamin Disraeli: Experience is the child of Thought, and Thought is the child of Action.

Isadora Duncan: What one has not experienced, one will never understand in print.

Albert Einstein: Ethical axioms are found and tested not very differently from the axioms of science. Truth is what stands the test of experience.

Ralph Waldo Emerson: Only so much do I know, as I have lived.

Empedocles: Each believes naught but his experience

English Proverb: He who would climb the ladder must begin at the bottom

Erasmus: Experience is the common schoolhouse of fools and ill men.—Men of wit and honesty are otherwise instructed.

F. Scott Fitzgerald: The inevitable shallowness that goes with people who have learned everything from experience.

John Florio: Experience is the mother of all things.

John Florio: Experience sometimes is perilous.

Sir Robert Foster: Happy is he that by other men's harms takes heed.

Benjamin Franklin: Experience keeps a dear school; but fools will learn in no other, and scarce in that; for it is true, we may give advice, but we cannot give conduct.

French Proverb: Appetite comes with eating.

James Froude: Experience teaches slowly, and at the cost of mistakes.

James Froude: Experience is no more transferable in morals than in the art.

Thomas Fuller: Experience is the father of wisdom, and memory the mother.

Thomas Fuller: Experience is good, if not bought too dear.

Thomas Fuller: Experience teacheth fools, and he is a great one that will not learn by it.
Thomas Fuller: All things are difficult before they are easy.
John Gay: His head was silver'd over with age, / And long experience made him sage.
German Proverb: He who has once burnt his mouth always blows his soup.
Matthew Green: Experience joined with common sense, / To mortals is a providence.
Matthew Green: Experience holds the cautious glass, / To shun the breakers, as I pass, / And frequent throws the wary lead, / To see what dangers may be hid.
Nathaniel Hawthorne: Nobody will use other people's experience, nor has any of his own till it is too late to use it.
Heinrich Heine: Experience is a good school. But the fees are high.
Sir Arthur Helps: Experience is the extract of suffering.
Patrick Henry: I have but one lamp by which my feet are guided, and that is the lamp of experience. I know of no way of judging the future but by the past.
Don Herold: Some people have had nothing else but experience.
Herbert Hoover: about the time we think we can make ends meet, somebody moves the ends.
Aldous Huxley: Experience taches only the teachable,
Aldous Huxley: Experience is not what happens to a man, it's what a man does with what happens to him.
Henrik Ibsen (Norwegian dramatist, 1828-1906): The spectacles of experience; through them you will see clearly a second time.
William Ralph Inge: Experience is a good teacher, but her fees are very high
Italian/Belgian Proverb: Experience is the comb that nature gives us when we are bald.
William James: Experience is remolding us every moment, and our mental reaction on any given thing is really a resultant of our experience of the whole world up to that date.
Thomas Jefferson: We Americans sip our hot soup. The French gulp it. (Speaking of the violent French Revolution).
Jewish Proverb: On black earth, the best corn grows. (Simple folk often have the best hearts).
Ben Jonson: Judgment is forced upon us by experience.
Franklin P. Jones: Experience is that marvelous thing that enables you to recognize a mistake when you make it again.
John Keats: A proverb is no proverb to you till life has illustrated it.
Lamartine: Experience is the only prophecy of wise men.
Ann Landers: Experience is what you get when you don't get what you wanted.
Vernon Sanders Law: Experience is the worst teacher, it gives the test before presenting the lesson.
Barry LePatner: Good judgment comes from experience, and experience comes from bad judgment.
Sir Roger L'Estrange: Experience is the mistress of natives as well as of fools.
Livy: Experience is the teacher of fools.
John Locke: No man's knowledge here can go beyond his experience.
James Russell Lowell: One thorn of experience is worth a whole wilderness of warning.
John Lyly: Experience is the mistress of fools.
John Lyly: A bird child dreadeth the fire.
Charles Mackay: Every man's experience of today, is that he was a fool yesterday and the day before yesterday. – Tomorrow he will most likely be of exactly the same opinion.
Manilius: Experience is forever sowing the seed of one thing after another.
Menander: The school of hard knocks is an accelerated curriculum.
Thomas Middleton: Does not he return wisest that comes home wipt with his own follies?
Midrash: Deuteronomy Rabbah: Only the one who eats the dish knows how it tastes.
Alfred de Musset: Experience is the name men give to their follies or their sorrows.
Napoleon I: The true wisdom of nations is experience.
John Newton: Experience is the Lord's school, and they who are taught by Him usually learn by the mistakes they make that in themselves they have no wisdom; and by their slips and falls, that they have no strength.
Friedrich Nietzsche: Dreadful experiences raise the question whether he who experiences them is not something dreadful also.

John Boyle O'Reilly: Who heeds not experience, trust him not.

Sir William Osler: The value of experience is not in seeing much, but in seeing wisely.

Sir William Osler: We are constantly misled by the ease with which our minds fall into the ruts of one or two experiences.

Isabel Paterson: In youth we learn how little we can do for ourselves; in age how little we can do for others. The wisdom of experience is incommunicable.

Wendell Phillips: Experience is a safe light to walk by, and he is not a rash man who expects success in the future by the same means which secured it in the past.

Plautus (Roman poet, 184 B.C.): That man is wise to some purpose who gains his wisdom at the expense and from the experience of another.

Plautus: Draw from others peoples' dangers the lesson that may profit yourself.

Pliny the Elder: The best plan is, as the common proverb has it, to profit by the folly of others.

Alexander Pope: Sad experience leaves no room for doubt.

Marcus Fabius Quintilian (Roman rhetorician, 40-118 AD): In almost everything, experience is more valuable than precept.

Francois Auguste Rene Rodin: Nothing is a waste of time if you use the experience wisely.

William Shakespeare (*As You Like It*, Act IV, i): Jacques: Yes, I have gained my experience. Rosalind: And your experience makes you sad. I had rather have a fool to make me merry than experience to make me sad; and to travel for it too!

William Shakespeare (*Hamlet*, Act I, iii): I shall the effect of this good lesson keep, / As watchman to my heart.

William Shakespeare (*The Lover's Complaint*, l. 155): But, ah, who ever shunned by precedent / The destined ill she must herself assay?

William Shakespeare (*Merry Wives of Windsor*, Act II, i): Unless experience be a jewel; that I have purchased at an infinite rate.

William Shakespeare (*Much Ado About Nothing*, Act IV, i): What we have we prize not to the worth, / Whiles we enjoy it; but being lack'd and lost, / Why then we rack the value; then we find / The virtue, that possession would not show us / While it was ours.

William Shakespeare (*Much Ado About Nothing*, Act V, i): Men / Can counsel, and speak comfort to that grief / Which they themselves not feel; but tasting it, / Their counsel turns to passion, which before / Would give preceptial medicine to rage, / Fetter strong madness in a silken thread, / Charm ache with air, and agony with words.

William Shakespeare (*The Two Gentlemen of Verona*, Act I, iii): Experience is by industry achieved / And perfected by the swift course of time.

William Shakespeare (*The Two Gentlemen of Verona*, Act II, iv): His years but young, but his experience old; / His head unmellow'd, but his judgement ripe.

William Shakespeare (*Sonnet*, L): My grief lies onward, and my joy behind.

George Bernard Shaw: Men are wise in proportion, not to their experience, but to their capacity for experience.

Stan Smith (Hall of fame tennis player): Experience tells you what to do; confidence allows you to do it.

Joseph Lincoln Steffens: You can't put the facts of experience in order while you are getting them, especially if you are getting them in the neck.

Publius Syrus (Roman poet, 1st century B.C.): Each succeeding day is the scholar of that which went before it.

Publius Syrus: Happy is he who gains wisdom from another's mishap.

Will Rogers: It's not what we don't know that hurts, it's what we know that ain't so.

Will Rogers: There are three kinds of men. The one that learns by reading. The few who learn by observation. The rest of them have to pee on the electric fence for themselves.

Will Rogers: A man only learns in two ways, one by reading, and the other by association with smarter people.

Joseph Roux: What is experience? A poor little hut constructed from the ruins of the palace of gold and marble called our illusions.

Joseph Roux: Our experience is composed rather of illusions lost than of wisdom acquired.

Bertrand Russell: Every man, wherever he goes, is encompassed by a cloud of comforting convictions, which move with him like flies on a summer day.

Vernon Sanders: Experience is a hard teacher because she gives the test first, the lesson afterwards.

Jean-Paul Sartre: The more sand has escaped from the hourglass of our life, the clearer we should see through it.

Pete Seeger: Education is when you read the fine print. Experience is what you get if you do not.

J.P. Senn: Experience is the successive disenchantment of the things of life.—It is reason enriched by the spoils of the heart.

William Shakespeare (*As You Like It*, Act IV, i): Jacques: Yes, I have gained my experience. Rosalind: And your experience makes you sad. I had rather have a fool to make me marry than experience to make me sat; and to travel for it too!

William Shakespeare (*King Lear*, Act II, iv): To willful men / The injuries that they themselves procure / Must be their school masters.

William Shakespeare (*The Merchant of Venice*, Act IV, i): What, would'st thou have a serpent sting thee twice?

George Bernard Shaw: We learn from experience that men never learn anything from experience.

George Bernard Shaw: Everything happens to everybody sooner or later if there is time enough.

Percy Bysshe Shelley: I know the past, and thence will assay to glean a warning for the future, so that man may profit by his errors, and derive experience from his folley.

Sir Philip Sidney: All is but lip-wisdom which wants (lacks) experience.

Ben Sirach, Ecclesiasticus: Without experience there can be little wisdom.

Robert Louis Stevenson: There are not words enough in all Shakespeare to express the merest fraction of a man's experience in an hour.

Madam Swetchine (Russian mystic, 1857): We are often prophets to others, only because we are our own historians.

Tacitus: Experience teaches.

Terence: You shall know by experience.

Terence (Roman poet, 150 B.C.): No man was ever so completely skilled in the conduct of life, as not to receive new information from age and experience.

Saint Teresa of Avila: To reach something good it is very useful to have gone astray, and thus acquire experience.

Terrence (Roman poet, 150 B.C.): No man was ever endowed with a judgment so correct and judicious, but that circumstances, time, and experience, would teach him something new, and apprise him that of those things with which he thought himself the best acquainted, he knew nothing; and that those ideas which in theory appeared the most advantageous were found, when brought into practice, to be altogether impracticable.

Tibullus: Fortunate thou who are taught by another's suffering to avoid thy own.

Mark Twain: We should be careful to get out of an experience only the wisdom that is in it – and stop there; lest we be like the cat that sits down on a hot stove-lid again – and that is well; but also she will never sit down on a cold one any more.

Turkish Proverb: Experience is a precious gift, only given a man when his hair is gone.

UA: Good judgment comes from experience, and experience comes from poor judgment.

UA: Once bit, twice shy.

UA: Some of the most well-trodden roads lead nowhere.

UA: The man who has been bitten by a snake is afraid of a piece of rope.

UA: Once a man has been burned by the hot, he blows on the cool.

UA: No one can know where the shoe pinches except the one who walks in it.

UA: The best preacher is the human heart; the best teacher is time; the best book is the world; the best friend is God.

Virgil: Believe one who has proved it. Believe an expert.

John Wesley: When I was young I was sure of everything; in a few years, having been mistaken a thousand times, I was not half so sure of most things as I was before; at present, I am hardly sure of anything but what God has revealed to me.

Oscar Wilde: A burnt child loves the fire.

Oscar Wilde: Experience is of no ethical value. Experience is merely the name everyone gives to their mistakes.

David T. Wolf: Idealism is what precedes experience; cynicism is what follows.

Yiddish Proverb: As we live, so we learn.

Edward Young (English poet, 1765): Experience, if wisdom's friend, her best; if not, her foe.

EXPERTS

Uncle Anthony: Ya know that all the big experts in Major League Baseball – the so called voices of baseball experience the managers and coaches of the ball clubs – all said in a 1918 sports poll that he'd be more valuable to himself and his team (Boston Red Sox at the time) if Babe Ruth only pitched every fourth day and forgot about playing everyday and hitting baseballs for homeruns!

Uncle Anthony: That expert guy should get the "Golden Giraffe Award" for sticking his neck out so far.

Uncle Anthony: If these so called efficiency experts are so smart about running a business, how come they're working for somebody else?

Uncle Anthony: Y'know, an engineer will tell you that aerodynamically the bumblebee design is a disaster: too much body weight, too little wing span. It just can't fly ... BUT IT DOES DON'T IT!

Aunt Mary Carlo: An accountant is jes' somebody hired to 'splain dat you didn't make da money ya did.

Aunt Mary Carlo: Deez IME's ("Independent" or Defense Medical Exams) are like Medical Blind Dates!

Aunt Mary Carlo (about IME exams): I had longer "visits" with the guy at the Garden State toll booth!

Joey Adams (comedian): Science is really going at a rapid pace. Now it's only a hundred years behind the comic strips.

Aesop: Never trust the advice of a man in difficulties.

Isaac Asimov: Part of the inhumanity of the computer is that, once it is competently programmed and working smoothly, it is completely honest.

David Ball: Our expert gives "scientific CONCLUSIONS" and the opposition's experts give "mere OPINIONS."

St. Bernard of Clairvaux: Believe an expert; believe one who has had experience. (*Experto credite*).

Bible: Acts 2:13: These men are full of new wine.

Bible: 1 Corinthians 13:9: We know in part, and we prophesy in part.

Bible: Ecclesiastes 1:18: He that increseth knowledge increseth sorrow.

Bible: Ezekiel 14:9: If the prophet be decieved when he hath spoken a thing, I the Lord have decieved that prophet, and I will stretch out my hand upon him, and will destroy him.

Bible: Mark 6:4: A prophet is not without honour, but in his own country, and among his own kin, and in his own house.

Bible: Matthew 7:15: Beware of false prophets, which come to you in sheep's clothing, but inwardly they are ravening wolves.

Bible: Matthew 13:57: A prophet is not without honour, save in his own country.

Bible: 2 Peter 2:1: There shall be false teachers among you.

Ambrose Bierce: ARCHITECT, n. One who drafts a plan of your house, and plans a draft of your money.

Ambrose Bierce: CLAIRVOYANT, n. A person, commonly a woman, who has the power of seeing that which is invisible to her patron – namely, that he is a blockhead.

Ambrose Bierce: CONNOISSEUR, n. A specialist who knows everything about something and nothing about anything else.

Ambrose Bierce: DENTIST, n. A prestidigitator who, putting metal into your mouth, pulls coins out of your pocket.

Ambrose Bierce: ERUDITION, n. Dust shaken out of a book into an empty skull.

Ambrose Bierce: IMPARTIAL, adj. Unable to perceive any promise of personal advantage from espousing either side of a controversy or adopting either of two conflicting opinions.

Ambrose Bierce: INVENTOR, n. A person who makes an ingenious arrangement of wheels, levers and springs, and believes it civilization.

Ambrose Bierce: LAUREATE, adj. Crowned with leaves of the laurel. In England the Poet Laureate is an officer of the sovereign's court, acting as dancing skeleton at every royal feast and singing-mute at every royal funeral....

Niels Bohr: An expert is a man who has made all the mistakes which can be made in a very narrow field.

Judge Curtis Bok (Pennsylvania Supreme Court 1897-1962): Expert opinion, which is only an ordinary guess in evening clothes. *Kerstetter, Inc v. Commonwealth*, 404 Pa. 168, 171 (1961).

Louis Brandeis: Two and two will always make four, despite reports of presidents and financial advisers who insist on stretching it into five.

Nicholas Murray Butler: An expert is one who knows more and more about less and less

Samuel Butler: The public do not know enough to be experts, yet know enough to decide between them.

Sir Winston Churchill: We are all worms, but I do believe I am a glowworm.

Confucius: When nature exceeds culture, we have the rustic. When culture exceeds nature, we have the pedant.

Bob Dylan: You don't need to be a weatherman to know which way the wind blows.

Albert Einstein (famous lament): Fate has punished me for my contempt for authority by making me an authority myself.

Ralph Waldo Emerson: A great man will find a great subject, or which is the same thing, make any subject great.

Ralph Waldo Emerson: The office of the scholar is to cheer, to raise, and to guide man by showing them facts amidst appearances.

Ralph Waldo Emerson: How we hate this solemn Ego that accompanies the learned, like a double, wherever he goes.

Ralph Waldo Emerson: A scholar is a man with this inconvenience, that, when you ask him his opinion of any matter, he must go home and look up his manuscripts to know.

Michael Ferrara: An expert does not need to know more than anyone else. He just has to be better organized and use slides.

Benjamin Franklin: Tim was so learned that he could name a horse in nine languages: so ignorant that he bought a cow to ride on.

Sigmund Freud (after he met Albert Einstein, 1927): Einstein understands as much about psychology as I do about physics.

Thomas Fuller: The world would perish were all man learned.

Thomas Fuller: There is much more learning than knowing in the world.

Donald R. Gannon: Where facts are few, experts are many.

George Francis Gilette: (By 1940) the theory of relativity will be considered a joke.

Malcolm Gladwell (from his book *The Tipping Point: How Little Things Can Make a Big Difference*, explaining the difference between a "maven" and an "expert"): The maven, ... such as the "Market Mavens" talk about subjects they study and become expert at because they like helping you, ... they are more socially motivated. Experts like to talk about subjects because they like the subject. [EDITOR: This seems to me to apply to the difference between most treating doctors and the insurance defense doctor who conducts a very brief exam]

William Hazlitt: It is the vice of scholars to suppose that there is no knowledge in the world but that of books.

Robert A. Heinlein: Always listen to experts. They will tell you what cannot be done, and why. Then do it.

Oliver Wendell Holmes Jr.: I know of no teachers so powerful and persuasive as the little army of specialists. They carry no banners, they beat no drums; but where they are men learn that bustle and push are not the equals of quiet genius and serene mastery.

Oliver Wendell Holmes Sr.: The world's great men have not commonly been great scholars, nor its great scholars great men.

Oliver Wendell Holmes Sr.: A poet on Pegasus, reciting his own verses, is hardly more to be dreaded than a mounted specialist.

Oliver Wendell Holmes Sr.: Do not be bullied out of your commonsense by a specialist; two to one, he is a pedant.

Tommy Holmes (1952 Braves' Triple A team manager and baseball "expert" about Hank Aaron): That kid can't play baseball. He can't pull the ball.

Aldous Huxley: Specialized meaninglessness has come to be regarded, in certain circles, as a kind of hallmark of true science.

Holbrook Jackson: Pedantry is the dotage of knowledge.

Judge Wilfred Jayne (New Jersey judge 1888-1961): The testimony relating to this footing of the case has been profuse and illuminating. The experts, as too often happens, disagree leaving the problem, as Tennyson might say, dark with excessive brightness. *International Pulverizing Corp. v. Kidwell*, 7 N.J. Super., 345, 354 (1950).

Judge Wilfred Jayne (New Jersey judge 1888-1961): Experience has disclosed that both optimism and pessimism may be found to exist in the minds of expert witnesses. *In re Port of New York Authority*, 28 N.J. Super. 575, 580 (1953)

Jewish Saying: The wisest of men can fool himself.

Immanuel Kant: Science is organized knowledge. Wisdom is organized life.

John Maynard Keynes: Economists (EDITOR: and others) have not yet earned the right to be listened to attentively.

Alfred A. Knopf: An economist [EDITOR: or really ANY EXPERT] is a man who states the obvious in terms of the incomprehensible.

Louis Kronenberger: The essence of the expert is that his field shall be very special and narrow: one of the ways in which he inspires confidence is too rigidly limit himself to the little toe; he would scarcely venture an off-the-record opinion on an infected little finger.

Walter Savage Landor: Two evils, of almost equal weight, may befall the man of erudition: never to be listened to, and to be listened to always.

Nikolai Lenin: Whenever the cause of the people is entrusted to professors it is lost.

Antonio Machado: Whenever learning breeds specialists, the sum of human culture is enhanced thereby. That is the illusion and consolation of specialists.

Groucho Marx (in the 1933 film *Duck Soup*): Why, a four-year-old child could understand this report. Run out and find me a four-year-old child. I can't make head or tail of it.

Jackie Mason: Did you ever hear of a kid playing accountant—even if he wanted to be one?

Midrash: A scholar (or expert) without sensibility is less than an ant.

Wayne C. Minnick (American educator): There is an old story of blind men trying to describe an elephant. One felt the elephant's leg and declared that the creature was like a tree, another felt the enormous side and said the elephant was like a wall, while a third, feeling the tail, was positive the animal was like a rope. Each man had a notion of reality that was limited by the number and kind of attributes he had perceived.

Molière: Don't appear so scholarly, pray. Humanize your talk, and speak to be understood. Do you think a Greek names gives more weight to your reasons?

Molière: Difficulty is a coin the learned make use of like jugglers, to conceal the inanity of their art.

Michael A. Musmanno (Justice of Pennsylvania Supreme Court, 1959): A theory without factual data to support it has no more weight in a courtroom than in a scientific laboratory.

Michael A. Musmanno (Justice of Pennsylvania Supreme Court, 1959): When, in the reconstruction of a scientific phenomenon, every plausible explanation for the accepted result is ruled out but one, it is idle to argue that there could possibly be still another explanation which lies in the realm of the unknowable and unascertainable and then expect a jury to base its verdict on that mysterious something which exists only in the misty shadowlands of shrouded mystery and supernatural supposition.

Lawrence Peter: Make three correct gases consecutively and you will establish a reputation as an expert.

Pablo Picasso: Computers are useless. They can only give you answers.

Robert M. Pirsig: One geometry (EDITOR: or ONE MEDICINE/ECONOMICS/ETC) cannot be more true than another; it can only be more *convenient.* Geometry is not true, it is advantageous.

P.J. Plauger: My definition of an expert in any field is a person who knows enough about what's really going on to be scared.

Lester J. Pourciau: There is no monument dedicated to the memory of a committee.

Will Rogers: An economist's guess is liable to be as good as anybody else's.

Will Rogers: Invest in inflation. It's the only thing going up.

Will Rogers: The fellow who can only see a week ahead is always the popular fellow, for he is looking with the crowd. But the one that can see years ahead, he has a telescope but he cant make anybody believe he has it.

Bertrand Arthur William Russell: A stupid man's report of what a clever man says can never be accurate, because he unconsciously translates what he hears into something he can understand.

Bertrand Arthur William Russell: Even when the experts all agree, they may well be mistaken.

Lord Salisbury: No lesson seems to be so deeply inculcated by the experience of life as that you never showed trust experts. If you believe the doctors, nothing is wholesome; if you believe the theologians, nothing is innocent; if you believe the soldiers, nothing is safe.

Arthur Schlesinger Jr.: People who claw their way to the top are not likely to find very much wrong with the system that enabled them to rise.

Arthur Schopenhauer: Talent hits a target no one else can hit; genius hits a target no one else can see.

William Shakespeare (*Antony and Cleopatra*, Act I, ii): In nature's infinite book of secrecy, / A little I can read.

William Shakespeare (*As You Like It*, Act I, ii): Touchstone: The more pity, that fools may not speak wisely, what wise men do foolishly. Celia: By my troth, thou say'st true; for since the little wit that fools have was silenced, the little foolery that wise men have makes a great show.

William Shakespeare (*As You Like It*, Act V, i): The fool doth think he is wise, but the wise man knows himself to be a fool.

William Shakespeare (*I Henry IV*, Act IV, iii): Greatness knows itself.

William Shakespeare (*II Henry IV*, Act II, ii): Well, thus we play the fools with the time, and the spirits of the wise sit in the clouds and mock us.

William Shakespeare (*I Henry VI*, Act V, i): I always thought, / It was both impious and unnatural, / That such immanity and bloody strife / Should reign among professors of one faith.

William Shakespeare (*Julius Caesar*, Act I, ii): Why, man, he doth bestride the narrow world, / Like a Colossus; and we petty men / Walk under his huge legs, and peep about / To find ourselves dishonorable graves.

William Shakespeare (*Julius Caesar*, Act I, ii): Now, in the name of all the gods at once, / Upon what meat doth this, our Caesar feed, / That he has grown so great?

William Shakespeare (*Love's Labour's Lost*, Act V, ii): Figures pedantical.

William Shakespeare (*Lucrese*, Line 1006): The mightier the man, the mightier is the thing / That makes him honour'd, or begets him hate; / For greatest scandal waits on greatest state.

William Shakespeare (*Macbeth*, Act III, i): There is none but he / Whose being I do fear: and under him / My genius is rebuk'd; as it is said, / Mark Antony's was by Caesar.

William Shakespeare (*Merchant of Venice*, Act I, iii): The devil can site scripture for his own purpose! An evil soul producing holy witness is like a villain with a smiling cheek."

William Shakespeare (*Othello*, Act II, iii): Your name is great / In mouths of wisest censure.

William Shakespeare (*Richard III*, Act I, iii): They that stand high have many blasts to shake them; / And if they fall they dash themselves to pieces.

William Shakespeare (*The Taming of the Shrew*, Act III, i): How fiery and forward our pedant is!

William Shakespeare (*Twelfth Night*, Act II, iii): Some are born great, some achieve greatness, / And some have greatness thrust upon them.

William Shenstone: The vacant skull of a pedant generally furnishes out a throne and a temple for vanity.

John Sladek: The future, according to some scientists, will be exactly like the past, only far more expensive.

Benjamin Stolberg: An expert is a person who avoids small error as he sweeps on to the grand fallacy.

Thomas Sowell: Much of the social history of the Western world over the past three decades has involved replacing what worked with what sounded good.

Shunryu Suzuki: In the beginner's mind there are many possibilities. In the expert's mind there are few.

Edward Teller: If there ever was a misnomer, it is "exact science." Science has always been full of mistakes. The present day he is no exception. And our mistakes are good mistake; they require a genius to correct them. Of course, we do not see our own mistakes.

Henry David Thoreau: Men have become the tools of their tools.

Kelvin Throop III: Isn't it interesting that the same people who laugh at science fiction listen to weather forecasts and economists?

Lily Tomlin as Ernestine: We don't care. We don't have to. We're the phone company.

Mark Twain: In religion and politics [EDITOR: and medical "junk-science"] people's beliefs and convictions [EDITOR: and some professional expert "opinions"] are in almost every case gotten at second-hand, and without examination, from authorities who have not themselves examined the questions at issue but have taken them at second- hand from other non-examiners, whose opinions about them were not worth a brass farthing.

UA: Those who can't sing can still be experts on singing.

Peter Ustinov: If the world should blow itself up, the last audible voice would be that of an expert saying it can not be done!"

Hendrik Van Loon (*The Story of Mankind*, 1922): (Erasmus) had travelled a great deal and knew whereof he wrote. Or as it has evolved: He knows whereof he speaks/spoke/writes/wrote.

Maggie Vesper (my daughter): That expert should get "The Pinocchio Award" for all the lies he told.

Virgil: Believe one who has proved it. Believe an expert.

Chris Watson (Atlantic City Press article "That's Not All, Folks! Lessons Learned From Cartoons Over Into Adult Situations"): Foghorn Leghorn, that pompous rooster-about-town, taught me how to spot vanity and pretentiousness. Because he had a valuable diploma from Chicken Tech (I kid you not!), I listened when he spoke. Like the time he gave a math lesson to Little Henery Hawk. "To nuthins is nuthin," Foghorn said. "To half nuthins is a whole nuthin." This sage advice is held me in good stead when I've felt the compulsion to buy something worthless off a sale table.

Oscar Wilde: The public is wonderfully tolerant. It forgives everything except genius.

EXPLANATION (See EXCUSES)

FACTS (See also EVIDENCE; FRAUD; HONESTY; LIES/LIARS)

Uncle Anthony: Don't think only honest men will look you in the eyes, a good liar can stare you down all day long.

Uncle Anthony: The facts stuck out like lettuce from (one your mom's Italian hoagies) or an over packed BLT!

Aunt Mary Carlo: Ignoring the facts, don't change the facts.

Joseph Addison: Facts are plain spoken; hopes and figures are its aversion.

Aesop: Never trust the advice of a man in difficulties.

Dr. Robert Anthony: Things are not what they seem, they are what they are.

Isaac Asimov: Part of the inhumanity of the computer is that, once it is competently programmed and working smoothly, it is completely honest.

Bernard Baruch: Every man has a right to his opinion, but no man has a right to be wrong in his facts.

Bible: Hebrews 11:1: Faith is the substance of things hoped for, the evidence of things not seen.

Bible: John 4:48: Except ye see signs and wonders, ye will not believe.

Bible: John 5:39: Search the scriptures.

Bible: John 19:22: Pontious Pilate: "What I have written I have written.

Bible: John 20:27: (Jesus to the Apostle Thomas): Reach hither thy hand, and thrust it into my side: and be not faithless, but believing.

Bible: 2 Kings 7:2: Thou shalt see it with thine eyes, ...

Bible: Numbers 20:10: Hear now, ye rebels; must we fetch you water out of this rock?

Ambrose Bierce: IMAGINATION, n. A warehouse of facts, with poet and liar in joint ownership.

Ambrose Bierce: REALISM, n. The art of depicting nature as it is seen by toads. The charm suffusing a landscape painted by a mode, or a story written by a measuring-worm.

Ambrose Bierce: REALITY, n. The dream of a mad philosopher. That which would remain in the cupel if one should assay a phantom. The nucleus of a vacuum.

Ambrose Bierce: REALLY, adv. Apparently.

Edmund Burke: Facts are to the mind what food is to the body.

Robert Burns: But facts are chiels that winna ding, / An downa be disputed.

John Burroughs: To treat your facts with imagination is one thing, but to imagine your facts is another.
George Canning: There is nothing I know of so sublime as a fact.
Anton J. Carlson: Let us keep our mouths shut and our pens dry until we know the facts.
Thomas Carlyle: Conclusive facts are inseparable from inconclusive except by a head that already understands and knows.
Thomas Carlyle: I grow daily to honor facts more and more, and theory less and less.
Sir Winston Churchill: I pass with relief from the tossing sea of Cause and Theory to the firm ground of Result and Fact.
Sir Winston Churchill: This is one of those cases in which the imagination is baffled by the facts.
Samuel Taylor Coleridge: Facts are not truths; they are not conclusions; they are not even premises, but in the nature and parts of premises.
Walter Cronkite (CBS TV *Evening News* anchorman): "...and that's the way it is ..."
Samuel McChord Crothers: The trouble with facts is that there are so many of them.
Dizzy Dean: I'm through talking about things folks ain't seeing.
John Dewey: We can have facts without thinking, but we cannot have thinking without facts.
Charles Dickens: I have known of vast quantity of nonsense talked about bad men not looking you in the face. Don't trust that conventional idea. Dishonesty will stare honesty out of countenance, any day in the week, if there is anything to be got by it.
Benjamin Disraeli: There are three kinds of lies: lies, damned lies, and statistics.
John Foster Dulles: Natural science has outstripped moral and political science. That is too bad; but it is a fact, and the fact does not disappear because we close our eyes to it.
Tyron Edwards: Facts are God's arguments; we should be careful never to misunderstand or pervert them.
Albert Einstein: If the facts don't fit the theory, change the facts.
Albert Einstein (in 1930 the Nazis Party in Germany and America published *"100 Authorities Against Einstein"* to disprove his theory of relativity, to which Einstein quipped): It would not take 100 authorities to prove relativity wrong, one single fact would do the trick."
Ebenezer Eliot: Facts are stubborn things.
Paul Eldridge: In the spider-web of facts, many a truth is strangled.
Jane (or Jean) Elliot: Facts are stubborn things.
Ralph Waldo Emerson: No facts are to me sacred; none are profane. I simply experiment, an endless seeker, with no past at my back.
Nathaniel Emmons: Any fact is better established by two or three good testimonies than by a thousand arguments.
Justice Felix Frankfurter: To some lawyers, all facts are created equal.
William S. Gilbert (*The Mikado*, Act II): Her terrible tale / You can't assail, / With truth it quite agrees: / Her taste exact / For faultless fact / Amounts to a disease.
Stephen Jay Gould: Facts do not 'speak for themselves', they are read in the light of theory.
Nathaniel Hawthorne: From principles is derived probability, but truth or certainty is obtained only from facts.
Werner Heisenberg: What happens depends on our way of observing it or on the fact that we observe it.
Eric Hoffer: Facts are counterrevolutionary.
Oliver Wendell Holmes, Jr.(*Oration before Harvard Law School Association*, 1886): The main part of intellectual education is not the acquisition of facts, but learning how to make the facts live.
Oliver Wendell Holmes, Sr.: This is not a matter for polite presumptions; we must look facts in the face.
Oliver Wendell Holmes, Sr.: Sin has many tools, but a lie is the handle which fits them all.
Richard Hooker (English theologian, 1554?-1600): In matters of fact, they say there is some credit to be given to the testimony of men, but not in matters of judgment.
Aldous Huxley: Facts do not cease to exist because they are ignored.
Thomas Henry Huxley: A world of facts lies outside and beyond the world of words.
Thomas Henry Huxley: Truly it has been said, that to a clear eye the smallest fact is a window through which the Infinite may be seen.
Robert H. Jackson (*Advocacy Before the Supreme Court: Suggestions for Effective Case Presentations*, 37 A.B.A.J. 801, 1951): The purpose of a hearing is that the Court may learn what it does not know and

it knows least about the facts. It may sound paradoxical, but most contentions of law are won or lost on the facts. They often incline a judge to one side or the other.

William James: As a rule we disbelieve all the facts and theories for which we have no use.

Samuel Johnson: When speculation has done its worst, two and two still make four.

Samuel Johnson: We are inclined to believe those whom we do not know because they have never deceived us.

Omar Khayyam: A hair perhaps divides the false from true.

Vladimir Lenin: A lie told often enough becomes the truth.

James Russell Lowell (*Bigelow Papers*, Ser. 2, No. 4): Though the the'ry's fust-rate, the facts wun't coincide: / Facs are contrary 'z mules, an' ez hard in the mouth .

Mary McCarthy: In science, all facts, no matter how trivial or banal, enjoy democratic equality.

Daniel Patrick Moynihan: Everyone is entitled to his own opinion, but not his own facts.

Michael A. Musmanno (Justice of Pennsylvania Supreme Court, 1959): A theory without factual data to support it has no more weight in a courtroom than in a scientific laboratory.

Michael A. Musmanno (Justice of Pa. Supreme Court, 1959): What is trivial is strictly a matter of comparison. Even an earthquake of sizable proportions is trivial against an atomic blast which lays waste half a continent.

Michael A. Musmanno (Justice of the Sup. Ct. of Pennsylvania, 1959): The Majority Opinion says very little about the facts in the case so that it will be necessary to enumerate them because the facts in any case constitute the anatomy over which the skin of a decision is snugly draped. I think, by reciting the facts, we will see that the Majority's decision fits very badly the contours of the body of the controversy at hand.

Myson of Chen (600B.C.): We should not investigate facts by the light of these arguments, but arguments by the light of facts.

Jawaharlal Nehru: Facts are facts and will not disappear on account of your likes.

Friedrich Wilhelm Nietzsche: There are no eternal facts as there are no eternal truths.

Friedrich Wilhelm Nietzsche: There are no facts, only interpretations.

Austin O'Malley: Facts are carpet-tacks under the pneumatic tires of theory.

Norman Vincent Peale: Any fact facing us is not as important as our attitude toward it, for that determines our success or failure.

Shimon Peres: If a problem has no solution, it may not be a problem, but a fact—not to be solved, but to be coped with over time.

George Denison Prentice: Some people have a peculiar faculty for denying facts.

Clarence Belden Randall: Facts, as such, never settled anything. They are working tools only. It is the implications that can be drawn from the facts that count, and to evaluate these requires wisdom and judgment that are unrelated to the computer approach to life.

Ronald Reagan: Facts are stupid things.

David Reuben, M.D. (title of his 1970 book *Everything You Always Wanted to Know About Sex But Were Afraid to Ask*, later made into 1972 Woody Allen film of the same): Everything You Always Wanted to Know About – But Were Afraid to Ask.

La Rochefoucauld: There is nothing more horrible than the murder of a beautiful theory by a brutal gang of facts.

La Rochefoucauld: Some disguised deceits counterfeit truth so perfectly that not to be taken in by them would be an error of judgment.

Will Rogers: All I know is what I read in the papers....

Franklin D. Roosevelt: Repetition does not transform a lie into the truth

Bertrand Russell: The degree of one's emotion varies inversely with one's knowledge of the facts—the less you know the hotter you get.

George Santayana: I believe in general in a dualism between facts and the ideas of those facts in human heads.

Dorothy Sayers: Facts are like cows. If you look them in the face hard enough they generally run away."

Arthur Schnitzler: To have no occasion for lying does not yet mean to be honest.

Walter Scott: O what a tangled web we weave, when first we practice to deceive!

William Shakespeare (*All's Well That Ends Well*, Act III, vii): Is wicked meaning in a lawful deed / And lawful meaning in a lawful act, / Where both not sin, and yet a sinful fact.

William Shakespeare (*Hamlet*, Act II, ii): If circumstances lead me, I will find / Where truth is hid, though it were hid indeed / Within the centre.

William Shakespeare (*I Henry VI*, Act IV, i): This fact was infamous / And ill beseeming any common man.

Charles Haddon Spurgeon: When facts were weak, his native cheek brought him serenely through.

Publilius Syrus (42 B.C.): Even false becomes true when the chief says so.

Marleau (or Marlo) Thomas: Never face facts; if you do you'll never get up in the morning.

Harry S. Truman: We must have strong minds, ready to accept facts as they are.

John Tyndall: It is as fatal as it is cowardly to blink facts because they are not to our taste.

Mark Twain: Get the facts first. You can distort them later.

Mark Twain: You cannot depend on your eyes when you're imagination is out of focus.

Mark Twain: It is easier to manufacture seven facts out a whole cloth than one emotion.

Mark Twain: News is history in its first and best form, its vivid and fascinating form... history is the pale and tranquil reflection of it.

Mark Twain: There is something fascinating about science. One gets such wholesale returns of conjecture of such a trifling investment of fact.

UA: From principles is derived probability; but truth, or certainty, is obtained only from facts.

UA: One fact is better than one hundred analogies.

UA (catchphrase on NBC-TVs *Rowan and Martin's Laugh-In*, 1967-73): Look that up in your Funk and Wagnall (American dictionary)!

Sir John Vaughan (Chief Justice, Common Pleas, England, 1603-1674): Without a known fact, it is impossible to know the law on that fact. *Bushel's Case*, Jones (T.) 13, 1670.

Maggie Vesper (my daughter): That expert should get "The Pinocchio Award" for all the lies he told.

Gore Vidal: It is the spirit of the age to believe that any fact, no matter how suspect, is superior to any imaginative exercise, no matter how true.

Jane Wagner: After all, what is reality anyway? Nothin' but a collective hunch.

Jack Webb (producer, director, star of TV series *Dragnet*, 1951-58, charcter of Los Angeles Police Sgt. Joe Friday): All we want is the facts, ma'am ... **just the facts ma'am** (Editor: don't give us your opinions, just the unvarnished details or facts of what happemed).

Jack Webb (producer, director, star of TV series *Dragnet*, 1951-58, charcter of Los Angeles Police Sgt. Joe Friday, radio announcement on first radio show in 1949): Ladies and gentlemen, the story you are about to hear is true. **Only the names have been changed to protect the innocent.**

Jessamyn West: We want the facts to fit the preconceptions. When they don't, it is easier to ignore the facts than to change the preconceptions.

Walter Winchell (1930's Sunday Night Radio Show): "Good evening Mr. & Mrs. America and all the ships at sea, let's go to press! ... FLASH! ... ITEM! ... ITEM! ... SCOOP! ... SCOOP! ... stay with me, I'll be right back in a flash ..."

Edward Livingston Youmans: Every fact that is learned becomes a key to other facts.

FAILURE (See also SUCCESS)

Uncle Anthony: Show me a good loser, and I'll show you a loser.

Uncle Anthony: It is easier to know how to do something then it is to actually do it.

Uncle Anthony (and my father Rocco): You can't win them all, but with very little effort you can lose them all.

Uncle Anthony: It ain't failure that's a crime – it's low aim!

Uncle Anthony: Some guys fail 'cause they "psych-out" themselves – they over analyse and plan so much in advance that they convince themselves they can't win.

Aunt Mary Carlo: For those guys, every morning is "the dawn of a new error."

Aunt Mary Carlo: He's a genius –he really is – he can do jes about anythin' except make a livin'!

Aunt Mary Carlo: The only time he knows where he's goin' is when he takes Exlax (a laxitive)!

Aunt Mary Carlo: When ya lose (an' ya will lose sometimes) don't lose da lesson!
Cindy Adams: Success has made failures of many men.
Douglas Adams: A common mistake people make when trying to design something completely foolproof is to underestimate the ingenuity of complete fools.
George Ade: Anybody can win unless their happens to be a second entry.
Minna Thomas Antrim: Three failures denote uncommon strength. A weakling has not enough grit to fail thrice.
Red Auerbach: Show me a good loser, and I'll show you a loser.
P.T. Barnum: I'd rather be kicked, than not noticed at all.
P.T. Barnum: There's a sucker born every minute. (EDITOR: A "sucker" was a name given to person from the upper mid-West, early settlers who purified their drinking water by sucking it through straws. Also there is the term "innocent as a suckling." NOTE: This phrase actulally originated in the 1880s from "Paper Collar Joe," a New York City con artist named Joseph Bessemer who really said: "There was a sucker born every minute, but none of them ever died."
Yogi Berra: Someone's got to win and someone's got to lose, and that was us.
Bible: Apocrypha, Ecclesiasticus 20:22: There is that destroyeth his own soul through bashfulness.
Bible: Ecclesiastes 4:10: Woe to him that is alone when he falleth; for he hath not another to help him up.
Bible: Luke 12:48: Unto whomsoever much is given, of him shall be much required.
Bible: Luke 20:17; Mark 12:10; Matthew 21:42; Psalms 118:22: The stone which the builders rejected is become the head of the corner.
Bible: Mark 10:31; Matthew 19:30; Matthew 20:16: Many that are first shall be last; and the last first.
Bible: Phillippians 2:16: I have not run in vain, neither laboured in vain.
Bible: Proverbs, 11:28: He that trusteth in his riches shall fall.
Bible: Proverbs 13:19: The desire accomplished is sweet to the soul.
Bible: Proverbs 16:18: Pride goeth before destruction, and an haughty spirit before a fall.
Bible: Psalms 37:29: The righteous shall inherit the land.
Bible: Psalms 69:19: Thou hast known my reproach, and my shame, and my dishonour.
Bible: 1 Samuel 1:27: How are the mighty fallen, and the weapons of war perished!
Bible: 2 Samuel 1:19: The beauty of Israel is slain upon thy high places; **how the mighty have fallen!**
Bible: 2 Samuel 1:25: **How the mighty have fallen** in the midst of battle!
Bible: 2 Samuel 1:27: **How the mighty have fallen,** and the weapons of war perished!
Bible: Titus 1:15: Unto the pure all things are pure.
Ambrose Bierce: ABSTAINER, n. A weak person who yields to the temptation of denying himself a pleasure.
Ambrose Bierce: PERSEVERANCE, n. A lowly virtue whereby mediocrity achieves an inglorious success.
Ambrose Bierce: SAINT, n. A dead sinner revised and edited.
Marlon Brando (in the 1954 film *On the Waterfront*): I could have had class. I could have been a contender.
George Burns: I'd rather be a failure at something I love than a success at something I hate.
Truman Capote: Failure is the condiment that gives success its flavor.
George Washington Carver: 99% of failures come from people who have a habit of making excuses.
Anton Chekhov: Dividing people into successes and failures means looking upon human nature from the narrow, preconceived point of view.... Are you a failure or not? Am I? Napolean? Your servant Vasili? Where is the criterion? One must be God to be able to distinguish successes from failures and not make mistakes.
Lord Chesterfield: It is undoubted truth that the less one has to do, the less time one finds to do it.
Chinese Proverb: Everyone pushes a falling fence.
Sir Winston Churchill: Success is going from failure to failure without loss of enthusiasm
Count Galeazzo Ciano: As always, victory finds a hundred fathers, but defeat is an orphan.
James Bryant Conant: Behold the turtle: He only makes progress when he sticks his neck out.
Charles Horton Cooley: Failure sometimes enlarges the spirit. You have to fall back upon humanity and God.
Bill Cosby: I don't know the key to success, but the key to failure is trying to please everybody.

Cyrus H. Curtis: There are two kinds of men who never amount to much: those who cannot do what they are told and those who can do nothing else.

Jefferson Davis (President of the Conferacy, 1864): If the Confederacy fails, there should be written on its tombstone: **Died of a theory.**

Sammy Davis, Jr.: Most of the trouble with most people in America who become successful is that they can really and truly get by on bullshit alone. They can survive on it.

John Dewey: Failure is instructive. The person who really thinks learns quite as much from his failures as from his successes.

Benjamin Disraeli: Every man has a right to be conceited until he is successful.

Benjamin Disraeli: Failure, when sublime, is not without its purpose.

Benjamin Disraeli: Every man has a right to be conceited until he is successful.

Mike Ditka: Success is not permanent, and failure is not fatal.

Leo Durocher: Show me a good loser and I'll show you an idiot.

Leo Durocher (1946 statement about the New York Giants baseball team, and title of his 1975 autobiography): Nice guys finish last.

Amelia Earhart: In soloing – as in other activities – it is far easier to start something than it is to finish it.

Thomas Edison: Show me a thoroughly satisfied men—and I will show you a failure.

Thomas Edison: Opportunity is missed by most people because it is dressed in overalls and looks like work.

Ralph Waldo Emerson: A weed is just a plant whose virtues have not yet been discovered.

William Feather: There are two kinds of failures: those who fought and never did, and those who did and never thought.

Errol Flynn: Any man who has $10,000 left when he dies is a failure.

Henry Ford: Failure is the only opportunity to begin again more intelligently.

Anatole France: If 50 million people say a foolish thing it is still a foolish thing.

Al Frankin: They dropped the ball ... while failing to connect the dots!

Al Frankin: "A TSUNAMI OF STUPIDITY!"

Al Frankin: They (politicians): used "Weekend With Bernie Strategy" = don't tell him or anyone he's dead!

John W. Gardner: One of the reasons mature people stop learning is that they become less and less willing to risk failure.

J. Paul Getty: A man may fail many times, but he is not a failure until he begins to blame somebody else.

Jean Giraudoux: Only the mediocre are always at their best.

David Grayson: We fail more often by timidity than by over-daring.

Julius Charles Hare: Half the failures in life arise from pulling in one's horse as he is leaping.

Joseph Heller: He was a self-made man who owed his lack of success to nobody.

Lillian Hellman: Is it age, or was it always my nature, to take a bad time, block out the good times until any success became an accident and failure seemed the only truth?

Conrad Hilton: I encourage boldness because the danger of our seniority and pension plans tempt a young man to settle in a rut named security rather than find his own rainbow.

Eric Hoffer: Absolute faith corrupts as absolutely as absolute power.

Herbert Hoover: About the time we think we can make ends meet, somebody moves the ends.

Bob Hope: ON HIS NEVER WINNING AN OSCAR: Welcome to the Academy Awards or, as it's called at my home, "Passover."

Bob Hope: ON HIS EARLY FAILURES: I would not have had anything to eat if it was not for all that stuff the audience threw at me.

Kin Hubbard: It's hard to tell which gets knocked the most, the success or the failure, but it's mighty close.

Elbert Hubbard: The line between failure in success is so fine that we scarcely know when we pass it; so fine that we are often on the line and do not know it.

Kin Hubbard: Whoever wrote "to win success we must deserve it" must have been the same fellow who gave out the statement that two can live as cheaply as one.

Victor Hugo: Friend is sometimes a word devoid of meaning; enemy, never.

Aldous Huxley: A chip on the shoulder is a sure sign that there is more wood higher up.

Lee Iacocca: The trick is to make sure you don't die waiting for prosperity to come.

Italian Proverb: Success has many parents, but failure is an orphan.

Italian Proverb: We cannot direct the wind, but we can adjust the sails.
Italian Proverb: It is a foolish sheep that makes the wolf its confessor.
Italian Proverb: Stumbling is not the same as falling.
Jewish Saying: When a *nebekh* leaves the room, you feel as if someone came in.
Jewish Saying: A *shlemiel* is always knocking things up a table, and the nebekh always picks them up.
Michael Jordan: I can except failure, everybody fails that something, but I cannot except not trying.
Rudyard Kipling: We have forty million reasons for failure, but not a single excuse.
Latin Proverb: To do two things at once is to do neither.
Robert E. Lee: We have fought this fight as long, and as well as we know how. We have been defeated. For us, as a Christian people, there is now but one course to pursue. We must accept the situation.
Wladziu Valentino Liberace (to his critics): What you said hurt me very much. I cried all the way to the bank.
Listerine mouthwash ad (1920's): Often/always a bridesmaid, but never a bride.
Vince Lombardi: If you can accept losing, you can't win. If you can walk, you can run. No one is ever hurt. Hurt is in your mind.
Groucho Marx: He may look like an idiot, but don't let that fool you. You really is an idiot.
W. Somerset Maugham: It is cruel to discover one's mediocrity only when it is too late.
H. L. Mencken: Science, at bottom, is really anti-intellectual. It always distrusts pure reason, and demands the production of objective fact.
Michel de Montaigne: There are some defeats more triumphant than victories.
Jack Nicklaus: Achievement is largely the product of steadily raising one's levels of aspiration and expectation.
Sioux Chief "Old Lodge Skins" (after June 25-26, 1876 Battle of Little Big Horn): Yes, my son, is finished now... there is no permanent winning or losing when things move as they should in a circle. But the white men, who live in squares and straight lines do not believe as I do. To them it is everything or nothing.... Winning is all they care about. And if they can do that by scratching a pen across a paper or saying something into the wind, they are much happier.
Robert Orben: There are days when it takes all you've got just to keep up with the losers.
Cynthia Ozick: I'm not afraid of facts, I welcome facts *but a congeries of facts is not equivalent to an idea.* This is the essential fallacy of the so-called "scientific" mind. People who mistake facts for ideas are incomplete thinkers; they are gossips.
Leroy "Satchel" Paige (Hall of Fame baseball pitcher): Don't look back, somebody might be gaining on you.
Mary Pickford: The thing that we call "failure" is not the falling down, but the staying down.
Pliny the Younger (Latin pleader and letter writer, 62-113 AD): An object in possession seldom retains the same charm that it had in pursuit.
Charles F. Richter (from the 1932 Richter Scale of measuring earthquakes): On a scale of one to ten ....
Preacher Roe (1940's Brooklyn Dodger "dipsy doo" pitcher): Some days you eat the bear. Some days the bear eats you. ... Yesterday, the bear ate us.
Will Rogers: Do the best you can, and don't take life too serious.
Will Rogers: The worst thing that happens to you may be the best thing for you if you don't let it get the best of you.
Will Rogers: The fellow that can only see a week ahead is always the popular fellow, for he is looking with the crowd. But the one that can see years ahead, he has a telescope but he can't make anybody believe that he has it.
Anna Eleanor Roosevelt: No one can make you feel inferior without your consent.
Theodore Roosevelt: It is hard to fail, but it is worse never to have tried to succeed. In this life we get nothing save by effort.
Leo Rosten: NEBEKH (NEBBECH): In the vocabulary of character types, woven out of pity, candor and insight, *nebekh* stands (along with nudnick, shlemiel, shlimazl, shnuk, shmendrick, yold, Chaim Yankel, shlepper) in that pantheon of special Yiddish words coined to describe the ineffectuals of this world (For definitions, see... The Joys of Yiddish,...) *"Nebekh"* is both a noun and an interjection. As a noun, it means an innocuous nonentity, a helpless, hapless soul—first cousin to a *shlemiel.* But whereas one may

dislike a *shlemiel* it is hard to feel anything but sympathy for a *nebekh*. As an interjection, *nebekh* means "alas... too bad... unfortunately..." expressing affectionate dismay, regret, or commiseration.

Leo Rosten: SCHLEMIEL: "... a *schlemiel*, though closely related to a *shlimaz*, is more precisely a simpleton, a gull, a pipsqueak; clumsy, submissive, uncomplaining, naïve; a Casper Milquetoast writ large—and in Yiddish.

Leo Rosten: SHLEMAZL: "The word comes from the German *schlimm* ("bad") and the Hebrew *mazl* ("lock"), but a *shlemazl* is thought of as more than simply unlucky. He is a chronic loser, Patsy, fall-guy, pigeon.... a *shlemazl* also may be characterized in psychiatric nomenclature as one predisposed to be victimized, one "accident prone." So *shlemazl* conveys the idea of one doomed (innocently) to fail and (perhaps) masochistically inclined to cooperate with the inequitable fates.

Leo Rosten: When a *shlemazl* (luckless one) buys a suit with two pair of pants he promptly burns to hole in the jacket; if he sold umbrellas, it would stop raining; if he sold candles, the son would never set; and if he made coffins, people would stop dying.

Rudy Ruettiger (motivational speaker, Notre Dame football player, ND Class of 1973; his true story is the movie *Rudy*): The only thing you can control is the effort, and you owe it to yourself to persevere and do whatever you decide to do with passion. Don't ask for permission to be successful. Go make it happen.

Bertrand Russell: Nothing is so exhausting as indecision, and nothing so futile.

Bertrand Russell: A stupid man's report of what a clever man says can never be accurate, because he unconsciously translates what he hears into something he can understand.

Rosalind Russell: Flops are part of life's menu and I have never been a girl to miss out on any of the courses.

Rosalind Russell: Success is a public affair. Failure is a private funeral.

Historian William W. Sears (about Civil War General George B. McClellan): He was so fearful of losing, he would not risk winning.

Thomas Sowell: Much of the history of the Western world over the past three decades has involved replacing what worked with what sounded good.

William Shakespeare (*I Henry IV*, Act V, i): With the losers let it sympathize; / For nothing can seem foul to those that win.

William Shakespeare (*III Henry VI*, Act II, i): Didst thou never hear / That things ill got had ever bad success?

William Shakespeare (*III Henry VI*, Act III, iii): And if thou fail us, all our hope is done

William Shakespeare (*Macbeth*, Act I, vii): If we should fail? – We fail! / But screw screw your courage to the sticking-place, / And we'll not fail.

William Shakespeare (*Measure for Measure*, Act IV, ii): Thus fail not to do your office, as you will answer it at your peril.

William Shakespeare (*The Merchant of Venice*, Act III, ii): Have all his ventures fail'd? / What, not one hit?

William Shakespeare (*Richard III*, Act I, i): Now is the winter of our discontent / Made glorious summer by this sun of York; / And all the clouds, that lower'd upon our house, / In the deep bosom of the ocean buried.

William Shakespeare (*Richard III*, Act I, iii): They that stand high have many blasts to shake them; / And, if they fall, they dash themselves to pieces..

William Shakespeare (*Twelfth Night*, Act II, v): Some are born great, some achieve greatness, and some have greatness thrust upon 'em.

Ashton Stevens: No one runs downhill as fast as a thoroughbred.

Frank Swinnerton: The man who fails because he aims astray or because he does not aim at all is to be found everywhere.

Herbert Bayard Swope: I cannot give you the formula for success, but I can give you the formula for failure, which is – try to please everybody.

Thomas Szasz: The stupid never forgive nor forget; the naïve forgive and forget; the wise forgive but do not forget.

Albert von Szent-Gyorgyi: Discovery consists of seeing what every body has seen and thinking what nobody has thought.
Albert von Szent-Gyorgi: Discovery is said to be an accident meeting a prepared mind.
Alfred Lord Tennyson: He makes no friend who never made a foe.
James Thurber: You might as well fall flat on your face as lean over backward too far.
Grant Tinker: Oddly enough, success over a period of time is more expensive than failure.
Alvin Toffler: The illiterate of the 21st century will not be those who cannot read and write, but those who cannot learn, unlearn, and relearn.
Mark Twain: Put all your eggs in one basket—and watch the basket.
Mark Twain: Keep away from people who try to belittle your ambitions. Small people always do that, but the really great make you feel that you, too, can become great.
UA: Defeat is not bitter, if you don't swallow it.
UA: A diamond is a piece of coal that stuck to the job.
UA: A man can fail many times, but he is not a failure until he begins to blame somebody else.
UA: The higher a monkey climbs up a tree, the more visible his ass.
Daniel Webster: A strong conviction that something must be done is the parent of many bad measures.
Rudy Westmoreland: He fails from "ANALYSIS PARALYSIS" – he overanalyzes, overthinks and overplans every problem or potential situation so that as a result the problem is never solved and/or the advantage (if any) is lost.
Rudy Westmoreland: Your case ain't dead yet ... but the buzzards are circling.
Oscar Wilde: Anybody can sympathize with the sufferings of a friend, but it requires a very fine nature to sympathize with a friend's success.
Billy Wilder, Charles Brackett, and D.M. Marshman, Jr. (1950 film *Sunset Boulevard*): Joe Gillis: "You used to be in pictures. You used to be big." Norma Desmond: "I am big. It's the pictures that got small."
Lin Yutang: Peace of mind is that mental condition in which you have accepted the worst.

FALSEHOOD (See LIES)

FAMILY (See ANCESTRY)

FATHER (See PARENT)

FAULT (SEE NEGLIGENCE)

FEAR (See COURAGE)

FEES

Uncle Anthony: Y'know your legal lawyer opinion ain't worth nothin' unless you get paid for it.
Uncle Anthony: I saw that guy's name listed in the Yellow Pages as an antitrust lawyer, I don't trust any lawyers!
Aunt Mary Carlo: Yeah, da last ting my lawyer tinks about is money ... just before he goes ta bed.
Aunt Mary Carlo: Yeah, my lawyer always wants cash – I call him "DA DOUGH NUT!"
Francis Bacon (*Speech*, upon taking his seat in Chancery as Lord Keeper, 1617): As for lawyers' fees, I must leave it to the conscience and merit of the lawyer.
Bible: Genesis 29:15: Laba to Jacob: Because thou art my brother, shouldest thou therefore serve me for nought? Tell me, what shall thy wages be?
Bible: Matthew 20:7: Whatever is right, that shall ye receive.
Bible: Proverbs 12:14: The recompense of a man's hands shall be rendered unto him.
Bible: Psalms 39:6: He heapeth up riches, and knoweth not who shall gather them.
Bible: 1 Timothy 5:18: The laborer is worthy of his reward.
Ambrose Bierce: ACCOMPLICE, n. One associated with another in a crime, having guilty knowledge and complicity, as an attorney who defends a criminal, knowing him guilty. This view of the attorney's

position in the matter has not hitherto commanded the assent of attorneys, no one having offered them a fee for assenting.

Ambrose Bierce: PRICE, n. Value, plus a reasonable sum for the wear and tear of conscience in demanding it.

Jimmy Breslin: Lawyers charge a fortune to handle a bond offering. You know what it takes to handle a bond offering? The mental capabilities of a filing cabinet.

Henry Brinklow (1545): The lawyer can not understond the matter tyl he fele his mony.

Les Brown, American Speaker, Author, Trainer, Motivator Lecturer: When you want something, you have to be willing to pay your dues.

Harry Browne, American Financial Advisor, Writer: Everything you want in life has a price connected to it. There's a price to pay if you want to make things better, a price to pay just for leaving things as they are, a price for everything.

Warren Burger: Is not unprofessional to give free legal advice, but advertising that the first visit will be free is a bit like a fox telling chickens he will not bite them until they cross the threshold of the henhouse.

Samuel Butler: In law, nothing is certain but the expense.

Sir Winston Churchill: If the railway makes greater profits, it is usually because it carries more goods and more passengers. If a doctor or a lawyer enjoys a better practice, it is because the doctor attends more patients and more exacting patients, and because the lawyer pleads more suits in the courts and more important suits. At every stage the doctor or the lawyer is giving service in return for his fees, and if the service is too poor or the fees are too high, other doctors and other lawyers can come freely into competition. There is constant service, there is constant competition; there is no monopoly, ... no injury to the public interest, ... no impediment to the general progress.

Clarence Darrow (asked by a client: "How can I ever thank you?" Darrow relied): My dear, since the Phoenicians invented money there has only been one way to do that.

Judge Learned Hand: The public needs the equivalent of Chevrolets as well as Cadillacs.

Reginald L. Hine (English solicitor and writer, 1883-1949, *Confessions of an Un-Common Attorney*, 1945): I dislike sending in professional charges to friendly people, but we have a saying here that offices like individuals have to live.

Barten Holyday: A man may as well open an oyster without a knife, as a lawyer's mouth without a fee.

Irish Proverb: Sweet is the wine but sour is the payment

Alan Liebowitz: I can think of no other business where you are rewarded for inefficiency. No matter what you sell, the fewer hours of labor that go into the product, the more you make. With lawyers its backwards—the more time you take, the more inefficient you are, the greater your profit.

Abraham Lincoln: A lawyer's time and advice are his stock in trade.

Abraham Lincoln (*Notes for a Law Lecture*, 1850): The matter of fees is important, far beyond the mere question of bread and butter involved. Properly attended to, fuller justice is done to both lawyer and client. An exorbitant fee should never be claimed. As a general rule never take your whole fee in advance, nor any more than a small retainer. When fully paid before hand, you are more than a common mortal if you can feel the same interest in the case, as if something was still in prospect for you, as well as for your client. And when you lack interest in the case the job will very likely lack skill and diligence in the performance.

Abraham Lincoln (*Letter to George Floyd*, 1856): I have just recieved yours of the 16th, with check on Flagg & Savage for twenty-five dollars. You must think I am a high-priced man. You are too liberal with your money. Fifteen dollars is enough for the job. I send you a receipt for fifteen dollars, and return to you a ten dollar bill.

Moliere: There's no praise to beat the sort you put in your pocket.

Michael A. Musmanno (Justice of Pennsylvania Supreme Court, 1959): The Contingent Fee: Without contingent fees in the practice of law, considerable portions of the court houses throughout the land, innumerable law offices and other parts of the legal machinery of the nation would be mantled with cobwebs. // If it were not for contingent fees, indigent victims of tortious accidents would be subject to the unbridled, self-willed partisanship of their tortfeasors. The person who has, without fault on his part, been injured and who, because of his injury, is unable to work, and has a large family to support, and has no money to engage a lawyer, would be at the mercy of the person who disabled him because, being in a superior economic position, the injuring person could force on his victim, desperately in need of money to keep the candle of life burning in himself and his dependent ones, a wholly unconscionably meager sum in settlement, or even refuse to pay him anything at all. Any society, and especially a democratic one, worthy of respect in the spectrum of civilization, should never tolerate such a victimization of the weak by the mighty. // Of course, an excessive contingent fee could not be enforced in law just as an excessive fixed fee might be unenforceable if it took inequitable advantage of the payer or in any way offended against public policy. // Contingent fees are not limited to personal-injury cases. Even in contract, equity, criminal and other legal actions, fees are often graduated according to the success to be achieved by the lawyer. Such an agreement, when voluntarily entered into, not only does not offend against the law and morals but it often provides an incentive which might make for better work on the part of the lawyer. A fee which is not absolutely fixed at the initiation of the relationship between the lawyer and his client is bound to be in the nature of a contingent fee, and it is absurd to say the lawyer and his client cannot enter into a fair arrangement whereby the lawyer is paid a little more for winning a case than for losing it. (Richette v. Pennsylvania Railroad, 410 Pa. 6).

Will Rogers: I see a good deal of talk from Washington about lowering taxes. I hope they do get 'em lowered enough so people can afford to pay 'em.

Will Rogers: The only way you can beat the lawyers is to die with nothing.

Theodore Roosevelt: Lawyering is about money making, not about achieving social justice.

Russian Proverb: Law is a flag, and gold is the wind that makes it wave.

Diane Sawyer: It seems for a lot of lawyers, padding the bill is a creative challenge.

William Shakespeare (*King Lear*, Act I, i): Kill thy physician, and the fee bestow / Upon thy foul disease.

William Shakespeare (*King Lear*, Act I, iv): 'Tis like the breath of an unfee'd lawyer; you gave me nothing for 't.

William Shakespeare (*Love's Labour's Lost*, Act IV, iii): To things of sale a seller's praise belongs.

William Shakespeare (*The Merchant of Venice*, Act IV, i): Take some remembrance of us, as a tribute, / Not as a fee

William Shakespeare (*Richard III*, Act III, v): As if the golden fee for which I plead / Were for myself.

William Shakespeare (*Romeo and Juliet*, Act I, iv): O! then, I see, Queen Mab hath been with you.... / She is the fairies' midwife, and she comes ... O'er lawyers' fingers, who strait dream on fees, O'er ladies' lips.

William Shakespeare (*Timon of Athens*, Act II, i): Importune him for moneys; be not ceas'd / With slight denial; nor then silenc'd, when - / "Commend me to your master" – and the cap / Plays in the right hand thus; - but tell him / My uses cry me.

Mark Twain: A lawyer one day spoke to him (Mark Twain) with his hands in his pockets. "Is it not a curious sight to see a lawyer with his hands in his *own* pockets?" remarked the humorist in his quiet drawl.

Mark Twain: The lack of money is the root of all evil.

Mark Twain: Some men worship rank, some worship heroes, some worship power, some worship God, & over these ideals they dispute & cannot unite – but they all worship money.

Mark Twain: No one ever went broke under-estimating the taste of the American public.

Mark Twain: Don't go around saying the world owes you a living, the world owes you nothing. It was here first.

UA: The contingent fee is the poor man's key to the courthouse door.

UA (Inscribed on walls of University of Bologna, Italy, 13th Century): While in bed the sick man's lying, / While in court your client's cause you're trying, / That's the time to get your fee. / For, when the sick man has recovered, / And the lawsuit's won or smothered, / He will never think of thee.

Rudy Westmoreland: Always live better than your clients, so that they won't object to the fees you demand.

FOLLY/FOOL(S) (See also FAILURE; IGNORANCE; NEGLIGENT)

Uncle Anthony: No matter how foolish,, there's always something more foolish that we coulda done.

Uncle Anthony: I think he's a GROSS ignoramus/idiot – he's 144 times worse than an ordinary ignoramus/idiot.

Uncle Anthony: There are well dressed foolish ideas, just as there are well dressed fools.
Uncle Anthony: That pompous ass knows everything – it's a shame he doesn't know anything!
Aunt Mary Carlo: I 'tink he's a life member of NAPWETD = the Nat'l Assoc of People Without Enough To Do!
Aunt Mary Carlo: Y'know 'dat song Sinatra sings – Fools Rush In Where Wisemen Fear to Tread – well – dontcha be in such a rush!
Aunt Mary Carlo: He ain't nobody's fool, nah, he couldn't get nobody to adopt him!
Aeschylus: Verily a prosperous fool is a heavy load.
Aeschylus: It is a profitable thing, if one is wise, to seem foolish.
Sholom Aleichem: You can tell when a fool speaks: he grinds much and produces little.
Sholom Aleichem: The wish to be wiser than everybody else is the biggest foolishness.
Arabian Proverb: A fool may be known by six things: anger, without cause; speech, without profit; change, without progress; inquiry, without object; putting trust in a stranger, and mistaking foes for friends.
Aristotle: There is a foolish corner even in the brain of the sage.
Aristotle: (One who) contributes nothing worth hearing and takes offense at everything.
Bible: Apocrypha, Ecclesiasticus 22:11: Weep for the dead, for he lacks the light; and weep for the fool, for he lacks intelligence; weep less bitterly for the dead, for he has attained rest; but the life of the fool is worse than death.
Bible: 1 Corinthians, 1:27: God hath chosen the foolish things of the world to confound the wise.
Bible: 1 Corinthians 3:18: If any man among you seemeth to be wise in this world, let him become a fool, that he may be wise.
Bible: 2 Corinthians 11:19: For ye suffer fools gladly, seeing ye yourselves are wise.
Bible: Ecclesiastes 10:1: Dead flies cause the ointment of the apothecary to send forth a stinking savour: so doth a little folly him that is in reputation for wisdom and honour.
Bible: Ecclesiastes 10:12: The words of a wise man's mouth are gracious; but the lips of a fool will swallow up himself.
Bible: Ephesians 5:15: Walk circumspectly, not as fools, but as wise.
Bible: Matthew 7:26: Every one that heareth these sayings of mine, and doeth them not, shall be likened unto a foolish man, which built his house upon the sand.
Bible: Proverbs 1:7: Fools despise wisdom and instruction.
Bible: Proverbs 1:22: Scorners delight in their scorning, and fools hate knowledge.
Bible: Proverbs: 12:15: The way of a fool is right in his own eyes: but he that harkeneth unto counsel is wise.
Bible: Proverbs 13:20: He that walketh with wise men shall be wise: but a companion of fools shall be destroyed.
Bible: Proverbs 14:29: He that is slow to wrath is of great understanding: but he that is hasty of spirit exalteth folly.
Bible: Proverbs 15:21: Folly is joy to him that is destitute of wisdom.
Bible: Proverbs, 17:12: Let a man meet a bear robbed of her cubs, rather than a fool in his folly.
Bible: Proverbs 17:28: Even a fool, when he holdeth his peace, is counted wise: and he that shutteth his lips is esteemed a man of understanding.
Bible: Proverbs, 18:7: A fool's mouth is his destruction.
Bible: Proverbs 22:15: Foolishness is bound in the heart of a child; but the rod of correction shall drive it far from him.
Bible: Proverbs, 26:5: Answer a fool according to his folly.
Bible: Proverbs 26:7: Like a lame man's legs that hang limp is a proverb in the mouth of a fool.
Bible: Proverbs, 26:11: As a dog returneth to his vomit, so a fool returneth to his folly.
Bible: Proverbs 29:11: A fool uttereth all his mind: but a wise man keepeth it in till afterwards.
Bible: Psalms 14:1 and 53:1: The fool hath said in his heart, There is no God.
Bible: Psalms 74:22: The foolish man reproacheth Thee daily.
Bible: Romans 1:22: Professing themselves to be wise, they became fools.
Bible: Titus 3:9: Avoid foolish questions.
Ambrose Bierce: APRIL FOOL, n. The March fool with another month added to his folly.
Ambrose Bierce: ASS, n. A public singer with a good voice but no ear....

Ambrose Bierce: CRAFT, n. A fool's substitue for brains.

Ambrose Bierce: FOOL, n. A person who pervades the domain of intellectual speculation and diffuses himself through the channels of moral activity. He is omnific, omniform, omnipercipient, omniscient, omnipotent. He it was who invented letters, printing, the railroad, the steamboat, the telegraph, the telegraph, the platitude and the circle of the sciences. He created patriotism and taught the nations war—founded theology, philosophy, law, medicine and Chicago. He established monarchical and republican government.... And after the rest of us shall have retired for the night of internal oblivion he will sit up to write the history of human civilization.

Ambrose Bierce: FOOLISHNESS, n. A statement or belief manifestly inconsistent with one's own opinion.

Ambrose Bierce: IGNORAMOUS, n. A person unacquainted with certain kinds of knowledge familiar to yourself, and having certain other kinds that you know nothing about.

Ambrose Bierce: INTIMACY, n. A relation into which fools are providentially drawn for their mutual destruction.

Ambrose Bierce: JESTER, n. An officer formerly attached to a king's household, whose business it was to amuse the court by ludicrous action and utterances, the absurdity being attested by his motley costume. The king himself being attired with dignity it took the world some centuries to discover that his own conduct and decrees were sufficiently ridiculous for the amusement not only of his court but of all mankind. The jester was commonly called a fool, but the poets and romancers have ever delighted to represent him as a singularly wise and witty person. In the circus of today the melancholy ghost of the court fool effects the dejection of humbler audiences with the same jests wherewith in life he gloomed the marble hall, panged the patrician sense of humor and tapped the tank of royal tears....

Ambrose Bierce: RASCAL, n. A fool considered under another aspect.

Ambrose Bierce: RASCALITY, n. Stupidity militant. The activity of a clouded intellect.

Ambrose Bierce: RASH, adj. Insensible to the value of our advice....

Ambrose Bierce: VANITY, n. The tribute of a fool to the worth of the nearest ass....

Josh Billings: A learned fool is one who has read everything and simply remembered it.

William Blake (*Proverbs of Hell*, 1790): The hours of folly are measured by the clock, but of wisdom no clock can measure.

Geoffrey Chaucer: A fool cannot be still.

Chinese Proverb: He who asks is a fool for five minutes, but he who does not ask remains a fool forever.

Chinese Proverb: If a fool be associated with a wise man all his life, he will perceive the truth as little as a spoon perceives the taste of truth.

Chinese Proverb: Whom Heaven at his birth has endowed as a fool, 'tis a waste of instruction to teach.

Charles Churchill: Fool beckons fool, and dunce awakens dunce.

Sir Winston Churchill: The greatest lesson in life is to know that even fools are right sometimes.

Sir Winston Churchill: No folly is more costly than the folly of intolerant idealism.

Sir Winston Churchill: Opening amenities are often opening inanities.

John Ciardi: The Constitution gives every American the inalienable right to make a damn fool of himself.

Cuban Saying: People who are resentful [EDITOR: negative, envious, etc. ... even some pro-insurance tort reformers] are like people who take poison and hope the other guy dies.

Demacatus: (One who) could never hold his peace; for too much talking is ever the indice of a fool.

Albert Einstein (August 1920 apologizing to a friend about his newspaper article in rebuttal to the Anti-relativity group rally and meeting in Berlin Philharmonic Hall): Don't be too severe with me. Everyone must from time to time make a sacrifice on the altar of stupidity to please the diety and mankind, and I did so thoroughly with my article.

George Eliot: One who expects things to happen that never can happen.

English Proverb: Six hours' sleep for a man, seven for a woman and eight for a fool.

James Finlayson (Scot actor, who appeared in 1930's Laurel and Hardy films, said it long before Homer Simpson in the TV series *The Simpsons*): DOH (or D'OH)!

Anatole France: If fifty million people say a foolish thing, it is still a foolish thing.

Benjamin Franklin: As Charms are nonsense, Nonsense is a Charm.

Benjamin Franklin: Most fools think they are only ignorant.

Benjamin Franklin: Wise men learn by others' harms, fools scarcely by their own.

Benjamin Franklin: The wise man draws more advantage from his enemies, than the fool from his friends.
Thomas Fuller: Fools grow without watering.
Thomas Fuller: A fool can dance without a fiddle.
Thomas Fuller: To make a trade of laughing at a fool is the highway to become one.
Jerry Garcia: It's pretty clear now that what looked like it might have been some kind of counterculture is, in reality, just the plain old chaos of undifferentiated weirdness.
German Proverb: Nothing looks so like a man of sense as a fool who holds his tongue.
German Proverb: Luck sometimes visits a fool, but never sits down with him.
Johann Wolfgang von Goethe: There is nothing worse than aggressive stupidity.
Goethe: The fools and the wise are equally harmless; it is a half wise and a half foolish who are the most to be feared.
Goethe: Of the whole rabble of thieves, the fools are the worst: for they rob you of both time and peace of mind.
John Hay: The use of proverbs is characteristic of an unlettered people. They are invaluable treasures to dunces with good memories.
John Haywood (1546): There is no fool to the old fool.
George Herbert: "(A fool is one)... that thinks not that another thinks."
Edgar Watson Howe: Don't be mean to the fool; put a penny in his cup, as you do for the blind beggar.
Elbert Hubbard: Every man is a damn fool for at least five minutes every day; wisdom consists in not exceeding the limit.
Irish Proverb: There is no fool who has not his own kind of sense.
Jewish Proverb: Someone who is clever—to himself
Jewish Saying: A person who grows without the help of rain.
Ben Jonson: No precepts will profit a fool.
Ben Jonson: To be a fool born is a disease incurable.
Walter Kerr: Half the world is composed of idiots, the other half of people clever enough to take indecent advantage of them
Elizabeth "Libby" Kinghorne: Some people always have their heads up their butts, but he is so single minded and biased that his head is always up his butt and always facing the same direction!
Francois de La Rochefoucauld: He who lives without folly isn't so wise as he thinks.
Frank Leahy: Egotism is the anesthetic that chills the pain of stupidity.
John Lilly (1592): There is no fool like an old fool.
John Locke: Folly consists in drawing of false conclusions from just principles, by which it is distinguished from madness, which draws just conclusions from false principles.
James Russell Lowell: There's nothing we read of in torture's inventions / Like a well-meaning dunce with the best of intentions.
Herman Melville: There's no folly of the beasts of the earth which is not infinitely outdone by the madness of men.
Wilson Mizner: A fellow who is always declaring he's no fool usually has his suspicions.
Molière: They learned fool is more foolish than an ignorant fool.
Lady Mary Wortley Montagu: I believe more follies are committed out of compliance to the world, than in following our own inclinations.
Montesquieu: To succeed in this world, one must have the appearance of a fool and be wise.
William Penn: To be a man's own fool is bad enough; but the vain man is everybody's.
Alexander Pope (*An Essay on Criticism*): Fools rush in where angels fear to tread.
John W. Raper: A woman never forgives anybody who tries to keep her from making a fool of herself over a man.
Agnes Repplier: People who cannot recognize a palpable absurdity are very much in the way of civilization.
Mary Roberts Rinehart: The great God endows His children variously. To some He gives intellect – and they move the earth. To some He allots heart – and the beating pulse of humanity is theirs. But to some He gives only a soul, without intelligence – and these, who never grow up, but remain always His children, are God's fools, kindly, elemental, simple, as if from His palette the Artist of all has taken one colour instead of many.

Will Rogers: A fool and his money are soon elected.

Will Rogers: There are three kinds of men. The one that learns by reading. The few who learn by observation. The rest of them have to pee on the electric fence for themselves.

Will Rogers: When ignorance gets started it knows no bounds.

Will Rogers: There is nothing so stupid as the educated man if you get him off the thing he was educated in.

Will Rogers: If Stupidity got us into this mess, then why can't it get us out?

Will Rogers: Everybody is ignorant, only on different subjects.

Carl Sagan: Skeptical scrutiny is the means, in both science and religion, by which deep insight can be winnowed from deep nonsense.

George Santayana: The best human intelligence is still decidedly barbarous; it fights in heavy armor and keeps a fool at court.

George Santayana: The more general the folly of mankind, the more likely is the critic himself to share it, especially as folly is a thing that folly is prone to impute.

Seneca: What fools these mortals be!

William Shakespeare (*As You Like It*, Act I, ii): Always the dulness of the fool is the whetstone of the wits.

William Shakespeare (*As You Like It*, Act II, vii): A fool! I met a fool i' the forest, / A motley fool; a miserable world: / As I do live by food, I met a fool; / Who laid him down, and bask'd him in the sun.

William Shakespeare (*As You Like It*, Act II, vii): O noble fool! / A worthy fool! Motley's the only wear.

William Shakespeare (*As You Like It*, Act IV, i): I had rather have a fool to make me merry, / than experience to make me sad; and to travel for it too.

William Shakespeare (*As You Like It*, Act V, i): The fool doth think he is wise, but the wise man knows himself to be a fool.

William Shakespeare (*Comedy of Errors*, Act IV, iv): I am an ass, indeed; you may prove it by my long ears. I have served him from the hour of my nativity to this instant, and have nothing at his hands for my service but blows; when I am cold, he heats me with beating.

William Shakespeare (*Cymbeline*, Act II, iii): Fools are not mad folks.

William Shakespeare (*Hamlet*, Act III, i): Let the doors be shut upon him; that he may play the fool nowhere but in's own house.

William Shakespeare (*II Henry IV*, Act II, ii): Well, thus we play the fools with the time; and the spirits of the wise sit in the clouds, and mock us.

William Shakespeare (*II Henry IV*, Act V, v): How ill white hairs become a fool and jester.

William Shakespeare (*Henry V*, Act III, vii): A fool's bolt is soon shot.

William Shakespeare (*King John*, Act IV, ii): To gild refined gold, to paint the lilly, / To throw a perfume on the violet, / To smooth the ice, or add another hue / Unto the rainbow, or with taper-light / To seek the beauteous eye of heaven to garnish, / Is wasteful, and ridiculous excess.

William Shakespeare (*Merchant of Venice*, Act III, v): The fool hath planted in his memory / An army of good words; and I do know / A many fools, that stand in better place, / Garnish'd like him, that for a trickey word / Defy the matter.

William Shakespeare (*A Midsummer-Night's Dream*, Act III, ii): What fools these mortals be!

William Shakespeare (*Othello*, Act V, ii): O murderous coxcomb! What should such a fool / Do with so good a wife?

William Shakespeare (*Pericles*, Act II, iv): To wisdom he's a fool that will not yield.

William Shakespeare (*Twelfth Night*, Act V, i): This fellow's wise enough to play the fool; / And to do that well craves a kind of wit.

William Shakespeare (*Twelfth Night*, Act V, i): Marry, sir; they praise me, and make me an Ass of me; now my foes tell me plainly I am an ass; so that, by my foes, Sir, I profit in the knowledge of myself.

William Shakespeare (*Two Gentlemen of Verona*, Act V, iv): I hold him but a fool, that will endanger / His body for a girl that loves him not.

George Bernard Shaw: Do you think that the things people make fools of themselves about are any less real than the things they behave sensibly about? They are more true: they are the only things that are true.

Frank Sinatra (one of my favorite ballads): Fools rush in where wise men fear to tread.

Spanish Proverb: (A fool) Every man in some man's opinion.

Spanish Proverb: What the fool does in the end, the wise man does in the beginning.
Spanish Proverb: It is better to be born a beggar than a fool.
Alfred Lord Tennyson: Ah! there's no fool like the old one.
Mark Twain: The country is a fool, I think.
Mark Twain: Hain't we got all the fools in town on our side? And ain't that a big enough majority in any town?
Mark Twain: Let us be thankful for the fools. But for them the rest of us could not succeed.
Mark Twain: *April 1.* This is the day upon which we are reminded of what we are on the other three hundred and sixty four.
Mark Twain: I am a great & sublime fool. But then I am God's fool, & all His works must be contemplated with respect.
Mark Twain: In the first-place God made idiots. This was for practice. Then he made proofreaders.
Mark Twain: In the first-place God made idiots. This was for practice. Then He made School Boards.
UA: When the body or tongue out races the brain.
UA: A combination of laziness and they dislike or enforced knowledge.
Voltaire: O Heaven! He who thinks himself wise is a great fool.
Bill Watterson: Sometimes I think the surest sign that intelligent life exists elsewhere in the universe is that none of it has tried to contact us.
Welsh Proverb: A spoon does not know the taste of soup, nor a learned fool the taste of wisdom.

FORSEEABLE/FORSEEABILITY

Uncle Anthony: I only wish my foresight was as good as my hindsight.
Aunt Mary Carlo: Y'know dat old expression – "What ya don't know won't hoit (hurt) ya"? Well, if dats true den he's practically indestructable.
Aesop: Affairs are easier of entrance than on exit; and it is but common prudence to see our way out before we venture in.
Aristotle: One swallow does not make a summer; neither does one fine day.
Francis Bacon: Prudence is of no service unless it be prompt.
Francis Bacon: He that cannot see well, let him go softly.
Bible: Apocrypha, Ecclesiasticus 7:36: Whatsoever thou takest in hand, remember the end, and thou shalt never do amiss.
Bible: Ecclesiastes 11:4: He that observeth the wind shall not sow; and he that regardeth the clouds shall not reap.
Bible: Luke 12:39; Matthew 24:43: If the good man of the house had known what hour the thief would come, he would have watched.
Bible: Mark 13:35: Watch ye therefore: for ye know not when the master of the house cometh.
Bible: Proverbs, 14:15: The prudent man looketh well to his going.
Bible: Proverbs 22:3: A prudent man forseeth the evil, and hideth himself: but the simple pass on, and are punished.
Bible: Proverbs 27:1: Boast not thyself of tomorrow; for thou knowest not what a day may bring forth.
Ambrose Bierce: DESTINY, n. A tyrant's authority for crime and a fool's excuse for failure.
Ambrose Bierce: FUTURE, n. That period of time in which our affairs prosper, our friends are true and our happiness is assured.
Ambrose Bierce: PREDESTINATION, n. The doctrine that all things occur according to programme....
Ernest Bramah: Where the road bends abruptly take short steps.
Ernest Bramah: Do not adjust your sandals while passing through a melon field; nor yet arrange your hat beneath an orange tree.
George William Bramwell (English judge, 1808-1892): We call it extraordinary, but in truth it is not an extraordinary storm which happens once in a century, or in fifty or twenty years; on the contrary it would be extraordinary if it did not happen. There is a French saying "that there is nothing so certain as that which is unexpected." In like manner, there is nothing so certain as that something extraordinary will happen now and then. *Ruck v. Williams,* 3 H. & N. 308 (Ex. 1858).

Edmund Burke: Early and provident fear is the mother of safety.
Samuel Butler: Look before you ere you leap, / For as you sow, ye are like to reap.
Sir Thomas Buxton: In life, as in chess, forethought wins.
Caesar Augustus: Make haste slowly.
Carlyle: Shakespeare says, we are creatures that look before and after, the more surprising that we do not look round a little and see what is passing under our very eyes.
Lewis Carrol (*Alice's Adventures in Wonderland*, 1865): "I've got a right to think," said Alice ... "Just about as much right," said Duchess, "as pigs have to fly."
Richard Cecil: To have too much forethought is the part of a wretch; to have too little is the part of fool.
Cervantes: Let every man look before he leaps.
Cervantes: Let us not throw the rope after the bucket.
Cervantes: It is the part of a wise man to keep himself today for tomorrow, and not to venture all his eggs in one basket.
Cervantes: They had best not stir the rice, though it sticks to the pot.
Geoffrey Chaucer: Advisement is good before the need.
Lord Chesterfield: Achilles, though invulnerable, never went to battle but completely armed.
Chinese Proverb: Forethought is easy, repentance hard.
Chinese Proverb: He who could foresee affairs three days in advance would be rich for thousands of years.
Chinese Proverb: If you are planning for a year, sow rice; if you are planning for a decade, plant trees; if you are planning for a lifetime, educate people.
Chinese Proverb: One generation plants the trees; another gets the shade.
Brock Chisholm: You can only cure retail but you can prevent wholesale.
Sir Winston Churchill (summer 1938, letter to his wife Clementine about FDR's willingness to help Britain with new U.S. Neutrality Laws and "Cash & Carry" and "Lend Lease"): Apparently you always have to have a disaster before anything sensible can be done which would prevent it.
Sir Winston Churchill: Politics is the ability to foretell what is going to happen tomorrow, next week, next month and next year. And to have the ability afterwards to explain why it didn't happen.
Winston Churchill: It is a mistake to try to look too far ahead. The chain of destiny can only be grasped one link at a time.
Cicero: By prudence,... we understand the practical knowledge of things to be sought, and of things to be avoided.
Cicero: I prefer silent prudence to loquacious folly.
Sir Edward Coke: Precaution is better than cure.
William Coleridge: As a man without forethought scarcely deserves the name of a man, so forethought without reflection is but a phrase for the instinct of the beast.
Charles Caleb Colton: Accustom yourself to submit on every occasion to a small present evil, to obtain a greater distant good. This will give decision, tone, and energy to the mind, which, thus disciplined, will often reap victory from defeat, and honor from repulse.
Charles Caleb Colton: Human foresight often leaves its proudest possessor only a choice of evils.
Confucius: If a man take no thought about what is distant, he will find sorrow near at hand.
Oliver Cromwell: Put your trust in God, my boys, and keep your powder dry.
Dante: The arrow seen before cometh less rudely.
Sir John Denham: When any great design thou dost intend, / Think on the means, the manner, and the end.
Franklin Edgerton: Forethought and Ready-wit both prosper in peace; Come-what-will perishes.
Albert Einstein: I never think of the future – it comes soon enough.
Queen Elizabeth I: I hope you will remember that he who seeketh two strings to one bow, he may shoot strong but never straight.
Epictetus: In every affair consider what precedes and follows, and then undertake it.
Euripides: Chance fights ever on the side of the prudent.
Euripides: The man who knows when not to act / Is wise. To my mind, bravery is forethought.
Benjamin Franklin (1736): Don't throw stones at your neighbors, if your own windows are glass.
Benjamin Franklin: He that scatters thorns, let him not go barefoot.

Benjamin Franklin: Speak with contempt of none, from slave to king; / The meanest bee hath, and will use, a sting.

Benjamin Franklin: Great Estates may venture more, / But little Boats must keep near Shore.

Thomas Fuller: A stitch in time may save nine.

Thomas Fuller: A danger foreseen is half avoided.

Edward Gibbon 1737-1794, British Historian: The laws of probability, so true in general, so fallacious in particular.

Goethe: He who does not stretch himself according to the coverlet finds his feet uncovered.

Justice Ellen Goodman (Maryland Supreme Court, 1985): The manufacturer or marketer of a Saturday Night Special knows or ought to know that he is making or selling a product principally to be used in criminal activity.

Greek Proverb: If you go into a labyrinth, take a clew with you (referring to the "clew" or ball of thread used by the Greek hero Theseus to find his way out of the labyrinth of King Minos of Crete).

Greek Proverb: In baiting a mousetrap with cheese, always leave room for the mouse.

Arthur Guiterman: The Boldest Farmer heeds the Cautious Rule / To stand Behind the Bull, Before the Mule.

George Herbert: Everyone stretcheth his legs according to his coverlet.

George Herbert (1640): Whose house is of glass must not throw stones at another.

George Herbert: He that goes barefoot must not plant thorns.

John Heywood: Look ere you leap.

John Heywood: Good riding at two anchors, men have told, / For if one fail, the other may hold.

Irish Proverb: If you do not sow in the spring you will not reap in the autumn.

Japanese Proverb: Darkness reigns at the foot of the lighthouse.

Thomas Jefferson: Take things always by their smooth handle.

Ben Jonson: Thou shouldst have looked before thou hadst leapt.

John F. Kennedy: The time to repair the roof is when the sun is shining.

John Lyly: Have more strings to thy bow than one; it is safe riding at two anchors.

Philip Massinger (English poet, 1640): Happy those who knowing they are subject to uncertain changes, are prepared and armed for either fortune; a rare principle, and with much labor learned in wisdom's school.

Thomas Middleton: Better to go on foot than ride and fall.

Midrash: Midrash Proverbs: If you don't plow in summer, what will you eat in winter?

Molière: Prudence is always in season.

Michael A. Musmanno (Justice of Pennsylvania Supreme Court, 1959): Forseeability: The fall of a telephone pole is not an act of God: It cannot be asserted that it was the hand of God which pushed over pole No. 16 to break Bowman's back. Snow fell, as it falls every winter in the temperate zone, and provident people anticipate this type of atmospheric precipitation by taking necessary precautions against its inflicting excessive damage. Sometimes all the ingenuity and industry of man cannot avail against the turmoil and turbulence of the elements, but it is not enough in order to escape responsibility, for the owner of an instrumentality which inflicts damage, to assert that the instrumentality was propelled by the Supreme Being and that, therefore, he can shake the clinging snow of responsibility off his hands. The defendant in the present case knew that pole No. 16 carried 28 wires and that these wires formed a grill which would receive and hold on to snow, especially if it was wet. It thus became a question of fact for the jury to determine whether the company could anticipate what should be the strength of the pole to sustain the total weight of the snow. To this requirement of knowledge there would be attached to question of suitable inspection.... In any event no person called into court to answer for a tort may find exoneration from the act of negligence charged to him by asserting that it was not he but the Supreme Being which inflicted the wound and the hurts of which the plaintiff complains. The loose use of the name of the Deity in the realm of the law should not be a matter of our approval.

William Painter: He that looketh not before he leapeth / May chance to stumble before he sleepeth.

Pennsylvania Dutch Proverb: You can't catch chickens from fried eggs.

Publilius Syrus: That should be considered long which can be decided but once.

Publilius Syrus: The wise man avoids evil by anticipating it.

Sir Walter Raleigh: Prevention is the daughter of intelligence.
Rainer Maria Rilke: Nothing in the world can one imagine beforehand, not the least thing. Everything is made up of so many unique particulars that cannot be foreseen.
Anthony Robbins: "The Niagara Falls Syndrome" – The Niagara Falls Syndrome means that most people make decisions without evaluating the consequences in advance.
Will Rogers: The fellow who can only see a week ahead is always the popular fellow, for he is looking with the crowd. But the one that can see years ahead, he has a telescope but he can't make anybody believe he has it.
Will Rogers: Plans get you into things but you got to work your way out.
Seneca: It is only the surprise and newness of the thing which makes terrible that misfortune, which by premeditation might be made easy to us; for what some people make light by sufferance, others do by foresight.
Johann Schiller (German poet, 1805): Whoever fails to turn aside the ills of life by prudent forethought, must submit to the course of destiny.
William Shakespeare (*Hamlet*, Act IV, iv): Looking before and after.
William Shakespeare (*Hamlet*, Act IV, v): We know what we are, but know not what we may be.
William Shakespeare (*Hamlet*, Act V, ii): There's a divinity that shapes our ends, / Rough-hew them how we will.
William Shakespeare (*III Henry VI*, Act V, iii): Every cloud engenders not a storm.
William Shakespeare (*Julius Caesar*, Act V, i): O that a man might know / The end of this day's business ere it come!
William Shakespeare (*Macbeth*, Act V, v): To-morrow and to-morrow, and to-morrow, / Creeps in this petty pace from day to day, / To the last syllable of recorded time; / And all our yesterdays have lighted fools / The way to dusty death.
William Shakespeare (*Troilus and Cressida*, Act III, ii): To fear the worst oft cures the worse.
William Shakespeare (*Twelfth Night, Act II*, v): Ay, and you had any eye behind you, you might see more detraction at your heels than fortunes before you.
George Bernard Shaw: People who live in glass houses have no right to throw stones.
Lee Simonson: Any event, once it has occurred, can be made to appear inevitable by a competent historian.
Logan Pearsall Smith: Only those who get into scrapes with their eyes open can find the safe way out.
Thomas Sowell: Much of the history of the Western world over the past three decades has involved replacing what worked with what sounded good.
Spanish Proverb: A forewarned man is worth two.
Spanish Proverb: More grows in the garden than the gardener knows he has sown.
Spanish Proverb: Tomorrow is often the busiest day of the week.
C. H. Spurgeon: Beware of a mule's hind foot, a dog's tooth, and a woman's tongue.
Talmud: Woe to him who makes a door before he has a house, or builds a gate and has no yard.
Terrance: I think you'd better to have two strings to my boat.
Thucydides: A few things are brought to a successful issue by impetuous desire, but most by calm and prudent forethought.
Thomas Tusser: Look ere you leap, see ere you go, / It may be for thy profit so.
Mark Twain: The serene confidence which a Christian feels in four aces.
William Tyndale: Look ere thou leap, whose literal sense is, / Do nothing suddenly or without advisement.
UA: The man who lives without a plan will die without a shroud.
UA: Fortune is more powerful than foresight.
UA: Better measure ten times before you cut, or you may have to cut ten times before you measure.
Virgil: I have anticipated all things, and traversed them in thought.

FRAUD (See also FACT; LIES/LIARS)

Uncle Anthony: Advertising is a fraud; it's a kind of voodoo science that freezes people's brains long enough to get money from them.
Uncle Anthony: I think if he ever had his conscience taken out – it'd be a very minor surgery.

Uncle Anthony: He's such a phoney his false teeth got cavities.
Uncle Anthony: I think he majored in alibi-ology.
Uncle Anthony: Some people call it embezzelment; Enron called it "profit sharing."
Aunt Mary Carlo: He never goes back on his word ... without talkin' to his lawyer first.
Aunt Mary Carlo: He really t'inks his baloney is whachacallit – "food fer thought."
Aunt Mary Carlo: He's so cheap he could skin a flint!
Aunt Mary Carlo: He's the original "Flim Flam Man."
Aunt Mary Carlo: Dats a real "Heads I win, tails you lose" proposition he made.
St. Augustine: I have met with many that would deceive; who would be deceived, no one.
Francis Bacon: Like strawberry wives, they laid two or three great strawberries at the mouth of their pot, and all the rest were little ones.
Gamaliel Bailey: The first and worst of all frauds is to cheat oneself. All sin is easy after that.
P.T. Barnum: There is a sucker born every minute.
Bible: Apocrypha, 1 Esdras 4:22: Great is truth and strongest of all
Bible: James 1:8: A double minded man is unstable in all his ways.
Bible: John 8:32: The truth shall make you free.
Bible: Proverbs 11:1: A false balance is abomination to the Lord: but a just weight is his delight.
Bible: Proverbs 26:18: As a mad man who casteth firebrands, arrows, and death, So is the man that deceiveth his neighbor, and saith, Am I not in sport?
Bible: Psalms 101:7: He that worketh deceit shall not dwell within my house: he that telleth lies shall not tarry in my sight.
Ambrose Bierce: Don't steal; thou't never thus compete / Successfully in business. Cheat.
Ambrose Bierce: HAND, n. A singular instrument worn at the end of a human arm and commonly thrust into somebody's pocket.
Ambrose Bierce: DEFAME, v. To lie about another. To tell the truth about another.
Ambrose Bierce: FIB, n. A lie that has not cut its teeth. An habitual liar's nearest approach to truth: the perigee of his eccentric orbit.
Ambrose Bierce: LIAR, n. A lawyer with a roving commission.
Hugo Black (1937): Laws are made to protect the trusting as well as the suspicious.
Harold Burns (New York City Building Commissioner, on the confusion of housing and building law, 1963): One might risk establishing the following mathematical formula for bribery, namely OG = PLR x AEB: The opportunity for graft equals the plethora of legal requirements multiplied by the number of architects, engineers and builders.
Benjamin Cardozo: Fraud includes the pretense of knowledge when knowledge there is none. Ultramares Corp. v. Touche, 255 N.Y. 170 (1931)
Geoffrey Chaucer: (A fraud) is The smiler with the knife under the cloak.
Sir Winston Churchill: A lie gets halfway around the world before the truth has a chance to get its pants on.
Sir Winston Churchill: I had no idea of the enormous and unquestionably helpful part that humbug plays in the social life of great peoples dwelling in a state of democratic freedom.
Sir Winston Churchill: Craft is common both to skill and deceit.
Sir Edward Coke: He is not cheated who knows he is being cheated.
Charles Caleb Colton: He that has no real esteem for any of the virtues, can best assume the appearance of them all.
Danish Proverb: He is most cheated who cheats himself.
John Dryden: Idiots only may be cozened twice.
Dutch Proverb: One sprinkles the most sugar where the tart is burnt.
Ralph Waldo Emerson: The abomination of desolution is not a burned town, nor a country wasted by war, but the discovery that the man who has moved you is an enthusiast upon calculation.
English Saying: Fraud and cunning are the weapons of the weak.
Benjamin Franklin: He will cheat without scruple, who can without fear.
Benjamin Franklin: There is no kind of dishonesty into which otherwise good people more easily and frequently fall than that of defrauding the government.
French Proverb: To a cheat, a cheat and a half.

Thomas Fuller: Fraud is always in a terrible hurry.

Baltasar Gracian: To be duped is not always the result of stupidity, but sometimes of virtue.

Justice Heath (English judge 1803): Fraud may consist as well in the suppression of what is true as in the representation of what is false.

Latin legal phrase: He is not deemed to give consent who was under a mistake.

Latin legal phrase: No one can bring an action upon his own fraud.

Nathaniel Lindley (English judge, 1828-1921): No court has ever attempted to define fraud. Allcard v. Skinner, 36 Ch. 145 (1887)

Niccolo Machiavelli: Though fraud in all other actions be odious, yet in matters of war it is laudable and glorious, and he who overcomes his eneemies by strategem is as much to be praised as he who overcomes them by force.

Lord Edward MacNaughten (English judge, 1830-1913): Fraud is infinite in variety; sometimes it is audacious and unblushing; sometimes it pays a sort of homage to virtue, and then it is modest and retiring; it would be honesty itself if it could only afford it. Reddaway v. Banham, A.C. 199 (1896)

Don Juan Manuel: He who praises you for what you lack wishes to take from you what you have.

James Clark McReynolds (Assoc Justice US Supreme Court, 1862-1946): The statute enjoins truth; this label exhales deceit. US v Schider, 246 US 519, 62 L ed 863, 38 S Ct 369 (1918)

Laurence J. Peter: Originality is the fine art of remembering what you hear but forgetting where you heard it.

Plautus: Frauds are not frauds, unless you make a practice of deceit.

Will Rogers: The income tax has made liars out of more Americans than golf.

Russian Proverb: The wolf will hire himself out very cheaply as a shepherd.

William Shakespeare (*II Henry IV*, Act I, ii): There's neither honesty, manhood, nor good fellowship in thee.

William Shakespeare (*II Henry VI*, Act III, ii): Beguiles him, as the mournful crocodile / With sorrow snares relenting passengers; / Or as the snake, roll'd in a flowering bank, / With shining checker'd slough, doth sting a child, / That, for the beauty, thinks it excellent.

William Shakespeare (*III Henry VI*, Act V, iv): A quicksand of deceit.

William Shakespeare (*Henry VIII*, Act IV, ii): His promises were, as he then was, mighty; / But his performance, as he is now, nothing.

William Shakespeare (*Macbeth*, Act I, iii): The instruments of darkness tell us truths; / Win us with honest trifles, to betray us / In deepest consequence.

William Shakespeare (*Merchant of Venice*, Act I, iii): The devil can cite Scripture for his purpose.

William Shakespeare (*Merchant of Venice*, Act I, iii): An evil soul, producing holy witness, / Is like a villain with a smiling cheek; / A goodly apple rotten at the heart: / O, what a goodly outside falsehood hath!

William Shakespeare (*Merchant of Venice*, Act II, vii): All that glitters is not gold.

William Shakespeare (*Merchant of Venice*, Act III, ii): The world is still deciev'd with ornament. / In law, what plea so tainted and corrupt, / But, being season'd with a gracious voice, / Obscures the show of evil? In religion, / What damned error, but some sober brow / Will bless it, and approve it with a text, / Hiding the grossness with fair ornament?

William Shakespeare (*Richard III*, Act II, ii): Ah, that deceit should steal such gentle shapes, / And with a virtuous visor hide deep vice.

William Shakespeare (*Romeo and Juliet*, Act III, ii): O, that deceit should dwell / In such a gorgeous palace!

William Shakespeare (*Timon of Athens*, Act IV, iii): Thus much of this, will make / Black, white; foul, fair; wrong, right; / Base, noble; old, young; coward, valiant. / Ha, you gods! Why this?

William Shakespeare (*Two Gentlemen of Verona*, Act II, vii): His heart as far from fraud as heaven from earth.

William Shakespeare (*Winter's Tale*, Act IV, iii): My revenue is the silly cheat.

Mark Twain: Talking of patriotism what humbug it is; it is a word which always commemorates a robbery. There isn't a foot of land in the world which doesn't represent the ousting and re-ousting of a long line of successive "owners," who each in turn, as "patriots," with proud swelling hearts defended it against the next gang of "robbers" who came to steal it and *did*—and became swelling-hearted patriots in *their* turn.

UA (about lack of originality/plagerism): I may milk a lot of cows, but I churn my own butter.

FRIEND/FRIENDSHIP

Uncle Anthony: "A FOREVER FRIEND" Y'know, sometimes in life, if yer lucky, ya find a special friend. Somebody who changes your life just by bein' a part of it. Somebody who makes ya laugh 'til you can't stop and yer sides hurt. Somebody who makes ya believe that there really is good in dis world. Somebody who convinces ya that there really is an unlocked door – an opportunity – just waiting for ya to open it. This is a **forever friendship**. When yer down and the world seems cold and dark and empty, yer forever friend lifts yer spirits up and makes that cold, dark and empty world suddenly seem all warm and bright and full. Your forever friend gets ya through the hard times, the sad times, the bad times, and the confused times. If ya turn and walk away, yer forever friend will always follow ya. If ya lose your way, yer forever friend will help guide ya and cheer ya on. Yer forever friend holds yer hand and tells ya that everything is gonna be okay. And if yer lucky enough and ya find such a friend, you feel happy and 100% complete because ya don't need t'worry. Ya got a forever friend, and forever means deres no end to it.

Uncle Anthony: A best friend is like a brother (or sister) that God forgot to give ya.

Uncle Anthony: Family and friends are the most important part of your life. You gotta treasure all the tears, and all the laughs, but most importantly, treasure the memories.

Uncle Anthony (from an old Italian family saying): Yer friends are like branches of a tree - we all get older and grow in different directions, but our roots remain as one big tree. Each of our lives will always be a special part of the other's.

Uncle Anthony: The best thing in life is when yer family becomes yer friends, and yer friends become yer family.

Uncle Anthony: He don't want a friend (or yer friendship) – all he wants is somebody to listen to him!

Aunt Mary Carlo: Y'know love is just a friendship dat's been set on fire.

Aunt Mary Carlo: Friends are like quiet angels 'dat sit on our shoulders and lift our wings when we forget howda fly.

Aunt Mary Carlo: True friendship is felt, not said. Dere's nuttin' needs to be said wit a true friendship.

Aunt Mary Carlo: I believe in angels, da kind Heaven sends. I'm surrounded by angels, but I call dem my best friends.

Aunt Mary Carlo: Yer friends are like da stars... ya don't always see 'em, but y'know dere always dere.

Ali ibn-Abi-Talib (602 AD - 661 AD, *A Hundred Sayings*): He who has a thousand friends has not a friend to spare, And he who has one enemy will meet him everywhere.

Aristotle: What is a friend? A single soul dwelling in two bodies.

Aristotle (384 BC - 322 BC, *Eudemian Ethics*): Misfortune shows those who are not really friends.

Aristotle (*Nichomachean Ethics*): Without friends no one would choose to live, though he had all other goods.

W. H. Auden: Between friends differences in taste or opinion are irritating in direct proportion to their triviality.

Saint Augustine (354-430, Numidian-born Bishop of Hippo, Theologian): I want my friend to miss me as long as I miss him.

Saint Augustine: If two friends ask you to judge a dispute, don't accept, because you will lose one friend; on the other hand, if two strangers come with the same request, accept because you will gain one friend.

Jane Austen (1775-1817): Friendship is certainly the finest balm for the pangs of disappointed love.

Francis Bacon (British philosopher, essayist, statesman, 1561-1626): The worst solitude is to have no real friendships.

Ethel Barrymore (American actress, 1879-1959): The best time to make friends is before you need them.

Sarah Bennett: A friend is a person who know what you are saying, even if you're not talking.

Ludwig Van Beethoven: Never forget the days I spent with you. Continue to be my friend, as you will always find me yours.

Bible: Apocrypha: A faithful friend is the medicine of life.

Bible: Apocrypha, Ecclesiasticus 9:10: A new friend is like new wine; when it has aged you will drink it with pleasure.

Bible: Apocrypha, Ecclesiasticus 9:10: Forsake not an old friend, for a new one does not compare with him.

Bible: John 15:13: Greater love hath no man than this, that a man lay down his life for his friends.

Bible: Proverbs 19:4: Wealth maketh many friends.

Bible: Proverbs 27:6: Faithful are the wounds of a friend; but the kisses of an enemy are deceitful.

Bible: Proverbs: 27:17: Iron sharpeneth iron; so a man sharpeneth the countenance of his friend.

Bible: Psalms 16:11: You have made known to me the path of life; you will fill me with joy in your presence.

Ambrose Bierce (*The Devil's Dictionary*): FRIENDSHIP, *n.* A ship big enough to carry two in fair weather, but only one in foul. The sea was calm and the sky was blue; / Merrily, merrily sailed we two. / (High barometer maketh glad.) / On the tipsy ship, with a dreadful shout, / The tempest descended and we fell out. / (O the walking is nasty bad!)

Ambrose Bierce *(The Devil's Dictionary*): ACQUAINTANCE, n. A person whom we know well enough to borrow from, but not well enough to lend to. A degree of friendship called slight when its object is poor or obscure, and intimate when he is rich and famous.

Ambrose Bierce: DISTRESS, n. A disease incurred by exposure to the prosperity of a friend.

Lawana Blackwell, (*The Courtship of the Vicar's Daughter, 1998*): It isn't kind to cultivate a friendship just so one will have an audience.

Arthur Brisbane (*The Book of Today*): A good friend can tell you what is the matter with you in a minute. He may not seem such a good friend after telling.

Buddha (568-488 BC, Founder of Buddhism): A good friend who points out mistakes and imperfections and rebukes evil is to be respected as if he reveals a secret of hidden treasure.

Buddha: The rule of friendship means there should be mutual sympathy between them, each supplying what the other lacks and trying to benefit the other, always using friendly and sincere words.

Lois McMaster Bujold (*Ethan of Athos, 1986*): A good friend of my son's is a son to me.

Lois McMaster Bujold (*A Civil Campaign, 1999*): Adversity does teach who your real friends are.

Lois McMaster Bujold (*Diplomatic Immunity, 2002*): If you make it plain you like people, it's hard for them to resist liking you back.

Lord Byron (1788-1824, British Poet): I have always laid it down as a maxim—and found it justified by experience – that a man and a woman make far better friendships than can exist between two of the same sex—but then with the condition that they never have made or are to make love to each other.

Melina Campos: Memories last forever, never do they die. Friends stay together, never say goodbye.

Albert Camus: Don't walk in front of me, I may not follow. / Don't walk behind me, I may not lead. / Just walk beside me and be my friend.

Truman Capote (American writer): Friendship is a pretty full-time occupation if you really are friendly with somebody. You can't have too many friends because then you're just not really friends.

Dale Carnegie: You can make more friends in two months by becoming interested in other people than you can in two years by trying to get other people interested in you.

Miguel De Cervantes (1547-1616, Spanish Novelist, Dramatist, Poet): A man must eat a peck of salt with his friend, before he knows him.

Coco Chanel (1883-1971, French Couturier): My friends, there are no friends.

Pierre Charron: The advice of friends must be received with a judicious reserve; we must not give ourselves up to it and follow it blindly, whether right or wrong.

Agatha Christie (1891-1976, British Mystery Writer): Every murderer is probably somebody's old friend.

Jennie Jerome Churchill (1854-1921, Anglo-American Mother of Sir Winston Churchill): Treat your friends as you do your pictures, and place them in their best light.

Sir Winston Churchill: Meeting Franklin Roosevelt was like opening your first bottle of champagne; knowing him was like drinking it.

Sir Winston Churchill: No lover ever studied every whim of his mistress as I did those of President Roosevelt [FDR].

Cicero (106 BC - 43 BC, *On Friendship, 44 B.C.*): Friendship make prosperity more shining and lessens adversity by dividing and sharing it.

Cicero (*De Amicitia*): The shifts of Fortune test the reliability of friends.

Cicero: Friendship improves happiness and abates misery, by the doubling of our joy and the dividing of our grief.

Samuel Taylor Coleridge(1772-1834, British Poet, Critic, Philosopher): Friendship is a sheltering tree.

Samuel Taylor Coleridge: And though thou notest from thy safe recess old friends burn dim, like lamps in noisome air love them for what they are; nor love them less, because to thee they are not what they were.

Colette (1873-1954, *The Pure and the Impure, 1932*): It is wise to apply the oil of refined politeness to the mechanisms of friendship.

John Churton Collins: In prosperity our friends know us; in adversity we know our friends.

Charles Caleb Colton: True friendship is like sound health; the value of it is seldom known until it be lost.

Confucius (551 BC - 479 BC, *The Confucian Analects*): Have no friends not equal to yourself.

Fr. Jerome Cummings: A friend is one who knows us, but loves us anyway.

Czech Proverb: Do not protect yourself by a fence, but rather by your friends.

Czech Proverb: Many a friend was lost through a joke, but none was ever gained so.

Bridget Davis: I hope we'll be friends forever, together we'll always be. I don't think you understand just how much you mean to me. And one day when we part our ways, we'll think back to the past and think about how happy we are 'cause our friendship will always last.

Marlene Dietrich (actress, 1901-1992): It's the friends you can call up at four a.m. that matter.

Bryon Douglas (*That Was Then, This Is Now* by S.E. Hinton): If you have two friends in your lifetime, you're lucky. If you have one *good* friend, you're more than lucky.

Charles W. Eliot: Books are the quietest and most constant of friends... and the most patient of teachers.

Ralph Waldo Emerson (1803-1882): The ornament of a house is the friends who frequent it.

Ralph Waldo Emerson: The only way to have a friend is to be one.

Ralph Waldo Emerson: Friendship should be surrounded with ceremonies and respects, and not crushed into corners.

Dame Edna Everage: My mother used to say that there are no strangers, only friends you haven't met yet. She's now in a maximum security twilight home in Australia.

Irwin Federman: People love others not for who they are, but for how they make us feel.

Kellina Filbin: The friendship isn't worth the tears unless the friend is.

Amanda Ford: It can be hard to break the friendship code of secrecy and make your friend mad at you, but you must do what you feel in your heart is right.

Arlene Francis: Trouble is a sieve through which we sift our acquaintances. Those too big to pass through are our friends.

Benjamin Franklin: Tart words make no friends; a spoonful of honey will catch more flies than a gallon of vinegar.

Benjamin Franklin: Thou canst not joke an enemy into a friend, but thou may'st a friend into an enemy.

French Proverb: Hatred watches while friendship sleeps.

Thomas Fuller (1608-1661): Purchase not friends by gifts; when thou ceasest to give, such will cease to love.

Sharita Gadison: Some friends come and go like a season. Others are arranged in our lives for good reason.

Baltasar Gracian: A wise man gets more use from his enemies than a fool from his friends.

Oliver Wendell Holmes, Sr. (1809-1894, *The Autocrat of the Breakfast-Table, 1858*): Don't flatter yourself that friendship authorizes you to say disagreeable things to your intimates. The nearer you come into relation with a person, the more necessary do tact and courtesy become. Except in cases of necessity, which are rare, leave your friend to learn unpleasant things from his enemies; they are ready enough to tell them.

Elbert Hubbard (1856-1915): Never explain—your friends do not need it and your enemies will not believe you anyway.

Elbert Hubbard: Your friend is the man who knows all about you, and still likes you.

Victor Hugo: Friend is sometimes a word devoid of meaning; enemy, never.

Irish Proverb: Both your friend and your enemy think you will never die.

Italian Proverb: Have you fifty friends? – it is not enough. Have you one enemy? – it is too much.

Italian Proverb: Words in haste do friendships waste.

Japanese Proverb: When the character of a man is not clear to you, look at his friends.

Saint Jerome (374 AD-419 AD, *Letter*): The friendship that can cease has never been real.

Cindy Jew: Remember, the greatest gift is not found in a store nor under a tree, but in the hearts of true friends.

Jewish Saying: Who finds a faithful friend, finds a treasure.

Samuel Johnson (1709-1784): If a man does not make new acquaintances as he advances through life, he will soon find himself alone. A man should keep his friendships in constant repair.

Franklin P. Jones (*Saturday Evening Post, November 29, 1953*): Nothing changes your opinion of a friend so surely as success - yours or his.

Thomas Jones (1892-1969): Friends may come and go, but enemies accumulate.

Carl Jung (1875-1961): The meeting of two personalities is like the contact of two chemical substances: if there is any reaction, both are transformed.

Amanda Kunkle: True friends are hard to find, difficult to leave, and impossible to forget.

Charles Lamb: Thou through such a mist dost show us, / That our best friends do not know us.

Jay Leno (comedian, 1950 -): Go through your phone book, call people and ask them to drive you to the airport. The ones who will drive you are your true friends. The rest aren't bad people; they're just acquaintances.

Joe E. Lewis (comedian): A friend in need is a pest!

Abraham Lincoln: The best way to destroy an enemy is to make him a friend.

Abraham Lincoln: I never encourage deceit; and falsehood, especially if you have got a bad memory, is the worst enemy a fellow can have. The fact is, truth is your truest friend, no matter what the circumstances are.

Listerine mouthwash ad (1920'2): Even your closest (best) friends won't tell you.

Matt Markham: Thick and thin, tall and small, fast and slow. / Tell me who is always there for you. I am sure you know. / Your best friend, of course, don't let him or her go."

Tim McGraw: We all take different paths in life, but no matter where we go, we take a little of each other everyhwere.

Bernard Meltzer: A true friend is someone who thinks that you are a good egg even though he knows that you are slightly cracked.

Randy K. Milholland (*Something Positive Comic, 08-16-05*): It's a lot like nature. You only have as many animals as the ecosystem can support and you only have as many friends as you can tolerate the bitching of.

Randy K. Milholland (*Something Positive Comic, 11-07-05*): Sometimes the measure of friendship isn't your ability to not harm but your capacity to forgive the things done to you and ask forgiveness for your own mistakes.

Randy K. Milholland (*Something Positive Comic, 09-07-06*): The only thing that lasts longer than a friend's love is the stupidity that keeps us from knowing any better.

Lucy Maud Montgomery: True friends are always together in spirit.

Nigerian Proverb: Hold a true friend with both your hands.

Katie Obenchain: Don't pity the girl with one true friend. Envy her. Pity the girl with just a thousand acquaintances.

Kellie O'Connor: Friends are always friends no matter how far you have to travel back in time. If you have memories together, there is always a piece of your friendship inside your heart.

Georgia O'Keeffe (artist, 1887-1986): Nobody sees a flower - really - it is so small it takes time - we haven't time - and to see takes time, like to have a friend takes time.

Molly Oliver: A friend shares the good times and helps out by listening during the bad times.

Willie Pep (former featherweight boxing champion): First your legs go. Then you lose your reflexes. Then you lose your friends.

Lawrence J. Peter: You can always tell a real friend; when you've made a fool of yourself he doesn't feel you've done a permanent job.

Plato (427 BC - 347 BC, *Dialogues, Phaedrus*): Friends have all things in common.

Maude V. Preston: There isn't much that I can do, but I can share an hour with you, and I can share a joke with you....as on our way we go.

Sandy Ratliff: A true friend is someone you can disagree with and still remain friends. For if not, they weren't true friends in the first place.

Will Rogers (American entertainer, famous for his pithy and homespun humour, 1879-1935): A stranger is just a friend I haven't met yet.

Russian Proverb: An enemy will agree, but a friend will argue.

Saadi (1184-1291): Reveal not every secret you have to a friend, for how can you tell but that friend may hereafter become an enemy. And bring not all mischief you are able to upon an enemy, for he may one day become your friend.

Sallust (86 BC-34 BC, *The War with Catiline*): To like and dislike the same things, that is indeed true friendship.

William Shakespeare (1564-1616): We are advertis'd by our loving friends.

William Shakespeare (*The Taming of the Shrew*, Act I, ii): And do as adversaries do in the law—Strive mightily, but eat and drink as friends.

Socrates (469 BC - 399 BC): Get not your friends by bare compliments, but by giving them sensible tokens of your love.

Publilius Syrus (~100 BC), *Maxims*): Prosperity makes friends, adversity tries them.

Publilius Syrus (~100 BC), *Maxims*): Treat your friend as if he might become an enemy.

Mr. Spock (TV show and movie, *Star Trek*, Starship Enterprise's Executive Officer, to Captain Kirk): Jim, you have been and shall always be my friend ... live long and prosper.

Dr. Wilhelm Stekhel: The child is surrounded by so much authority, so much school, so much dinity, so much law, that it would have to break down under the weight of all these restraints if it were not saved from such a fate by meeting with a friend.

Jeremy Taylor: Never be a judge between thy friends in any matter where both set their hearts upon the victory. If strangers or enemies be litigants, whatever side thou favorest, thou gettest a friend; but when friends are the parties thou losest one.

Madame de Tencin: Never refuse any advance of friendship, for if nine out of ten bring you nothing, one alone may repay you.

Alfred Lord Tennyson (English poet, 1809-1892): He makes no friend who never made a foe.

Texas: 28th state; "Texas" comes from the Caddo Indian word, *Tejas*, meaning friends or allies; Friendship is state motto.

William Thackery: I vow and believe that the cigar has been one of the greatest creature comforts of my life—a kind companion, a gentle stimulant, an amiable anodyne, a cementer of friendship.

Thucydides (471 BC - 400 BC, *Peloponnesian War*): We secure our friends not by accepting favors but by doing them.

Harry S. Truman: If you want a friend in Washington, get a dog.

Mark Twain: It takes your enemy and your friend, working together, to hurt you to the heart; the one to slander you and the other to get the news to you.

Mark Twain: Grief can take care of itself, but to get the full value of joy you must have somebody to divide it with.

Mark Twain: The best way to cheer yourself up is to try to cheer somebody else up.

Mark Twain: Good friends, good books and a sleepy conscience: this is the ideal life.

UA: Some people come into our lives and quickly go. Some stay for awhile and leave footprints on our hearts. And we are never, ever the same.

UA: If I could reach up and hold a star for every time you made me smile, the entire evening sky would be in the palm of my hand.

UA: The best preacher is the human heart; the best teacher is time; the best book is the world; the best friend is God.

UA: Friends are the pillars on your porch. Sometimes they hold you up, sometimes they lean on you, and sometimes it's just enough to know that they are standing by.

George Washington: Be courteous to all, but intimate with few, and let those few be well tried before you give them your confidence. True friendship is a plant of slow growth, and must undergo and withstand the shocks of adversity before it is entitled to the appellation.

Rebecca West (1892-1983): There was a definite process by which one made people into friends, and it involved talking to them and listening to them for hours at a time.

Walt Whitman (1819-1892): I no doubt deserved my enemies, but I don't believe I deserved my friends.

Elie Wiesel: Friendship marks a life even more deeply than love. Love risks degenerating into obsession, friendship is never anything but sharing.

Oscar Wilde: I always like to know everything about my new friends, and nothing about my old ones.

Oscar Wilde: I choose my friends for their good looks, my acquaintances for their good characters, and my enemies for their intellects. A man cannot be too careful in the choice of his enemies.

Oscar Wilde: Anybody can sympathize with the sufferings of a friend, but it requires a very fine nature to sympathize with a friend's success.

Oscar Wilde: He has no enemies, but is intensely disliked by his friends.

Oprah Winfrey: Lots of people want to ride with you in the limo, but what you want is someone who will take the bus with you when the limo breaks down.

Gretchen Witter (Sasha Alexander, *Dawson's Creek*): ...And you help each other realize that all the things you want to be...you already are.

Nick Zeigler: While everybody else shakes my hand, you hold it.

FRUGALITY (See CHEAP)

GAMES (See also GOLF)

Uncle Anthony: There ain't nothing like the smell of a baseball glove or a real grass ball field.

Uncle Anthony: Ya gotta see how this guy plays to be depreciated.

Uncle Anthony: Sports is beautiful – it's cut, dry and honest. You always know when you win. You're not some kinda actor or speech maker – you don't gotta worry about whether your "performance" was good or not. You win or you lose.

Aunt Mary Carlo: Y'know, life's too short for soma dez games!

Aunt Mary Carlo: My son, Sonny, he played Macbeth – Macbeth lost!

Franklin Pierce Adams: Ruthlessly pricking our gonfalon bubble, / Making a Giant hit into a double—/ Words that are heavy with nothing but trouble: / "Tinkers to Evers to Chance."

Marty Adler (Brooklyn Dodgers fan on the team's move from Brooklyn to Los Angeles, 1957): When I was 4, I learned that Santa Claus didn't exist. When I was 9, I found out my father didn't know everything. When the Dodgers left I was 20, and things have never been the same.

Red Auerbach (legendary Boston Celtic coach and general manager): Basketball is like war in that offensive weapons are developed first, and it always takes a while for the defense to catch up.

Russell Baker: In America, it is sport that is the opiate of the masses.

Jacques Barzun (historian): Whoever would understand the heart and mind of America had better learn baseball.

Buzzy Bavasi (baseball executive, then with the Brooklyn Dodgers): He (Red Barber) reminds me of the Arabian horse – every race horse in the world is descended from the Arabian. Every announcer learns something from Red.

Mark Beltaire: Almost the only place in life for sacrifice is really appreciated.

Bible: 1 Corinthians 9:24: Run, that ye may obtain.

Bible: 1 Corinthians 9:24: They which run in a race run all, but one receiveth the prize.

Bible: Ecclesiastes 9:11: The race is not to the swift, not the battle to the strong, neither yet bread to the wise, nor riches to men of understanding, nor yet favour to men of skill; but time and chance happeneth to them all.

Bible: Hebrews 12:1: Let us run with patience the race that is set before us.

Bible: St. Paul's Letter to the Corinthians: **"Run to win."** [EDITOR: And: don't you know that while all the runners in the stadium take part in the race, only one wins the prize. **Run to win!**]

Bible: 2 Timothy 4:7: I have fought a good fight, I have finished my course, I have kept the faith.

Ambrose Bierce: ENTERTAINMENT, n. Any kind of amusement whose inroads stop short of death by objection.

Ambrose Bierce: OLYMPIAN, adj. Relating to a mountain in Thessaly, once inhabited by gods, now a repository of yellowing newspapers, beer bottles and mutilated sardine cans, attesting the presence of the tourist and his appetite.

Ambrose Bierce: POKER, n. A game said to be played with cards for some purpose to this lexicographer unknown.

Ambrose Bierce: RECREATION, n. A particular kind of dejection to relieve a general fatigue.

Earl Blank (Army football coach 1941-1858): You don't develop good teeth by eating mush.

Humphrey Bogart: A hot dog at the (baseball) game beats roast beef (or steak) at the Ritz.

Jimmy Braddock, aka "The Cinderella Man," Jersey James, The Bear of North Bergen, The Bergen Battler: Keep your left hand high and your keester off the canvas.

Bill Bradley (former NBA All-Star player with the Champion New York Knickerbockers and US Senator): There has never been a great athelete who died not knowing what pain is.

Bill Bradley: The taste of defeat has a richness of experience all its own.

Terry Bradshaw (NFL Hall of Fame QB for 4-Time Super Bowl Champion Pittsburgh Steelers – 1975, 1976, 1979, 1980): This isn't nuclear physics, it's a game. How smart do you really have to be?

Ralph Branca (RHP for the Brooklyn Dodgers, coming in to relieve starting pitcher Don Newcombe, in the bottom of 9th inning of Game #3 of the 1951 best of 3 game NL Playoffs; with Brooklyn ahead 4-2, and one out, and two NY Giants on base and Bobby Thomson coming up to bat, said to Newcombe): "Don't worry about it big fella, I'LL TAKE CARE OF EVERYTHING." (See Russ Hodges below)

Lou Brock (Baseball Hall of Fame outfielder with Chicago Cubs and St. Louis Cardinals): Show me a guy who's afraid to look bad, and I'll show you a guy you can beat.

Heywood Hale Broun (writer/sportscaster): Sports do not build character. They reveal it.

Drew "Bundini" Brown (cornerman and assistant trainer to Muhammad Ali): Float like a butterfly, sting like a bee.

Bear Bryant (legendary University of Alabama football coach): Most coaches study the films when they lose. I study them when we win – to see if I can figure out what I did right.

Sir Richard Burton: And who, 'mid e'en the Fools, but feels that half the joy is in the race.

Walter Camp (legendary Yale football coach): There is no substitute for hard work and effort beyond the call of mere duty. That is what strengthens the soul and ennobles one's character.

Roy Campanella (Brooklyn Dodgers 1957): You gotta be a man to play baseball for living but you gotta have a lot of little boy in you, too.

Bruce Catton: The greatest conversation piece ever invented is America.

Sir Winston Churchill: Play the game for more than you can afford to lose... only then will you learn the game.

Howard Cosell (quoting a popular saying about the Washington Senators): Washington, first in war, first in peace, last in the American League.

Howard Cosell: I have found most baseball players to be afflicted with tobacco-chewing minds.

Baron Pierre De Coubertin (modern Olympic Games founder, who in 1894 organized an International Congress which agreed to hold games every four years-called the "Olympiad," and in 1896 held the first Modern Olympic games since 393 A.D. in Athens in 1896, and whose words have become the Olympic Creed): The important thing in the Olympic Games is not to win but to take part; the important thing in life is not the triumph (or conquering) but the struggle (or fighting well). [EDITOR: The Olympic Motto is *"Citius, altius, fortius" or "SWIFTER, HIGHER, STRONGER"*]

Jack Dempsey (Heavyweight Champion): I was a pretty good fighter, but it was the writers who made me great.

Joe DiMaggio: A ballplayer's got to keep hungry to become a big leaguer. That's why no boy from a rich family ever made the big leagues.

Angelo Dundee (legendary Boxing Hall of Fame trainer of 15 world champions including Muhammad Ali and Sugar Ray Leonard): Notice who is in the locker room after you lose, not after you win.

Finley Peter Dunne: In me younger days 'twas not considered rayspictable f'r to be an athlete. An athlete was always a man that was not strong enough f'r wurruk. Fractions dhruve him fr'm school an' th' vagrancy laws dhruv him to baseball.

Leo Durocher (title of his book, 1975): *"Nice Guys Finish Last."*

Leo Durocher: Give me some scratching, diving, hungry ballplayers who come to kill you.

Leo Durocher: Ballplayers are superstitious breed, nobody more than eye, and while you are winning you'd murder anybody tried to change or sweatshirt, let alone your uniform.

Leo Durocher: Managing a ballclub is the most vulnerable job in the world.... If you don't win, you're going to be fired. If you do win, you've only put off the day you're going to be fired. And no matter what you do, you're going to be second-guessed. The manager is the only person in the ballpark who has to call it right now. Everybody else can call it after it's over.

H.J. Dutiel: A game which consists of tapping all with a piece of wood, then running like a lunatic.

General Dwight Eisenhower: I had occassion because of my position (Supreme Allied Commander, Europe during WWII): To be on the lookout for natural leaders. I noted with satisfaction how well exfootball players seemed to fulfill leadership qualifications; among others: Bradley, Keys, Patton, Simpson, VanFleet, Harmon, Hobbes, Juet, Patch, and Pritchart, and many others measured up. I cannot recall a single exfootballer with whom I came in contact who failed to meet every requirement. Personally, I think this was more than coincidental. I believe that football, almost more than any other sport, tends to install into men the feeling that victory comes through hard, almost slavish work, team play, self-confidence, and an enthusiasm that amounts to dedication.

Gerald Ford (former US President): If it's a cliche to say athletics build character as well as mucle, then I subscribe to the cliche.

George Foreman (two-time heavyweight boxing champ): Boxing is sort of like jazz. The better it is, the less amount of people can appreciate it.

George Foster: I don't know why people like the home run so much. A home run is over as soon as it starts.... The triple is the most exciting play of the game. The triple is like meeting a woman who excites you, spending the evening talking and getting more excited, then taking her home. It drags on and on. You're never sure how it's going to turn out.

Larry Fox (NY Sports writer, commenting on William D. Eckert, USAF General retired, when he was named by the baseball owners as MLB Commissioner, serving from 1965-1968): Geez, they went and got the Unknown Soldier!

Benjamin Franklin: Games lubricate the body and the mind.

French Proverb: It is a poor sport that is not worth the candle.

Joe Garagiola (former baseball player and Hall of Fame broadcaster): Baseball gives you every chance to be great. Then it puts every pressure on you to prove that you haven't got what it takes. It never takes away the chance, and it never eases up on the pressure.

Joe Garagiola: It's pitching, hitting a defense that wins. Any two can win. All three make you unbeatable.

Joe Garagiola: Baseball is a drama with an endless run and an ever-changing cast.

Frank Gifford (New York Giants halfback and sports announcer): Pro football is like nuclear warfare. There are no winners, only survivors.

George Gissing: Everyone knows that horse-racing is carried on mainly for the delight and profit of fools, ruffians, and thieves.

Larry Goetz (umpire, 1955): In a way an umpire is like a woman. He makes quick decisions, never reverses them, and doesn't think you're safe when you're out.

Baltasar Gracian: In a game where the players are equally matched it is a great advantage to have the first move.

Billy Graham (Christian evangelist): More than being concerned with who's going to win the Super Bowl, I feel the Lord is probably more concerned that they might find a day other than Sunday to play it on.

Frank Graham (news columnist, June 13, 1935): The incredible has happened, and James J. Braddock [EDITOR: aka "The Cinderella Man" or "Jersey Jim"] is the Heavy weight Champion of the World. Nothing like this has ever happened before in the long history of the prize ring. It just goes to show you how far a stout heart will take a fellow provided he has a good left hand to go with it."

Wayne Gretzky (NHL Hall of Fame hockey player): You miss 100% of the shots you never take.

Dr. Daniel Hanley (US Olympic team physician): By itself, practice does not make perfect. Those of us with a ten-year-old son practicing the trumpet may understand that.

Russ Hodges (Wednesday, Oct 3, 1951 at 3:58 PM – 34,320 fans at The Polo Grounds for Game #3 of the National League Playoffs between NY Giants and Brooklyn Dodgers; Russ Hodges on WMCA Radio announces "The Shot Heard Round the World" in bottom of 9th inning, two Giants on base, Brooklyn ahead 4-2 with one out, as 3B Bobby Thomson swings on a 0-1 fastball thrown by Ralph Branca, the Brooklyn relief pitcher who relieved starting pitcher Don Newcombe): "Branca throws. There's a long drive to left field ... it's gonna be ... I believe ... THE GIANTS WIN THE PENNANT! THE GIANTS WIN THE PENNANT! THE GIANTS WIN THE PENNANT! THE GIANTS WIN THE PENNANT! Bobby Thomson hit it into the lower deck of the left field stands. THE GIANTS WIN THE PENNANT! And they're going crazy! They're going crazy! OOHOOOH!" (See Ralph Branca above)

Lou Holtz (legendary college football coach): Coaching is nothing more than eliminating mistakes before you get fired.

Lou Holtz: The man who complains about the way the ball bounces is likely the one who dropped it.

Lou Holtz: If you don't make a total commitment to whatever you're doing, then you start looking to bail out the first time the boat starts leaking. It's tough enough getting that boat to shore with everybody rowing, let alone when a guy stands up and starts putting his life jacket on.

President Herbert Hoover: The rigid volunteer rules of right and wrong in sports are second only to religious faith in moral training.

Bob Hope: ON GOLF: Golf is my profession. Show business is just to pay the green fees.

Bob Hope: ON GIVING UP HIS BOXING CAREER: I ruined my hands in the ring ... the referee kept stepping on them.

Elbert Hubbard: The new definition of a heathen is a man who has never played baseball.

Catfish Hunter (after pitching a rare World Series loss): The sun don't shine on the same dog's ass every day!

Rogers Hornsby (National League batting champion, St. Louis Cardinals): Any ballplayer that don't sign autographs for little kids ain't an American. He's a Communist.

Don Hutson (NFL Hall of Fame wide reciever for the Green Bay Packers): For every pass I caught in a game, I caught a thousand in practice.

Keith Jackson (former ABC college football TV announcer): A football was a "prolate spheroid."

Keith Jackson: Sports, more than any other activity, has proven that a truly democratic society owes the individual nothing more than an opportunity.

Reggie Jackson: I don't want to be a hero; I don't want to be a star. It just works out that way.

Reggie Jackson (Hall of Fame baseball player) (spring-training 1977): This team (New York Yankees), it all flows from me. I've got to keep it going. I'm the straw that stirs the drink.

Emory Jones (CHL St. Louis Braves hockey team general manager): Hockey players are like mules. They have no fear of punishment and no hope of reward.

Harry Kalas (Philadelphia Phillies Hall of Fame broadcaster, immediately after Phillies 6-1 win over the Washington Nationals, at Citizens' Bank Ballpark, Phila., PA to come from 7 games behind with 17 games to play on September 12, and beat out the NY Metropolitans or Mets for The Greatest Comeback in Major League Baseball history, clinch the NL East Division Championship on the last day of the season, September 30, 2007, sang the song *"High Hopes"*): Once there was a little ole ant, thought he'd move a rubber tree plant; everyone knows an ant can't move a rubber tree plant, BUT HE HAD HIGH HOPES, HE HAD HIGH HOPES, HE HAD HIGH APPLE PIE IN THE

SKY HOPES! So anytime you're feelin' low, 'stead of lettin' go, just remember that ant ... whoops there goes another rubber tree plant!

William Henry "Wee Willie" Keeler (1872 -1923, born in Brooklyn, NY; right fielder who played professionally from 1892 to 1910, primarily for the Baltimore Orioles and Brooklyn Superbas – later called Dodgers - in the National League, and the New York Highlanders – later named Yankees - in the American League. A remarkable hitter, who helped perfect the "Baltimore Hop;" compiled a .341 batting average over his career, currently 14th all time; hit over .300 16 times in 19 seasons, and hit over .400 once; one of the smaller players to play the game, standing approximately 5'7" (some sources say he was only 5'4") and weighing 140 pounds, hence his nickname; elected to the Baseball Hall of Fame in 1939, among the shortest players ever elected to the Hall of Fame): Keep your eye clear, and HIT'EM WHERE THEY AIN'T! (EDITOR: "they" being the opposing fielders)

Jack Kemp (AFL-NFL quaterback 1957-1969, 1996 Republican Vice Presidential nominee): Pro football gave me a good sense of perspective to enter politics. I'd been booed, sheered, cut, sold, traded and hung in effigy.

John F. Kennedy: We are inclined to think that we if we watch a football game or a baseball game, we have taken part in it.

Rudyard Kipling: Then ye contented your souls / With the flannelled fools at the wicket or the muddied oafs at the goals.

Rudyard Kipling: In all time of our distress, / And in our triumph too / The game is more than the player of the game, / And the ship is more than the crew!

Sandy Koufax: The older I get, the better I used to be.

Kenesaw Mountain Landis (statement issued August, 1921, after a Cook County jury found eight members of the Chicago White Sox not guilty of fixing the 1919 World Series): Regardless of the verdict of juries, no player that throws a ball game, no player that entertains proposals or promises to throw a game, no player that sits in a conference with a bunch of crooked players and gamblers where the ways and means of throwing games are discussed, and does not promptly tell his club about it, will ever again play professional baseball.

Tom Landry (legendary Dallas Cowboys football coach): A team that has character doesn't need stimulation.

Tommy Lasorda (former Los Angeles Dodgers baseball manager): Managing is like holding a dove in your hand. Squeeze too hard and you kill it; not hard enough and it flies away.

Latin Proverb: Without danger the game grows cold.

Abe Lemons (longtime college basketball coach at Oklahoma City University and University of Texas): One day of practice is like one day of clean living. Doesn't do you any good.

Fred Lieb: Records are made to be broken.

Abraham Lincoln (Abe's mother was a good wrestler; the family would set up sucker bets by Saying: "I bet you can't even take one of our women." Abe's father, Tom Lincoln, would set up wrestling matches for Abe, but would get irritated when Abe shook hands before and after a fight, to which Abe said): Do I not destroy my enemies when I make them my friends?

Bill Linderman: Rodeoing is about the only sport you can't fix. You'd have to talk to the bulls and horses, and they wouldn't understand you.

Vince Lombardi (legendary Green Bay Packers coach): If they can't put up with my pressure, how are they going to stand the pressure from 60,000 people?

Vince Lombardi: Football is blocking and tackling. Everything else is mythology.

Vince Lombardi: Coaches who can outline plays on a blackboard are a dime a dozen. The ones who win get inside their players and motivate.

Vince Lombardi: This is a game (football) for madmen.

Knrad Lorenz (Austrian ethologist): Few lapses of self-control are punished as immediately and severely as loss of temper during a boxing bout.

Robert Lynd: Almost any game with any ball is a good game.

Robert Lynd: It may be that games are silly. But, then, so are human beings.

"Easy" Ed Macauley (Hall of Fame basketball player): When you are not practicing, remember, someone somewhere is practicing, and when you meet him he will win.

Billy Martin (New York Yankee player and manager): I'm not the greatest Yankee, but I am the proudest.

Pepper Martin (St. Louis Cardinal "Gas House Gang" baseball player): You can take an ol' mule and feed him and train him and get him in the best shape of his life, but you ain't going to win the Kentucky Derby.

Christy Mathewson (Hall of Fame New York Giants baseball pitcher): You can learn little from victory. You can learn everything from defeat.

Joe McCarthy (Hall of Fame baseball manager of New York Yankees): Give a boy a bat and a ball and a place to play and you'll have a good citizen.

Montaigne: The game is not worth the candle.

Joe Montana (aka "Joe Cool," NFL Hall of Fame Quarterback, NFL 1979-1994, 4-Time Super Bowl Champion, NCAA National Champion with Notre Dame): Sure I got nervous and lost confidence, but I was also good at hiding my emotions.

Sir Sterling Moss (legendary British Grand Prix winner): To achieve anything in this game (racing), you must be prepared to dabble on the boundary of disaster.

Jim Murray (*The Babe Ruth Story*): What makes a star?.... A star is not something that flashes through the sky. That's a comet. Or a meteor. A star is something you can steer ships by. It stays in place and gives off a steady glow; it is fixed, permanent. A star works at being a star. And that's how you tell a star in baseball (EDITOR: & LAW or any profession)

Marina Navratilova (women's tennis player): The moment of victory is much too short to live for that and nothing else.

Henry Newbolt: To love the game beyond the prize.

Mike Newlin (former NBA basketball player): The problem with many athletes is they take themselves seriously and their sport lightly.

Chuck Noll (NFL Hall of Fame coach of the Pittsburgh Steelers): The most interesting thing about this sport, at least to me, is the activity of preparation – any aspect of preparing for the games. The thrill isn't in the winning, it's in the doing.

Jack Norworth (*"Take Me Out to the Ball Game,"* 1908; words by Jack Norworth; music by Albert Von Tiltzer): Take me out to the ballgame, / Take me out with the crowd. / Buy me some peanuts and cracker-jack—/ I don't care if I never get back.

George Orwell: Serious sport has nothing to do with fair play. It is bound up with hatred, jealousy, boastfulness, disregard of all rules and sadistic pleasure in witnessing violence: in other words it is war minus the shooting.

Danny Ozark (Philadelphia Phillies manager): Half this game is ninety percent mental.

Satchel Paige (Hall of Fame baseball pitcher): Don't look back. Somethin' might be gainin' on you.

Willie Pep (former featherweight boxing champion): First your legs go. Then you lose your reflexes. Then you lose your friends.

Bum Phillips (former NFL head coach): The only discipline that lasts is self-discipline.

Bum Phillips (former NFL head coach): My idea of discipline is not makin' guys do something, it's getting 'em to do it. There's a difference in bitchin' and coachin'.

Dr. Robert Ray (orthopedic surgeon): If God had intended man to engage in strenuous sports, He would have given us better knees.

Mike Reid (former NFL Pro Bowl defensive end): The most intangible aspect of winning and losing is the human heart.

Grantland Rice: For when the One Great Scorer comes to write against your name, / He marks—not that you won or lost in goes to you—but how you played the game.

Grantland Rice (Oct 18, 1924): "Outlined against the blue, gray October sky the Four Horsemen rode again." (Notre Dame QB Harry Stuhldreber, FB Elmer Layden, RHB Don Miller, LHB Jim Crowley)

Branch Wesley Rickey (lawyer, and legendary baseball executive): Problems are the price you pay for progress.

Branch Wesley Rickey: Luck is the residue of design.

Branch Wesley Rickey: "Addition by subtraction" (EDITOR: June 28, 1907 – Branch W. Rickey – 3rd string catcher for NY Highlanders – later named Yankees - allowed the Washington Nationals – later named Senators - to STEAL 13 BASES = a Major League RECORD FOR 1 GAME)

David Riesman (sociologist): The road to the boardroom leads through the locker room.

Will Rogers: Baseball is a skilled game. It's America's game—it, and high taxes.

Will Rogers: The income tax has made liars out of more Americans than golf.

Will Rogers: I guess there is nothing that will get your mind off everything like golf. I have never been depressed enough to take up the game, but they say you get so sore at yourself you forget to hate your enemies.

Will Rogers: Legalize racing in every State. Sure people will bet, but they get to see the horses run and you certainly can't see General Motors and General Electric and General Utility run when you bet on them.

Franklin D. Roosevelt: Sport is the very fiber of all we stand for. It keeps our spirits alive.

Theodore Roosevelt (1905 speaking about how he liked football played): Don't flinch, don't foul, and hit the line hard!

Lee Rose (University of North Carolina at Charlotte basketball coach): I would like to deny the statement that I think basketball is a matter of life and death. I feel it's much more important than that.

Rosey Rosewell (Pittsburgh Pirates' sportscaster whenever a Pirate hit a home run in the old Forbes Field): Open the window, Aunt Minnie—here it comes!

Darrell Royal (longtime University of Texas football coach): A coach isn't as smart as they say when he wins, or as stupid when he loses.

Darrell Royal: Breaks balance out. The sun don't shine on the same ol' dog's rear end every day.

Rudy Ruettiger (mptivational speaker, Notre Dame football player, ND Class of 1973; his true story is in the movie *Rudy*): The only thing you can control is the effort, and you owe it to yourself to persevere and do whatever you decide to do with passion. Don't ask for permission to be successful. Go make it happen.

Eddie Sachs (race car driver): Your car moves faster than you can think.

Antoine de Saint-Exupery: But games always cover something deep and intense, else there would be no excitement in them, no pleasure, no power to stir us.

William Shakespeare (*Coriolanus*, Act I, i): What work's, my countrymen, in hand? where go you / With bats and clubs?

William Shakespeare (*Cymbeline*, Act III, iii): The game is up.

William Shakespeare (*I Henry IV*, Act I, iii): Before the game is afoot, thou still let'st slip.

William Shakespeare (*Henry V*, Act III, i): The game's afoot...

William Shakespeare (*Henry VIII*, Act I, iii): The faith they have in tennis, and tall stockings.

William Shakespeare (*King Lear*, Act I, iv): You base foot-ball player.

William Shakespeare (*Love's Labour's Lost*, Act IV, ii): The gentles are at their game...

Bill Shankly (Scottish soccer manager): Some people think football (soccer) is a matter of life and death – I can assure them it is much more important than that.

George Bernard Shaw: He hates chess. He says it is a foolish expedient for making idle people believe they are doing something very clever, when they are only wasting their time.

Red Smith (legendary sports writer): Fighters fight.

Red Smith: The baseball mind is a jewel in the strict sense—that is to say, a stone of special value, rare beauty, and extreme hardness. Cut, polished and fixed in the Tiffany setting of a club owner's skull, it resists change as a diamond resists erosion.

Stan Smith (Hall of fame tennis player): Experience tells you what to do; confidence allows you to do it.

Herbert Spencer: To play billiards well is a sign of a missspent youth.

Amos Alonzo Stagg (legendary University of Chicago football coach): No coach ever won a game by what he knows, it's what his players have learned.

Saul Steinberg: Baseball is an allegorical play about America, a poetic, complex, and subtle play of courage, fear, good luck, mistakes, patience about fate, and sober self-esteem.... It is impossible to understand America without a thorough knowledge of baseball.

Casey Stengel (Hall of Fame baseball manager): You done splendid.

Casey Stengel (commenting on Pittsburgh Pirates' Bill Virdon's key eighth-inning hit in the seventh game of the 1960 World Series): Maybe God can do something about such a play; man cannot.

Casey Stengel (speaking to his barber after his team, the Brooklyn Dodgers in 1935 lost a doubleheader): Don't cut my throat. I may want to do that later myself.

Casey Stengel (announcing his retirement as manager of the New York Yankees in 1960): I'll never make the mistake of being seventy again.

Casey Stengel (about New York Yankee pitcher Bob Turley): He don't smoke, drink, chase women ... and he don't win!

Casey Stengel: Every day in baseball you see something you never saw before. (EDITOR: Casey's 1962 NY Metropolitans – Mets – lost more games – 120, en route to 40-120 record, and became THE WORST TEAM in modern MLB History)

Casey Stengel: I had many years that I was not so successful as a ballplayer, as it is a game of skill.

Casey Stengel: Now, there's three things you can do in a baseball game. You can win, or you can lose, or it can rain.

John L. Sullivan (in 1905, speaking about football, after 1904, THE most violent/dirty season in college football history 21 fatalities and 200+ serious injuries "reported"; and the 1905 season - 18 deaths + 149 reported serious injuries): Football? There's murder in that game. Sparing, it doesn't compare in roughness and danger with football. In sparing, you know what you are doing. You know what your opponent is trying to do, and he's right there in front of you, and there's only one. But in football, say, there's twenty-one people trying to do you!

Jonathan Swift: Most sorts of diversion in men, children, and other animals, are an imitation of fighting.

Fran Tarkenton (former NFL quaterback): I've been playing this game for eighteen years, and I haven't yet figured a way to get into the end zone when you're on your rear end.

Ernest Lawrence Thayer (poem "Casey at the Bat," *San Francisco Examiner*, June 1888): There was ease in Casey's manner as he stepped into its place; / There was pride in Casey's bearing, and a smile on Casey's face. / And when, responding to the cheers, he lightly doffed his hat, / No stranger in the crowd could doubt 'twas Casey at the bat. /... Oh, somewhere in this favored land the sun is shining bright; / The band is playing somewhere, and somewhere hearts are light, / And somewhere men are laughing, and somewhere children shout; / But there is no joy in Mudville - mighty Casey has struck out.

Joe Theisman (former NFL football quarterback, TV sports analyst): 'The word "genius" isn't applicable in football. A genius is a guy like Norman Einstein.

Jack Thompson (former NFL quarterback): It's amazing what the human body can do when chased by a bigger human body.

Jim Thorpe (1912 Summer Olympics, Stockholm, Sweden, in the Decathalon he won 4 gold medals – in the 1,500 meters, 100 meter hurdles, shot putt, and high jump, and a bronze medal in javalin; King Gustov of Sweden presented him with a gold medal, wreath, bonze bust of King Gustov, and a jeweled gold-silver chalice shaped like a Viking ship from the Tsar of Russia for the winner of the Decathalon, and the King of Sweden said: "Sir, you are the greatest athlete in the world): "Thanks, king."

Jim Thorpe (enroute to 1912 Summer Olympic in Stockholm, while lounging in a deck chair on "The Finland" asked by a reporter): What are you doing? Jim: I'm practicing the long jump. I just jumped 23 feet 8 inches. I think that will win it.

Jim Thorpe (to football coach Pop Warner): Hell, Pop, what's the use of going through 'em when I can run around 'em?

Jim Thorpe: I played (football at Carlisle) with the heart of an amateur – for the pure hell of it.

Jim Thorpe (Saturday, Nov 9, 1911, in a famous football game where Jim kicked a 48 yard field goal to win 18-15, Carlisle's first ever win over Harvard): Give me the ball and get out of my way – I mean to do some real running.

Jim Thorpe (said to his daughter Grace who asked: "Dad, which sport did you like best?" before he died in 1953): I liked hunting and fishing best (EDITOR: because he could do them alone).

Louis Toaneema (Carlisle Indian School track team mate of Jim Thorpe, 1912 Olympic medal winner, and one of America's greatest long-distance runners, to his doubting track coach Pop Warner): Me run fast good ... all Hopis run good.

Lee Trevino (PGA golfer): You don't know what pressure is until you play for five bucks with only two in your pocket.

John Tunis (writer): Losing is the great American sin.

Mark Twain (about football): This is a sport which makes the body's liver curl with enjoyment.

Mark Twain (about baseball, 1889, at Delmonico's Restaurant, NYC with Teddy Roosevelt, Albert Goodwill Spaulding and the American baseball team that toured Australia in 1888): (Baseball is) the very symbol, the outward and visible expression of the drive and push and rush and struggle of this raging, tearing and booming of the 19th century.

UA (Attributed to young fan confronting "Shoeless Joe" Jackson of the Chicago White Sox, after hearing that Jackson had conspired with gamblers to fix the 1919 World Series): Say it ain't so, Joe!

Bill Veeck: Rooting for the Yankees is like rooting for U.S. steel.

Bill Veeck: An island of surety in a changing world.

Bill Veeck: This is a game to be savored, not gulped. There's time to discuss everything between pitches or between innings.

Bill Veeck: The baseball is not the sport of the wealthy, it is the sport of the wager earner.

Bill Veeck: Baseball's unique possession, the real source of our strength, is the fan's memory of the times his daddy took into the game to see the great players of his youth. Whether he remembers it or not, the excitement of those hours, the step they represented in his own growth and the part those afternoons—even *one* afternoon—played in his relationship with his own father is bound up in his feeling toward the local ball club and toward the game. When he takes his own son to the game, as his father once took him, there is a spanning of the generations that is warm and rich and—if I may use the word—lovely.

George Vecsey (in his book *BASEBALL*): There's as many names for home runs as Eskimos have for snow.

Dick Vitale (Special Commentary in Introduction of *Numbelievable! The Dramatic Stories Behind the Most Memorable Numbers in Sports History*): When an athelete is "in the zone" – totally focused, mentally and physically prepared – he or she can put up special performances.... Being in the zone leads to greatness ... truly remarkable stuff that you never expected to see.... This chapter is about atheletes that are awesome, baby, with a capital A!

Darrell Waltrip (former NASCAR racer, and sports analyst): If the lion didn't bite the tamer every once in a while, it wouldn't be exciting.

George Washington: Gambling is the child of avarice, the brother of iniquity, and the father of mischief.

Glen Scobey "Pop" Warner (1894 Cornell graduate, a lawyer in Buffalo, NY, coached Cornell, then 13 seasons with the Carlisle Indian Industrial School; then coached Pittsburgh, Stanford, and Temple, retired 1938 with 341-118-33 record): Whenever I see one of those All America teams I cannot help but think what an eleven could have been selected from those REAL ALL AMERICANS who blazed such a trail of glory.

George F. Will: Football is a mistake. It combines the two worst elements of American life – violence and committee meetings.

John Wooden (legendary UCLA basketball coach): Be quick, but never hurry.

John Wooden (legendary UCLA basketball coach): Ability may get you to the top, but it takes character to keep you there.

John Wooden (legendary UCLA basketball coach): Be more concerned with your character than with your reputation, because your character is what you really are, while your reputation is merely what others think you are.

Phil Woosnam (North American Soccer League Commissioner): The rules (of soccer) are very simple. Basically it's this: If it moves, kick it; if it doesn't move, kick it until it does.

Yiddish Proverb: The first winner is the last loser.

Steve Zorn (former NFL quaterback on the art of scrambling): You have to know when and how to go down. The key is to have a fervent desire to be in on the next play.

GENERALITY/GENERALIZATION (See REASON/LOGIC)

GENIUS (See EXPERTS)

GIRLS (See CHILDREN)

GOLF

Uncle Anthony: I think he likes being a bad golfer - the worse he plays the better he remembers his few good shots.

Uncle Anthony: Golf is a game that starts with a golf ball and ends up with a high ball.

Uncle Anthony: They did MRI studies of good and bad golfers – they found the bad golfers had more brain waves than the good golfers. It's just like baseball – the bad golfers/hitters think too much!

Aunt Mary Carlo: To me all yer doin' is beatin' 'round the bush.

Al Barkow: A golf spectator is satisfied when he gets to see, at least a few times during the course of his long day, a ball struck with consumate power and amazing control; a ball sent soaring from the standing start, then floating to earth and stopping within a prescribed swatch of lawn. It is an awesome sensation, not unlike watching a rocket launch

Patty Berg: If I were a man I wouldn't have half a dozen Tom Collinses before going out to play golf, then let profanity substitute for proficiency on the golf course.

Ambrose Bierce: PASTIME, n. A device for promoting dejection. Gentie exercise for intellectual debility.

Max Beerbohm: The most... perfect expression of national stupidity.

Yogi Berra: If I ever hit a ball that far, I want somebody else to go run after it.

Haywood Hale Broun: Golf is not, on the whole, a game for realists. By its exactitude of measurement it invites the attention of perfectionists.

Billy Casper: Golfers are the greatest worriers in the world of sports.... In fast-action sports, like football, baseball, basketball, or tennis, there is little time to worry compared to the time a golfer has on his hands between shots.

Sir Winston Churchill: Golf is like chasing a quinine pill around a cow pasture.

Sir Winston Churchill: Golf is a game whose aim is to hit a very small ball into an even smaller hole, with weapons singularly ill-designed for the purpose.

Finley Peter Dunn: In a gin'ral way, all I can say about it is that it's a kind iv game iv ball that ye play with ye'er own worst inimy, which is ye'ersilf.

Abba Eban: Playing the game I have learned the meaning of humility. It has given me an understanding of the futility of human effort.

King Edward VII (1901-1910, of the House of Saxcova-Gerter): aka Prince Albert Edward; "Bertie"; "Edward The Peacemaker," [EDITOR: Edwarde was a bit of golf fanatic: he had golf courses rebuilt whenever he played a bad round. He gave the name to "The Edwardian Age"; he called the US "The Land of Dangerous Republicans and Democrats."

Jean Giraudoux: A golf course is the epitome of all that is purely transitory in the universe, a space not to dwell in, but to get over as quickly as possible.

Walter Hagen (Hall of Fame golfer): Make the hard ones look easy and the easy ones look hard.

Ben Hogan: Did you ever consider hitting it closer to the hole?

John Hogben: It seems that the most reticent of men on other subjects no sooner takes to golf than eloquence descends upon him.

Bob Hope: If you watch a game, it's fun. If you play it, it's recreation. If you work at it, it's golf.

Samuel Johnson: The playthings of childhood.

Bobby Jones (legendary golfer): It is nothing new or original to say that golf is played one stroke at a time. But it took me many years to realize it.

Bobby Jones: Sometimes this game (golf) cannot be endured with a club in one's hand.

John F. Kennedy: It is true that my predecessor (Dwight Eisenhower) did not object as I do to pictures of one's golfing skill in action. But neither, on the other hand, did he ever bean a Secret Service agent.

Stephen Leacock: Golf may be played on Sunday, not being a game within the view of the law, but being a form of moral effort.

Harper Lee (why she does most of her creative thinking while golfing): In Monroeville (Alabama), well, they're Southern people, and if they know you're working at home they think nothing of walking right in for coffee. But they woudn't dream of interrupting you on the golf course.

Eric Linklater: All I've got against it (golfing) is that it takes you so far from the clubhouse.

A.A. Milne: Golf is so popular simply because it is the best game in the world at which to be bad.

Byron Nelson: Putting affects the nerves more than anything. I would actually get nauseated over three-footers, and there were tournaments when I couldn't keep a meal down for four days.

Jack Nicklaus: The longer you play, the better chance the better player has of winning.

Jack Nicklaus: I'll be honest about it. I want to win more than (Bobby) Jones. That's what you play for, to separate yourself from the crowd.

Paul O'Neil: Golf is essentially an exercise in masochism conducted out of doors; it affords opportunity for a certain swank, it induces a sense of kinship in its victims, and it forces them to breathe fresh air, but it is, at bottom, an elaborate and addictive rite calculated to drive them crazy for hours on end and send them straight to the whiskey bottle after that.

Arnold Palmer: It's a funny thing. The more I practice, the luckier I get.

Arnold Palmer: The most rewarding things you do in life are often the ones that look like they cannot be done.

Arnold Palmer: Concentration comes out of a combination of confidence and hunger.

Arnold Palmer: I never quit trying. I never felt like I didn't have a chance.... The fact that people think of me as playing hard and charging from behind is a great feeling for me. I was, and still today am, about the effort to succeed, not just about the result. That's what keeps me going. I still test myself. I still exercise. I still eat right. And that's contributed a great deal to the enjoyment I'm getting out of my later years.

Westbrook Pegler: The most useless outdoor game ever devised to waste the time and try the spirit of man.

Gary Player (PGA golfer): When you play for fun, it's fun. But when you play golf for a living, it's a game of sorrows. You're never happy.

Tom Puritzer: It was one of those days you dream about. Every hole seemed to be six inches wide.

James Reston: A plague invented by the Calvinistic Scots as a punishment for man's sins.

Bobby Riggs: Golf matches are not won on the fairways or greens. There are won on the tee—the first tee.

Chi Chi Rodriguez: I'm playing like Tarzan – and scoring like Jane.

Will Rogers: The Income Tax has made more Liars out of the American people than golf has.

Will Rogers: I guess there is nothing that will get your mind off everything like golf. I have never been depressed enough to take up the game, but they say you get so sore at yourself you forget to hate your enemies.

Bertrand Russell: The place of the father in the modern suburban family is a very small one, particularly if he plays golf.

Henry H. Shires: The only game which has a moral purpose and is definitely tinged with a touch of the spiritual.

Adlai Stevenson: Some of us worship in churches, some in synagogues, some on golf courses.

Louise Suggs: If a woman can walk, she can play golf.

Lee Trevino: We all choke, and the man who says he doesn't choke is lying like hell.

Lee trevino (held up his 2-iron during a lightning storm and said): Even God can't hit a 2-iron!

Mark Twain: Golf is a good walk spoiled.

Mark Twain: It's good sportsmanship to not pick up lost golf balls while they are still rolling.

UA: The game that turns the cows out of the pasture and lets the bull in.

UA: A game where the ball lies poorly and the player well.

UA: A sport in which many impressive scores are attained by a lead pencil.

Pat Ward-Thomas: Every great golfer has learned to think positively, to assume the success and not the failure of a shot, to disregard misfortune and to accept disaster, and never to indulge the futility of remorse and blame. These are the hardest lessons of all.

Glen Scobey "Pop" Warner (legendary football coach at Carlisle Indian Industrial School): You play the way you practice.

Earl Wilson: A lot of walking, broken by disappointments and bad arithmetic.

Woodrow Wilson: A game in which one endeavors to control the ball with implements ill adapted for that purpose.

P.G. Wodehouse: The least thing upset him on the links. He missed short putts because of the uproar of butterflies in the adjoining meadow.

GOVERNMENT/POLITICS

Uncle Anthony: I can't vote for a party led by a man thinks that charisma is December 25.

Uncle Anthony: Thomas, you really think that the Bill of Rights could get through Congress today? It would never get "out of committee."

Uncle Anthony: They oughta call it the campaign "HEDGEQUARTERS."

Aunt Mary Carlo: I tink he's refusin' to answer any questions 'cause dey may tend to eliminate him.

Aunt Carlo: He's really good at talkin' in coicles (circles) and still standin' "four-square" on somet'in.

John Adams (*Draft Massachusetts Constitution: Declaration of Rights, Art. XXX*, 1779): To the end it may be a government of laws, and not of men.

John Adams: In my many years I have come to a conclusion that one useless man is a shame, two is a law firm, and three or more is a Congress.

Henry Adams: The work of internal government has become the task of controlling the thousands of fifth-rate men.

Alain: The first rule in a handbook of government is idleness.

Jack Anderson: I believe our country is strong enough to be criticized.

Aristotle: Good laws, if they are not obeyed, do not constitute good government.

Aristotle: It is better for a city to be governed by a good man than even by good laws.

Aristotle: If liberty and equality, as thought by some, are chiefly to be found in democracy, they will be best attained when all persons alike share in government to the utmost.

Aristotle (*Politics*, III, 16): He who bids the law rule may be deemed to bid God and Reason alone rule, but he who bids man rule adds an element of the beast; for desire is a wild beast, and passion perverts the minds of rulers, even when they are the best of men.

Francis Bacon: When any of the four pillars of government, religion, justice, counsel, and treasure, are badly shaken or weakened, men had need to pray for fair weather.

Alben W. Barkley: A bureaucrat is a Democrat who holds some office that a Republican wants.

Frederic Bastiat: Government is the great fiction, through which every body endeavors to live at the expense of everybody else.

James Bavard (Civil Libertarian): Democracy must be something more than two wolves and a sheep voting on what to have for dinner.

Stephen Vincent Benet (1937 short story *The Devil and Daniel Webster*): It's a story they tell in the "Border Country" where Massacusetts joins Vermont and New Hampshire. Yes, Daniel Webster's dead, or at least they buried him, but everytime there is a thunder storm around Marshfield (Daniel Webster's country homestead) they say you can hear his rolling voice in the hollows of the sky. And they say if you go to his grave and speak loud and clear: "Dan'l Webster! Dan'l Webster!" the ground will begin to shiver and the trees begin to shake, and after a while you'll hear a deep voice Saying: **"Neighbor, how stands the Union?"** Then, you better answer: "The Union stands as she stood, rock bottomed and copper sheathed, one and indivisible." Or, he's liable to rear right out of the ground. At least that's what I was told when I was a youngster.

Bible: Mark 12:17: Render to Caesar the things that are Caesar's, and to God the things that are God's.

Bible: I Peter 2:17: Fear God. Honour the king.

Bible: Proverbs 14:34: Righteousness exalteth a nation.

Bible: Psalms 118:9: It is better to trust in the Lord than to put confidence in princes.

Bible: Romans 13:1: Let every soul be subject unto the higher powers.

Bible: Romans 13:1:The powers that be are ordained of God.

Bible: II Samuel 23:3: He that ruleth over men must be just, ruling in the fear of God.

Ambrose Bierce: ARISTOCRACY, n. Government by the best men. (In this sense the word is obsolete; so is that kind of government.) Fellows that wear downy hats and clean shirts – guilty of education and suspected of bank accounts.

Ambrose Bierce: CAPITAL, n. The seat of misgovernment....

Ambrose Bierce: COMMONWEALTH, n. An administrative entity operated by an incalculable multitude of political parasites, logically active but fortuitously efficient.

Ambrose Beirce: CONGRESS, n. A body of men who meet to repeal laws.

Ambrose Bierce: DICTATOR, n. The chief of a nation that prefers the pestilence of despotism to the plague of anarchy.

Ambrose Bierce: EXECUTIVE, n. An officer of the Government, whose duty it is to enforce the wishes of the legislative power until such time as the judicial department shall be pleased to pronounce them invalid and of no effect.

Ambrose Bierce: HOUSELESS, adj. Having paid all taxes on household goods.

Ambrose Bierce: KING, n. A male person commonly known in America as a "crowned head," although he never wears a crown and has usually no head to speak of.

Ambrose Bierce: PEROGATIVE, n. A sovereign's right to do wrong.

Ambrose Bierce: QUEEN, n. A woman by whom the realm is ruled when there is a king, and through whom it is ruled when there is not

Ambrose Bierce: QUORUM, n. A suffiecient number of members of a deliberative body to have their own way and their own way of having it. In the United States Senate a quorum consists of the chairman of the Committee on Finance and a messenger from the White House; in the House of Representatives, of the Speaker and the devil.

Ambrose Bierce: REFERENDUM, n. A law for submission of proposed legislation to a popular vote to learn the nonsensus of public opinion.

Ambrose Bierce: REPRESENTATIVE, n. In national politics, a member of the Lower House in this world, and without discernible hope of promotion in the next.

Ambrose Bierce: REPUBLIC, n. A nation in which, the thing governing and the thing governed being the same, there is only a permitted authority to enforce an optional obedience. In a republic the foundation of public order is the ever lessening habit of submission inherited from ancestors who, being truly governed, submitted because they had to. There are so many kinds of republics as there are gradations between the despotism whence they came and the anarchy whither they lead.

Ambrose Bierce: REVOLUTION, n. In politics, an abrupt change in the form of misgovernment. Specifically, in American history, the substitution of the rule of an Administration for that of a Ministry, whereby the welfare and happiness of the people were advanced by a full half-inch. Revolutions are usually accompanied by a considerable effusion of blood, but are accounted worth it – this appraisement being made by beneficiaries whose blood had not the mischance to be shed. The French revolution is of incalculable value to the Socialist of to-day; when he pulls the string actuating its bones its gestures are inexpressibly terrifying to gory tyrants suspected of fomenting law and order.

Ambrose Bierce: SENATE, n. A body of elderly gentlemen charged with high duties and misdemeanors.

Chester Bowles: Government is too big and important to be left to the politicians.

Louis Dembitz Brandeis: Accountancy – that is government.

Louis D. Brandeis: Government is not an exact science.

Louis D. Brandeis: The doctrine of separation of powers was adopted by the Convention of 1787, not to promote efficiency but to preclude the exercise of arbitrary power. The purpose was, not to avoid friction, but, by means of the inevitable friction incident to the distribution of the governmental powers among three departments, to save the people from autocracy. (dissenting opinion) *Myers v. US*, 272 US 53, 71 L ed 160, 47 S Ct 21 (1926)

Louis D. Brandeis: Our government is the potent, the omnipresent teacher. For good or for ill, it teaches the whole people by its example.... If the Government becomes a lawbreaker, it breeds contempt for law; it invites every man to become a law unto himself; it invites anarchy. To declare that in the administration of the criminal law the end justifies the means – to declare that the Government may commit crimes in order to secure the conviction of a private criminal – would bring terrible retribution. Against that pernicious doctrine this court should resolutely set its face. (dissenting opinion) Olmstead v. US, 277 US 438, 72 L ed 944, 48 S Ct 564 (1928)

Wernher von Braun: We can lick gravity, but sometimes the paperwork is overwhelming.

David Brin: It is said that power corrupts, but actually it's more true that power attracts the corruptible. The sane are usually attracted by other things than power.

Mel Brooks (comic, producer and star of movie *The History of the World Part II*): It's good to be the king!

Jerry Brown: The great problem in government is that it never goes bankrupt.

William F. Buckley, Jr.: Liberals claim to want to give a hearing to other views, but then are shocked and offended to discover that there are other views.

Edmund Burke: And having looked to Government for bread, on the first scarcity they will turn and bite the hand that fed them.

Thomas Carlyle: Government is emphatically a machine: to the discontented a "taxing machine," to the contented a "machine for securing property."

Douglas Casey: Foreign aid might be defined as a transfer of money from poor people in rich countries to rich people in poor countries.

Donald Cattie: The "Art of Taxation" is the art of plucking the goose so as to get the greatest amount of feathers with the least amount of squawking.

William Ellery Channing: The office of Government is not to confer happiness, but to give men opportunity to work out happiness for themselves.

Sir Winston Churchill: When one is in office one has no idea how damnable things can feel to the ordinary rank and file of the public.

Sir Winston Churchill: I contend that for a nation to try to tax itself into prosperity is like a man standing in a bucket and trying to lift himself up by the handle.

Sir Winston Churchill: The nation will find it very hard to look up to the leaders who are keeping their ears to the ground.

Sir Winston Churchill: The inherent vice of capitalism is the unequal sharing of the blessings. The inherent blessing of socialism is the equal sharing of misery.

Sir Winston Churchill: Many forms of Government have been tried, and will be tried in this world of sin and woe. No one pretends that democracy is perfect or all-wise. Indeed, it has been said that democracy is the worst form of Government except all those others that have been tried from time to time.

Sir Winston Churchill: At the bottom of all the tributes paid to democracy is the little man walking into the little booth with a little pencil, making a little cross on a little bit of paper.

Sir Winston Churchill: Socialism is like a dream. Sooner or later you wake up to reality.

Sir Winston Churchill: The whole history of the world is summed up in the fact that, when nations are strong, they are not always just, and when they wish to be just, they are no longer strong.

Henry Clay (Kentucky lawyer, statesman, 1777-1852): Self-government is the natural government of man.

Henry Clay: Government is a trust, and the officers of the government are trustees; and both the trust and the trustees are created for the benefit of the people.

Cadwallader Colden (17th Century Irish-born American politician): All associations are dangerous to good Government ... and associations of Lawyers the most dangerous of any next to the Military.

Confucius: To govern means to rectify.

James Fennimore Cooper: The tendency if democracy is, in all things, to mediocrity.

Declaration of Independence: Whenever any Form of Government becomes destructive... it is the Right of the People to alter or abolish it.

Dionysius of Halicarnassus (20 B.C.): A good government produces citizens distinguished for Kurdish, love of justice, and every other good quality; a bad government makes them cowardly, rapacious, and the slaves of every foul desire.

Benjamin Disraeli: No government can be long secure without a formidable opposition.

Ralph Waldo Emerson: Government has been a fossil; it should be a plant.

Felix Frankfurter: Government is itsself an art, one of the subtlest of the arts. It is the art of making men live together in peace with reasonable happiness.

Benjamin Franklin: There is no kind of dishonesty into which otherewise good people more easily and frequently fall than that of defrauding the government.

Donald M. Fraser: Under current law, it is a crime for a private citizen to lie to a government official, but not for the government to lie to the people.

David Friedman: The direct use of force is such a poor solution to any problem, it is generally employed only by small children and large nations.

Milton Friedman: The government solution to a problem is usually as bad as the problem.

John Gardner: The hallmark of our age is the tension between related aspirations and sluggish institutions.

James A. Garfield: All free governments are managed by the combined wisdom and folly of the people.

German Proverb: Even a fool can govern if nothing happens.

Jean Giraudoux: Government defines the physical aspects of man by means of the Printed Forum, so that for every man in the flesh there is an exactly corresponding man on paper.

William Godwin: Society is produced by our wants, and government by our wickedness.

Barry Goldwater: A government that is big enough to give you all you want is big enough to take it all away.

Barry Goldwater: I fear Washington and centralized government more than I do Moscow.

Learned Hand (*The Deficiencies of Trials to Reach the Heart of the Matter*, 3 Lectures on Legal Topics, Assn Bar of City of N.Y., 1926): A government of laws without men is as visionary as a government of men without laws; the solution will always be a compromise based on experience.

Warren G. Harding: Government after all is a very simple thing.

Thomas Hardy (English poet and novelist, 1840-1928): The offhand decision of some commonplace mind in high office at a critical moment influences the course of events for a hundred years.

James Harrington (English political theorist, 1611-1677, *Oceana*): And these I conceive to be the principles upon which Aristotle and Livy (injuriously accused by Hobbes for not writing out of nature) have grounded their assertion that a **"Commonwealth is an empire of laws and not of men."**

Oliver Wendell Holmes, Jr.: Men must turn square corners when they deal with the Government. *Rock Island, A. & L. R. Co. v. US*, 254 US 141, 65 L ed 188, 41 S Ct 55 (1920)

Oliver Wendell Holmes, Jr.: Taxes are what we pay for civilized society. *Compania General De Tabacos v. Collector of Internal Revenue*, 275 US 87, 100 L ed 177, 48 S Ct 100 (1927)

Oliver Wendell Holmes, Jr.: The power to tax is not the power to destroy while this Court sits. *Panhandle Oil Co. v. Mississippi ex rel.*, Knox, 277 US 218, 72 L ed 857, 48 S Ct 451 (1928)

David Hume: Nothing appears more surprising to those who consider human affairs with a philosophical eye than the easiness with which the many are governed by the few.

Hubert Humphrey: The impersonal hand of government can never replace the helping hand of a neighbor.

Aldous Huxley: Government is an affair of sitting not hitting. You rule with the brains and the buttocks, never the fists.

William Ralph Inge: A nation is a society united by delusions about its ancestry and by common hatred of its neighbors.

Robert H. Jackson: (Government employees) .... are subject to that very human weakness, especially displayed in Washington, which leads men into "crook the pregnant hinges of the knee where thrift may follow fawning."

Edward Jacobs (attorney for former Atlantic City mayor, Bob Levy, who resigned as mayor on October 10, 2007, after only 22 months in office, because of an ongoing federal probe into his military record, about which he lied about being a Green Beret, medical problems and media attention over his disappearance from the public and his city hall office): You can't fool with the federal government. They won two world wars, and they print their own money.

Thomas Jefferson: The whole of government consists in the art of being honest.

Thomas Jefferson: The execution of the laws is more important than the making of them

Thomas Jefferson: Each generation... has a right to choose for itself the form of government it believes most promotive of its own happiness.

Thomas Jefferson: Were we directed from Washington when to sow, and when to reap, we should soon want bread.

Thomas Jefferson: The will of the people is the only legitimate foundation of any government, and to protect its free expression should be our first object.

Thomas Jefferson: The spirit of resistance to Government is so valuable on certain occasions that I wish it to be always kept alive.

Thomas Jefferson: A government big enough to give you everything you want, is strong enough to take everything you have.

Thomas Jefferson: The functionaries of every government have propensities to command at will the Liberty and property of their constituents.

Thomas Jefferson: But it is not the consolidation, or concentration, of powers, but by their distribution that good government is affected.

Jewish Saying: Co-rulers become over-rulers.

Samuel Johnson (*Dictionary*): EXCISE: A hateful tax levied upon commodities and adjudged not by the common judges of property, but wretches hired by those to whom excise is paid.

Samuel Johnson: I would not give half a guinea to live under one form of government rather than another.

William Johnson (South Carolina lawyer, Assoc Justice US Supreme Court, 1771-1834): The science of government is the most abstruse of all sciences; if, indeed, that can be called a science, which has but few fixed principles, and practically consists in little more than the exercise of a sound discretion, applied to the exigencies of the state as they arise. It is the science of experiment. *Anderson v. Dunn*, 6 Wheat 204, 5 L ed 242 (1821)

John F. Kennedy: My brother Bob doesn't want to be in government – he promised Dad he'd go straight.

John F. Kennedy: My experience in government is that when things are non-controversial, beautifully coordinated and all the rest, it must be that there is not much going on.

Henry Kissinger: 90% of the politicians give the other 10% a bad reputation.

Henry Kissinger: The illegal we do immediately. The unconstitutional takes a little longer.

Sir Wilmot Lewis (English journalist, 1877-1950): Legislation in the United States is a digestive process by Congress with frequent regurgitations by the Supreme Court.

Abraham Lincoln: No man is good enough to govern another man without that other's consent.

Abraham Lincoln: While the people retain their virtue and vigilance, no administration, by any extreme of wickedness or folly, can very seriously injure the government in the short space of four years.

Abraham Lincoln: You can fool some of the people all of the time, and all of the people some of the time, but you cannot fool all of the people all of the time.

Abraham Lincoln: A house divided against itself cannot stand—I believe this government cannot endure permanently half slave and half free.

Niccolo Machiavelli: All well-governed states and wise princes have taken care not to reduce the nobility to despair, nor the people to discontent.

James Madison (*The Federalist No. 51*, 1788): If men were angels, no government would be necessary. If angels were to govern men, neither external nor internal controuls on government would be necessary. In framing a government which is to be administered by men over men, the great difficulty lies in this: You must first enable the government to controul the governed: and in the next place, oblige it to control itself.

George Mason (1787): An aristocratic body (like the aspiring nature or insidious screw of the judicial aristocracy), like the screw in mechanics, works its way by slow degrees, holds fast to whatever it gains, and should ever be suspected of an encroaching tendency.

George McGovern: The longer the title, the less important the job.

H.L. Mencken: Unquestionably, there is progress. The average American now pays out twice as much in taxes as he formerly got in wages.

H.L. Mencken: Under democracy one-party always devotes its chief energies to trying to prove that the other party is unfit to rule—and both commonly succeed, and both are right.

Edward R. Murrow: When politicians complain that TV turns the proceedings into a circus, it should be made clear that the circus was already there, and that TV has merely demonstrated that not all the performers are well-trained.

Michael A. Musmanno (Justice of Pa. Supreme Court, 1959): It is simply unthinkable that in a government of the people, the government should withhold from one of the people evidence which could prove one innocent of a crime against all the people.

Tsar Nicholas I: I do not rule Russia; ten thousand clerks do.

P.J. O'Rourke: Giving money and power to government is like giving whiskey and car keys to teenage boys.

P.J. O'Rourke: A little government and a little luck are necessary in life, but only a fool trusts either of them.

George Orwell (book "1984"): Big Brother is watching you.

Thomas Paine: The more perfect civilization is, the less occasion it has for government, but the more it does to regulate its own affairs, and govern itself.... All the great laws of society are laws of nature.

Thomas Paine: Government, even in its best state, is but a necessary evil; in its worst state, an intolerable one.

Drew Pearson: Government is only as good as the men in it.

William Penn: Governments rather depend upon men than men upon governments.

William Penn: If men be good, government cannot be bad.

Amos R. E. Pinchot: Today the nations of the world may be divided into two classes – the nations in which government fears the people, and the nations in which the people fear the government.

Plato (*Laws* IV, 715): I see that the State in which the law is above the rulers ... has salvation.

Polybius: That form of government is the best that includes monarchy, aristocracy, and democracy.

Lester J. Pourciau: There is no monument dedicated to the memory of a committee.

Ronald Reagan: One way to make sure crime does not pay would be to let the government run it.

Ronald Reagan: The most terrifying words in the English language are: I'm from the government and I'm here to help.

Ronald Reagan: Today, if you invent a better mousetrap, the government comes along with a better mouse.

Ronald Reagan: Politics is supposed to be the second oldest profession. I have come to realize that it bears a very close resemblance to the first.

Ronald Reagan: The best minds are not in government. If any were, business would hire them away.

Ronald Reagan: Government's view of the economy could be summed up in a few short phrases: if it moves, tax it. If it keeps moving, regulate it. And if it stops moving, subsidize it.

Ronald Reagan: The trouble with our liberal friends is not that they're ignorant; it's just that they know so much that isn't so.

Ronald Reagan: If we ever forget that we're one nation under God, then we will be a nation gone under.

Ronald Reagan: I have wondered at times about what the Ten Commandments would have looked like if Moses had run them through the U.S. Congress.

Ronald Reagan: The taxpayer: That's someone who works for the federal government but doesn't have to take the civil service examination.

Ronald Reagan: Government is like a baby: An alimentary canal with a big appetite at one end and no sense of responsibility at the other.

Ronald Reagan: The nearest thing to eternal life we will ever see on this earth is a government program.

Ronald Reagan: I've laid down the law, though, to everyone from now on about anything that happens: no matter what time it is, wake me, even if it's in the middle of a Cabinet meeting.

James Reston: A government is the only known vessel that leaks from the top.

James Reston: Rudyard Kipling recommended that the leaders of nations study the art of "judicious leaving alone." Chief Justice Berger has a warning sign on his desk: L.I.S. – Let It Simmer.

Joseph Rickaby: All real government is what may be called a Pentegerontamphitrapezy, i.e. five (more or less) old (more or less) gentlemen (more or less) sitting around a table.

Hyman Rickover: Trying to make things work in government is sometimes like trying to sew a button on to a custard pie.

Tom Robbins: Disbelief in magic can force a poor soul into believing in government and business.

John D. Rockefeller, Jr.: I believe that the law was made for man and not man for the law; that government is the servant of the people and not their master.

Will Rogers: There's no trick to being a humorist when you have the whole government working for you.

Will Rogers: This country has come to feel the same when Congress is in session as when the baby gets hold of a hammer.

Will Rogers: The business of government is to keep the government out of business—that is, unless business needs government aid.

Will Rogers: About all I can say for the United States Senate is that it opens with a prayer and closes with an investigation.

Will Rogers (*Autobiography of Will Rogers*, Feb 18, 1923, re Congress): The Capitol Comedy Company of Washington.

Will Rogers: When everybody has got money they cut taxes, and when they're broke they raise 'em. That's statesmanship of the highest order.

Will Rogers: Noah must have taken into the Ark two taxes, one male and one female, and did they multiply bountifully! Next to guinea pigs, taxes must be the most prolific animals.

Will Rogers: The Income Tax has made more Liars out of the American people than golf has.

Will Rogers: I don't want to complain, but every time they build a tax structure, the first thing they nail is me.

Will Rogers: No Voter in the World ever voted for nothing; in some way he has been convinced that he is to get something for that vote. His vote is all that our Constitution gives him, and it goes to the highest bidder.

Will Rogers: I see a good deal of talk from Washington about lowering taxes. I hope they do get 'em lowered enough so people can afford to pay 'em.

Will Rogers: There is not a man in the country that can't make a living for himself and family. But he can't make a living for them and his government, too, the way his government is living. What the government has got to do is live as cheap as the people.

Will Rogers: Government spending? I don't know what it's all about. I don't know any more about this thing than an economist does, and, God knows, he doesn't know much.

Will Rogers: It's a good thing we don't get all the government we pay for.

Will Rogers: Be thankful we're not getting all the government we're paying for.

Will Rogers: If I studied all my life, I couldn't think up half the number of funny things passed in one session of congress.

Will Rogers: I bet after seeing us, George Washington would sue us for calling him "father."

Will Rogers: I don't make jokes. I just watch the government and report the facts.

Will Rogers: If you make any money, the government shoves you in the creek once a year with it in your pockets, and all that don't get wet you can keep.

Will Rogers: I don't care how little your country is, you got a right to run it like you want to. When the big nations quit meddling, then the world will have peace.

Will Rogers: I have a scheme for stopping war. It's this - no nation is allowed to enter a war till they have paid for the last one.

Will Rogers: Now if there is one thing that we do worse than any other nation, it is try and manage somebody else's affairs.

Will Rogers: Ohio claims they are due a president as they haven't had one since Taft. Look at the United States, they have not had one since Lincoln.

Will Rogers: On account of being a democracy and run by the people, we are the only nation in the world that has to keep a government four years, no matter what it does.

Will Rogers: Anything important is never left to the vote of the people. We only get to vote on some man; we never get to vote on what he is to do.

Will Rogers: Diplomats are just as essential to starting a war as Soldiers are for finishing it. You take Diplomacy out of war and the thing would fall flat in a week.

Will Rogers: Diplomacy is the art of saying "Nice doggie" until you can find a rock.

Will Rogers: Prohibition is better than no liquor at all.

Will Rogers: The man with the best job in the country is the vice-president. All he has to do is get up every morning and say, "How is the president?"

Will Rogers: The only difference between death and taxes is that death doesn't get worse every time Congress meets.

Will Rogers: Things in our country run in spite of government, not by aid of it.

Will Rogers: Baseball is a skilled game. It's America's game—it, and high taxes.

Will Rogers (1936 - Two years after FDR won the presidency, Rogers hit both his friend in the White House and big business over the misadministration of FDR's National Recovery Administration - the arm of the New Deal intended to shorten the work week, establish a minimum wage, and let workers organize; but, some selfish industries were successfully lobbying for exemptions from the law): The NRA looked like a good bet at the time, but part of it, in fact maybe over half of it, has proven to be nonpractical. It had all the right ideas but we are still just too selfish to see that exactly the right thing is done for the good of everybody.

Franklin D. Roosevelt (*Radio Address*, March 9, 1937): Last Thursday I described the American form of Government as a three-horse team provided by the Constitution to the American people so that their field might be plowed. The three horses are, of course, the three branches of Government – the Congress, the Executive and the Courts. Two of the horses are pulling in unison today; the third is not. Those who have intimated that the President of the United States is trying to drive that team, overlook the simple fact that the President, as Chief Executive, is himself one of the three horses. / It is the American people themselves who are in the driver's seat. / It is the American people themselves who want the furrow plowed. / It is the American people themselves who expect the third horse to pull in unison with the other two.

Theodore Roosevelt: The government is us; we are the government, you and I.

Theodore Roosevelt (April 19, 1906): Behind the ostensible government sits enthroned an invisible government owing no allegiance and acknowledging no responsibility to the people. To destroy this invisible government, to befoul the unholy alliance between corrupt business and corrupt politics is the first task of the statesmanship of the day.

Bertrand Russell: Government can easily exist without law, but law cannot exist without government.

John Seldon (English lawyer and writer, 1584-1654, *Table-Talk: Power-State*): They that govern most make least noise; you see, when they row in a barge, they that do the drudgery work slash and puff and sweat but he that governs sits quietly at the stern and scarce is seen to stir.

William Shakespeare (*Coriolanus*, Act I, vi): A man busied about decrees; / Condemning some to death, and some to exile; / Ransoming him, or pitying, thret'ning the other.

William Shakespeare (*I Henry IV*, Act I. ii): Let men say we be men of good government.

William Shakespeare (*III Henry VI*, Act IV, vi): Now join your hands, and with your hands your hearts, / That no dissension hinder government.

William Shakespeare (*Henry VIII*, Act II, iv): Wife-like government, / Obeying in commanding.

William Shakespeare (*Richard III*, Act I, i): Why this it is, when men are rul'd by women.

George Bernard Shaw: Democracy is a device that ensures we shall be governed no better than we deserve.

George Bernard Shaw: The art of government is the organization of idolatry.

Gen. William Tecumseh Sherman (Union General during Civil War, best remembered for his 1864 destructive march through Georgia or his "march to the sea"; speaking in 1868 about settling "The Indian Question"): (The West needed to be a place where) things reassuingly could be counted, taxed and governed.

Thomas Sowell: Much of the social history of the Western world over the past three decades has involved replacing what worked with what sounded good.

Adlai Stevenson: He is the kind of politician who would cut down a redwood tree, then mount the stump and make a speech for conservation.

Jonathan Swift: For in reason, all government without the consent of the governed is the very definition of slavery.

Talmud: Don't live in a city run by scholars.

Talmud: The real guardians of the state are the teachers.

Henry David Thoreau: Why does (the government) always crucify Christ, and excommunicate Copernicus and Luther, and pronounce Washington and Franklin rebels?

Tolstoy: Government is an association of men who do violence to the rest of us.

Mark Twain: That government is not best which best secures mere life and property – there is a more valuable thing – manhood.

Mark Twain: Suppose you were an idiot and suppose you were a member of Congress. But I repeat myself.

Mark Twain: The only difference between a tax man and a taxidermist is that the taxidermist leaves the skin.

Mark Twain: No man's life, liberty, or property is safe while the legislature is in session.

Mark Twain: All kings is mostly rapscallions.

Voltaire (1764): In general, the art of government consists of taking as much money as possible from one party of the citizens to give to the other.

George Washington: The basis of our political systems is the right of the people to make and to alter their constitutions of government.

Woodrow Wilson (*Constitutional Government in the United States*, 1908): There never was such a government. Constitute them how you will, governments are always governments of men, and no part of any government is better than the men to whom that part is entrusted. The gauge of excellence is not the law under which officers act, but the conscience and intelligence with which they apply it, if they apply it at all. And the courts do not escape the rule. So far as the individual is concerned, a constitutional government is as good as its courts; no better, no worse.

Bernard Woolley: Two kinds of chair correspond with the two kinds of minister: one sort folds up instantly and the other sort goes round and round in circles.

GREATNESS (See SUCCESS)

GREED (See CHEAP/CHEAPNESS)

GRIEF & SORROW (See also PAIN)

Uncle Anthony: There's nothing worse than the grief of a parent for a child who dies.

Aunt Mary Carlo: Y'know 'dat gospel song – Nobody Knows the Trouble I Seen – well, 'dat's true.

Louisa May Alcott: When a man has a great sorrow, he should be indulged in all sorts of vagaries till he has lived it down.

Amelia Barr: It is only in sorrow bad weather masters us; in joy we face the storm and defy it.

Henry Ward Beecher: Sorrow makes men and sincere.

Bible: 2 Corinthians 7:10: Godly sorrow worketh repentence to salvation not to be repented of.

Bible: Ecclesiastes 7:3: Sorrow is better than laughter: for by the sadness of the countenance the heart is made better.

Bible: Isaiah 53:4: Surely he hath borne our griefs, and carried our sorrows.

Bible: John 16:20: Ye shall weep and lament, but the world will rejoice; and ye shall be sorrowful, but your sorrow shall be turned into joy.

Bible: Lamentations 1:12: Is it nothing to you, all ye that pass by? Behold, and see if there be any sorrow like unto my sorrow.

Bible: Psalms 30:5: Weeping may endure for a night, but joy cometh in the morning.

Ambrose Bierce: PAIN, n. An uncomfortable frame of mind that may have a physical basis in something that is being done to the body, or may be purely mental, caused by the good fortune of another.

Chinese Proverb: A day of sorrow is longer than a month of joy.

Chinese Proverb: One joy scatters a hundred griefs.

Chinese Proverb: Sorrow is born of excessive joy.

Sir Winston Churchill: We have a lot of anxieties, and one cancels out another very often.

Sir Winston Churchill: Death and sorrow will be the companions of our journey; hardship our garment; constancy and valor our only shield.

Cicero: No grief is so acute but that time ameliorates it,

William Cowper: Grief is itself a medicine.

Greg Cusimano: You know, nothing arrives more slowly and passes more quickly than having fun. And nothing arrives more quickly and passes more slowly than misery.

Dante Alighieri: There is no greater grief than to remember days of joy when misery is at hand.

Emily Dickinson: Parting is all we know of heaven, / And all we need of hell.

Queen Elizabeth I (in a letter to her cousin Mary, Queen of Scots, in 1567 concerning "The Gunpowder Conspiracy" – assassination of 21-year-old King of the Scots, Henry Stuart, Lord Darney, by gunpowder/blowing up his house): "My ears have been so deafened, and my understanding so griefull, and my heart so afrighted to hear the dreadful news of ... the abomidable murder of your mad husband and my killed cousin that I scarcely have the wits to write about it ..."

Queen Elizabeth I (Queen of England): We all stand as equals to pain and sorrow.

Ralph Waldo Emerson: Tragedy is in the eye of the observer, and not in the heart of the sufferer.

Ralph Waldo Emerson: No man ever stated his griefs as lightly as he might. Allow for exaggeration in the most patient and sorely ridden hack that ever was driven.

Ralph Waldo Emerson: The chamber of flame in which the martyr passes is more magnificent than the royal apartment from which majesty looks out on his sufferings.

William Faulkner: *Yes*, he thought, *between grief and nothing I will take grief.*

Jon Gay: A moment of time may make us unhappy forever.

Bret Harte: If of all words of tongue and pen, / The saddest are, "It might have been," / More sad are these we daily see, / "It is, but it hadn't ought to be."

Oliver Wendell Holmes, Sr.: There are a good many real miseries in life that we cannot help smiling at, but they are the smiles that make wrinkles and not dimples.

Elbert Hubbard: If you suffer, thank God! – it is a sure sign that you are alive.

Washington Irving: The sorrow for the dead is the only sorrow from which we refuse to be divorced. Every other wound we seek to heal, every other affliction to forget; but this wound we consider it a duty to keep open, this affliction we cherish and brood over in solitude.

William James: In the deepest heart of all of us there is a corner in which the ultimate mystery of things works sadly.

Sara Orne Jewett: A lean sorrow is hardest to bear.

Jewish Saying: No one knows the sorrow of another.

Jewish Saying: The deeper the sorrow, the less voice it has.

Jewish Saying: Sorrows create ailments; happiness cures them.

Alphonse de Lamartine: Grief knits two hearts in closer bonds than happiness ever can; common sufferings are far stronger links than common joys.

Latin Proverb: Light griefs can speak; but deeper ones are dumb.

George Henry Lewes: The only cure for grief is action.

Henry Wadsworth Longfellow: There is no grief like the grief that does not speak.

Henry Wadsworth Longfellow: Into each life some rain must fall.

Henry Wadsworth Longfellow: Oh, fear not in a world like this, / And thou shalt know erelong, / Know how sublime a thing it is / To suffer and be strong.

Henry Wadsworth Longfellow: Believe me, every man has his secret sorrows, which the world knows not; and oftentimes we call a man cold when he is only sad.

Henry Wadsworth Longfellow: If we could read the secret history of our enemies, we should find in each man's life sorrow and suffering enough to disarm all hostility.

Henry Wadsworth Longfellow: A feeling of sadness comes o'er me / That my soul cannot resist: / A feeling of sadness and longing, / That is not akin to pain, / And resembles sorrow only / As the mist resembles rain.

Henry Wadsworth Longfellow: Be still, sad heart! And cease repining; / Behind the clouds is the sun still shining; / Thy fate is the common fate of all, / Into each life some rain must fall. / Some days must be dark and dreary.

James Russell Lowell: Sorrow, the great idealizer.

Minquass Saying: The soul would have no rainbow, If the eyes had no tears.

Suzanne Moarny: In extreme youth, in our most humiliating sorrow, we think we are alone. When we are older we find that others have suffered too.

Sir (or Saint) Thomas More: Earth has no sorrow that Heaven cannot heal.

Jim M. Perdue (*Who Will Speak For The Victim? A Practical Treatise on Plaintiff's Jury Argument*, State Bar of Texas, 2002): Broken hearts are much more difficult to heal than broken bones.... Grief is not peculiar to the human being. A cow that loses her calf will despair for a period of time. A cat that loses a kitten will search for it for a few days. But a man or woman who loses a loved one will never forget.

Jean Paul Richter: Sorrows are like thunderclouds—in the distance they look black, over our heads scarcely gray.

Will Rogers: Last year we said, 'Things can't go on like this', and they didn't, they got worse.

William Shakespeare (*A Comedy of Errors*, Act V, i): Grief hath changed me since you saw me last.

William Shakespeare (*Cymbeline*, Act III, ii): Let that grieve him: / Some griefs are med'cinable.

William Shakespeare (*Hamlet*, Act IV, v): When sorrows come, they come not as single spies, / But in battalions!

William Shakespeare (*I Henry IV*, Act II, iv): A plague of sighing and grief.

William Shakespeare (*II Henry IV*, Act V, ii): Be sad, good brothers / Sorrow so royally in you appears, / That I will deeply put the fashion on.

William Shakespeare (*Henry V*, Act IV, iv): The saying is true, / "The empty vessel makes the greatest sound."

William Shakespeare (*Henry V*, Act IV, vi): I had not so much of man in me, / And all my mother came into mine eyes, / And gave me up to tears.

William Shakespeare (*III Henry VI*, Act V, iv): What I should say / My tears gainsay; for every word I speak, / Ye see, I drink the waters of mine eyes.

William Shakespeare (*Henry VIII*, Act II, iv): I am about to weep; but thinking that / We are a queen, (or long have dream'd so) certain / The daughter of a king, my drops of tears / I'll turn to sparks of fire.

William Shakespeare (*Henry VIII*, Act III, ii): I did not think to shed a tear / In all my miseries; but thou hast forc'd me / Out of my honest truth to play the woman.

William Shakespeare (*Henry VIII*, Act V, i): He has strangled / His language in his tears.

William Shakespeare (*Julius Caesar*, Act III, ii): If you have tears, prepare to shed them now.

William Shakespeare (*King John*, Act III, i): I will instruct my sorrow to be proud.

William Shakespeare (*King John*, Act III, i): Here I and sorrow sit: / Here is my throne, bid kings come bow to it.

William Shakespeare (*King Lear*, Act II, iv): Down, climbing sorrow.

William Shakespeare (*King Lear*, Act II, iv): The tempest in my mind / Doth from my senses take all feelings else, / Save what beats there.

William Shakespeare (*King Lear*, Act II, iv): Let not women's weapons, water-drops, / Stain my man's cheek!

William Shakespeare (*King Lear*, Act II, iv): No, I'll not weep:- / I have full cause of weeping; but this heart / Shall break into a hundred thousand flaws, / Or ere I'll weep,

William Shakespeare (*King Lear*, Act IV, i): Bad is the trade that must play fool to sorrow.

William Shakespeare (*King John*, Act IV, iii): Trust not those cunning waters of his eyes, / For villainy is not without such rheum; / And he, long traded in it, makes it seem / Like rivers of remorse and innocency.

William Shakespeare (*Love's Labour's Lost*, Act V, ii): Honest plain words best pierce the ear of grief.

William Shakespeare (*Macbeth*, Act IV, iii): Give sorrow words; the grief that does not speak / Whispers the o'erfraught heart and bids it break.

William Shakespeare (*Macbeth*, Act IV, iii): Each new moon, / New widows howl, new orphans cry; new sorrows / Strike heaven on the face, that it resound / As if it felt with Scotland, and yell'd out / Like syllable of dolour.

William Shakespeare (*Macbeth*, Act V, vii): Your cause of sorrow / Must not be measur'ed by his worth, for then / It hath no end.

William Shakespeare (*Measure forMeasure*, Act III, i): The miserable have no other medicine / But only hope.

William Shakespeare (*Much Ado About Nothing*, Act I, i): LEONATO: Did he break into tears? / MESSENGER: In great measure. / LEONATO: A kind overflow of kindness: There are no faces truer than those that are so washed.

William Shakespeare (*Much Ado About Nothing*, Act III, ii): Every one can master a grief but he that has it.

William Shakespeare (*Much Ado About Nothing*, Act V, i): Men / Can counsel and speak comfort to that grief / Which they themselves not feel; but tasting it, / Their counsel turns to passion.
William Shakespeare (*Othello*, Act II, i): I am not merry, but I do beguile / The thing I am seeming otherwise.
William Shakespeare (*Othello*, Act IV, i): If that the earth could teem with woman's tears, / Each drop she falls would prove a crocodile.
William Shakespeare (*Pericles*, Act I, iv): One sorrow never comes but brings an heir, / That may succeed as his inheritor.
William Shakespeare (*Richard II*, Act I, ii): Sorrow ends not when it seemeth done.
William Shakespeare (*Richard II*, Act I, iii): What is six winters? They are quickly gone. - / To men in joy; but grief makes one hour ten.
William Shakespeare (*Richard II*, Act III, iv): Joy being altogether wanting, / It doth remember me the more of sorrow.
William Shakespeare (*Richard II*, Act IV, i): Still my griefs are mine: / You may my glories and my state depose, / But not my griefs; still am I king of those.
William Shakespeare (*Richard II*, Act IV, i): 'Tis very true, my grief lies all within; / And these external manners of laments / Are merely shadows to the unseen grief.
William Shakespeare (*Richard III*, Act I, iv): Sorrow breaks seasons and reposing hours; / Makes the night morning, and the noontide night.
William Shakespeare (*Richard III*, Act IV, i): Eighty odd years of sorrow have I seen, / And each hour's joy wracked with a week of teen.
William Shakespeare (*Richard III*, Act IV, iv): If sorrow can admit society, / Tell o'er your woes again by viewing mine.
William Shakespeare (*Romeo and Juliet*, Act III, ii): These griefs, these woes, these sorrows make me old.
William Shakespeare (*Titus Andonicus*, Act II, v): Sorrow conceal'd, like an oven stopp'd, / Doth burn the heart to cinders.
William Shakespeare (*Titus Andronicus*, Act III, i): To weep with them that weep doth ease some deal, / But sorrow flouted at is double death.
William Shakespeare (*Titus Andronicus*, Act V, iii): Nor can I utter all our bitter grief, / But floods of tears will drown my oratory.
William Shakespeare (*Twelfth Night*, Act I, i): Eye-offending brine.
William Shakespeare (*Two Gentlemen of Verona*, Act III, ii): A little time, my lord, will kill that grief.
J.H. Vincent: There can be no rainbow without a cloud and a storm.
Johann Friedrich von Schiller: Great souls suffer in silence.
Spanish Proverb: Do not rejoice at my grief, for when mine is old, yours will be new.
Alfred, Lord Tennyson: Sorrow's crown of sorrow is remembering happier things.
Henry David Thoreau: If misery loves company, misery has company enough.
Turkish Proverb: He that conceals his grief finds no remedy for it.
Mark Twain: Adam and Eve had many advantages, but the principal one was that they escaped teething.
Mark Twain: Noise proves nothing. Often a hen who has laid an egg cackles as if she had laid an asteroid.
Mark Twain: Grief can take care of itself, but to get the full value of a joy you must have somebody to divide it with.
UA: Sorrow will pay no debt.
John Greenleaf Whittier: For of all sad words of tongue or pen, / The saddest are these: "It might have been!"

HABIT (See CONSISTENCY/MISTAKE)

HAPPY/HAPPINESS (See COMEDY)

HARDSHIP (See TROUBLE)

HEALTH (See also DOCTOR)

Uncle Anthony: Y'know what's worse than being unhealthy or hurt? It's being unhealthy or hurt with no hope of ever gettin' better again.
Aunt Mary Carlo: He's got so many cavities in his mouth he talks wit an echo!
Aunt Mary Carlo: De only way she'd get any color in 'er face if she sticks out her tongue.
Sherwood Anderson: A man needs a purpose for real health.
Arabian Proverb: He who has health has hope, and he who has hope has everything.
Franklin Pierce Adams: Health is the thing that makes you feel that now is the best time of the year.
J. B. Bates: I don't eat anything that has a face on it.
Rona Barrett: The healthy, the strong individual, is the one who asks for help when he needs it. Whether he's got an abscess on his knee or in his soul.
Bruce Barton: If you want to know if your brain is flabby feel of your legs.
Bible: James 2:26: The body without the spirit is dead.
Bible: Matthew 6:25: Take no thought of your life, what ye shall eat, or what ye shall drink; nor yet for your body, what ye shall put on. Is not the life more than meat, and the body than raiment?
Bible: Proverbs 30:8: Give me neither poverty nor riches; feed me with food convenient for me.
Bible: 1 Timothy 4:8: Bodily exercise profiteth little; but godliness is profitable unto all things.
Ambrose Bierce: HEART, n. An automatic, muscular blood-pump. Figuratively, this organ is said to be the seat of emotions and sentiments – a very pretty fancy which, however, is nothing but a survival of a once universal belief....
Ambrose Bierce: WIDOW, n. A pathetic figure that the Christian world has agreed to take humorously, although Christ's tenderness towards widows was one of the most marked features of his character.
Josh Billings: When a man loses his health, then he first begins to take good care of it.
Eubie Blake: If I had known I was going to live this long, I'd have taken better care of myself.
David Brenner: A vegetarian is a person who won't eat anything that can have children.
Chinese Proverb: Back to the draught is face to the grave.
Chinese Proverb: When disease returns, no medicine can cure it.
Sir Winston Churchill: I have taken more out of alcohol than alcohol has taken out of me.
Emile Coue (French psychologist and originator of "Self-Mastery Through Conscious Auto-Suggestion" in 1920's): Every day and in every way I am getting better and better.
Adelle Davis: Thousands upon thousands of persons have studied disease. Almost no one has studied health.
Mary Baker Eddy: Health is not a condition of matter, but of the Mind; nor can the material senses bear reliable testimony on the subject of health.
Mary Baker Eddy: Sickness is a belief, which must be annihilated by the divine Mind.
Ralph Waldo Emerson: Health is the first muse, and sleep is the condition to produce it.
Ralph Waldo Emerson: Give me health and a day and I will make the pomp of emperors ridiculous.
Benjamin Franklin: To lengthen thy Life, lessen thy Meals.
Benjamin Franklin: Been not sick too late, nor well too soon.
Benjamin Franklin: Be sober and temperate, and you will be healthy.
Nathaniel Hawthorne: A bodily disease which we look upon as whole and entire within itself, may, after all, be but a symptom of some ailment in the spiritual part.
Edgar Watson Howe: There is only one thing people like that is good for them: a good night's sleep.
Italian Proverb: Illness tells us what we are.
Thomas Jefferson: The sovereign invigorator of the body is exercise, and of all the exercises walking is best.
Thomas Jefferson: The most uninformed mind with a healthy body is happier than the wisest valetudinarian.
Jewish Saying: Too much is unhealthy.
Jewish Saying: What a fat belly costs, I wish I had; what it does, I wish on my enemies.
Jewish Saying: What soap is for the body, tears are for the soul.
Jewish Saying: Love is the best medicine.
Jewish Saying: No medicines heal sick souls.

Fletcher Knebel: Smoking is one of the leading causes of statistics.
Will Kommen: If you look like your passport photo, you are too ill to travel.
Krishnamurti: It is no measure of health to be well adjusted to a profoundly sick society.
Latin Proverb: Eat well, drink in moderation, and sleep sound, in these three good health abound.
Latin Proverb: *Mens sana in corpore sano* = Healthy mind in a healthy body.
Lebanese Proverb: Hygiene is two thirds of health.
Abe Lemon: I don't jog. If I die, I want to be sick.
Martial (Roman epigrammist, 1st century AD): Life is not to live, but to be well.
Jackie Mason: It's no longer a question of staying healthy. It's a question of finding a sickness you like.
Henry Maudsley: The sorrow which has no vent in tears may make other organs weep.
Jonathan Miller: Illness is not something a person has. It's another way of being.
John Henry Cardinal Newman: Health of body and mind is a great blessing, if we can bear it.
Robert Orben: Quit worrying about your health. It'll go away.
P.J. O'Rourke: If you think health care is expensive now, wait until you see what it costs when it's free!
Jon Poppy: Long-range studies imply that doing something with other people, especially something for them, is the most powerful of all stimuli to longeveity and health.
Will Rogers: Lord, let me live until I die.
George Santayana: It is true that I am carrying out various methods of treatment recommended by doctors and dentists in the hope of dying in the remote future in perfect health.
Arthur Schopenhauer: The greatest mistake a man can make is to sacrifice health for any other advantage.
William Shakespeare (*II Henry IV,* Act IV, v): Health, alack, with youthful wings is flown / From this bare wither'd trunk.
William Shakespeare (*King Lear*, Act II, iv): Maybe he is not well: / Infirmity doth still neglect all office, / Whereto our health is bound.
William Shakespeare (*Macbeth*, Act III, iv): Now, good digestion wait on appetite, / And health on both!
William Shakespeare (*Sonnet*, CXL): Testy sick men, when their deaths be near, / No news but health from their physicians know.
William Shakespeare (*A Winter's Tale,* Act IV, iv): He has his health and ampler strength indeed / Than most have of his age.
George Bernard Shaw: All sorts of bodily diseases are produced by half-used minds.
Sir Philip Sidney: The ingredients of health and long life, are great temperance, open air, easy labor, and little care.
Spanish Proverb: A man too busy to take care of his health is like a mechanic too busy to take care of his tools.
Talmud: Three things drain a man's health: worry, travel, and sin.
Talmud: A Fox does not die from breathing the dust of his own den.
Talmud: Eat a third and drink a third, but leave the remaining third of your stomach emptied: for then, if anger over take two, there will be room for your rage.
Talmud: Six things are good omens for the sick: sneezing, perspiring, open bells, the mission of seamen, sleep – and a dream.
Henry David Thoreau: Measure your health by your sympathy with morning and Spring.
Henry David Thoreau: Must be out-of-doors enough to get experience of wholesome reality, as a ballast to thought and sentiment. Health requires this relaxation, this aimless life.
Mark Twain: He had had much experience of physicians, and said, "The only way to keep your health is to eat what you don't want, drink what you don't like, and do what you'd druther not."
Mark Twain: I have never taken any exercise, except for sleeping and resting, and I never intend to take any. Exercise is loathsome.
Mark Twain: Be careful about reading health books. You may die of a misprint.
UA: Those who do not find time for exercise will have to find time for illness.
Yiddish Proverb: Your health comes first; you can always hang yourself later.

HONESTY (See also FACT; LIES/LIARS; TRUTH/UNDERSTANDING)

Uncle Anthony: He's so honest he looks like Abe Lincoln.
Uncle Anthony: He's so upright he's uptight!
Aunt Mary Carlo: Honesty ain't jus "da best policy" – it's da *only policy* you can have with people.
Arabian Proverb: Examine what is said, not him who speaks.
Bible: Deuteronomy 5:6;Exodus 20:2: (8th Commandment) Thou shalt not bear false witness against thy neighbor.
Bible: Job 31:5: If I walked with vanity, or if my foot hath hasted to deceit; Let me be weighed in an even balance, that God may know mine integrity.
Bible: Leviticus 19:11: Ye shall not steal, neither deal falsley, neither lie one to another.
Bible: Proverbs 11:1: A false balance is abomination to the Lord: but a just weight is his delight.
Bible: Proverbs 11:3: The integrity of the upright shall guide them.
Bible: Psalms 7:8: Judge me, O Lord; according to my righteousness, and according to mine integrity that is in me.
Bible: Romans 12:17: Provide things honest in the sight of all men.
Bible: 1 Thessalonians 4:12: Walk honestly.
Ambrose Bierce: HONORABLE, adj. Afflicted with an impediment in one's reach. In legislative bodies it is customary to mention all members as honorable; as "the honorable gentleman is a scurvy cur.
Ambrose Bierce: TRUTH, n. An ingenious compund of desirability and appearance. Discovery of truth is the sole purpose of philosophy, which is the most ancient occupation of the human mind and has a fair prospect of existing with increasing activity to the end of time.
Ambrose Bierce: TRUTHFUL, adj. Dumb and illiterate.
Benjamin Cardozo: There is an accuracy that defeats itself by the overemphasis of details.... The sentence may be so overloaded with all its possible qualifications that it will tumble down of its own weight.
Sir Winston Churchill: A lie gets halfway around the world before the truth has a chance to get its pants on.
Sir Winston Churchill: It is a fine thing to be honest, but it is also very important to be right.
Cicero: One deserves no praise for being honest when no one tries to corrupt.
Oliver Cromwell: A few honest man are better than numbers.
Daniel Defoe: Fools out of favour grudge at knaves in place, / And men are always honest in disgrace.
English Proverb: Honesty is the best policy.
French Proverb: The surest way to remain poor is to be an honest man.
Thomas Fuller: No man ever repented of his honesty.
Thomas Fuller: Of all crafts, to be an honest man is the master craft.
Thomas Fuller: Honest men fear neither the light nor the dark.
Thomas Fuller: Honest men and knaves may possibly wear the same cloth.
Oliver Wendell Holmes, Jr.: Delusive exactness is a source of fallacy throughout the law.
Thomas Jefferson: Every honest man will suppose honest acts flow from honest principles.
Samuel Johnson: Honesty is not greater where elegance is less.
Samuel Johnson: A man who only does what every one of the society to which he belongs would do, is not a dishonest man.
Samuel Johnson: Integrity without knowledge is weak and useless, and knowledge without integrity is dangerous and dreadful.
Ben Jonson: If he were / To be made honest by an act of Parliament / I should not alter my faith in him.
Juvenal: Integrity is praised and starves.
Rudyard Kipling: But he couldn't lie if you paid him, and he'd starve before he stole.
John Lyly: He that loseth his honesty, hath nothing else to lose.
John Lyly: The measure of life is not length, but honesty.
O'Henry: He injects a few sweet raisins of (EDITOR: truth/honest) conversation into the tasteless dough of our existence.
Ovid: It is annoying to be honest to no purpose.
Alexander Pope: An honest man's the noblest work of God.
Will Rogers: I have just enough white in me to make my honesty questionable.

Will Rogers: Things ain't what they used to be and never were.

Will Rogers: All I know is just what I read in the papers, and that's an alibi for my ignorance.

Will Rogers: "Ability is all right but if it is not backed up by honesty and public confidence you will never be a (successful person). The best a man can do is to arrive at the top in his chosen profession. I have always maintained that one profession is deserving of as much honor as another provided it is honorable." August 17, 1924.

Will Rogers: Shrewdness in Public Life all over the World is always honored, while honesty in Public Men is generally attributed to Dumbness and is seldom rewarded.

Seneca: Never too late is trod the path to honesty.

William Shakespeare (*All's Well that Ends Well*, Act I, iii): Though honestly be no puritan, yet it will do no hurt; it will wear the surplice of humility over the black gown of a big heart.

William Shakespeare (*All's Well that Ends Well*, Act III, v): No legacy is so rich as honesty.

William Shakespeare (*As You Like It*, Act V, iv): Rich honesty dwells like a miser, sir, in a poor house; as your pearl in your foul oyster.

William Shakespeare (*Hamlet*, Act I, iii): This above all: to thine own self be true, / And it must follow, as the night the day, / Thou canst not then be false to any man.

William Shakespeare (*Hamlet*, Act II, ii): HAMLET: What's the news? ROSENCRANTZ: None, my lord; but that the world's grown honest. HAMLET: Then is dooms-day near.

William Shakespeare (*Hamlet*, Act II, ii): Ay, sir; to be honest, as this world goes, is to be one man picked out of ten thousand.

William Shakespeare (*Hamlet*, Act III, i, HAMLET to OPHELIA): Ha, ha! Are you honest? / OPHELIA: My lord? / HAMLET: Are you fair? / OPHELIA: What means your lordship? HAMLET: That if you be honest and fair, your honesty should admit no discourse to your beauty.

William Shakespeare (*Hamlet*, Act III, i): I am myself indifferent honest.

William Shakespeare (*Hamlet*, Act IV, iv): Rightly to be great / Is not to stir without great argument, / But greatly to find quarrel in a straw / When honour's at the stake.

William Shakespeare (*I Henry IV*, Act I, ii): There is neither honesty, manhood, nor good fellowship in thee.

William Shakespeare (*Julius Caesar*, Act IV, iii): There is no terror, Cassius, in your threats; / For I am arm'd so strong in honesty / That they pass by me as the idle wind.

William Shakespeare (*The Merry Wives of Windsor*, Act I, iv): An honest maid as ever broke bread.

William Shakespeare (*Much Ado About Nothing*, Act III, i): An old man, sir, and his wits are not so blunt, as, God help, I would desire they were; but, in faith, honest as the skin between his brows.

William Shakespeare (*Much Ado About Nothing*, Act III, iv): I thank God I am as honest as any man living that is an old man and no honester then I.

William Shakespeare (*Much Ado About Nothing*, Act III, v): An honest soul... as ever broke bread.

William Shakespeare (*Othello*, Act III, iii): Take note, take note, O world, / To be direct and honest is not safe.

William Shakespeare (*Othello*, Act III, iii): Honesty is a fool / And loses that it works for.

William Shakespeare (*Richard III*, Act IV, iii): An honest tale speeds best, being plainly told.

William Shakespeare (*Timon of Athens*, Act I, iii): I do proclaim / One honest man - mistake me not – but one; / No more, I pray – and he's a steward.

William Shakespeare (*Timon of Athens*, Act II, ii): At many times I brought in my accounts; / Laid them before you; you would throw them off, / And say, you found them in mine honesty.

William Shakespeare (*Timon of Athens*, Act III, i): Everyman has his fault, and honesty is his.

William Shakespeare (*The Two Gentlemen of Verona*, Act II, vii): His heart as far from fraud as heaven from earth.

William Shakespeare (*The Winter's Tale*, Act IV, iii): Ha, ha! What a fool Honesty is! and Trust, / his sworn brother, a very simple gentlemen!

William Shakespeare (*The Winter's Tale*, Act IV, iv): Though I am naturally honest, I am so sometimes by chance.

George Bernard Shaw: I am afraid we must make the world honest before we can honestly say to our children that honesty is the best policy.

Socrates: Integrity is better than charity. The gods approve of the depth and not of the tumult of the soul.
Talmud: Magilla, 16a: As my mouth, so my heart.
David Tuvill (1638): Honesty is the best policy.
Mark Twain: I was gratified to be able to answer promptly, and I did. I said I didn't know.
Mark Twain: A pretty air in an opera is prettier there than it could be anywhere else, I suppose, just as an honest man in politics shines more than he would elsewhere.

HUMOR (See COMEDY)

HUSBANDS (See MARRIAGE; MAN)

HYPOCRACY (See PRINCIPLE)

IDEAS (See THINKING/THOUGHT)

IDIOCY/IDIOT (See CONSISTENCY; FAILURE; FOOL; IGNORANCE)

IGNORANCE/INCOMPETENCE (See also CONSISTENCY; FAILURE; FOOL; INSULTS; NEGLIGENCE)

Uncle Anthony: Why is it that the people who know the least know it the loudest?
Uncle Anthony: For those guys, every morning is "the dawn of a new error."
Uncle Anthony: She's got a terrific stairway, but nuttin' upstairs.
Uncle Anthony: An intelligent idea dies quick in his head – it can't stand solitary confinement!
Uncle Anthony: They're always given ya a piece of their mind – an they can least afford it.
Uncle Anthony: I think he's a GROSS ignoramus/idiot – he's 144 times worse than an ordinary ignoramus/idiot.
Aunt Mary Carlo: He's like a blotter – he takes everytin in, but then gets it ass-backwards!
Aunt Mary Carlo: She must have a sixth sense – I don't see dat she's got de udder five woikin (working).
Aunt Mary Carlo: He keeps loinin (learning) more and more about less and less, pretty soon he'll know everythin' about nuttin'!
Aunt Mary Carlo: I tink he's recoverin' from an accident – a thought just struck 'em!
Aunt Mary Carlo: I read dat light travels at 186,000 miles per second – well, it ain't reached his mind yet!
Aunt Mary Carlo: I tink he ran inta an accident dat started out ta happen to somebody else.
Aunt Mary Carlo: Yer Uncle picked a horse he was sure would win ina walk – problem was da udder horses ran.
Arabic Proverb: When a learned man errs, he errs with a learned error.
Aristotle: The difference between an educated and an uneducated man is the same difference as between being alive and being dead.
Isaac Asimov: Violence is the last refuge of the incompetent.
Yogi Berra: You've gotta be careful if you don't know where you're going because you might not get there.
Aneurin Bevan: This island (England) is made up mainly of coal and surrounded by fish. Only an organizing genius could produce a shortage of coal and fish at the same time.
Bible: 1 Corinthians 8:2: If any man think that he knoweth anything, he knoweth nothing yet as he ought to know.
Bible: Job 35:16: He multiplieth words without knowledge.
Bible: John 12:35: He that walketh in darkness knoweth not whither he goeth.
Bible: Matthew 7:6: Neither cast ye pearls before swine, lest they trample them under their feet, and turn again and rend you.
Bible: Matthew 13:13: They seeing see not; and hearing they hear not, neither do they understand.
Bible: Matthew 15:14: If the blind lead the blind, both shall fall into the ditch.
Bible: 1 Peter 2:15: With well doing ye may put to silence the ignorance of foolish men.
Bible: Proverbs 19:2: That the soul be without knowledge, it is not good.

Ambrose Bierce: IDIOT, n. A member of a large and powerful tribe whose influence in human affairs has always been dominant and controlling.

Ambrose Bierce: IGNORAMOUS, n. A person unacquainted with certain kinds of knowledge familiar to yourself, and having certain other kinds that you know nothing about.

Ambrose Bierce: ILLUMINATI, n. A sect of Spanish heretics of the later part of the sixteenth century; so called because they were light weights – *cunctationes illuminati.*

Ambrose Bierce: IMBECILITY, n. A kind of divine inspiration, or sacred fire affecting censorious critics of this dictionary (*The Devil's Dictionary).*

Ambrose Bierce: RELIGION, n. A daughter of Hope and Fear, explaining to Ignorance the nature of the Unknowable.

Gamaliel Bradford: Ignorance is the curse of the age we live in. We talk about the dark ages. When was there one so dark as this? We have smothered ourselves, buried ourselves, in the vast heap of information which all of us have and none of us has.

Lois McMaster Bujold: The will to be stupid is a very powerful force, but there are always alternatives.

Burmese Proverb: A man with little learning is like a frog who thinks its puddle is a great sea.

George Carlin: Most people don't know what you're doing. And a lot of them are really good at it.

Thomas Carlyle: A man doesn't know what he knows until he knows what he does not know.

Chinese Proverb: Ignorance is the night of the mind.

Chinese Proverb: A wise man makes his own decisions, an ignorant man follows the public opinion.

Sir Winston Churchill: A fanatic is one who can't change his mind and won't change the subject.

Victor Cousin: Ignorance is the primary source of all misery and vice.

Quentin Crisp: The English think that incompetence is the same thing as sincerity.

John Dewey: Genuine ignorance is... profitable because it is likely to be accompanied by humility, curiosity, and open-mindedness; whereas ability to repeat catch phrases, cant terms, familiar propositions, gives the conceit of a learning and coats the mind with a varnish, waterproof to new ideas.

Will Durant: Education is the progressive discovery of our own ignorance.

Albert Einstein: Only two things are infinite, the universe and human stupidity, and I'm not sure about the former.

English Proverb: He that hath a head of wax must not walk in the sun.

Sam Ewing: Every year education gets more expensive, but ignorance costs even more.

Enrico Fermi: It is no good to try to stop knowledge from going forward. Ignorance is never better than knowledge.

Henry Ford: What we call evil is simply ignorance bumping its head in the dark.

Benjamin Franklin: A learned blockhead is a greater blockhead than an ignorant one.

Galileo Galilei: I have never met a man so ignorant that I could not learn something from him.

James Cardinal Gibbons: A young levite once remarked to his professor: "God can dispense with my learning." "Yes," was the reply, "but He has still less need of your ignorance."

Johann Wolfgang von Goethe: There is nothing worse than aggressive stupidity.

Thomas Gray (English poet, 1716-1771; *Ode to a Distant Prospect of Eton College*): Where ignorance is bliss, 'tis folly to be wise.

Philip G. Hamerton: Men are qualified for their work by knowledge, but they are also negatively qualified for it by their ignorance.... If we have any kind of efficiency, very much of it is owing to our narrowness, which is favourable to a powerful individuality.

Hasidic Saying: For the ignorant, old age is winter; for the learned, old age is the harvest.

Sir Arthur Helps: How exactly proportioned to a man's ignorance of the subject is the noise he makes about it at a public meeting.

Frank McKinney Hubbard ("Kin Hubbard"): 'Taint what a man don't know that hurts him; it's what he knows that just ain't so.

Hungarian Proverb: An ox remains an ox, even if driven to Vienna.

Aldous Huxley: A chip on the shoulder is a sure sign that there is more wood higher up.

Aldous Huxley: The pleasures of ignorance are as great, in their way, as the pleasures of knowledge.

Robert Jackson: The price of freedom of religion, or of speech, or of the press, is that we must put up with a good deal of rubbish.

Japanese Proverb: Darkness reigns at the foot of the lighthouse.

Thomas Jefferson: Ignorance is preferable to error; and he is less remote from the truth who believes nothing, than he who believes what is wrong.

Jewish Proverb: The greatest luck of an *am ha-arets* (ignoramus) is this: he doesn't know that he doesn't know. (*am ha-arets*: Hebrew: "people of the soil;" described in the Talmud as one who does not respect the Law; Maimonides says "a boor in whom is neither learning nor moral virtue; an ignoramus)

Jewish Saying: When a *nebekh* leaves the room, you feel as if someone came in.

Jewish Saying: A *shlemiel* is always knocking things off a table, and the nebekh always picks them up.

Jewish Saying: Ony the ignorant are really poor.

Jewish Saying: Even a blind hen sometimes finds a grain.

Jewish Saying: Wiseman, grown older, grown wiser; ignorant men, grown older, grown more foolish.

Jewish Saying: Some are so stupid they must search for a notch in a saw.

Jewish Saying: Drunkards can sober up, but the stupid remains stupid.

Jewish Saying: The stupid do not even understand stupidity.

Jewish Saying: Educating the stupid does not teach them how to be smart.

Jewish Saying: When the smart talk to the stupid, both act like fools.

Jewish Saying: No one is as deaf as the man who will not listen.

Jewish Saying: A dream uninterpreted is like a letter unopened.

Arte Johnson (as a bespectacled Nazi soldier with thick German accent on *Rowan and Martin's Laugh-In* in the 1960's): Verrrrry Interrrrresting ... but stupid!

Lynden B. Johnson: If two men agree on everything, you may be sure that one of them is doing the thinking.

Martin Luther King, Jr.: Nothing in the world is more dangerous than sincere ignorance and concientious stupidity.

Latin Proverb: Hay is more acceptable to an ass than gold.

Frank Leahy: Egotism is the anesthetic that chills the pain of stupidity.

Doris Lessing: In university they don't tell you that the greater part of the law is learning to tolerate fools.

Michael A. Musmanno (Justice of Pa. Supreme Court, 1959): How all this can be done in this age of a supposedly more sensitive appreciation of the rights of the accused is a riddle, wrapped in a mystery, enveloped in an enigma, and concealed in a labyrinth of inexplicability.

Dorothy Parker (speaking about Harold Ross, Editor of the New Yorker): His ignorance was an Empire State Building of ignorance. You had to admire it for its size.

Laurence J. Peter: Against logic there is no armor like ignorance.

Plato: We can easily forgive a child who is afraid of the dark; the real tragedy of life is when men are afraid of the light.

Edgar Allan Poe: I have great faith in fools; self-confidence, my friends call it.

Alexander Pope: Some people will never learn anything because they understand everything too soon.

Ronald Reagan (speaking about his critics): They sort of remind me of the fellow who was asked which was worse, ignorance or apathy, and he said, "I don't know and I don't care."

J.K. Rowling: Indifference and neglect often do much more damage then outright dislike.

Will Rogers: Everyone is ignorant, only on different subjects.

Will Rogers: It ain't what a man don't know that hurts him; it's what he knows that just ain't so.

Will Rogers: An ignorant person is one who doesn't know what you have just found out.

Will Rogers: When ignorance gets started it knows no bounds.

Will Rogers: There is nothing so stupid as the educated man if you get him off the thing he was educated in.

Will Rogers: If Stupidity got us into this mess, then why can't it get us out?

Will Rogers: America is becoming so educated that ignorance will be a novelty. I will belong to the select few.

Will Rogers: Shrewdness in Public Life all over the World is always honored, while honesty in Public Men is generally attributed to Dumbness and is seldom rewarded.

Leo Rosten: NEBEKH (NEBBECH): In the vocabulary of character types, woven out of pity, candor and insight, *nebekh* stands (along with nudnick, shlemiel, shlimazl, shnuk, shmendrick, yold, Chaim Yankel, shlepper) in that pantheon of special Yiddish words coined to describe the ineffectuals of this world (For definitions, see... The Joys of Yiddish,...) *"Nebekh"* is both a noun and an interjection. As a noun, it means an innocuous nonentity, a helpless, hapless soul—first cousin to a *shlemiel.* But whereas one may dislike a *shlemiel* it is hard to feel anything but sympathy for a *nebekh*. As an interjection, *nebekh* means "alas... too bad... unfortunately..." expressing affectionate dismay, regret, or commiseration.

Leo Rosten: SCHLEMIEL: "... a *schlemiel*, though closely related to a *shlimaz*, is more precisely a simpleton, a gull, a pipsqueak; clumsy, submissive, uncomplaining, naïve; a Casper Milquetoast writ large—and in Yiddish.

Leo Rosten: SHLEMAZL: "The word comes from the German *schlimm* ("bad") and the Hebrew *mazl* ("lock"), but a *shlemazl* is thought of as more than simply unlucky. He is a chronic loser, Patsy, fall-guy, pigeon.... a *shlemazl* also may be characterized in psychiatric nomenclature as one predisposed to be victimized, one "accident prone." So *shlemazl* conveys the idea of one doomed (innocently) to fail and (perhaps) masochistically inclined to cooperate with the inequitable fates.

Leo Rosten: When a *shlemazl* (luckless one) buys a suit with two pair of pants he promptly burns to hole in the jacket; if he sold umbrellas, it would stop raining; if he sold candles, the sun would never set; and if he made coffins, people would stop dying.

Russian Proverb: There is plenty of sound in an empty barrel.

Arthur Schopenhauer: Every person takes the limits of their own field of vision for the limits of the world.

William Shakespeare (*Henry VI,* Act I, ii): Ignorance is the curse of God, Knowledge the wing wherewith we fly to heaven.

William Shakespeare (*Henry V,* Act IV, iv): The saying is true, / "The empty vessel makes the greatest sound."

William Shakespeare (*Love's Labour's Lost,* Act I, i): That unlettered, small-knowing soul.

William Shakespeare (*Love's Labour's Lost,* Act IV, ii): O thou monster ignorance, how deformed dost thou look!

William Shakespeare (*Much Ado About Nothing,* Act III, iii): Well, for your favour, sir, why, give God thanks, and make no boast of it; and for your writing and reading, let that appear when there is no need of such vanity.

William Shakespeare (*Much Ado About Nothing,* Act IV, i): O, what men dare do! What men may do! What men daily do, not knowing, what they do!

William Shakespeare (*Twelfth Night,* Act IV, ii): There is no darkness but ignorance.

William Shakespeare (*Twelfth Night,* Act IV, ii): Madam, thou errest: I say, there is no darkness, but ignorance; in which thou art more puzzled, than the Egyptians in their fog.

William Shakespeare (*The Winter's Tale,* Act I, ii): One good deed dying tongueless / Slaughters a thousand waiting upon that.

George Bernard Shaw: He knows nothing; he thinks he knows everything. That points clearly to a political career.

George Bernard Shaw: When a stupid man is doing something he is ashamed of, he always declares that it is his duty.

Ben Sirach: Don't make fun of the ignorant: you may be maligning your ancestry.

Logan Pearsall Smith: Uncultivated minds are not full of wild flowers, like uncultivated fields. Villainous weeds grow in them, and they are full of toads.

Sydney Smith: Have the courage to be ignorant of a great number of things, in order to avoid the calamity of being ignorant of everything.

Sophocles: Ignorant men / Don't know what good they hold in their hands until / They've flung it away.

Edith Sitwell: I am patient with stupidity, but not with those who are proud of it.

Thomas Szasz: The stupid never forgive nor forget; the naïve forgive and forget; the wise forgive but do not forget.

Talmud: The ignorant think less clearly as they grow older; scholars think more clearly as they age.

Leo Tolstoy: In all types of activity it is important to know how to stop before what you do not know and not to think that you know what you do not know.

Mark Twain: Let us be thankful for the fools. But for them the rest of us could not succeed.

Mark Twain: Don't you know, there are some things that can beat smartness and foresight? Awkwardness and stupidity can. The best swordsman in the world doesn't need to fear the second best swordsman in the world; no, the person for him to be afraid of is some ignorant antagonist who has never had a sword in his hand before; he doesn't do the thing he ought to.

Bill Veeck: I have discovered, in twenty years of moving around a ball park, that the knowledge of the game is usually in inverse proportion to the price of the seats.

Bill Veeck: The Mets achieved total incompetence in a single year, while the Browns worked industriously for almost a decade to gain equal proficiency.

Gore Vidal: Half of the American people have never read a newspaper. Half never voted for president. One hopes it is the same half.

Edward Bennett Williams (past owner of Washington Senators, who welcomed the former Baseball Commissioner Peter Ueberroth to his first MLB baseball owners meeting saying): Welcome to the den of village idiots!

Woodrow Wilson: You get a great deal more light on the street than you do in the closet. You get a good deal more light by keeping your ears open among the rank and file of your fellow citizens than you do in any private conference whatever.

W.B. Yeats: I myself know the sense of strain that comes when one speaks to ignorant or, still worse, half-ignorant men. There is a perpetual temptation not merely to over-simplification but to exaggeration, for all ignorant thought is exaggerated thought.

INDICTMENT (See ALLEGATION)

INDUSTRIOUSNESS (See WORK)

INFERENCE (See EVIDENCE)

INJURY (See DAMAGES; JUSTICE; PAIN; WRONGDOING)

INSPIRATION (See MOTIVE/MOTIVATION)

INSULTS … WITH CLASS (See also IGNORANCE)

Uncle Anthony: Give him enough rope and he'll wind up hanging you.

Uncle Anthony: He ain't a complete idiot – some parts are missing.

Uncle Anthony: Some speakers are a "Baltimore hop": they're a legitimate hit, but more style and bounce than substance.

Uncle Anthony: He/she/they treated me just like family ... LIKE THE GAMBINO FAMILY!!"

Uncle Anthony: They broke the mold BEFORE they made him.

Uncle Anthony: He was not a missile drawn to heat of a new idea.

Uncle Anthony: Y'know, he should wipe his mouth after speaking ... there's still a little bullsh-t left around his lips!

Uncle Anthony: Don't let the door hit ya where the Good Lord split ya!

Uncle Anthony: The closest that guy ever got to buying his wife jewelry was buying her onion rings!

Aunt Mary Carlo: I hear ya changed yer mind ... whaddidyado with the diaper?

Aunt Mary Carlo: Don't let yer mind wander ... it's too small to be let out on its own

Aunt Mary Carlo: You're not (acting) yourself today ... and I noticed the improvement immediately!

Aunt Mary Carlo: If you have something to say, raise your hand ... and place it over yer mouth!

Aunt Mary Carlo: I don't know what yer problem is ... but I bet it's something very hard to pronounce!

Aunt Mary Carlo: Shhhh! Listen ... that's the sound of nobody caring what you think!

Aunt Mary Carlo: Did you guys eat an extra bowl of STUPID this morning?!

Aunt Mary Carlo: I'd 'tink da cops'd say dat his "identy theft" outta be classified as a petty offence!

Aunt Mary Carlo: When dey talk about he's gotta "BROADBAND" – 'dere talkin about his pants NOT HIS RADIO!

Joey Adams (speaking about President Jimmy Carter): Jimmy's basic problem is that he is supercautious. He looks before and after he leaps.

Fisher Ames: The gentleman puts me in mind of an old hen which persists in setting after her eggs are taken away. (speaking about an opposing counsel)
Albanian Saying: After shaking hands with a Greek, count your fingers.
Fred Allen: What's on your mind, if you will allow the overstatement?
Clive Anderson (speaking about Jeffrey Archer): Is there no beginning to your talents?
Julie Andrews: She needs open heart surgery, and they should go in through her feet.
Arab Curse: May your left ear wither and fall into your right pocket.
Tom Arnold: Roseanne Barr went on Saturday Night Live and said I had a three-inch penis. Well, even a 747 looks small if it is landing in the Grand Canyon!
Lady Asquith (about Sir Strafford Cripps): He has a brilliant mind until it is made up.
Margo Asquith (about David Lloyd George): He can't see a belt without hitting below it.
Kenneth Baker (about David own): He has conferred on the practice of desolation though our up of statesmanship.
Arthur James Balfour (speaking about Sir Winston Churchill): I thought he was a young man of promise, but it appears he is a young man of promise is.
Lucille Ball: Katharine Hepburn is not really stand-offish. She ignores everyone equally
Tallulah Bankhead (to Tennessee Williams after seeing the film of Orpheus Descending): Darling, they have positively ruined your perfectly dreadful play.
Tallulah Bankhead (speaking to young actress): If you really want to help the American theater Darling, be an audience.
Tallulah Bankhead (writing to a critic): I am sitting in the smallest room of the house. Your review is before me. Soon it will be behind me.
Tallulah Bankhead (speaking about Bette Davis): Betty and I are good friends. There's nothing I would not say were face—both of them.
J. M. Barrie: She was a large woman who seemed not so much dressed as upholstered.
John Barrymore: I have previous engagement which I shall make as soon as possible.
Louise Beale: Love thy neighbor as yourself, but choose your neighborhood.
Alan Bennett (speaking about Arianna Stassinopoulos): She was so boring you fall asleep halfway through her name.
Ingrid Bergman (speaking about Sir Winston Churchill): He would rather make love to a word than to a woman.
Bernhardt: Oscar Wilde: Do you mind if I smoke? Sarah Bernhardt: I don't care if you burn!
Aneurin Bevan (about Harold McMillan): The Prime Minister has an absolute genius for putting flamboyant labels on empty luggage.
Aneurin Bevan (about Clement Atlee): He brings to the fierce struggle of politics the tepid enthusiasm of a lazy summer afternoon at a cricket match.
Aneurin Bevan (speaking about Sir Winston Churchill): The mediocrity of his thinking is concealed by the majesty of his language.
Bible: Apocrypha, Ecclesiasticus 28:17: The blow of the whip raises a welt, but a blow of the tongue crushes bones.
Bible: 1 Corinthians 10:12: Let him that thinketh he standeth take heed lest he fall.
Bible: Ecclesiastes 7:21: Take no heed unto all words that are spoken; lest thou hear thy servant curse thee.
Bible: Isaiah 5:21: Woe unto them that are wise in their own eyes, and prudent in their own sight!
Bible: Romans 2:1: Wherein thou judgest another, thou condemnest thyself.
Ambrose Bierce (about Oscar Wilde): The sovereign of insufferable. He had nothing to say and he said it.
Ambrose Bierce: IMPIETY, n. Your irreverence toward my diety.
Ambrose Bierce: REPARTEE, n. Prudent insult in retort. Practiced by gentlemen with a constitutional aversion to violence, but a strong disposition to offend. In a war of words, the tactics of the North American Indian.
Ambrose Bierce: WASHINGTONIAN, n. A Potomac tribesman who exchanged the privilege of governing himself for the advantage of good government. In justice to him it should be said that he did not want to.

Ambrose Bierce: WEREWOLF, n. A wolf that was once, or is sometimes, a man.All werewolves are of evil disposition, having assumed a bestial form to gratify a bestial appetite, but some, transformed by sorcery, are as humane as is consistent with an acquired taste for human flesh.

Ambrose Bierce: YANKEE, n. In Europe an American. In the Northern States of our Union, a New Englander. In the Southern States the word is unknown. (See DAMYANK.)

Paltney Bigelow (about Theodore Roosevelt): An excellent specimen of genus AMERICANUS EGOTISTICUS.

Stephen Bishop: I feel so miserable without you, it's almost like having you here.

Marlon Brando (speaking about Montgomery Clift): He acts like he's got a mixmaster up his ass and does not want anyone to know it.

John Bright: Disraeli is a self-made man who worships his creator.

Bellamy Brooks: Egotism is the anesthetic given by a kindly nature to relieve the pain of being a damned fool.

William F. Buckley, Jr.: Liberals claim to want to give a hearing to other views, but then are shocked and offended to discover that there are other views.

Julie Burchill (speaking about Camille Paglia): The 'g' is silent—that is the only thing about her that is.

Richard Burton (giving advice to fellow actors): If you are going to make rubbish, be the best rubbish in it.

George H.W. Bush (about Michael Dukakis): He is the Stealth candidate. His campaign jets from place to place, but no issue show up on the radar screen.

Sir Thomas Buxton: I once met a man who had forgiven an injury. I hope some day to meet a man who has forgiven an insult.

Carlisle Indian Industrial School insult: May Cerberus bite you when you reach the Styxx.

Johnny Carson (speaking about Rona Barrett): She doesn't need a steak knife—she cuts her food with her tongue.

Angela Carter: She looked like $1 million, I must admit, even if in well-used notes.

James Carville: As with mosquitoes, horse flies, and most blood sucking parasites, Kenneth Starr was spawned in stagnant water.

John Cassavetes: Ricardo Montalban is to improvised acting what Mount Rushmore is to animation.

Chinese Ancient Curse: May your every wish be granted.

Sir Winston Churchill: NANCY ASTOR: Winston, if you were my husband, I should flavor your coffee with poison. **Sir Winston Churchill:** Madam, if I were your husband I should drink it.

Sir Winston Churchill: He has all the virtues I dislike and none of the vices I admire.

Sir Winston Churchill: GEORGE BERNARD SHAW to Winston Churchill: "I am enclosing two tickets to the first night of my new Play, bring a friend... if you have one." WINSTON CHURCHILL, in response: "Cannot possibly attend first night, will attend second...if there is one."

Sir Winston Churchill (about Woodrow Wilson): The spacious philanthropy which he exhaled upon Europe stopped quite sharply at the coasts of his own country.

Sir Winston Churchill (about Stanley Baldwin): He occasionally stumbles over the truth, but he always hastily picks itself up and hurries long as if nothing had happened.

Sir Winston Churchill (about Clement Atlee): He is a sheep in sheep's clothing.

Sir Winston Churchill (about Clement Atlee): A modest little man with much to the modest about.

Sir Winston Churchill (about Lord Charles Beresford): He is one of those orators of whom it was well said: "Before they get up, they do not know what they are going to say; when they are speaking, they do not know what they are saying; and when they have sat down, they do not know what they have said."

Sir Winston Churchill (about William Gladstone): Mr. Gladstone read Homer for fun, which I thought served him right.

Sir Winston Churchill (about Ramsay Macdonald, January 28, 1931): I have waited 50 years to see the boneless wonder (Ramsay Macdonald) sitting on the Treasury Bench.

Sir Winston Churchill (about Field Marshal Montgomerie): In defeat unbeatable: in victory unbearable.

Sir Winston Churchill (about the German emperor, during WWI, Kaiser William II): At every crisis the Kaiser crumpled. In defeat he fled; in revolution he abdicated; in exile he remarried.

Sir Winston Churchill: Member of Parliament (MP) to Winston Churchill: Must you fall asleep while I'm speaking? WINSTON CHURCHILL reply: No, it is purely voluntary.

Sir Winston Churchill (In a heated controversy with the judge): The JUDGE said to Churchill: "Young man, you are extremely offensive." CHURCHILL replied: "Yes, we both are. But I am trying to be, and you can't help yourself."

Sir Winston Churchill: The English never draw a line without blurring it.

Sir Winston Churchill: I may be drunk, Miss, but in the morning I will be sober and you will still be ugly.

Sir Winston Churchill: We have always found the Irish a bit odd. They refuse to be English.

Henry Clay: He said he spoke for posterity... and he seemed resolved to speak until the arrival of his audience.

Hillary Rodham Clinton (speaking about Bill Clinton): He is a hard dog to keep on the porch.

Jean Cocteau: "We must believe in luck. For how else can we explain the success of [X, or] those we don't like."

Irvin S. Cobb: "I've just learned about his illness. Let's hope it's nothing trivial."

Cyril Connolly (speaking about George Orwell): He would not blow his nose without moralizing on the conditions in the handkerchief industry.

Sherwin L. Cook: Calvin Coolidge's perpetual expression was that of someone smelling something burning on a stove.

Noel Coward (speaking about Randolph Churchill): He is utterly unspoiled by failure.

Noel Coward (speaking to Claudette Colbert): I would ring your neck—if you had won!

Joan Crawford (speaking about Judy Garland): I did not know her well, but after watching her in action I did not want to.

Clarence Darrow (responding to a news reporter's criticism of his appearance): I go to better tailors than any of you and I pay more for my clothes. The only difference is that you probably do not sleeping in yours.

Clarence Darrow: I have never killed a man, but I have read many obituaries with great pleasure.

Clarence Darrow (about William Jennings Bryan, 1925): He is "The Idol of Morondom!"

Bette Davis (speaking about Joan Crawford): She always cries a lot. Her tear ducts must be close to her bladder.

Bette Davis: She was the original good time that was had by all.

Charles de Gaulle: The graveyards are fulll of indispensable man.

Charles de Gaulle (speaking about Sir Winston Churchill): When I am right, I get angry. Churchill gets angry when he is wrong. We are angry at each other much of the time.

Benjamin Disraeli (speaking about Gladstone): A misfortune is if Gladstone fell into the Thames; a calamity would be if someone pulled him out.

Benjamin Disraeli (about Sir Robert Peel): The right honorable gentleman's file is like the silver fittings on a coffin.

Benjamin Disraeli (about Sir Robert Peel): The right honorable gentleman is reminiscent of a poker. The only difference is the poker gives off the occasional signs of warmth.

Alice K. Dormann: I wouldn't take his word for good morning till I looked out and saw the sun.

Will Durst: Walter Mondale has all the charisma of a speed bump.

Queen Elizabeth I (1549, regarding Lord Admiral Thomas Seymour, allegedly her lover, beheaded for treason): "This day died a man with much wit and very little judgement."

English Saying: The Spaniard is a bad servant but a worse master.

English saying (during "The Battle of Britain" of WWII when Joseph Kennedy fled London): I thought my daffodils were yellow before I met Joe Kennedy. (Joseph Kennedy was US Ambassador to England in 1940).

English saying (by and about women): The difference between Gladstone and Disraeli is: Mr. Gladstone took me to a theater play and at the end of the evening I was convinced *HE* was the most sophisticated, intelligent, and charming person in the world; Mr. Disraeli took me to the opera and at the end of the evening I was convinced *I* was the most sophisticated, intelligent and charming person in the world.

Clifton Fadiman (speaking about Clare Booth Luce): No woman of her time has gone further with less mental equipment.

William Faulkner (about Ernest Hemingway): He has never been known to use a word that might send a reader to the dictionary.

Henry Fielding: There is an insolence which none but those who themselves deserve contempt can bestow, and those who deserve no contempt can bear.

W.C. Fields: Charlie McCarthy: Mr. Fields, I read in the paper were you consumed 2 qts. of liquor a day. What would your father think about that? WC Fields: he'd think I was a sissy!

James Elroy Flecker: Thy impudence hath a monstrous beauty likened to the hind quarters of an elephant.

Michael Foote (about Norman Tebbit): It is not necessary that every time he rises he should give us his famous imitation of a semi-housetrained polecat.

Glenn Ford (speaking about Joan Crawford): She had perfect posture, but it was rather intimidating. She looked as if she had swallowed a yardstick.

Sigmund Freud: The first human being who hurled an insult instead of a stone was the founder of civilization.

David Frost: He has left his body to science—and science is contesting the will.

Zsa Zsa Gabor: News reporter: how many husbands have you had? Zsa Zsa. Gabor: you mean, apart from my own?

Ava Gardner (speaking about Clark Gable): He's the kind of guy who, if you say, "Hi Clark how are you?", he gets stuck for an answer.

Judy Garland (speaking about Lana Turner): She's a nice girl, but it's like sitting in a room with a beautiful vase.

David Lloyd George: Someone introduced him as a man of quite small stature. Lloyd George remarked: in North Wales, we measure a man from his chin up. You evidently measure from his chin down.

David Lloyd George: He would make a drum out of the skin of his mother in order to sound his own praises.

German Saying: The Russian knows the way, yet he asks for directions.

German Saying: An ass in Germany is a professor in Rome.

German Saying: He who would eat in Spain must bring his kitchen along.

William S. Gilbert: She may very well be past 40—in the dark and with a light behind her.

Barry Goldwater (about Senator William Scott): If he were any dumber, he would be a tree.

Kelsey Grammer: I'm not saying you have a fat face, I just keep wondering how long you are going to store those nuts in your mouth for winter.

General Ulysses Simpson Grant (American general and US President, 1822-1885; Responding to an officer's remark that a certain officer had been through 10 campaigns, General Grant remarked): So is that mule over yonder, but he's still a jackass!

Horace Greeley: A congressman told me that he was a self-made man. That's certainly relieved the Almighty of a great responsibility.

Gypsy Curse: May you wander over the face of the earth forever, never sleep twice in the same bed, never drink water twice from the same well, and never cross the same river twice in a year.

Moses Hadas: "Thank you for sending me a copy of your book; I'll waste no time reading it."

Alexander Hamilton (Referring to his opponent Theophilis Parsons): I have known gentlemen to split a hair, and I may have tried to do it myself. But I never before saw any one decimate a hair and count the pieces before the court.

Bob Hawke (about Malcolm Fraser): He is the cutlery man of Australian politics. He was born with the silver spoon is mouth, speaks with a forked tongue, and knives his colleagues in the back.

Lillian Hellman (speaking about Norma Shearer): She had a face unclouded by thought.

Ernest Hemingway (about William Faulkner): "Poor Faulkner. Does he really think big emotions come from big words?"

John Heywood (*The Proverbs of John Heywood,* 1546): Butter would not melt in her mouth.

Alfred Hitchcock: Mary Anderson: what you think is my best side? Alfred Hitchcock: my dear, you are sitting on it.

Oliver Wendell Holmes, Jr.: I could carve out of a banana a judge with more backbone than that.

Polly Holliday (as the Southern-born waitress Flo Castelberry, in the American TV sit com *Alice*, 1976-1980): Kiss my grits!

Sam Houston (referring to Thomas Jefferson Green): He has all the characteristics of a dog – except loyalty.

Howard Hughes (speaking about Clark Gable): His years make him look like a taxicab with both doors open.

Howard Hughes (speaking to Robert Mitchum): You are like a pay toilet, aren't you? You don't give a shit for nothing.

Aldus Huxley: A chip on the shoulder is a sure indication that there is more wood higher up.

Washington Irving: A sharp tongue is the only edged tool that grows keener with constant use.

Molly Ivins: I have been attacked by Rush Limbaugh on the air, an experience somewhat akin to being gummed by a newt. It doesn't actually hurt, but it leaves you with slimy stuff on your ankle.

Molly Ivins (about Dick Armey): If ignorance ever goes to $40 a barrel, I want drillin' rights on that man's head.

Molly Ivins: Last week, I began a sentence saying, "If (X) had any imagination ..." and then I hit myself. Silly me.

Molly Ivins (about the state of Texas): I dearly love (X), but I consider that a harmless perversion on my part, and discuss it only with consenting adults.

Irish Traditional Curse: May the curse of Mary Malone and her nine blind illegitimate children chase you so far over the hills of Damnation that the Lord himself can't find you with a telescope.

Irish Saying: As sluttish and slatternly as an Irishwoman bred in France.

Italian Proverb: He who puts up with insult invites injury.

Clive James (speaking about John McEnroe): He has hair like badly turned broccoli.

Douglas Jerrod: Sir, you are like a pin, but without either its head or its point.

Sir George Jessel (English judge, 1824-1883, Reply to Attorney General Coleridge when asked if he had any doubts regarding a recent issue under discussion, Jessel admitted that the story was true but rebuked what AG's misquotation of what Jessel ahd said by adding): "Coleridge, with his constitutional inaccuracy has told it wrong. I can never have said 'Often wrong.' **I may be wrong, and often am, but never in doubt.**

Jewish Saying: The eggs want to be smarter than the hens.

Lyndon B. Johnson (speaking about the Association of American States): They couldn't pour piss out of their shoe if the instructions were written on the heel!

Samuel Johnson: He is not only dull himself, he is the cause of dullness in others.

Samuel Johnson: Whatever be the motive of an insult it is always best to overlook it; for folly scarcely can deserve resentment, and malice is punished by neglect.

Junius: Oppression is more easily borne than insult.

Darold Knowles (Oakland A's pitcher commenting on "hot dog" label pinned on teammate Reggie Jackson): There isn't enough mustard in the world to cover Reggie Jackson.

Pauline Kael (speaking about Robert Redford): He has turned alarmingly blind—he's gone past Platinum, he must be into plutonium—his hair seems corrugated with his teeth.

Pauline Kael: Bob Hoskins is just a testicle with legs.

Paul Keating: He is simply a shiver looking for a spine to run up.

Robert S. Kerr (speaking about Dwight D. Eisenhower): He is the only living unknown soldier.

Walter Kerr: He had delusions of adequacy.

Burt Lancaster (speaking about Kirk Douglas): Kirk would be the first to tell you that he is a difficult man; I would be the second.

Burt Lancaster: A bore is a man who, when you ask him how he is, tells you.

Elsa Lancaster (speaking about Maureen O'Hara): She looked as though butter would not melt in her mouth – or anywhere else for that matter.

Ring Lardner (about President William Taft): He looked at me as if I was a side dish he had not ordered.

Gypsy Rose Lee: She has everything now that she had 20 years ago—except now it's a lower.

Andrew Lang: He uses statistics as a drunken man uses lamp-posts...for support rather than illumination.

Frank Leahy: Egotism is the anesthetic that tells the pain of stupidity.

Jack E. Leonard: There's nothing wrong with you that reincarnation won't cure.

Oscar Levant (speaking about Zsa Zsa Gabor): She is the only person who ever left the Iron Curtain wearing it.

Oscar Levant: When I can't go to sleep, I read a book by Steve Allen

Oscar Levant (speaking to George Gershwin): Play us a medley of your hit.

Oscar Levant (speaking about Phyllis Diller): I treasure every moment that I do not see her.

Oscar Levant (speaking about Dwight D. Eisenhower): Once he makes up his mind, he is full of indecision.

Abraham Lincoln: General McClellan is a pleasant and scholarly gentlemen. He is an admirable engineer, but he seems to have special talent for stationary engines.

Abraham Lincoln: (General George B. McClellan) had the amazing ability to imagine any sort of hallucinations.

Abraham Lincoln: The trouble with General Hooker is that he has got his headquarters where his hind quarters ought to be.

Abraham Lincoln: He can compress the most words into the smallest idea of any man I know.

David Lloyd George: When they circumcised Herbert Samuel, they threw away the wrong bit.

David Lloyd George (about Ramsey McDonald): Sufficient conscience to bother him, but not sufficient to keep him straight.

Alice Roosevelt Longworth (referring to Douglas MacArthur): Never trust a man who combs his hair strait from his left armpit.

Mary Lowry: There are very few people who don't become more interesting when they stop talking.

J. Russell Lynes: The only gracious way to except an insult is to ignore it; if you can't ignore it, top it; if you can't top it, laugh at it; if you can't laugh at it, it is probably deserved.

Niccolo Machiavelli: I hold it to be a proof of great prudence for men to abstain from threats and insulting words toward an enemy, for neither ... diminishes the strength of the enemy; but the one makes him more cautious, and the other increases his hatred of you and makes him more persevering in his efforts to injure you.

Billy Martin (NY Yankee manager in 1978 describing Reggie Jackson and George Steinbrenner): The two of them deserve each other. One's a born liar, the other's convicted.

Dean Martin: There is a statue of Jimmy Stewart in the Hollywood Wax Museum, and a statue talks better than he does.

Groucho Marx: I never forget a face, but in your case I will be glad to make an exception.

Groucho Marx: I've had a perfectly wonderful evening. But this wasn't it.

Harpo Marx (speaking about Alexander Woollcott): He looked like something that had gotten loose from a Macy's Thanksgiving Day Parade.

Walter Matthau (playing Max Goldman in the movie *Grumpier Old Men*): Why don't you do the world a favor? Pull your lip over your head and swallow.

Mary McCarthy (speaking about Lillian Hellman): Every word she writes is a lie, including "and" and "the."

Harold McMillan (about Anthony Eden): He is forever poised between a cliché and an indiscretion.

Golda Meir: Don't be humble: you're not that great.

Andrea Michaels (speaking about Nancy Reagan): She has agreed to be the first artificial heart donor.

A. A. Milne: Bores can be divided into two classes: those who have their own particular subject, and those who do not need a subject.

Margaret Mitchell (last scene, 1939 film, *Gone With the Wind*, Scarlett O'Hara is finally abandoned by her husband Rhett Butler): Scarlett: "Where shall I go? What shall I do?" Rhett: "Frankly, my dear, I don't give a damn!"

Bob Monkhouse (speaking about Jeffrey Archer): The last time I was in Spain I got through six Jeffrey Archer novels. I must remember to take enough toilet paper with the next time.

Greg Nettles (NY Yankee third baseman in 1970's commenting on a George Steinbrenner tirade): When I was a kid, I wanted to play baseball and join the circus. With the Yankees, I've been able to do both.

David Niven (speaking of fellow actor George Sanders): He was a giant grizzly of a man, who had a face, even his twenties, which looked as though he had rented it on a long-term lease and had lived in it so long he did not want to move out.

Jack Paar: I am fond of Steve Allen, but not as much as he is.

Walter H. Page (about Woodrow Wilson): The air currents of the world never ventilated his mind.

Dorothy Parker (Speaking of Clare Booth Luce being kind to her inferiors): Whereof wherever does she find them?

Dorothy Parker (one learning that Calvin Coolidge had died): How can they tell?

Dorothy Parker (speaking about Katharine Hepburn): She ran the whole gamut of the motions from A to B.

Dorothy Parker: After a young snobbish man observed, "I simply cannot bear fools." Ms. Parker replied: "Apparently your mother could."

Dorothy Parker: Someone observed that a woman was outspoken. Ms. Parker replied: "By whom?"

Steven Pearl: I can't believe that out of 100,000 sperm, you were the quickest.

Polish Saying: The devil seduced Eve in Italian. Eve mislead Adam in Bohemian. The Lord scolded them both in German. Then the angel drove them from paradise in Hungarian.

Polish Saying: Did hogs feed here or did Lithuanians have a feast here?

John Randolph (on Edward Livingston): He is a man of splendid abilities, but utterly corrupt. He shines and stinks like a rotten mackerel by moonlight.

Ronald Reagan: The trouble with our liberal friends is not that they're ignorant; it's just that they know so much that isn't so.

Robert Redford: He has the attention span of a lightning bolt.

Thomas Brackett Reed: They never open their mouths without subtracting from the sum of human knowledge.

Thomas Brackett Reed: I will say to this gentleman that if I ever "made light" of his remarks, it is more than he ever made of them himself.

James Reston (about Richard Nixon): He inherited some good instincts from his Quaker forebears, but by diligent hard work, he overcame them.

Don Rickles: You look at Ernest Borgnineand you think yourself: was there anybody else hurt in that accident?

Joan Rivers (Speaking about Marie Osmond): She is so pure even Moses could not part her knees.

Joan Rivers: Joan Collins has had so many men, she is known in the United States as the British Open.

Joan Rivers (speaking about Yoko Ono): If I found her in my pool, I would punish my dog.

Joan Rivers: That is the kind of face you find hanging over your door in Africa.

Will Rogers: Calvin Coolidge did not say much, but when he did ... he did not say much.

Will Rogers: Shrewdness in Public Life all over the World is always honored, while honesty in Public Men is generally attributed to Dumbness and is seldom rewarded.

Theodore Roosevelt (about John Tyler): He has been called a mediocre man, but this is unwarranted flattery.

Theodore Roosevelt: He had no more backbone than a chocolate éclair.

Russian Proverb: A single Russian hair outweighs half a Pole.

Russian Proverb: There are only two types of Chinese—those who give bribes and those who take them.

Saki (of Ralph Waldo Emerson): Waldo is one of those people who would be enormously improved by death.

Saki: George Bernard Shaw has discovered himself, and given ungrudgingly of his discovery to all the world.

Arthur's Schlesinger: I liked your book, Liz. Who wrote it for you? Liz Carpenter: I'm glad you liked it, Arthur. Who read it to you?

Seneca: It is often better not to see an insult than to avenge it.

William Shakespeare (*As You Like It*, Act III, ii): I do desire we may be better strangers.

William Shakespeare (*Coriolanus*, Act V, iv): The tartness of his face sours ripe grapes.

William Shakespeare (*Hamlet*, Act III, ii): Call me what instrument you will, though you can fret me, you cannot play upon me.

William Shakespeare (*III Henry VI*, Act V, i): I had rather chop this hand off at a blow, / And with the other fling it at thy face, / Than bear so low a sail to strike to thee.

William Shakespeare (*Julius Caesar*, Act IV, iii): I had rather be a dog, and bay the moon; / Than such a Roman.

William Shakespeare (*King Lear*, Act IV, ii): Get thee glass eyes; / And, and like a scurvy politician, seem / To see the things thou dost not.

George Bernard Shaw (speaking about Isadora Duncan): A woman whose face looked as if it had been made of sugar and someone had licked it.

R. B. Sheridan: From the silence which prevails I conclude that Lauderdale has been making a joke.

Michael Simkins: You know why actors don't look out the window in the morning? Because they would have nothing to do in the afternoon.

John Simon (speaking about Doris Day): The only real talent she possesses is that of being absolutely sanitary: her personality is untouched by any human emotions, her brow is unclouded by any human thought, and her form is unsmudged by the slightest evidence of any femininity.

Mort Sol (speaking about Johnny Carson): He is an anaesthetist—Prince Valium.

Barbara Stanwyck: Egotism is usually just a case of mistaken non-entity.

John Stark: His performance was so wooden you want to spray him with Liquid Pledge.

Casey Stengel (Former NY Mets manager at a team birthday party for "Marvelous Marv" Throneberry): They didn't give him a cake. They were afraid he'd drop it.

Charles, Count Talleyrand: "In order to avoid being called a flirt, she always yielded easily."

Mother Teresa (born Agnes Gonxha Beiaxhiu, 1910-1997, Humanitarian, Nobel Peace Prize 1979, from *"A Simple Path"*; found on the wall at Shishu Bhavan, an orphanage in Calcutta, India, and on a Sign In Mother Teresa's Office): DO IT ANYWAY: People are unreasonable, illogical, and self-centered, / LOVE THEM ANYWAY // If you do good, people will accuse you of selfish, ulterior motives, / DO GOOD ANYWAY // If you are successful, you win false friends and true enemies, / SUCCEED ANYWAY // The good you do will be forgotten tomorrow, / DO GOOD ANYWAY // Honesty and frankness make you vulnerable, / BE HONEST AND FRANK ANYWAY // What you spent years building may be destroyed overnight, / BUILD ANYWAY // People really need help but may attack you if you help them, / HELP PEOPLE ANYWAY // Give the world the best you have and you'll get kicked in the teeth, / GIVE THE WORLD THE BEST YOU'VE GOT ANYWAY.

Forrest Tucker: He loves Nature in spite of what it did to him.

Turkish Proverb: An Englishman will burn his bed to catch a flea.

Mark Twain: You take the lies out of him, and he'll shrink to the size of your hat; you take the malice out of him, and he'll disappear.

Mark Twain: He is useless on top if the ground; he ought to be under it, inspiring the cabbages.

Mark Twain: I didn't attend the funeral, but I sent a nice letter saying I approved of it.

Mark Twain: Why do you sit there looking like an envelope without any address on it?

Mark Twain (speaking about empire-builder Cecil Rhodes): I admire him, I freely confess it. And when his time comes I shall buy a piece of the rope for a keepsake.

Kenneth Tynan: She was a garden gnome expelled from Eden.

UA: An egotist is someone who would usually be me-deep in conversation.

UA: One nice thing about egotists is that they don't talk about other people.

UA: He is a bull who carries his own china shop with him.

UA: An actor is the only ham that cannot be cured.

UA (about Byron "Ban" Bancroft Johnson, first President of The American League in Major League Baseball): Looked like he was weaned on an icicle.

UA: Johnson had more learning, but Shakespeare had more luck.

UA: You're just jealous because the voices only talk to me.

John Updike: A healthy male adult bore consumes one half times his own weight in other people's patience.

Harriet Van Horn (speaking about Joan Crawford): She would have made an exemplary prison matron, possibly at Buchenwald. She had the requisite sadism, paranoia and taste for violence.

Queen Victoria (speaking about Gladstone): He speaks to me as if I was a public meeting.

Mae West: His mother should have thrown him away and kept the stork.

Wexford Curse: May the grass grow at your door and the fox build his nest on your hearthstone.
May the light fade from your eyes, so you never see what you love.
May your own blood rise against you, and the sweetest drink you take be the bitterest cup of sorrow.
May you die without benefit of clergy;

May there be none to shed a tear at your grave, and may the hearthstone of hell be your best bed forever.

Oscar Wilde: After someone remarked that they would never talk about things when they did not know the facts, Wilde flashed: "that must limit your conversation frightfully."

Oscar Wilde: He has no enemies, but is intensely disliked by his friends.

Oscar Wilde: Some cause happiness wherever they go; others, whenever they go.

Oscar Wilde: Frank Harris is invited to all of the great houses in England—once.

Oscar Wilde: The gods bestowed on Max Beerbohm the gift of perpetual old age.

Billy Wilder: He has Van Gogh's ear for music.

George Will: His ego is so big he has applied for statehood.

Rabbi Stephen S. Wise: To a snobbish member of the Daughters of the American Revolution who proudly stated "My ancestors witnessed the signing of the Declaration of Independence," Dr. Wise replied, " That is very well. My ancestors witnessed the signing of the Ten Commandments."

P.G. Woodhouse: He was a tubby little chap who looked as if he had been poured into his clothes and had forgotten to say when.

Alexander Woollcott (about Mrs. Patrick Campbell): What enchanted me was her unwavering and ingenious rudeness to everyone there who could possibly have been of assistance to her... her failure to be politic took on the proportions of a magnificent gesture. She was like a sinking ship firing on the rescuers.

Alexander Woollcott (speaking about Dorothy Parker): She was a combination of Little Nell and Lady Macbeth.

Alexander Woollcott: There is absolutely nothing wrong with Oscar Levant that a miracle cannot fix.

Henny Youngman: Zsa Zsa has been married so many times she has rice marks on her face.

INSURANCE

Uncle Anthony: In every insurance policy ya gotta be sure ya read the fine print ... or else yer gonna be left bare a—d and with no protection.

Uncle Anthony: Gettin' insurance is lie payin' for a disaster on an installement plan.

Uncle Anthony: I thought my group insurance was fine 'til I found I couldn't collect unless the whole group got sick.

Aunt Mary Carlo: Those companies love to take yer money – but just try to get them to pay some out.... They won't cover their own bets!

Aunt Mary Carlo: He applied for an insurance policy soz if he bumped his head he'd get a "lump sum."

Aunt Mary Carlo: His insurance agent said his company paid over $5 million for broken arms and legs and backs; he asked "What do they do wit 'em all?"

Fred Allen: The insurance policy was a guarantee that, no matter how many necessities a person had to forego all through life, death was something to which he could look forward.

Cecil Beaton: Americans have an abiding belief in their ability to control reality by purely material means... airline insurance replaces the fear of death with the comforting prospect of cash.

Bible: Ecclesiastes 5:5: Better it is that thou shouldest not vow, than that thou shouldest vow and not pay.

Bible: Proverbs 11:15: He that is surety for a stranger shall smart for it.

Ambrose Bierce: INSURANCE: An ingenious modern game of chance in which the player is permitted to enjoy the comfortable conviction that he is beating the man who keeps the table....

Bertolt Brecht: When the praying does no good, insurance does help.

George Gordon Byron: 'Tis said that persons living on annuities / Are longer lived than others.

Benjamin Cardozo: The attempted distinction between accidental results and accidental means will plunge this branch of law into a Serbonian Bog. _Landress v. Phoenix Mut. Ins. Co._, 291 US 491, 78 L ed 934, 54 S Ct 461 (1934) [EDITOR: **Serbonian Bog** = "A gulf profound, as that Serbonian bog / Betwixt Damiata and Mount Casius old, / Where armies whole have sunk. Milton, *Paradise Lost*, Bk 2, 1.]

Sir Winston Churchill (March 2, 1943): National compulsory insurance for all classes for all purposes **from the cradle to the grave.**

William T. Costello: This is the Hartford heresy. Economic, material security, life insurance, endowments, annuities take the place of a providential destiny, so that ultimate values are not built upon a rock whose name is Peter, but upon a rock whose name is Prudential.

Charles Dickens: Buy an annuity cheap, and make your life interesting to yourself and everybody else that watches the speculation.

Philip Hamburger: Everybody in Des Moines is insured—against fire, flood, theft, hog cholera, death, crop failure, rickets. Name it, and Des Moines has the insurance to cover it.

David Letterman: Rising (high) insurance rates are what really killed off the dinosaurs.

Michael A. Musmanno (Justice of Sup. Ct. of Pennsylvania, 1959): An insurance company which insures against rain in Bombay during the summer months cannot complain if its treasury is liquidated by a flood of claims in July.

Michael A. Musmanno (Justice of the Sup. Ct. of Pennsylvania, 1959): Next to the daily rising of the sun, nothing is so warming and comforting to the American family as the realization of every member thereof that by periodical payment of stated sums from their hard-earned wages they have engaged the services of a powerful and unfailing friend who will protect them against the rain of sickness, the hail of accident, the snows of debility, the storms of fire and theft, and the hundreds of other mishaps and contingencies which can darken and sadden the life of any happy home. Insurance policies contain much fine print. They are to be read with human understanding and not through the glasses of super-technical interpretation.

Michael A. Musmanno (Justice of the Sup. Ct. of Pennsylvania, 1959): Diminutive type grossly disproportionate to that used in the face body of a contract cannot be ignored; it has its place in law, and, where space is at a premium, it allows for instruction, guidance and protection which might otherwise be lost, but where it is used as an ambush to conceal legalistic spears to stab other rights agreed upon, it will receive rigorous scrutinization by the courts for the ascertainment of the true meaning which may go beyond the literal import.

Michael A. Musmanno (Justice of Pennsylvania Supreme Court, 1959): The clause in the policy on which the insurance company defendant builds its assertion of non-liability... would most assuredly never take a prize in a school of expression for clear and crystalline prose. Ambiguity runs through it like ink poured into a fishbowl, clouding the identity of its swimming occupants. From this clouding bowl of language the insurance company fishes up the conclusion that the exclusion clause was intended to allow coverage only in the event of certain factors which are absent here. The insurance company maintains that the bleary paragraph excludes coverage in any case where the beneficiary receives worker's compensation.... If such an exclusion had been stated in language clear to anyone who reads, it is possible that a lesser number of persons would have wanted to buy the insurance policy because worker's compensation is so much a part of a workman's economic status that no worker would want to willingly forgo its benefits. Under those circumstances the company would have quite probably sold fewer policies. Aside from the morality involved in permitting ambiguous language to entice insurance buyers, only to drop them into a pit of non-recoverability when claims are made under the policy, the insurance company cannot maintain its position because of the law which specifically states that where ambiguity clouds interpretation, a contract in controversy must be interpreted against its authors. The person who writes with ink which spreads and simultaneously produces two conflicting versions of the same proposition cannot complain if the person affected by both propositions chooses to accept that which is more helpful to him and which is against the interests of the contract writer. (Frances Sykes, Adm. v. Nationwide Insurance Company, 413 Pa. 640).

Ralph Nader: For almost 70 years the life insurance industry has been a smug sacred cow feeding the public a steady line of sacred bull.

Will Rogers: Asking Europe to disarm is like asking a man in Chicago to give up his life insurance.

Don C. Seitz: Hartford is a gay combination of Life Insurance and Death, for here the former had a pioneer foundation that has brought in great accumulations of cash, while Samuel Colt's "revolver" has grown into "Browning guns" and many forms of deadly repeaters that wipe out a regiment at a discharge.

Mary Beth Senkewicz (former Senior executice at National Association of Insurance Commissioners): The bottom line is that insurance companies make money when they don't pay claims. They'll do anything to avoid paying, because if they wait long enough, they know the policyholders will die.

William Shakespeare (*The Merchant of Venice,* Act I, iii): Yes, Shylock, I will seal unto this bond.

William Shakespeare (*The Merchant of Venice,* Act IV, i): This bond doth give thee here no jot of blood; / The words expressly are "a pound of flesh:" / Take then thy bond, take thou thy pound of flesh.

Gerry Spence (in his 1989 Penguin Books *With Justice For None)*: The insurance company is the God of Money ... The insurance-compay lawyers come to court not to ascertain the truth or to search for justice, but to fight for money, and they will do whatever is necessary to keep it.

Gerry Spence: Like the irresistible force of a glacier, the (insurance) industry has carved out huge immunities for itself in Congress, and is this country's ONLY major industry not subject to the nation's antitrust laws.

Mark Twain: They inwardly resolved that so long as they remained in the business, their piracies should not again be sullied with the crime of stealing.

INTELLIGENCE (See TRUTH/UNDERSTANDING)

INTERPRETATION (See WORDS)

ISSUES/PROBLEMS

Uncle Anthony: Today people call their problems a "challenge," but ya still gotta work at solving 'em no matter what label ya stick on 'em.

Uncle Anthony: I don't know what the hell yer "issues" are, but I got lots of unanswered questions.

Uncle Anthony: When yer at da edge of a cliff, sometimes "progress" is takin' a step backwards.

Aunt Mary Carlo: He's really straitforward in da way he dodges da issues.

Aunt Mary Carlo: I tink he approaches every question wit an open mouth.

Aunt Mary Carlo: He's a real acrobat – he can straddle any fence an' still keep his ear to da ground.

Aesop: Never trust the advice of a man in difficulties.

Henri-Frederic Amiel: The man who insists on seeing with perfect clearness before he decides, never decides.

Dr. Robert Anthony: If you find a good solution and become attached to it, the solution may become your next problem.

Isaac Asimov: If knowledge can create problems, it is not through ignorance that we can solve them.

Bible: Job 5:7: Man is born into trouble, as the sparks fly upwards.

Bible: Mark 3:25: If a house be divided against itself, that house cannot stand.

Bible: Matthew 26:41: The spirit indeed is willing, but the flesh is weak.

Ambrose Bierce: DELIBERATION, n. The act of examining one's bread to determine which side it is buttered on.

Ambrose Bierce: DECIDE, v.i. To succumb to the preponderance of one set of influences over another set....

Ambrose Bierce: INDECISION, n. The chief element of success; "for whereas," said Sir Thomas Brewbold, "there is but one way to do nothing and divers ways to do something, whereof, to a surety, only one is the right way, it followeth that he who from indecision standeth still hath not so many chances of going astray as he who pusheth forwards" – a most clear and satisfactory exposition of the matter....

Ambrose Bierce: INDIFFERENT, adj. Imperfectly sensible to distinctions among things.

Robert Bramson, Ph.D. (book *Coping With Difficult People*): The Seven Categories or Groups of Difficult People:

1. Hostile/Aggressive Trio = Sherman Tanks, Snipers, and "Exploders"
2. Indecisives
3. Complainers
4. Negativists
5. Clams
6. Expert Know-It-Alls = Bulldozers & Hot Air Balloons
7. Super Agreeables

Nancy Cattie: "Ground-truthing" is what we do whenever we conduct a focus group, jury project or mock trial. Ground-truthing is what mapping services like Map Quest and Google Maps or in-car navigation systems like On-Star do to verify and update every area on the GPS with current street-by-street data by actually driving on the streets, roads and highways.

William Ellery Channing: Difficulties are meant to rouse, not discourage. The human spirit is to grow strong by conflict.

G.K. Chesterton: It isn't that they can't see the solution, it is that they can't see the problem.

Chinese Proverb: He who rouses a sleeping tiger exposes himself to danger.

Sir Winston Churchill (November 12, 1936): [The government] goes on in strange paradox, decided only to be undecided, resolved to be irresolute, adamant for drift, solid for fluidity.

Sir Winston Churchill: In my belief: you cannot deal with the most serious things in the world unless you also understand the most amusing.

Calvin Coolidge: Nothing in this world can take the place of persistence. Talent will not; nothing is more common than unsuccessful people with talent. Genius will not; unrewarded genius is almost a proverb. Education will not; the world is full of educated derelicts. Persistence and determination alone are omnipotent. The slogan "press on" has solved and always will solve the problems of the human race.

Anthony J. D'Angelo: Focus 90% of your time on solutions and only 10% of your time on problems.

Anthony J. D'Angelo: When solving problems, dig at the roots instead of just hacking at the leaves.

Philip K. Dick: Don't try to solve serious matters in the middle of the night.

William J. Donnelly (*The Confetti Generation: How the New Communications Technology Is Fragmenting America*, 1986): There is little doubt about the revolutionary potential of the new electronic media in our society and culture.... at some very early point, nearly everyone between the ages of ten and forty-nine today will have at least two new electronic media in their homes: (1) a random acess information system (home computer, videotext, optical videodisc); and (2) a fickle access enetertainment system (cable television, pay television, videocassette, video game)...The new media encompasses a quantum leap in the ability to store and retrieve information; a quantum leap in the availability of mimetic entertainment that is readily internalized; a quantum leap in services that provide controlled, individualized, remote transactions; and a quantum leap in speed, to the point of warping our sense of time...together, they will produce and define **THE CONFETTI GENERATION.**

William J. Donnelly (*The Confetti Generation: How the New Communications Technology Is Fragmenting America*, 1986): To appreciate the living experience of the Confetti Generation, we should ask ourselves a few simple questions. When ideas and experiences float down upon us like confetti – and just as cheaply – how do we expect to choose?....The electronification of our lives that began with television and the use of computers ... wil become pervasive and microspecific... That is our destination, but what is our destiny? ... In THE CONFETTI GENERATION, we will be living undirected lives and life-styles. We will think and act not only for ourselves, but by ourselves, isolated from the common experiences and judgments of others... we are about to think and choose and live differently than ever before in history.

Sir Arthur Conan Doyle (The Sherlock Holmes phrase that suggests the answer is obvious to anyone of with the smallest amount of intelligence): Doctor John H. Watson: "Amazing, Holmes!" Sherlock Holmes: "Elementary, my dear Watson, elementary."

Albert Einstein: The significant problems we face cannot be solved at the same level of thinking we were at when we created them.

Albert Einstein: The problems that exist in the world today cannot be solved by the level of thinking that created them.

Ralph Waldo Emerson: We do what we must, and call it by the best names.

Errol Flynn: My problem lies in reconciling my gross habits with my net income.

Malcolm Forbes: It's so much easier to suggest solutions when you don't know much about the problem.

Andrew Franken: When you're ready to do something about a problem, almost anything can help. When you're not ready, no amount of workshops, counselling or programs will effect a change. The rule is: "When a student is ready, the teacher appears."

Benjamin Franklin: There are no gains without pains.

Thomas Fuller: All things are difficult before they are easy.

Galileo Galilei: I think that in the discussion of natural problems we ought to begin not with the Scriptures, but with experiments, and demonstrations.

John Galsworthy: Idealism increases in direct proportion to one's distance from the problem.

Baltasar Gracian: Attend easy tasks as if they were difficult, and difficult as if they were easy; in the one case that confidence may not fall asleep, in the other that it may not be dismayed.

Etty Hillesum: We are always in search of the redeeming formula, the crystalizing thought.

Edward Hodnett: A good problem statement often includes: (a) what is known, (b) what is unknown, and (c) what is sought.

Robert Maynard Hutchins: To solve a problem it is necessary to think. It is necessary to think to even decide what facts to collect.

Italian Proverb: We cannot direct the wind, but we can adjust the sails.

Walt Kelly (cartoonist, the possum Pogo, in *The Pogo Papers*, 1953): "... we shall meet the enemy, ... and not only may he be ours, he may be us."

Charles Kettering: A problem well stated is a problem half solved.

Rudyard Kipling: I keep six honest serving men; / They taught me all I knew. / Their names are: What and Why and When, / and How and Where and Who.

Ann Landers: I don't believe you have to be a cow to know what milk is.

Abraham Lincoln: When you have got an elephant by the hind legs and he is trying to run away, it is best to let him run.

Allard Lowenstein: The question should be, is it worth trying to do, not can it be done.

Ralph Marston: It doesn't matter how much you want. What really matters is how much you want it. The extent and complexity of the problem does not matter was much as does the willingness to solve it.

Groucho Marx: There is no sweeter sound than the crumbling of one's fellow man.

H.L. Mencken: There is always an easy solution to every human problem: it is neat, plausible, and wrong!

John Peer: The information we need is not available. The information we want is not what we need. The information we have is not what we want.

John Peer (The Rule of Accuracy): When working toward the solution of a problem, it always helps if you know the answer.

Shimon Peres: If a problem has no solution, it may not be a problem, but a fact—not to be solved, but to be coped with over time.

Branch Rickey (lawyer, and legendary baseball executive): Problems are the price you pay for progress.

La Rochefoucauld: We all have the strength to endure the misfortunes of others.

Will Rogers: If I could kick the person in the tail that causes me the most problems I could not sit down for a week.

Will Rogers: Last year we said, 'Things can't go on like this', and they didn't, they got worse.

Will Rogers: If you find yourself in a hole, stop digging.

Theodore Rubin: The problem is not that there are problems. The problem is expecting otherwise and thinking that having problems is a problem.

William Shakespeare (*Hamlet,* Act III, i): To be, or not to be: that is the question.

William Shakespeare (*Hamlet,* Act III, i): Puzzles the will / And makes us rather bear those ills we have / Than fly to others that we know not of.

William Shakespeare (*Twelfth Night,* Act IV, ii): More puzzled than the Egyptians in their fog.

William Shakespeare (*Winter's Tale,* Act I, ii): If ever fearful / To do a thing, where I the issue doubted.

Charles M. Shultz: No problem is so formidable that you can't walk away from it.

Mother Teresa: I know God will not give me anything I can't handle. I just wish that He didn't trust me so much.

Mark Twain: Life does not consist mainly—or even largely—of facts and happenings. It consists mainly of the storm of thoughts that is forever blowing through one's head.

UA (the $64 question was the highest award on the CBS radio quiz show Take It or Leave It in 1940's in which the prize doubled every time a contestant got the right answer – 1-2-4-8-16-32-64; the TV show from 1955-1957 was): The Sixty Four Thousand Dollar Question. Or, alternately referred to as The Sixty Four Dollar Question.

UA (originally a popular Black Power campaign phrase in 1960's; referring to grit-like nits or small lice that are hard to get out of one's hair; also a Shirley Ellis 1963 song "The Nitty Gritty"): Let's get down to the nitty gritty.

Chris Watson (Atlantic City Press article "That's Not All, Folks! Lessons Learned From Cartoons Over Into Adult Situations"): ....And Daffy Duck, my favorite of them all (don't laugh unless you tell me yours) showed me there is always more than one way to look at the situation. Daffy's illogical universe had its own logic. That crazy duck taught me to value my idiosyncrasies even when others frowned on them.

JUDGES (See also JUDGMENT; JUSTICE; LAW)

Aesop (c. 560 B.C., *Fables*): A swallow had built her nest under the eaves of a Court of Justice. Before her young ones could fly, a serpent glided out of his hole and ate them all up. When the poor bird returned to her nest and found it empty, she began a pitiable wailing. A neighbor suggested, by way of comfort, that she was not the first bird who had lost her young. "True," she replied, "but it is not only my little ones that I mourn, but that I should have been wronged in that very place where the injured fly for justice."

Uncle Anthony: Some of these guys in the black togas ... do they live anywhere near our planet?

Uncle Anthony: In court the "benchwarmer" is the boss.

Aunt Mary Carlo: You can show off the best briefs, but still lose yer shirt!

Aunt Mary Carlo: Dat judge wouldn't even listen to both side of a phonograph record.

Aunt Mary Carlo: When HE wants yer opinion. HE gives it to ya.

Dean Acheson: At least one role in presenting the foreign policy statement will have the merit which John G. Johnson found in staying at the bar instead of accepting President Cleveland's offer of a place on the Supreme Court. "I would rather talk to the damned fools," he said, "then listen to them."

Maxwell Anderson: When did the judge ever think? He's paid not to.

Aristotle: The arbitrator has regard to equity and the judge to law.

Francis Bacon (philosopher, writer, Lord Chancellor of England, 1561-1626, *Essays: Of Judicature, 1625*): Judges must beware of hard constructions and strained inferences; for there is no worse torture than the torture of laws.

Francis Bacon (*De Augmentis Scientiarum*, bk 8): Decided cases are the anchors of the law, as laws are of the state.

Francis Bacon: A judge is one more learned than witty, more reverend than plausible, and more advised than confident. Above all things, integrity is their portion and proper virtue.

Francis Bacon (*Essays: Of Judicature,* 1625): Judges ought to remember that their office is *Ius dicere* and not *Ius dare:* to interpret law, and not to make law.

Francis Bacon (*Essays: Of Judicature,* 1625): Judges ought to be more learned than witty, more reverent than plausible, and more advised than confident. Above all things, integrity is their portion and proper virtue.

Francis Bacon (*Essays: Of Judicature,* 1625): Patience and gravity of hearing is an essential part of justice; and an overspeaking judge is no well-tuned cymbal. (EDITOR: How many times have I been interrupted by such an off-tuned cymbal!)

Francis Bacon (*Essays: Of Judicature*, 1625): A judge ought to prepare his way to a just sentence, as God useth to prepare his way, by raising valleys and taking down hills: so when there appeareth on either side an high hand, violent prosecution, cunning advantages taken, combination, power, great counsel, then is the virtue of a judge seen, to make inequality equal; that he may plant his judgment as upon an even ground.

Francis Bacon (*Speech, Star Chamber*, 1617, to the judges): A popular judge is a deformed thing: and *plaudite's* are fitter for players than magistrates:

Francis Bacon (letter to Duke of Buckingham, 1616): Judges must be chaste as Caesar's wife. Nither to be, nor so much as suspected in the least to be unjust.

Phantly Roy Bean (the "Hangin' Judge," c. 1825 – 1903, an eccentric U.S. saloon-keeper and Justice of the Peace who called himself "The Law West of the Pecos." According to legend, Judge Roy Bean

held court in his saloon along the Rio Grande in Vinegarroon, in a desolate stretch of the Chihuahuan Desert of West Texas; a sign erected by Roy Bean in 1889 at his store/saloon in Vinegarroon, Texas, establishing himself without authority, save his two six-guns and indominatable spirit, as Law in the lawless domain between El Paso and Pecos River): VINEGARROON: Roy Bean ... Barrel Whiskey ... Justice of the Peace ... Law West of the Pecos.

Melvin Belli: Now, the law is good but some of these judges just don't know how to handle it in court. They simply don't have the experience. There are an awful lot of "C" law students practicing law and sitting on the bench.

Jeremy Bentham (English lawyer, utilitarian philosopher, 1748-1832, *Scotch Reform*, 5 Works 13): Fiction (in law) a wilful falsehood, uttered by a judge, for the purpose of giving to injustice the colour of justice.

Bible: Acts 23:3: Then said Paul unto him, God shall smite thee, thou whited wall: for sittest thou to judge me after the law, and commandest me to be stricken contrary to the law?

Bible: Daniel 5:27: Thou are weighed in the balances, and art found wanting.

Bible: Deuteronomy 1:17: There shall be no difference of persons, Ye shall hear the small as well as the great: neither shall you respect any man's person, because it is the judgment of God. And if any thing seem hard to you, refer it to me, and I will hear it.

Bible: Deuteronomy 16:18: Thou shalt appoint judges and magistrates in all thy gates, which the Lord thy God shall give thee, in all thy tribes: that they may judge the people with just judgment.

Bible: Deuteronomy 16:19: Thou shalt not accept person nor gifts: for gifts blind the eyes of the wise, and change the words of the just.

Bible: Exodus 18:21, 22: Moreover thou shalt provide out of all the people able men, such as fear God, men of truth, hating covetousness.... And let them judge the people at all seasons: and it shall be, that every great matter they shall bring unto thee, but every small matter they shall judge: so shall it be easier for thyself, and they shall bear the burden with thee.

Bible: Exodus 23:7: The innocent and the just you shall not put to death, nor shall you acquit the guilty.

Bible: Job 9:24: The earth is given into the land of the wicked: He covereth the faces of the judges thereof.

Bible: John 7:51: Nicodemus: "Doth our law judge any man, before it hear him, and know what he doeth?

Bible: Judges 2:17; 1 Chronicles 5:25: They would not harken unto their judges, but they went a whoring after other gods.

Bible: Judges 4:4: And there was at that time Deborra, a prophetess, the wife of Lapidoth, who judged the people.

Bible: Kings 7:16: And he (Samuel) went every year about to Bethel, and Galgal, and Masphath, and he judged Israel in the aforesaid places.

Bible: Leviticus 19:5: Thou shalt not respect the person of the poor, not honour the person of the mighty: but in righteousness shalt thou judge thy neighbor.

Bible: Leviticus 19:15: Ye shall do no unrighteousness in judgment: thou shalt not respect the person of the poor, nor honor the person of the mighty: but in righteousness shalt thou judge thy neighbor.

Bible: Luke 6:37: Out of thine own mouth will I judge thee.

Bible: Matthew 7:1: Judge not, that ye be not judged.

Bible: Proverbs 31:9: Open thy mouth, judge righteously, and plead the cause of the poor and needy.

Bible: Romans 2:1: Wherein thou judgest another, thou condemnest thyself.

Ambrose Bierce: DECIDE, v.i. To succumb to the preponderance of one set of influences over another set.

Ambrose Bierce: DELIBERATION, n. The act of examining one's bread to determine which side it is buttered on.

Ambrose Bierce: JUDGE, *n.* A person who is always interfering in disputes in which he has no personal interest.

Ambrose Bierce: PRECEDENT, n. In Law, a previous decision, rule or practice which, in the absence of a definite statute, has whatever force and authority a Judge may choose to give it, thereby greatly simplifying his task of doing as he pleases. As there are precedents for everything, he has only to ignore those that make against his interest and accentuate those in line of his desire. Invention of precedent elevates the trial-at-law from the low estate of a fortuitous ordeal to the noble attitude of a dirigible arbitrament.

Ambrose Bierce: PRESIDE, v. To guide the action of a deliberative body to a desirable result. In Journalese, to perform upon a musical instrument; as, "he presided at the piccolo."

Ambrose Bierce: JUSTICE, n. A commodity which in a more or less adulterated condition the State sells to the citizen as a reward for his allegiance, taxes and personal service.

Hugo L. Black (Supreme Court Justice): Our Constitution was not written in the sands to be washed away by each wave of new judges blown in by each successive political wind.

Harry A. Blackmun (Supreme Court Justice): We are all eccentrics. We're nine prima donnas.

Harry A. Blackmun: We (on the Supreme Court) never have the hours and the moments to put our feet on the windowsills and reflect a bit.

Harry A. Blackmun (Supreme Court Justice): Who is to say that five men 10 years ago were right whereas five men looking the other direction today are wrong.

Sir Wiiliam Blackstone (English lawyer, *Commentaries*, bk 1): They are the depositories of the laws; the living oracles, who must decide in all cases of doubt, and who are bound by an oath to decide according to the law of the land.

Curtis Bok: It has been said that a judge is a member of the Bar once knew a governor.

Henry de Bracton (English judge, d. 1268, *De Legibus et Consuetudinibus Angliae*): Laws and customs ... are often abusively perverted by the foolish and unlearned who ascend the judgment seat before they have learnt the laws.

Louis Brandeis: On the question of public policy it is no disrespect to the Supreme Court to say that the majority of the court were mistaken. There's no reason why five gentlemen of the Supreme Court should know better what public policy demands than five gentlemen of Congress.

Louis Brandeis: If we would guide by the light of reason, we must let our minds be bold. Jay Burns Baking Co. v Bryan, 264 US 504, 68 L ed 813, 44 S Ct 412 (1924)

William J. Brennan, Jr. (New Jersey judge, Assoc Justice US Supreme Court): We current justices read the Constitution in the only way we can – as 20th-century Americans.

William Jethro Brown (Autralian lawyer and writer, 1868-1930, *Customary Law in Modern England*, 5 Col. L. R. 561, 1905): What judges do and what they profess to do are not always the same, and the latter is only evidence of the former, - often very misleading evidence.

Jean De La Bruyere: The duty of a judge is to render justice; his art is to delay it.

Pearl S. Buck: Once the *what* is decided, the *how* always follows. We must not make the *how* an excuse for not facing and accepting the *what.*

Lord John Campbell (Chief Judge, Queen's Bench, Lord Chancellor of Great Britain, 1779-1861): It is of great consequence that the public should know what takes place in Court; and the proceedings are under the control of the Judges. The inconvenience therefore arising from the chance of injury to private character is infinitesimally small as compared to the consequence of publicity. Davison v Duncan, 7 E. & B. 229 (1857)

Benjamin Cardozo (*Nature of the Judicial Process*, 1921): It is when the colors do not match, when the references in the index fail, when there is no decisive precedent, that the serious business of the judge begins.

Benjamin Cardozo (*Growth of the Law*, 1924): Judges have at last awakened, or at all events a number of them not wholly negligible, to the treasures buried in the law reviews.

Benjamin Cardozo (*Nature of the Judicial Process*, 1921): The great tides and currents which engulf the rest of men, do not turn aside their course, and pass the judges by.

Benjamin Cardozo (*Nature of the Judicial Process*, 1921): We do not pick our rules of law full-blossomed from the trees.

Benjamin Cardozo (*Nature of the Judicial Process*, 1921): The judge, even when he is free, is not wholly free. He is not to innovate at pleasure. He is not a knight-errant, roaming at will in pursuit of his own ideal of beauty or of goodness. He is to draw his inspiration from consecrated principles. He is not to yield to spasmodic sentiment, to vague and unregulated benevolence. He is to exercise a discretion informed by tradition, methodized by analogy, disciplined by system, and subordinated to "the primordial necessity of order in the social life." Wide enough in all conscience is the field of discretion that remains.

Benjamin Cardozo (*Law and Literature*, 1931): Write an opinion, and read it a few years later when it is dissected in the briefs of counsel. You will learn for the first time the limitations of the power of speech, or, if not those of speech in general, at all events your own.

Benjamin Cardozo (*Law and Literature*, 1931): The picture cannot be painted if the significant and the insignificant are given equal prominence. One must know how to select. All these generalities are as easy as they are obvious, but, alas! The application is an ordeal to try the souls of men.

Benjamin Cardozo (*Law and Literature*, 1931): We have one judge even now who can vie with the best of his English brethren, past as well as present, in the art of packing within a sentence the phosphorescence of a page. If I begin to quote from the opinions of Mr. Justice Holmes, I hardly know where I shall end.

Miguel De Cervantes: He who has the judge for his father goes into court with an easy mind.

Cicero (*De Legibus*, III): It may truly be said that the magistrate is the speaking law, and the law a silent magistrate.

Champ Clark (US Congressman): I will tell you about judges. You can take the most mild-mannered and tender-hearted man you ever saw, make him a judge for life, and his disposition to tyrannize over people will grow with what he feeds on.

Charles E. Clark (US Court of Appeals Judge): A judge is merely a lawyer who has been benched.

Roy M. Cohn: I don't want to know what the law is, I want to know who the judge is.

Sir Edward Coke (Lord Chief Justice of England, 1552-1634, *Second Institute 161*): The laws sometimes sleep, never die.

Sir Edward Coke (*First Institute* 130, oft repeated as "Judges are the speaking law"): The law is the rule, but it is mute. The king judgeth by his judges, and they are the speaking law.

Sir Edward Coke: Judges do not answer questions of fact, juries do not answer questions of law.

Sir Edward Coke: He threatens the innocent who spares the guilty.

Peter Cook: All in all I'd rather have been a judge than a miner. And what's more, being a miner, as soon as you are too old and tired and sick and stupid to do the job properly, you have to go. Well, the very opposite applies with judges.

Edward S. Corwin (American educator, political scientist and writer, 1878-1963, *Standpoint in Constitutional Law*, 17 B.U.L.Rev. 513, 1937): A friend of mine ... called upon Justice (Holmes) shortly after his retirement from the Court and asked him whether he had been guided by any one principle in the decision of constitutional cases. "Young man," said he, fixing my friend's eye sternly, "Young man, I discovered about 75 years ago that I wasn't God Almighty."

Mario Cuomo: If this country wanted its Supreme Court to reflect the immediate social or political wishes of the nation's people, it would provide for the election of the Court. And if the founding fathers had wanted it that way, they could have said so—or at least hinted at it. They did just the opposite. They designed a system that tried to immunize the Court from the changing moods and passions of the people.

Dante (*Paradise*, Canto 20): O mortal men! Be wary how ye judge.

Declaration of Independence (Ninth specification): He has made judges dependent on his will alone, for the tenure of their offices, and the amount and payment of their salaries.

Alan Dershowitz: Judges are the weakest link in our system of justice, and they are also the most protected.

Edward J. Devitt (Minnesota, Chief Judge U.S. District Court, *Ten Commandments for the New Judge*, 47 A.B.A.J. 1175, 1961): "1. Be Kind.... 2. Be Patient.... 3. Be Dignified..... 4. Don't Take Yourself Too Seriously.... 5. Remember That a Lazy Judge Is a Poor One.... 6. Don't Be Dismayed When Reversed.... 7. Remember There Are No Unimportant Cases.... 8. Don't Impose Long Sentences.... 9. Don't Forget Your Common Sense.... 10. Pray for Divine Guidance....

William O. Douglas (US Supreme Court Justice): A lifetime diet of the law alone turns judges into dull, dry husks.

Finley Peter Dunne (*Observations by Mr. Dooley: The Law's Delays*): "If I had me job to pick out," said Mr. Dooley, "I'd be a judge. I've looked over all th' others an that's the on'y wan that suits. I have th' judicyal timperamint. I hate wurruk."

Leo Durocher: I never questioned the integrity of an umpire – their eyesight, yes.

Ralph Waldo Emerson: The judge weighs the arguments and puts a brave face on the matter, and, since there must be a decision, decides as he can, and hopes he has done justice.

English Proverb (Herbert, *Jacula Prudentum*, 1651): A good judge conceives quickly, judges slowly.

English Saying: To get a handle = means to be appointed a judge and have a "handle" or gavel.

Martin Erdmann: Appellate Division judges are the whores who became madams.

Euripedes: A man's most valuable trait is a judicious sense of what not to believe.

Brendan Francis: Some persons are very decisive when it comes to avoiding decisions.

Felix Frankfurter: Like all human institutions, the Supreme Court must earn reverence through the test of truth.

Felix Frankfurter: By the very nature of the functions of the Supreme Court, each member of it is subject only to his own sense of the trusteeship of what are perhaps the most revered traditions in our national system.

Felix Frankfurter (*Supreme Court in the Mirror of Justice*, 105 U. of Pa. L. Rev. 781, 1957): One is entitled to say without qualification that the correlation between prior judicial experience and fitness for the functions of the Supreme Court is zero.

Felix Frankfurter (*The Commerce Clause*, 1937): No judge writes on a wholly clean slate.

Felix Frankfurter (*Chief Justices I Have Known*, 39 Va. L. Rev. 883, 1953, referring to US Supreme Court Chief Justice Charles Evans Hughes): To see him preside was like witnessing Toscanini lead an orchestra.

Sigmund Freud: When making a decision of minor importance, I have always found it advantageous to consider all the pros and cons. In vital matters, however, such as the choice of a mate or a profession, the decision should come from the unconscious, from somewhere within ourselves. In the important decisions of personal life, we should be governed, I think, by the deep inner needs of our nature.

Erich Fromm: Each time we make a decision it is determined by the good or evil forces, respectively, which are dominant.

Thomas Fuller: It is the justice's clerk that makes the justice.

Thomas Fuller: When a judge puts on his robes he puts off his relations to any, and, like Melchisedech, becomes without predigree.

William S. Gilbert (*Trial by Jury*): Though homeward as you trudge, / You declare my law is fudge. / Yet of beauty I'm a judge.

Judge Henry Gildersleeve (New York Criminal Courts on the subject of the death sentence): I never sentence a man to death. God does that. I only arrange the date.

Martin L. Haines (retired New Jersey Assignment Judge): Is it wrong to be an "activist" judge? Should we be appalled when a judge makes law? Is law to be made by legislators, and only legislators? The answer to all three questions is "no." Were the answer the opposite, judges would be unable to resolve novel issues, to the great disadvantage of many litigants. The term "legislating"—making law—as used here, needs definition. It includes any decision of a judge creating new law; a judicial interpretation of existing law; a substantive judicial answer to a novel question; and a judicial decision holding a statute to be unconstitutional. A word of caution. A law, statutory or judge-made, set aside because it ignores controlling law, never reflected existing law; its elimination does not make law, it reaffirms existing law.... Passionate objectors to judicial activism ignore reality and longstanding practice. That judges legislate—and do so for good reasons—is no secret. The activism has been so thoroughly exposed, discussed and accepted that it is hard to understand continuing criticisms so frequently aired by critics of every stripe.... Activism can be excessive and deserving of criticism. In response to *Bush v. Gore*, 531 U.S. 98 (2000) (the decision that made George W. Bush president) 650 legal scholars signed an advertised statement charging the court—appropriately—with judicial activism. Most judicial legislation, however, is not wholesale and not excessive; dictated by circumstance, it is interstitial, realistic and necessary.

Alexander Hamilton (*The Federalist*, No. 22): Laws are a dead letter without courts to expound and define their true meaning and operation.

Learned Hand: Nor is it desirable for a lower court to embrace the exhilarating opportunity of anticipating a doctrine which may be in the womb of time, but whose birth is distant. *Spector Motor Service Inc. v. Walsh*, 139 F. 2d 809 (1944)

Sefer Hasidim: The judge who knows other judges have erred, but agrees because he does not want to shame them, will end in *Gehenna* (Hell).

Lord Justice Hewitt of the Old Bailey Court (to a man sentenced to a long term of imprisonment): The man: "You can see I am old and never can live to serve this long sentence, Your Lordship." Lord Justice: "Then serve as much of it as you can."

Oliver Wendell Holmes, Jr. (*Law and the Court*, in *Speeches* 102, 1913): Judges are apt to be naif [naïve], simple-minded men, and they need something of Mephistopheles.

Oliver Wendell Holmes Jr.: I recognize without hesitation that judges do and must legislate, but they can do so only interstitially; they are confined from molar to molecular motions.

Oliver Wendell Holmes Jr. (*Law and the Courts*, 1913): I do not think the United States would come to an end if we lost our power to declare an Act of Congress void. I do think the Union would be imperiled if we could not make that declaration as to the laws of the several States.

Oliver Wendell Holmes Jr.: We ought to remember the great caution shown by the Constitution in limiting the power of the States, and should be slow to construe the clause in the Fourteenth Amendment as committing to the Court, with no guide but the Court's own discretion, the validity of whatever laws the States may pass. *Baldwin v Missouri*, 281 US 586, 74 L ed 1056, 50 S Ct 436 (1930)

Benjamin Hooks (Chairman, NAACP): If you took the brains of the majority of the United States Supreme Court and put them into the head of a bird, the bird would fly backward for ever and ever and ever.

Horace (13 B.C.): A good and faithful judge prefers what is right to what is expedient.

Andrew Horn (14th century English author or editor of *Mirror of Justice*, died 1328): Women, serfs, those under the age of twenty-one, open lepers, idiots, attorneys, lunatics, deaf mutes, those excommunicated by a bishop and criminal persons are inelegible for appointment to the bench.

Charles Evans Hughes (*The Supreme Court of the United States*, 1928): Judges are constantly sustaining the validity of legislation which as legislators they would probably condemn.

Charles Evans Hughes (Chief Justice US Supreme Court, speaking on occassion of the 150th anniversary of the U S Supreme Court, 1940): We do not write on a blank sheet. The Court has its jurisprudence, the helpful repository of the deliberate and expressed convictions of generations of sincere minds addressing themselves to exposition and decision, not with the freedom of casual critics or even of studious commentators, but under the pressure and within the limits of a definite official responsibility.

Washington Irving: Young lawyers attend the courts, not because they have business there but because they have no business anywhere else.

Robert H. Jackson: On your first appearance before the Court, do not waste your time or ours telling us so. We are likely to discover for ourselves that you are a novice but will think none the less of you for it. Every famous lawyer had his first day at our bar, and perhaps a sad one. It is not ingratiating to tell us you think it is an overwhelming honor to appear, for we think of the case as the important thing before us, not the counsel. Some attorneys use time to thank us for granting the review, or for listening to their argument. Those are not intended as favors and it is good taste to accept them as routine performance of duty. Be respectful, of course, but also be self-respectful, and neither disparage yourself nor flatter the Justices. We think well enough of ourselves already.

Thomas Jefferson (*Letter to William Charles Jarvis*, 1820): You seem ... to consider the judges as the ultimate arbiters of all constitutional questions; a very dangerous doctrine indeed, and one which would place us under the despotism of an oligarchy. Our judges are as honest as othe men, and not more so. They have, with others, the same passions for party, for power, and the privilege of their corps. Their maxim is *"boni judicis est amplaire jurisdictionem,"* and their power the more dangerous, as they are in office for life, and not responsible, as the other functionaries are, to the elective control. The constitution has erected so such single tribunal, knowing that to whatever hands confided, with the corruptions of time and party, its members would become despots.

Thomas Jefferson: Knowing that religion does not furnish grosser bigots than law, I expect little from old judges.

Thomas Jefferson: For Heaven's sake discard the monstrous wig which makes the English judges look like rats peeping through bunches of oakum.

Jewish Proverb: Don't blame the judge for the law.

Irving R. Kaufman (New York lawyer, Judge of US District and US Court of Appeals): Courtrooms contain every symbol of authority that a set designer could imagine. Everyone stands up when you come in. You wear a costume identifying you as, if not quite divine, someone special.

Christine Kellett (Dickinson Law School professor): They were political animals before they got to the Supreme Court, and they don't change when they get there.

Lord Kilmuir (Lord Chancellor of Great Britain, 1901-1967, *Judicial Qualities*, 36 New Zeal. L. J. 112, 1960): There is much to be said for the view that a kindly and patient man who is not a profound lawyer will make a far better judge ... than an ill-tempered genius.

Bill Klem (Major League Baseball umpire): It ain't nothin' till I call it.

Karl Kraus: A weak man has doubts before a decision: a strong man has them afterwards.

Nikolai Lenin: There are no more reactionary people in the world than judges.

Jay Leno: You know, it's almost time to turn back the clock. That's right, the Supreme Court's back in session.

Sir Wilmot Lewis (English journalist, 1877-1950): Legislation in the United States is a digestive process by Congress with frequent regurgitations by the Supreme Court.

Abraham Lincoln (At time of appointing Salmon P. Chase as Chief Justice of the US Supreme Court): We wish for a Chief Justice who will sustain what has been done in regard to emancipation and the legal tenders. We cannot ask a man what he will do, and if we should, and he would answer us, we should despise him for it. Therefore we must take a man whose opinions are known.

Henry T. Lummus (Judge Supreme Court, Massachusetts, 1876-1960, *The Trial Judge*, 1937): There is no certain harm in turning a politician into a judge. He may be or become a good judge. The curse of the elective system is the converse, that it turns almost every judge into a politician.

Nicolo Machiavelli: There should be many judges, for a few will always do the will of few.

Frederic William Maitland (English lawyer, legal historian, 1850-1906, *From the Old Law Courts to the New*, 1883): Judges and lawyers took to wigs when other men in a frivilous moment took to them; unfortunately they retained the silliest adornment that human head has yet invented for itself when even physicians and bishops had recovered their wonted sobriety.

Katherine Mansfield: Now who is to decide between "Let it be" and "Force it?"

Dewey "Pigmeat" Markham (a black vaudeville veteran revived the old vaudeville catchphrase in sketches on NBC-TV's *Rowan and Martin's Laugh-In* in the late 1960's, often with Sammy Davis, Jr. saying): Here come de judge!

John Marshall (Supreme Court Chief Justice): The acme of judicial distinction means the ability to look a lawyer straight in the eyes for two hours and not hear a damned word he says.

John Marshall: I have always thought, from my earliest youth till now, that the greatest scourge an angry Heaven ever inflicted upon an ungrateful and sinning people was an ignorant, a corrupt, or a dependent judiciary.

John Marshall: It is emphatically the province and duty of the judicial department to say what the law is. Marbury v. Madison, 1 Cranch 137, 2 L ed 60 (1803)

George Mason (1787): An aristocratic body (like the aspiring nature or insidious screw of the judicial aristocracy), like the screw in mechanics, works its way by slow degrees, holds fast to whatever it gains, and should ever be suspected of an encroaching tendency.

Baron de Montesquieu (French lawyer and philosopher, 1689-1755): There is no liberty if the power of judging been not separated from the legislative and executive powers.

Baron de Montesquieu (*Spirit of the Laws*, bk 11): Judges are no more than the mouth that pronounces the words of the law, mere passive beings, incapable of moderating either its force or rigor.

Mother Teresa: If you judge people, you have no time to love them.

H. L. Mencken: Judge - A law student who marks his own examination papers.

Midrash: He who passes judgment on full is himself judged a full.

Michael A. Musmanno (Justice of the Pennsylvania Supreme Court , 1959): A judicial decision should be a searchlight before it becomes a guillotine.

Michael A. Musmanno (Justice of Pennsylvania Supreme Court, 1959): Trial Judges should be extremely wary about drawing word pictures with crayons taken from a box of sheer speculation.

Michael A. Musmanno (Justice of Pennsylvania Supreme Court, 1959): The law does not deal with phantoms nor does it require the performance of meaningless gestures. A trial judge is not expected to pour words on the wheel of an empty millstream. To charge on a nonexistent issue is to light a smoking torch which can only cast flickering shadows on legitimate evidence, thus doing mischief to both parties in litigation and making possible a verdict founded not on fact but on distorted perspectives.

Michael A. Musmanno (Justice of Pennsylvania Supreme Court, 1959): No judge should ever been visibly wrought up in the presence of the jury. He should never hurl thunderbolts of Olympian judgment when there is always the danger that one of them may strike the constitutional rights of the accused. When a judge becomes wrathful on the bench, the fury of his ire may sweep into the jury box and, in consequence, the jury may generate against the target of his rage a resentment which is not kindled from the evidence.

Michael A. Musmanno (Justice of Pennsylvania Supreme Court, 1959): Every decision rendered by a Court becomes a pier for the bridge over which future litigants must pass. To the extent that the bridge is weakened by a bad decision, to that extent an innocent person in the future may plunge through the bridge into the sea of unjust conviction, degradation, shame and disaster.

Michael A. Musmanno ((Justice of Pennsylvania Supreme Court, 1959): A reading of the Court's charge, as it appears in the record, will show that it is as chaotic as a cavalry charge. It advances, retreats, reverses, crosses and recrosses the field of discussion until all sense of direction, purpose, and objective is lost in a mass of riderless words.

Michael A. Musmanno (Justice of the Sup. Ct. of Pennsylvania, 1959): When a judge slashes the neutrality of his charge with a partisan attack, any unctuous words which follow cannot heal, in the little time still remaining of the trial, the wounds he has inflicted.

Michael A. Musmanno ((Justice of Pennsylvania Supreme Court, 1959): Judges unquestionably know more about logic and legal principles than brakemen, engineers and yardmasters, but they do not know as much about running a railroad as railroaders. With every deference to my brethren, I must say that they approach their deliberation of this case over a strange track of logic.

Michael A. Musmanno (Justice of Pennsylvania Supreme Court, 1959): Throughout the entire length of the Judge's charge,..., the defendant's case traveled on a big wheel, while the plaintiffs' rode a small wheel. The defendant's case strode on strong legs, the plaintiffs' case stumbled on short legs. The defendant's case was trumpeted with a brass horn, the plaintiffs' case squeaked through a piccolo. The Trial Judge's charge was unilateral, partisan, partial, warped, unequal, in equitable and unjust.... In this case he threw impartiality to the winds and neutrality to the hounds as he rode the steed of partisnship with the vigor and determination of the cavalry officer. He was apparently determined to see a verdict for the defendant and nothing could thwart him. Facts, law, reason disappeared under the thundering hooves of his partisan charge—and what was inevitable became reality. The jury brought in the verdict desired by the Judge—and Mrs. Bizich fell down the stairs of injustice and unfairness. She never had a chance once the Trial Judge mounted the courser of his charge.

Michael A. Musmanno (Justice of Pennsylvania Supreme Court, 1959): Although the administration of justice has undergone many changes since the first tribal chieftain climbed to the top of a boulder to sit in judgment on his fellow tribesman, all civilizations since then have attested that anyone entrusted with the awesome responsibility of deliberating on the fate of others must be patient, considerate, reflective and temperate—ever holding the scales of justice with an equalizing hand. The Judge in this case, unfortunately, was impatient, inconsiderate, intemperate and, throughout the trial rested his arm on that side of the scale assigned to the prosecution. Under his domination the proceedings were no longer a trial by jury as it has come down through the venerating centuries. He used the courtroom as a stage for a solo performance of judicial despotism. The repertoire of his tyranny was limited only by the number of those who appeared before the footlights of his unrestrained ire and sarcasm.

Michael A. Musmanno ((Justice of Pennsylvania Supreme Court, 1959): Without intending any disrespect I cannot help feeling that the description of the mechanical door involved in this case, as given in the Majority Opinion, sounds like the description of complicated invention in a Rube Goldberg cartoon,... As the majority opinion progresses, its logic oscillates from the transverse centerline of precedent until the tension of the facts is overcome by the concomitant force of spring barrel technicality and finally the decision comes to rest in a closed position with the plaintiff lying prostrate outside the doors of the courthouse and the right to jury trial mingling with the dust beside her.

Jawaharlal Nehru: No one expects the judge to embrace every offender and invite him to dinner, but a human element in a trial and sentence would certainly improve matters. The judges are too impersonal, distant, and too little aware of the consequences of the sentences they award. If their awareness could be increased, as well as a sense of fellow-feeling with the prisoner, it would be a great gain. This can only come when the two belong to more or less the same class.

Kenneth P. Nolan: I assume you know enough not to trust any adversary. We're in a business, after all. My third grade teacher Mrs. Lynch always insisted that we be polite. So the proper statement is that judges are different. Nonetheless, I don't trust them. I just blame it on my New York paranoia, having been raised on the philosophy that, on any given subway car, there sits at least one axe murderer. Do not underestimate the power of the robe.... Their agenda is moving cases, satisfying court administration and, if you get in the way, some can chew you up and spit you out with looks, tone of voice, and rulings.

George W. Norris (US Senator): The people can change Congress but only God can change the Supreme Court.

Harry Philo: You can tell the philosophy of a judge by whether or not he/she likes (has compassion for) people.

Plato (*Republic*, bk 3): The judge should not be young; he should have learned to know evil, not from his own soul, but from late and long observance of the nature of evil in others: knowledge should be his guide, not personal experience.

Sir Frederick Pollock (English lawyer, writer, legal historian, 1847-1937, *Judicial Caution and Valour*, 45 L.Q.R. 293, 1929): The problem of judicial interpretation is to hold a just middle way between excess of valour and excess of caution.

Sir Frederick Pollock: Judges are philologists of the highest order. Ex parte Davis, 5 W.R. 522 (1857)

Justice Stewart G. Pollock (retired Justice of NJ Supreme Court (Speech at University of Tulsa College of Law: "Lawyers and Judges as Catchers in the Rye") (in JD Salinger's 1951 book, *The Catcher in the Rye*, the novel's main character, Holden Caulfield, tells his sister Phoebe that what he wanted most to be was a man forever coming to the rescue of children who, while playing a game in a field of rye, become so excited that they unwittingly start to run off a cliff. Holden longs to save them—the catcher in the rye): "The lesson that I draw from the conversation between Holden and Phoebe addresses something more compelling than abstract legal analysis, as important as is such analysis. For me, the dialogue illustrates the crucial battle being waged for the soul of the legal profession. Holden Caulfield has figured out, perhaps without realizing it, what state court judges do. In today's world, state courts are the catchers in the rye. For some many people, state courts are all that stand between them and the edge of the cliff. That cliff endangers the poor, the homeless, and the jobless. It threatens public school children in impoverished school districts with an inadequate education. It imposes intolerable conditions on people living in penal and mental institutions. The cliff condemns anyone who falls over its edge to poverty, ignorance and isolation. Ultimately, it puts us all at peril of living in a world of lawless ness and injustice. Injustice, like any precipice, does not distinguish between those who do and do not deserve to fall over its edge.... To conclude, I invite you to join me and Holden Caulfield in the rye "on the edge of the cliff." It may be, as Holden said, "crazy," but what better way to spend your life than "to catch everybody if they start to go over the cliff... "—to be a catcher in the rye.

Alexander Pope: The hungry judges soon the sentence sign, / And wretches hang that jurymen may dine.

Roscoe Pound (American lawyer, dean Harvard Law School, legal writer, 1870-1964): There is strong aversion to straight-forward change of any important legal doctrine. The cry is interpret it. But such interpretation is spurious. It is legislation.

Lewis F. Powell Jr. (Supreme Court Justice): For the most part... we function as nine small independent law firms.

Lewis F. Powell Jr. (Supreme Court Justice): In an era of "sound bites" and instant opinion polls it is dangerous to apply broad labels to a single Supreme Court term.

Ronald Reagan: I will appoint the first woman to the Supreme Court.

Chief Justice William H. Rehnquist: The right to one's day in court is meaningless if the judge who hears the case lacks the talent, experience and temperament that will enable him to protect imperiled rights and to render a fair decision.

Darlene Ricker: Judges are, in many respects, like parents. You have to give them a good enough reason to do what you want.

Will Rogers: Good judgment comes from experience, and a lot of that comes from bad judgment.

Will Rogers: When you're throwin' your weight around, be ready to have it thrown around by somebody else.

Franklin D. Roosevelt: We want a Supreme Court which will do justice under the Constitution—not over it. In our courts we want a government of laws and not of men.

Theodore Roosevelt: The decisions of the courts on economic and social questions depend on their economic and social philosophy.

Theodore Roosevelt (after Oliver Wendell Holmes' dissent in *Northern Secur. Co. v. US*, 193 US 197, 48 L ed 679, 24 S Ct 436, 1904): I could carve out of a banana, a judge with more backbone than that.

Russian Proverb: The thing to fear is not the law but the judge.

Arthur M. Schlesinger, Jr.: The Supreme Court is becoming a wholly owned subsidiary of the rich and powerful, instead of the impartial and compassionate tribunal it has been.

William Shakespeare (*Cymbeline,* Act IV, ii): Why should we be tender / To let an arrogant piece of flesh threat us, / Play judge and executioner all himself?

William Shakespeare (*I Henry,* Act II, iv): Between two hawks, which flies the higher pitch, / Between two dogs, which hath the deeper mouth, / Between two blades, which bears the better temper, / Between two horses, which doth bear him best, / Between two girls, which hath the merriest eye, / I have, perhaps, some shallow spirit of judgment: / But in these nice sharp quillets of the law, / Good faith, I am no wiser than a daw.

William Shakespeare (*Henry VIII,* Act III, i): Heaven is above all yet; there sits a Judge, / That no King can corrupt.

William Shakespeare (*Measure for Measure,* Act II, ii): Thieves for their robbery have authority / When judges steal themselves.

William Shakespeare (*Measure for Measure,* Act II, ii): The marshall's truncheon, nor the judge's robe, / Become them with one half so good a grace / As mercy does.

William Shakespeare (*Measure for Measure,* Act III, ii): He who the sword of heaven will bear / Should be as holy as severe; / Pattern in himself, to know, / Grace to stand, and virtue go; / More nor less to others paying, / Than by self offenses weighing. / Shame to him, whose cruel striking / Kills for faults of his own liking!

William Shakespeare (*The Merchant of Venice,* Act II, ix): To offend and judge, are different offices, / And of opposed natures.

William Shakespeare (*The Merchant of Venice,* Act IV, i): O wise and upright judge! / How much more elder art thou than thy looks!

William Shakespeare (*The Merchant of Venice,* Act IV, i): SHYLOCK: It does appear you are a worthy judge; / You know the law; your exposition / Hath been most sound: I charge you by the law, / Proceed to judgment.

William Shakespeare (*The Merchant of Venice,* Act IV, i): A Daniel come to judgment! Yea a Daniel! / O wise young judge, how I do honour thee!

William Shakespeare (*The Merchant of Venice,* Act IV, i): The quality of mercy is not strained; / It droppeth as the gentle rain from heaven / Upon the place beneath. It is twice blessed - / It blesseth him that gives, and him that takes.

William Shakespeare (*Merry Wives of Windsor,* Act I, i): He's a justice of peace in his country, simple though I stand here.

William Shakespeare (*Richard III,* Act I, iv): What is my offence? / Where is the evidence that doth accuse me? / What lawful quest have given their verdict up / Unto the frowning judge?

Seneca: A judge is unjust who hears one side of a case, even though he decides it justly.

Socrates: Four things belong to a judge: to hear courteously, to answer wisely, to consider soberly, and to decide impartially.

Harlan Fiske Stone (New York lawyer, Chief Justice US Supreme Court, 1872-1946): While unconstitutional exercise of power by the executive and legislative branches is subject to judicial restraint, the only check upon our own exercise of power is our own sense of self- restraint.

Joseph Story: When I examine a question, I go from headland to headland, from case to case; Marshall (EDITOR: referring to Chief Justice John Marshall) has a compass, puts out to sea, and goes directly to the result.

Publilius Syrus 1st Century BC, Roman Writer: The judge is condemned/found guilty when a criminal is acquitted.

Tacitus: Judges are best in the beginning; they deteriorate as time passes.

Talmud: When a judge sits in judgment over a fellow man, he should feel as if a sword is pointed at his own heart.

Talmud: A habitual borrower is unfit to be a judge.

Harry S. Truman: Whenever you put them in on the Supreme Court he ceases to be your friend.

Mark Twain: Those people.... early stricken of God, intellectually – the departmental interpreters (Editor: Judges and/or Supreme Court Justices) of the laws in Washington ... can always be depended on to take any reasonably good law and interpret the common sense all out of it.

Mark Twain: The administration of the law can never go lax where every individual sees to it that it grows not lax in his own case, or in cases which fall under his (EDITOR: The Judge's) eyes.

UA (EDITOR: one of the earliest references to the "sobriety" of judges' catch phrase, *Terence Made English*, 1694): I thought myself as sober as a judge.

UA (EDITOR: derisive term applied to last-minute appointments by President John Adams pursuant to the Judiciary Act of 1801 which created six new federal circuit courts with sixteen new judges, appointed on last day of Adams' term of office): Midnight Judges.

UA (Attributed to Sir Francis Buller, an English judge, 1745-1800, who in dictum announced that a husband may beat his wife with a stick no thicker than his thumb, but no substantial evidence of such an opinion exists): JUDGE THUMB.

Morris K. Udall (US Congressman, contrasting Supreme Court Justices and Ku Klux Klan members): One puts on black robes to scare the hell out of white people, while the other puts on white robes to scare the hell out of blacks.

Joseph A. Wapner: The ability of the judge to put himself into the shoes of the men and women who appear before him is the heart of being a decent judge.

Earl Warren (*The Law and the Future*, 52 Fortune 107, 1955): Our judges are not monks or scientists, but participants in the living stream of our national life steering the law between the dangers of rigidity on the one hand and of formlessness on the other.

H.G. Wells: The lawgiver, of all beings, most owes the law allegiance. He of all men should behave as though the law compelled him. But it is the universal weakness of mankind that what we are given to administer we presently imagine we own.

Benjamin Whichcote: The judge is nothing but the law speaking.

JUDGMENT (See also JUDGES)

Uncle Anthony: There's no such thing as a "judgment call" between a right way and a wrong way!

Uncle Anthony: That guy's scarry – he's stuck for an answer when someone says "Hello."

Aunt Mary Carlo: Yeah, he uses "good judgment" – he finds out which way the crowd is goin' den he jumps out in front and waves his flag.

Apocrypha, Ecclesiasticus, 11:28: Judge none blessed before his death: for a man shall be known in his children.

Yogi Berra: When you come to a fork in the road, take it!

Bible: Daniel 5:27: Thou are weighed in the balances, and art found wanting.

Bible: Luke 6:37: Judge not, and ye shall not be judged: condemn not, and ye shall not be condemned: forgive, and ye shall be forgiven.

Bible: Luke 19:22: Out of thine own mouth will I judge thee.

Bible: Mark 6:11; Matthew 10:15: It shall be more tolerable for Sodom and Gomorrha in the day of judgment than for that city.

Bible: Matthew 7:3: And why beholdest thou the mote that is in thy brother's eye, but considereth not the beam that is in thine own eye? Or how wilt thou say to thy brother, Let me pull out the mote out of thine eye; and, behold, a beam is in thine own eye? Thou hypocrite, first cast out the beam out of thine own eye; and then shalt thou see clearly to cast out the mote of thy brother's eye.

Bible: Psalms 19:9: The judgments of the Lord are true and righteous altogether. More to be desired are they than gold, yea than much fine gold: sweeter also than honey and the honeycomb.

Bible: Revelations, 6:17: The great day of His wrath is come; and who shall be able to stand?

Bible: Revelations, 14:7: Fear God, and give glory to Him; for the hour of His judgment is come.

Bible: Revelations, 20:12: I saw the dead, small and great, stand before God.

Bible: Revelations, 20:13: Death and hell delivered up the dead which were in them: and they were judged every man according to their works.

Bible: Revelations, 20:15: Whosoever was not found written in the book of life was cast into the lake of fire.

Ambrose Bierce: DECIDE, v.i. To succumb to the preponderance of one set of influences over another set.

Ambrose Bierce: DELIBERATION, n. The act of examining one's bread to determine which side it is buttered on.

Josh Billings: No man has yet lived long enough in this world to doubt the infallibility of his own judgment.

Giosue Borsi: When the judge is unjust he is no longer a judge but a transgressor.

Edmund Burke: The wise determine from the gravity of the case; the irritable, from sensibility to oppression; the high-minded, from disdain and indignation at abuse of power in unworthy hands.

G. K. Chesterton: To have a right to do a thing is not at all the same as to be right in doing it.

Sir Winston Churchill: What most people call bad judgment, is judgment which is different from theirs.

Sir Winston Churchill: It is not open to the cool bystander ... to set himself up as an impartial judge of events which would never have occurred had he outstretched a helping hand in time.

Caleb Colton: To judge by the event is an error that all commit; for in every instance, courage, if crowned with success, is heroism; if clouded by defeat, temerity.

Epictetus: As the touchtone which tries gold, but is not itself tried by gold, such is he who has the true standard of judgment.

Euripedes: A man's most valuable trait is a judicious sense of what not to believe.

Felix Frankfurter: When an issue is squarely and fully presented to the Court and its disposition is essential to the result reached in a case, the issue is decided, whether the Court says much or little, whether the opinion is didactic or elliptical. (dissenting opinion) Federal Maritime Board v Isbrandtsen Co., 356 US 481, 2 L ed 2d 926, 78 S Ct 851 (1958)

Felix Frankfurter (*Mr. Justice Brandeis and the Constitution*, 45 Harv. L. Rev. 33, 1931): To quote from Mr. Justice Brandeis' opinions is not to pick plums from the pudding but to pull threads from a pattern. He achieves not by epigrammatic thrust but through powerful exposition.

Felix Frankfurter (*Mr. Justice Brandeis and the Constitution*, 45 Harv. L. Rev. 33, 1931): To consider Mr. Justice Holmes' opinions is to string pearls.

Robert Frost: The most terrible thing is your own judgment.

Andre Gide: In order to judge properly, one must get away somewhat from what one is judging, after having loved it. This is true of countries, of persons, and of oneself.

Malcolm Gladwell: If we are to improve the quality of the decisions we make, we need to accept the mysterious nature of our snap judgments.

William Hazlitt: The seat of knowledge is in the head; of wisdom, in the heart.—We are sure to judge wrong if we do not feel right.

Richard Hill: Fools measure actions after they are done, by the event; wise men beforehand, by the rules of reason and right. The former look to the end to judge of the act. Let me look to the act, and leave the end to God.

Joan of Arc (The Trial of Jeanne d'Arc, 1431): You say you are my judge; I do not know if you are; but take good heed not to judge me ill, because you would put yourself in great peril.

Ben Jonson: Judgment is forced upon us by experience.

Joseph Joubert: There are some minds like either convex or concave mirrors, which represent objects such as they receive them, but they never receive them as they are.

Sir Roger L'Estrange: Men are not to be judged by their looks, habits, and appearances; but by the character of their lives and conversations, and by their works.—It is better to be praised by one's own works than by the words of another.

Henry Wadsworth Longfellow: We judge ourselves by what we feel capable of doing; others judge us by what we have done.

John Lubbock: Our duty is to believe that for which we have sufficient evidence, and to suspend our judgment when we have not.

Alexander Pope: It is with our judgments as with our watches: no two go just alike, yet each believes his own.

Will Rogers: Good judgment comes from experience, and a lot of that comes from bad judgment.

Theodore Roosevelt: Nine-tenths of wisdom consists in being wise in time.

Donald Rumsfeld: Listening to both sides does not necessarily bring about a correct judgment.

William Shakespeare (*All's Well That Ends Well*, Act II, i): He that of greatest works is finisher / Oft does them by the weakest minister: / So holy writ in babes hath judgment shown / When judges have been babes.

William Shakespeare (*Antony and Cleopatra*, Act I, v): My salad days when I was green in judgment.

William Shakespeare (*Antony and Cleopatra*, Act III, ii): I see, men's judgments are / A parcel of their fortunes; and things outward / Do draw all inward quality after them, / To suffer all alike.

William Shakespeare (*Hamlet*, Act I, iii): Give every man thy ear, but few thy voice; / Take each man's censure, but reserve thy judgement.

William Shakespeare (*Hamlet*, Act I, v): No reckoning made, but sent to my account / With all my imperfections on my head.

William Shakespeare (*Hamlet*, Act III, ii): Blest are those / Whose blood and judgement are so well commingled / That they are not a pipe for fortune's finger / To sound what stop she please.

William Shakespeare (*II Henry VI*, Act III, iii): Forbear to judge for we are sinners all.

William Shakespeare (*Henry VIII*, Act I, ii): What we oft do best, / By sick interpreters, once, weak ones, is / Not ours, or not allow'd; what worst, as oft, / Hitting a grosser quality, is cried up / For our best act.

William Shakespeare (*Julius Caesar*, Act III, ii): O judgement! Thou art fled to brutish beasts, / And men have lost their reason!

William Shakespeare (*King Lear*, Act I, i): Answer my life my judgement.

William Shakespeare (*Measure for Measure,* Act II, ii): Why, all the souls that were, were forfeit once; / And He that might the vantage best have took / Found out the remedy. How would you be, / If He, which is the top of judgement, should / But judge you as you are?

William Shakespeare (*The Merchant of Venice*, Act IV, i): I stand for judgment: answer: shall I have it?

William Shakespeare (*The Merchant of Venice*, Act I, iii): I charge you by the law, / Whereof you are a well deserving pillar, / Proceed to judgment.

William Shakespeare (*The Merchant of Venice*, Act IV, i): A Daniel come to judgment! Yea, a Daniel.

William Shakespeare (*The Merchant of Venice*, Act IV, i): What judgement shall I dread, doing no wrong?

William Shakespeare (*Richard III*, Act I, iv): The urging of that word, judgment, hath bred a kind of remorse in me.

Sir Philip Sidney: In forming a judgment, lay your hearts void of fore-taken opinions; else, whatsoever is done or said will be measured by a wrong rule; like them who have the jaundice, to whom everything appeareth yellow.

Robert Southey: How little do they see what really is, who frame their hasty judgment upon that which seems.

Jeremy Taylor: Never be a judge between thy friends in any matter where both set their hearts upon the victory. If strangers or enemies be litigants, whatever side thou favorest, thou gettest a friend; but when friends are the parties thou losest one.

Terence: Human nature is so constituted, that all see and judge better in the affairs of other men than in their own.

Mark Twain: In this topsy-turvy, crazy, illogical world, Man has made laws for himself. He has fenced round with them, mainly with the idea of keeping communities together, and gain for the strongest. No woman was consulted in the making of laws. And nine-tenths of the people who are daily obeying – or fighting against – Nature's laws, have no real opinion. Opinion means deduction, after weighing the matter, and deep thought upon it. They simply echo feeling, because for generations forbears have laid something down as an axiom. They do not investigate or weigh for themselves. The axiom of the forbears was, "It is immoral to follow God's law, unless bound by man's law and wedding ring."

Mark Twain: Those people.... early stricken of God, intellectually – the departmental interpreters (Editor: Judges and/or Supreme Court Justices) of the laws in Washington ... can always be depended on to take any reasonably good law and interpret the common sense all out of it.

Mark Twain: The administration of the law can never go lax where every individual sees to it that it grows not lax in his own case, or in cases which fall under his (Editor: The Judge's) eyes.

Duke of Wellington (Arthur Wellesley, British general, 1769-1852): I mistrust the judgment of every man in a case in which his own wishes are concerned.

Richard Whately: The judgment is like a pair of scales, and evidences like the weights; but the will holds the balances in its hand; and even a slight jerk will be sufficient, in many cases, to make the lighter scale appear the heavier.

Richard Wheatley: In our judgment of human transactions, the law of optics is reversed; we see the most indistinctly the objects which are close around us.

Woodrow Wilson: One cool judgment is worth a thousand hasty councils. The thing to be supplied is light, not heat.

JURY

Uncle Anthony: You should never tell anybody what they're gonna find or decide ... just help 'em make the right choices for the right reasons.

Uncle Anthony: Ya don't have to spend money on some high fallootin' psychologists or consultants to help you to pick a jury that likes yer client or your case – go get a good cab driver or a good old waitress – they know people – they know whose gonna like you, your client, and your case.

Aunt Mary Carlo: I tink a jury's got the right to be proud of demself when dey get done dere job, just like you.

John Adams (Second President of U.S.) (1771): It is not only his (the juror's) right, but his duty...to find the verdict according to his own best understanding, judgment, and conscience, though in direct opposition to the direction of the court.

John Adams (1774): Representative government and trial by jury are the heart and lungs of liberty. Without them we have no other fortification against being ridden like horses, fleeced like sheep, worked like cattle and fed and clothed like swine and hounds.

John Quincy Adams (Massachusetts lawyer, President of US; 1767-1848; 1839): The struggle for American independence was for chartered rights, for English liberties, for trial by jury, habeas corpus and *Magna Carta*.

Samuel Adams (1772): The Magna Carta is a constrained declaration of our original, inherent, indefeasible natural rights as citizens.

Ellen Alderman & Caroline Kennedy, *In Our Defense: The Bill of Rights in Action,* (1991): Historically, the right to a civil jury has been one of the most prized and excepted of all those in the Bill of Rights. It was included in the original Jamestown Charter of 1607, and by 1776 all 13 colonies protected the right in some form.... (Since this) right was secured in 1791, the Supreme Court has repeatedly recognized that the right to a civil jury has "so from a place in our history," and "is so fundamental and sacred to the citizen" that it must be" jealously guarded by the courts."

Ellen Alderman & Caroline Kennedy, *In Our Defense: The Bill of Rights in Action* (1991): Historically the right to a civil jury has been one of the most prized and accepted of all those in the Bill of Rights.

Albert Averbach, *Tampering With the Jury System* (1956): Since it was first recognized in the *Magna Carta*, trial by jury has been a prized shield against oppression. It is a right treasured by the American people.

Steven E. Barkan ("Jury Nullification in Political Trials," Social Problems, 31, No. 1, 38, Oct. 1983): "Jury acquittals in the colonial, abolitionist, and post-bellum eras of the United States helped advance insurgent aims and hamper government efforts at social control. Wide spread jury acquittals or hung juries during the Vietnam War might have had the same effect. But the refusal of judges in trials of anti war protesters to inform juries of their power to disregard the law helped ensure convictions, which in turn frustrated anti-war goals and protected the government from the many repercussions that acquittals or hung juries would have brought."

Sydney Biddle Barrows: If the district attorney wanted, a grand jury would indict a ham sandwich.

Dave Barry: We operate under a jury system in this country, and as much as we complain about it, we have to admit that we know of no better system, except possibly flipping a coin.

Judge David Bazelon (U.S. v. Dougherty, 473 F.2d 1113, 1140, D.C. Circ. 1972): "The drafters of legal rules cannot anticipate and take account of every case where a defendant's conduct is 'unlawful' but not blameworthy, any more than they can draw a bold line to mark the boundary between an accident and negligence. It is the jury—as spokesman for the community's sense of values—that must explore that subtle and elusive boundary."

Judge David Bazelon (*"The Adversary Process: Who Needs It?,"* 12th Annual James Madison Lecture, NY University School of Law, April, 1971, reprinted in 117 Cong. Rec. 5852, 5855, daily ed. April 29, 1971): It's easy for the public to ignore an unjust law, if the law operates behind closed doors and out of sight. But when jurors have to use a law to send a man to prison, they are forced to think long and hard about the justice of the law. And when the public reads newspaper accounts of criminal trials and convictions, they too may think about whether the convictions are just. As a result, jurors and spectators alike may bring to public debate more informed interest in improving the criminal law. Any law which makes many people uncomfortable is likely to attract the attention of the legislature. The laws on narcotics and abortion come to mind and there must be others. The public adversary trial thus provides an important mechanism for keeping the substantive criminal law in tune with contemporary community values.

Jeremy Bentham (English philosopher, 1832): The law of England has established trial by judge and jury in the conviction that it is the mode best calculated to ascertain the truth.

Sidney Bernard: Jury duty is a bog of quicksand on the path to justice.

Bible: John 7:51: Nicodemus: "Doth our law judge any man, before it hear him, and know what he doeth?

Bible: Proverbs 31:9: Open thy mouth, (and) judge righteously, ...

Ambrose Bierce: In the McFarland case the defendant set up the plea of insanity, and succeeded in proving himself a fool. And he was acquitted by a jury of his peers.

Ambrose Bierce: DELIBERATION, n. The act of examining one's bread to determine which side it is buttered on.

Ambrose Bierce: INADMISSIBLE, adj. Not competent to be considered. Said of certain kinds of testimony which juries are supposed to be unfit to be entrusted with, and which judges, therefore, rule out, even of proceedings before themselves alone. Hearsay evidence is inadmissable because the person quoted was unsworn and is not before the court for examination; yet most momentous actions, military, political, commercial and of every other kind, are daily undertaken on hearsay evidence. Revelation is hearsay evidence; that the Scriptures are the word of God we have only the testimony of men long dead whose identity is not clearly established and who are not known to have been sworn in any sense. Under the rules of evidence as they now exist in this country, no single assertion in the Bible has in its support any evidence admissible in a court of law. It cannot be proved that the battle of Blenheim ever was fought, that there was such a person as Julius Caesar, such an empire as Assyria. / But as records of courts of justice are admissible, it can easily be proved that powerful and malevolent magicians once existed and were a scourge to mankind. The evidence (including confession) upon which certain women were convicted of witchcraft and executed was without a flaw; it is still unimpeachable. The judges' decisions based on it were sound in logic and in law. Nothing in any existing court was ever more thoroughly proved than the charges of witchcraft and sorcery for which so many suffered death. If there were no witches, human testimony and human reason are alike destitute of value.

Justice Hugo Black, United States Supreme Court (1939): The founders of our government thought that trial by civil jury was an essential bulwark of civil liberty.

Justice Hugo Black (Smith v. Texas, 1940): "It is part of the established tradition in the use of juries as instruments of public justice that the jury be a body truly representative of the community. For racial discrimination to result in the exclusion from jury service of otherwise qualified groups not only violates our Constitution and the laws enacted under it, but is at war with our basic concepts of a democratic society and a representative government.... "If there has been discrimination, whether accomplished ingeniously or ingenuously, the conviction cannot stand."

Justice Hugo Black: The jury injects a democratic element into the law. This element is vital to the effective administration of criminal justice, not only in safeguarding the rights of the accused, but in encouraging popular acceptance of the laws and the necessary general acquiescence in their application. It can hardly be denied that trial by jury removes the great burden from the shoulders of the judiciary. Martyrdom does not come easily to a man who has been found guilty as charged by twelve of his neighbors and fellow citizens. (dissenting opinion) *Green v. US*, 356 US 165, 2 L ed 672, 78 S Ct 632, 1958.

Sir William Blackstone (English lawyer, 1723-1780, *Commentaries*, bk 3,): The trial by jury has been, and I trust ever will be, looked upon as the glory of the English law. And if it has so great an advantage over others in regulating civil property, how much must that advantage be heightened when it is applied to criminal cases!

Sir William Blackstone (*Commentaries on the Laws of England,* 1765-1769): "Every new tribunal, erected for the decision of facts, without the intervention of a jury...is a step towards establishing aristocracy, the most oppressive of absolute governments."

Sir William Blackstone (*Commentaries*, bk 3): That principal criterion of truth in the law of England.

Sir William Blackstone (1768): Trial by jury is the principal bulwark of our liberties.

Morris J. Bloomstein, (*Verdict: The Jury System,* 1968): Those twelve citizens in the jury box are the cornerstone of our judicial process.

Judge George H. Boldt (U.S. federal court judge, U.S. V. Beck, Feb., 1959): Jury service honorably performed is as important in the defense of our country, its Constitution and laws, and the ideals and standards for which they stand, as the service that is rendered by the soldier on the field of battle in time of war.

Boston, Resolution of the Town of Boston (1765): The most essential rights of the British subjects are representative government and trial by jury. These are the very pillars of the British Constitution founded in the common rights of mankind.

Stanley F. Brewster (*Twelve Men in a Box,* 1934): Jury trial offers the most satisfactory means of settlement of civil disputes and is looked upon today by American citizens as one of the most precious rights secured by our forefathers.

Henry Peter Brougham, Lord Chancellor of England (1828): What individual can so well assess the amount of damages which a plaintiff ought to recover for an injury he has received than an intelligent jury?

William Jennings Bryan: The essence of democracy is found in the right of the people to have what they want. There is more virtue in the people themselves, than can be found anywhere else.

William J. Campbell: Today, the grand jury is the total captive of the prosecutor, who, if he is candid, will concede that he can indict anybody, any time, for almost anything, before any grand jury.

Henry Care, (*English Liberties* 1680): Trial by jury ranks among the choicest of our fundamental laws and whosoever shall openly suppress or craftily undermine it is an enemy and traitor to his king and country.

Lewis Carrol, (*Alice in Wonderland*): "I'll be the judge, I'll be the jury," said cunning old Fury; "I'll try the whole cause, and condemn you to death."

Lewis Carrol, (*Alice in Wonderland*): "No! No! Sentence first—verdict afterwards."

D.H. Chamberlain (*American System of Trial by Jury,* 1887): Trial by jury presents the foremost feature of the system of jurisprudence under which the English race has gained its liberties, and through which those liberties will in the future be preserved.

Samuel Chase (1804): The jury has the right to determine both the law and the facts.

G.K. Chesterton (1909): Our civilization has very justly decided that when it wishes anything done which is really serious, it collects twelve of the ordinary men of an English jury.

G. K. Chesterton: When it wishes anything done which is really serious, it collects twelve of the ordinary men standing round. The same thing was done, if I remember right, by the Founder of Christianity.

Sir Winston Churchill: Trial by jury, the right of every man to be judged by his equals is among the most precious gifts that England bequeathed to America.

Sir Winston Churchill: The jury system has come to stand for all we mean by English justice, because so long as a case has to be scrutinized by 12 honest men (and women), defendant and plaintiff alike have a safeguard from arbitrary perversion of the law.

Sir Winston Churchill: This system (jury trials) which provides for fair and impartial juries in all civil or criminal actions " endures to this day" and acts as a guarantee that "law flows from the people."

Sir Winston Churchill: It is impossible to obtain a conviction for sodomy from an English jury. Half of them don't believe that it can physically be done, and the other half are doing it.

Joseph Coate (ABA President, 1898): All attempts to tinker or tamper with trial by jury in civil causes should be discouraged as disastrous to the public welfare.

Harold H. Corbin (*The Jury on Trial,* 1928): The jury's homely experience, its touch with human affairs and its contact in everyday society endow it with a special ability to see and know what the real facts are.

Cynthia J. Cohen (*Whatever Happened to the Seventh Amendment?* 1991): The civil jury was intended to serve as a means of political expression for average citizens. No other political institution can fulfill this role. Unless we find new respect for the Seventh Amendment, one of the basic elements of our democracy may be lost.

Sir Edward Coke, Chief Justice of Common Pleas (1628): Trial by jury is a wise distribution of power which exceeds all other modes of trial.

Charles T. Coleman (*Origin of Trial by Jury,* 1919): The jury system appeals with peculiar force to the great masses of common people.... It shields individual rights from the encroachment of government power; it imbues the ordinary citizen with an important part in the administration of governmental affairs; and it makes the people the of a state the keepers of the conscience of the laws of that state. But above all, the jury system is especially dear to the heart of the masses, because service on the jury is the simple transfiguring ceremony which the shoulder of every citizen, whatever the accident of his birth or station, tingles with that matchless precept of the law that all men are born free, equal and independent.

Continental Congress, Declaration of the First Continental Congress (1774): The colonies are entitled to the great and inestimable privilege of being tried by their peers.

James Fenimore Cooper: Juries ... have the effect ... of placing the control of the law in the hands of those who would be most apt to abuse it.

Alfred C. Coxe (*The Trials of Jury Trials,* 1901): Trial by jury is the best system yet devised. Its foundations are laid deep in the hearts of liberty-loving Anglo-Saxons. Without it, the Republic would be deprived of one of its most effective weapons against absolutism, intolerance and greed.

Peter W. Culley (*In Defense of Civil Juries,* 1983): The civil jury is firmly embedded in our system of justice. It is difficult to conceive of a better mechanism for establishing standards to which members of the community must conform.

Greg Cusimano: It is not that the jury will believe it if they see it, instead it is if they believe it they will see it.

Greg Cusimano: The jury's eye follows the action.

Greg Cusimano: Sometimes juries don't treat my wife's husband very well.

Clarence Darrow: I never saw twelve men in my life, that if you could get them to understand a human case, were not true and right.

Clarence Darrow (Debate with Judge Alfred J. Talley, Oct. 27, 1924): "Why not reenact the code of Blackstone's day? Why, the judges were all for it—every one of them—and the only way we got rid of those laws was because juries were too humane to obey the courts. "That is the only way we got rid of punishing old women, of hanging old women in New England—because, in spite of all the courts, the juries would no longer convict them for a crime that never existed."

Delaware Declaration of Rights (1776): Trial by jury is one of the greatest securities of the lives, liberties and estates of the people.

Delphin M. Delmas (*The Democracy of Justice,* 1918): Trial by jury is the most enduring of all institutions which have flourished among the English-speaking peoples. No other institution ever struck its roots so deep into their hearts. Its decay would mark the decadence, and its overthrow be the end of popular government.

Lord Denman, (O'Connel v. R., 1884): "Every jury in the land is tampered with and falsely instructed by the judge when it is told it must take (or accept) as the law that which has been given to them, or that they must bring in a certain verdict, or that they can decide only the facts of the case."

Charles Dickens (*Pickwick Papers*): "I wonder what the foreman of the jury, whoever he'll be, has got for breakfast, said Mr. Snodgrass.... "Ah!" said Perker, "I hope he's got a good one." "Why so?" inquired Mr. Pickwick. "Highly important – very important, my dear Sir," replied Perker. "A good, contented, well-breakfasted juryman, is a capital thing to get hold of. Discontented or hungry jurymen, my dear Sir, always find for the plaintiff." (EDITOR: I wish jurors were that predictable)

John Dickinson (Delaware, 1788): Trial by jury is the cornerstone of our liberties. We must guard it with jealous circumspection against those new and arbitrary methods of trial which may imperceptibly undermine it. Trial by jury is our birthright; who in opposition to the genius of United America, shall dare to attempt its subversion?

Paula Di Perna (*Faces of American Justice*, 1984): The concept of the jury system is as close as any society has ever come to true democracy.

William J. Donnelly (*The Confetti Generation: How the New Communications Technology Is Fragmenting America*, 1986): There is little doubt about the revolutionary potential of the new electronic media in our society and culture.... at some very early point, nearly everyone between the ages of ten and forty-nine today will have at least two new electronic media in their homes: (1) a random acess information system (home computer, videotext, optical videodisc); and (2) a fickle access entertainment system (cable television, pay television, videocassette, video game)...The new media encompasses a quantum leap in the ability to store and retrieve information; a quantum leap in the availability of mimetic entertainment that is readily internalized; a quantum leap in services that provide controlled, individualized, remote transactions; and a quantum leap in speed, to the point of warping our sense of time...together, they will produce and define **THE CONFETTI GENERATION.**

William J. Donnelly (*The Confetti Generation: How the New Communications Technology Is Fragmenting America*, 1986): To appreciate the living experience of the Confetti Generation, we should ask ourselves a few simple questions. When ideas and experiences float down upon us like confetti – and just as cheaply – how do we expect to choose?....The electronification of our lives that began with television and the use of computers ... wil become pervasive and microspecific... That is our destination, but what is our destiny? ... In **THE CONFETTI GENERATION**, we will be living undirected lives and life-styles. We will think and act not only for ourselves, but by ourselves, isolated from the common experiences and judgments of others... we are about to think and choose and live differently than ever before in history.

Justice William O. Douglas (United States Supreme Court, 1954): Representative government and trial by jury are invaluable rights without which a people cannot be free and happy.

Finley Peter Dunne (*The Power of the Press*, 1906): Th' lawyers make th' law; th' judges make th' errors, but th' iditors make th' juries.

Finley Peter Dunne (*Mr Dooley on Making a Will: On Criminal Trials*): In due time twelve men iv intilligence who have r-read th' pa-papers an' can't remimber what they've r-read, or who can't r-read, or ar-re out iv wurruk, ar-re injooced to sarve, an' th' awful wheels iv justice begins to go round.

Finley Peter Dunne (*Mr. Dooley in Peace and War: On Expert Testimony*): Whin th' case is all over, the jury'll pitch th' tistimony out iv th' window, an' consider three questions: "Did Lootgert look as though he'd kill his wife? Did his wife look as though she ought to be kilt? Isn't it time we wint to supper?"

Lester P. Edge (*Jury System? Yes.*, 1925): The jury system is as fundamental as freedom of speech, habeas corpus, due process of law, or any of the other guarantees of the Bill of Rights.

Ralph Waldo Emerson (*Spiritual Laws*): I have heard an experienced counsellor say that he never feared the effect upon a jury of a lawyer who does not believe in his heart that his client ought to have a verdict. If he does not believe it, his unbelief will appear to the jury, despite all his protestations, and will become their unbelief.

J. Kendall Few (*In Defense of Trial by Jury*, at p. 9): In his *History of Trial by Jury*, William Forsythe wrote that "few subjects have exercised the ingenuity and baffled the research of the historian more than the origin of the jury." Its origin, he says "is lost in the night of time." Rene Wormser traced the jury to Solon, Athenian statesman of 638-588 B.C. Maximus A. Lesser concluded that an institution resembling the modern jury originated among the Greeks at the earliest civilized period and was brought to England by the Romans. Matthew Hale attributed the antiquity of trial by jury to the early Britons and later, to the Saxons long before the Norman Conquest. William Blackstone noted that many are apt to impute its invention to "the superior genius of Alfred the Great" (871-899 A.D.), but concluded that trial by jury "hath been used time out of mine in this nation and seems to have been co-eval with the first civil government thereof."// The more modern view is represented by Pollock and Maitland, traced the history of the modern jury to the Frankish Inquest of the 9th century, later brought to England by William the Conqueror in 1066 A.D. Likewise, William Holdsworth concluded that "though there may be more than one origin for the jury (and) though England may have been prepared for its introduction, it was definitely introduced by the Norman Kings."// According to Forsythe's *History of Trial by Jury*, this ancient institution "does not owe its existence to any positive law," but arose "silently and gradually" out of the usages of society. An institution similar in nature to the modern jury can be traced to the laws of King Ethelred around 977 A.D. A Saxon court was directed to be held in every local area in which 12 nights and a representative of the Crown swore upon a sacred object "that they will accuse no innocent man, nor conceal any guilty one." Although Stenton's *Anglo-Saxon England* acknowledges that "the sworn jury is unknown to pure old English law" and concludes that "the Norman kings established the jury as a regular part of the machinery of English government," he found sufficient evidence of the use of institutions resembling juries by the Saxons to believe that the ultimate establishment of the jury as a recognized institution resulted as much from old English practice as it did from the Norman Conquest. // Regardless of its origin, the one point upon which all historians appear to agree is that our modern jury system owes much of its impetus to the laws of Henry II (1154-1189), great-grandson of William the Conqueror, and to the *Magna Carta* of King John in 1215 A.D.

J. Kendall Few: (As early as 2000 B.C.) A form of jury called the *Kenbet* existed in ancient Egypt with eight jurors, four from each side of the Nile. Also, according to Forsythe, in the Swedish *Nambd*, which existed "from time immemorial," there are "many curious points of resemblance" to the English jury. Similar institutions also existed in other Scandinavian countries.

J. Kendall Few: The most significant provision of the *Magna Carta* was Article 39 which provided that "no free man shall be seized, or imprisoned, or dispossessed... excepting by the judgment of his peers." For more than seven centuries, this article has been construed as a guarantee of the right of trial by jury both in civil and criminal cases.

William Forsythe (*History of Trial by Jury,* 1852): The right of being tried by his fellow citizens who simply decide according to what they believe to be the truth gives every man a conviction he will be dealt with impartially and inspires him to mete out to others the same measure of equity that is dealt to himself.

Sir John Fortescue, Chief Justice of the Kings Bench (1468): Trial by jury is the most rational and effective method for discovering the truth.

Jerome Frank: Only a very foolish lawyer will dare guess the outcome of a jury trial.

Antonia Fraser (her book "*The Lives of The Kings & Queens of England*"): THE ONE ESSENTIAL VIRTUE of a biography [EDITOR: or a jury] is BALANCE. Two Aspects of Balance = (1) Vital assessment of the evidence. One single question the researcher (EDITOR: or juror) must ask himself in assessing the evidence = HOW & WHY did this come into existence. (Note: the 2 categories of Historical Evidence = (A) That produced for historian's attention, and (B) That produced for some other purpose), and (2) Proper balance of the subject in the age in which the subject lived....Another DUTY of Biographer (EDITOR: and a JUROR) is to sift through and dispel MYTHS

Antonia Fraser: The HISTORIAN'S (EDITOR: JUROR's) DUTY is to:

1. Relate what happened (and what will happen)
2. Grasp the particular and the general or universal
3. Probabilities
4. BALANCE: (A) How & Why, and (B) Relate to the Age or "Totality of Circumstances"
5. BALANCE 2 TYPES of EVIDENCE: (A) Self serving, (B) Produced for other reasons
6. Dispel the MYTHS (EDITOR: Example: Tort Reform Myths)

M. D.A. Freeman (*The Jury on Trial,* 1981): The jury represents democratic self-government. Attacks on the jury system are attacks on the foundations of our political culture.

Robert Frost: A jury consists of 12 persons chosen to decide who has the better lawyer.

Jacob Fuchsberg: The average juror ... wraps himself in civic virtue. He's a judge now. He tries to act the part and do the right thing.

Thomas Fuller: A fox should not be of the jury at a goose's trial.

Elbridge Gerry (Massachusetts, 1787-1788): The jury is adapted to the investigation of truth beyond any other system the world can produce. A tribunal without juries would be a Star Chamber in civil cases.

John F. Geeting (*Trial by Jury Must be Preserved,* 1907): Trial by jury has withstood the reign of tyrants, survived the overthrow of dynasties, and remains as one of the best expressions of free government. This heritage, coming from our liberty-loving ancestors, is one of the foundation stones of our commonwealth.

William S. Gilbert (*Trial by Jury*): Now, Jurymen, hear my advice - / All kinds of vulgar prejudice / I pray you set aside: / With stern judicial frame of mind / From bias free of every kind, / This trial must be tried.

Justices Gray and Shiras (US SUPREME COURT, Dissenting opinion, Sparf and Hansen v. U.S., 156 U.S. 51, 154-155 (1894)): "Within six years after the Constitution was established, the right of the jury, upon the general issue, to determine the law as well as the fact in controversy, was unhesitatingly and unqualifiedly affirmed by this court, in the first of the very few trials by jury ever had at its bar, under the original jurisdiction conferred upon it by the Constitution."

Justices Gray and Shiras (US SUPREME COURT, Dissenting opinion, Sparf and Hansen v. U.S., 156 U.S. 51, 154-155 (1894)): "The report shows that, in a case in which there was no controversy about the facts, the court, while stating to the jury its unanimous opinion upon the law of the case, and reminding them of 'the good old rule, that on questions of fact it is the province of the jury, on questions of law it is the province of the court to decide,' expressly informed them that 'by the same law, which recognizes this reasonable distribution of jurisdiction,' the jury 'have nevertheless a right to take upon themselves to judge of both, and to determine the law as well as the fact in controversy.'"

Justices Gray and Shiras (US SUPREME COURT, Dissenting opinion, Sparf and Hansen v. U.S., 156 U.S. 51, 174 (1894)): "...It is a matter of common observation, that judges and lawyers, even the most upright, able and learned, are sometimes too much influenced by technical rules; and that those judges who are...occupied in the administration of criminal justice are apt, not only to grow severe in their sentences, but to decide questions of law too unfavorably to the accused." The jury having the undoubted and uncontrollable power to determine for themselves the law as well as the fact by a general verdict of acquittal, a denial by the court of their right to exercise this power will be apt to excite in them a spirit of jealousy and contradiction..."

Justices Gray and Shiras (UNITED STATES SUPREME COURT, Dissenting opinion, Sparf and Hansen v. U.S., 156 U.S. 51, 174 (1894)): "...[A] person accused of crime has a twofold protection, in the court and the jury, against being unlawfully convicted. If the evidence appears to the court to be insufficient in law to warrant a conviction, the court may direct an acquittal...But the court can never order the jury to convict; for no one can be found guilty, but by the judgment of his peers."

Justices Gray and Shiras (UNITED STATES SUPREME COURT, Dissenting opinion, Sparf and Hansen v. U.S., 156 U.S. 51, 176 (1894)): "But, as the experience of history shows, it cannot be assumed that judges will always be just and impartial, and free from the inclination, to which even the most upright and learned magistrates have been known to yield from the most patriotic motives, and with the most honest intent to promote symmetry and accuracy in the law of amplifying their own jurisdiction and powers at the expense of those entrusted by the Constitution to other bodies. And there is surely no reason why the chief security of the liberty of the citizen, the judgment of his peers, should be held less sacred in a republic than in a monarchy."

John Guinther (*The Jury in America,* 1988): The civil jury performs a guardian role against oppression; it helps protect us against those who would threaten our health and safety and sets standards for responsibility and fair dealing.

Lord Chief Justice Matthew Hale (English Judge, 1609-1676; 2 Hale P C 312, 1665): "...it is the conscience of the jury that must pronounce the prisoner guilty or not guilty."

Lord Chief Justice Matthew Hale (2 Hale P C 312) (1665): "...it was impossible any matter of law could come in question till the matter of fact were settled and stated and agreed by the jury, and of such matter of fact they [the jury] were the only competent judges."

Connor Hall (*The Present Day Jury,* 1924): In most cases there is a better chance of justice from a jury of ordinary men than from any substitute.

Henry Hallam (*The Constitutional History of England,* 1827): The sacred privilege of trial by jury is the unadulterated voice of the people which should be heard in the sanctuaries of justice as fountains springing fresh from the lap of earth.

Alexander Hamilton (1787): The civil jury is a valuable safeguard to liberty.

Alexander Hamilton (1804): Jurors should acquit even against the judge's instruction...."if exercising their judgement with discretion and honesty they have a clear conviction that the charge of the court is wrong."

Alexander Hamilton (defense counsel for John Peter Zenger, accused of seditious libel, 7 Hamilton's Works (ed. 1886), 336-373): "That in criminal cases, nevertheless, the court are the constitutional advisors of the jury in matter of law; who may compromise their conscience by lightly or rashly disregarding that advice, but may still more compromise their consciences by following it, if exercising their judgments with discretion and honesty they have a clear conviction that the charge of the court is wrong."

Trent Hammerstein (book *Stealth Juror: The Ultimate Defense Against Bad Laws & Government Tyranny*): A stealth juror is an ordinary citizen serving on a jury who understands and is not afraid to judge not only the evidence in a case but the very law upon which the prosecution is based (sometimes referred to as "jury nullification"). If the law itself is bad or unfair, he secretly works to acquit any defendant being persecuted for a nonviolent, victimless crime. He must remain undercover because he represents a direct threat to the power of judges and prosecutors. He is the last champion of justice in the American courtroom (EDITOR: I prefer to call such a lying juror as a snake in the grass).

Judge Learned Hand (U.S. ex rel. McCann v. Adams, 126F.2d774, 775-76 (2d Circ. Ct, 1942): "...[T]he institution of trial by jury especially in criminal cases has its hold upon public favor chiefly for two reasons. The individual can forfeit his liberty to say nothing of his life only at the hands of those who, unlike any official, are in no wise accountable, directly or indirectly, for what they do, and who at once separate and melt anonymously in the community from which they came. Moreover, since if they acquit their verdict is final, no one is likely to suffer of whose conduct they do not morally disapprove; and this introduces a slack into the enforcement of law, tempering its rigor by the mollifying influence of current ethical conventions. A trial by any jury...preserves both these fundamental elements and a trial by a judge preserves neither..."

Justice John Marshall Harlan (United States Supreme Court, 1900): Trial by jury is a fundamental guarantee of the rights and liberties of the people. English speaking people have for centuries regarded it as vital to personal security and the men of the Revolutionary period universally claimed it as the birthright of free men.

W. S. Holdsworth (*A History of English Law,* 1927): The jury system has for some hundreds of years been constantly bringing the rules of law to the touchstone of contemporary commonsense.

Oliver Wendell Holmes Jr (Horning v. District of Columbia, 249 U.S. 596 (1920): The jury has the power to bring in a verdict in the teeth of both law and facts.

Oliver Wendell Holmes Jr: Trial by jury is a rough scales at best; the beam ought not to tip for motes and straws.

Oliver Wendell Holmes Jr: (Frank v. Mangum, 237 US 309, 347, 1915,): "It is our duty to declare lynch law [to be] as little valid when practiced by a regularly drawn jury as when administered by one elected by a mob intent on death."

Oliver Wendell Holmes Jr: (Frank v. Mangum, 237 US 309, 347 (1915)): "Mob law does not become due process of law by securing the assent of a terrorized jury."

Oliver Wendell Holmes, Jr., (I Holmes-Pollock Letters, (Howe, Mark DeWolfe, ed., Cambridge, Mass: Harvard University Press, 1946, p.74): "The man who wants a jury has a bad case....The use of it is to let a little popular prejudice into the administration of law—(in violation of their oath)."

Elbert Hubbard: The jury is a collection of sedentary owls.

Elbert Hubbard: Jury - The stupidity of one brain multiplied by twelve.

David Hume, English philosopher (1762): Trial by jury is the best institution calculated for the preservation of liberty and the administration of justice that ever was devised by the wit of man.

Justice Ward Hunt, United States Supreme Court (1873): Twelve jurors know more of the common affairs of life than does one man, and they can draw wiser and safer conclusions than a single judge.

Justice Robert H. Jackson (Morisette v. United States, 342 U.S. 246): But juries are not bound by what seems inescapable logic to judges.

Justice Robert H. Jackson: (Douglas v. Jeannette, 319 US 157, 182 (1943): Civil liberties had their origin and must find their ultimate guaranty in the faith of the people.

Justice Robert H. Jackson (Dennis v. U.S., 339 US 162, 94 L.ed. 734, 70 S Ct 519, 1950): So long as accused persons who are Republicans, Dixiecrats, Socialists, or Democrats must put up with such a jury, it will have to do for Communists.

Rudolph Janata (President, Defense Research Institute (DRI), 1974): The cost of the jury system is insignificant. The delay caused by the jury system is minimal. The value of the jury system is immeasurable.

John Jay (1774): We claim all the benefits secured by the English Constitution, particularly the inestimable right of trial by jury.

John Jay (1794): The jury has a right to judge both the law as well as the fact in controversy.

Thomas Jefferson (*Letter to Thomas Paine,* 1789): I consider trial by jury as the only anchor ever yet imagined by man, by which a government can be held to the principles of its constitution.

Thomas Jefferson (First Inaugural Address 1801): The wisdom of our sages and the blood of our heroes has been devoted to the attainment of trial by jury. It should be the creed of our political faith.

President Thomas Jefferson (1801): Trial by jury is part of the bright constellation which leads to peace, liberty and safety.

Thomas Jefferson: To consider the judges as the ultimate arbiters of all constitutional questions is a very dangerous doctrine indeed, and one which would place us under the despotism of an oligarchy.

Thomas Jefferson (1789): The new Constitution has secured these [individual rights] in the Executive and Legislative departments: but not in the Judiciary. It should have established trials by the people themselves, that is to say, by jury.

Justice William Johnson (United States Supreme Court, 1833): Trial by jury is among the most inestimable privileges of an American citizen. It is a fundamental right which protects the lowest individual for which our union exists.

Charles W. Joiner (*Civil Justice and the Jury,* 1962): Trial by jury involves a carefully developed series of checks and balances equaled in no other method of trial.

Harry Kalvin, Jr. (Director, Chicago Jury Project, 1964): In the course of many years of study I have become increasingly impressed with the humanity, strength, sanity, and responsibility of the civil jury.

Joseph T. Karcher (*The Case for the Jury System,* 1969): For almost eight centuries trial by jury remains the best, safest, surest and perhaps the only bulwark to protect the basic rights of the average citizen. It is still the "Lamp of Liberty" and it must be preserved.

Irving Kaufman (American Judge, 1973): The institution of trial by jury is almost 1000 years old. But it may not last another 50 unless we can show the public that it is an efficient tool for the administration of justice.

Justice Kent (New York Supreme Court 3 Johns Cas., 366-368 (1803)): "The true criterion of a legal power is its capacity to produce a definitive effect, liable neither to censure nor review. And the verdict of not guilty in a criminal case, is, in every respect, absolutely final. The jury are not liable to punishment, nor the verdict to control. No attaint lies, nor can a new trial be awarded. The exercise of this power in the jury has been sanctioned, and upheld in constant activity, from the earliest ages." [Quoted in Sparf and Hansen v. U.S., 156 U.S.51, 148-149. (1894), Gray, Shiras dissenting.]

Richard H. Kuhlman (*Jury Trial, Progress & Democracy,* 1981): The competence of the common man and the validity of the jury trial are two basic, closely related notions upon which American democracy has always rested.

William Kunstler (quoted in Franklin M. Nugent, *"Jury Power: Secret Weapon Against Bad Law,"* revised from Youth Connection, 1988): "Unless the jury can exercise its community conscience role, our judicial system will have become so inflexible that the effect may well be a progressive radicalization of protest into channels that will threaten the very continuance of the system itself. To put it another way, the jury is...the safety valve that must exist if this society is to be able to accommodate its own internal stresses and strains...[I]f the community is to sit in the jury box, its decision cannot be legally limited to a conscienceless application of fact to law."

Thomas F. Lambert, Jr. (Suffolk University Law Professor, 1963): Jury trial represents courthouse democracy, the preservation of our founded experience in direct citizen participation in government.

Richard Henry Lee, Virginia (1787): The right of trial by jury is a fundamental right of free and enlightened people and an essential part of a free government. Trial by jury in civil cases and a trial by jury in criminal cases stay and on the same footing: they are the common rights of Americans.

Maximus A. Lesser (1894): Trial by jury has served as a potent promoter of the dispensation of justice for which no more perfect substitute has ever been devised.

Abraham Lincoln (Inaugural Address, 1861): Why should there not be a patient confidence in the ultimate justice of the people? Is there any better or more equal hope in the world?

Abraham Lincoln: A jury too often has at least one member more ready to hang the panel than to hang the traitor.

John Locke (*Second Treatise of Government*): "Yet the legislative being only a fiduciary power to act for certain ends, there remains still in the people a supreme power to remove or alter the legislative, when they find the legislative act contrary to the trust reposed in them....And thus the community perpetually retains a supreme power of saving themselves from the attempts and designs of any body, even of their legislators, whenever they shall be so foolish or so wicked as to lay and carry on designs against the liberties and properties of the subject."

John Locke (*Fundamental Constitutions of Carolina,* 1669): No cause, whether civil or criminal, of any freeman, shall be tried in any court of judicature, without a judgment of his peers.

James Madison (1789): Trial by jury in civil cases is as essential to security to secure the liberty of the people as any one of the pre-existing rights of nature...."

James Madison: In suits at common law between man and man, the trial by jury, as one of the best securities to the rights of the people, law to remain in violent.

James Madison (the Seventh Amendment adopted along with the Bill of Rights on September 25, 1789): "In suits at common law, where the valuing controversy shall exceed $20, **the right of trial by jury shall be preserved,** and no fact tried by jury shall be otherwise examined by any court of United States than according to the rules of the common law."

Frederick William Maitland (*Collected Papers,* 1912): For a long time past English man have been proud of their trial by jury, proud to see the nations of Europe imitating as best they might this "palladium of English liberties," this "bulwark of the British Constitution.

John Marshall, Virginia (1780): It has been urged that the exclusion of trial by jury would prostrate our rights, but I hope that in this country, where impartiality is so admired, the laws will direct facts to be ascertained by jury.

Justice Thurgood Marshall (<u>Peters v. Kiff,</u> 407 US 493, 502 (1972)): "Illegal and unconstitutional jury selection procedures cast doubt on the integrity of the whole judicial process. They create the appearance of bias in the decision of individual cases, and they increase the risk of actual bias as well."

Maryland Ratification Convention Committee (1788): Trial by jury in all cases is the boasted birthright of Englishmen and their descendents, and the palladium of civil liberty.

Massachusetts Constitution (1780): In civil suits the parties have right to trial by jury and this method of procedure shall be held sacred.

Charles S. May (1875): The jury system is the handmaid of freedom. It takes on the spirit of liberty, and grows with the progress of constitutional government. Rome, Sparta and Carthage fell because they did not know it, let not England and America fall because they threw it away.

Sir John Maynard, Sergeant at Law (1689): Trial by jury is our fence and protection against all frauds and surprises and against all storms of power.

Jefferson F. Meagher (*A Fair Trial for Trial by Jury,* 1964): Created for the protection of individual rights and freedoms over the long pull of history, trial by jury has become one of the hallmarks of our civilization. To abolish trial by jury is to rupture a vital artery in the bloodstream of the democratic process.

H.L. Mencken: Jury: Twelve men of limited information and intelligence, chosen precisely because of their lack of intellectual resilience.

Newton Minow: In today's world a peer is not a hermit.

Robert Morgenthau: I would rather have my fate in the hands of 23 representative citizens of the country than in the hands of a politically appointed judge.

Gouverneur Morris (on the Colonial Trial of John Peter Zenger, 1735): The jury trial of Peter Zenger was the germ of American freedom, the morning star of liberty which revolutionized America.

Michael A. Musmanno (Justice of Pennsylvania Supreme Court, 1959): No juror has the right to enter the jury box with a personal ax to grind, a blade to sharpen, or a row to hoe. Every juror must be as neutral as the rays of the sun which light up hill and dale with equal impartiality, he must be as unprejudiced as the falling snow, he must be as unbiased as the angel of truth. A juror should have only one obligation, only one duty, and only one objective, and that is to look always to the Truth, as the needle of the compass points always to the North. And as the compass can not be affected by the elements, the mind of the juror should not be influenced by thoughts of reward or the infliction of revenge, or, as in this case, by the possible motivation of brandishing red or menace.

Michael A. Musmanno (Justice of Pennsylvania Supreme Court, 1959): The Jury Decides The Value of Intangibles: It is generally supposed that love, affection, and devotion are abstract terms which have no palpable reality and therefore cannot be translated into money. In the spiritual world this undoubtedly is true, but where a trespass action for a demonstrated wrongful act is involved, these terms, because of the inexorable law of necessity, must find practical transmutation. The music produced by a symphony orchestra and the fragrances which emanate from a flower garden also fall into the world of the incorporeal, but they are nonetheless very real and can be the subject of material compensation if they cease to exist because of the disruption of the means which bring them into existence. The mere presence of a mother who cooks and serves a meal adds an enjoyment which is something beyond what one tastes in the food prepared by a hired housekeeper, no matter how conscientious and able that housekeeper may be. The extinguishment of that enjoyment is something which goes into the accounting of the person who extinguished it. The affectionate greeting, the tender solace, the never-failing inspiration are all part of a wife's companionship and a mother's care, which disappear with the intervention of death, and there is no reason why the person responsible for the death should not be required to pay for those lost treasures, as much as he is required to pay the wages of the strange housekeeper, the employed seamstress, the new cook or the hired tutor. Who is to compute the financial counterpart of these cherished resources which have been laid in ruins? The answer is, the jury. Who is to appraise the hurt and the haunting emptiness of a home when the mother has permanently departed, even though all the curtains are in place and every piece of furniture is still in use? The answer is again, the jury, who, from the testimony, may visualize the decedent and re-create in their minds what she brought to the household which was dependant upon her. (dissenting opinon, Neuberg v. Bobowiez, 401Pa. 146).

New Hampshire House of Representatives (1776): The citizens of New Hampshire are entitled to their great, inestimable and inherent right of trial by jury.

North Carolina Constitution (1776): The ancient mode of trial by jury in civil cases is one of the best securities of the rights of the people, and ought to remain sacred and inviolable.

Thomas Paine (1777): Every free government should include a Bill of Rights containing the great principles of natural and civil liberty unalterable by human power. The right of redress by an appeal to public justice includes the right to trial by jury, a civil right common to both parties.

Theophilus Parsons (A leading supporter of the Constitution at the Convention of 1788, Parsons declined President Adams' nomination to be Attorney General and became Chief Justice of Massachusetts). (2 Elliot's Debates, 94; 2 Bancroft's History of the Constitution, p. 267): "The people themselves have it in their power effectually to resist usurpation, without being driven to an appeal to arms. An act of usurpation is not obligatory; it is not law; and any man may be justified in his resistance. Let him be considered as a criminal by the general government, yet only his fellow citizens can convict him; they are his jury, and if they pronounce him innocent, not all the powers of Congress can hurt him; and innocent they certainly will pronounce him, if the supposed law he resisted was an act of usurpation."

Theophilus Parsons (2 Elliot's Debates, 94; 2 Bancroft's History of the Constitution, p. 267): "If a juror accepts as the law that which the judge states then that juror has accepted the exercise of absolute authority of a government employee and has surrendered a power and right that once was the citizen's safeguard of liberty,—For the saddest epitaph which can be carved in memory of a vanished liberty is that it was lost because its possessors failed to stretch forth a saving hand while yet there was time."

Pennsylvania Constitution (1776): In civil suits the parties have right to trial by jury, which ought to be held sacred.

Perry & Cooper (*Sources of our Liberties,* 1959): In the earliest colonies the jury system became a fundamental feature of the administration of American justice.

Frederick Pollock (*The History of English Law,* 1899): The right of trial by jury is the palladium of our liberties.

Roscoe Pound (former Dean of Harvard Law School, 1942): The jury has grown up as a representative of the local community whose representative character appealed to democratic America. It seemed to Americans important to preserve the jury as a bulwark of political liberty.

Charles Pratt, Lord Camden, Chancellor of England (1792): Trial by jury is the foundation of our free Constitution: take that away and the whole fabric will soon moulder into dust.

Eli K. Price (*Discourse on Trial by Jury,* 1863): The institution of trial by jury has been consecrated in the affections of the only nations of the earth truly free, and that security should forever be regarded as an inappreciable inheritance.

John Proffatt (*A Treatise on Trial by Jury,* 1877): The English colonists settled here with a deep-rooted regard for trial by jury. They brought it with them and establish it and cherished it as one of their dearest privileges. Ever since the *Magna Carta*, the right of trial by jury has been esteemed as a peculiarly dear and inestimable privilege by the English race.

Chief Justice William H. Rehnquist (Parklane Hosiery v. Shore, U.S. Supreme Court 1979): The founders of our Nation considered trial by jury in civil cases an important bulwark against tyranny and corruption, a safeguard too precious to be left to the whim of the sovereign, or for that matter the judiciary.

Will Rogers: A jury should decide a case the minute they are shown it, before the lawyers have had a chance to mislead them.

Will Rogers: No Voter in the World ever voted for nothing; in some way he has been convinced that he is to get something for that vote. His vote is all that our Constitution gives him, and it goes to the highest bidder.

Elihu Root (New York lawyer, statesman, Nobel Peace Prize Winner, 1845-1937, 1894): Trial by Jury is one of the most important, most vital, most sacred of the institutions which maintain our free and popular government. It serves to bring the people into immediate participation in the administration of law and makes its administration tolerable.

Donald K. Ross, Public Relations Director, Defense Research Institute (DRI) (1965): The right of trial by jury was gained through the blood of revolution and is part of the Constitution which has truly made this is the land of the free.

Clinton Rossiter (*Seedtime of the Republic,* 1953): Is difficult to exaggerate the esteem in which the American columnists held representative government and trial by jury. Few Americans believed that they could ever be improved upon as instruments of popular control of government. They are the means of defending all other fundamental rights.

Stanley E. Sacks (*Preservation of the Civil Jury System,* 1965): The civil jury is one of our best safeguards against tyranny and injustice, an ingenious and cherished element of Anglo-American jurisprudence, a bulwark of liberty and a cornerstone of democracy.

George Santayana (*Dominations and Powers,* 1951): Trial by jury, where property, reputation and life are at stake, the jurors are chosen by lot, and democracy appears unalloyed.

Alan Scheflin & Jon Van Dyke (*"Jury Nullification: the Contours of a Controversy,"* 1980): "The arguments for opposing the nullification instruction are, in our view, deficient because they fail to weigh the political advantages gained by not lying to the jury...What impact will this deception have on jurors who felt coerced into their verdict by the judge's instructions and who learn, after trail, that they could have voted their consciences and acquitted? Such a juror is less apt to respect the legal system."

Alan Scheflin & Jon Van Dyke (*"Jury Nullification: the Contours of a Controversy,"* 1980):): "If juries were restricted to finding facts, cases with no disputed factual issues would be withheld from the jury. But such cases are presented to the jury. By its general verdict of innocence, the jury may free a person without its verdict being subject to challenge. The judge cannot ask jurors to explain their verdict, nor may the judge punish the jurors for it. Although judges now generally tell jurors they must obey the judge's instructions on the law, the jurors may not be compelled to do so. If the jury convicts, however, the defendant is entitled to a broad range of procedural protections to ensure that the jury was fair and honest. // When a jury acquits a defendant even though he or she clearly appears to be guilty, the acquittal conveys significant information about community attitudes and provides a guideline for future prosecutorial discretion in the enforcement of the laws. Because of the high acquittal rate in prohibition cases during the 1920s and early 1930s, prohibition laws could not be enforced. The repeal of these laws is traceable to the refusal of juries to convict those accused of alcohol traffic."

Bernard Schwartz (*Roots of the Bill of Rights* (1980): Trial by jury in all cases is the boasted birthright of Englishmen and their descendents, and the palladium of liberty.

Austin Wakeman Scott, President of Rutgers College (1918): In the American colonies there was great popular enthusiasm for trial by jury as bulwark of liberty. So highly prized by our ancestors, they put it beyond the power of the legislature to abolish.

William Seagle (Washington DC lawyer, legal writer, *The History of Law,* 1946): Trial by jury has been the subject of countless eulogies as the very citadel of freedom.

Justice Theodore Sedgwick, Massachusetts (1813): Trial by jury is the most cherished institution of free and intelligent government that the world has ever seen.

Arthur Schlesinger (*The Birth of the Nation,* 1968): In the minds of the American colonists, trial by jury was the firmest barrier of English liberty; it survives today as the voice of the people.

William Shakespeare (*HenryVIII,* Act III, ii): How innocent I was / From any private malice in his end, / His noble jury and foul cause can witness.

William Shakespeare (*Henry VIII,* Act V, iii): If your will pass, I shall both find your lordship judge and juror, / You are so merciful.

William Shakespeare (*Measure for Measure,* Act II, i): 'Tis one thing to be tempted, Escalus, / Another thing to fall. I not deny, / The jury, passing on the prisoner's life, / May in the sworn twelve have a thief or two / Guiltier than him they try.

William Shakespeare (*Twelfth Night*, Act III, ii): They have been grand-jurymen since before Noah was a sailor.

Marc Shar: "It's not that jurors accept the Story that fits the Facts – It's that they accept the Facts that fit the Story."

John Shay (*A Defense of the Jury System,* 1929): The right of trial by jury is as fundamental to democracy as the rights of suffrage or the freedom of worship, press and speech. It cannot be surrendered without an equal loss of our faith in the fundamental principles upon which our government is founded.

Herbert Spencer: A jury is a group of twelve people of average ignorance.

Herbert Spencer (1820-1903, British Philosopher): A jury consists of twelve persons chosen to decide who has the better lawyer.

Samuel Spencer, North Carolina (1788): Juries are called the bulwarks of our rights and liberty; and no country can ever be enslaved as long as those cases which affect their lives and property are to be decided, in a great measure, by the consent of 12 honest, disinterested men.

Lysander Spooner, Massachusetts Lawyer (*An Essay on the Trial by Jury,* 1852, p. 11): "For more than six hundred years—that is, since Magna Carta, in 1215, there has been no clearer principle of English or American constitutional law, than that, in criminal cases, it is not only the right and duty of juries to judge what are the facts, what is the law, and what was the moral intent of the accused; but that it is also their right, and their primary and paramount duty, to judge of the justice of the law, and to hold all laws invalid, that are, in their opinion, unjust or oppressive, and all persons guiltless in violating, or resisting the execution of, such laws."

Lysander Spooner (1852): A jury ensures to us that first and indispensable requisite of a judicial tribunal, integrity.

Lysander Spooner (*An Essay on the Trial by Jury,* 1852): "Our American constitution have provided five...separate tribunals, to wit, representatives, senate, executive, jury, and judges; and have made it necessary that each enactment shall pass the ordeal of all these separate tribunals, before its authority can be established by the punishment of those who choose to transgress it. "

Lysander Spooner (*An Essay on the Trial by Jury,* 1852): "The authority to judge what are the powers of the government, and what are the liberties of the people, must necessarily be vested in one or the other of the parties themselves—the government, or the people; because there is no third party to whom it can be entrusted. If the authority be vested in the government, the government is absolute, and the people have no liberties except such as the government sees fit to indulge them with."

Lysander Spooner (*An Essay on the Trial by Jury,* 1852): "This preposterous doctrine, that "ignorance of the law excuses no one," is asserted by courts because it is an indispensable one to the maintenance of absolute power in the government."

Lysander Spooner (*An Essay on the Trial by Jury,* 1852): "...there can be no legal right to resist the oppressions of the government, unless there be some legal tribunal, other than the government, and wholly independent of, and above, the government, to judge between the government and those who resist its oppressions...."

Lysander Spooner (*An Essay on the Trial by Jury,* 1852): "The bounds set to the power of the government, by the trial by jury, as will hereafter be shown, are these—that the government shall never touch the property, person, or natural or civil rights of an individual, against his consent, (except for the purpose of bringing them before a jury for trial,) unless in pursuance and execution of a judgment, or decree, rendered by a jury in each individual case, upon such evidence, and such law, as are satisfactory to their own understandings and consciences, irrespective of all legislation of the government."

The Stamp Act Congress (1765): Trial by jury is the inherent and invaluable right of every American.

J. E. R. Stephens (*The Growth of Trial by Jury,* 1896): The very essence of trial by jury is its principle of fairness. Twelve men of ordinary ability are just as capable of deciding today on the effect of evidence as they were in the infancy of the institution.

Justice Joseph Story, United States Supreme Court (1833): The inestimable privilege of trial by jury is conceded by all to be essential to political and civil liberty. It is justly dear to the American people, has always been an object of deep interest and solicitude and every encroachment upon it has been watched with great jealousy.

James Bradley Thayer, Harvard law professor (1898): Nothing among the English was more ancient than the practice of popular justice. The jury system is characterized by its intrinsic fairness and as the most rational way of determining questions of fact.

Alexis de Tocqueville: The institution of the jury, if confined to criminal cases, is always in danger; but when once it is introduced into civil proceedings, it defies the aggressions of time and man.

Alexis de Tocqueville: Juries, above all civil juries, help every citizen to share something of the deliberations that go on in the judge's mind; and it is these very deliberations which best prepare the people to be free.

Alexis de Tocqueville (*Democracy in America,* 1835).: The civil jury is the most effective form of sovereignty of the people. It defies the aggressions of time and man. During the reigns of Henry VIII (1509-1547) and Elizabeth I (1558-1603), the civil jury did in reality save the liberties of England.

Joseph Towers (*The Rights and Duties of Juries,* 1764): The right of trial by jury cannot be guarded with too much vigilance, nor defended with too much ardor. If the people surrender it, their other rights will inevitably follow.

Mark Twain: We have a criminal jury system which is superior to any in the world; and its efficiency is only marred by the difficulty of finding twelve men every day who don't know anything and can't read.

Mark Twain: The most ingenious and infallible agency for defeating justice that human wisdom could contrive.

Mark Twain: When the peremptory challenges were all exhausted, a jury of twelve men were impaneled—a jury who swore that they had neither heard, read, talked about, nor expressed an opinion concerning a murder which the very cattle in the corrals, the Indians in the sage-brush, and the stones in the street were cognizant of!

Mark Twain (*Roughing It*, v. 2, ch. 7, 1872): The jury system puts a ban upon intelligence and honesty, and a premium upon ignorance, stupidity, and perjury.

Mark Twain: If there wasn't a penalty for laughing in court, the jury would never be able to hear the evidence.

Mark Twain: The humorist who invented trial by jury played a colossal practical joke upon the world, but since we have the system we ought to try and respect it. A thing which is not thoroughly easy to do, when we reflect that by command of the law a criminal juror must be an intellectual vacuum, attached to a melting heart and perfectly macaronian bowels of compassion.

Yale Law Journal (Note in *"The Changing Role of the Jury in the Nineteenth Century,"* Yale Law Journal, 74, 170, 1964): "It is useful to distinguish between the jury's right to decide questions of law and its power to do so. The jury's power to decide the law in returning a general verdict is indisputable. The debate of the nineteenth century revolved around the question of whether the jury had a legal and moral right to decide questions of law."

Yale Law Journal (Note in *"The Changing Role of the Jury in the Nineteenth Century,"* Yale Law Journal, 74, 172, 1964): "Underlying the conception of the jury as a bulwark against the unjust use of governmental power were the distrust of 'legal experts' and a faith in the ability of the common people. Upon this faith rested the prevailing political philosophy of the constitution framing era: that popular control over, and participation in, government should be maximized. Thus John Adams stated that 'the common people...should have as complete a control, as decisive a negative, in every judgment of a court of judicature' as they have, through the legislature, in other decisions of government."

Yale Law Journal (Note, supra, Yale Law Journal, 74, 172, 1964): "Since natural law was thought to be accessible to the ordinary man, the theory invited each juror to inquire for himself whether a particular rule of law was consonant with principles of higher law. This view is reflected in John Adams' statement that it would be an 'absurdity' for jurors to be required to accept the judge's view of the law, 'against their own opinion, judgment, and conscience.'"

Yale Law Journal (Note, supra, Yale Law Journal, 74, 174, 1964): "During the first third of the nineteenth century,...judges frequently charged juries that they were the judges of law as well as the fact and were not bound by the judge's instructions. A charge that the jury had the right to consider the law had a corollary at the level of trial procedure: counsel had the right to argue the law its interpretation and its validity to the jury."

Sir John Vaughan, Lord Chief Justice ("Bushell's Case," 124 Eng Reports 1006; Vaughan Reports 135, 1670): "...without a fact agreed, it is impossible for a judge or any other to know the law relating to the fact nor to direct [a verdict] concerning it. Hence it follows that the judge can never direct what the law is in any matter controverted."

Vermont Constitution (1777): In civil actions the parties have right to trial by jury which ought to be held sacred.

Tom Vesper: In a 2000 study quoted by Jim Lees Aalmost 30% of people polled are not willing to award money damages for pain and suffering under any circumstances . . .and that is regardless of the law given to them by the judge.@ In 1998 I coined a phrase and wrote of a "new attitude" infecting civil juries in America - "Seinfield Syndrome: The Indifference of Otherwise Nice Jurors," Trial, Oct 1998, p.38-43. By now you may have seen TV reruns or heard of "The Seinfeld Show's Final Episode." Jerry, Kramer, George and Elaine were a humorous but all too real mug shot of character traits in today's young, upwardly mobile jurors. The Seinfeld cast was convicted of **CRIMINAL INDIFFERENCE.** From that 1998 television finale I adopted a new phrase for the Generation X and Y Juror attitudes: the "Seinfeld Syndrome." However, criminal indifference is not now limited to people between the ages "20 to 40 something." I am sad to report that this virus has spread! It now typifies the social conscience (or lack thereof) of many jurors, despite their age. More jurors have an irrational indifference to anyone's plight except those most horribly, objectively proven, undeniably, and catastrophically damaged plaintiffs. Even in catastrophic, totally disabled or wrongful death cases they refuse/resist awarding monetary compensation for intangible, yet legally compensable damages. To them "money solves nothing." I have heard jurors say that anyone seriously injured should be "fairly made whole" by getting "lost wages and medical bills paid . . . and that's all! Any out of pocket, special (economic) damages yes, but nothing for pain and suffering (non-economic damages)!"

Tom Vesper (2006, *Seinfeld Revisited* paper): In revisiting this Center for Disease Control subject I regret how our fellow professionals in personal injury law - medical professionals - have intentionally and repeatedly instigated phony "crisis" (seemingly on an annual basis) in their malpractice insurance premiums in order to lobby state legislatures and Congress to impose "caps" on "non-economic" damages any malpractice victim can recover. This national campaign to "cap damages" has brought out the very worst in some treating doctors. In order to insure they do not pay more for liability coverage, some doctors are willing to sacrifice their own patients' rights to full and fair recovery under tort law. This public debate, which festered for several years in New Jersey starting sometime in 2004, has seen doctors making "house calls" to voters to vote against any politician who does not endorse caps on damages. The immediate and long term effects of this "debate" are obvious: jury tampering and indoctrination. Potential jurors are led to believe that "windfall, jackpot, or runaway" verdicts are hurting the civil justice system and everyone in the country who "soon won't be able to find a doctor to deliver babies!" Potential jurors repeatedly read and hear how $350,000 (or whatever amount) is "more than enough to compensate anyone if their out of pocket "economic" damages are left uncapped and unlimited. Over and over, doctors are becoming the infected spores and carriers of the plague I call "THE SEINFELD SYNDROME."

Virginia Declaration of Rights (1776): The civil jury trial is preferable to any other and ought to be held sacred.

Virginia Bill of Rights (1788): In suits between man and man, the ancient trial by jury is one of the greatest securities to the rights of the people.

Chief Justice Earl Warren, United States Supreme Court (1962): Those who serve upon our juries have maintained a standard of fairness and excellence and demonstrated a vision toward the administration of justice that is a wellspring of inspiration.

Emory Washburn (*Study and Practice of Law,* 1871): To forgo the good sense, practical experience and unbiased instincts of an impartial jury would do violence to history and injustice to the cause of personal liberty.

George Washington (1788): There was not a member of the Constitutional Convention who had the least objection to what is contended for by the advocates for a Bill of Rights and trial by jury.

Paul B. Weiss (*Reforming Tort Reform,* 1989): Undermining and eroding Seventh Amendment guarantees is unacceptable, intolerable, and repugnant to the concept of Constitutional government.

Francis L. Wellman (*Gentlemen of the Jury,* 1924): The ancient and honorable institution of trial by jury has been universally considered the bulwark of our system of jurisprudence. It is a great popular university which has done a large part to perpetuate our American democracy.

Justice Byron White (1975): The purpose of a jury is to guard against the exercise of arbitrary power—to make available the common sense judgement of the community as a hedge against the overzealous or mistaken prosecutor and in preference to the professional or perhaps over conditioned or biased response of a judge.

Justice Byron White (Duncan v. Louisiana, 391 US 145, 155 (1968)): "A right to jury trial is granted to criminal defendants in order to prevent oppression by the Government."

Justice Byron White (Duncan v. Louisiana, 391 US 145, 156 (1968)): "Those who wrote our constitutions knew from history and experience that it was necessary to protect against unfounded criminal charges brought to eliminate enemies and against judges too responsive to the voice of higher authority."

Justice Byron White (Duncan v. Louisiana, 391 US 145, 156 (1968)): "Providing an accused with the right to be tried by a jury of his peers gave him an inestimable safeguard against the corrupt or overzealous prosecutor and against the compliant, biased, or eccentric judge. If the defendant preferred the common-sense judgment of a jury to the more tutored but perhaps less sympathetic reaction of the single judge, he was to have it."

Justice Byron White (Taylor v. Louisiana, 419 US 522, 530 (1975)): "The purpose of a jury is to guard against the exercise of arbitrary power—to make available the commonsense judgment of the community as a hedge against the overzealous or mistaken prosecutor and in preference to the professional or perhaps overconditioned or biased response of a judge."

Dean John Henry Wigmore, Northwestern Law School (1929): Trial by jury must be preserved. It is the best system ever invented for a free people in the world's history. It supplies that flexibility of legal rules which is essential to justice and popular contentment.

John Henry Wigmore: Trial by jury must and shall be preserved! Amidst the throng of crude sacrilegisms... that assail us nowadays in the legal sanctuary, none is more shortsighted, none more dangerous, than the proposal to abolish trial by jury.

John Henry Wigmore: We are good friends of jury trial. We believe in it as the best system of trial ever invented for a free people in the world's history. In spite of all suggestions to substitute the trained judge of fact, we believe that a system of trying facts by a regular judicial official, known beforehand and therefore accessible to the arts of corruption and chicanery, would be fatal to justice. The grand solid merit of jury trial is that the jurors of fact are selected at the last moment from a multitude of citizens. They cannot be known beforehand, and they melt back into the multitude after each trial.

John Henry Wigmore (1929): The writer believes that... (trial by jury) possesses four merits that can never be possessed by a judge trial.... 1. Prevention of Popular Distrust of Official Justice.... Hence, the popular attitude toward the administration of justice should be one of respect and competence. Bureaucratic, purely official justice, can never receive such confidence. The one way to secure it is to give the citizen-body itself a share in the administration of justice. And that is what jury-trial does.... 2. Provision for Necessary Flexibility in Legal Rules. Law and justice are from time to time inevitably in conflict. That is because law is a general rule...; while justice is the fairness of this precise case under all its circumstances. And as a rule of law only takes account of broadly typical conditions and is aimed on average results, law and justice every so often do not coincide.... Now this is where the jury comes in. The jury, in the privacy of his retirement, adjusts the general rule of law to the justice to the particular case. Thus the odium of inflexible rules of law is avoided, and popular satisfaction is preserved... That is what jury trial does. It supplies that flexibility of legal rules which is essential to put to justice and popular contentment.... 3. Education of the Citizenry in Administration of Law. In a democracy, where the operation of law frequently becomes a political issue, it is important that the body of citizens should have general acquaintance with court method.... Jury-duty will bring all respectable citizens sooner or later to have acquaintance with court methods, and in such a way as to compel serious thought and give the needed scrap of judiciary education common to all.... 4. Improve Quality of a Verdict Based on Reconciliation of Varied Temperaments and Minds.... Ask any twelve intelligent friends any question of opinion or fact, calling for serious thought.... Will it ever happen that you do not glean from at least two or three of the twelve some argument or detail or judgment that the others... had failed to mention?... (T)he conduct of human life has to be based on elusive averages or generalities, whether in politics, law, medicine, engineering, commerce or ethics. And when it comes to applying the generalities to concrete cases, the only safe machinery, that is dependable in the long run, is a machinery that embodies an average judgment, i.e., the reconciliation of several judgments taken at random.

Edward Willes (English judge): I admit the jury has the power of finding a verdict against the law, and so they have of finding a verdict against evidence, but I deny that they have the right to do so. *Rex v. Shipley*, 4 Doug. 73 (1784)

B. R. Wise, Australian King's Counsel (1948): The more I see of trial by judge, the more highly I think of trial by jury.

Judge Wiseman (U.S. v. DATCHER, 830 F.Supp. 411, 413, M.D. Tennessee, 1993): "Judicial and prosecutorial misconduct still occur, and Congress is not yet an infallible body incapable of making tyrannical laws."

Judge Wiseman (U.S. v. DATCHER, supra, at 415): "...a defendant's right to inform the jury of that information essential to prevent oppression by the Government is clearly of constitutional magnitude."

Judge Wiseman (U.S. v. DATCHER, supra, at 415-416): "There is no statutory proscription against making the jury aware of possible punishment. Instead, courts that have disallowed juror awareness of sentencing contingencies have peremptorily resorted to the factfinding - sentencing dichotomy to justify this denial. For example, the Eighth Circuit, in United States v. Goodface, merely stated that 'the penalty to be imposed upon a defendant is not a matter for the jury' and so it was proper not to inform the jury of a mandatory minimum term. See 835 F.2d at 1237. No further justification is given. In making this facile distinction, the courts have created an artificial, and poorly constructed, fence around the jury's role."

Judge Wiseman (U.S. v. DATCHER, supra, at 417): "The Supreme Court has not mandated that juries be in the dark on the issue of sentence. Those courts so ruling have done so on unconvincing grounds. The power of jury nullification historically has extended to sentencing decisions, and it rightfully should extend to such decisions. This court finds no precedential rationale for rejecting the defendant's motion."

Judge Wiseman (U.S. v. DATCHER, supra, at 417): "...this remedy [jury nullification] is one that should be reserved for only those cases where criminal law and community norms greatly diverge."

Sam M. Wolfe (*A Defense of the Jury,* 1911): Trial by jury is essentially a child of freedom. Where the scepter of the tyrant rules, it has no home. It is the greatest safeguard of liberty, and greatest protector of its privileges.

Rene A. Wormser (*The Law,* 1949): Trial by jury is one of our treasured legacies. To date, no finer or more just system of law has been devised anywhere.

Melvyn Zerman: It is the "ordinariness" of the jury that finally emerges as its unique strength.

JUSTICE

Uncle Anthony (After hearing about another delaying tactic by the insurance defense): I always heard that Justice was blind, but I didn't think she was lame too! I seen her blindfolded, but where's her crutches? She needs crutches!

Uncle Anthony: Y' know sometimes those wheels of justice seem to be square... they don't move!

Uncle Anthony: Sometimes justice is too good to some people and not good enough for others.

Aunt Mary Carlo: If yer gonna be the judge and the jury, ya might as well be the executioner too!

Aeschylus (6th Century B.C. Greek dramatist): Wrong must not to win by technicalities.

Arab Proverb: One hour of justice is worth a hundred of prayer.

Aristotle (*Ethica Nicomachea*, bk 5, ch 10): [Ethics is] a correction of law where it is defective owing to its universality.

Aristotle (*Rhetoric*, bk 1, ch 13): Equity is that idea of justice, which contravenes the written law.

St. Augustine (*City of God*, bk IV, c. 4): Set aside justice, and what are kingdoms but enterprises of robbery.

Francis Bacon (*Speech*, upon taking his seat as Lord Keeper, 1617): Fresh justice is the sweetest.

Simone de Beauvoir: Justice can never be done in the midst of injustice.

Bible: Amos 5:7: You that turn judgment into wormwood, and forsake justice in the land.

Bible: Amos 5:24: Let judgment run down as water, and righteousness as a mighty stream.

Bible: Amos 5:24: Instead, I want to see a mighty flood of justice, a river of righteous living that will never run dry.

Bible: Colossians 4:1: Masters, give unto your servants that which is just and equal.

Bible: Deuteronomy 1:17: Ye shall hear the small as well as the great.

Bible: Isaiah 59:4: None calleth for justice, nor any pleadeth for truth: they trust in vanity, and speak lies; they conceive mischief, and bring forth iniquity.

Bible: Matthew 7:12: Whatsoever ye would that men should do to you, do ye even so to them.

Bible: Micah 6:8: What doth the Lord require of thee, but to do justly, and to love mercy, and to walk humbly with thy God?

Bible: Proverbs 4:18: The path of the just is as the shining light, that shineth more and more unto the perfect day.

Bible: Psalms 82:3: Defend the poor and fatherless; do justice to the afflicted and needy.

Bible: Psalms 126:5: They that sow in tears shall reap in joy.

Bible: 2 Samuel 23:3: He that ruleth over men must be just.

Ambrose Bierce: INJURY, n. An offense next in degree of enormity to a slight.

Ambrose Bierce: INJUSTICE, n. A burden which of all those that we load upon others and carry ourselves is lightest in the hands and heaviest upon the back.

Ambrose Bierce: JUSTICE, n. A commodity which in a more or less unadulterated condition the State sells to the citizen as a reward for his allegiance, taxes, and personal service.

Bernard Bosanquet: A community in which there is injustice must be full of pain and bad conscience in as far as its mind is active.

Louis Brandeis: Equity does not demand that its suitors shall have led blameless lives. Loughran v. Loughran, 292 US 216, 78 L ed 1219, 54 S Ct 684 (1934)

Lenny Bruce: They call it the Halls of Justice because the only place you get justice is in the halls

Edmund Burke: A good person once said that where mystery begins religion ends. Cannot I say, as truly at least, of human laws, that where mystery begins, justice ends?

Samuel Butler: Justice, though she's painted blind, is to the weaker side incline.

Samuel Butler: Justice is my being allowed to do whatever I like. Injustice is whatever prevents my doing so.

Albert Camus: Absolute freedom balks at justice. Absolute justice denies freedom.

Justice Benjamin N. Cardozo: Justice, though due to the accused, is due to the accuser also. The concept of fairness must not be strained till it is narrowed to a filament. We are to keep the balance true. Snyder v. Massachusetts, 291 US 97, 78 L ed 674, 54 S Ct 330, 1934.

Benjamin N. Cardozo (Chief Justice of New York Court of Appeals): Equity does not act for every shadowy or unsubstantial wrong. Nann v. Raimist, 255 N.Y. 307 (1931)

Benjamin N. Cardozo: Justice, though due to the accused, is due to the accuser too.

Jane Welsh Carlyle: When one has been threatened with a great in justice, one accepts a smaller as a favor.

Jimmy Carter: But law is not the private property of warriors, nor is justice the exclusive province of judges and juries. In the final analysis, true justice is not a matter of courts and Waldenbooks, but of a commitment in each of us to liberty and mutual respect.

G.K. Chesterton: To have a right to do a thing is not at all the same as to be right in doing it.

Chinese Proverb: Though the sword of justice is sharp, it will not slay the innocent.

Sir Winston Churchill: Justice cannot be a hit or miss system. We cannot be content with an arrangement where our system of... laws applies only to those who are willing to keep them.

Sir Winston Churchill: One ought to be just before he is generous.

Cicero: The fundamentals of justice are that no one shall suffer wrong, and that the public good be served.

Cicero: Extreme justice is extreme injustice.

Cicero: Let the punishment match the offense.

Ramsey Clark (US Attorney General): A right is not what someone gives you; it's what no one can take from you.

Sir Edward Coke (*Second Institute* 48): It is the worst oppression, that is done by colour of justice.

Charles Horton Cooley: People who live in a narrow circle are kind, but rarely just. Only an open and varied life educates us to share many points of view, and so to become capable of justice.

Bill Cosby: Parents are not interested in justice; they are interested in quiet.

Earl William Cowper (Lord Chancellor of Great Britain, died 1723): Equity acts in personam. Toller v. Carteret, 2 Vern. 494 (1705)

William Cowper: He who will have equity, or comes hither for equity, must do equity. Demandray v. Metcalf, Prec. Ch. 419 (1715)

Greg Cusimano: Justice will only be achieved when those who are not denied justice feel as indignant as those who are.

Clarence Darrow: There is no such thing as justice—in or out of court.

Daniel Defoe: Justice is the end of government.

Daniel Defoe: Justice is always violent to the party offending, for every man is innocent in his own eyes.

Benjamin Disraeli: Justice is truth in action.

George Eliot: Justice is like the Kingdom of God—it is not without us as a fact, it is within us as a great yearning.

Ralph Waldo Emerson: Truth is the summit of being; justice is the application of it to affairs.

Sir James Eyre (English judge, 1734-1799): A man must come into a court of equity with clean hands. Dering v. Earl of Winchelsea, 1 Cox Eq. 318 (1787)

Ferdinand I (Holy Roman Emperor): Let justice be done, though the world perish.

John Galsworthy (English novelist and playwright, *Justice*, Act II): Justice is a machine that, when some one has once given it the starting push, rolls on of itself.

William Ewart Gladstone (English statesman, 1809-1898): Justice delayed is justice denied.

Hannah Green (*I Never Promised You a Rose Garden*, 1964): "Look here," Furii said. "I never promised you a rose garden. I never promised you perfect justice..."

Barry Goldwater: Extremism in defense of liberty is no vice, and moderation in pursuit of justice is no virtue.

Alexander Hamilton: I think the first duty of society is justice.

Learned Hand (*Address before the Legal Aid Society of New York*, 1951): If we are to keep our democracy there must be one commandment: **Thou shalt not ration justice.**

Learned Hand: Justice, I think, is the tolerable accommodation of the conflicting interests of society, and I do not believe there is any royal road to attain such accommodations concretely.

Lillian Hellman: Since when do you have to agree with people to defend them from injustice?

Joseph H. Hertz (British-born Hungarian Rabbi): Whereas in Greek the idea of justice was akin to harmony, in Hebrew it is akin to holiness.

Oliver Wendell Holmes, Jr.: This is a court of law, young man, not a court of justice.

J. Edgar Hoover (Washington, DC lawyer, Director of FBI): Justice is incidental to law and order.

Horace: Though justice moves slowly, it's seldom fails to overtake the wicked.

Italian Proverb: Everyone loves justice in the affairs of another.

Jesse Jackson (American clergyman and civil rights leader): White folks don't want peace; they want quiet. The price you pay for peace is justice. Until there is justice, there will be no peace and quiet.

Justice Robert H. Jackson: Questioning is an indispensable instrumentality of justice. (dissenting opinion) Ashcraft v. Tennessee, 322 US 143, 88 L ed 1192, 64 S Ct 921, 1944

Justice Robert H. Jackson: The most odious of all oppressions are those which mask as justice. (concurring opinion) Krulewitch v. US, 336 US 440, 93 L ed 790, 69 S Ct 716, 1949

Thomas Jefferson (*First Inaugural Address, March 4, 1801*): Equal and exact justice to all men, of whatever state or persuasion, religious or political.

Thomas Jefferson: The sword of the law should never fall but on those whose guilt is so apparent as to be pronounced by their friends as well as foes.

Justinian I (Emperor of Byzantine): Justice is the earnest and constant will to render to every man his due. The precepts of the law are these: to live honorably, to injure no other man, to render to every man his due.

Justinian (*Institutes* 1, 1, 3; Bract. Fols. 3, 3b): *Honeste vivere, Alterum non laedere, Suum cuique tribere* = Live honorably/honestly, injure no one, and give each their due.

John F. Kennedy: The achievement of justice is an endless process.

Robert F. Kennedy: Justice delayed is democracy denied.

Martin Luther King Jr.: Injustice anywhere is a threat to justice everywhere.

Walter Savage Landor (English essayist and poet, 1775-1864): Delay of justice is injustice.

James Madison (*The Federalist No. 51*, 1788): Justice is the end of government. It is the end of civil society. It ever has been, and ever will be pursued, until it be obtained, or until liberty be lost in the pursuit.

Magna Carta (ch 40, 1215): To no one will we sell, to no one will we refuse or delay right or justice.

Frederick William Maitland (English lawyer and legal historian, 1850-1906, *Lectures on Equity* 18, 1909): Equity without common law would have been a castle in the air, an impossibility.

Earl of Mansfield (William Murray, Chief Justice, King's Bench, England, 1705-1793): Let justice be done though the heavens fall.

H.L. Mencken: Injustice is relatively easy to bear; what stings is justice.

Thomas Middleton: Justice may wink a while, but see at last.

Midrash, *Genesis Rabba*,49:20: Abraham said to God: "If you want the world to exist, you cannot insist upon complete justice; if it is complete justice you want, the world cannot endure."

Michael A. Musmanno (Justice of the Sup. Ct. of Pennsylvania, 1959): As much as the law world may assume that law consists of a game in the abracadabra of words, and as much as that assumption may have been true in Shakespearean days, it is reassuring to note that the law of today aims at realities and the achievement of a justice which will appeal to the reason of the most of unlettered man on the street. Law is simply justice in action.

Nachman of Bratslav: Arbitration is justice blended with charity.

Napoleon I (Emperor of France): There is no authority without justice.

New Jersey Supreme Court Justices Long, Zazzali & Albin: Buono v. Scalia, 179 NJ 131, 150 (2004): "Our courts exist so that innocent victims may be made whole for the injuries they have sustained at the hands of others."

Friedrich Nietzsche: Distrust all those who talk much of their justice! Verily, in their souls not only honey is lacking.

North American Proverb: Without justice, courage is weak.

Austin O'Malley: The perfection of justice implies charity, because we have a right to be loved.

George Orwell (*Animal Farm*, 1945): All animals are equal, but some animals are more equal than others.

Thomas Otway (17th century English dramatist, *Venice Preserved*, Act I, i, 1682): Justice is lame as well as blind among us.

Plato (*Republic*, bk 1): Justice is but the interest of the stronger.

Sir Frederick Pollock (English lawyer, writer, legal historian, 1847-1937, *The Expansion of the Common Law 82*, 1904): Enormous offences call for a greater axe.

Richard Pryor: Justice is: JUST US.

Richard Pryor: In Life there is no justice. There's "JUST US."

John W. Raper: Justice is what we get when the decision is in our favor.

Rashi: If you see wicked men perverting justice, do not say: "Since they are many, I must follow after them."

La Rochefoucauld: The love of justice is simply, in the majority of men, the fear of suffering in justice.

Jeanne-Marie Roland (18th-century French revolutionary): It would have cost me more trouble to escape from injustice, than it does to submit to it.

Will Rogers: We will never have true civilization until we have learned to recognize the rights of others.

Will Rogers: We don't give our criminals much punishment, but we sure give 'em plenty of publicity.

Will Rogers (1934, about special interests avoiding laws to help unemployed): If we are really all in this together, then we ought to act like it: Some industry can't come in and say, "Ours is special and unique business. You can't judge it by the others." Well no committee come into Jerusalem looking for Moses and saying "Ours is a special business." Moses just went up on the mountain with a letter of credit and some instructions from the Lord, and He just wrote 'em out, and they applied to the steel men, the oil men, the bankers, the farmers, and even the United States Chamber of Commerce. And he said, "Here they are, Brothers, you can take 'em and live by 'em, or else."

Theodore Roosevelt: To submit tamely and meekly to theft or any other injury is to invite almost certain repetition of the offense.

Isaac Rosenfeld: No man suffers injustice without learning, vaguely but surely, what justice is.

Russian Proverb: Clemency is the support of justice.

Seneca: A kingdom founded on injustice never lasts.

William Shakespeare (*All's Well That Ends Well*, Act I, iii): There is more owing her than is paid; and more shall be paid her than she'll demand.

William Shakespeare (*Hamlet*, Act IV, v): Where the offence is, let the great axe fall.

William Shakespeare (*I Henry IV*, Act I, ii): He will give the devil his due.

William Shakespeare (*II Henry VI*, Act III, ii): What stronger breast-plate than a heart untainted? / Thrice is he arm'd that hath his quarrel just, / And he but naked. Though lock'd up in steel, / Whose conscience with injustice is corrupted.

William Shakespeare (*III Henry VI*, Act III, iii): For though usurpers sway the rule a while, / Yet heavens are just, and time suppresseth wrongs.

William Shakespeare (*Henry VIII*, Act III, ii): Be just, and fear not.

William Shakespeare (*Henry VIII*, Act V, i): And not ever / The justice and the truth o' the question carries / The due o' the verdict with it: At what ease / Might corrupt minds procure knaves as corrupt / To swear against you? Such things have been done.

William Shakespeare (*King Lear*, Act III, vi): Thou robed man of justice, take thy place; / And thou, his yoke-fellow of equity, / Bench by his side.

William Shakespeare (*King Lear*, Act IV, ii): This shows you are above, / Your justicers; that these our nether crimes / So speedily can venge!

William Shakespeare (*King Lear*, Act IV, vi): Through tatter'd clothes small vices do appear; / Robes and ferr'd gowns hide all. Plate sin with gold, / And the strong lance of justice hurtless breaks; / Arm it in rags, a pygmy's straw does pierce it.

William Shakespeare (*King Lear*, Act V, iii): The Gods are just, and of our pleasant vices / Make instruments to scourge us.

William Shakespeare (*Macbeth*, Act I, vii): This even-handed justice / Commends the ingredients of our poison'd chalice / To our own lips.

William Shakespeare (*Measure for Measure*, Act I, iii): Liberty plucks justice by the nose.

William Shakespeare (*Measure for Measure*, Act II, i): What's open made / To justice, that justice seizes. What know the laws, / That thieves do pass on thieves? 'Tis very pregnant, / The jewel that we find we stoop and take it, / Because we see it; but what we do not see / We tread upon and never think of it.

William Shakespeare (*Measure for Measure*, Act II, ii): The law hath not been dead, though it hath slept.

William Shakespeare (*Measure for Measure*, Act II, ii): I show it most of all, when I show justice; / For then I pity those I do not know, / Which a dismiss'doffence would after gall; And do him right, that, answering one foul wrong, / Lives not to act another.

William Shakespeare (*Measure for Measure*, Act II, ii): How would you be, / If He, which is the top of judgment, should / But judge you as you are? O, think on that; / And mercy then will breathe within your lips, / Like man made new.

William Shakespeare (*The Merchant of Venice*, Act IV, i): But mercey is above this sceptred sway, / It is enthroned in the hearts of kings, / It is an attribute to God himself / And earthly power doth then show likest God's / When mercy seasons justice.

William Shakespeare (*The Merchant of Venice*, Act IV, i): As thou urgest justice, be assur'd / Thou shalt have justice more than thou desir'st.

William Shakespeare (*The Merchant of Venice*, Act IV, i): He shall have merely justice, and his bond.

William Shakespeare (*The Merchant of Venice*, Act IV, i): This bond is forfeit; / And lawfully by this the Jew may claim / A pound of flesh.

William Shakespeare (*Othello*, Act V, ii): O, I were damn'd beneath all depth in Hell, / But that I did proceed upon just grounds / To this extremity.

William Shakespeare (*Othello*, Act V, ii): I have done the state some service, and they know it; / No more of that; I pray you, in your letters, / When you shall these unlucky deeds relate, / Speak of me as I am; nothing extenuate, / Nor set down aught in malice.

William Shakespeare (*The Rape of Lucrece*, l. 1687): Sparing justice feeds iniquity.

William Shakespeare (*Richard II*, Act I, i): Impartial are your eyes, and ears; / Were he my brother, nay, my kingdom's heir, / Now by my sceptre's awe I make a vow, /Such neighbor nearness to our sacred blood / Should nothing privilege him, nor partialize / The unstopping firmness of my upright soul.

William Shakespeare (*Romeo and Juliet*, Act III, i): Mercy but murders, pardoning those that kill.

Gloria Steinem: Law and justice are not always the same. When they aren't, destroying the law may be the first step toward changing it.

Gerry Spence (from his 1989 book *With Justice For None*): Like us, our young lawyers search, not for justice but for what someone called the "twin Holy Grails of American life – money and success." Skillfully, designedly, our young have made themselves salable to corporate America as replacement parts for the legal machine that grinds away in corporate law firms at lush hourly rates. The new lawyers flock to our large cities and descend in hordes on Wall Street and Washington, D.C. There many will spend their lives dotting i's and crossing t's in high-floor cubbyholes – human sacrifices to the profit gods of their corporate employers. Already, only a fortnight past puberty, they scorn such sentimental idealism as justice. "Justice?" They laugh. "What is justice? But *this* is a dollar." Our young, I fear, only bear our own familiar stripes.

Justice Potter Stewart: Fairness is what justice really is.

Joseph Story (Massachusetts lawyer, Assoc. Justice of US Supreme Court, legal writer, 1779-1845, *Equity Jurisdiction,* section 77, 1836): [EDITOR: Roscoe Pound credited Joseph Story with the wording of this often repeated legal maxim] He who seeks equity must do equity.

J.G. Sueme: Whoever suffers from the malady of being unable to endure any injustice, must never look out of the window, but stay in his room with the door shut. He would also do well, perhaps, to throw away his mirror.

Madame Swetchine: Men are always invoking justice; and it is justice which should make them tremble.

Theognis (6th century Greek poet): Every virtue is included in the idea of justice, and every just man is good.

Henry David Thoreau: It costs us nothing to be just.

Mark Twain: If we only had some God in the country's laws, instead of being in such a sweat to get him into the Consitution, it would be better all around.

Mark Twain: You see, he knew his own laws just as other people so often know the laws, not by effects. They take a meaning, and get to be very vivid, when you come to apply them to yourself.

UA (Inscriptions on US Supreme Court Building, Washington, DC. Neither is a direct quotation from any identified source): Equal Justice under Law. Justice the Guardian of Liberty.

UA (Inscription, US Department of Justice Building, Washington, DC, 5th Floor – Attorney General's Rotunda): The United States wins its case whenever justice is done one of its citizens in the courts.

Domitius Ulpian (Roman jurist, legal writer, 170-228 AD, *Digest*, Justinian, i, I, 10): Justice is the constant and perpetual will to allot to every man his due.

Tom Vesper: The 3 Acts of the Penitent (and perhaps modern-day tortfeasors?) (according to 1616 Council of Trent):

1. Contrition
2. Confession = Public Abduration
3. Satisfaction = prayer, fasting and Alms giving

George Washington: The Federal judiciary must be considered THE KEYSTONE of our political fabric"

Daniel Webster (*Funeral Oration on Mr. Justice Story*, 1845): Justice Sir, is the great interest of man on earth. It is the ligament which holds civilized beings and civilized nations together. Wherever her temple stands, and so long as it is duly honored, there is a foundation for social security, general happiness and the improvement and progress of our race. And whoever labors on this edifice with usefulness and distinction, whoever clears its foundations, strengthens its pillars, adorns its entablatures, or contributes to raise its august dome still higher in the skies, connects himself, in name and fame and character, with that which is and must be as durable as the frame of human society.

John Webster (English dramatist, 1580-1625): The weakest arm is strong enough that strikes, with the sword of justice.

Simone Weil: One must always be ready to change sides with justice, that fugitive from the winning camp.

Simone Weil: Justice consists in seeing that no harm is done to men. Whenever a man cries inwardly, "Why am I being hurt?", harm is being done to him. He is often mistaken when he tries to define the harm, and why and by whom it is being inflicted upon him. But the cry itself is infallible.

Simone Weil: Justice. To be ever ready to admit that another person is something quite different from what we read when he is there (or when we think about him). Or rather, to read in him that he is certainly something different, perhaps something completely different from what we read in him.

Walt Whitman: Judging from the main portions of the history of the world so far, justice is always in jeopardy.

Woodrow Wilson: Unless justice be done to others it will not be done to us.

Yevgeny Yevtushenko (Russian poet): Justice is like a train that's nearly always late.

Yiddish Proverb: Rather suffer and injustice then commit one.

KINDNESS (See COMPASSION)

KNOWLEDGE/REALITY (See also MAXIMS; TRUTH/UNDERSTANDING)

Uncle Anthony: Everybody has to face reality. But lots of people don't wanna face other people's reality.

Uncle Anthony (1964, aka "The Year of the Blue Snow"): I ain't no pessimist – I'm just a realist.... The Phillies ain't gonna win the pennant!

Uncle Anthony: The more you know about baseball or football or anything the more you can see the plays and the strategies and the game plans unfold.... The more you know the better yer eyesight gets.

Uncle Anthony: That pompous ass knows everything – it's a shame he don't know anything!

Uncle Anthony: I think he's a GROSS ignoramus/idiot – he's 144 times worse than an ordinary ignoramus/idiot.

Aunt Mary Carlo: Da more ya know, da less ya know.

Aunt Mary Carlo: Reality ain't any less real 'cause somebody don't see it.

Aunt Mary Carlo: He's like a blotter – he takes everytin in, but then gets it ass-backwards!

Aunt Mary Carlo: He ain't nobody's fool, nah, he couldn't get nobody to adopt him!

James T. Adams: Scientific knowledge is constantly changing. A discovery of one year receives confirmation the next or is thrown aside.

Joseph Addison: A great deal of knowledge, which is not capable of making a man wise, has a natural tendency to make him vain and arrogant.

Sherwood Anderson: I am constantly amazed at how little painters know about painting, writers about writing, merchants about business, manufacturers about manufacturing. Most men just drift.

Thomas Arnold: Real knowledge, like everything else of value, is not to be obtained easily. It must be worked for, studied for, thought for, and, more than all, must be prayed for.

Francis Bacon (*Med. Sacrae: de Haeresibus*): Knowledge is power.

Francis Bacon: Knowledge is not a couch whereon to rest a searching and restless spirit; or a terrace for a wandering mind to walk up and down with a fair prospect; or a tower of state for a proud mind to raise itself upon; or a sort of commanding ground for strife and contention; or a shop for profit and sale; but a rich storehouse for the glory of the Creator, and the relief of man's estate.

Francis Bacon: Reading maketh a full man; conference, a ready man: histories make men wise; poets, witty; the mathematics, subtle; natural history, deep; moral philosophy, grave; logic and rhetoric, able to contend.

Francis Bacon: It is in knowledge as it is in plants; if you mean to use the plant, it is no matter for the root; if you mean it to grow, it is safer to rest upon routes than upon slips.

Henry Ward Beecher: The love of knowledge in a young mind is almost a warrant against the infirm excitement of passions and vices.

George Berkeley: He that would make real progress in knowledge, must dedicate his age as well as youth, the latter growth as well as the first fruits, at the altar of truth.

Bible: Apocrypha, Ecclesiasticus 34:23: When one builds and another tears down, what do they gain but toil?

Bible: Colossians 1:9: Be filled with knowledge of his will in all wisdom and spiritual understanding.

Bible: 1 Corinthians 8:1: Knowledge puffeth up, but charity edifieth.

Bible: Ecclesiastes 1:18: He that increseth knowledge increaseth sorrow.

Bible: Ecclesiastes 11:4: He that observeth the wind shall not sow; and he that regardeth the clouds shall not reap.

Bible: Hosea 4:6: My people are destroyed for lack of knowledge: because thou hast rejected knowledge, I will also reject thee.

Bible: Jeremiah 4:22: They are wise to do evil, but to do good they have no knowledge.

Bible: Proverbs 1:7: The fear of the Lord is the beginning of knowledge.

Ambrose Bierce: MIND, n. A mysterious form of matter secreted by the brain. Its chief activity consists in the endeavor to ascertain its own nature, the futility of the attempt being due to the fact that it has nothing but itself to know itself with. From the Latin *mens*, a fact unknown to that honest shoe-seller, who, observing that his learned competitor over the way had displayed the motto "*Mens conscia recti*," emblazoned his own shop front with the words "Men's, womes's and children's conscia recti."

Ambrose Bierce: REALISM, n. The art of depicting nature as it is seen by toads. The charm suffusing a landscape painted by a mole, or a story written by a measuring-worm.

Ambrose Bierce: REALITY, n. The dream of a mad philosopher, That which would remain in the cupel if one should assay a phantom. The nucleus of a vacuum.

Earnest Boas: In the present state of medical knowledge a pronouncement of the sentence of "incurable" on a patient places a serious responsibility on the physician and implies a greater knowledge than he possesses.

Lord Bolingbroke: The shortest and the surest way of arriving at real knowledge is to unlearn the lessons we have been taught, to remount the first principles, and take nobody's word about them.

Louis Brandeis: Knowledge is essential to understanding; and understanding should precede judging. Jay Burns Baking Co. v. Bryan, 264 US 504, 68 L ed 813, 44 S Ct 412 (1924)

Sir Thomas Brown: The wise carry their knowledge, as they do their watches, not for display, but for their own use.

Sir Thomas Brown: I envy no man that knows more than myself, but pity them that know less.

Edward George Bulwer: He fancies himself enlightened, because he sees the deficiencies of others; he is ignorant, because he has never reflected on his own.

Thomas Carlyle: Properly, there is no other knowledge but that which is got by working; the rest is yet all a hypothesis of knowledge; a thing to be argued of in schools; a thing floating in the clouds, in endless logic-vortices, till we try and fix it.

Joyce Cary: It is the tragedy of the world that no one knows what he doesn't know – and the less a man knows, the more sure he is that he knows everything.

Philip Chesterfield: Knowledge is a comfortable and necessary retreat and shelter for us in advanced age, and if we do not plant it while young, it will give us no shade when we grow old.

Chinese Proverb: Learning is a treasure which accompanies its owner everywhere.

Chinese Proverb: Poverty is the common fate of scholars.

Sir Winston Churchill: The more knowledge we possess of the opposite point of view, the less puzzling it is to know what to do.

Sir Winston Churchill: If you have knowledge, let others light their candles with it.

Richard Cecil: The first step to knowledge is to know that we are ignorant.

Sir Edward Coke: When a great learned man, who is long in making, dieth, much learning dieth with him.

Jeremy Collier: Those who come last enter with advantage.—They are born to the wealth of antiquity.—The materials for judging are prepared, and the foundations of knowledge are laid to their hands.—Besides, if the point was tried by antiquity, antiquity would lose it, for the present age is really the oldest, and has the largest experience to plead.

Confucius: The essence of knowledge is, having it to apply it; not having it, to confess your ignorance.

William Cowper: Knowledge dwells in heads replete with thoughts of other men; wisdom, in minds attentive to their own.

George William Curtis: The sure foundations of the state are laid in knowledge, not in ignorance; and every sneer at education, at culture, at book learning, which is the recorded wisdom of the experience of mankind, is the demagogue's sneer at intelligent liberty, inviting national degeneracy and ruin.

Benjamin Disraeli: The more extensive a man's knowledge of what has been done, the greater will be his power of knowing what to do.

Tryon Edwards: If you would thoroughly know anything, teach it to others.

Tryon Edwards: It was said of one of the most intelligent man who ever lived in New England, that when asked how he came to know so much about everything, he replied, By constantly realizing my own ignorance, and never being afraid or ashamed to ask questions.

Albert Einstein: Imagination is more important than knowledge.

Ralph Waldo Emerson: People disparage knowing and the intellectual life, and urge doing. I am very content with knowing, if only I could know. That is an august entertainment, and would suffice me a great while. To know a little would be worth the expense of this world.

English Proverb: Better the devil you know than the devil you don't know.

Frederick William Ferrar: "Knowledge, without commonsense," says Lee, "is folly; without method, it is waste; without kindness, it is fanaticism; without religion, it is death." But with common sense, it is wisdom; with method, it is power; with charity, it is beneficence; with religion, it is virtue and life and peace.

Benjamin Franklin: genius without education is like silver in the mine.

Erich Fromm: We know ourselves, and yet even with all the efforts we make, we do not know ourselves. We know our fellow man, and yet we do not know him, because we are not a thing, and our fellow man is not a thing. The further we reach into the depths of our being, or someone else's being, the more the goal of knowledge eludes us.

Robert Fuller: If you have knowledge, let others light their candles at it.

Robert Fuller: He that sits of many arts, drinks of none.

William Gladstone: To comprehend a man's life it is necessary to know not merely what he does, but also what he purposely leaves undone. There is a limit to the work that can be got out of a human body or a human brain, and he is a wise man who wastes no energy on pursuits for which he is not fitted; and he is still wiser who, from among the things that he can do well, chooses and resolutely follows the best.

George W. Goethals: Knowledge of our duties is the most essential part of the philosophy of life. If you escape duty you avoid action. The world to man's results.

Goethe: We know accurately only when we know little; with knowledge doubt increases.

Goethe: What is not fully understood is not possessed.

Goethe: Man is not born to solve the problem of the universe, but to find out what he has to do; and to restrain himself within the limits of his comprehension.

Lord Halifax: The struggle for knowledge has a pleasure in it like that of wrestling with a fine woman.

Robert Henri: No knowledge is so easily found as when it is needed.

George Herbert: Knowledge is but folly unless it is guided by grace.

Charles Hodge: In many things a comprehensive survey of a subject is the shortest way of getting at a precise knowledge of a particular division of it.

Oliver Wendell Holmes, Jr.: A page of history is worth a volume of logic.

Oliver Wendell Holmes, Jr.: To be master of any branch of knowledge, you must master those which lie next to it; and thus to know anything you must know all.

Oliver Wendell Holmes, Jr.: Knowledge and timber should not be much used until they are seasoned.

Oliver Wendell Holmes Jr.: The best part of our knowledge is that which teaches us where knowledge leaves off and ignorance begins.

Thomas H. Huxley: If a little knowledge is dangerous where is the man who has so much as to be out of danger?

Thomas H. Huxley: For the aims of my own career, I want to promote the increase of natural knowledge, and to forward the application of scientific methods of investigation to all the problems of life, in the conviction that there is no alleviation for the sufferings of mankind except veracity of thought and action, and the resolute facing of the world as it is, when the garment of make-believe is stripped off.

William James: The art of being wise is the art of knowing what to overlook.

Japanese Proverb: Learning without wisdom is a load of books on an ass's back.

Jewish Saying: With knowledge, one is nowhere lost.

Jewish Saying: Men study so much they don't have time to know.

Jewish Saying: To know a trade is to own a kingdom.

Ben Jonson: The seeds of knowledge may be planted in solitude, but must be cultivated in public.

Ben Jonson: Knowledge is more than equivalent to force. The master of mechanics laughs at strength.

Ben Jonson: There is nothing so minute, or in considerable, that I would not rather know it than not.

Ben Jonson: Knowledge always desires increase; it is like fire, which must first be kindled by some external agent, but which will afterward propagate itself.

Ben Jonson: When a king asked Euclid, whether he could not explain his art to him in a more compendious manner, he was answered, that there was no royal way to geometry. Other things may be seized by might, or purchased with money; but knowledge is to be gained only by study, and study to be prosecuted only in retirement.

Juvenal: All wish to possess knowledge, but few, comparatively speaking, are willing to pay the price.

Kenyan Proverb: He who does not know one thing knows another.

Latin Proverb: What one knows it is sometimes useful to forget.

Gottfried Leibnitz: The knowledge we have acquired ought not to resemble a great shop without order, and without an inventory; we ought to know what we possess, and be able to make it serve us in our need.

Walter Lippmann: There is but one bond of peace that is both permanent and enriching: the increasing knowledge of the world in which experiment occurs.

John Locke: A taste of every sort of knowledge is necessary to form the mind, and is the only way to give the understanding its due improvement to the full extent of its capacity.

Thomas Macaulay: Charles V said that a man who knew four languages was worth four men; and Alexander the Great so valued learning, that he used to say he was more indebted to Aristotle for giving him in knowledge, than to his father Philip for giving him life.

Thomas Macaulay: Every generation enjoys the use of a vast hoard at bequeathed to it by antiquity, and transmits that hoard, augmented by fresh acquisitions, to future ages.

Henry Mackenzie: Knowledge is said to be power: and it is power in the same sense that wood is fuel. Wood on fire is fuel. Knowledge on fire is power. There is no more power in knowledge then there is in the stones or stars, unless there be a spirit and life in the knowledge which give it its energy. In proportion as men have this spiritual power they become strong in the world.

Menander: "Know thyself" means this, that you get acquainted with what you know, and what you can do.

Menander: In many things it is not well to say, "Know thyself"; it is better to say, "Know others."

Midrash: When wine comes in, knowledge goes out.

Henry Miller: As soon as one begins to look deeply into any subject one realizes how very little is known, how very, very much is conjecture, hypothesis, surmise and speculation.... When it comes to vital instruction, almost everything that has been written for our edification can be junked.

Robert Andrews Milliken: Fullness of knowledge always and necessarily means some understanding of the depths of our ignorance, and that is always conducive to both humility and reverence.

John Milton: The end of all learning is to know God, and out of that knowledge to love and imitate him.

John Milton: To know that which before us lies in daily life, is the prime wisdom; what is more is fume, or emptiness, or fond impertinence, and renders us, in things that most concern, unpracticed and unprepared.

Montaigne: To know by rote is no knowledge; it is only a retention of what is entrusted to the memory. That which a man truly knows may be disposed of without regard to the author, or reference to the book from whence he had it.

Austin O'Malley: Never carry your shotgun for your knowledge at half-cock.

Thomas W. Palmer: The expression, "Knowledge is power," he is used by Lord Bacon; but it had its origin long before his time, in the saying of Solomon, that "a wise man is strong: yea, a man of knowledge increaseth strength."

Thomas W. Palmer: Socrates said that a knowledge of our own ignorance is the first step toward true knowledge. – And Coleridge said, We cannot make another comprehend our knowledge until we first comprehend his ignorance.

Thomas W. Palmer: "Knowledge," says Bacon, "is power"; but mere knowledge is not power; it is only possibility. Action is power; and its highest manifestation is when it is directed by knowledge.

Alexander Pope (*An Essay on Criticism*): A littel learning is a dangerous thing.

Persian Proverb: Doubt is the key of knowledge.

Persian Proverb: Knowledge is a wild thing and must be hunted before it can be tamed.

Jane Porter: Imparting knowledge is only lighting other men's candle at our lamp, without depriving ourselves of any flame.

Francois Rabelais: Knowledge without conscience is the ruination of the soul.

François Rabelais: It is wise to get knowledge and learning from every source—from a sot, a pot, a fool, a winter-mitten, or an old slipper.

Rutherford Rogers: We're drowning in information and starving for knowledge.

Will Rogers: All I know is what I read in the papers.

Bertrand Russell: A stupid man's report of what a clever man says can never be accurate, because he unconsciously translates what he hears into something he can understand.

Marilyn vos Savant: To acquire knowledge, one must study; but to acquire wisdom, one must observe.

Arthur Schopenhauer: Talent hits a target no one else can hit; genius hits a target no one else can see.

Arthur Schopenhauer: Every person takes the limits of their own field of vision for the limits of the world.

John Robert Seeley: A grain of real knowledge, of genuine uncontrollable conviction, will outweigh a bushel of adroitness; and to produce persuasion there is one golden principal of rhetoric not put down in the books—to understand what you are talking about.

William Shakespeare (*Epigram on King James I*): Crowns have their compass—length of days their date—/ Triumphs their tomb—felicity, her fate—/ Of nought but earth can earth make us partaker, / But knowledge makes a king most like his Maker.

William Shakespeare (*Hamlet*, Act II, ii): I know a hawk from a handsaw.

William Shakespeare (*Hamlet*, Act IV, v): We know what we are, but know not what we may be.

William Shakespeare (*II Henry VI*, Act IV, vii): Ignorance is the curse of God, space last day's Knowledge of the winning wherewith we fly to happen.

William Shakespeare (*Love's Labour's Lost*, Act I, i): Too much to know, is, to know naught but fame.

William Shakespeare (*Love's Labour's Lost*, Act I, i): BIRON: What is the end of study? / KING: Why, that to know, which else we should not know. / BIRON: Things hid and barr'd, you mean, from common sense? / KING: Ay, that is study's god-like recompense.

William Shakespeare (*Macbeth*, Act I, iii): If you can look into the seeds of time, / And say, which grain will grow, and which will not, / Speak then to me.

William Shakespeare (*The Merchant of Venice*, Act III, ii): An unlesson'd girl, unschool'd, unpractis'd; / Happy in this, she is not yet so old / But she may learn.

Charles Simmons: Accurate knowledge is the basis of correct opinions; the want of it makes the opinions of most people of little value.

Sydney Smith: Most men want knowledge, not for itself, but for the superiority which knowledge confers; and the means they employ to secure this superiority are as wrong as the ultimate object, for no man can ever end with being superior, who will not begin with being inferior.

Sydney Smith: Every increase of knowledge may possibly render depravity more depraved, as well as it may increase the strength of virtue. It is in itself only power; and its value depends on its application.

Spanish Proverb: He who knows nothing, doubts nothing.

Gerry Spence: I would rather have a mind opened by wonder than one closed by belief.

Lawrence Sterne: The desire of knowledge, like the thirst of riches, increases ever with the acquisition of it.

Lawrence Stern: Nothing in this life, after health and virtue, is more estimable than knowledge,—nor is there anything so easily attained, or so cheaply purchased,—the labor, only sitting still, and the expense but time, which, if we do not spend, we cannot save.

Talmud: A light for one is a light for a hundred.

Mark Twain: One should be careful to get out of an experience only the wisdom that is in it—and stop thee; lest we be like the cat that sits down on a hot stove lid.. She will never sit down on a hot stove lid again—and that's all well and good; but she will also never sit down on a cold one anymore."

John Tyndall: Does your doctor know anything?—I don't mean about medicine, but about things in general?—Is he a man of information and good sense?—If he does not know anything but medicine, the chance is that he does not know much about that.

John Tyndall: Knowledge once gained casts a light beyond its own immediate boundaries.

Vincent Van Gogh: I believe one gets more sound ideas when thoughts arise from direct contact with things than when one looks at them with the set purpose of finding certain facts in them

Alec Waugh: Strength exists only as the opposite of weakness, and supreme knowledge of one subject presupposes as supreme an ignorance of others.

Daniel Webster: The world is governed more by appearance than by realities, so that is fully as necessary to seem to know something as it is to know it.

Daniel Webster: It is the glorious prerogative of the empire of knowledge, that what it gains it never loses. On the contrary, it increases by the multiple of its own power: all its ends becomes means; all its attainments help to new conquests.

Daniel Webster: Knowledge, in truth, is the great sun in the firmament. Life and power are scattered with all its beams.

Daniel Webster: Knowledge is the only foundation, both of the love and the principles of human liberty.

Daniel Webster: Knowledge has, in our time, triumphed, and is triumphing, over prejudice and over bigotry. The civilized and Christian world is fast learning a great lesson that difference of nation does not imply necessary hostility, and that all contact need not be war. The whole world is becoming a common field for intellect to act in. Energy of mind, genius, power, wheresover it exists, may speak out in any tongue, and the world will hear it.

Richard Whately: The dangers of knowledge are not to be compared with the dangers of ignorance. Man is more likely to miss his way in darkness than in twilight; in twilight than in full sun.

Richard Whately: The word knowledge, strictly employed, implies three things, viz., truth, proof, and conviction.

Edwin Percy Whipple: Knowledge, like religion, must be "experienced" in order to be known.

Thomas Wolfe: This is what knowledge really is. It is finding out something for oneself with pain, with joy, with exultancy, with labor, and all the little ticking, breathing moments of our lives, until it is ours as that only is ours which is rooted in the structure of our lives.

Edward Young: Your learning, like the lunar beam, affords light but not heat; it leaves you undevoutt, and frozen at heart, while speculation shines.

LANGUAGE (See WORDS)

LAUGHTER (See COMEDY)

LAW (See JUDGE, LAWYERS, LITIGATION)

Uncle Anthony: Seems to me that if ys got just a little bitta money, that's about how much law ya get.

Aunt Mary Carlo: Der oughta be a law ...

Brooks Adams: Law is merely the expression of the will of the strongest for the time being, and therefore laws have no fixity, but shift from generation to generation.

John Adams: in my many years I have come to a conclusion that one useless man is a shame, two is a law firm, and three or more is a Congress.

John Quincy Adams: I told (John Marshall) it was law logic—and artificial system of reasoning, exclusively used in the courts of justice, but good for nothing anywhere else.

Anacharsis (600 B.C.): Laws are like cobwebs, for any trifling or powerless thing falls into them, they hold it fast; but if a thing of any size falls into them, it breaks the mesh and escapes.

St. Thomas Aquinas (Italian scholastic philosopher c. 1225-1274, *Summa Theologica*, I-II): We must say that the natural law, as to the first common principles, is the same for all, both as to rectitude and as to knowledge. But as to certain matters of detail, which are conclusions, as it were of those common principles, it is the same for all in the majority of cases, both as to rectitude and as to knowledge; and yet in some few cases it may fail, both as to rectitude, by reason of certain obstacles (just as natures subject to generation and corruption fail in some few cases on account of some obstacle), and as to knowledge, since in some the reason is perverted by passion, or evil habit, or an evil disposition of nature.

St. Thomas Aquinas (*Summa Theologica*, I-II): Every human law has just so much of the character of law as it is derived from the law of nature. But if in any point it differs from the law of nature, it is no longer a law but a corruption of law.

St. Thomas Aquinas: Law is a regulation in accord with reason, issued by a lawful superior for the common good.

John Arbuthnot 1667-1735, Grampian-Born Physician and Writer: Law is a bottomless pit.

Hannah Arendt 1906-1975, German-born American Political Philosopher: No civilization would ever have been possible without a framework of stability, to provide the wherein for the flux of change. Foremost among the stabilizing factors, more enduring than customs, manners and traditions, are the legal systems that regulate our life in the world and our daily affairs with each other.

Aristotle (*Politics*, bk2, 8, 384-322 BC): As in other sciences, so in politics, it is impossible that all things should be precisely set down in writing; for enactments must be universal, but actions are concerned with particulars.

Aristotle (*Rhetoric*, bk 1, ch 15): To seek to be wiser than the laws is precisely what good laws forbid.
Aristotle (*Politics, III*, 16, 322 B.C.): The law is reason free from passion.
Aristotle: Even when laws have been written down, they ought not always to remain unaltered.
Aristotle: Law is order, and good law is good order.
Aristotle: Law is a pledge that citizens of a state will do justice to one another.
Aristotle: Good law means good order.
Aristotle: Even when laws have been written down, they ought not always to remain unaltered.
Aristotle: The best laws should be constructed as to leave as little as possible to the decision of the judge.
Aristotle: Whereas the law is passionless, passion must ever sway the heart of man.
Aristotle: Therefore he who bids the law rule may be deemed to bid God and Reason alone the rule, but he who bids man rule adds an element of the beast; for desire is a wild beast, and passion perverts the minds of rulers, even when they are the best of men.
Asoka ?-238 B.C., Buddhist Emperor of India: I have enforced the law against killing certain animals and many others, but the greatest progress of righteousness among men comes from the exhortation in favor of non-injury to life and abstention from killing living beings.
Association of Trial Lawyers of America (ATLA) Mission Statement: Seek justice for all . . . Champion the cause of those who deserve redress for injury to personal property . . . Promote the public good through concerted efforts to secure safe products, a safe work place, a clean environment, and quality healthcare . . . Further the rule of law in a civil justice system, and protect the rights of the accused . . . Advance the common law and the finest traditions of jurisprudence . . . and uphold the honor and dignity of the legal profession and the highest standards of ethical conduct and integrity.
Norman Augustine: Bulls do not win bullfights; people do. People do not win people fights; lawyers do.
St. Augustine: Necessity has no law.
Benjamin Austin (writing under the pen name "Honestus," 1819): Is it not a disgrace to a free republic that the citizens should dread appealing to the laws of their country?
Azarias: Laws are not invented. They grow out of circumstances.
Sir Francis Bacon (1561-1626, British Philosopher, Essayist, Lord Chancellor of England): Judges ought to be more leaned than witty, more reverent than plausible, and more advised than confident. Above all things, integrity is their portion and proper virtue.
Sir Francis Bacon: There are in nature certain foundations of justice, whence all civil laws are derived but as streams.
Sir Francis Bacon: I am of a mind that said, "Better is it to live where nothing is lawful, than where all things are lawful."
Sir francis Bacon: Moses the lawgiver, and God's first pen.
Sir James Bacon (1798-1895, Vice-Chancellor of Great Britain): That unfortunate statute (the Statute of Frauds), the misguided application of which has been the cause of so many frauds.
Walter Bagehot 1826-1877, British Economist, Critic: Our law very often reminds one of those outskirts of cities where you cannot for a long time tell how the streets come to wind about in so capricious and serpent-like a manner. At last it strikes you that they grew up, house by house, on the devious tracks of the old green lanes; and if you follow on to the existing fields, you may often find the change half complete.
David Ball: Theater informs trial principally because each is: (1) a live human event; (2) a collaborative activity in which none of the individuality of the separate people is lost; (3) not about you, but about the person to whom you are talking, about the other person, not yourself.
Dave Barry: Our second completely true news item was sent to me by Mr. H. Boyce Connell Jr. of Atlanta, Ga., where he is involved in a law firm. One thing I like about the South is, folks there care about tradition. If somebody gets handed a name like "H. Boyce," he hangs on to it, puts it on his legal stationery, even passes it to his son, rather than do what a lesser person would do, such as get it changed or kill himself.
Henry Ward Beecher: Laws are not masters, but servants, and he rules them, who obeys them.
Henry Ward Beecher 1813-1887, American Preacher, Orator, Writer: Laws and institutions, like clocks, must occasionally be cleaned, wound up, and set to true time.

Henry Ward Beecher: Laws and institutions are constantly tending to gravitate. Like clocks, they must be occasionally cleansed, and wound up, and set to true time.

Henry Ward Beecher: A law is valuable not because it is law, but because there is right in it.

Melvin Belli: There is never a deed so foul that something couldn't be said for the guy; that's why there are lawyers.

Melvin Belli: Now, the law is good but some of these judges just don't know how to handle it in court. They simply don't have the experience. There are an awful lot of "C" law students practicing law and sitting on the bench.

Jeremy Bentham (1748-1832, British Philosopher, Jurist, Political Theorist): Every law is an infraction of liberty.

Jeremy Bentham: Lawyers are the only persons in whom the ignorance of the law is not punished.

Jeremy Bentham: Right... is the child of law.

Jeremy Bentham (*Principles of the Civil Code*): Property and law are born and must die together.

Bible: Corinthians 6:7: There is utterly a fault among you, because ye go to law one with another.

Bible: Exodus 12:49; Leviticus 24:22; Numbers 9:14: Ye shall have one manner of law, as well for the stranger, as for one of your own country.

Bible: Galatians 5:14: All the law is fulfilled in one word, even in this; Thou shalt love thy neighbor as thyself.

Bible: Isaiah 10:1-2: Woe to those who enact unjust statutes and who write oppressive decrees, depriving the needy of judgment and robbing my peoples' poor of their rights, making widows their plunder, and orphans their prey."

Bible: John 7:51: Nicodemus: "Doth our law judge any man, before it hear him, and know what he doeth?

Bible: Luke 16:17: It is easier for heaven and earth to pass, than one tittle of the law to fail.

Bible: Proverbs, 29:18: "... he that keepeth the law, happy is he."

Bible: Romans 2:13: Not the hearers of the law are just before God, but the doers of the law shall be justified.

Bible: Romans 3:28: A man is justified by faith without the deeds of the law.

Bible: Romans 13:8: He that loveth another hath fulfilled the law.

Bible: St. Paul, Galatians 5:14: For the whole law is fulfilled in one word: Thou shalt love thy neighbor as thyself.

Bible: St. Paul, Romans 2:14: When the Gentiles who have no law do by nature what the Law prescribes, these having no law are a law unto themselves. They show the work of the Law written in their hearts. Their conscience bears witness to them, even when conflicting thoughts accuse or defend them.

Bible: St. Paul, Romans 4:15: For where there is no law, neither is there transgression.

Bible: 1 Timothy 1:7: Desiring to be teachers of the Law, when they understand neither what they say nor the things about which they make assertion.

Bible: 1 Timothy 1:8: The law is good, if a man use it lawfully.

Bible: 1 Timothy 1:8: This is the love of God, that we keep his commandments.

Bible: 1 Timothy 1:8-9: The law is not made for a righteous man, but for the lawless and disobedient, for the ungodly and for sinners.

Ambrose Bierce: CAPITAL PUNISHMENT: A penalty regarding the justice and expediency of which many worthy persons – including all the assassins – entertain grave misgivings.

Ambrose Bierce: HABEAS CORPUS. A writ by which a man may be taken out of jail when confined for the wrong crime.

Ambrose Bierce: LAWFUL, adj. Compatible with the will of a judge having jurisdiction.

Ambrose Bierce (*The Devil's Dictionary*, 1911): PRECEDENT: From The Lunarian Astonished, - Pfeiffer & Co., Boston, 1803: LUNARIAN: Then when your Congress has passed a law it goes directly to the Supreme Court in order that it may at once be known whether it is constitutional? TERRESTRIAN: Oh no; it does not require the approval of the Supreme Court until having perhaps been enforced for many years somebody objects to its operation against himself—I mean his client. The President, if he approves it, begins to execute it at once. LUNARIAN: Ah, the executive power is a part of the legislative. Do your policemen also have to approve the local ordinances that they enforce? TERRESTRIAN: Not yet—at least not in their character of constables. Generally speaking, though, all laws require the approval of those whom they are intended to restrain. LUNARIAN: I see. The death warrant is not valid until signed by the murderer. TERRESTRIAN: My friend, you put it too strongly; we are not so consistent. LUNARIAN: But this system of maintaining an expensive judicial machinery to pass upon the validity of laws only after they have long been executed, and then only when brought before the court by some private person—does it not cause great confusion? TERRESTRIAN: It does. LUNARIAN: Why then should not your laws, previously to being executed, be validated, not by the signature of your President, but by that of the Chief Justice of the Supreme Court? TERRESTRIAN: There is no precedent for any such course. LUNARIAN: Precedent. What is that? TERRESTRIAN: It has been defined by five hundred lawyers in three volumes each. So how can any one know?

Ambrose Bierce: OATH, n. In law, a solemn appeal to the Diety, made binding upon the conscience by the penalty for perjury.

Ambrose Bierce: PRECEDENT, n. In Law, a previous decision, rule or practice which, in the absence of a definite statute, has whatever force and authority a Judge may choose to give it, thereby greatly simplifying his task of doing as he pleases. As there are precedents for everything, he has only to ignore those that make against his interest and accentuate those in the line of his desire. Invention of the precedent elevates the trial-at-law from the low estate of a fortuitous ordeal to the noble attitude of a dirigible arbitrament.

Ambrose Bierce: TECHNICALITY, n. In an English court a man named Home was tried for slander in having accused a neighbor of murder. His exact words were: "Sir Thomas Holt hath taken a cleaver and stricken his cook upon the head, so that one side of the head fell upon one shoulder and the other side upon the other shoulder." The defendant was acquitted by instruction of the court, the learned judges holding that the words did not charge murder, for they did not affirm the death of the cook, that being only an inference.

Otto Von Bismarck 1815-1898, Prussian Statesman, Prime Minister: Laws are like medicines: they usually cure the disease only by setting up another that is lesser or more transient.

Otto von Bismark: Laws are like sausages. It is better not to see them being made.

Justice Hugo Black: Morality cannot be legislated but behavior can be regulated. Judicial decrees may not change the heart, but they can restrain the heartless.

Sir William Blackstone (English lawyer, 1723-1780, *Commentaries*, bk 1): The law of nature, being coequal with mankind, and dictated by God himself, is of course superior in obligation to any other. It is binding over all the globe, in all countries, and at all times: no human laws are of any validity, if contrary to this; and such of them as are valid derive all their force, and all their authority, mediately or immediately, from this original.

Blackstone: Law is the embodiment of the moral sentiment of the people.

William Blake: One law for the lion and one for the ox is oppression.

Lord Bolingbroke (Viscount Henry St. John, English stateman and political writer, 1678-1751): Law,—in its nature the noblest and most beneficial to mankind, in its abuse and debasement the most sordid and most pernicious.

George H. Bolt: The term "rule of law," like the phrases "love of God" and "brotherhood of man," is a short and simple expression of one of the few most sublime concepts that the mind and spirit of man has yet achieved.

Louis Brandeis: A lawyer who has not studied economics and sociology is very apt to become a public enemy.

Louis Brandeis: Crime is contagious. If the government becomes a law breaker, it breeds contempt for law.

Louis Brandeis: If we desire respect for the law, we must first make the law respectable.

Bertolt Brecht 1898-1956, German Dramatist, Poet: The law was made for one thing alone, for the exploitation of those who don't understand it, or are prevented by naked misery from obeying it.

William J. Brennan (Roth v. United States, 1957): The law is not an end in itself, nor does it provide ends. It is preeminently a means to serve what we think is right.

Benjamin Brewster: A lawyer starts life giving $500 worth of law for $5 and ends giving $5 worth for $500.

Reese Brown: Clearly, police officers cannot break the law to enforce it.

Lord Henry Peter Brougham 1778-1868, Scottish Whig Politician: He found law dear and left it cheap.

Lord Henry Peter Brougham 1778-1868, Scottish Whig Politician: A lawyer is a gentlemen that rescues your estate from your enemies and then keeps it to himself.

James Bryce: Of the faults traditionally attributed to democracy one only is fairly chargeable on the United States... the disposition to be lax in enforcing laws disliked by any large part of the population.

Edmund Burke 1729-1797, British Political Writer, Statesman: Bad laws are the worst form of tyranny.

Edmund Burke: In effect, to follow, not to force the public inclination; to give a direction, a form, a technical dress, and a specific sanction, to the general sense of the community, is the true end of legislature.

Edmund Burke: There are two, and only two, foundations of law ... equity and utility.

Edmund Burke: There is but one law for all, namely, that law which governs all the law, the law of our Creator, the law of humanity, justice, equity – the law of nature and of nations.

Edmund Burke: People crushed by laws, have no hope but to evade power. If the laws are their enemies, they will be enemies to the law; and those who have must to hope and nothing to lose will always be dangerous.

Edmund Burke: Law and arbitrary power are in eternal enmity.

Edmund Burke: Laws, like houses, lean on one another.

Edmund Burke: Law is beneficence acting by rule.

Aaron Burr (New York lawyer, VP of US, 1756-1836): Law is whatever is boldly asserted and plausibly maintained.

Samuel Butler 1612-1680, British Poet, Satirist: In law, nothing is certain but the expense.

Samuel Butler: A lawyer's dream of heaven; every man reclaimed his property at the resurrection, and each tried to recover it from all his forefathers.

Samuel Butler: In law, nothing is certain but the expense.

Helen M. Cam: As soon as you begin to say ''We have always done things this way—perhaps that might be a better way,'' conscious law-making is beginning. As soon as you begin to say We do things this way—they do things that way—what is to be done about it?'' men are beginning to feel towards justice, that resides between the endless jar of right and wrong.

John Campbell (British judge, 1854): Hard cases, it is said, make hard law.

Truman Capote: Even an attorney of moderate talent can postpone doomsday year after year, for the system of appeals that pervades American jurisprudence amounts to a legalistic wheel of fortune, a game of chance, somewhat fixed in the favor of the criminal, that the participants play interminably.... But at intervals the wheel does pause to declare a winner—or, though with increasing rarity, a loser.

Benjamin N. Cardozo (*Commencement Address to First Graduating Class 1928*, 13 St. John's Law Rev. 231, 1939): Our Lady of the Common Law – I say it with the humility that is due from an old and faithful servant – our Lady in these days is no longer an easy one to please. She has become insatiate in her demands. Not law alone, but almost every branch of human knowledge, has been brought within her ken, and so within the range of sacrifice exacted of her votaries. Those who would earn her best rewards must make their knowledge as deep as the science and as broad and universal as the culture of their day. She will not be satisfied with less.

Benjamin N. Cardozo: More truly characteristic of dissent is a dignity, an elevation, of mood and thought and phrase. Deep conviction and warm feeling are saying their last say with knowledge that the cause is lost. The voice of the majority may be that of force triumphant, content with the plaudits of the hour, and recking little of the morrow. The dissenter speaks to the future, and his voice is pitched to a key that will carry through the years.

Benjamin Cardozo: The law, like the traveler, must be ready for the morrow. It must have the principle of growth.

Jerome E. Carlin: The best trained, most technically skilled and ethically most responsible lawyers are reserved for the upper reaches of business and society. This leaves the least competent, least well-trained, and least ethical lawyers to the lower income individuals.

Julius Ceasar: All bad precedents begin with justifiable measures.

Miguel De Cervantes 1547-1616, Spanish Novelist, Dramatist, Poet: When the severity of the law is to be softened, let pity, not bribes, be the motive.

Judge Chambre (1739-1823) Beale v. Thompson, (1803): The great object of the law is to encourage commerce.

Sebastien-Roch Nicolas De Chamfort 1741-1794, French Writer, Journalist, Playwright: Some things are easier to legalize than to legitimate.

Raymond Chandler (1888-1959, American Author): The kind of lawyer you hope the other fellow has.

Raymond Chandler (1888-1959, American Author): The law isn't justice. It's a very imperfect mechanism. If you press exactly the right buttons and are also lucky, justice may show up in the answer. A mechanism is all the law was ever intended to be.

Carrie Chapman Catt: No written law has ever been more binding than unwritten custom supported by popular opinion.

George Chapman (*Revenge for Honour,* Act III, scene ii): I am ashamed the law is such an ass.

Stuart Chase: The violation of some laws is a normal part of the behavior of every citizen.

Edward Potts Cheney: The law locks up both man and woman, Who steals the goose off the common, But lets the greater felon loose, Who steals the common from the goose.

G. K. Chesterton: When it wishes anything done which is really serious, it collects twelve of the ordinary men standing round. The same thing was done, if I remember right, by the Founder of Christianity.

Chinese Proverb: Laws control the lesser man. Right conduct controls the greater one.

Chinese Proverb: Win your lawsuit and lose your money.

Chinese Proverb: Going to law is losing a cow for the sake of a cat.

Rufus Choate (Massachusetts lawyer, statesman, 1799-1859; To the Court requesting a precedent for his position during a trial): "I will look, your Honor, and endeavor to find a precedent, if you require it; though it would seem to be a pity that the Court should lose the honor of being the first to establish so just a rule."

Sir Winston Churchill (re the Nuremberg trials): Humanity, not legality, must be our guide.

Sir Winston Churchill: If you have ten thousand regulations you destroyed all respect for the law.

Sir Winston Churchill: The jury system has come to stand for all we mean by English justice. The scrutiny of 12 honest jurors provides defendants and plaintiffs alike a safeguard from arbitrary perversion of the law.

Sir Winston Churchill: There is scarcely anything more important in the government of men than the exact – I will even say the pedantic – observance of the regular forms by which the guilt or innocence of accused persons is determined.

Marcus T. Cicero (c. 106-43 BC, Great Roman Orator, Politician): The magistrates are the ministers for the laws, the judges their interpreters, the rest of us are servants of the law, that we all may be free.

Cicero (*De Re Publica*, III, xxii): There is in fact a true law – namely, right reason – which is in accordance with nature, applies to all men, and is unchangeable and eternal. By its commands this law summons men to the performance of their duties; by its prohibitions it restrains them from doing wrong.... The man who will not obey it will abandon his better self, and in denying the true nature of a man, will thereby suffer the severest of penalties, though he has escaped all the other consequences which men call punishment.

Cicero: We are in bondage to the law so that we may be free.

Cicero: Extreme law is extreme injustice.

Cicero: Law stands mute in the midst of arms.

Cicero: The welfare of the people is the chief law.

Cicero: Law is nothing else but right reason, calling us imperiously to our duty, and prohibiting every violation of it.

Cicero: The magistrate is a speaking law, but the law is a silent magistrate.

Cicero: The laws put the safety of all above the safety of one

Cicero: Law is the highest reason, implanted in Nature, which commands what ought to be done and forbids the opposite.

Cicero: Reason is the mistress and queen of all things.

Ramsey Clark: Who will protect the public when the police violate the law?

Felix S. Cohen: Jurisprudence, in effect, is a special branch of the science of transcendental nonsense.

Morris Cohen: Law is a formless mass of isolated decisions.

Roy Cohn: I don't want to know what the law is, I want to know who th ejudge is.

Sir Edward Coke (Lord Chief Justice of England, 1552-1634): For a man's house is his castle.

Sir Edward Coke (Inscription on rings given to friends): Law is the safest helmet.

Sir Edward Coke (*First Institute*): Reason is the life of the law; nay, the common law itself is nothing else but reason.

Sir Edward Coke (*First Institute*): The reason of the law is the life of the law; for though a man can tell the law, yet, if he know not the reason thereof, he shall soon forget his superficial knowledge. But when he findeth the right reason of the law, and so bringeth it to his natural reason, that he comprehendeth it as his own, this will not only serve him for the understanding of that particular case, but of many others.

Sir Edward Coke (*First Institute*): The knowledge of the law is like a deep well, out of which each man draweth according to the strength of his understanding.

Sir Edward Coke (*Calvin's Case*, 7 Rep. 12, 1608): The law of nature is that which God at the time of creation of the nature of man infused into his heart, for his preservation and direction; and this is *lex aeterna*, the moral law, called also the law of nature.

Sir Edward Coke: A cursory and tumultuary reading doth ever make a confused memory, a troubled utterance, and an uncertain judgment.

Sir Edward Coke: How long soever it hath continued, if it be against reason, it is of no force in law.

Sir Edward Coke: The house of everyone is to him as his castle and fortress, as well for his defense against injury and violence as for his repose.

Sir Edward Coke: They [corporations] cannot commit treason, nor be outlawed nor excommunicate, for they have no souls.

Charles Caleb Colton (1780-1832, British Writer): Law and equity are two things which God has joined, but which man hath put asunder.

Henry S. Commager: If you pass a bad law you find out and correct it; some damage is done but not irreparable damage; the same group who passed the laws say, "Come, we made fools of ourselves and we will now repeal that law.

Calvin Coolidge 1872-1933, 30th President of the US: I sometimes wish that people would put a little more emphasis on the observance of the law than they do upon its enforcement.

Calvin Coolidge: One with the law is a majority.

Calvin Coolidge: Free government has no greater menace than disrespect for authority and continual violation of law. It is the duty of a citizen not only to observe the law but to let it be known that he is opposed to its violation.

Ramsey Clark: Who will protect the public when the police violate the law?

Grover Cleveland (NY lawyer, US President, 1837-1908): No man has yet been hanged for breaking the spirit of the law.

James Fenimore Cooper: As [a citizen] is a "law-maker," he should not be a "law-breaker," for he ought to be conscious that every departure from the established ordinances of society is an infraction of his rights. His power can only be maintained by the supremacy of the laws, as in monarchies, the authority of the king is asserted by obedience to his orders. The citizen in lending a cheerful assistance to the ministers of the law, on all occasions, is merely helping to maintain his own power. This feature in particular, distinguishes the citizen from the subject."

James Fenimore Cooper: [Responding to a statement that "laws should be considerate of the poor":] Not more so than of the rich. The laws should be equal and just; and the poor are the last people who ought to wish them otherwise, since they are certain to be the losers when any other principle governs....No class suffers so much by a departure from the rule, as the rich have a thousand other means of attaining their ends, when the way is left clear to them, by setting up any other master than the right."

Dr. Frank Crane: All sorts of substitute for wisdom are used by the world. When the court doesn't know, it consults precedent. The court that made the precedent guessed at it. Yesterday's guess, grown gray and wearing a big wig, becomes today's justice.

Quentin Crisp 1908-, British Author: The law is simply expediency wearing a long white dress.

Norm Crosby: When you go into court you are putting your fate into the hands of twelve people who weren't smart enough to get out of jury duty.

Charles Curtis: Bias and prejudice are attitudes to be kept in hand, not attitudes to be avoided.

Czech Proverb: It is not the thief who is hanged, but one who was caught stealing.
Clarence Darrow (1857-1938, American Lawyer): The trouble with law is lawyers.
Dorothy Salisbury Davis: The law is above the law, you know.
Daniel Defoe: Law is but a heathen word for prayer.
Patrick Devlin: You're law chaps will be glad to hear that I shall present a point of law uncorrupted by any merits.
Charles Dickens (1812-1870, British Novelist): If there were no bad people, there would be no good lawyers.
Charles Dickens (*Oliver Twist, ch. 51)*: "If the law supposes that," said Mr. Bumble, "the law is a ass, a idiot."
Charles Dickens (*Oliver Twist, ch. 51)*: "That is no excuse," replied Mr. Brownlow. "You were present on the occassion of the destruction of these trinkets, and, indeed, are the more guilty of the two, in the eye of the law; for the law supposes that your wife acts under your direction." / "If the law supposes that," said Mr. Bumble, ... "the law is a ass – a idiot. If that's the eye of the law, the law's a bachelor; and the worst I wish the law is, that his eye may be opened by experience – by experience."
Charles Dickens: Keep out of Chancery. It's being ground to bits in a slow mill; it's being roasted at a slow fire; it's being stung to death by single bees; it's being drowned by drops; it's going mad by grains.
Charles Dickens: The one great principle of English law is to make business for itself.
Denis Diderot 1713-1784, French Philosopher: The decisions of law courts should never be printed: in the long run, they form a counter authority to the law.
David Dinkins: I haven't committed a crime. What I did was fail to comply with the law.
Benjamin Disraeli (1804-1881, British Statesman, Prime Minister): When men are pure, laws are useless; when men are corrupt, laws are broken.
John Dryden: Self-defense is nature's eldest law.
William Orville Douglas (Assoc. Justice US Supreme Court, *The Dissent, a Safeguard of Democracy*, 32 J. Am. Jud. Soc. 105, 1948): The law is not a series of calculating machines where the definitions and answers come tumbling out when the right levers are pushed.
William O. Douglas: I would rather create a precedent than find one."
Isadora Duncan (1878-1927, American Dancer): We may not all break the Ten Commandments, but we are certainly all capable of it. Within us lurks the breaker of all laws, ready to spring out at the first real opportunity.
Finley Peter Dunne (Illinois humorist, 1867-1936): A law, Hinnissy, that might look like a wall to you or me wud look like a triumphal arch to th' expeeryenced eye iv a lawyer. (EDITOR: Often this is misquoted – and perhaps properly so – as: "What looks like a stone wall to a layman is a triumphal arch to a corporation lawyer.")
Finley Peter Dunne: Laws are-re made to throuble people an' the more throuble they make th' longer they stay on th' stachoo book.
Albert Einstein: Our defense is not in armaments, nor in science, nor in going underground. Our defense is in law and order.
Dwight D. Eisenhower 1890-1969, 34th President of the US: The clearest way to show what the rule of law means to us in everyday life is to recall what has happened when there is no rule of law.
President Dwight D. Eisenhower (1952): Should any political party attempt to abolish social security, unemployment insurance, and eliminate labor laws and farm programs, you would not hear of that party again in our political history. There is a tiny splinter group, of course, that believes that you can do these things. Among them are a few Texas oil millionaires, and an occasional politician or businessman from other areas. Their number is negligible and they are stupid."
George Eliot 1819-1880, British Novelist: When one wanted one's interests looking after whatever the cost, it was not so well for a lawyer to be over honest, else he might not be up to other people's tricks.
Ralph Waldo Emerson: People say law but they mean wealth.
Ralph Waldo Emerson (1803-1882, American Poet, Essayist): The law is only a memorandum.
Ralph Waldo Emerson: Any laws but those we make for ourselves are laughable.
Ralph Waldo Emerson: Good men must obey the laws too well.

Ralph Waldo Emerson: No law can be sacred to me but that of my nature. Good and bad are but names very readily transferable to that or this; the only right is what is after my own constitution; the only wrong what is against it.

Ralph Waldo Emerson: The good lawyer is not the man who has an eye to every side and angle of contingency, and qualifies all his qualifications, but who throws himself on your part so heartily, that he can get you out of a scrape.

Ralph Waldo Emerson: The laws of each are convertible into the laws of any other.

Ralph Waldo Emerson: The wise know that foolish legislation is a rope of sand, which perishes in the twisting.

Nicholas Emery (Whitney v. Stearns, 16 Me. 394, 397, 1839): A cent or a pepper corn, in legal estimation, would constitute a valuable consideration.

Friedrich Engels (1820-1895, German Social Philosopher): Some laws of state aimed at curbing crime are even more criminal.

English Proverb (Ray's *Proverbs*, 1678): Possession is eleven points of the law and they say there are but twelve.

English Proverb: He that goes to law holds a wolf by the tail.

English Proverb (Ray's *Proverbs*, 1678): In a thousand pounds of law there's not an ounce of love.

English Proverb: Law, logic and Switzers may be hired to fight for anybody.

English Proverb: It is a bad cause that none dare speak in.

Epictetus: As physicians are the preservers of the sick, so are the laws of the injured.

Desiderius Erasmus (c.1466-1536, Dutch Humanist): Amongst the learned the lawyers claim first place, the most self-satisfied class of people, as they roll their rock of Sisyphus and string together six hundred laws in the same breath, no matter whether relevant or not, piling up opinion on opinion and gloss on gloss to make their profession seem the most difficult of all. Anything which causes trouble has special merit in their eyes.

Henry Fielding (1707-1754, British Novelist, Dramatist): Where the law ends tyranny begins.

Anatole France: The law, in its majestic equality, forbids all men to sleep under bridges, to beg in the streets, and to steal bread—the rich as well as the poor.

Felix Frankfurter: The eternal struggle in the law between constancy and change is largely a struggle between history and reason, between past and reason and present needs.

Felix Frankfurter: It is a fair summary of history to say that the safeguards of liberty have frequently been forged in controversies involving not very nice people."

Felix Frankfurter: We recognize that stare decisis embodies an important social policy. It represents an element of continuity in law, and is rooted in the psychologic need to satisfy reasonable expectations. But stare decisis is a principle of policy and not a mechanical formula of adherence to the latest decision, however recent and questionable, when such adherence involves collision with a prior doctrine more embracing in its scope, intrinsically sounder, and verified by experience...This Court, unlike the House of Lords, has from the beginning rejected a doctrine of disability at self-correction.

Felix Frankfurter: Ours is the accusatorial as opposed to the inquisitorial system. *Watts v. Indiana*, 338 US 49, 93 L ed 1801, 69 S Ct 1347 (1949)

Benjamin Franklin: Laws too gentle are seldom obeyed; too severe, seldom executed.

Benjamin Franklin: Where there is Hunger, Law is not regarded; and where Law is not regarded, there will be Hunger.

Douglas M. Fraser: Under current law, it is a crime for a private citizen to lie to a government official, but not for a government official to lie to the people.

David Frost: This is what has to be remebered about the law; beneath that cold, harsh, impersonal exterior beats a cold, harsh, impersonal heart.

Robert Frost (1875-1963, American Poet): A successful lawsuit is the one worn by a policeman.

Robert Frost: A jury consists of twelvepersons chosen to decide who has the better lawyer.

James A. Froude (1818-1894, British Historian): Our human laws are more or less imperfect copies of the external laws as we see them.

Thomas Fuller: Ill manners occasion good laws, as the handsome children of ugly parents.

Thomas Fuller: Possession is nine points of the law.

Mahatma Gandhi (1869-1948, Indian Political, Spiritual Leader): An unjust law is itself a species of violence. Arrest for its breach is more so.

King George III: Lawyers know the law no better than other people; they only know where to find it.

Edward Gibbon: The laws of the nation form of the most instructive portion of its history.

Grant Gilmore: The worse the society, the more laws there will be. In Hell there will be nothing but laws, and due process will be meticulously observed.

William E. Gladstone (1809-1888, British Liberal Prime Minister, Statesman): Good laws make it easier to do right and harder to do wrong.

Glaser and Way: The trouble with any unwritten law is that you don't know where to go to erase it.

Goethe: Law alone can give us freedom.

Goethe: Law is mighty, necessity is mightier.

Johann Wolfgang Von Goethe (1749-1832, German Poet, Dramatist, Novelist): We eagerly get hold of a law that serves as a weapon to our passions.

Arthur Goldberg: If law is not made more than a policeman's nightstick, American society will be destroyed.

Emma Goldman (1869-1940, American Anarchist): No great idea in its beginning can ever be within the law. How can it be within the law? The law is stationary. The law is fixed. The law is a chariot wheel which binds us all regardless of conditions or place or time.

Oliver Goldsmith: Law grinds the poor, and rich men rule the law.

Oliver Goldsmith (1728-1774, Anglo-Irish Author, Poet, Playwright): The English laws punish vice; the Chinese laws do more, they reward virtue.

Nadine Gordimer (1923-, South African Author): In a democracy—even if it is a so-called democracy like our white-Totalitarianist one—the greatest veneration one can show the rule of law is to keep a watch on it, and to reserve the right to judge unjust laws and the subversion of the function of the law by the power of the state. That vigilance is the most important proof of respect for the law.

William T. Gossett (President, American Bar Association): The rule of law can be wiped out in one misguided, however well-intentioned, generation.

Ulysses S. Grant (*Inaugural Address*, March 4, 1869): Laws are to govern all alike – those opposed as well as those who favor them. I know no method to secure the repeal of bad or obnoxious laws so effective as their stringent execution.

Hugo Grotius (Dutch jurist and statesman, 1583-1645): *De Jure Belli ac Pacis*, bk 1, ch 1, 1625): The law obliges us to do what is proper, not simply what is just.

Frank Hague (Mayor of Jersey City, N.J., 1927): I am the law.

Matthew Hale: Christianity is part of the Common Law of England.

Edward F. Halifax 1881-1959, British Conservative Statesman: If the laws could speak for themselves, they would complain of the lawyers.

Edith Hamilton: When the freedom they wished for most was freedom from responsibility then Athens ceased to be free and was never free again.

Learned Hand: There is something monstrous in commands couched in invented and unfamiliar language; an alien master is worst of all. The language of the law must not be foreign to those who are to obey it.

Learned Hand: If the prosecution of crime is to be conducted with so little regard for that protection which centuries of English law have given to the individual, we are indeed at the dawn of a new era; and much that we have deemed vital to our liberties is a delusion.

Learned Hand: Without it we cannot live; only with it can we insure the future which by right is ours. The best of man's hopes are enmeshed in its success; when it fails they must fail; the measure in which it can reconcile our passions, our wills, our conflicts, is the measure of our opportunity to find ourselves.

Vaclav Havel 1936-, Czech Playwright, President: The law is only one of several imperfect and more or less external ways of defending what is better in life against what is worse. By itself, the law can never create anything better. Establishing respect for the law does not automatically ensure a better life for that, after all, is a job for people and not for laws and institutions.

Heraclitus: The people should fight for the law as for their city wall.

John Harrington: New lords, new laws.

Benjamin Harrison (23rd President of the United States): To the law we bow with reverence. It is the one king that commands our allegiance. We shall change our king when his rule is oppressive.

Sir Arthur Helps: No man can imagine, not Swift himself, things more shameful, absurd, and grotesque than the things which do take place daily in the law.

Thomas Hobbs: The first and fundamental law of Nature... is "to seek peace and follow it." The second, the sum of the right of Nature... is, "by all means we can to defend ourselves."

Abbie Hoffman: Expedience, not justice, is the rule of contemporary American law.

J.G. Holland: Laws are the very bulkwarks of liberty; they define every man's rights, and defend the individual liberties of all men.

Oliver Wendell Holmes Jr. (Chief Justice Supreme Court of Massachusetts, Assoc Justice US Supreme Court, 1841-1935): Law is a plant that lives long before it throws out bulbs.

Oliver Wendell Holmes Jr.: It is perfectly proper To regarded study the law simply as a great anthropological document.

Oliver Wendell Holmes Jr.: It cannot be helped, it is as it should be, that the law is behind the times.

Oliver Wendell Holmes Jr: Every opinion tends to become a law.

Oliver Wendell Holmes Jr: Mob law does not become due process of law by securing the assent of a terrorized jury.

Oliver Wendell Holmes Jr (*Common Law*, 1881): The life of the law has not been logic: it has been experience. The felt necessities of the time, the prevelant moral and political theories, intuitions of public policy, avowed or unconscious, even the prejudices which judges share with their fellow-men, have had a good deal more to do than the syllogism in determining the rules by which men should be governed.

Oliver Wendell Holmes Jr: Law is not a science, but is essentially empirical.

Oliver Wendell Holmes Jr (*Path of the Law*, 10 Harv. L. Rev. 457, 1897): The prophesies of what the courts will do in fact, and nothing more pretentious, are what I mean by the law.

Oliver Wendell Holmes Jr (*Path of the Law*, 10 Harv. L. Rev. 457, 1897): If you want to know the law and nothing else, you must look at it as a bad man, who cares only forthe material consequences which such knowledge enables him to predict, not as a good one, who finds his reason for conduct, whether inside the law or outside of it, in the vaguer sanctions of conscience.

Oliver Wendell Holmes, Jr.: When I talk of law I talk as a cynic. I don't care a damn if twenty professors tell me that a decision is not law if I know that the courts will enforce it.

Oliver Wendell Holmes Jr: Most rights are qualified.

Oliver Wendell Holmes, Jr.: But the word "right" is one of the most deceptive of pitfalls; it is so easy to slip from a qualified meaning in the premise to an unqualified one in the conclusion. Most rights are qualified. " American Bank & Trust Co. v. Federal Reserve Bank of Atlanta, 256 U.S. 350, 358 (1921)

Oliver Wendell Holmes, Jr: General propositions do not decide concrete cases.

Oliver Wendell Holmes Jr.: Lawyers spend a great deal of their time shoveling smoke.

Oliver Wendell Holmes, Jr:.The law is not the place for the artist or the poet. The law is the polling of thinkers.

Oliver Wendell Holmes, Jr: It is perfectly proper to regard and studied the law simply as a great anthropological document.

Oliver Wendell Holmes, Jr: It cannot be helped, it is as it should be, that the law is behind the times.

Oliver Wendell Holmes, Jr (*Path of the Law*, 10 Harv. L. R. 457, 1897): The law is the witness and external deposit of our moral life. Its history is the history of the moral development of the race.

Oliver Wendell Holmes, Jr: The standards of the law are standards of general application. The law takes no account of the infinite varieties of temperament, intellect, and education which make the internal character of a given act so different in different men. It does not attempt to seeing men as God sees them...

Oliver Wendell Holmes, Jr: Pretty much all law consists in forbidding men to do some things that they want to do.

Oliver Wendell Holmes, Jr: Great cases like hard cases make bad law. For great cases are called great not by reason of their real importance in shaping the law of the future but because of some accident of immediate overwhelming interest which appeals to the feelings and distorts the judgment. These immediate interests exercise a kind of hydraulic pressure which makes what previously was clear seem doubtful, and before which even well-settled principles of law will bend.

Oliver Wendell Holmes, Jr.: The very considerations which judges most rarely mention, and always with an apology, are the secret root from which the law draws all the juices of life. I mean, of course, considerations of what is expedient for the community concerned.

Oliver Wendell Holmes, Jr.: I have been mad with work. First, a stinker of a case that frightened me, and then, as 500 times before, gradually sank to the dimensions of a poodle, no longer diaboloic except for the longwindedness and confused argument of counsel.

Oliver Wendell Holmes, Jr. (*Path of the Law*, 10 Harv. L. R. 457, 1896): Theory is the most important part of the dogma of the law, as the architect is the most important man who takes part in the building of a house.

Oliver Wendell Holmes, Jr.: I have said to my brethren many times that I hate justice, which means that I know if a man begins to talk about that, for one reason or another he is shirking thinking in legal terms.

Oliver Wendell Holmes, Sr., 1809-1894, American Author, Poet: This is a court of law young man, not a court of justice.

Barton Holyday: A man may as well open an oyster without a knife, as a lawyer's mouth without a fee.

Herbert Hoover: If the law is upheld only by government officials, than all law is at an end.

Horace (Latin poet): Of what use are laws, inoperative through public immorality?

Samuel Horsley: The mass of people have nothing to do with the laws but to obey them.

Elbert Hubbard: Laws, that do not embody public opinion can never be enforced.

Elbert Hubbard: Law: 1. A scheme for protecting the parasite and prolonging the life of the rogue, averting the natural consequences which would otherwise come to them. 2. The crystallization of public opinion.

Hubert H. Humphrey: There are not enough jails, not enough policemen, not enough courts to enforce a law not supported by the people.

Elbert Hubbard: Law is simply a matter of the length of the judge's ears.

Charles Evans Hughes: The United States is the greatest law factory the world has ever known.

Hubert H. Humphrey 1911-1978, American Democratic Politician, Vice President: We should have learnt by now that laws and court decisions can only point the way. They can establish criteria of right and wrong. And they can provide a basis for rooting out the evils of bigotry and racism. But they cannot wipe away centuries of oppression and injustice—however much we might desire it.

Aldous Huxley: There is no such thing as "natural rights"; there are only adjustments of conflicting claims.

Aldous Huxley: The law of diminishing returns holds good in almost every part of our human universe.

Michael Isenberg: Rulers were made to be broken.

Irish Proverb: It is better to exist unknown to the law.

Irish Proverb: Necessity knows no law.

Italian Proverb: Laws catch flies but let hornets go free.

Italian Proverb: He that goes to law holds a wolf by the ears.

Thomas Jefferson: The execution of the laws is more important than the making of them.

Thomas Jefferson (when considering punishment): The patch should fit the hole.

Thomas Jefferson: I consider trial by jury as the only anchor ever yet imagined by man, by which government can be held to the principles of its constitution."

Thomas Jefferson (First Inaugural Address 1801): The wisdom of our sages and the blood of our heroes has been devoted to the attainment of trial by jury. It should be the creed of our political faith.

Thomas Jefferson: Ignorance of the law is no excuse in any country. If it were, the laws would lose their effect, because it can always be pretended.

Thomas Jefferson (List of Colonists' Grievances against King George III, Declaration of Independence, July 4, 1776): He has obstructed the Administration of Justice, by refusing his Assent to Laws for establishing Judiciary powers. / He has made Judges dependent on his Will alone, for the tenure of their offices, and the amount and payment of their salaries. / He has combined with others to subject us to a jurisdiction foreign to our constitution, and unacknowledged by our laws; giving his Assent to their Acts of pretended Legislation: . . . For depriving us in many cases, of the benefits of Trial by Jury.

Thomas Jefferson: I should apologize, perhaps, for the style of this bill. I dislike the verbose and intricate style of the English statutes, and in our revised code I endeavored to restore it to the simple one of the ancient statues, in such original bills as I drew in that work. I suppose the reformation has not been acceptable, as it has been little followed. You, however, can easily correct this bill to the taste of my brother lawyers, by making every other word a "said" or "aforesaid," and saying everything over two or three times, so that nobody but we of the craft can untwist the diction, and find out what it means; and that, too, not so plainly but that we may conscientiously divide one half on each side. Mend it, therefore, in form and substance to the orthodox taste, and make it what it should be; or, if you think it radically wrong, try something else, and let us make a beginning in some way. No matter how wrong, experience will amend it as we go along, and make it effectual in the end.

Thomas Jefferson (1743-1826, 3rd President of the US): It is the trade of lawyers to question everything, yield nothing, and talk by the hour.

Thomas Jefferson: Certainly one of the highest duties of the citizen is a scrupulous obedience to the laws of the nation. But it is not the highest duty.

Sir George Jessel (Speech in House of Commons, 1869): Only in a sense was it true that our Common Law was not based on the Roman law, for we had used the Roman law as the Turks used the remains of the splendid temples of antiquity. We had pulled out the stones and used them in constructing buildings which we called our own.

Lyndon B. Johnson: A rioter with a Molotov cocktail in his hands is not fighting for civil rights any more than a Klansman with a sheet on his back and mask on his face. They are both more or less what the law declares them: lawbreakers, destroyers of constitutional rights and liberties and ultimately destroyers of a free America.

Samuel Johnson: The law is the last result of human wisdom acting upon human experience for the benefit of the public.

Samuel Johnson, 1709-1784, British Author: Laws teach us to know when we commit injury and when we suffer it.

Samuel Johnson, 1709-1784, British Author: I would be loath to speak ill of any person who I do not know deserves it, but I am afraid he is an *attorney.*

Samuel Johnson, 1709-1784, British Author: Lawyers know life practically. A bookish man should always have them to converse with.

Franklin P. Jones: Anybody who thinks talk is cheap should get some legal advice.

Sir William Jones (English lawyer and author, 1746-1794): Law like all human systems, will ever advance nearer to perfection, and ever fall short of it.

Sir William Jones: As the law is a jealous science, and will not have any partnership with the Eastern Muses, I must absolutely renounce their acquaintance for ten or twelve years to come.

Sir William Jones: And sovereign Law, that state's collected will O'er thrones and globes elate, Sits empress, crowning good, repressing ill.

Justinian I: The precepts of the law are these: to live honorably, to injure no other men, to render every man his due.

Decimus Junius Juvenal (Roman satirical poet, 40-125 A.D., *Satires*): *Hoc volo, sic ubeo, sit pro ratione voluntas*: It's my will, my command, let that for reason stand.

Lord Kames (Scottish judge, 1696-1782, *Historical Law Tracts: Preface*): Law in particular becomes then only a rational study, when it is traced historically, from its first rudiments among savages, through successive changes, to its highest improvements in a civilized society.

Lord Kames (Scottish judge, 1696-1782, *Historical Law Tracts*): Law treated historically becomes an entertaining study; entertaining not only to those whose profession it is, but to every person who hath any thirst for knowledge.

Immanuel Kant: "So act that your principle of action might safely be made a law for the whole world."

Joshua Karton: The actor (and lawyer) who uses every part of him/herself becomes irresistible.

John Keats 1795-1821, British Poet: I think we may class the lawyer in the natural history of monsters.

Florynce R. Kennedy: Every form of bigotry can be found in ample supply in the legal system of our country. It would seem that Justice (usually depicted as a woman) is indeed blind to racism, sexism, war, and poverty.

John F. Kennedy: Certain other societies may respect the rule of force—we respect the rule of law.

John F. Kennedy (Innaugural Address 1961): If a beachhead of cooperation may push back the jungles of suspicion, let both sides join in creating a new endeavor – not a new balance of power, but a new world of law, where the strong are just and the weak secure and the peace preserved.

Robert F. Kennedy 1925-1968, American Attorney General, Senator: Whenever men take the law into their own hands, the loser is the law. And when the law loses, freedom languishes.

Robert F. Kennedy: Each time a man stands up for an ideal, / or acts to improve the lot of others, / or strikes out against injustice, / he sends forth a tiny ripple of hope."

Coretta Scott King: When laws cease to have usefulness to society, they should be changed, not enforced. All one has to do is to think of the jimcrow laws of most states in the South not so many years ago to know what I mean.

Martin Luther King Jr. 1929-1968, American Black Leader, Nobel Prize Winner, 1964: Law and order exist for the purpose of establishing justice, and ... when they fail in this purpose they become the dangerously structured dams that block the flow of social progress.

Martin Luther King, Jr.: It may be true that the law cannot make a man love me. But it can keep him from lynching me, and I think that's pretty important.

Rudyard Kipling (*The Law of the Jungle*): Now these are the Laws of the Jungle, and many and mighty are they; / But the head and the hoof of the Law and the haunch and the hump is – OBEY!

Rudyard Kipling: Leave to live by no man's leave, underneath the Law...

Joan Kiser: The sins of the fathers are often visited upon the sons-in-law."

Edward I. Koch: America is a nation of laws... The law is not always an easy friend, because the law does not play favorites. But for those who seek justice in a society of responsible citizens, the law will always be an ally.

Ted Koskoff, highly regarded personal injury attorney, Bridgeport, CT.: "WHAT IS A LAWYER?" If I were to ask what is a lawyer, not of Blackstone, but of you, you might say, or I might say,

If you are a lawyer, you stand between the abuse of governmental power and the individual.
If you are a lawyer, you stand between the abuse of corporate power and the individual.
If you are a lawyer, you stand in between the judicial abuse of power and the individual.
If you are a lawyer, you are helping to mold the rights of individuals for generations to come.

And, if you think of some of the people who have filled this mold, your thoughts would, I think, inevitably turn to certain people and you would see these people as I see them.

He undertook the defense of John Peter Zanger to protect his right to publish what he chose, free of censorship and interference. His name was Alexander Hamilton and he was a lawyer.

You would see him at the trial of Captain Preston, defending him at a political trial which arose out of the Boston Massacre. His name was John Adams and he was a lawyer.

You would see him at the miracle in Philadelphia, the constitutional convention of 1787, fighting for the Bill of Rights which was to become the creed of American Freedom. His name was James Madison. He was a lawyer.

You would see him presiding over the Supreme Court, as the architect of the real powers of the Court. His name was John Marshall. He was a lawyer.

And I know you would see him at Gettysburg with tears in his eyes, gaunt and morose, rededicating our country to the proposition that all men are created equal. His name was Abraham Lincoln. He was a lawyer.

I know we all see him, an elemental man fighting for one cause or another in Dayton Tennessee, preaching the legitimacy of evolution. His name was Clarence Darrow and he was a lawyer.

You would see him speaking to us from his wheelchair, lifting our spirits, making us stronger with his inspirational philosophy, "The only thing we have to fear is fear itself." His name was Franklin Delano Roosevelt and he was a lawyer.

You might see him in the Senate Hearing Room in Washington uttering that anguished cry for decency. His name was Joseph Welch and he was a lawyer.

And then you would think of the precious monuments that they had left to their lives and of Milton's wonderful comment on Shakespeare that, "thou and I wonder in astonishment that thou hast left thyself a monument."

Then you might think, what kind of monument will I leave? Not one of brick and mortar or stone, but of thought, because only thoughts live.

Finally, you would probably think of that marvelous admonition of Holmes, when nearly a hundred years ago, he said, "I think of this life as action and passion. It is required of man that he should share the passion and action of his time at the peril of being judged not to have lived."

William M. Kunstler: I know the law. It is used to oppress those who threaten the ruling class. The judicial decree has replaced the assassination... I stay with the law only because the law is maneuverable, it can be manipulated.

Jean De La Bruyere 1645-1696, French Writer: Avoid lawsuits beyond all things; they pervert your conscience, impair your health, and dissipate your property.

Jean De La Bruyere 1645-1696, French Writer: The court is like a palace of marble; it's composed of people very hard and very polished.

Suzanne Lafollette 1893-1983, American Feminist, Writer: Laws are felt only when the individual comes into conflict with them.

Charles Lamb 1775-1834, British Essayist, Critic: He is no lawyer who cannot take two sides.

Latin Maxim: Inability suspends the law.

Latin Maxim: No one is bound to the impossible.

Latin Maxim: The law does not seek to compel a man to do that which he cannot possibly perform.

Latin Maxim: What is inconsistent with and contrary to reason is not permitted in law.

Latin Maxim: Rights are lost by disuse.

Latin Maxim: The laws assist those who are vigilant, not those who sleep over their rights.

Latin Maxim: When a greater right belongs to a man, the lesser right bought to be included.

Harper Lee, To Kill a Mockingbird (1960): But there is one way in this country in which all men are created equal-there is one human institution that makes a pauper the equal of a Rockefeller, the stupid man the equal of an Einstein, and the ignorant man the equal of any college president. That institution, gentlemen, is a court. It can be the Supreme Court of the United State or the humblest J.P. court in the land, or this honorable court which you serve. Our courts have their faults, as does any human institution, but in this country our courts are the great levelers, and in our courts all men are created equal.

Stanislaw Lec: Thoughts, like fleas, jump from man to man, but they don't bite everybody."

Robert A. Leflar: The law does not exist for the lawyers though there are some of us who seem to think that it does. The law is for all the people and the lawyers are only its ministers.

N.Y. Chief Justice Irving Lehman (Chief Judge NY Court of Appeals, 1876-1945): The law draws a distinction between a criminal act and yielding to a vice. It does not treat alike the spider who spins the web and the fly enmeshed in it. *Bamman v. Erickson*, 288 N.Y. 133 (1942)

Doris Lessing: In university they don't tell you that the greater part of the law is learning to tolerate fools.

Alex Levin: The reason there is so little crime in Germany is that it's against the law.

Sir Wilmot Lewis (English journalist, 1877-1950): Legislation in the United States is a digestive process by Congress with frequent regurgitations by the Supreme Court.

Gerald F. Lieberman (American Writer): It is unfair to believe everything we hear about lawyers, some of it might not be true.

Abraham Lincoln 1809-1865, 16th President of the US: A jury too often has at least one member more ready to hang the panel than to hang the traitor.

Abraham Lincoln: Let reverence for the laws be breathed by every American mother to the lisping babe that prattles on her lap. Let it be taught in schools, in seminaries, and in colleges. Let it be written in primers, spelling books, and in almanacs. Let it be preached from the pulpit, proclaimed in legislative halls, and enforced in the courts of justice. And, in short, let it become the political religion of the nation.

Walter Lippmann 1889-1974, American Journalist: A country survives its legislation. That truth should not comfort the conservative nor depress the radical. For it means that public policy can enlarge its scope and increase its audacity, can try big experiments without trembling too much over the result. This nation could enter upon the most radical experiments and could afford to fail in them.

Walter Lippmann: The real law in the modern State is the multitude of little decisions made daily by millions of men.

John Locke: Whenever Law ends, Tyranny begins.

Virginia Long (Justice of New Jersey Supreme Court, speaking about professionalism): We've come a long way ... How did we get from Atticus Finch to Richard Fish (on the TV series *Alley McBeal*)?

King Louis XIV of France: Laws are the sovereigns of sovereigns.

Livy: No law perfectly suits the convenience of every member of the community; the only consideration is, whether upon the whole it be profitable to the greater part.

Lycophron: Law is a pledge that the citizens of a state will do justice to one another.

Machiavelli: The principal foundations of all states are good laws and good aims; and their cannot be good laws where there are not good aims.

Charles Macklin (English dramatist, 1697?-1797): Law is a sort of hocus-pocus science.

Charles Macklin: The law is a sort of hocus-pocus science, that smiles in yer face while it picks yer pocket: and the glorious uncertainty of it is of more use to the professors than the justice of it.

Archibald Macleish 1892-1982, American Poet: The business of the law is to make sense of the confusion of what we call human life—to reduce it to order but at the same time to give it possibility, scope, even dignity.

Charles A. Madison: Law is merely the expression of the will of the strongest for the time being, and therefore laws have no fixity, but shift from generation to generation.

Calvert Magruder: The power of a sonorous phrase to command uncritical acceptance has often been encountered in the law.

Frederic William Maitland (*Bracton's Notebook, Introduction*, 1887): English lawyers seem from the outset to treat Roman law much as our church treats the Apocrypha; it is instructive but not authoritative.

Herbert Marcuse: Law and order are always and everywhere the law and order which protect the established hierarchy.

John Marshal, Marbury v. Madison, 5 U.S. (1 Cranch) 137, 163 (1803): The government of the United States has been emphatically termed a government of laws, and not of men. It will certainly cease to deserve this high appellation, if the laws furnish no remedy for the violation of a vested legal right.

Harriet Martineau 1802-1876, British Writer, Social Critic: Laws and customs may be creative of vice; and should be therefore perpetually under process of observation and correction: but laws and customs cannot be creative of virtue: they may encourage and help to preserve it; but they cannot originate it.

Bert Masterson: Someone has tabulated that we have 35 million laws on the books to enforce the Ten Commandments.

Milton Mayer: From Antigone through Martin Luther to Martin Luther King the issue of liberty has turned on the exercise of a higher law than that of the State.

James Clerk Maxwell: The only laws of matter are those that our minds must fabricate and the only laws of mind are fabricated for it by matter.

William Mcilvanney: Who thinks the law has anything to do with justice? It's what we have because we can't have justice.

Margaret Mead: The contempt for law and the contempt for the human consequences of lawbreaking of from the bottom to the top of American society.

H. L. Mencken 1880-1956, American Editor, Author, Critic, Humorist: Say what you will about the Ten Commandments, you must always come back to the pleasant fact that there are only ten of them.

H.L. Mencken: The law is a sort of hocus-pocus science that smiles in your face while it picks your pocket.

John Stuart Mill 1806-1873, British Philosopher, Economist: All that makes existence valuable to any one depends on the enforcement of restraints upon the actions of other people.

Cecil B. De Mille 1881-1959, American Film Producer and Director: It is impossible for us to break the law. We can only break ourselves against the law.

Dennis Miller: The frightening reality is every day this society seems to make its legal decisions in much the same way the Archies picked their vacation spots—blindfold Jughead, give him a dart, and spin the globe.

Kate Millet: It is further irony that our legal ethic prosecutes those who are forced (economically or psychologically) to offer themselves for sale as objects, but condones the act of buying persons as objects.

John Milton: Litigious terms, fat contentions, and flowing fees.

John Milton: Our reason is our law.

John Milton (English poet and writer, 1608-1674, *Paradise Lost*, XII): Law can discover sin, but not remove.

Addison Mizner: Ignorance of the law excuses no man from practicing it.

Michel Eyquem De Montaigne 1533-1592, French Philosopher, Essayist: It would be better to have no laws at all, than to have too many.

Michel De Montaigne: Nothing is more subject to change than the laws.

Charles Louis de Montesquieu: Laws should not be changed without good reason.

Charles De Montesquieu 1689-1755, French Jurist, Political Philosopher: The severity of the laws prevents their execution.

Charles De Montesquieu: The spirit of moderation should also be the spirit of the lawgiver

Charles De Montesquieu: There is no nation so powerful, as the one that obeys its laws not from principals of fear or reason, but from passion.

Charles De Montesquieu: Useless laws weaken the necessary laws.

Thomas Moore 1779-1852, Irish Poet: I would uphold the law if for no other reason but to protect myself.

Sir Thomas More (1478-1535, British Chancellor, Canonized 1935): Lawyers—a profession it is to disguise matters.

Abraham Myerson: In a democracy only those laws which have their bases in folkways or the approval of strong groups have a chance of being enforced.

Gunnar Myrdal: We must observe the moralistic attitude toward law in America, expressed in the common belief that there is a higher law.

New Testament, *Romans* 2:14: Render therefore to all their dues: tribute to whom tribute is due; custom to whom custom; fear to whom fear, honour to whom honour. Owe no man any thing, but to love one another: for he that loveth another hath fulfilled the law.

Richard Nixon: While technically I did not commit a crime, an impeachable offense... these are legalisms, as far as the handling of this matter is concerned; it was so botched up, I made so many bad judgments. The worst ones, mistakes of the heart, rather than the head. But let me say, a man in that top job - he's got to have a heart, but his head must always rule his heart."

Richard Nixon: "When the president does it, that means it is not illegal."

Louis Nizer: "... defeat is education. It is a step to something better."

Louis Nizer: (Preparation) is the be-all of good trial work. Everything else—Felicity of expression, improvisational brilliance—is a satellite around the sun. Through preparation is that sun.

Louis Nizer, British Born American Lawyer, Writer: In cross examination, as in fishing, nothing is more ungainly than a fisherman pulled into the water by his catch.

Christopher North: Laws were made to be broken.

Virginia Ostman: If lawyers are disbarred and clergymen defrocked, doesn't it follow that electricians can be delighted, musicians denoted, cowboys deranged, models deposed, tree surgeons debarked, and dry cleaners depressed.

Ouida 1838-1908, British Writer: Petty laws breed great crimes.

Ovid: Laws were made that the stronger might not in all things have his way.

Robert Owen: Courts of law, and all the paraphernalia and folly of law cannot be found in a rational state of society.

Thomas Paine: "But where, say some, is the king of America? I'll tell you. Friend,... let a crown be placed..., by which the world may know,... that in America the law is king. For in absolute governments the king is the law, so in free countries the law ought to be king; and there ought to be none other ...."

Blaise Pascal 1623-1662, French Scientist, Religious Philosopher: Law, without force, is impotent.

Harry Philo: The Law is never settled until it is settled right; the Law is never right until it is just; the Law is never just until it serves society to the fullest.

William Pitt (Earl of Chatham, English statesman, 1708-1778, In Debate in House of Lords on right of John Wilkes to take his seat in House of Commons, January 9, 1770): Unlimited power is apt to corrupt the minds of those who possess it; and this I know, my Lords, **that where law ends, there tyranny begins.**

Plato: No law or ordinance is mightier than understanding."

Plato: Law, being a tyrant, compels many things to be done contrary to nature.

Edgar Allan Poe: I am beginning to think ... that "the people have nothing to do with the laws but to obey them"

Sir Frederick Pollock (English lawyer, writer, legal historian, 1847 - 1937): Even habitual disobedience in some things is consistent with the rule of law: it is certain that only a minority of motorists observe the statutory speed limit on a clear road, but England is not therefore in a state of anarchy.

Sir Frederick Pollock (English lawyer, writer, legal historian, *Oxford Lectures and Discourses*, 1890): There you shall see in very truth how the spark, fostered in our own land by Glanvill and Bracton, waxed into a clear flame under the care of Brian and Choke, Littleton and Fortescue, was tended by Coke and Hale, and was made a light to shine round the world by Holt and Mansfield, and the Scotts, and others whom living men remember. You shall understand how great a heritage is the law of England, whereof we and our brethern across the ocean are partakers, and you shall deem treaties and covenants a feeble bond in comparison of it; and you shall know with certain assurance that, however arduous has been your pilgrimage, the achievement is a full answer. So venerable, so majestic,is this living temple of justice, that immemorial yet freshly growing fabric of the Common Law, that the least of us is happy who hereafter may point to so much as one stone thereof, and say, The work of my hands is there.

Hart Pomerantz: Law school taught me one thing; how to take two situations that are exactly the same and show how they are different.

Alexander Pope 1688-1744, British Poet, Critic, Translator: Curse on all laws, but those that love has made.

Roscoe Pound (*A Hundred Years of American Law*, 1937): There is no law without lawyers.

Roscoe Pound (*Interpretations of Legal History*, 1923): The law must be stable, and yet it can not stand still.

Roscoe Pound: Law is experience developed by reason and applied continually to further experience.

Roscoe Pound: The law is the highest inheritance the sovereign people has, for without the law there would be no sovereign people and no inheritance.

Adam Clayton Powell Jr.: A man's respect for law and order exists in precise relationship to the size of his paycheck.

Lewis F. Powell Jr. (Supreme Court Justice): Consider the reason of the case, for nothing is law that is not reason.

Proverb: Fools and obstinate men make lawyers rich.

Proverb: Lawyers and painters can soon make what's black, white.

Proverb: Lawyers and woodpeckers have long bills.

Proverb: Possession is nine tenths of the law.

Proverb: The law helps those who watch, not those who sleep.

Proverb: The more laws the less justice

Proverb: Where the law is uncertain there is no law.

Mario Puzo: A lawyer with a briefcase can steal more than hundred men with guns.

Ronald Reagan: I've been told that since the beginning of civilization, millions and millions of laws have not improved on the Ten Commandments one bit.

Ronald Reagan (40th President of the United States): We have the means to change the laws we find unjust or onerous. We cannot, as citizens, pick and choose the laws we will or will not obey.

Ronald Reagan: We have the means to change the laws we find unjust or onerous. We cannot, as citizens, pick and choose the laws we will or will not obey.

James A. Reed, in 67 Congressional Record 10,708 (1926): What we need to do is to stop passing laws. We have enough laws now to govern the world for the next 10,000 years. Every crank who has a foolish notion that he would like to impose upon everybody else hastens to some legislative body and demands that it be graven upon the statutes. Every fanatic who wants to control his neighbor's conduct is here or at some other legislative body demanding that a law be passed to regulate that neighbor's conduct.

Alison Reppy (American law school dean, legal writer, 1893-1958, *Common-Law Pleading,* 2 N.Y. Law Forum 1, 1956): The law is what it is today because of what the law was yesterday; it cannot escape its ancestry, and it, too, must progress against the background of its history.

Seneca Rhetor: *Quaedam iura non scripta sed omnibus scriptis certiora sunt.* ~ Some laws are unwritten but they are better established than all written ones.

Henry M. Robert: Where there is no law, but every man does what is right in his own eyes, there is the least of real liberty.

Will Rogers: I don't see why a man shouldn't pay an inheritance tax. If a Country is good enough to pay taxes to while you are living, it's good enough to pay in after you die. By the time you die you should be so used to paying taxes that it would just be almost second nature to you.

Will Rogers: The minute you read something you can understand, you can almost be sure it was drawn up by a lawyer.

Will Rogers: We are always saying let the law take its course, but what we mean is "Let the law take our course."

Will Rogers: The ony way to solve the Traffic problems of the Country is to pass a law that only paid-for Cars are allowed to use the Highways. That would make traffic so scarce we could use our Boulevards for Children play grounds.

Will Rogers: Talking about Prohibition is like whittling used to be—it passes the time but don't get you nowhere.

Theodore Roosevelt 1858-1919, 26th President of the US: No man is above the law and no man is below it; nor do we ask any man's permission when we require him to obey it. Obedience to the law is demanded as a right; not asked as a favor.

Theodore Roosevelt: No people is wholly civilized where a distinction is drawn between stealing an office and stealing a purse.

Theodore Roosevelt: It is difficult to make our material condition better by the best law, but it is easy enough to ruin it by bad laws.

Theodore Roosevelt: The decisions of the courts on economic and social questions depend on their economic and social philosophy.

Donald Rumsfeld: Listening to both sides does not necessarily bring about a correct judgment.

Bertrand Russell: Government can easily exist without law, but law cannot exist without government.

Russian Proverb: Law is a flag, and gold is the wind that makes it wave.

Marquis De Sade 1740-1814, French Author: Are not laws dangerous which inhibit the passions? Compare the centuries of anarchy with those of the strongest legalism in any country you like and you will see that it is only when the laws are silent that the greatest actions appear.

Marquis De Sade 1740-1814, French Author: Those laws, being forged for universal application, are in perpetual conflict with personal interest, just as personal interest is always in contradiction with the general interest. Good for society, our laws are very bad for the individuals whereof it is composed; for, if they one time protect the individual, they hinder, trouble, fetter him for three quarters of his life

Bernard Joseph Saurin 1706-1781, French Dramatist: The law often permits what honor prohibits.

Dorothy L. Sayers 1893-1957, British Author: Lawyers enjoy a little mystery, you know. Why, if everybody came forward and told the truth, the whole truth, and nothing but the truth straight out, we should all retire to the workhouse.

Leslie Scarman: Law reform is far too serious a matter to be left to the legal profession.

Eric Schnapper: Lawyering is within the relatively narrow category of occupations where borderline dishonesty is fairly lucrative. In many instances, the very art of a lawyer is a sort of calculated this regard of the law or at least no ordinary notions of morality.

Diane B. Schulder: Law is a reflection and a source of prejudice. It both enforces and suggests forms of bias.

Sir Walter Scott (*Guy Mannering*): It is the pest of our profession that we seldom see the best side of human nature. People come to us with every selfish feeling newly pointed and grinded.... In civilized society, law is the chimney through which all that smoke discharges itself, that used to circulate through the whole house and put every one's eyes out; no wonder, therefore, that the vent itself should sometimes get a little sooty.

Scottish Proverb: It is an ill cause that lawyers think shame o'

Seneca: Laws do not persuade because they threaten.

Victor Serge: I followed his argument with the blank uneasiness which one might feel in the presence of a logical lunatic.

Eric Sevareid (CBS evening News, April 3, 1972): Years ago, despairing citizens used to say, "their oughta be a law." There is a law. There are lots of laws. What there oughta be is severe—and equal—in Forstmann of laws. In one area after another of our public life we are seeing a reversion to that frontier phenomenon—citizens taking the law into their own hands, not to enforce it themselves, but to force the official enforcers to enforce it.

Sir Walter Scott 1771-1832, British Novelist, Poet: A lawyer without history or literature is a mechanic, a mere working mason; if he possesses some knowledge of these, he may venture to call himself an architect.

William Shakespeare (*Coriolanus*, Act II, i): You wear out a good wholesome forenoon in hearing a cause between orange-wife and fosset-seller; and then rejourn the controversy of three pence to a second day of audience.

William Shakespeare (*Coriolanus*, Act III, i): He hath resisted law, / And therefore law shall scorn him further trial.

William Shakespeare (*Hamlet*, Act III, i): The law's delay.

William Shakespeare (*Hamlet*, Act III, iii): In the corrupted currents of this world / Offence's gilded hand may shove by justice, / And oft 'tis seen the wicked prize itself / Buys out the law: but 'tis not so above; / There is no shuffling, there the action lies / In his true nature; and we ourselves compell'd, / Even to the teeth and forehead of our faults, / To give in evidence.

William Shakespeare (*Hamlet*, Act V, i): FIRST CLOWN: Argal, he that is not guilty of his own death shortens not his own life. / SECOND CLOWN: But is this law? / FIRST CLOWN: Ay, marry is't; crowner's quest law.

William Shakespeare (*I Henry IV*, Act I, ii): But, I prithee, sweet wag, shall there be gallows standing in England when thou art king? – and resolution thus fobbed as it is with the rusty curb of old father antic, the law.

William Shakespeare (*II Henry IV*, Act IV, i): A rotten case abides no handling.

William Shakespeare (*I Henry VI*, Act II, iv): Faith, I have been a truant in the law, / And never yet could frame my will to it; / And therefore frame the law unto my will.

William Shakespeare (*II Henry VI*, Act I, iii): Let him have all the rigour of the law.

William Shakespeare (*II Henry VI*, Act IV, ii): Is not this a lamentable thing, that of the skin of an innocent lamb should be made parchment; that parchment, being scribbled o'er, should undo a man?

William Shakespeare (*Henry VI*, Part II, Act IV, ii): Jack Cade, a notorious criminal, who is described by his "peers" as a sheep thief punished by burning off his hand, is addressing his gang of ne'er do wells, plotting to dispatch the king and all his court and live free of any law or order; he advocates burning down the Inns of Court; he laments that an innocent lamb should have his skin torn off to make parchment on which is scribbled law, and he is sorely vexed at the obstacles in his path to plunder. Dick Butcher, one of Cade's gang says: "The first thing we do, let's kill all the lawyers.

William Shakespeare (*Henry VIII*, Act III, ii): Press not a falling man too far; 'tis virtue: / His faults lie open to the laws; let them, / Not you, correct him.

William Shakespeare (*King John*, Act III, i): When law can do no right, / Let it be lawful that law bar no wrong.

William Shakespeare (*Measure for Measure*, Act I, iii): We have strict statutes and most biting laws.

William Shakespeare (*Measure for Measure*, Act I, iv): He... follows close the rigour of the statute, / To make him an example.

William Shakespeare (*Measure for Measure*, Act II, i): We must not make a scarecrow of the law, / Setting it up to fear the birds of prey, / And let it keep one shape, till custom make it / Their perch and not their terror.

William Shakespeare (*Measure for Measure*, Act II, ii): The law hath not been dead, though it hath slept.

William Shakespeare (*Measure for Measure*, Act III, i): Has he affections in him, / That thus can make him bite the law by the nose?

William Shakespeare, (*The Merchant of Venice*, Act I, ii): Portia: "The brain may devise laws for the blood; but a hot temper leaves over a cold decree!"

William Shakespeare, (*The Merchant of Venice*, Act III, ii): In law, what plea so tainted and corrupt / But, being seasoned with a gracious voice, / Obscures the show of evil.

William Shakespeare (*The Merchant of Venice,* Act IV, i): It must not be; there is no power in Venice / Can alter a decree established: 'Twill be recorded for a precedent, / And many an error by the same example / Will rush into the state.

William Shakespeare (*Othello*, Act I, iii): The bloody book of law / You shall yourself read in the bitter letter.

William Shakespeare (*Richard II*, Act II, iii): I am a subject / And challenge law: attorneys are denied me; / And therefore personally I lay my claim / To my inheritance.

William Shakespeare (*Richard III*, Act I, iv): Before I be convict by course of law, / To threaten me with death is most unlawful.

William Shakespeare (*Romeo and Juliet*, Act I, i): Abraham: Do you bite your thumb at us, sir? Sampson: Is the law of our side, if I say ay?

William Shakespeare (*Timon of Athens*, Act III, ii): They have been grand jury-men since before Noah was a sailor.

William Shakespeare (*Timon of Athens*, Act III, v): We are for law: he dies.

William Shakespeare (*Timon of Athens*, Act III, v): It pleases time and fortune, to lie heavy / Upon a friend of mine, who, in hot blood, / Hath stepp'd into the law; whish is past depth / To those that, without head, plunge into't.

William Shakespeare (*Timon of Athens*, Act IV, iii): The laws, your curb and whip, in their rough power / Have uncheck'd theft.

William Shakespeare (*Twelfth Night,* Act III, iv): Still you keep o' the windy side of the law.

George Bernard Shaw (1856-1950, Irish-born British Dramatist): Whenever you wish to do anything against the law, Cicely, always consult a good solicitor first.

George Bernard Shaw: Our laws make law impossible; our liberties destroy all freedom; our property is organized robbery; our wisdom is administered by inexperienced dupes, our power wielded by cowards and weaklings, and our honor false in all its points. I am an enemy of the existing order for good reasons.

Ruth Shays: If you got the say-so, you want to keep it, whether you are right or wrong. That's why they have to keep changing the laws—so they don't unbenefit any of these big white men.

Bishop Fulton J. Sheen (Roman Catholic Bishop of New York, and Rochester, writer, orator, *Sermon at Red Mass*, 1965): A sign of the loss of freedom is the new compassion which extends pity not to the raped but to the rapist.

Edgar A. Shoaff: The two leading recipes for success are building a better mousetrap and finding a bigger loophole.

Sidney Smith: When I hear any man talk of unalterable law, the only affect it produces upon me is to convince me that he is an unalterable fool.

Sophocles: Laws can never be enforced unless fear supports them.

Sophocles: Nobody has a more sacred obligation to obey the law than those who make the law.

Alexander Solzhenitsyn 1918-, Russian Novelist: I have spent all my life under a Communist regime, and I will tell you that a society without any objective legal scale is a terrible one indeed. But a society with no other scale but the legal one is not quite worthy of man either.

Spanish Proverb: He who goes to law for a sheep loses his cow.

Spanish Proverb: Laws, like the spider's web, catch the fly and let the hawk go free.

Robert D. Sprecht: Under any conditions, anywhere, whatever you are doing, there is some ordinance under which you can be booked.

Konstantin Stanislavisky 1863-1968, Russian Actor, Theatre director, Teacher: Our demands are simple, normal, and therefore they are difficult to satisfy. All we ask is that an actor on the stage live in accordance with natural laws.

Elizabeth Cady Stanton 1815-1902, American Social Reformer and Women's Suffrage Leader: To make laws that man cannot, and will not, obey, serves to bring all law into contempt.

Elizabeth Cady Stanton: A very wise father once remarked, that in the government of his children, he forbade as few things as possible; a wise legislation would do the same. It is folly to make laws on subjects beyond human prerogative, knowing that in the very nature of things they must be set aside. To make laws that man can not and will not obey, serves to bring all law into contempt. It is very important in a republic, that the people should respect the laws, for if we throw them to the winds, what becomes of civil government?

Gloria Steinem: Law and justice are not always the same. When they aren't, destroying the law may be the first step toward changing it.

Adlai Ewing Stevenson: As citizens of this democracy, you are the rulers and the ruled, the law-givers and the law-abiding, the beginning and the end."

Supreme Court Justice Potter Stewart: We dedicated ourselves to a powerful idea—organic law rather than naked power. There seems to be universal acceptance of that idea in the nation.

E. Ralph Stewart: Of course there is a different law for the rich and poor; otherwise, who would go into business?

Max Stirner 1806-1856, German Satiric Philosopher: The state calls its own violence law, but that of the individual crime.

Joseph Story: He who seeks equity must do equity.

Joseph Story (his inauguration speech as Dean Professor of Law, Harvard Univ., 1829): (The law) is a jealous mistress, and requires a long and constant courtship. It is not to be won by trifling favors, but by lavish homage."

John Stossel: America has a legal system that is the laughing stock in the civilized world.

Sutrakritanga: All breathing, existing, living, sentient creatures should not be slain nor treated with violence, nor abused, nor tormented, nor driven away. This is the pure unchangeable law.

Jonathan Swift 1667-1745, Anglo-Irish Satirist: I said there was a society of men among us, bred up from their youth in the art of proving by words multiplied for the purpose, that white is black, and black is white, according as they are paid. To this society all the rest of the people are as slaves.

Jonathan Swift: Laws are like cobwebs, which may catch small flies, but let wasps and hornets break through.

Publilius Syrus 1st Century BC, Roman Writer: The judge is found guilty when a criminal is acquitted.

Publius Cornelius Tacitus 55-117 AD, Roman Historian: In a state where corruption abounds, laws must be very numerous.

Publius Cornelius Tacitus: The more corrupt the state, the more laws.

Talmud, *Avoda zava,:* Fish die when they are out of water, and people die without law and order.

Talmud, *Breakhot*: See how people act, and that is the Law.

Talmud, *Sanhedrin*: Judgment delayed is judgment voided.

Talmud, *Shabbat*: What is hateful to you, do not to your fellow: that is the whole Law; all the rest is interpretation.

Tennyson (*In Memorian, xxxv*): Within the dusty purlieus of the law.

Terence: Extreme law is often extreme injustice.

St. Thomas Aquinas (*Summa Theologica*, I-II, q. 90): It is nothing other than a certain rule of reason for the purpose of the common good, laid down by him who is entrusted with the welfare of the community and promulgated.

Henry David Thoreau 1817-1862, American Essayist, Poet, Naturalist: I say, break the law.

Henry David Thoreau: It is not desirable to cultivate a respect for law, so much as a respect for right.

Henry David Thoreau: The lawyer's truth is not Truth, but consistency or a consistent expediency.

Henry David Thoreau: Whatever the human law may be, neither an individual nor a nation can commit the least act of injustice against the obscurest individual without having to pay the penalty for it.

Henry David Thoreau: The law will never make men free; it is men who have got to make the law free.

Henry David Thoreau: Law never made men a whit more just.

Henry David Thoreau: Are laws to be enforced simply because they were made?

Alexis De Tocqueville 1805-1859, French Social Philosopher: Scarcely any political question arises in the United States that is not resolved, sooner or later, into a judicial question.

Alexis de Tocqueville: In the United States, every one is personally interested in enforcing the obedience of the whole community to the law; for as the minority may shortly rally the majority to its principles, it is interested in professing that respect for the decrees of the legislator which it may soon have occasion to claim for its own. However irksome an enactment may be, the citizen of the United States complies with it, not only because it is the work of the majority, but because it is his own, and he regards it as a contract to which he is himself a party.

Alexis de Tocqueville: All the sovereigns who have chosen to govern by their own authority, and to direct society instead of obeying its directions, have destroyed or enfeebled the institution of the jury. The Tudor monarchs sent to prison jurors who refused to convict, and Napoleon caused them to be selected by his agents.

Alexis de Tocqueville: The institution of the jury, if confined to criminal causes, is always in danger; but when once it is introduced into civil proceedings, it defies the aggressions of time and man. If it had been as easy to remove the jury from the customs as from the laws of England, it would have perished under the Tudors, and the civil jury did in reality at that period save the liberties of England.

Alexis de Tocqueville: The best laws cannot make a constitution work in spite of morals; morals can turn the worst laws to advantage. That is a commonplace truth, but one to which my studies are always bringing me back. It is the central point in my conception. I see it at the end of all my reflections.

June L. Trapp: The due process of law as we use it, I believe, rests squarely on the liberal idea of conflict and resolution.

Benjamin Ricketson Tucker 1854-1939, American Philosophical Anarchist: We enact many laws that manufacture criminals, and then a few that punish them.

Mark Twain 1835-1910, American Humorist, Writer: To succeed in the other trades, capacity must be shown; in the law, concealment of it will do.

Mark Twain: If you laid all of our laws end to end, there would be no end.

Mark Twain: Laws are sand, customs are rock. Laws can be evaded and punishment escaped, but an openly transgressed custom brings sure punishment.

Mark Twain: We have a criminal jury system which is superior to any in the world; and its efficiency is only marred by the difficulty of finding twelve men every day who don't know anything and can't read.

Mark Twain: Let me make the superstitions of the nation and I care not who makes its laws or its songs either.

Mark Twain: If we only had some God in the country's laws, instead of being in such a sweat to get him into the Consitution, it would be better all around.

Mark Twain: You see, he knew his own laws just as other people so often know the laws, not by effects. They take a meaning, and get to be very vivid, when you come to apply them to yourself.

Mark Twain: It would not be possible for Noah to do in our day what he was permitted to do in his own... The inspector would come and examine the Ark, and make all sorts of objections.

Mark Twain: We have an insanity plea that would have saved Cain.

Mark Twain: Really, what we want now, is not laws against crime, but a law against insanity.

Mark Twain: The laws of Nature, that is to say the laws of God, plainly made every human being a law unto himself, we must steadfastly refuse to obey those laws, and we must steadfastly stand by the conventions which ignore them, since the statutes furnish us peace, fairly good government, and stability, and therefore are better for us than the laws of God, which would soon plunge us into confusion and disorder and anarchy if we should adopt them.

Mark Twain (On reading statutes) (*Roughing It*, while on his way to Nevada to be secretary to his brother, Governor of the Teritory, Twain read the U.S. Rev. Statutes): I had many an exciting day ... reading the statutes and the dictionary and wondering how the characters would turn out.

Oscar W. Underwood: When a people lose respect for one bad law, it is but a short step before they include the good laws with the bad and are shortly in rebellion against all law.

Cornelius Vanderbilt: What do I care about the law? Hain't I got the power?

Voltaire: It is necessity which makes laws, and force which makes them observed.

Voltaire: I was never ruined but twice – once when I lost a lawsuit, once when I won.

Voltaire: In crossing France, laws changed as often as one changed horses.

Earl Warren: In civilized life, law floats on a sea of ethics.

Earl Warren: It is the spirit and not the form of law that keeps justice alive.

Earl Warren: Where the weak or assert the rights that have been so long denied them, those in power inevitably resist on the basis of the necessity for tranquility.

Daniel Webster: The law, - it has honored us, may we honor it.

Joseph Weintraub, (Chief Justice, New Jersey Supreme Court, 1973): More automobile accidents in New Jersey occur on yellow legal pad's (used by lawyers) than on the highways in New Jersey.

Orson Welles 1915-1985, American Film Maker: The law and the stage – both are a form of exhibitionism.

Alfred North Whitehead: There are no natural laws. There are only temporary habits of nature.

Grover Whelan (Police Commissioner of NYC 1928-1930): There's a lot of law at the end of a nightstick.

Oscar Wilde: The study of law is sublime, and its practice vulgar.

Alexander S. Williams (Inspector of Police, NYC during 1870's): There is more law in the end of a policeman's nightstick than in a decision of the Supreme Court.

Earl Wilson 1907-, American newspaper columnist: Somebody figured it out—we have 35 million laws trying to enforce Ten Commandments.

Woodrow Wilson: The law that will work is merely the summing up in legislative form of the moral judgment that the community has already reached.

Woodrow Wilson: What we seek is the reign of law, based upon the consent of the governed and sustained by the organized opinion of mankind.

Woodrow Wilson: The worst enemy of the law is the man who knows only the technical details.

Andrew Young: (The law) is designed to protect the power and privilege of those who write the law and to ward off any values or vision that threatens it.

Brigham Young 1801-1877, American Mormon Leader: I want to live perfectly above the law, and make it my servant instead of my master.

S. C. Yuter: Law is the backbone that keeps man erect.

Frank Zappa: The United States is a nation of laws—badly written and randomly enforced.

LAWSUITS (See LITIGATION)

LAWYERS (See also LAW; LITIGATION)

Uncle Anthony: I know why you guys use 'dem big fifty cent words (instead of 5 and dimers) it's 'cause the bigger the words sound, the bigger the fee you can charge.

Uncle Anthony: I knew it! Some scientist says you got the same blood cells as truck drivers! You got too much caffiene! (In fact psychologist Dr. James Dabbs, Jr. at Georgia State University in 1990 did a study and found that trial lawyers do have high levels of testosterone which causes overly aggressive/antisocial behavior in juvenile delinquents, certain violent criminals, and truck drivers).

Uncle Anthony: Y'know what ya get when ya cross a Mafioso with a lawyer? Ya get "an offer ya can't understand!"

Aunt Mary Carlo: In my generation we looked at lawyers as professionals, because lawyers look at themselves and the law as a profession. Today lawyers look at themselves as businessmen, and that's what people see.

Aunt Mary Carlo: A lawyer (or law student) is a person who approaches all problems with an open mouth.

Aunt Mary Carlo: Y'know why most lawyers get their offices on the top floors of all 'dose big buildings? ... 'Cause 'dats as close to Heaven as 'der ever gonna get!

Aunt Mary Carlo: He never goes back on his word ... without talkin' to his lawyer first.

Roger Abrams (Dean of Rutgers Law School-Newark, New Jersey): We can redefine what it means to be lawyer. We can promote and behave in accordance with the premise that a lawyer is not a value-neutral champion of a client's interests. A lawyer's responsibility as an "officer of the court" means more than simply protecting the process of justice; it means seeking justice in court and outside of court. Some might think this is just tilting at windmills, but if lawyers do not do it, who will? Lawyers, just because they are lawyers, are not immoral, but many, at times, seem amoral. As a result, we forfeit our power and our responsibility to improve society and seek justice. Every so often you actually hit the windmill.

John Adams (in the play "1776"): I have come to the conclusion that one useless man is called a disgrace, two men are called a law firm, and three or more become a Congress.

John Quincy Adams: Whoever tells the best story wins.

Joseph Allegretti (book *The Lawyer's Calling*): The lesson of Thomas More's life is not that he refused to sign the Kings oath, but that he was willing to draw a line somewhere. He was not willing to surrender his whole self to anyone or anything.

Woody Allen: Some men are heterosexual and some men are bisexual and some men don't think about sex at all ... you know, they become lawyers.

Norman Augustine: Bulls do not win bullfights; people do. People do not win people fights; lawyers do.

Francis Bacon (philosopher, writer and Lord Chancellor of England, 1561-1626, *Maxims of the Law, Preface*): I hold every man a debtor to his profession; from the which as men of course do seek to receive countenance and profit, so ought they of duty to endeavour themselves by way of amends, to be a help and ornament thereunto.

Howard H. Baker Jr. (United States Senator): I'll tell you what my daddy told me after my first trial. I thought I was just great. I asked him, "How did I do?" He paused and said, "You've got to guard against speaking more clearly than you think."

Dave Barry: Our second completely true news item was sent to me by Mr. H. Boyce Connell Jr. of Atlanta, Ga., where he is involved in a law firm. One thing I like about the South is, folks there care about tradition. If somebody gets handed a name like "H. Boyce," he hangs on to it, puts it on his legal stationery, even passes it to his son, rather than do what a lesser person would do, such as get it changed or kill himself.

John R. Bartlett, *Dictionary of Americanisms* (1859): "Lake lawyer"—the Western Mud-fish... Dr. Kirtland says it is...called the lake lawyer, from its 'ferocious looks and voracious habits'.

John R. Bartlett, *Dictionary of Americanisms* (1859): "Lawyer"—.the black-necked Stilt... On the New Jersey coast it is some~times called lawyer on account of its 'long bill'

William G. Bassler (Judge of U.S. District Court in New Jersey): (Hans) Holbein's painting corroborates what Joseph G. Allegretti observed in his book, *The Lawyer's Calling*: "The lesson of Thomas More's life is not that he refused to sign the king's oath, but that he was willing to draw a line somewhere. He was not willing to surrender his whole self to anyone or anything." And that is why More is a man for this season. He stands in stark contrast to those in our profession who today champion unrestricted advocacy and unquestioned loyalty to the client's interests even if those interests may be morally repugnant. Unfortunately, and with serious consequences to our profession, the ideal of a lawyer is a hired gun is replacing the ideal of a lawyer as independent counselor.

William G. Bassler (Judge of U.S. District Court in NJ): In (Robert) Bolt's play (*A Man For All Seasons*, More is being chastised by his wife for having upset the king on his visit to More's home in Chelsea. The dialogue goes like this: "Alice: Be ruled! If you won't ruled him, be ruled! More: I neither could nor would rule my king. But there's a little, little, area. It's very little—less to him than a tennis court, where I must rule myself." To a profession that in many ways seems to have lost its bearings, ... More reminds us that if we cannot be master of our fate, we can at least be the captain of our soul. So today, in our time, More invites us to look, in solitude and in silence, for that area within where we and we alone should rule and where we can find and hold fast our self, our soul and our God.

William F. Baxter: I've never met a litigator who didn't think he was winning—right up until the moment the guillotine dropped.

Charles Becton: I cannot envision a calling with a greater need for passion—strong commitment to some goal—than trying cases for wrongfully injured people. Without passion, there can be no compassion.

Melvin Belli: I'm not an ambulance chaser. I'm usually there before the ambulance.

Melvin Belli: Getting kicked out of the American Bar Association is like getting kicked out of the Book-of-the-Month Club.

Melvin Belli: There is never a deed so foul that something couldn't be said for the guy; that's why there are lawyers.

Harry Bender: Imagine the appeals and dissents if lawyers had written the Ten Commandments.

Jeremy Bentham (English lawyer, utilitarian philosopher, 1748-1832, *Commonplace Book*, 10 Works 74): It is as impossible for a lwayer to wish men out of litigation, as for a physician to wish them in health.

Jeremy Bentham (1821): The duty of an advocate is to take fees, and in return for those fees to display to the utmost advantage whatsoever falshoods the solicitor has put into his brief.

Jeremy Bentham: The only persons in whom ignorance of the law is not punished.

Jeremy Bentham: Lawsuits generally originate with the obstinate and the ignorant, but they do not end with them; and that lawyer was right who left all his money to the support of an asylum for fools and lunatics, saying that from such he got it, and to such he would bequeath it.

Jeremy Bentham: Lawyers are the only persons in whom the ignorance of the law is not punished.

Milton Berle: Most attorneys practice law because it gives them a grand and glorious feeling. You give them a grand – and they feel glorious.

David E. Bernstein: By all reasonable measures, the American tort system is a disaster. It resembles a wealth-redistribution lottery more than an efficient system designed to compensate those injured by the wrongful actions of others.

Bible: Corinthians 6:7: There is utterly a fault among you, because ye go to law one with another.

Bible: Hosea 10:13: Ye (Editor: trial lawyers) have plowed wickedness, ye have reaped iniuquity.

Bible: Job 16:21: O that one might plead for a man with God, as a man pleadeth for his neighbor.

Bible: Luke 11:46: Woe to you lawyers also! Because you load men with oppressive burdens and you yourselves with one of your fingers do not touch the burdens.

Bible: Luke, 11:52: Woe unto you, lawyers! for ye have taken away the key of knowledge: ye entered not in yourselves, and them that were entering in ye hindered.

Bible: Proverbs 31:9: Open thy mouth, ... and plead the cause of the poor and needy.

Bible: 1 Timothy 1:8: The law is good, if a man use it lawfully.

Ambrose Bierce: Death is not the end. There remains the litigation over the estate.

Ambrose Bierce: ACCOMPLICE, n. One associated with another in a crime, having guilty knowledge and complicity, as an attorney who defends a criminal, knowing him guilty. This view of the attorney's position in the matter has not hitherto commanded the assent of attorneys, no one having offered them a fee for assenting.

Ambrose Bierce: ATTORNEY, n. A person legally a[pointed to mismanagaae one's affairs which one has not himself the skill to rightly mismanage.

Ambrose Bierce: LL.D. Letters indicating the degree, Legumptionorum Doctor, one learned in laws, gifted with legal gumption. Some suspicion is cast upon this derivation by the fact that the title was formerly LL.d., and conferred only upon gentlemen distinguished for their wealth.

Ambrose Bierce: DICE, n. Small polka-dotted cubes of ivory, constructed like a lawyer to lie on any side, but commonly the wrong one.

Ambrose Bierce: FORMA PAUPERIS. [Latin] In the character of a poor person - a method by which a litigant without money for lawyers is considerately permitted to lose his case.

Ambrose Bierce: IN FORMA PAUPERIS. [Latin] In the character of a poor person—a method by which a litigant without money for lawyers is considerately permitted to lose his case. When Adam long ago in Cupid's awful court (for Cupid ruled ere Adam was invented) sued for Eve's favor, says an ancient law report, He stood and pleaded unhabilimented. "You sue _in forma pauperis_, I see," Eve cried; "Actions can't here be that way prosecuted." So all poor Adam's motions coldly were denied: He went away—as he had come—nonsuited. G.J."

Ambrose Bierce (1842-1914): HOMICIDE, n. The slaying of one human being by another. There are four kinds of homocide: felonious, excusable, justifiable, and praiseworthy, but it makes no great difference to the person slain ..., [but] is for the advantage of the lawyers.

Ambrose Bierce: INNOCENCE, *n.* The state or condition of a criminal whose counsel has fixed the jury.

Ambrose Bierce: JUDGE, *n.* A person who is always interfering in disputes in which he has no personal interest.

Ambrose Bierce: LAWYER, n. One skilled in the circumvention of the law.

Ambrose Bierce: LAWSUIT, n. A machine which you go into as a pig and come out as a sausage.

Ambrose Bierce: LIAR, n. A lawyer with a roving commission.

Ambrose Bierce: QUIVER, n. A portable sheath in which the ancient statesman and the aboriginal lawyer carried their lighter arguments

Logan E. Bleckley (American Judge): Some people think that a lawyer's business is to make white black; but his real business is to make white in spite of the stained and soiled condition which renders its true color questionable. He is simply an intellectual washing machine.

Roy Blount Jr. (American writer): Doctors and lawyers must go to school for years and years, often with little sleep and with great sacrifice to their first wives.

Henry George Bohn: Fools and obstinate men make lawyers rich.

Curtis Bok: It has been said the a judge is a member of the bar who once knew a Governor.

George Borrow (English novelist, 1803-1881; *Wild Wales*): The law is a profession which abounds with honourable men, and in which I believe there are fewer scamps, than in any other. The most honourable men I have known have been lawyers; they were men whose word was their bond, and who would have preferred ruin to breaking it.

Louis Dembitz Brandeis (Associate Justice U.S. Supreme Court, 1856-1941, The Opportunity in the Law, 39 Am. L. Rev. 559): Instead of holding a position of independence, between the wealthy and the people, prepared to curb the excesses of either, able lawyers have, to a large extent, allowed themselves to become adjuncts of great corporations and have neglected their obligation to use their powers for the protection of the people. We hear much of the "corporate lawyer," and far too little of **the "people's lawyer."** The great opportunity of the American bar is and will be to stand as it did in the past, ready to protect also the interests of the people.

Louis D. Brandeis: A lawyer who has not studied economics and sociology is very apt to become a public enemy.

Louis D. Brandeis: Your law may be perfect, your knowledge of human affairs may be such as to enable you to apply it with wisdom and skill, and yet without individual acquaintance with men, their haunts and habits, the pursuit of the profession becomes difficult, slow, and expensive. A lawyer who does not know men is handicapped.

Richard Brautigan: The [trial attorney] was in his late forties, tall, reddish, and looked as if life had given him an endless stream of two-timing girl friends, five-day drunks and cars with bad transmissions.

Richard E. Brennan (from "Reflections on Matrimonial Motion Day," poem, 1996): I wonder if they ever think of their wedding days, / The bright dresses, the tender words, the promises and dreams. / As they witness the end of their marriages / And engage in settlement talks and schemes.... /"Sell the house"; "Split the stuff we acquired through the years"; / "Start anew, move again, forget the former ways." / But I wonder as I watched them with their lawyers, / Do they ever think about their wedding days?

David J. Brewer (Supreme Court Justice): America is the paradise of lawyers.

Henry Brinklow (1545): The lawyer can not understond the matter tyl he fele his mony.

Lord Henry P. Brougham: A lawyer is a gentleman who rescues your estate from your enemies and keeps it for himself.

Lord Henry P. Brougham (1778-1868, Scottish Whig Politician): A lawyer is a gentlemen that rescues your estate from your enemies and then keeps it to himself.

Lenny Bruce: In the Halls of Justice, the only justice is in the halls.

Eugene E. Brussell: One who defends you at the risk of your pocketbook, reputation and life

Jean De La Bruyere: Avoid lawsuits beyond all things; they pervert your conscience, impair your health, and dissipate your property.

Art Buchwald: It is not the bad lawyers who are screwing up the justice system in this country—it's the good lawyers. If you have two competent lawyers on opposite sides, a trial that should take three days could easily last six months.

Warren Burger (US Supreme Court Chief Justice): Doctors... still retain a high degree of public confidence because they are perceived as healers. Should lawyers not be healers? Healers, not warriors, healers, not procures? Healers, not hired guns?

Edmund Burke: It is not, what a lawyer tells me I may do; but what humanity, reason, and justice, tell me I ought to do.

Raymond Burr (as TV lawyer Perry Mason): I'd rather have my hand cut off than betray the interests of a client.

Robert Burton (1577-1640): Our wrangling lawyers . . . are so litigious and busy here on earth, that I think they will plead their clients' causes hereafter, - some of them in hell.

Samuel Butler: A lawyer's dream of heaven: every man reclaimed his own property at the resurrection, and each tried to recover it from all his forefathers.

Samuel Butler: In law, nothing is certain but the expense.

Benjamin N. Cardozo (Associate Justice U.S. Supreme Court, 1870-1938): Membership in the bar is a privilege burdened with conditions. *Matter of Rouss*, 221 N.Y. 81 (1917).

Benjamin N. Cardozo (Associate Justice U.S. Supreme Court, 1870-1938, *Law and Literature*, 1931): The quest is greater than what is sought, the effort finer than the prize, or, rather, that the effort *is* the prize – the victory cheap and hollow were it not for the rigor of the game.

Jimmy Carter: "The law is not the private property of lawyers, nor is justice the exclusive province of judges and juries. In the final analysis, true justice is not a matter of courts and law books, but of a commitment in each of us to liberty and mutual respect."

Stephen Carter (*Civility*): Civility is the sum of the many sacrifices we are called on to make for the sake of living [practicing law] together.

Joseph H. Choate: You cannot live without lawyers, and certainly you cannot die without them.

Rufus Choate (Massachusetts lawyer and statesman, 1799-1859): The lawyer's vacation is the space between the question put to a witness and his answer.

Sir Winston Churchill (regarding Gandhi with contempt, he described the 'Mahatma' as a dangerous charlatan): It is alarming and also nauseating to see Mr. Gandhi, a seditious Middle Temple lawyer, now posing as a fakir of a type well known in the East, striding half-naked up the steps of the Vice regal palace, while he is still organising and conducting a campaign of civil disobedience, to parley on equal terms with the representative of King-Emperor.

Cicero (*Brutus*, I, 2, on the death of Hortensius): I grieved because there was taken away from me, not, as many thought, a rival, who stood in the way of my reputation, but a partner and companion, in a glorious calling.

Cicero: The greatest orator among the lawyers, the greatest lawyer among orators.

Cicero: For the house of a great lawyer is assuredly the oracular seat of the whole community.

Cicero: (Gaius Acquilius) so just and virtuous a man that he seems to be a lawyer by nature rather than training.

Morris Cohen: No [attorney], however conservative, can stand before a [court] day after day and refrain from saying more than he knows.

Sir Edward Coke (Lord Chief Justice of England): No man can be a compleat Lawyer by universality of knowledge without experience in particular Cases, nor by bare experience without universality of knowledge; he must be both speculative and active, for the science of the laws, I assure you, must joyn hands with experience.

Sir Edward Coke (*First Institute*): Six hours to sleep, as many to righteous law; / Four to your prayers, and two to fill your maw; / The rest bestow upon the sacred Muses.

Samuel Taylor Coleridge: He saw a lawyer killing a viper, On a dunghill hard by his own stable, And the Devil smiled, for it put him in mind, Of Cane and his brother Abel.

Samuel Taylor Coleridge (*Table Talks: Duties and Needs of an Advocate*): Legal studies ... sharpen, indeed, but like a grindstone narrow whilst they sharpen.

Columbian Magazine, April, 1788: They have a proverb here [in London], which I do not know how to account for; in speaking of a difficult point, they say, it would puzzle a Philadelphia lawyer.

Peter Cook: All in all I'd rather have been a judge than a miner. And what's more, being a miner, as soon as you are too old and tired and sick and stupid to do the job properly, you have to do. Well, the very opposite applies with judges.

William D. Cooper (1836): Lawyer—a long bramble full of thorns, so called because 'when once they gets a holt an ye, ye doant easy get shut of 'em'.

Philip Corboy: A personal-injury lawyer is in a position to level the playing field and help people under our legal system.

Abraham Cowley (1663): A cowardly ranting Soldier, an ignorant charlatanical Doctor, a fooling Cheating Lawyer...have always been, and still are the Principal Subjects of all Comedies.

William Cowper: A lawyer's dealings should be just and fair; / Honesty shines with great advantage there.

Amanda Cross: One hires lawyers as on hires plumbers, because one wants to keep one's hands off the beastly drains.

Moses Crowell: It is a secret worth knowing that lawyers rarely go to law.

John Crowne, *Henry VI*, IV(1681): Must Justice starve because we want a Lawyer's forked distinctions to feed her neatly with?

Mario Cuomo (1986): I am a trial lawyer.... Matilda says that at dinner on a good day I sound like an affidavit.

Greg Cusimano: A common mistake among lawyers is believing that trying cases makes one a Trial Lawyer— which is as faulty as believing that having a guitar makes one a guitarist.

Greg Cusimano: A great lawyer's value is not handling great cases, but in making ordinary cases great.

Greg Cusimano: Never doubt the fact that committed trial lawyers can change our nation for the better. In fact, they have.

John J. Curtin Jr.: Anyone who believes a better day dawns when lawyers are eliminated bears the burden of explaining who will take their place. Who will protect the poor, the injured, the victims of negligence, the victims of racial discrimination and the victims of racial violence?

Clarence Darrow: The only real lawyers are trial lawyers, and trial lawyers try cases to juries.

Clarence Darrow 1857-1938, American Lawyer: The trouble with law is lawyers.

Clarence Darrow: To be an effective criminal defense council, an attorney must be prepared to be demanding, outrageous, irreverent, blasphemous, a rogue, a renegade, and a hated, isolated and lonely person.... few love a spokesman for the despised and the damned.

Clarence S. Darrow: I have lived my life, and I have fought my battles, not against the weak and the poor - anybody can do that - but against power, against injustice, against oppression, and I have asked no odds from them, and I never shall.

Dale Dauten: Criticizing lawyers for lawsuits is like criticizing linebackers for knocking people down.

John W. Davis: In the heart of every lawyer, worthy of the name, there burns a deep ambition so to bear himself that the profession may be stronger by reason of his passage through its ranks, and that he may leave the law itself a better instrument of human justice than he found it.

Thomas Dekker (1622): The devil hates a civil lawyer, as a soldier does peace

Benjamin DeMott (*"Seduced by Civility"*): When you are in an argument with a thug, there are things much more important than civility....Civility is what slaveholders called for when abolitionists marched.

Alan M. Dershowitz: A criminal trial is anything but a pure search for truth. When defense attorneys represent guilty clients—as most do, most of the time—their responsibility is to try, by all fair and ethical means, to prevent the truth about their clients and killed from emerging. Failure to do so... is now practice.

Charles Dickens (1812-1870, British Novelist): If there were no bad people, there would be no good lawyers.

Charles Dickens (*David Copperfield*, ch. 39): "How do you like the law, Mr. Micawber?" "My dear Copperfield," he replied, "to a man possessed of the higher imaginative powers the objection to legal studies is the amount of detail they involve. Even in our professional correspondence," said Mr. Micawber, glancing at some letters he was writing, "the mind is not at liberty to soar to any exalted form of expression. Still, it is a great pursuit, a great pursuit."

Charles Dickens (*Little Dorrit*, bk 2, ch 12): We lawyers are always curious, always inquisitive, always picking up odds and ends for our patchwork minds, since there is no knowing when and where they may fit into some corner.

Charles Dickens (*Uncommercial Traveller: Chambers*, ch 14): I myself was uncommercially preparing for the Bar – which is done, as everybody knows, by having a frayed old gown put on in a pantry by an old woman in a chronic state of St. Anthony's fire and dropsey, and, so decorated, bolting a bad dinner in a party of four, whereof each individual mistrusts the other three.

Benjamin Disraeli (*Vivian Grey*, 1826): To be a great lawyer, I must give up my chance of being a great man.

Benjamin Disraeli: The legal mind chiefly consists in illustrating the obvious, explaining the self-evident and axpatiating on the common-place.

Harry Edwards (Chief Judge of U.S. Court of Appeals for D.C. Circuit): In the October 1992 edition of the *Michigan Law Review*, I expressed deep concerns about legal education and the legal profession. I argued that many law schools have abandoned their proper place by emphasizing abstract theory at the expense of practical scholarship and pedagogy. And many law firms have also abandoned their proper place by pursuing profit above all else. Since publishing the article, I have been literally inundated with letters,.... Indeed, since 1992, there have been a number of major books ruing the state of the legal profession: among them are *The Lost Lawyer*, by the dean of the Yale Law School, Anthony Kronman; *The Betrayed Profession*, by distinguished practitioner, Sol Linowitz; and *A Nation Under Lawyers,* by a Harvard Law School Professor Mary Ann Glendon. What is interesting about the three accounts is how similar they are in chronicling the problems of the legal profession. All see a profession in crisis. They decry the modern law firm: its preoccupation with money, its tendency to make lawyers mere technicians, and its rejection of the notion that lawyers should council clients regarding ends.

Lord John Scott Eldon (1st Earl of Eldon, Lord Chancellor of Great Britain, 1751-1838, Reply to Wilberforce's query as to what advice he would give students who wanted to be great in the practice of law, *3 Life of Wilberforce 9*, 1801): To succeed as a lawyer, a man must work like a horse and live like a hermit.

Lord John Scott Eldon: There is nothing does a young lawyer so much good as to be half starved: it has a fine effect.

Ralph Waldo Emerson: The good judge is not he who does hair-splitting justice to every allegation, but who, aiming at substantial justice, rules something intelligible for the guidance of suitors. The good lawyer is not the man who has an eye to every side and angle of contingency, and qualifies all his qualifications, but who throws himself on your part so heartily that he can get you out of a scrape.

Ralph Waldo Emerson: The good lawyer is not the man who has an eye to every side and angle of contingency, and qualifies all his qualifications, but who throws himself on your part so heartily, that he can get you out of a scrape.

Ralph Waldo Emerson: Lawyers are a prudent race though not very fond of liberty.

Ralph Waldo Emerson: The good lawyer is not the man who has an eye to every side and angle of contingency, and qualifies all his qualifications, but who throws himself on your part so heartily, that he can get you out of a scrape.

English Proverb: The Devil makes his Christmas pies of lawyers' tongues and clerks' fingers.

English Proverb: The three learned professions live by roguery on the three parts of man. The doctor mauls our bodies, the parson starves our soul, and the lawyer ensnares our minds.

English Proverb: Two attorneys can live in a twon where one cannot.

English Saying: The three proverbial roads to success at the bar – influence, a book, or a miracle.

English Proverb (Thomas Fuller's *Proverbs*, 1732): The king can make a serjeant, but not a lwayer.

Epictetus: As physicians are the preservers of the sick, so are the lawyers of the injured.

Desiderius Erasmus (c.1466-1536, Dutch Humanist): Amongst the learned the lawyers claim first place, the most self-satisfied class of people, as they roll their rock of Sisyphus and string together six hundred laws in the same breath, no matter whether relevant or not, piling up opinion on opinion and gloss on gloss to make their profession seem the most difficult of all. Anything which causes trouble has special merit in their eyes.

Erasmus (referring to English lawyers and their lack of knowledge outside their profession): A most learned profession of profoundly ignorant men.

Senator Sam Ervin: There was a young lawyer who showed up at a revival meeting and was asked to deliver a prayer. Unprepared, he gave a Prayer straight from his lawyer's heart: "stir up much strife amongst the people, Lord," he prayed, "lest thy servant perish."

W.C. Fields: The only thing a lawyer won't question is the legitimacy of his mother.

Atticus Finch (in Harper Lee's To Kill a Mockingbird): Never, never, never on cross examination, ask a witness a question you don't already know the answer to, was a tenet I absorbed with my baby food. Do it, and you'll often get an answer you don't want.

Marlin Fitzwater: Everyone ought to take every opportunity to blast lawyers.

Percy Foreman (American trial lawyer): You don't approach a case with the philosophy of applying abstract justice – you go into win.

G. G. Foster (1849): He must wait next day for the visits of the 'shyster' lawyers, a set of turkey-buzzards whose touch is pollution and whose breath is pestilence

Justice Felix Frankfurter: Future lawyers should be more aware that law is not a system of abstract logic, but the web of arrangements, rooted in history but also in hopes, for promoting to a maximum the full use of a nation's resources and talents.

Benjamin Franklin (*Poor Richard's Almanac for 1734*): Necessity knows no law; I know some attorneys of the same.

Benjamin Franklin (1734): Necessity knows no law; I know some attorneys of the same.

Benjamin Franklin: A countryman between two lawyers is like a fish between two cats.

Benjamin Franklin: God works wonders now and then. Behold: a lawyer, an honest man.

Benjamin Franklin: Lawyers, Preachers, and Tomtits Eggs, there are more of them hatch'd than come to perfection."

Monroe Freedman (Law Professor, Hofstra University, author of *Understanding Lawyers' Ethics*, Matthew Bender; "Brandeis' Lawyer for the Situation" article): At every conference on lawyer's ethics and professionalism, someone is bound to say that lawyers should abandon adversary zeal and adopt instead Justice Louis Brandeis' ideal of **"lawyer for the situation."** We are rarely told just what it means to be a lawyer for situation—only that it is somehow superior to being the lawyer for a client....Consider, first, the following case. Lennox is in financial trouble and has several creditors. Lawyer A., of the firm of A & B represents Creditor No. 1. Lawyer B, of the same firm, then becomes attorney for Creditor No. 2. Neither Creditor gives its informed consent for this conflict of interest. Lawyer B. than meets up with his client (Creditor No. 2) and with Lennox (the debtor), who is unrepresented. B questions Lennox, obtaining information from him that is both confidential and damaging. B then suggests that he "act for Mr. Lennox in this matter." Lennox asks whether that means that B would be "acting as my council." B replies ambiguously, "Not altogether as your council, but as a trustee of your property." Both Lennox and Creditor No. 2 understand that B has become Lennox's lawyer. Pursuant to B's advice, Lennox signs documents transferring all of his assets—his personal property as well as the company's to an assignee for the benefit of creditors. The assignee is none other than B's partner, Lawyer A. B does not tell Lennox that making the assignment gives his creditors the right to throw him into bankruptcy. The firm of A&B then institute involuntary bankruptcy proceedings against Lennox, citing the assignment as their grounds. Lennox retains a new lawyer, who confronts B with his conduct. B tells the new lawyer, "I did not intend to act personally for Mr. Lennox, nor did I agree to." The new lawyer replies, "Yes, but you advised him to make the assignment. For whom were you council when you advised him to do that, if not for (Lennox)?" B answers, "I should say I was council for the situation."... The facts of the case, including the quotations, are based directly on Louis Brandeis' representation of Jim Lennox in 1907.... Justice Brandeis was an admirable person, lawyer, and judge. The Lennox episode was a rare lapse. Those who promote the phrase "lawyer for the situation" as an ideal for the profession cannot be aware of the unfortunate case that originally gave rise to it. In fatuously repeating the phrase, however, they do no service either to Brandeis or to lawyers' ethics.

French Proverb: No lawyer will ever go to Heaven so long as there is room for more in Hell.

French Proverb: Lawyers and soldiers are the Devil's playmates.

French Proverb: A good lawyer is a bad neighbor.

Abraham Fraunce (1588): It cannot bee, sayde one great Tenurist, that a good scholler should euer prooue good Lawyer.

David Frost: This is what has to be remebered about the law; beneath that cold, harsh, impersonal exterior beats a cold, harsh, impersonal heart.

Robert Frost: A jury consists of twelve persons chosen to decide who has the better lawyer.

Thomas Fuller (English clergyman and author, 1608-1661, *The Holy State:* *The Good Advocate*, 1642): Lawyers, like bread, are best when they are young and new.

Mahatma Gandhi (1869-1948, Indian Political, Spiritual Leader): An unjust law is itself a species of violence. Arrest for its breach is more so.

Lord Gardiner (b. 1900, former Lord Chancellor of Great Britain): "I really went to the Bar because I thought it would be easier to go on the stage after failing at the Bar than to go to the Bar after failing on the stage."

Erle Stanley Gardner (California lawyer, writer of detective fiction; under his pseudoname A.A. Fair, *Some Women Won't Wait: Forward*): Two classes of people have poor public relations – mothers-in-law and attorneys-at-law.

Karl Friedrich Gauss: I mean the word proof not in the sense of the lawyers, who set two half proofs equal to a whole one, but in the sense of a mathematician, where half proof = 0, and it is demanded for proof that every doubt becomes impossible.

John Gay: A fox may steal your hens, sir . . . . If lawyer's hand is fee'd, sir He steals your whole estate.

John Gay 1688-1732, British Playwright, Poet: A fox may steal your hens, Sir, a whore your health and pence, Sir, your daughter rob your chest, Sir, your wife may steal your rest, Sir, a thief your goods and plate. But this is all but picking, with rest, pence, chest and chicken; it ever was decreed, Sir, if lawyer's hand is fee d, Sir, he steals your whole estate.

John Gay: I know you lawyers can, with ease, twist words and meanings as you please.

Edward Gibbon 1737-1794, British Historian: The laws of probability, so true in general, so fallacious in particular.

William S. Gilbert (*H.M.S. Pinafore*, Act I): When I was a lad I served a term / As office boy to an Attorney's firm. / I cleaned the windows and I swept the floor, / And I polished the handle on the big front door. / I polished that handle so carefullee / That now I am the Ruler of the Queen's Navee!

Jean Giraudoux: We all know here that the law is the most powerful of schools for the imagination. No poet ever interpreted nature as freely as a lawyer interprets the truth.

William E. Gladstone 1809-1888, British Liberal Prime Minister, Statesman: Good laws make it easier to do right and harder to do wrong.

Johann Wolfgang Von Goethe 1749-1832, German Poet, Dramatist, Novelist: We eagerly get hold of a law that serves as a weapon to our passions.

Goldin, H. E., *Dictionary of American Underworld Lingo* (1950): The lip (lawyer) took a hundred skins (dollars) and never showed (appeared) in court.

William Goldsmith (1768): Lawyers are always more ready to get a man into troubles than out of them.

Oliver Goldsmith: Lawyers are always more ready to get a man into troubles than out of them.

Samuel Goldwyn: It is hard to say whether the doctors of law or of divinity have made the greater advances in the lucrative business of mystery.

Ned Good: There are no "little cases" – there are only "little lawyers."

Albert Gore Jr. (45th vice president of United States): When you have the facts on your side, argue the facts. When you have law on your side, argue the law. When you have neither, holler.

Cary Grant: Divorce is a game played by lawyers.

Arthur Greebler: If you're a litigating attorney, always discuss tactics with the client at the trial. Not only will the surprise your adversary but your client as well.

Lord Wilfrid Arthur Greene (English Judge, 1883-1952): Definition of a lawyer's function: To protect his clients from being persuaded by persons whom they do not know to enter into contracts which they do not understand to purchase goods which they do not want with money which they have not got.

Sarah Grimke: It would be as wise to set up an accomplished lawyer to saw wood as a business as to condemn an educated and sensible woman to spend all her time boiling potatoes and patching old garments. Yet this is the lot of many a one who incessantly stitches and boils and bakes, compelled to thrust back out of sight the aspirations which fill her soul.

George Hathaway: Lawyers like to throw around jargon and flowery language because it makes them feel self-important and prestigious.

Herbert, George (1640) (also French, Spanish and Italian Proverb): Lawyers houses are built on the heads of fools.

German Proverb: When two dogs fight for a bone, and the third runs off with it, there's a lawyer among the dogs.

Cary Grant: Divorce is a game played by lawyers.

Edward F. Halifax: If the laws could speak for themselves, they would complain of the lawyers.

James Gibbons Haneker: Lawyers earn a living by the sweat of browbeating others.

Arthur G. Hayes: When there is a rift in the lute, the business of the lawyer is to widen the rift and gather the loot.

George Herbert: Go not for every grief to the physician, nor for every quarrell to the lawyer, nor for every thirst to the pot.

Cullen Hightower: Don't expect other nations to have a democracy like ours - they don't have enough lawyers.

Adolph Hitler: I shall not rest until every German sees that it is a shameful thing to be a lawyer.

Matthew A. Hodel (American lawyer): Any culture that has had its Jeffersons, Lincolns, and Darrows also must have a healthy notion of the lawyer's role in society.

Matthew A. Hodel: My thesis is that the truly successful lawyer finds a good heart more useful than sharp fangs.

Samuel Hofstadter & Shirley Levittan (*Lest the Constable Blunder*, 20 Record of Assn of NYC Bar 629, 643; referring to *Gideon v. Wainwright* 372 US 335, 9 L ed 2d 799, 83 S Ct 792, 1963, and the book *Gideon's Trumpet* by Anthony Lewis): Gideon's Trumpet has been heard throughout the land by all potential defendants.

Oliver Wendell Holmes Jr: Lawyers spend a great deal of their time shoveling smoke.

Oliver Wendell Holmes, Jr.: You know my division of able lawyers into kitchen knives, razors, and stings.

Oliver Wendell Holmes, Jr: When lawyers take what they would give And doctors give what they would take.

Oliver Wendell Holmes, Jr.: The glory of lawyers, like that of men of science, is more corporate than individual.

Oliver Wendell Holmes, Jr. (*The Law. Speeches 17*, 1913): Every calling is great when greatly pursued.

Oliver Wendell Holmes, Jr. (*Path of the Law,* 10 Harvard L. Rev. 457, 1897): Law is the business to which my life is devoted, and I should show less than devotion if I did not do what in me lies to improve it, and, when I perceive what seems to me the ideal of its future, if I hesitated to point it out and to press toward it with all my heart.

Oliver Wendell Holmes, Jr. (*Path of the Law,* 10 Harvard L. Rev. 457, 1897): For the rational study of the law the black-letter man may be the man of the present, but the man of the future is the man of statistics and the master of economics.

Oliver Wendell Holmes, Jr. (*Profession of the Law, Speeches 22*, 1913): Of course, the law is not the place for the artist or the poet. The law is the calling of thinkers.

Oliver Wendell Holmes, Jr. (*Profession of the Law, Speeches 23*, 1913): A man may live greatly in the law as well as elsewhere; that there as well as elsewhere his thought may find its unity in an infinite perspective; that there as well as elsewhere he may wreak himself upon life, may drink the bitter cup of heroism, may wear his heart out after the unattainable.

Oliver Wendell Holmes, Jr.: The training of lawyers is a training in logic. The process of analogy, discrimination, and deduction are those in which they are most at home. The language of judicial decision is mainly the language of logic. And the logical method and form flatter that longing for certainty and for repose which is in every human mind. But certainty generally is illusion, and repose is not the destiny of man.

Oliver Wendell Holmes, Jr.(Review of Holdsworth's *History of English Law*, 25 L.Q.R. 412, 1909): Alongside the practioners to whom the law is a rag-bag from which they pick out the piece and colour that they want, there have been some students who have striven to make their knowledge organic.

Oliver Wendell Holmes, Jr.: I can but envy the felicity of the generation to whom it is made so easy to see the subject [of law] as a whole. When I began, the law presented itself as a ragbag of details.

Oliver Wendell Holmes, Sr.(on his son's plans to attend law school): "What's the use of that, Wendell, a lawyer can't be a great man!"

Oliver Wendell Holmes, Sr. (*Lines Recited at Berkshire Jubilee*): Come, you of the law, who can talk if you please, / Till the man in the moon will allow it's a cheese.

Oliver Wendell Holmes, Sr. (*Poet at the Breakfast Table*): The lawyers are the cleverest men, the ministers are the Most Learned, and the doctors are the most sensible.

Barton Holyday: A man may as well open an oyster without a knife, as a lawyer's mouth without a fee.

Andrew Horn (14th century English): Women, serfs, those under the age of twenty-one, open lepers, idiots, attorneys, lunatics, deaf mutes, those excommunicated by a bishop and criminal persons are inelegible for appointment to the bench.

R.T. House (1912 article on the 100th anniversary of the Paris Bar Association): Lawyers and magistrates wore a long scarlet robe trimmed with ermine (which was generally of feline origin, whence Rabelais's qualification "furred cats," which is synonymous with "pettifoggers").

Elbert Hubbard: Lawyers are men whom we hire to protect us from lawyers.

Elbert Hubbard, *The Roycroft Dictionary and Book of Epigrams* (1923): Lawyer: 1. A person who takes this from that, with the result that That hath not where to lay his head. 2. An unnecessary evil. 3. The only man in whom ignorance of the law is not punished.

Judge Burrell Ives Humphreys (Judge of New Jersey Appellate Division): Make no mistake. You are not in a failed or failing profession. You are not in a business. You are members of a proud calling – one whose place in history and place today is that of honor and trust and integrity. Lawyers are persons who would rather light a candle than curse the darkness. You will have the opportunity ... to light many a candle. Make the most of it.

Lamar Hunt (one of a million "Lawyer Jokes"): The best description of "utter waste" would be a busload of lawyers to go over a cliff with three empty seats.

Lee Iacocca: There are more lawyers in just Washington, D.C. than in all of Japan. They've got about as many lawyers as we have sumo-wrestlers.

Henrik Ibsen (Norwegian dramatist, 1828-1906, *A Doll House*, Act I): A barrister's profession is such an uncertain thing, especially if he won't take unsavory cases.

Harold L. Ickes (American lawyer, US government official, 1874-1952; referring to Wendell Wilkie as the Republican presidential nominee, *3 Secret Diary 396, Dec 21, 1940*): A simple barefoot Wall Street lawyer.

Washington Irving: Young lawyers attend the courts, not because they have business there but because they have no business anywhere else.

Washington Irving, The History of New York 261-62 (1868) (1809): "Let me not be thought as intending anything derogatory to the profession of the law, or to the distinguished members of that illustrious order. Well am I aware that we have in this ancient city innumerable worthy gentlemen, the knights-errant of modern days, who go about redressing wrongs and defending the defenseless, not for the love of filthy lucre, nor the selfish cravings of renown, but merely for the pleasure of doing good. Sooner would I throw this trusty pen into the flames and cork up my ink bottle forever, than infringe even for a nail's breadth upon the dignity of these truly benevolent champions of the distressed. On the contrary, I allude merely to those caitiff scouts who, in these latter days of evil, infest the skirts of the profession, as did the recreant Cornish knights of yore the honorable order of chivalry, - who under its auspices, commit flagrant wrongs, - who thrive by quibbles, by quirks and chicanery, and like vermin increase the corruption in which they are engendered."

Italian Proverb: A lawsuit is a fruit tree planted in a lawyer's garden.

Rufus Isaacs (Lord Reading, Lord Chief Justice of England, 1860-1935): The bar is not a bed of roses, - it is either all bed and no roses, or all roses and no bed.

Robert H. Jackson (Supreme Court Justice): I used to say that, as Solicitor General, I made three arguments of every case. First came the one I planned as I thought—logical, coherent, complete. Second was the one actually presented—interrupted, incoherent, disjointed, disappointing. The third was the utterly devastating argument that I thought of after going to bed that night.

Robert H. Jackson (*Functions of the Trust Co.*, 52 N.Y. S. Bar Rept. 144, 1929): The office of lawyer ... is too delicate, personal and confidential to be occupied by a corporation.

Robert H. Jackson: On your first appearance before the Court, do not waste your time or ours telling us so. We are likely to discover for ourselves that you are a novice but will think none the less of you for it. Every famous lawyer had his first day at our bar, and perhaps a sad one. It is not ingratiating to tell us you think it is an overwhelming honor to appear, for we think of the case as the important thing before us, not the counsel. Some attorneys use time to thank us for granting the review, or for listening to their argument. Those are not intended as favors and it is good taste to accept them as routine performance of duty. Be respectful, of course, but also be self-respectful, and neither disparage yourself nor flatter the Justices. We think well enough of ourselves already.

Japanese Proverb: Only painters and lawyers can change white to black.

Peter R. Jarvis and Bradley F. Tellam: We believe that there are four main components of modern professionalism: 1. An orientation that is respectful of clients. 2. An orientation that is respectful of staff. 3. An enlightened view of civility civility and courtesy. 4. The exercise of objectivity.

Leon Jaworski: When dictators and tyrants seek to destroy the freedoms of men, their first target is the legal profession and through it the rule of law.

Thomas Jefferson (1743-1826, 3rd President of the US): [A] lawyer without books would be like a workman without tools.

Thomas Jefferson: Other branches of science, and especially history, are necessary to form a lawyer.

Thomas Jefferson: It is the trade of lawyers to question everything, yield nothing, and talk by the hour.

Thomas Jefferson: It is well known that on every question the lawyers are about equally divided,... and were we to act but in cases where no contrary opinion of a lawyer can be had, we should never act.

Thomas Jefferson: Were we to act but in cases where no contrary opinion of a lawyer can be had, we should never act.

Thomas Jefferson: Never fear the want of business. A man who qualifies himself well for his calling never fails of employment in it.

Thomas Jefferson: The study of law qualifies a man to be useful to himself, to his neighbors, and to the public. It is the most certain stepping stone to preferment in the political line.

F. Ross Johnson, former CEO of RJR Nabisco: The only thing I expect out of lawyers is that they be back in their coffins by sunup.

Samuel Johnson (1709-1784, British Author): I would be loath to speak ill of any person who I do not know deserves it, but I am afraid he is an *attorney.*

Samuel Johnson: Lawyers know life practically. A bookish man should always have them to converse with.

Samuel Johnson: A lawyer has no business with the justice or injustice of the cause which he undertakes, unless his client asks his opinion, and then he is bound to give it honestly. The justice of injustice of the cause is to be decided by the judge.

Franklin P. Jones: Anybody who thinks talk is cheap should get some legal advice.

Sir William Jones (English lawyer and author, 1746-1794, *Letter to Lord Chief Justice Wilmot*, 1771): I do not see why the study of the law is called dry and unpleasant; and I very much suspect that it seems so to those only who would think any study unpleasant which required a great application of the mind and exertion of the memory.

Ben Jonson: I oft have heard him say how he admir'd / Men of your large profession, that could speak / To every cause, and things mere contraries, / Till they were hoarse again, yet all be law.

Junius (pseudonym, possibly of Sir Philip Francis): As to lawyers, their profession is supported by the indiscriminate defence of right and wrong.

Lucille Kaelin: A lawyer's relationship to justice and wisdom... is on a par with the piano tuner's relationship to a concert. He neither composes the music, nor interprets it—he merely keeps the machinery running.

Joshua Karton: The actor (and lawyer) who uses every part of him/herself becomes irresistible.

John Katzenbach: A lot of defense lawyers take the facts of the case and twist them around and try, in effect, to create a lie out of some truth.

George S. Kaufman: It sounds a little grand, I know, to say 'my lawyers' in the plural, but I didn't start out that way. I started with one lawyer, but you know what happens. One moves in and pretty soon there are seven, all in the same office. They get together all day long and say to each other, "What can we postpone next?" The only thing they don't postpone, of course, is their bill, which arrives regularly. You've heard about the man who got the bill from his lawyer which said, "For crossing the street to speak to you and discovering it was not you ... twelve dollars."

Irving R. Kaufman: The trial lawyer does what Socrates was executed for: making the worse argument appear the stronger.

Irving R. Kaufman (US Court of Appeals Judge): No other profession is subject to the public contempt and derision that sometimes befalls lawyers... the bitter fruit of public in comprehension all the law itself and its dynamics.

John Keats: I think we may class all lawyers in the natural history of monsters.

James Keller: A Seattle lawyer once interrupted his lengthy cross-examination of a witness and exclaimed, "Your Honor, one of the jurors is asleep." "You put him to sleep," replied the judge. "Suppose you wake him up."

Florynce Rae Kennedy (American lawyer and civil rights activist): Most lawyers are like whores. They serve the client puts the highest fee on the table.

Florynce Rae Kennedy (American lawyer and civil rights activist): Ours is a prostitute society. The system of justice, and most especially the legal profession, is a whorehouse serving those best able to afford the luxuries of justice offered to preferred customers. The lawyer, in these terms, is analogous to a prostitute. The difference between the two was simple. The prostitute is honest—the buck is her aim. The lawyer is dishonest—he claims that justice, service to mankind is his primary purpose. The lawyer's deception of the people springs from his actual moneymaking role; he represents the client who puts the highest fee on the table.

John F. Kennedy: I see nothing wrong with giving Robert some legal experience as Attorney General before he goes out to practice law.

Robert F. Kennedy: Courage is the most important attribute of a lawyer. It is more important than competence or vision. It can never be an elective in any law school. It can never be de-limited, dated or outworn, and it should pervade the heart, the halls of justice and the chambers of the mind.

Jean Kerr, *Time Magazine*, Arpil 14, 1969: A lawyer is never entirely comfortable with a friendly divorce, anymore than a good mortician wants to finish his job and then have the patient sit up on the table.

Soren Kierkegaard: Sin is: before God, or with the conception of God, in despair not to will to be oneself, or in despair to will to be oneself. Thus sin is intensified weakness or intensified defiance: sin is the intensification of despair. The emphasis is on before God, or with a conception of God; it is the conception of God that makes sin dialectically, ethically, and religiously what lawyers call 'aggravated' despair.

Alexander King (1965): There is a general prejudice to the effect that lawyers are more honourable then politicians but less honourable than prostitutes. That is an exaggeration.

Ted Koskoff, highly regarded personal injury attorney, Bridgeport, CT.: "WHAT IS A LAWYER?" If I were to ask what is a lawyer, not of Blackstone, but of you, you might say, or I might say,

If you are a lawyer, you stand between the abuse of governmental power and the individual.
If you are a lawyer, you stand between the abuse of corporate power and the individual.
If you are a lawyer, you stand in between the judicial abuse of power and the individual.
If you are a lawyer, you are helping to mold the rights of individuals for generations to come.

And, if you think of some of the people who have filled this mold, your thoughts would, I think, inevitably turn to certain people and you would see these people as I see them.

He undertook the defense of John Peter Zanger to protect his right to publish what he chose, free of censorship and interference. His name was Alexander Hamilton and he was a lawyer.

You would see him at the trial of Captain Preston, defending him at a political trial which arose out of the Boston Massacre. His name was John Adams and he was a lawyer.

You would see him at the miracle in Philadelphia, the constitutional convention of 1787, fighting for the Bill of Rights which was to become the creed of American Freedom. His name was James Madison. He was a lawyer.

You would see him presiding over the Supreme Court, as the architect of the real powers of the Court. His name was John Marshall. He was a lawyer.

And I know you would see him at Gettysburg with tears in his eyes, gaunt and morose, rededicating our country to the proposition that all men are created equal. His name was Abraham Lincoln. He was a lawyer.

I know we all see him, an elemental man fighting for one cause or another in Dayton Tennessee, preaching the legitimacy of evolution. His name was Clarence Darrow and he was a lawyer.

You would see him speaking to us from his wheelchair, lifting our spirits, making us stronger with his inspirational philosophy, "The only thing we have to fear is fear itself." His name was Franklin Delano Roosevelt and he was a lawyer.

You might see him in the Senate Hearing Room in Washington uttering that anguished cry for decency. His name was Joseph Welch and he was a lawyer.

And then you would think of the precious monuments that they had left to their lives and of Milton's wonderful comment on Shakespeare that, "thou and I wonder in astonishment that thou hast left thyself a monument."

Then you might think, what kind of monument will I leave? Not one of brick and mortar or stone, but of thought, because only thoughts live.

Finally, you would probably think of that marvelous admonition of Holmes, when nearly a hundred years ago, he said, "I think of this life as action and passion. It is required of man that he should share the passion and action of his time at the peril of being judged not to have lived."

Charles Lamb, *The Old Benchers of Middle Temple* (1823): Lawyers, I suppose, were children once.

Charles Lamb, *Lexicon balatronicum:* *a dictionary of buckish slang, university wit, and pickpocket eloquence* (1811): Sea Lawyer—a shark

Charles Lamb: He is no lawyer who cannot take two sides.

Prof. Thomas F. Lambert Jr.: The trial lawyer's mission is "to comfort the afflicted and afflict the comfortable," and the performance of that mission offers attorneys the unique opportunity to escape "the only awful kind of aging, the slow desertion of ideals."

Prof. Thomas F. Lambert Jr.: Those who work with their hands are laborers; those who work with their hands and heads are craftsmen; those who work with their hands, heads, and hearts are artists. Trial lawyers are artists.

Doris Lessing: In university they don't tell you that the greater part of the law is learning to tolerate fools.

Gerald F. Lieberman: It is unfair to believe everything we hear about lawyers, some of it might not be true.

Abraham Lincoln: I am only a mast-fed lawyer.

Abraham Lincoln: A lawyer's time and advice are his stock in trade.

Abraham Lincoln (*Notes for a Law Lecture*, 1850): Extemporaneous speaking should be practiced and cultivated. It is the lawyer's avenue to the public.... And yet there is not a more fatal error to young lawyers than relying too much on speech-making. If anyone upon his rare powers of speaking, shall claim an exemption from the drudgery of the law, his case is a failure in advance.

Abraham Lincoln: In law it is good policy never to plead what you need not, lest you oblige yourself to prove what you cannot.

Abraham Lincoln: There is a vague popular belief that lawyers are necessarily dishonest. I say vague because when we consider to what extent confidence and honors are reposed in and conferred upon lawyers by the people, it appears improbable that their impression of dishonesty is very distinct and vivid. Yet the impression is common, almost universal. Let no young man choosing the law for a calling for a moment yield to the popular belief—resolve to be honest at all events; and if in your own judgment you cannot be an honest lawyer, resolve to be honest without being a lawyer. Choose some other occupation, rather than one in the choosing of which you do, in advance, consent to be a knave.

Abraham Lincoln: The leading rule for the lawyer, as for the man of every other calling, is diligence. Leave nothing for tomorrow which can be done today.

Abraham Lincoln: A lawyer who believes his gifts of speech exempt him from the drudgery of the law will be a failure in advance.

Abraham Lincoln: Discourage litigation. Persuade your neighbors to compromise whenever you can. Point out to them how the nominal winner is often a real loser—in fees, expenses, and waste of time. As a peacemaker the lawyer has a superior opportunity of being a good man. There will still be business enough. Never stir up litigation. A worse man can scarcely be found than one who does this.... A moral tone ought to be infused into the profession which should drive such man out of it.

London Review, November 8, 1862: There is, however, one subject which Mr. Trollope pursues with unremitting zeal. He cannot bear a lawyer. They are all rogues, not by nature, but by profession.

Louis XII, King of France: Lawyers use the law as shoemakers use leather: rubbing it, pressing it, and stretching it with their teeth, all to the end of making it fit for their purposes.

Carl Lumholtz, *Among Cannibals:* *account of four years travels in Australia and of camp life with the Aborigines of Queensland* (1890): The stem and leaves are studded with the sharpest thorns, which continually cling to you and draw blood, hence its not very polite name of lawyer-palm.

Kip Lurie, *Adam's Rib* (1949): Lawyers should never marry other lawyers. This is called "inbreeding," from which comes idiot children and more lawyers.

Timothy Lytton (Albany Law School professor): This year (2007) marks the fifth anniversary of The Boston Globe's Pulitzer Prize-winning coverage of clergy sexual abuse. The Pulitzer citation praised the Globe for its "courageous, comprehensive coverage of sexual abuse by priests, an effort that pierced secrecy, stirred local, national, and international reaction and produced changes to the Roman Catholic Church." Yet while the news media have received well-deserved recognition for their part in exposing the abuse and focusing attention on the need for institutional reform, little attention has been paid to the underlying role played by lawsuits. There's an unsung hero in this story, the plaintiff's lawyer. Although the tort system is more often maligned than celebrated, it was the work of plaintiffs' lawyers that brought the scandal to light in the first place. Pleadings, discovery documents, and depositions in hundreds of cases during the course of more than two decades have provided most of the information underlying media coverage of the scandal. Lawsuits have fed journalists a steady supply of compelling stories of both personal suffering and official wrongdoing, and they have provided a defense against potential libel claims and political cover to criticize powerful church officials.... Clergy sexual abuse litigation is, in short, a poster child for the policy-making benefits of tort litigation.

MacNelly's comic strip *"Shoe"* (9/16/79) (proposes an effective solution to the problem of the increasing number of attorneys: "Today's topic is lawyers ... something has to be done about lawyers...."They're everywhere! Writing laws, opinions, regulations - and all of them in a language that's so ridiculous we have to hire other lawyers to translate. You can't do anything these days before you talk to a lawyer. By mastering the art of gobbledygook, lawyers have amassed incredible influence and power... It's time to cut these guys down to size. And I say start at the root of the problem — shorten their (8 inch x 14 inch legal sized) pads!

Patrick Mahoney ("Barbed Wit and Malicious Humor"): At the end of the last century there was a flourishing firm of lawyers in New York named Ketchum and Cheetham. Oddly enough, the first names of the partners were Isaac and Uriah, so they could have headed their company I. Ketchum and U. Cheetham! Even in the present time there is a noted firm of lawyers in a midwestern City owning the delicious combination of Dilly, Daly and Dolittle."

Frederic W. Maitland (English lawyer, legal historian, 1850-1906): Taught law is tough law.

Frederic W. Maitland (*English Law and the Renaissance*, 1901): Law schools make tough law.

Frederic W. Maitland (*From the Old Law Courts to the New*, 1883): Judges and lawyers took to wigs when other men in a frivilous moment took to them; unfortunately they retained the silliest adornment that human head has yet invented for itself when even physicians and bishops had recovered their wonted sobriety.

Mignon McLaughlin: It took man thousands of years to put words down on paper, and his lawyers still wish he wouldn't.

David Melinkoff (UCLA law professor): Lawyers as a group are no more dedicated to justice and public service than a private public utility is dedicated to giving light.

David Mellor: Lawyers are like rhinoceroses: thick skin, shortsighted, and always ready to charge.

Henry Louis Mencken: Lawyer: One who protects us against robbery by taking away the temptation.

H.L. Mencken: Judge - A law student who marks his own examination papers.

H.L. Mencken: Their professional aim and function is not to get at the truth, but simply to carry on combats between ancient rules.

Mexican curse: May your life be filled with lawyers.

John Stuart Mill: Men are men before they are lawyers, or physicians, or merchants, or manufacturers; and if you make them capable and sensible men, they will make themselves capable and sensible lawyers or physicians.

Edna St. Vincent Millay: I am not so afraid of lawyers as I used to be. They are lambs in wolves clothing.

John J. Miller: Laws are only words, words written on paper, words that change on society's whim and are interpreted differently daily by politicians, lawyers, judges, and policemen. Anyone who believes that all laws should always be obeyed would have made a fine slave catcher. Anyone who believes that all laws are applied equally, despite race, religion, or economic status, is a fool.

Adison Mizner: Ignorance of the law excuses no man—from practicing it.

Baron de Montesquieu, Charles Louis de Secondat (French lawyer and philosopher, 1689-1755): Sometimes a man who deserves to be looked down upon because he is a fool is despised only because he is a lawyer.

St. Thomas More (1478-1535, British Chancellor, Canonized in 1915): Lawyers—a profession it is to disguise matters.

St. Thomas More (*Utopia*, bk. 2, 1516): Furthermore they utterly exclude and banish all attorneys, proctors, and sergeants at the law; which craftily handle matters, and subtly dispute of the laws. As for lawyers, a class of men whose trade it is to manipulate cases and multiply quibbles, they wouldn't have them in the country.

St. Thomas More (*Utopia*, bk 2): They have no lawyers among them, for they consider them as a sort of people whose profession it is to disguise matters.

St. Thomas More Society: A Lawyer's Prayer: Saint Thomas More, counselor and advocate, learned in law, chancellor of charity and jurist of justice, merry martyr, scholar and canonized saint. May the Lord of law and of all lawyers make me, at your request, a little more like you than I was yesterday. Pray that for the greater glory of God and in the pursuit of His Justice, I may be able in argument, accurate in anlysis, strict in study, correct in conclusion, candid with clients, honest with adversaries, faithful in my library. Stand beside me in Court, so that today I shall not, in order to win a point, lose my soul. Pray that each may find in me, what they have a right there to seek: humor and humility, cheerfulness and charity, an approach to wisdom, counselor, sound consolation and a little bit of the shadow of you. Saint Thomas, brother lawyer, who by your membership have proven our profession both honorable and compatible with true sanctity. Pray for us now engaged in the struggle to imitate the Divine Master. Lord Chancellor, stand retained by us before the Infinite Lord Justice Who will preside when we are to be tried.

J.P. Morgan: I don't know if I want a lawyer to tell me what I cannot do. I hire him to tell me how to do what I want to do.

Peter Morrison: I don't know of any other industry, except the movie business, that has so many stars. Every lawyer thinks he's special.

John Mortimer (English lawyer): My father told me that all you need to succeed in the law is a certain amount of common sense and clean fingernails.

Patrick Murray: A Lawyer will do anything to win a case, sometimes he will even tell the truth.

Ralph Nader & Wesley J. Smith (book, *No Contest: Corporate Lawyers and the Perversion of Justice in America*, 1996): "(Power lawyers) ... crush the powerless populace and smaller businesses to ensure that their clients prevail... Simply stated, these attorneys are masterminds of choreographing contests that are, in fact, no contest at all. To many corporate lawyers such deeds are their finest hour."

John Naisbitt (American writer): Lawyers are like beavers: they get in the mainstream and damn it up.

New Jersey Lawyer Editorial (7 NJL 858, 1998): "So Ya Wanna Be a Trial Lawyer: .... A recently published study (funded by a National Science Foundation grant) in the *Journal of Applied Social Psychology* reported that trial lawyers have 30% higher testosterone levels than lawyers who stay out of the courtroom, levels similar to those found in blue-collar workers. And not just male trial lawyers: The study found that male and female trial lawyers had significantly higher testosterone levels than nontrial lawyers of the same gender.... their findings (derived by comparing saliva samples from 97 Atlanta trial and nontrial lawyers with each other and with samples taken in earlier studies from blue- and white-collar workers)... authors then analyzed 37 United States Supreme Court arguments by 74 lawyers, half of whom were ATLA members and half characterized as "appellate lawyers," to determine if the trial lawyers used fewer cognitive mechanisms, reflecting less complex thought. The "observed pattern" was that they did, making them "less skilled... at the subtle arguments that judges seem to appreciate in appeals court... The last sentence of the study abstract summarizes the authors' interpretation of their findings: "high levels of testosterone are associated with energy, dominance, persistence, combativeness, and focused attention, qualities that are useful both in trial lawyering and blue-collar work."... in fairness to the authors, the study is expressly "not intended as an insult" to either group and is, in certain aspects, complementary to trial lawyers... (but) If the legal economy goes bust, plumbers and electricians will still be in demand.

Louis Nizer: Most lawyers who win a case advise their clients, "We have won," and when justice has frowned upon their cause ... "You have lost."

Louis Nizer: "... defeat is education. It is a step to something better."

Louis Nizer: (Preparation) is the be-all of good trial work. Everything else—Felicity of expression, improvisational brilliance—is a satellite around the sun. Through preparation is that sun.

Louis Nizer: In cross-examination, as in fishing, nothing is more ungainly than a fisherman pulled into the water by his catch.

Kenneth Nolan: Clients are like the Seven Dwarfs – greedy, dopey, angry, shifty – they come in all types. "Funny people are everywhere," to paraphrase Dr. Seuss, and they always worm their way into your office. All clients should be met with healthy skepticism. Some deserve private investigation, others jail, but the worse are those who proclaim: "Money isn't important. It's the principle. I want my day in court. Kick that one out of your office. Take him by the scruff of the neck and throw him onto Main Street.

Roger North (English lawyer and writer, 1653-1734, *On the Study of Laws*): Sir Henry Finch used to say, study all the morning, and talk all the afternoon.

Roger North (*On the Study of Laws*): I have heard Serjeant Maynard say the law is *ars bablativa*, meaning that all the learning in the world will not set a man up in bar practice without a faculty of a ready utterance of it.

Sandra Day O'Connor (Supreme Court Justice): I have watched with great sadness the decline in the esteem held by our society of lawyers. There must be a rediscovery of civility in the profession.

Walter K. Olson (Senior Fellow, Manhattan Institute): More Americans are terrified of being bit, bashed, or brutalized by attorneys. No wonder they vent their anxiety in cathartic one-liners. Should we non-lawyers stop telling the one about the skid marks, or the good start, or the researchers who turned to dissecting lawyers because they got emotionally attached to white rats?

Paul O'Neil: No splints yet invented will heal a lawyer's broken reputation

Paul O'Neil, *Life Magazine*, June 22, 1959: A criminal lawyer, like a trapeze performer, is seldom more than one slip from an awful fall. [speaking of criminal defense lawyer Edward Bennett Williams]

John J. Osborne Jr.: Lawyers shake papers at each other the way primitive tribes shake spears.

Virginia Ostman: If lawyers are disbarred and clergymen defrocked, doesn't it follow that electricians can be delighted, musicians denoted, cowboys deranged, models deposed, tree surgeons debarked, and dry cleaners depressed.

Sir Thomas Overbury (English poet, 1581-1613, *Characters: An Honest Lawyer*): An Honest Lawyer – a trusted Pilot, a true priest of justice, one who wears the conscience as well as the gowne, weighs the cause as well as the gold, and knows, but never uses, the nice snapperadoes of Practice.

Edward J. Packard, Jr., *Columbia Forum*, Spring 1967: Law students are trained in the case method, and to the lawyer everything in life looks like a case.

Tom Paine (to George Washington): The world will be puzzled to decide whether you have abandoned good principles, or whether you ever had any.

Angie Papadakis: In almost every case, you have to read between the lies.

Laurence J. Peter: A lawyer is a man who helps you get what is coming to him.

Plato: The lawyer is always in a hurry.

Sir Frederick Pollock (*Oxford Lectures and Discourses*, 1890): There you shall see in very truth how the spark, fostered in our own land by Glanvill and Bracton, waxed into a clear flame under the care of Brian and Choke, Littleton and Fortescue, was tended by Coke and Hale, and was made a light to shine round the world by Holt and Mansfield, and the Scotts, and others whom living men remember. You shall understand how great a heritage is the law of England, whereof we and our brethern across the ocean are partakers, and you shall deem treaties and covenants a feeble bond in comparison of it; and you shall know with certain assurance that, however arduous has been your pilgrimage, the achievement is a full answer. So venerable, so majestic, is this living temple of justice, that immemorial yet freshly growing fabric of the Common Law, that the least of us is happy who hereafter may point to so much as one stone thereof, and say, The work of my hands is there.

Hart Pomerantz (American lawyer): Law school taught me one thing: how to take two situations that are exactly the same and show how they are different.

Carl Poplar (EDITOR: outstanding New Jersey trial lawyer, my former boss, and esteemed co-counsel, who during oral argument, while defense counsel stood and glared threateningly at him said, without turning to address this rude and overly dramatic and demonstrative adversary, calmly to the trial judge): I am being starred at. Should I be concerned? I am being stared at. I believe her stare fulfills me.

Roscoe Pound (*A Hundred Years of American Law*, 1937): There is no law without lawyers.

Roscoe Pound (*Annual Survey of American Law: Dedication*, 1947, the name bestowed upon Roscoe Pound): The Schoolmaster of the American Bar.

Thomas Reed Powell (Vermont and Massachusetts lawyer, professor and dean, Harvard Law School, legal writer, 1880-1956): If you can think of something which is connected with something without thinking of the something it is connected to, you have a legal mind.

William L. Prosser (California lawyer, law school dean, legal writer): Your lawyer in practice spends a considerable part of his life in doing distasteful things for disagreeable people who must be satisfied, against an impossible time limit and with hourly interruptions, from other disagreeable people who want to derail the train; and for his blood, sweat and tears he receives in the end a few unkind words to the effect that it might have been done better, and a protest at the size of his fee.

***Punch*, 1847:** He fareth best who loveth best / All fees both great and small / For the Bench declare that etiquette / Of the Bar is "pocket All."

Mario Puzo (Don Corleone in The Godfather): A lawyer with a briefcase can steal more than 100 men with guns.

Josiah Quincy (Massachusetts lawyer, American patriot, one-time mayor of Boston and President of Harvard University, 1774-1775, recalled an anecdote which Daniel Webster gave at a dinner): ".... upon the importance of doing small things thoroughly and with the full measure of one's ability. This Webster illustrated by an account of some petty insurance case that was brought to him when a young lawyer in Portsmouth. Only a small amount was involved, and a twenty-dollar fee was all that was promised. He saw that, to do his clients full justice, a journey to Boston, to consult the law library, would be desirable. He would be out of pocket by such an expedition, and for his time he would receive no adequate compensation. After a little hesitation he determined to do his very best, cost what it might. He accordingly went to Boston looked up the authorities, and gained the case. Years after this, Webster, then famous, was passing through New York City. An important insurance case was to be tried the day after his arrival, and one of the counsel had been suddenly taken ill. Money was no object, and Webster was begged to name his terms and conduct the case. " 'I told them,' Mr. Webster said, 'that it was preposterous to prepare a legal argument at a few hours' notice. They insisted, however, that I should look at the papers; and this after some demur, I consented to do. Well, it was my old twenty-dollar case over again, and as I never forget anything, I had all the authorities at my fingers' ends. The Court knew that I had no time to prepare, and was astonished at the range of my acquirements. So, you see, I was handsomely paid both in fame and money for that journey to Boston; and the moral is that good work is rewarded in the end, though, to be sure, one's self-approval should be enough.'"

Jane Bryant Quinn: Lawyers are... operators of the toll bridge across which anyone in search of justice must pass.

Janet Reno: The good lawyer is the great salesman.

Deborah L. Rhode (*In the Interests of Justice Reforming the Legal Profession*): As one participant in an ABA seminar on civility acknowledged, at her firm, "We pride ourselves on being assholes. It's part of the firm culture."

Charles Rhyne (World Conference on World Peace Through Law, 1963): What we lawyers want to do is to substitute courts for carnage, dockets for rockets, briefs for bombs, warrants for warheads, mandates for missiles...

Ann Richards: I'm against an income tax because all the rich people hire lawyers and accountants to be sure that they don't pay income tax.

David Riesman: To be sure, most lawyers today recognize that their most important work is done in the office, not in the courtroom; the elaborate masked ritual of the courtroom holds attraction only for the neophyte and layman.

Mary Roberts Rinehart: I never saw a lawyer yet who would admit he was making money.

R. Rinkle: A man without money needs no more fear a crowd of lawyers than a crowd of pickpockets.

Fred Rodell (law professor, Yale University): It is pretty hard to find a group less concerned with serving society and more concerned with serving themselves than the lawyers.

Fred Rodell: There are two things wrong with almost all legal writing. One is its style. The other is its content.

Will Rogers: Make crime pay. Become a Lawyer.

Will Rogers: The only way you can beat the lawyers is to die with nothing.

Will Rogers: The minute you read something you can't understand, you can almost be sure it was drawn up by a lawyer.

Will Rogers: Lawyers make a living out of trying to figure out what other lawyers have written.

Will Rogers: A jury should decide a case the minute they are shown it, before the lawyers have had a chance to mislead them.

Will Rogers: Of course people are getting smarter nowadays; they are letting lawyers instead of their conscience be their guidance.

Will Rogers (1949): The banker, the lawyer, and the politician are still our best bets for a laugh. Audiences haven't changed at all, and neither has the three above professions.

Will Rogers: The minute you read something and you can't understand it, you can be sure it was written by a lawyer. Then, if you give it to another lawyer to read and he don't know just what it means, then you can be sure it was drawn up by a lawyer. If its in a few words and is plain, and understandable only one way, it was written by a non-lawyer.

Will Rogers: Every time a lawyer writes something, he is not writing for posterity. He is writing so endless others of his craft can make a living out of trying to figure out what he said. 'Course perhaps he hadn't really said anything, that's what makes it hard to explain.

Will Rogers: Personally I don't think you can make a lawyer honest by an act of the Legislature. You've got to work on his conscience. And his lack of conscience is what makes him a lawyer.

Will Rogers: I have always noticed at any time a man can't come in and settle with you without bringing his lawyer, why, look out for him.

Will Rogers: Lawyers are like a lot of crafts that many of us live by, great, but useless. One level-headed man could interpret every law there is. If you commit a crime, you either did, or you didn't, without habeas corpus, change of venue, or any other legal shindig. But Lord, if we go into things that are useless, why, two-thirds of the world would have to turn to manual labor. That's really the only essential thing there is.

Theodore Roosevelt: Lawyering is about money making, not about achieving social justice.

Theodore Roosevelt: A man who never graduated from school might steal from a freight car. But a man who attends college and graduates as a lawyer might steal the whole railroad.

Theodore Roosevelt: The great lawyer who employs his talent and his learning in the highly emunerative task of enabling a very wealthy client to override or circumvent the law is doing all that in him lies to encourage the growth in the country of a spirit of dumb anger against all laws and of disbelief in their efficacy.

Elihu Root: About half the practice of a decent lawyer consists in telling would-be clients that they are damned fools and should stop.

Ellis Rubin: Being a lawyer is about serving justice. That's not only our greatest calling, it's our only calling.

Rumpole of The Bailey: "Criminal trial lawyers are like TAXI CABS – they stop for anyone who hails them for money"

Carl Sandburg: Why is there always a secret singing when a lawyer cashes in? Why does the hearse horse snicker hauling a lawyer away?

Carl Sandburg (1916): Let us be honest; the lady was not a harlot until she married a corporation lawyer who picked her from a Ziegfeld chorus.

Carl Sandburg: A lawyer for the defense clears his throat and holds himself ready if the word is "Guilty" to enter motion for a new trial, speaking in a soft voice, speaking in a voice slightly colored with bitter wrongs mingled with monumental patience, speaking with mythic Atlas shoulders of many preposterous, unjust circumstances

Lord Leslie Scarman (English lawyer): Law reform is far too serious a matter to be left to the legal profession.

Gordon Schaber: The practice of law in most courtrooms today is about as modern as performing surgery in a barbership.

Bob Schmitt: The average lawyer is esentially a mechanic who works with a pen instead of a ball-peen hammer. Machinists' unions require an apprencticeship, not an advanced degree.

Eric Schnapper: Lawyering is within the relatively narrow category of occupations where borderline dishonesty is fairly lucrative. In many instances, the very art of a lawyer is a sort of calculated disregard of the law or at least of ordinary notions of morality.

Scotland (Rules of Court, ch 1, 1532): No advocate without very good cause shall refuse to act for any person tendering a reasonable fee under pain of deprivation of his office of advocate.

Sir Walter Scott (1771-1832, British Novelist and poet, *Guy Mannering,* ch 37): A lawyer without history or literature is a mechanic, a mere working mason; if he possesses some knowledge of these, he may venture to call himself an architect.

Sir Walter Scott (*Guy Mannering*): It is the pest of our profession that we seldom see the best side of human nature. People come to us with every selfish feeling newly pointed and grinded.... In civilized society, law is the chimney through which all that smoke discharges itself, that used to circulate through the whole house and put every one's eyes out; no wonder, therefore, that the vent itself should sometimes get a little sooty.

William Shakespeare (*Hamlet,* Act V, i): Why might not that be the skull of a lawyer? / Where be his quiddities now, his quillets, / his cases, his tenures, and his tricks?

William Shakespeare, (*Henry VI,* Part II, Act IV, ii): Jack Cade, a notorious criminal, who is described by his "peers" as a sheep thief punished by burning off his hand, is addressing his gang of ne'er do wells, plotting to dispatch the king and all his court and live free of any law or order; he advocates burning down the Inns of Court; he laments that an innocent lamb should have his skin torn off to make parchment on which is scribbled law, and he is sorely vexed at the obstacles in his path to plunder. Dick Butcher, one of Cade's gang says): "The first thing we do, let's kill all the lawyers." (EDITOR: Read in its full context, and not on some AMA T-shirt, these words show that Shakespeare knew that a tyrant could never set up a totalitarian form of government unless he first got rid of all the lawyers).

William Shakespeare (*II Henry VI,* Act IV, ii): The first thing we do, let's kill all the lawyers.

William Shakespeare (*King Lear,* Act I, iv): 'Tis like the breath of an unfee'd lawyer; you gave me nothing for it.

William Shakespeare (*Love's Labour's Lost,* Act II, i): Bold of your worthiness, we single you / As our best-moving fair solicitor.

William Shakespeare (*Measure for Measure,* Act II, iv): O perilous mouths, / That bear in them one and the self-same tongue, / Either of the condemnation or approof; / Bidding the law make court'sy to their will; / Hooking both right and wrong to the appetite, / To follow as it draws.

William Shakespeare (*The Merchant of Venice,* Act III, ii): The world is still deceiv'd with ornament: / In Law, what plea so tainted and corrupt, / But, being season'd with a gracious voice, / Obscures the show of evil?

William Shakespeare (*The Taming of the Shrew,* Act I, ii): And do as adversaries do in law, / Striving mightily, but eat and drink as friends.

William Shakespeare (*Timon of Athens*, Act III, v): It pleases time and fortune, to lie heavy / Upon a friend of mine, who, in hot blood, / Hath stepp'd into the law; whish is past depth / To those that, without head, plunge into't.

George Bernard Shaw (British dramatist and novelist, 1856-1950, *The Doctor's Dilemma*, Act I): All professions are conspiracies against the laity.

Norm Sherman (American lawyer): Good law schools teach you to think like lawyers. But the top law schools teach young people to think; just to think. And that makes a potentially great lawyer.

John R. Silber: The lawyers' contribution to the civilizing of humanity is evidenced in the capacity of lawyers to argue furiously in the courtroom, then sit down as friends over a drink or dinner. This habit is often interpreted by the layman as a mark of their ultimate corruption. In my opinion, it is their greatest moral achievement: It is a characteristic of humane tolerance that is most desperately needed at the present time.

Gaius Silius: If no one paid a fee for lawsuits, there would be less of them! As it is, feuds, charges, malevolence and slander are encouraged. For just as physical illness brings revenue to doctors, so a diseased legal system entices advocates.

Ann Sleeper, *Devil's Advocates: The Unnatural History of Lawyers* (1989): The startling thing is that lawyers don't seem to like to laugh at themselves, or even get mildly amused about their profession.

Elliott Dunlap Smith (Illinois lawyer, educator, writer): The law is the only profession which records its mistakes carefully, exactly as they occurred, and yet does not identify them as mistakes.

Sir Thomas Smith (English statesman, professor of law and writer, Vice-Chancellor, *De Republica Anglorum*, bk 1, ch 20, 1583): As for gentlemen, they be made good cheape in England. For whosoever studieth the lawes of the realme, who studieth in the universities, who professeth liberall sciences, and to be shorte, who can live idly and without manuall labour, and will beare the port, charge, and countenance of a gentleman, he shall be called master, for that is the title which men give to esquires and other gentlemen, and shall be taken for a gentleman.

William Henry Smyth, *Sailor's Word-book*, (1867): Sea-lawyer—an idle litigious 'long-shorer, more given to question orders than to obey them. One of the pests of the navy as well as of the mercantile marine.

Paul Somerson: Ever negotiate with lawyers at a huge company? If they saw you drowning 100 feet from the shore, they'd through you a 51-foot rope and say they went more than halfway.

Spanish Proverb: A peasant between two lawyers is like a fish between two cats.

Spanish Proverb: It is better to be a mouse in a cat's mouth than a man in a lawyer's hands.

Stuart M. Speiser: "KICKING IN OF ROTTEN DOORS" The economist John Kenneth Galbraith observed that most revolutions resulting in human progress have come about through the kicking in of rotten doors. So it has gone in the saga of the underdog's progress in American tort cases, which some observers have described as a litigation revolution. Those of us who happen to be in the practice when the empowerment of the Equalizers (American trial lawyers in the beginnings of ATLA's history) took place in the last half of the 20th century would like to think of ourselves as the architects or master builders of a brand new legal system. But in truth we were more like a band of hikers wearing hobnail boots. Rather than erecting glittering new edifices, the real contribution of the Equalizers has been to use our hobnail boots to kick in the doors there were kept locked over the centuries to protect the powerful against the enforcement of the existing laws by the underdogs.

Gerry Spence: I think good lawyers are good actors. But acting is telling the truth. It is revealing to the audience the truth about the person whose role the actor is playing.

Gerry Spence (from his 1989 book *"With Justice For None"*): ".... everywhere we hear the same old cry: "Too many lawyers." Former Chief Justice Burger thought so. So does the established bar. We are told there are too many lawyers out there scrambling over each other to make a dollar. The specter we are shown is horrible – hungry lawyers drumming up business, inventing new rights, and encouraging groundless litigation. Yet today there are not too many lawyers, but *too few* – too few of the right kind; too few who are trained fighters; too few who will represent the people. There are too few warriors and too few committed to a just cause.

Gerry Spence (from his 1989 book *"With Justice For None"*): Like us, our young lawyers search, not for justice but for what someone called the "twin Holy Grails of American life – money and success." Skillfully, designedly, our young have made themselves salable to corporate America as replacement parts for the legal machine that grinds away in corporate law firms at lush hourly rates. The new lawyers flock to our large cities and descend in hordes on Wall Street and Washington, D.C. There many will spend their lives dotting i's and crossing t's in high-floor cubbyholes – human sacrifices to the profit gods of their corporate employers. Already, only a fortnight past puberty, they scorn such sentimental idealism as justice. "Justice?" They laugh. "What is justice? But *this* is a dollar." Our young, I fear, only bear our own familiar stripes.

Herbert Spencer 1820-1903, British Philosopher: A jury consists of twelve persons chosen to decide who has the better lawyer.

***Sporting Magazine* (1794):** A water-lawyer, or, in plainer terms a shark was caught last month near Workington.

Adlai Stevenson: It's not a profession at all, but rather a business service station and repair shop.

Robert Louis Stevenson (*Weir of Hermiston*): To be wholly devoted to some intellectual exercise is to have succeeded in life; and perhaps only in law and the higher mathematics may this devotion be maintained, suffice to itself without reaction, and find continual rewards without excitement.

John Stossel: America has a legal system that is the laughing stock in the civilized world.

Lloyd Paul Stryker: Trying a case the second time is like eating yesterday morning's oatmeal.

Lloyd Paul Stryker: A trial is still an ordeal by battle. For the broadsword there is the weight of evidence; for the battle-axe the force of logic; for the sharp spear, the blazing gleam of truth; for the rapier, the quick and flashing knife of wit.

Brendan Sullivan, Iran Contra hearings, July 9, 1987: I'm not a potted plant. I'm here as the lawyer. That's my job. [on being told to allow his client Lt. Col. Oliver L. North to object for himself if he wished to do so]

Robert Smith Surtees (English solicitor, noelist 1805-1864): There are three sorts of lawyers - able, unable and lamentable.

Jonathan Swift (*Gulliver's Travels: Houyhnhnms*): There was a society of men among us, bred up from their youth in the art of proving, by words multiplied for the purpose, that white is black and black is white, according as they are paid.

Gaius Cornelius Tacitus*:* No commodity was so publicy for sale as the perfidy of lawyers.

William Makepiece Thackeray (English novelist, 1811-1863, *Letter* to his mother, 1832): This lawyer's preparatory education is certainly one of the most cold blooded, prejudiced pieces of invention that ever a man was slave to.... A fellow should do and think of nothing else than LAW.

Henry David Thoreau: The lawyer's truth is not Truth, but consistency or a consistent expediency.

Alexis de Tocqueville (French political writer, 1805-1859, *Democracy in America*): As the lawyers constitute the only enlightened class which people do not mistrust (NOTE: BOY, HAVE TIMES CHANGED!!), they are naturally called upon to occupy most of the public stations. They fill the legislative assemblies, and they conduct the administration; they consequently exercise a powerful influence upon the formation of the law, and upon its execution.

Alexis de Tocqueville: A French observer is surprised to hear how often an English or an American lawyer quotes the opinions of others, and how little he alludes to his own; ... This abnegation of his own opinion, and this implicit deference to the opinion of his forefathers, which are common to the English and American lawyer, this servitude of thought which he is obliged to profess, necessarily give him more timid habits and more conservative inclinations in England and America than in France.

John Kennedy Toole: They can't sue me for a half million for a letter I didn't write." "Oh no? Somebody like Adelman could. I can just see that lawyer he's got. Crippled from chasing ambulances. Mutilated from being caught in fires he's started for insurance money.

Robert Townsend: Lawyers take to politics like bears take to honey.

Arthur Train: Whatever their failings as a class may be, and however likely to lose their immortal souls, lawyers do not generally lose papers.

Mark Twain: If there wasn't a penalty for laughing in court, the jury would never be able to hear the evidence.

Mark Twain: What chance has the ignorant, uncultivated liar against the educated expert? What chance have I... against a lawyer?

Mark Twain: A lawyer one day spoke to him (Mark Twain) with his hands in his pockets. "Is it not a curious sight to see a lawyer with his hands in his *own* pockets?" remarked the humorist in his quiet drawl.

Mark Twain: They all laid their heads together like as many lawyers when they are gettin' ready to prove that a man's heirs ain't got any right to his property.

Mark Twain (1873): There is no display of human ingenuity, wit, and power, so fascinating as that made by trained lawyers in the trial of an important case, nowhere else is exhibited such subtlety, acumen, address, eloquence.

Mark Twain (deleted dedication of Mark Twain's book "Roughing It"): To the Late Cain, This Book is Dedicated, Not on account of respect for his memory, for it merits little respect; not on account of sympathy with him, for his bloody deed placed him without the pale of sympathy, strictly speaking; but out of a mere human commiseration for him in that it was his misfortune to live in a dark age that knew not the beneficent Insanity Plea.

Harrison Tweed: I have a high opinion of lawyers. With all their faults, they stack up well against those in every other occupation or profession. They are better to work with or play with or fight with or drink with than most other varieties of mankind.

UA: If it weren't for lawyers, we wouldn't need them

UA: Be frank and explicit with your lawyer. It is his business to confuse the issue afterwards.

UA: A lawyer is someone willing to spend every cent you own to prove he's right.

UA: Lawyer: An individual whose principal role is to protect his clients from others of his profession.

UA: "They have a proverb here [in London], which I do not know how to account for ; - in speaking of a difficult point, they say, it would puzzle **a Philadelphia lawyer**." Found in "A Humorous Description of the Manners and Fashions of London; in a Letter from a Citizen of America to his Correspondent in Philadelphia," 2 Columbian Magazine 181, 182 (1788) This is the earliest usage of the phrase Philadelphia lawyer to mean "a shrewd lawyer expert in legal technicalities." There is little doubt this term was inspired by Philadelphia trial attorney Andrew Hamilton's successful defense of John Peter Zenger in a New York court in 1735. Zenger's New York lawyers were disbarred by the court. Andrew Hamilton, then 80 years old, came from Philadelphia to successfully defend him. Remarks on the trial by two lawyers, defending the arguments of The Crown, repeatedly use the expression in a disparaging manner.

UA: Oath administered to new attorneys: "I do solemnly swear or affirm: I will support the Constitution of the United States and the Constitution of this State, and I will faithfully perform the duties of attorney at law. / I will exhibit, and I will seek to maintain in others, the respect due courts and judges. / I will, to the best of my ability, abide by the Model Rules of Professional Conduct and any other standards of ethics proclaimed by the courts, and in doubtful cases I will attempt to abide by the spirit of those ethical rules and precepts of honor and fair play. / I will not reject, from any consideration personal to myself, the cause of the impoverished, the defenseless, or the ppressed. / I will endeavor always to advance the cause of justice and to defend and to keep inviolate the rights of all persons whose trust is conferred upon me as an attorney at law."

Arthur Vanderbilt (New Jersey lawyer, educator, law reformer, Chief Justice of NJ Supreme Court, 1888-1957): The elements that constitute the practice of law "in the grand manner—the only way it is worth practicing,... (Are) a lifetime's involvement with public service was an essential involvement depended not on a single and a career called by office, but a continuing obligation of service throughout one's professional lifetime... (and) The attorney whose professional thoughts begin and end with his own private clients is a pitiful mockery of what a great lawyer really is. Training for public service is a lifetime career.

Thorstein Veblen (American educator and author, 1857-1929, *Higher Learning in America*, 1918): The law school belongs in the modern university no more than a school of fencing or dancing.

Bill Veeck: We're doing this whole thing backward. Attorneys should wear numbers on their backs, and box scores should have entries for writs, dispositions, and appeals.

Bill Veeck: Three strikes and you're out – even if (attorney) Edward Bennett Williams defends you.

Bill Veeck, *The Hustler's Handbook* (1965): Next to the confrontation between two highly trained, finely honed batteries of lawyers, jungle warfare is a stately minuet.

Bill Veeck: Greed vs. greed makes for the kind of lawsuits that are settled between the lawyers as soon as both sides decide to take what they can get. Principle vs. principle is a holy war, and no holy war has ever been settled out of court.

Gaius Verres (governor of Sicily, 114-50 B.C.): What I steal the first year goes to increase my own fortune, but the profits of the second year go to lawyers and defense counsels, and the whole of the third year's take, the largest, is reserved for judges.

Tom Vesper (paraphrasing the movie *Dragonheart*): The "OLD CODE" of the Knights of the Round Table are applicable to all trial lawyers: A Knight is sworn to Honor; / His heart knows only Virtue; / His sword defends the Helpless; / His might upholds the Weak; / His word speaks only Truth; / His wrath undoes the Wicked.

Voltaire (French writer, 1694-1778, *Dictionnaire Philosophique*): An *advocat* is a man who, not having money enough to buy one of those brilliant offices on which the universe has its eyes fixed, studies for three years the laws of Theodosius and Justinian so as to know the custom of Paris, and who at length having got matriculated has the right of pleading for money, if he has a loud voice.

Kurt Vonnegut, Jr.: Beware of the [attorney] who works hard to learn something, learns it, and finds himself no wiser than before. He is full of murderous resentment of [attorneys] who are ignorant without having come by their ignorance the hard way.

Tom Waites (2002): There's a leak, there's a leak, in the boiler room / The poor, the lame, the blind / Who are the ones that we kept in charge? / Killers, thieves, and lawyers / God's away, God's away, God's away / On business, business / God's away, God's away, God's away / on business.

Tom Waites: There are a few things I never could believe / A woman when she weeps / A merchant when he swears / A thief who says he'll pay / A lawyer when he cares / A snake when he is sleeping / A drunkard when he prays.

Tom Waites: Everybody knows that the game was rigged / Justice wears suspenders and a powdered wig. "Sins of the Father" on *Real Gone*, 2004

Edward Ward: A good lawyer is a great liar. *Washington Post*, March 25, 1977: President Carter has made it clear that he understands how complex the income tax laws are. To head IRS, he has picked a Philadelphia lawyer.

Daniel Webster (*Speech, Charleston, SC Bar*, 1847): After twenty-five years' observation, I can give it as the condensed history of most, if not all, good lawyers, that they lived well and died poor.

Daniel Webster: Lawyers on opposite sides of the case are like the two parts of shears; they cut what comes between them, but not each other.

Daniel Webster: I have given my life to law and politics. Law is uncertain and politics are utterly vain.

Daniel Webster (When advised not to become a lawyer because the profession was overcrowded): "There is always room at the top."

Daniel Webster: Our profession is good if practiced in the spirit of it; it is damnable fraud and inequity when its true spirit is supplied by a spirit of mischief-making and money getting.—The love of fame is extinguished; every ardent wish for knowledge repressed; conscience put in jeopardy, and the best feelings of the heart indurated by the mean, money catching, abominable practices, which cover with disgrace some of the modern practitioners of law.

Daniel Webster: Accuracy and diligence are much more necessary to a lawyer than great comprehension of mind, or brilliancy of talent.—His business is to refine, define, split hairs, look into authorities, and compare cases.—A man can never gallop over the fields of law on Pegasus nor fly across them on the wing of oratory.—If he would stand on terra firma, he must descend.—If he would be a great lawyer, he must first consent to become a great drudge.

Orson Welles: The law and the stage – both are a form of exhibitionism.

H.G. Wells (*The Work, Wealth and Happiness of Mankind*, 1931): When every inequity of the lawyers of the past has been admitted, we still find that there were abundant gentlemen of the long robe (barristers or trial lawyers), haunted, even if they were not inspired and pervaded, by the spirit of righteousness. The illumination they shed may not always have been a beacon, but at any rate the wick never ceased altogether to glow, and down the centuries we see a succession of these unloved men boring away in their tedious frowsty courts, really struggling in that dim mediaeval light to import some semblance of justice, some thought for the common weal, into the limitless greed of robber barons, the unqualified imperatives of feudal chiefs and the grasping cunning of baser sort.

Caspar Weinberger: We have too many lawyers chasing too many dollars through too many lawsuits, and it is time to do something about it.

Joseph Weintraub, (Chief Justice, New Jersey Supreme Court, 1973): More automobile accidents in New Jersey occur on yellow legal pad's (used by lawyers) than on the highways in New Jersey.

John Wesley, *Journal*, Oct. 1, 1764: I breakfasted..with Mr. B, a black swan, an honest lawyer!

Daniel R. White (American writer): Law school has been described as a place for the accumulation of learning. First-year students bring some in; third-year students take none away. Hence it accumulates.

Oscar Wilde: Lawyers have been known to wrest from reluctant juries triumphant verdicts of acquittal for their clients, even when those clients, as often happens, were clearly and unmistakably innocent.

John Wilson (English playwright, 1627-1696, *The Cheats*, act 1, sc. Iv, 1664): A modest lawyer! - A silent woman! – A paradox in nature.

Thomas Wilson, *The Art of Rhetorique* (1553): The lawyer never dieth a begger. The lawyer can never want a livyng till the earth want men.

Woodrow Wilson: I used to be a lawyer, but now I am a reformed character.

Woodrow Wilson: The worst enemy of the law is the man who knows only the technical details.

Woodrow Wilson (*The Lawyer and the Community*, 35 A.B.A.R. 419, 435, 1910): You are not a mere body of expert business advisers in the field of civil law or a mere body of expert advocates for those who get entangled in the meshes of the criminal law. You are servants of the public, of the state itself. You are under bonds to serve the general interest, the integrity and enlightenment of law itself, in the advice you give individuals. It is your duty also to advise those who make the laws, - to advise them in the general interest, with a view to the amelioration of every undesirable condition that the law can reach, the removal of every obstacle to progress and fair dealing that the law can remove, the lightening of every burden the law can lift and the righting of every wrong the law can recify.

Stephen Wright: I broke a mirror in my house and I'm supposed to get seven years bad luck but my lawyer thinks he can get five.

William Wycherley (English dramatist, 1640-1716, *The Plain Dealer, Act V, i,* 1677): That litigious pettifogger.

William Wycherley (*The Plain Dealer,* 1677): I shall no more mind you, than a hungry judges does a cause, after the clock has struck one. A man without money needs no more fear a crowd of lawyers than a crowd of pickpockets.

Evelle Younger: An incompetent lawyer can delay the trial for months or years. A competent lawyer can delay one even longer.

Lin Yutang, Chinese-American Philosopher: Where there are too many policemen, there is no liberty. / Where there are too many soldiers, there is no peace. / Where there are too many lawyers, there is no justice.

Warren Zevon: Send lawyers, guns and money, the shit has hit the fan.

LEADER/LEADERSHIP (See POLITICS/POLITICIANS)

LEARNING (See TEACHING)

LEGISLATION (See GOVERNMENT; LAW; POLITICS)

LEGISLATOR(S) (See POLITICS)

LIABILITY (See NEGLIGENCE)

LIBEL (See LIES)

LIES/LIARS/LYING (See also FACT/LIES; HONESTY)

Uncle Anthony: A good liar can lie with a straight, smiling, honest face.
Uncle Anthony: Sometimes, y'gotta read between the lies.
Uncle Anthony: I think he majored in alibi-ology.
Uncle Anthony: Honesty may be the best policy, but I don't think there are enough policyholders.
Uncle Anthony: He's so two-faced, he stands up in both the top and bottom halves of the seventh inning.
Aunt Mary Carlo: He's one of dem professional reformers dat takes da pie (money) otta the piety.
Aunt Mary Carlo: He's da kinda guy dat not only wants his cake t'eat – but your and your cookies too.
Aunt Mary Carlo: When he slaps ya on yer back, it's soz ta make sure ya swallow what he told ya.
Aunt Mary Carlo: Somebody should build him a partition between his imagination an his facts.
Aunt Amry Carlo: Da only way he's not a bald-faced liar is 'cause he's growed a moustache.
Aunt Mary Carlo: A liar don't have to say nuthin' to be a liar.
Don Adams (in the *Get Smart* TV series created by Mel Brooks and Buck Henry, 1965-70, secret agent Maxwell Smart used this line whenever anyone did not accept one of his fabrications and he was trying to come up with a more acceptable alternativee): Would you believe . . .?
Aeschylus: God is not averse to untruth in a holy cause.
Scott Adams: There's a reason that executives lie – the alternative is worse!
Aesop: Never trust the advice of a man in difficulties.
Kingsley Amis: The real trouble with liars ... was there could never be any guarantee against their occasionally telling the truth.
Margot Asouth: She tells enough white lies to ice a wedding cake.
Francis Bacon: Hurl your calumnies boldly; something will be sure to stick.
Francis Bacon: A mixture of a lie doth ever add pleasure. Doth any man doubt that if it were taken of men's minds vain opinions, flattering hopes, false valuations, imaginations as one would, and the like, but it would leave the minds of a number of men poor shrunken things, full of melancholy and indisposition, and unpleasing to themselves.
Gamaliel Bailey: The first and worst of all frauds is to cheat one's self. All sin is easy after that.
Dave Barry: The most powerful force in the universe is gossip.
Lyman Beecher: Never chase a lie. Let it alone, and it will run itself to death.
Bishop Berkely: It is impossible that a man who is false to his finds and neighbors should be true to the public.
Bible: Corinthians 15:33: Evil communications corrupt good manners.
Bible: Exodus 20:2: ...Thou shalt not bear false witness against thy neighbour.
Bible: Exodus 23:1: Thou shalt not raise a false report: put not thine hand with the wicked to be an unrighteous witness.
Bible: James 4:11: He that speaketh evil of his brother, and judgeth his brother, speaketh evil of the law, and judgeth the law.
Bible: Leviticus 19:11: Ye shall not steal, neither deal falsely, neither lie one to another.
Bible: Luke 3:14: Do violence to no man, neither accuse any falsely.
Bible: Luke, 11:52: Woe unto you, lawyers! for ye have taken away the key of knowledge: ye entered not in yourselves, and them that were entering in ye hindered.
Bible: Matthew 5:11: Blessed are ye, when men shall revile you, and persecute you, and shall say all manner of evil against you falsely, for my sake.
Bible: 1 Peter 4:15: Let none of you suffer as ... a busybody in other men's matters.
Bible: Proverbs 10:18: He that hideth hatred with lying lips, and he that uttereth a slander, is a fool.
Bible: Proverbs 18:8: The words of a talebearer are as wounds, and they go down into the innermost parts of the belly.
Bible: Proverbs 19:5: A false witness shall not be unpunished, and he that speaketh lies shall not escape.
Bible: Proverbs 19:22: A poor man is better than a liar.
Bible: Proverbs 26:20: Where no wood is, there the fire goeth out: so where there is no talebearer, the strife ceaseth.
Bible: Proverbs 26:28: A lying tongue hateth those that are afflicted by it.

Bible: Proverbs 27:6: Faithful are the wounds of a friend; but the kisses of an enemy are deceitful.

Bible: Psalms 62:9: Surely men of low degree are vanity, and men of high degree are a lie.

Bible: Psalms 101:5: Who so privily slandereth his neighbor, him will I cut off.

Bible: 1 Timothy 4:7: Refuse profane and old wives' fables.

Ambrose Bierce: DEFAME, v.t. To lie about another. To tell the truth about another.

Ambrose Bierce: ENCOMIAST, n. A special (but not particular) kind of liar.

Ambrose Bierce: FIB, n. A lie that has not cut its teeth. An habitual liar's nearest approach to truth: the perigee of his eccentric orbit....

Ambrose Bierce: IMAGINATION, n. A warehouse of facts, with poet and liar in joint ownership.

Ambrose Bierce: LIAR, n. A lawyer with a roving commission.

Ambrose Bierce: PREVARICATOR, n. A liar in the caterpillar state.

Josh Billings: There are people so addicted to exaggeration they can't tell the truth without lying.

William Blake: A truth that's told with bad intent. Beats all the lies you can invent.

Hans Blix: You can put up a sign on the door "beware of the dog" without having a dog.

Robert Bolt: The law is not a "light" for you or any man to see by; the law is not an instrument of any kind. The law and is a causeway upon which so long as he keeps to it a citizen may walk safely.

Daniel Boorstin: "Truth" has been displaced by "believability."

Edmund Burke: Laws, like houses, lean on one another.

Harold Burns (New York City Building Commissioner, on the confusion of housing and building law, 1963): One might risk establishing the following mathematical formula for bribery, namely OG = PLR x AEB: The opportunity for graft equals the plethora of legal requirements multiplied by the number of architects, engineers and builders.

Robert Burns (Scottish poet, 1759-1796): Dost not know that old Mansfield who writes like the Bible / Says the more 'tis a truth, sir, the more 'tis a libel.

Samuel Butler: I do not mind lying, but I hate inaccuracy.

Lord George Noel Gordon Byron: What is a lie? 'Tis but / The truth in masquerade.

James Callaghan: A lie can be half-way round the world before the truth has got its boots on.

Paul Campos (Law professor, University of Colorado, 2002): Karaoke is a charming Japanese form of entertainment in which customers at bars and restaurants sing popular songs while accompanied by a machine that duplicates all aspects of the music, other than the lead vocal track of the songs the customers perform.... now karaoke has migrated to America, in both a literal and metaphorical sense. More and more, we find ourselves living in a karaoke culture. Recent charges of plagiarism against historians Stephen Ambrose and Doris Kearns Goodwin provide excellent examples of the trend. Ambrose and Goodwin have both been caught plagiarizing several passages from more obscure authors within the pages of their own best-selling books. Both have defended themselves by claiming the plagiarisms were "unintentional"..... the kind of mistakes that Ambrose and Goodwin claimed to have made are extremely unlikely to occur when an author has actually written a book that appears under his or her name. Unintentional plagiarism is a product of something much more disturbing than an inadvertent failure to properly mark this or that passage as a quotation. It takes place when the putative "author" is really just a front for the work of others, specifically, of the "research assistants" who in many such cases are writing the books that appear under the names of their famous employers .... In a karaoke culture, authorship becomes what lawyers refer to as "a term of art."

Benjamin Cardozo (Chief Judge, NY Court of Appeals, Assoc Justice of US Supreme Court, 1870-1938): Many things that are defamatory may be said with impunity through the medium of speech. Not so, however, when speech is caught upon the wing and transmuted into print. What gives the sting to the writing is its permanence of form. The spoken word dissolves, but the written one abides and "perpetuates the scandal." _Ostrowe v. Lee_, 256 N.Y. 36 (1931)

Chinese Proverb: A rumor goes in one ear and out many mouths.

Sir Winston Churchill: It is a fine thing to be honest, but it is also very important to be right.

Sir Winston Churchill: Truth is so precious she must often be attended by a bodyguard of lies.

Sir Winston Churchill: There are a terrible lot of lies going about the world, and the worst of it is that half of them are true.

Cicero: It is a true saying that one falsehood leads easily to another.

Czech Proverb: Better a lie that heals than a truth that wounds.

Demosthenes (Greek orator, statesman, 385?-322 BC): The easiest thing of all is to deceive one's self; for what a man wishes he generally believes to be true, while things often turn out quite differently.

Demosthenes: Nothing is more easy than to deceive one's self, as our affections are subtle persuaders.

John Dryden: Some truth there was, but dash'd and brew'd with lies, / To please the fools and puzzle all the wise, / Succeeding times did equal folly call, / Believing nothing, or believing all.

Ralph Waldo Emerson: The louder he talked of his honor, the faster we counted our spoons.

Ralph Waldo Emerson: We do what we must, and call it by the best names.

English Saying: (This maxim was applicable to the criminal law of defamation prior to Lord Campbell's Libel Act of 1843, which permitted truth to be given in evidence on the subject of malice. This maxim is attributed to both Lord Mansfield and Lord Ellenborough, although not found in any reports): The greater the truth the greater the libel.

Greg Evans: Anger at lies lasts forever. Anger at truth cannot last.

Mike Ficaro (American lawyer): Liars are like snakes. Sooner or later they shed their skin. The cross examiner's job is to make a few small incisions that will help them do this right in front of the jury. Cross examination is a process in which you loosen the witness's skin.

Al Frankin: They (politicians): used "Weekend With Bernie Strategy" = don't tell him or anyone he's dead!

Al Frankin (his book, *Lies, and the Lying Liars Who Tell Them*): " … they fight with lies. We can't do that. We have to fight them with the truth. Our added entertainment value will have to come from being funny, and attractive, and passionate, and idealistic, but also smart and not milk toasty. We've got to be willing to throw their lies in their face. F you... no F you! That's how were gonna win this thing. Truth to power!"

Goethe: Unlike grownups, children have little to deceive themselves.

Oliver Goldsmith (*She Stoops to Conquer*): Tony Lumpkin: Ask me no questions, and I'll tell you no fibs.

Rev. Billy Graham: Everybody has a little bit of Watergate in him.

Phillip Guedella: The Lord Chief Justice of England recently said that the greater part of his judicial time was spent investigating collisions between propelled vehicles, each on its own side of the road, each sounding its horn and each stationary.

Theodor Haecker: When men no longer have the least fear of saying something untrue, they very soon have no fear whatsoever of doing something unjust.

John Heywood: Children and fools cannot lye.

Adolf Hitler: In the size of a lie is always contained a certain factor of credulity, since the great masses of the people... will more easily fall victims to a great lie than to a small one.

Buddy Holly (1957 song): That'll be the day!

Oliver Wendell Holmes: Pretty much all the honest truthtelling there is in the world is done by children.

Irish Proverb: Time is a great story teller.

Italian Proverb: If a man deceives me once, shame on him; if he deceives me twice, shame on me.

Robert Jackson: The price of freedom of religion, or of speech, or of the press, is that we must put up with a good deal of rubbish.

Thomas Jefferson: He who permits himself to tell a lie once finds it much easier to do it a second and a third time till at length it becomes habitual.

Jewish Saying: He only lies twice a year: in summer and in winter.

Jewish Saying: A liar is like a mute: neither tells the truth.

Jewish Saying: You may go a long way through lies—but not back.

Jewish Saying: A half-truth is a whole lie.

Jewish Saying: Better the ugly truth than a beautiful lie.

Jewish Saying: A lie one must not tell, and some truths you should not tell.

Jewish Saying: You mustn't tell a lie, but you are not bound to always tell the truth.

Jewish Saying: A liar tells his story so often that he begins to believe it himself.

Jewish Saying: Truth shows in the eyes; lies stay behind them (the eyes).

Jewish Saying: The tongue is a dangerous enemy.

Jewish Saying: What is candor to your face is slander behind your back.

Jewish Saying: An angry tongue is worse than a wicked hand.

Jewish Saying: It is better to speak good of yourself than bad about others.
Jewish Saying: Some men are prone to steal, but all men seem prone to slander.
Jewish Saying: If you think of yourself, you will not speak badly of others.
Latin Proverb: Men's faces are not to be trusted.
Latin Proverb: The face is the portrait of the mind; the eyes, its informers.
Abraham Lincoln: I never encourage deceit; and falsehood, especially if you have got a bad memory, is the worst enemy of fellow can have. The fact is, truth is your truest friend, no matter what the circumstances are.
Lyly: Children and fools speak true.
Maimonides: Do you think of thing proved because it is in a book; the liar, who deceives men with his time, does not hesitate to deceive them with his pan.
Billy Martin (NY Yankee manager in 1978 describing Reggie Jackson and George Steinbrenner): The two of them deserve each other. One's a born liar, the other's convicted.
Larry McMurtry: The United States broke 378 Treaties with the Indians.
H.L. Mencken: Legend is a lie that has attained the dignity of age.
H.L. Mencken: The men the American public admire most extravagantly are the most daring liars; the men they detest most violently are those who try to tell them the truth.
Midrash: Even if all of a slander is not believed, half of it is.
Henry Miller: One can be absolutely truthful and sincere even though admittedly the most outrageous liar. Fiction and invention are of the very fabric of life.
Phil Miller: Some people would rather climb a tree to yell a lie than stand on the ground and say the truth.
John Milton: The best apology against false accusers is silence and sufferance, and honest deeds set against dishonest words.
Montaigne: It is not without good reason said that he who has not a good memory should never take upon him the trade of lying.
Thomas Moore (Irish poet, *A Case of Libel. Odes on Cash, Corn, etc.*, 1779-1852): And oh, 'twas nuts to the Father of Lies, / (As this wily fiend is named in the Bible) / To find it settled by laws so wise, / That the greater the truth, the worse the libel.
Moses Hayyim Luzzatto: To some men, lying is a profession.
Ethel Watts Mumford (*The Limmerick Up to Date Book*, "Appearances Deceitful," 1903): There was a young lady from Skye, / With a shape like a capital I; / She said, "It's too bad! / But then I can pad," / Which shows you that figures can lie.
Rebbe Nachman of Bratslav (teacher and spiritual leader, founder of Breslov Hasidic dynasty; 1772-1810): He who has no confidence of others also does, and he who utters falsehoods has no confidence.
Rebbe Nachman of Bratslav: Lies are usually caused by an undue fear of men.
Richard Nixon: They think that whenever anyone in the White House now tells a lie, I get a royalty.
Louis B. Nizer: Some people will believe anything if you whisper it to them.
George Orwell (*1984*, 1949): *Doublethink* means the power of holding two contradictory beliefs in one's mind simultaneously, and accepting both of them.
George Orwell: Political language ... is designed to make lies sound truthful and murder respectable, and to give an appearance of solidity to pure wind.
George Orwell: In a time of universal deceit telling the truth is a revolutionary act.
Robert Pollock (Scottish poet, 1827): Slander, the foulest whelp of sin.
Alexander Pope: Blunt truths cause more mischief then nice falsehoods do.
Alexander Pope: He who tells a lie is not sensible to how great a task he undertakes: for he must be forced to invent twenty more to maintain that one.
Cuthbert W. Pound (Chief Judge, NY Court of Appeals, 1864-1935): The question is not so much who was aimed at, as who was hit. Corrigan v. Bobbs-Merril Co., 228 NY 58 (1920)
Portuguese Proverb: He who serves two masters has to lie to one.
Quintillian: To be a liar, memory is necessary.
Quintilian: A liar must be good at remembering.
Stanley J. Randall: The closest to perfection a person ever comes is when they fill out a job application.
Twiggy Rathbone: Flattery is the floating cockroach in the milk of human kindness.

Will Rogers: Rumor travels Faster, but it don't stay put as long as Truth.
Franklin D. Roosevelt: Repetition does not transform a lie into the truth
Bertrand Russell: No one gossips about other people's secret virtues.
Russian Insult: He lied like an eyewitness.
Saki: A little inaccuracy sometimes saves tons of explanation.
Sir Walter Scott: O, what a tangled web we weave, / When first we practice to deceive.
William Shakespeare (*All's Well that Ends Well*, Act IV, iii): PAROLLES: He will lie, sir, with such volubility, that you would think truth were a fool.
William Shakespeare (*The Comedy of Errors*, Act III, i): Slander lives upon succession, / For ever housed where it gets possession.
William Shakespeare (*Cymbeline*, Act III, iv): Slander, / Whose edge is sharper than the sword, whose tongue / Outvenoms all the worms of Nile, whose breath / Rides on the posting winds and doth belie / All corners of the world.
William Shakespeare (*Cymbeline*, Act III, iv): Though those that are betrayed / Do feel the treason sharply, yet the traitor / Stands in worse case of woe.
William Shakespeare (*Cymbeline*, Act III, vi): To lapse in fulness . Is sorer than to lie for need; and falsehood / Is worse in kings than beggars.
William Shakespeare (*Hamlet*, Act II, i): Your bait of falsehood takes this carp of truth.
William Shakespeare (*Hamlet*, Act III, i): Be thou as chaste as ice, as pure as snow, thou shalt not escape calumny.
William Shakespeare (*Hamlet*, Act III, ii): HAMLET: 'Tis as easy as lying.
William Shakespeare (*Hamlet*, Act IV, i): Slander, / Whose whisper o'er the world's diameter, / As level as the cannon to his blank, / Transports his poison'd shot.
William Shakespeare (*I. Henry IV*, Act II, iv): PRINCE HENRY: These lies are like the father that begets them: gross as a mountain, open, palpable.
William Shakespeare (*I. Henry IV*, Act V, iv): FALSTAFF: Lord, Lord, how this world is given to lying!
William Shakespeare (*I. Henry IV*, Act V, iv): PRINCE HENRY: For my part, if a lie may do thee grace, / I'll gild it with the happiest terms I have.
William Shakespeare (*Introduction to II Henry IV*, 15): Rumour is a pipe / Blown by surmises, jealousies, conjectures.
William Shakespeare (*II Henry IV*, Act III, i): Rumour doth double, like the voice and echo, / The numbers of the feared.
William Shakespeare (*II Henry IV*, Act III, ii): FALSTAFF: Lord, Lord, how subject we old men are to this vice of lying!
William Shakespeare (*King John*, Act IV, ii): Whose tongue soe'er speaks false, / Not truly speaks; who speaks not truly, lies.
William Shakespeare (*The Merchant of Venice*, Act I, iii): The devil can cite Scripture for his purpose. / An evil soul producing holy witness / Is like a villain with smiling cheek, / A goodly apple rotten at the heart.
William Shakespeare (*The Merchant of Venice*, Act I, iii): O, what a goodly outside falsehood hath!
William Shakespeare (*Much Ado About Nothing*, Act III, i): Done to death by slanderous tongues, / Was the Hero that here lies.
William Shakespeare (*Othello*, Act V, ii): Emilia: You told a lie, an odious, damned lie: / Upon my soul, a lie, a wicked lie.
William Shakespeare (*Romeo and Juliet,* Act IV, i): JULIET: That is no slander, sir, which is a truth; / And what I spake, I spake it to my face.
William Shakespeare (*Twelfth Night*, Act III, iv): Thou liest in thy throat.
Percy Bysshe Shelley: You lie—under a mistake, / For this is the most civil sort of lie / That can be given to a man's face. I now / Say what I think.
Sophocles: A lie never lives to be old.
Spanish Proverb: Whoever gossips to you will gossip about you.
Adlai Stevenson: I offer my opponents a bargain: if they will stop telling falsehoods about us, I will stop telling the truth about them.

Adlai Stevenson: Flattery is like a cigarette—it's all right so long as you don't inhale.

Jonathan Swift (English satirist, 1667-1745): I mean you lie—under a mistake.

Jonathan Swift (*Journal of a Modern Lady*): Convey a libel in a frown, / And wink a reputation down.

Publilius Syrus (42 B.C.): Even false becomes true when the chief says so.

Talmud: A lie has no fee (No leg to stand on).

Talmud: The man who slanders hurts three people: the man slandered, the man to whom the slander is uttered – and himself.

Talmud: It is a duty to say what should be heard, and a duty not to say what should not be heard.

Talmud: A good man who speaks evil is like a palace next to a than tannery: one defect destroys all the grandeur

Talmud: Slander is in the same category with murder.

Talmud: Slander is worse than weapons; for weapons heard from near, slander from afar.

Talmud: Hot coals, cooled on the outside, cool within; but slander, cooled outwardly, does not cool inside.

Alfred Lord Tennyson: That a lie which is half a truth is ever the blackest of lies; / That a lie which is all a lie may be met and fought with outright; / But a lie which is part a truth is a harder matter to fight.

Alfred Lord Tennyson: What is it all but a trouble of ants in the gleam of a million million of suns? / Lies upon this side, lies upon that side.

Mark Twain: One of the most striking differences between a cat and a lie is that a cat has only nine lives.

Mark Twain: It is easier to manufacture seven facts out of whole cloth than one emotion.

Mark Twain (*The Adventures of Huckleberry Finn*, Chapter 26, 1884): You can't pray a lie.

Mark Twain: It takes your enemy and your friend, working together, to hurt you to the heart; the one to slander you and the other to get the news to you.

Mark Twain: The history of our race, and each individual's experience, are sown thick with evidence that a truth is not hard to kill and a lie told well is immortal.

Mark Twain: Often the surest way to convey misinformation is to tell the strict truth.

Mark Twain: There was things which he stretched, but mainly he told the truth.

Mark Twain: At bottom he was probably fond of them, but he was always able to conceal it.

Mark Twain: An experienced, industrious, ambitious, and often quite picturesque liar.

Mark Twain: Adam was but human – this explains it all. He did not want the apple for the apple's sake, he wanted it only because it was forbidden.

Mark Twain: If you don't read the newspaper you are uninformed, if you do read the newspaper you are misinformed.

UA: Gossiping and lying go together.

UA: Crafty men deal in generalizations.

UA: A gossip is a person who will never tell a lie if the truth will do more damage.

UA (about lack of originality/plagerism): I may milk a lot of cows, but I churn my own butter.

Paul Valery: That which has always been accepted by everyone, everywhere, is almost certain to be false.

Maggie & Catie Vesper: Always tell the truth – there's less to remember.

Horace Walpole: There are three persons you should never deceive: your physician, your confessor, and your lawyer.

Barbara Walters: Show me someone who never gossips, and I'll show you someone who isn't interested in people.

George Washington (referring to his critics): "Hyperbolic prejudices conjured up by designing men to work their own purposes upon terrified imaginations."

George Washington: "No nation (or man) is to be trusted farther than it is bound by its (his) interests"

Isaac Watts: And he that does one fault at first, / And lies to hide it, makes it two.

Joseph Weintraub (Chief Justice, New Jersey Supreme Court, 1973): More automobile accidents in New Jersey occur on yellow legal pad's (used by lawyers) than on the highways in New Jersey.

Walter Winchell: Gossip is the art of saying nothing in a way that leaves practically nothing unsaid.

Yiddish Proverb: A half-truth is a whole lie.

Zohar: If you wish to strengthen a lie, mix a little truth in with it.

Zohar: God will except repentance for all sins except one: giving another man a bad name.

LIFE (See also AGE/AGING)

Uncle Anthony: Life ain't about how long you can reach, or how far you can run, or how high you can jump; but how often you can bounce back.
Uncle Anthony: You know, Thomas, when you gripe about things ain't being what they used to be, don't forget to include yourself.
Uncle Anthony: Life is 10% what you make of it, and 90% how you take it.
Uncle Anthony: Y'know, life is likea roll of toilet paper ... the closer you get to the end, the faster it goes!
Uncle Anthony: The game of life ain't so much about holding a good hand as much as playing a poor hand well.
Aunt Mary Carlo; (my aunt from Brooklyn): Life is too short to dance with ugly men!
Aunt Mary Carlo: Life is tough, and you gotta be tougher!
Aunt Mary Carlo (about "Life's Milestones"): Ya get to a time in life when yer scorecard starts to fill up y'know? (that is, your friends and acquaintances start to die before you do)
African Proverb: Every morning a lion wakes up and knows it must out run the slowest gazelle; every morning a gazelle wakes up and knows it must outrun the fastest lion. Whether you are a gazelle or a lion, when you wake up, you better start running!
Woody Allen: Life is full of misery, loneliness, and suffering – and it's over much too soon.
Maya Angelou: Life loves to be taken by the lapel and told, "I'm with you kid. Let's go."
Marcus Aurelius: The art of living is more like wrestling than dancing.
Donald Barthelme: The best way to live is by not knowing what will happen to you at the end of the day.
Bible: Job 8:9: We are but of yesterday, and know nothing, because our days upon the earth are a shadow.
Bible: Job, 12:2: With the ancient is wisdom; and in length of days understanding.
Bible: Job, 32:9: Great men are not always wise: neither do the aged understand.
Bible: Proverbs, 16:31: The hoary head is a crown of glory, if it be found in the way of righteousness.
Bible: Psalms 103:15: As for man, his days are as grass: as a flower in the field, so he flourisheth.
Ambrose Bierce: LIFE, n. A spiritual pickle preserving the body from decay. We live in daily apprehension of its loss; yet when lost it is not missed....
Ambrose Bierce: OPERA, n. A play representing life in another world, whose inhabitants have no speech but song, no motions but gestures and no postures but attitudes.
Ambrose Bierce: Life is war; and to live is to be a soldier. Those who cannot face up to this are just civilians. None of us are getting out (of life) alive. It is the civilian who will be picked off first, either by war, or nature or himself.
Josh Billings: Life consists not in holding good cards, but in playing those you hold well.
Margaret Bonnano: It is only possible to live happily ever after on a day-to-day basis.
Jimmy Buffett: It takes no more time to see the good side of life than to see the bad.
Lois McMaster Bujold: If you can't do what you want, do what you can.
Samuel Butler: Life is like playing a violin in public and learning the instrument as one goes on.
James Branch Cabal (The Silver Stallion): The optimist proclaims that we live in the best of all possible worlds; and the pessimist fears this is true.
Joseph Campbell: "FOLLOW YOUR BLISS."
Albert Camus: If, after all, men cannot always make history have a meaning, they can always act so that their own lives have one.
Albert Camus: There is no fate that cannot be surmounted by scorn.
Benjamin Cardozo: Life has relations not capable always of division into inflexible compartments. The moulds expand and shrink. <u>Glanzer v. Shepard</u>, 233 N.Y. 236 (1922)
Dale Carnegie: You can make more friends in two months by becoming interested in other people then you can in two years by trying to get other people interested in you.
Johnny Carson: If life was fair, Elvis would be alive and all the impersonators would be dead.
Allan K. Chalmers: The grand esentials of happiness are: something to do, something (EDITOR: and someone) to love, and something to hope for.
Chinese Proverb: Better to light a candle than to curse the darkness.
Chinese Proverb: There are many paths to the top of the mountain, but the view is always the same.

Sir Winston Churchill: We make a living by what we get. We make a life by what we give.

Sir Winston Churchill: Without a measureless and perpetual uncertainty, the drama of human life would be destroyed.

Sir Winston Churchill: The influence of each human being on others in this life is a kind of immortality.

Frank A. Clark: If you can find a path with no obstacles, it probably doesn't lead anywhere.

Dr. Logan Clendening: If you do everything you should do, and do not do anything you should not do, you will, according to the best available statistics, live exactly eighteen hours longer than you would otherwise.

Marquis de Condorcet: Enjoy your own life without comparing it with that of another.

Alyce P. Cornyn-Selby: A perfect method for adding drama to life is to wait until the deadline looms large.

Madam Marie Curie: Nothing in life is to be feared, it is only to be understood. Now is the time to understand more, so that we may fear less.

Greg Cusimano: Some say I'm in a rut, but I think I'm in a groove.

Greg Cusimano: We often spend too much time making a living, and not enough time making a life.

Clarence Darrow: This is life and all there is of life; to play the game, to play the cards we get; play them uncomplainingly and play them to the end. The game may not be worth the while. Mistakes may not be worth the winning. But the playing of the game is the forgetting of self, and we should be game sports and play bravely to the end.

Peter DeVries: Life is a zoo in a jungle.

Diogenes: A man should live with his superiors as he does with his fire; not too near, lest he burn; not too far, lest he freeze

Frederick Douglas (asked by a young man "what should be done with my life?"): Agitate, agitate, agitate!

Norman Douglas: Nothing ages a man like living always with the same woman.

Isadora Duncan: Life is a dream, and it is well that it is so, or who could survive some of its experiences?

Marie Dressler: By the time we hit fifty, we have learned our hardest lessons. We have found out that only a few things are really important. We have learned to take life seriously, but never ourselves.

Umberto Eco: The real hero is always a hero by mistake; he dreams of being an honest coward like everybody else.

Irwin Edman: Life is always at some turning point.

Albert Einstein (to his youngest son Edward, aka "TeTe," after a failed love affair with an older woman): Life is like riding on a bicycle, to keep your balance, you must keep moving.

Albert Einstein (1934): Striving for social justice is the most valuable thing to do in life.

Albert Einstein: I never think of the future – it comes soon enough.

Epictetus: First say to yourself what you would be; and then do what you have to do.

Richard Evans: Don't let life discourage you; everyone who got where he is had to begin where he was.

Malcolm Forbes: By the time we've made it, we've had it!

French Proverb: Life is an onion which one peels crying.

R. Buckminster Fuller: Now there is one outstandingly important fact regarding Spaceship Earth, and that is that no instruction book came with it.

John Galsworthy: I shall pass through this world but once; any good things, therefore, that I can do, or any kindness that I can show to any human being, or dumb animal, let me do it now. Let me not deter it or neglect it, for I shall not pass this way again.

William Goldman: Life isn't fair. It's just fairer than death, that's all.

Frederick Goodyear: Long life is the right mode for some people and not for others – just as some people write books in ten volumes and others epigrams in two lines – and the two works may be of exactly equal value.

Ruth Gordon: I'm sure the best way to be happy is to live well beyond your means.

Learned Hand (*Proceedings in Memory of Mr. Justice Brandeis*, 317 U.S. xi, 1942): A man's life, like a piece of tapestry, is made up of many strands which interwoven make a pattern; to separate a single one and look at it alone, not only destroys the whole, but gives the strand itself a false value.

Jack Handey: I hope life isn't a big joke, because I don't get it.

Tom Hanks (as the the hero of the 1994 film *Forrest Gump*): My momma always said life is like a box of chocolates ... you never know what you're gonna get.

Janet Harris: "... with the beginnings of middle years, we face an identity crisis for which nothing in our past has prepared us."

Helen Hayes: The hardest years in life are those between 10 and 70.

Nelson Henderson: The true meaning of life is to plant trees under whose shade you do not expect to sit.

Oliver Wendell Holmes, Jr.: Life is painting a picture, not doing a sum.

Oliver Wendell Holmes, Jr.: Life is an end in itself, and the only question as to whether it is worth living is whether you have enough of it.

Oliver Wendell Holmes, Jr.: "... all life is an experiment. Every year if not every day we have to wager our salvation upon some prophecy based upon imperfect knowledge.

Oliver Wendell Holmes, Jr.: Life is like an artichoke, each day, week, month, year, gives you one little bit which you nibble off—but precious little compared with what you throw away.

Oliver Wendell Holmes, Jr.: One of the eternal conflicts out of life is made up is that between the effort of every man to get the most he can for his services, and that of society, disguised under the name of capital, to get his services for the least possible return.

Oliver Wendell Holmes, Jr.: The joy of life is to put out one's power in some natural and useful or harmless way. There is no other. And the real misery is not to do this.

Oliver Wendell Holmes, Jr. (*Common Law*, 1881): A ship is the most living of inanimate things.

Oliver Wendell Holmes, Sr,: With most men life is like backgammon – half skill and half luck.

Herbert Hoover: About the time we think we can make ends meet, somebody moves the ends.

Vernon Howard: You have succeeded in life when all you really want is only what you really need.

Kin Hubbard: It is pretty hard to tell what does bring happiness; poverty and wealth have both failed.

Aldous Huxley (*Brave New World*): Each one of us goes through life in a bottle (EDITOR: pre-conditioning of the human persona through our environment).

Irish Saying: What way are you? (EDITOR: this lyrically metaphysical query probes "where is your life going?")

Italian Proverb: We cannot direct the wind, but we can adjust the sails.

Holbrook Jackson: No man is ever old enough to know better.

Mick Jagger: It's all right letting yourself go as long as you can get yourself back.

William James: Is life worth living? It depends on the liver.

William James: The greatest use of life is to spend it for something that will outlast it.

Carl Jung: The meeting of two personalities is like the contact of two chemical substances: if there is any reaction, both are transformed.

Carl Jung: The nearer we approach to the middle of life, and the better we have succeeded in entrenching ourselves in our personal standpoints and social positions, the more it appears as if we had discovered the right course and the right ideals and principles of behavior.... We wholly overlook the essential fact that the achievements which society rewards are won at the cost of diminution of personality. Many – far too many – aspects of life which should also have been experienced lie in the lumberroom among dusty memories. Sometimes, even, they are glowing coals under grey ashes.

Carl Jung: Protection and security are only valuable if they do not cramp life excessively; and in the same way the superiority of consciousness is desirable only if it does not suppress and exclude too much of our existence. As always, life is a voyage between Scylla and Charybdis.

Carl Jung: Great talents are the most lovely and the most dangerous fruits on the tree of humanity. They hang upon the most slender twigs that are easily snapped off.

Danny Kaye: Life is a great big canvas; throw all the paint on it you can.

John F. Kennedy: Change is the law of life. And those who look only to the past or present are certain to miss the future.

Ken Keys: A loving person lives in a loving world. A hostile person lives in a hostile world. Everyone you meet is your mirror.

Martin Luther King Jr.: Our lives begin to end the day we become silent about things that matter.

Yolanda King (oldest daughter of Corletta Scott King and Martin Luther King, Jr): We must keep reaching across the table and, in the tradition of Martin Luther King, Jr. and Coretta Scott King, feed each other.

Elizabeth "Libby" Kinghorne (Executive Director of Atlantic Provinces Trial Lawyers Association; advice given to both my daughter Maggie and me in PEI, Canada): The guy who is nice to you, but not nice to the waiter - is not a nice guy!

Charles Kingsley: We act as if comfort and luxury are the chief requirements of life, when all that we need to make as happy is something to be enthusiastic about.

Soren Kierkegaard: My life is absolutely meaningless. When I consider the different periods into which it falls, it seems like the word *Schnur* in the dictionary, which means in the first place a string, in the second a daughter-in-law. The only thing lacking is that the word *Schnur* should mean in the third place a camel, in the fourth, a dust-brush.

Ursula K. LeGuin: The only thing that makes life possible is permanent, intolerable uncertainty—not knowing what comes next.

Michael Landon: Somebody should tell us, right at the start of our lives, that we are dying. Then we might live life to the limit, every minute of every day.

Sir Edwin Landseer (1838 painting entitled): The Life's in the Old Dog Yet.

Latin Saying: *vita non est vivere sed valere vita est*: life is more than merely staying alive.

D.H. Lawrence: I believe that one has to be seventy before one is full of courage. The young are always half-hearted.

D.H. Lawrence: Well – life itself is life – even the magnificent frost-foliage on the window. While we live, let us live.

Doris Lessing: Growing up is after all only the understanding that one's unique and incredible experience is what everyone shares.

W.M. Lewis: The tragedy of life is not that it ends too soon, but that we wait so long to begin it.

Anne Morrow Lindbergh (*Gift from the Sea*, 1955): Perhaps middle-age is, or should be, a period of shedding shells; the shell of ambition, the shell of material accumulations and possessions, the shell of ego.

Anne Morrow Lindbergh: People "died" all the time in their lives. Parts of them died when they made the wrong kinds of decisions – decisions against life. Sometimes they died bit by bit until finally they were just living corpses walking around. If you were perceptive you could see it in their eyes; the fire had gone out.... But you always knew when you made a decision life. When you denied life you were warned. The cock crowed, always, somewhere inside of you. The door clicked and you were safe inside – safe and dead.

John Lithgow: Time sneaks up on you like a windshield on a bug.

Henry Wadsworth Longfellow: *Psalm of Life*, Full Text: "Tell me not, in mournful numbers, / 'Life is but an empty dream!' / For the soul is dead that slumbers, / And things are not what they seem. / Life is real! Life is earnest! / And the grave is not its goal; / 'Dust thou art, to dust returnest,' / Was not spoken of the soul. / Not enjoyment, and not sorrow, / is our destined end or way; / But to act, that each tomorrow / Finds us further than today. / Art is long, and Time is fleeting, / And our hearts, though stout and brave, /Still, like muffled drums, are beating / Funeral marches to the grave. / In the world's broad field of battle, / In the bivouac of life, / Be not like dumb, driven cattle! / Be a hero in the strife! / Trust no Future, howe'er pleasant! / Let the dead Past bury its dead! / Act, - act in the living Present! / Heart within, and God o'erhead! / Lives of great men all remind us / We can make our lives sublime, And, departing, leave behind us / Footprints on the sands of time; / Footprints, that perhaps another, / Sailing o'er life's solemn main, /A forlorn and shipwrecked brother, / Seeing, shall take heart again. / Let us, then, be up and doing, / With a heart for any fate; / Still achieving, still pursuing, / Learn to labour and to wait."

Earl Mac Rauch: Remember, no matter where you go, there you are.

W. Somerset Maugham: It's a funny thing about life: If you refuse to accept anything but the best, you very often get it.

Harvey Milk: Isn't it strange that as technology advances, the quality of life frequently declines?

Edna St. Vincent Millay: It is not true that life is one damn thing after another – it is one damn thing over and over.

Henry Miller: All growth is a leap in the dark, a spontaneous unpremeditated act without the benefit of experience.

Christopher Morley: Life is a foreign language; all men mispronounce it.

Christopher Morley: There is only one success – to be able to spend your life in your own way.

John Mortimer (spoken by Rumpole of The Bailey): "Life with (X) becomes a never ending Wagnerian Ring Cycle.

Michael A. Musmanno (Justice of Pa. Supreme Court, 1959): Seventy-five is Not the End of Productivity: It is a mistaken assumption that because one is eligible to Social Security benefits at 65, this age represents the end of the line for productive work on the part of the average person. Longevity is not so rare in modern life that it must be dismissed as bizarre. The advances made in medical science, the widely publicized rules of health and better living have all contributed to a constantly increasing lifespan which one has the right to enjoy free of pain and suffering caused by tortious happenings. Therefore, it is error to say that at 65 one can no longer work remuneratively and therefore must be cast on the economic ash heap. There is no reason dogmatically to assume that, given reasonable health, one can not for some years continue as efficiently after the 65th milestone has been reached as for the few years which preceded that heretofore awesome marker. The ripened experience, the matured intellect, the self-control, the storehouse of knowledge gathered through the years also contribute to the efficiency of the human mechanism that it may continue to produce after 65 years with an effectiveness that no employer or society at large should want unthinkingly to discard. (Cuneo v. Philadelphia Transportation Co., 405 Pa. 532).

Bill Naughton (1966 song, stage show, radio play and film *Alfie*): What's it [EDITOR: life] all about, Alfie?

Anais Nin: Those who cannot live fully often become destroyers of life.

Kathleen Norris: In spite of the cost of living, it's still popular.

Sean O'Casey: All the world's a stage and most of us are desperately unrehearsed.

Sean O'Casey: Well, I have found life an enjoyable, enchanting, active, and sometimes a terrifying experience, and I've enjoyed it completely. A lament in one ear, maybe, but always a song in the other. And to me life is simply an invitation to live.

Lewis Orr: Science will never be able to reduce the value of a sunset to arithmetic. Nor can it reduce friendship to a formula. Laughter and love, pain and loneliness, the challenge of accomplishment in living, and the depth of insight into beauty and truth: these will always surpass the scientific mastery of nature.

P.R. Regamey: Life has its own hidden forces which you can only discover by living.

Mary Roberts Rhinehart: A little work, a little sleep, a little love and it is all over.

Paul Rodriguez: Life is not a box of chocolates, it's like a jar of jalapenos—you never know what's going to burn your ass.

Will Rogers: Half our life is spent trying to find something to do with the time we have rushed through life trying to save.

Will Rogers: Don't let yesterday use up too much of today.

Eleanor Roosevelt: I think that somehow, we learn who we really are and then live with that decision.

Eleanor Roosevelt: Life has got to be lived – that's all there is to it. At 70, I would say the advantage is that you take life more calmly. You know that "this, too, shall pass!"

Theodore Roosevelt: The poorest way to face life is to face it with a sneer.

Margaret Lee Runbeck: Happiness is not a station in your route, but a manner of traveling.

John Ruskin: Every increased possession loads us with new weariness.

Bertrand Russell: The time you enjoy wasting is not wasted time.

David Russell: The hardest thing in life is to know which bridge to cross and which to burn.

Carl Sandburg: I am an idealist. I don't know where I'm going, but I'm on my way!

George Santayana: I agree that the last years of life are the best, if one is a philosopher.

George Santayana: There is no cure for birth and death save to enjoy the interval.

Arthur Schopenhauer: If we were not all so interested in ourselves, life would be so uninteresting that none of us would be able to endure it.

Charles Schultz: The secret of life is to replace one worry with another

Charles Schultz: There's a difference between a philosophy and a bumper sticker.

Dr. Martin Seligman, et als (a scientific study shows): THE determinant ... THE critical determining element in life and business success is resilience in the face of adversity.

William Shakespeare (*All's Well That Ends Well,* Act IV, iii): The web of our life is of a mingled yarn, good and ill together.

William Shakespeare (*As You Like It,* Act II, vii): All the world's a stage, / And all the men and women merely players.

William Shakespeare (*As You Like It,* Act II, vii): Last scene of all, / That ends this strange, eventful history, / Is second childishness and mere oblivion, / Sans teeth, sans eyes, sans taste, sans everything.

William Shakespeare (*Comedy of Errors,* Act V, i): Though now this grained face of mine be hid / In sap-consuming winter's drizzle snow, / And all the conduits of my blood froze up, / Yet hath my night of life some memory.

William Shakespeare (*I Henry IV,* Act V, ii): The time of life is short! / To spend that shortness basely were too long.

William Shakespeare (*II Henry IV*, Act I, ii): Your lordship, though not clean past your youth, hath yet some smack of age in you, some relish of the saltness of time.

William Shakespeare (*III Henry VI,* Act II, v): Minutes, hours, days, weeks, months, and years. / Pass'd over to the end they were created, / Would bring white hairs unto a quiet grave. Ah, what a life were this!

William Shakespeare (*Henry VIII,* Act IV, iv): O father Abbot, / An old man, broken with the storms of State, / Is come to lay his weary bones among ye; / Give him a little earth for charity.

William Shakespeare (*King John,* Act III, iv): Life is as tedious as a twice-told tale / Vexing the dull ear of a drowsy man.

William Shakespeare (*King Lear,* Act II, iv): I confess that I am old; Age is unnecessary.

William Shakespeare (*King Lear,* Act II, iv): O, heavens, / If you do love old men, if your sweet sway / Allow obedience, if you yourselves are old, / Make it your cause.

William Shakespeare (*King Lear,* Act II, iv): You see me here, you gods, a poor old man, / As full of grief as age; wretched in both.

William Shakespeare (*King Lear,* Act IV, vii): Pray, do not mock me: / I am a very foolish fond old man, / Fourscore and upward; and to deal plainly, / I fear I am not in my perfect mind.

William Shakespeare (*Macbeth,* Act II, iii): The wine of life is drawn, and the mere lees / Is left this vault to brag of.

William Shakespeare (*Macbeth,* Act V, iii): My way of life / Is fallen into the sear, the yellow leaf: / And that which should accompany old age, / As honor, love, obedience, troops of friends, / I must not look to have; but, in their stead, / Curses not loud, but deep, mouth-honor, breath, / Which the poor heart would fain deny, and dare not.

William Shakespeare (*The Passionate Pilgrim,* l. 157): Crabbed age and youth cannot live together: / Youth is full of pleasance, age is full of care; / Youth like summer morn, age like winter weather; / Youth like summer brave, age like winter bare. / Youth is full of sport, age's breath is short; / Youth is nimble, age is lame; Youth is hot and bold, age is weak and cold; Youth is wild, age is tame. / Age, I do abhor thee; youth, I do adore thee.

William Shakespeare (*Richard II,* Act II, i): More are men's ends mark'd than their lives before: / The setting sun, and music at the close, / As the last taste of sweets, is sweetest last, / Writ in remembrance more than things long past.

William Shakespeare (*Sonnets*, No. iii): Thou art thy mother's glass, and she in thee / Calls back the lovely April of her prime: So thou through windows of thine age shall see, / Despite of wrinkles this thy golden time.

George Bernard Shaw: A life spent making mistakes is not only more honorable but more useful than a life spent doing nothing.

George Bernard Shaw: This is the true joy of life, the being used for a purpose recognized by yourself as a mighty one; the being thoroughly worn out before you are thrown on the scrap heap; the being a force of Nature instead of a feverish little clod of ailment and grieving, complaining that the world will not devote itself to making you happy.

George Bernard Shaw: Life does not cease to be funny when people die any more than it ceases to be serious when people laugh.

J. Walker Smith (President of Yankelovich, a marketing firm in Chapel Hill, N.C.): Used to be we simply lived in our houses. Then the '80's came, and we "cocooned." Now, we are "hiving." Hiving entails making connections to others from within our homes; the home is "command central" for a variety of activities involving other people, including work and socializing. Borrowing from the metaphor of a beehive, abuzz with activity, hiving represents engagement, interaction and connection with the outside environment.

C.P. Snow: The pursuit of happiness is a most ridiculous phrase; if you pursue happiness you'll never find it.

Socrates: Remember that there is nothing stable in human affairs; therefore, avoid undue elation in prosperity, or undue depression in adversity.

Sophocles: Nobody loves life like him who is growing old.

August Strindberg: People are constantly clamoring for the joy of life. As for me, I find the joy of life in the hard and cruel battle of life – to learn something is a joy to me.

Roland "Cooks Books" Suarez (slogan and emblem painted on his taxi, "Atlantic City's Goodwill Amabassador," popular entertainer and taxi driver in Atlantic City, NJ, stabbed to death March 31, 1985): Every day is a miracle.

Kathleen Sutton: When you can't get what you want, it's time to start wanting what you have.

Dylan Thomas: Isn't life a terrible thing, thank God?

Eckhart Tolle: Realize deeply that the present moment is all you ever have.

Mark Twain: When we remember we are all mad, the mysteries disappear and life stands explained.

Mark Twain: Let us endeavour so to live that when we come to die even the undertaker will be sorry.

Mark Twain: When I reflect upon the number of disagreeable people who I know have gone to a better world, I am moved to lead a different life.

Evelyn Underhill: After all it is those who have a deep and real inner life who are best able to deal with the "irritating details of outer life."

Horace Walpole: The whole secret of life is to be interested in one thing profoundly and in a thousand things well.

Martha Washington: The greater part of our happiness or misery depends on our dispositions and not on our circumstances.

Chris Watson (Atlantic City Press article "That's Not All, Folks! Lessons Learned From Cartoons Over Into Adult Situations"): Wile E. Coyote taught me to never give up – that life is more process than achievement.

Thomas J. Watson: Life itself is a matter of salesmanship.

Rudy Westmoreland: Living well is the best revenge.

Oscar Wilde: We live in an age when unnecessary things are our only necessities.

Oscar Wilde: The Book of Life begins with a man and woman in a garden. It ends with Revelations.

Oscar Wilde: Selfishness is not living as one wishes to live; it is asking others to live as one wishes to live.

Margery Williams (*"The Velveteen Rabbit"*): "What is real?" asked the Rabbit one day, ... "Real isn't how you are made," said the Skin Horse. "it's a thing that happens to you. When a child loves you for a long, long time, not just to play with, but really loves you, then you become real." "Does it hurt?" asked the Rabbit. "Sometimes," said the Skin Horse, for he was always truthful. "When you are Real you don't mind being hurt."

W.B. Yeats: When I think of all the books I have read, and of the wise words I have heard spoken, and of the anxiety I have given to parents and grandparents, and of the hopes I have had, all life weighed in the scales of my own life seems to me a preparation for something that never happens.

Lin Yutang: Peace of mind is that mental condition in which you have accepted the worst.

LISTENING **(See TEACHING)**

LITERATURE **(See BOOKS)**

LITIGATION

Uncle Anthony: You know Thomas, lawsuits burn up not just your time and money, but also your friends.

Aunt Mary Carlo: Sometimes it seems like them litigators are tryin' to beat each udder an' not solve da case.

Thomas H. Allen (American lawyer): We've produced a system of ending disputes rather than digging up truths.

John Arbuthnot (English physician and writer, 1667-1735, *Law is a Bottomless Pit (History of John Bull)*, 1712): Law is a bottomless pit! It is a cormorant, a harpy that devours everything!

Aristotle: (Hippodamus) maintained that there are three subjects of lawsuits—insult, injury and homicide.

Melvyn Belli: Lawsuits help insure that Americans have good life. We protect our rights by litigating if anyone attempts to trample on them. We have always been like that. One of the colonial flags included a rattlesnake with the legend, "Don't Tread On Me." That's the American mind of today as expressed by trial lawyers.

Jeremy Bentham: Lawsuits generally originate with the obstinate and the ignorant, but they do not end with them; and that lawyer was right who left all his money to the support of an asylum for fools and lunatics, saying that from such he got it, and to such he would bequeath it.

Warren Berger (Supreme Court Justice): The courtrooms of America all too often have Piper Cub advocates trying to handle the controls of Boeing 747 litigation.

Bible: 1 Corinthians 6:7, St. Paul: There is utterly a fault among you, because ye have lawsuits one with the another.

Bible: Matthew 5:40: If any man will sue thee at the law, and take away thy tunic, let him have thy cloak also.

Ambrose Bierce (from *The Devil' Dictionary, 1906*): COURT FOOL: The plaintiff.

Ambrose Bierce: LAWSUIT, n. A machine which you go into as a pig and come out as a sausage.

Ambrose Bierce: LITIGANT, A person about to give up his skin for the hope of retaining his bones.

Ambrose Bierce: LITIGATION, n. A machine which you go into as a pig and come out of as a sausage.

Ambrose Bierce: OPPOSE, v. To assist with obstructions and objections.

Josh Billings (pseudonym of Henry Wheeler Shaw, American humorist, 1818-1885, *Sollum Thoughts*): Going tew law iz like skinning a new milch cow for the hide, and giving the meat tew the lawyers.

Jerry Brown: The volume of paper expands to fill the available briefcases.

Jean De La Bruyere: Avoid lawsuits beyond all things; they pervert your conscience, impair your health, and dissipate your property.

Robert Burton (English clergyman and writer, 1577-1640, *Anatomy of Melancholy: Democritus to the Reader*, 1621): He that goes to law (as the proverb is) holds a wolf by the ear.

Chinese Proverb: A lawsuit is a piece of paper blown by the wind into a law court which may in the end only be drawn out again by two oxen.

Chinese Proverb: Going to law is losing a cow for the sake of a cat.

Chinese Proverb: Win your lawsuit and lose your money.

Chinese Proverb: Winning a cat you lose a cow.

Cicero: The litigious spirit is more often found with ignorance than with knowledge of law.

Confucius (500 B.C.): I can try a lawsuit as well as other men, but the most important thing is to prevent lawsuits.

Confucius: We should make it our aim that there may be no lawsuits at all.

Ernest Conine (American journalist): As a people we must somehow get over the notion that the solution to every problem is a lawsuit.

Danish Proverb: One goes to court with one lawsuit and comes home with two.

Dale Dalton (American newspaper columnist): Criticizing lawyers for lawsuits is like criticizing linebackers for knocking people down.

Alan Dershowitz: More lawsuits may not be good for large corporations, but they are good for justice and society, especially if brought by the powerless against the powerful.

English Proverb: I shall make him water his horse at Highgate (by suing someone in England you caused them to take a journey to London).

English Proverb: A lean compromise is better than a fat lawsuit.

English Proverb: He that goes to law holds a wolf by the tail.

English Proverb: Fond of lawsuits, little wealth; fond of doctors, little health.

English Proverb (Ray, *Proverbs*, 1678): Sue a beggar and catch a louse.

English Proverb (Ray, *Proverbs*, 1678): He'll go to law for the wagging of a straw.

English Proverb (Herbert, *Jacula Prudentum*, 1651): Lawsuits consume time, and money, and rest, and friends.

Owen Felltham (English writer, 1623): To go to law is for two persons to kindle a fire, at their own cost, to war with others, and singe themselves to cinders.

Felix Frankfurter (Massachuesetts lawyer, Associate Justice US Supreme Court, 1882-1965): Litigation is the pursuit of practical ends, not a game of chess. Indianapolis v. Chase Nat. Bank, 314 US 63, 86 L ed 48, 62 S Ct 15 (1941).

Gypsy curse: May you have lawsuit in which you know you are right.

Learned Hand (Judge US District Court and Circuit Court, 1872-1961, *Deficiencies of Trials to Reach the Heart of the Matter*, 3 Lectures on Legal Topics, Ass'n Bar City of NY 89): I must say that, as a litigant, I should dread a lawsuit beyond almost anything else short of sickness and death.

Charles Evans Hughes (Supreme Court Justice): The United States is the greatest law factory the world has ever known.

Italian Proverb: A lawsuit is a fruit tree planted a lawyer's garden.

Italian Proverb: Sue a beggar and get a louse.

Wilfred Jayne (New Jersey judge, 1888-1961): It would also seem evident that each of the parties to this litigation possesses ample independent financial means. It sometimes seems that litigation is pursued only to experience a rapturous warmth from the heat of battle. Schulter v. Schulter, 23 N.J. Super. 409, 413 (1952)

J. Michael Jordan (R.J. Reynolds Tobacco Company lawyer, in his memo about how the tobacco company won dismissals of nine cigarette cases in California: he credited an aggressive legal posture that made cases burdensome and expensive to plaintiffs): To paraphrase General Patton, the way we won those cases was not spending all of RJ Reynolds' money, but by making sure that the other son-of-a-bitch spent all of his."

Irving R. Kaufman (US Court of Appeals Judge): The judicial system is the most expensive machine ever invented for finding out what happened and what to do about it.

Jean De La Bruyere 1645-1696, French Writer: Avoid lawsuits beyond all things; they pervert your conscience, impair your health, and dissipate your property.

Abraham Lincoln: Never stir up litigation. A worse man can scarcely be found than one who does this.

Timothy Lytton (Albany Law School professor): This year (2007) marks the fifth anniversary of The Boston Globe's Pulitzer Prize-winning coverage of clergy sexual abuse. The Pulitzer citation praised the Globe for its "courageous, comprehensive coverage of sexual abuse by priests, an effort that pierced secrecy, stirred local, national, and international reaction and produced changes to the Roman Catholic Church." Yet while the news media have received well-deserved recognition for their part in exposing the abuse and focusing attention on the need for institutional reform, little attention has been paid to the underlying role played by lawsuits. There's an unsung hero in this story, the plaintiff's lawyer. Although the tort system is more often maligned than celebrated, it was the work of plaintiffs' lawyers that brought the scandal to light in the first place. Pleadings, discovery documents, and depositions in hundreds of cases during the course of more than two decades have provided most of the information underlying media coverage of the scandal. Lawsuits have fed journalists a steady supply of compelling stories of both personal suffering and official wrongdoing, and they have provided a defense against potential libel claims and political cover to criticize powerful church officials.... Clergy sexual abuse litigation is, in short, a poster child for the policy-making benefits of tort litigation.

John Milton: Litigious terms, fat contentions, and flowing fees.

Napolean (Parkes, *History of Court of Chancery*, 1828): Lawsuits are an absolute leprosy, a social cancer. My code has singularly diminished lawsuits, by placing numerous causes within the decision of every individual. But there still remained much for the legislator to accomplish. Not that he could hope to prevent men from quarrelling: that they have done in all ages; but he might have prevented a third party in society, from living upon the quarrels of the two others, and even stirring up disputes, to promote their own interest. It was therefore my intention to establish the rule that lawyers should never receive fees, except when they gain causes.

Angie Papadakis: In almost every case, you have to read between the lies.

Harry Philo: Whatever you think the case is worth and the costs will be to litigate, cut the case value in half and multiply the out-of-pocket costs by three.

Frederick Pollock (English Judge): We lawyers know well, and may cite high authority for it if required, that life would be intolerable it every man insisted on his legal rights to the full.

David Porter: Litigation is the basic legal right which guarantess every corporation its decade in court.

J. Danforth Quayle (44th Vice President of the United States): It's becoming increasingly clear that litigation is threatening our national economic viability. Sheer numbers tell the story. (Editor's note: these "sheer numbers" have been thoroughly discredited).

Jane Bryant Quinn (American journalist): A poor man may still be able to get into heaven, but after Reaganization, he may not be able to get into court.

Will Rogers: Lawyers make a living out of trying to figure out what other lawyers have written.

Salvatore Satta (1902-1975, Italian Jurist, Novelist): The most important thing in their lives was to have a lawsuit going. It was not a question of winning or losing it, and indeed it was vital to do neither, for otherwise the suit would be over and done with. A lawsuit was part of the personality, if not the only visible sign of it, to such an extent that there was often no real animosity between the litigants, because they both needed each other.

Gordon Schaber: The practice of law in most courtrooms today is about as modern as performing surgery in a barbership.

William Shakespeare (*Hamlet*, Act III, iii): In the corrupted currents of this world / Offence's gilded hand may shove by justice, / And oft 'tis seen the wicked prize itself / Buys out the law: but 'tis not so above; / There is no shuffling, there the action lies / In his true nature; and we ourselves compell'd, / Even to the teeth and forehead of our faults, / To give in evidence.

William Shakespeare (*II Henry IV*, Act IV, i): A rotten case abides no handling.

William Shakespeare (*II Henry VI*, Act I, iii): Let him have all the rigour of the law.

Spanish Proverb: A happy death is better than a lawsuit.

Spanish Proverb: He who goes to law for a sheep loses his cow.

William B. Spann (President, American Bar Association, 1978): Fairness and honesty are finding it increasingly hard to prevail in a judicial system clogged with frivolous lawsuits.

Jonathan Swift (1667-1745, Anglo-Irish Satirist): Come, agree, the law's costly.

Mark Twain: They all laid their heads together like as many lawyers when they are gettin' ready to prove that a man's heirs ain't got any right to his property.

Mark Twain (1873): There is no display of human ingenuity, wit, and power, so fascinating as that made by trained lawyers in the trial of an important case, nowhere else is exhibited such subtlety, acumen, address, eloquence.

Mark Twain (deleted dedication of Mark Twain's book "Roughing It"): To the Late Cain, This Book is Dedicated, Not on account of respect for his memory, for it merits little respect; not on account of sympathy with him, for his bloody deed placed him without the pale of sympathy, strictly speaking; but out of a mere human commiseration for him in that it was his misfortune to live in a dark age that knew not the beneficent Insanity Plea.

Gore Vidal: Litigation takes the place of sex at middle age.

Rudy Westmoreland: Being "upside down" in real estate means you got more invested in the property than you can resell it for, it's the same as a plaintiff client's case in which you've spent more than the case can be settled for.

LIVING (See AGE; LIFE)

LOGIC (See REASON/LOGIC)

LOSING/LOSERS (See FAILURE)

LOST ENJOYMENTS OF LIFE (See AGING)

LYING (See LIES)

MAJORITY

Uncle Anthony: Sometimes a majority just means that all the a-holes/idiots/fools are on the same side.
Uncle Anthony: In a lynch mob there is only one vote against hanging.
Uncle Anthony: Birds of a feather flock together ... then they crap on your car.
Aunt Mary Carlo: If you t'ink dere's good in everybody, you ain't met everybody.
Aunt Mary Carlo: If yer wrong, gettin' some udder people to agree wit ya, don't make ya right.
Aunt Mary Carlo: A whole crowd of people can still make a mistake.
James Bavard (Civil Libertarian): Democracy must be something more than two wolves and a sheep voting on what to have for dinner.
Henry Ward Beecher: A man in the right, with God on his side, is in the majority though he be alone.
Henry Ward Beecher: A man who puts himself on the ground of moral principle, though the whole world be against him, is mightier than them all; for the orb of time becomes such a man's shield, and every step brings him nearer to the hand of omnipotence.—Take ground for truth, and justice, and rectitude, and piety, and fight well, and there can be no question as to the result.—We are to feel that right is itself a host.—Never be afraid of minorities, so that minorities are based on principles.
Bible: Exodus 23:2: Thou shalt not follow a multitude to do evil.
Bible: Isaiah 17:12: The multitude of many people, which make a noise like the noise of the seas.
Ambrose Bierce: MAGNITUDE, n. Size. Magnitude being purely relative, nothing is large and nothing small. If everything in the universe were increased in bulk one thousand diameters nothing would be any larger than it was before, but if one thing remained unchanged all the other would be larger than they had been. To an understanding familiar with the relativity of magnitude and distance the spaces and masses of the astonomer would be no more impressive than those of the microscopist. For anything we know to the contrary, the visible universe may be a small part of an atom, with its component ions, floating in the life-fluid (luminiferous ether) of some animal. Possibly the wee creatures peopling the corpuscles of our own blood are overcome with the proper emotion when contemplating the unthinkable distance from one of these to another,
Ambrose Bierce: MULTITUDE, n. A crowd; the source of political wisdom and virtue. In a republic, the object of the statesman's adoration....
Ambrose Bierce: RABBLE, n. In a republic, those who exercise a supreme authority tempered by fraudulent elections. The rabble is like the sacred Simurgh, of Arabian fable – omnipotent on condition that it do nothing. (The word is Aristocratese, and has no exact equivalent in our tongue, but means, as nearly as may be, "soaring swine."
Edmund Burke: This minority is great and formidable. I do not know whether, if I aimed at the total overthrow of a kingdom, I should wish to be encumbered with a large body of partisans.
Edmund Burke: When bad men combine, the good must associate; else they will fall one by one, an unpitied sacrifice in a contemptible struggle.
Edmund Burke: Because half a dozen grasshoppers under a fern make the field rating with their importunate chink... do not imagine that those who make the noise are the only inhabitants of the field.
Benjamin N. Cardozo: More truly characteristic of dissent is a dignity, an elevation, of mood and thought and phrase. Deep conviction and warm feeling are saying their last say with knowledge that the cause is lost. The voice of the majority may be that of force triumphant, content with the plaudits of the hour, and recking little of the morrow. The dissenter speaks to the future, and his voice is pitched to a key that will carry through the years.
Thomas Carlyle (1795-1881, Scottish essayist and historian): Popular opinion is the greatest lie in the world.
G.K. Chesterton (1874-1936, English journalist): To be in the weakest camp is to be in the strongest school.
Sir Winston Churchill: There is no such thing as public opinion. There is only published opinion.

James Fenimore Cooper: The minority of the country is never known to agree, except in it in its efforts to reduce and oppress the majority.

Jefferson Davis: Neither current events nor history show that the majority rules, or ever did rule.

Eugene V. Debs: When great changes occur in history, when great principles are involved, as a rule the majority is wrong.

Benjamin Disraeli: A majority is always the best repartee.

Frederick Douglass: One and God make a majority.

Ralph Waldo Emerson: Shall we judge a country by the majority, or by the minority? By the minority, surely.

Ralph Waldo Emerson: All history is a record of the power of minorities, and of minorities of one.

Ralph Waldo Emerson: It is easy in the world to live after the world's opinion; it is easy in solitude after our own; but the great man is he who in the midst of the crowd keeps with perfect sweetness the independence of solitude.

Anatole France: If fifty million people say a foolish thing, it is still a foolish thing.

William Ewart Gladstone: Decision by majorities is as much an expedient as lighting by gas.

William Gladstone: The oppression of a majority is detestable and odious: the oppression of a minority is only by one degree less detestable and odious.

Albert Guinon: If everyone is against you, it means you are absolutely wrong—or absolutely right.

William Hazlitt: The majority, compose them how you will, are a herd, and not a very nice one.

Oliver Wendell Holmes, Sr: The history of most countries has been that of majorities—mounted majorities, clad in iron, armed with death, treading down the tenfold more numerous minorities.

Edgar Watson Howe: I not only believe majority rule is just, I believe it is best. All men know more than a few; all experience is better than new and untried theory.

Lawrence Houseman: Minority is no disproof: / Wisdom is not so strong and fleet / As never to have known defeat.

Henrik Ibsen: The minority is always in the right.

Henrik Ibsen: The majority never has right on its side.

Henrik Ibsen: The most dangerous foe to truth and freedom in our midst is the compact majority. Yes, the damned, compact, liberal majority.

President Andrew Jackson: One man with courage can be a majority.

Thomas Jefferson (first inaugural address, March 4, 1801): Bear in mind this sacred principle, that though the will of a majority is in all cases to prevail, that will come to be rightful, must be reasonable; that the minority possessed their equal rights, which equal laws must protect, and to violate which would be oppression.

Thomas Jefferson: I readily... suppose my opinion wrong, when opposed by the majority.

Thomas Jefferson: It is my principle that the will of the majority should always prevail.

Thomas Jefferson: One man with courage is a majority.

John F. Kennedy: Public Opinion is not the same as "Public Interest."

Mark R. Kosieradzki, Esq. (my good friend, *Deposition Notebook* co-author, and great personal injury trial lawyer from Minnesota): The trouble with going with the flow is, you might wind up getting sucked down the drain.

Latin Proverb: When one dog barks another will join it.

Harper Lee: The one thing that doesn't abide by majority rule is a person's conscience.

Abraham Lincoln (First Inaugural Address, 1861): If by the mere force of numbers a majority should deprive a minority of any clearly written constitutional right, it might, in a moral point of view, justify revolution – certainly would if such a right or a vital one.

Walter Lippmann: The principle of majority rule is the mildest form in which force of number can be exercised. It is a pacific substitute for civil war.

James Russel Lowell: That cause is strong which has not a multitude, but one strong man behind it.

Horace Mann: We go to the major vote, and if the majority are in saying, the sand must go to the hospital.

Midrash, *Genesis Rabba*: If one man says, "You're a donkey," don't mind; if two say so, be worried; if three say so, get a saddle.

John Stuart Mill: If all mankind minus one were of one opinion and only one person were of the contrary opinion, mankind would be no more justified in silencing that person than he, if he had the power, would be justified in silencing mankind... if the opinion is right, they are deprived of the opportunity of exchanging error for truth; if wrong, they lose, what is almost as great a benefit, the clearer perception and livelier impression of truth, produced by its collision with error.

Napoleon I: Ten persons who speak make more noise than ten thousand who are silent.

Robert Craggs Nugent: Safer with multitudes to stray, / Than tread alone a fairer way: / To mingle with the erring throng, / Than boldly speak ten millions wrong.

P.J. O'Rourke: There's a whiff of the lynch mob or the lemming migration about any overlarge concentration of like-thinking individuals, no matter how virtuous their cause.

Wendell Phillips: One, of God's side, is a majority.

Wendell Phillips: Governments exist to protect the rights of minorities. The loved and the rich need no protection,—they have many friends and few enemies.

Lester J. Pourciau: there is no monument dedicated to the memory of a committee.

Marcel Proust: The artist penetrates under the crust of consensus.

Thomas B. Reed: One, with God, is always a majority, but many a martyr has been burned at the stake while the votes were being counted.

James Reston: A resolute minority has usually prevailed over an easy-going or wobbly majority whose prime purpose was to be left alone.

William H. Rehnquist: Somewhere "out there," beyond the walls of the courthouse, run currents and tides of public opinion which lap at the courtroom door.

Leonard H. Robbins: How a minority, / Reaching majority, / Seizing authority, / Hates a minority!

Will Rogers (Jan. 27, 1924): They are having quite an argument over (Treasury Secretary) Mellon's Tax Bill. Mr. Mellon wants to cut the surtax on the rich, and leave it as is on the poor, as there is more poor than rich. I suppose the majority will win.

Will Rogers: "This country is not where it is today on account of any one man. It is here on account of the real common sense of the Big Normal Majority."

Charles Victor Roman: If the majority rules, then the earth belongs to colored people.

Andy Rooney: I don't think being a minority makes you a victim of anything except numbers. The only things I can think of that are truly discriminatory are things like the United Negro College Fund, Jet Magazine, Black Entertainment Television, and Miss Black America. Try to have things like the United Caucasian College Fund, Cloud Magazine, White Entertainment Television, or Miss White America; and see what happens...Jesse Jackson will be knocking down your door.

Franklin D. Roosevelt: No democracy can long survive which does not accept as fundamental to its very existence the recognition of the rights of minorities.

Theodore Roosevelt: The only tyrannies from which men, women and children are suffering in real life are the tyrannies of minorities.

Theodore Roosevelt: I don't know the way people do feel, I only know the way they ought to feel.

Russian Proverb: Seven never wait for one.

Johann Schiller: The voice of the majority is no proof of justice.

Johann Schiller: Votes should be weighed, not counted.

Arthur Schopenhauer: We forget that three quarters of ourselves to be like other people.

William Shakespeare (*As You Like It*, Act II, vii): All the world's a stage, / And all the men and women merely players.

William Shakespeare (*Coriolanus*, Act II, iii): Ingratitude Is monstrous, and for the multitude to the ingrateful, were to make a monster of the multitude.

William Shakespeare (*Coriolanus*, Act II, iii): He himself stuck not to call us the many-headed multitude.

William Shakespeare (*Coriolanus*, Act IV, i): The beast With many heads butts me away.

William Shakespeare (*II Henry IV: Induction*, 1. 18): The blunt monster with uncounted heads, / The still-discordant wavering multitude.

William Shakespeare (*II Henry VI*, Act IV, viii): Was ever feather so lightly blown to and fro as this multitude?

William Shakespeare (*III Henry VI,* Act III, i): Look, as I blow this feather from my face, / And as the air blows it to me again, / Obeying with my wind when I do blow, / And yielding to another when it blows, / Commanded always by the greater gust; / Such is the lightness of you common men.

William Shakespeare (*Julius Caesar,* Act I, ii): That tag-rag people.

William Shakespeare (*The Merchant of Venice*, Act II, ix): I will not choose what many men desire, / Because I will not jump with common spirits, / And rank me with the barbarous multitudes.

Charles Simons: The smallest number, with God and truth on their side, are weightier than thousands.

Ralph W. Sockman: The test of courage comes when we are in the minority. The test of tolerance comes when we are in the majority.

Herbert Spencer: The fact disclosed by a survey of the past that majorities have been wrong, must not blind us to the complementary fact that majorities have usually not been entirely wrong.

Jonathan Swift: A majority, with a good cause, are negligent and supine.

Talleyrand: There is one body that knows more than anybody, and that is every body.

Henry David Thoreau: Any man more right than his neighbor constitutes a majority of one.

Mark Twain: Whenever you find that you are on the side of the majority, it is time to reform.

Mark Twain: Hain't we got all the fools in town on our side? And ain't that a big enough majority in any town?

Mark Twain: The vast majority of the race, whether savage or civilized, are secretly kind-hearted and shrink from inflicting pain, but in the presence of the aggressive and pitiless minority they don't dare to assert themselves.

Oscar W. Underwood: The great mass of the people are in more danger of having their rights invaded and their liberties destroyed by the overweening influence of organized minorities, who have fanatical or selfish interests to serve, than by the force of an unthinking or cruel majority.

Virgil: It never troubles the wolf how many the sheep may be.

Yiddish Proverb: If all pulled in one direction, the world would keel over.

MAN (See MEN)

MARRIAGE

Uncle Anthony: There are two secrets to keep your marriage happy: 1. Whenever you're wrong, admit it and say so right away, and 2. Whenever you're right, shut the hell up!

Uncle Anthony: I think somebody who's been married many years knows more about marriage than somebody who's been married many times.

Uncle Anthony: Hey, ya know what "Hierogomy" means? It means yer wife is right – you married a god!

Aunt Mary Carlo: The thing about "two being made one" in marriage is who's gonna be the one?

Alfred Adler: Most married couples conduct themselves as if each party were afraid that the other one could see that it was the weaker.

Sholem Aleichem: A man enters the *khupe* (marriage canopy) living, and comes out a corpse

Woody Allen: I tended to place my wife under a pedestal.

Woody Allen: I'm very old-fashioned. I believe that people should stay married for life, like pigeons and Catholics.

Dr. Robert Anthony: The one who loves the least controls the relationship.

Karen Armstrong (*A Short History of Myth*, Chapter III: The Neolithic Period: The Mythology of the Farmer, c. 8,000 to 4,000 BCE): **HIEROGOMY** is a sacred marriage ... sexual congress of heaven and earth.... The soil is female, and the seeds are divine seman .... the plow is a sacred phallus that opened the womb of Earth.... (EDITOR: therefore farming was a form of ritualistic marriage).

Sir James Richard Atkin (English judge, 1867-1944): The common law does not regulate the form of agreements between spouses. Their promises are not sealed with seals and sealing wax. The consideration that really obtains for them is that natural love and affection which counts for so little in these cold Courts. Balfour v. Balfour, 2 K.B. 571 (1919)

St. Augustine of Hippo: Humble wedlock is far better than proud virginity.

Jim Backus: Many a man owes his success to his first wife and his second to his success.

Francis Bacon: A man finds himself seven years older the day after his marriage.
Joseph Barth: Marriage is our last best chance to grow up.
Milton Berle: A good wife always forgives her husband when she's wrong.
Bible: Amos 3:3: Can two walk together, except they be agreed?
Bible: 1 Corinthians 7:9: It is better to marry than to burn.
Bible: 1 Corinthians 7:33: He that is married careth for the things that are of the world, how he may please his wife. She that is married careth for the things of the world, how she may please her husband.
Bible: Ephesians 5:31: For this cause shall a man leave his father and mother, and shall be joined unto his wife, and they shall be one flesh.
Bible: Genesis 2:18: It is not good that the man should be alone.
Bible: Mark 12:25: When they shall rise from the dead, they neither marry, nor are given in marriage; but are as the angels which are in heaven.
Bible: Matthew 19:6: What therefore God hath joined together, let not man put assunder.
Bible: Proverbs 18:22: Whoso findeth a wife findeth a good thing.
Bible: Proverbs 21:9 and 25:24: It is better to dwell in a corner of the housetop, than with a brawling woman in a wide house.
Ambrose Bierce: AFFIANCED, n. An acclimatizing process preparing the soul for another and bitter world.
Ambrose Bierce: BRIDE, n. A woman with a fine prospect of happiness behind her.
Ambrose Bierce: BRUTE, n. See HUSBAND.
Ambrose Bierce: FRIENDSHIP, n. A ship big enough to carry two in fair weather, but only one in foul.
Ambrose Bierce: HELPMATE, n. A wife, or bitter half....
Ambrose Bierce: HUSBAND, n. One who, having dined, is charged with the care of the plate.
Ambrose Bierce: INCOMPATIBILITY, n. In matrimony a similarity of tastes, particularly the taste for domination. Incompatibility may, however, consist of a meek-eyed matron living just around the corner. It has even been known to wear a moustache.
Ambrose Bierce: MARRIAGE, n. The state or condition of a community consisting of a master, a mistress and two slaves, making in all, two.
Ambrose Bierce: UXORIOUSNESS, n. A perverted affection that has strayed to one's own wife.
Ambrose Bierce: WEDDING, n. A ceremony at which two persons undertake to become one, one undertakes to become nothing, and nothing undertakes to become supportable.
David Bissonette: I recently read that love is entirely a matter of chemistry. That must be why my wife treats me like toxic waste.
Richard E. Brennan (from "Reflections on Matrimonial Motion Day," poem, 1996): I wonder if they ever think of their wedding days, / The bright dresses, the tender words, the promises and dreams. / As they witness the end of their marriages / And engage in settlement talks and schemes.... /"Sell the house"; "Split the stuff we acquired through the years"; / "Start anew, move again, forget the former ways." / But I wonder as I watched them with their lawyers, / Do they ever think about their wedding days?
Pearl Buck: A good marriage is one which allows for change and growth in the individuals and in the way they express their love.
Ken Burns (in his PBS Special *The Civil War*): Because slaves could not legally marry, old Negro preachers in the antebellum South would change the marriage vows to **"till death or distance do us part."**
Albert Camus: Married couples: the man tries to shine before a third person. Immediately his wife says: "But you're just the same ... " and tries to bring him down, to make him share her mediocrity.
Chinese Proverb: A wife is sought for her virtue, a concubine for her beauty.
Chinese Proverb: An ugly wife and a lean piece of ground protect the house.
Sir Winston Churchill: My most brilliant achievement was my ability to be able to persuade my wife to marry me.
Sir Winston Churchill: My wife and I tried to breakfast together, but we had to stop or our marriage would have been wrecked.
Coke (*Case of Swans*, 7 Rep. 17, 1592): The cock swan is an emblem or representation of an affectionate and true husband to his wife above all other fowls; for the cock swan holdeth himself to one female

only, and for this cause nature hath conferred on him a gift beyond all others; that is, to die so joyfully, that he sings sweetly when he dies.

Czech Proverb: Do not choose your wife at a dance, but in the field among the harvesters.

Rodney Dangerfield: My wife and I were happy for twenty years. Then we met.

Lord Charles John Baron Darling (Justice, King's Bench, England, 1849-1936; *Scintillae Juris: Of Evidence*): If a man stays away from his wife for seven years, the law presumes the separation to have killed him; yet, according to our daily experience, it might well prolong his life.

Charles Dickens (*Oliver Twist*, ch. 51): (You are) "the more guilty of the two in the eye of the law; for the law supposes that your wife acts under your direction." "If the law supposes that," said Mr. Bumble, squeezing his hat emphatically in both hands, **"the law is a ass – a idiot.** If that's the eye of the law, the law's a bachelor; and the worst I wish the law is, that his eye may be opened by experience."

Dr. Rudolf Dreikus: Everyone is deeply interested in maintaining the faults of his partner.

Dr. Rudolf Dreikus: The complaints which anyone voices against his mate indicate exactly the qualities which stimulated attraction before marriage.

Dumas: Woman inspires us to great things, and prevents us from achieving them.

Dutch Proverb: One should not think about it too much when marrying or taking pills.

Mrs. Elza Einstein (Albert Einstein's second wife): I manage him, but I never let him know I manage him.

English Proverb: Sorrow for a husband is like a pain in the elbow, sharp and short.

Jules Feiffer: We want playmates we can own.

Edna Ferber: Men often marry their mothers.

Benjamin Franklin: Keep thy eyes wide open before marriage, and a half shut afterwards.

Sigmund Freud: The great question... which I have not been able to answer... is, "What does a woman want?

Warren H. Goldsmith: There's one consolation about matrimony. When you look around you can always see somebody who did worse.

Paul Goodman: If very many marriages could simply let themselves dissolve after a few years, the partners would suddenly become brighter, rosier, and younger.

Sacha Guitry: When a man steals your wife, there is no better revenge than to let him keep her.

Nathaniel Hawthorne: Methinks this birth-day of our married life is like a cape, which we now have doubled, and find a more infinite ocean of love stretching out before us. God bless us and keep us; for there is something more awful in happiness than in sorrow – the latter being earthly and finite, the former composed of the texture and substance of eternity, so that spirits still embodied may well tremble at it.

John Heywood (*The Proverbs of John Heywood*): More things belong to marriage than four bare legs in a bed.

James K. Hines (Georgia judge, 1852-1932): While the husband is still declared by statute to be the head of the family, he, like the King of England, is largely a figurehead. Curtis v. Ashworth, 165 Ga 782 (1928)

Oliver Wendell Holmes, Jr. (2 *Holmes-Pollock Letters* 243, 1929): For sixty years she made life poetry for me.

David Hopkinson: I believe that we all should wise up and recognize that a marriage is a small business and that married couples are business partners.

Kin Hubbard: Just because a girl's married ain't no sign she hasn't loved and lost.

Henrik Ibsen: Marriage is something you have to give your whole mind to.

Irish Proverb: If you want to be criticized, marry.

Wilfred Jayne (New Jersey judge, 1888-1961): Mrs. Barber is the kind of wife who stands by her husband in all the troubles he would not have had if he had not married her. Bondarchuk v. Barber, 135 N.J. Eq. 334 (1944).

Jewish Legend: God is considered the supreme *shadkhn* (matchmaker): Forty days before a Jewish child is born, its mate is selected in heaven.

Jewish Saying: An old man who marries a young wfe grows younger—but she grows older.

Jewish Saying: It is better for a woman to have one husband, though he be useless, than wealthy children.

Jewish Saying: When a Man is too good for this world, it's too bad for his wife.

Jewish Saying: When a young man marries, he divorces his mother.
Jewish Saying: Even a bad match can beget good children.
Jewish Saying: The man who marries for money earns it.
Jewish Saying: By day they fight, but bed at night.
Jewish Saying: Husband and wife are one flesh, but have different purses.
Jewish Saying: A third person may not interfere between two who sleep on the same pillow.
Jewish Saying: Better break the engagement than the marriage.
Jewish Saying: Marriage is made in Heaven; but second marriages are arranged by people.
Jewish Saying: For dying or marrying, there's always time.
Jewish Saying: The ceremony lasts an hour, but the troubles last a lifetime.
Samuel Johnson (Boswell, *Life of Johnson*, 1776): I believe marriages would in general be as happy, and often more so if they were all made by the Lord Chancellor, upon a due consideration of characters and circumstances, without the parties having any choice in the matter.
Hemant Joshi: After marriage, husband and wife become two sides of a coin; they just can't face each other, but still they stay together.
Carl Jung: The meeting of two personalities is like the contact of two chemical substances: if there is any reaction, both are transformed.
Carl Jung: Unlived life is a destructive and irresistible force working quietly but relentlessly. The result is that the married woman begins to doubt marriage. The unmarried woman believes in it, because she desires marriage.
Soren Kierkegaard: If you marry, you will regret it; if you do not marry, you will also regret it.
Sam Kinison: "I don't worry about terrorism. I was married for two years."
D.H. Lawrence: A man, proceeding from his known self, likes a woman because she is in sympathy with what he knows. He feels that he and she know one another. They marry. And then the fun begins.
Latin Saying: *Sponsalia de presente* = in presence of witnesses; both parties "contract" a true contract for marriage/sex
Groucho Marx: The husband who wants a happy marriage should learn to keep his mouth shut and his checkbook open.
James Holt McGavran: There's a way of transferring funds that is even faster than electronic banking. It's called marriage.
H.L. Mencken: No matter how happily a woman may be married, it always pleases her to discover that there is a nice man who wishes that she were not.
Montaigne: I see no marriages which sooner fail than those contracted on account of beauty and amorous desire.
Patrick Murray: "I've had bad luck with both my wives. The first one left me, and the second one didn't."
Ogden Nash (American poet, 1902-1971, *A Word to Husbands*): To keep your marriage brimming with love in the loving cup, / Whenever you're wrong admit it. Whenever you're right, shut up.
Ogden Nash: Two secrets to keep your marriage brimming: 1. Whenever you're wrong, admit it, and 2. Whenever you're right, shut up.
Ovid: If you would marry suitably, marry your equal.
Theodore Parker: Marriages are best made of dissimilar material.
Channing Pollock: Marriage is the greatest educational institution on earth.
Alexander Pope: Men dream in courtship, but in wedlock wake.
Joan Rivers: Trust your husband, adore your husband, and get as much as you can in your own name.
Will Rogers: I see by the papers that they are going to do away with all the nuisance taxes. That means that a man can get a marriage license for nothing.
Helen Rowland: Love, the quest; marriage, the conquest; divorce, the inquest.
Helen Rowland: Courtship is a republic; marriage, a monarchy; divorce, a soviet.
Lord Charles Russel (First Baron Russell of Killowen, Lord Chief Justice of England, 1832-1900): What was once a holy estate enduring for the joint lives of the spouses, is steadily assuming the characteristics of a contract for a tenancy at will. Fender v. St. John-Midmay, A.C. 1, 34 (1938)
Jean-Paul Sartre: In love, one and one are one.

Sir Walter Scott: From my experience, not one in twenty marries the first love; we build statues of snow, and weep to see them melt.

Scottish Proverb: Never marry for money. Ye'll borrow it cheaper.

John Selden (English lawyer and writer, *Table-Talk: Marriage*, 1584-1654): Of all actions of a man's life, his marriage does least concern other people, yet of all actions of our life 'tis most meddled with by other people.

William Shakespeare (*All's Well That Ends Well*, Act V, iii): If you shall marry, / You give away this hand, and that is mine; / You give away Heaven's vows, and those are mine; / You give away myself, which is known mine.

William Shakespeare (*As You Like It*, Act IV, i): Men Are April when they woo, December when they wed: maids are May when they are maids, but the sky changes when they are wives.

Shakespeare (*Comedy of Errors*, Act II, ii): I will fasten on this sleeve of thine: / Thou art an elm, my husband, I, a vine.

William Shakespeare (*Comedy of Errors,* Act III, ii): Ill deeds are doubled with an evil word.

William Shakespeare (*Cymbeline*, Act III, iv): Men's vows are women's traitors! All good seeming, / By thy revolt, O husband, shall be thought / Put on for villany; not born, where 't grows; / But worn, a bait for ladies.

William Shakespeare (*Hamlet*, Act I, ii): Ere yet the salt of most unrighteous tears / Had left the flushing in her galled eyes, / She married.

William Shakespeare (*Hamlet,* Act II, ii): Unpack my heart with words, / And fall a cursing, like a very drab.

William Shakespeare (*Hamlet,* Act II, ii): POLONIUS: What do you read, my Lord? / HAMLET: Words, words, words!

William Shakespeare (*Hamlet*, Act III, i): I say, we will have no more marriages. Those that are married already, all but one, shall live; the rest shall keep as they are. To a nunnery, go.

William Shakespeare (*Hamlet*, Act III, i): If thou wilt needs marry, marry a fool; for wise men know well enough what monsters you make of them.

William Shakespeare (*Hamlet*, Act III, ii): The instances that second marriage move, / Are base respects of thrift, but none of love.

William Shakespeare (*Hamlet,* Act III, iii): My words fly up, my thoughts remain below: / Words without thoughts, never to heaven go.

William Shakespeare (*Hamlet*, Act III, iv): Make marriage vows / As false as dicers' oaths.

William Shakespeare (*Henry V,* Act IV, iii): Familiar in his mouth as household words.

William Shakespeare (*Henry V*, Act V, ii): God, the best maker of all marriages, / Combine your hearts in one.

William Shakespeare (*I Henry VI,* Act V, v): What is wedlock forced but a hell, / An age of discord and continual strife? Whereas the contrary bringeth bliss / And is a pattern of celestial peace.

William Shakespeare (*III Henry VI*, Act IV, i): Hasty marriage seldom proveth well.

William Shakespeare (*Henry VIII: Prologue*, 1.32): A man may weep upon his wedding day.

William Shakespeare (*Henry VIII*, Act II, ii): He counsels a divorce: a loss of her, / That, like a jewel, has hung twenty years / About his neck, yet never lost her lustre; / Of her, that loves him with that excellence / That angels love good men with; even of her / That when the greatest stroke of fortune falls, / Will bless the king.

William Shakespeare (*Henry VIII,* Act III, ii): 'Tis well said again; / And 'tis a kind of good deed, to say well: / And yet words are no deeds.

William Shakespeare (*Julius Caesar*, Act II, i): O ye gods, / Render me worthy of this noble wife!

William Shakespeare (*Julius Caesar*, Act IV, iii): O Cassius, you are yoked with a lamb / That carries anger as the flint bears fire; Who, much enforced, shows a hasty spark, / And straight is colod again.

William Shakespeare (*Julius Caesar,* Act V, i): Good words are better than bad strokes.

William Shakespeare (*King John,* Act II, i): He is the half part of a blessed man / Left to be finished by such as she; / And she a fair divided excellence, / Whose fullness of perfection lies in him. / O, to such silver currents, when they join, / Do glorify the banks that bound them in!

William Shakespeare (*King John,* Act II, ii): Zounds! I was never so bethump'd with words; / Since I first call'd my brother's father, dad.

William Shakespeare (*Love's Labour's Lost,* Act V, i): He draweth out the thread of his verbosity finer than the staple of his argument.

William Shakespeare (*Love's Labour's Lost,* Act V, ii): (Marriage is) A world-without-end bargain.

William Shakespeare (*The Merchant of Venice*, Act II, ix): The ancient saying is no heresy, / Hanging and wiving go by destiny.

William Shakespeare (*The Merchant of Venice,* Act III, ii): Madam, you have bereft me of all words, / Only my blood speaks to you in my veins.

William Shakespeare (*The Merchant of Venice*, Act III, ii): Happy in this, she is not yet so old / But she may learn; happier than this, / She is not bred so dull but she can learn; / Happiest of all, is, that her gentle spirit / Commits itself to yours to be directed, / As from her lord, her governor, her king.

William Shakespeare (*The Merchant of Venice,* Act III, ii): As are those dulcet sounds in break of day / That creep into the dreaming bridegroom's ear / And summon him to marriage.

William Shakespeare (*The Merchant of Venice,* Act V, i): A light wife doth make a heavy husband.

William Shakespeare (*The Merry Wives of Windsor*, Act I, i): I will marry her, sir, at your request; but if there be no great love in the beginning, yet heaven may decrease in upon better acquaintance.... I hope, upon familiarity will grow more contempt: I will marry her; that I am freely dissolved, and dissolutely.

William Shakespeare (*Much Ado About Nothing*, Act I, i): An' thou wilt needs thrust thy neck into a yoke, wear the print of it, and sigh away Sundays.

William Shakespeare (*Much Ado About Nothing,* Act II, i): Wooing, wedding, and repenting, is as a Scotch jig, a measure, and a cinque pace.

William Shakespeare (*Much Ado About Nothing*, Act II, i): I would not marry her, though she were endowed with all that Adam had left him before he transgressed; she would have made Hercules have turned spit: yea and have cleft his club to make the fire too.... I would to God some scholar would conjure her; for certainly while she is here, a man may live as quiet in hell, as in a sanctuary.

William Shakespeare (*Much Ado About Nothing*, Act II, iii): No: the world must be peopled. When I said, I would die a bachelor. I did not think I should live till I were married.

William Shakespeare (*Othello,* Act I, iii): But words are words; I never yet did hear / That the bruis'd heart speaks to you in my veins.

William Shakespeare (*Othello*, Act I, iii): Most potent, grave, and reverend signiors, / My very noble and approv'd good masters, / That I have ta'en away this old man's daughter, / It is most true; true, I have married her; / The very head and front of my offending / Hath this extent, no more.

William Shakespeare (*Othello,* Act III, iii): I know thou'rt full of love and honesty, / And weigh'st thy words before thou giv'st them breath.

William Shakespeare (*Othello*, Act IV, iii): Let husbands know, / Their wives have sense like them: they see, and smell, / And have their palates both for sweet and sour, / As husbands have.

William Shakespeare (*Richard II,* Act I, iii): How long a time lies in one little word? / Four lagging winters, and four wanton springs, / End in a word: Such is the breath of kings.

William Shakespeare (*Richard II,* Act II, i): The tongues of dying men / Enforce attention, like deep harmony: / Where words are scarce, they are seldom spent in vain; / For they breathe truth, that breathe their words in pain.

William Shakespeare (*Romeo and Juliet*, Act IV, v): She's not well married that lives married long / But she's best married that dies married young.

William Shakespeare (*Taming of the Shrew*, Act II, i): If she deny to wed, I'll crave the day / When I shall ask the banns, and when be married.

William Shakespeare (*The Taming of the Shrew*, Act III, ii): I will be master of what is mine own. / She is my goods, my chattels; she is my house, / My household stuff, my field, my barn, / My horse, my ox, my ass, my anything.

William Shakespeare (*The Taming of the Shrew*, Act III, ii): Who woo'd in haste, and means to wed at leisure.

William Shakespeare (*The Taming of the Shrew*, Act III, ii): What mockery will it be, / To want the bridegroom, when the priest attends / To speak the ceremonial rites of marriage.

William Shakespeare (*The Taming of the Shrew*, Act IV, i): She shall watch all night; / And, if she chance to nod, I'll rail and bawl, / And with the clamour keep her still awake. / This is the way to kill a wife with kindness.

William Shakespeare (*The Taming of the Shrew*, Act IV, iii): O, monstrous arrogance! Thou liest, thou thread, / Thou thimble, / Thou yard, three-quarters, half-yard, quarter, nail, / Thou flea, thou nit, thou winter cricket thou: / Brav'd in mine own house with a skein of thread! / Away, thou rag, thou quantity, thou remnant; / Or I shall so be-mete thee with thy yard, / As thou shalt think on prating whilst thou liv'st! / I tell thee, I, that thou hast marr'd her gown.

William Shakespeare (*The Taming of the Shrew*, Act V, ii): Thy husband commits his body / To painful labour, both by sea and land; .... And craves no other tribute at thy hands, / But love, fair looks, and true obedience, - / Too little payment for so great a debt.

William Shakespeare (*Twelfth Night*, Act II, iv): Then let thy love be younger than thyself, / Or by affection cannot hold the bent: / For women are as roses, whose fair flower / Being once display'd, doth fall that very hour.

William Shakespeare (*Twelfth Night*, Act IV, iv): Now go with me, and with this holy man, / Into the chantry by: / And underneath that consecrated roof / Plight me the full assurance of your faith.

William Shakespeare (*Two Gentlemen of Verona*, Act II, iii): She is mine own; / And I as rich in having such a jewel / As twenty seas, if all their sand were pearl, / The water nectar, and the rocks pure gold.

George Bernard Shaw: What God hath joined together no man shall put asunder: God will take care of that.

GB Shaw: Marriage is popular because it combines the maximum of temptation with the maximum of opportunity.

Wilfred Sheed: Even the God of Calvin never judged anyone as harshly as married couples judged each other.

Simone Signoret: It is threads, hundreds of tiny threads, which sew people together through the years. That's what makes a marriage last more than passion or sex.

Carrie Snow: Why get married and make one man miserable when I can stay single and make thousands miserable.

Socrates: By all means marry. If you get a good wife, you'll be happy. If you get a bad one, you'll become a philosopher.

Gloria Steinem: The surest way to be alone is to get married.

Robert Louis Stevenson: Marriage is one long conversation chequered by disputes.

Jonathan Swift: The reason why so few marriages are happy is because young ladies spend their time in making nets, not in making cages.

Talmud: When a man marries, his sins decrease.

Talmud: If you must sell everything... marry your daughter to a scholar.

Talmud: Forty days before the creation of a child, a voice proclaims in heaven: "So-and-so's daughter for so-and-so's son!"

Talmud: The female (child) should be married first, for the shame of a woman is > the shame of a man.

Talmud: It was the custom (in ancient Judea) to plant a cedar tree when a boy was born, and to plant a Pinewood when a girl was born; and when they were married, the canopy was made of branches woven from both trees.

Talmud: It is as hard to arrange a good marriage as it was to divide the Red Sea.

Talmud: No marriage contract is made without a quarrel.

Talmud: Women want to be married more than men do.

Talmud: Females should be married before males, for the shame of a woman is greater than that of a man.

Alfred Lord Tennyson: As the husband is, the wife is.

Dennis Thatcher (husband of Margaret): Who wears the pants in this house? I do, and I also wash and iron them.

Henry David Thoreau: There is more of good nature than of good sense at the bottom of most marriages.

Mark Twain: If I were settled I would quit all nonsense & swindle some girl into marrying me. But I wouldn't expect to be *"worthy"* of her. I wouldn't *have* a girl that *I* was worthy of. *She* wouldn't do. She wouldn't be respectable enough.

Mark Twain: Separately, foreign marriages and whiskey are bad; mixed, they are fatal.

UA (Attributed to Sir Francis Buller, an English judge, 1745-1800, who in dictum announced that a husband may beat his wife with a stick no thicker than his thumb, but no substantial evidence of such an opinion exists): JUDGE THUMB.
UA: I had some words with my wife, and she had some paragraphs with me.
UA: The most effective way to remember your wife's birthday is to forget it once...
UA: Marriage is the only war where one sleeps with the enemy.
UA: A man inserted an 'ad' in the classifieds: "Wife wanted." Next day he received a hundred letters. They all said the same thing: "You can have mine."
UA: First Guy (proudly): "My wife's an angel!" Second Guy: "You're lucky, mine's still alive."
UA: When a man asks you for advice you can figure he isn't married.
Shirley Valentine: Marriage is like the Middle East – no solutions.
King Vidor (1928 film *The Crowd*): Marriage isn't a word ... it's a *sentence!*
Henny Youngman: "Some people ask the secret of our long marriage. We take time to go to a restaurant two times a week. A little candlelight, dinner, soft music and dancing. She goes Tuesdays, I go Fridays."
Henny Youngman: You know what I did before I married? Anything I wanted to.
J.B. Yeats: I think a man and a woman should choose each other for life, for the simple reason that a long life with all its accidents is barely enough for a man and a woman to understand each other; and in this case to understand is to love. The man who understands one woman is qualified to understand pretty well everything.

MAXIMS (See CHARLEY CHAN)

G.M. "Max" Abbott: She is the kind of person who would bitch if you hung her with a new rope.
Uncle Anthony: The way to get to wisdom ain't by gettin' smarter in school, but by watchin' and listenin' to a wise man.
Uncle Anthony: Didja ever notice how a really wise person can say somptin in just a couple words.
Uncle Anthony: Usin' a good short sentence is like hittin' a homerun with a short compact swing of 'da bat.
Uncle Anthony: Shakespeare said that ... I think ... and if he didn't HE SHOULDA!
Aunt Mary Carlo: Yer mom didn't need to make no speech – she'd wise us up wit' just a couple words.
Aunt Mary Carlo: Y'now a good line is like an orphan – it ain't got no parent. Anybody can adopt it an give it dere own name if it's a good quote, or ya can say it's somebody else's baby if it's a dud.
William R. Alger: Aphorisms are portable wisdom, the quintessential extracts of thought and feeling.
Peter Anderson: Stealing someone else's words frequently spares the embarrassment of eating your own.
Francis Bacon: The genius, wit, and spirit of a nation are discovered in its proverbs.
Francis Bacon: There is some degree of licentiousness and error in forming axioms.
Francis Bacon: This delivering of knowledge in distinct and disjointed aphorisms doth leave the wit of man more free to turn and toss, and to make use of that which is so delivered to more several purposes and applications.
Francis Bacon: Nor do apothegms only serve for ornament and delight, but also for action and civil use, as being the edge tools of speech, which cut and penetrate the knots of business and affairs.
Francis Bacon: Certainly apothegms are of excellent use. They are "mucrones verborum," pointed speeches. Cicero prettily called them "salinas," salt pits, that you may extract salt out of and sprinkle it where you will. They serve to be interlaced in continued speech. They serve to be recited upon occasion of themselves. They serve, if you take out the colonel of them and make them your own.
Bible: Deuteronomy, 28:37: Thou shalt become an astonishment, a proverb, and a byword, among all nations.
Bible: Ecclesiasticus, 8:8: Despise not the discourse of the wise, but acquaint thyself with their proverbs; for of them thou shalt learn instruction.
Bible: Ezek. 16:44: Every one that useth proverbs shall use this proverb against thee.
Bible: Matthew 10:16: Be ye therefore wise as serpents, and harmless as doves.
Bible: Proverbs 19:20: Hear counsel, and recieve instruction; that thou mayest be wise in thy latter end.
Bible: Proverbs 26:7: Like a lame man's legs that hang limp is a proverb in the mouth of a fool.

Ambrose Bierce: ADAGE, n. Boned wisdom for weak teeth.

Ambrose Bierce: APHORISM, n. Predigested wisdom....

Ambrose Bierce: EPIGRAM, n. A short, sharp saying in prose or verse, frequently characterized by acidity or acerbity and sometimes by wisdom. Following are some of the more notable epigrams of the learned and ingenious Dr. Jamrach Holobom: "We know better the needs of ourselves than of others. To serve oneself is economy of administration. / In each human heart are a tiger, a pig, an ass and a nightingale. Diversity of character is due to their unequal activity. / There are three sexes; males, females and girls. / Beauty in women and distinction in men are alike in this: they seem to the unthinking a kind of credibility. / Women in love are less ashamed than men. They have less to be ashamed of. / While your friend holds you affectionately by both your hands you are safe, for you can watch both his."

Ambrose Bierce: QUOTATION, n. The act of repeating erroneously the words of another. The words erreously repeated....

Ambrose Bierce: SAW, n. A trite popular saying, or proverb. (Figurative and colloquial.) So called because it makes its way into a wooden head. Following are examples of old saws fitted with new teeth. "A penny saved is a penny to squander. A man is known by the company he organizes. A bad workman quarrels with the man who calls him that. A bird in the hand is worth what it will bring. Better late than before anybody has invited you. Example is better than followingit. Half a loaf is better than a whole one if there is much else. Think twice before you speak to a friend in need. What is worth doing is worth the trouble of asking somebody to do it. Least said is soonest disavowed. He laughs best who laughs least. Speak of the Devil and he will hear about it. Of two evils choose the least. Strike while your employer has a big contract. Where there's a will there's a won't.

Ambrose Bierce: WITTICISM, n. A sharp and clever remark, usually quoted, and seldom noted; what the Philistine is pleased to call a "joke."

Cervantes: There are but few proverbial sayings that are not true, for they are all drawn from experience itself, which is the mother of all sciences.

Cervantes: A proverb is a short sentence drawn from long experiences.

Chamfort: The majority of those who put together collections of verses or epigrams resemble those who eat cherries or oysters: they begin by choosing the best and end up eating everything.

Lord Chesterfield: Most maxim-mongers have preferred the prettiness to the justness of a thought, and the turn to the truth.

Lord Chesterfield: Proverbial expressions and trite sayings are the flowers of the rhetoric of a vulgar man.... A man of fashion never has recourse to proverbs and vulgar aphorisms.

Sir Winston Churchill (Nov. 9, 1914 speech): "The maxim of the British people is **'Business as usual.'**"

Sir Winston Churchill: Mean narrow maxims which enslave mankind, ne'er from its bias warp thy settled mind.

Sir Winston Churchill: Apt analogies are among the most formidable weapons of the rhetorician

Sir Winston Churchill: It is a good thing for an uneducated man to read a book of quotations.

Sir Winston Churchill: It is a good thing for an uneducated man to read books of quotations. *Bartlett's Familiar Quotations* is an admirable work, and I studied it intently. The quotations when engraved upon the memory give you good thoughts. They also make you anxious to read the authors and look for more.

Sir Winston Churchill: I am reminded of the professor who, in his declining hours, was asked by his devoted pupils for his final counsel. He replied, "Verify your quotations."

Robert Peter Tristram Coffin: Proverbs are not merely decorations on life. They have life itself in them. They are the bedrock substance of living, built up, by many people and many years. They are the beginnings of all literature, the first metaphors and similes, the first comedies and tragedies. They are the first poetry we have.

Samuel Coleridge: A maxim is a conclusion from observation of matters of fact, and is merely speculative; a principle carries knowledge within itself, and is prospective.

Samuel Coleridge: Exclusively of the abstract sciences, the largest and worthiest portion of our knowledge consists of aphorisms, and the greatest and best of men is but an aphorism.

Samuel Coleridge: A man of maxims only, is like a Cyclops with one eye, and that in the back of his head.

Samuel Coleridge: What is an epigram? A dwarfish whole, / Its body brevity, and wit its soul.

David H. Comins: People will accept your ideas much more readily if you tell them Benjamin Franklin said it first.

Joseph Conrad: Proverbs are art—cheap art. As a general rule that are not true; unless indeed they happen to be made mere platitudes.

Charles Dickens: Proverbs or easily made in cold blood.

Denis Diderot: Pithy sentences are like sharp nails which force truth upon our memory.

Sir Kenelm Digby: Syllogisms do breed or rather are all the variety of man's life. They are the steps by which we walk in all our businesses.

Benjamin Disraeli: Proverbs were bright shafts in the Greek and Latin quivers.

Benjamin Disraeli: Proverbs were anterior to books, and formed the wisdom of the vulgar, and in the earliest ages were the unwritten laws of morality.

Isaac D'Israeli: The wise make proverbs and fools repeat them.

Isaac D'Israeli: The feathered arrow of an epigram has sometimes been wet with the heart's blood of its victim.

Dutch Proverb: Proverbs are the daughters of daily experience.

Tryon Edwards: Sense, brevity, and point are the elements of a good proverb.

Ralph Waldo Emerson: Never utter the truism, but live it among men.

Ralph Waldo Emerson: Much of the wisdom of the world is not wisdom.

Ralph Waldo Emerson: Proverbs, like the sacred books of each nation, are the sanctuary of the intuitions.

Ralph Waldo Emerson: Proverbs are the literature of reason, or the statements of absolute truth, without qualification. Like the sacred books of each nation, they are the sanctuary of its institutions.

Ralph Waldo Emerson: I hate quotations. Tell me what you know.

English Proverb: A proverb is the child of experience.

English Proverb: Old saws speak truth.

English Proverb: Common proverbs seldom lie.

English Proverb: Solomon made a book of proverbs, but a book of proverbs never made a Solomon.

Erasmus: Apothegms are in history, the same as pearls in the sand, or gold in the mind.

Joseph Farrell: Epigram and truth are rarely commensurate. Truth has to be somewhat chiselled, as it were, before it will fit into an epigram.

Benjamin Franklin: These proverbs, which contained the wisdom of many ages and nations, I assembled and formed into a connected discourse prefixed to the Almanack of 1757, as the harangue of a wise old man to the people attending an auction.

French Proverb: The maxims of men disclose their hearts.

Thomas Fuller: A proverb is much better decocted into few words.

Thomas Fuller: Constant popping off of proverbs will make thee a byword thyself.

Gaelic Proverb: Don't quote your proverb until you bring your ship into port.

German Proverb: A country can be judged by the quality of its proverbs.

Lilius Gyraldus: The epigram has been compared to a scorpion, because as the sting of the scorpion lieth in the tail, the force of the epigram is in the conclusion.

Thomas Hardy: Don't you go believing in sayings, Pecotee; they are all made by men, for their own advantage.

William Hazlitt: To repeat what has been said a thousand times is commonplace.

Hindu Saying: Proverbs are a treasury of precepts which can extricate a man from any predicament.

George Herbert: Stories and sayings they will well remember.

Charles Hodge: The value of a maxim depends on fourth things: its intrinsic excellence or the comparative correctness of the principle it embodies; the subject to which it relates; the extent of its application; and the comparative ease with which it may be applied in practice.

J. G. Holland: The proverbs of a nation furnish the index to its spirit, and the results of its civilization.

John Andrew Holmes: A ten-word epigram to be accurate needs a ten-page footnote, yet what it lacks in accuracy it makes up in nimbleness.

Horace: There are words and maxims whereby you may soothe the pain and cast much of the malady aside.

James Howell: The People's Voice the voice of God we call; And what are proverbs but the Peoples Voice?

Aldous Huxley: Proverbs are always platitudes until you have personally experienced the truth of them.

Moses Ibn-Ezra: A proverb has three characteristics: few words, right sense, fine image.

Italian Proverb (also a German Proverb): A country can be judged by the quality of its proverbs.

William James: I don't see how an epigram, being a bolt from the blue, with no introduction or cue, ever gets itself writ.

Jewish Saying: Acquaint yourself with the proverbs of the wise, for by them shalt thou be instructed.

Samuel Johnson: In all pointed sentences, some degree of accuracy must be sacrificed to conciseness.

Samuel Johnson: He is a benefactor of mankind who contracts the great rules of life into short sentences, that may be easily impressed on the memory, and so recur habitually to the mind.

Samuel Johnson: The excellence of aphorisms consists not so much in the expression of some rare or abstruse sentiment, as in the comprehension of some useful truth in few words.

Samuel Johnson: We frequently fall into error and folly, not because the true principles of action are not known, but because for a time they are not remembered; he may, therefore, justly be numbered among the benefactors of mankind who contracts the great rules of life into short sentences that may easily be impressed on the memory, and taught by frequent recollection to occur habitually to the mind.

Samuel Johnson: Classical quotation is the parole of literary men all over the world.

Joseph Joubert: Maxims are to the intellect what laws are to actions: they do not enlighten, but guide and direct, and through themselves blind, are protecting.

Joseph Joubert: I would fain coin wisdom, mould it, I mean, into maxims, proverbs, sentences, that can easily be retained and transmitted.

Joseph Joubert: A maxim is the exact and noble expression of an important and unquestionable truth.

Joseph Joubert: Proverbs may be said to be the abridgments of wisdom.

John Keats: A proverb is no proverb to you till life has illustrated it.

John Keats: Nothing ever becomes real till it is experienced – Even a proverb is no proverb to you till your life has illustrated it.

Rudyard Kipling: As I pass through my incarnations in every age and race, I make my proper prostrations to the Gods of the Market Place; peering through reverent fingers, I watch them flourish and fall, and Gods of the Copybook Headings (Maxims), I notice, outlast them all.

Jacob Klatzkin: The aphorism should be a light vessel holding a heavy load.

John Casper Lavater: The proverbial wisdom of the populace in the street, on the roads, and in the markets, instructs the ear of him who studies man more fully than a thousand rules ostentatiously displayed.

Thomas Locke: General observations drawn from particulars are the jewels of knowledge, comprehending great store in a little room.

James Russell Lowell: Though old the thought and oft exprest, / 'Tis his at last who says it best.

Thomas Macaulay: Few of the many wise apothegms which have been plundered from the time of the seven sages of Greece to that of poor Richard, have prevented a single foolish action.

Thomas Macaulay: Nothing is so useless as a general maxim.

Sir James Mackintosh (Scottish lawyer, historian, 1765-1832): Maxims are the condensed good sense of nations.

Daniel March: The proverb condenses the meaning and power of a thousand words into one short and simple sentence, and it is the more effective because it carries so much force in so compact a form.

Daniel March: Simple words, short maxims, homely truths, old sayings, are the masters of the world. In them is the hiding of the power that forms the character, controls conduct, and makes individuals and nations what they are. Great reformations, great revolutions in society, great eras in human progress and improvement, start from good words, right words, sound words, spoken in the fitting time, and finding their way to human hearts as easily as the birds find their homes.

Daniel March: Proverbs are in the world of thought what gold coin is in the world of business—great value in small compass, and equally current among all people. Sometimes the proverb may be false, the coin counterfeit, but in both cases the false proves the value of the true.

Martial: (Marcus Valerius Martialis, better known as Martial, Latin poet from Hispania – Iberian Peninsula, and known for his twelve books of Epigrams; 40AD – 102AD): Epigram's need no crier, but are content with their own tongue.

William Matthews: All maxims have their antagonist maxims; all proverbs should be sold in pairs, a single one being but a half-truth.

W. Somerset Maugham: Anyone can tell the truth, but only very few of us can make epigrams.

Midrash: Let not a simple parable seem trivial in your eyes, for through it you acquire an insight into the complex law.

Montaigne: Most men are rich in borrowed sufficiency: a man may very well say a good thing, give a good answer, cite a good sentence, without at all seeing the force of either the one or the other.

Christopher Morley: Such is epigram, requiring / Wit, occasion, and good luck.

Moses Ibn Ezra: A proverb has three characteristics: few words, good sense, and a fine image.

William Motherwell: The study of proverbs may be more instructive and comprehensive than the most elaborate scheme of philosophy.

Theodore Munger: Proverbs are but rules, and rules do not create character.—They prescribe conduct, but do not furnish a full and proper motive.—They are usually but half-truths, and seldom contain the principle of the action they teach.

Theodore Munger: Proverbs are the condensed wisdom of long experience, in brief, epigrammatic form, easily remembered and always ready for use.—They are the alphabet of morals; they are commonly prudential watchwords and warnings, and so lean toward a selfish view of life.

James A. Murray: Nothing hits harder, or sticks longer in the memory, than an apothegm.

Friedrich Nietzsche: A good aphorism is too hard for the tooth of time, and is not worn away by all the centuries, although it serves as food for every epoch.

Coventry Patmore: The most ardent love is rather epigrammatic than lyrical.

Coventry Patmore: The highest and deepest thoughts do not "voluntary move harmonious numbers," but rather run to grotesgue epigram and doggerel.

William Penn: The wisdom of nations lies in their proverbs, which are brief and pithy. Collect and learn them; they are notable measures of directions for human life; you have much in little; they save time in speaking; and upon occasion may be the fullest and safest answers.

Persian Proverb: Epigrams succeed where epics fail.

Andrew Ramsay: Apothegms to thinking minds are the seeds from which spring vast yields of new thought, that may be further cultivated, unified, and enlarged.

John Ray: Proverbs are the wisdom of the streets.

Leo Rosten: MISHLE: Hebrew: "proverbs." This is the name in Hebrew for the Book of Proverbs.

Leo Rosten: The Power of Proverbs: Men quote proverbs the better to express themselves. Adages are the wit of the inarticulate. Proverbs are the gospel of the poor. Folk sayings are the college of the masses. More important: Proverbs are what a people—any people—believe, cherish, and teach their young. They are those gleanings of knowledge and experience with which the dead dower each generation of the living. Shakespeare has a phrasing that runs: "Weak patch grief with proverbs." I think we do more than that. We patch our ignorance and our impotence with them, two.... indeed, the Proverbs is often reason laid bare, arguments stripped of fat, complexity clarified beyond this interpretation.

Leo Rosten: You may retort that proverbs often contradict one another (as any reader of anthologies,... soon discovers). The sagacity that advises us to look before we leap promptly warns us that if we hesitate we are lost; that absence makes the heart grow fonder, but out of sight, out of mind. What can we believe? Simply that life as is full of contradictions, that proverbs reflect and express them, and that many apothegms are more witty than true.

Leo Rosten: Proverbs, said Emerson, are "the sanctuary of our institutions. But they are more: they are the precious distillation of what man has learned from centuries of experience. Aristotle considered apothegms the product of intellectual maturity and, recognizing their enormous power, declared it "unbecoming" for the young to utter maxims!

Leo Rosten: The Talmud, (is) that monumental compendium of 1200 years of dialectics (from the 5th century before, to the 8th century of, the Christian Era) and commentaries, discussion and debate on the Torah (the first five books of the Old Testament) and the post-Biblical sages, is an inexhaustible treasure trove of pithy sagacities (in Aramaic) on every conceivable aspect of faith, life, law, man, virtue, evil, customs, morals and mores. The names of over 2000 rabbi-teachers appear in the Talmud; so far as I know, no one has counted the apothegms.

Joseph Roux: A fine quotation is a diamond on the finger of a man of wit, and a pebble in the hand of a fool.

Joseph Roux: A maker of maxims is synonymous with a pessimist.

Lord John Russell: The wisdom of many, and the wit of one.

Lord John Russell: A proverb is one man's wit and all men's wisdom.

George Santayana: Almost every wise saying has an opposite one, no less wise, to balance it.

Seneca: Precepts or maxims are great weight; and a few useful ones at hand do more toward a happy life than whole volumes that we know not where to find.

Anthony Ashley Cooper, Lord of Shaftsbury: As a malicious censure, carefully worded and pronounced with assurance, is apt to pay us with mankind for truth with, so a purulent maxim in bold expressions, though without any justness of one, is readily received for true philosophy.

William Shakespeare (*As You Like It*, Act II, vii): Full of wise saws and modern instances.

William Shakespeare (*Hamlet*, Act III, ii): The proverb is something musty.

Wayne Shakespeare (*I Henry IV*, Act I, ii): He was never yet a breaker of proverbs.

William Shakespeare (*King Lear*, Act I, v): Thou shouldst not have been old till thou hadst been wise.

William Shakespeare (*King Lear*, Act II, iv): When a wise man gives thee better counsel, give me mine again.

William Shakespeare, (*Love's Labour's Lost*, Act IV, i): An old saying, that was a man when King Pepin of France was a little boy.

William Shakespeare (*Much Ado About Nothing*, Act V, i): Patch grief with proverbs.

William Shakespeare (*Romeo and Juliet*, Act I, iv): For I am proverb'd with a grandsire phrase.

Karl Shapiro: The proverbist knows nothing of the two sides of a question. He knows only the roundness of the answers.

Sir Henry Sidney: If you hear a wise sentence or an apt phrase, commit it to your memory.

Charles Simmons: Sensible men show their sense by saying much in few words.—If noble actions are the substance of life, good sayings are its ornament and guide.

Ben Sirach: A parable from a fool is worthless because he tells it at the wrong time.

Sophocles: A short saying oft contains much wisdom.

Robert South: The Scripture vouches Solomon for the wisest of men; and his proverbs prove him so. The seven wise men of Greece, so famous for their wisdom all the world over, acquired all that fame each of them by a single sentence, consisting of two or three words.

Robert Louis Stevenson: There is a strong feeling in favor of cowardly and prudential proverbs.... Most of our pocket wisdom is conceived for the use of mediocre people, to discourage them from ambitious attempts, and generally console them in their mediocrity

Robert Louis Stevenson: Man is a creature who lives not upon bread alone, but principally by catchwords.

Jonathan Swift: The two maxims of any great man at court are, always to keep his countenance, and never to keep his word.

Jonathan Swift: It is hard to form a maxim against which an exception is not ready to start up: as "where the minister grows rich, the public is proportionately poor"; as "in a private family the steward always thrives the fastest when the lord is running out."

Sir William Temple: Books and proverbs receive their chief value from the stamp and esteem of ages through which they have passed.

Alfred Lord Tennyson: Jewels five words long, that on the stretched forefinger of all-time sparkle forever.

John Tillotson: The short sayings of wise and good men are of great value, like the dust of gold, or the sparks of diamonds.

Mark Twain: What are the proper proportions of a maxim? A minimum of sound to a maximum of sense.

Mark Twain: It is more trouble to make a maxim than it is to do right.

Mark Twain: One good thing Adam had—when he said a good thing he knew nobody had said it before.

UA: Proverbs are the cream of the nation's thought.

Henry Van Dyke: Epigrams are worth little for guidance to the perplexed, and less for comfort to the wounded.

Hendrik Wilhelm Van Loon: Somewhere in the world there is an epigram for every dilemma.

Vauvenargues: The maxims of men reveal their characters.

Maggie & Catie Vesper: Words of "T-Shirt Wisdom":

Never judge a day by the weather.
The best things in life are not things.

Always tell the truth – there's less to remember.
Speak softly and wear a loud shirt.
Goals are deceptive—the unaimed arrow never misses.
He who dies with the most toys... still dies.
Age is relative—when you're over the hill, you pick up speed.
There are two ways to be rich—make more or desire less.
Beauty is eternal—looks mean nothing.
No rain—no rainbows.

Richard Whately (Archbishop of Dublin, 1863): Proverbs are somewhat analogous to those medical formulas which, being in frequent use, are kept ready made up in the chemists' shops, and which often save the framing of a distinct prescription.

MEDICINE (See DOCTORS)

MELANCHOLY (See EMOTIONAL DISTRESS)

MEMORY

Uncle Anthony: If you really want to improve your memory, just lend somebody some money.
Uncle Anthony: Sometimes we got the best memory of the things we most wanna forget.
Aunt Mary Carlo: I'll never ferget ... whatzizname? ... or whaddycallit?
Aeschylus: Memory is the mother of all wisdom.
Sholem Asch: Not the power to remember, but it's very opposite, the power to forget, is a necessary condition for our existence.
St. Basil: Memory is the cabinet of imagination, the treasury of reason, the registry of conscience, and the council chamber of thought.
Bible: Apocrypha, Ecclesiasticus 9:10: Forsake not an old friend, for a new one does not compare with him.
Bible: Apocrypha, Ecclesiasticus 9:10: A new friend is like new wine; when it has aged you will drink it with pleasure.
Bible: Romans 14:5: Let every man be fully persuaded in his own mind.
Ambrose Bierce: MIND, n. A mysterious form of matter secreted by the brain. Its chief activity consists in the endeavor to ascertain its own nature, the futility of the attempt being due to the fact that it has nothing but itself to know itself with. From the Latin *mens*, a fact unknown to that honest shoe-seller, who, observing that his learned competitor over the way had displayed the motto "*Mens conscia recti*," emblazoned his own shop front with the words "Men's, women's and children's conscia recti."
Ambrose Bierce: RECOLLECT, v. To recall with additions something not previously known.
Ambrose Bierce: REFLECTION, n. An action of the mind whereby we obtain a clearer view of our relation to the things of yesterday and are able to avoid the perils that we shall not again encounter.
Lewis Carroll: "The horror of that moment," the King went on, "I shall never, never forget!" / "You will, though," the Queen said, "if you don't make a memorandum of it."
Chinese Proverb: The palest ink is better than the best memory.
Sir Winston Churchill: It is a good thing for an uneducated man to read books of quotations. The quotations, when engraved upon the memory, give you good thoughts. They also make you anxious to read the authors and look for more
Sir Winston Churchill: Although present on the occasion, I have no clear recollection of the events leading up to it.
Sr Winston Churchill: Those who forget history are bound to repeat it
Cicero: Memory is the treasury and guardian of all things.
Cicero: Memory is the receptacle and sheath of all knowledge.
Joseph Conrad: In plucking the fruit of memory one runs the risk of spoiling its bloom.
Dante: There is no greater sorrow than to recall, in misery, the time when we were happy.
George Eliot: Some call her Memory, / And some Tradition; and her voice is sweet, / With deep mysterious accords.

English Proverb: Last ship, best ship.

English Saying (about celebration of the plot against King James I and plan to blow up Parliament on November 5, 1605 = Guy Faux Day): Please to remember, the 5th of November, / Gunpowder, treason and plot. / I see no reason why gunpowder treason / Should ever be forgot!

Thomas Fuller: Memory (is) a purse,—if it be overfull that it cannot shut, all will drop out of it. Take heed of a gluttonous curiosity to feed on many things, lest the greediness of the appetite of thy memory spoil the digestion thereof.

Thomas Fuller: Method is the mother of memory.

Thomas Fuller: That which is bitter to endure may be sweet to remember.

German Proverb: How sweet to remember the trouble that is past!

Lillian Hellman: Nothing, of course, begins at the time you think it did.

John Heywood (*The Proverbs of John Heywood*, 1546): Went in one ear and out the other.

Thomas Hobbes: Imagination and memory are but one thing which for divers considerations have divers names.

Oliver Wendell Holmes, Sr.: Memory is a net; one finds it full of fish when he takes it from the brook; but a dozen miles of water have run through it without sticking.

Horace: The jar will long retain the fragrance with which it was steeped when new.

Jewish Saying: Two things get weaker with time: your teeth in your memory.

Jewish Saying: What's good, we remember; what's bad, we feel.

Samuel Johnson: The true art of memory is the art of attention.

Rudyard Kipling: The tumult and the shouting dies; / The captains and the kings depart: / Still stands Thine ancient sacrifice, / An humble and a contrite heart. / Lord God of Hosts, be with us yet, / Les we forget—lest we forget!

Ben Jonson: Memory, of all the powers of the mind, is the most delicate and frail.

Samuel Johnson: The true art of memory is the art of attention.

François Duc de La Rochefoucauld: Everyone complains of his lack of memory, but nobody of his want of judgment.

Henry Wadsworth Longfellow: Nothing now is left But a majestic memory.

John Milton: The bitter memory space last space Of what he was, what is, and what must be.

Montaigne: Experience teaches us that a good memory is generally joined to a weak judgment.

John Mortimer: RUMPOLE'S RUBRIC: "Spectacles, testicles, wallet & watch."

Friedrich Nietzsche: Many a man fails to become a thinker for the sole reason that his memory is too good.

Ovid: When time has assuaged the wounds of the mind, he who unseasonably reminds us of them, opens them afresh.

Dorothy Parker: Women and elephants never forget.

Plutarch: Memory: what wonders it performs in preserving and storing up things gone by, or rather, things that are!

Robin Post: (book *Brothers in Battle – Best of Friends: William "Wild Bill" Guarnere and Edward "Babe" Heffron, Two WWII Paratroopers from the Original Band of Brothers (101st Airborne Div, Easy Company) Tell Their Story):* On Sept 17, 1944 the US Army 101st Division, aka "Screaming Eagles," liberated Holland from the Nazis, during Operation "Market Garden." Matthew VanLeicht and the "Dutch Airborne Friends" have arranged EVERY YEAR since 1944 to have the Dutch town of Eindhoven, and others celebrate "REMEMBER SEPTEMBER" on Sept 17.

Jean Paul Richter: Recollection is the only paradise from which we cannot be turned out.

Will Rogers: We know lots of things we didn't use to know but we don't know any way to prevent 'em from happening.

Will Rogers: "When you write down the good things you ought to have done, and leave out the bad things you did do, that's memoirs."

William Shakespeare (*Alls Well That Ends Well*, Act V, iii): Praising what is lost / Makes the remembrance dear.

William Shakespeare (*The Comedy of Errors*, Act V, i): Yet hath my night of life some memory, / My wasting lamps some fading glimmer left.

William Shakespeare (*Hamlet*, Act I, iii): 'Tis in my memory lock'd, / And you yourself shall keep the key of it

William Shakespeare (*Hamlet*, Act I, v): Remember thee? / Ay, thou poor ghost, while memory holds a seat / In this distracted globe. Remember thee? / Yea, from the table of my memory / I'll wipe away all trivial fond records.

William Shakespeare (*Hamlet*, Act III, ii): Purpose is but the slave to memory.

William Shakespeare (*Hamlet*, Act III, ii): Die two months ago, and not forgotten yet? / Then there's hope a great man's memory may outlive his life half a year.

William Shakespeare (*Hamlet*, Act IV, v): There's rosemary, that's for remembrance.

William Shakespeare (*King Lear*, Act IV, vi): Briefly thyself remember.

William Shakespeare (*Macbeth,* Act I, vii): Memory, the warder of the brain, / shall be a fume.

William Shakespeare (*Macbeth,* Act IV, iii): I cannot but remember such things were, / That were most precious to me.

William Shakespeare (*Merchant of venice*, Act I, i): I should not see the sandy hour-glass run, / But I should think of shallows and of flats; / And see my wealthy Andrew dock'd in sand, / Vailing her high-top lower than her ribs, / To kiss her burial.

William Shakespeare (*Much Ado About Nothing,* Act IV, i): The idea of her life shall sweetly creep / Into his study of imagination, / And every lovely organ of her life / Shall come apparell'd in more precious habit, / More moving-delicate and full of life, / Into the eye and prospect of his soul.

William Shakespeare (*Othello*, Act II, iii): I remember a mass of things, but nothing distinctly; a quarrel, but nothing wherefore.

William Shakespeare (*Richard II*, Act II, ii): I count myself in nothing else so happy, / As in a soul rememb'ring my good friends; / And, as my fortune ripens with thy love, / It shall be still thy true love's recompense.

William Shakespeare (*Richard II*, Act III, iv): THE GARDENER speaks about the QUEEN, wife of KING RICHARD II, DUCHESS OF GLOUCESTER, who leaves with her ladies in waiting after he has just reported the "black tidings" that King Richard II was deposed): Here did she fall a tear; here in this place / I'll set a bank of rue, sour herb of grace: / Rue, even for ruth, here shortly shall be seen, / In the remembrance of a weeping queen.

William Shakespeare (*Romeo and Juliet*, Act III, ii): It presses to my memory, / Like damned, guilty deeds to sinners' minds.

William Shakespeare (*Sonnets*, No. 30): When to the sessions of sweet silent thought / I summon up remembrance of things past, / I sigh the lack of many in thing I sought, / And with old woes new whale my dear time's waste.

William Shakespeare (*The Tempest,* Act V, i): Let us not burden our remembrance with / A heaviness that's gone.

William Shakespeare (*The Tempest,* Act V, i): How sharp the point of this remembrance is!

William Shakespeare (*Two Gentlemen of Verona*, Act V, iv): O thou that dost inhabit in my breast, / Leave not the mansion so long tenantless; / Lest, growing ruinous, the building fall, / And leave no memory of what it was.

William Shakespeare (*Winter's Tale*, Act I, ii): Looking on the lines / Of my boy's face, my thoughts I did recoil / Twenty-three years; and saw myself unbreech'd, / In my green velvet coat; my dagger muzzled, / Lest it should bite its master, and so prove, / As ornaments oft do, too dangerous.

R.B. Sheridan: The Right Honorable gentleman is indebted to his memory for his jests and to his imagination for his facts.

Alfred Lord Tennyson: This is truth the poet sings / a sorrow's crown of sorrows is remembering happy happier things.

Martin Farquhar Tupper: Memory is not wisdom; idiots can by rote repeat volumes. Yet what is wisdom without memory?

Mark Twain: It isn't so astonishing, the number of things that I can remember, as the number of things I can remember that aren't so.

UA (English Saying about celebration of the plot against King James I and plan to blow up Parliament on November 5, 1605 = Guy Faux Day): Please to remember, the 5th of November, / Gunpowder, treason and plot. / I see no reason why gunpowder treason / Should ever be forgot!
UA: Writing things down is the best secret of a good memory.
UA: What was hard to endure is sweet to recall. Good memories have ill judgments.
UA: Memory of happiness makes misery woeful.
UA: Sorrow remembered sweetens present joy.
UA: That which is better to endure may be sweet to remember.
UA: The true art of memory is the art of attention.
Virgil: Perchance someday the memory of this sorrow space Will even bring delight.

MEN

Uncle Anthony (from the musical *Robin and the Seven Hoods*): Any man who loves his mother is man enough for me.
Uncle Anthony: Didja hear about whaddatheycallit a "MANCATION?" It's where guys go off someplace with the guys – in my time we called 'em a bachelor's party or just a drinking binge.
Uncle Anthony: I like a man who's the same Saturday night as on Sunday morning.
Aunt Mary Carlo: I tink he's lookin' for a well formed not a well informed woman.
Aunt Mary Carlo: He's so old, he's forgot why he's still chasin' women.
W.H. Auden: Whether, as some psychologists believe, some women suffer from penis envy, I am not sure. I am quite certain, however, that all males without exception suffer from penis rivalry, and that this trait has now become a threat to the future existence of the human race.
Bible: Apocrypha, Ecclesiasticus 13:25: A man's heart changes his countenance, either for good or for evil.
Bible: 1 Corinthians 15:47: The first man is of the earth, earthy.
Bible: Genesis 1:27: So God created man in his own image, in the image of God created he him; male and female created he them.
Bible: Genesis 2:7: The Lord God formed man of the dust of the ground, and breathed into his nostrils the breath of life; and man became a living soul.
Bible: Deuteronomy 8:3: Man doth not live by bread only.
Bible: Isaiah 64:8: We are the clay, and thou (Lord) our potter.
Bible: Jeremiah 17:5: Thus saith the Lord; Cursed be the man that trusteth in man.
Bible: Job 4:17: Shall a man be more pure than his maker?
Bible: Job 5:7: Man is born into trouble, as the sparks fly upwards.
Bible: Job 14:1: Man that is born of a woman is of few days, and full of trouble. He cometh forth like a flower, and is cut down: he fleeth also as a shadow and continueth not.
Bible: Psalms 8:4: What is man, that thou art mindful of him? Thou hast made him a little lower than the angels.
Bible: Psalms 62:9: Surely men of low degree are vanity, and men of high degree are a lie.
Bible: Psalms 103:15: As for man, his days are as grass: as a flower of the field, so he flourisheth.
Bible: Psalms 139:14: I am fearfully and wonderfully made.
Ambrose Bierce: CIRCUS, n. A place where horses, ponies and elephants are permitted to see men, women and children acting the fool.
Ambrose Bierce: CURIOSITY, n. An objectionable quality of the female mind. The desire to know whether or not a woman is cursed with curiosity is one of the most active and insatiable passions of the masculine soul.
Ambrose Bierce: HUSBAND, n. One who, having dined, is charged with the care of the plate.
Ambrose Bierce: MALE, n. A member of the unconsidered, or negligible sex. The male of the human race is commonly known (to the female) as Mere Man, The genus has two varieties: good providers and bad providers.
Ambrose Bierce: MAN: An animal (whose) ... chief occupation is extermination of other animals and his own species, which, however, multiplies with such insistent rapidity as to infest the whole habitable earth and Canada.

Ambrose Bierce: MAN, n. An animal so lost in rapturous contmplation of what he thinks he is as to overlook what he indubitably ought to be....

Ambrose Bierce: MISS, n. A title with which we brand unmarried women to indicate that they are in the market. Miss, Missis (Mrs.) and Mister (Mr.) are the three most distinctly disagreeable words in the language, in sound and sense. Two are corruptions of Mistress, the other of Master. In the general abolition of social titles in this our country they miraculously escaped to plague us. If we must have them let us be consistent and give one to the unmarried man. I venture to suggest MUSH, abbreviated to Mh.

Ambrose Bierce: MOUTH, n. In man, the gateway to the soul; in woman, the outlet of the heart.

Ambrose Bierce: OCCIDENT, n. The part of the world lying west (or east) of the Orient. It is largely inhabited by Christians, a powerful subtribe of the Hypocrites, whose principal industries are murder and cheating, which they are pleased to call "war" and "commerce." These, also, are the principal industries of the Orient.

Ambrose Bierce: For every man there is something in the vocabulary that would stick to him like a second skin. His enemies have only to find it.

Irma Bombeck: Man is the only creature endowed with the ability and power of laughter … and is he not also the only creature worth laughing at?

Myron Brenton: It's fallacious to go in for a so-called masculine activity in order to arrive at a masculine attitude. The two just aren't synonymous, although it's characteristic of men caught in the masculinity trap to confuse activity with attitude.

Myron Brenton: The problems besetting men have many names. Call them boredom and restlessness and discontent and frustration. In some men they're intense and consistent. In the majority of men they're much more vague and sporadic. There's a feeling that the job, the wife, the sex, the kids, or the leisure time – in short, the good life – is ... well ... good, but not *that* good. Real fulfillment, one senses, is a long way around the corner.

Heywood Broun: Men build bridges and throw railroads across deserts, and yet they contend successfully that the job of sewing on a button is beyond them.

Pearl Buck: It takes a brave man to face a brave woman, and man's fear of woman's creative energy has never found an expression more clear than in the old German clamor, renewed by the Nazis, of "*Kinder, Kuchen* and *Kirche*" for women.

Samuel Butler: Man is the only animal that laughs and has a state legislature.

Albert Camus: A single sentence will suffice for modern man: He fornicated and read the papers.

Chinese Proverb: The man who strikes first admits that his ideas have given out.

Sir Winston Churchill: I like pigs. Dogs look up to us. Cats look down on us. Pigs treat us as equals.

Sir Winston Churchill: Too often the strong, silent man is silent only because he does not know what to say, and is reputed strong only because he has remained silent.

Sir Winston Churchill: Great and good are seldom the same man.

Stephen Craine (*War is Kind, and Other Lines*, XXI, 1899): A man said to the Universe: "Sir, I exist." "However," replied the Universe, "the fact has not created in me a sense of obligation."

Ellen DeGeneres: The only thing that scares me more than space aliens is the idea that there aren't any space aliens. We can't be the best that creation has to offer.

Benjamin Disraeli: Every man has a right to be conceited until he is successful.

Will Durst: Men are superior to women. For one thing, they can urinate from a speeding car.

Ralph Waldo Emerson: A man is known of the books he reads.

English Proverb: Sorrow for a husband is like a pain in the elbow, sharp and short.

English Proverb: Six hours' sleep for a man, seven for a woman and eight for a fool.

William Faulkner: I believe that Man will not merely endure, he will prevail. He is immortal not because he alone among creatures has an inexhaustible voice, but because he has a soul, a spirit capable of compassion and sacrifice and endurance.

Edna Ferber: Men often marry their mothers.

Malcolm Forbes: Men who never get carried away should be.

Ben Franklin: Many men die at twenty-five and aren't buried until they are seventy-five.

French Proverb: If you would understand men, study women.

French Proverb: The best thing about a man is his dog.

Sigmund Freud (1932 Letter to Albert Einstein): You surmise that Man has in him an active instinct for hatred and destruction. I entirely agree. Psychoanalysts have come to the conclusion that two types of human instincts were woven together: those that conserve and unify which we call "erotic" and secondly the instincts to destroy and kill which we assimilate as the "aggressive" or "destructive" instincts. Each of these instincts is every bit as indispensible as its opposite, and all of the phenomena of life derive from their activity, whether they work in concert or opposition ... The upshot of these observations is that there is no likelihood of our being able to suppress humanity's aggressive tendencies..."

Ibn Gabirol: There are four types of men in this world: / The man who knows, and knows that he knows: he is wise, so consult him. / The man who knows, but doesn't know that he knows: help him not forget what he knows. / The man who knows not, and knows that he knows not: teach him. / Finally, there is the man knows not but pretends that he knows: he is a fool, so avoid him.

German Proverb: When a boy is growing he has a wolf in his belly.

Greek Proverb: Though boys throw stones at frogs in sport, the frogs do not die in sport, but in earnest.

Hasidic Saying: Man is endowed by nature with two eyes: one to see his neighbors' virtues, the other to see his own faults.

Hasidic Saying: In everyone there is something precious, found in no one else; so honor each man for what is hidden within him—for what he alone has done and none of his fellows.

Hasidic Saying: The man who believes he can live without others is mistaken; and the man who thinks others can live without him is more mistaken.

John Oliver Hobbes: Men are all the same. They always think that something they are going to get is better than what they have got.

John Oliver Hobbes: Men don't understand, as a rule, that women like to get use to them by degrees.

Oliver Wendell Holmes, Jr. (February 4, 1901, the 100th anniversary of the day John Marshall took his seat as Chief Justice of the United States): A great man represents a great ganglion in the nerves of society, or, to vary the figure, a strategic point in the campaign of history, and part of his greatness consists in his being *there*.

Elbert Hubbard: One machine can do the work of fifty ordinary man. No machine can do the work of one extraordinary man.

Ibsen (Pere Gint): THE BUTTON MAKER: " ... men, like buttons are designed with a definite shape and function – to hold things together with order and harmony.

Italian Proverb: The right man comes at the right time.

William James: Man, biologically considered ... is the most formidable of all the beasts of prey, and, indeed, the only one that preys systematically on its species.

Jewish Saying: It is easier to know ten countries than one man.

Jewish Proverb: Every man has his own *meshugas* (craziness).

Jewish Proverb: To know a man you must ride in the same cart with him.

Jewish Saying: Every man is blind—to himself.

Jewish Saying: A bachelor is a man who comes to work each morning from a different direction.

Jewish Saying: An old man who marries a young wife grows younger—but she grows older.

Jewish Saying: It is better for a woman to have one husband, though he be useless, than wealthy children.

Jewish Saying: When a Man is too good for this world, it's too bad for his wife.

Jewish Saying: A Man is what he is, not what he used to be.

Jewish Saying: All virtues in one man are nowhere to be found.

Jewish Saying: A Man is weaker than a straw and stronger than iron.

Jewish Saying: Animals have long tongues and can't speak; men have shortcomings and dare not.

Jewish Saying: The world is full of troubles, but each man feels only his own.

Jewish Saying: Men should take care not to make women weep, for God counts their tears.

Jewish Saying: Man's brains are his jewels; women's jewels are her brains.

Sayings of the Jewish Fathers: There are four types among men: / The ordinary one says: "What is mine is mine, and what is yours is yours." / The queer one says: "What is mine is yours, and what is yours is mine." / The saintly one says: "What is mine is yours, and what is yours is yours." / The wicked one says: "What is mine is mine, and what is yours is also mine.

Sayings of the Jewish Fathers: There are four types of temperaments: easy to provoke and easy to calm—here the fault is canceled by the virtue; hard to provoke, but hard to calm—here the virtue is canceled by the fault; hard to provoke, and easy to calm—this is the temperament of a good man; easy to provoke but hard to calm—this is the temperament of the wicked.

Sayings of the Jewish Fathers: The bashful man cannot learn, the ill-tempered man cannot teach, and the one who preoccupies himself with worldly affairs cannot impart wisdom.

Lynden B. Johnson: If two men agree on everything, you may be sure that one of them is doing the thinking.

Carl Jung: The meeting of two personalities is like the contact of two chemical substances: if there is any reaction, both are transformed.

Martin Luther King. Jr.: Our science has outrun our spiritual power. We have guided missiles and misguided men.

Andrew Kirkpatrick (Chief Justice NJ Supreme Court): Man with all his wisdom, **toils for heirs he knows not who.** Nevison v. Taylor, 8 N.J.L. 43, 46 (1824)

Alan Jay Lerner and Frederick Loewe (in 1956 opening New York show of their Broadway musical *My Fair Lady*, in the song *"I'm an Ordinary Man,"* Professor Henry Higgins answers his friend Colonel Pickering's warning that a bachelor living in the same house with a young woman calls for a man of character with regard to women): HIGGINS: No man has good character where women are concerned. He has learned, he assures his friend Colonel Pickering, that he will never let a woman in his life:

Alan Jay Lerner and Frederick Loewe (in 1956 opening New York show of their Broadway musical *My Fair Lady*, in the song *"A Hymn to Him,"* Professor Henry Higgins asks his friend Colonel Pickering why Eliza Doolittle has left): HIGGINS: What in all in Heaven can have prompted her to go? / After such a triumph at the ball? / What could have depressed her? / What could have possessed her? / I cannot understand the wretch at all. // Women are irrational, that's all there is to that! / Their heads are full of cotton, hay and rags! / They're nothing but exasperating, irritating, / Vacillating, calculating, agitating, / Maddening and infuriating hags! // Pickering, **why can't a woman be more like a man?** / Hm? Yes, why can't a woman be more like a man? // Men are so honest, so thoroughly square, / Eternally noble, historically fair; / Who when you win will always give your back a pat. / Why can't a woman be like that? / Why does everyone do what the others do? / Can't a woman learn to use her head? / Why do they do everything their mothers do? / Why don't they grow up, like their fathers instead? // Why can't a woman take after a man? / Men are so pleasant, so easy to please; / Whenever you're with them, you're always at ease. / Would you be slighted if I didn't speak for hours? PICKERING: Of course not. HIGGINS: Would you be livid if I had a drink or two? PICKERING: Nonsense. HIGGINS: Would you be wounded if I never sent you flowers? PICKERING: Never. HIGGINS: Well, why can't a woman be like you? /// .... Why can't a woman be more like a man? / If I were a woman who'd been to a ball, / Been hailed as a princess by one and by all; / Would I start weeping like a bathtub overflowing? / Carry on as if my home were in a tree? / Would I run off and never tell me where I'm going? / Why can't a woman be like me?"

Maimonides: There is no such thing as two men exactly alike—nor two thoughts.

Maimonides: By nature we like the familiar and dislike the strange.

Maimonides: Man like the opinions to which they have been accustomed from their youth; they defended them, and shun contrary views: and this is one of the things that prevents men from finding truth, for they cling to the opinions of habit.

Stella Terrill Mann: Whatever God's dream about man may be, it seems certain it cannot come true unless man cooperates.

Midrash: Ecclesiastes Rabbah, 1:2: At one, man is a king, adored by all; at two, he is like a pig, wallowing in dirt; at ten, he skips like a goat; at twenty, he neighs like a horse; married, he works like an ass; when a father, he snarls like a dog; and when old, he dodders like an ape.

Larry Miller: To women, we are like big dogs that talk.

Robin Morgan: Do not accept rides from strange men, and remember that all men are strange.

Ogden Nash (American poet, 1902-1971, *Portrait of the Artist as a Prematurely Old Man*): It is common knowledge to every schoolboy and even every Bachelor of Arts, / That all sin is divided into two parts. / One kind of sin is called a sin of commission, and that is very important, / And it is what you are doing when you are doing something you oughtant, / And the other kind of sin is just the opposite and is called / a sin of omission and is equally bad in the eyes of all / right-thinking people, from Billy Sunday to Buddha, And it consists of not having done something you shuddha. / .... The moral is that it is probably better not to sin at all, / but if some kind of sin you must be pursuing, / Well, remember to do it by doing rather than by not doing.

Ogden Nash (American poet, *The Perfect Husband*): He tells you when you've got on too much lipstick, / And helps you with your girdle when your hips stick.

Abot de Rabbi Nathan: A man is a world in miniature.

Abot de Rabbi Nathan: One man is equivalent to all creation.

Carrie Nations (1846-1911, temperance leader and founding member of the Women's Christian Temperance Union, she accompanied by hymn-singing women, would march into bars in Kansas and Missouri and sing and pray, while smashing bar fixtures and stock with a hatchet. Between 1900 and 1910, she was arrested 30 times for "hatchetations," as she came to call her deeds): Men are nicotine-soaked, beer-besmirched, whiskey-greased, red-eyed devils.

Friedrich Nietzsche: Man is more an ape than many of the apes.

Kathleen Norris: Men are more conventional than women and much slower to change their ideas.

Sioux Chief "Old Lodge Skins" (after June 25-26, 1876 Battle of Little Big Horn): Yes, my son, is finished now... there is no permanent winning or losing when things move as they should in a circle. But the white men, who live in squares and straight lines do not believe as I do. To them it is everything or nothing.... Winning is all they care about. And if they can do that by scratching a pen across a paper or saying something into the wind, they are much happier.

Dorothy Parker (American satirist and poet): I require three things in a man. He must be handsome, ruthless, and stupid.

Dorothy Parker (American satirist and poet, 1893-1967, *Men*): They hail you as their morning star / because you are the way you are. / If you return the sentiment, / They'll try to make you different; / And once they have you, safe and sound, / They want to change you all around. / Your moods and ways they put a curse on; / They'd make of you another person. / They cannot let you go your gait; / They influence and educate, / They'd alter all that they admired. / They make me sick, they make me tired.

Dorothy Parker (American satirist and poet, *Tombstones in the Starlight, III. The Very Rich Man*): He'd have the best, and that was none too good; / No barrier could hold, before his terms. / He lies below, correct in cypress wood, / And entertains the most exclusive worms.

Blaise Pascal: Man is equally incapable of seeing the nothingness from which he emerges and the infinity in which he is engulfed.

Jules Renard: The only man who is really free is the one who can turn down an invitation to dinner without giving an excuse.

Will Rogers: God made man a little lower than the angels, and he has been getting a little lower ever since.

Will Rogers: Nothing makes a man or body of men as mad as truth. If there is no truth in it they laugh if off.

Motitz Rosenthal: A man is young if a girl can make him happy or unhappy; he enters middle age when a woman can make him happy but not unhappy; he becomes old when a woman can make him neither happy nor unhappy.

Helen Rowland: The average man takes all the natural taste out of his food by covering it with ready-made sauces, and all the personality out of a woman by covering her with his ready-made ideals.

Helen Rowland: Every man wants a woman to appeal to his better side, his nobler instincts and his higher nature – and another woman to help him forget them.

Red Skelton: All men make mistakes, but married men find out about them sooner.

Mort Sahl: The bravest thing that men do is love women.

Francoise Sagan: I like men to behave like men – strong and childish.

William Shakespeare (*As You Like It,* Act IV, i): Men have died from time to time, and worms have eaten them, but not for love.

William Shakespeare (*Hamlet*, Act I, ii): He was a man, take him for all in all, / I shall not look upon his like again.

William Shakespeare (*Hamlet*, Act II, ii): What a piece of work is a man! How noble in reason! how infinite in faculty! in form and moving how express and admirable! in action how like an angel! in apprehension how like a god! the beauty of the world! the paragon of animals! And yet, to me, what is this quintessence of dust? man delights not me: no, nor woman neither.

William Shakespeare (*Hamlet*, Act III, ii): I have thought some of Nature's journeymen had made men and not made them well, they imitated humanity so abominably.

William Shakespeare (*Hamlet*, Act III, ii): Give me that man / That is not passion's slave, and I will wear him / In my heart's core, ay, in my heart of heart, / As I do thee.

William Shakespeare (*Hamlet*, Act III, iv): A combination, and a form, indeed, / Where every god did seem to set his seal, / To give the world assurance of a man.

William Shakespeare (*Hamlet*, Act IV, iv): What is a man / If his chief good, and market of his time, / Be but to sleep and feed?

William Shakespeare (*Hamlet*, Act IV, iv): What is a man / If his chief good, and market of his time, / Be but to sleep and feed? A beast, no more.

William Shakespeare (*Henry VIII*, Act V, ii): Men that make / Envy, and crooked malice, nourishment, / Dare bite the best.

William Shakespeare (*Julius Caesar*, Act I, ii): Let me have men about me that are fat, / Sleek-headed men, such as sleep o'nights. / Yond Cassius has a lean and hungry look. / He thinks too much. Such men are dangerous.

William Shakespeare (*Julius Caesar*, Act I, ii): Men at some time are masters of their fates, / The fault, dear Brutus, is not in our stars, / But in ourselves, that we are underlings.

William Shakespeare (*Julius Caesar*, Act I, iii): The foremost man of all this world.

William Shakespeare (*Julius Caesar*, Act III, ii): You are not wood, you are not stones, but men.

William Shakespeare (*Julius Caesar*, Act V, v): His life was gentle, and the elements / so mixed in him that Nature might stand up, / And say to all the world "This was a man!"

William Shakespeare (*King Lear*, Act III, iv): Is man no more than this?

William Shakespeare (*King Lear*, Act IV, ii): O, the difference of men and man?

William Shakespeare (*Macbeth*, Act III, i): FIRST MURDERER: We are men, my liege. MACBETH: Ay, in the catalog ye go for men.

William Shakespeare (*Measure for Measure*, Act II, ii): But man, proud man, / Drest in a little brief authority, / Most ignorant of what he's most assur'd, / His glassy essence, like an angry ape, good to good / Plays such fantastic tricks before high heaven, / As make the angels weep.

William Shakespeare (*The Merchant of Venice*, Act I, ii): God made him, and therefore let him pass for a man.

William Shakespeare (*A Midsummer Night's Dream*, Act I, ii): A proper man as one shall see in a summer's day.

William Shakespeare (*A Midsummer Night's Dream,* Act III, ii): Lord, what fools these mortals be!

William Shakespeare (*Much Ado About Nothing,* Act III, iii): Are you good men and true?

William Shakespeare (*Othello*, Act II, iii): But men are men; the best sometimes forget.

William Shakespeare (*The Rape of Lucrece,* St. 178): Men have marble, women waxen, minds.

William Shakespeare (*Richard II*, Act V, v): Now hath Time made me his numbering clock: / My thoughts are minutes; and, with sighs, they jar / Their watches on into mine eyes, the outward watch, / Where to my finger, like a dial's point, / Is pointing still, in cleansing them from tears. / The sounds that tell what hour it is. / Are clamorous groans, that strike upon my heart, / Which is the bell.

William Shakespeare (*Romeo and Juliet*, Act I, iii): Why, he's a man of wax.

William Shakespeare (*Romeo and Juliet*, Act III, ii): There's no trust, / No faith, no honesty in men; all perjured, / All forsworn, all naught, all dissemblers.

William Shakespeare (*Sonnets*, No. 121): All men are bad, and in their badness reign.

William Shakespeare (*The Tempest,* Act V, i): How beauteous mankind is! O brave new world / That has such people in it!

William Shakespeare (*Timon of Athens*, Act I, ii): I wonder men dare trust themselves with men.

William Shakespeare (*Troilus and Cressida*, Act III, iii): Men, like butterflies, / Show not their mealy wings but to the summer.

William Shakespeare (*Troilus and Crissida*, Act IV, v): Every man is odd.

William Shakespeare (*Two Gentlemen of Verona*, Act V, iv): O heavens! were man / But constant, he were perfect; that one error / Fills him with faults.

Sir Thomas Smith (English statesman, professor of law and writer, Vice-Chancellor, *De Republica Anglorum*, bk 1, ch 20, 1583): As for gentlemen, they be made good cheape in England. For whosoever studieth the lawes of the realme, who studieth in the universities, who professeth liberall sciences, and to be shorte, who can live idly and without manuall labour, and will beare the port, charge, and countenance of a gentleman, he shall be called master, for that is the title which men give to esquires and other gentlemen, and shall be taken for a gentleman.

Spanish Proverb: The man who does not love a horse cannot love a woman.

Gloria Steinman: Some of us are becoming the men we wanted to marry.

Gloria Steinman: I have yet to hear a man ask for advice on how to combine marriage and a career.

Talmud: Why was man created on the last day? So that he can be told, when pride takes hold of him: God created the gnat before thee.

Talmud: Even one ear of corn is not exactly like another.

Talmud: He is the kind of man who first prepares the bandage, then inflicts the wound.

Talmud: Four kinds of man are intolerable: an arrogant poor man, a deceitful rich man, a lecherous old man, and the head of a synagogue who lords it over his congregation.

Talmud: For types of men may be thought of as dead: the poor, the blind, the leprous, and the childless.

Talmud: Men are like weasels: they hoard and know not for what purpose.

Talmud: Like fish, like men: the greater swallow the smaller.

Talmud: It is easier to appease a male than a female—because the first man was created out of dust, which is soft, but the first woman was created out of bone, which is hard.

Talmud: Women want to be married more than men do.

Talmud: Females should be married before males, for the shame of a woman is greater than that of a man.

Mark Twain: Man is the Only Animal that Blushes. Or needs to.

Mark Twain: Adam was but human – this explains it all. He did not want the apple for the apple's sake, he wanted it only because it was forbidden.

Mark Twain: All that I care to know is that a man is a human being—that is enough for me; he can't be any worse.

Mark Twain: Man is the Religious Animal. He is the only Religious Animal. He is the only animal that has the True Religion—several of them.

Mark Twain: Of all God's creatures there is only one that cannot be made the slave of the lash. That one is the cat. If man could be crossed with a cat it would improve man, but it would deteriorate the cat.

Mark Twain: I believe that our Heavenly Father invented man because he was disappointed in the monkey.

Mark Twain: God made man, without man's consent, and made his nature, too; made it vicious instead of angelic, and then said, Be angelic, or I will punish you and destroy you. But no matter, God is responsible for everything man does, all the same; He can't get around that fact. There is only one Criminal, and it is not man.

Mark Twain: To create man was a fine and original idea; but to add the sheep was tautology.

Mark Twain: Man was made at the end of the week's work, when God was tired.

Mark Twain: Biographies are but the clothes and buttons of the man—the biography of the man himself cannot be written.

Mark Twain: Clothes make the man. Naked people have little or no influence in society.

Mark Twain: He is the only animal that loves his neighbor as himself, and cuts his throat if his theology isn't straight.

Mark Twain: A round man cannot be expected to fit a square hole right away. He must have time to modify his shape.

Mark Twain: A man cannot be comfortable without his own approval.

Mark Twain: I have no respect for any man who can spell a word only one way.

Mark Twain: The universal brotherhood of man is our most precious possession, what there is of it.

Mark Twain: We are offended and resent it when people do not respect us; and yet no man, deep down in the privacy of his heart, has any considerable respect for himself.

Mark Twain: Emperors, kings, artisans, peasants, big people, little people – at bottom we are all alike and all the same; all just alike on the inside, and when our clothes are off, nobody can tell which of us is which.

Mark Twain: There are many humorous things in the world, among them the white man's notion that he is less savage than the other savages.

Gloria Upham: Talking with a man is like trying to saddle a cow. You work like hell, but what's the point?

Jimmy "Beau James" Walker (Mayor of NYC): It takes only one or two reasons for me to like a man, but it takes a hundred for me to dislike him.

George Washington: "No nation (or man) is to trusted farther than it (he) is bound by its (his) interests."

Arthur K. Watson: Show me a man with both feet on the ground and I'll show you a man who can't put his pants on.

Mae West: His mother should have thrown him away and kept the stork.

Oscar Wilde: Nowadays, all the married men live like bachelors, and all the bachelors like married men.

UA: A strong man stands up for himself; a stronger man stands up for others.

Zohar: The ideal man has the strength of the man and the compassion of a woman.

MERCY (See COMPASSION)

MERIT (See CHARACTER; WORTH)

MILITARY

Uncle Anthony: Hell, we wasn't retreating. We was just backing up to get a good running start to charge.

Uncle Anthony: Wars don't decide who's right, just who's left!

Uncle Anthony: Whether it's a WMD (weapon of mass destruction) or IED (improvised explosive device), you're still SOL (sh-t out of luck)!

Aunt Mary Carlo: Dat sergeant's got a waterproof voice – nobody can drown him out.

Aunt Mary Carlo: He'd (any Democrat President) start a war at da drop of a hat – and he'd drop da hat himself!

Harold Adamson and Jimmy McHugh (1943 song title): Comin' In On a Wing and a Pray'r.

Acronym used by Military Pilots: A.B. and H.A. = After Burner and Haul Ass

Acronym used by USMC: BOHICA = Bend Over, Here It Comes Again

Acronym used by Military: CIA = Christians in Action

Acronym used by Military: DILLIGAS or DILLIGAF = Do I look Like I give a shit or f—k?

Acronym used by USMC: FUBAR = Fouled (or F—ed) Up Beyond All Recognition

Acronym used by USMC: FUBIJAR or FUPIJAR = F—k you buddy or pal! I am just a reserve!

Acronym used by Military: GF = Goat F—k

Acronym used by Military: MFWIC = Mother F—er! Who's/ what's in charge?!

Acronym used by Military: POOMA = Pull Out Of My Ass

Acronym used by Military: REMF = Rear Echelon Mother F—er

Acronym used by Military: RF = Rat F—!

Acronym used in WWII: SNAFU = Situation Normal, All Fouled (or F—ed Up

American Eagle Squadron Motto (first of the RAF, then a USAAC unit during WWII): LET US TO THE BATTLE!

Aristotle: In the choice of a general, we should regard his skill rather than his virtue – for few have military skill, but many have virtue.

Francis Bacon: The best armor is to keep out of gunshot.

Union General Nathaniel Banks (at 1862 Civil War Battle of Winchester, VA, as Union troops ran in retreat): Stop, men! Don't you love your Country?! (To which one of his men replied) "Yes, by God! And I'm trying to get back to it just as fast as possible!"

Confederate Gen. Bernard Bee (of the South Carolina Brigade, 1861, at the First Battle of Bull Run/Monasa, went up to Gen. Thomas J. Jackson: "General, they're beating us back!" Gen Jackson: "Sir, we'll give them the bayonet!" Gen. Bee's last words (before he was mortally wounded): "There is Jackson, **STANDING LIKE A STONE WALL**, let us determine to die here, and we will conquer. Follow me!"

Bible: Isaiah 2:4: He shall judge among the nations, and shall rebuke many people; and they shall beat their swords into plowshares, and their spears into pruninghooks: nation shall not lift up sword against nation, neither shall they learn war any more.

Bible: Isaiah 33:7: The ambassadors of peace shall weep bitterly.

Bible: James 4:2: Ye fight and war, yet ye have not, because ye ask not.

Bible: Jeremiah 51:20: Thou art my battle axe and weapons of war: for with these will I break in pieces the nations.

Bible: Joshua 1:9 (The US Army Rangers' "Shield of Strength"): "I will be strong and courageous. I will not be terrified or discouraged, because the Lord my God is with me wherever I go."

Bible: Matthew 5:39: Whosoever shall smite thee on thy cheek, turn to him the other also.

Bible: Psalms 120:7: I am for peace: but when I speak, they are for war.

Bible: 2 Timothy 2:4: No man that warreth entangleth himself with the affairs of this life; that he may please him who hath chosen him to be a soldier.

Ambrose Bierce: ADMIRAL, n. That part of a war-ship which does the talking while the figure-head does the thinking.

Ambrose Bierce: BARRACK, n. A house in which soldiers enjoy a portion of that of which it is their business to deprive others.

Ambrose Bierce: CORPORAL, n. A man who occupies the lowest rung of the military ladder.

Ambrose Bierce: DRAGOON, n. A soldier who combines dash and steadiness in so equal measure that he makes his advances on foot and retreats on horseback.

Ambrose Bierce: EPAULET, n. An ornamental badge, serving to distinguish a military officer from the enemy – that is to say, from the officer of the lower rank to whom his death would give promotion.

Ambrose Bierce: NON-COMBATANT, n. A dead Quaker.

Ambrose Bierce: OFFENSIVE, adj. Generating disagreeable emotions or sensations, as the advance of an army against its enemy.

Ambrose Bierce: PRIVATE, n. A military gentleman with a field-marshal's baton in his knapsack and an impediment in his hope.

Ambrose Bierce: REAR, n. In American military matters, that exposed part of the army that is nearest to Congress.

Ambrose Bierce: RECRUIT, n. A person distinguishable from a civilian by his uniform and from a soldier by his gait....

Ambrose Bierce: REVEILLE, n. A signal to sleeping soldiers to dream of battlefields no more, but get up and have their blue noses counted. In the American army it is ingeniosly called "rev-e-lee," and to that pronunciation our countrymen have pledged their lives, their misfortunes and their sacred dishonour.

Ambrose Bierce: RIOT, n. A popular entertainment given to the military by innocent bystanders.

Ambrose Bierce: VALOR, n. A soldierly compound of vanity, duty and the gambler's hope.

Ambrose Bierce: WAR, n. A by-product of the arts of peace. The most menacing political condition is a period of international amity. The student of history who has not been taught to expect the unexpected may justly boast himself inaccessible to the light. "In time of peace prepare for war" has a deeper meaning that is commonly discerned; it means, not merely that all things earthly have an end—that change is the one immutable and eternal law—but that the soil of peace is thickly sown with seeds of war and singularly suited to their germination and growth. It was when Kubla Khan had decreed his "stately pleasure dome"—when, that is to say, there were peace and fasting in Xanadu – that he "heard from far / Ancestral voices prophesying war." One of the greatest poets, Coleridge was one of the wisest of men, and it was not for nothing that he read us this parable. Let us have little less of "hands across the sea," and a little more of that elemental distrust that is the security of nations. War loves to come like a thief in the night; professions of eternal amity provide the night.

Omar Bradley: I am convinced that the best service they retired general can perform is to turn in his tongue along with his suit, and to most all his opinions.

Bertolt Brecht: War is like love; it always finds a way.

Confed Maj Gen John C. Breckenridge (Town of New Market, in the Shenandoah Valley, May 15, 1864, issuing the order for the VMI Cadets into the Battle of New Market where 10 cadets were killed and 47 wounded in the Wheat Field, aka "The Field of Lost Shoes"): Put the boys in and may God forgive me for the order

Brig. Gen Mark Brown (October 2007, discussing the fact that in WWII an American GI went to war with about 35 pounds of gear costing $170 in 2006 inflation-adjusted dollars, which rose to $1,100 by the 1970's and Viet Nam War, and today has 75 pounds of gear costing $17,500, and US Army estimates are $28,000 to $60,000 by the middle of the next decade): The ground soldier was perceived to be a relatively inexpensive instrument of war ... now, the Pentagon spends 100 times more than it did in WWII to outfit a soldier for war.

General Benjamin F. "The Beast" Butler (a Union General also nicknamed "Spoons" for allegedly pocketing silverwear, named by President Lincoln as Military Governor of occupied New Orleans on May 1, 1862, after its capture during the Civil War, issued his infamous General Order #28 to the townsfolk as a result of his occupying Union soldiers being routinely insulted by New Orleans women, and after one woman in The French Quarter dumped her chamber pot onto Admiral David Glasgow Farragut): As the officers and soldiers of the United States have been subject to repeated insults from the women calling themselves ladies of New Orleans ... it is ordered that hereafter when any female shall by word, gesture or movement insult or show contempt for any officer or solder of the United States, she shall be regarded and held liable to be treated as a woman of the town plying her avocation.

Ken Burns (narrated in part by Shelby Foote, 1989 PBS Series *The Civil War*): Lt. Gen. U.S. Grant had what men called **"4 O'Clock in the Morning Courage,"** that is, you could wake him up at 4 o'clock in the morning and he would be calm.

Ken Burns (1989 PBS Series *The Civil War*, Unnamed Confederate boy soldier during the westward retreat of Gen. Lee's Army of Northern Virginia from Petersburg along the Appomatox River with Gen. Grant in pursuit, during the Battle of Sailor's Creek, April 6, 1864, running away was asked why he was running, he replied): I'm running 'cause I can't fly!

Ken Burns (1989 PBS Series *The Civil War;* after the April 6, 1865 Battle of Sailor's Creek, an Unnamed Confederate officer urged Gen. Lee to surrender his 25,000 troops of the Army of Northern Virginia to Gen. U.S. Grant, whose 125,000 troops had them nearly surrounded near the village of Appomatox Court House, Lee asked "what the country would think" of him if he did not fight on, the officer replied): The country be damned! There is no country! There has been no country for a year or more. You are the country to these men!

Ken Burns (1989 PBS Series *The Civil War*, Unnamed surrendering Confederate told his captors during General William Tecumseh Sherman's march to the Sea, June 1864): Sherman (aka "Cump" or "Uncle Billy") will never go to Hell! He'll flank the Devil and make Heaven in spite of the guards!"

Ken Burns (1989 PBS Series *The Civil War*)(July 18, 1863, just 3 days after the New York City Civil War Draft Riots ended with deaths of free blacks, 650 men of the all black 54th Massachusetts Regiment, under command of Union Col. Robert Gould Shaw assaulted the Confederate Battery (Fort) Wagner, SC, in an ill-advised, unsuccessful, bloody charge): It is not too much to say that if this Massachusetts 54th had faltered when this trial (the doomed charge) came, 200,000 troops for which it was a pioneer would never have been put into the field. But it did not falter. It made Fort Wagner such a name for the colored race as Bunker Hill has been for 90 years to the white Yankees.

Joshua Lawrence Chamberlain (34-year-old commander of 20th Regiment of Infantry of Maine Volunteers, 5th Corps of Army of the Potomac; during the Civil War he was wounded 6 times, cited for bravery 4 times, promoted to Brigadier General by Gen US Grant for heroism at the Battle of Petersburg; promoted to Maj Gen for heroism at "5 Forks"; Medal of Honor recieved for his heroism at Little Round Top, during the Battle of Gettysburg; on Tuesday, June 30, 1863, one day before the Battle of Gettysburg began, 120 mutineers from a disbanded Maine unit –

mostly Maine logging men – quit, Chamberlain motivated 114 of the mutineers to fight by telling them): Some of us volunteered to fight for the Union; some came in mainly because we were bored at home and this looked like it might be fun; some came because we were ashamed not to; many of us came because it was the right thing to do. All of us have seen men die; most of us never saw a black man back home. We think on that too, but Freedom is not just a word. This is a different kind of army. If you look at history you'll see men fight for pay, or women, or some other kind of loot. They fight for land or because a king makes them, or just because they like killing. But we're here for something new. I don't ... this hasn't happened much in the history of the world. We're an army going out to set other men free. This is Free Ground. All the way from here to the Pacific Ocean. No man has to bow. No man born to royalty. Here, we judge you by what you do, not by what your father was. Here, you can be something. Here's a place to build a home. It isn't the land. There's always more land. It's the idea that we all have value. You and me. We're worth something more than dirt. I never saw dirt I'd die for. But I'm not asking you to come join us and fight for dirt. What we're all fighting for in the end is each other!

Joshua Lawrence Chamberlain (Union Officer in Charge of the 20th Maine Regiment during the Civil War, July 2, 1863, Day # 2 of The Battle of Gettysburg, spoke to his 360 men on Little Round Top, as the 15th Alabama Regiment under Col. William C. Oates attacked): Stand firm you boys from Maine! For not once in a century are men permitted to bear such responsibilities for freedom and justice, for God and humanity, as are now placed upon you."

Chinese Proverb: Though the left hand conquer the right, no advantage is gained.

Sir Winston Churchill (about Field Marshal Montgomerie): In defeat unbeatable: in victory unbearable.

Sir Winston Churchill: History is written by the victors.

Sir Winston Churchill: War is a game that is played with a smile. If you can't smile, grin. If you can't grin, keep out of the way till you can.

Sir Winston Churchill: Don't talk to me about naval tradition. It's nothing but rum, sodomy and the lash.

Sir Winston Churchill: No one can guarantee success in war, but only deserve it.

Sir Winston Churchill (July 4, 1918 speech at Central Hall, Westminster at a meeting of Anglo-Saxon Fellowship): When I have seen during the past few weeks the splendor of American manhood striding forward on all the roads of France and Flanders I have experienced emotion which words cannot describe. A presence in Europe of a million American soldiers is an event that seems to transcend the limits of purely mundane things, and fills us with the deepest awe. Winston Churchill (1895, as a British Lieutenant, assigned to observe the rebellion in Cuba, upon recieving The Red Cross of the Spanish Order of Military Merit First Class for his "distinguished comportment in military action" in Cuba, between the rebels and the Spanish ruler Campos, speaking to NY World nespaper): The most remarkable fact seems to be that two armies will shoot at each other for hours and no one will get hit....I believe that statisticians say that in a battle it takes 2,000 bullets to kill a man. When the calculations are arranged I think it will be found that in the Cuban War it took 2,000 bullets to miss each individual combatant.

Sir Winston Churchill (Secretary of State, British War Office, 1919, on authorizing use of chemical weapons against Iraqis in the first of 6 invasions of Iraq by agents of Anglo Iranian Oil [British Petroleum] in the last 100 years): I do not understand this squeamishness about the use of gas. I am strongly in favour of using [it] against uncivilised tribes.

Sir Winston Churchill (October 1, 1939): I cannot forecast to you the action of Russia. It is **a riddle wrapped in a mystery inside an enigma**: but perhaps there is a key. That key is Russian national interests.

Sir Winston Churchill (May 13, 1940): "I have nothing to offer but **blood, toil, tears and sweat...."**

Sir Winston Churchill (May 13, 1940): What is our policy? ... to wage war against a monstrous tyranny, never surpassed in the dark, lamentable catalogue of human crime.

Sir Winston Churchill (June 4, 1940 speech to Parliament on the final day of "The Miracle of Dunkirk"; see Joseph Kennedy above): "We shall not flag or fail. We shall go on to the end. We shall fight in France, we shall fight on the seas and oceans, we shall fight with growing confidence and growing strength in the air, we shall defend our island, whatever the cost may be. We shall fight on the beaches, we shall fight on the landing grounds, we shall fight in the fields and in the streets, we shall fight in the hills; **WE SHALL NEVER SURRENDER!"**

Sir Winston Churchill (June 18, 1940, 4 days after Nazis marched into Paris and 4 days before the French surrendered ignominiously in the same railroad car where the 1918 Armistice was signed by Germany at the end of WWI in the Forest of Compiegne, in the "railroad headquarters" of former French Marshal Foch,): The Battle of Britain is about to begin.... The whole fury and might of the enemy must very soon be turned on us. Hitler knows that he will have to break us in this island or lose the war.... Let us therefore brace ourselves to our duties, and so bear ourselves that, if the British Empire and its Commonwealth, last for a thousand years, man will say, **"THIS WAS THEIR FINEST HOUR!"**

Sir Winston Churchill (August 20, 1940, three days after William "Billy" Fisk, the first American to die in combat in WWII, and the first of seven Americans to join the RAF during the Battle of Britain, died of massive burns after landing his shot up and burning Hurricane fighter, saying "I think I can save the kite"): Never in the field of human conflict has so much been owed by so many to so few.

Sir Winston Churchill (February 9, 1941, Addressing President Franklin D. Roosevelt): Give us the tools and we will finish the job.

Sir Winston Churchill (December 30, 1941, Address to the Canadian Parliament): When I warned them (the French Government) that Britain would fight on alone whatever they did, their generals told their Prime Minister and his divided Cabinet, "In three weeks England will have her neck wrung like a chicken." Some chicken! Some neck!

Sir Winston Churchill (November 10, 1942 - On the Battle of Egypt): Now this is NOT THE END. It is not even the beginning of the end. But it is, perhaps, the END OF THE BEGINNING.

Sir Winston Churchill (Nov 1945, after FDR had been asked what WWII should be called, "WSC" said at Joint Meeting of the Belgium Senate): "THE UNNECESSARY WAR" – if the United States had taken an active part in the League of Nations, and if the League of Nations had been prepared to use concerted force, even had it been only European force to prevent the rearmament of Germany there was no need for further serious bloodshed.

Sir Winston Churchill (1946): "There was no greater exhibition of power in history than the American Army fighting the Battle of the Ardenne with its left hand and advancing from island to island towards Japan with its right.

Sir Winston Churchill (March 5, 1946 – his famous "FULTON SPEECH," Westminster College, Fulton, Missouri): From Stettin in the Baltic, to Trieste in the Adriatic, **AN IRON CURTAIN** (a phrase he had first used one year before in a telegram on June 4, 1945, VE Day, to President Truman) has descended across the Continent. Behind that line lie all the capitols of the ancient states of Central and Eastern Europe – Warsaw, Berlin, Prague, Vienna, Budapest, Belgrade, Bucharest, and Sophia – all lie in the Soviet sphere.

Sir Winston Churchill: In War: Resolution. In Defeat: Defiance. In Victory: Magnanimity. In Peace: Goodwill.

Sir Winston Churchill: If you go on with this nuclear arms race, all you are going to do is make the rubble bounce.

Sir Winston Churchill: War is mainly a catalogue of blunders.

Sir Winston Churchill: When you are winning a war almost everything that happens can be claimed to be right and wise.

Sir Winston Churchill: Nothing is so exhilarating as being shot at without result.

Sir Winston Churchill (June 26, 1954): To jaw-jaw- is always better than to war-war.

Sir Winston Churchill: A prisoner of war is a man who tries to kill you and fails, and then asks you not to kill him.

Sir Winston Churchill: When you have to kill a man it costs nothing to be polite, on formal declaration of war

Sir Winston Churchill: Never, never, never believe any war will be smooth and easy, or that anyone who embarks on the strange voyage can measure the tides and hurricanes he will encounter. The statesman who yields to war fever must realize that once the signal is given, he is no longer the master of policy but the slave of unforeseeable and uncontrollable events.

Sir Winston Churchill: In war: resolution. In defeat: defiance. In victory: magnanimity. In peace: goodwill.

Sir Winston Churchill: Those who can win a war well can rarely make a good peace and those who could make a good peace would never have won the war.

Sir Wiston Churchill: Wars are not won by evacuations.

Sir Winston Churchill: One day President Roosevelt told me that he was asking publicly for suggestions about what the war (WWII) should be called. I said at once **"THE UNNECESSARY WAR."**

Sir Winston Churchill: In war you do not have to be nice—you only have to be right.

Count Galeazzo Ciano: As always, victory finds a hundred fathers, but defeat is an orphan.

Marcus Tullius Cicero: An unjust peace is better than a just war.

Blake Clark: Being in the army is like being in the Boy Scouts, except that the Boy Scouts have adult supervision.

Karl Von Clausewitz: In war more than anywhere else in the world things happen differently from what we had expected, and look differently when near from what they did at a distance.

Karl von Clausewitz: To secure peace is to prepare for war.

Calvin Coolidge: The nation which forgets its defenders will it will be itself forgotten.

Pierre Corneille: When there is no peril in the fight there is no glory in the triumph.

Edouard Daladier: The weakness of democracies is that once a general has been built up in public opinion it becomes impossible to remove him.

Jefferson Davis (President of the Conferacy, 1864): If the Confederacy fails, there should be written on its tombstone: Died of a theory.

John Dryden: War is the trade of kings.

Albert Einstein (in 1932 at The Geneva Convention, which he criticized as "a travesty" because of debates over the size of aircraft carriers and "arms control"): One does not make war less likely to occur by formulating rules of warfare.

Albert Einstein (an avowed "militant pacifist," around the same time he wrote his famous July 16, 1939 letter to Presdent FDR warning of the Nazis developement of an atomic bomb): Organized power can be opposed only by organized power.

Albert Einstein: That a man can take pleasure in marching in fours to the strains of a band is enough to make me despise him.

Dwight D. Eisenhower: The necessary and wise subordination of the military to civil power (must) be sustained.

Dwight D. Eisenhower: In the councils of government we must guard against the acquisition of unwarranted influence, whether sought or unsought, by the military-industrial complex.

Dwight David Eisenhower: We are going to have peace even if we have to fight for it.

Dwight D. Eisenhower (General, Supreme Allied Commander, Europe WWII, June 5, 1944, "D-Day minus one"): Soldiers, Sailors and Airmen of the Allied Expeditionary Force: You are about to embark upon the Great Crusade, toward which we have striven these many months. The eyes of the world are upon you. Good luck! And let us all beseech the blessing of Almighty God upon this great and noble undertaking.

President Dwight Eisenhower (in his 1961 "Cross of Iron" Farewell Address): "(Cold War fears have produced) ... a military industrial complex that distorted our priorities and transfered the decision making process from the people to a scientific, technological elite .... (The hidden costs of the "Cold War" are) .... every gun that is made, every warship launched, every rocket fired, signifies in the final sense a theft from those who hunger and are not fed, those who are cold and are not clothed. This world in arms is not spending money alone, it is spending the sweat of its laborers, the genius of its scientists, the hopes of its children. The cost of one heavy bomber is this: a modern brick school in more than 30 cities; it is 2 electric power plants, each serving a town with a population of 60,000; it is 2 fine, fully equipped hospitals; it is some 50 miles of a concrete highway. We pay for a single fighter with a half-million bushels of wheat; we pay for a single destroyer with new homes that could have housed more than 8,000 people. This, I repeat is the best way of life to be found on the road the world has been taking. This is not a way of life at all, in any true sense. Under the cloud of threatening war **it is humanity hanging from a cross of iron.**

Dwight D. Eisenhower: I think that people want peace so much that one of these days governments had better get out of the way and let them have it.

Dwight D. Eisenhower: When you appeal to force, there's one thing you must never do – lose.

English Proverb: When the sword of rebellion is drawn, the sheath should be thrown away.

English WWII Saying: "Balls Up" is the British equivalent for SNAFU or FUBAR

Admiral David Glasgow Farragut (Union naval hero of the Civil War, during his attack upon the Confederate naval base at Mobile, Alabama, as his ships entered Mobile Bay, which was guarded by two forts and filled with "torpedoes" or mines, after one ship struck a mine and the next ship stopped, he shouted): DAMN THE TORPEDOES! GO AHEAD!

Shelby Foote (Writer and narrator of Ken Burns' 1989 PBS Series *The Civil War*): Before The (Civil) War it was said "the United States ARE." Gramatically it was spoken that way, and thought of as a collection of independent states. After The War it was always "The United States IS," as we say today without any self consciousness at all. And that sums up what The War accomplished – IT MADE US AN IS.

Nathan Bedford Forrest, Confederate Civil War Lieutenant General (aka "The Wizard of the Saddle" for his cavalry raids and tactical genius): Get there fustest with the mostest.

General Nathan Bedford Forrest (1864 Civil War battle at Parkers Crossroads, TENN, when surprised during a raid by a Union attack in the rear of his forces, he successfully ordered his men): Split in two and charge both ways!

General Nathan Bedford Forrest: Hit 'em in the end!

General Nathan Bedford Forrest: Keep 'em scared.

Anatole France: War will disappear only when men shall take no part whatever in violence and shall be ready to suffer every persecution that their abstention will bring them. It is the only way to abolish war.

Frederick the Great (talking about espionage/spying): It is pardonable to be defeated, but not to be taken by surprise.

French Saying: One bad general is better than two good ones.

German phrase (used during WWII by Axis captors referring to "Tommy Atkins" - nickname for a British soldier): For you, Tommy (Atkins), the war is over!

Barry Goldwater: Thank heaven for the miltary-industrial complex. Its ultimate aim is peace for our time.

General Ulysses S. Grant (aka "Unconditional Surrender" Grant to the Union during the Civil War): The art of war is simple enough. Find out where your enemy is. Get at him as soon as you can. Strike at him as hard as you can and as often as you can, and keep moving on.

General Ulysses S. Grant (at the Battle of Cold Harbor, Virginia, May – June 1864, he called for reinforcements from the men from Washington DC called "Bandbox Soldiers" or "Parade Soldiers," they were 2nd Connecticutt Heavy Artillery and 7th New York Heavy Artillery, hence the expression): "He Called for the Heavy Artillery/Calling in the Heavy Artillery"

W.E.B. Griffin and William E. Butterworth IV (book The Double Agents): The "Pins on the Map Syndrome" is the use of an asset management tool [pins on a map]; the syndrome has come to mean that the more pins you have placed on your map, the more power and prestige [you think] you have.

Tom Hanks & Steven Spielberg (co-producers, HBO Special movie *"Band of Brothers"*about the men of Easy Company, 101st US Army Airborne in WWII for 434 days after D-Day): Was I a hero? No, but I served in the company of heroes.

George Herbert (*Outlandish Proverbs*): War is death's feast.

President Herbert Hoover: Older men declare war. But it is the youth that must fight and die.

Horace: It is courage, courage, courage, that raises the blood of life to crimson splendor. Live bravely and present a brave front to adversity.

James Hornfischer ("*SHIP OF GHOSTS: The Story of the USS Houston, FDR's Legendary Lost Cruiser, And the Epic Saga of Her Survivors*): Faith and hope are unclassified vitamins (speaking about POW's in WWII).

Elbert Hubbard: A soldier is a slave—he does what he is told to do—everything is provided for him—his head is a superfluity. He is only a stick used by men to strike other men.

Saddam Hussein (January 1991, start of the Gulf War): The great, the jewel and mother of all battles has begun.

Italian Proverb: It is the boldness of the soldier that makes the general great

General Thomas J. "Stonewall" Jackson:

Thomas Jefferson: The Creator has not thought proper to mark those in the forehead who are of the stuff to make good generals. We are first, therefore, to seek them blindfold, and then let them learn the trade at the expense of great losses.

Jewish Saying: Soldiers are braver after eating.

Jewish Saying: Soldiers do the fighting and generals are called heroes.

Oliver Wendell Holmes: The prize of the general is not a bigger tent, but command.

Confederate General Thomas "Stonewall" Jackson (also called "Old Blue Light," his motto): Once you get 'em running, you stay right on top of 'em! (EDITOR: That way a small force can defeat a much larger force)

Confederate General Thomas "Stonewall" Jackson: Always mystify, mislead, and surprise the enemy. And when you strike and overcome him, never let up in the pursuit. Never fight against heavy odds if you can hurl your force on only a part of your enemy and crush it. A small army may thus destroy a large one. And repeated victory will make it invincible.

Confederate General Thomas "Stonewall" Jackson (during the First Battle of Bull Run or Monasas in 1861 his instruction to his troops started the "Rebel Yell"): Yell like the Furries!

Confederate General Thomas "Stonewall" Jackson (during his successes in his Shenandoah Valley Campaign in 1862): He who does not see the Hand of God in this (Confederate victories) is blind sir! Blind!

Confederate General Thomas "Stonewall" Jackson: It is a man's entire duty to pray and to fight.

Japanese Imperial Navy (WWII Motto): Across the sea, corpses in the water; / Across the mountain, corpses in the field / I shall die only for the Emperor / I shall never look back.

Japanese Proverb (used during WWII to justify the Kamakaze): It is better to be a smashed gem than a tile that is whole.

Jean Jaures: There is, then, over the affairs of the army a universal conspiracy of silence, of childlike mysteries, of clannishness, routine, and intrigue.

Jewish Saying: Better to be a dog in peace than a soldier at war.

John Paul Jones: I do not wish to have command of any ship that does not sail fast, for I intend to go in harm's way.

James J. Kilroy (WW II American GI graffiti slogan): Kilroy was were.

Kurdish Proverb: Those who do not go to war roar like lions

Confederate Gen Evander Law (Old Cold Harbor, Virginia, May – June 1864, after 5,000 Union troops slaughtered in less than 20 minutes): Not war, but murder.

Robert E. Lee (after General Thomas "Stonewall" Jackson's left arm was amputated from "friendly fire" wounds at the Battle of Chancellorsville, VA, 1863): He (General Jackson) has lost his left arm. I have lost my right.

Robert E. Lee: Our army would be invincible if it could be properly organized and officered. There never were such men in an army before. They will go anywhere and do anything if properly led. But there is the difficulty – proper commanders—and where can they be obtained?

Robert E. Lee: It is well that war is so terrible, or we should grow too fond of it.

Robert E. Lee (Palm Sunday, April 9, 1865, after surrendering his 25,000 soldiers of the Army of Northern Virginia to Gen. U.S. Grant and his 125,000 Union soldiers, Lee rode back to his men, dismounted his horse, Traveller, and before entering his tent said): Boys, I have done the best I could for you. Go home now. And if you make as good citizens as you have soldiers you will do well. And I shall always be proud of you. Good bye and God bless you all.

Robert E. Lee: Soldiering has one great trap – to be a good soldier you must love the army. But, to be a good officer you must be willing to order the death of the thing you love. That is a very hard thing to do. No other profession requires it... That is one reason there are so very few good officers, although there are many good men. We don't fear our own deaths, you and I (Lee and Longstreet). We protect ourselves out of military necessity not fear. You, sir, do not protect yourself enough, and must give thought to it. I need you. But the point is, we are not afraid to die. We are prepared for our own deaths and for the deaths of commrades. We learn that at the Point. But, I have seen this happen. We are not prepared for as many deaths as we have to face. Inevitably, as the war goes on, there comes a time. We are never prepared for so many to die. So you understand. No one is. We expect some chosen few; we expect an occassional empty chair, a toast to dear departed comrades; victory celebrations for most of us, a hallowed death for a few; but the war goes on and the men die. The price gets ever higher. Some officers can pay no longer. We are prepared to lose some of us.... But never all of us. Surely not all of us. But that is the trap. You can hold nothing back when you attack. You must commit yourself totally; and yet if they all die a man must ask himself: will it have been worth it?

Abraham Lincoln: It often requires more courage to dare to do right than to fear to do wrong.

Abraham Lincoln (Second Inagural Address 1865): Fondly do we hope, fervently do we pray that this mighty scourge of war may speedily pass away. Yet if God wills that it continue until all the wealth piled by the bondsman's 250 years of unrequited toil should be sunk, and until every drop of blood drawn with the lash shall be paid by another drawn with sword as was said 3,000 years ago, so still it must be said. The judgments of the Lord are true and righteous altogether.... **with malice toward none, with charity for all, with firmness in the right as God gives us to see the right, let us strive on to finish the work we are in**; to bind up the Nation's wounds, to care for him who shall have borne the battle, and for his widow, and his orphan; to do all which may achieve and cherish a just and lasting peace among ourselves and with all nations.

Abraham Lincoln (after learning of General Philip Henry Sheridan's famous 20-mile ride from Winchester to Cedar Creek on October 18, 1864, to successfully rally his troops who had been surprised by Confederate General Jubal Early, and drive the Rebel forces from the Shenandoah Valley): General Sheridan, when this particular war began I thought a cavalryman should be at least 6 feet 4 inches high. But I have changed my mind. **5 feet 4 will do in a pinch.**

Abraham Lincoln (after learning in March 1863 that General John Singleton Moseby's Confederate Rangers had raided Fairfax Courthouse, VA, and captured 2 captains, 30 privates and Union Brigadier General Edwin Stotten): For that I am sorry, for I can make Brigadier Generals, but I can't make horses.

Abraham Lincoln (about the bragging of his Union General Joseph "Fighting Joe" Hooker, before the 1863 Battle of Chancellorsville – and Hooker's retreat): The hen is the wisest of all animal creation because she never cackles until after the egg is laid.

Charles Lindbergh (Nov 1939, after Hitler invaded Poland on September 1, 1939, Lindbergh wrote an article for Reader's Digest, *"Aviation, Geography and Race,"* arguing for US isolation and staying out of WWII): We should be as impersonal as a surgeon with his knife.

Frank Loesser (1942 song title; the origin and authorship of the phrase may have been Naval Chaplain Lt. Howell M. Forgy, on the cruiser *USS New Orleans*, or Naval Chaplain Capt. W.H. Maguire, both at Pearl Harbor, Dec. 7, 1941): Praise the Lord and pass the ammunition!

Lt. Gen. James Longstreet (speaking to a foreign dignitary about the "tactics" used during the Civil War of having massive numbers of troops charge into fortified positions): Tactics? Tactics? Tactics (of General Robert E. Lee) are "Old Napolean and Chivary" – See the enemy and attack the enemy!"

Lt. Gen. James Longstreet (speaking to Gen. Robert E. Lee on Day #3 of Battle of Gettysberg, July 3, 1863, referring to Lee's plan): General, it is my considered opinion that a frontal assault here (Pickett's Charge) would be a disaster!

General Douglas MacArthur: A general is just as good or just as bad as the troops under his command.

Genral Douglas MacArthur (1942, MacArthur was evacuated from the Phillipines to Australia): I SHALL RETURN!

General Douglas MacArthur (when MacArthur landed on Leyte Island, Phillipines, Oct 20, 1944 or "A-Day" – "D-day" had already been assigned to General Eisenhower for the June 6, 1944 Normandy invasion): I have returned, rally to me.

General Douglas MacArthur (speech to Congress, 1951): The world has turned over many times since I took the oath on the Plain at West Point, and the hopes and dreams have long since vanished. But I still remember the refrain of one of the most popular barrick ballads of that day, which proclaimed, most proudly, that **"Old soldiers never die. They just fade away."** And like the soldier of the ballad, I now close my military career and just fade away—an old soldier who tried to do his duty as God gave him the light to see that duty.

Poet Archibald MacCleesh (tribute to Edward R. Murrow, Dec 2, 1941 at Testimonial Dinner at Waldrof Astoria, NYC for his heroic live radio broadcasts during and in the midst of the Battle of Britain and the Nazi bombing of London): You laid the dead of London at our doors, and we knew that the dead were our dead without more emotion than needed be. You have destroyed the superstition that what is done beyond 3,000 miles of water is not really done at all. There were some people in this country who did not want the people of America to hear the things you had to say.

Groucho Marx: Military intelligence is a contradiction in terms.

Groucho Marx: Military justice is to justice what military music is to music.

Leutenant Commander Joseph Matoush (7th Marine Regiment Chaplain, 0700 Sunday 24 Feb 1991. in Kuwait, "Task Force Ripper" = 4,000 Marines about to begin a 3-day blitz against Sadam Hussein's Royal Guard troops, paraphrasing Shakespeare's *Henry V*): "We few, we happy few, we band of brothers. For he who sheds his blood with me shall be my brother .... and if Shakespeare were alive today, he'd probably add – LET'S GO KICK SOME ASS!"

Brigadier General Anthony C. McAuliffe (Artillery commander and Acting Division Commander of the 101st Airbourne Division, during the Battle of the Bulge, while surrounded in Bastogne in the Ardennes region of Belgium near the border of Luxembourg, December 22, 1944, after Lt. Gen. Heinz Kokott "the German commander" sent a party under white flag offering an "honorable surrender" ultimatum with the alternative of "annihilation," General McAuliffe wrote this note: "To the German Commander: **NUTS!** – The American Commander."

Gen. George B. McClellan (THE OVERLY CAUTIOUS Civil War General, called "The Virginia Creeper," relieved of command by President Lincoln, Historian William S. Sears said "(McClellan) was so fearful of losing he would not risk winning."): The true course in conducting military operations is to make NO MOVEMENT UNTIL THE PREPARATIONS ARE COMPLETE.

Phyllis McGinley (American poet, *The Conquerors*): .... Though doubtless now our shrewd machines / Can blow the world to smithereens / More tidily and so on, / Let's give our ancestors their due. / Their ways were coarse, their weapons few. / But ah! How wondrously they slew / With what they had to go on.

British Field Marshall Lord Montgomery (speech to House of Lords, 1962): Rule 1, on page 1 of the book of war, is: "Do not march on Moscow" ... (Rule 2) is: "Do not go fighting with your land armies in China."

Napolean Bonaparte: Generals should mess (eat) with the common soldiers. The Spartan system was a good one.

Napolean Bonaparte (June 18, 1815, on the second day of The Battle of Waterloo, to his generals): I tell you now that Wellington is a bad general, that the English are bad soldiers, and that the whole thing (this battle) will be a picnic!.... Gentlemen, if my orders are carried out well, tonight we shall sleep in Brussels.

Lord Horatio Nelson (killed in action at the Battle of Trafalgar, October 21, 1805, delivered this message to his men): "England expects that every man will do his duty."

Lord Horatio Nelson: In case signals can neither not be seen nor perfectly understood, **no Captain can do wrong if he places his ship alongside the enemy.**

Admiral Chester Nimitz (October 25, 1944 in message to Admiral William"Bull" Halsey during the Battle of Leyte Gulf): "Where is Task Force 34 RR (EDITOR: RR means the rest was "padding" or irrelevant) ... **THE WORLD WONDERS."**

Admiral Chester Nimitz (about the U.S. Marines during WWII Battle of Iwo Jima, 1945): On that tiny Pacific Island (Iwo Jima) uncommon valor was a common virtue.

Sioux Chief "Old Lodge Skins" (after June 25-26, 1876 Battle of Little Big Horn): Yes, my son, is finished now... there is no permanent winning or losing when things move as they should in a circle. But the white men, who live in squares and straight lines do not believe as I do. To them it is everything or nothing.... Winning is all they care about. And if they can do that by scratching a pen across a paper or saying something into the wind, they are much happier.

General George S. Patton: The object of war is not to die for your country but to make the other bastard die for his.

General George S. Patton: Battle is the most magnificent competition in which a human being can indulge. It brings out all that is best; it removes all that is base.

General George S. Patton: In 40 hours I shall be in battle, with little information, and on the spur of the moment will have to make momentous decisions. But I believe that one's spirit enlarges with responsiblity and that, with God's help, I shall make them and make them right.

General George S. Patton: I love war and responsibility and excitement. Peace is going to be hell on me.

William Penn: No man is fit to command another that cannot command himself.

Polybius: A good general not only sees the way to victory; he also knows when victory is impossible.

Confederate General George E. Pickett (at 3 PM on July 3, 1863, Day #3 of The Battle of Gettysburg, as he ordered his 3 Divisions of 13,000 men to start out of the woods and up to "The Stone Wall, " 1 ½ mile away, attacking the center of the Union line of General George Meade dug in on Cemetary Ridge, aka "Pickett's Charge"): Up men and to your posts! Don't forget today that you are from Ole Virginia! (A Confederate Lieutenant cried out to his men during this famous and bloody charge): Home boys! Home! Remember home is over beyond those hills!

Col. William Prescott (June 17, 1775 at the Battle of Bunker Hill): Men, you are all marksmen – don't one of you fire until you see the whites of their eyes."

Chesty Puller: "Hell, we Marines didn't retreat (from the Chosen Reservoir in Korea), we just fought in the opposite direction!"

Ernie Pyle: War makes strange giant creatures out of us little routine men who inhabit the earth.

RAF (Royal Air Force Motto during WWII): PER ARDUA ET ASTRA = through hardship to the stars.

RAF (WWII Battle Cry taken from the motto of RAF Squadron 609): TALLY HO!

RAF (WWII saying): "Scramble to Pancake" = take off to landing or beginning to end

Ronald Reagan: Here's my strategy on the Cold War: We win, they lose.

Ronald Reagan: "Of the four wars in my lifetime, none came about because the U.S. was too strong."

Ronald Reagan: "No arsenal, or no weapon in the arsenals of the world, is as formidable as the will and moral courage of free men and women."

General Matthew B. Ridgway: Physical courage is never in short supply in the fighting army. Moral courage sometimes is.

Will Rogers: You can't say civilization don't advance—in every war they kill you a new way.

Will Rogers: Diplomats are just as essential to starting a war as soldiers are for finishing it.... You take diplomacy out of war, and the thing would fall flat in a week.

Will Rogers: The way we got in the last war was through notes. We send so many that nations can't tell which one we mean. Our wars ought to be labeled, "Entered on account of too much penmanship."

Franklin D. Roosevelt: You cannot organize militarism and at the same time expect reason to control human destinies.

Franklin D. Roosevelt: More than an end to war, we want an end to the beginnings of all wars.

Franklin D. Roosevelt (When told that a US Navy submarine commander, Captain Lowe, had responded to FDR's urgent demand for an immediate and inspirational American counter punch after the Japanese December 7, 1941 attack on Pearl Harbor, and had come up with the "outside the box" and unprecedented idea for Colonel Jimmy Doolittle's bombing raid on Tokyo by launching B-25 US Army Air Corps bombers from a US Navy carrier, the USS Hornet on April 18, 1942): "I like sub commanders. **They don't have time for bullshit – and neither do I!**" [EDITOR: This sums up my admiration for most of my fellow plaintiff trial bar, who, because they work on contingent "results oriented" fees do not waste time like some lawyers who unethically "churn" and charge clients huge hourly fees.)

Theodore Roosevelt (about the short 1898 Spanish American War): The trouble with that war was there was not enough war to go around.

Russian saying (about WWI Russian logistics): The Supreme Russian Command ("The Russian Steamroller") ordered, …but the Railroad decided!

Michael Ryan (surviving member of Easy Company, 506 Parachute Infantry Regiment, 101st Airborne Division, US Army in a letter quoted in the HBO Special Series and movie *"A Band of Brothers"*):

"I cherish the memories of a question my grandson asked me the other day when he said: "Grandpa, were you a hero in the war (WWII)?" Grandpa said: "No, ... but I served with a company of heroes."

Col. Robert Lee Scott, Jr. ("Flying Tiger," US Army Air Corps, WWII, author of *God Is My Co-Pilot*): They who scorned the thought of any strength except their own to lean on, learned at length / how Fear can sabotage the bravest heart. / When human weakness answering to the prod of Terror calls: / Help us! Oh, God! / Then silence lets the silent voice be heard / Bringing its message like a spoken word: / BELIEVE! ... BELIEVE IN ME! Cast out your fear! / Oh, I'm not up there beyond the sky, / But here, right in your heart. / I am the strength you seek. / BELIEVE! ... and, THEY BELIEVED!!

Historian William W. Sears (about Civil War General George B. McClellan): He was so fearful of losing, he would not risk winning.

William Shakespeare (*All's Well That Ends Well*, Act II, i): Worthy fellows; and like to prove most sinewy swordsmen.

William Shakespeare (*All's Well That Ends Well*, Act II, iii): War is no strife / To the dark horse, and the detested wife.

William Shakespeare (*As You Like It*, Act II, vii): Then a soldier; / Full of strange oaths and bearded like the pard, / Jealous in honour, sudden and quick in quarrel, / Seeking the bubble reputation / Even in the cannon's mouth.

William Shakespeare (*Hamlet*, Act I, i): O, farewell, honest soldier.

William Shakespeare (*I Henry IV*, Act II, iii): We must have bloody noses – and cracked crowns, / And pass them current too. – Gods me, my horse!

William Shakespeare (*I Henry IV*, Act IV, ii): Food for powder, food for powder; they'll fill a pit as well as better: tush, man, mortal men, mortal men.

William Shakespeare (*Henry V*, Act III, i): In peace, there's nothing so becomes a man / As modest stillness, and humility: / But when the blast of war blows in our ears, / They imitate the action of the tiger. / Stiffen the sinews, summon up the blood.

William Shakespeare (*Henry V*, Act III, i): Once more unto the breach, dear friends, once more / Or close the wall up with our English dead .... I see you stand like greyhounds in the slips, / Straining from the start. The game's afoot: / Follow your spirit; and upon this charge / Cry "God for Harry, England, and Saint George!"

William Shakespeare (*Henry V*, Act III, vii): Give them great meals of beef and iron and steel, they will eat like wolves and fight like devils.

William Shakespeare (*Henry V*, Act IV, i): There are few die well that die in battle.

William Shakespeare (*Henry V*, Act IV, iii; The English Camp, on St. Crispin's Day, Oct 25, 1415 at Battle of Agincourt: The Agincourt Speech or "St Crispin's Day Speech"): WESTMORELAND: O that we now had here / But one thousand of those men in England / That do not work to-day? / HENRY V: What's he that wishes so? / My cousin Westmoreland? {No, my fair cousin: / If we are mark'd to die, we are enow / To do our country loss; and if to live, / The fewer men, the greater share of honour. / God's will, I pray thee wish not one man more. / By Jove, I am not covetous for gold, / Nor care I who doth feed upon my cost; / It yearns me not if men my garments wear; / Such outward things dwell not in my desires. / But if it be a sin to covet honour, / I am the most offending soul alive. / No, faith, my coz, wish not a man from England:} / God's peace, I would not lose so great an honour, / As one man more, methinks, would share from me, / For the best hope I have. O, do not wish one more! / Rather proclaim it, Westmoreland, through my host, / That he which hath no stomach to this feast, / Let him depart, hiss passport shall be drawn, / And crowns for convoy put into his purse: / We would not die in that man's company / That fears his fellowship, to die with us. / This day (Oct 25, 1415) is call'd the feast of Crispian: / He that outlives this day, and comes safe home, / Will stand a tip-toe when this day is named, / And rouse him at the name of Crispian. / He that shall live this day, and see old age, / Will yearly on the vigil feast his neighbors, / And say, "To-morrow is Saint Crispian:" / Then will he strip his sleeve, and show his scars, / [And say "These wounds I had on Crispin's day."] / Old men forgot; yet all shall be forgot, / But he'll remember with advantages / What feats he did that day: then shall our names, / Familiar in his mouth as household words, / Harry the king, Bedford and Exeter, / Warwick and Talbot, Salisbury and Gloucester, / Be in their flowing cups freshly remember'd. / This story shall the good man teach his son; / And Crispin Crispian shall ne'er go by, / From this day to the ending of the world, / But we in it shall be remembered; / We few, we happy few, we band of brothers; / For he to-day that sheds his blood with me / Shall be my brother; be he ne'er so base, / This day shall gentle his condition: / And gentlemen in England, now a-bed, / Shall think themselves accurs'd they were not here: / And hold their manhoods cheap, while any speaks / That fought with us upon Saint Crispin's day.

William Shakespeare (*Henry V*, Act IV, iii): He which hath no stomach to this fight / Let him depart; his passport shall be made.

William Shakespeare (*I Henry VI*, Act III, ii): A braver soldier never couched lance, / A gentler heart did never sway in court.

William Shakespeare (*I Henry VI*, Act V, iii): I am a soldier and unapt to weep / Or to exclaim on fortune's fickleness.

William Shakespeare (*III Henry VI*, Act IV, vii): Drummer, strike up, and let us march away.

William Shakespeare (*Julius Caesar*, Act III, i): Caesar's spirit, ranging for revenge, / With Ate by his side, come hot from hell, / Shall in these confines, with a monarch's voice, / Cry "Havock," and let slip the dogs of war.

William Shakespeare (*Julius Caesar*, Act IV, iii): I said, an elder soldier, not a better: / Did I say "better"?

William Shakespeare (*King John*, Act V, ii): I drew this gallant head of war, / And cull'd these fiery spirits from the world, / To outlook conquest, and to win renown / Even in the jaws of danger and of death.

William Shakespeare (*Macbeth*, Act V, i): Fie, my lord, fie! A soldier and afear'd?

William Shakespeare (*Macbeth*, Act V, viii): God's soldier be he! / Had I as many sons as I have hairs, / I would not wish them to a fairer death: / And so, his knell is knoll'd.

William Shakespeare (*Othello*, Act I, i): Mere prattle, without practice, / Is all his soldiership.

William Shakespeare (*Othello*, Act II, i): You may relish him more in the soldier, than in the scholar.

William Shakespeare (*Othello*, Act II, iii): He is a soldier fit to stand by Caesar, / And give direction.

William Shakespeare (*Othello,* Act II, iii): "tis the soldier's life / To have their balmy slumbers wak'd with strife.

William Shakespeare (*Richard III*, Act V, iii): Fight, gentlemen of England! Fight boldly, yeomen! / Draw, archers, draw your arrows to the head! / Spur your proud horses hard, and ride in blood; / Amaze the welkin with your broken staves!

William Shakespeare (*Sonnets*, No. 25): The painful warrior famoused for fight, / After a thousand victories once foil'd. / Is from the book of honour razed quite, / And all the rest forgot for which he toil'd.

William Shakespeare (*Troilus and Cressida*, Act I, iii): May that soldier a mere recreant prove, / That means not, hath not, or is not in love!

George Bernard Shaw: I never expect a soldier to think.

General Philip Henry Sheridan (on October 18, 1864 made his famous 20-mile ride from Winchester to Cedar Creek to successfully rally his troops who had been surprised by Confederate General Jubal Early, and drive the Rebel forces from the Shenandoah Valley; while he rode past them, his men stopped to cheer him): God damn you! Don't cheer me, fight!

Lt. Gen Philip Henry Sheridan (during the Plains Wars of 1874-75): The only good Indians I ever saw were dead.

General William Tecumseh Sherman (1864, referring to his All Out & Total War against civilians and his campaign to capture Atlanta and "March to the Sea" and Savanah): My aim was to whip the rebels; to humble their pride; to follow them to their innermost recesses; to make them fear and dread us. **War is cruelty. There's no use trying to reform it. The crueler it is the sooner it will be over.**

General William Tecumseh Sherman (1864, referring to his All Out & Total War against civilians and his campaign to capture Atlanta and "March to the Sea" and Savanah): Gentlemen, you cannot qualify war in harsher terms than I will. We cannot change the hearts of these people of the South, but **we can make war so terrible and make them so sick of war that generations will pass away before they again appeal to it.**

General William Tecumseh Sherman (aka "Uncle Billy"): War is all hell.

General William T. Sherman: The legitimate object of war is a more perfect peace.

Gen. William Tecumseh Sherman (1868, addressing the "The Indian Question"): (The West needed to be a place where) things reassuingly could be counted, taxed and governed.

Shel Silverstein: I will not play tug o' war. I'd rather play hug o' war. Where everyone hugs instead of tugs, Where everyone giggles and rolls on the rug, Where everyone kisses, and everyone grins, and everyone cuddles, and everyone wins.

Baruch Spinoza: Peace is not an absence of war, it is a virtue, a state of mind, a disposition for benevolence, confidence, justice.

Major General James Ewell Brown "J.E.B." or "Jeb" Stuart (noted Confederate cavalry leader, gained his widest fame for his daring reconnaissance, "riding circles around" the Union army during "the Seven Days' Battle" in 1862; mortally wounded at Yellow Tavern, he died in 1864 protecting Richmond, VA from attack by General Philip Henry Sheridan's cavalry; 1833-1864; his War Credo): DIE GAME!

Talmud: Man of the sword cannot claim to be men of the Book.

C. M. Talleyrand: War is much too serious a thing to be left to military men.

Alfred Lord Tennyson: Theirs not to make reply, / Theirs not to reason why, / Theirs but to do and die: / Into the valley of Death / Rode the six hundred.

Robert Toombs (former US Senator from Georgia in an 1861 letter complaining of the lack of creative thinking leaders): The (Confederate) Army is dy$ing. I don't mean the poor fellows who go under the soil; but the army as an army is dying. Set this down in your book and set opposite to it its epitath: **DIED OF WEST POINT!** We have patched a new government with old cloth. We have tied the living with the dead.

Harry S. Truman: If there is one basic element in our Constitution, it is civilian control of the military.

Mark Twain: My kind of loyalty was loyalty to one's country, not to its institutions or its officeholders.

Mark Twain: "By and by when each nation has 20,000 battleships and 5,000,000 soldiers we shall all be safe and the wisdom of statesmanship will stand confirmed."

Sun Tzu: In peace prepare for war, in war prepare for peace. The art of war is of vital importance to the state. It is matter of life and death, a road either to safety or to ruin. Hence under no circumstances can it be neglected.

Sun Tzu ("*THE ART OF WAR*," 2nd Century): The 13 Lessons of War:

Sun Tzu ("*THE ART OF WAR*," 2nd Century is divided into 13 chapters or *P'ien*): The 13 Lessons of War:

1. Laying Plans: the five key elements that define competitive position (mission, climate, ground, leadership, and methods) and how to evaluate your competitive strengths against your competition.
2. Waging War: deals with how to understand the economic nature of competition and how success requires making the winning play, which in turn, requires limiting the cost of competition and conflict.
3. Attack by Stratagem: defines the source of strength as unity, not size, and the five ingredients needed to succeed in any competitive situation.
4. Tactical Dispositions: explains the importance of defending existing positions until you can advance them and how you must recognize opportunities, not try to create them.
5. Energy: explains the use of creativity and timing in building your competitive momentum.
6. Weak Points & Strong: explains how your opportunities come from the openings in the environment caused by the relative weakness of your competitors in a given area.
7. Maneuvering: explains the dangers of direct conflict and how to win those confrontations when forced upon you.
8. Variation in Tactics: focuses on the need for flexibility in your responses. It explains how to respond to shifting circumstances successfully.
9. The Army on the March: describes the different situations in which you find yourselves as you move into new competitive arenas and how to respond to them. Much of it focuses on evaluating the intentions of others.
10. Terrain: looks at the three general areas of resistance (distance, dangers, and barriers) and the six types of ground positions that arise from them. Each of these six field positions offer certain advantages and disadvantages.

11. The Nine Situations: describe nine common situations (or stages) in a competitive campaign, from scattering to deadly, and the specific focus you need to successfully navigate each of them.
12. The Attack by Fire: explains the use of weapons generally and use of the environment as a weapon specifically. It examines five targets for attack, five types of environmental attack, and the appropriate responses to such attack.
13. The Use of Spies: discusses the importance of developing good information sources, specifically the five types of sources and how to manage them.

UA (about Civil War General George B. McClellan, nicknamed "Little Mack, The New Napolean, and The Virginia Creeper" for his conservative mode of operation): He had a particular facility for realizing hallucinations.

UA (WWI poet about the all-black 808th Regiment, American Expeditionary Forces, named "The Pioneers," their insignia was a pick, shovel and a rifle, they were the forerunners of combat engineers): They sleep in pup tents in the cold, / and work in mud and mire; / They fill up shell holes in the roads, / Always under fire. / Far o'er the lines the scout plane goes, / directing the barrage. / Just as Zero Hour draws near / Or just before the charge, / As o'er the top the dough boy goes / To put the Hun to tears; / But who went out and cut the wire? / The hungry Pioneers. // They buried beaucoup heroes and carried beaucoup shells / From every dump on every front; / The kind of work that tells. / A heavy pack on every back / On every truck in France. / They never won the Crois de Guere; / They never had the chance. / As a the heavy trucks whirled by / They worked to calm their fears. / Who was it made the roads so smooth? / The same old Pioneers.

UA (WWII slogan): Tell it to the Marines!

UA (WWII gravesite epitaph for a fallen Marine on Iwo Jima): "Tell them: for their tomorrow's we gave our today's."

UA WWII Vet: Combat service is like a sentence placed on you – you may get out of jail, but you never get over the sentence (combat experience) … you go to the grave with it.

UA: Scatological Phrase of "SHIT HOT" (meaning very competent/proficient at some military skill).

UA: Did you get a commission while in the Army? No, I got paid a straight salary.

UA: He was so dumb he saluted refrigerators because they were made by General Electric... and jeeps because they were made by General Motors.

UA (16 February 1940, 299 British seamen freed from German supply ship *Altmark* in a Norwegian fjord by British destroyer *Cossack's* boarding party, one of whom said): "... the Navy's here."

UA: What is the Marine Corps for? For? The Marines are FOREVER!

UA: He was a West Pointer, but he looked more like an Irish setter.

UA (WWI British soldiers aka "Tommies"): "Sapper" was a trench digger; **THE SAPS** were the tunnels or tunnel diggers.

UA (WWII poet on Corregidor during Japanese invasion of the Philipines 1941-42): We're the battling bastards of Bataan / No mama, no papa, no Uncle Sam / No aunts, no uncles, no cousins, no nieces, / No pills, no planes or artillery pieces / And NOBODY GIVES A DAMN!"

UA (WWII GI Joke): I fell into the mud up to my ankles … I fell up to my knees … yeah but I fell HEAD FIRST!

UA: "Up the Haws Pipe" = up from enlisted ranks to officer rank

UA: If your dick was as sharp as your tongue, you'd have to put a serial number on it and keep it locked up in your wall locker!

UA: I'm gonna put my foot up your ass up to my knee!

UA (Army GI): I'm gonna put my foot so far up his ass that his Adam's Apple will be my big toe!

UA (Navy CPO): I've pissed more salt water than you puppies have sailed over!

UA (Marine & Navy Fighter Pilots): Air Combat: One vs. Six is a "target rich environment."

UA (Marine & Navy Fighter Pilots): Remember in Flying that you never have to much fuel unless you are on fire.

UA (Marine & Navy Fighter Pilots): When we start or take-off on the ship we are going flying or swimming…There ain't no stopping the catapault.

UA (Navy Fighter Pilots): Watching Marine Aviators trying to come aboard a carrier at night is always exciting.

UA (Marine & Navy Fighter Pilots): Always turn into a fight, never run from one.

UA (Marine & Navy Fighter Pilots): Listen up, if we miss the target today, we gotta go back tomorrow.

UA (Marine & Navy Fighter Pilots): The best way to win a fight is through a well-planned ambush.

UA (Marine & Navy Fighter Pilots): Always remember the fighter airplane you fly was built by the lowest bidder.

UA (Marine & Navy Fighter Pilots): Yeah, though I fly through the valley of the shadow of death I shall fear no evil since I am the meanest S.O.B in the Valley!

UA (Marine & Navy Fighter Pilots): Remember if you crash do not burn…Keep Pensacola Green

UA (1st US Army "The Big Red One" Division's Motto): No Mission Too Difficult; No Sacrifice Too Great.

US (1st US Army "The Big Red One" Division Saying): DO IT FIRST!

UA: "IN HACK" = to be in trouble or in the brig or some kind of detention

UA: FUBAR = F-d Up Beyond All Recognition

UA: SNAFU = Situation Normal, All Fouled Up

UA: "Balls Up" = British SNAFU or FUBAR

UA (Marine NCO): You don't know horse shit from peanut butter!

UA (Marine NCO in Viet Nam): If they ever gave the world an enema – they'd stick the tube in here!

UA: "The Fabian Choice" - **THE FABIAN STRATEGY** = Roman General Fabius Contater defeated the Carthaginians by withdrawing each time Carthage armies showed up (EDITOR: Gen. George Washington adopted this strategy in 1775).

UA (WWII prayer for and about the fallen RAF fliers): Lord, hold them in thy mighty hand / Above the ocean and the land; / Like wings of eagles mounting high / Along the pathways of the sky.

US Military Oath: I do solemnly swear that I will support and defend the Constitution of the United States against all enemies, foreign and domestic; that I will obey the orders of the President of the United States and the orders of the officers appointed over me, according to regulations and the Uniform Code of Military Justice. So help me God.

US Navy (cable to Admiral William "Bull" Halsey, April 18, 1943 when Japanese Admiral Yamamoto's plane was shot down and the infamous admiral who engineered the Pearl Harbor attack was killed): "POP GOES THE WEASEL"

UA: (1863, while Gen Robert E. Lee and Lt. Gen James Longstreet were talking about Darwin's book and Darwinism: a Confederate soldier nearby said): "Well, maybe you are come from an ape, and maybe I am come from an ape, but General Lee ... HE DIDN'T COME FROM NO APE!"

Alfred Victor de Vigny: The army is a good book in which to study human life. One learns there to put his hand to everything. The most delicate and rich are forced to see poverty and live with it; to understand distress; and to know how rapid and great are the revolutions and changes of life.

George Washington: Mar 16, 1783 meeting for ALL 500 officers in The Newburg Building ("The Temple" auditorium), Washington's "NEWBURG ADDRESS": Let me conjure you in the name of our common country, as you value your own sacred honor, as you respect the rights of humanity, and as you regard to military and national character of America to express your utmost horror and detestation of the man who wishes, under any specious pretenses, to overturn the liberties of our country, and who wickedly attempts to open the floodgates of civil discord and deluge our rising empire in blood."

George Washington (at start of his "Newburg Address," see above): Forgive me, gentlemen, I have not only grown gray but almost blind in the service of my country.

George Washington (May 28, 1754 at Je Montville Glen, the "Battle (or massacre by the British of the French and their Indian allies) of J'Montville," followed by the British defeat at Fort Necessity, Pennsyvannia): I heard the sound of bullets whistle, and ... there was something charming in the sound.

Evelyn Waugh: Punctuality is the virtue of the bored.

Lord Duke of Wellington (June 19, 1815 at the little Belgium town of Waterloo, south of Brussels, where Napolean Bonaparte lost in 9 hours what he had built in 9 years): Hard pounding gentlemen, let us see who pounds the longest. (EDITOR: that is, fight a war of attrition).

Rebecca West: Before a war, military science seems like a real science, like astronomy; but after a war, it seems more like astrology.

Oscar Wilde: As long as war is regarded as wicked, it will always have its fascination. When it is looked upon as vulgar, it will cease to be popular.

George Will: When asked in 1997 to describe the kind of conflict for which Marines were training, Gen. Charles Krulak, then the Corps' commandant, replied with one word: "Chechnya." He meant ethnic and sectarian conflict in an urban context. He spoke of "the three-block war" in which a marine wraps a child in a blanket, then is a buffer between warring factions, then engages in combat, within three city blocks.

U.S. Army Captain Lloyd S. Williams (WWI, June 1918, after arrival at the Western front and advised by French to retreat): Retreat? Hell, no, we just got here!

Woodrow Wilson: Let it be your pride, therefore, to show all men everywhere not only what good soldiers you are, but also what good men you are, keeping yourselves fit and straight in everything, and pure and clean through and through. Let us set for ourselves a standard so high that it will be a glory to live up to it, and then let us live up to it and add a new laurel to the crown of America.

MISCHIEF (See TROUBLE)

MISER (See CHEAP)

MISERY (See EMOTIONAL DISTRESS; GRIEF & SORROW)

MISINFORM/MISINFORMATION (See FRAUD; LIES/LIARS; TRUTH)

MISTAKES (See CONSISTENCY; and NEGLIGENCE)

MONEY (See also CHEAP)

Uncle Anthony: There's always too much month at the end of the money.

Uncle Anthony: Money will never buy you friends, but if you get a lot of it you will have a better class of enemies.

Uncle Anthony: If you want to see a short winter, just borrow some money due in the spring.

Uncle Anthony: Y'know those guys just think/hear **CHA-CHING, CHA-CHING** when they talk about clients' cases.

Uncle Anthony: Didja ever notice that when ya put the 2 words "The" and "IRS" together it spells "THEIRS."

Aunt Mary Carlo: He started out with nothing, and he still has most of it.

Aunt Mary Carlo: Suppose 'dat guy hadda pay taxes on what he thought he was worth.

Aunt Mary Carlo: Ya know what dey say - a penny saved is a government oversight.

Aunt Mary Carlo: Money don't buy class.

Bud Abbott and Lou Costello (1943 movie *It Ain't Hay*): "...and that ain't hay!"

Charles Francis Adams: Failure seems to be regarded as the one unpardonable crime, success as the all redeeming virtue, the acquisition of wealth as the single worthy aim of life.

Franklin P. Adams: There are plenty of good five cents a guards in this country. The trouble is a caustic water. What this country really needs is a good five cent nickel.

Joey Adams: Bankruptcy is a legal proceeding in which you put your money in your pants pocket and give your coat to the creditors.

Marty Allen: A study of economics usually reveals that the best time to buy anything is last year.

Woody Allen: Money is not everything, but it is better than having one's health.

Woody Allen and Mickey Rose (1969 film title): Take the money and run.

Marian Anderson: Where there is money, there is fighting.

Sherwood Anderson: There is a kind of shrewdness many men have that enables them to get money. It is the shrewdness of the fox after the chicken. A low order of mentality often goes with it.

Aristotle (*Politics*, bk 2, ch. 6): Poverty is the parent of revolution and crime.

Armenian Proverb: When your fortune increases, the columns of your house appear to be crooked.

Francis Bacon: The ways to enrich are many, and most of them are foul.

P. T. Barnum: Money is a terrible master but an excellent servant.

P.T. Barnum: I proved successful at getting money and getting rid of it.

PT Barnum (1844, PT Barnum writing about the Scottish royalty in a paper entitled "Practice versus Precept."): Money is not the standard of merit. What a miserable, disgraceful and pitiful state of society it is that elevates a booby or a tyrant to its highest summit provided he has more gold than others. While a good heart or a wise head is trampled in the dust if their owner happens to be poor.

Jules Bertillon: If all the rich men in the world divided up their money amongst themselves there wouldn't be enough to go around.

Bible: Ecclesiastes: He that loveth money will not be satisfied with money.

Bible: Ecclesiastes 5:12: The sleep of a labouring man is sweet, whether he eat little or much: but the abundance of the rich will not suffer him to sleep.

Bible: Ecclesiastes 9:16: The poor man's wisdom is despised, and his words are not heard.

Bible: Exodus 22:25: If thou lend money to any of my people that is poor by thee, thou shalt not be to him as an usurer, neither shalt thou lay upon him usury.

Bible: Luke 6:24: Woe unto you that are rich! For ye have received your consolation. Woe unto you that are full! For ye shall hunger.

Bible: Luke 6:34: If ye lend to them of whom ye hope to receive, what thanks have ye?

Bible: Matthew 5:42: Give to him that asketh thee, and from him that would borrow of thee turn not thou away.

Bible: Matthew 6:21: Where your treasure is, there will your heart be also.

Bible: Matthew 19:21: If thou wilt be perfect, go and sell that thou hast, and give to the poor, and thou shalt have treasure in heaven.

Bible: Matthew 19:24: It is easier for a camel to go through the eye of a needle, than for a rich man to enter the kingdom of God.

Bible: Proverbs 19:4: Wealth maketh many friends.

Bible: Proverbs 22:7: The borrower is servant to the lender.

Bible: Proverbs 23:5: Riches certainly make themselves wings; they fly away as an eagle toward heaven.

Bible: Proverbs 28:11: The rich man is wise in his own conceit; but the poor that hath understanding searcheth him out.

Bible: Proverbs 28:20: A faithful man shall abound with blessings: but he that maketh haste to be rich shall not be innocent.

Bible: Psalms 39:6: He heapeth up riches, and knoweth not who shall gather them.

Bible: Psalms 49:16: Be not thou afraid when one is made rich, when the glory of his house is increased; For when he dieth he shall carry nothing away: his glory shall not descend after him.

Bible: Psalms 112:5 A good man sheweth favour, and lendeth: he will guide his affairs with discretion.

Bible: 1 Samuel 2:7: The Lord maketh poor, and maketh rich: he bringeth low, and lifteth up.

Bible: 1 Timothy 6:10: The love of money is the root of all evil.

Bible: Tutus 1:11: Teaching things which they ought not, for filthy lucre's sake.

Ambrose Bierce: ACQUAINTANCE, n. A person whom we know well enough to borrow from, but not well enough to lend to. A degree of friendship called slight when its object is poor or obscure, and intimate when he is rich or famous.

Ambrose Bierce: CREDITOR, n. One of a tribe of savages dwelling beyond the Financial Straits and dreaded for their desolating incursions.

Ambrose Bierce: DEBT, n. An ingenious substitute for the chain and whip of the slave-driver....

Ambrose Bierce: DEPENDENT, adj. Reliant upon another's generosity for the support which you are not in a position to exact from his fears.

Ambrose Bierce: DISTRESS, n. A disease incurred by exposure to the prosperity of a friend.

Ambrose Bierce: DISTANCE, n. The only thing that the rich are willing for the poor to call theirs, and keep.

Ambrose Bierce: FINANCE, n. The art or science of managing revenues and resources for the best advantage of the manager. The pronunciation of this word with the i long and the accent on the first syllable is one of America's most precious discoveries and possessions.

Ambrose Bierce: FORGETFULNESS, n. A gift from God bestowed upon debtors in compensation for their destitution of conscience.

Ambrose Bierce: IMPROVIDENCE, n. Provision for the needs of today from the revenues of tomorrow.

Ambrose Bierce: IMPUNITY, n. Wealth.

Ambrose Bierce: INCOME, n. The natural and rational guage and measure of respectability, the commonly accepted standards being artificial, arbitrary and fallacious; ....

Ambrose Bierce: IN FORMA PAUPERIS. [Latin] In the character of a poor person—a method by which a litigant without money for lawyers is considerately permitted to lose his case....

Ambrose Bierce: MISFORTUNE, n. The kind of fortune that never misses.

Ambrose Bierce: MONEY, n. A blessing that is of no advantage to us excepting when we part with it....

Ambrose Bierce: OWE, v. To have (and to hold) a debt. The word formerly signified not indebtedness, but possession; meant "own," and in the minds of debtors there is still a good deal of confusion between assets and liabilities.

Ambrose Bierce: POVERTY, n. A file provided for the teeth of the rats of reform. The number of plans for its abolition equals that of the reformers who suffer from it, plus that of the philosophers who know nothing about it. Its victims are distinguished by possession of all the virtues and by their faith in leaders seeking to conduct them into a prosperity where they believe these to be unknown.

Ambrose Bierce: PRICE, n. Value, plus a reasonable sum for wear and tear of conscience in demanding it.

Ambrose Bierce: QUOTIENT, n. A number showing how many times a sum of money belonging to one person is contained in the pocket of another – usually about as many times as it can be got there.

Ambrose Bierce: RESPECTABILITY, n. The offspring of a liason between a bald head and a bank account.

Ambrose Bierce: RICH, adj. Holding in trust and subject to an accounting the property of the indolent, the incompetent, the unthrifty, the envious and the luckless. That is the view that prevails in the underworld, where the Brotherhood of Man finds its most logical development and candid advocacy. To denizens of the midworld the word means good and wise.

Ambrose Bierce: RICHES, n. A gift from Heaven signifying, "This is my beloved son, in whom I am well pleased." - John D. Rockefeller. The reward of toil and virtue. – J.P. Morgan. The savings of many in the hands of one. – Eugene Debs. To these excellent definitions the inspired lexicographer feels that he can add nothing of value.

Ambrose Bierce: TARIFF, n. A scale of taxes on imports, designed to protect the domestic producer against the greed of his consumer.

Ambrose Bierce: WALL STREET, n. A symbol of sin for every devil to rebuke. That Wall Street is a den of thieves is a belief that serves every unsuccessful thief in place of a hope in Heaven. Even the great and good Andrew Carnegie has made his profession of faith in the matter.

Ambrose Bierce: A penny saved is a penny to squander.

American Proverb: He that marries for money will earn it.

Bion: He has not acquired a fortune; the fortune has acquired him.

Lewis D. Brandeis: We can have democracy in this country or we can have great wealth concentrated in the hands of a few, but we can't have both.

British saying (a take-off of the phrase "full amount"): The full monty.

Norman O. Brown: All currency is neurotic currency.

James F. Byrnes (South Carolina lawyer, statesman, Associate Justice, U.S. Supreme Court): Poverty and immorality are not synonymous. _Edwards v. California_, 314 US 160, 86 L.Ed 119, 62 S Ct 164 (1941).

Albert Camus: Novel: the man who realizes that one needs to be rich in order to live, who devotes himself completely to the acquisition of money, who succeeds, lives and dies *happy*.

Andrew Carnegie: Thrift is the great fortune maker. It draws the line between the savage and the civilized man.

Douglas Casey: Foreign aid might be defined as a transfer of money from poor people in rich countries to rich people in poor countries.

Cato: Luxury and avarice – these pests have been the ruin of every state.

Miguel de Cervantes: There were only two families in the world, my old grandmother used to say, the Haves and the Have-Nots.

Chase Manhattan Bank ad: A reminder to everyone spending money like there's no tomorrow. There is a tomorrow.

Chinese Proverb: Riches take away more pleasures than they give.

Chinese Proverb: With money you are a dragon; with no money, a worm.

Chinese Proverb: Wealth infatuates as well as beauty.

Sir Winston Churchill: The process of the creation of new wealth is beneficial to the whole community.

Sir Winston Churchill: You don't make the poor richer by making the rich poorer.

Cicero: Money, the sinews of war.

Edward Clarke: The best way to realize the pleasure of feeling rich is to live in a smaller house than your means would entitle you to have.

Confucius: When wealth is centralized the people are dispersed; when wealth is dispersed the people are brought together.

Alistair Cooke (in the epilogue of his *America*, 1973): "...an Italian immigrant, when asked to say what forty years of American life had taught him – There is no free lunch."

Croatian Proverb: Without money one cannot go anywhere, not even to church.

e. e. cummings: I am living so far beyond my income that we may almost be said to be living apart.

Danish Proverb: If you have no money, be polite.

Eugene V. Debs: (Wealth) The savings of many in the hands of one.

Peter De Vries: The rich aren't like us; they pay less taxes.

Senator Everett Dirksen: One billion here, one billion there—pretty soon it adds up to real money.

Bob Dylan: What's money? A man is a success if he gets up in the morning and goes to bed at night and in between does what he wants to do.

English Proverb (17th century): Speak not of my debts unless you mean to pay them.

English Proverb: God help the rich man, let the poor man beg!

English Proverb: God help the rich, the poor can look after themselves.

Paul Erdman: The entire essence of America is the hope to first make money – then make money with money – then make lots of money with lots of money.

Frantz Fanon: The people came to realize that wealth is not the fruit of labor but the result of organized protected robbery.

William Feather: A budget tells us what we can't afford, but it doesn't keep us from buying it.

Sigmund Freud: Happiness is the deferred fulfillment of a prehistoric wish. That is why wealth brings so little happiness; money is not an infantile wish.

Brendan Francis: True, you can't take it with you, but then that's not the place where it comes in so handy.

Brendan Francis: A man who has money may be anxious, depressed, frustrated and unhappy, but one thing he's not – and that's broke.

Benjamin Franklin: Creditors have better memories and debtors.

French Proverb: One beggar at the door is enough.

French Proverb: Fortune is a woman; if you neglect her today do not expect to regain her tomorrow.

French Proverb: Fortune is blind, but not invisible.

French Proverb: Riches run after the rich, and poverty runs after the poor.

Senator J.W. Fulbright: Priorities are reflected in the things we spend money on. Far from being a dry accounting of bookkeepers, a nation's budget is full of moral implications; it tells what a society cares about and what it does not care about; it tells what its values are.

John Kenneth Galbraith: In economics the majority is always wrong.

John Kenneth Galbraith: People of privilege will always risk their complete destruction rather than surrender any material part of their advantage.

J. Paul Getty: Money is like manure. You have to spread it around or it smells.

J. Paul Getty: If you can count your money, you don't have a billion dollars.

Sir Philip Gibbs: It is better to give them to lend, and it costs about the same.

Sen. James Hammond of South Carolina (1858): What would happen if no cotton was furnished for three years? England would topple headlong and carry the whole civilized world with her, save the South. No. You dare not make war on cotton. No power on earth dares to make war on it. **COTTON IS KING!**

Vernon Lewis Harrington: We must have a political state powerful enough to deal with corporate wealth, but how are we going to keep that state with its augmenting power from being captured by the force we want it to control?

Ernest Haskins: Save a little money each month and at the end of the year you will be surprised at how little you have.

Leona Helmsley: Only little people pay taxes.

Robert Heinlein: Taxes are not levied for the benefit of the taxed.

Lillian Hellman: Maybe money is unreal for most of us, easier to give away than things we want.

John Heywood (*The Proverbs of John Heywood*, 1546): Beggars shouldn't be choosers.

Oliver Wendell Holmes, Sr.: Put not your trust in money, but put your money in trust.

Bob Hope: ON HIS FAMILY'S EARLY POVERTY: Four of us slept in the one bed. When it got cold, mother threw on another brother.

Bob Hope: ON HIS SIX BROTHERS: That's how I learned to dance. Waiting for the bathroom.

Horace: Make money, money by fair means if you can, if not, by any means money.

Kin Hubbard: We may not know when we're well off, but investment salesmen get on to it somehow.

Hubert H. Humphrey: I learned more about the economy from one South Dakota dust storm than I did in all my years at college.

Julian Huxley: We all know how the size of sums of money appears to vary in a remarkable way according as they are being paid in the our paid out.

Indian Proverb: To lend is to buy a quarrel.

Italian Saying: Public money is like holy water; everyone helps himself.

Italian Proverb: Better give a penny then lend twenty.

Andrew Jackson: It is to be regretted that the rich and powerful too often bend the acts of government to their selfish purposes.

Holbrook Jackson: Only the rich preach content to the poor.

Jewish Saying: The man who thinks that anything can be accomplished by money is likely to do anything for money.

Jewish Saying: Shrouds have no pockets.

Jewish Saying: Money really adds no more to the wise than clothes can to the beautiful.

Jewish Saying: Money can marry off even a grandmother.

Jewish Saying: Money is a soap that removes the worst stains.

Jewish Saying: The world rests on three things: Money, Money, and money.

Jewish Saying: The Torah gives light, but warmth comes from money.

Jewish Saying: It is easier to make money than to keep it.

Jewish Saying: Money goes to money.

Jewish Saying: To have money is good; to have control of money is still better.

Jewish Saying: The rich have heirs, not children.

Dr. Samuel Johnson: You never find people laboring to convince you that you may live very happily upon a plentiful fortune.

Samuel Johnson: There are few ways in which a man can be more innocently employed than in getting money.

Jim Kitchens: We were so pore, that when Christmas mornin' came, me and my little brother wouldn't a-had nothing to play with if it hadn't a-been for our little old peters! (**The Story of a Bogue Chitto Christmas**, as originally told him by Smithie Buie. Bogue Chitto is a small, unincorporated community in southern Lincoln County, Mississippi, near the Pike County Line. Mr. Smithie (pronounced *Smitty*) Buie, often told how hard times were during the Great Depression, when he was growing up at Bogue Chitto. Jim told it to his three sons, and if they were having a lean year at the law firm, he'd say, **"Well, Boys, it looks like we're going to have a Bogue Chitto Christmas this year."**)

Lancastrian Proverb: Rags to riches to rags.

Stephen Leacock: Money ruins life: I mean, to have to think of it, to take account of it, to know that it is there. Men apart from money, men in an army, men of an expedition of exploration, emerge to a new life. Money is gone.

Liberace (flamboyant pianist, in his 1973 autobiography): When the reviews are bad I tell my staff that they can join me **as I cry all the way to the bank.**

Jacques Lipchitz: Real richness is in how you spend your money.

Robert Lynn: The rich never feel so good as when they are speaking of their possessions as responsibilities.

Dwight MacDonald: A foundation is a large body of money surrounded by people who want some.

Elizabeth Marbury: The richer your friends, the more they will cost you.

John P. Marquand: I know a fellow who's as broke as the Ten Commandments.

Jackie Mason: I have enough money to last me the rest of my life, unless I buy something.

Grouho Marx: Money is a good thing to have. It frees you from doing things you dislike. Since I dislike doing nearly everything, money is handy.

Karl Marx: The Irish famine of 1846 killed more then one million people, but it killed poor devils only. To the wealth of the country it did not the slightest damage.

Karl Marx: My power is as great as is the power of money. The qualities of money are my – the possesor's – qualities and potentialities. What I *am* and *can do,* therefore, is by no means determined by my individuality. I *am* ugly, but I can buy the *most beautiful* woman. So I am not *ugly*, for the effect of *ugliness*, its repulsive power, is eliminated by money.

Andrew Mellon: Prosperity of the middling and lower orders depends upon the fortunes and light taxes of the rich.

H.L. Mencken: The chief value of money lies in the fact that one lives in a world in which it is overestimated.

Moliere: There's no praise to beat the sort you put in your pocket.

Ogden Nash: Bankers Are Just Like Anybody Else, Except Richer.

C. Northcote Parkinson: Expenditure rises to meet income.

Polish Proverb: If you love him, don't lend him.

Joyce Carol Oates: The only people who claim that money is not important are people who have enough money so that they are relieved of the ugly burden of thinking about it.

Sean O'Casey: Money does not make you happy but it quiets the nerves.

Seth Parker: Some folks seem to get the idea that they're worth a lot of money just because they have it.

Plato: If I keep my good character, I shall be rich enough.

Plutarch: It is the higher accomplishment to use money well than to use arms; but not to need it is more noble than to use it.

Marcel Proust: "His/her hand is a crucible in which money melts"

John Jacob Rascom (founder and creator of GM, financer and capitalist, NYC mover & shaker, wrote an article in 1928 *Good Housekeeping* magazine entitled: **"Everybody Ought To Be Rich"** ... less than one year before October 29, 1929, aka "Black Tuesday," the Stock Market Crash which started The Great Depression! (EDITOR: The last happy whistle of the canary before the mine shaft exploded!)

Ronald Reagan: Money can't buy you happiness but it will get you a better class of memories.

Tim Robbins: There is a certain Buddhistic calm that comes from having... money in the bank.

Will Rogers: The income tax has made liars out of more Americans than golf. And

Will Rogers: The budget is a mythical bean bag. Congress votes mythical beans into it, and then tries to reach in and pull real beans out.

Will Rogers: An economist's guess is liable to be as good as anybody else's.

Will Rogers: Let Wall Street have a nightmare and the whole country has to help get them back in bed again.

Will Rogers: Ten men in our country could buy the whole world and ten million can't buy enough to eat.

Will Rogers (1949): The banker, the lawyer, and the politician are still our best bets for a laugh. Audiences haven't changed at all, and neither has the three above professions.

Will Rogers: In a real estate man's eye, the most expensive part of the city is where he has a house to sell.

Will Rogers: If the other fellow sells cheaper than you, it is called dumping. 'Course, if you sell cheaper than him, that's mass production.

Will Rogers: Money and women are the most sought after and the least known about of any two things we have.

Will Rogers: It's not what you pay a man, but what he costs you that counts.

Will Rogers: Buy land. They ain't making any more of the stuff.

Will Rogers: Don't gamble; take all your savings and buy some good stock and hold it till it goes up, then sell it. If it don't go up, don't buy it.

Will Rogers: I can remember way back when a liberal was generous with his own money

Will Rogers: I wonder if it isn't just cowardice instead of generosity that makes us give tips.

Will Rogers: Legalize racing in every State. Sure people will bet, but they get to see the horses run and you certain can't see General Motors and General Electric and General Utility run when you bet on them.

Will Rogers: There is no income tax in Russia. But there's no income.

Will Rogers: The nation is prosperous on the whole, but how much prosperity is there in a hole?

Will Rogers: They call it the Latin Quarter because nobody there is Latin and nobody has a quarter.

Will Rogers: America is a great country, but you can't live in it for nothing.

Will Rogers (in a 1931 appeal for the unemployed, who then numbered 25 percent of our population): You know, not a one of us has anything that these people that are without now haven't contributed to what we've got. There is not an unemployed man in the country that hasn't contributed to the wealth of every millionaire in America.

Franklin D. Roosevelt: The hopes of the Republic cannot forever tolerate either undeserved poverty or self-serving wealth.

Billy Rose: Never invest your money in anything that eats or needs repairing.

John Ruskin: It is physically impossible for a well-educated intellectual or brave man to make money the chief object of his thoughts.

Russian Proverb: Some people are masters of money, and some its slaves.

Paul Samuelson: If we made an income pyramid out of child's blocks, with each layer portraying $1000 of income, the peak would be far higher than the Eiffel Tower, but almost all of us would be within the yard of the ground.

Carl Sandburg: Money is power, freedom, a cushion, the root of all evil, the sum of blessings.

May Sarton: Being very rich as far as I am concerned is having a margin. The margin is being able to give.

Scottish Proverb: A penny saved is a penny gained.

William Shakespeare (*Cymbeline*, Act III, vi): All gold and silver rather turn to dirt! / As 'tis no better reckon'd, but of those / Who worship dirty gods.

William Shakespeare (*Hamlet*, Act I, iii): Neither a borrower, nor a lender be: / For loan oft loses both itself and friend; / And borrowing dulls the edge of husbandry.

William Shakespeare (*I Henry IV*, Act II, iv): But, by the Lord, lads, I am glad you have the money.

William Shakespeare (*I Henry VI*, Act V, iv): Decrepit miser; base, ignoble wretch; / I am descended of a gentler blood.

William Shakespeare (*Macbeth*, Act IV, iii): This avarice / Strikes deeper, grows with more pernicious root.

William Shakespeare (*Macbeth*, Act IV, iii): There grows, / In my most ill-compos'd affection, such / A stanchless avarice, that, were I king, / I should cut off the nobles for their lands.

William Shakespeare (*Measure for Measure*, Act III, i): If thou art rich, thou art poor; / For, like an ass whose back with ingots bows, / Thou bear'st thy heavy riches but a journey, / And death unloads thee.

William Shakespeare (*The Merry Wives of Windsor*, Act II, ii): Money is a good soldier sir, and will on.

William Shakespeare (*The Merry Wives of Windsor*, Act II, ii): If money go before, all ways do lie open.

William Shakespeare (*Othello*, Act I, iii): Put but money in thy purse.... Fill thy purse with money.

William Shakespeare (*Othello*, act III, iii): Who steals my purse steals trash.

William Shakespeare (*Romeo and Juliet,* Act V, i): There is thy gold; worse poison to men's souls.

William Shakespeare (*The Taming of the Shrew*, Act I, ii): Nothing comes amiss, so money comes withal.

William Shakespeare (*The Taming of the Shrew*, Act I, ii): Why, give him gold enough and marry him to a puppet, or an aglet-baby; or an old trot with ne'er a tooth in her head, though she have as many diseases as two-and-fifty-horses! Why, nothing comes amiss, so money comes withal.

William Shakespeare (*Venus and Adonis*, 1. 767): Foul-cankering rust the hidden treasure frets, / But gold that's put to use more gold begets.

George Bernard Shaw: Lack of money is the root of all evil.

George Bernard Shaw: Money is indeed the most important thing in the world; and all sound and successful personal and national morality should have this fact for its basis.

George Bernard Shaw: The seven deadly sins.... Food, clothing, firing, rent, taxes, respectability and children. Nothing can lift those seven millstones from man's neck but money; and the spirit cannot soar until the millstones are lifted.

Percy Bysshe Shelley: Wealth is a power usurped by the few to compel the many to labor for their benefit.

Adam Smith: The rich, in particular, are necessarily interested to support that order of things which can alone secure them in the possession of their own advantages.

Southern Expression (used by Phil Miller of Tennessee): They've got enough money to burn a wet mule.

Roger Starr: Money is the most egalitarian force in society. It confers power on whoever holds it.

Gertrude Stein: Money is always there, but the pockets change; it is not in the same pockets after a change, and that is all there is to say about money.

Robert Louis Stevenson: The price we have to pay for money is paid in liberty.

Rex Stout: Nothing is more admirable than the fortitude with which millionaires tolerate the disadvantages of their wealth.

Talmud: There is no money for provisions, but there is for waste.

Mother Teresa: Let us not be satisfied with just giving money. Money is not enough, money can be got, but they need your hearts to love them. So, spread your love everywhere you go.

Mother Teresa: It is a poverty to decide that a child must die so that you may live as you wish.

Mother Teresa: Our life of poverty is as necessary as the work itself. Only in heaven will we see how much we owe to the poor for helping us to love God better because of them.

Mother Teresa: We think sometimes that poverty is only being hungry, naked and homeless. But, the poverty of being unwanted, unloved and uncared for is the greatest poverty. We must start in our own homes to remedy this kind of poverty.

Mother Teresa: Being unwanted, unloved, uncared for, forgotten by everybody, I think that is a much greater hunger, a much greater poverty than the person who has nothing to eat.

Mother Teresa: Loneliness and the feeling of being unwanted is the most terrible poverty.

Mother Teresa: Loneliness is the most terrible poverty.

Joseph A. Thomas: the upper crust is a bunch of crumbs held together by dough.

Henry David Thoreau: You may raise money enough to tunnel a mountain, but you cannot raise money enough to hire a man who is minding his own business.

Tolstoy: Money is a new form of slavery, and distinguishable from the old simply by the fact that it is impersonal – that there is no human relations between master and slave.

Tolstoy: He who has money has in his pocket those who have none.

Mark Twain: There are two times in a man's life when he should not speculate: when he can't afford it, and when he can.

Mark Twain: I'm opposed to millionaires, but it would be dangerous to offer me the position.

Mark Twain: We Americans worship the almighty dollar! Well, it is a worthier god than Heredity Privilege.

Mark Twain: A banker is a fellow who lends you his umbrella when the sun is shining, but wants it back the minute it begins to rain.

Mark Twain: We (Americans) are the lavishest and showiest and most luxury-loving people on the earth; and at our masthead we fly one true and honest symbol, the gaudiest flag the world has ever seen.

Mark Twain: I wish to become rich, so that I can instruct the people and glorify honest poverty a little, like those kind-hearted, fat, benevolent people do.

Mark Twain: The lack of money is the root of all evil.

Mark Twain: Some men worship rank, some worship heroes, some worship power, some worship God, & over these ideals they dispute & cannot unite – but they all worship money.

Mark Twain: No one ever went broke under-estimating the taste of the American public.

Mark Twain: Don't go around saying the world owes you a living, the world owes you nothing. It was here first.

UA: Economists are people who work with numbers but don't have the personality to be accountants.
UA: It is difficult to save money when your neighbors keep buying things you can't afford.
UA: The only business that makes money without advertising is the United States mint.
UA: My father lost money on everything my brother ever made. My brother made... mistakes.
UA: Would you be happy if you have all the money you wanted? I would be happy if I have all the money my creditors wanted.
UA: Before you borrow money from a friend, decide which you need more.
UA: Always borrow from a pessimist—he never expects it back.
UA: The drive-in bank was established so that the real owner of the car could get to see it once in awhile.
UA: Better a steady dime than a rare dollar
UA: The wages of sin are unreported.
UA: Jesus saves, (but) Moses invests.
UA (often described as the real estae agents' mantra; Answer to the question: What are the three most important factors in determining the selling price of a property?): **Location, location, location.**
UA (Wisconsin expression): "Spondulicks" = old Mid-Western word for cash
Jesse Unruh: Money is the mother's milk of politics.
Gore Vidal: The more money an American accumulates, the less interesting he becomes.
Katherine Whitehorn: The easiest way for your chidren to learn about money is for you not to have any.
Thomas Wolfe: With money I'll throttle the beast-blind world between my fingers. Without it I am strapped; weakened; my life is a curse and a care.
Alexander Woollcott: A broker is a man who runs your fortune into a shoestring.
Herman Wouk: Income taxes are the most imaginative fiction written today.
Yiddish Proverb: If rich people could hire other people to die for them, the poor could make a wonderful living.
Yiddish Saying: You can tell what God thinks of money by looking at some of the people he gives it to.
Yiddish Proverb: To be rich is not everything, but it certainly helps.
Henny Youngman: I had plastic surgery last week. I cut my credit cards.

MOTHER (See PARENT)

MOTIVE/INSPIRATION (See also COURAGE; MILITARY)

Uncle Anthony: A lot of things in life are like a wheelbarrow – Nuthin' happens until you start pushing.
Uncle Anthony: Let me give ya an example of motivation – take eggs an' bacon – the hen was involved, but the pig was really committed to the thing.
Uncle Anthony: Businessmen invest money for one reason – to make more money – they call it profit. Governments and charities invest for political or charitable reasons. Private corporations do it for lots of profit dollars. So, you gotta expect a certain amount of greed since profit is the prime motive.
Aunt Mary Carlo: I tink he went an bought himself an alarm clock dat don't ring – it applauds!
Aunt Mary Carlo: All she needs to boost her ego/confidence is a swivel chair.
Aesop: Never trust the advice of a man in difficulties.
African Proverb: Every morning a lion wakes up and knows it must out-run the slowest gazelle; every morning a gazelle wakes up and knows it must outrun the fastest lion. Whether you are a gazelle or a lion, when you wake up, you better start running!
Erna Asp: Instead of crying over spilt milk, go milk another cow.
Sir James Matthew Barrie: Never ascribe to an opponent motives meaner than your own.
Sarah Bernhardt's Personal Motto: "Devise comen" = "DESPITE ALL ODDS"
Bible: Colossians: Set your affection on things above, not on things on the earth.
Bible: Hebrews 10:35: Cast not away therefore your confidence, which hath great recompence of remorse.
Bible: Isaiah 14:3: The Lord shall give thee rest from thy sorrow, and from thy fear.
Bible: Isaiah 35:3: Strengthen ye the weak hands, and confirm the feeble knees.
Bible: Isaiah 40:31: They that wait on the Lord shall renew their strength; they shall mount up with wings as eagles; they shall run, and not be weary, and they shall walk, and not faint.

Bible: Mark 9:35: If any man desire to be first, the same shall be last of all, and servant of all.

Bible: Matthew 26:41: The spirit indeed is willing, but the flesh is weak.

Bible: Philippians 4:11: I have learned, in whatever state I am, therewith to be content.

Bible: Proverbs 15:27: He that is greedy of gain troubleth his own house.

Bible: Proverbs 24:5: A wise man is strong; yea, a man of knowledge increaseth strength.

Bible: Psalms 23:4: Yea, though I walk through the valley of the shadow of death, I will fear no evil: for thou art with me; thy rod and thy staff they comfort me.

Bible: Psalms 46:1: God is our refuge and our strength, a very present help in trouble.

Ambrose Bierce: AIM, n. The task we set our wishes to.

Ambrose Bierce: AMBITION, n. An overmastering desire to be villified by enemies while living and made ridiculous by friends when dead.

Ambrose Bierce: CUI BONO? (Latin). What good would that do *me*?

Ambrose Bierce: PLAN, v.t. To bother about the best method of accomplishing an accidental result.

Ambrose Bierce: POCKET, n. The cradle of motive and the grave of conscience. In woman this organ is lacking; so she acts without motive, and her conscience, denied burial, remains ever alive, confessing the sins of others.

Ambrose Bierce: TENACITY, n. A certain quality of the human hand in its relation to the coin of the realm. It attains its highest development in the hand of authority and is considered a serviceable equipment for a career in politics....

Ambrose Bierce: ZEAL, n. A certain nervous disorder afflicting the young and inexperienced. A passion that goeth before a sprawl....

Jacob M. Braude: Life is a grindstone; whether it grinds you down or polishes you depends on what you're made of.

Jacob Braude: Always behave like a duck - keep calm and unruffled on the surface, but paddle like the devil underneath.

Pearl Buck: The secret of joy in work is contained in one work—excellence. To know how to do something well is to enjoy it.

Buddha: If a man speaks or acts with pure thought, happiness follows him like a shadow that never leaves him.

Lois McMaster Bujold: If you can't do what you want, do what you can.

Charles Bukowski: You begin saving the world by saving one man at a time; all else is grandiose romanticism or politics.

Leo Burnett: When you reach for the stars you may not quite get one, but you won't come up with a handful of mud either.

Edwin Hubbel Chapin: Through every rift of discovery some seeming anomaly drops out of the darkness, and falls, as a golden link, into the great chain of order.

Paddy Chayevsky (wrote the 1976 film *Network*, in which Peter Finch as a TV pundit exhorts his viewers): "I want you to get up right now and go to the window, open it and stick your head out and yell: **'I'm as mad as hell, and I'm not going to take this any more!'"**

Chinese Proverb: Better to light a candle than to curse the darkness.

Chinese Proverb: Want a thing long enough and you don't.

Sir Winston Churchill (May 13, 1940): "Blood, toil, tears and sweat...."

Sir Winston Churchill: Never give in. Never, never, never, never, in nothing great or small, large or petty, never give in except to convictions of honour and good sense. Never yield to force; never yield to the apparently overwhelming might of the enemy.

Sir Winston Churchill: Before you can inspire with emotion, you must be swamped with it yourself. Before you can move their tears, your own must flow. To convince them, you must yourself believe.

Sir Winston Churchill: Still, if you will not fight for the right when you can easily win without bloodshed, if you will not fight when your victory will be sure and not so costly, you may come to the moment when you will have to fight with all the odds against you and only a precarious chance for survival. There may be a worse case. You may have to fight when there is no chance of victory, because it is better to perish than to live as slaves.

Sir Winston Churchill: Today we may say aloud before an awe-struck world: 'We are still masters of our fate. We are still captain of our souls.

Sir Winston Churchill: have never accepted what many people have kindly said, namely that I have inspired the nation. It was the nation and the race dwelling all around the globe that had the lion heart. I had the luck to give the roar.

Marcus Tullius Cicero (Roman lawyer, statesman, philosopher, 106-43 BC, *Pro Roscio Amerino*, xxx, 84): The illustrious Lucius Cassius, whom the Roman people considered the wisest and most conscientious of judges, was in the habit of asking repeatedly in trials, "who had profited by it?" (*L. Cassius ille quem populus Romanus verissimum et sapientissimum iudicem putabat, indentidem in causis quaerere solebat, "cui bono" fuisset.*)

Cicero: To who's good? (Cui buno?)

Cicero: It is a shameful thing to be weary of inquiry when what we search for is excellent.

Greg Cusimano: We need straight line logic for direction and passion for motivation.

Walt Disney: Around here, however, we don't look backwards for very long. We keep moving forward, opening up new doors and doing new things, because we're curious ... and curiosity keeps leading us down new paths.

Benjamin Disraeli: Nurture your mind with great thoughts; to believe in the heroic makes heroes.

Mike Ditka: You never really lose until you quit trying.

Dwight D. Eisenhower (General, Supreme Allied Commander, Europe WWII, June 5, 1944, "D-Day minus one"): Soldiers, Sailors and Airmen of the Allied Expeditionary Force: You are about to embark upon the Great Crusade, toward which we have striven these many months. The eyes of the world are upon you. Good luck! And let us all beseech the blessing of Almighty God upon this great and noble undertaking.

Ralph Waldo Emerson: We sing as we are bid. Our inspirations are very manageable and tame. Death and Sin have whispered in the ear of our wild horses and they have become drays and hacks.

Henry Ford: Failure is the only opportunity to begin again more intelligently.

Brendan Francis: Inspirations never go in for long engagements; they demand immediate marriage to action.

Anne Frank: How wonderful it is that nobody need wait a single moment before starting to improve the world.

Robert Frost: The world is full of willing people, some willing to work, the rest willing to let them.

Thomas Fuller: All things are difficult before they are easy.

Sir John Eardley Wilmot (English Chief Justice, 1767): The end directs and sanctifies the means.

Mohandas Karamchand (Mahatma) Gandhi: Numerous examples have convinced me that God ultimately saves him whose motive is pure.

Gandhi: The moment there is suspicion about a person's motives, everything he does becomes tainted.

Johann Wolfgang von Goethe: Divide and rule, a sound motto. Unite and lead, a better one.

Baltasar Gracian: Attend easy tasks as if they were difficult, and difficult as if they were easy; in the one case that confidence may not fall asleep, in the other that it may not be dismayed.

Wayne Gretzky: You miss 100% of the shots you never take.

John Heywood (*The Proverbs of John Heywood*, 1546): Nothing is impossible to a willing heart.

Oliver Wendell Holmes: A man may have as bad a heart as he chooses, if his conduct is within the rules.

Oliver Wendell Holmes: Philosophy does not furnish motives, but it shows men that they are not fools for doing what they already want to do.

James Hornfischer ("*SHIP OF GHOSTS: The Story of the USS Houston, FDR's Legendary Lost Cruiser, And the Epic Saga of Her Survivors*): Faith and hope are unclassified vitamins.

Thomas Jefferson: I have a great believer in luck, and I find the harder I work the more I have of it.

Samuel Johnson: The morality of an action depends upon the motive from which we act.

Samuel Johnson: The two great movers of the human mind are the desire of good, and the fear of evil.

Abba Kovner (WWII Polish-Jewish freedom fighter to his fellow ghetto residents): Do not go like sheep to the slaughter!

Frankie Lane (theme song for TV series *Rawhide*): Move 'em on, head 'em up, head 'em up, move 'em on, / Move 'em on, head 'em up ... Rawhide!

Ann Landers: There are really only three types of people: those who make things happen, those who watch things happen, and those who say, What happened?

Edward Law, Lord Ellenborough (English Chief Justice, 1817): It is a principal of law, that a person intends to do that which is the natural effect of what he does.

Legal maxim: Acts indicate the intention.

Legal maxim: Outward actions are a clue to hidden secrets

Allard Lowenstein: The question should be, is it worth trying to do, not can it be done.

George Leigh Mallory (in 1923, during a lecture tour asked why he wanted to be the first to climb Mt. Everest, he replied with his famous quote, which was repeated by Sir Edmund Hillary regarding his own successful attempt in 1953): "Because it's there."

Karl Marx: The road to Hell is paved with good intentions.

Michelangelo: Lord, grant that I may always desire more than I accomplish.

Moliere: The road is long from the intention to the completion.

Adolph Monod: Between the great things we cannot do and the small things we will not do, the danger is that we shall do nothing.

Mother Teresa (born Agnes Gonxha Beiaxhiu, 1910-1997, Humanitarian, Nobel Peace Prize 1979, from *"A Simple Path"*; found on the wall at Shishu Bhavan, an orphanage in Calcutta, India, and on a Sign In Mother Teresa's Office): DO IT ANYWAY: People are unreasonable, illogical, and self-centered, / LOVE THEM ANYWAY // If you do good, people will accuse you of selfish, ulterior motives, / DO GOOD ANYWAY // If you are successful, you win false friends and true enemies, / SUCCEED ANYWAY // The good you do will be forgotten tomorrow, / DO GOOD ANYWAY // Honesty and frankness make you vulnerable, / BE HONEST AND FRANK ANYWAY // What you spent years building may be destroyed overnight, / BUILD ANYWAY // People really need help but may attack you if you help them, / HELP PEOPLE ANYWAY // Give the world the best you have and you'll get kicked in the teeth, / GIVE THE WORLD THE BEST YOU'VE GOT ANYWAY.

Edward R. Murrow (legendary broadcast journalist, born Egbert Roscoe Murrow, in Pole Cat Creek, Gilford County, NC, raised and educated in Washington state, 1908-1965): "Let's get up off our fat surpluses!"

Frederick Nietzsche: At times one remains faithful to a cause only because its opponents do not cease to be insipid.

Lawrence Olivier (motivational speech in WWII England): "URGENCY, SPEED, COURAGE! Our Watchwords shall be: Urgency in all our decisions, Speed in the execution of all our plans, Courage in the face of all our enemies … and may God bless our cause!"

Thomas Paine: It is error only, and not truth, that shrinks from inquiry.

Knute Rockne (at half-time of football game with Army, Notre Dame the coach recalled for his team what George Gipp, a former star who died young had said): "Rock, someday when things look real tough for Notre Dame, ask the boys to go out there and win one for me." Hence, the expression: **Win one for the Gipper!**

Will Rogers: Even if you are on the right track, you'll get run over if you just sit there.

Will Rogers: We live in an age of "urge." We do nothing till somebody shoves us.

Eleanor Roosevelt: No one can make you feel inferior without your consent.

Eleanor Roosevelt: The thing always to remember is that you must do the thing you think you cannot do

Arthur Schopenhauer: Talent hits a target no one else can hit; genius hits a target no one else can see.

Frank Scully: Why not go out on a limb? Isn't that we're the fruit is?

Seneca: It is not the incense, or the offering which is acceptable to God, but the purity and devotion of the worshipper.

William Shakespeare (*All's Well That Ends Well*, Act V, iii): All impediments in fancy's course / Are motives of more fancy.

William Shakespeare (*Antony and Cleopatra,* Act II, ii): To this good purpose, that so fairly shows, / Dream of impediment.

William Shakespeare (*Hamlet*, Act II, ii): The very substance of the ambitious is merely the shadow of a dream.

William Shakespeare (*Hamlet*, Act III, ii): Purpose is but the slave to memory, / Of violent birth, but poor validity.

William Shakespeare (*Hamlet*, Act V, ii): Purposes mistook Fall'n on the inventors' heads.

William Shakespeare (*Henry V*, Act III, i): Once more unto the breach, dear friends, once more / Or close the wall up with our English dead.

William Shakespeare (*Henry V*, Act IV, iii; The English Camp, on St. Crispin's Day, Oct 25, 1415 at Battle of Agincourt: The Agincourt Speech or "St Crispin's Day Speech"): WESTMORELAND: O that we now had here / But one thousand of those men in England / That do not work to-day? / HENRY V: What's he that wishes so? / My cousin Westmoreland? {No, my fair cousin: / If we are mark'd to die, we are enow / To do our country loss; and if to live, / The fewer men, the greater share of honour. / God's will, I pray thee wish not one man more.

William Shakespeare (*Henry V*, Act IV, iii; The English Camp, on St. Crispin's Day, Oct 25, 1415 at Battle of Agincourt: The Agincourt Speech or "St Crispin's Day Speech"): HENRY V: We few, we happy few, we band of brothers; / For he to-day that sheds his blood with me / Shall be my brother; be he ne'er so base, / This day shall gentle his condition: / And gentlemen in England, now a-bed, / Shall think themselves accurs'd they were not here: / And hold their manhoods cheap, while any speaks / That fought with us upon Saint Crispin's day.

William Shakespeare (*II Henry VI*, Act III, i): Virtue is chok'd with foul ambition.

William Shakespeare (*Julius Caesar*, Act I, iii): Man may construe things after their fashion, / Clean from the purpose of the things themselves.

William Shakespeare (*Julius Caesar*, Act III, i): Ambition's debt is paid.

William Shakespeare (*Julius Caesar*, Act III, ii): The noble Brutus / Hath told you Caesar was ambitious: / If it were so, it was a grievous fault; / And grievously hath Caesar answered it.

William Shakespeare (*King Lear*, Act I, i): We shall express our darker purpose.

William Shakespeare (*Macbeth*, Act I, v): No compunctious visitings of nature / Shake my fell purpose.

William Shakespeare (*Macbeth*, Act I, vii): I have no spur / To prick the sides of my intent, but only / Vaulting ambition; which o'erleaps itself, / And falls on the other -

William Shakespeare (*Romeo and Juliet*, Act V, iii): The time and my intents are savage-wild, / More fierce and more inexorable far / Than empty tigers or the roaring sea.

William Shakespeare (*Twelfth Night*, Act II, iii): My purpose is, indeed, a horse of that colour.

William Shakespeare (*Macbeth*, Act II, ii): Infirm of purpose!

William Shakespeare (*Macbeth*, Act IV, i): The flighty purpose never is o'ertook, / Unless the deed go with it.

George Bernard Shaw: The people who get on in this world are the people who get up and look for the circumstances they want and, if they can't find them, make them.

George Bernard Shaw: No more inspiration in her than in a plate of muffins.

General William T. Sherman (In the Civil War Battle of Altoona, Georgia, October 5, 1864, he semaphored from Keneshaw Mountain to General John M. Corse: "Sherman says hold fast. We are coming." Or as it later evolved: "Hold the fort (I am coming)."

Socrates: Are you not ashamed of heaping up the greatest amount of money and honor and reputation, and caring so little about wisdom and truth and the greatest improvement of the soul.

Socrates: My belief is that to have no wants is divine.

Benedict Spinoza: As long as a man imagines that he cannot do a certain thing, it is impossible for him to do it.

John Steinbeck (1939 novel *The Grapes of Wrath*): I know this – a man got to do what he got to do.

U.S. Army General "Vinegar Joe" Stilwell (WWII motto): Illegitimi(s) non carborundum. Or translated: Don't let the bastards grind you down.

Clement Stone: There is little difference in people... the little difference is attitude. The big difference is whether it is positive or negative.

Kathleen A. Sutton: When you can't have what you want, it's time to start wanting what you have.

Mother Teresa: We can do no great things—only small things with great love.

J. Arthur Thomson: The most powerful factors in the world are clear ideas in the minds of energetic men of goodwill.

Henry David Thoreau: Why should we be in such a desperate haste to succeed, and in such desperate enterprises? If a man does not keep pace with his companions, perhaps it is because he hears a different drummer.

Donald Trump: As long as you're going to think anyway, think big.

Mark Twain: To do something, say something, see something, before *anybody* else—these are things that confer a pleasure compared with which other pleasures are tame and commonplace, other ecstasies cheap and trivial.

Mark Twain: A man has no business to be depressed by a disappointment, anyway; he ought to make up his mind to get even.

Mark Twain: When I reflect upon the number of disagreeable people who I know have gone to a better world, I am moved to lead a different life.

U.S. Olympic Team slogan (first used at the 1980 Winter Olympis, Lake Placid, NY): Go for gold!

U.S. Postal Service (Pony Express, c. 1860 slogan): The mail must get through.

Jimmy Valvanno (aka "Jimmy V," legendary college basketball coach): "Never give up! Don't ever give up!"

Virgil: The boldest motive is the public good.

Albert von Szent-Gyorgyi: Discovery consists of seeing what everybody has seen and thinking what nobody has thought.

Oscar Wilde: Whenever a man does a thoroughly stupid thing, it is always from the noblest motives.

William Wordsworth (poem To The Planet Venus, aka The Vesper Star. the Morning Star and the Evening Star): "What strong allurement draws, what spirit guides thee Vesper?"

W.B. Yeats: You ask if inspiration can be lost; no, when creation has started (then it goes on like the child in the womb).

Yiddish Proverb: What you can't acquire, don't desire.

Dan Zadra: Worry is a misuse of imagination.

NEGLECT/NEGLIGENCE

Uncle Anthony: You can be sincere and still be very stupid.

Uncle Anthony: For those guys, every morning is "the dawn of a new error."

Uncle Anthony: There's never enough time (and money) to plan and prepare properly, but there's always enough time and money to fix all the mistakes caused by piss poor planning.

Uncle Anthony: Y'know the "50-50-90 Rule?" Anytime you got a 50-50 chance of getting something right, there's a 90% probability you'll get it wrong.

Uncle Anthony: Y'know the 3 R's – reading, 'riting and 'rithmatic? Well, I think ya should remember these three R's: Respect for yourself; Respect for others; and Responsibility for your actions.

Aunt Mary Carlo (she would substitute any great center fielder in the same mold as "Willie (Mays), Mickey (Mantle) and The Duke (Snider): Y'know even Willie Mays dropped the ball once in a while.

Aunt Mary Carlo: Instead of "Let's get ready to rumble" their motto musta been "Let's get ready to STUMBLE!"

Aunt Mary Carlo: I think he stopped to think, and forgot to start again.

Aunt Mary Carlo: Ya know, stupidity is NOT a handicap ... so park somewheres else!

African Proverb: Do not look where you fell, but where you slipped.

African Proverb: No one tests the depth of a river with both feet.

Tallulah Bankhead: The only thing I regret about my life is the length of it. If I had to live my life again, I would make all the same mistakes, only sooner.

Richard Bentley: The fortuitous or casual concourse of atoms.

Yogi Berra: If the world was perfect, it wouldn't be.

Yogi Berra: We made too many wrong mistakes.

Bible: Colossians 3:25: He that doeth wrong shall receive for the wrong which he hath done: and there is no respect of persons.

Bible: Deuteronomy 24:16: Every man shall be put to death for his own sin.

Bible: Ecclesiastes 12:13: Fear God, and keep his commandments: for this is the whole duty of man.

Bible: John 9:41: If ye were blind, ye should have no sin: but now ye say, We see; therefore your sin remaineth.

Bible: Luke 12:48: Unto whomsoever much is given, of him shall much be required.

Bible: Luke 17:10: We have done that which was our duty to do.

Bible: Luke 20:25: Render therefore unto Caesar the things which are Caesar's, and unto God the things which be God's.

Bible: Matthew 6:3: When thou doest alms, let not thy left hand know what thy right doeth.

Bible: Matthew 7:14: Straight is the gate, and narrow is the way, which leadeth unto life, and few there be that find it.

Bible: Proverbs 3:27: Withhold not good from them to whom it is due, when it is in the power of thine hand to do it.

Bible: Proverbs 26:27: Whoso diggeth a pit shall fall therein.

Bible: Romans 4:12: Every one of us shall give account of himself to God.

Bible: Romans 13:7: Render therefore to all their dues: tribute to whom tribute is due; custom to whom custom; fear to whom fear; honour to whom honour.

Ambrose Bierce: ACKNOWLEDGE, v.t. To confess. Acknowledgment of one another's faults is the highest duty imposed by our love of truth.

Ambrose Bierce: DULLARD, n. A member of the reigning dynasty in letters and life. The Dullards came in with Adam, and being both numerous and sturdy have overrun the habitable world. The secret of their power is their insensibility to blows; tickle them with a bludgeon and they laugh with a platitude. The Dullards came originally from Boeotia, whence they were driven by stress of starvation, their dulness having blighted the crops. For some centuries they infested Philistia, and many of them are called Philistines to this day. In the turbulent times of the Crusades they withdrew thence and gradually overspread all Europe, occupying most of the high places in politics, art, literature, science and theology. Since a detachment of Dullards came over with the Pilgrims in the *Mayflower* and made a favorable report of the country, their increase by birth, immigration, and conversion has been rapid and steady. According to the most trustworthy statistics the number of adult Dullards in the United States is but little short of thirty millions, including the statisticians. The intellectual centre of the race is somewhere about Peoria, Illinois, but the New England Dullard is the most shockingly moral.

Ambrose Bierce: DUTY, n. That which sternly impels us in the direction of profit, along the line of desire....

Ambrose Bierce: HURRY, n. The dispatch of bunglers.

Ambrose Bierce: PEDESTRIAN, n. The variable (and audible) part of the roadway for an automoblie.

Ambrose Bierce: POSITIVE: being mistaken at the top of one's voice.

Ambrose Bierce: RESPONSIBILITY, n. A detachable burden easily shifted to the shoulders of God, Fate, Fortune, Luck or one's neighbor. In the days of astrology it was customary to unload it upon a star.

Josh Billings: Most men would rather be charged with malice than with making a blunder.

Lord Charles Synge Christopher Bowen (English Judge, 1835-1894, defined the "Reasonable Man" as): The man on the Clapham omnibus.

Joseoh P. Bradley (New Jersey lawyer, Assoc. Justice US Supreme Court, 1813-1892): The event is always a great teacher. *The Nevada*, 106 US 154, 27 L ed 149, 1 S Ct 234 (1882)

William Baliol Brett, Viscount Esher (English judge, 1815-1899): Whenever one person is by circumstances placed in such a position with regard to another that every one of ordinary sense who did think would at once recognize that if he did not use ordinary care and skill in his own conduct with regard to those circumstances he would cause danger of injury to the person or property of the other, a duty arises to use ordinary care and skill to avoid such danger. *Heaven v. Pender*, 11 Q.B.D. 503 (1883).

Edmund Burke: A wise and salutary neglect.

Edmund Burke: No one could make a greater mistake than he who did nothing because he could do only a little.

Burma-Shave jingle/road side ad: If daisies are your favorite flower, keep pushin' up those miles per hour!

Samuel Butler: From a worldly point of view there is no mistakes so great as that of being always right.

Augustus Caesar: Hasten slowly.

Benjamin N. Cardozo (Chief Judge NY Ct of Appeals, Assoc. Justice US S Ct, 1870-1938, quoting Pollock, *Torts, 11th ed*): Negligence is not actionable unless it involves the invasion of a legally protected interest, the violation of a right. "Proof of negligence in the air, so to speak will not do." Palsgrave v. Long Island R.R. Co., 248 N.Y. 339, 341 (1928)

Benjamin N. Cardozo: Standards of prudent conduct are declared at times by courts, but they are taken over from the facts of life. Pokora v. Wabash R. Co., 292 US 98, 78 L ed 1149, 54 S Ct 580 (1934)

Benjamin N. Cardozo: Looking back at the mishap with the wisdom born of the event, we can see that the mechanic would have done better if he had given warning of the change of pose. Extraordinary prevision might have whispered to him at the moment that the warning would be helpful. What the law exacted of him, however, was only the ordinary prevision to be looked for in a busy world. Breene v. Sibley, et al., 257 N.Y. 190 (1931)

Benjamin N. Cardozo: The hand once set to a task may not always be withdrawn with impunity though liability would fail if it had been applied at all.

Sir Winston Churchill: Perhaps it is better to be irresponsible and right, than to be responsible and wrong.

Confucius: A man who has committed a mistake and doesn't correct it is committing another mistake.

Gregory S. Cusimano: To err is human. To blame it on somebody else is more human.

Danish Proverb: Faults are thick where love is thin.

Charles Dickens: Accidents will occur in the best regulated families.

Charles Dickens: Fortuitous combination of circumstances.

Amelia Earhart: In soloing – as in other activities – it is far easier to start something than it is to finish it.

Albert Einstein (August 1920 apologizing to a friend about his newspaper article in rebuttal to the Anti-relativity group rally and meeting in Berlin Philharmonic Hall): Don't be too severe with me. Everyone must from time to time make a sacrifice on the altar of stupidity to please the diety and mankind, and I did so thoroughly with my article.

T.S. Eliot: Half the harm that is done in this world is due to people who want to feel important. They don't mean to do harm, but the harm does not interest them.

Owen Feltham: Negligence is the rust of the soul, that corrodes through all her best resolves.

Saint Francis de Sales: The business of finding fault is very easy, and that of doing better very difficult.

Al Franken: Appreciate your mistakes for what they are: precious life lessons that can only be learned the hard way. Unless it's a fatal mistake, which at least, others can learn from.

Benjamin Franklin: Most fools think they are only ignorant.

Benjamin Franklin: A little neglect may breed great mischief; for want of a nail the shoe was lost; for want of the shoe the horse was lost, and for want of the horse the rider was lost, being overtaken and slain by the enemy, all for want of a little care about a horse-shoe nail.

French Proverb: Only he who does nothing makes a mistake.

Gaelic Proverb: If the best man's faults were written on his forehead, it would make him pull his hat over his eyes.

German Proverb: An error no wider than a hair will lead a hundred miles away from the goal.

Johann Wolfgang von Goethe: There is nothing worse than aggressive stupidity.

Greek Proverb: There's many a slip 'twixt the cup and the lip.

Greek Proverb: It is disgraceful to stumble against the same stone twice.

Sir Frederic Arthur Greer (English Judge, writing about "The Reasonable Man"): The person concerned is sometimes described as "the man in the street" or "the man in the Chapham omnibus," or, as I recently read in an American author, "the man who takes the magazines home, and in the evening pushes the lawn mower in his shirt sleeves." Hall v. Brooklands Auto Racing Club, 1 K.B. 205, 224 (1933).

Joseph Hall: The best ground, untilled and neglected, soonest runs out into rank weeds.—A man of knowledge that is either negligent or uncorrected cannot but grow wild and godless.

Edith Hamilton: When the freedom they wished for most was freedom from responsibility then Athens ceased to be free and was never free again.

Frederich Hebbel: There are persons who always find a hair in their plate of soup for the simple reason that, when they sit down before it, they shake their heads until one falls in.

Hebrew Proverb: Love him who tells you your faults in private.

Hebrew Proverb: He is great whose faults can be numbered.

John Heywood (*The Proverbs of John Heywood*, 1546): Haste makes waste.

Oliver Wendell Holmes, Jr (*Common Law*, 109, 1881): A blind man is not required to see at his peril.

Italian Proverb: Any man may make a mistake; none but a fool will persist in it.

Molly Ivins: I believe in practicing prudence at least once every two or three years.

Thomas Jefferson: We Americans sip our hot soup. The French gulp it. (Speaking of the violent French Revolution)

J. Jenkins: To air is human, but when the eraser wears out ahead of the pencil, you are overdoing it.

Ben Jonson: He that thinks he can afford to be negligent, is not far from being poor

Samuel Johnson: He that thinks he can afford to be negligent, is not far from being poor.

Franz Kafka: There art two cardinal sins from which to all others spring: impatience and laziness.

Sir William Rann Kennedy (English judge, 1846-1915): This is the classic quotation in "EGGSHELL" SKULL CASES; that is, the tortfeasor must take his victim as he finds him): If a man is negligently run over or otherwise negligently injured in his body, it is no answer to the sufferer's claim for damages that he would have suffered less injury, or no injury at all, if he had an unusually thin skull or an unusually weak heart. Dulieu v. White & Sons, 2 K.B. 669, 679 (1901)

Rudyard Kipling: I never made a mistake in my life; at least, never one I could not explain away afterwards.

Henry Lamm (Assoc & Chief Justice Supreme Court, Missouri, 1846-1927; early statement of "contributory negligence"): We are admonished that hard cases are the quicksands of the law. Neither equity nor the law relieves those who seek aid in Court merely to avoid the effects of their own negligence.... Negligence always has misfortune for a companion. Lipscomb v. Talbott, 243 Mo 1, 36 (1912)

Francois de La Rochefoucauld: Almost all our faults are more pardonable than the methods we resort to to hide them

D.H. Lawrence: If only one could have two lives: the first, in which to make one's mistakes, which seem as if they *had* to be made; and the second in which to profit by them.

Abraham Lincoln: You cannot escape the reponsibility of tomorrow by evading it today.

Henry Wadsworth Longfellow: It takes less time to do a thing right than it does to explain why you did it wrong.

Baron Hugh Pattison Macmillan (Scottish Judge, 1873-1952): The categories of negligence are never closed. Donoghue v. Stevenson, A.C. 562, 619 (1932)

Norman Mansbridge (in a 1938 *Punch* cartoon – two policemen are shown standing outside a cinema that is showing "The Mansion Murder" and on the poster it asks: "Who killed the duke?" One policeman says to the other): I guessed **the butler did it.**"

W. Somerset Maugham: Only a mediocre person is always at his best.

W. Somerset Maugham: It is cruel to discover one's mediocrity only when it is too late.

William McFee: People don't ever seem to realize that doing what's right is no guarantee against misfortune.

John Stuart Mill: A person may cause evil to others not only by his actions but by his inaction, and in either case he is justly accountable to them for the injury.

Dennis Miller: "He was about as hip to (or honest about) the situation (or disaster) he had caused as the Captain of the Titanic, who said as his ship was sinking: "Ice? What ice? I didn't see any ice? Did you see any ice?"

Henry Miller: To be a victim of one's own mistakes is bad enough, but to be a victim of the other fellow's mistakes as well is too much.

Newton Minow: We've gotten to the point where everybody's got a right and nobody's got a responsibility.

Mohammedan Proverb: When God wishes a man well, He gives him insight into his faults.

Molière: A learned fool is more foolish than an ignorant fool.

Michael A. Musmanno (Justice of Pennsylvania Supreme Court, 1959): "Accidents": Accidents do not ordinarily happen at a leisurely pace or with the retardation of a slow motion picture. Cars move and stop, move again, lights change, there are sweeping glances and suddenly the air is shaken with the ugly noises of clashing and grinding steel, tin, glass, and often human bone and flesh.

Michael A. Musmanno (Justice of the Sup. Ct. of Pennsylvania, 1959): A person who goes into a store to help enrich the store's owner has the right to expect that after entering the establishment, the door will not violently return to strike him down like an avenging fury.

Michael A. Musmanno (Justice of the Sup. Ct. of Pennsylvania, 1959): What is contributory negligence? It's simply means doing what one should not do, or failing to act as one should. The standard of performance as to what one should or should not do is intended to be that conduct which one expects in a reasonably prudent person. What is a reasonably prudent person? It is not a perfect man with perfect vision, hearing, perspective, intuition, foresight and hindsight. The reasonably prudent person whom the court decisions uphold as an exemplar of virtue is not a composite of Einstein, Lindbergh,, Dr. Salk and Admiral Byrd. So far as the gasoline world is concerned, a reasonably prudent person is one who, with ordinary faculties, comports himself according to the gauge of the average individual who has no desire to harm anyone else on the highway—and much less and self.... In another case this Court placed the gem of revelation in the brooch of logic when it said that "having one's car under control means that in any situation *reasonably likely to arise* he will be able to stop his car before doing injury to any person or property." Applying that principle to the facts in this case, it cannot be said that it was reasonably likely that the plaintiff would find a parked car in a tunnel where it had no right to stop at all. Thus., it turns out in the end that the plaintiff is forfeiting the verdict which was awarded him by a jury of his peers because he has eyes which are like everybody else's, because he is denied the gift of prophecy to determine what an unknown truck driver will do in a darkened cavern beyond his view, and because he is simply average motorist without powers of divinnation, without mechanical magic, and without luck.

Michael A. Musmanno (Justice of Pennsylvania Supreme Court, 1959): "Split-second decisions": Why would it be unfair to hold the bus driver responsible because he had to make a split-second decision? That was his job. A good motorist must so have his wits about him that he can make split-second decisions, especially if he is the driver of a passenger bus which, because of its size alone, makes it an easy target of the road. A split-second decision is by no means an unheard-of thing, nor even unusual. Every ballplayer at bat must make a split-second decision as to whether he should swing or not each time the ball comes hurtling toward him. For a prizefighter the difference between delivering a knockout blow and finding himself on the canvas floor counting constellations no rocket can ever reach is the matter of a split-second decision. Dynamite engineers in setting off a blast must time their decision by split-seconds. Every airplane pilot is trained to make split-second decisions. Thus, it is not too much to expect of a motorist that he should know what to do when confronted with what was a not unusual or even an infrequent situation. A slight movement to the right (perhaps only the matter of a few inches or a foot or two) by the bus driver would have avoided contact with the car, and that avoidance would have saved the bus from tumbling over the embankment, imperiling life and limb of every passenger.

Michael A. Musmanno (Justice of the Sup. Ct. of Pennsylvania, 1959): Faith in one's fellow man is not negligence: The average person going about his affairs with reasonable care is not required by law to approach every phase of his daily routine with suspicion and distrust. It is not contributory negligence per se to oppose faith in one's fellow man. It is not contributory negligence for one to assume that his neighbor will not, for no reason at all, throw a boulder in his path or place a snare at his feet. (Seng v. American Stores Co., 384 Pa. 338)

Michael A. Musmanno (Justice of Pennsylvania Supreme Court, 1959): Law does not require in a moment of extreme peril and overwhelming fright, a pedestrian should do the precise thing which posthumous investigation decides would have been the perfect course for him to follow.

Michael A. Musmanno (Justice of Pennsylvania Supreme Court, 1959: Backing up a truck where, it is known, people are congregated is conduct as morally reprehensible and legally culpable as pulling the trigger of a shotgun without first ascertaining whether the gun is loaded.

Michael A. Musmanno (Justice of Pennsylvania Supreme Court, 1959): What is an accident? Everyone knows what an accident is until the word comes up in Court. Then it becomes a mysterious phenomenon, and, in order to resolve the enigma, witnesses are summoned, experts testify, lawyers argue, treatises are consulted and even when a conclave of 12 world knowledgeable individuals agree as to whether a certain set of facts made out an accident, the question may not yet be settled and it must be reheard in an appellate court. An accident, simply stated, is merely an unanticipated event; it is something which occurs not as the result of natural routine but as the culmination of forces working without design, coordination or plan. And the more disorganized the forces may be, the more confusedly they may operate, and the more indiscriminately haphazard their clashing and intermingling, the more perfect is the resulting accident.

Michael A. Musmanno (Justice of the Supreme Court of Pennsylvania, 1959): Credibility in a trial is what a compass is to a ship, an altimeter to an airplane, a sight to a rifle, and a scale to a customer in a butcher shop. Without a standard for measuring direction, height, accuracy or weight, how does one know what is true or not true? How can we determine negligence unless we first decide that we can believe the person who is telling the story of alleged negligence or non-negligence? Without credibility to back up any story told from the witness stand, the witness's testimony is as meaningless as a sack of feathers thrown to the winds.

Michael A. Musmanno (Justice of Pennsylvania Supreme Court, 1959): Forseeability: The fall of a telephone pole is not an act of God: It cannot be asserted that it was the hand of God which pushed over pole No. 16 to break Bowman's back. Snow fell, as it falls every winter in the temperate zone, and provident people anticipate this type of atmospheric precipitation by taking necessary precautions against its inflicting excessive damage. Sometimes all the ingenuity and industry of man cannot avail against the turmoil and turbulence of the elements, but it is not enough in order to escape responsibility, for the owner of an instrumentality which inflicts damage, to assert that the instrumentality was propelled by the Supreme Being and that, therefore, he can shake the clinging snow of responsibility off his hands. The defendant in the present case knew that pole No. 16 carried 28 wires and that these wires formed a grill which would receive and hold on to snow, especially if it was wet. It thus became a question of fact for the jury to determine whether the company could anticipate what should be the strength of the pole to sustain the total weight of the snow. To this requirement of knowledge there would be attached to question of suitable inspection.... In any event no person called into court to answer for a tort may find exonerated from the act of negligence charged to him by asserting that it was not he but the Supreme Being which inflicted the wound and the hurts of which the plaintiff complains. The loose use of the name of the Deity in the realm of the law should not be a matter of our approval.

Michael A. Musmanno (Justice of Pennsylvania Supreme Court, 1959): Pedestrian Responsibility: The Law does not require a pedestrian, pursuing his careful way, to keep his eyes glued to the pavement over which he walks, as if he were looking for lost gold pieces. (O'Toole v. Dunmore Borough, 404 PA. 479).

Michael A. Musmanno (Justice of Pennsylvania Supreme Court, 1959): Pedestrian is not the King of Diamonds: When a pedestrian crosses a street, looking to both right and left, he cannot, like the King of Diamonds, look in both directions simultaneously. In the physical act of surveying the scene at his left the right side blacks out, and when he directs his attention to the right the left does not exist visually.

Michael A. Musmanno (Justice of the Sup. Ct. of Pennsylvania, 1959): A Dangerous Store Floor: It needs little argumentation to convince the impartial mind that a one-fourth-inch thickness of wax on a smooth surface can precipitate a pedestrian's fall as effectively as thrusting a loose roller skate under his striding feet. Where potatoes are on sale, the more potatoes the merchant sells the greater is the success of the day for him. Thus, where the commodities which are sold or of such size and shape that to carry them away the encompassing package limits the purchaser's view of his immediate path ahead, nothing could be more necessary to the safety of the store patron than that flooring beneath his feet be maintained in a firm and safe condition. The goods and wares in most stores are so displayed on shelves, and the advertisements which proclaim the virtues of those goods and wares are so hung on the walls, that the floors is about the last place to which the customer's attention is directed. Hence, there is need for particular care in keeping the walking area free of obstruction and uncoated with unctuous, greasy and oleaginous concoctions.

Michael A. Musmanno (Justice of the Pennsylvania Sup. Ct., 1959): A Drunk is a Bull in a China Shop: An intoxicated person amid a group of people is a constant source of danger and hurt to those about him. He is the proverbial bull in a china shop and, of course, it is clear that when the owner of a bull is sued for damages done by his animal he cannot expect to escape liability by demanding proof as to how the bull smashed the china. He is liable for allowing the bull to be abroad unrestrained, unfettered and uncontrolled. The proprietor of an establishment whose employees pour inflammable liquid into a vessel already too full cannot plead ignorance of results when the vessel explodes from contact with the slightest spark.

Michael A. Musmanno (Justice of the Sup. Ct. of Pennsylvania, 1959): Selling Liquor to an Intoxicated Person: Since an intoxicated person is and can be an instrument of danger to others, especially if he is operating a motor vehicle, the Legislature of Pennsylvania declared by the Act of 1951, that it shall be unlawful for any person to sell liquor to one already intoxicated. The first prime requisite to de-toxicate one who has, because of alcohol, lost control over his reflexes, judgment and sense of responsibility to others, is to stop pouring alcohol into him. This is a duty which everyone owes to society and to law entirely apart from any statute. The person who would put into the hands of an obviously demented individual a firearm with which he shot an innocent third person would be amenable in damages to that third person for unlawful negligence. An intoxicated person behind the wheel of an automobile can be as dangerous as an insane person with a firearm. He is as much a hazard to the safety of the community as a stick of dynamite that must be defused in order to be rendered harmless. To serve an intoxicated person more liquor is to light the fuse.

Michael A. Musmanno (Justice of the Sup. Ct. of Pennsylvania, 1959): Life is Worth More Than Mere Cement: No railroad has the right to build its tracks in such a manner and over such a route that it kills people and yet escape responsibility on the theory that it would cost too much to erect the necessary barriers of safety. As lightly as human life is sometimes regarded in the economic and military wars of the age, it has not dropped to so cheap a level that it can be compared in value to the cost of the few mixersful of cement. (Fuller v. Pennsylvania Railroad, 371 Pa. 330).

Michael A. Musmanno (Justice of Pennsylvania Supreme Court, 1959): Danger Warnings: If one's hearing is such that he can only hear a locomotive warning when he is being attentive to hearing it, he may be run down by the locomotive which blows the whistle. A warning of danger, if it is to be of any use, must be such that it warns the person who is not thinking of danger. The warning must be of such a character that its appearance, audible or visual, startles the listener whether he is on the alert or not. By the same token, the absence of that startling experience is also an event to be remembered, especially when the presence or absence of the warning is immediately associated with the tragic occurrence which focuses the memory of on all phenomena which proceeded it.... This court continues to draw a distinction between so-called "positive" testimony and so-called "negative" testimony and, in doing so, makes a shambles, in this respect, of logic, ratiocination and elementary common sense. Testimony is neither negative nor positive. It may be credible testimony or incredible testimony, but it is not negative or positive. A "no" answer is just as positive as a "yes" answer since it describes a given posture of affairs. The absence of law and order is just as positive a situation as the presence of it. (dissenting opinion, Burd v. Pennsylvania Railroad, 401 PA. 284).

Michael A. Musmanno (Justice of Pennsylvania Supreme Court, 1959): Millions of Other People Were Not Injured: The Majority Opinion states that 1,297,802 "human bodies" had ridden the course "and absorbed the abruptness of this curve without injury." There was not a word or syllable in the testimony to support this statement; 1,297,802 persons did not testify that they had not been injured. This volunteered conclusion of the Majority is founded on the statement of the defendant's witness that there was no record of accident during the period in question. This is far from stating that no accident occurred or that no one had been injured. Many people could have sustained substantial jolts which did not seriously disable them. Others may have until later and then they did not connect them with the roller coaster ride. Others may have known they were injured by the roller coaster ride but preferred not to litigate. In addition, it does not matter how many rode without injury. The question is: Was there anything wrong with the Blue Streak on the day, hour and minute that the plaintiff was injured?... Moreover, before the fact of the multitudinous rides can be compared to the single ride involved in this case, there must be proof that the conditions in the million rides were exactly similar to the one's present in the instant case, as, for instance that there were three passengers in the front seat as in this case,... that the weight of the passengers in the front seat, in all the million rides was the same as that on the Wood ride, that the heights of the persons in the front seat in all the other rides tallied with the heights of the persons of this ride. There would have to be a determination also as to whether the passengers all the other rides were aware that they were coming to an abrupt bend. Also, did the passengers of the other rides brace themselves when they came to the bend or did they all slide over and crush the person on the outside seat, as happened in this case? There are innumerable variables which have to be considered before one can base a conclusion on a multiplicity of events as against the one which is in focus. A million pedestrians may pass over a defect in the sidewalk and not been injured, but the 1,000,001st traveler may fall into the hole or trip over the defect and, if the facts reveal that the hole was caused by the negligence of the municipality, the injured person is entitled to a recovery, regardless of the army which had good luck to pass unscathed over the danger which reached up and pulled down that 1,000,001st traveler to his doom. If cases of this kind are to be decided on mere numbers instead of cause-and-effect, and logic and reason, there can be no need for a judicial inquiry. A computer will suffice, an IBM machine can dictate the verdict, a unifax can displace the jury and eventually the judge himself, all of which, of course, is absurd. (dissenting opinion, George Wood v. Conneaut Lake Park Inc., 417 Pa. 58).

Michael A. Musmanno (Justice of Pennsylvania Supreme Court, 1959): The Fiery Dragon of Electricity: Enigmatic as is the basic element of electricity, no one with the slightest mental equipment is ignorant of its vast potentialities for destruction. The degree of care required to protect people from this devastating element is no less than that required to prevent poisonous reptiles from breaking loose from their restraining enclosures. As the proprietor of ferocious beasts may not, by pleading excessive cost for confining them, escape liability for the loss of life occasioned by his savage wards, so also the owner of high-voltage machinery may not avoid responsibility, on the excuse of expense, for the devastation caused through his failure to adequately contain the fiery dragon of electricity. (Cooper v. Heintz Manufacturing Co., 385 Pa. 298).

Michael A. Musmanno (Justice of Pennsylvania Supreme Court, 1959): Feasibility Defense by Power Company: If the wires or the towers supporting them had been painted or illuinated, they would have been visible to the pilot and he would have avoided them. This Court has said that "when human life is at stake, the rule of due care and diligence requires everything that gives reasonable promise of its preservation to be done, regardless of difficulties or expense." In comparison to the benefit of saving human life, the cost of a few cans of pain and a few electric bulbs would be negligible. And since the defendant company is engaged in the very manufacture and creation of electric current, the cost of the current needed to supply the desired illumination would be as insignificant as the cost of a few biscuits and a bakery. (Yoffee v. Pennsylvania Power Co., 385 Pa. 520).

Michael A. Musmanno (Justice of Pennsylvania Supreme Court, 1959): Child "Trespassing" on Railroad Land: What are the ordinary and natural things to be expected of children? The obvious answer is that they will act like children. The playful instincts of boys of tender age are as much a part of the demonstrated forces of nature as the snows of January, the winds of March and the roses of June. To speak, in this afternoon of the universe, of these elementary and fundamental concepts, which were already accepted fact in the dawn of creation, would be sheer superfluity. And yet it would seem that this truism can at times be overlooked by sages of the law who would attribute to infants the reflection of graybeards, while at the same time excusing the neglect of adults who act with the irresponsibility of children.... The Majority, however, in discussing this phase of the case refuses to restrict the locus" to 67th Street where the accident occurred and where the Jungle was located, but speaks of fencing in vast distances and immeasurable areas over the 275 miles of electrified main tracks. There is no argument in logic so wearisome as that which seeks to prove a point by an irrelevant comparison or one so exaggerated in scope as to make it wholly foreign to the discussion. It is like equating an ant hill with Mount Everest because they are both protuberances from the earth's surface, or comparing a flea with an eagle because they both fly, or a monkey with an elephant because they both eat peanuts. It is absurd to say that because the railroad would be required to fence away the Jungle (20 to 30 ft. long) from the tracks, it would be compelled to fence the whole length of its 275 miles of electrified main tracks or even to fence areas where children have been seen playing beside the right-of-way or climbing on cars. Liability only arises where there is a known dangerous practice which a railroad company can avoid.... The argument that the railroad's treasury takes precedence over the value of human life runs counter to everything that has been advocated and done in America in the way of social and economic progress. In every progressive step of the laws of safety, there have been those who protested because of the cost involved in installing and maintaining the innovation. But we have seen how safety and greater appreciation of the precious commodity of existence advanced, notwithstanding. When a dangerous curve wrecks a train, railroad architects and civil engineers consider at once ways of straightening out the track so as to avoid future wrecks. When a hillside caves in, burying a train and its passengers beneath an avalanche of death and crippling injuries, the mountain is trussed up with bands of steel and fortified with masonry. When a flood washes a train into a swollen river the tracks are raised in future indentations balked. Tunnels are bored through mountain sides, interlocking systems are developed, bridges are thrown across chasms and ravines, all at huge expenditures of money, and all for safety, all for progress, and eventually for greater profit to the railroads too, because no railroad can hope to become successful if it's tracks are strewn with the skeletons and limbs of victims of brutal indifference to humanity. (Dugan v. Pennsylvania Railroad, 37 PA. 39).

Michael A. Musmanno (Justice of Pennsylvania Supreme Court, 1959): Doctors and Bus Drivers: I stand second to none in my boundless admiration for the medical profession. In my estimation, statesman, industrialists, inventors and philosophers are inconsequential, so far as contributing to human happiness is concerned, as against the doctor who is dedicated to health—the sweetest desideratum in life because without health one has not the strength to squeeze the orange of existence to obtain the elixir of the joy of living. But after having paid my sincere tribute to doctors, I would not place them on a marble pedestal of impeccability and infallibility. They are human and therefore subject to all the foibles and weaknesses of the flesh which occasionally manifest themselves through indifference or carelessness in a particular field which requires the maximum of competence, attention and care. And if one doctor is negligent, the rest of the medical world need not feel that this constitutes an adverse appraisement of their own skill and their own supreme dedication to the welfare of man. Dr. Bradlow testified that he made two attempts to negotiate the curve in the patient's esophagus and that he encountered resistance. In spite of this plunged ahead... (and) forced the gastroscope through the esophagus wall. If a passenger in a bus is injured when the bus does not take a curve in the highway, the passenger does not need to prove, in order to make out a prima facia case against a common carrier, that the driver was drunk, the steering wheel was defective, or that the wheels of the vehicle were out of a line. He shows that the bus did not turn with the road and on that fact alone, he has a case in court. It is then up to the bus company to demonstrate that it used due care in that it employed a sober driver, that its steering wheel had been tested, and so on. And so, in the state of the law as the Majority now announces it with this decision, the legal profession is informed that we require a higher responsibility of care from a bus driver who travels over a wide macadamized highway than we require of a doctor who embarks on a journey through the narrow darkened passages of the alimentary canal. (dissenting, Demchuk v. Bralow, 404 Pa. 100).

Michael A. Musmanno (Justice of Pennsylvania Supreme Court, 1959): Inadequate Warning: A (railroad) crossing bell which sounds so closely in time to the actual arrival of a train, that one on the track may not escape being struck, is not a bell of warning but a knell of doom. (Meade v. Pennsylvania Railroad, 375 PA. 325).

Michael A. Musmanno (Justice of Pennsylvania Supreme Court, 1959): OSHA & Workers Working Near Hazards: This is like saying that a hole into which a pedestrian walks caused the pedestrian no harm, since it was the fall not the hole which broke his neck. No one in this case has advanced the droll proposition that the platform, in its inert, isolated and unused state, hurt or even could hurt anybody. Even a tiger will not harm anybody who stays away from him. An unguarded elevator shift will not injure anyone unless he steps into the shaft. // The purpose of the Health and Safety Act (OSHA) is something far more intelligent than that ascribed to it by the defendant. The drafters of that Act well knew that workers who were engaged in a task which takes them to perilous heights may easily overlook, in the preoccupation over discharging their tasks, the absence of a railing at the spot where they may be immediately engaged. Thus, the workers must be protected, not against foolhardiness, but against the most natural and human reaction, namely, that of concentration on the instant details of their job to the exclusion of a constant overall survey of the locale in which they are working. In addition, it cannot be doubted that a worker's efficiency will be lowered and the productiveness of his labors considerably diminished if he must continuously have an eye on the distance intervening between him and the brink of the surface his pressing chore requires him to occupy. // The defendant maintains that the ledge in question could not be a platform until the railing was installed. This argument completely misses the objective of the Safety Act, which is to protect the workmen while they work. If the railing is not to be added until the construction job has been completed and uncounted workmen have fallen to their injury or death in the meanwhile, the Act, whose very intendment is aimed at protecting workmen, becomes a mockery. The Act specifically refers to "building construction," and it says that platforms shall have railings "so as to avoid accident hazards to workers or the public." (Emphasis supplied.) (Windusch v. Babcock and Wilcox Co., 412 Pa. 558)

Michael A. Musmanno (Justice of Pa. Supreme Court, 1959): STOP, LOOK, and LISTEN – For What? A railroad company that places a crossing at a point where it cannot be seen by the traveler until he is practically committed to passing over it, cannot use the stop, look and listen sign as a badge of immunity from liability for accidents occurring as the result of non-visibility. Of what value is it to stop if stoppage does not allow the traveler to see the train, and of what value is it to listen, if the railroad fails to sound warning signals which perilous crossings demand? // The railroad company in the case before us knew or should have known of the physical obstructions here enumerated, which, by chance arrangement formed a visual barrier to the traveler so that he could not see far enough down the track to be adequately warned of an approaching train. Everyone knows that a small object in the immediate foreground of one's vision can completely black out an enormous object in the distance. A butterfly winging by a yard away can easily hide from view and elephant 100 feet away. Lifting one's hand to the sky can shut off from view the prodigious, fiery sun. // A railroad company may, in some instances have no choice as to location of crossings, since many factors enter into determining a right-of-way, but where, as here, physical conditions visually blanket the speeding train until several short seconds before it sweeps, like a steel and iron tornado, into a crossing, a due responsibility for the safety of mankind dictates that something be done to alert the public of the omnipresent danger—over and above that of asking it to stop, look and listen.

Michael A. Musmanno (Justice of Pa. Supreme Court, 1959): Presumption of Due Care to Avoid Death: There is a presumption in law that a person killed in an accident exercised due care to avoid being killed. This is a sensible rule because although it is inevitable that everyone must eventually turn in his bat and glove, no one actually wants to hasten the end of the ballgame.

Michael A. Musmanno (Justice of Pa. Supreme Court, 1959): Where there are no playgrounds, a boy's instinct for play will exert itself even on the lip of a volcano; and boys must be accepted as boys and not as graybearded savants.

Michael A. Musmanno (Justice of Pa. Supreme Court, 1959): Once a train of violence is begun, one event leads to another with the fluency, rapidity and explosiveness of Chinese firecrackers.

Kathleen Norris: If we do not always see our own mistakes and omissions we can always see those of our neighbors.

Harry Philo: The Law is never settled until it is settled right, the Law is never right until it is just, the law is never just until it serves society to the fullest.

Sir John Pratt (Lord Chief Justice of England, 1657-1725): Torts are infinitely various, not limited or confined, for there is nothing in nature but may be an instrument of mischief. Chapman v. Pickersgill, 2 Wils. K.B., 145, 146 (1762)

Duc de La Rochefoucauld: If we had no faults we should not take so much pleasure in noting those of others.

La Rochefoucauld: Happy people rarely correct their faults.

Will Rogers: People who fly into a rage always make a bad landing.

Russian Proverb: Make peace with men and quarrel with your faults.

Eddie Sachs (NASCAR race car driver): Your car moves faster than you can think.

George Santayana: Habit is stronger than reason.

Scottish Proverb: Wink at small faults, for you have great ones yourself.

William Shakespeare (*Antony and Cleopatra*, Act III, vii) (haste makes waste): Cleopatra: Celerity is never more admired / Than by the negligent.

William Shakespeare (*Hamlet,* Act I, iv): More honour'd in the breach than the observance.

Willaim Shakespeare (*Hamlet*, Act V, ii): Hamlet: Sir, in this audience, / Let my disclaiming from a purpos'd evil / Free me so far in your most generous thoughts, / As that I have shot my arrow o'er the house, / And hurt my brother.

William Shakespeare (*Henry V*, Act II, iv): Self-love, my liege, is not so vile a sin / As self-neglecting.

William Shakespeare (*III Henry VI*, Act V, iv): Wise men ne'er sit and wail their loss, / But cheerly seek how to redress their harms.

William Shakespeare (*Julius Caesar*, Act V, iii): O hareful error, melancholy's child! / Why dost thou shew to the apt thoughts of men / The things that are not? O error, soon conceiv'd, / Thou never com'st unto a happy birth, / But kill'st the mother that engender'd thee.

William Shakespeare (*King Lear*, Act II, ii): A lily-livered, action-taking knave.

William Shakespeare (*Merry Wives of Windsor*, Act II, ii): This is the short and long of it.

William Shakespeare (*Othello*, Act I, iii): Wherein I spake of most disastrous chances, / Of moving accidents by flood and field.

William Shakespeare (*Othello,* Act V, ii): One that loved not wisely but too well, -

William Shakespeare (*Romeo and Juliet*, Act II, ii): What's in a name? That which we call a rose by any other name would smell as sweet.

William Shakespeare (*Romeo and Juliet,* Act II, iii): Wisely and slow; they stumble that run fast.

William Shakespeare (*Romeo and Juliet,* Act II, vi): Friar Laurence: Too swift arrives as tardy as too slow.

William Shakespeare (*Timon of Athens*, Act I, i): The strain of man's bred out Into baboon and monkey.

William Shakespeare (*Troilus and Cressida*, Act V, ii): The error of our eye directs our mind: / What error leads must err.

William Shakespeare (*Twelfth Night*, Act III, iv): Thou liest in thy throat.

William Shakespeare (*Winter's Tale*, Act I, ii): A servant grafted in my serious trust / And therein negligent.

William Shakespeare (*Winter's Tale*, Act I, ii): In every one of these no man is free, / But that his negligence, his folly, fear, / Among the infinite doings of the world, / Sometimes puts forth....

William Shakespeare (*Winter's Tale*, Act IV, iii): Florizel: As the unthought-on accident is guilty / Of what we wildly do, so we profess / Ourselves to be the slaves of chance, and flies / Of every wind that blows.

Thomas Sowell: Much of the history of the Western world over the past three decades has involved replacing what worked with what sounded good.

Spanish Proverb: More grows in the garden than the gardener knows he has sown.

Herbert Spencer: The ultimate result of shielding men from the effects of folly is to fill the world with fools.

Gertrude Stein: Everybody knows if you are too careful you are so occupied in being careful that you are sure to stumble over something.

Justice Storrs (Supreme Court of Connecticut. 1844): "An injury is a wrong; and for the redress of every wrong there is a remedy: a wrong is a violation of one's right; and for the vindication of every right there is a remedy."

William Thackery: A fool can no more see his own folly that he can see his ears.

Harry S. Truman (U.S. President 1945-53): The buck stops here.

Mark Twain: Don't you know, there are some things that can beat smartness and foresight? Awkwardness and stupidity can. The best swordsman in the world doesn't need to fear the second best swordsman in the world; no, the person for him to be afraid of is some ignorant antagonist who has never had a sword in his hand before; he doesn't do the thing he ought to.

Mark Twain: I have no respect for any man who can spell a word only one way.

Mark Twain: Name the greatest of all the inventors. Accident.

Mark Twain: Intemperate temperance injures the cause of temperance, while temperate temperance helps it in its fight against intemperate intemperance.

UA: We are responsible for the effort (or lack thereof), not the outcome.

UA: The difference between genius and stupidity is that genius has its limits.

Tom Vesper: The 3 Acts of the Penitent (and perhaps modern-day tortfeasors?) (according to 1616 Council of Trent):

1. Contrition
2. Confession = Public Abduration
3. Satisfaction = prayer, fasting and Alms giving

Johann Christopher Friedrich von Schiller: What the reason of the ant laboriously drags into a heap, the wind of accident will collect in one breath.
Rudy Westmoreland: He who laughs last, thinks slowest.
Rudy Westmoreland: Nothing is "foolproof" to a sufficiently talented fool.
Oscar Wilde: Whenever a man does a thoroughly stupid thing, it is always from the noblest motives.

NEGOTIATION (See also COMPROMISE)

Uncle Anthony: If the guy who writes the check (the insurance adjuster) ain't interested, you can mediate or meditate or do whatever dance you do, but ain't you wasting your time?
Uncle Anthony: Ain't a good settlement better than a good trial?
Aunt Mary Carlo: I tink da most important ting ya can do in any situation is keep yer mout shut and LISTEN!
Aunt Mary Carlo: Don't fall in love wit any deal yer negotiatin' – always be ready to walk out.
Bible: James 1:19: Be swift to hear, slow to speak, slow to wrath.
Bible: Matthew 5:9: Blessed are the peacemakers: for they shall be called the children of God.
Bible: Proverbs 15:1: A soft answer turneth away wrath.
Bible: Zech. 11:12: If ye think good, give me my price; and if not, forbear.
Ambrose Bierce: AIM, n. The task we set our wishes to.
Ambrose Bierce: COMPROMISE, n. Such an adjustment of conflicting interests as gives each adversary the satisfaction of thinking he has got what he ought not to have, and is deprived of nothing except what was justly his due.
Ambrose Bierce: ULTIMATUM, n. In diplomacy, a last demand before resorting to concessions....
Ambrose Bierce: PROJECTILE, n. The final arbiter in international disputes. Formerly these disputes were settled by physical contact of the disputants, with such simple arguments as the rudimentary logic of the times could supply – the sword, the spear, and so forth. With the growth of prudence in military affairs the projectile came more and more into favor, and is now held in high esteem by the most courageous. Its capital defect is that it requires personal attendance at the point of propulsion.
Ed Brodow: "Brodows' Law" = If you want a deal too badly you lose the ability to say no.
Ed Brodow: WHAT you give up is not as important as HOW you give it up.
Ed Brodow: NEVER underestimate the importance of your negotiation ability. The way you negotiate really does matter. Among the factors that may influence the outcome of your negotiations:

1. How well you read the other side's situation and manage its expectations
2. Where you open
3. What concessions you make
4. How you respond to the other side's tactics
5. And, the point at which you decide to make a deal or walk away

Ed Brodow: There are 5 Destructive Assumptions to effective negotiation:

1. The "Average Person" is not tough enough to win at negotiation with e.g. Donald Trump
2. Negotiation is all or nothing – either Winner or Loser (Columbo is better role model than Donald Trump)
3. Only "Good Talkers" make good negotiators ... NO! LISTENING is critical
4. Assertive people are selfish & rude – take care of #1
5. Women do not negotiate as effectively as men

Ed Barrow: The 10 Character Traits for The Profile for a Successful Negotiator:

1. "Negotiation Consciousness" = be assertive/challenging DO NOT accept all opponents position
2. "LISTENING" = Key trait
3. Ability to ask good questions – like detectives
4. High aspirations = self-fulfilling prophesy
5. Patience – Asia, Middle East, S. America look at time differently = like Italian Sunday dinner
6. Flexibility = every negotiator makes assumptions = Asian "face saving"
7. Focus on satisfaction = "one hand washes the other" NOT mean How can I win
8. Willingness to take risks = REASONABLE RISKS e.g. histrionics can be effective

9. Solving the problem
10. Willingness to WALK AWAY: aka, Brodows' Law = If you want a deal too badly you lose the ability to say no.

Ed Brodow: The 16 RULES FOR CONCESSION MAKING – to maximize your satisfaction production:

1. Open with an "Extreme Position" – give yourself room to give away CAVEAT: "too extreme" = turnoff. You get 3 benefits = a. Lowers expectations, b. Leaves room for concessions, c. Maybe you'll get surprised;
2. Q: How "extreme" should opening position be? A. As long as you can provide "reasonable justification" then no position is "too extreme";
3. Make small concessions – large concessions reflect weakness/desperation;
4. Vary the size of concessions – DO NOT PROJECT A PATTERN so that "bottom line" is predictable;
5. Do not make the "First Move";
6. Never accept the FIRST OFFER – opposition must feel "satisfied" they pushed PL to "bottom line";
7. You do not have to "MATCH" opposition's concessions dollar for dollar;
8. Make "Straw Demands";
9. To "Counter straw demands" you must collect info about opponent's real needs to cut through the straw;
10. Claim "Limited Authority";
11. Offer "Peripheral Concessions" – make a list;
12. NEVER "Split the difference" – when you do this you concede ½ the difference – that is, a smart negotiator will hold out for ANOTHER ½ concession;
13. GET SOMETHING IN RETURN – NEVER make "Unilateral Concessions" – you negotiate vs self. The BEST TIME to ask for concession is after you make/offer one;
14. Make opposition work for concessions;
15. Leave something small on table – that is, "save face";
16. Don't GET CARRIED AWAY – remember rules are made to be broken.

Ed Brodow: 3 COMMON SENSE RULES for WIN-WIN Negotiations:

1. Change your behavior from adversarial to cooperative
2. Develop trust by LISTENING
3. Explore options for mutual satisfaction

Robert Browning: The common problem, yours, mine, every one's, / Is – not too fancy what were fair in life / Provided it could be,—but, finding first / What may be, then find how to make it fair / Up to our means.

Edmund Burke: All government – indeed, every human benefit and enjoyment, every virtue and every prudent act – is founded on compromise and barter.

Edmund Burke: The concessions of the weak are the concessions of fear.

George Canning: And finds, with keen, discriminating sight, / Black's not so black,—nor white so *very* white.

Cervantes: He who buys and lies feels it in his purse.

Neville Chamberlain (British Prime Minister, September 30, 1938, the day after returning from Munich, after conferring with Hitler and Mussolini): My good friends, this is the second time in our history that there has come back from Germany to Downing Street peace with honor. I believe it is peace for our time. We thank you from the bottom of our hearts. And now I recommend you to go home and sleep quietly in your beds.

Lord Chesterfield: To please people is a great step toward persuading them.

Sir Winston Churchill (June 27, 1954): Better to jaw-jaw than to war-war.

Charles de Gaulle: Treaties are like roses and young girls. They last while they last.

Charles Dickens: Here's the rule for bargains: "Do other men, for they would do you." That's the true business precept.

Tryon Edwards: Compromise is but the sacrifice of one right or good in the hope of retaining another,—too often ending in the loss of both.

Albert Einstein: Sometimes one pays most for the things one gets for nothing.

Joseph Ellis (his book *"His Excellency: George Washington"*): James Madison was called "The Big Knife" because "he cut so many deals."

Row Waldo Emerson: Every compromise was surrender and invited new demands.

Ralph Waldo Emerson: Everything yields. The very glaciers are viscous, or regelate into conformity, and the stiffest patriots falter and compromise.

English Proverb: "Let us agree not to step on each other's feet," said the cock to the horse.

Ludwig Erhard: A compromise is the art of dividing a cake in such a way that everyone believes he has the biggest piece.

Thomas Fuller: A man loseth his time that comes early to a bad bargain.

Thomas Fuller: It is a silly bargain where nobody gains.

Baltazar Gratian: Never contend with a man who has nothing to lose.

Joseph Grynbaum: An ounce of mediation is worth a pound of arbitration and a ton of litigation!

George Herbert: On a good bargain think twice.

George Herbert: A lean compromise is better than a fat lawsuit.

Holbrook Jackson: Sacrifice is a form of bargaining.

Samuel Johnson: Life cannot subsist in society but by reciprocal concessions.

Rudyard Kipling: And that is called paying the Dane-geld; / But we've proved it again and again, / That if once you have paid him the Dane-geld / You never get rid of the Dane.

Rudyard Kipling: Man, a bear in most relations – worm and savage otherwise,—/ Man propounds negotiations, Man accepts the compromise. / Very rarely will he squarely push the logic of a fact. / To its ultimate conclusion in unmitigated act.

Allard Lowenstein: The question should be, is it worth trying to do, not can it be done.

Nelson Mandela (statement from prison, 1985): Only free men can negotiate. Prisoners cannot enter into contracts.

John Milton (*Paradise Lost*, 1667: referring to the debate by Satan in the palace of Pandemonium, to decide whether to launch an attack to recover Heaven): Thus Belial, with words clothed in reason's garb, / Counseled ignoble ease, and peaceful sloth, / Not peace.

Molière: Heaven forbids, it is true, certain gratifications, but there are ways and means of compounding such matters.

Gerard J. O'Brien: The advantage of a settlement is that the defense can never appeal.

Lawrence J. Peter: If you don't know where you're going, you'll probably wind up somewhere else.

Plautus: The bargain is not a bargain, or what was not a bargain is a bargain, just as you please.

Mario Puzo (in his novel *The Godfather*, Don Corleone, played by Marlon Brando in the film, says): He's a businessman. I'll make him an offer he can't refuse.

John Ray: Make every bargain clear and plain, / That none may afterwards complain.

Charles Reade: 'Tis ill luck to go back upon a bargain.

Will Rogers: I have always noticed at any time a man can't come in and settle with you without bringing his lawyer, why, look out for him.

John Romano: These guys who say they don't like to settle are either lying to themselves or losing sight of the best interests of their clients.

George Schultz: Negotiations are a euphemism for capitulation if the shadow of power is not cast across the bargaining table.

William Shakespeare (*Cymbeline*, Act I, iv): Lest the bargain should catch cold and starve.

William Shakespeare (*I Henry IV*, Act III, i): But in the way of bargain, mark ye me, / I'll cavil on the ninth part of a hair.

William Shakespeare (*I Henry VI,* Act V, iv): Now the matter grows to compromise, / Stand'st thou aloof?

William Shakespeare (*King John,* Act V, i): Send fair-play orders and make compromise.

William Shakespeare (*Love's Labor's Lost,* Act III, i): To sell a bargain well is as cunning as fast and loose.

William Shakespeare (*Richard II*, Act II, i): But basely yielded upon compromise / That which his noble ancestors achieved with blows.

William Shakespeare (*Troilus and Cressida*, Act IV, i): Fair Diomed, you do as chapmen do, / Dispraise the thing that you desire to buy; / But we in silence hold this virtue well, /we'll not commend what we intended to sell.

Sydney Smith: All great alterations in human affairs are produced by compromise.

Lee Steinberg (sports agent): If you got your foot on someone else's neck, at some point in the future that person will have his foot on your neck.

Charles Sumner: From the beginning of our history the country has been afflicted with compromise. It is by compromise that human rights have been abandoned. I insist that this shall cease. The country needs a repose after all its trials; it deserves repose. And repose can only be found in everlasting principles.

Algernon Charles Swinburne: Is not Compromise of old a god among you?

Publius Syrus: Everything is worth what its purchaser will pay for it.

Donald Trump: I aim high and then I just keep pushing and pushing and pushing to get what I'm after.

Mark Twain: The timid man yearns for full value and demands a tenth. The bold man strikes for double value and compromises on par.

Thomas J. Watson: Life itself is a matter of salesmanship.

NONSENSE (See COMMON SENSE; FOLLY; TRUTH/UNDERSTANDING)

NORM/NORMAL

Uncle Anthony: Exceptions ain't always provin' the rule, I think it shows up the rule fer bein' a bad rule.

Uncle Anthony: Standards is like flags for all of us to follow, and everybody forgets or loses sight of dem flags/standards and goes their own way.

Aunt Mary Carlo: Everybody's abnormal about sometin'.

Alan Bennett: Standards are always out of date. That is what makes them standards.

Bible: 1 Corinthians 14:40: Let all things be done decently and in order.

Bible: Ecclesiastes 3:1: To every thing there is a season, and a time to every purpose under the heaven.

Bible: 1 Peter 4:4: They think it strange that ye run not with them to the same excess of riot.

Bible: Philippians 3:16: Let us walk by the same rule, let us mind the same thing.

Bible: Romans 12:2: Be not confirmed to this world.

Ambrose Bierce: ABNORMAL, adj. Not conforming to standard. In matters of thought and conduct, to be independent is to be abnormal, to be abnormal is to be detested.

Ambrose Bierce: MORAL, adj. Conforming to a local and mutable standard of right. Having the quality of general expediency.

Charlotte Bingham: And the only way to avoid playing the game is never to belong to a club, class, set, or trade union. As soon as you do, you're accepting someone else's rules, and as soon as you do that, you start looking down on the other chap with different rules.

Robert Burton: No rule is so general, which admits not some exception.

Samuel Butler: For nothing goes for sense or light, / That will not with old rules jump right.

Lord Byron: You will recollect that "exceptions only prove the rule."

Benjamin Cardozo: Standards of prudent conduct are declared at times by courts, but they are taken over by the facts of life. Pokora v. Wabash R. Co., 292 US 98, 78 L ed 1149, 54 S Ct 580 (1934).

Sir Winston Churchill (speaking of the First Lord of the Admiralty, Sir Samul Hoare): We received ... the assurance that there is no foudation whatever for the statement that we are "vastly behind" with our Air Force programme. It is clear from his words that we are behind, and the only question is, what meaning does the First Lord attach to the word "vastly"? ... One does not know what his standard is. His standards change from time to time....

Cicero: If the exception make this thing unlawful, necessarily it is lawful where there is no exception.

Charles Darrow (1929 *Monopoly* game he invented): Do not pass go.

Charles Dickens: "Do other men, for they would do you." That's the true business precept. All others are counterfeits.

Sir Arthur Conan Doyle: An exception disproves the rule.

George Eliot: (She) was strict in adherence to her own rules of propriety.

Ralph Waldo Emerson: Conformity is the ape of harmony.

Henry Ford: If you think of "standardization" as the best that you know today, but which is to be improved tomorrow – you get somewhere.

Margaret Fuller: Nature provides exceptions to every rule.

Thomas Fuller: There is no useful rule without an exception.

Augustus William Hare: *The exception proves the rule* ... has often been greatly abused.... The exception in most cases merely proves the rule to be a bad one.

William Hazlitt: Rules and models destroy genius and art.

Joseph Heller: Orr was crazy and could be grounded. All he had to do was ask; and as soon as he did, he would no longer be crazy and would have to fly more missions... Yossarian was moved very deeply by the absolute simplicity of this clause of Catch-22 and let out a respectful whistle.

Thomas Heywood (1608): A general concourse of wise men! ... if the general rule have no exceptions, thou wilt have an empty consistory.

Robert F. Kennedy (Attorney General of U.S., 1961): Laws can embody standards; governments can enforce laws – but the final task is not a task for government. It is a task for each and every one of us. Every time we turn our heads the other way we see the law flouted – when we tolerate what we know to be wrong – when we close our eyes and ears to the corrupt because we are too busy, or too frightened – when we fail to speak up and speak out – we strike a blow against freedom and decency and justice.

Suzanne LaFollette: To institutionalize (EDITOR: or standardize) means in great degree to mechanize.

Legal Maxim: An exception proves the validity of a rule concerning things not excepted. Or: The exception proves the rule.

Marcus Aurelius: In reading and writing, you cannot lay down rules until you have learnt to obey them. Much more so in life.

W. Somerset Maugham: The normal is what you find but rarely. The normal is an ideal. It is a picture that one fabricates of the average characteristics of men, and to find them all in a single man is hardly to be expected.

John Stuart Mill: To do as one would be done by, and to love one's neighbor as one's self, constitute the ideal perfection of utilitarian morality.

Edith Ronald Mirrielees: Experience shows that exceptions are as true as rules.

G.F. Northall: By line and rule works many a fool.

Cole Porter (1934 song and musical show title): Anything goes!

Will Rogers: "Whoever wrote the Ten Commandments made 'em short. They may not always be kept but they can be understood. They are the same for everyone."

Scottish Proverb: No rule so good as rule of thumb, if it hit.

Quintilian (Marcus Fabius Quintilianus, 1st century AD): Rules and precepts are of no value without natural capacity.

W.W. Skeat: *Exceptio probat regulum* ... means, "The exception tests the rule."

Publilius Syrus: You cannot put the same shoe on every foot.

William Shakespeare (*All's Well That Ends Well*, Act I, i): Little can be said in 't; 'tis against the rule of nature.

William Shakespeare (*Antony and Cleopatra*, Act II, iii): I have not kept my square; but that to come / Shall be done by the rule.

William Shakespeare (*Comedy of Errors*, Act II, ii): By what rule, sir? - / Marry, sir, by a rule as plain as the plain bald pate of father Time himself.

William Shakespeare (*II Henry VI*, Act I, i): Whose bookish rule hath pull'd fair Englamd down.

William Shakespeare (*Taming of the Shrew*, Act III, i): I am not so nice, / To change true rules for old inventions.

William Shakespeare (*Troilus and Cressida*, Act I, iii): The heavens themselves, the planets, and this centre, / Observe degree, priority, and place, / Insisture, course, proportion, season, form, / Office, and custom, in all line of order.

George Bernard Shaw: The golden rule is that there are no golden rules.

George Bernard Shaw: Do not do unto others as you would they should do unto you. Their tastes may not be the same.

Gertrude Stein: She always says she dislikes the abnormal, it is so obvious. She says the normal is so much more simply complicated and interesting.

Gertrude Stein: What is the use of thinking if after all there is to be organization (EDITOR: or fixed standards).

Henry David Thoreau: When I read some of the rules for speaking and writing the English language correctly ... I think / Any fool can make a rule / And every fool will mind it.

Henry David Thoreau (Walden, 1854): If a man does not keep pace with his companions, perhaps it is because he hears a different drummer. Let him step to the music which he hears, however measured or far away." Or (as used nowadays): **Marching to a different drummer.**

Mark Twain: Adam was but human – this explains it all. He did not want the apple for the apple's sake, he wanted it because it was forbidden.

Tennessee Williams: My suit is pale yellow. My nationality is French, and my normality has been often subject to question.

UA: If anything can go wrong, it will.

Gore Vidal: In its slow way, our society is beginning to shed many of its superstitions about the sexual act. The idea that there is no such thing as "normality" is at last penetrating the tribal consciousness, although the religiously inclined still regard non-procreative sex as "unnatural," while the statistically inclined regard as "normal" only what the majority does.

John Wilson (1664): The exception proves the rule.

John M. Woolsey: The meaning of the word "obscene" as legally defined by the Courts is: tendency to stir the sex impulses or to lead to sexually impure and lustful thoughts.... Whether a particular book would tend to excite such impulses and thoughts must be tested by the Court's opinion as to its effect on a person with average sex instincts. .... It is only with normal persons that the law is concerned. *U.S. v. One Book Called "Ulysses,"* (1933).

William Wordsworth: A few strong instincts, and a few plain rules.

NUISANCE (See TROUBLE)

OBSCENITY (See PROFANITY)

OLD AGE (See AGE/AGING)

OPINIONS (See also EXPERTS; JUDGMENT)

Uncle Anthony: The other guys (or opposition) offer mere "opinions," but I (or our experts) present well reasoned and supported conclusions of fact.

Aunt Mary Carlo: Some guys really can't tell da difference between der opinions and facts.

Aristotle: Some men are just as sure of the truth of their opinions as are others of what they know.

Peter Arno (1940 cartoon in the New Yorker magazine showing an official with a rolled-up engineering plan under his arm, walking away from a recently crashed airplane, saying): "Well, back to the old drawing board."

Thomas Arnold: It is common to men to err; but it is only a fool that perseveres in his error; a wise man alters his opinion, a fool never.

Thomas Arnold: Differences of opinion give me but little concern; but it is a real pleasure to be brought into communication with anyone who is in earnest, and really looks to God's will as his standard of right and wrong, and judges of actions according to their greater or less conformity.

Brooks Atkinson: We tolerate differences of opinion in people who are familiar to us. But differences of opinion in people we do not know sound like heresy or plots.

Bible: 1 Corinthians 10:12: Let him who thinketh he standeth take heed lest he fall.

Bible: 1 Corinthians 13:9: We know in part, and we prophesy in part.

Bible: Habakkuk 2:2: Write the vision, and make it plain upon the tables, that he may run that readeth it.

Bible: Hebrews 13:9: Be not carried about with divers and strange doctrines.

Bible: Hosea 12:10: I have multiplied visions, and used similitudes.

Bible: Matthew 6:34: Take therefore no thought for the morrow: for the morrow shall take thought for the things of itself.

Bible: Matthew 7:15: Beware of false prophets, which come to you in sheep's clothing, but inwardly they are ravening wolves.

Bible: Proverbs 27:1: Boast not thyself of to morrow; for thou knowest not what a day may bring forth.

Bible: Proverbs 29:18: Where there is no vision, the people perish.

Ambrose Bierce: ABSURDITY, n. A statement of belief manifestly inconsistent with one's own opinion.

Ambrose Bierce: DELUSION, n. The father of a most respectable family, comprising Enthusiasm, Affection, Self-denial, Faith, Hope, Charity and many other goodly sons and daughters....

Ambrose Bierce: FLOP, v. Suddenly to change one's opinions and go over to another party. The most notable flop on record was that of Saul of Tarsus, who has been severely criticised as a turn-coat by some of our partisan journals.

Ambrose Bierce: IMPARTIAL, adj. Unable to perceive any promise of personal advantage from espousing either side of a controversy or adopting either of two conflicting opinions.

Ambrose Bierce: OUTCOME, n. A particular type of disappointment. By the kind of intelligence that sees in an exception a proof of the rule the wisdom of an act is judged by the outcome, the result. This is immortal nonsense; the wisdom of an act is to be judged by the light that the doer had when he performed it.

Ambrose Bierce: PREDILECTION, n. The preparatory stage of disillusion.

Ambrose Bierce: PRESIDE, v. To guide the action of a deliberative body to a desirable result. In Journalese, to perform upon a musical instrument; as, "he presided at the piccolo."

Ambrose Bierce: PROSPECT, n. An outlook, usually forbidding. An expectation, usually forbidden.....

Charles Synge Christopher Bowen (English judge, 1835-1894): *Obiter dicta*, like the proverbial chickens of destiny, come home to roost sooner or later in a very uncomfortable way to the Judges who have uttered them, and are a great source of embarrassment in future cases. Cooke v. New River Co., 38 Ch. D. 56 (1888)

Baron George Wilshere Bramwell (English Judge, 1802-1892): The matter does not appear to me now as it appears to have appeared to me then.

Sir Thomas Browne: I could never divide myself from any man upon the difference of an opinion, or be angry with his judgment for not agreeing with me in that from which perhaps within a few days I should dissent myself.

Elizabeth Barrett Browning: Men get opinions as boys learn to spell, / By reiteration chiefly.

Joseph Butler: An obstinate man does not hold opinions—they hold him.

Samuel Butler: The more unpopular an opinion is, the more necessary is it that the holder should be somewhat punctilious in his observance of conventionalities generally.

Benjamin Cardozo: Often a liberal antidote of experience supplies a sovereign cure for a paralyzing abstraction built upon a theory.

Benjamin Cardozo: Opinion has a significance proportioned to the sources that sustain it. Petrogradsky M.K. Bank v. National City Bank, 253 N.Y. 23, 35 (1930)

Benjamin Cardozo (*Nature of the Judicial Process*, 1921): Dicta are not always ticketed as such, and one does not recognize them always at a glance.

Thomas Carlyle: Popular opinion is the greatest lie in the world.

Sir Winston Churchill: Please be good enough to put your conclusions and recommendations on one sheet of paper in the very beginning of your report, so I can even consider reading it.

Sir Winston Churchill: I pass with relief from the tossing sea of Cause and Theory to the firm ground of Result and Fact.

Cicero: No liberal man would be imputed a charge of unsteadiness to another for having changed his opinion.

Claud Cockburn: Never believe anything until it has been officially denied.

Clarence Darrow: The world is made up for the most part of morons and natural tyrants, sure of themselves, strong in their own opinions, never doubting anything.

Jefferson Davis (President of the Conferacy, 1864): If the Confederacy fails, there should be written on its tombstone: Died of a theory.

Leonardo da Vinci: The greatest deception men suffer is from their own opinions.

Rene Descartes: One cannot conceive (EDITOR: or opine) anything so strange and so implausible that it has not already been said by one philosopher or another.

Benjamin Disraeli: Predominant opinions are generally the opinions of the generation that is vanishing.

Albert Einstein (June 1933 lecture at Oxford "On the Method of Theoretcal Physics"): To truly understand the methods and philosophies of physicists, don't listen to their words, fix your attention on their deeds.

Earl of Eldon, Lord Chancellor of Great Britain (1751-1838): I feel myself bound to state that I must, when I decided that case, have seen it in a point of view, in which, after most laborious consideration, I cannot see it now.

Ralph Waldo Emerson: We are of different opinions at different hours, but we always may be said to be at heart on the side of truth.

Ralph Waldo Emerson: Lidian says that the only sin which people never forgive in each other is a difference of opinion.

Ralph Waldo Emerson: It is easy in the world to live after the world's opinion; it is easy in solitude to live after our own; but the great man is he who, in the midst of the crowd, keeps with perfect sweetness the independence of solitude.

Ralph Waldo Emerson: A man cannot utter two or three sentences without disclosing to intelligent ears precisely where he stands in life and thought, whether in the kingdom of the senses and the understanding, or in that of ideas and imagination, or in the realm of intuitions and duty.

John Erskine: Opinion is that exercise of the human will which helps us to make a decision without information.

Euripides: If all men saw the fair and wise the same / men would not have debaters' double strife.

Euripides: A man's most valuable trait is a judicious sense of what not to believe.

Anatole France: If fifty million people say a foolish thing, it is still a foolish thing.

Benjamin Franklin: The eyes of other people are the eyes that ruin us. If all but myself were blind, I should want neither fine clothes, fine houses, nor fine furniture.

Andre Gide: An opinion, though it is original, does not necessarily differ from the accepted opinions; the important thing is that it does not try to conform to it.

George Francis Gilette: (By 1940) the theory of relativity will be considered a joke.

Goethe: It is with true opinions which one has the courage to utter, as with pawns first advanced on the chessboard; they may be beaten, but they have inaugurated a game which must be won.

Baltazar Gracian: Everything is good or everything is bad according to the votes they gain.

Horace Greeley: I do not regret having braved public opinion, when I knew it was wrong and was sure it would be merciless.

Sacha Guitry: What probably distorts everything in life is that one is convinced that one is speaking the truth because one says what one think.

Lord Halsbury (Lord Chancellor of Great Britain, 1823-1921): A case is only an authority for what it actually decides. I entirely deny that it can be quoted for a proposition that may seem to follow logically from it. Such a mode of reasoning assumes that the law is necessarily a logical code, whereas every lawyer must acknowledge that the law is not always logical at all. *Quinn v. Leathem*, A.C. 495 (1901)

Philip Hamerton (English author, 1894): The opinions of men who think are always growing and changing, like living children.

Learned Hand (Judge of U.S. District and Ciruit Courts, 1872-1961): We now think that we were then wrong and that the decision must be overruled for reasons we shall state. Metallizing Eng. Co. v. Kenyon, 153 F. 2d 516, 518 (1946)

Sydney Harris: Any philosophy (EDITOR: or opinion) that can be put "in a nutshell" belongs there.

Heinrich Heine: The men of the past had convictions, while we moderns have only of opinions.

Oliver Wendell Holmes, Jr. (2 *Holmes-Pollock Letters* 173, 1925): I am hard at work ... preparing small diamonds for people of limited intellectual means.

Oliver Wendell Holmes Jr.: A man's opinions are generally of much more value than his arguments.

Oliver Wendell Holmes Jr.: With effervescent opinions, as with the not yet forgotten champagne, the quickest way to let them go flat is to let them get exposed to the air.

Oliver Wendell Holmes Sr.: A man's opinions are generally of much more value than his arguments.

Edgar Watson Howe: When half the people believe one thing, and the other half another, it is usually safe to accept either opinion.

Joseph C. Hutcheson (Texas lawyer, Judge US District & Circuit Courts): I recognize,...that the rule of stare decisis binds us to follow that court (U.S. Supreme) in respect of things decided by it. I know of no rule of stare "dictis" which binds us to follow it in respect of things merely said by it. Hercules Gasoline Co. v Comm'r, 147 F. 2d 972 (1945)

Thomas Henry Huxley: There is no greater mistake than the hasty conclusion that opinions are worthless because they are badly argued.

Thomas Huxley: The great tragedy of Science—slaying of a beautiful hypothesis by an ugly fact.

Thomas Jefferson: Error of opinion may be tolerated where reason is left free to combat it.

Joseph Joubert: Those who never retract their opinions love themselves more than they love truth.

La Bruyere: It is often easier as well as more advantageous to conform to other men's opinions than to bring them over to ours.

Walter Savage Landor: We listen to those whom we know to be of the same opinions as ourselves, and we call them wise for being of it; but we avoid such as differ from us.

La Rochefoucauld: We credit scarcely any persons with good sense except those who are of our opinion.

Georg Christoph Lichtenberg: One must judge men not by their opinions, but by what their opinions have made of them.

John Locke: New opinions are always suspected, and usually opposed, without any other reason but because they are not already common.

Lucretius: Fly no opinion because it is new, but strictly search, and after careful view, reject it if false, embrace it if 'tis true.

S.E. Luria: Significant advances in science often have a peculiar quality: they contradict obvious, commonsense opinions.

Maimonides: Men cling to the opinions of habit

Horace Mann: Do not think of knocking out another person's brains because he differs in opinion from you. It would be as rational to knock yourself on the head because you differ from yourself ten years ago.

John Marshall (statesman and Chief Justice US Supreme Court, 1755-1835): It is a maxim, not to be disregarded, that general expressions, in every opinion, are to be taken in connection with the case in which those expressions are used. If they go beyond the case, they may be respected, but ought not to control the judgment in a subsequent suit, except when the very point is presented for decision. Cohens v Virginia, 6 Wheat 264 (1821)

John Stuart Mill: In the human mind, one-sidedness has always been the rule, and many-sidedness the exception. Hence, even in revolutions of opinion, one part of the truth usually sets while another rises.

John Stuart Mill: If Mankind minus one were of one opinion, then Mankind is no more justified in silencing the one, than the one – if he had the power – would be in silencing Mankind.

John Milton: Where there is much desire to learn, there of necessity will be much arguing, much writing, many opinions; for opinions in good men is but knowledge in the making.

Montaigne: There never was in the world two opinions alike, no more than two hairs or two grains. The most universal quality is diversity.

Montaigne: Every opinion is of force enough to cause itself to be espoused at the expense of life.

Montaigne: The relish of good and evil depends in great measure upon the opinion we have of them.

John Morley: Our opinions are less important than the spirit and temper with which they possess us, and even good opinions are worth very little unless we hold them in a broad, intelligent, and spacious way.

Michael A. Musmanno (Justice of Pennsylvania Supreme Court, 1959): A theory without factual data to support it has no more weight in a courtroom than in a scientific laboratory.

Michael A. Musmanno (Justice of Pa. Supreme Court, 1959): Trial Judges should be extremely wary about drawing word pictures with crayons taken from a box of sheer speculation.

Michael A. Musmanno (Justice of the Sup. Ct. of Pennsylvania, 1959): There is no excuse for groping in the darkness of conjecture when a simple lifting of the blind will reveal the circumstances of reality.

Michael A. Musmanno (Justice of the Pennsylvania Supreme Court, 1959): The reasoning of the Majority which defeats the plaintiff's verdict, fairly and squarely won in the assizes, is a reasoning which would upset any decision because it uses theory for facts and suspicion for logic. The river of conjecture flowing on to the sea of presumption can carry on its boundless bosom fleets of hypotheses and armadas of surmise, but they will never reach the port of reality and never sail into the harbor of objective revelation.

Michael A. Musmanno (Justice of Pennsylvania Supreme Court, 1959): When, in the reconstruction of a scientific phenomenon, every plausible explanation for the accepted result is ruled out but one, it is idle to argue that there could possibly be still another explanation which lies in the realm of the unknowable and unascertainable and then expect a jury to base its verdict on that mysterious something which exists only in the misty shadowlands of shrouded mystery and supernatural supposition.

Friedrich Nietzsche: One often contradicts an opinion when it is really only the tone in which it has been presented that is unsympathetic.

Friedrich Nietzsche: It is hard enough to remember my opinions, without also remembering my reasons for them.

Austin O'Malley: Facts are carpet-tacks under the pneumatic tires of theory.

William Penn: It is safer to learn than teach; and who conceals his opinion has nothing to answer for.

William Penn: In all things reason should prevail; it is quite another thing to be stiff, than to be steady in opinion.

Wendell Phillips: Truth is one forever absolute, but no opinion is truth filtered through the moods, the blood, of the spectator.

Luigi Pirandello (Italian dramatist, novelist and short story writer, Nobel Prize in Literature in 1934; 1867-1936): Refusing to have an opinion is a way of having won, isn't it?

Robert M. Pirsig: One geometry (EDITOR: or ONE MEDICINE/ECONOMICS/ETC) cannot be more true than another; it can only be more *convenient.* Geometry is not true, it is advantageous.

Alexander Pope: To observations which ourselves we make, / We grow more partial for the observer's sake.

Cuthbert W. Pound (Assoc Judge, Chief Judge, New York Court of Appeals, 1864-1935): As this State has always permitted foreign judgments to be impeached for fraud, the preceding fifty-four pages of the opinion may be regarded as magnificent dictum, entitled to the utmost respect, but not determinative of the question. Johnston v Compagnie Generale Transatlantique, 242 N.Y. 381(1926) (Referring to the opinion of Mr. Justice Gray in Hilton v Guyot, 159 US 113, 40 L ed 57, 15 S Ct 1027, 1895)

Thomas Brackett Reed: Copernicus... did not publish his book (on the nature of the solar system) until he was on his deathbed. He knew how dangerous it is to be right when the rest of the world is wrong.

Will Rogers: Broad-minded is just another way of saying a fellow's too lazy to form an opinion.

Will Rogers: When you straddle a thing it takes a long time to explain it.

Will Rogers: A difference of opinion is what makes horse racing and missionaries.

Seneca: Provided we look to and satisfy our consciences, no matter for opinion; let me deserve well though I hear ill.

Socrates: Wind puffs up empty bladders; opinion, fools

Sir Philip Sidney: Among the best men are diversities of opinion; which should no more, in true reason, breed hatred, than one that loves black should be angry with him that is clothed in white; for thoughts are the very apparel of the mind.

William Shakespeare (*Antony and Cleopatra*, Act I, ii): On the sudden / A Roman thought hath struck him.

William Shakespeare (*Hamlet*, Act V, i): Nay, an thou 'lt mouth, / I'll rant as well as thou.

William Shakespeare (*Henry V*, Act I, i): List his discourse of war, and you shall hear / A fearful battle render'd you in music: / Turn him to any cause of policy, / The Gordian knot of it he will unloose, / Familiar as his garter: that, when he speaks, / The air, a charter'd libertine, is still, / And the mute wonder lurketh in men's ears, / To steal his sweet and honey'd sentences.

William Shakespeare (*I Henry VI*, Act V, i): I always thought, / It was both impious and unnatural, / That such immanity and bloody strife / Should reign among professors of one faith.

William Shakespeare (*Henry VIII*, Act III, ii): I am afraid His thinkings are below the moon.

William Shakespeare (*Henry VIII*, Act IV, ii): To add great honours to his age / Than man could give him, he died fearing God.

William Shakespeare (*Julius Caesar*, Act I, ii): Yond Cassius has a lean and hungry look; / He thinks too much: such men are dangerous.

William Shakespeare (*Julius Caesar,* Act II, i): His silver hairs / Will purchase us a good opinion, / And buy men's voices to commend our deeds.

William Shakespeare (*Macbeth,* Act I, iii): Stands not within the prospect of belief.

William Shakespeare (*Macbeth,* Act I, vii): We will proceed no further in this business. / He hath honour'd me of late; and I have bought / Golden opinions from all sorts of people, / Which would be worn now in their newest gloss, / Not cast aside so soon.

William Shakespeare (*Macbeth,* Act II, ii): You do unbend your noble strength, to think / So brainsickly of things.

William Shakespeare (*Pericles,* Act II, ii): Opinion's but a fool, that makes us scan, / The outward habit by the inward man.

William Shakespeare (*Richard III,* Act III, vii): Divinely bent to meditation; / And in no worldly suit would he be moved, / To draw him from his holy exercise.

Sydney Smith: It is always considered as a piece of impertinence in England, if a man of less than two or three thousand a year has any opinions at all upon important subjects.

Paul Smokov (North Dakota rancher who forecasts the weather by looking at pig spleens, said in 2007): The spleens are 85% correct, according to my figures. (Weathermen) aren't any better.

Spanish Proverb: Three Spaniards, four opinions.

Jonathan Swift: If a man should register all his opinions upon love, politics, religion, learning, etc., beginning from his youth, and so go on to old age, what a bundle of inconsistencies and contradictions would appear at last.

Talmud: Judge a man only by his own deeds and words; the opinions of others can be false.

Edward Teller: If there ever was a misnomer, it is "exact science." Science has always been full of mistakes. The present day he is no exception. And our mistakes are good mistakes; they require a genius to correct them. Of course, we do not see our own mistakes.

Mark Twain: In all matters of opinion our adversaries are insane.

Mark Twain: You tell me whar a man gits his corn pone, en I'll tell you what his 'pinions is.

Mark Twain: Loyalty to petrified opinions never yet broke a chain or freed a human soul in *this* world—and never *will.*

Mark Twain: In religion and politics (Editor: and in some medical "junk-science"?) people's beliefs and convictions [Editor: and "opinions"?] are in almost every case gotten at secondhand, and without examination, from authorities who have not themselves examined the questions at issue but have taken them at second- hand from other non-examiners, whose opinions about them were not worth a brass farthing.

UA (*The Old Judge*, quoted on title page of Birrel, *Obiter Dicta*, 1885): An obiter dictum, in the language of the law, is a gratuitous opinion, and individual impertinence, which, whether it be wise or foolish, right or wrong, bindeth none – not even the lips that utter it.

USMC Acronym: S.W.A.G. = Scientific/Silly Wild Assed Guess

Marquis de Vauvenargues: When a thought is too weak to be expressed simply, it should be rejected.

Ralph Venning: To maintain an opinion because it is thine, and not because it is true, is to prefer thyself above the truth.

Voltaire: The history of human opinion is scarcely anything more than the history of human errors.

Alec Waugh: If we knew where opinion ended and fact began, we should have discovered, I suppose, the absolute.

Richard Whately: A confident expectation that no argument will be adduced that will change our opinions is very different from a resolution that none ever shall. We may print but not stereotype our opinions.

Virginia Woolf: But it is just when opinions universally prevail and we have added lip service to their authority that we become sometimes most keenly conscious that we do not believe a word that we are saying.

OPPRESSION (See CIVIL RIGHTS)

ORATORY/SUCCINCTNESS/SPEECH

Uncle Anthony: You got two eyes, two ears and only one mouth, that's 'cause God wanted you to watch out and listen up twice as much as you open your mouth to talk.

Uncle Anthony: Some guys don't have a lot to say, but ya gotta listen a long time to find that out.

Uncle Anthony: When you're in it up to your ears – KEEP YOUR MOUTH SHUT!

Uncle Anthony: he can stay longer in one hour than most people do in one week.

Uncle Anthony: The real art of conversation is not only learning how to say the right thing at the right time, but also learning to leave unsaid the wrong thing at the tempting moment.

Aunt Mary Carlo: He don't monopoloze a subject; he monotonizes it!

Aunt Mary Carlo: Canyabeatdat! She get upset when somebody tries to talk while she's interruptin'.

Aunt Mary Carlo: When dere's nuttin' more to be said, he's still sayin it!?

Aunt Mary Carlo: Its amazzin' how she comes inta a room voice first.

Sholem Aleichem: If a horse with four legs can sometimes stumble, how much more then a man with only one tongue.

Saint Ambrose: Let us have a reason for beginning, and let our end be within due limits. For a speech that is wearisome only stirs up anger.

Arabic Saying: The best orator is one who can make men see with their ears.

Francis Bacon: Every man speaks more virtuously that he either thinks or act.

Howard H. Baker Jr. (United States Senator): I'll tell you what my daddy told me after my first trial. I thought I was just great. I asked him, "How did I do?" He paused and said, "You've got to guard against speaking more clearly than you think."

Stanley Baldwin: The Speaker's eye: the most elusive organ that Nature ever created.

Stephen Vincent Benet (1937 short story *The Devil and Daniel Webster*): "... They said when he (Daniel Webster) stood up to speak stars and stripes came right out of the sky. And once he spoke against a river and made it sink into the ground. They said when he walked the woods with his fishing rod, "Kill All," trout would jump out of the streams into his pocket because they knew it was no use putting up a fight against him. And when he argued a case he could turn on the harps of the blessed and the shaking of the earth underground. That was the kind of man he was.

Sarah Bernhardt: Acting is (EDITOR: and TRIAL ADVOCACY) like style – it does not improve, it merely changes.

Bible: Apocrypha, Ecclesiasticus 32:8: Let thy speech be short, comprehending much in few words.

Bible: Colossians 4:6: Let your speech be always with grace, seasoned with salt.

Bible: James 1:19: Be swift to hear, slow to speak, slow to wrath.

Bible: Proverbs 17:28: Even a fool, when he holdeth his peace, is counted wise: and he that shutteth his lips is esteemed a man of understanding.

Bible: Proverbs 26:5: Answer a fool according to his folly, lest he be wise in his own conceit.

Bible: Proverbs 26:16: The sluggard is wiser in his own conceit than seven men that can render a reason.

Bible: Proverbs 27:2: Let another man praise thee, and not thine own mouth; a stranger, and not thine own lips.

Bible: Proverbs 28:11: The rich man is wise in his own conceit; but the poor that hath understanding searcheth him out.

Bible: Proverbs 29:11: A fool uttereth all his mind.

Bible: Romans 12:16: Mind not high things, but condescend to men of low estate. Be not wise in your own conceit.

Bible: 1 Samuel 2:3: Talk no more so exceeding proudly; let not arrogancy come out of your mouth: for the Lord is a God of knowledge, and by him actions are weighed.

Bible: 1 Thessalonians 4:11: Study to be quiet, and do your own business.

Ambrose Bierce: BORE, n. A person who talks when you wish him to listen.

Ambrose Bierce: CONVERSATION, n. A fair for the display of the minor mental commodities, each exhibitor being too intent upon the arrangement of his own wares to observe those of his neighbor.

Ambrose Bierce: ELOQUENCE, n. The art of orally persuading fools that white is the color that it appears to be. It includes the gift of making any color appear white.

Ambrose Bierce: END, n. The position farthest removed on either hand from the Interlocutor....

Ambrose Bierce: HOMILETICS, n. The science of adapting sermons to the spiritual needs, capacities and conditions of the congregation....

Ambrose Bierce: LECTURER, n. One with his hand in your pocket, his tongue in your ear and his faith in your patience.

Ambrose Bierce: LOQUACITY, n. A disorder which renders the sufferer unable to curb his tongue when you wish to talk.

Ambrose Bierce: MENDACIOUS, adj. Addicted to rhetoric.

Ambrose Bierce: MOUTH, n. In man, the gateway to the soul; in woman, the outlet of the heart.

Amborse Bierce: ORATORY, n. A conspiracy between speech and action to cheat the understanding. A tyranny tempered by stenography.

Ambrose Bierce: PERIPATETIC, adj. Walking about. Relating to the philosophy of Aristotle, who, while expounding it, moved from place to place in order to avoid his pupil's objections. A needless precaution – they knew no more of the matter than he.

Ambrose Bierce: PERORATION, n. The explosion of an oratorical rocket. It dazzles, but to an observer having the wrong kind of nose its most conspicuous peculiarity is the smell of the several kinds of powder used in preparing it.

Ambrose Bierce: PLEONASM, n. An army of words escorting a corporal of thought.

Ambrose Bierce: ROSTRUM, n. In Latin, the beak of a bird or the prow of a ship. In America, a place from which a candidate for office energetically expounds the wisdom, virtue and power of the rabble.

Ambrose Bierce: TALK, v.t. To commit an indiscretion without temptation, from an impulse without purpose.

Ambrose Bierce: Speak when you are angry and you will make the best speech you will ever regret.

Ambrose Bierce: Least said is soonest disavowed.

Josh Billings: I don't care how much a man talks, if he only says it in a few words.

Lord Birkett: I do not object to people looking at their watches when I am speaking – but I strongly object when they start shaking them to make certain they are still going.

Louis Brandeis: If there be time to expose through discussion of falsehood and fallacies, to avert the evil by the process of education, the remedy to be applied is more speech, not enforced silence.

Louis Brandeis (to a long-winded lawyer who asked for some latitude): I don't mind your latitude. What I object to is your LONG-itude.

William Jennings Bryan: I'd rather see a sermon any day than hear one.

Warren E. Burger: Free-speech carries with it some freedom to listen.

Leo Buscaglia: Don't look over people's shoulders. Look in their eyes. Don't talk at your children. Take their faces in your hands and talk to them. Don't make love to a body, make love to a person.

George Bush, Sr. (acceptance speech for Republican presidential nomination in 1988): Read my lips!

Lord Byron: His speech was a fine sample, on the whole, / Of the rhetoric, which learn'd call rigmarole.

Cato the Elder: I think the first virtue is to restrain the tongue; he approaches nearest to gods who knows how to be silent, even though he is in the right.

Paul Chatfield: Oratory is the power to talk people out of their sober and natural opinions.

Chinese Proverb: Although there exist many thousand subjects for elegant conversation, there are persons who cannot meet a cripple without talking about feet.

Sir Winston Churchill: Short words are best and old words when short are best of all.

Sir Winston Churchill: Some people's idea of (free-speech) is that they are free to say what they like, but if anyone says anything back, that is an outrage.

Sir Winston Churchill: I got into my bones the essential structure of the ordinary British sentence – which is a noble thing.

Sir Winston Churchill: I dreamed last night I was speaking before the House of Lords. Then I woke up and found I was!

Sir Winston Churchill: There are two things that are more difficult than making an after-dinner speech: climbing a wall which is leaning toward you and kissing a girl who is leaning away from you.

Sir Winston Churchill: Everybody is in favor of free speech. Hardly a day passes without its being extolled, but some people's idea of it is that they are free to say what they like, but if anyone says anything back, that is an outrage

Cicero: Nothing is so unbelievable that oratory cannot make it acceptable.

Cicero: All speaking of merit is characterized by nervousness.

Henry Clay speaking to General Alexander Smyth of Virginia: General Smyth: "you, sir, speak for the present generation; but I speak for posterity." Henry Clay: "Yes, General, and you seem resolved to speak until the arrival of your audience."

Charles Caleb Colton: Men are born with two eyes, but only one tongue, in order that they should see twice as much as they say."

Charles Caleb Colton: When you have nothing to say, say nothing.

William Connor: To say that he was not at a loss for a word is one of the great understatements of all time. He was not at a loss for 500,000 words and we heard them, every one.

Calvin Coolidge: I have never been hurt by anything I did not say.

Calvin Coolidge: a Washington society woman sitting next to President Coolidge said: Mr. President, you are so silent. I made a bet today that I can get more than two words out of you." President Coolidge said: "you lose."

Thomas Corwin (an American politician): But Corwin's Law was established in advice he gave a budding Speaker: "Never make people laugh. If you would succeed in life, you must be solemn, solemn as an ass. All the great monuments are built over solemn asses."

Degas: The preparation of a painting is something that requires the same or as much cunning, treachery and deceit as the preparation of a crime. (EDITOR: ACTING = PAINTING = TRIAL ADVOCACY)

Benjamin Disraeli: Be frank and explicit. That is the right line to take when you wish to conceal your own mind and to confuse the minds of others.

William O. Douglas: Free-speech is not to be regulated like diseased cattle and impure butter. The audience... that hissed yesterday may applaud today, even for the same performance.

Hansell B Duckett: What this country needs is more free speech worth listening to.

Albert Einstein: If A is a success in life, then A equals x plus y plus z. Work is x; y is play; and z is keeping your mouth shut.

Albert Einstein (at boring speech at dinner in DC in 1921): I have just developed a new Theory of Eternity.

Queen Elizabeth I's motto: "*Video et tacheo*" = I see, but I say nothing.

Ralph Waldo Emerson: Speeches power: speech is to persuade, to convert, to compel.

Ralph Waldo Emerson: In perfect eloquence, the hearer would lose the sense of dualism, of hearing from another; would cease to distinguish between the orator and himself.

Ralph Waldo Emerson: The least effect of the oration is on the prator; yet it is something; a faint recoil; a kicking of the gun.

English Proverb (18th century): To talk without thinking is to shoot without aiming.

Evan Esar: Eloquence is the art of saying as little as possible but making it sound as much as possible.

Edward Everett to Abraham Lincoln at Gettysburg: "I should be glad if I could flatter myself that I came as near to the central idea of the occasion in two hours as you did in two minutes."

Gerald Ford: When a man is asked to make a speech, the first thing he has to decide is what to say.

Felix Frankfurter: It must never be forgotten, however, that the Bill of Rights was the child of the Enlightenment. That of the guarantee of free-speech Lady Faith in the power of an appeal to reason by all the peaceful means for gaining access to the mind... but utterance in a context of violence and lose its significance as an appeal to reason and become part of an instrument of force. Such utterance was not meant to be sheltered by the Constitution.

Benjamin Franklin: Here comes the orator with his flood of words and his drop of reason.

Benjamin Franklin: The heart of a fool is in his mouth, but the mouth of a wise man is in his heart.

German Proverb: Beware of a silent dog and still water.

Andre Gide: I notice once more how unsuitable real passion is to eloquence.

Ruth Gordon: The best impromptu to speeches are those written well in advance.

Gian Vincenzo Gravina: A bore is a man who deprives you of solitute without providing you with company.

Learned Hand: ... I had rather take my chance that some traitors will escape detection than spread abroad a spirit of general suspicion and distrust, which accepts rumor and gossip in place of undismayed and unintimidated inquiry. I believe that that community is already in process of dissolution where each man begins to eye his neighbor as a possible enemy, where nonconformity with the accepted decree, political as well as religious, is a mark of disaffection; where denunciation, without specification or backing, takes the place of evidence; where orthodoxy chokes freedom of dissent; where Faith in the eventual supremacy of reason has become so timid that we dare not enter our convictions in the open lists, to win or lose.

Adolf Hitler: All epoch-making revolutionary events have been produced not by written but by spoken word.

Thomas Hobbes: A democracy in effect is no more than an aristocracy of orators, interrupted sometimes with a temporary monarchy of one orator.

John Andrew Holmes (brother of Oliver Wendell Holmes): Speech is conveniently located midway between thought and action, where it often substitutes for both.

Oliver Wendell Holmes, Jr.: Long wind hasn't given out on this side any more than on yours, nor so much, though the tendency is towards shorter opinions. I abhor, loathe and despise these long discourses, and agree with Carducci the Italian poet who died some years ago that a man who takes half a page to say what can be said in a sentence will be damned.

Oliver Wendell Holmes Jr: Nothing conduces to brevity like a caving in of the knees. (Therefore, it is better to stand when writing)

Oliver Wendell Holmes, Sr: Eloquence may set fire to reason.

Oliver Wendell Holmes Jr: The most stringent protection of free speech would not protect a man from falsely shouting fire in a theater and causing a panic.

Oliver Wendell Holmes Jr: The question in every case is whether the words are used in such circumstances and are of such a nature as to create a clear and present danger.

Oliver Wendell Holmes Jr: I... probably take the extremist of view in favor of free speech, (in which, in the abstract, I have no very enthusiastic believe, though I hope I would die for it)...

Kin Hubbard: Why don't th' feller who says, "I'm not a speechmaker," let it go at that instead o' givin' a demonstration?

Irish Proverb: A silent mouth is melodious.

Irish Proverb: It is the quiet pigs that eat the meal.

Italian Proverb: Half a brain is enough for him who says little.

Italian Proverb: A closed mouth catches no flies.

Italian Proverb: Silence was never written down.

George Jessel: The human brain starts working the moment you were born and never stops and to you stand up to speak in public.

George Jessel: My advice to speech makers is if you haven't struck oil in the first three minutes, stop boring!

Jewish Saying: If a horse had anything to say, he would speak up.

Jewish Saying: The heart of fools is in their mouth; the mouth of the wise is in their heart.

Al Jolson (in the first full-length motion picture, *The Jazz Singer*, 1927): You ain't heard nothin' yet!

Franklin P. Jones: The difference between news and gossip lies in whether you raise your voice or lower it.

Elizabeth Kenny: He who angers you, conquers you.

Latin Proverb (also called *Verb. Sap.*, an abbreviation of *Verbum sapienti sat est*): A word to the wise is enough.

Tom Lehrer: I wish people who had trouble communicating would just shut up.

Fran Liebowitz: The opposite of talking isn't listening. The opposite of talking is waiting.

Abraham Lincoln: He can compress the most words into the smallest ideas better than any man I have ever met.

Abraham Lincoln: Better to remain silent and be thought a fool than to speak out and remove all doubt.

Abraham Lincoln: I like to see a man speaking like he's fighting a swarm of bees

Abraham Lincoln (Nov. 19, 1863 Gettysburg Address, he told an aide that his 2 minute, 272 word, 10 sentence speech was a failure): That speech won't scow (an Illinois expression for a plow being unable to crack the surface of the ground)

Abraham Lincoln (Nov. 19, 1863, Gettysburg, PA): Four score and seven years ago our fathers brought forth on this continent a new nation, conceived in Liberty, and dedicated to the proposition that all men are created equal. Now we are engaged in a great civil war, testing whether that nation, or any nation, so conceived and so dedicated, can long endure. We are met on a great battle-field of that war. We have come to dedicate a portion of that field, as a final resting place for those who here gave their lives that that nation might live. It is altogether fitting and proper that we should do this. // But, in a larger sense, we can not dedicate—we can not consecrate—we can not hallow—this ground. The brave men, living and dead, who struggled here, have consecrated it, far above our poor power to add or detract. The world will little note, nor long remember what we say here, but it can never forget what they did here. It is for us the living, rather, to be dedicated here to the unfinished work which they who fought here have thus far so nobly advanced. It is rather for us to be here dedicated to the great task remaining before us — that from these honored dead we take increased devotion to that cause for which they gave the last full measure of devotion — that we here highly resolve that these dead shall not have died in vain — that this nation, under God, shall have a new birth of freedom — and that government of the people, by the people, for the people, shall not perish from the earth.

Stanley Link: Eloquence: Saying the proper thing and stopping.

Walter Lippman: The compulsion of politicians to talk too much is in our day a very big obstacle to accomplishing what they all say they want to do.

Clare Booth Luce: The politicians were talking themselves red, white and blue in the face.

Charles Luckman: The trouble with America is that there are far too many wide-open spaces surrounded by teeth.

Thomas Macaulay: The object of oratory alone is not truth, but persuasion.

Lord Mancroft: A speech is like a love affair. Any fool can start it but to end it requires considerable skill.

Chief Justice John Marshall: To listen well is as powerful a means of communication and influence as to talk well.

H. L. Mencken: I never lecture, not because I am shy or a bad speaker, but simply becasue I detest the sort of people who go to lectures and don't want to meet them.

John Stuart Mill: If all mankind minus one were of one opinion and only one person were of the contrary opinion, mankind would be no more justified in silencing that person than he, if he had the power, would be justified in silencing mankind... if the opinion is right, they are deprived of the opportunity of exchanging error for truth; if wrong, they lose, what is almost as great a benefit, the clearer perception and livelier impression of truth, produced by its collision with error.

John Milton: Give me the liberty to know, to utter, and to argue freely according to conscience, above all liberties.

Christopher Morley: Beware the conversationalist who adds "in other words." He is merely starting afresh.

John Mortimer (spoken by Rumpole of The Bailey): Like a very old grammaphone record my conversation with (X) seemed to be stuck in a groove.

Edmund Muskie: In Maine we have saying that there's no point in speaking unless you can improve on silence.

Lawrence Olivier: I know not when I act and when not, or more accurately, when I lie and when I do not"

Plato: Rhetoric is the art of ruling the minds of men.

President Ronald Reagan (adaptation of Al Jolson's phrase, above, used in successful 1984 re-election campaign): You ain't seen nothin' yet!

Joan Rivers: An eloquent male is one who can describe Dolly Parton without using his hands.

François de la Rochefoucauld: Eloquence: saying the proper thing and stopping.

Will Rogers: Never miss a good chance to shut up.

Will Rogers: We do more talking progress than we do progressing.

Will Rogers: More words ain't good for anything in the world only to bring on more argument.

Will Rogers: Nobody wants his cause near as bad as he wants to talk about his cause.

Will Rogers: You could be the World's greatest orator and if you don't say anything while orating, they are going to walk out on you after a while.

Leo Rosten: MEGILLAH: Hebrew: "scroll, roll volume..." (1) The Scroll of Esther, which is Red and synagogues during Purim. (2) The tenth tractate in MO'ED, the second order of the Mishnah, which describes the time and manner of the public reading of the Scroll of Astor during the feast of Purim, and also describes the public reading of other portions of Scripture.... (3) In popular usage, anything very long, verbose, a rigmarole.

James Roosevelt: My father gave me these hints on speech-making: "Be sincere, be brief... be seated."

Russian Proverb: He need not search his pockets for words.

Russian Proverb: There is plenty of sound in an empty barrel.

Carl Sandburg: Slang is a language that rolls up its sleeves, spits on its hands, and goes to work.

Carl Sandburg: Look out how you use proud words. When you let proud words go, it is not easy to call them back. They wear long boots, hard boots.

George Santayana: To be brief is almost a condition of being inspired.

George Santayana: Eloquence is a republican art, as conversation is an aristocratic one.

William Shakespeare (*All's Well That Ends Well*, Act V, iii): Whose words all ears took captive.

William Shakespeare (*Antony and Cleopatra*, Act III, x): To try thy eloquence, now 'tis time.

William Shakespeare (*Comedy of Errors*, Act III, ii): Be not thy tongue thy own shame's orator.

William Shakespeare (*Coriolanus*, Act III, ii): Action is eloquence.

William Shakespeare (*Hamlet*, Act I, iii): Give every man thine ear, but few thy voice.

William Shakespeare (*Hamlet*, Act II, ii): Brevity is the soul of wit.

William Shakespeare (*II Henry VI*, Act I, i): Nephew, what means this passionate discourse, / This preoration with such circumstance?

William Shakespeare (*Henry V*, Act I, i): List his discourse of war, and you shall hear / A fearful battle render'd you in music.

William Shakespeare (*Henry V*, Act III, ii): Men of few words are the best men.

William Shakespeare (*Julius Caesar*, Act III, ii): I am no orator, as Brutus is; / But, as you know me all, a plain blunt man,... / For I have neither wit, nor words, nor worth, / Action, nor utterance, nor power of speech, / To stir men's blood: I only speak right on.

William Shakespeare (*Julius Caesar*, Act IV, iii): Hear me, for I will speak.

William Shakespeare (*King John*, Act III, iii): I had a thing to say, - / But I will fit it, with some better time.

William Shakespeare (*King Lear*, Act V, iii): Her voice was ever soft, / Gentle, and low – an excellent thing in woman.

William Shakespeare (*A Lover's Complaint*, Line 120): So on the tip of his subduing tongue, / All kinds of arguments and questions deep, / All replication prompt, and reason strong, / For his advantage still did wake and sleep: / To make the weeper laugh, the laugher weep, / He had the dialect and different skill.

William Shakespeare (*Love's Labour's Lost*, Act I, i): A man in all the world's new fashion planted, / That hath a mint of phrases in his brain.

William Shakespeare (*Love's Labour's Lost*, Act II, i): That aged ears play truant at his tales, / And younger hearings are quite ravished; / So sweet and voluble is his discourse.

William Shakespeare (*Merry Wives of Windsor*, Act II, ii): This is the short and long of it.

William Shakespeare (*Much Ado About Nothing*, Act II, i): She speaks poignards, and every word stabs.

William Shakespeare (*Othello*, Act I, iii): Rude am I in my speech, / And little bless'd with the set phrae of peace; / For since these arms of mine had seven years' pith, / Till now some nine moons wasted, they have us'd / Their dearest action in the tented field; / And little of this great world can I speak, / More than pertains to feats of broil and battle; / And therefore little shall I grace my cause, / In speaking for myself.

William Shakespeare (*Richard II*, Act I, iii): My tongue's use is to me no more, / Than an unstringed viol, or a harp.

William Shakespeare (*Richard II*, Act II, iii): Our fair discourse hath been as sugar / Making the hard way sweet and delectable.

William Shakespeare (*Richard III*, Act I, iii): Talkers are no good doers.

William Shakespeare (*Richard III*, Act III, v): Fear not, my lord, I'll play the orator.

William Shakespeare (*Richard III*, Act III, v): Doubt not, my lord; I'll play the orator, / As if the golden fee, for which I plead, / Were for myself.

William Shakespeare (*Richard III*, Act IV, iv): An honest tale speeds best being plainly told.

William Shakespeare (*Romeo and Juliet*, Act III, ii): Every tongue, that speaks / But Romeo's name, speaks heavenly eloquence.

William Shakespeare (*Taming of the Shrew*, Act II, i): Say, she be mute, and will not speak a word; / Then I'll commend her volubility, / And say she uttereth piercing eloquence.

William Shakespeare (*Twelfth Night*, Act I, v): I would be loath to cast away my speech; for, besides that it is excellently well penn'd, I have taken great pains to con it.

William Shakespeare (*Venus and Adonis*, l. 805): More I could tell, but more I dare not say; / The text is old, the orator too green.

William Shakespeare (*Venus and Adonis*, St. 25): Bid me discourse, I will enchant thine ear, / Or, like a fairy, trip upon the green.

George Bernard Shaw: My method is to take the utmost trouble to find the right thing to say, and then to say it with the utmost levity.

Sidney Smith: He has occasional flashes of silence, that make his conversation perfectly delightful.

Spanish Proverb: Who knows most speaks least.

Sir Josiah Stamp: I don't mind a bit having you look at your watches to see what time it is, but it really annoys me when you put them up to your years to see if they are still running.

Adlai Stevenson: Man does not live by words alone, despite the fact that sometimes he has to eat them.

Adlai Stevenson: I sometimes marvel at the extraordinary docility with which Americans submit to speeches.

Jonathan Swift: One of the best rules in conversation is, never to say a thing which any of the company can reasonably wish had been left unsaid.

Talmud: Let thine ears (too) hear what thine mouth speaketh.

Talmud, Berakoth, 4a: Teach your tongue to say "I do not know," lest you invent something.

Talmud, Niddah, 3b: Set a fence around your words.

Mother Teresa: Kind words are short and easy to speak, but their echoes are truly endless.

Henry David Thoreau: I should not talk so much about myself if there were anybody else whom I knew as well.

Lilly Tomlin as Ernestine: Have I reached the person to whom I am speaking?

Spencer Tracey: Acting isn't an important job in the scheme of things – plumbing is!

Mark Twain: The difference between a good speech and a great speech, is the difference between lightning and a lightning bug.

Mark Twain: A powerful agent is the right word. Whenever we come upon one of those intensely right words in a book or newspaper the resulting effect is physical as well as spiritual, and electically prompt.

Mark Twain: It usually takes me more than three weeks to prepare a good impromptu speech.

Mark Twain: It is by the goodness of God that in our country we have those three unspeakably precious things: freedom of speech, freedom of conscience, and the prudence never to practice either of them.

Mark Twain: The right word may be effective, but no word was ever as effective as a rightly timed pause.

Mark Twain: It is better to keep your mouth shut and appear stupid than to open it and remove all doubt.

Mark Twain: The language (German) which enables a man to travel all day in one sentence without changing cars.

Mark Twain: To say a compliment well is a high art and few possess it.

Mark Twain: There is nothing you can say in answer to a compliment. I have been complimented myself many times, and they always embarass me – I always feel that they have not said enough.

Mark Twain: When you cannot get a compliment in any other way, pay yourself one.

Mark Twain: There are five types of actresses: Bad, Fair, Good, Great … and Sarah Bernhardt

UA: After all is said and done, more is said than done.

UA: Diplomacy: Thinking twice before saying nothing.

John Updike: A healthy male adult bore consumes, each year, one and a half times his own weight in other people's patience.

Arthur T. Vanderbilt (Chief Justice of New Jersey Supreme Court, 1888-1957; a frequent expression used by this court and law reformer): Judicial reform is no sport for the short-winded.

Gore Vidal: Today's public figures can no longer write their own speeches or books, and there is some evidence that they can't read them either.

Voltaire: I disapprove of what you say, but I will defend to the death your right to say it.

Voltaire: Men use thought only to justify their wrongdoings and speech only to conceal their thoughts.

Voltaire: The secret of being a bore is to tell everything.

John Wayne: Talk low, talk slow, and don't say too much.

Dame Rebecca West: There is no such thing as conversation. It is an illusion. There are intersting monologues, that is all.

Walt Whitman: O the orator's joys! / To inflate the chest, to roll the thunder of the voice out from the ribs and throat, / To make the people rage, weep, hate, desire, with yourself, / To lead America – to quell America with a great tongue.

Woodrow Wilson: The man with power but without conscience, could, with an eloquent tongue... put this whole country into a flame.

J.B. Yeats: I always think a great orator convinces us not by the force of reasoning, but because *he is visibly enjoying the beliefs which he wants us to accept.*

Yiddish Proverb: If you are bitter at heart, sugar in the mouth will not help you.

Zohar: From a man's mouth you can tell who he is.

PAIN (See also EMOTIONAL DISTRESS; DAMAGES; GRIEF/SORROW)

Uncle Anthony: Y'know I respect a man who ENDURES and tries to live and cope with his pain as opposed to some whiner who SUFFERS and bellyaches about his PAIN AND SUFFERING.

Uncle Anthony: You can't choose how you feel, but you can choose what you do about it.

Aunt Mary Carlo: Physical pain and mental pain (or whatchacallit "sufferin'" an "mental anguish"), dey are really different; but dey both hurt, just dey hurt us different ways.... Sometimes doctors fix da physical pain, not da mental.

Francis Bacon: it is as natural to die as to be born; and to a little infant, perhaps, the one is as painful as the other.

Gamaliel Bailey: Night brings out stars, as sorrow shows us truths.

Henry Ward Beecher: God washes the eyes by tears until they can behold the invisible land where tears shall come no more.

Henry Ward Beecher: Tears are often the telescope by which men see far into heaven.

Henry Ward Beecher: Affliction comes to us all not to make us sad, but sober, not to make us sorry, but wise; not to make us despondent, but by its darkness to refresh us, as the night refreshes the day; not to impoverish, but to enrich us, as the plow enriches the field; to multiply our joy, as the seed, by planting, is multiplied a thousand-fold.

Jeremy Bentham: Nature has placed mankind under the government of two sovereign masters, pain and pleasure. It is for them to point out what we ought to do, as well as to determine what we shall do. On the one hand, the standard of right and wrong; on the other, the chain of causes and effects, are fastened to their throne.

Marilyn & Alan Bergman (Song: "The Way We Were"): What's too painful to remember, we just choose to forget."

Subhadra Bhikshu: To be born is to suffer: to grow old is to suffer: to die is to suffer: to lose what is loved is to suffer: to be tied to what is not loved is to suffer: to endure what is distasteful is to suffer. In short, all the results of individuality, of separate self-hood, necessarily involve pain or suffering.

Bible: 2 Corinthians 1:7: As ye are partakers of the sufferings, so shall ye be also of the consolation.

Bible: Hebrews 9:22: Without shedding of blood is no remission.

Bible: Isaiah 26:17: Like as a woman with child, that draweth near the time of her delivery, is in pain, and crieth out in her pangs; so have we been in thy sight, O Lord.

Bible: Isaiah 48:10: I have chosen thee in the furnace of affliction.

Bible: Isaiah 53:7: He was oppressed, and he was afflicted, yet he opened not his mouth.

Bible: Job 7:4: When I lie down, I say, When shall I arise, and the night be gone? And I am full of tossings to and fro unto the dawning of the day.

Bible: Lamentations 1:22: My sighs are many, and my heart is faint.

Bible: Matthew 26:39: Let this cup pass from me.

Bible: Revelations 9:6: In those days shall men seek death, and shall not find it; and shall desire to die, and death shall flee from them.

Ambrose Bierce: COMFORT, n. A state of mind produced by contemplation of a neighbor's uneasiness.

Ambrose Bierce: AFFLICTION, n. An acclimatizing process preparing the soul for another and bitter world.

Ambrose Bierce: PAIN, n. An uncomfortable frame of mind that may have a physical basis in something that is being done to the body, or may be purely mental, caused by the good fortune of another.

Buddha: Pain is the outcome of sin.

Bulgarian Proverb: One does not get crucified, one crucifies oneself.

Byron: What deep wounds ever closed without a scar?

Sir Winston Churchill: Criticism may not be agreeable, but it is necessary. It fulfils the same function as pain in the human body.

Marcus Tullius Cicero: Friendship improves happiness and abates misery, by the doubling of our joy and the dividing of our grief.

Florence Earle Coates ("The House of Pain," 1927): Ah me! The Prison House of Pain! – what lessons there are bought! - / Lessons of a sublimer strain than any elsewhere taught.

Susan Coolidge ("The Cradle Tomb in Westminster Abbey," 1905): "Men die, but sorrow never dies; / The crowding years divide in vain, / And the wide world is knit with ties / Of common brotherhood in pain."

Caleb Colton: Afflictions sent by providence melt the constancy of the noble minded, but confirm the obduracy of the vile, as the same furnace that liquefies the gold, hardens the clay.

Chinese Proverb: The gem cannot be polished without friction, nor man perfected without trials.

Howard Cosell: Courage takes many forms. There is physical courage, there's moral courage. Then there is a still higher type of courage – the courage to brave pain, to live with it, to never let others know of it and to still find joy in life; to wake up in the morning with enthusiasm for the day ahead.

Leonardo da Vinci: The greater the sensitivity, the greater the suffering.

Queen Elizabeth I (Queen of England): We all stand as equals to pain and sorrow.

Emily Dickinson: After great pain, a formal feeling comes.

Emily Dickinson: Pain has an element of blank; / It cannot recollect / When it began, or if there were / A day when it was not. // It has no future but itself, / Its infinite realms contain / Its past, enlightened to perceive / New periods of pain.

English Proverb: Only the wearer knows where the shoe pinches

Brendan Francis: If the pleasures that an age offers are insipid, passionate souls will seek pain.

Benjamin Franklin: There are no gains without pains.

Gaviscon Antiacid ad: Nobody's heartburn is like your heartburn.

Baltasar Gracian: Pain may be caused by many things which, if their advantageous aspect had been considered, might have given rise to satisfaction.

Thomas Gray: To each his suff'rings, all are men, Condemn'd alike to groan; The tender for another's pain; Th' unfeeling for his own

Joseph Hall: The most generous vine, if not pruned, runs in and out into many superfluous stems and grows at last weak and fruitless: so doth the best man if he be not cut short in his desires, and pruned with afflictions.

Felicia Hemans: Strength is born in the deep silence of long-suffering hearts; not amid joy.

King Henry II (of Saint Thomas Beckett 1170): Will no one revenge me of the injuries I have sustained from one turbulent priest?

Matthew Henry: Extraordinary afflictions are not always the punishment of extraordinary sins, but sometimes the trial of extraordinary graces.—Sanctified afflictions are spiritual promotions.

Katharine Hepburn: Life is to be lived. If you have to support yourself, you had bloody well better find some way that is going to be interesting. And you don't do that by sitting around wondering about yourself.
Hindu Proverb: He who has come through the fire will not fade in the sun.
Horace: Fools, through false shame, conceal their open wounds.
Irish Proverb: Patience is poultice for all wounds.
Irish Proverb: The wearer best knows where the shoe pinches.
Jewish Saying: The greatest pains are those you can't tell others.
Jewish Saying: A toothache makes you forget a headache.
Jewish Saying: The one who suffers alone suffers most.
Jewish Saying: From happiness to suffering is a step; from suffering to happiness seems an eternity.
Jewish Saying: Suffering creates nervous ailments; happiness cures them.
Jewish Saying: Suffering (sorrow) makes bones thin.
Jewish Saying: Garments conceal the suffering underneath.
Jewish Saying: The paths to a cemetery are paid with suffering.
Jewish Saying: We can understand neither the suffering of the good nor the prosperity of the wicked.
Samuel Johnson: Those who do not feel pain seldom think that it is felt.
Helen Keller: Although the world is full of suffering, it is also full of the overcoming of it.
Letitia Elizabeth Landon: Forgiveness is rarely perfect except in the breasts of those who have suffered.
Letitia Elizabeth Landon: We need to suffer that we may learn to pity.
Livy: Wounds cannot be cured unless probed and dressed.
Henry Wadsworth Longfellow: Know how sublime a thing it is to suffer and to be strong.
Sir John Lubbock: To render ourselves insensible to pain we must forfeit also the possibility of happiness.
Lord Macaulay: The Puritan hated bear-baiting, not because it gave pain to the bear, but because it gave pleasure to the spectators.
Somerset Maugham: The world is quickly bored by recital of misfortunes, and willingly avoids the sight of distress.
Jonathan Miller: Illness (or pain) is not something a person has. It's another way of being.
Addison Mizner: Misery loves company, but company does not reciprocate.
Miguel de Molinos: With the wind of tribulation God separates, in the floor of the soul, the wheat from the chaff.
Edward Moore (The Foundling, 1747): This is adding insult to injuries.
Michael A. Musmanno (Justice of the Sup. Ct. of Pennsylvania, 1959): The Corrugations of Pain: This court, solely from the cold, printed page, unwrinkled by the corrugations of pain that the jury and the trial judge saw on the face of the victim of the accident which caused this lawsuit, has decided to reduce his verdict from $14000 to $8000. By what authority is this done?.... Testimony at the trial indicated that the plaintiff's back injury has considerably decreased his ability to attend to domestic duties at home. A man's services around the house have been so much a subject for light humor and cartoon that the seriousness and efficacy of his domestic toil did not always receive the acknowledgement they deserve. The difference between a bare adobe and a comfortable home depends to a great extent on the householder's skill with hammer, saw, hoe, mower, rake and paint brush. And if the man is so injured that he cannot perform as physical domiciliary duties, he has been deprived of something which is as definitely a loss as a paring down of earnings. (Duffy v. Monongahela Con. R.R., 371 Pa. 361).
Michael A. Musmanno (Justice of the Sup. Ct. of Pennsylvania, 1959): Subjective vs. Objective Signs of Pain: It is the defendant's theses that it is impossible for doctor to know whether a patient is in pain or not. Defendant's council in his brief categorically declares that there is a "unanimity of view that pain is completely subjective." We know of no such unanimity. There is no authoritative medical work which asserts that pain is wholly and always subjective. There is not a doctor who would not declare that a person will suffer pain if he holds his hand over a blazing torch, or loses a finger in a grinding machine, or takes poison which throws him into bodily contortions with accompanying grimaces, cries, twitching and bloodshot eyes. There are very few absolutes in medicine as perhaps there are few, if any, in the law, but the fact is that pain can be very objective, and it can be detected by persons other than the one who states he feels it. There are symptoms of pain that write their story on one's countenance as clearly

as lightning scribbles in the sky its fiery message of nature's discomfiture. (Laurelli v. William Shapiro, 416 Pa. 308).

Michael A. Musmanno (Justice of the Sup. Ct. of Pennsylvania, 1959): The Plaintiff Returned to Work: ... The defendant contends further that the Trial Judge failed to explain to the jury "the difference between permanent, chronic and recurrent disability." In the first place, the words explain themselves. In second place, the issue was not only the impairment of earning power but the continuity of disabling pain. Even though one could with gritting teeth and aching body apply himself to remunerative employment, he would still be entitled to compensation for the physical anguish inflicted upon him by a tortfeasor. There is something more to life than earning one's bread and eating it salted with the agony of ceaseless pain. (Laurelli v. William Shapiro, 416 Pa. 308).

Michael A. Musmanno (Justice of the Sup. Ct. of Pennsylvania, 1959): At an initial glance the sum of $15,000 for pain, suffering and inconvenience might seem rather substantial because these items are sometimes regarded as of less gravity than others usually encompassed in personal injury verdicts. However, pain, suffering and inconvenience in this case cover some very serious disablements even though they may not conspicuously exhibit themselves to the casual observer. The defendant contends that since these physical impairments are not related to earning power they are not the subject of damages. The object of a trespass action involving personal injuries, where the plaintiff has proved his case, is to compensate him for what he has lost as a result of the defendant's negligence. The loss of well-being is as much a loss as an amputation. The inability to enjoy what one has heretofor keenly appreciated is a pain which can be equated with the infliction of a positive hurt. The conscious loss of a benefit to which one is entitled hurts as much as a festering wound. (The plaintiff suffered the complete loss of hearing, sense of smell, and the loss of the sense of taste and the pleasure of eating. Corcoran v. McNeal, 400 Pa. 14).

Michael A. Musmanno (Justice of the Sup. Ct. of Pennsylvania, 1959): A Permanent Cripple: A permanent cripple is an object of constant pity and a subject for repeated discard. He awakens sympathy but not assistance; he arouses compassion but not employment. In the economic world he is the last one to be employed and the first one to be discharged. In the race of life for the awards of comfort, promotion and happiness, he always arrives last. In the words of John Davidson:

In anguish we uplift
A new on the unhallowed song;
The race is to the swift;
The battle to the strong.

The Majority has decided that $35,000 is an excessive verdict, but, after deduction for medical expenses it will be none too much as the plaintiff limps across the span of life left to him in the arduous years of this fast-moving 20th century which has little or no time for cripples. (Shields v. Larry Construction Co., 370 Pa. 582).

Friedrich Nietzsche: As deeply as a man looketh into life, so deeply also doth he look into suffering.

Ben Okri: The most authentic thing about us is our capacity to create, to overcome, to endure, to transform, to love and to be greater than our suffering.

John Oldham: A wound, though cured, yet leaves behind a scar.

John Patrick: Pain makes man think. Thought makes man wise. Wisdom makes life endurable.

Jim M. Perdue (*Who Will Speak For The Victim? A Practical Treatise on Plaintiff's Jury Argument*, State Bar of Texas, 2002): Physical pain is our ageless enemy. Its allies are fear, despair, and agony. From the dawn of time, we have fought to avoid it, paid great sums to elude it, resorted to both science and religion to control it, and died to escape from its tyranny. It is a cruel master, choosing as its victims the helpless and the sick, who are least able to bear its oppression. It is in attendance at every human birth, loves to prey on children, and plagues us in our last minutes of life. It has destroyed marriages, authored family ruin, and pillaged lifelong friendships. It writes the scripts for suicide and euthanasia. In severe cases, it breeds compassiuon; in lesser ones, indifference.

Jim M. Perdue (*Who Will Speak For The Victim? A Practical Treatise on Plaintiff's Jury Argument*, State Bar of Texas, 2002): The words used to describe pain are countless. Words such as tormenting, burning, excruciating, agonizing, severe, cruel, harsh, throbbing, horrendous, gnawing, and grinding all have been used to characterize it; but to one afflicted by it, no words are adequate. Though beyond verbal description, its boundaries are easily defined. It is encapsulated within flesh, bone, muscle, nerves, tissues, and vital organs.

Jim M. Perdue (*Who Will Speak For The Victim? A Practical Treatise on Plaintiff's Jury Argument*, State Bar of Texas, 2002): Physical pain can be the greatest form of agony and torment. It is the scourge of life and death's extreme disgrace. It is a perfect form of misery and the worst of all evils. It forces even the innocent to lie, and it overturns all patience.

Jim M. Perdue (*Who Will Speak For The Victim? A Practical Treatise on Plaintiff's Jury Argument*, State Bar of Texas, 2002): Show me a man in severe pain, and I will show you a person who has lost all track of time – a man who cannot remember when the pain began. He knows only that his pain is now, that it is harsh, and that his life is a blur.

Jim M. Perdue (*Who Will Speak For The Victim? A Practical Treatise on Plaintiff's Jury Argument*, State Bar of Texas, 2002): Show me a man in severe pain, and I will show you someone who has looked into hell. To the person in pain, hell is the compass point on his chart of life. Although theologians, philosophers, and scholars may debate whether there is a hell after death, the ideological squabble is meaningless to the person in pain. His injury and its effects have become his "window into hell," through which he sees the torment of the ages .... Pain is the tool of torturers, the scourge of humankind, and the means by which we can create a hell on earth. A man in severe pain has, to his own satisfaction, long ago settled the theological debate concerning the existence of hell.

Jim M. Perdue (*Who Will Speak For The Victim? A Practical Treatise on Plaintiff's Jury Argument*, State Bar of Texas, 2002): Isn't it strange that the only place where pain becomes cheap is in the courthouse? We spend billions of dollars a year in this country in quest for cures for diseases, in quest of means to alleviate pain.... When corporations fight among themselves, there is never any quarrel about the fact that the loss of profits, loss of business, or loss of property is worth millions of dollars. Yet when we talk about the individual and the pain and agony that irresponsible conduct can bring, it is only then – in the courtroom – that pain becomes cheap.

Jim M. Perdue (*Who Will Speak For The Victim? A practical Treatise on Plaintiff's Jury Argument*, State Bar of Texas, 2002): Pain is something that a person lives with because he cannot hire a substitute to take his place. If someone could suffer for those in pain, what would be the hourly rate?

Jim M. Perdue (*Who Will Speak For The Victim? A Practical Treatise on Plaintiff's Jury Argument*, State Bar of Texas, 2002): We all know that fear magnifies pain and mental anguish in a person of any age. But a child cannot build the same bridge over troubled waters as can an adult. Children lack the armor of maturity – an aquired stoic attitude that what cannot be endured must somehow be tolerated. They have been taught that pain means punishment or discipline; in a child, needless and accidental pain may plague the conscience as well as the soul.... Pain and anguish do not come to children in reduced doses like baby aspirin. The torture of broken bones and ravaged flesh may be the same for a child as an adult, but it is magnified many times by the child's fear, which lies beyond the reach of any remedy – any pill, treatment or therapy.

Pope Pious VII (Eugenio Pacelli): Bodily pain affects man as a whole down to the deepest layers of his moral being. It forces him to face again the fundamental questions of his fate, of his attitude toward God and fellow men, of his individual and collective responsibility and of the sense of his pilgrimage on earth.

Margaret Preston: Pain is no longer pain when it is past.

Adelaide Proctor: Tell her that the lesson taught her / Far outweighs the pain.

Jean Paul Richter: The very afflictions of our earthly pilgrimage are presages of our future glory, as shadows indicate the sun.

Will Rogers (in a 1931 appeal for the unemployed, who then numbered 25 percent of our population): These people that you are asked to aid, they are not asking for charity, they are naturally asking for a job. But if you can't give them a job, why the next best thing you can do is see that they have food and the necessities of life.

Will Rogers (EDITOR: his line between pain and laughter was "barbed-wire thin"): You have to have a serious streak in you, or you can't see the funny side of the other fellow.

Edna St. Vincent Millay ("Time does not bring relief"): Who told me time would ease me of my pain!

John Selden: Pleasure is nothing else but the intermission of pain, the enjoying of something I am in great trouble for till I have it.

William Shakespeare (*All's Well that Ends Well*, Act II, i): His cicatrice, an emblem of war, here on his sinister cheek.

William Shakespeare (*All's Well that Ends Well*, Act IV, v): A scar nobly got, or a noble scar, is a good livery of honour.

William Shakespeare (*III Henry VI*, Act II, ii): The wound that bred this meeting here / Cannot be cured by words.

William Shakespeare (*Julius Caesar*, Act III, ii): Show you sweet Caesar's wounds, poor, poor dumb mouths, / And bid them speak for me.

William Shakespeare (*Julius Caesar,* Act III, ii): Put a tongue / In every wound of Caesar that should move / The stones of Rome to rise and mutiny.

William Shakespeare (*King Lear*, Act IV, vi): Henceforth I'll bear / Affliction till it do cry out itself, / Enough, enough, and die.

William Shakespeare (*King Lear*, Act IV, vii): Thou art a soul in bliss; but I am bound / Upon a wheel of fire; that mine own tears / Do scald like molten lead.

William Shakespeare (*Measure forMeasure*, Act III, i): The miserable have no other medicine / But only hope.

William Shakespeare (*Much Ado About Nothing*, Act V, i): There was never yet philosopher that could endorse a toothache patiently, however they have writ the style of gods, and made a pish at chance and sufferance.

William Shakespeare (*Othello*, Act II, iii): What wound did ever heal but by degrees?

William Shakespeare (*Romeo and Juliet*, Act I, ii): One fire burns out another's burning; / One pain is lessened by another's anguish.

William Shakespeare (*Romeo and Juliet*, Act II, ii): He jests at scars that never felt a wound.

William Shakespeare (*Romeo and Juliet*, Act III, iii): Affliction is enamour'd of thy parts, / And thou art wedded to calamity.

William Shakespeare (*Troilus and Cresida*, Act III, ii): One touch of nature makes the whole world kin.

William Shakespeare (*The Two Gentlemen of Verona*, Act V, iv): The private wound is deepest.

William Shakespeare (*The Rape of Lucrece*, 1.213): Who buys a minute's mirth to wail a week? Or sells eternity to get a toy? For one sweet grape who will the vine destroy?

Edward Shepard: The soul that suffers is stronger than the soul that rejoices.

Ben Sirach: One days of happiness makes us forget suffering, and one days suffering makes us forget all our past happiness.

Laurence Sterne: Pain and pleasure, like light and darkness, succeed each other; and he only who knows how to accomodate himself to their returns, and can wisely extract the good from the evil, knows how to live.

Bert Leston Taylor: A bore is a man who when you ask him how he is, tells you.

Mark Twain: Adam and Eve had many advantages, but the principal one was that they escaped teething.

Mark Twain: Noise proves nothing. Often a hen who has laid an egg cackles as if she had laid an asteroid.

Mark Twain: To forget pain is to be painless; to forget care is to be rid of it; to go abroad is to accomplish both.

Bill Veeck: Suffering is overrated. It doesn't teach you anything.

Izaak Walton: Affliction is a divine diet which though it be not pleasing to mankind, yet Almighty God hath often imposed it as a good, though bitter, physic, to those children who souls are dearest to him.

George Washington: "The People must FEEL before they can SEE."

H. G. Wells: Humanity either makes, or breeds, or tolerates all its afflictions, great or small.

Oscar Wilde: Behind joy and laughter there may be a temperment, coarse, hard and callous. But behind sorrow there is always sorrow. Pain, unlike pleasure, wears no mask.

Margery Williams (*"The Velveteen Rabbit"*): "What is real?" asked the Rabbit one day, ... "Real isn't how you are made," said the Skin Horse. "it's a thing that happens to you. When a child loves you for a long, long time, not just to play with, but really loves you, then you become real." "Does it hurt?" asked the

Rabbit. "Sometimes," said the Skin Horse, for he was always truthful. "When you are Real you don't mind being hurt."

Yiddish Proverb: The greatest pain is that which you can't tell others.

PARABLE (See also ADVICE; CHARLEY CHAN; MAXIMS)

PARENT

Uncle Anthony (about my father Rocco): Thomas, you gotta learn what everybody else in the family says about your dad – "Don't knock the Rock!"

Uncle Anthony: Your dad may not have read as many books as you and your friends, but he knows a helluva lot more about life and being a good man than all you young guys put together.

Uncle Anthony: Y'know, growing up I never remember seeing our mother sleep.

Uncle Anthony: There ain't no such thing as "a nonworking mother."

Aunt Mary Carlo: Y'know, it ain't easy being a mother – if it was more guys would do it.

African Proverb: A man's mother is his other God.

Sholem Aleichem: Adam was the luckiest man: he had no mother-in-law.

Sherwood Anderson: You hear it said that fathers want their sons to be what they feel they cannot themselves be, but I tell you it also works the other way. A boy wants something very special from his father.

Thomas D. Bailey: There must be such a thing as a child with average ability. What you can't find is a parent who will admit that it is his child. ... Start a program for gifted children, and every parent demands that his child be enrolled.

Roseanne Barr: I figure if the kids are alive at the end of the day, I've done my job.

Henry Ward Beecher: What the mother sings to the cradle goes all the way down to the coffin.

Henry Ward Beecher: We never know the love of our parents for us till we have become parents.

Henry Ward Beecher: There is no slave out of heaven like a loving woman; and, of all loving women, there is no such slave as a mother.

Bible: Colossians 3:21: Fathers, provoke not your children to anger, lest they be discouraged.

Bible: Ephesians 6:1: Children, obey your parents in the Lord: for this is right. Honour thy father and mother; which is the first commandment with promise.

Bible: Exodus 20:12; Matthew 19:19: (5th Commandment) Honour thy father and thy mother.

Bible: Proverbs 1:8: My son, hear the instruction of thy father, and forsake not the law of thy mother.

Bible: Proverbs 13:24: He that spareth his rod hateth his son.

Bible: Proverbs 15:20: A wise son maketh a glad father: but a foolish man despiseth his mother.

Bible: Proverbs 17:21: He that begetteth a fool doeth it to his sorrow.

Bible: Proverbs 19:26: He that wasteth his father, and chaseth away his mother, is a son that causeth shame, and bringeth reproach.

Bible: Proverbs 23:22: Hearken unto thy father that begat thee, and despise not thy mother when she is old.

Ambrose Bierce: CHILDHOOD, n. The period of human life intermediate between the idiocy of infancy and the folly of youth – two removes from the sin of manhood and three from the remorse of age.

Ambrose Bierce: LOW-BRED, adj. "Raised" instead of brought up.

Robert Bly: When a father, absent during the day, returns home at six, his children receive only his temperament, not his teaching.

Heywood Broun: She leads away from aces and neglects to keep jump bids alive. But she is still my mother.

Pearl S. Buck: Some are kissing mothers and some are scolding mothers, but it is love just the same, and most mothers kiss and scold together.

Pearl Buck: The concept of "Momism" is male nonsense. It is the refuge of a man seeking excuses for his own lack of virility.

Bulgarian Proverb: The father is the guest in the house.

Chinese Proverb: The father in praising his son extols himself.

Chinese Proverb: The old pearl-oyster produces a pearl.

Sir Winston Churchill: Saving is a fine thing. Especially when your parents have done it for you.

Czech Proverb: Don't be a lion in your own house.

Danish Proverb: A rich child often sits in a poor mother's lap.

Bette Davis: Discipline is a symbol of caring to a child. He needs guidance. If there is love, there is no such thing as being too tough with a child. A parent must also not be afraid to hang himself. If you have never been hated by your children, you have never been a parent.

Midge Decter: All they wished for her was that she should turn herself into a little replica of them.

Emily Dickinson: I never had a mother. I suppose a mother is one to whom you hurry when you are troubled.

Marian Wright Edelman: Parents have become so convinced that educators know what is best for the children that they forget that they themselves are really the experts.

Barbara Ehrenreich: While everything else in our lives has gotten simpler, speedier, more microwavable and user-friendly, child raising seems to have expanded to fill the time no longer available for it.

Barbara Ehrenreich: No culture on earth outside of mid-century suburban America has ever deployed one-woman per child without simultaneously assigning her such major productive activities as weaving, farming, gathering, temple maintenance, and tent building. The reason is that full-time, one-on-one child raising is not good for women or children.

Hilda Cole Espy: Men derive more genuine undutiful amusement and companionship from youngsters than do women.

Euripides: Lucky that man / whose children make his happiness in life / and not his grief, the anguished disappointment of his hopes.

Euripides: Here all mankind is equal: / rich and poor alike, they love their children.

Euripides: All men know their children / Mean more than life. If childless people sneer - / Well, they've less sorrow. But what lonesome luck!

Jules Feiffer: I grew up to have my father's looks, my father's speech patterns, my father's posture, my father's walk, my father's opinions and my mother's contempt for my father.

Brendan Francis: Parents may fairly be criticized for anything, with one exception – their children's behavior.

French Proverb: A father is a banker provided by nature.

Sigmund Freud: I could not point to any need in childhood as strong as that for a father's protection.

Sigmund Freud: A man who has been the indisputable favorite of his mother keeps for life the feeling of a conqueror, that confidence of success that often induces real success.

Robert Frost: The father is always a Republican toward his son, and his mother's always a Democrat.

Robert Frost: You don't have to deserve your mother's love. You have to deserve your father's. He's more particular.

English King George V (1910-1936) George Frederick Ernest Albert; "The Sailor King": My father was frightened of his mother; I was frightened of my father; and I'm damn well going to see that my children are frightened of me!

Ellen Goodman: There is no shower for a woman when she completes the trimester of her life spent as a full-time mother. There is no midwife to help that woman deliver a healthy adult.

Harry Graham (*Ruthless Rhymes*, 1899): Father, chancing to chastise/ His daughter Sue, / Said: I hope you realize / That **this hurts me more than you.**

Gypsy Proverb: You have to dig deep to bury your Daddy.

Amy Heckerling: Babies don't need fathers, but mothers do. Someone who is taking care of a baby needs to be taken care of.

Lillian Hellman: My mother was dead for five years before I knew that I had loved her very much.

Theodore Hesburgh: The most important thing a father can do for his children is love their mother.

Jane Howard: Parents, however old they and we may grow to be, serve among other things to shield us from a sense of our doom. As long as they are around, we can avoid the fact of our mortality; we can still be innocent children.

Victor Hugo: The most ferocious animals are disarmed by caresses to their young.

Irish Proverb: As the big hound is, so will the pup be.

Holbrook Jackson: A mother never realizes that her children are no longer children.

Japanese Proverb: A father's goodness is higher than the mountains; a mother's goodness is deeper than the sea.

Jewish Proverb: God could not be everywhere and therefore he made mothers.

Jewish Saying: A child without a mother is like a door without a knob.

Jewish Saying: A mother has glass eyes (she cannot see her children's faults).

Jewish Saying: A mother understands what a child does not say.

Jewish Saying: One mother achieves more than 100 teachers.

Jewish Saying: A mother is a veil: she hides her children's failings

Jewish Saying: The warmest bed of all is Mother's.

Jewish Saying: Mothers have big aprons—to cover the faults of the children.

Jewish Saying: The best fork is Mother's hand.

Jewish Saying: There is no such thing as a bad mother.

Jewish Saying: A mother-in-law and a daughter-in-law in one house are like two cats in a bag.

Jewish Saying: The mother-in-law and the daughter-in-law should not ride in the same cart.

Pope John XXIII (1960): It is easier for a father to have children than for children to have a real father.

Jean Kerr: The real menace in dealing with a five-year-old is that in no time at all you begin to sound like a five-year-old.

Latin Proverb: To the ass, or the sow, their own offspring appears the fairest in creation.

Robert Lynd: Happy is the child whose father acquits himself with credit in the presence of his friends.

Robert Lynd: Happy is the father whose child finds his attempts to amuse it amusing.

Margaret Mead: It is not that women have less impulse than men to be creative and productive. But through the ages having children, for women who wanted children, has been so satisfying that it has taken some special circumstances – spinsterhood, barrenness, or widowhood – to let women give their whole minds to other work.

Karl A. Menninger: No one but doctors and mothers know what it means to have interruptions.

Midrash: Exodus Rabbah, 46:5: He who raises a child is to be called its father, not the man who only gave it birth.

Midrash: A father suffers for the troubles of his son.

Moroccan Proverb: In the eyes of its mother every beetle is a gazelle.

Zero Mostel: My mother was a wit, but never a sentimental one. Once, when somebody in our house stepped on our cat's paw, she turned to the cat and said sternly, "I *told* you not to go around barefoot!"

National Urban League slogan: Don't make a baby if you can't be a Father.

Friedrich Nietzsche: What the father hath hid cometh out in the son; and oft have I found in the son the father's revealed secret.

Anais Nin: I never could dance around you, my father: No one ever danced around you. As soon as I left you, my father, the whole world swung into a symphony.

Tillie Olsen: More than in any other human relationship, overwhelmingly more, motherhood means being instantly interruptible, responsive, responsible.

William Penn: Men are generally more careful of the breed of their horses and dogs than of their children.

Ronald Reagan: Insanity is hereditary ... you catch it from your kids.

Will Rogers: I bet after seeing us, George Washington would sue us for calling him "father."

Eleanor Roosevelt: The kind of man who thinks that helping with the dishes is beneath him will also think that helping with the baby is beneath him, and then he certainly is not going to be a very successful father.

Bertrand Russell: The fundamental defect of fathers is that they want their children to be a credit to them.

Bertrand Russell: The place of the father in the modern suburban family is a very small one, particularly if he plays golf.

Russian Proverb: If you live without being a father you will die without being a human being.

George Santayana: Parents lend children their experience and a vicarious memory; children endow their parents with a vicarious immortality.

Mack Sennett: We never make sport of religion, politics, race, or mothers. A mother never gets hit with a custard pie. Mothers-in-law – yes. But mothers – never.

William Shakespeare (*The Comedy of Errors*, Act I, i): (Children are) The pleasing punishment that women bear.

William Shakespeare (*Cymbeline*, Act II, v): We are all bastards; / And that most venerable man which I / Did call my father, was I know not where / When I was stamp'd; some coiner with his tools / Made me a counterfeit.

William Shakespeare (*Hamlet*, Act I, ii): So loving to my mother / That he might not beteem the winds of heaven / Visit her face too roughly.

William Shakespeare (*Henry V*, Act IV, vi): And all my mother came into mine eyes, / And gave me up to tears.

William Shakespeare (*King Lear*, Act II, iv): Fathers that wear rags / Do make their children blind; / But fathers that bear bags / Shall see their children kind.

William Shakespeare (*King John*, Act III, iv): O lord! My boy, my Arthur, my fair son! / My life, my joy, my food, my all the world! / My widow-comfort, and my sorrow's cure.

William Shakespeare (*The Merchant of Venice*, Act II, ii): It is a wise father who knows his own child.

William Shakespeare (*The Merchant of Venice,* Act II, ii): O heavens, this is my true-begotten father!

William Shakespeare (*A Midsummer-Night's Dream*, Act I, i): To you your father should be as a god; / One that composed your beauties, yea, and one / To whom you are but as a form in wax / By him imprinted and within his power / To leave the figure or disfigure it.

William Shakespeare (*Othello*, Act I, i): Who would be a father?

William Shakespeare (*Richard II,* Act III, iv): Unruly children make their sire Stoop.

William Shakespeare (*Richard III*, Act III, i): He's all the mother's, from the top to toe.

William Shakespeare (*Richard III*, Act IV, iv): A grandam's name is little less in love, / Than is the doting title of a mother.

William Shakespeare (*Richard III*, Act IV, iv): Your children were vexation to your youth, / But mine shall be a comfort to your age.

George Bernard Shaw: Parentage is a very important profession; but no test of fitness for it is ever imposed in the interest of the children.

John Lancaster Spalding: Women are aristocrats, and it is always the mother who makes us feel that we belong to the better sort.

Spanish Proverb: An ounce of mother is worth a pound of clergy.

Gertrude Stein: Once an angry man dragged his father along the ground through his own orchard. "Stop!" cried the groaning old man at last, "Stop! I did not drag my father beyond this tree."

John Steinbeck: Father and son are natural enemies and each is happier and more secure in keeping it that way.

Gloria Steinem: It's clear that most American children suffer too much mother and too little father.

Publilius Syrus: An angry father is most cruel toward himself.

Talmud: Whoever teaches his son teaches not only his son but also his son's son—and so on to the end of generations.

Talmud: Should a father tell his son to throw gold into the sea, the son should obey.

Talmud: Even a rabbi should rise (in the presence of his pupils) when his father enters.

Baal Shem Tov: When a father complains that his son has taken to evil ways, what should he do? Love him more than ever.

Harry S. Truman: I have found the best way to give advice to children is to find out what they want and then advise them to do it.

Mark Twain: When I was a boy of fourteen, my father was so ignorant I can hardly stand to have the old man around. When I got to be twenty-one, I was astonished at how much he had learned in seven years.

Mark Twain: My father and I were always on the most distant terms when I was a boy – a sort of armed neutrality, so to speak. At irregular intervals this neutrality was broken, and suffering ensued; but I will be candid enough to say that the breaking and suffering were always divided with strict impartiality between us – which is to say, my father did the breaking and I did the suffering.

UA: When a father helps a son, both smile; when a son must help his father, both cry.

UA: Fathers are always trying to make their sons good Jews; when will they try to be good Jews instead of leaving the task to their sons?

UA: No man in the world loves one more than one's father.

Frank Lloyd Wright (speaking about his six children with his first of three wives, Kitty): I had a fatherly feeling for a building, but never for my children.

Leon Rene Yankwich (California lawyer, Chief Judge US District Court, Southern District of California): There are no illegitimate children – only illegitimate parents.

Zohar: Honor your father and mother, even as you honor God; for all three were partners in your creation

PARTIES (See POLITICS)

PAST (See ANCESTRY)

PEACE (See COMPROMISE)

PERCEPTION (See APPEARANCE)

PHILOSOPHY (See ATTITUDE; THINKING)

PITY (See COMPASSION)

PLAGERISM (See FRAUD)

PLAN/PLANNING (See PREPARATION)

PLEADING (See ALLEGATION)

POLICE

Uncle Anthony: Sometimes the cops look a lot like the robbers.

Uncle Anthony: When I grew up the "cop on the corner" was part of the neighborhood. We recognized each other a block away and knew each other's first name. Now, cops ride around in cars and I can't even see their faces.

Aunt Mary Carlo: Y'know, not all cops is bad, but some of dem are worse den da hoods dey hunt, and some of dem work fer da hoods.... dere on da take, dere on da "payroll."

Ugo Betti: A vague uneasiness: the police. It's like when you suddenly understand you have to undress in front of the doctor.

Bible: Ezekiel 7:23: The land is full of bloody crimes, and the city is full of violence.

Bible: Proverbs 20:26: A wise king scattereth the wicked.

Bible: Psalms 59:2: Deliver me from the workers of iniquity, and save me from bloody men.

Ambrose Bierce: POLICE, n. An armed force for protection and participation.

Ambrose Bierce: SHERIFF, n. In America the chief executive officer of a county, whose most characteristic duties, in some Western and Southern States, are the catching and hanging of rogues.

Reese Brown: Clearly, police officers cannot break the law to enforce it.

Gelett Burgess (1907): If you happen to want a policeman, there's never one within miles. (Now more popularly stated: "You can never find a cop when you need one.")

George Carlin: I think the cops have every right to shoot your sorry ass if you're running from them... I also think they have the right to pull you over if you're breaking the law, regardless of what color you are. And, no, I don't mind having my face shown on my drivers license. I think it's good!

Hal Chadwick: One reason for our high crime rate is that the long arm of the law is often shorthanded.

Raymond Chandler: He did not know the right people. That is all a police record means.

Sir Winston Churchill: You see these dictators on their pedestals, surrounded by the bayonets of their soldiers and the truncheons of their police. Yet in their hearts there is unspoken – unspeakable! – fear. They are afraid of words and thoughts!

Ramsey Clark: Who will protect the public when the police violate the law?

Joseph Conrad: The terrorist and the policeman both come from this same basket. Revolution, legality – countermoves in the same game; forms of idleness at bottom identical.

Richard M. Daley (1968 Democratic convention in Chicago): The police are here not to create disorder. They are here to preserve disorder.

Sir Arthur Conan Doyle: Detection is, or ought to be, an exact science, and should be treated in the same cold and unemotional manner.

Finley Peter Dunne: A polisman goes afther vice as an officer iv th' law an' comes away as a philosopher.

Finley Peter Dunne: There's more joy over wan sinner rayturned to th' station thin f'r ninety an' nine that've rayformed.

Robert Frost 1875-1963, American Poet: A successful lawsuit is the one worn by a policeman.

James Garrison (District Attorney, New Orleans, 1977): This won't be the first time I've arrested somebody and then built my case afterward.

W. S. Gilbert (*The Pirates of Penzance*, 1879): Ah, take one consideration with another, a policeman's lot is not a happy one.

W.S. Gilbert: When constabulary duty's to be done, / The policeman's lot is not a happy one!

Arthur Goldberg: If law is not more than a policeman's nightstick, American society will be destroyed.

Michael Harrington: For the middle class, the police protect property, give directions, and help old ladies. For the urban poor, the police are those who arrest you.

Alfred Hitchcock: I am not against the police; I'm just afraid of them.

Juvenal: Who shall guard the guardians themselves?

Nicholas Katzenbach: What society fails to realize is that the tension between the police and the judiciary has always been fundamental to our constitutional system. It is intentional and constitutes the real difference between a free society and a police state.

Robert F. Kennedy: Every society gets the kind of criminal it deserves. What is equally true is that every community gets the kind of law enforcement it insists on.

Burr W. Leyson: The dependence of the average citizen on the police is evident daily. Let almost anything happen that is out of the ordinary and their first reaction is "call a cop!"

Miles F. McDonnell: In the age of modern advanced technology, when the criminal can avail himself of every new invention, law enforcement officers are denied even the simplest of electronic devices, even though they will be under the supervision of the Courts. The result is like asking a champion boxer to fight a gorilla and insisting that the boxer abide by the Marquis of Queensberry Rules, while the gorilla is limited only by the law of the jungle.

Dr. Karl Menninger: There is no question that the police are misunderstood, looked down upon, unfairly treated, ridiculed, criticized, overburdened, underestimated, and generally given a bad go of it in America.

Michael A. Musmanno (Justice of the Supreme Court of Pennsylvania, 1959): A policeman is a soldier of peace, the symbol of an orderly community. When the tranquility is disturbed, when violence threatens, when accidents spill their cargoes of pain and confusion, it is the policeman who works and battles to bring back normalcy and harmony, it is the policeman who summons medical care and mechanical aid, it is the policeman who restores confidence and well-being to the distraught neighborhood... William Schwenk Gilbert said: "the policeman's lot is not a happy one." But there is no reason why that unhappiness should be added to by the forces of the very law, to uphold which the policeman fears no storm or darkness, flinches from no danger or menace, fights against visible and invisible foe, and stands ready, at any time, if necessary, to give his life. The cumulative dangers and hardships which these three men of the law have sustained over a collective incumbency of 61 years entitle them to a showing of kindness which they have undoubtedly often displayed toward others, in entire keeping with the majesty of the law and the dignity of man, which, all combined, make America the land of true and understanding justice. (Bell Appeal, 396 Pa. 592).

Joseph Orton (English playwright): Reading is not an occupation we encourage among police officers. We try to keep paperwork down to a minimum.

Will Rogers: They used to take your horse and if they were caught they got hung for it. Now they take your car and if they are caught it's a miracle.

Andy Rooney: I think the police should have every right to shoot your sorry ass if you threaten them after they tell you to stop. If you can't understand the word "freeze" or "stop" in English, see the above lines.

William Shakespeare (*All's Well That Ends Well*, Act II, iv): There is no fettering of authority.

William Shakespeare (*The Comedy of Errors*, Act IV, ii): A fiend, a fury, pitiless and rough; / A wolf, nay, worse, a fellow all in buff; / A back-friend, a shoulder-slapper, one that countermands / The passages of alleys, creeks and narrow lands; / A hound that runs counter and yet draws dryfoot well; / One that before the judgement carries poor souls to hell.

William Shakespeare (*The Tempest*, Act V, i): Thou art pinch'd for't now.

George Bernard Shaw: Criminals do not die by the hands of the law. They die by the hands of other men.

Herbert Spencer: Policemen are soldiers who act alone; soldiers are policemen who act in unison.

Mark Twain: A crowded police court docket is the surest of all signs that tree is brisk and money plenty.

Mark Twain: An average English word is four letters and a half. By hard, honest labor I've dug all the large words out of my vocabulary and shaved it down till the average is three and a half.... I never write "metropolis" for seven cents, because I can get the same money for "city." I never write "policeman," because I can get the same price for "cop." I never write "valetudinarian" at all, for not even hunger and wretchedness can humble me to the point where I will do a word like that for seven cents; I wouldn't do it for fifteen.

Grover Whalen (Police Commissioner, New York City, 1928-1930): There's a lot of law at the end of a nightstick.

Orlando W. Wilson: No police department can remain free of corruption in a community where bribery flourishes in public office and private enterprise; a corrupt police department in an otherwise corruption-free society is a contradiction in terms.

John Minor Wisdom (American judge): If police efficiency were an end in itself, the police would be three to point and accused on the rack. Police efficiency must yield to constitutional rights.

Arthur Woods (former New York City Police Commissioner): The policeman on post is in all truth the court of first instance; he is a de facto judge just as truly as any ermined magistrate, and a wise policeman can be guide, philosopher and friend as he carries on his daily, hourly court.

POLITICS/POLITICIANS (See also GOVERNMENT)

Uncle Anthony: Where are our leaders in this country? Where are the Washingtons, the Jeffersons, and the Jacksons? I'll tell you where they are—they're all playing professional football and basketball.

Uncle Anthony: Talk is cheap, except when politicians do it.

Aunt Mary Carlo: At da very start of his campaign he came out shootin' from his lip!

Aunt Mary Carlo: When dis guy asks ya to vote fer him an good government – he's really askin' ya t'vote twice!

Edward Abbey: What is the difference between a prostitute and a congressman? A congressman makes more money.

Dean Acheson: I will undoubtedly have to seek what is happily known as gainful employment, which I am glad to say does not describe holding public office.

Lord Acton (1887): Power tends to corrupt and absolute power corrupts absolutely.

Lord Acton: There is no worse heresy than that the office sanctifies the holder of it.

Franklin P. Adams: When the political columnists say "Every thinking man" they mean themselves, and when candidates appeal to "Every intelligent voter" they mean everybody who is going to vote for them.

Henry Adams: Practical politics consists in ignoring facts.

Henry Adams: You can't use tact with a Congressman. A Congressman is a hog. You must take a stick and hit him on the snout.

Saul Alinsky: When people agree on certain political ideas and want the power to put them into practice, they organize and call it a political party.

John Arbuthnot: All political parties die at last of swallowing their own lies.

Aristophanes: You have all the characteristics of a popular politician: a horrible voice, bad breeding and a vulgar manner.

Aristotle (*Politics*, bk2, 8, 384-322 BC): As in other sciences, so in politics, it is impossible that all things should be precisely set down in writing; for enactments must be universal, but actions are concerned with particulars.

Aristotle: Man is by nature a political animal.

W. H. Auden: Political history is far too criminal a subject to be a fit thing to teach children.

P. T. Barnum: My ambition is to be a poor politician.

Maurice Barres: The politician is an acrobat. He keeps his balance by saying the opposite of what he does.

Bible: Exodus 23:2: Thou shalt not follow a multitude to do evil

Bible: Isaiah 17:12: The multitude of many people, which make a noise like the noise of the seas.

Bible: Isaiah 33:7: The ambassadors of peace shall weep bitterly.

Bible: Job 12:2: Job to his friends: No doubt but ye are the people, and wisdom shall die with you.

Bible: 1 Samuel 15:24: Saul to Samuel: I feared the people, and obeyed their voice.

Ambrose Bierce: ALDERMAN, n. An ingenious criminal who covers his secret thieving with a pretence of open marauding.

Ambrose Bierce: ADMINISTRATION, n. An ingenious abstraction in politics, designed to receive the kicks and cuffs due to the premier or president.

Ambrose Bierce: ALLIANCE, n. In international politics, the union of two thieves who have their hands so deeply inserted in each other's pocket that they cannot separately plunder a third.

Ambrose Bierce: ARENA, n. In politics, an imaginary rat-pit in which the statesman wrestles with his record.

Ambrose Bierce: BOUNDARY, n. In political geography, an imaginary line between two nations, separating the imaginary rights of one from the imaginary rights of another.

Ambrose Bierce: CONSERVATIVE, n. A statesman who is enamored of existing evils, as distinguished from the Liberal, who wishes to replace them with others.

Ambrose Bierce: CONSUL, n. In American politics, a person who having failed to secure an office from the people is given one by the Administration on condition that he leave the country.

Ambrose Bierce: CORSAIR, n. A politician of the seas.

Ambrose Bierce: DELEGATION, n. In American politics, an article of merchandise that comes in sets.

Ambrose Bierce: DIPLOMACY, n. The patriotic art of lying for one's country.

Ambrose Bierce: IDIOT, n. A member of a large and powerful tribe whose influence in human affairs has always been dominant and controlling.

Ambrose Bierce: INCUMBENT, n. A person of the liveliest interst to the outcombents.

Ambrose Bierce: INFLUENCE, n. In politics, a visionary *quo* given in exchange for a substantial *quid.*

Ambrose Bierce: MUGWUMP, n. In politics one afflicted with self-respect and addicted to the vice of independence. A term of contempt.

Ambrose Bierce: NEPOTISM, n. Appointing your grandmother to office for the good of the party.

Ambrose Bierce: NIHILIST, n. A Russian who denies the existence of anything but Tolstoi. The leader of the school is Tolstoi.

Ambrose Bierce: NOMINATE, v. To designate for the heaviest political assessment. To put forward a suitable person to incur the mudgobbing and deadcatting of the opposition.

Ambrose Bierce: NOMINEE, n. A modest gentleman shrinking from the distinction of private life and diligently seeking the honorable obscurity of public office.

Ambrose Bierce: OPPOSITION, n. In politics the party that prevents the Government from running amuck by hamstringing it.

Ambrose Bierce: PLEBISCITE, n. A popular vote to ascertain the will of the sovereign.

Ambrose Bierce: POLITICS, n. A strife of interests masquerading as a contest of principles.

Ambrose Bierce: POLITICIAN, n. An eel in the fundamental mud upon which the superstructure of organized society is reared. When he wriggles he mistakes the agitation of his tail for the trembling of the edifice. As compared with the statesman, he suffers the disadvantage of being alive.

Ambrose Bierce: POPULIST, n. A fossil patriot of the early agricultural period, found in the old red soapstone underlying Kansas; characterized by an uncommon spread of ear, which some naturalists contend gave him the power of flight, though Professors Morse and Whitney, pursuing independent lines of thought, have ingeniously pointed out that had he possessed it he would have gone elsewhere. In the picturesque speech of his period, some fragments of which have come down to us, he was known as "The Matter with Kansas."

Ambrose Bierce: PRESIDENCY, n. The greased pig in the field game of American politics.

Ambrose Bierce: PRESIDENT, n. The leading figure in a small group of men and women – and of whom only – it is positively known that immense numbers of their countrymen did not want any of them for President....

Ambrose Bierce: RADICALISM, n. The conservatism of tomorrow injected into the affairs of today.

Ambrose Bierce: RECOUNT, n. In American politics, another throw of the dice, accorded to the player against whom they are loaded.

Ambrose Bierce: SUFFRAGE, n. Expression of opinion by means of a ballot.The right of suffrage (which is held to be both a privilege and a duty) means, as commonly interpreted, the right to vote for the man of another man's choice, and is highly prized. Refusal to do so has the bad name of "incivism." The incivilian, however, cannot be properly arraigned for his crime, for there is no legitimate accuser. If the accuser is himself guilty he has no standing in the court of opinion; if not, he profits by the crime, for A's abstention from voting gives greater weight to the vote of B. By female suffrage is meant the right of a woman to vote as some man tells her to. It is based on female responsibility, which is somewhat limited. The woman most eager to jump out of her petticoat to assert her rights is first to jump back into it when threatened with a switching for misusing them.

Ambrose Bierce: VOTE, n. The instrument and symbol of a freeman's power to make a fool of himself and a wreck of his country.

Josh Billings (pseudonym of Henry Wheeler Shaw, in *Josh Billings' Wit and Humour*, 1874): The Politishun's golden rule ... **Vote early and vote often.**

Otto von Bismarck: Politics ruins the character.

Daniel Boorstin: Our national politics has become a competition for images or between images, rather than between ideals.

James Bovard (Civil Libertarian, 1994): Democracy must be something more than two wolves and a sheep voting on what to have for dinner.

Marlon Brando: Acting is as old as mankind.... Politicians are actors of the first order.

H.H. Breckenridge: Recollect that you were not made for the party, but the party for you.

David Brin: It is said that power corrupts, but actually it's more true that power attracts the corruptible. The sane are usually attracted by other things than power.

David Brinkley: This is the first convention of the space age – when a candidate can promise the moon and mean it.

Lenny Bruce: Communism is like one big phone company.

Art Buchwald: I always wanted to get into politics, but I was never light enough to make the team.

William F. Buckley, Jr.: Liberals claim to want to give a hearing to other views, but then are shocked and offended to discover that there are other views.

William F. Buckley Jr.: I would rather in trust the government of United States to the first 400 people listed in the Boston telephone directory then to the faculty of Harvard University.

Charles Bukowski: You begin saving the world by saving one man at a time; all else is grandiose romanticism or politics.

Benjamin Butler: The Democratic Party is like a man riding backward in a carriage. It never sees a thing until it has gone by.

Robert Byrne: Democracy is being allowed to vote for the candidate you dislike leased.

Simon Cameron: An honest politician is one who when he is bought will stay bought.

Albert Camus: I am unsuited to politics since I am unable to wish for or accept my opponents' death.

Albert Camus: Politics, and the fate of mankind, are shaped by men without ideals and without greatness. Men who have greatness within them don't go in for politics.

Joe Cannon: In politics one must deal with skunks, but no one should be fool enough to allow the skunks to choose the weapons.

Sir Winston Churchill: Politics is not a game. It is an earnest business.

Sir Winston Churchill: It would be a great reform in politics if wisdom could be made to spread as easily and as rapidly as folly.

Sir Winston Churchill: I have always felt that a politician is to be judged by the animosities he excites among his opponents.

Sir Winston Churchill: In war you can be killed only once. In politics, many times.

Sir Winston Churchill: It has been said that democracy is the worst form of government except all others that have been tried.

Sir Winston Churchill: A WOMAN said: "There are two things I dislike about you – your politics and your face." CHURCHILL replied: "My dear, do not disturb yourself. You are not likely to come into contact with either."

Sir Winston Churchill: Politics are almost as exciting as war, and quite as dangerous. In war you can only be killed once, but in politics many times.

Sir Winston Churchill: (Political skill) is the ability to foretell what is going to happen tomorrow, next week, next month, and next year. And to have the ability afterwards to explain why it didn't happen.

Sir Winston Churchill: The inherent vice of capitalism is the unequal sharing of the blessings. The inherent blessing of socialism is the equal sharing of misery.

Sir Winston Churchill: A communist is like a crocodile: when it opens its mouth you cannot tell whether it is trying to smile or preparing to eat you up.

Sir Winston Churchill: We must beware of trying to build a society in which nobody counts for anything except a politician or an official, a society where enterprise gains no reward and thrift no privileges.

Sir Winston Churchill: The best argument against democracy is a five-minute conversation with the average voter.

Cicero: Persistence in one opinion has never been considered a merit in political leaders.

James Freeman Clarke: A politician thinks of the next election – a statesman, of the next generation.

Samuel Taylor Coleridge: In politics, what begins in fear usually ends in folly.

Alan Corenk: Democracy consists of choosing your dictators, after they've told you what you think it is you want to hear.

Richard Daley: The party permits ordinary people to get ahead. Without the party, I couldn't be a mayor.

Charles De Gaulle: In order to become the master, the politician poses as the servant.

Charles de Gaulle: Politics are too serious a matter to be left to politicians.

Benjamin Disraeli: Better they should wonder why you do not speak, than why you do.

Benjamin Disraeli: Damn your principles! Stick to your party.

Benjamin Disraeli: Party is organized opinion.

Benjamin Disraeli: In politics there is no honour.

Benjamin Disraeli: The practice of politics in the East may be defined by one word – dissimulation.

Frank Dane: Get all the fools on your side and you can be elected to anything.

Clarence Darrow: When I was a boy I was told that anybody could become president; I'm now beginning to believe it.

Charles de Gaulle: Since politicians never believe what they say, they are always astonished when others do

Charles Dudley: Politics makes strange bedfellows.

Walter Dwight: Politicians speak for their parties, and parties never are, never have been, never will be wrong.

Abba Eban: Men and nations behave wisely once they have exhausted all other alternatives.

Bob Edwards: Now I know what a statesman is; he's a dead politician. We need more statesmen.

Dwight D. Eisenhower: Politics should be the part-time profession for every citizen.

President Dwight D. Eisenhower (1952): Should any political party attempt to abolish social security, unemployment insurance, and eliminate labor laws and farm programs, you would not hear of that party again in our political history. There is a tiny splinter group, of course, that believes that you can do these things. Among them are a few Texas oil millionaires, and an occasional politician or businessman from other areas. Their number is negligible and they are stupid."

Erik H. Erikson: American politics is not, as is that of Europe, "a prelude to civil war"; it cannot become either entirely irresponsible or entirely dogmatic; and it must not try to be logical. It is a rocking sea of checks and balances in which uncompromising absolutes must drown.

Eugene Field: Some statesmen go to Congress and some go to jail. It is the same thing after all.

Malcolm Forbes: Few businessmen are capable of being in politics – they don't understand the democratic process – they have neither the tolerance nor the depth it takes – democracy is not a business.

Brendan Francis: Politicians, like prostitutes, are held in contempt, but what man does not run to them when he requires their services?

Al Frankin: They (politicians): used "Weekend With Bernie Strategy" = don't tell him or anyone he's dead!

Benjamin Franklin: The first mistake in public business is the going into it.

John Kenneth Galbraith: politics consists of choosing between the disastrous and the unpalatable.

John Kenneth Galbraith: Nothing is so admirable in politics as a short memory.

John Kenneth Galbraith: Politics is not the art of the possible. It consists in choosing between the disastrous and the unpalatable.

Kahlil Gibran: He brings disaster upon his nation who never sows a seed, or lays a brick, or weaves a garment, but makes politics his profession.

William E. Gladstone: Politics are like a labyrinth, from the inner intricacies of which it is even more difficult to find the way of escape, than it was to find the way into them.

Johann Wolfgang von Goethe: In politics as on the sickbed, people toss from one side to another, thinking they will be more comfortable.

Baltazar Gracian: Fate often makes up for the eminence by the inferiority of the officeholder.

Larry Hagman: My definition of a redundancy is an airbag in a politician's car.

Frank Hague (Mayor of Jersey City, N.J., 1927): I am the law.

Wayne G. Haisley: Politics makes strange bedfellows rich.

Rutherford B. Hayes: "Practical politics" means selfish ends promoted by base means.

Rutherford B. Hayes (his March 1877, Inaugural Speech): He serves his party best who serves his country best.

Arthur Garfield Hays (an American lawyer): More lawyers (considering the number who play the game intensively) have been ruined by politics than by liquor, women, or the stock market.

Matthew Green: Or to some coffee-house I. stray, / For news, the manna of a day, / And from the hipp'd discourses gather / That politics go by the weather.

Gilbert Highet: What is politics but persuading the public to vote for this and support that and endure these for the promise of those.

Sidney Hillman: Politics is the science of how who gets what, when and why.

Oliver Wendell Holmes: The prize of the general is not a bigger tent, but command.

Bob Hope: Ronald Reagan is not a typical politician because he does not know how to lie, cheat, and steal. He has always had an agent for that.

Bob Hope: ON PRESIDENTS: I have performed for 12 presidents and entertained only six.

Louis McHenry Howe: You cannot adopt politics as a profession and remain honest.

Kin Hubbard: Politics makes strange postmasters.

Kin Hubbard: Now and then an innocent man is sent to the legislature.

Aldous Huxley: Idealism is the noble toga that political gentlemen drape over their will to power.

Henrik Ibsen: It is inexcusable for scientists to torture animals; let them make their experiments on journalists and politicians.

Italian Proverb: Politicians and roosters crow about what they intend to do. The roosters deliver what is promised.

Molly Ivins: "....our very own dreaded Legislature is almost upon us. Jan. 9 and they'll all be here, leaving many a village without its idiot."

Molly Ivins: Good thing we've still got politics in (Texas)—finest form of free entertainment ever invented.

Molly Ivins: What stuns me most about contemporary politics is not even that the system has been so badly corrupted by money. It is that so few people get the connection between their lives and what the bozos do in Washington and our state capitols.

Thomas Jefferson: If the present Congress errs in too much talking, how can it be otherwise in a body to which the people send 150 lawyers?

Thomas Jefferson: Politics like religion, hold up the torches of martyrdom to the reformers of error.

Thomas Jefferson: If I could go to heaven but with a party, I would not go there at all.

Thomas Jefferson: No more good must be attempted then the public can bear.

Thomas Jefferson: I tremble for my country when I reflect that God is just.

Samuel Johnson: Politics are nothing more than a means of rising in the world.

Jack Kemp (AFL-NFL quaterback 1957-1969, 1996 Republican Vice Presidential nominee): Pro football gave me a good sense of perspective to enter politics. I'd been booed, sheered, cut, sold, traded and hung in effigy.

Jack Kemp: Republicans no longer worship at the shrine of a balanced budget.

John F. Kennedy: When we got into office, the thing that surprised me the most was that things were as bad as we had been saying they were.

John F. Kennedy: Forgive your enemies, but never forget their names.

John F. Kennedy: Mothers all want their sons to grow up to be President, but they didn't want them to become politicians in the process.

John F. Kennedy: I have just recieved the following wire from my generous Daddy: "Dear Jack – Don't buy a single vote more than is necessary. I'll be damned if I am going to pay for a landslide."

Henry William King: Men play at being God, but lacking God's experience they wind up as politicians.

W. M. Kiplinger: Public interest is a term used by every politician to support his ideas.

Jeane Kirkpatrick: Democrats can't get elected unless things get worse, and things won't get worse unless they get elected.

Henry Kissinger: 90% of the politicians give the other 10% a bad reputation.

Edward Koch: You punch me, I punch back. I do not believe it is good for one's self-respect to be a punching bag.

Karl Kraus: The secret of the demagogue is to make himself as stupid as his audience so that they believe they are as clever as he.

Nikita Khrushchev: Politicians are the same all over. They promise to build a bridge even where there is no river.

Alfonse de Lamartine: The more I see of the representatives of the people, the more I admire my dogs.

Ann Landers: A pompous senator asked: "So you're Ann Landers. Say something funny." Without hesitation she answered: "Well, you're a politician. Tell me a lie."

Edward Langley: What this country needs is more unemployed politicians.

Doug Larson: Instead of giving a politician the keys to the city, it might be better to change the locks.

Jay Leno (comedian and *The Tonight Show* TV host): Some comedians are like Democrat Presidents – they think they can handle everytthing themselves without any help

Jay Leno: The Republicans elect stupid presidents with brilliant staffs, and the Democrats elect brilliant presidents with stupid staffs.

Jay Leno: The reason there are two senators for each state is so that one can be the designated driver.

Jay Leno: I heard that the Senate voted for tougher regulations—when corporations buy a senator, they must now get a receipt.

Jay Leno: I looked up the word "politics" in the dictionary, and its actually a combination of two words: "poli" which means many, and "tics," which means "bloodsuckers."

Oscar Levant: The only difference between the Democrats and the Republicans is that the Democrats allow the poor to be corrupt, too.

G. Gordon Liddy: A liberal is someone who feels a great debt to his fellow man, which debt he proposes to pay off with your money.

Abraham Lincoln: Republicans are for both the man and the dollar, but in case of conflict the man before the dollar.

James Russell Lowell: He who is firmly seated in authority soon learns to think of security, and not progress, the highest lesson of statecraft.

Clare Booth Luce: Remember, whenever a Republican leaves one side of the aisle and goes to the other, it raises the intelligence quotient of both parties.

Clare Booth Luce: They say women talk too much. If you worked in Congress you know that the fillibuster was invented by men.

Clare Booth Luce: The politicians were talking themselves red, white and blue in the face.

Thomas Macaulay: Timid and interested politicians think much more about the security of their seats than about the security of their country.

Niccolo Machiavelli: Princes and governments are far more dangerous than other elements within a society.

Niccolo Machiavelli: The first method for estimating the intelligence of a ruler is to look at the men he has around him.

Boris Marshalov: Congree is so strange. A man gets up to speak and says nothing. Nobody listens – and then everybody disagrees.

Dwight D. Marrow: Any party which takes credit for the rain, must not be surprised if its opponents blamed for the drought.

Groucho Marx: Politics is the art of looking for trouble, finding it everywhere, diagnosing it incorrectly, and applying the wrong remedy.

Eugene McCarthy: The only thing that saves us from the bureaucracy is its inefficiency.

Eugene McCarthy: It is dangerous for a national candidate to say things that people might remember.

Eugene McCarthy: The function of liberal Republicans is to shoot the wounded after battle.

Eugene McCarthy: Being in politics is like being a football coach. You have to be smart enough to understand the game and dumb enough to think it's important.

H.L. Mencken: It is an accurate to say I hate everything. I am strongly in favor of common sense, common honesty, and common decency. This makes me forever ineligible for any public office.

H.L. Mencken: Under democracy one-party always devotes its chief energies to trying to prove that the other party is unfit to rule—and both commonly succeed, and both are right.

John Stuart Mill: A party of order or stability, and a party of progress or reform, are both necessary elements of a healthy state of political life.

Maureen Murphy: The reason there are so few female politicians is that it is too much trouble to put makeup on two faces.

Edward R. Murrow: When politicians complain that TV turns the proceedings into a circus, it should be made clear that the circus was already there, and that TV has merely demonstrated that not all the performers are well-trained.

Napoleon Bonaparte: In politics, an absurdity is not an impediment.

George Jean Nathan: Bad officials are elected by good citizens who do not vote

Reinhold Neibuhr: Man's capacity for justice makes democracy possible, but his inclination to injustice makes democracy necessary.

Richard Nixon: I would not like to be a political leader in Russia. They never know when they're being taped.

Lawrence O'Brien: We do not promise what we know can not be delivered by man, God, or the Democratic Party.

F.S. Oliver: With all the temptations and degradations that beset it, politics is still the noblest career that any man can choose.

Jacqueline Kennedy Onassis: You have to have been a Republican to know how good it is to be a Democrat.

Max O'Rell: To be a chemist you must study chemistry; to be a lawyer or physician you must study law or medicine; but to be a politician you need only to study your own interests.

George Orwell: Political language is designed to make it lies it sound truthful and murder respectable, and to give an appearance of solidity to pure wind.

Theodore Parker: Politics is the science of exigencies.

Francis Parkman: There are no political panaceas, except in the imagination of political quacks.

Lester Pearson: Politics is the skilled use of blunt object.

Pericles: Just because you do not take an interest in politics doesn't mean politics won't take an interest in you.

Dr. Laurence J. Peter: Political success is the ability, when the inevitable occurs, to get credit for it.

Plato: Those who are too smart to engage in politics are punished by being governed by those who are dumber.

Willis Player: A liberal is a person whose interests are at stake at the moment

P.J. Proudhon: All parties without exception, when they seek for power, are varieties of absolutism.

John O'Connor Power: The mules of politics: without pride of ancestry, or hope of posterity.

Ronald Reagan: Politics is supposed to be the second oldest profession. I have come to realize that it bears a very close resemblance to the first.

Ronald Reagan: Politics is not a bad profession. If you succeed, there are many rewards; if you disgrace yourself, you can always write a book.

Ronald Reagan: The best minds are not in government. If any were, business would hire them away.

Ronald Reagan: Politics is just like show business. You have a hell of an opening, coast for awhile, and then have a hell of a close.

Ronald Reagan: Professional politicians like to talk about the value of experience in government. Nuts! The only experience you gain in politics is how to be political.

Thomas B. Reed: A statesman is a successful politician who is dead.

Thomas B. Reed: Parties seldom follow their best men. They follow their average sense.

Will Rogers: If you've got half a mind to go into politics, that's all you'll ever need.

Will Rogers: Politics is applesauce.

Will Rogers: Politics has got so expensive that it takes lots of money to even get beat with.

Will Rogers: If you ever injected truth into politics you have no politics.

Will Rogers: Politicians, after all, are not over a year behind Public Opinion.

Will Rogers: A Congressman is never any better than his roads, and sometimes worse.

Will Rogers: If we have Senators and Congressmen there that can't protect themselves against the evil temptations of lobbyists, we don't need to change our lobbies, we need to change our representatives.

Will Rogers: The taxpayers are sending congressmen on expensive trips abroad. It might be worth it except they keep coming back!

Will Rogers (1949): The banker, the lawyer, and the politician are still our best bets for a laugh. Audiences haven't changed at all, and neither has the three above professions.

Will Rogers: The way to judge a good Comedy is by how long it will last and have people talk about it. Now Congress has turned out some that have lived for years and people are still laughing about them.

Will Rogers: Shrewdness in Public Life all over the World is always honored, while honesty in Public Men is generally attributed to Dumbness and is seldom rewarded.

Will Rogers: There's no trick to being a humorist when you have the whole government working for you.

Will Rogers: The man with the best job in the country is the vice-president. All he has to do is get up every morning and say, "How is the President?"

Will Rogers: Diplomats are just as essential to starting a war as Soldiers are for finishing it. You take Diplomacy out of war and the thing would fall flat in a week.

Will Rogers: The only real diplomacy ever performed by a diplomat is in deceiving their own people after their dumbness has got them into a war.

Will Rogers: Diplomats write Notes, because they wouldn't have the nerve to tell the same thing to each other's face.

Will Rogers: I belong to no organized party—I am a Democrat.

Will Rogers: I never said all Democrats were saloonkeepers. What I said was that all saloonkeepers were Democrats.

Will Rogers: Democrats never agree on anything, that's why they're Democrats. If they agreed with each other, they would be Republicans.

Will Rogers: The Democrats are having a lot of fun exposing the Republican campaign corruptions, but they would have a lot more fun if they knew where they could lay their hands on some of it themselves for next November.

Will Rogers: The Republicans have a habit of having three bad years and one good one, and the good one always happens to be election years.

Will Rogers: The 1928 Republican Convention opened with a prayer. If the Lord can see His way clear to bless the Republican Party the way it's been carrying on, then the rest of us ought to get it without even asking.

Will Rogers: The Republicans have their splits after the election and Democrats have theirs just before an election.

Will Rogers: There isn't any finer folks living than a Republican that votes the Democratic ticket.

Will Rogers: More men have been elected between Sundown and Sunup, than ever were elected between Sunup and Sundown.

Will Rogers: No Voter in the World ever voted for nothing; in some way he has been convinced that he is to get something for that vote. His vote is all that our Constitution gives him, and it goes to the highest bidder.

Will Rogers: Communism is like Prohibition, it's a good idea but it won't work.

Will Rogers: Communism to me is one-third practice and two-thirds explanation.

Will Rogers: And the thing about my jokes is, they don't hurt anybody. You can take 'em or leave 'em - you can say they're funny or they're terrible or they're good, or whatever, but you can just pass 'em by. But with Congress, every time they make a joke, it's a law! And every time they make a law, it's a joke!

Will Rogers: Our constitution protects aliens, drunks and U.S. Senators.

Will Rogers: A fool and his money are soon elected.

Will Rogers: Everything is changing. People are taking their comedians seriously and the politicians as a joke.

Will Rogers: Ohio claims they are due a president as they haven't had one since Taft. Look at the United States, they have not had one since Lincoln.

Will Rogers: Ancient Rome declined because it had a Senate, now what's going to happen to us with both a House and a Senate?

Will Rogers: Alexander Hamilton started the U.S. Treasury with nothing, and that was the closest our country has ever been to being even.

Will Rogers: About all I can say for the United States Senate is that it opens with a prayer and closes with an investigation.

Will Rogers: The more you observe politics, the more you've got to admit that each party is worse than the other.

Will Rogers: The more you read and observe about this Politics thing, you got to admit that each party is worse than the other. The one that's out always looks the best.

Will Rogers: There is no more independence in politics than there is in jail.

Will Rogers: There ought to be one day - just one - when there is open season on senators.

Will Rogers: This country has come to feel the same when Congress is in session as when the baby gets hold of a hammer.

Will Rogers: If all the time consumed in attending dinners and luncheons was consumed in some work, the production of this country would be doubled.

Will Rogers: Every time there is a big conference, they always have a war to go with it.

Will Rogers: Viva Diplomacy. Nobody is fooled, nobody is hurt.

Will Rogers: A diplomat is one that says something that is equally misunderstood by both sides, and never clear to either.

Will Rogers: We shouldn't elect a President; we should elect a magician.

Will Rogers: I hope some of the men who get the most votes will be elected.

Will Rogers: Washington, D.C., papers say, 'Congress is deadlocked and can't act.' I think that is the greatest blessing that could befall this Country.

Will Rogers: Once a man holds a public office he is absolutely no good for honest work.

Will Rogers: If all politicians fished instead of spoke publicly, we would be at peace with the world.

Will Rogers: Come pretty near having two holidays of equal importance in the same week—Halloween and election. And of the two, election provides us the most fun. On Halloween they put pumpkins on their heads and on election they don't have to.

Will Rogers: Politics ain't worrying this country one-tenth as much as where to find a parking space.

Will Rogers: If we got one-tenth of what was promised to us in these acceptance speeches there wouldn't be any inducement to go to Heaven.

Andy Rooney: I think tattoos and piercing are fine if you want them, but please don't pretend they are a political statement. And, please, stay home until that new lip ring heals. I don't want to look at your ugly infected mouth as you serve me French fries!

Theodore Roosevelt: The most successful politician is he who says what everybody is thinking most often and in the loudest voice.

Russian Proverb: Politics is a rotten egg; if broken, it stinks.

Mark Sahl: Liberals feel unworthy of their possessions. Conservatives feel they deserve everything that they have stolen.

Mort Sahl: A conservative does not want anything to happen for the first time; a liberal feels it should happen, but not now.

Mort Sahl: Reagan won because he ran against Jimmy Carter. Had he run unopposed, he would have lost.

John of Salisbury: With the rashness of ignorance the uninitiated dare to dabble in affairs of state.

William Shakespeare (*All'sWell That Ends Well*, Act II, iv): There is no fettering of authority.

William Shakespeare (*Hamlet*, Act I, iv): Something is rotten in the state of Denmark.

William Shakespeare (*Hamlet*, Act V, i): It might be the pate of a politician, ... one that would circumvent God.

William Shakespeare (*I Henry IV*, Act I, iii): This vile politician.

William Shakespeare (*II Henry IV*, Act III, i): Uneasy lies the head that wears a crown.

William Shakespeare (*Henry V*, Act I, i): Turn him to any cause of policy, / The Gordian knot of it he will unloose, / Familiar as his garter: that, when he speak, / The air, a charter'd libertine, is still.

William Shakespeare (*King Lear*, Act IV, vi): Get thee glass eyes; / And, like a scurvy politician, seem / To see the things thou dost not.

William Shakespeare (*King Lear*, Act IV, vi): Thou hast seen a farmer's dog bark at a beggar. / And the creature run from the cur: There, / There, thou might'st behold the great image of authority; / A dog's obey'd in office.

William Shakespeare (*Macbeth*, Act V, ii): Those he comands, move only in command, / Nothing in love: now does he feel the title / Hang loose about him, like a giant's robe / Upon a dwarfish thief.

William Shakespeare (*The Merchant of Venice*, Act II, ix): O, that estates, degrees, and offices, / Were not deriv'd corruptly! And that clear honour / Were purchased by the merit of the wearer!

William Shakespeare (*Richard II*, Act III, ii): Within the hollow crown / That rounds the mortal temples of a king / Keeps Death his court.

William Shakespeare (*Winter's Tale*, Act IV, iv): And though authority be a stubborn bear, yet he is oft led by the nose with gold.

George Bernard Shaw: You in America should trust to that volcanic political instinct which I have divined in you.

George Bernard Shaw: A government which robs Peter to pay Paul can always depend on the support of Paul.

George Bernard Shaw: Democracy substitutes election by the incompetent many for appointment by the corrupt few.

George Bernard Shaw: He knows nothing: he thinks he knows everything—that clearly points to a political career.

Frank Simonds: There is but one way for a newspaper man to look at a politician and that is down.

Adam Smith: "... that insidious and crafty animal, vulgarly called a statesman or politician, whose councils are directed by momentary fluctuations of affairs."

Socrates: If I had engaged in politics, O men of Athens, I should have perished long ago, and done no good either to you or to myself.

William Stanton: Republicans sleep in twin beds—some even in separate rooms. That is why there are more Democrats.

Adlai Stevenson: A politician is a man who approaches every problem with an open mouth.

Adlai Stevenson: If the Republicans will stop telling lies about the Democrats, we will stop telling the truth about them.

Adlai Stevenson: He is the kind of politician who would cut down a redwood tree, then mount the stump and make a speech for conservation.

Adlai Stevenson: Someone asked me how I felt. I was reminded of a story that a fellow townsman of ours used to tell – Abraham Lincoln. They asked him how he felt once after an unsuccessful election. He said he felt like a little boy who had stubbed his toes in the dark. He said that he was too old to cry, but it hurt too much to laugh.

Robert Louis Stevenson: Party is the madness of many, for the gain of a few.

Robert Louis Stevenson: Politics is perhaps the only profession for which no preparation is thought necessary.

Jonathan Swift: Be silent as a politician, for talking may beget suspicion.

Robert A. Taft: Every Republican candidate for President since 1936 has been nominated by the Chase National Bank.

C. M. Talleyrand: An important art of politicians is to find new names for institutions which under old names have become odious to the public.

Margaret Thatcher: In politics if you want anything said, ask a man; if you want anything done, ask a woman.

C.V.R. Thompson: Washington is the only place where sound travels faster than light.

Lily Tomlin: 98% of the adults in this country are decent, hard-working, honest Americans. It is the other lousy 2% that get all the publicity. But then—we elected them.

Alexis de Tocqueville (French political writer, 1805-1859, *Democracy in America*, Pt. 1, ch. 16): Scarcely any political question arises in the United States which is not resolved sooner or later into a judicial question.

Terry M. Townsend: One of the principal qualifications for a political job is that the applicant know nothing much about what he is expected to do. This

Leon Trotsky: Party is the historical organ by means of which a class becomes class conscious.

Harry S. Truman: A statesman is a politician who has been dead 10 or 15 years.

Harry S. Truman: If you want a friend in Washington, get a dog.

Harry S. Truman: The Republican Party either corrupts its liberals or expels them.

Mark Twain: There is no distinctly American criminal class—except Congress.

Mark Twain: In religion and politics people's beliefs and convictions are in almost every case gotten at second-hand, and without examination.

Mark Twain: The political and commercial morals of the United States are not merely food for laughter, they are an entire banquet.

Mark Twain: To my mind Judas Iscariot was nothing but a low, mean, premature Congressman.

Mark Twain: The chances are that a man cannot get into Congress now without resorting to arts and means that should render him unfit to go there.

Mark Twain: The radical invents the views. When he has worn them out the conservative adopts them.

Mark Twain (*A Connecticut Yankee in King Arthur's Court*, Chapter 22, 1889): Here I was, in a country where a right to say how the country should be governed was restricted to six persons in each thousand of its population.... I was become a stockholder in a corporation where nine hundred and ninety four of the members furnished all the money and did all the work, and the other six elected themselves a permanent board for direction and took all the dividends. It seemed to me that what the nine hundred and ninety four dupes needed was a new deal.

Mark Twain: Bill Styles... spoke of a low grade of legislative morals. "Kind of discouraging. You see, it's so hard to find men of a so high type of morals that they'll *stay bought*."

Mark Twain: My kind of loyalty was loyalty to one's country, not to its institutions or its officeholders.

Mark Twain: A pretty air in an opera is prettier there than it could be anywhere else, I suppose, just as an honest man in politics shines more than he would elsewhere.

Mark Twain: In statesmanship get formalities right, never mind about moralities.

UA: Politicians are like diapers – they should be changed regularly, and for precisely the same reason.

Jesse Unruh: Money is the mother's milk of politics.

Paul Valery: Politics is the art of preventing people from taking part in affairs which properly concern them.

Paul Valery: Politics is the art of preventing people from busying themselves with what is their own business.

Frank Vanderlip: A conservative is a person who does not think anything should be done for the first time.

Bill Vaughan: A statesman is any politician who is considered safe to name a school after.

Gore Vidal: Today's public figures can no longer write their own speeches or books, and there is some evidence that they can't read them either.

Gore Vidal: Half of the American people have never read a newspaper. Half never voted for president. One hopes it is the same half.

Kurt Vonnegut: thanks to TV and for the convenience of TV, you can only be one of two kinds of human beings, either a liberal or a conservative.

Daniel Webster: I have given my life to law and politics. Law is uncertain and politics are utterly vain.

Benjamin Whichcote: Among politicians the esteem of religion is profitable; the principles of it are troublesome.

George Will: Ronald Reagan has held the two most demanding jobs in the country—president of United States and radio broadcaster for the Chicago Cubs.

Harold Wilson: A week is a long time in politics.

Woodrow Wilson: Power consists in one's capacity to link his will with the purpose of others, to lead by reason and a gift of cooperation.

Woodrow Wilson: The trouble with the Republican Party is that it has not had a new idea for 30 years.

Henry Wotton: An ambassador is an honest man sent abroad to lie for his country.

POOR/POVERTY (See MONEY)

PORNOGRAPHY (See PROFANITY; SEX)

PRECEDENT

Uncle Anthony: Are "precedents" something you (lawyers and judges) decided were good a long time ago and you put 'em down like old coins in a chest in the cellar and never change them or is it something good like wine that gets better over time because you turn 'em over and shake 'em up every so often so the wine don't turn sour.

Aunt Mary Carlo: I guess ya need some kinda ruler ta set tings strait. But if da ruler's bent or crooked, ya gotta change dat precedent don'tcha?

William Henry Ashhurst: There is no magic in parchment or in wax.

Sir Francis Bacon: Set it down to thyself, as well to create good precedents, as to follow them.

Sir Francis Bacon: If it be that previous decisions must be rescinded, at least let them be interred with honour.

Bible: Acts 7:51: As your fathers did, so do ye.

Bible: Jeremiah 6:16: Ask for the old paths, where is the good way, and walk therein, and ye shall find rest for your souls.

Bible: 2 Kings 17:41: As did their fathers, so do they unto this day.

Bible: Matthew, 15:2; Mark, 7:3: The tradition of the elders.

Bible: Proverbs 22:28; Proverbs 23:10: Remove not the ancient landmark, which thy fathers have set.

Ambrose Bierce: PRECEDENT, n. In Law, a previous decision, rule or practice which, in the absence of a definite statute, has whatever force and authority a Judge may choose to give it, thereby greatly simplifying his task of doing as he pleases. As there are precedents for everything, he has only to ignore those that make against his interest and accentuate those in line of his desire. Invention of precedent elevates the trial-at-law from the low estate of a fortuitous ordeal to the noble attitude of a dirigible arbitrament.

Justice Louis Brandeis: *Stare decisis* is ordinarliy a wise rule of action. But it is not a universal, inexorable command. *Washington v. W.C. Dawson & Co.*, 264 US 219, 68 L ed 646, 44 S Ct 302 (1924)

Justice Louis Brandeis: The doctrine of *stare decisis* does not command that we err again when we have occasion to pass upon a different statute. *DiSanto v. Pennsylvania*, 273 US 34, 71 L ed 524, 47 S Ct 267 (1927)

Justice Louis Brandeis: *Stare decisis* is usually the wise policy, because in most matters it is more important that the applicable rule of law be settled than that it be settled right.... But in cases involving the Federal Constitution, where correction through legislative action is practically impossible, this Court has often overruled its earlier decisions. The Court bows to the lessons of experience and the force of better reasoning. (dissenting opinion) *Burnett v. Coronado Oil & Gas Co.*, 285 US 393, 76 L ed 815, 52 S Ct 443 (1932)

Benjamin Cardozo: Precedents drawn from the days of travel by stage coach do not fit the conditions of travel to-day. The principle that the danger must be imminent does not change, but the things subject to the principle do change. They are whatever the needs of life in a developing civilization require them to be. MacPherson v. Buick Motor Co., 217 N.Y. 382, 391 (1916)

Benjamin Cardozo (*Nature of the Judicial Process*, 1921): It is when the colors do not match, when the references in the index fail, when there is no decisive precedent, that the serious business of the judge begins.

Benjamin Cardozo (*Nature of the Judicial Process*, 1921): We do not pick our rules of law full-blossomed from the trees.

Benjamin Cardozo (*Nature of the Judicial Process*, 1921): The judge, even when he is free, is not wholly free. He is not to innovate at pleasure. He is not a knight-errant, roaming at will in pursuit of his own ideal of beauty or of goodness. He is to draw his inspiration from consecrated principles. He is not to yield to spasmodic sentiment, to vague and unregulated benevolence. He is to exercise a discretion informed by tradition, methodized by analogy, disciplined by system, and subordinated to "the primordial necessity of order in the social life." Wide enough in all conscience is the field of discretion that remains.

Benjamin Cardozo: The repetition of a catchword can hold analysis in fetters for fifty years and more.

Benjamin Cardozo: What has once been settled by a precedent will not be unsettled overnight, for certainty and uniformity are gains not lightly to be sacrificed.

Rufus Choate (Massachusetts lawyer, statesman, 1799-1859; to the Court requesting a precedent for his position during a trial; *Works of Choate*, 1862): I will look, your Honor, and endeavor to find a precedent, if you require it; though it would seem to be a pity that the Court should lose the honor of being the first to establish so just a rule.

Sir Winston Churchill: If we open a quarrel between the past and the present, we shall find we have lost the future.

Sir Winston Churchill: The farther back you can look, the farther forward you are likely to see.

Sir Winston Churchill: A nation that forgets its past is doomed to repeat it.

Sir Winston Churchill: A love for tradition has never weakened a nation, indeed it has strengthened nations in their hour of peril.

Sir Edward Coke (Lord Chief Justice of England, 1552-1634, 4 *Inst.* 109; referencing Chaucer, *The Parlement of Foules*: "For out of olde feldys, as men seith, / Cometh al this newe corn fro yere to yere."): We must pursue our ancient authors for out of the old fields must come the new corn.

William Cowper: To follow foolish precedents, and wink / With both our eyes, is easier than to think.

Dr. Frank Crane: All sorts of substitute for wisdom are used by the world. When the court doesn't know, it consults precedent. The court that made the precedent guessed at it. Yesterday's guess, grown gray and wearing a big wig, becomes today's justice.

Stephen Crane: Tradition, thou art for suckling children, /Thou art the enlivening milk for babies, / But no meat for men is in thee.

Sir George Croke (1560-1642, Judge of King's Bench): They said that those things which have been so often adjudged ought to rest in peace. Spicer v. Spicer, Cro. Jac. 527 (1620)

Benjamin Disraeli (Speech to House of Commons, Feb. 22, 1848): A precedent embalms a principle.

Baron Thomas Egerton Ellesmere (Lord Chancellor of England, 1540-1617, *Case of Proclamations*, 1611): Every precedent had first a commencement.

Sam Ervin, Jr. (Senate Watergate Hearings, 1973): An old lawyer in St. Louis made a speech sometime ago in which he said: "Do not waste your time looking up the law in advance, because you can find some Federal district court that will sustain any proposition you make."

F. Scott Fitzgerald: If you're strong enough, there *are* no precedents.

Sam Walter Foss: For men are prone to go it blind / Along the calf-paths of the mind, / And work away from sun to sun / To do what other men have done.... / But how the wise old wood-gods laugh, / Who saw the first primeval calf.... / For thus such reverence is lent / To well-established precedent.

Judge Jerome Frank (1889-1957, US Circuit Court Judge): We are not here compelled by Erie R. Co. v. Tompkins, 304 U.S. 64 ... to play the role of ventriloquist's dummy to the courts of some particular state. *Richardson v. Comm'r Int. Rev.,* 126 F. 2d 562 (1942)

Jerome Frank: Every lawyer of experience comes to know (more or less unconsciously) that in the great majority of cases, the precedents are none too good as bases of prediction. Somehow or other, there are plenty of precedents to go around.

Justice Felix Frankfurter (1882-1965): We recognize that stare decisis embodies an important social policy. It represents an element of continuity in law, and is rooted in the psychologic need to satisfy reasonable expectations. But stare decisis is a principle of policy and not a mechanical formula of adherence to the latest decision, however recent and questionable, when such adherence involves collision with a prior doctrine more embracing in its scope, intrinsically sounder, and verified by experience...This Court, unlike the House of Lords, has from the beginning rejected a doctrine of disability at self-correction. *Helvering v. Hallock,* 309 US 106, 121 L ed 604, 60 S Ct 444 (1940)

Goethe: Laws are inherited like diseases.

Farrer Herschell: The acts of today become the precedents of tomorrow.

Oliver Wendell Holmes (*Path of the Law*, 10 Harv. L.R. 457, 469, 1897): It is revolting to have no better reason for a rule of law than that so it was laid down in the time of Henry IV. It is still more revolting if the grounds upon which it was laid down have vanished long since, and the rule simply persists from blind imitation of the past.

Justice Robert Houghwout Jackson (1892-1954): I had supposed that our judicial responsibility is for the regularity of the law, not for the regularity of pedigrees. *Williams v. North Carolina*, 317 US 287, 324 L ed 279, 63 S Ct 207 (1942)

Robert H. Jackson: "... constitutional precedents ... have a mortality rate almost as high as their authors.

Junius: What yesterday was fact today is doctrine.

Junius: One precedent creates another.—They soon accumulate, and constitute law.—What yesterday was fact, today is doctrine.—Examples are supposed to justify the most dangerous measures; and where they do not suit exactly, the defect is supplied by analogy.

Karl Llewellyn (American lawyer, professor of law, author, 1893-1962, *The Bramble Bush*, 1930): Every doubtful point is regularly answered both ways by authority.... There is the Janus face of Precedent.

Frederic W. Maitland: The forms of action we have buried but they rule us from their graves.

Lord William Murray, Earl of Mansfield (Chief Justice, King's Bench, England, 1705-1793): The reason and spirit of cases make law; not the letter of particular precedents. Fisher v. Prince, 3 Burr. 1363, 1364, 1762

Alexander Pope: Who lasts a century can have no flaw; / I hold that Wit a classic, good in law.

Fred Rodell (Yale Law School professor): The law is like the Killy-loo bird – a creature that insists on flying backward because it didn't care where it was going but was mightily interested in where it had been.

Will Rogers: We know lots of things we didn't use to know but we don't know any way to prevent 'em from happening.

Will Rogers: When you write down the good things you ought to have done, and leave out the bad things you did do, that's memoirs.

Will Rogers: (The government) sent the Indians to Oklahoma. They had a treaty that said, "You shall have this land as long as grass grows and water flows." It was not only a good rhyme but looked like a good treaty, and it was till they struck oil. Then the Government took it away from us again. They said the treaty only refers to "Water and Grass; it don't say anything about oil." (1928)

Lawrence Sterne: Precedents are the band and disgrace of legislation. - They are not wanted to justify right measures, and are absolutely insufficient to excuse wrong ones. They can only be useful to heralds, dancing-masters, and gentleman ushers.

William Shakespeare (*I Henry IV*, Act II, iv): Step aside, and I'll show thee a precedent.

William Shakespeare (*II Henry*, Act II, iii): He was, indeed, the glass / Wherein the noble youth did dress themselves.

William Shakespeare (*A Lover's Complaint*, l. 155): But, ah, who ever shunn'd by precedent / The destined ill she must herself assay?

William Shakespeare (*Measure for Measure*, Act II, ii): Thieves for their robbery have authority, / When judges steal themselves.

William Shakespeare (*The Merchant of Venice*, Act IV, i): It must not be; there is no power in Venice / Can alter a decree established. / 'Twill be recorded for a precedent, / And many an error by the same example / Will rush into the state.

William Shakespeare (*Tempest*, Act II, i): Thy case, dear friend, / Shall be my precedent.

Jonathan Swift (*Gulliver's Travels: Houyhnhnms*, ch. 5): It is a maxim among these lawyers, that whatever has been done before may legally be done again; and therefore they take especial care to record all the decisions formerly made against common justice and the general reason of mankind. These, under the name of precedents, they produce as authorities to justify the most iniquitous opinions; and the judges never fail of directing accordingly.

Algernon Charles Swinburne: Is not Precedent indeed a King of men?

Tacitus: All things which are now regarded as of great antiquity were once new, and what we today maintain by precedents will hereafter become a precedent.

Talmud, *Shabbat*: Do not use the conduct of a fool as a precedent.

Alfred Lord Tennyson (English poet, 1809-1892; *You Ask me, Why*): A land of settled government, / A land of just and old renown, / Where Freedom slowly broadens down / From precedent to precedent.

Alfred Lord Tennyson: The lawless science of the law, that codeless myriad of precedent, that wilderness of single instances.

Mark Twain: To do something, say something, see something, before *anybody* else—these are things that confer a pleasure compared with which other pleasures are tame and commonplace, other ecstasies cheap and trivial.

Voltaire: The more ancient the abuse the more sacred it is.

PREJUDICE (See BIAS)

PREPARATION (See also WORK)

Uncle Anthony: Thomas, never forget the 7 Lucky P's: Proper Prior Preparation Prevents Piss Poor Performance!

Uncle Anthony: There's never enough time (and money) to plan and prepare properly, but there's always enough time and money to fix all the mistakes caused by piss poor planning.

Aunt Mary Carlo: When ya say to everybody "Let's git ready" nobody does, y'now why? 'Cause no one person is gonna be held responsible to "git ready."

Aunt Mary Carlo: Y'know the best way to screw up anything is to turn it over to a committee to plan.

Aunt Mary Carlo: Pray, prepare, then proceed!

Aesop: Little by little does the trick.

Aesop: Better one safe way than a hundred which you cannot reckon.

Albert von Szent-Gyorgi: Discovery is said to be an accident meeting a prepared mind.

Aristotle: When we deliberate it is about means and not ends.

Bible: Ezekiel 7:14: They have blown the trumpet, even to make all ready; but none goeth to the battle.

Bible: Ezekiel 38:7: Be thou prepared.

Bible: Isaiah, 38:1: Set the thine house in order.

Bible: Isaiah 40:3: Prepare ye the way of the Lord, make straight in the desert a highway for our God.

Bible: John 1:23: John the Baptist: I am the voice of one crying in the wilderness, Make straight the way of the Lord.

Bible: Joshua 3:5; Joshua 7:13: Sanctify yourselves against tomorrow.
Bible: Luke 3:4; Mark 1:3; Matthew 3:3: Prepare ye the way of the Lord, make His paths straight.
Bible: Luke, 7:35: Let your loins be girded about, and your lights burning.
Bible: Mark 13:35: Watch ye therefore: for ye know not when the master of the house cometh.
Bible: Matthew 24:44: Be ye also ready: for in such an hour as ye think not the Son of man cometh.
Bible: Proverbs 6:6: Go to the ant, thou sluggard; consider her ways, and be wise: Which having no guide, overseer, or ruler, Provideth her meat in summer, and gathereth her food in the harvest.
Bible: 1 Samuel 7:3: Prepare your hearts unto the Lord, and serve him only.
Bible: Song 3:8: Every man hath his sword upon his thigh because of fear in the night.
Ambrose Bierce: PLAN, n. To bother about the best method of accomplishing an accidental result.
Ambrose Bierce: PRESCRIPTION, n. A physician's guess at what will best prolong the situation with least harm to the patient.
Ambrose Bierce: PREVARICATOR, n. A liar in the caterpillar state.
Ambrose Bierce: PROPHECY, n. The art and practice of selling one's credibility for future delivery.
Ambrose Bierce: PROSPECT, n. An outlook, usually forbidding. An expectation, usually forbidden.....
Ambrose Bierce: PROJECTILE, n. The final arbiter in international disputes. Formerly these disputes were settled by physical contact of the disputants, with such simple arguments as the rudimentary logic of the times could supply – the sword, the spear, and so forth. With the growth of prudence in military affairs the projectile came more and more into favor, and is now held in high esteem by the most courageous. Its capital defect is that it requires personal attendance at the point of propulsion.
Boy Scouts of America Motto: Be Prepared.
Burtolt Brecht: If there are obstacles, the shortest line between two points may be the crooked line.
Daniel H. Burnham: Make no little plans: they have no magic to stir men's blood.
Robert Burns ("To a Mouse," 1785): The best-laid schemes o' mice an' men / Gang aft agley, / and lea'e us nought but grief an' pain, / For promis'd joy!
John Bunyon: Then Christian began to gird up his loins, and to address himself to his journey.
Robert Burton: The Commonwealth of Venice in their armoury have this inscription: "Happy is that city which in time of peace thinks of war."
Sir Thomas Buxton: In life, as in chess, forethought wins.
John Cage: All I know about method is that when I am not working I sometimes think I know something, but when I am working, it is quite clear I know nothing.
Cervantes: Forewarned, forearmed; to be prepared his half the victory.
Lord Chesterfield: There is time enough for everything in the course of the day if you do but one thing at once; but there is not time enough in the year if you will do two things at a time.
Sir Winston Churchill: I'm just preparing my impromptu remarks.
Sir Winston Churchill: There is in the act of preparing, the moment you start caring.
Sir Winston Churchill: Time needed to cancel is far shorter than time needed to plan
Confucius: If a man take no thought about what is distant, he will find sorrow near at hand.
John Dryden: Unforeseen, they say, is unprepared.
Friedrich Durrenmatt: The more human beings proceed by plan the more effectively they may be hit by accident.
Albert Einstein: I never think of the future – it comes soon enough.
Dwight D. Eisenhower: In preparing for battle I have always found that plans are useless, but planning is indispensable.
Ralph Waldo Emerson: There is always a best way of doing everything, if it be to boil an egg.
Ralph Waldo Emerson: The lawyers have always... some reserve of sovereignty, tantamount to the Rob Roy rule that might makes right. America should affirm and establish that in no instance should the guns go in advance of the perfect right.
English Proverb: Practice makes perfect.
Epictetus: We should be careful as to the play, but indifferent to the ball.
Euripides: Do not plan for ventures before finishing what's at hand.
Farquhar: 'Tis safest making peace with sword in hand.
Benjamin Franklin: Diligence is the mother of good luck.

Benjamin Franklin: Forewarned, forearmed.
French Proverb: Who carries a sword, carries peace.
Thomas Fuller: In fair weather prepare for foul.
Andre Gide: It is not always by plugging away at a difficulty and sticking at it that one overcomes it; but, rather, often by working on the one next to it. Certain people and certain things require to be approached on an angle.
Goethe: It is not enough to take steps which may someday lead to a goal; each step must be itself a goal and a step likewise.
Baltazar Gracian: Attempt easy tasks as if they were difficult, and difficult as if they were easy: in the one case that confidence may not fall asleep, in the other that it may not be dismayed.
Arthur Guiterman: While Honey lies in Every Flower, no doubt, / It takes a bee to get the Honey out.
Alan Harrington: We are all, it seems, saving ourselves for the Senior Prom. But many of us forget that somewhere along the way we must learn to dance.
George Herbert: A disarmed peace is weak.
George Herbert: The first blow is as much as two.
Irish Proverb: If you do not sow in the spring you will not reap in the autumn.
Oliver Goldsmith: The first blow is half the battle.
Randy James: Albert Einstein is dumber than the stupidest lawyer in the world if that lawyer is preparing him for or taking his deposition.
Samuel Johnson: Few things are impossible with diligence and skill... Great works are performed, not by strength, but perseverance.
Michael Jordan: The will to win doesn't mean anything, because everyone wants to win. **It's the will to prepare to win** that makes all the difference.
Abraham Lincoln: "If I were given 6 hours to chop down a tree, I would spend the first 5 hours sharpening my axe"
Edwin Markham: For all your days prepare, / And meet them all alike: / When you are the anvil, bear—/ When you are the hammer, strike.
Gen. George B. McClellan (THE OVERLY CAUTIOUS Civil War General, called "The Virginia Creeper," relieved of command by President Lincoln, Historian William S. Sears said "(McClelllan) was so fearful of losing he would not risk winning."): The true course in conducting military operations is to make NO MOVEMENT UNTIL THE PREPARATIONS ARE COMPLETE.
H.L. Mencken: There is no record in history of a nation that ever gained anything valuable by being unable to defend itself.
John Morley: The means prepare the end, and the end is what the means have made it.
Napoleon I: Unhappy the general who comes on the field of battle with a system.
Napoleon I: We often get in quicker by the back door than by the front.
Louis Nizer: (Preparation) is the be-all of good trial work. Everything else—Felicity of expression, improvisational brilliance—is a satellite around the sun. Thorough preparation is that sun.
Louis Nizer: Yes, there is such a thing as luck in trial law but it only comes at three o'clock in the morning... You'll still find me in the library looking for luck at three o'clock in the morning.
José Ortega y Gasset: The past is the *terra firma* of methods, of the roads which we believe we have under our feet.
Ovid: He who is not prepared today, will be less so tomorrow.
Ovid: The mightiest rivers lose their force when split up into several streams.
Laurence J. Peter: If you don't know where you are going, you will probably end up somewhere else.
Alexander Pope: Those oft are stratagems which errors seem, / Nor is it Homer nods, but we that dream.
Publilius Syrus: Amid a multitude of projects, no plan is devised.
Publilius Syrus: It is a bad plan that admits of no modification.
Publilius Syrus: Divide the fire, and you will the sooner put it out.
Publilius Syrus: To do two things at once is to do neither.
Publilius Syrus: Look for a tough wedge for a tough log.
Publilius Syrus: We should provide in peace what we need in war.
John Ray: One sword keeps another in the sheath.

Will Rogers: Plans get you into things but you got to work your way out.
Theodore Roosevelt: There is a homely adage which runs: "Speak softly and carry a big stick; you will go far." If the American nation will speak softly and yet build and keep at a pitch of the highest training a thoroughly efficient navy, the Monroe Doctrine will go far.
Theodore Roosevelt: Broomstick preparedness.
Bertrand Russell: When the journey from the means to end is not too long, the means themselves are enjoyed if the end is ardently desired.
Saint-Exupery: What sets us against one another is not our aims – they all come to the same thing – but our methods, which are the fruit of our varied reasoning.
Saki: In baiting a mousetrap with cheese, always leave room for the mouse.
Sallust: A good man would prefer to be defeated than to defeat injustice by evil means.
William Shakespeare (*All's Well That Ends Well*, Act II, i): Oft expectation fails, and most oft there / Where most it promises; and oft it hits, / Where hope is coldest and despair most fits.
William Shakespeare (*Cymbeline*, Act II, iv): A piece of work / So bravely done, so rich, that it did strive / In workmanship and value.
William Shakespeare (*Henry V*, Act II, iv): But that defences, musters, preparations, / Should be maintain'd, assembled and collected, / As were a war in expectation.
William Shakespeare (*Henry V*, Act II, iv): It is most meet we arm us 'gainst the foe; / For peace itself should not so dull a kingdom,... / But that defences, musters, preparations, / Should be maintained, assembled and collected, / As were a war in expectation.
William Shakespeare (*Henry VIII*, Act I, ii): Things done well, / And with a care, exempt themselves from fear; / Things done without example, in their issue / Are to be fear'd.
William Shakespeare (*Macbeth*, Act I, vii): If it were done, when 'tis done, then 'twere well / It were done quickly.
William Shakespeare (*MidsummerNight's Dream*, Act V, i): Now the hungry lion roars, / And the wolf behowls the moon; / Whilst the heavy ploughman snores, / All with weary tasks fore-done.
William Shakespeare (*Troilus and Cressida*, Act I, i): I have had my labour for my travel.
William Shakespeare (*Troilus and Cressida*, Act IV, ii): How my achievements mock me! / I will go meet them.
William Shakespeare (*Venus and Adonis*, l. 419): The colt that's back'd and burden'd being young, / Loseth his pride and never waxeth strong.
Spanish Proverb: A forewarned man is worth two.
Terence: Nobody ever drew up his plans for life so well but what the facts, and the years, and experience always introduce some modification.
Thucydides: Few things are brought to a successful issue by impetuous desire, but most by calm and prudent forethought.
Turkish Proverb: One arrow does not bring down two birds.
Mark Twain: Don't you know, there are some things that can beat smartness and foresight? Awkwardness and stupidity can. The best swordsman in the world doesn't need to fear the second best swordsman in the world; no, the person for him to be afraid of is some ignorant antagonist who has never had a sword in his hand before; he doesn't do the thing he ought to.
John Updike: Any activity becomes creative when the doer cares about doing it right, or better.
U.S. Coast Guard Motto: Semper Paratus ("Always Prepared")
George Washington: To be prepared for war is one of the most effectual means of preserving peace.

PRESUMPTION (See EVIDENCE)

PRINCIPLE/HYPOCRACY (See also ETHICS)

Uncle Anthony: One ounce of pretension is worth at least a pound of manure!
Aunt Mary Carlo: Yer mom an dad didn't teach ya tings to do jest on Sundays – ya do da right tings everyday.

Sir Arthur Adams: Don't stay away from church because there are so many hypocrites. There's always room for one more.

John Quincy Adams: Always vote for a principle, though you vote alone, and you may cherish the sweet reflection that your vote is never lost.

Alfred Adler: It is easier to fight for ones principles than to live up to them.

Francis Bacon: A bad man is worse when he pretends to be a saint.

Stanley Baldwin: I would rather be an opportunist and float, then go to the bottom with my principles around my neck.

Henry Ward Beecher: Expedients are for the hour; principles for the ages.

Hillary Belloc: The worst sort of hypocrite and liar is the man who lies to himself in order to feel at ease.

William Biederwolf: A man who hides behind the hypocrite is smaller than the hypocrite.

Bible: James 3:10: Out of the same mouth proceedeth blessing and cursing.

Bible: James 3:11: Doth a fountain send forth at the same place sweet water and bitter?

Bible: Job 8:13: The hypocrite's hope shall perish.

Bible: Job 20:5: The triumphing of the wicked is short, and the joy of the hypocrite but for a moment.

Bible: Job 27:8: What is the hope of the hypocrite, though he hath gained, when God taketh away his soul?

Bible: Luke 20:46; Mark 12:38; Matthew 23:5: Beware of the scribes, which love to go in long clothing, and love salutations in the marketplaces, And the chief seats in the synagogues, and the uppermost rooms at feasts.

Bible: Mark 7:6: This people honoureth me with their lips, but their heart is far from me.

Bible: Matthew 6:12: Forgive us our debts, as we forgive our debtors.

Bible: Matthew 7:5: Thou hypocrite, first cast out the beam out of thine own eye; and then shalt thou see clearly to cast out the mote out of thy brother's eye.

Bible: Matthew 23:5: All their works they do for to be seen of men.

Bible: Matthew 23:14: Woe unto you, scribes and Pharisees, hypocrites!

Bible: Matthew 23:24: Ye blind guides, which strain at a gnat, and swallow a camel.

Bible:aMatthew 23:27:: Woe unto you, scribes and Pharisees, hypocrites! for ye are like unto whited sepulchres, which indeed appear beautiful outward, but are within full of dead men's bones, and of all uncleanness.

Bible: Matthew 23:28: Ye also outwardly appear righteous unto men, but within ye are full of hypocrisy and iniquity

Bible: Proverbs 11:9: An hypocrite with his mouth destroyeth his neighbor.

Bible: Psalms 28:3: The workers of iniquity, which speak peace to their neighbors, but mischief is in their hearts.

Bible: Psalms 62:4: They bless with their mouth, but they curse inwardly.

Ambrose Bierce: BEHAVIOR, n. Conduct, as determined, not by principle, but by breeding.

Ambrose Bierce: CHRISTIAN, n. One who believes that the New Testament is a divinely inspired book admirably suited to the spiritual needs of his neighbor.

Ambrose Bierce: HYPOCRITE, n. One who, professing virtues that he does not respect, secures the advantage of seeming to be what he despises.

Ambrose Bierce: OCCIDENT, n. The part of the world lying west (or east) of the Orient. It is largely inhabited by Christians, a powerful subtribe of the Hypocrites, whose principal industries are murder and cheating, which they are pleased to call "war" and "commerce." These, also, are the principal industries of the Orient.

Ambrose Bierce: POLITENESS, n. The most acceptable hyprocrisy.

Benjamin N. Cardozo (*Nature of the Judicial Process*, 1921): The tendency of a principle (is) to expeand itself to the limit of its logic....

Richard Cecil: As a man loves gold, in that proportion he hates to be imposed upon by counterfeits; and in proportion as a man has regard for that which is above price and better than gold, he abhors that hypocrisy which is but its counterfeit.

GK Chesterton: To have a right to do a thing is not at all the same as to be right in doing it.

Chinese Proverb: If you want to see black-hearted people, look among those who never miss their prayers.

Willis Gaylord Clark: The most terrible of lies is not that which is uttered but that which is live.

Caleb Colton: If the devil ever laughs, it must be at hypocrites; they are the greatest dupes he has; they serve him better than any others, but receive no wages; nay, what is still more extraordinary, they submit to greater mortifications to go to hell, then the sincerest Christian to go to heaven.

Confucius: Better be poisoned in one's blood, then to be poisoned in one's principles.

Confucius: He who merely knows right principles is not equal to him who loves to them.

Albert Einstein: Never do anything against conscience, even if the state demands it.

Ralph Waldo Emerson: We do what we must, and call it by the best names.

Ralph Waldo Emerson: The value of a principle is the number of things it will explain; and there is no good theory of a disease which does not at once suggest a cure.

Zona Gale: The world consists almost exclusively of people who are one sort and who behave like another sort.

German Proverb: When the fox preaches, look to your geese.

Albert Goodrich: Some people speak as if hypocrites were confined to religion; but they are everywhere; people pretending to wealth when they have not a sixpence, assuming knowledge of which they are ignorant, shamming a culture they are far removed from, adopting opinions they do not hold.

Nathaniel Hawthorne: No man can, for any considerable time, wear one face to himself, and another to the multitude, without finally getting bewildered as to which is the true one.

William Hazlitt: Principle is a passion for truth and right.

Matthew Henry: Hypocrites do the devil's drudgery in Christ's livery.

William Dean Howells: We are companions in hypocrisy.

Elbert Hubbard: When a fellow says, "It ain't the money, but the principle of the thing," it's the money.

Friedrich Jacobi: I have all reverence for principles which grow out of sentiments; but as to sentiments which grow out of principles, you shall scarcely build a house of cards thereon.

Ben Jonson: No man is a hypocrite in his pleasures.

Ben Jonson: The hypocrite shows the excellence of virtue by the necessity he thinks himself under of seeming to be virtuous.

Ben Jonson: Hypocrisy is the necessary burden of villainy; affectation, part of the chosen trappings of folly; the one completes a villain, the other only finishes a fop. Contempt is the proper punishment of affectation, and detestation the just consequence of hypocrisy.

Martin Luther King: I refuse to accept the idea that the is-ness of man's present nature makes him morally incapable of reaching up for the ought-ness that forever confronts him.

Henry Liddon: The restless mind of man cannot but press a principle to the real limit of its application, even though centuries should intervene between the premises and the conclusion.

Abraham Lincoln: It has been my experience that folks who have no vices have very few virtues.

Henry Wadsworth Longfellow: Many men do not allow their principles to take root, but hold them up every now and then, as children do the flowers they have planted, to see if they are growing.

Groucho Marx: Those are my principles. If you don't like them, I have others.

Harpo Marx: Oscar Lamont was a man of principle. He never spawned off anybody he did not admire.

Somerset Maugham: You can't learn to soon at the most useful thing about a principle is that it can always be sacrificed to expediency.

Richard Miller: Some people try to use "Ecclesiastical Whiteout" – no one goes to church on prom night, only when they get caught making a big mistake or arrested for a crime, then all of a sudden they "find Jesus."

John Milton: Satan was the first that practiced falsehood under saintly show.

Austin O'Malley: If you cultivate piety as an end and not a means, you will become a hypocrite.

Pope Pius XI: Though economics, science, and moral discipline are guided each by its own principles in its own sphere, it is false that the two orders are so distinct and alien that the former in no way depends upon the latter.

Channing Pollock: The hypocrite was a man who stole the livery of the court of heaven to serve the devil in.

Robert Reisner: Sacred cows make great hamburgers.

Jean Paul Richter: Principles, like troops of the line, are undisturbed, and stand fast.

Will Rogers: So let's be honest with ourselves and not take ourselves too serious, and never condemn the other fellow for doing what we are doing every day, only in a different way.

Will Rogers: (Rogers was asked by a piano manufacturer to write a short testimonial for their instruments. Unwilling to endorse a product he could not put to the test, Rogers simply replied) "Dear Sirs, I guess your pianos are the best I ever leaned against. Yours truly, Will Rogers."

Will Rogers: (The government) sent the Indians to Oklahoma. They had a treaty that said, "You shall have this land as long as grass grows and water flows." It was not only a good rhyme but looked like a good treaty, and it was till they struck oil. Then the Government took it away from us again. They said the treaty only refers to "Water and Grass; it don't say anything about oil." (1928)

Frederick William Robertson: A principle is one thing; a maxim or rule is another.—A principle requires liberality; a rule says, "one tenth."—A principle says, "forgive"; a rule defines "seven times."

Rochefoucauld: Hypocrisy is the homage that vice pays to virtue.

Walter Scott: A man may with more impunity be guilty of an actual breach, either of real good breeding or good morals, than appear ignorant of the most minute points of fashionable etiquette.

John Robert Seeley: Principles last forever; but special rules pass away with the things and conditions to which they refer.

William Shakespeare (*The Comedy of Errors*, Act III, ii): Apparel vice like virtue's harbinger; / Bear a fair presence, though your heart be tainted; / Teach sin the carriage of a holy saint.

William Shakespeare (*Hamlet*, I, ii): Frailty, thy name is woman.

William Shakespeare (*Hamlet,* Act I, ii): With an auspicious and a dropping eye, / With mirth in funeral, and with dirge in marriage, / In equal scale waiting delight and dole.

William Shakespeare (*Hamlet*, Act I, iv): Something is rotten in the state of Denmark.

William Shakespeare (*Hamlet*, Act I, v): One may smile and smile and be a villain still.

William Shakespeare (*Hamlet,* Act III, i): 'Tis too much proved—that with devotion's visage / And pious action, we do sugar o'er / The devil himself.

William Shakespeare (*Hamlet*, Act III, i): God hath given you one face, and you / Make yourself another.

William Shakespeare (*Hamlet*, Act III, ii): I will speak daggers to her, but use none; / My tongue and soul in this be hypocrites.

William Shakespeare (*Hamlet*, Act III, ii): The lady doth protest too much.

William Shakespeare (*III Henry VI*, Act III, ii): Why, I can smile, and murder whiles I smile, / And cry "Content" to that which grieves my heart; / And wet my cheeks with artificial tears, / And frame my face to all occasions.

William Shakespeare (*III Henry VI*, Act III, ii): Why I can smile and murder while I smile.

William Shakespeare (*Julius Caesar*, Act V, i): Thinking, by this face, / To fasten in our thoughts that they have courage; / But 'tis not so.

William Shakespeare (*King Lear*, Act I, i): I want that glib and oily art / To speak and purpose not.

William Shakespeare (*King Lear*, Act III, ii): Thou similar man of virtue / That art incestuous.

William Shakespeare (*King Lear*, Act IV, vi): Thou rascal beadle, hold thy bloody hand! / Why dost thou lash that whore? Strip thine own back; / Thou hotly lust'st to use her in that kind / For which thou whipp'st her.

William Shakespeare (*King Lear*, Act IV, vi): Behold yond simpering dame,... / That minces virtue, and does shake the head / To hear of pleasure's name; /The fitchew, nor the soiled horse, goes to 't / With a more riotous appetite.

William Shakespeare (*Love's Labour's Lost*, Act IV, iii): Now step I forth to whip hypocrisy.

William Shakespeare (*Macbeth,* Act I, v): To beguile the time, / Look like the time;... look like the innocent flower, / But be the serpent under it.

William Shakespeare (*Macbeth*, Act I, vii): Away, and mock the time with their fairest show; / False face must hide what a false heart doth know.

William Shakespeare (*Macbeth,* Act II, iii): There's daggers in men's smiles.

William Shakespeare (*Measure for Measure,* Act III, i): O, 'tis the cunning livery of hell, / The damned'st body to invest and cover / In phrenzie guards!

William Shakespeare (*Measure for Measure*, Act III, ii): O, what may man within him hide, / Though angel on the outward side!

William Shakespeare (*The Merchant of Venice*, Act I, iii): The devil can cite Scripture for his purpose. / An evil soul, producing holy witness, / Is like a villain with the smiling cheek, / A goodly apple rotten at the heart: / O, what a goodly outside falsehood hath!

William Shakespeare (*Much A do About Nothing*, Act I, i): He is no less than a stuffed man.

William Shakespeare (*Much Ado About Nothing*, Act IV, i): O, what authority and show of truth / Can cunning sin cover itself the itself withal!

William Shakespeare (*Othello*, Act II, iii): When devils will the blackest sins put on, / They do suggest at first with heavenly shows.

William Shakespeare (*Richard III*, Act I, iii): But then I sigh; and, with a piece of Scripture, / Tell them that God bids us do good for evil: / And thus I clothe my naked villainy / With old odd ends, stolen out of holy writ; / And seem a saint, when most I play the devil.

William Shakespeare (*Richard III*, Act III, v): So smooth he daub'd his vice with show of virtue,... / He liv'd from all attainder of suspects.

William Shakespeare (*Romeo and Juliet*, Act III, i): A plague o' both your houses.

William Shakespeare (*Romeo and Juliet*, Act III, ii): O serpent heart, hid with a flow'ring face! / Did ever a dragon keep so fair a cave?

William Shakespeare (*Tempest*, Act V, i): How camest thou in this pickle?

Jonathan Swift: The hypocrite pays tribute to God that he may impose upon man.

Jonathan Swift: Hypocrisy is much more eligible than open infidelity and vice, it wears the livery of religion, and is cautious of giving scandal.

David Thomas: The principles now implanted in thy bosom will grow, and one day reach maturity; and in that maturity thou wilt find thy heaven or thy hell.

J. Arthur Thomson: The most powerful factors in the world are clear ideas in the minds of energetic men of goodwill.

John Tillotson: It is hard to personate and act a part long; for where truth is not at the bottom nature will always be endeavoring to return, and will peep out and betray herself one time or another.

Mark Twain: The Moral Sense teaches us what is right, and how to avoid it – when unpopular.

Mark Twain: Barring that natural expression of villainy which we all have, the man looked honest enough.

Mark Twain: Good breeding consists in concealing how much we think of ourselves and how little we think of other people.

Mark Twain: Prosperity is the best protector of principle.

Oscar Wilde: I hope you have not been leading a double life, pretending to be wicked and being really good all the time. That would be hypocrisy.

PROBABILITY (See EVIDENCE; FACTS/LIES)

PROBLEMS/PROBLEM SOLVING (See ISSUES/PROBLEMS; TROUBLE)

PROFANITY

Uncle Anthony: I promised your mother I wouldn't curse, and I won't, but he is a son of a bitch!

Aunt Mary Carlo: Cursing is just what you say when you don't know what to say.

Arabic Proverb: A thousand curses never tore a shirt.

Kenneth Bartlett: A meaningless use of words which allows the speaker to vocalize and exercise his tone code. Since he has reached the linguistic stage of development he swears. Otherwise he would coo.

Bible: Colossians 3:8: Put off all these; anger, wrath, malice, blasphemy, filthy communication out of your mouth.

Bible: Exodus 20:2; Deuteronomy 5:11: (3rd Commandment): Thou shalt not take the name of the Lord thy God in vain; for the Lord will not hold him guiltless that taketh His name in vain.

Bible: Leviticus 24:15: Whosoever curseth his God shall bear his sin.

Bible: Matthew 5:44: Bless them that curse you.

Bible: Proverbs 17:5: Whoso mocketh the poor reproacheth his Maker.

Bible: Psalms 109:17: As he loved cursing, so let it come unto him: as he delighted not in blessing, so let it be far from him.

Ambrose Bierce: CURSE, v.t. Energetically to belabor with a verbal slap-stick. This is an operation which in literature, particularly in the drama, is commonly fatal to the victim. Nevertheless, the liability to a cursing is a risk that cuts but a small figure in fixing the rates of life insurance.

Ambrose Bierce: DAMN, v. A word formerly much used by the Paphlagonians, the meaning of which is lost. By the learned Dr. Dolabelly Gak it is believed to have been a term of satisfaction, implying the highest possible degree of mental tranquility. Professor Groke, on the contrary, thinks it expressed an emotion of tumultuous delight, because it so frequently occurs in combination with the word *jod* or *god*, meaning "joy." It would be with great diffidence that I should advance an opinion conflicting with that of either of these formidable authorities.

Ambrose Bierce: RIBALDRY, n. Censorious language by another concerning oneself.

Ambrose Bierce: RIBROASTER, n. Censorious language by oneself concerning another. The word is of classical refinement, and is even said to have been used in a fable by Georgius Coadjutor, one of the most fastidious writers of the fifteenth century – commonly, indeed, regarded as the founder of the Fastidiotic School.

William J. Brennan, Jr. (New Jersey judge, Associate Justice U.S. Supreme Court): Some American courts adopted this standard [Regina v. Hicklin] but later decisions have rejected it and substituted this test: whether to the average person, applying contemporary community standards, the dominant theme of the material taken as a whole appeals to prurient interest. Roth v. United States, 354 US 476, 1 L.Ed 2d 1498, 77 S Ct 1304 (1957) (NOTE: see Lord Cockburn below)

Ambrose Bierce: Take not God's name in vain; select / A time when it will have effect.

Edward Bulwer-Lytton (Baron Lytton): Curses are like young chickens, and still come home to roost.

Samuel Butler: A kind of prayers.

E.H. Chapin: Profaneness is a brutal vice. / He who indulges in it is no gentlemen. / I care not what his stamp may be in society, or what clothes he wears, or what culture he boasts. / Despite all his refinement, the light and habitual taking of Gods name in vain, betrays a course and brutal will.

E.H. Chapin: Profanity never did any man the least good. No man is the richer, or happier, or wiser, for it. It commends no one to any society. It is disgusting to the refined; abominable to the good; insulting to those with whom we associate; degrading to mind; unprofitable, needless, and injurious to society.

Chinese Proverb: A man should not curse the crocodile while crossing the river.

Sir Winston Churchill: Under certain circumstances, profanity provides a relief denied even to prayer.

Cicero: The more you are averse to base actions, the more you should keep yourself from license in language.

Sir Alexander (Lord) Cockburn (English judge, 1802-1880, in his oft quoted "obscenity standard"): I think the test of obscenity is this, whether the tendency of the matter charged as obscenity is to deprave and corrupt those whose minds are open to such immoral influences, and into whose hands a publication of this sort may fall. Now, with regard to this work it is quite certain that it would suggest to the minds of the young of either sex, or even to persons of more advanced years, thoughts of a most impure and libidinous character. Regina v. Hicklin, 3 Q.B. 360, 371 (1868).

Cyril Connolly: The garlic in the salad of taste.

William Cowper: It chills my blood to hear the blest Supreme rudely appealed to one each trifling theme. / Maintain your rank, vulgarity despise. / To swear is neither brave, polite, nor wise.

Finley Peter Dunne (Mr. Dooley): But th' best thing about a little judicyous swearin' is that it keeps th' temper. 'Twas intinded as a compromise between runnin' away an' fightin'. Befure it was invinted they was on'y th' two ways out iv an argymint.

Tryon Edwards: Profanity is both an unreasonable and an unmanly sin, a violation alike of good taste and good morals; an offensive against both man and God. / Some sins are productive of temporary profit or pleasure; but profaneness is productive of nothing unless it be shame on earth, and damnation in hell. It is the most gratuitous of all kinds of wickedness—a sort of pepper-corn acknowledgment of the sovereignty of the devil over those who indulge it.

Ralph Waldo Emerson: I confess to some pleasure from the stinging rhetoric or a rattling oath.

English Proverb: He who says what he likes shall hear what he does not like.

W.S. Gilbert: When you are lying awake with a dismal headache, and repose is tabooed by anxiety, / I conceive you may use any language you choose to indulge in without impropriety.

W. S. Gilbert: Bad language or abuse / I never, never use, / Whenever the emergency; / Though "Bother it" I may / Occasionally say, / I never, never use a big, big D.

Robert Hall: Swearing is properly a superfluity of haughtiness, and can only be considered as a sort of pepper-corn sent, in acknowledgment of the devil's right of superiority.

John M. Harlan, (Kentucky lawyer, Assoc Justice US Supreme Court): One man's vulgarity is another man's lyric. Cohen v. California (1971).

George Herbert: Take not His name, who made thy mouth, in vain; / It gets thee nothing, and hath no excuse.

George Herbert: Who spits against Heaven, it falls in his face.

George Herbert: When thou dost tell another's jest, therein / Omit the oaths, which true wit cannot need.

D.H. Lawrence (On a publisher's rejection of *Sons and Lovers*, 1912): Curse the blasted, jelly-boned swines, the slimy, the belly-wriggling invertebrates, the miserable sodding rotters, the flaming sods, the snivelling, dribbling, dithering, palsied, pulseless lot that make up England today.

D.H. Lawrence (*Pornography and Obscenity*, 1929): What is pornography to one man is the laughter of genius to another.

D.H. Lawrence: Words that make you squint in print.

Horace Mann: The devil tempts men through their ambition, their cupidity or their appetite, until he comes to the profane swearer, whom he catches without any bait or reward.

Montaigne: When I swear after my own fashion, it is only by God; the directest of all oaths.

Alexander Pope: And each blasphemer quite escape the rod, / Because the insult's not on man but God?

Quintilian: To swear at all, except when absolutely necessary, is unbecoming to a man of sense.

Will Rogers: We cuss Congress, and we joke about 'em, but they are all good fellows at heart, and if they wasn't in Congress, why, they would be doing something else against us that might be even worse.

Sir Walter Scott: Dinna curse him, sir; I have heard it said that a curse was like a stone flung up to the heavens, and most likely to return on the head of him that sent it.

William Shakespeare (*Comedy of Errors*,Act III, ii): Ill deeds are doubled with an evil word.

William Shakespeare (*As You Like It*, Act II, vii): Full of strange oaths.

William Shakespeare (*Cymbeline*, Act V, v): Foam'd at the mouth, and swore.

William Shakespeare (*Cymbeline*, Act II, i): A whoreson some jackanapes must take me up for swearing; as if I borrowed mine oaths of him and might not spend them at my pleasure.... When a gentleman is disposed to swear, it is not for any standers-by to curtail his oaths, ha?

William Shakespeare (*Hamlet,* Act II, ii): Why, what an ass am I! This is most brave, / That I, the son of a dear father murdere', / Prompted to my revenge by heaven and hell, / Must, like a whore, unpack my heart with words, / And fall a-cursing, like a very drab, / A scullion!

William Shakespeare (*I Henry IV*, Act III, i): Swear me, Kate, like a lady as thou art, / A good mouth-filling oath, and leave "in sooth," / And such protests of pepper-gingerbread, / To velvet-guards and Sunday-citizens.

William Shakespeare (*III Henry VI*, Act V, vi): Down, down to hell; and say I sent thee thither.

William Shakespeare (*Measure for Measure,* Act II, ii): That in the captain's but a choleric word, / Which in the Soldier is flat blasphemy.

William Shakespeare (*The Merchant of Venice*, Act III, ii): Swearing till my very roof was dry.

William Shakespeare (*The Tempest*, Act I, ii): You taught me language; and my profit on 't /Need to Is, I know how to curse.

William Shakespeare (*Twelfth Night*, Act III, iv): It comes to pass oft that a terrible oath, with a swaggering accent sharply twanged off, gives manhood more approbation than ever proof itself would have earned him.

William Shakespeare (*Romeo and Juliet*, Act III, i): A plague on both your houses! / They have made worms' meat of me.

Sir Philip Sidney: Blasphemous words betray the vain foolishness of the speaker.

Robert Southey: Curses are like young chickens, they always come home to roost.

Justice Potter Stewart: I shall not today attempt further to define the kinds of material I understand to be embraced within [the term hard-core pornography]; and perhaps I shall never succeed in intelligibly doing so. But I know it when I see it… Jacobellis v. Ohio (1964)
Jonathan Swift: A footman may swear, but he cannot swear like a lord. He can swear as often, but can he swear with equal delicacy, propriety and judgment?
Jeremy Taylor: Nothing is a greater, or more fearful sacrilege than to prostitute the great name of God to the petulancy of an idle tongue.
Mark Twain: In certain trying circumstances, urgent circumstances, desperate circumstances, profanity furnishes a relief denied even to prayer.
Mark Twain: When angry, count four; when very angry, swear.
Mark Twain: Let us swear while we may, for in heaven it will not be allowed.
UA (Term used to replace vulgarity in the transcripts of the White House recordings of conversations related to the Watergate affair, April, 1974): Expletive deleted.
George Washington: The foolish and wicked practice of profane cursing and swearing is a vice so mean and low, that every person of sense and character detests and despises it.
Robert Zwickey: A phrase of resurrected adolescence in adulthood.

PROOF (See FACTS/LIES; and EVIDENCE)

PROVERB (See ADVICE; CHARLEY CHAN; MAXIMS)

PROXIMATE CAUSE (SEE CAUSATION)

PRUDENCE (See NEGLIGENCE; RISK)

PSYCHIC INJURY (See EMOTIONAL DISTRESS; GRIEF/SORROW)

PUBLIC/PUBLIC OPINION (See MAJORITY)

QUALITY OF LIFE (See AGE/AGING)

QUESTIONS (See ALLEGATIONS; CRITICS; DISCOVERY; ISSUES)

QUOTATIONS/QUOTES (See ADVICE; CHARLEY CHAN; MAXIM)

READ/READING (See BOOKS; TEACHING; WORDS)

REASON/LOGIC

Uncle Anthony: You can't use reason with a bigot – his mind has been sucked dry of any reasons for years.
Uncle Anthony: You can't use reason or logic on only half of what you hear – both sides gotta be considered.
Aunt Mary Carlo: Some people talk about usin' dere reasonin' abilities or logic – I tink everybody uses dere gut.
Aristotle: The law is reason free from passion.
John Quincy Adams (as Secretary of State to William Wert, Attorney General, 1819): I told him (John Marshall) it was law logic – an artificial system of reason, exclusively used in the courts of justice, but good for nothing anywhere else.
Isaac Asimov: Part of the inhumanity of the computer is that, once it is competently programmed and working smoothly, it is completely honest.
Francis Bacon: Logic and rhetoric make men able to contend. Logic differeth from rhetoric as the fist from the palm; the one close, the other at large.
Joan Baez: Hypothetical questions get hypothetical answers.

Bible: 1 Corinthians 4:4: I know nothing by myself.

Bible: 1 Corinthians 8:2: If any man think that he knoweth any thing, he knoweth nothing yet as he ought to know.

Bible: Ecclesiastes 3:1: To every thing there is a season, and a time to every purpose under the heaven.

Bible: Isaiah 1:18: Come now, and let us reason together, saith the Lord.

Bible: Job 34:4: Let us choose to us judgment: let us know among ourselves what is good.

Bible: Proverbs 4:5: Get wisdom, get understanding: forget it not.

Bible: Proverbs 10:14: Wise men lay up knowledge.

Bible: Proverbs 14:6: Knowledge is easy unto him that understandeth.

Bible: Proverbs 15:14: The heart of him that hath understanding seeketh knowledge.

Bible: Romans 16:19: I would have you wise unto that which is good, and simple concerning evil.

Ambrose Bierce: LOGIC, n. The art of thinking and reasoning in strict accordance with the limitations and incapacities of the human misunderstanding....

Ambrose Bierce: RATIONAL, adj. Devoid of all delusions save those of observation, experience and reflection.

Ambrose Bierce: REASON, v.i. To weigh probabilities in the scales of desire.

Ambrose Bierce: REASON, n. Propensitate of prejudice.

Ambrose Bierce: REASONABLE, adj. Accessible to the infection of our own opinions. Hospitable to persuasion, dissuasion and evasion.

Ambrose Bierce: SYLLOGISM, n. A logical formula consisting of a major and a minor assumption and an inconsequent. (See LOGIC.)

Louis Brandeis: Two and two will always make four, despite reports of presidents and financial advisers who insist on stretching it into five.

Louis Brandeis: If we would guide by the light of reason, we must let our minds be bold.

Rita Mae Brown: If the world were a logical place, men would ride side saddle.

Alexis Carrel: Logic never attracts men to the point of carrying them away.

G.K. Chesterton: Do not ever take a fence down until you know the reason why it was put up.

Sir Winston Churchill: True genius resides in the capacity for evaluation of uncertain, hazardous, and conflicting information.

Sir Winston Churchill: Our difficulties and our dangers will not be removed by closing our eyes to them.

Cicero: Reason is the mistress and queen of all things.

Charles Caleb Colton: Logic and metaphysics make use of more tools than all the rest of the sciences put together, and they do the least work.

Greg Cusimano: We need straight line logic for direction and passion for motivation.

Bernard Augustine De Voto: The mind has its own logic but does not often let others in on it.

Thomas Robert Dewar: Minds are like parachutes; they only function when they are open.

William Drummond: He who will not reason, is a bigot; he who cannot is a fool; and he who dares not is a slave.

Lord Dunsany: Logic, like whiskey, loses its beneficial effect when taken in too large quantities.

Albert Einstein (1927 to Max Born with whom he sparred for 3 decades about Quantum Mechanics): Quantum mechanics is certainly imposing, but an inner voice tells me it is not yet the real thing. The theory says a lot, but it does not really bring us any closer to the secrets of the Old One. I at any rate am convinced that **He (GOD) DOES NOT PLAY DICE.**

Werner Erhard: What is is and what isn't isn't.

Al Franken: When you encounter seemingly good advice that contradicts other seemingly good advice, ignore them both.

Felix Frankfurter: The eternal struggle in the law between constancy and change is largely a struggle between history and reason, between past reason and present needs.

Benjamin Franklin: If you will not hear reason, she will surely rap your knuckles.

Galileo Galilei: I do not feel obligated to believe that that same God who has endowed us with sense, reason, and intellect had intended us to forgo their use.

Andre Gide: I dream of new harmonies – a subtler, franker art of words, not rhetorical, not seeking to prove anything. Oh, who will deliver my mind from the heavy chains of logic? My sincerest emotion is distorted as soon as I express it.

Greek Proverb: You cannot reason with a hungry belly; it has no ears.

Dick Gregory: I never believed in Santa Claus because I knew no white dude would come into my neighborhood after dark.

Learned Hand: Indeed, nothing is so likely to lead us astray as abject reliance upon canons of any sort; so much the whole history of verbal interpretation teaches, if it teaches anything.

Burton Hillis: There's a mighty big difference between good, sound reasons and reasons that sound good.

Oliver Wendell Holmes, Jr.: A page of history is worth a volume of logic. *New York Trust co. v. Eisner*, 256 US 345, 65 L ed 963, 41 S Ct 506 (1921)

Oliver Wendell Holmes, Jr.: To generalize is to omit. *Donnell v. Herring-Hall-Marvin Safe Co.*, 208 US 267, 52 L ed 481, 28 S Ct 288 (1908)

Oliver Wendell Holmes, Jr.: Reason means truth and those who are not governed by it take the chance that some day the sunken fact will rip the bottom out of their boat.

Burton Hillis: There's a mighty big difference between good, sound reasons and reasons that sound good.

Thomas Henry Huxley: Logical consequences are the scarecrows of fools and the beacons of wise men.

Italian Proverb: Reason lies between the spur and the bridle.

Thomas Jefferson: Reason and free enquiry are the only effectual agents against error.

Joseph Joubert: Logic works; metaphysics contemplates.

Decimus Junius Juvenal (Roman satirical poet, 40-125 A.D., *Satires*): *Hoc volo, sic ubeo, sit pro ratione voluntas*: It's my will, my command, let that for reason stand.

Joseph Krutch: Logic is the art of going wrong with confidence.

D.H. Lawrence: One truth does not displace another. Even apparently contradictory truths do not displace one another. Logic is far too coarse to make the subtle distinctions life demands.

Don Marquis: We have noticed a disposition on the part of the human race always to take its logic with a chaser.

John Milton: Reason is but choosing.

Sir Thomas More (the story that Sir Thomas More, when asked by an author his opinion of an impertinent book, desired him by all means to put it into verse and bring it to him again. This being done, Sir Thomas looking upon it said): Yea, now it is somewhat like; now it is rhyme; before, it was **neither rhyme nor reason.**

Michael A. Musmanno (Justice of Pennsylvania Supreme Court, 1959): There is no argument in logic so wearisome as that which seeks to prove a point by an irrelevant comparison or one so exaggerated in scope as to make it wholly foreign to the discussion. It is like equating an ant hill with Mount Everest because they are both protuberances from the earth's surface, or comparing a flea with an eagle because they both fly, or a monkey with an elephant because they both eat peanuts. (Dugan v. Pennsylvania Railroad, 37 PA. 39).

John Henry Cardinal Newman: Men may argue badly, but they reason well; that is, their professed grounds are no sufficient measures of their real ones.

John Henry Cardinal Newman: Reason, or the exercise of reason, is a living spontaneous energy within, not an art.

John Henry Cardinal Newman: All men have reason, but not all men can give a reason.

Friedrich Nietzsche: Reason is only a tool.

Blaise Pascal: The heart has its reasons which reason does not know.

Blaise Pascal: We are usually convinced more easily by reasons we have found ourselves than by those which have occurred to others.

Charles Sanders Peirce: Truly, that reason upon which we so plume ourselves, though it may answer for little things, yet for great decisions is hardly surer than a toss-up.

Charles Sanders Peirce: The very first lesson that we have a right to demand that logic shall teach us is, how to make our ideas clear; and a most important one it is, depreciated only by minds who stand in need of it.

Charles Sanders Peirce: Few persons care to study logic, because everybody conceives himself to be proficient enough in the art of reasoning already. But I observe that this satisfaction is limited to one's own ratiocination, and does not extend to that of other men.

Shimon Peres: If a problem has no solution, it may not be a problem, but a fact—not to be solved, but to be coped with over time.

Laurence J. Peter: Against logic, there is no armor like ignorance.

Terry Pratchett: The trouble with having an open mind, of course, is the people will insist on coming along and trying to put things in it.

Ayn Rand: Ever since Kant divorced reason from reality, his intellectual descendents have been diligently widening the breach.

James Harvey Robinson: Most of our so-called reasoning consists in finding arguments for going on believing as we already do.

Will Rogers: "I got no "Philosophy." I don't even know what the word means. The Fourth Reader, (McGuffy's) is as far as I ever got in schools. I am not bragging on it, I am thoroughly ashamed of it for I had every opportunity. Everything I have done has been by luck, no move was premeditated. I just stumbled from one thing to another. I may be making the wrong use of any little talent (if any) that I accidentally have. I don't know."

Will Rogers: Lawyers are like a lot of crafts that many of us live by, great, but useless. One level-headed man could interpret every law there is. If you commit a crime, you either did, or you didn't, without habeas corpus, change of venue, or any other legal shindig. But Lord, if we go into things that are useless, why, two-thirds of the world would have to turn to manual labor. That's really the only essential thing there is.

Bertrand Russell: A stupid man's report of what a clever man says can never be accurate, because he unconsciously translates what he hears into something he can understand.

George Santayana: Habit is stronger than reason.

Franz Schubert: Reason is nothing but the analysis of belief.

Sir Walter Scott: When a man has not a good reason for doing a thing, he has one good reason for letting it alone.

John Seldon (English lawyer and writer, 1584-1654, *Table Talk: Reason*): The reason of a thing is not to be inquired after, till you are sure the thing itself be so. We commonly are at "What's the reason of it?" before we are sure of the thing. It was an excellent question of my Lady Cotton, when Sir Robert Cotton was magnifying of a shoe which was Moses' or Noah's, and wondering at the strange shape and fashion of it; "but Mr. Cotton," says she, "are you sure it is a shoe?"

William H. Seward: Doth not the idiot eat? Doth not the idiot drink? Doth not the idiot know his father and mother?... Think you he does this for nothing? He does it all because he is a man, and because, however imperfectly, he exercises his reason.

William Shakespeare (*The Comedy of Errors*, Act II, ii): ANTIPHOLUS OF SYRACUSE: Shall I tell you why? DROMO OF SYRACUSE: Ay, sir, and wherefore; for they say every why hath a wherefore.

William Shakespeare (*Hamlet*, Act I, v): There are more things in heaven and earth, Horatio, / Than are dreamt of in your philosophy.

William Shakespeare (*Hamlet*, Act III, iv): And reason pandars will.

William Shakespeare (*Henry V*, Act V, v): There is occasions and causes why and wherefore in all things.

William Shakespeare (*Julius Caesar*, Act IV, iii): Good reasons must, of force, give place to better.

William Shakespeare (*Julius Caesar*, Act V, i): But since the affairs of men rest still incertain, / Let 's reason with the worst that may befall.

William Shakespeare (*King John*, Act III, iv): Strong reasons make strong actions.

William Shakespeare (*The Merchant of Venice*, Act I, i): His reasons are as two grains of wheat hid in two bushels of chaff: you shall seek all day ere you find them, and when you have them, they are not worth the search.

William Shakespeare (*A Midsummer-Night's Dream*, Act II, ii): The will of man is by his reason swat'd.

William Shakespeare (*Pericles*, Act I, i): It fits thee not to ask the reason why.

William Shakespeare (*Romeo and Juliet*, Act III, iii): adversity's sweet milk, philosophy.

William Shakespeare (*The Taming of the Shrew*, Act I, i): My reasons are both good and weighty.

George Bernard Shaw: The power of accurate observation is commonly called cynicism by those who have not got it.

Percy Bysshe Shelley: Reason is founded on the evidence of our senses.

Sydney Smith: Never try to reason the prejudice out of a man. It was not reasoned into him, and cannot be reasoned out.

Gloria Steinem: Logic is in the eye of the eye of the logician.

Texas Saying (about likelihood): When you hear approaching hoof beats you don't think zebra, you gotta think horses.

Mark Twain: Life does not consist mainly—or even largely—of facts and happenings. It consists mainly of the storm of thoughts that is forever blowing through one's head.

Mark Twain: Don't you know, there are some things that can beat smartness and foresight? Awkwardness and stupidity can. The best swordsman in the world doesn't need to fear the second best swordsman in the world; no, the person for him to be afraid of is some ignorant antagonist who has never had a sword in his hand before; he doesn't do the thing he ought to.

UA: The mind is like the stomach. It is not how much you put into it that counts, but how much it digests.

Voltaire: Doubt is not a pleasant mental state, but certainty is a ridiculous one.

Jimmy "Beau James" Walker (Mayor of NYC): It takes only one or two reasons for me to like a man, but it takes a hundred for me to dislike him.

Chris Watson (AC Press article "That's Not All, Floks! Lessons Learned From Cartoons Over Into Adult Situations"): ....And Daffy Duck, my favorite of them all (don't laugh unless you tell me yours) showed me there is always more than one way to look at the situation. Daffy's illogical universe had its own logic. That crazy duck taught me to value my idiosyncrasies even when others frowned on them.

Theodore White: Asked why he robbed banks, the notorious American bank robber Willie Sutton is reputed to have remarked, "Because that's where the money is."

Alfred Whitehead: In formal logic, a contradiction is the signal of defeat. But in the evolution of real knowledge it marks the first step in progress towards a victory.

Oscar Wilde: I can stand brute force, but brute reason is quite unbearable. There is something unfair about its use. It is hitting below the intellect.

Oscar Wilde: The fatal errors of life are not due to man's being unreasonable. An unreasonable moment may be one's finest. They are due to man's being logical.

Woodrow Wilson (speaking about Warren Harding): He has a bungalow mind—nothing upstairs.

Woodrow Wilson: Power consists in one's capacity to link his will with the purpose of others, to lead by reason and a gift of cooperation.

W.B. Yeats: People who lean on logic and philosophy and rational exposition end by starving the best part of the mind.

REMEDY (See DAMAGES; LAW)

REPUTATION (See CHARACTER)

RESPONSIBILITY (See NEGLIGENCE)

RIDICULE (See COMEDY; INSULTS)

RISK

Uncle Anthony: Sometimes taking bigger risks make the rewards even sweeter.

Uncle Anthony: It's one thing to take risks with your own life, but taking risks with others is a damn serious crime.

Aunt Mary Carlo: There are guys who are "brinksmen" – they practice "brinksmanship" – they keep pushin' deals up to the brink of what is illegal.

Francis Bacon: If the danger seems slight, then truly it is not slight.

Richard Baxter: Dangers bring fears, and fears more dangers bring.

Bible: 1 Corinthian 11:19: With the jeopardy of their lives they brought it.
Bible: 1 Corinthians 15:30: Why stand we in jeopardy every hour?
Bible: Ezekiel 17:20: I will spread My net upon him, and he shall be taken in My snare.
Bible: Matthew 10:16: I send you forth as sheep in the midst of wolves: be ye therefore wise as serpents, and harmless as doves.
Bible: 1 Peter 5:8: Be sober, be vigilant; because your adversary the devil, as a roaring lion, walketh about, seeking whom he may devour.
Bible: Proverbs 6:28: Can one go upon hot coals, and his feet not be burned?
Bible: Proverbs 7:23: As a bird hasteth to the snare, and knoweth not that it is for his life.
Bible: Psalms 66:12: We went through fire and water.
Bible: 1 Samuel 20:3: There is but a step between me and death.
Ambrose Bierce: ACCOUNTABILITY, n. The mother of caution. "My accountability, bear in mind," / Said the Grand Vizier: "Yes, yes," Said the Shah: "I do – 'tis the only kind / Of ability you possess." Joram Tate.
Ambrose Bierce: DANGER, n. "A savage beast which, when it sleeps, / Man girds at and despises, / But takes himself away by leaps / And bounds when it arises. Ambat Delaso.
Ambrose Bierce: DARING, n. One of the most conspicuous qualities of a man in security.
Ambrose Bierce: SAFETY-CLUTCH, n. A mechanical device acting automatically to prevent the fall of an elevator, or cage, in case of an accident to the hoisting apparatus....
Edmund Burke: Dangers, being despised, grow great.
Byron: Where Mars might quake to tread.
Byron: I have not quailed to danger's brow / When high and happy—need I now?
Byron: For danger levels man and brute, / And all are fellows in their need.
Cervantes: Those who will play with cats must expect to be scratched.
George Chapman: Danger, the spur of all great minds.
George Chapman: Without danger the grant the game grows cold.
Chinese Proverb: He that is afraid to shake the dice will never throw a six.
Chinese Proverb: If you do not enter the tiger's den, you cannot get his cubs.
Sir Winston Churchill: True genius resides in the capacity for evaluation of uncertain, hazardous, and conflicting information.
Sir Winston Churchill: This is no time for ease and comfort. It is the time to dare and endure.
Sir Winston Churchill: Danger—if you meet it promptly and without flinching—you will reduce the danger by half. Never run away from anything. Never!
Sir Winston Churchill: This report, by its very length, defends itself against the risk of being read.
Charles Caleb Colton: Mystery magnifies danger as the fog the sun.
Pierre Corneille: To win without risk is to triumph without glory.
Abraham Cowley: Where one danger's near, / The more remote, though greater, disappear. / So, from the hawk, birds to man's succour flee, / So from fired ships, man leaps into the sea.
E. E. Cummings: We do not believe in ourselves until someone reveals that deep inside us is valuable, worth listening to, worthy of our trust, sacred to our touch. Once we believe in ourselves we can risk curiosity, wonder, spontaneous delight or any experience that reveals the human spirit.
Dennis Dugan: In order to find the edge, you must risk going over the edge.
Albert Einstein: The fear of death is the most unjustified of all fears, for there's no risk of accident for someone who's dead.
T.S. Eliot: Only those who will risk going too far can possibly find out how far one can go.
Havelock Ellis: However well organized the foundations of life may be, life must always be full of risks.
Ralph Waldo Emerson: The Wiseman in the storm praise God, not for safety from danger, but for deliverance from fear.
English Proverb: Danger and the light grow on one's stall.
Euripides: A man who has been in danger / When he comes out of it forgets his fears, / And sometimes he forgets his promises.
Admiral David Glasgow Farragut (Aug. 5, 1864 at the Civil War Battle of Mobile Bay): Damn the torpedoes – full speed ahead!

John Fletcher: Great things through greatest hazards are attained /And then they shine.
Richard Frank: Dangers foreseen are the sooner prevented.
Thomas Fuller: He that fears danger in time seldom feels it.
Thomas Fuller: Danger is next door to security.
Thomas Fuller: He that bringeth himself into needless dangers, dieth the devil's martyr.
Thomas Fuller: Danger past, God is forgotten.
German Proverb: The silent dog is the first to bite.
Andre Gide: One doesn't discover new lands without consenting to lose sight of the shore for a very long time.
Goethe: In comradeship is danger countered best.
George Herbert: Without danger we cannot get beyond danger.
Homer: All on a razor's edge it stands, either woeful ruin or life.
Victor Hugo: Great perils have this beauty, that they bring to light the fraternity of strangers.
William James: It is only by risking our persons from one hour to another that we live at all.
Japanese Proverb: The nail that sticks up will be hammered down.
Jewish Saying: Don't sell the hide of a bear that is still in the woods.
Jewish Saying: If you fight a wave, it overpowers you; let it roll over you.
Flavius Josephus: Great successes never come without risks.
John F. Kennedy: Any danger spot is tenable if men—brave men—will make it so.
Charles Lindbergh (May 13, 1932, 73 days after his baby son was kidnapped, one day after body found on Mt. Rose Rd. 2 miles from Hopewell, near Mercer County, NJ): You can guard against the high percentage of chance, but not chance itself.
Lucan: The mere apprehension of a coming peril has put many into a situation of the utmost danger.
Harold Macmillan: To be alive at all involves some risk.
Walter Mattheau as Oscar Madison (movie "The Odd Couple"): There's no such thing as a sure thing. That's why they call it gambling.
Midrash: A man should not hide all is money in one corner.
Milton: Ye see our danger on the utmost edge / Of hazard, which admits no long debate.
Milton: Danger will wink on opportunity.
Michael A. Musmanno (Justice of Pa. Supreme Court, 1959): Where there are no playgrounds, a boy's instinct for play will exert itself even on the lip of a volcano; and boys must be accepted as boys and not as graybearded savants.
Jawaharlal Nehru: The ploicy of being too cautious is the greatest risk of all.
John Henry Cardinal Newman: We are so constituted, that if we insist upon being as sure as is conceivable, in every step of our course, we must be content to creep along the ground, and can never soar.
Anais Nin: And the day came when the risk to remain tight in a bud was more painful than the risk it took to blossom.
M.P. "Pappy" Papadakis: Out here at the wreckage sight "acceptable risk" doesn't seem so acceptable.
M.P. "Pappy" Papadakis: Have you asked the widow what she thinks about acceptable risk.
General George S. Patton: Take calculated risks. That is quite different from being rash.
Jean Paul Richter: A timid person is frightened before a danger, a coward during the time, and a courageous person afterward.
Will Rogers (Saturday Evening Post, May 19, 1928): "The fellow that furnished the resources ought to have a fair divvy of the loot, and (Ambassador Dwight) Morrow feels they should have it. You know, sometimes the fellow who is putting in his money feels that he ought to have the big end. But, after all, when he gets through he has got his profit and his Investment out. But the one with nothing but the resources, when they are gone, his original investment is blowed up. Nature only put so many resources in the ground and when you happen to own some of 'em, why, you got to nurse your investment along."
Rousseau: Every man has a right to risk his own life in order to preserve it. Has it ever been said that a man throws himself out of the window to escape from a fire is guilty of suicide?
Russian Proverb: Fear the goat from the front, the horse from the rear, and man from all sides.
Russian Proverb: The tallest blade of grass is the first to be cut by the scythe.

Frank Scully: Why not go out on a limb? Isn't that where the fruit is?

Historian William W. Sears (about Civil War General George B. McClellan): He was so fearful of losing, he would not risk winning.

Seneca: Constant exposure to dangers will breed contempt for them.

Seneca: Blind panic is incapable of providing even for its own safety, for it does not avoid danger, but runs away. Yet we are more exposed to danger when we turn our backs.

Seneca: No one can with safety expose himself often to danger. The man who has often escaped is caught at last.

Seneca: The danger that is nearest we least dread.

Madame de Sevigne: There is no person who is not dangerous for someone.

William Shakespeare (*Hamlet,* Act V, i): For, though I am not splenitive and rash, / Yet have I something in me dangerous.

William Shakespeare (*I Henry IV*, Act I, iii): Send danger from the east unto the west, / So honour cross it from the north to south.

William Shakespeare (*Julius Caesar*, Act I, ii): Beware the ides of March.

William Shakespeare (*Julius Caesar*, Act III, i): Caesar: The ides of March are come. / Soothsayer: Ay, Caesar; but not gone.

William Shakespeare (*Julius Caesar,* Act IV, iii): There is no terror, Cassius, in your threats, / For I am arm'd so strong in honesty / That they pass by me as the idle wind, / Which I respect not.

William Shakespeare (*King John*, Act III, iv): He that stands upon a slippery place / Makes nice of no vile hold to stay him up.

William Shakespeare (*King Lear*, Act III, iv): Thou'ldst shun a bear; / But if thy flight lay toward the raging sea, / Thou'ldst meet the bear i' the mouth.

William Shakespeare (*The Merchant of Venice*, Act III, v): When I shun Scylla, your father, I fall in Charybdis, your mother.

William Shakespeare (*Venus and Adonis*, l. 690): Danger deviseth shifts; wit waits on fear.

William Shakespeare (*Venus and Adonis,* 1593, 788): The path is smooth that leadeth on to danger.

Alexander Smith: Everything is sweetened by risk.

Gertrude Stein: Everybody knows if you are too careful you are so occupied in being careful that you are sure to stumble over something.

Adlai E. Stevenson: In America, anyone can become president. That's one of the risks you take.

Publilius Syrus: Danger comes the sooner when despised.

Publilius Syrus: A danger is never overcome without danger.

Talmud: Better a little pumpkin in your hand than a big one in the field.

Thucydides: When tremendous dangers are involved, no one can be blamed for looking to his own interest.

Mark Twain: Well, then, says I, what's the use you learning to do right, when it's troublesome to do right and ain't no trouble to do wrong, and the wages is just the same?

Mark Twain: The serene confidence which a Christian feels in four aces.

Mark Twain: Don't you know, there are some things that can beat smartness and foresight? Awkwardness and stupidity can. The best swordsman in the world doesn't need to fear the second best swordsman in the world; no, the person for him to be afraid of is some ignorant antagonist who has never had a sword in his hand before; he doesn't do the thing he ought to.

Elie Wiesel: Friendship marks a life even more deeply than love. Love risks degenerating into obsession, friendship is never anything but sharing.

Flip Wilson: You can't expect to hit the jackpot if you don't put a few nickels in the machine.

Jeanette Winterson: What you risk reveals what you value.

UA: Danger itself is the best remedy for danger.

UA: He that would sail without danger must never come on the main sea.

UA (1989, British TV program entitled): Don't Try This At Home.

Vincent Van Gogh: The fishermen know that the sea is dangerous and the storm terrible, but they have never found these dangers sufficient reason for remaining ashore.

RUMORS (See LIES)

SADNESS (See EMOTIONAL DISTRESS; GRIEF/SORROW)

SAFETY (See RISK)

SCIENCE & TECHNOLOGY (See also COMPUTERS; EXPERTS)

Uncle Anthony: You don't try a case or fight a war (or win an argument) with a computer, you stand up and slug it out face to face in the courtroom or on the battlefield.

Uncle Anthony: Wit all that technology stuff ya still can't make a will or do a sales contract for five bucks?

Aunt Mary Carlo: Thomas, wit' all 'dis machinery, are you really a better lawyer? You still gotta talk to people don'tcha?

Edward Abbey: That which today calls itself science gives us more and more information, an indigestible glut of information, and less and less understanding.

James T. Adams: Scientific knowledge is constantly changing. A discovery of one year receives confirmation the next or is thrown aside.

Charles M. Allen: If the human race wants to go to hell in a basket, technology can help it get there by jet. It won't change the desire or the direction, but it can greatly speed the passage.

Sherwood Anderson (1926): The machine (herded) men into towns and cities, the age of the factory.... Men all began to dress alike, eat the same foods, read the same kind of newspapers and books. Minds began to be standardized as were the clothes men wore.

Isaac Asimov: The most exciting phrase to hear in science, the one that heralds new discoveries, is not "Eureka!" (I found it!) but "That's funny ..."

Leo Baeck: Every answer given arouses new questions. The progress of science is matched by an increase in the hidden and mysterious.

Arthur Balfour: Science is the greatest instrument of social change... the most vital of all revolutions which have marked the development of modern civilizations.

Jacques Barzun: It is not clear to anyone, least of all the practitioners, how science and technology in their head along the course do or should influence ethics and law, education and the government, art and social philosophy, religion and the life of the affections. Yet science has an all pervasive energy, for it is at once a mode of thought, a source of strong emotion, and a faith as fanatical as any in history.

Jacques Barzun: For the educated, the authority of science rested on the strictness of its method; for the mass, it rested on its powers of explanation.

Henry Ward Beecher: A tool is but the extension of a man's hand, and a machine is but a complex tool. He that invents a machine augments the power of a man and the well-being of mankind.

Bible: Ecclesiastes 1:9: There is no new thing under the sun.

Ambrose Bierce: BOTANY, n. The science of vegetables – those that are not good to eat, as well as those that are. It deals largely with their flowers, which are commonly badly designed, inartistic in color, and ill-smelling.

Ambrose Bierce: ETHNOLOGY, n. The science that treats of the various tribes of Man, as robbers, thieves, swindlers, dunces, lunatics, idiots and ethnologists.

Ambrose Bierce: GRAVITATION, n. The tendency of all bodies to approach one another with a strength proportioned to the quality of matter they contain – the quantity of matter they contain being ascertained by the strength of their tendency to approach one another. This is a lovely and edifying illustration of how science, having made A the proof of B, makes B the proof of A.

Ambrose Bierce: INVENTOR, n. A person who makes an ingenious arrangement of wheels, levers and springs, and believes it civilization.

Ambrose Bierce: NEWTONIAN, adj. Pertaining to a philosophy of the universe, invented by Newton, who discovered that an apple will fall to the ground, but was unable to say why. His successors and disciples have advanced so far as to be able to say when.

Ambrose Bierce: OBSERVATORY, n. A place where astronomers conjecture away the guesses of their predecessors.

Murray Bookchin: Once regarded as the herald of enlightenment in all spheres of knowledge, science is now increasingly seen as a strictly instrumental system of control. Its use as a means of social manipulation and its role in restricting human freedom now parallel in every detail its use as a means of natural manipulation.

Daniel Boorstin: Just as the American's love affair with his land produced pioneering adventures and unceasing excitement in the conquest of the continent, so to his latter-day romance with the Machine produced pioneering adventures—of a new kind... there were no boundaries to a machine-made a world.

Hal Borland: Consider the wheelbarrow. It may lack the grace of an airplane, the speed of an automobile, the initial capacity of a freight car, but its humble wheel marked out the path of what civilization we still have. Particularly that phase of civilization which leads down Main Street, through the front gate, around the house and into the back garden.

Kenneth E. Boulding: Society produces technology and technology produces society in an endless mesh of action and interaction.

Omar Bradley (1948): We have grasped the mystery of the atom and rejected the Sermon on the Mount.

Jacob Bronowski: That is the essence of science: ask an impertinent question, and you are on the way to the pertinent answer.

John Burroughs: To treat your facts with imagination is one thing, to imagine your facts is quite another.

Benjamin Cardozo: Often a liberal antidote of experience supplies a sovereign cure for a paralyzing abstraction built upon a theory.

Rachel Carson: We live in a scientific age, yet we assume that knowledge of science is the prerogative of only a small number of human beings, isolated and priestlike in their laboratories. This is not true. The materials of science are the materials of life itself. Science is part of the reality of living; it is the what, the how and the why for everything in our inexperience.

Erwin Chargaff: Science is wonderfully equipped to answer the question "How?" But it gets terribly confused when you ask the question "Why?"

Noam Chomsky: As soon as questions of will or decision or reason or choice of action arise, human science is at a loss.

Sir Winston Churchill: The latest refinements of science are linked with the cruelties of the Stone Age.

Barry Commoner: The gap between brute power and human need continues to grow, as the power fattens on the same faulty technology that intensifies the need.

Barry Commoner: Despite the dazzling successes of modern technology and the unprecedented power of modern military systems, they suffer from a common and catastrophic fault. While providing us with a bountiful supply of food, with great industrial plants, with high-speed transportation, and with military weapons of unprecedented power, they threaten our very survival.

Karl Taylor Compton: In recent times, modern science has developed to give mankind, for the first time in the history of the human race, a way of securing a more abundant life which does not simply consist in taking away from someone else.

e. e. cummings: Take the so called standard of living. What do most people mean by "living"? They don't mean living. They mean the latest and closest pleural approximation to singular prenatal passivity which science, in its finite but unbounded wisdom, has succeeded in selling their wives.

John Dewey: Science through its physical technological consequences is now determining the relations which human beings, severally and in groups, sustain to one another. If it is incapable of developing moral techniques which will also determine these relations, the split in modern culture goes so deep that not only democracy but all civilized values are doomed.

John Dewey: Every great advance in science has issued from a new audacity of imagination.

J. Frank Dobie: Putting on the spectacles of science in expectation of finding the answer to everything looked at signifies inner blindness.

Rene Dubos: Most of the dangerous aspects of technological civilization arise, not from its complexities, but from the fact that modern man has become more interested in the machines and industrial goods themselves than in their use to human ends.

John Foster Dulles: Natural science has outstripped moral and political science. That is too bad; but it is a fact, and the fact does not disappear because we close our eyes to it.

Will Durant: Every science begins as philosophy and ends as art.

Freeman Dyson: Science and technology, like all original creations of the human spirit, are unpredictable. If we had a reliable way to label our toys good and bad, it would be easy to regulate technology wisely. But we can rarely see far enough ahead to know which road leads to damnation. Whoever concerns himself with big technology, either to push it forward or to stop it, is gambling in human lives.

Anthony Eden: Every succeeding scientific discovery makes greater nonsense of old-time conceptions of sovereignty.

Albert Einstein (to friend Max Born): Physics should represent a reality in time and space, free from SPOOKY ACTION AT A DISTANCE.

Alice Embree: America's technology has turned in upon itself; its corporate form makes it the servant of profits, not the servant of human needs.

Albert Einstein: Why does this magnificent applied science which saves work and makes life easier bring us so little happiness? The simple answer runs: Because we have not yet learned to make sensible use of it.

Albert Einstein: The whole of science is nothing more than a refinement of every day thinking.

Albert Einstein: Concern for man himself and his fate must always form the chief interest of all technical endeavors.... Never forget this in the midst of your diagrams and equations.

Albert Einstein: Science can only ascertain what <u>is</u>, but not what <u>should be</u>, and outside of its domain value judgments of all kinds remain necessary.

Albert Einstein: Science without religion is lame, religion without science is blind.

Milton S. Eisenhower: Modern man worships at the temple of science, but science tells him only what is possible, not what is right.

Loren Eisley: In the end, science as we know it has two basic types of practitioners. One is the educated man who still has a controlled sense of wonder before the universal mystery, whether it hides in a snail's eye or within the light that impinges on that delicate organ. The second kind of observer is the extreme reductionist who is so busy stripping things apart that the tremendous mystery has been reduced to a trifle, to intangibles not worth troubling one's head about.

Alice Embree: America's technology has turned in upon itself; its corporate form makes it the servant of profits, not the servant of human needs.

Doug Ferrari: MTV is the lava lamp of the 1980's.

Abraham Flexner: Science, in the very act of solving problems, creates more of them.

Eric Fromm: The danger of the past was that men became slaves. The danger of the future is that men may be, robots.

J. William Fulbright: Science has radically changed the conditions of human life on Earth. It has expanded our knowledge and our power but not our capacity to use them with wisdom.

John Kenneth Galbraith: It is a commonplace of modern technology that problems have solutions before there is knowledge of how they are to be solved.

George Francis Gilette: (By 1940) the theory of relativity will be considered a joke.

Goethe: Goethe: Science and art along to the whole world, and before them vanish the barriers of nationality.

Ellen Goodman: Once upon a time we were just plain people. But that was before we began having relationships with mechanical systems. Get involved with the machine and sooner or later you are reduced to a factor.

Ellen Goodman: Throughout my childhood, it was clear that (phone) lines were not for conversation but for announcements. We were as likely to reach out and touch someone by telephone as we were to communicate by using a cattle prod. Casual phoning was as rare as casual sex.

Michael Harrington: If there is technological advance without social advance, there is, almost automatically, an increase in human misery.

Al Harwitz: The modern marvels of modern technology include the development of a soda can which, when discarded, will last forever—and a $7,000 car which, when properly cared for, will rust out in two or three years.

Frank Herbert: The function of science fiction is not always to predict the future but sometimes to prevent it.

Philip Hilts: In all human activities, it is not ideas or machines that dominate; it is people. I have heard people speak of "the effect of personality on science." But this is a backward thought. Rather, we should talk about the effect of science on personalities. Science is not the dispassionate analysis of impartial data. It is the human, and thus passionate, exercise of skill and sense on such data. Science is not an exercise in objectivity, but, more accurately, an exercise in which objectivity is prized.

Mahlon Hoagland: As children we all possess a natural, uninhibited curiosity, a hunger for acts what they, which seems to die slowly as we age—suppressed, I suppose, by the high-value replays on conformity and by the need not to appear ignorant. It betokens a conviction that somehow science is innately incomprehensible. It precludes reaching deeper, thereby denying the profound truth that understanding enriches experience, that explanation vastly enhances the beauty of the natural world in the eye of the beholder.

Mahlon Hoagland: It is often the scientist's experience that he sense is the nearness of truth when... connections are envisioned. A connection is a step toward simplification, unification. Simplicity is indeed often the sign of truth and a criterion of beauty.

Elbert Hubbard: One machine can do the work of fifty ordinary man. No machine can do the work of one extraordinary man.

Edwin Powell Hubble: Equipped with his five senses, man explores the universe around him and calls the adventure Science.

Thomas Hughes: Modern technology was made in America.

Thomas Hughes: By 1900 (Americans) had reached the promised land of the technological world, the world as artifact. In doing so they had acquired trades that have become characteristically American. A nation of machine makers and system builders, they became imbued with a drive for order, system, and control.

Aldous Huxley (*Brave New World*; spoken by one of the biologically engineered and mass produced "Epsilon" leaders): "All our science is just a cookery book, with an othodox theory of cooking that nobody is allowed to question, and a list of recipes that mustn't be added to except by special permission from the Head Cook. I'm the Head Cook now, but I was an inquisitive young scullion once...."

Thomas Huxley: The great tragedy of Science—slaying of a beautiful hypothesis by an ugly fact.

Robert Johnson: Science cannot bear the thought that there is an important natural phenomenon which it cannot hope to explain even with unlimited time and money.

Helen Keller: Science may have found a cure for most evils; but it has found no remedy for the worst of them all – the apathy of human beings.

John F. Kennedy: Every time you scientists make a major invention, we politicians have to invent an institution to cope with it—and almost invariably, these days, it must be an international institution.

Martin Luther King Jr.: Our scientific power has outgrown our spiritual power. We have guided missiles and misguided men.

Charles Lamb: Can we unlearn the arts that pretend to civilize, and then burn the world? There is a march of science; but who shall be the drums for its retreat?

Paul Langevin (on Albert Einstein's move to Princeton New Jersey, from Germany in 1933): It's as important in event as would be the transfer of the Vatican from Rome to the new world. The Pope of Physics has moved in. The United States will now become the center of the natural sciences.

Louis H. Lapham: Without meaning to belittle the wonders of science, I do not think they can absolve mankind of suffering, desire, madness, and death.

H.W. Lewis: It is a curious paradox that aversion of future harm seems more important than the promise of future benefit. That was not always true. Those who are unwilling to invest in the future have not earned one.

David E. Lilienthal: The machine that frees a man's back of drudgery does not thereby make his spirit free. Technology has made us more productive, but it does not necessarily enrich our lives. In two years it can build us great dams, but only great people make a valley great. There is no technology of goodness. Men must make themselves spiritually free.

Charles A. Lindbergh: At the end of the first half-century of engine-driven flight, we are confronted with the stark fact that the historical significance of aircraft has been primarily military and destructive.

Walter Lippmann: You cannot endow even the best machine with initiative; the jolliest steamroller will not plant flowers.

Louis Lozowick: The history of America is a history of gigantic engineering feats and colossal mechanical construction.

S.E. Luria: Significant advances in science often have a peculiar quality: they contradict obvious, commonsense opinions.

S.E. Luria: Everyone knows that in the research there are no final answers, only insights that allow one to formulate new questions.

S.E. Luria: The world of science may be the only existing participatory democracy.

Norman Mailer: Television pollutes identity.

Judith Martin (Miss Manners' *Guide for the Turn of the Millennium*, 1989): *Call Waiting.* One of Miss Manners' least favorite devices, this is like a child screaming for attention while one is on the telephone. It is possible that the scream is "There's a fire in the kitchen," but demands to pay attention to a ringing telephone while you are already on the telephone constitute the rude policy of "Last come, first served."

Louise Mattage: Well I'll tell you what a phone is for. It's for not looking someone in the eyeball and saying I love you.

Karl Marx: Bourgeous scientists make sure that their theories are not dangerous to God or to capital.

H. L. Mencken: Science, at bottom, is really anti-intellectual. It always distrusts pure reason, and demands the production of objective fact.

Harvey Milk: Isn't it strange that as technology advances, the quality of life frequently declines?

Newton Minow (1961): When television is good, nothing – not the theater, not the magazines or newspapers – nothing is better. But when television is bad, nothing is worse. I invite you to sit down in front of your television set when your station goes on the air and stay there without a book, magazine, newspaper, profit-and-loss sheet, or rating book to distract you, and keep your eyes glued to that set until the station signs off. I can assure you that you will observe a vast wasteland.

George Moore: The world is dying of machinery; that is the great disease, that is the great disease, that is the plague that will sweep away and destroy civilization; man will have to rise against it sooner or later.

Lewis Mumford: By his very success in inventing laborsaving devices, modern man has manufactured an abyss of boredom that only the privileged classes in earlier civilizations have ever fathomed.

Lewis Mumford: What is important to realize is that automation... is an attempt to exercise control, not only of the mechanical process itself, but of the human being who once directed it: turning him from an active to a passive agent, and finally illuminating him altogether.

Lewis Mumford: For those of us who have thrown off the myth of the machine, the next move is ours: for the gates of the technocratic prison will open automatically, despite their rusty ancient hinges, as soon as we choose to walk out.

Richard M. Nixon (1959): Television is not so effective now as it was in 1952. The novelty has worn off. There is a very early point of diminishing returns in using television. Both parties did too much of it in the 1956 campaign. People probably got tired of seeing favorite programs thrown off for political speeches.

David Noble: Modern technology has lost its magic. No longer do people stand in awe, thrilled by the onward rush of science, the promise of a new day. Instead, the new is suspect. It arouses our hostility as much as it used to excite our fancy. With each breakthrough there are recurrent fears and suspicion. How will the advance further pollute our lives; modern technology is not merely what it first appears to be. Behind the white coats, the disarming jargon, the elaborate instrumentation, and at the core of what has often seemed an automatic process, one finds what Dorothy found in Oz: modern technology is human after all.

Sir William Olser: In science, the credit goes to the man who convinces the world, not to the man to whom the idea first occurs.

J. Robert Oppenheimer: In some sort of crude sense which no vulgarity can quite extinguish, no humor, no overstatement can quite extinguish, the physicists have known sin; and this is a knowledge which they cannot lose.

J. Robert Oppenheimer: The open society, the unrestricted access to knowledge, the unplanned and uninhibited association of men for its furtherance—these are what may make a vast, complex, ever growing, ever-changing, even more specialized and expert technological world, nevertheless a world of human community.

J. Robert Oppenheimer: Both the man of science and the man of art live always at the edge of mystery, surrounded by it. Both, as the measure of their creation, have always had to do with the harmonization of what is new with what is familiar, with the balance between novelty and synthesis, with the struggle to make partial order in total chaos.... This cannot be an easy life.

Lewis Orr: Science will never be able to reduce the value of a sunset to arithmetic. Nor can it reduce friendship to a formula. Laughter and love, pain and loneliness, the challenge of accomplishment in living, and the depth of insight into beauty and truth: these will always surpass the scientific mastery of nature.

Cynthia Ozick: I'm not afraid of facts, I welcome facts *but a congery of facts is not equivalent to an idea.* This is the essential fallacy of the so-called "scientific" mind. People who mistake facts for ideas are incomplete thinkers; they are gossips.

Heinz Pagels: Science provides a vision of reality seen from the perspective of reason, a perspective that sees the vast order of the universe, living and nonliving matter, as a material system governed by rules that can be known by the human mind. It is a powerful vision, formal and austere but strangely silent about many of the questions that deeply concerned us. Science shows us what exists but not what to do about it.

Abraham Pais (on particle physics in early 1950's): It was a wonderful mass at that time. Wonderful! Just great! It was so confusing—physics at its best, when everything is confused and you know something important lies just around the corner.

Charles Sanders Peirce: There is one thing even more vital to science than intelligent methods; and that is, the sincere desire to find out the truth, whatever it may be.

Arno Penzias: Either we've seen the birth of the universe, or we've seen a pile of pigeon shit.

Robert M. Pirsig: One geometry cannot be more true than another; it can only be more *convenient.* Geometry is not true, it is advantageous.

Robert M. Pirsig: One geometry (EDITOR: or ONE MEDICINE/ECONOMICS/ETC) cannot be more true than another; it can only be more *convenient.* Geometry is not true, it is advantageous.

Ronald Reagan: I guess television just has more power than any of us know.

Al Ries: Today: communication itself is the problem. We have become the world's first overcommunicated society. Each year we send more and receive less.

Will Rogers: Nothing you can't spell will ever work.

Will Rogers: America is a nation that conceives many odd inventions for getting somewhere but it can think of nothing to do once it gets there.

Will Rogers: Technocracy wants to do everything by machinery... Machinery is doing just fine. If it can't kill you, it will put you out of work.

Will Rogers: Just flew in from Santa Barbara and found a real, legitimate use for my polo field. We landed on it.

Will Rogers: There has been and will be lots of fine pilots lost in developing aviation to such a point that it will be safe for a lot of folks less useful to the world than these fine young fellows are.

Will Rogers: If there is a safer mode of transportation (EDITOR: than the airplane) I have never found it."

Bertrand Russell: If science could operate unchecked, it would soon produce a single world state.

Carl Sagan: There is a lurking fear that some things are "not meant" to be known, that some inquiries are too dangerous for human beings to make.

Carl Sagan: Skeptical scrutiny is the means, in both science and religion, by which deep insight can be winnowed from deep nonsense.

Arthur L. Samuel: A machine is not a genie, it does not work by magic, it does not possess a will, and (Norbert) Wiener to the contrary, nothing comes out which has not been put in, barring of course, and in frequent case of malfunctioning. Oh... The "intentions" which the machine seems to manifest are the intentions of the human programmer, as specified in advance, or they are subsidiary intentions derived from these, following rules specified by the programmer.... The machine will not and cannot do any of these things until it has been instructed as to how to proceed.... To believe otherwise is either to believe in magic or to believe that the existence of man's will. It is an illusion and that man's actions are as mechanical as the machine's.

William Shakespeare (*All's Well That Ends Well,* Act V, iii): Plutus himself, / That knows the tinct and multiplying medicine, / Hath not in nature's mystery more science / Than I have in this ring.

William Shakespeare (*As You Like It,* Act IV, iii): This is a man's invention, and his hand.

William Shakespeare (*Hamlet,* Act I, v): There are more things in heaven and earth, Horatio, / Than are dreamt of in your philosophy.

William Shakespeare (*Henry V,* Act V, ii): (We) do not learn for want of time / The sciences which should become our country.

William Shakespeare (*Julius Caesar,* Act IV, iii): Of your philosophy you make no use, / If you give place to accidental evils.

William Shakespeare (*Love's Labour's Lost,* Act I, i): Small have continual plodders ever won / Save base authority from others' books. / These earthly godfathers of heaven's lights / That give a name to every fixed star / Have no more profit of their shining nights / Than those that walk and wot not what they are. / Too much to know is to know nought but fame; And every godfather can give a name.

William Shakespeare (*The Taming of the Shrew,* Act III, i): I am not so nice / To change true rules for old inventions.

William Shakespeare (*Tempest,* Act V, i): O brave new world, That has such people in't!

Jean Shepherd (*In God We Trust, All Others Pay Cash,* 1966): I have long had a suspicion that an entire generation of Americans grew up feeling inferior to just the *names* of the guys on the radio. Pierre Andre. Harlow Wilcox. Vincent Pelletier. Truman Bradley. Westbrook Van Voorhees. Andre Baruch. Norman Brokenshire. There wasn't a Charlie Schmidlap in the lot.

B.F. Skinner: The real problem is not whether machines think but whether men do.

CP Snow: Scientists have it within them to know what a future-directed society feels like, for science itself, in its human aspect, is just that.

Adlai Stevenson: Technology while adding daily to our physical ease, grows daily another loop of fine wire around our souls. It contributes hugely to our mobility, which we must not confuse with freedom. The extensions of our senses, which we find so fascinating, are not adding to the discrimination of our minds, since we need increasingly to take the reading of a needle on the dial to discover whether we think something is good or bad, or right or wrong.

Adlai Stevenson: There is no boredom or misery to equal the pursuit of distraction alone. We do not slip into happiness. It is strenuously sought and earned. A nation glued to the television screen is not simply at a loss before the iron pioneers of the new collective society. It isn't even having a good time.

Gertrude Stein: Everybody gets so much information all day long that they lose their common sense.

Thomas Szasz: Formerly, when religion was strong and science weak, men mistook magic for medicine; now, when science is strong and religion weak, men mistake medicine for magic.

Booth Tarkenton: Mystics always hope that science will someday overtaken them.

Edward Teller: If there ever was a misnomer, it is "exact science." Science has always been full of mistakes. The present day he is no exception. And our mistakes are good mistakes; they require a genius to correct them. Of course, we do not see our own mistakes.

Alvin Toffler: Our technological powers increase, but the side effects and potential hazards also escalate.

Alvin Toffler: That great, growing engine of change—technology.

Alvin Toffler: Technology feeds on itself. Technology makes more technology possible.

Alvin Toffler: Each new machine or technique, in a sense, changes all existing machines and techniques, by permitting us to put them together into new combinations. The number of possible combinations rises exponentially as the number of new machines or techniques rises arithmetically. Indeed, each new combination may, itself, be regarded as a new super-machine.

Robert Trivers: I want to change the way people think about their everyday lives. How you think is going to affect who you marry, what kind of relationship you establish, weather and in what manner you reproduce. That's day-to-day thinking, right? But they don't even teach courses on that stuff.... life *is* intrinsically biological. It's absurd not to use our best biological concept.

Mark Twain: (Christian nations are the most enlightened and progressive) in spite of their religion, not because of it. The Church has opposed every innovation and discovery from the day of Galileo down to our own time, when the use of anesthetics in child-birth was regarded as a sin because it avoided the biblical curse pronounced against Eve.

Mark Twain: There is something fascinating about science. One gets such wholesale returns of conjecture of such a trifling investment of fact.

Mark Twain: All the modern inconveniences.

Johann Von Newman: In mathematics you don't understand things; you get used to them.

James D. Watson: Science seldom proceeds in the straightforward logical manner imagined by outsiders. Instead, it steps forward (and sometimes backward) are often very human events in which personalities and cultural traditions play major roles.... (Science moves with) the spirit of and it venture characterized both by youthful arrogance and by the belief that the truth, once found, would be simple as well as pretty.

Jonathan Weiner: Specialization has gotten account of hand. There are more branches in the tree of knowledge then there are in the tree of life. A petrologist studies rocks; a pedologist studies soils. The first one sieves the soil and froze away the rocks. The second one picks up the rocks and brushes off the soil. Out in the field, they bump into each other only like Laurel and Hardy, by accident, when they are both backing up.

Victor Weisskopf: Science is an important part of the humanities because it is based on an essential human trait: curiosity about the how and why of our environment. We must foster wonder, joy of insight.

Victor Weiskopf: The history of physics shows that deeper insights into the nature of things are best achieved with distance from daily experience.

Victor Weiskopf: Some people maintain that scientific insight has eliminated the need for meaning. I do not agree. The scientific worldview established the notion that there is a sense and purpose in the development of the universe when it recognized the evolution from the primal explosion to matter, life, and humanity. In humans, nature begins to recognize itself.

Orson Welles (concluding remarks on the Mercury Theater of the Air radio production of "The War of the Worlds," Oct. 30, 1938): Remember please, for the next day or so, the terrible lesson you learned tonight: That grinning, glowing, globular invader of your living room is an inhabitant of the Punkin Patch, and if your doorbell rings and nobody's there, that was no Martian—its Halloween!

Rebecca West: Before a war, military science seems like a real science, like astronomy; but after a war, it seems more like astrology.

Harvey Wheeler: The goal is to understand the plan of creation, period.

Oscar Wilde: The evil that machinery is doing is not merely in the consequences of its work but in the fact that it makes men themselves machines also.

Edward O. Wilson: The audaciously disruptive tendencies of our species run deep and are poorly understood. They are so difficult to probe and manage as to suggest an archaic biological origin. We run a risk if we continue to diagnose them as byproducts of history and suppose that maybe he erased with simple economic and political remedies.

Edward O. Wilson: Important science is not just any similarity glimpsed for the first time. It offers analogues that map the gateways to one explored terrain.

Edward O. Wilson: To a considerable degree science consists in originating the maximum amount of information with the minimum expenditure of energy. Beauty is the cleanness of line in which formulations, along with symmetry, surprise, and congruence with other prevailing beliefs.

Robert Wilson: As a builder of accelerators, I could thrill to what appeared to me to be a medieval physicist responding to a very challenging physical problem. I saw the similarity between the cathedral and the accelerator. The one structure was intended to reach a soaring height in space; the other is intended to reach a comparable height in energy.

E. B. White (1939): One of the chief pretenders to the throne of God is radio itself, which has acquired a sort of omniscience. I live in a strictly rural community, and people here speak of "The Radio" in the large sense, with an over-meaning. When they say "The Radio" they don't mean a cabinet, an electrical phenomenon, or a man in a studio, they refer to a pervading and somewhat godlike presence which has come into their lives and homes.

Frank Lloyd Wright (speaking about television): Chewing gum for the eyes.

Chen Ning Yang: We did not know how to make the theory fit experiment. It was our judgment, however, that the beauty of the idea alone merited attention.

SEARCH (See DISCOVERY)

SETTLEMENT (See COMPROMISE)

SEX

Uncle Anthony: Sex education in school? I guess it's better than learning in the back seat of a car.
Aunt Mary Carlo: Fer a girl wit no principle, she draws alotta interest.
Aunt Mary Carlo: She may call 'erself a "Miss" but she don't miss a lot.
Aunt Mary Carlo: I tink she's been run around more desks in dat office den da vacuum cleaner.
Woody Allen: Having sex is like playing bridge. If you don't have a good partner, you'd better have a good hand.
Woody Allen: My brain is my second favorite organ.
Woody Allen: Sex is dirty only when it is done right.
Woody Allen: The difference between sex and love is that sex relieves tension and love causes it.
Woody Allen: Her figure described a set of parabolas that could cause cardiac arrest in a yak.
Tallulah Bankhead: I am not promiscuous, you know. Promiscuity implies that attraction is not necessary.
Matt Barry: Leaving sex to the feminists is like letting your dog vacation at the taxidermist.
Bible: Exodus 20:2: Thou shalt not commit adultery.... Thou shalt not covet thy neighbour's house, thou shalt not covet thy neighbour's wife, nor his manservant, nor his ox, nor his ass, nor any thing that is thy neighbour's.
Bible: Matthew 5:28: Whosoever looketh on a woman to lust after her hath committed adultery with her already in his heart.
Bible: Matthew 5:32; Mark 10:11: But I say unto you, that whosoever shall put away his wife, saving for the cause of fornication, causeth her to commit adultery: and whosoever shall marry her that is divorced commiteth adultery.
Bible: Proverbs 6:24: Keep thee from the evil woman, from the flattery of the tongue of a strange woman.
Bible: Proverbs 6:25: Lust not after her beauty in thine heart; neither let her take thee with her eyelids.
Bible: Proverbs 6:28: Can one go upon hot coals, and his feet not be burned?
Bible: Proverbs 7:22: He goeth after her straightway, as an ox goeth to the slaughter.
Bible: Proverbs 31:3: Give not thy strength unto women, nor thy ways to that which destroyeth kings.
Ambrose Bierce: ARDOR, n. The quality that distinguishes love without knowledge.
Ambrose Bierce: CUPID, n. The so-called god of love. This bastard creation of a barbarous fancy was no doubt inflicted upon mythology for the sins of its dieties. Of all unbeautiful and inappropriate conceptions this is the most reasonless and offensive. The notion of symbolizing sexual love by a semi-sexless baby, and comparing the pains of passion to the wounds of an arrow – of introducing this pudgy homunculus into art grossly to materialize the subtle spirit and suggestion of the work – this is eminently worthy of the age that, giving its birth, laid it on the doorstep of posterity.
Ambrose Bierce: LOVE, n. A temporary insanity curable by marriage or by the removal of the patient from the influences under which he incurred the disorder. This disease, like *caries* and many other ailments, is prevalent only among civilized races under artificial conditions; barbarous nations breathing pure air and eating simple food enjoy immunity from its ravages. It is sometimes fatal, but more frequently to the physician than to the patient.
Ambrose Bierce: SALACITY, n. A certain literary quality frequently observed in popular novels, especially in those written by women and young girls, who give it another name and think that in introducing it they are occupying a neglected field of letters and reaping an overlooked harvest. If they have the misfortune to live long enough they are tormented with a desire to burn their sheaves.
Charles Boyer (in the film *Algiers*, said to Hedy Lamarr): Come with me to the Casbah!
Malcolm Bradbury: If God meant for us to have group sex, He'd have given us more organs.
George Burns: Sex at age 90 is like trying to shoot pool with a rope. Even putting my cigar in its holder is a thrill.
George Burns: Sex is one of the nine reasons for reincarnation. The other eight are unimportant.

Barbara Bush (Former US First Lady): Clinton lied. A man might forget where he parks or where he lives, but he never forgets oral sex, no matter how bad it is.

Clairol ad slogan (for hair-colouring, 1955): Does she or dosen't she? ... only her hairdresser knows for sure.

Albert Camus: Women in the street. The warm beast of desire that lies curled up in our loins and stretches itself with a fierce gentleness.

Truman Capote: The good thing about masturbation is that you don't have to dress up for it.

Sir Winston Churchill: It is impossible to obtain a conviction for sodomy from an English jury. Half of them don't believe that it can physically be done, and the other half are doing it.

Tom Clancy: I believe that sex is one of the most beautiful, natural, wholesome things that money can buy.

C. Everett Coop (former Surgeon General): Do not have sex with people you do not know and whose state you cannot attest to.

Billy Crystal: Women need a reason to have sex. Men just need a place.

Rodney Dangerfield: Last time I made love to my wife nothing was happeneing, so I said to her, "What's the matter? You can't think of anybody either?"

Rodney Dangerfield: Bisexuality immediately doubles your chances for a date on Saturday night.

Rodney Dangerfield: My wife gives good headache.

Robert De Niro: According to a new survey, women say they feel more comfortable undressing in front of men than they do undressing in front of other women. They say that women are too judgmental, where, of course, men are just grateful.

Marlene Dietrich: In America, sex is an obsession; in other parts of the world it is a fact.

Will Durst: How did sex come to be thought of as dirty in the first place? God must have been a Republican.

Albert Einstein: I can remember when the air was clean and sex was dirty.

English Proverb: A maid that laughs is half taken.

Euphemisms: For a listing of sexual euphemisms, see **From A to Z, by Richard & Kitty's World of Sex Euphemisms www.starma.com and www.wikipedia.com**

Brendan Francis: The big difference between sex for money and sex for free is that sex for money usually costs a lot less.

Sigmund Freud: Sometimes a cigar is just a cigar.

Eleanor Glynn (wrote in a news column in 1928): "The IT GIRL – Clara Bow, had IT (sex appeal)"

Guy Godin: Celibacy is not hereditary.

Lewis Grizzard: Kinky sex is the use of duck feathers. Perverted sex involves the whole duck.

Robert Heinlein: Everybody lies about sex.

Robert Heinlein: Sex should be friendly. Otherwise stick to mechanical toys; it's more sanitary.

Robert Heinlein: All cats are not gray after midnight.

Joseph Heller: Erogenous zones are either everywhere or nowhere.

Ernest Hemingway (in the novel *For Whom the Bell Tolls*, 1940): Did thee feel the earth move? Or (nowadays): Did the earth move for you?

Dustin Hoffman: There's a new medical crisis. Doctors are reporting that many men are having allergic reactions to latex condoms. They say they cause severe swelling. So what's the problem?

Italian Proverb: Bed is the poor man's opera.

Glenda Jackson: If I have to cry, I think of my sex life. If I have to laugh, I think of my sex life.

Steve Jobs (Founder, Apple Computers): My girlfriend always laughs during sex—no matter what she's reading.

Garrison Keillor: Sex is good, but not as good as fresh sweet corn.

Alan King: If you want to read about love and marriage you've got to buy two separate books.

Henry Kissinger: Power is the ultimate aphrodisiac.

John Kobal: Mae West had a voice like a vibrating bed.

Ann Landers: Women complain about sex more often than men. Their gripes fall into two major categories: (1) Not enough. (2) Too much.

Lynn Lavner: There are a number of mechanical devices which increase sexual arousal, particularly in women. Chief among these is the Mercedes-Benz 380SL.

Gloria Leonard: The difference between pornography and erotica is the lighting.

Victor Lownes: a promiscuous person is someone who is getting more sex than you are.

Steve Martin: You know "that look" women get when they want sex? Me neither.

Chico Marx: I wasn't kissing her, I was whispering in her mouth.

H.L. Mencken: Men have a much better time of it than women; for one thing they marry later; for another thing they die earlier.

Jim McGinn: McGinn's Law: Just about everything takes longer than they say it does, except sex.

Cynthia Nelms: In sex as in banking there is a penalty for early withdrawal.

Jack Nicholson: My mother never saw the irony in calling me a son-of-a-bitch.

Leonard Orman: When I was growing up, my friends wanted to have sex with anything that moved. I thought that was the wrong attitude. "Why limit yourself?" I told them.

Joan Rivers: It's been so long since I made love, I can't remember who gets tied up.

Will Rogers: In Hollywood you can see things at night that are fast enough to be in the Olympics in the day time.

Will Rogers: I never expected to see the day when girls would get sunburned in the places they now do.

Don Rose: The reason people sweat is so they don't catch fire when making love.

Jerry Seinfeld: There's very little advice in men's magazines, because men think, I know what I'm doing. Just show me somebody naked.

Gary Shandling: I once made love for an hour and fifteen minutes, but it was the night the clocks were set ahead.

William Shakespeare (*As You Like It*, Act II, iv): If thou remembers not the slightest folly / That ever love did make thee run into, / Thou hast not lov'd.

William Shakespeare (*As You Like It*, Act III, ii): Love is merely a madness, and, I tell you, deserves as well a dark horse and a whip as madmen do.

William Shakespeare (*As You Like It*, Act III, ii): It is as easy to count atoms as to resolve the propositions of a lover.

William Shakespeare (*As You Like It*, Act V, ii): It is to be all made of fantasy.

William Shakespeare (*II Henry IV*, Act II, iv): I'll canvas thee between a pair of sheets.

William Shakespeare (*I Henry VI*, Act II, ii): Like to a pair of loving turtle-doves, / That could not live asunder day or night.

William Shakespeare (*Love's Labour's Lost*, Act I, ii): Love is a familiar; Love is a devil: there is no evil angel but Love.

William Shakespeare (*Love's Labour's Lost*, Act IV, iii): It adds a precious seeing to the eye.

William Shakespeare (*Love's Labour's Lost*, Act V, iii): And when Love speaks, the voice of all the gods / Make heaven drowsy with the harmony.

William Shakespeare (*The Merchant of Venice*, Act II, vi): But love is blind, and lovers cannot see / The pretty follies that themselves commit.

William Shakespeare (*A Midsummer-Night's Dream*, Act I, i): The course of true love never did run smooth.

William Shakespeare (*A Midsummer-Night's Dream*, Act I, i): O, then, what graces in my love do dwell, / That he hath turned a heaven unto a hell!

William Shakespeare (*A Midsummer-Night's Dream*, Act I, i): Things base and vile, holding no quality, / Love can transpose to form and dignity: / Love looks not with the eyes, but with the mind; / And therefore is wing'd Cupid painted blind: / Nor hath Love's mind of any judgment taste; / Wings and no eyes figure unheedy haste: / And therefore is Love said to be a child, / Because in choice he is so oft beguil'd.

William Shakespeare (*Romeo and Juliet*, Act I, i): Love is a smoke raised with the fume of sighs; / Being purged, a fire sparkling in lovers' eyes; / Being vex'd, a sea nourish'd with lovers' tears: / What is it else? a madness most discreet, / A choking gall and a preserving sweet.

William Shakespeare (*Romeo and Juliet*, Act II, ii): With love's light wings did I o'erperch these walls, / For stony limits cannot hold love out, / And what love can do that dares love attempt.

William Shakespeare (*Romeo and Juliet*, Act II, v): Love's heralds should be thoughts, / Which ten times faster glide than the sun's beams, / Driving back shadows over louring hills: / Therefore do nimble-pinion'd doves draw love, / And therefore hath the wind-swift Cupid wings.

William Shakespeare (*The Two Gentlemen of Verona,* Act I, i): Love is your master, for he masters you: / And he that is so yoked by a fool, / Methinks, should not be chronicled for wise.

William Shakespeare (*The Two Gentlemen of Verona,* Act II, iv): Even as one heat another heat expels, / Or as one nail by strength drives out another, / So the remembrance of my former love / Is by a newer object quite forgotten.

William Shakespeare (*Twelfth Night*, Act III, i): Love sought is good, but given unsought is better.

William Shakespeare (*Venus and Adonis*, l. 575): Were beauty under twenty locks kept fast, / Yet love breaks through and picks them all at last.

William Shakespeare (*Venus and Adonis*, l. 799): Love comforteth like sunshine after rain, / But Lust's effect is tempest after sun; / Love's gentle spring doth always fresh remain, / Lust's winter comes ere summer half be done: / Love surfeits not. Lust like a glutton dies; / Love is all truth, Lust full of forged lies.

Sydney Smith: As the French say, there are three sexes – men, women, and clergymen.

Rod Stewart: Instead of getting married again, I'm going to find a woman I don't like and just give her a house.

Sharon Stone: Women might be able to fake orgasms. But men can fake whole relationships.

Mark Twain: (Man) has imagined the heaven, and has left entirely out of it the supremest of all his delights, the one ecstasy that stands first and foremost in the heart of every individual of his race—and of ours—sexual intercourse! It is as if a lost and perishing person in a roasting desert should be told by a rescuer he might choose and have all longed for things but one, and he should elect to leave out water!

Jane Wagner: To me the term "sexual freedom" means freedom from having to have sex.

Jane Wagner: People don't need sex so much as they need to be listened to.

Mae West: I've been in more laps than a napkin.

Mae West: A hard man is good to find.

Mae West (1933 film She Done Him Wrong, she says to a very young underciver policeman, played by Gary Cooper): "Come up and see me sometime? Why don't you?"

Robin Williams: Ah, yes, divorce, from the Latin word meaning to rip out a man's genitals through his wallet.

Robin Williams: See, the problem is that God gives men a brain and a penis, and only enough blood to run one at a time.

SIN (See EVIL; WRONGDOING)

SKEPTIC/SKEPTICISM (See CRITICS)

SLANDER (See LIES/LIARS; HONESTY)

SMILE/SMILING (See COMEDY)

SMOKING (See CIGARS)

SOPHISTRY (See ADVERSARY/ARGUMENT)

SORROW (See EMOTIONAL DISTRESS; GRIEF & SORROW)

SPEECH(ES)/SPEAKER(S) (See ORATORY/SUCCINCTNESS)

SPORTS (See GAMES; GOLF)

STANDARD (See NORM)

STATES of THE UNITED STATES & PROVINCES AND TERRITORIES OF CANADA

STATES of THE UNITED STATES

ALABAMA

Alabama: 22nd state (1819); nicknames: Yellowhammer State, The Heart of Dixie; Capitol: Montgomery
Audemus jura nostra defendere: We dare to defend our rights. (State motto)
Alabama named after the Alibamu Indians, early farmers who cleared thickets to plant crops. *Alibamu* meant "thicket clearers" or "vegetation gatherers."
J. S. Buckingham (1839): Alabama ... seems to have a bad name even among those who reside in it.
Carl Carmer ("Stars Fell on Alabama," 1934): They (the black conjure women) say that on the memories of the oldest slaves their fathers knew there was one indelible imprint of an awful event – a shower of stars over Alabama. Many an Alabamian to this day reckons dates from "the year the stars fell" – though he and his neighbor frequently disagree as to what year of our Lord may be so designated. All are sure, however, that once upon a time stars fell on Alabama, changing the land's destiny.
Carl Carmer: Birmingham is not like the rest of the state. It is an industrial monster sprung up in the midst of a slow-moving pastoral. It does not belong.... Birmingham is a new city in an old land.
Carl Carmer: Mobile stands in the heart, loveliest of cities. I have made many journeys down the Black Warrior and I have always found happiness at its mouth.... The old city rests apart, remembering the five flags that have flown over her. Spain and France and England and the Old South, grown harmonious through the mellowing of time, are echoes in the streets.
Carl Carmer: Mobile is a city of intimacies that have stood the test of time.
Henry Miller: I have never once thought of work in connection with the word Mobile. *Not anybody working.* A city surrounded with shells, the empty shells of bygone fiestas. Bunting everywhere, and the friable relics of yesterday's carnival. Gaiety always in retreat, always vanishing, like clouds brushing a mirror. In the center of this glissando, Mobile itself, very prim, very proper, Southern and not Southern, listless but upright, slatternly and yet respectable, bright but not wicked. Mozart for the Mandolin. Not Segovia feathering Bach. Not grace and delicacy so much as anemia. Fever cooled, Musk. Fragrant ashes.
Stephen Foster (1848): I came to Alabama with a banjo on my kneee, I'm goin' to Lou'siana, my true love for to see. It rain'd all night the day I left, the weather it was dry; The sun so hot I froze to death; Suzanna, don't you cry. **Oh! Suzana, oh, don't you cry for me,** For I'm goin' to Lou'siana with my banjo on my knee.

ALASKA

Alaska: 49th State (1959); Nicknames: The Last Frontier State, Land of the Midnight Sun; Captol: Juneau
North to the Future (State motto)
Alaska comes from Aleut word *Alyeska* meaning "Great Land"
Athabascans named the highest mountain "Denali" meaning "High One" (today named Mt. McKinley)
Dwight D. Eisenhower (speech in Anchorage, 1960): Thinking back to my boyhood, Alaska, for all of us... was synonymous with the gold and glamour of the Yukon and Klondike: the home of sourdoughs and Eskimos.... We thought of it as the cruel Artic region.... The change in less than a century heartens as we view the future. The future is bound to be a bright, useful one. You are no longer an Arctic frontier. You constitute a bridge to the continent of Asia and all its people.
Jack London: Nature has many tricks wherewith she convinces man of his finity... but the most tremendous, the most stupefying of all, is the passive phase of the White Silence. All movement ceases, the sky clears, the heavens are as brass; the slightest whispers seem sacrilege, and man becomes timid, affrighted at the

sound of his own voice. Sole speck of life journeying across the ghostly wastes of a dead world, he trembles at his audacity, realizes that his is a maggot's life, nothing more.

Jack London: As for the hardship, it cannot be conveyed by printed page or word of mouth. No man may know who has not undergone. And those who have undergone, out of their knowledge, claim that in the making of the world God grew tired, and when He came to the last barrowload, "just dumped it anyhow," and that was how Alaska happened to be.

John McPhee: A handful of people clinging to a subcontinent.

Ernie Pyle: I had always been skeptical about this all-night-daylight business. It was my believe that it would be an inferior brand, pumped up by the Chamber of Commerce, and not really what an honest man would call day light at all. But, as usual, I was wrong. We had actual day light all night long. (This was in June.) True, it wasn't so light at midnight as at noon. But you could stand out in the open at midnight, anywhere on the whole mainland of Alaska, and read a newspaper with ease.

Ernie Pyle: The Eskimos are a gentle people. I like gentle people, because there are so many in the world who are not gentle. Sometimes in a big-city I just sit all day in my room, with my head down, afraid to go out and talk to tough people. I expect Eskimos have spells like that too.

"Seward's Icebox" or "Seward's Folly" – the name applied to Alaska after Secretary of State William H. Seward signed a treaty with Russia for $7,200,000 in 1867.

Catie Vesper: Alaska means "The Great Land" in Aleut ... and they're right! It is GREAT!

ARIZONA

Arizona: 48th state (1912); Nicknames: Grand Canyon State, Valentine State (became a state on Valentine's Day 1912, and Baby State because for 47 years it was the youngest state; Capitol: Phoenix

Ditat Deus: God enriches (the state motto).

Arizona comes from the Tohono O'odham (Papago) Indian word *arizonac* meaning "small spring;" or another theory is it comes from the Aztec word *arizuma* meaning "silver-bearing."

George Horatio Derby: A very, very wicked soldier died there once, and of course went straight to the hottest corner of predation—and the next day he telegraphed back for his blankets.

Charles Kuralt: Most of those old settlers told it like it was, rough and rocky. They named their towns Rimrock, Rough Rock, Round Rock, and Wide Ruins, Skull Valley, Bitter Springs, Wolf Hole, Tombstone. It's a tough country. The names of Arizona towns tell you all you need to know.

Charles Kuralt: I don't know about you, but I am suspicious of Pleasantville, New York. I am sure that Sawmill, Arizona, is more my kind of town. Or Window Rock or Hermits Rest or Turkey Flat or Grasshopper Junction. I can settle down here, just for the pleasure of having folks at home say, "Oh, don't you know what happened to old Charles? Lives now in Jackrabbit, Arizona. Just down the road from Cow Lick and Bumble Bee."

John Steinbeck: Across the Colorado River from Needles, the dark and jagged ramparts of Arizona stood up against the sky, and behind them the huge tilted plain rising toward the backbone of the continent again.

Travel slogan (c. 1935): Come to Arizona, where Summer spends the Winter ... and where Hell spends the Summer.

ARKANSAS

Arkansas: 25th state (1836); Nickname: Natural State; Capitol: Little Rock

Regnat populus: let the people rule: (state motto).

Arkansas: from French word for the Quapaws – "Arkansas Indians," *Arkansas* is the French version of a Quapaw word meaning "south wind" or "downstream people."

Davy Crockett: If I could rest anywhere it would be in Arkansas where the men are of the real half-horse and alligator breed such as grows nowhere else on the face of the universal earth.

Howard W Odum (1929): Biggest fool I ever saw Come from the state of Arkansas; Put his shirt on over his coat, Button his britches up round his throat.

Glenn Shirley: There is no Sunday west of St. Louis and no God west of Fort Smith.

Mark Twain: So the duke said these Arkansas lunkheads couldn't come up to Shakespeare; what they wanted was low comedy—and maybe something rather worse than low comedy, he reckoned. He said he could size their style. So next morning he got some big sheets of wrapping paper and some black paint, and drawed off some handbills.... at the bottom was the biggest line of all, which said: LADIES AND CHILDREN NOT ADMITTED. "There," says he, "if that line don't fetch them, I don't know Arkansas!"

CALIFORNIA

California: 31st state (1850); Nicknames: Golden State. Capitol: Sacramento
Eureka: I have found it. (state motto)
California named after the "island called California ... that abounds with gold and precious stones." California was the mythical island paradise in Garci Ordonez Montalvo's 16th century book, *Las Sergas de Esplandian.*
Fred Allen: California is a great place—if you happen to be an orange.
Candice Bergen: Hollywood is like Picasso's bathroom.
James Bryce: California more than any other part of the Union, is a country by itself, and San Francisco a capital.
"Californioes" were Natives of California before and after Mexico surrendered California to the US in 1848.
Truman Capote: It's a scientific fact that if you stay in California, you lose one point of IQ every year.
Jimmy Carter: Whatever starts in California unfortunately has an inclination to spread.
Joan Didion: The West Coast of Iowa.
W.C. Fields: California is the only state in the union where you can fall asleep under a rose bush in full bloom and freeze to death.
F. Scott Fitzgerald: It (Hollywood) is a mining town in lotus land.
F. Scott Fitzgerald: Every California girl has lost at least one overy and none of them has read *Madame Bovary.*
D.W. Griffith: It's a shame to take this country away from the rattlesnakes.
Molly Haskell: The propaganda arm of the American Dream machine, Hollywood.
O. Henry: East is East, and West is San Francisco, according to Californians. Californians are a race of people; they are not merely inhabitants of a State.
Christopher Isherwood: California is a tragic country—like Palestine, like every Promised Land.
Carey McWilliams: A circus without a tent.
H. L. Mencken (describing Los Angeles, 1925): Nineteen suburbs in search of a metropolis.
Dan Quayle (former Vice President of US): I love California. I practically grew up in Phoenix.
Will Rogers: I attended a dinner the other morning given for the Old Settlers of California. No one was allowed to attend unless he had been in the State 2 and one half years.
Will Rogers: When the Oakies left Oklahoma and moved to California, it raised the I.Q. of both states.
Will Rogers: In Hollywood the woods are full of people that learned to write but evidently can't read. If they could read their stuff, they'd stop writing.
Will Rogers: In Hollywood you can see things at night that are fast enough to be in the Olympics in the day time.
Will Rogers: The movies are the only business where you can go out front and applaud yourself.
Will Rogers: I'm not a real movie star. I've still got the same wife I started out with twenty-eight years ago.
San Francisco was once a small port town named "Urabuena"
George Santayana: I am struck in California by the deep and almost religious affection which people have for nature, and by the sensitiveness they show to its influences; not merely poetically, but also athletically, because they like to live as nature lives. It is a relief from business and the genteel tradition.
R. Z. Sheppard: The San Francisco Bay Area is the playpen of countercultures.
Gertrude Stein: What was the use of my having come from Oakland it was not natural to have come from there yes write about it if I like or anything if I like but not there, there is no there there.
John Steinbeck: If Carmel's founders should return, they could not afford to live there, but it wouldn't go that far. They would be instantly picked up as suspicious characters and deported over the city line.
Mark Twain: All scenery in California requires <u>distance</u> to give it its highest charm.

Mark Twain: Twenty-four years ago I was strangely handsome; in San Francisco in the rainy season I was often mistaken for fair weather.

Mark Twain: The coldest winter I ever spent was a summer in San Francisco.

Frank Lloyd Wright: If you tilt the whole country sideways, Los Angeles is the place where everything loose will fall.

COLORADO

Colorado: 38th state (1876); Nickname: Centennial State. Capitol: Denver

Nil sine Numine: Nothing without Providence. (State motto)

Colorado named by Spanish explorers after the Colorado River. *Colorado* means "colored red."

Eugene Cervi: What's good, thrilling, exciting about Colorado was produced by God – not the Denver Chamber of Commerce.

John Gunther: Water is blood in Colorado. Touch water, and you touch everything; about water the state is as sensitive as a carbuncle.

Rudyard Kipling: After some hours we reached the level plain, and later the city of Denver .... The pulse of that town was too like the rushing mighty wind in the Rocky Mountain tunnel. It made me tired because complete strangers desired me to do something to mines which were in mountains, and to purchase building blocks upon inaccessible cliffs; and once, a woman urged that I should supply her with strong drinks. I had almost forgotten that such attacks were possible in any land, for the outward and visible signs of public morality in American towns are generally safeguarded. For that I respect this people.

Donald Culross Peattie: The Grand Canyon is carven deep by the master hand; it is the gulf of silence; widened in the desert; it is all time inscribing the naked rock; it is the book of earth.

Theodore Roosevelt: Passing through your wonderful mountains and canons I realize that this state is going to be more and more the playground for the entire Republic .... You will see this the real Switzerland of America.

CONNECTICUT

Connecticut: 5th state (1788); Nickname: Constitution State from having the first written constitution in the New World and the Connecticut Compromise or great Compromise of the Constitutional Convention. Capitol: Hartford

Qui transtulit sustinet: He who transplanted sustains . (State motto)

Connecticut: from an Indian word *Quinnehtukgut* meaning "beside the long tidal river."

P.T. Barnum: Connecticut is "The Land of Steady Habits."

Thomas Jefferson: Connecticut in her blue-laws, layingit down as a principle, that the laws of God should be the law of the land.

Bill Moyers: Liberals have always been eunuchs in the court of Connecticut.

Odell Shepard: Taken as a group, they (Connecticut peddlers) were probably no less honest than itinerant salesmen are wont to be, but the point is that they were probably no more so. Aggressive, pervasive, with a foot in every American door, they gave the country at large its first clear notions of the New England character, and there are some parts of the country, one fears, that have not yet revised the opinions then formed. The word "Yankee" came to mean "Connecticut Yankee," and throughout the Old South, long before Abolition days, it came to be pronouncd "Damyank."

Mark Twain: I asked him how far we were from Hartford. He said he had never heard of the place; which I took to be a lie, but allowed it to go at that. At the end of an hour we saw a far-away town sleeping in a valley by a winding river; and beyond it on a hill, a vast fortress, with towers and turrets, the first I had ever seen out of a picture. "Bridgeport?" said I, pointing. "Camelot," said he.

Mark Twain: There is a sumptuous variety about the New England weather that compels the stranger's admiration—and regret.... In the spring I have counted one hundred and thirty-six different kinds of weather inside of four-and-twenty hours.

Mark Twain: If you don't like the weather in New England, just wait a few minutes.

UA (c. 1774): The land of steady habits.

Yankee = from Dutch word (Jhankee) meaning "Pirate"

DELAWARE

Delaware: 1st state (1787); Nicknames: The First State, Diamond State, and Blue Hen State. Capitol: Dover
Liberty and Independence. (State motto)
Delaware named for Sir Thomas West, Lord De La Warr

James Warner Bellah: Know the mold – and you will understand the people of the state. Hardheaded with money. Courteous, to minimum requirements, with no urban frills. Completely self-sufficient in private living. Fine judges of good food and drink – in the castles of their own homes, which accounts for the indifferent public eating places throughout the state to this day. Honest at heart – but watch yourself carefully in all business transactions, for Delawareans are, of ancient times, close traders. Comfortably cynical in all basic philosophy. And utterly unchangeable, come hell, high water, the Du Pont overlordship, or thermonuclear reaction.

James Warner Bellah: Delaware has fought and bucked, hated, reviled, admired and fawned upon, ignored and courted the Du Ponts, but in the end, it has invariably bowed to Du Pont's benevolent paternalism.

Beverly Bove (Wilmington, DEL trial lawyer): This is such a small state – everyone here is **dated, mated or related.**

John James Ingalls: A state that has three counties when the tide is out, and two when the tide is in.

Thomas Jefferson: Delaware will probably remain what it ever has been, a mere county of England, conquered indeed, and held under by force, but always disposed to counter-revolution.

John Lofland: Delaware is like a diamond, diminutive, but having within it inherent value.

James Phelan and Robert Pozen: There are two political parties in delaware: the DuPonts and the anti-DuPonts, with the proviso that many DuPonts are members of the anti-DuPont family.

DISTRICT OF COLUMBIA

District of Columbia has been a Federal District since 1800; Nicknames: Nation's Capital, A Capital City
Justitia omnibus: Justice to all. (motto)

Washington, the city that makes up the entire District of Columbia, was named for our nation's first president, George Washington, who chose the site and planner/engineer Pierre-Charles L'Enfant whom he supervised.

Dean Acheson: Washington is like a self-sealing tank on a military aircraft. When a bullet passes through, it closes up.

James Bryce (1888): The United States is the only great country in the world which has no capital .... By Capital I mean a city which is not only the seat of political government, but is also by the size, wealth, and character of its people the head and center of its country.

Francis X. Clines: A show of police force worthy of a banana republic is the latest attraction on the cobbled streets of Georgetown.

Dwight D. Eisenhower: There are a number of things wrong with Washington. One of them is that everyone has been too long away from home.

Ralph Waldo Emerson: Washington, where an insignificant individual may trespass on a nation's time.

Barbara Howar: The cocktail party remains a vital Washington institution, the official intelligence system.

John F. Kennedy: Washington is a city of Southern efficiency and Northern charm.

Alexander Mackay: (In Washington) is to be seen in constant whirl the balance-wheel, such as it is, of the most complicated political machine on earth.

Sally Quinn: Washington is, for one thing, the news capital of the world. And for another, it is a company town. Most of the interesting people in Washington wither work for the government or write about it.

Elliot L. Richardson: Washington is ... a city of cocker spaniels. It's a city of people who are more interested in being petted and admired, loved, than rendering the exercise of power.

Dylan Thomas: Washington isn't a city, it's an abstraction.

Mark Twain: Why, when I think of the multitudes of clerks and congressmen – whole families of them – down there slaving away and keeping the country together, why then I know in my heart there is something so good and motherly about Washington, that grand old benevolent National Asylum for the Helpless.

Artemus Ward: It is easy enough to see why a man goes to the poor house or the penitentiary. It's becawz he can't help it. But why he should woluntarily go and live in Washington, is intirely beyond my comprehension, and I can't say no fairer nor that.

Artemus Ward: Washington, D.C., is the Capital of "our once happy country" – if I may be allowed to koin a frase! The D.C. stands for Desprit Cusses, a numerosity which abounds here.

Woodrow Wilson: A friend of mine says that every man who took office in Washington either grew or swelled, and when I give a man an office, I watch him carefully to see whether he is swelling or growing.

Woodrow Wilson: Things get very lonely in Washington sometimes. The real voice of the great people of America sometimes sounds faint and distant in that strange city. You hear politics until you wish that both parties were smothered in their own gases.

FLORIDA

Florida: 27th state (1845); Nickname: The Sunshine State. Capitol: Tallahasee

In God We Trust. (State motto)

Florida named by Spanish explorer Juan Ponce de Leon *La Florida* or "the Flowery Land."

Lenny Bruce: Miami Beach is where neon goes to die.

Federal Writers' Project (1939): Physically and socially, Florida has its own North and South, but its northern area is strictly southern and its southern area definitely northern.

Sidney Lanier: What business have healthy people with climates?

Budd Schulberg: Florida is the world's greatest amusement park.

Budd Schulberg: The billion-dollar-a-year tourist trade, the fusion of the Old South and the restless North is rapidly producing a new kind of state which is neither Southern nor Northern, Middle Western nor Western, yet with discernible elements of all four. In fact, Florida is to the United States today what the United States was to Europe a hundred years ago – a melting pot, a frontier, a place to improve your health or your luck.

Edmund Wilson: Miami is ... of an unimaginable awfulness – much like other American seaside resorts but on an unprecedented scale: acres of cheap white shops, mountain ranges of white hotels. After lunch, I had a taxi drive me over to Miami Beach. It goes on for miles – thousands of hotels and houses and monotonous lines of palms. I can't imagine how people live here or why so many of them come: it all seems a great insipid vacuum – less amusing than Southern California, because there is no touch of fantasy about anything.

GEORGIA

Georgia: 4th state (1788); Nicknames: Peach State, Empire State of the South, Cracker State, Goober State. Capitol: Atlanta

Wisdom, Justice, Moderation. (State motto)

Georgia named in honor of King George II of England

Jimmy Carter (inaugural address as Governor of Georgia, 1971): I am determined that at the end of this administration we shall be able to stand up anywhere in the world – in New York, California, or Florida – and say, "I'm a Georgian," and be proud of it.

Federal Writers' Project: The average Georgian votes the Democratic ticket, attends the Baptist or Methodist church, goes home to midday dinner, relies greatly on high cotton prices, and is so good a family man that he flings wide his doors to even the most distant of his wife's cousins' cousins.

John Gunther: I heard it said that the "architecture" of Atlanta is rococola. The pun is bad, but what the city would be like without Coca-Cola is hard to conceive .... In Atlanta alone Coca-Cola has made at least a thousand millionaires.

Henry Miller: Savannah is a living tomb about which there still clings a sensual aura as in old Corinth.

HAWAII

Hawaii: 50th state (1959); Nickname: The Aloha State. Capitol: Honolulu on island of Oahu

Ua mau ke ea o ka aina i ka pono: The life of the land is perpetuated by righteousness. (State motto)

Hawaii according to legend named in honor of legendary Polynesian chief Hawai'i-loa, said to have discovered the islands; another story is that early Polynesian settlers named the islands after their far-off South Pacific homeland, which in ancient times had been called *Hawaiki.*

Sanford B. Dole: I cannot help feeling that the chief end of this meeting is plantation profits, and the prosperity of the country, the demands of society, the future of the Hawaiian race only comes secondarily if at all.

Francois du Plessix Gray: The spiritual destiny of Hawaii has been shaped by a Calvinist theory of paternalism enacted by the descendants of the missionaries who had carried it there: a will to do good for unfortunates regardless of what the unfortunates thought about it.

Francois du Plessix Gray: The vast Pacific ocean would always remain the islanders' great solace, escape and nourishment, the amniotic fluid that would keep them hedonistic and aloof, guarded, gentle and mysterious.

Thomas Hamilton: The *nicest* thing about Hawaii is that when we select a beauty queen at the university we don't have just *one* beauty queen. We have a Polynesian beauty queen, a Chinese beauty queen, a Japanese beauty queen, a Filipino beauty queen, a Portugese beauty queen, a Puerto Rico beauty queen, a Negro beauty queen, *and* a Caucasian beauty queen. Six, eight beauty queens all in a row. *That's* what I like best about Hawaii.

Lydia Kamekeha Liliuokalani: The Hawaiian people have been from time immemorial lovers of poetry and music, and have been apt in improvising historic poems, songs of love, and chants of worship, so that praises of the living or wails over the dead were with them but the natural expression of their feelings.

Mark Twain: No alien land in all the world has any deep strong charm for me but that one, no other land could so longingly and so beseechingly haunt me, sleeping and waking, through half a lifetime, as that one has done.

Mark Twain: The loveliest fleet of islands that lies anchored in any ocean.

IDAHO

Idaho: 43rd state (1890); Nickname: Gem State. Capitol: Boise

Esto perpetua: May she endure forever. (State motto)

Idaho invented by George M. Willing in 1860 tried to convince Congress to adopt the name *Idaho* for the new territory, saying it meant "gem of the mountains" in Indian language. In 1863 the invented name was adopted.

Ernest Day: We're a user-oriented society in Idaho. And the users – the miners, loggers and grazers – all camp at the same campfire.

John Gunther: Idaho is torn, above all, between two other states; between the pull of Washington in the north, that of Utah in the south. Half of Idaho belongs to Spokane, I heard it said, and the other half to the Mormon church.

John Gunther: I asked an Idaho patriot why the potatoes were so big. Answer: "We fertilize 'em with cornmeal, and irrigate them with milk."

Idaho football cheer: Dice 'em, hash 'em, boil 'em, mash 'em! Idaho, Idaho, Idaho!

Ernie Pyle: There were two small hotels in Ketchum, and a group of nice cabins built around a hot-water pool. The business section consisted of one block; two grocery stores, three restaurants, one drugstore, and twelve combination saloons and gambling halls. These were called "clubs." Gambling was not legal in Idaho, and neither was liquor by the drink, but nobody in Ketchum paid any attention. Everything was wide open.

ILLINOIS

Illinois: 21st state (1818); Nicknames: Land of Lincoln, and Prairie State. Capitol: Springfield
State Sovereignty – National Union. (State motto)
Illinois is from French word *Illiniwek*, the name of a group of Indians who lived in Illinois; *Illiniwek* means "the men" or "the superior men."

Clyde Brion Davis: Illinois is perhaps the most American of all the states. It's the U.S.A. in a capsule. Here our virtues and our faults are most exaggerated and magnified. Here somehow the heroes seem more heroic, the villains more villainous, the buffoons more comic. Here violence is more unrestrained, and the capacity for greatness is as limitless as the sweep of the unending cornfields.

John Gunther: Chicago is the greatest and most typically American of all cities. New York is bigger and more spectacular and can outmatch it in other superlatives, but it is a "world" city, more European in some respects than American.

Carl Sandburg: Here is the difference between Dante, Milton, and me. They wrote about hell and never saw the place. I wrote about Chicago after looking the town over for years and years.

Studs Terkel: Chicago is not the most corrupt American city, it's the most theatrically corrupt.

INDIANA

Indiana: 19th state (1816); Nickname: Hoosier State. Capitol: Indianapolis
The Crossroads of America. (State motto)
Indiana is named for the people who lived there; *Indiana* means "Land of the Indians."

Roger Branigin: Indianans have an ability to see sin at a distance but never at their very feet. Indianapolis is shocked by vice in East Chicago; Bloomington is horrified by what goes on in Terre Haute or South Bend, and so on.

Paul Dresser (song 1897): Oh the moonlight's fair tonight along the Wabash, From the fields there comes the breath of new-mown hay; Thro' the sycamores the candle lights are gleaming, On the banks of the Wabash far away.

Ralph Waldo Emerson: When an Eastern man is cheated by a Hoosier he is said to be *Wabashed.*

Thomas Marshall: I came form Indiana, the home of more first-rate second-class men than any State in the Union.

Kurt Vonnegut: Indianapolis ... where the practice of the arts was regarded as an evasion of real life by means of parlor tricks.

IOWA

Iowa: 29th state (1846); Nickname: Hawkeye State. Capitol: Des Moines
Our Liberties We Praise and Our Rights We Will Maintain. (State motto)
Iowa named for a tribe of Indians who lived in the area who the Sioux called *Iowa*; the word *Iowa* has been variously interpreted to mean "one who puts to sleep" or "beautiful land"

Harvey Arden: Iowa is top-choice America, America cut thick and prime.

John Gunther: Iowa spells agriculture, and agriculture in this part of the world spells corn. This is the heart of agrarian America.

Philip Hamburger: Everybody in Des Moines is insured – against fire, flood, theft, hog cholera, death, crop failure, rickets. Name it, and Des Moines has the insurance to cover it.

Philip Hamburger: In Des Moines, a man's eyes will light up at the mere mention of the word "corn."

Donald Kaul: Iowa is graced by absolutely marvelous people. I lnow you hear that all the time, but it's true. They are clean, brave, thrifty, reverent, loyal, honest and able to brush after every meal.

Catherine Ann McLollum: Iowa winters were very cold and I well remember seeing the coal oil frozen in the lamps in the morning.

Phil Strong: The gold mines and the diamond mines of the world are cheap and trivial compared to the produce that Iowa breeds out of its land every year. Iowa could buy out the world's diamond production every year with hunks of ham and buckets of lard. Iowa would still have most of its produce left.

Phil Strong: The character of Iowa is essentially bucolic in the best senses of the world (and, to be quite honest, occasionally in some of the worst).

KANSAS

Kansas: 34th state (1861); Nicknames: Sunflower State, Wheat State, Jayhawker State, Midway. Capitol: Topeka

Ad astra per aspera: To the stars through difficulties. (State motto)

Kansas is named after the Indians the Sioux called the *Kansa*, meaning "people of the south wind."

Carl Lotus Becker: To understand why people say "Dear old Kansas!" is to understand that Kansas is no mere geographical expression, but a state of mind, a religion, and a philosophy in one.

Henry Ward Beecher: There is no monument under heaven on which I would rather have my name inscribed than on this goodly state of Kansas.

Roger Butterfield: Raise less corn and more Hell.

Pearl S. Buck: Kansas, in sum, is one of our finest states and lives a sane, peaceful, and prosperous life.

Foster Dwight Coburn: Happy is the man who wakens to find he has wandered from Kansas only in a dream.

John James Ingalls: Kansas is the navel of the nation. Diagonals drawn from Duluth to Galveston, from Washington to San Francisco, from Tallahassee to Olympia, from Sacramento to Augusta, intersect it in its center.

Mary Elizabeth Lease: Raise less corn and more *Hell.*

Alfred M. "Alf" Landon (1936): We oreferred the comparatively simple but more intelligent life of Kansas to Washington. There are some intelligent people in Washington. More of 'em in Kansas.

William H. Seward: If I wander in my affection for freedom, I shall come up here (to Kansas) and renew it. Men will yet come to Kansas as they came of old to Jerusalem.

William Allen White: Kansas is the child of Plymouth Rock.

KENTUCKY

Kentucky: 15th state (1792); Nickname: Bluegrass State. Capitol: Frankfort

United We Stand, Divided We Fall. (State motto)

Kentucky is a Commonwealth ("for the good of all") Several Indian groups had a word sounding like Kentucky; several translations include: "dark and bloody group," "great meadows" and "land of tomorrow."

Harry Caudill: We are the nation's perennial problem child.

Harry Caudill: We have a myth our economy is based on coal. It isn't; it's based on poverty.

Stephen Collins Foster (song, 1853): The sun shines bright in the old Kentucky Home.

Kentucky toast: Here's to old Kentucky, The State where I was born, Where the corn is full of kernels, And the Colonels full of corn.

James H. Mulligan: The moonlight is softest, in Kentucky; Summer days come oftest, in Kentucky; Friendship is the strongest, Love's fires glow the longest, Yet a wrong is always wrongest, In Kentucky.

Harriet Beecher Stowe: Great, tall, raw-boned Kentuckians, attired in hunting-shirts, and trailing their loose joints over a vast extent of territory, with the easy lounge peculiar to the race.

Zachary Taylor (to the 2nd Kentucky Regiment at Battle of Buena Vista, Mexico, 1847): Hurrah for Old Kentucky! That's the way to do it. Give 'em hell, damn 'em.

LOUISIANA

Louisiana: 18th state (1812); Nickname: Pelican State. Capitol: Baton Rouge

Union, Justice, and Confidence. (State motto)

Louisiana named by French explorer Rene-Robert Cavelier, Sieur de La Salle in honor of French King XIV.

John James Audubon: But where is that favored land? – It is in this great continent. – It is, reader, in Louisiana that these bounties of nature are in the greatest perfection.

Alistair Cooke: In 1803 Louisiana was an unmanned, undefended empire embracing the whole watershed of the Mississippi and comprising the present states of Louisiana, Arkansas, Oklahoma, Missouri, both Dakotas, Iowa, Nebraska, Kansas, Minnesota, Colorado, Wyoming, and Montana – a third of North America.

Mark Duffy: In Louisiana we don't bet on football games ... We bet on whether a politician is going to be indicted or not.

Thomas Jefferson: In Louisiana the live-oak is the king of the forest, and the magnolia is its queen; and there is nothing more delightful to one who is fond of the country than to sit under them on a clear, calm spring morning like this.

Huey P. Long (Louisiana lawyer and Governor, 1893-1935; in 1929 a reporter asked: "Governor, do you mean to tell us that you bought and paid for our Representative?"): I have sir; just like you would a load of potatoes.

George Sessions Perry: It (New Orleans) is a town where an architect, a gourmet, or a roue is in hog heaven.

Kevin Reilly (1985): As a society, we're a banana republic. What we ought to do is declare bankruptcy, secede from the union and declare ourselves a banana republic and file for foreign aid. We're just about as illiterate and just about as progressive as a Latin American country.

Will Rogers: In Louisiana they vote by electricity. It's a marvelous way to vote, but Huey (Long) runs the switchboard, so it don't matter which button the boys press, all the answers come out yes.

Mark Twain: Sir Walter Scott is probably responsible for the Capitol building; for it is not conceivable that this little sham castle would ever have been built if he had not run the people mad, a couple of generations ago, with his medieval romances .... It is pathetic enough that a whitewashed castle, with turrets and things – materials all ungenuine within and without, pretending to be what they are not – should ever have been built in this otherwise honorable place; but it is much more pathetic to see this architectural falsehood undergoing restoration and perpetuation in our day, when it would have been so easy to let dynamite finish what a charitable fire began, and then devote this restoration money to the building of something genuine.

MAINE

Maine: 23rd state (1820); Nickname: Pine Tree State; Capitol: Augusta

Dirigo: I direct. (State motto)

Maine is said to be named for former French province of Maine; or derived from "the main" or "mainland."

James A. Farley (after 1936 presidential election): As Maine goes, so goes Vermont.

Groucho Marx: There are only two things that ever make the front page in Maine papers. One is a forest fire and the other is when a New Yorker shoots a moose instead of the game warden.

Political maxim: As Maine goes, so goes the nation.

Thomas Brackett Reed: Here's to the state of Maine, the land of the bluest skies, the greenest earth, the richest air, the strongest, and what is better, the sturdiest men, the fairest, and what is best of all, the truest women under the sun.

Will Rogers: Did you ever see a place that looks like it was built just to enjoy? Well, this whole state of Maine looks that way. If it's not a beautiful lake, it's a beautiful tree, or a pretty green hay meadow. And beautiful old time houses, with barns built right in with the kitchens.

John Steinbeck (quoting a Maine native): Don't ever ask directions of a Maine native.... Somehow we think it is funny to misdirect people and we don't smile when we do it, but we laugh inwardly. It is our nature.

Henry David Thoreau: This is what you might call a brand-new country; the only roads were of Nature's making, and the few houses were camps. Here, then, one could no longer accuse institutions and society, but must front the true source of evil.

E. B. White: I am lingering in Maine this winter, to fight wolves and foxes. The sun here is less strong than Florida's, but so is the spirit of development.

MARYLAND

Maryland: 7th state (1788); Nickname: Old Line State, Free State; Capitol: Annapolis

Fatti maschii, parole femine: Manly deeds, womanly words. (State motto)

Maryland named in honor of Queen Henrietta Maria, wife of King Charles I of England.

Henry Adams: In truth, he had never seen a finished landscape; but Maryland was raggedness of a new kind.

Francis F. Beire (1968): For more than a century Baltimore was known throughout the nation under the unsavory name of "Mobtown." The title owed its origin to the speed and frequency with which the citizenry found excuse to riot.

Henry James: You have never seen, on the lap of nature, so large a burden so neatly accommodated. Baltimore sits there as some quite robust but almost unnaturally good child might sit on the green apron of its nurse, with no concomitant crease or crumple, no uncontrollable "mess," by the nursery term, to betray its temper.

Gerald W. Johnson: I firmly believe that Maryland is the most improbable state in the Union.

Theodore McKelden: America in Miniature.

H. L. Mencken: A Baltimorean is not merely John Doe, an isolated individual of *Homo sapiens*, exactly like every other John Doe. He is John Doe of a certain place – of Baltimore, of a definite *house* in Baltimore.

H. L. Mencken (1926): The old charm, in truth, still survives in the town (Baltimore), despite the frantic efforts of the boosters and boomers who, in late years, have replaced all its ancient cobblestones with asphalt, and bedizened it with Great White Ways and suburban boulevards, and surrounded it with stinking steel plants and oil refineries, and increased its population from 400,000 to 800,000.

MASSACHUSETTS

Massachusetts: 6th state (1788); Nickname: Bay State; Capitol: Boston

Ense petit placidam sub libertate quietem: By the sword we seek peace, but peace only under liberty. (State motto)

Massachusetts, a Commonwealth is named for an Indian tribe called the Massachusett that lived in Massachusetts Bay area; the name is believed to mean "near the great hill" referring to the Great Blue Hill south of Boston.

Fred Allen: I have just returned from Boston. It is the only thing to do if you find yourself up there.

Calvin Coolidge: Have faith in Massachusetts!

Calvin Coolidge: (The Puritans) were a very wonderful people.... If they were narrow it was not a blighting and destructive narrowness, but a vital and productive narrowness.

e. e. cummings: the Cambridge ladies who live in furnished souls are beautiful and have comfortable minds.

T.S. Eliot: The society of Boston was and is quite uncivilized but refined beyond the point of civilization.

Ralph Waldo Emerson: Massachusetts is Italy upside down.

Henry Wadsworth Longfellow: Down to the Plymouth Rock, that had been to their feet as a doorstep Into a world unknown, - the corner-stone of a nation!

Herman Melville: Nantucket! Take out your map and look at it – a mere hillock, and elbow of sand; all beach, without a background. Some gamesome weights will tell you that they have to plant weeds there, they don't grow naturally; that pieces of wood in Nantucket are carried about like bits of the true cross in Rome; that one blade of grass makes an oasis, three blades in a day's walk a prairie.

Wendell Phillips: The rock underlies all America: it only crops out here.

Mark Twain: The difference between New York and Boston is that in New York people ask how much you make, but in Boston people ask how much you know.

Mark Twain (quoting an "American joke"): In Boston they ask, How much does he know? In New York, How much is he worth? In Philadelphia, Who were his parents?

Mark Twain: There is a sumptuous variety about the New England weather that compels the stranger's admiration—and regret.... In the spring I have counted one hundred and thirty-six different kinds of weather inside of four-and-twenty hours.

Mark Twain: If you don't like the weather in New England, just wait a few minutes.

Daniel Webster (1830): I shall enter of no encomium upon Massachusetts; she needs none. There she is. Behold her, and judge for yourselves. There is her history; the world knows it by heart. The past, at least, is secure. There is Boston and Concord and Lexington and Bunker Hill; and there they will remain forever.

H. G. Wells: One feels in Boston, as one feels in no other part of the States, that the intellectual movement has ceased.

John Greenleaf Whittier (1843): No slave-hunt in our borders, - no pirate on our strand! No fetters in the Bay State – no slave upon our land!

MICHIGAN

Michigan: 26th state (1837); Nicknames: Wolverine State, Water Wonderland; Capitol: Lansing (1847) (first Capitol – Detroit)

Si quaeris peninsulam amoenam circumspice: If you seek a pleasant peninsula, look around you. (State motto)

Michigan is named for Lake Michigan, which the Chippewa called *Michigama*, meaning "great lake or large lake."

Leonard Lanson Cline: The only state in the union boasting a spare part.

Woody Guthrie: There was a rich man and he lived in Detroitium, Glory hallelujah, heirojarum. And all the workers he did eploitium, Glory hallelujah, heirojarum.

Henry Miller: The capitol of the new planet – the one, I mean, which will kill itself off – is of course Detroit.

George Sessions Perry: You can slip up on Detroit in the dead of night, consider it from any standpoint, and it's still hell on wheels.

John Steinbeck: I had forgotten how rich and beautiful is the countryside – the deep topsoil, the wealth of great trees, the lake country of Michigan handsome as a well-made woman, and dressed and jeweled. It seemed to me that the earth was generous and outgoing here in the heartland, and perhaps the people took a cue from it.

MINNESOTA

Minnesota: 32nd state (1858); Nicknames: Gopher State, North Star State, Land of 10,000 Lakes, Land of Sky-Blue Waters, and Bread and Butter State; Capitol: St. Paul

E'etoile du nord: The star of the north. (State motto)

Minnesota is from a Dakota word meaning "sky-tinted water.":

Fredrika Bremer (1853): What a glorious new Scandinavia might not Minnesota become! ... The climate, the situation, the character of the scenery, agrees with our people better than that of any other of the American states, and none of them appear to me to have a greater or more beautiful future before them than Minnesota.

Garrison Keillor: Where all the women are strong, all the men are good looking, and all the children above average.

Garrison Keillor: May your soul be forever tormented by fire and your bones be dug up by dogs and dragged through the streets of Minneapolis.

James Proctor Knott (1871): Duluth! The word fell upon my ear with a peculiar and indescribable charm, like the gentle murmur of a low fountain stealing forth in the midst of roses; or the soft, sweet accents of an angel's whisper in the bright, joyous dream of sleeping innocence.

Charles Kuralt: Minnesotans are just different, that's all. On the day of which I speak, with the wind-chill factor hovering at fifty-seven below, hundreds of them could be perceived through the slits in my ski mask out ice fishing on this frozen lake. It was cold out there, bitter, biting, cutting, piercing, hyperborean, marmoreal cold, and there were all these Minnesotans running around outdoors, happy as lambs in the spring.

Charles Kuralt: The state seal shows a farmer, a waterfall, a forest, and an Indian riding into the sunset. It should be changed to ice cubes rampant on a field of white, a grinning, barefoot Swede in a Grain Belt Beer T-shirt riding a snowmobile, and a sivering visitor whose stricken breath is freezing into ice crystals.

Calvin Trillin: "Home of the Late April Slush."

MISSISSIPPI

Mississippi: 20th state (1817); Nickname: The Magnolia State; Capitol: Jackson

Virtute es armis: By valor and arms. (State motto)

Mississippi takes its name from the Mississippi River; Mississippi is a Choctaw Indian word meaning "Great Water" or "Father of Waters."

Mississippi: the word comes from the Algonquian words for "Great River" Mississippi River is called "The Father of Waters"

Charles Dickens: But what words shall describe the Mississippi, great father of rivers, who (praise to Heaven) has no young children like him! An enormous ditch, sometimes two or three miles wide, running liquid mud, six miles an hour: its strong and frothy current choked and obstructed everywhere.

William Faulkner: Mississippi begins in the lobby of a Memphis, Tennessee, hotel and extends south to the Gulf of Mexico. It is dotted with little towns concentric about the ghosts of the horses and mules once tethered to the hitch-rail enclosing the county courthouse and it might almost be said to have only two directions, north and south, since until a few years ago it was impossible to travel east or west in it unless you walked or rode one of the horses or muless.

Bern Keating: Mississippians are serenely confident that they have the most colorful history of any state. Never mind that almost all of it concerns one lost concern or another.

Abraham Lincoln (after capture of Vicksburg, MISS, July 4, 1863): The Father of Waters again goes unvexed to the sea.

Bob Parris Moses: When you're in Mississippi, the rest of America doesn't seem real. And when you're in the rest of America, Mississippi doesn't seem real.

Mark Twain: The Mississippi is a just and equitable river; it never tumbles one man's farm overbroad without building a new farm just like it for that man's neighbor. This keeps down hard feelings.

Mark Twain: The Mississippi is well worth reading about. It is not a commonplace river, but on the contrary is in all ways remarkable. Considering the Missouri its main branch, it is the longest river in the world – four thousand three hundred miles. It seems safe to say that it is also the crookedest river in the world, since in one part of its journey it uses up one thousand three hundred miles to cover the same ground that a crow would fly over in six hundred and seventy-five.

MISSOURI

Missouri: 24th state (1821); Nickname: Show Me State; Capitol: Jefferson City

Sallus populi suprema lex esto: The welfare of the people shall be the supreme law. (State motto)

Missouri is from the Illinois language means "people of the big canoe" or "town of the big canoe."

Elbert Hubbard: Be from Missouri, of course; but for God's sake forget it occasionally.

William Least Heat Moon: A Missourian gets used to Southerners thinking him a Yankee, a Northerner considering him a cracker, a Westerner sneering at his effete Easterness, and the Easterner taking him for a cowhand.

Jonathan Raban: Old, genteel St. Louis – T.S. Eliot's city – thought of itself as a slice of cultivated Europe. It seemed mystified as to how it had landed here, stranded on the wrong side of the big American river.

Harry S. Truman: In all the years since I left the White House, I have wondered why so many people come from so far away and take so much trouble to look at the house where I live. Perhaps it is because once a man has been President he becomes an object of curiosity like those other notorious Missouri characters, Mark Twain and Jesse James.

Mark Twain: The first time I ever saw St. Louis I could have bought it for $6 million, and it was the mistake of my life that I did not do it.

Willard D. Van diver (1899): I am from Missouri, you've got to show me. *

* Note: one popular story is that the origin of the phrase "show me" comes from when Missouri miners went to work in Colorado mines and they used the phrase repeatedly to show their unfamiliarity with local mine operations.

MONTANA

Montana: 41st state (1889);Nickname: Treasure State, Bug Sky Country, and Last Best Place; Capitol: Helena

Oro y plata: Gold and silver. (State motto)

Montana is derived from the Spanish word for "mountainous."

John Gunther: Butte is the toughest, bawdiest town in America, with the possible exception of Amarillo, Texas.... I heard it called "the only electric-lit cemetery in the United States."

John Gunther (1947): Montana is as big as Illinois, Michigan, and Indiana. It is bigger than Italy and Japan. To say that it is the third American state in size does not, perhaps, make its enormousness tangible; say instead that one out of every twenty-five American square miles is Montanan.

Joseph Kinsey Howard (1943 book title): *"High, Wide, and Handsome"*

John Kinsey Howard: Butte is the black heart of Montana, feared and distrusted .... Butte is a sooty memorial to personal heroism, to courage and vigor even in rascality; and it is a monument to a wasted land.

Donald Culross Peattie: Colorado is high, having more peaks within its borders than any other state. Wyoming is wide, with the breadth of the plains between the Big Horns and the Grand Tetons. California is handsome, with a splendor of success. It takes all three adjectives to describe Montana.

John Steinbeck: Montana seems to me to be what a small boy would think Texas is like from hearing Texans.

John Steinbeck: It seemed to me that the frantic bustle of America was not in Montana. Its people did not seem afraid of shadows in a John Birch Society sense. The calm of the mountains and the rolling grasslands had got into the inhabitants.

John Steinbeck: I am in love with Montana. For other states I have admiration, respect, recognition, even some affection, but with Montana it is love .... It seems to me that Montana is a great splash of grandeur. The scale is huge but not overpowering. The land is rich with grass and color, and the mountains are the kind I would create if mountains were put on my agenda.

NEBRASKA

Nebraska: 37th state (1867); Nickname: Cornhusker State, Treeplanter's State Capitol:
Equality Before the Law. (State motto)
Nebraska comes from the Oto Indian word *Nebrathka*, which means "flat water" describing the Platte River. In 1843, Lt. John C. Fremont suggested the name be used for the territory that included what is now Nebraska.

John C. Fremont (writing about the Platte River, which flows east into Missouri, and has been called "the Mile-Wide and Inch-Deep."): The names given by the Indians are always remarkably appropriate: and certainly none was ever more so than that which they have given to this stream – the Nebraska, or Shallow River.

Philip Hamburger: When an Omaha man (or boy) speaks of a steak, one expects him to pull from his pocket a series of treasured snapshots of steaks.

Rudyard Kipling (1891): Omaha, Nebraska, was but a halting place on the road to Chicago, but it revealed to me horrors that I would not willingly have missed. The city to casual investigations seemed to be populated entirely by Germans, Poles, Slavs, Hungarians, Croats, Magyars, and all the scum of Eastern European States, but it must have been laid out by the Americans. No other people would cut the traffic of a main street with two streams of railway lines, each some eight or nine tracks wide, and cheerfully drive tramcars across the metals. Every now and again they have horrible railway crossing accidents at Omaha, but nobody seems to think of building an overhead bridge. That would interfere with the vested interests of the undertakers.

Charles Kuralt: Barns back east have weather vanes on them to show which way the wind is blowing, but out here there's no need .... Farmers just look out the window to see which way the barn is leaning. Some farmers ... attach a logging chain to a stout pole. They can tell the wind direction by which way the chain is blowing. They don't worry about high wind until the chain starts whipping around and the links begin snapping off. Then they know it's likely the wind will come up before morning.

Wright Morris: There is no obstruction but the sky.

Robert Louis Stevenson (1892): We were at sea—there is no other adequate expression—on the plains of Nebraska.... It was a world almost without a feature; an empty sky, an empty earth; front and back, the line of railway stretched from horizon to horizon, like a cue across a billiard-board; one either hand, the green plain ran till it touched the skirts of heaven.

David Wagoner: The Platte River is famous for being a mile wide and an inch deep, and it's both sometimes. But there's other times – like this stretch along South Fork – when it narrowed up and deepened down and hurried along looking siltier and soupier than usual, too thick to drink and too runny to eat.

Artemus Ward: The Platte River would be a good river if set on edge.

NEVADA

Nevada: 36th state (1864); Nicknames: Silver State, Sagebrush State, and Battle Born State; Capitol: Carson City
All for Our Country. (State motto)
Nevada is from a Spanish word *Nevada* meaning "snowy" or "snow-clad."

Alistair Cooke: at it occurred to some charitable people (moving west in 1849) who could still me use as they staggered that you couldn't get word back to a man's family that he had died nowhere. So they created place names, and wherever the trail turned or there was a new this To they marked a steak and planted it.... I have an old, yellowing automobile map that still peppers the wilderness of Nevada with such names and has Fortitude, Desolation, Last Yes.

John Gunther: Look at Utah and Nevada from an airplane. They are indistinguishable. You could not possibly tell where one stops and the other begins. Yet the two states differ so enormously that they might belong to different worlds. Utah is a creature of the Mormon Church.... Nevada was settled... by miners and prospectors and gamblers who found California too tame. Utah is the most staid and respectable of states; Nevada is, by common convention at least, the naughtiest.

John Gunther (1947): Nevada is mostly desert, mountains, and fabulous natural resources. It is one of the friendliest states I know, and it lives on four things, mining, livestock, divorce trade, and gambling.

John McPhee: Neon looks good in Nevada. The tawdiness is refined out of it in so much wide black space.

Mark Twain: If an unknown individual arrived, they did not inquire if he was capable, honest, industrious, but – had he killed his man? If he had not, he gravitated to his natural and proper position, that of a man of small consequence; if he had, the cordiality of his reception was graduated according to the number of his dead.

Mark Twain: The cheapest and easiest way to become an influential man and be looked up to by the community at large was to stand behind a bar, where a cluster-diamond pin, and sell whiskey. I am not sure but that the saloonkeeper held a shade higher rank than any other member of society.

NEW ENGLAND STATES

Charles Francis Adams: Of the great vice of this New England people is their adoration of Mammon. And rooted as it is in the character, the tree has now attained immense luxuriance and bids fair to overshadow us all.

Cleveland Amory: The New England conscience... does not stop you from doing what you shouldn't—it just stops you from enjoying it.

Henry Ward Beecher: The one great poem of New England is her Sunday.

Ambrose Beirce: YANKEE, n. In Europe, an American. In the Northern States of our Union, a New Englander. In the Southern states the word is unknown. (See Damyank.)

Calvin Colton: New England is a legitimate child of *Old* England.... It is England and Scotland again in miniature and in childhood.

Emily Dickinson: How condescending to descend / And be of Buttercups the friend / In a New England Town.

John Gunther: Of course what the man from Mars will find out first about New England is that it is neither new nor very much like England.

Oliver Wendell Holmes Sr.: He comes of the *Brahmin caste of New England.* This is a harmless, inoffensive, untitled aristocracy.

Fanny Kemble: Those New England States, I do believe, will be the noblest country in the world in a little while. They will be the salvation of that very large great body with a very little soul, the rest of the United States; they are the pith and marrow, heart and core, head and spirit of that country.

Rudyard Kipling: Oliver Wendell Holmes says that Yankee schoolmarms, the cider, and the salt codfish of the Eastern states are responsible for what he calls a nasal accident.

Joseph Wood Krutch: The most serious charge which can be brought against New England is not Puritanism but February.

Harriet Martineau: I believe no one attempts to praise the climate of New England.

Cotton Mather: The New Englanders are a people of God, settled in those which were once the Devil's territories.

Phyllis McGinley: The East is a montage.... It is old and is young, very green in summer, very white in winter, gregarious, withdrawn and at once both sophisticated and provincial.

Editor Allan Poe: The Hottentots and Kickapoos are very well in their way. The Yankees alone are preposterous.

John Steinbeck: There are enough antiques for sale along the roads of New England alone to furnish the houses of a population of fifty million.

Mark Twain: The people of New England are by nature patient and forbearing but there are some things which they will not stand. Every year they kill a lot of poets for writing about "Beautiful Spring." These are generally casual visitors who bring their notions of spring from somewhere else.

Mark Twain: There is a sumptuous variety about the New England weather that compels the stranger's admiration – and regret.... In the spring I have counted one hundred and thirty-six different kinds of weather inside of four-and-twenty hours.

Barrett Wendell: I wonder if anybody ever reach the age of thirty-five in New England without wanting to kill himself.

George E. Woodberry: All well-brought-up New England boys who are specially intellectual or sensitive want to save the world.

Thomas Wolfe: You are a New Englander and quieter about it, but every American has this exultant feeling at times – the way snow comes in New England and the way it spits against the window at night and the sounds of the world get numb ... and there was the train for Boston in the middle of it, black, warm, fast, and all around the lonely and tragic beauty of New England.

NEW HAMPSHIRE

New Hampshire: 9th state (1788); Nickname: Granite State; Capitol: Concord

Live Free or Die. (State motto)

New Hampshire colony named by Captain John Mason in 1629 for his native county of Hampshire in England.

Stephen Vincent Benet ("The Devil and Daniel Webster" 1937): If two New Hampshire men aren't a match for the devil, we might as well give the country back to the Indians.

Ralph Waldo Emerson: The God who made New Hampshire / Taunted the lofty land / With little man.

Gerald Ford: I like your nickname, the "Granite State." It shows the strength of character, firmness of principle and restraint that have long characterized New Hampshire.

Robert Frost: She's one of the two best states in the Union. Vermont's the other.

Ralph D. Paine: Politically New Hampshire is as unproductive as an abandoned farm.

Maxfield Parrish: I live in New Hampshire so I can get a better view of Vermont.

Mark Twain: There is a sumptuous variety about the New England weather that compels the stranger's admiration – and regret.... In the spring I have counted one hundred and thirty-six different kinds of weather inside of four-and-twenty hours.

Mark Twain: If you don't like the weather in New England, just wait a few minutes.

NEW JERSEY

New Jersey: 3rd state; Nickname: The Garden State; Capitol: Trenton

Liberty and Prosperity. (State motto)

New Jersey was named for the Isle of Jersey in the English Channel.

Uncle Anthony: Did New Jersey invent traffic circles? I never saw so many circles to drive around than in Jersey.

Aunt Mary Carlo: I don't care whatchasay - Joisey has DA BEST TOMATOES!!

Woody Allen: The curtain rises on a vast primitive wasteland, not unlike certain parts of New Jersey.

Ambrose Bierce: Mousquetaire: n., A long glove covering a part of the arm. Worn in New Jersey. But "mousquetaire" is a might poor way to spell muskeeter.

Ambrose Bierce: Hangman: n., An officer of the law charged with duties of the highest dignity and utmost gravity, and held in hereditary disesteem by a populace having a criminal ancestry. In some of the American States his functions are now performed by an electrician, as in New Jersey, where executions by electricity have recently been ordered – the first instance known to this lexicographer of anybody questioning the expediency of hanging Jeseymen

Struthers Burt (1945): New Jersey has always been a useful "no man's land" between the arrogance of New York and the obstinacy of Pennsylvania. The time it takes to traverse it diagonally permits a cooling off, coming or going.

Raymond J. Donovan: If you're in the contracting business in this country, you're suspect. If you're in the contracting business in New Jersey, you're indictable. If you're in the contracting business in New Jersey and are Italian, you're convicted.

Albert Einstein (described Princeton, NJ): "A quaint ceremonius village of puny demi-gods on stilts.

Albert Einstein (describing Princeton, NJ): Young and fresh - a pipe yet unsmoked.

Federal Writers' Project (1939): Like China, New jersey absorbs the invader.

Benjamin Franklin: New Jersey resembles a beer barrel, tapped at both ends, with all the beer running into Philadelphia and New York.

John McPhee: Of the great unbroken city that will one day reach at least from Boston to Richmond, this section (New Jersey) is already built.

Dennis Miller: If some unemployed punk in New Jersey, can get a cassette to make love to Elle McPherson for $19.95, this virtual reality stuff is going to make crack look like Sanka.

Raymond Sokolov: Manhattan is a narrow island off the coast of New Jersey.

Andy Warhol: The mosquito is the state bird of New Jersey.

Woodrow Wilson: We have always been inconvenienced by New York on the one hand and Philadelphia on the other.

UA: What Exit (on the N.J. Turnpike which runs north and south through New Jersey) do you live at?

UA: An Ode to New Jersey

New Jersey is a peninsula.

Highlands, New Jersey has the highest elevation along the entire eastern seaboard, from Maine to Florida.

New Jersey is the only state where all of its counties are classified as metropolitan areas.

New Jersey has more race horses than Kentucky.

New Jersey has more Cubans in Union City (1 sq. mi.) than Havana, Cuba

New Jersey has the most dense system of highways and railroads in the US.

New Jersey has the highest cost of living.

New Jersey has the highest cost of auto insurance.

New Jersey has the highest property taxes in the nation.

New Jersey has the most diners in the world and is sometimes referred to as the Diner Capital of the World

New Jersey is home to the original mystery pork parts chub (no,not spam) Taylor Ham or Pork Roll.

Home to the less mysterious, but the best, Italian hot dogs and Italian sausage w/peppers and onions.

North Jersey has the most shopping malls in one area in the world, with 7 major shopping malls in a 25 square mile radius.

New Jersey is home to the Statue of Liberty and Ellis Island.

The Passaic River was the site of the first submarine ride by inventor John P. Holland.

New Jersey has 50+ resort cities &towns, some of the nations' most famous: Asbury Park, Wildwood, Atlantic City (once called "The World's Favorite Playground"), Avalon, Seaside Heights, Long Branch & "Old Historic" Cape May.

New Jersey has the most stringent testing of our coastline for Water Quality Control than any other seaboard state in US.

New Jersey is a leading technology &industrial state and is the largest chemical producing state in the nation when you include pharmaceuticals.

Jersey tomatoes are known the world over as being the best you can buy.

New Jersey is the world leader in blueberry and cranberry production (and here you thought Massachusetts?)

Here's to New Jersey - the toast of the country! In 1642, the first brewery in America opened in Hoboken.

New Jersey rocks! The famous Les Paul invented the first solid body electric guitar in Mahwah in 940.

New Jersey is a major seaport state with the largest seaport in the US, located in Elizabeth. Nearly 80% of what our nation imports comes through Elizabeth Seaport first.

New Jersey is home to one of the nation's busiest airports at Newark Liberty International.

George Washington slept here. Several important Revolutionary War battles were fought on New Jersey soil, led by General George Washington.

The light bulb, phonograph (record player) and motion picture projector, were invented by Thomas Edison in his Menlo Park, NJ laboratory.

We also boast the first town ever lit by incandescent bulbs.
The first seaplane was built in Keyport, NJ.
The first airmail (to Chicago) was started from Keyport, NJ.
The first phonograph records were made in Camden, NJ.
New Jersey is home to the Miss America Pageant held in Atlantic City.
The game Monopoly, played all over the world, named the streets on their playing board after the actual streets in Atlantic City, Ventnor, and Margate City, which are on the Island of Absecon.
And, Atlantic City has the longest boardwalk in the world.
New Jersey has the largest petroleum containment area outside of the Middle East countries.
The first Indian reservation was in New Jersey, in the Watchung Mountains.
New Jersey has the tallest water-tower in the world. (Union, NJ!!!)
New Jersey had the first Medical Center, in Jersey City.
The Pulaski SkyWay, from Jersey City to Newark, was the first skyway highway
NJ built the first tunnel under a river, the Hudson. (Holland Tunnel).
The first baseball game was played in Hoboken, NJ, which is also the birthplace of Frank Sinatra.
The first intercollegiate football game was played in New Brunswick in 1889. (Rutgers College played Princeton.)
The first Drive-in Movie theater was opened in Camden, NJ, (but they're all gone now!)
New Jersey is home to both of "NEW YORK'S " ProFootball Teams (Giants or "Gents" and the Jets)!
The first radio station and broadcast was in Paterson, NJ.
The first FM radio broadcast was made from Alpine, NJ, by Maj.Thomas Armstrong.
All New Jersey natives: Sal Martorano, Jack Nicholson, Bruce Springsteen, Bon Jovi, Jason Alexander, Queen Latifa, Susan Sarandon, Connie Francis, Shaq, Judy Blume, Aaron Burr, Joan Robertson, Ken Kross, Dionne Warwick, Sarah Vaughn, Bud Abbott, Lou Costello, Alan Ginsberg, Norman Mailer, Marilynn McCoo, Flip Wilson, Alexander Hamilton, Whitney Houston, Eddie Money,Linda McElroy, Eileen Donnely, Grover Cleveland, Woodrow Wilson, Walt Whitman, Jerry Lewis, Tom Cruise, Richard Wojewodzki, Joyce Kilmer, Bruce Willis, Caesar Romero,Lauryn Hill, Ice-T, Nick Adams, Nathan Lane, Sandra Dee, Danny DeVito, Richard Conti, Joe Pesci,Joe Piscopo, Robert Blake,John Forsyth, Meryl Streep, Loretta Swit, Norman Lloyd, Paul Simon,Jerry Herman, Gorden McCrae,Kevin Spacey, John Travolta, Phyllis Newman, Anne Morrow Lindbergh, Eva Marie Saint, Elisabeth Shue, Zebulon Pike, James Fennimore Cooper, Admiral Wm.Halsey,Jr., Dave Thomas(Wendy's), William Carlos Williams, Ray Liotta, Robert Wuhl, Paul Robeson, Ernie Kovacs, Joseph Macchia and of course.........Frank Albert Sinatra and "Uncle Floyd" Vivino.
You know you're from Jersey when....
You don't think of fruit when people mention "The Oranges."
You know that it's called Great Adventure, not Six Flags.
A good, quick breakfast is a hard roll with butter.
You've known the way to Seaside Heights since you were seven.
You've eaten at a Diner, when you were stoned or drunk, at 3a.m.
You know that the state isn't one big oil refinery.
At least three people in your family still love Bruce Springsteen and you know the town Jon Bon Jovi is from.
You know what a "jug handle" is.
You know that WaWa is a convenience store.
You know that the state isn't all farmland.
You know that there are no "beaches" in New Jersey -there's the shore and you don't go to the shore, you go "down the Shore." And when you are there, you're not "at the shore," you are "down the Shore."
You know how to properly negotiate a Circle.

You knew that the last sentence had to do with driving.
You know that this is the only "New..."state that doesn't require
"New" to identify it (like, try...Mexico,...York, ...Hampshire - doesn't work, does it?)
You know that a "White Castle" is the name of BOTH a fast food chain AND a fast food sandwich
You consider putting mayo on a corned beef sandwich a sacrilege.
You don't think "What exit?" is very funny.
You know that people from the 609 area code are "a little different"... Yes they are!
The Jets-Giants game has started fights at your school or localbar.
You live within 20 minutes of at least three different malls.
You refer to all highways and interstates by their numbers.
Every year you have at least one kid in your class named Tony.
You know the location of every clip shown in the Sopranos opening credits.
You've gotten on the wrong highway trying to get out of the mall.
You know that people from North Jersey go to Seaside Heights, and people from Central Jersey go to Belmar and people from South Jersey go to Wildwood. It can be no other way.
You weren't raised in New Jersey—you were raised in either North Jersey, Central Jersey or South Jersey.
You don't consider Newark or Camden to actually be part of the state.
You remember the stores Korvette's, Two Guys, Rickel's, Channel, Bamberger's and Orbach's.
You also remember Palisades Amusement Park.
You've had a Boardwalk cheese steak and vinegar fries.
You start planning for Memorial Day weekend in February.
And finally...
You've NEVER, NEVER pumped your own gas.

NEW MEXICO

New Mexico: 47th state; Nickname: Land of Enchantment; Capitol: Santa Fe
It Grows as It Goes. (State motto)
New Mexico was named by the 16th century Spanish explorers who hoped to find gold and wealth equal to Mexico's Aztec treasures.
Alistair Cooke: In the spring of 1943 a very small dribble of odd-looking tourists arrived at Santa Fe, New Mexico, the first capital of New Spain in North America .... They were a secret team of refugees and native Americans and British scientists wh had gathered at Santa Fe before being driven off thirty miles northwest to Los Alamos. There, in the lonekiness of the desert, they would brew the Apocalypse.
Federal Writers' Project (1940): Space is a keystone of the land – vast, limitless stretches of plain, desert, and lofty mountains, with buttes and mesas and purple distances to rest the eye.
John Gunther: That New Mexico, which has given life to art from ancient Indian rain dances to a story like D. H. Lawrence's "The Woman Who Rode Away," should also have given birth to the atomic bomb, is perhaps an irony that measures the gamut of our civilization.
John Gunther: It looks rather like Nevada, but its higher, ruggeder, more dramatic. Half the mountains seem to have their tops blown off.

NEW YORK

New York: 11th state (1788); Nickname: The Empire State, The Excelsior State; Capitol: Albany
Excelsior: Ever upward. (State motto)
New York named in honor of James Stuart, Duke of York and Albany (later King James II of England)
Aunt Mary Carlo: Manhatten is where women who don't have it go to see women who do.
Sherwood Anderson: I think you know that when an American stays away from New York too long something happens to him. Perhaps he becomes a little provincial, a little dead and afraid.
Louis Auchincloss: New York has absolutely everything today except the past.
W.T. Ballard: You can take a boy out of Brooklyn, but you can never get Brooklyn out of the boy.
Jack Barry: the trouble with New York is it's so convenient to everything I can't afford.
Saul Bellow: What is barely hinted at in other American cities is condensed and enlarged in New York (City).
Meyer Berger: Each man reads his own meaning into New York.
Irving Berlin: Everybody ought to have a lower Est Side in their life.
Ambrose Bierce: Mammon, n. The god of the world's leading religion. His chief temple is in the holy city of New York.
James W. Blake (The Sidewalks of New York, 1894): East Side, WestSide, all around the town, / The tots sang "Ring-a-rosie," "London Bridge is falling down"; / Boys and girls together, me a Mamie O'Rourke, / Tripped the light fantastic on the sidewalks of New York.
Bill Bradley: I like the rough impersonality of New York, where human relations are oiled by jokes, complaints, and confessions – all made with the assumption of never seeing the other person again. I like New York because there are enough competing units to make it still seem a very mobile society. I like New York because it engenders high expectations simply by its pace.
Truman Capote: New York is the only city-city.
John J. Chapman (1909): The present in New York is so powerful that the past is lost.
George M. Cohan (song title, 1904): "Give My Regards to Broadway"
e. e. cummings (1932): absolutely posolutely dead / like coney island in the winter.
Charles Dickens: The beauty and freshness of this calm retreat (West Point), in the very dawn and greenness of summer – it was then the beginning of June – were exquisite indeed. Leaving it upon the sixth, and returning to New York, to embark for England on the succeeding day, I was glad to think that among the last memorable beauties which had glided past us, and softened in the bright perspective, were those whose pictures, traced by no common hand, are fresh in most men's minds; not easily to grow old, or fade beneath the dust of Time: The Kaatskill Mountains, Sleepy Hollow, and the Tappaan Zee.
Ralph Waldo Emerson: New York is a sucked orange.
James Frakes: Hell is New York City with all the escape hatches sealed.
Charlotte Perkins Gilman (1935): New York ... that unnatural city where every one is an exile, none more so than the American.
Roy Goodman: Prostitution is the only business that isn't leaving the city.
Pete Hamill: The city of right angles and tough, damaged people.
Moss Hart: The only credential the city asked was the boldness to dream. For those who did, it unlocked its gates and its treasures, not caring who they were or where they came from.
O. Henry: Little old Bagdad-on-the-Subway.
O. Henry: The Yappian Way.
O. Henry: You'd think New York people was all wise, but no. They don't get a chance to learn/ Everything's too compressed. Even the hayseeds are baled hayseeds. But what else can you expect from a town that's shut off from the world by the ocean on one side and New Jersey on the other?
Elbert Hubbard: New York: The posthumous revenge of the Merchant of Venice.
Robert G. Ingersoll (1876): Tammany Hall bears the same relation to a penitentiary as a Sunday-school to the church.

Washington Irving: Whoever has made a voyage up the Hudson must remember the Kaatskill mountains. They are a dismembered branch of the great Appalachian family, and are seen away to the west of the river, swelling up to a noble height, and lording it over the surrounding country.

Washington Irving ("Salmagundi," 1807-08): The renowned and ancient city of Gotham

Thomas Jefferson: New York, like London, seems to be a cloaca of all the depravities of human nature.

Rudyard Kipling: The more one studied it, the more grotesquely bad it grew – bad in its paving, bad in its streets, bad in its street-police, and but for the kindness of the tides, would be worse than bad in its sanitary arrangements.

John Vliet Lindsay: New York has total depth in every area. Washington has only politics; after that, the second biggest thing is white marble.

John Vliet Lindsay: Not only is New York the nation's melting pot, it is also the casserole, the chafing dish, and the charcoal grill.

Walter Lippmann: Robinson Crusoe, the self-sufficient man, could not have lived in New York City.

Edmund Love: New York attracts the most talented people in the world in the arts and professions. It also attracts them to other fields. Even the bums are talented.

Mignon McLaughlin: A car is useless in New York, essential everywhere else. The same with good manners.

H.L. Mencken: Every great wave of popular passion that rolls up on the prairies is dashed to spray when it strikes the hard rocks of Manhattan.

H.L. Mencken: New York is not all bricks and steel .... It is the place where all the aspirations of the Western World meet to form one vast master aspiration.... It is the icing on the pie called Christian Civilization.

Christopher Morley: The nation's thyroid gland.

Ogden Nash (1931): The Bronx? / No thonx.

Ogden nash (1964): I wrote those lines, "The Bronx? No Thonx"; / I shudder to confess them. / Now I'm an older, wiser man / I cry, "The Bronx? God bless them!"

Albert Bigelow Paine (1901): The Great White Way.

Will Rogers: Hardly a day goes by, you know, that some innocent bystander ain't shot in New York City. All you got to do is be innocent and stand by and they're gonna shoot you. The other day, there was four people shot in one day – four innocent people – in New York City, Amazing. It's kind of hard to find four innocent people in New York. That's why a policeman don't have to aim. He just shoots anywhere. Whoever he hits, that's the right one.

Jerry Rubin: Every person on the streets of New York is a type. The city is one big theater where everyone is on display.

Emmanuel Savas: Genghis Khan conquered Asia with an army one half the size of New York City's civil service.

Gail Sheehy: The upper EastSide of Manhattan ... is the province of Let's Pretend.

Betty Smith ("A Tree Grows in Brooklyn," 1943): There's a tree that grows in Brooklyn. Some people call it the Tree of heaven. No matter where its seed falls, it makes a tree which struggles to reach the sky.

John Steinbeck: Niagara Falls is very nice. It's like a large version of the old Bond sign on Times Square. I'm very glad I saw it, because from now on if I am asked whether I have seen Niagara Falls I can say yes, and be telling the truth for once.

Mark Twain (quoting an "American joke"): In Boston they ask, How much does he know? In New York, How much is he worth? In Philadelphia, Who were his parents?

UA: Wall Street is a thoroughfare that begins in a graveyard and ends in a river.

Kurt Vonnegut: Skyscraper National Park.

Oscar Wilde: I was disappointed with Niagara – most people must be disappointed with Niagara. Every American bride is taken there, and the sight of the stupendous waterfall must be one of the earliest, if not the keenest disappointments in American married life.

Thomas Wolfe: One belongs to New York instantly, one belongs to it as much in five minutes as in five years.

Israel Zangwell ("The Melting Pot," 1908): We plant a tub and call it Paradise .... New York is the great stone desert.

NORTH CAROLINA

North Carolina: 12th state (1789); Nicknames: Tar Heel State, Old North State; Capitol: Raleigh
Esse quam videri: To be rather than seem. (State motto)
North Carolina - in 1629, a huge tract of land included what would become North and South Carolina was named *Carolana* (Latin for Charles) in honor of King Charles I of England. The spelling was later changed to Carolina. North and South Carolina became separate colonies in 1712.
Sam J. Ervin, Jr: In my honest and unbiased judgment, the Good Lord will place the Garden of Eden in North Carolina when He restores it to earth. He will do this because He will have so few changes to make in order to achieve perfection.
Federal Writers' Project (1939): A vale of humility (NC) between two mountains of conceit (VA & SC).
Ovid Williams Pierce: North Carolina begins with the brightness of sea sands and ends with the loneliness of the Smokies reaching in chill and cloud to the sky.
Christian Reid (title of her 1876 novel): The Land of the Sky.
UA: If God isn't a Tarheel why is the sky Carolina blue?
UA: First at Bethel, furthest at Gettysburg, and last at Appomattox.

NORTH DAKOTA

North Dakota: 39th state (1889); Nicknames: Flickertail State, Peace Garden State, Sioux State, Rough Rider State; Capitol: Bismark
Liberty and Union, Now and Forever, One and Inseparable. (State motto)
North Dakota from the Dakota Indians who roamed the northern plains. Tribes joined together in friendship, and *Dahkota* means "allies" in their language. The Dakota were also known as Sioux.
Mart Connolly: I like the democracy of North Dakota, the state without a millionaire and with fewest paupers; where rich and poor find a common meeting ground in the fight for improvements in the home state .... There is something of the broadness of its prairies in the mental makeup of its people. A radical is not so radical nor a conservative so conservative in this rather free-and-easy non-eastern state.
Federal Writers' Project (1938): Freely admitted is the rural character of the State, and there is seldom an attempt to cover native crudities with a veneer of eastern culture.
Clifton Johnson (1910): All this country is still youthful. Man has not labored long enough there to thoroughly humanize it, and often you continue to find a savor of the desert or wilderness .... The long broad slope between the Rocky Mountains and the Mississippi River which includes North Dakota is destined to be in most ways an ideal farming section that for extent and fertility will be unrivaled the world over.
Theodore Roosevelt: I would never have been President if it had not been for my experiences in North Dakota.
John Steinbeck: If you will take a map of the United States and fold it in the middle, eastern edge against western, and crease it sharply, right in the crease will be Fargo .... That may not be a very scientific method for finding the east-west middle of the country, but it will do.

OHIO

Ohio: 17th state (1803); Nickname: The Buckeye State; Capitol: Columbus
With God, All Things Are Possible. (State motto)
Ohio is named for the Ohio River; the Iroquois word *oheo* means "something great," "great river," or "beautiful."
Louis Bromfield: Ohio is the farthest west of the east and the farthest north of the south.
Charles Dickens: Cincinnati is a beautiful city; cheerful, thriving, and animated. I have not often seen a place that commends itself so favorably and pleasantly to a stranger at the fiirst glance as this does: with its clean houses of red and white, its well-paved roads, and footways of bright tile. Nor does it become less prepossessing on a closer acquaintance. The streets are broad and airy, the shops extremely good, the private residences remarkable for their elegance and neatness.

John Gunther: Basically, Ohio is nothing more or less than a giant carpet of agriculture studded by great cities.

John Gunther: I know of no other metropolis with quite so impressive a record in the practical application of good citizenship to government.

OKLAHOMA

Oklahoma: 46th state (1907); Nicknames: The Sooner State, Boomer State, Land of Six Countries, America's Frontier Lake State; Capitol: Oklahoma City

***Labor omnia vincit*:** Work conquers all things. (State motto)

Oklahoma is a combination of two Choctaw words – *okla*, meaning "people," and *hummus*, meaning "red"; thus Oklahoma means "red people."

Alastair Cooke: In 1889 the last big track of Indian land was declared open for settlement, in Oklahoma. The claimants and the speculators mounted their horses and lined up like trotters waiting for a starting gun. The itchy ones jumped the gun and were ever after known as Sooners—and Oklahoma was thereafter called the Sooner State.

John Gunther: The state that Oklahoma most resembles is of course Texas, if only because it too does everything with color and originality, but tell an Oklahoman that his State is a "dependency" of Texas and he will bite your eyes out.

John Gunther: During a single day (during the Dust Bowl disaster of 1935), I heard, fifty million tons of soil were blown away. People sat in Oklahoma City, with the sky invisible for three days in a row, holding dust masks over their faces and wet towels to protect their mouths at night, while the farms blew by.

John Gunther: Tulsa, "oil capital of the world," as it calls itself, is a tough, get-rich-quick, heady town about as sensitive as corduroy.

Oscar Hammerstein II (Oklahoma, 1943): Oklahoma, / Where the wind comes sweepin' down the plain, / And the wavin' wheat / Can sure smell sweet / When the wind comes right behind the rain.

Ernie Pyle: Oklahoma City is an especially friendly town. People have a pride about their town – not a silly civic pride, but that same feeling that exists in San Fransisco and New Orleans. They just wouldn't live anywhere else, that's all.

Will Rogers: When the Oakies left Oklahoma and moved to California, it raised the I.Q. of both states.

John Steinbeck: Okie use' ta mean you was from Oklahoma. Now it means you're a dirty son-of-a-bitch. Okie means you're scum. Don't mean nothing itself, it's the way they say it.

OREGON

Oregon: 33rd state (1859); Nickname: Beaver State; Capitol: Salem

The Union. (State motto)

Oregon, sometimes spelled *Origan* or *Ouragon,* was an early name for the river now called the Columbia.

Uncle Anthony: "The Holy Road" was another name for "The Oregon Trail"- I'm sure that ain't what the Indians called it.

William O. Douglas: Packed tight in a New York City subway, I have closed my eyes and imagined I was walking the ridge high above Cougar Lake. That ridge has the majesty of a cathedral.

John Gunther (1947): Oregon was settled by New Englanders in the first instance, and has a native primness, a conservatism, much like that of New Hampshire or Vermont. It is, indeed, one of the most astonishing things in America that Portland, Oregon, should be almost indistinguishable from Portland, Maine.

E. J. Kahn, Jr.: Oregonians ... tend to be small-townish, middle-of-the-roadish, and Waspish. They're also fairly prudish about some things. *Last Tango in Paris* is not advertised in the big family newspapers, and when the society columns mention a cocktail party, it is usually called a reception.

Rudyard Kipling: Portland produces lumber and jig-saw fittings for houses, and beer and buggies, and bricks and biscuit; and, in case you should miss the fact, there are glorified views of the town hung up in public places with the value of the products set down in dollars. All this is excellent and exactly suitable to the opening of a new country; but when a man tells you it is civilization, you object.

Rudyard Kipling: Portland is so busy that it can't attend to its own sewage or paving, and the four-story brick blocks front cobble-stones and plank sidewalks and other things much worse. I saw a foundation being dug out. The seage of perhaps twenty years ago, had thoroughly soaked into the soil, and there was a familiar and Oriental look about the compost that flew up with each shovel-load. Yet the local papers, as was just and proper, swore there was no place like Portland, Oregon, U.S.A.

H.L. Mencken: Oregon is seldom heard of. Its people believe in the Bible, and hold that all radicals should be lynched. It has no poets and no statesmen.

Neal R. Pierce: If any West Coast city could be said to have a monopoly on propriety and an anxiousness to "keep things as they are," it is Portland, a town of quiet old wealth, discreet culture, and cautious politics.

UA Pioneer on the Oregon Trail: The cowards never started – and the weak died along the way.

Phillip Wyle: Oregon is only an idea. It is in no scientific way a reality.

PENNSYLVANIA

Pennsylvania: 2nd state (1787); Nickname: Keystone State, Quaker State; Capitol: Harrisburg

Virtue, Liberty and Independence. (State motto)

Pennsylvania is a Commonwealth; the name means "Penn's Woods," was given to the land by King Charles II of England in honor of Admiral William Penn, father of Pennsylvania's founder William Penn.

Henry Adams (1918): The Pennsylvania mind, as minds go, was not complex; it reasoned little and never talked, but in practical matters it was the steadiest of all American types; perhaps the most efficient; certainly the safest.

Stephen Birmingham: But in Philadelphia, Philadelphians feel, the Right Thing is more natural and more firmly bred in them than anywhere else.

Rocky Blier (Pittsburgh Steeler running back): Pittsburgh? They call it a shot-and-beer twon. Hard-working guys with stumpy legs. A team with mean-looking black uniforms. Nothing squeaky-clean about Pittsburgh.

Charles Dickens: (Philadelphia) is a handsome city, but distractingly regular. After walking about it for an hour or two, I felt that I would have given the world for a crooked street.

Charles Dickens: Pittsburgh is like Birmingham in England; at least its townspeople say so. Setting aside the streets, the shops, the houses, wagons, factories, public buildings, and population, perhaps it may be. It certainly has a great quantity of smoke hanging around it, and is famous for its ironworks.

W.C. Fields (proposed inscription for his tombstone): On the whole I'd rather be in Philadelphia.

Thomas Jefferson: The cradle of tolerance and freedom of religion.

Pennsylvania Democratic Committee (1803): Pennsylvania is the keystone of the democratic arch.

S. J. Perelman: Philadelphia, a metropolis sometimes known as the City of Brotherly Love, but more accurately as the City of Bleak November Afternoons.

Henry Spencer (1882): Six months' residence here would justify suicide.

Mark Twain (quoting an "American joke"): In Boston they ask, How much does he know? In New York, How much is he worth? In Philadelphia, Who were his parents?

RHODE ISLAND

Rhode Island: 13th state (1790); Nicknames: Ocean State, Little Rhody; Capitol: Providence

Hope. (State motto)

Rhode Island: The origin of its name is disputed. One theory: name came form Giovanni da Verrazano after coming upon Block Island in 1524 the navigator supposedly wrote it was "about the size of the island of Rhodes" – a Greek island in the Aegean Sea. Others claim the Dutch explorer Adriaen Block discovered an island in Narragansett Bay in 1614 and called it *Roodt Eylandt,* meaning "red island," because of its red clay soil. *Rhode Island* was the name given to Aquidneck Island, the largest island in Narragansett Bay, and site of Portsmouth and Newport. Roger Williams named his settlement *Providence* in 1636 for

God's providence. The first charter for the colony (1644) was for "the Proidence Plantations in Narragansett Bay." The Island of Rhode Island grew in importance, and the second charter (1663) called the colony "Rhode Island and Providence Plantations;" the state has retained that lengthy title.

Alistair Cooke: Newport had once been a haven for religious dissenters out of Massachusetts and later a capital port of the slave trade. One hundred years after theDeclaration that "all men are created equal," there began to gather in Newport a colony of the rich, determined to show that some Americans were conspicuously more equal than others.

Joan Didion: What Newport turns out to be, then, is homiletic, a fantastically elaborate stage setting for an American morality play in which money and happiness are presented as antithetical.

John Gunther: The uniqueness of Rhode Island lies in its size; (James) Bryce wrote that it might become the first American "city-state." Everybody is packed close together; almost everybody knows everybody else. An administrator – the governor, say – is at the beck and call of anybody; he must go and see for himself in an emergency, becasue everything is within fifty miles of his office.

Henry James: One views it as placed there, by some refinement in the scheme of nature, just as a touchstone of taste – with a beautiful little sense to be read into it by a few persons, and nothing at all to be made of it, as to its essence, by most others.

Mark Twain: There is a sumptuous variety about the New England weather that compels the stranger's admiration—and regret.... In the spring I have counted one hundred and thirty-six different kinds of weather inside of four-and-twenty hours.

Mark Twain: If you don't like the weather in New England, just wait a few minutes.

UA: Before the Revolutionary War, the colony was referred to as "Rogue Island"

Woodrow Wilson: Rhode Island was settled and is made up of people who found it unbearable to live anywhere else in New England.

SOUTH CAROLINA

South Carolina: 8th state (1788); Nickname: Palmetto State; Capitol: Columbia

Animis opibusque parati: Prepared in mind and resources. (State motto)

South Carolina - in 1629, a huge tract of land included what would become North and South Carolina was named *Carolana* (Latin for Charles) in honor of King Charles I of England. The spelling was later changed to Carolina. North and South Carolina became separate colonies in 1712.

George William Bagby (1977): Gentlemen, there are Hottentots and there are Cottontots. A cottontot I take to be a person who, growing nothing but cotton, has to buy every earthly thing that he uses or consumes, consequently rarely if ever saves anything, and finds himself at the last of the year the property of his commission merchant – himself the property of the Northern man.

Federal Writers' Project: South Carolinians are among the rare folk in the South who have no secret envy of Virginians.

William Francis Guess: We were taught to be South Carolinians, Ca-ro-li-ni-ans, mind you, and not, please God, the Tarheel slur, Calinians.

James Louis Petigru (1860): South Carolina is too small for a republic and too large for a lunatic asylum.

Johann David Schoepf: The manners of the inhabitants of Charleston are as different from those of the other North American cities as are the products of their soil.... There prevails here a finer manner of life, and on the whole there are more evidence of courtesy than in the northern cities.

SOUTH DAKOTA

South Dakota: 40th state (1889); Nicknames: Sunshine State, Coyote State, Land of Infinite Variety; Capitol: Pierre

Under God the People Rule. (State motto)

South Dakota: North and South Dakota were named for the Sioux Indians, who called themselves *Dahkota* meaning "allies."

Holger Cahill: You could shoot a cue ball from the southern boundary of the state all the way to Canada and halfway to the North Pole.

George Armstrong Custer: A part of hell with the fires burnt out.

Tom Brokaw: I guess it's the physical and cultural remoteness of South Dakota that compels evryone to memorize almost every South Dakotan who has left the state and achieved some recognition. As a child I would pore over magazines and newspapers, looking for some sign that the rest of the world knew we existed.

Kathleen Norris: What frightens me ... is that our nation's urban majority don't understand a place like South Dakota. They don't connect what they consider to be the country's "boondocks" with the food they need for survival .... Often I think we are all Indians here, in as much danger of losing our land as the Sioux of one hundred years ago. And if it happens, I fear we will meet with the same massive national indifference.

John Steinbeck: I was not prepared for the Bad Lands. They deserve this name. They are like the work of an evil child. Such a place the Fallen Angels might have built as a spite to Heaven, dry and sharp, desolate and dangerous, and for me filled with foreboding. A sense comes from it that does not like or welcome humans.

TENNESSEE

Tennessee: 16th state (1796); Nicknames: The Volunteer State (War of 1812), Big Bend State (for the bend in the Tennessee River), and The Hog and Hominy State; Capitol: Nashville

Tennessee – America at Its Best. (State motto)

Tennessee name was adapted from the name of the principal Cherokee village, *Tenasie.*

Pearl S. Buck: It appears to be a very American state, Tennessee, and inhabited by very American people.

Hodding Carter (1947): It grew from a brawling boomtown on the river to the state's largest city so hurriedly that it has hardly had time to assess itself. Energetic, clean and preoccupied with its almost incredible industrial expansion, Memphis seems—despite its Beale Street, it's heavy Negro population, it's Cotton carnival, and a commanding position as the deep South's cotton-trade Center, more like a bustling midwestern city than the mecca of Mississippi planters.

O. Henry: Take of London fog 30 parts; malaria 10 parts; gas leaks 20 parts; dew drops gathered in a brickyard at sunrise 25 parts; odor of honeysuckle 15 parts. Mix. The mixture will give you an approximate conception of a Nashville drizzle.

Charles Kuralt: What you need for breakfast, they say in East Tennessee, is a jug of good corn liquor, a thick beefsteak, and a hound dog. Then you feed the beefsteak to the hound dog.

Ernie Pyle: The way the government interferes with private business is enough to drive a fellow crazy. That old government moved into Tennessee and bought a lot of hilly land. Then they signed a proclamation making this land into the Great Smokies National Park. And thereby ruined the finest settlement of moonshiners in the U.S.A.

Mark Twain: I came South for my health, I will go back on the same errand, and suddenly, Tennesseean journalism is too stirring for me.

TEXAS

Texas: 28th state (1845); Nickname: The Lone Star State; Capitol: Austin

Friendship. (State motto)

Texas comes from the Caddo Indian word, *Tejas*, meaning friends or allies.

Battle cry at San Jacinto, Texas, April 21, 1836: Remember the Alamo!

Edna Ferber: It was part of the Texas ritual. We're rich as son-of-a-bitch stew but look how homely we are, just as plain-folksy as Grandpappy back in 1836. We know about champagne and caviar but we talk hog and hominy.

John Gunther: I like the story, doubtless antique, that I heard near San Antonio. A child asks a stranger where he comes from, whereupon his father rebukes him gently, "Never do that, son. If a man's from Texas, he'll tell you. If he's not, why embarrass him by asking?"

Pat Neff: Texas could wear Rhode Island as a watch fob.

Philip H. Sheridan: If I owned Texas and Hell, I would rent out Texas and live in Hell.

John Steinbeck: Writers facing the problem of Texas find themselves floundering in generalities, and I am no exception. Texas is a state of mind. Texas is an obsession. Above all, Texas is a nation in every sense of the word.... A Texan outside of Texas is a foreigner.

John Steinbeck: Like most passionate nations Texas has its own private history based on, but not limited by, facts. The tradition of the tough and virtuous frontiersman is true but not exclusive. It is for the few to know that in the great old days of Virginia there were three punishments for high crimes—death, exile to Texas, and imprisonment, in that order. And some of the deportees must have descendents.

UTAH

Utah: 45th state (1896); Nickname: The Beehive State; Capitol: Salt Lake City

Industry. (State motto)

Utah is named for the Ute Indians, who lived there; *Eutaw* means "dwellers in the tops of the mountains"

Edward Abbey: Alaska is our biggest, buggiest, boggiest state. Texas remains our largest unfrozen state. But mountainous Utah, if ironed out flat, would take up more space on a map than either.

Ralph Waldo Emerson: One must thank the genius of Brigham Young for the creation of Salt Lake City, - an inestimable hospitality to the Overland Emigrants, and an efficient example to all men in the vast desert, teaching how to subdue and turn it to a habitable garden.

Federal Writers Project (1941): The fertility of the land has been outstripped by the fertility of the people.

Federal Writers Project (1941): Even if there had been no background of Joseph Smith, Angel Moroni, and the Book of Moorman, Utahans would have been incomprehensible, misunderstood and lied about, because they set down in the book of Western history the most stubbornly cross-grained chapter it contains.... Utah has always had a way of doing things different. The rest of the country has never quite got over it.

John Gunther: Jews in Utah, being non-Mormon, are theoretically subject to classification as Gentiles, which gives rise to the well-known remark that "Utah is the only place in the world where Jews are gentiles."

Charles Kuralt: What's in the Great Salt Lake? ... Salt. Eight billion tons of salt, worth about fifty billion dollars. Also gypsum, magnesium, lithium, sulfur, boron, and potash .... Swimmers like the Great Salt Lake. Nonswimmers are absolutely knocked out by it because they can't sink. There is no record of anybody ever having gone swimming and drowned in the Great Salt Lake. The best life preserver, they say, is a ten-pound weight tied to your feet, to keep your feet down and your head up.

Mark Twain: (Salt Lake City) lies in the edge of a level plain as broad as the state of Connecticut, and crouches close down to the ground under a curving wall of mighty mountains whose heads are hidden in the clouds, and whose shoulders bear relics of the snows of winter all the summer long. Seen from one of these dizzy heights, twelve or fifteen miles off, Great Salt Lake City is toned down and diminished till it is suggestive of a child's toy village reposing under the majestic protection of the Chinese wall.

VERMONT

Vermont: 14th state (1791); Nickname: Green Mountain State; Capitol: Montpelier

Freedom and Unity. (State motto)

Vermont gets its name from the French words *vert* (green) and *mont* (mountain).

Pearl S. Buck: Vermont is a country unto itself. Indeed, for fourteen years after the Declaration of Independence, the State refused to join the Union and remained an independent republic.

Pearl S. Buck: All in all, Vermont is a jewel state, small but precious.

Calvin Coolidge: I love Vermont because of her hills and valleys, her scenery and invigorating climate, but most of all, because of her indomitable people. They are a race of pioneers who have almost beggared themselves to serve others. If the spirit of liberty should vanish in other parts of the union, and support of our institutions should languish, it could all be replenished from the generous store held by the people of this brave little state of Vermont.

John Gunther: Vermonters are really something quite special and unique.... This State bows to nothing; the first legislative measure it ever passed was "to adopt the laws of God... until there is time to frame better."

Noel Perrin: There is no cure for Vermont weather. It is consistent only in its inconsistency.

Will Rogers: Statistics prove that no Vermonter ever left the State unless transportation was furnished in advance. She is what you call a "Hard Boiled State." The principal ingredients are Granite, Rock Salt and Republicans. The last being the hardest of the three.

Mark Twain: There is a sumptuous variety about the New England weather that compels the stranger's admiration—and regret.... In the spring I have counted one hundred and thirty-six different kinds of weather inside of four-and-twenty hours.

Mark Twain: If you don't like the weather in New England, just wait a few minutes.

VIRGINIA

Virginia: 10th state (1788); Nickname: The Old Dominion; Capitol: Richmond

Sic semper tyrannis: Thus always to tyrants. (State motto)

Virginia is named for Queen Elizabeth I of England, known as the "Virgin Queen."

James A. Bland (1875): Carry me back to old Virginny, / There's where the cotton and the corn and taters grow.

John Davis (1803): The higher Virginians seem to venerate themselves as men.

Clifford Dowdey: The Virginia idea, it must be clearly understood, was not what is today called the American Dream. The Virginian did not dream of a democracy, with its literal meaning of the rule of the people. His dream was to found an aristocratic republic, in which superior individuals would emerge to rule the many.

Douglas Southall Freeman: All eastern Virginians are Shintoists under the skin. Genealogy makes history personal to them in terms of family. Kinship to the eigth degree usually is recognized .... A pleasant society it is, one that does not adventure rashly into new acquaintanceship but welcomes with a certain stateliness of manner those who come with letters from friends.

John Gunther: But what I like best (about Richmond),..., is the heroic (and heroically ugly) equestrian statue of George Washington, which was cast in Munich of all places, and which now stands in Capital Square. The general's eyes look sternly at the State House and his finger, like a flail, points to the penitentiary!

Thomas Jefferson: The good Old Dominion (Virginia), the blessed mother of us all.

Thomas Jefferson: Our society is neither scientific nor splendid, but independent, hospitable, correct and neighborly.

Robert E. Lee (1870): You can work for Virginia, to build her up again, to make her great again. You can teach your children to live and cherish her.

Virginia Moore: Virginia reeks of tobacco. Its odor saturates her like the coat of a veteran smoker. The brown stain of tobacco juice is on every page of her history.

Tom Robbins: In South Richmond, the mouse holes, lace curtains and Sears catalogs, even the bologney sandwiches and measles epidemics, always wore a faint odor of cured tobacco.

James Wooten: Wouldn't it be nice if when it (Arlington Cemetery) is all full, they'd just stop having wars. I mean, like you just say, "Well, I'm sorry but we can't get in this war because we don't have any more room left in Arlington."

WASHINGTON

Washington: 42nd state (1889); Nickname: Evergreen State; Capitol: Olympia

Alki (Chinook): By and by. (State motto)

Washington is named for George Washington.

William O. Douglas: The wildest, the most remote, and I think the most picturesque beach area of our whole coastline lies under a pounding surf along the Pacific Ocean in the state of Washington.

Paul Fountain: Rainier, from Puget Sound, is a sight for the gods, and when one looks upon him he feels that he is in the presence of the gods.

George Sessions Perry: In this city of hills and waterways, surrounded by visible, snowy mountain peaks, it is almost impossible to build a house without a view.

Neal R. Pierce: Washington is a puzzling state. We think of it as cool, pristine and evergreen. Yet the civilization around Puget Sound is industrial, cosmopolitan, intense, wracked by economic boom or bust.

Ernie Pyle: Everybody in Portland is crazy about Portland. They rave about it. They don't like chamber of commerce folders; they don't talk about their industries and their schools and their crops; they roar about what a wonderful place Portland is, just to live in.

John Steinbeck: I remembered Seattle as a town sitting on hills beside a matchless harborage – a little city of space and trees and gardens, its houses matched to such a background. It is no longer so .... This Seattle was not something changed that I once knew. It was a new thing. Set down there not knowing it was Seattle, I could not have told where I was. Everywhere frantic growth, a carcinomatous growth.

Thomas Wolfe: And unapproachable the great line of the Cascades with their snow-spired sentinels Hood, Adams, Jefferson, Three Sisters, etc., and out of the Bend at 3 and then through the vast and level pinelands—somewhat reminiscent of the South.

WEST VIRGINIA

West Virginia: 35th state (1863); Nicknames: Mountain State, Panhandle State; Capitol: Charleston

Montani semper liberi: Mountaineers are always free. (State motto)

West Virginia was formed from the western counties of Virginia, which was named for Queen Elizabeth I of England, known as the Virgin Queen.

John Denver (1971): Country roads, take me home / To the place I belong. / West Virginia, mountain momma / Take me home, country roads.

John Gunther (1947): The state is one of the most mountainous in the country; sometimes it is called the "Little Switzerland" of America, and I once heard an irreverent local citizen call it the "Afghanistan of the United States."

John Knowles (1960): We West Virginians are very tired of being considered inhabitants of just a dominion of the Old Dominion; we would like to make it clear that our state has been independent for ninety years. Some residents take a strong line about this and always refer to it in conversation as "WEST – By God – Virginia!"

John Knowles: On the map my state is probably the funniest-looking state in the Union; it resembles a pork chop with the narrow end splayed.

John Alexander Williams: Whether or not mountaineers were always free, they were almost always poor.

WISCONSIN

Wisconsin: 30th state (1848); Nicknames: Badger State, America's Dairyland; Capitol: Madison

Forward. (State motto)

Wisconsin is named for the Wisconsin River, whose Chippewa name is translated "the gathering of waters."

George Sessions Perry: Wisconsin's politics have traditionally been uproar politics – full of yammer, the squawk, the accusing finger, the injured howl. Every voter is an amateur detective, full of zeal to get out and nip a little political iniquity in the bud.

John Steinbeck: I had heard of the Wisconsin Dells but was not prepared for the weird country sculptured by the Ice Age, a strange, gleaming country of water and carved rock, black and green. To awaken here might make one believe it a dream of some other planet, for it has a non-earthly quality, or else the engraved record of a time when the world was much younger and much different

Frank Parker Stockbridge: By cheese factories and creameries they direct the stranger in rural Wisconsin, for cheese factories and creameries are the most striking landmarks of that country. His most striking impression is that the entire landscape of southern Wisconsin is as picturesquely suggestive of dairying as the skyline of Pittsburgh is of the steel industry.

WYOMING

Wyoming: 44th state (1890); Nicknames: Equality State, The Cowboy State; Capitol: Cheyenne.
Equal rights. (State motto)
Wyoming is from the Delaware Indian phrase *meche-weami-ing*, or "land of mountains and valleys alternating."
Federal Writers' Project (1941): Wyoming is a land of great open spaces with plenty of elbow room .... There are sections of the State where it is said you can look farther and see less than any other place in the world.
John Gunther: Here is America high, naked, and exposed; this is a massive upland almost like Bolivia.
John Gunther: Almost all the great western rivers are born in or near Wyoming: the Snake (which becomes the Columbia), the Green (Colorado), North Platte, and Yellowstone.
Rudyard Kipling: I have been through Yellowstone National Park in a buggy, in the company of an adventurous old lady from Chicago and her husband, who disapproved of (the) scenery as being "ongodly." I fancy it scared them.

TEN PROVINCES & THREE TERRITORIES OF CANADA

ALBERTA

Alberta (AB): formed in 1882; entered Confederation September 1, 1905; nicknames: Wild Rose Country; Wild Rose Province.
Capitol: Edmonton (The West Edmonton Mall is one of the largest indoor shopping and entertainment centers or "malls" in the world).
Motto: Strong and Free
Origin of Name: Named for English Queen Victoria's fourth daughter (she and her husband Prince Albert had nine children – four sons and five daughters) Princess Louise Caroline Alberta, the wife of the Governor General of Canada when the province was formed in 1882.
Edmonton: Name taken from Fort Edmonton, built in 1795 farther down the North Saskatchewan River than the present city. The fort was destroyed in 1807, but was relocated within the site of the present city limits by the Hudson's Bay Company some time before 1819. The fort is reputed to have been named by William Tomison for Edmonton, now part of metropolitan London, England, in honour of the birthplace of John Peter Pruden, a clerk of the Hudson's Bay Company.
Provincial Symbols: Animal: Rocky Mountain Bighorn Sheep; Bird: Great Horned Owl; Flower: Wild Rose; Tree: Lodgepole Pine
Alberta is one of Canada's three prairie provinces, bordered by the Rocky Mountains and its foothills on the west. The southern part of Alberta is mostly flat (hence "flatlanders" refers to prairie residents), with fields of grain. The north has rivers, lakes, forest and muskeg (or peat bog). Alberta gets more sun than any other province; in the southwest mild, warm winds called the "chinook," funnel through the mountains from the Pacific Ocean. Drilling for oil and natural gas, especially south-east of Calgary, has made the province wealthy (oil workers are called "rig pigs"), but grain farming and ranching are also important. "Head-Smashed-In Buffalo Jump" is a place south of Calgary where the Blackfoot people used to stampede buffalo over the cliff to their deaths and provide food and clothing.
UA: TOP 10 REASONS TO LIVE IN ALBERTA

1. The Rockies are between you and B.C.
2. Preston Manning goes to Ottawa a lot, so he isn't here
3. Tax on goods is 7 percent instead of approx. 20 percent
4. The Premier is a beer drinker with about grade 4 education
5. Flames vs. Oilers
6. Stamps vs. Eskies
7. You can exploit almost any natural resource you can think of
8. Eventually, it will be your town's turn to ban Video Casino games
9. The Americans below you are all in anti-government militia groups
10. You get red and white license plates so other Canadians can immediately identify the bad drivers on their roads

BRITISH COLUMBIA

British Columbia (BC): entered the Confederation July 20, 1871; nicknames: BC, Pacific Playground, "The Graveyard of the Pacific" (because of its dangerous coast), "Lotus Land"; Capitol: Victoria: was first known as Fort Victoria, the city, like the numerous other locations of the same name, commemorates Queen Victoria (1819-1900). The name was chosen by the Council of the Northern Department (Hudson's Bay Company) at Fort Garry, June 10, 1843.

Motto: heraldic motto is *Splendor sine occasu* = "splendor without end/diminishment;" long-time tourism motto has been "Super Natural BC"; "Beautiful BC; since BC got the 2010 Olympics, it's "The Best Place On Earth"

Origin of Name: BC used to be 2 colonies: Vancouver Island and BC, then amalgamated by Governor Douglas to head off Americans coming up for the 1849 gold rush. The southern part of the province was named "Columbia" after the river running through it. The "British" part was added to the name to avoid confusion with the South American country of Columbia. The northern part was originally called New Caledonia (aka Scotland). The entire province of British Columbia was SUPPOSED to be called "British Caledonia" until some bright spark in the Colonial Office pointed out that we already HAD a "Nova Scotia" – so "British Columbia" was chosen by Queen Victoria for the colony in 1858.

Provincial Symbols: Animal: White Spirit Bear; Bird: Steller's Jay; Flower: Pacific Dogwood; Tree: Red Cedar

B.C. is a province of contrasts, from its Pacific coastline to high mountain ranges inland to its flat grasslands in the northeast corner. Most of the year, you can golf, swim OUTDOORS and snow ski ON THE SAME DAY. The climate and vegetation are similarly varied. The coast has mild, wet climate, while parts of the interior are drier – even desert. Much of this province is mountainous and forested; B.C. produces one half of Canada's lumber. Most people live along the coast or in the mountain valleys, especially around Vancouver and Victoria. BC is home to more mammal and bird species than any other Canadian Province. Of 209 known terrestrial mammals in Canada, 119 live in BC. Of 462 known resident species of birds, 362 live in BC.

The final boundary of the 49th parallel resulted in a tiny bit of land just south being ceded to the USA. It's called "Point Roberts" and is a few acres, totally isolated by Canada – locals have to cross into Canada to drive to the rest of the USA. You can go by boat to Seattle (etc.) but that's mostly a drug-runner's route.

For decades the whole mainland of the province was "governed" by a few Mounties and a single judge – Sir Matthew Baillie Begbie – known as the "Hanging Judge," who rode alone through the wilderness from town to town. Not quite the "Wild West" – he defended himself against several murder attempts, held court wherever he found himself, and handed out the typically simple sentences of the time – most crimes being "capital."

UA: We built the Rockies to keep out those damned Albertans.

UA: He's as up-tight as a Squamish (Native Canadians) totem pole!

UA: TOP 10 REASONS TO LIVE IN BRITISH COLUMBIA

1. You don't have to worry if it is going to rain - it's already raining
2. Vancouver: 1.5 million people and two bridges to the 'burbs
3. The local hero is a pot-smoking snowboarder
4. The local wine doesn't taste like malt vinegar
5. Your $400,000 Vancouver home is 5 hours from downtown
6. You have a university with a nude beach
7. You can throw a rock and hit three Starbucks locations
8. You have a fleet of old rusted ships that you got for free from China
9. There's always some sort of forest protest going on somewhere
10. People here never get a tan - they rust

CANADA-GENERAL

Canada: "The Dominion of Canada" was formed in 1867 at Charlottetown, P.E.I., when the leaders of the two provinces of Upper or British Canada (which later became Ontario) and Lower, or French Canada (which later became Quebec) and Nova Scotia and New Brunswick known as the "Fathers of the Confederation" – John A. Macdonald and Georges Cartier in Canada, Samuel Tilley and Charles Tupper in New Brunswick and Nova Scotia, and others – agreed to form a united nation in the British North American Act ; The plaque outside the Confederation Chamber reads: "In the hearts and minds of the delegates who assembled in this room on September 1st, 1864 was born the Dominion of Canada. **Providence being their Guide, they builded better than they knew.** Nicknames: The Great White North, Canadialand, The 51st State (due to Canada's perceived similarity with the United States), **"A few acres of snow"** (a quotation by Voltaire about 18th-century Canada's perceived economic unworth as a colony); Soviet Canuckistan – (first use derogatorily by Pat Buchanan, from Canada's perceived anti-American and left-wing political alignment), America's Cousin, The True North Strong and Free (from the National Anthem of Canada), "O Canada" (Describing how many residents including THIS EDITOR AND HIS FAMILY see this beautiful nation and all its People), Canadia; Other Nicknames for Canadians: Canucks, Ice Heads.

Capitol: Ottowa

National Anthem: "God Save the Queen" (official); "O Canada" (unofficial)

Motto: From Sea to Sea

Origin of Name: Canada is named from the Huron-Iroquois word *kanata*, meaning "village" or "small community," referring to the area along the St. Lawrence River.

Animal: Beaver

Tree: Maple Tree

Canada is the second largest country in size in the world, but it does not have a big population (approximately 30 million); in fact, the city of Tokyo, Japan has almost as many people as all of Canada. Nearly 90% of all of Canada's population lives along its southern border with the United States. Canada is made up of ten provinces and three territories in the north. The country has two official languages: English and French.

Andy Barrie: We will explain the appeal of curling to you if you explain the appeal of the National Rifle Association to us.

Bible: Psalms 72: He shall have dominion also from sea unto sea, and from the river unto the ends of the earth.

President George W. Bush (during his first visit to Ottawa Nov. 30, 2004): I want to thank all the Canadians who came out today to wave to me - with all five fingers!

June Callwood: The beaver, which has come to represent Canada as the eagle does the United States and the lion Britain, is a flat-tailed, slow-witted, toothy rodent known to bite off it's own testicles or to stand under its own falling trees.

Al Capone: I don't even know what street Canada is on.

Sir Winston Churchill: There are no limits to the majestic future which lies before the mighty expanse of Canada with its verile, aspiring, cultured, and generous-hearted people.

Sir Winston Churchill: Canada is the linchpin of the English-speaking world.

Stompin' Tom Connors: If you don't believe your country should come before yourself, you can better serve your country by livin' someplace else.

Prime Minister Jean Chrétien (on finding no Iraqi "WMD's " or weapons of mass destruction): A proof is a proof. What kind of a proof? It's a proof. A proof is a proof. And when you have a good proof, it's because it's proven.

John Crosbie (on the state of Canada's military in 1983): Down in Newfoundland, we can hardly sleep for wondering when St. Pierre and Miquelon are going to invade.

Former Saskatchewan premier Tommy Douglas: Canada is like an old cow. The West feeds it. Ontario and Quebec milk it. And you can well imagine what it's doing in the Maritimes.

Lord Dufferin: A constitution nursed upon the oxygen of our bright winter atmosphere makes its owner feel as though he could toss about the pine trees in his glee.

Arnold Edinborough: Canada has never been a melting-pot; more like a tossed salad.

Will Ferguson: Many Canadian nationalists harbour the bizarre fear that should we ever reject royalty, we would instantly mutate into Americans, as though the Canadian sense of self is so frail and delicate a bud, that the only thing stopping it from being swallowed whole by the US is an English lady in a funny hat.

Will Ferguson: With or without the Royals, we are not Americans. Nor are we British. Or French. Or Void. We are something else. And the sooner we define this, the better.

Will Ferguson: The great themes of Canadian history are as follows: Keeping the Americans out, keeping the French in, and trying to get the Natives to somehow disappear.

Matthew Fisher: I'm not an American! I am a Canadian. I come from a "nice," thoroughly unrealistic country.

Walter Gordon: Americans as a nation do not know a great deal about Canada. This is our misfortune.

Thomas Chandler Haliburton (from Nova Scotia, wrote a series of books called *The Clockmaker*, 1836, *The Attache*, 1843, and *The Old Judge*, 1849, in which their chief character "SAM SLICK" is a "slicker" speaking the "down-east" dialect and selling clocks by his knowledge of "soft sawder" and "human natur." Sam Slick became famous throughout the English-speaking world and hence the term): "Slick," "city slicker" and "slickster."

Paul Henderson: Canadians don't have a very big political lever, we're nice guys.

Montreal Mayor Camillien Houde (in 1939 to King George VI): Your majesty, I thank you from the bottom of my heart, and Madame Houde thanks you from her bottom too.

C.D. Howe (in Washington, D.C. to resolve a shipping dispute): Gentlemen, we all must realize that neither side has any monopoly on sons of bitches.

Peter Jennings: Canadians have an abiding interest in surprising those Americans who have historically made little effort to learn about their neighbour to the North.

Stuart Keate: In any world menu, Canada must be considered the vichyssoise of nations, it's cold, half-French, and difficult to stir.

Former Toronto mayor Allan Lamport: Canada is the greatest nation in this country.

Andrew H. Malcom: It's going to be a great country when they finish unpacking it.

Marshall McLuhan: The huge advantage of Canada is its backwardness.

Marshall McLuhan: Canadians are the people who learned to live without the bold accents of the natural ego-trippers of other lands.

Helen Gordon McPherson: Canadians have been so busy explaining to the Americans that we aren't British, and to the British that we aren't Americans that we haven't had time to become Canadians.

Rick Mercer: The US is our trading partner, our neighbour, our ally and our friend... and sometimes we'd like to give them such a smack!

Desmond Morton: Canadians, like their historians, have spent too much time remembering conflicts, crises, and failures. They forgot the great, quiet continuity of life in a vast and generous land. A cautious people learns from its past; a sensible people can face its future. Canadians, on the whole, are both.

Farley Mowat: After all, we fought the Yanks in 1812 and kicked them the hell out of our country - but not with blanks.

Kevin Myers (*The Daily Telegraph*, London): As always, Canada will now bury its war dead, just as the rest of the world, as always, will forget its sacrifice, just as it always forgets nearly everything Canada ever does. It seems that Canada's historic mission is to come to the selfless aid both of its friends and of complete strangers, and then, once the crisis is over, to be well and truly ignored. Canada is the perpetual wallflower that stands on the edge of the hall, waiting for someone to come and ask her for a dance.

Peter Stoffer: You look at the history—the aboriginal people welcomed the first settlers here with open arms, fed us and took care of us ... that continues today, we welcome people from all nations to come in and share.

Former Prime Minister Pierre E. Trudeau (who caused a minor scandal when opposition MPs, Members of Parliament, claimed he had mouthed the words "f* o**" to them in the House of Commons in February 1971. Pressed by journalists, Trudeau later unconvincingly stated he may have said or mouthed):** "fuddle duddle or something like that." (The phrase then took on a humorous connotation of that event for Canadians).

Former Prime Minister Pierre Trudeau (addressing the Press Club in Washington, D.C. on March 25, 1969, describing Canada's relationship with the USA): Living next to you is in some ways like sleeping with an elephant. No matter how friendly and even-tempered is the beast, if I can call it that, one is affected by every twitch and grunt."

Former Prime Minister Pierre Trudeau (on being referred to as "that ass-hole" by former President Richard Nixon): "I've been called worse things by better people."

Former Prime Minister Pierre E. Trudeau: Canada is a country whose main exports are hockey players and cold fronts. Our main imports are baseball players and acid rain.

UA: What is a Canadian? A Canadian is a fellow wearing English tweeds, a Hong Kong shirt and Spanish shoes, who sips Brazilian coffee sweetened with Philippine sugar from a Bavarian cup while nibbling Swiss cheese, sitting at a Danish desk over a Persian rug, after coming home in a German car from an Italian movie... and then writes his Member of Parliament with a Japanese ballpoint pen on French paper, demanding that he do something about foreigners taking away our Canadian jobs.

UA: God Bless America, but God help Canada to put up with them!

UA: The Meaning of "Eh!" ... and other Canadian terms:

It is quite obvious that some people are having a tough time understanding Canadians, so the following will run through a very brief translation of the Canadian 'dialect' and hopefully ease some minds out there.

EH = pronounced AY (similar, but not the same as huh)

Eh is a useful word that is very important and is the basis of all Canadian communications. It is used in conjunction with other words, or simply by itself. The tone or the slight differences in exclamation also changes the meaning:-

Eh? = what did you say?
Eh? = what do you think?
EH? = something to say just to end a sentence.
Ehhhh!! = WOW!!
EH!? = what do you mean?
Eh?? = your joking!!!??
EH!! = Hello..(you off in the distance!!!)
Eh? want a doughnut or some Tim Bits?
Eh! = sure!!
Eh!Eh! = coffee double-cream too please!
Eh? = what you say when you realize you have no money to pay for it.
Eh..cmon, eh? = asking them to let you pay for it next time.
hey..eh! = want to go to the drive-in movie??
Eh...uhuh = yes sure!
Eh..y'know = I'll pick you up at 8:00 (8:30 in Newfoundland).
Eh..cmon!! = well that's early..but ok.
Eh..wanna? eh? = lets fool around ...
EHHHHHHH = sounds coming from the car.
hey..um..er eh... = I'm pregnant!
EH????????? = how did that happen?
EHHehhEHHehhEHHH = sounds from the delivery room.
EHHH-ehh, EHHH-ehh = baby's first cry.
Ehh..whadya think eh? = marry me.
Other interesting Canadian terms:-
hoser = a good friend..

take off! = you are kidding, no way, fly an airplane.
skates = what all canadians wear as first shoes (that's why we walk funny).
lumberjack = something in our genes..
Newfoundland screech = a nice (?) little distilled rum drink ....!
swish = a drink made from leftover screech barrels.
sixty-pounder = large bottle of Screech rum.
The Rock = Newfoundland.
Newfoundland = pronounced NOOFUNLAN.
Dory = Newfoundland cruise liner.
Toronto = pronounced Trawna.
Lotus Land = British Columbia (when it is not raining).
Lake Ontario = where all sewers drain into.
Two-Four = case of 24 bottles/cans of beer.
Yukon Dew Me = A drink.
Over by = no one has deciphered that term yet....
.... So if you hear a Canadian talking like this:-
Hey..eh..cmon eh hoser! y'know take off!! EH?? umm err well, hey, ok, eh!
It's very friendly! ...... and we really DON'T talk like that!

UA: Canadian Foods that are unique to Canada include:

- Bokkepootjes(we will not tell you what *they* are, if you don't know!) ('borrowed' from the Dutch)
- Bugger-in-a-bag (ditto)
- Butter tarts
- Cod tongues and/or cod cheeks
- Crispy Crunch bars
- Date squares
- Quebec yellow pea soup
- Maple syrup pie
- McIntosh toffee bars
- Montreal smoked meat and real Montreal bagels
- Nanaimo bars (we made 'em first)
- Newfie screech (rum)
- Pablum
- Poutine (pronounced "poo-teen," Acadian slang for mushy mess and is best described as a heart attack in a bowl; French fries, covered with fresh white cheddar cheese curds and French-Canadian dark, thick brown gravy, which is also called BBQ Chicken Gravy; served in a bowl; invented in Warwick, Quebec in 1957 by Fernand Lachance, it resembles American Gravy Cheese Fries, but tastes better/different; called "THE BEST junk food on earth")
- Red Rose tea (Only in Canada ....Pity!)
- Scrunchins (we will not tell you what *they* are, if you don't know!)
- Smarties
- Timbits (we will not tell you what *they* are, if you don't know!).

UA: Some other things that are really cool and unique in or about Canada:

Lacrosse is Canadian.
Hockey is Canadian.
Basketball is Canadian.
The size of Canadian footballs and football fields and, one less down.
Ogopogo is Canadian (Ogopogo, a distant and less-famous relative of the Loch Ness Monster, is said to sill live in Lake Okanagan, B.C.)
Molson's (beer) is Canadian. Stronger too!
The biggest flags ever seen at the Olympic closing ceremonies were Canadian (twice...and the second one was smuggled in against a rule that was made because of the first one).
Way better beer commercials here.

Much Music kicks MTV's butt.
Tim Horton's kicks Dunkin Donut's butt.
Maple Syrup kicks Mrs. Butterworth's butt (I don't know about Aunt Jemima).
In the War of 1812 we burned the White house and most of Washington.
Our "Civil War" was led by a drunken, and possibly insane William Lyon McKenzie.
Our Civil War was a bar fight that lasted a little less than an hour.
The only person arrested and hanged after our Civil War was an American mercenary who slept in and missed the whole fight, showing up just in time to get caught.
The Hudson Bay company once owned 1/11th of the Earth's surface.
The average dog sled team can kill and devour a grown human in less than three minutes.
We don't have much of a taste for powdered bear testicles, but we know who does, and we're willing to sell them.
We wear socks (black ones, if possible) with our sandals.
We knew plaid flannel was cool way before Seattle did.
We can out-drink most Americans.
We don't often marry our kinfolk.
The light bulb was actually invented by a Canadian. (Henry Woodward patented it in 1874). The patent was bought by some obscure American named Edison who improved upon the design and took credit for inventing it.
Other Canadian inventions include: the jolly jumper, duct tape, insulin, walkie talkies, roller skates, Superman, air-conditioned vehicles, acrylics, standard time (and daylight saving time), the paint-roller, the radio compass, snowmobiles, jet skis, improved zippers, and the handles on cardboard beer cases, etc.,etc., etc. (there are thousands more!)

UA: <u>You know you're Canadian if:</u>
You stand in "line-ups" or "queues" (in Victoria, BC) at the movie, not lines.
You're not offended by the term, "Homo Milk."
You understand the sentence, "Could you please pass me a serviette, I just spilled my <u>BOWL OF POUTINE</u>" !
You eat chocolate bars instead of candy bars.
You drink pop, not soda.
You had a Prime Minister who wasn't fluent in either of the official languages (English & French).
You know what it means to be 'on the pogey'.
You know that a mickey and 2-4's mean "Party at the camp, eh?!"
You can drink legally while still a teen in some provinces.
You talk about the weather with strangers and friends alike.
You don't know or care about the fuss with Cuba, it's just a cheap place to travel with very good cigars.
When there is a social problem, you turn to your government to fix it, instead of telling them to stay out of it.
You're not sure if the leader of your nation has EVER had sex and you don't WANT to know if he has!
You get milk in bags as well as cartons and plastic jugs.
Pike is a type of fish, not some part of a highway.
You drive on a highway, not a freeway.
You know what a Robertson screwdriver is.
You have Canadian Tire money in your kitchen drawers.
You know that Mounties "don't always look like that."
You dismiss all beers under 6% as "for children and the elderly."
You know that the Friendly Giant isn't a vegetable product line.
You know that Casey and Finnegan are not a Celtic musical group.
You drive with headlights on during the day (since 1989 all new cars have been fitted with "daytime running lights").
You participated in "Participaction."

You have an Inuit carving by your bedside with the rationale, "What's good enough protection for the Prime Minister is good enough for me."
You wonder why there isn't a 5 dollar coin yet.
Like any international assassin/terrorist/spy in the world, you possess a Canadian Passport.
You use a red pen on your non-Canadian textbooks and fill in the missing 'u's from labor, honor, color. etc.
You know the French equivalents of "free," "prize," and "no sugar added," thanks to your extensive education in bilingual cereal packaging.
You are excited whenever an American television show mentions Canada.
You make a mental note to talk about it at work the next day.
You can do all the hand actions to Sharon, Lois and Bram's "Skin-a-ma-rinky-dinky-doo" opus.
You can eat more than one maple sugar candy without feeling nauseous.
You were mad at the CBC when "The Beachcombers" were taken off the air.
You know who "Relic" is/was.
You know what a touque is and you own one and often wear it.
You have heard of ... and have some cherished memento of Bob and Doug McKenzie.
You still sing the "Great White North" theme song with pride ... "coo-ooh-coocoo-coo-ooh-coocoo."
You know Toronto is NOT a province.
You never miss "Coach's Corner" during Hockey Night in Canada.
Back bacon and Kraft Dinner are two of your favorite food groups.
If you live in some of the colder Canadian provinces, your car has a cord and plug sticking out of the grill ... it's a block heater for those sub-zero (in Celsius) days.
You only know three spices: salt, pepper and ketchup.
You design your Halloween costume to fit over a snowsuit.
The mosquitoes have landing lights.
You have more kilometres on your snow blower than your car.
You have 10 favorite recipes for moose meat.
Canadian Tire Store on any Saturday is busier than most toy stores at Christmas.
You live in a house that has no front step, yet the door is one meter above the ground.
You've taken your kids trick-or-treating in a blizzard.
Driving is better in the winter because the potholes are filled in with frozen snow and slush.
You think sexy lingerie is tube-socks and a flannel nightie with only 8 buttons.
You owe more money on your snowmobile than your car.
The local paper covers national and international headlines on 2 pages, but requires 6 pages for hockey.
At least twice a year, the kitchen doubles as a meat processing plant.
The most effective mosquito repellent is a shotgun.
Your snowblower gets stuck on the roof.
You think the start of deer season is a national holiday.
You head South to go to your cottage.
You frequently clean grease off your barbecue so the bears won't prowl on your deck.
You know which leaves make good toilet paper now that there are no more dollar bills.
The major parish fund-raiser isn't bingo, it's sausage making.
You find -40C a little chilly.
The trunk of your car doubles as a portable deep freeze.
You attend a formal event in your best clothes, your finest jewelry and your Sorels.
You can play road hockey on skates.
You know 4 seasons: Winter, Still Winter, almost Winter and Construction.
The municipality buys a Zamboni before a bus.
You understand the Labatt Blue commercials.
You perk-up when you hear the theme from "Hockey Night in Canada."
You pronounce the last letter of the alphabet "zed" instead of "zee."
and ... You end some sentences with "eh," ... eh? (See above for more "Eh" sayings).

MANITOBA

Manitoba (MB): entered Confederation July 15, 1870; nicknames: The Keystone Province, The Land of 100,000 Lakes, Friendly Manitoba; People who live in Manitoba and Saskatchewan get called "Gappers," because they live in the "gap" of the country.

Capital: Winnipeg: This name is from the Cree ***Winnipi*** and may be freely translated as "dirty water" or "murky water." The lake was designated as Sea Lake by Thompson in 1816. Metropolitan Winnipeg, an amalgamation of neighbouring municipalities, was created November 1, 1960, and reorganized as the city of Winnipeg, January 1, 1972.

Motto: Glorious and Free

Origin of Name: Likely from the Cree *Manitou bah*, meaning "the narrows of the Great Spirit." This refers to a narrow part of Lake Manitoba where waves on the rocks make a bell-like and wailing sound, thought to be the sound of Manitou beating a drum.

Provincial Symbols: Bird: Great Gray Owl; Flower: Prairie Crocus; Tree: White Spruce; EDITOR: The Northern Prairie SKINK is probably Canada's only lizard, and found, if at all in Manitoba.

Manitoba is one of three of Canada's prairie provinces; with flat prairie (hence "flatlander" refers to prairie residents) in its southern half and rocky with forest in its north. Manitobans have many different ethnic and cultural origins. The province has a large population of Mennonites, Ukranians, and the largest French-speaking community in Western Canada. "First Nations" or Native Americans or Indians – especially Cree and Assiniboine – make up about 7% of the population. More than half the population of Manitoba lives in Winnipeg. People who live in Manitoba and Saskatchewan get called "Gappers," because they live in the "gap" of the country.

Louis Riel (1844-1885) was a Metis leader who led the "Red River Rebellion" in Manitoba in 1869, to fight with the government of Canada to protect the land, language, religion, and way of life of his people. *Metis* is French for "mixed," and refers to a "mixing" of European and Native people (usually English and French traders who married Ojibwa or Cree women. Riel was hanged for treason after the North-West Rebellion in 1885.

UA: TOP 10 REASONS TO LIVE IN MANITOBA

1. You wake up one morning to find you suddenly have beach front property
2. Amusing town names like "Flin Flon" and "Winnipeg"
3. All your local bands make it big and move to Toronto
4. The only province to ever violently rebel against the Federal government
5. Hundreds of huge but horribly frigid lakes
6. Nothing compares to a wicked winter in Winter-peg
7. You don't need a car, just take the canoe to work
8. You can be an Easterner or a Westerner depending on your mood
9. Because of your license plate, you are still "friendly" even when you cut someone off
10. You have a naked gold-painted little boy on top of your Legislature Building

NEW BRUNSWICK

New Brunswick NB): entered the Confederation July 1, 1867; nicknames: The Picture Province, "The Acadian Coast" (Until 1775 the Acadians lived in a French colony called Acadia since 1660's, in an area which included the Maritime Provinces of Canada, part of Quebec and northern New England, the British forced them out), ;

Capital: Fredericton: Assigned by order-in-council, February 22, 1785 - "a town at St. Anne's Point, on the River Saint John, to be called Fredericktown after His Royal Highness Prince Frederick, Bishop of Osnaburg." The "k" and "w" were dropped shortly thereafter.

Motto: Hope Restored

Origin of Name: Named in 1784 to honor reigning King George III of England (who with his Prime Minister Lord North are the "men who lost America"), who was also the Duke of Brunswick.

Provincial Symbols: Bird: Black-Capped Chickadee; Flower: Purple Violet; Tree: Balsam Fir

New Brunswick is one of "The Maritime Provinces." It is 85% forested, with mountains in the north and rolling farmland along the St. John River Valley. It is Canada's only officially bilingual province, and many speak French. The main rivers are the Miramichi, Nepisguit, Restigouche and Saint John. Known as *"oa-lus-tuk"* or "beautiful river" to the Indians. The St. John River waters the fertile lands of the western part of the province over a distance of 725 km. Downstream, in the Madawaska area, it traces a natural boundary between the state of Maine and Canada. Twice a day, with the rising tide of the Atlantic Ocean, 100 billion tons of water stream past a rocky headland in the Bay of Fundy. The current created is practically equal to the flow of all the world's rivers over a 24-hour period. The eastern end of the Bay of Fundy has tides of nearly 15 m, the highest in the world, sufficient to completely submerge a four-story building!

UA: TOP 10 REASONS TO LIVE IN NEW BRUNSWICK

1. You are sandwiched between French Separatists and drunken Celtic fiddlers
2. One way or another, the government gets 98 percent of your income
3. You're poor, but not as poor as the Newfies are
4. When listing the 10 provinces, everyone forgets to mention yours
5. The economy is based on fish, cows and ferrying Ontario motorists to Boston
6. No one ever blames anything on New Brunswick
7. You have French people, but they don't want to leave you
8. Everybody has a grandfather who runs a lighthouse
9. Just as charming as Maine, but with more unemployed fishermen
10. You probably live in a small seaside cottage with no television

NEWFOUNDLAND AND LABRADOR

Newfoundland and Labrador (NF): entered Confederation March 31, 1949; nicknames: Newfoundland = "The Rock" (NOT to be confused with "The Rock" or hill in the oldest part of the city of Yellowkife, in North West Territory)

Capitol: St. John's (THE OLDEST CITY in North America, whose Water Street is THE OLDEST continually occupied STREET in North America and NOT to be confused with the city of St. John in New Brunswick): Derived from the supposed date of discovery - on the Feast of St. John the Baptist, 1497. The name has survived through a series of translations from the Portuguese (***São Joãom***) to the French (***b. de Saincte Jean***) to St. John's.

Motto: Seek Ye First The Kingdom Of God

Origin of Name: From "New Found Launda," which is what King Henry VII of England called the land discovered by John Cabot (aka Giovanni Caboto, EDITOR: honestly he WAS Italian) who captained English expeditions to the Canadian coast in 1497 and 1498.

Labrador: There remains an element of uncertainty, but most authorities credit the origin of the name Labrador to João Fernandes, a Portuguese explorer and lavrador, or "farmer," in the Azores.

Provincial Symbols: Animal (unofficial): Caribou; Bird: Atlantic Puffin; Flower: Pitcher Plant; Tree: Black Spruce

Newfoundland and Labrador is a province made up of two quite different parts – the island of Newfoundland (nicknamed "The Rock") and the mainland region of Labrador. Most of the population lives along the coast of Newfoundland. For years the traditional way of life was based on fishing, especially for cod. However, a ban on cod fishing put many out of work. Labrador is inhabited by Inuit and Innu Native people.

Newfoundland saying (and Screech toast): LONG MAY YER BIG JIB DRAW!

Newfoundland maritime greeting: "AERE'N?" (meaning, are there any fish out there?)

Newfoundland maritime reply: "NAER'N!" (nary a one) or "AYE!" (yes)

UA: TOP 10 REASONS TO LIVE IN NEWFOUNDLAND

1. The poorest province in Confederation but with the most social assistance
2. If Quebec separates, you will likely float off to sea

3. In the rare case when someone moves to the Rock, you can make them kiss a dead cod fish
4. The economy is based on fish, seafood, and fish-related products
5. If you do something really stupid, you have a built-in excuse
6. You understand the meaning of all the "Great Big Sea's" lyrics
7. The work day is about two and 1/2 hours long
8. You get credit for many great inventions, like solar-powered flashlight and screen door for submarines 9. If someone asks if you're from Nova Scotia, you are allowed to kick their pants10. It is socially acceptable to wear your hip waders on your wedding day.

NORTHWEST TERRITORIES

Northwest Territories (NT): entered Confederation July 15, 1870; nicknames: The Beautiful Land, The Land of the Dene (the Dene people have lived in N.W.T. for centuries, there are five Dene tribes and several Dene languages), N.W.T., Canada's Arctic (which also appears on Nunavut's license plates).

Capitol: Yellowknife (a name used by explorer Samuel Hearne in 1770's for the Dene people whom he called "Yellowknives" because they used copper knives)

Motto: (no official motto)

Origin of Name: The area was earlier known as the North-Western Territory because in 1870 it was in the north-west part of the continent.

Yellowknife: The community was established following the discovery of gold in 1934. The name is derived from the Athapaskan band of Amerindians, who possessed tools made from yellow copper. It is now capital of the Northwest Territories, and was incorporated as a city on January 1, 1970.

Provincial Symbols: Bird: Gyrfalcon; Flower: Mountain Avens; Tree: Tamarack

N.W.T. covers a huge area. Its southern part is in the "taiga zone," an area covered with short coniferous forests. Farther north are the vast treeless plains of tundra, dotted with hundreds of lakes and rivers. At some time in its history, the Northwest Territory has included all of Alberta, Saskatchewan, Nunavut and the Yukon, and most of Manitoba, Ontario and Quebec. Today, the Northwest Territory remains a large political subdivision in Canada, with 15% of the total area of the country. One of the most remarkable features of the Territory is the Mackenzie River, one of the world's longest at 4,241 km. The Mackenzie Mountains lie along the Yukon border to the west. Climate is dry with long, cold winters, and warm summers in the south. About half the population is Native peoples – Dene, Inuvialuit, Metis. Eight official languages are used in the N.W.T. Legislative Assembly (where the provincial government meets) in Yellowknife: Chipewyan, Cree, Dogrib, Gwitch'in, Inuktitut, Slavey, French, and English.

NOVA SCOTIA

Nova Scotia (NS): entered Confederation July 1, 1867; nicknames: Atlantic Playground, Canada's Ocean Playground; "Bluenosers" (refers to the famous sailing ship "The Bluenose" depicted on the Canadian dime and people from NS).

Capitol: Halifax: Founded June 21, 1749, and named for George Montagu Dunk, Earl of Halifax (1716-71), then President of the Board of Trade. Became the capital of Nova Scotia on July 14, 1749.

Motto: One Defends And The Other Conquers

Gaelic Saying: *"Ciad Mile Failte!"* means "one hundred thousand welcomes!"

Origin of Name: *"Nova Scotia"* is Latin for "New Scotland" It was nmaed by Sir William Alexander, who received a grant to the land from King James VI of Scotland.

Provincial Symbols: Bird: Osprey; Flower: Mayflower; Tree: Red Spruce

Nova Scotia is one of "The Maritime Provinces;" it is surrounded by water. Fishing villages dot the bays and inlets along its coast. Inland, it is mostly forested, although its Annapolis Valley is scenic farm country known for its apples. Rugged and mountainous Cape Breton Island lies at the north end of the province. About 80% of its population is of English, Scottish, or Irish descent.

UA: TOP 10 REASONS TO LIVE IN NOVA SCOTIA

1. You have the highest tides in the world, but you have to share them with New Brunsick
2. Your province is shaped somewhat (?) like male genitalia
3. Everyone is a fiddle player, or has one in the family
4. If someone asks if you're a Newfie, you are allowed to kick their pants
5. The local hero is a long-haired, fiddle playing ..... whatever ...
6. The province that produced Rita MacNeil, Nova Scotia's equivalent to Mama Cass
7. You are the reason Anne Murray makes tons of money
8. You can pretend you have Scottish heritage as an excuse to wear a kilt
9. The economy is based on fish, lobster, and fiddle music
10. Even though it smells like dead sea animals, Halifax is considered one of Canada's most beautiful cities

NUNAVUT TERRITORY

Nunavut (NU): formed and entered Confederation April 1, 1999; nicknames: Our Land, Land of the Umingmak (meaning "bearded one," the Inuit name for a muskox), Canada's Arctic (which appears on NWT's license plates).

Capital: Iqaluit: Located at the head of Frobisher Bay, this town (1980) was established in 1949 as *Frobisher Bay*, when the Hudson's Bay Company moved its post here from a site 70 km southeast. It became a municipal hamlet in 1971 and a village three years later. In December 1984 its residents voted 310 to 213 to rename the place Iqaluit, meaning "place of fish" in Inuktitut.

Motto: Nunavut, Our Strength

Origin of Name: Established in 1999 *"Nunavut"* means "our land" in Inuktitut, the Inuit language. English-speaking people used to call the Inuit "Eskimos." This is somewhat insulting, because "eskimo" is a Cree word for eating raw meat. Inuit means "the people" in Inuktitut. Onre Inuit is called an "Inuk."

Territorial Symbols: Bird: Rock Ptarmigan; Flower: Purple Saxifrage; Animal: Canadian Inuit Dog

Nunavut is Canada's newest territory, formed April 1, 1999. Biefore that it was part of the Northwest Territories. Like the N.W.T., its southern part has short, coniferous forests of the taiga, while its northern landscape is treeless tundra. Nunavut includes Arctic islands stretching up to the North Pole. This is the land of the Midnight Sun in summer, as well as long, dark winters with little sunlight. Its small population is mostly Inuit. There are three official languages: Inuktitut, French, and English. Inuktitut is the working language of the territorial government. Nunavut's system of government combines traditional Inuit ways with modern government systems.

ONTARIO

Ontario: entered the Confederation July 1, 1867; nicknames: Canada's Heartland; Yours to Discover.

Capitol: Toronto: Details surrounding exact origin are uncertain. For many years it was thought to stem from a Huron word translated as "a place of meeting"; however, recent scholarship indicates that it may be of Mohawk origin. The Mohawk descriptive phrase ***tkaronto*** was used to indicate the fishing weirs located at The Narrows near present day Orillia. Literally translated as "where there are trees standing in the water," the name was noted by Champlain in 1615. Over time it was to move 125 kilometres southward to the site of the city of Toronto (Rayburn, 1994). Listed as ***Tarantou*** (Sanson, 1656); in 1793 Governor John Graves Simcoe moved the capital from Newark (Niagara) to Toronto Bay and renamed it York. In 1834 the city was incorporated as Toronto. Contemporary Metropolitan Toronto comprises the cities of Toronto, North York, Scarborough, York, Etobicoke and the borough of East York.

Motto: Loyal She Began and Loyal She Remains

Origin of Name: Ontario: Is of Native origin from the Huron words, "onitari" for lake and "io" for beautiful; and the Iroquoian word *kanadario* meaning "sparkling water." It appeared in 1641 and was applied to the province in 1867.

Provincial Symbols: Bird: Common Loon; Flower: White Trillium; Tree: Eastern White Pine

Ontario is Canada's second largest province in land size and the one with the most people. Ontario has three main regions: the wet scrubby lowlands around Hudson Bay; the rocky Canadian Shield of northern Ontario; the lowlands around the Great Lakes and St. Lawrence River in the south (where most of the province's population and industry is located). Toronto is the headquarters for many Canadian businesses; Ottowa is the national capitol; Ottowa has the 124 mile long Rideau Canal hand built 1826-32 linking Ottowa River with Lake Ontario, which is the world's longest skating rink; and Niagra Falls, "The Canadian Falls" (which ARE BIGGER than "The American Falls" which curve into a horseshoe shape is one of Canada's major tourist attractions.

UA: TOP 10 REASONS TO LIVE IN ONTARIO

1. You think you live in the centre of the universe
2. Your $400,000 Toronto home is actually a bit of a dump
3. You and you alone decide who will win EVERY Federal election
4. There's no such thing as an Ontario Separatist
5. Your grandparents sold booze to the States during Prohibition
6. Lots of tourists come to Toronto because they mistakenly believe it's a really 'cool' city
7. The only province with hard-core American-style crime
8. MuchMusic's Speaker's Corner - rant and rave on national TV for a loonie
9. Baseball fans park on your front lawn and pee on the side of your house
10. Mike Harris: basically a more sober Ralph Klein

PRINCE EDWARD ISLAND

Prince Edward Island or PEI (PE): entered Confederation July 1, 1873; nickname: Home of Confederation, The Garden Province (because half of its land is under cultivation – excellent potatoes in its red soil)

Capital: Charlottetown: Listed as Charlotte Town on the Holland Survey map of 1765, the city was named for Queen Charlotte, (1744-1818), the consort of King George III. Incorporated as a town in 1855 and as a city in 1875.

Motto: The Small Under The Protection of The Great

Origin of Name: Named in 1799 to honor the son of English King George III (who together with his Prime Minister Lord North are the men "wholost America"), Prince Edward at that time was commander in chief of British North America.

Provincial Symbols: Bird: Blue Jay; Flower: Lady's Slipper; Tree: Red Oak

PEI is Canada's smallest, but most densely populated province – one of "The Maritime Provinces." It is mostly gently rolling farmland. It is known for its potatoes (ever heard the song *"Bud the Spud"* by Stompin' Tom Connors, who is from PEI?), which grow well in the rich, red soil and mild climate. Many tourists visit Green Gables in Cavendish, on the northern shore of PEI (which the author, Lucy Maud Montgomery, fictiously named "Avonlea"), the home of the fictional character in the novel and movies *Anne of Green Gables.* PEI is now linked to New Brunswick and the mainland of Canada 130 feet above and across the Northumberland Strait by the 8 mile long Confedration Bridge, aka "The Link," one of the longest bridges in the world.

UA: TOP 10 REASONS TO LIVE ON PRINCE EDWARD ISLAND

1. Even though more people live on Vancouver Island, you still got the big expensive bridge from the mainlend
2. You can walk right across the province in an hour
3. You were probably once an extra on "Road to Avonlea"
4. This is where all those tiny red potatoes come from
5. The economy is based on fish, potatoes and crappy CBC TV shows
6. Tourists arrive, see the "Anne of Green Gables" house, then promptly leave
7. You can drive right across the province in 10 minutes
8. It doesn't matter to you if Quebec separates
9. You don't share a border with the Americans, or with anyone for that matter
10. You can confuse ships by turning your porch lights on and off at night

QUEBEC

Quebec (QC): entered Confederation July 1, 1867; nicknames: La Belle Province; "Frogs"or "Peppers" for Québecois

Capital: Quebec City

Motto: *Je me souviens* = I Remember

Origin of Name: From the Algonquin word *quebecq* or *kebek* for "narrow passage" or "strait," or channel that narrows, referring to the narrow part of the St. Lawrence River at Quebec City. The name was applied first to the region of the modern city and the word is of undoubted Algonquin origin. Early spellings were: Quebecq (Levasseur, 1601); Kébec (Lescarbot, 1609); Quebec (Champlain, 1613). Champlain wrote of the location in 1632: "It...is a strait of the river, so called by the Indians" - a reference to the Algonquin word for "narrow passage" or "strait" to indicate the narrowing of the river at Cape Diamond. The term is common to the Algonquin, Cree, and Micmac languages and signifies the same in each dialect. Quebec: was named in 1763, after the Algonquin word for narrow passage.

Montreal, the world's second-largest French-speaking city (after Paris) was named for the "mont" or "mountain royal" the French explorer Samuel de Champlain found. The Gaspe or Gaspesie Peninsula (comes from a Native word *gaspeg*, meaning "where the world ends" is the tongue of land that sticks out of the St. Lawrence River into the Atlantic Ocean.

Provincial Symbols: Bird: Snowy Owl; Flower: Blue Flag; Tree: Yellow Birch

Quebec is Canada's largest province in land size. The north is part of the Canadian Shield; the Appalachian Mountains are along the southern border. In between are most of its people and cities in the lowlands of the St. Lawrence River. The official language in Quebec is French. The province's culture (laws, customs, music, food) is quite different from that found elsewhere in Canada. There has been ongoing debate about the idea of Quebec separating from the rest of Canada, but so far the majority of the population has always voted "no."

UA: TOP 10 REASONS TO LIVE IN QUEBEC

1. Every visitor assumes you can't speak English
2. Montreal smoked meat and bagels make life somewhat bearable
3. The only province to ever kidnap a Federal politician
4. You can take bets with your friends on which English neighbour will move to Ontario next
5. Other provinces and the Feds basically bribe you to stay in Canada
6. The Hell's Angles and the Rock Machine - great dances!
7. Your hockey team is made up entirely of mean French guys
8. The province with the oldest everything
9. NON-smokers are the outcasts here
10. You can blame all your problems on the "Anglo minorities"

SASKATCHEWAN

Saskatchewan (SK): entered the Confederation September 1, 1905; nicknames: Land of Living Skies, The Sunshine Capital of Canada (2,540 hours of sunshine per year out of a total 8,760); People who live in Manitoba and Saskatchewan get called "Gappers," because they live in the "gap" of the country.

Capital: Regina (which was originally named "Pile o' Bones" because there was a pile of buffalo bones beside the Wascana Creek, but the name was changed to *Regina* or "reigning queen" for the provincial capitol).

Motto: From Many Peoples, Strength

Origin of Name: From the Cree name for the Saskatchewan River, *kisiskatchanisipi*, meaning "swift-current" or "swift flowing river."

Regina: Assigned August 23, 1882, by the Governor General, the Marquess of Lorne (1845-1914), in honour of his wife's mother, Queen Victoria. Originally called "Pile O'Bones."

Provincial Symbols: Animal: White-tailed Deer; Bird: Prairie Sharp-Tailed Grouse; Flower: Western Red Lily; Tree: White Birch

Saskatchewan is flat prairie province (hence "flatlander" refers to prairie residents) and one of the world's gretest producers of wheat; it grows two-thirds of Canda's supply. Northern Saskatchewan is part of the Canadian Shield, covered in forests, lakes, rivers, and bogs. The province is the world's leadeing exporter of potash, a mineral used as fertilizer for crops. The RCMP or Royal Canadian Mounted Police, Canada's national police were first established in 1882 in Saskatchewan. The RCMP Training school is in Regina. Moose Jaw (NOT named for the animal, but from the Cree word *"moose gaw"* meaning "warm breezes"), west of Regina, is the Home of Canada's largest military jet-training base and "The Canadian Snowbirds" – the aerial acrobatic squadron of the Royal Canadian Air Force.

UA: TOP 10 REASONS TO LIVE IN SASKATCHEWAN

1. You never run out of wheat
2. Those cool Saskatchewan Wheat Pool hats
3. Cruise control takes on a whole new meaning here
4. Your province is really easy to draw
5. You never have to worry about roll-back if you have a standard transmission car
6. It takes you two weeks to walk to your neighbour's house
7. YOUR Roughriders survived
8. You can watch the dog run away from home for hours
9. People will always assume you live on a farm
10. Buying a huge John Deere mower makes sense

YUKON TERRITORY

Yukon Territory (YT): entered the Confederation June 13, 1898; nicknames: Canada's True North, Land of the Midnight Sun (north of Arctic Circle).

Capitol: Whitehorse: The capital of Yukon since 1953. Named for the Whitehorse Rapids which are said to resemble the mane of a white horse.

Motto: (no official motto)

Origin of Name: Likely from the word *yukunah* in the Gwitch'in language or the Loucheux Native word *Yuchoo*, both of which mean "great river" which refers to the Yukon River, site of the 1896 Klondike Gold Rush, which started on the Bonanza Creek, near Dawson City.

Territorial Symbols: Bird: Common Raven; Flower: Fireweed; Tree: Sub-Alpine/Sub-Arctic Fir

Yukon is triangular shaped and almost entirely covered by mountain ranges. Mount Logan, Canada's highest mountain (19,525 feet) is in the St. Elias Mountain Range in the southwest corner of the territory. The landscape of the southern part is taiga, with short, coniferous forests, while the north is tundra. Summers are short and warm; winters are long and cold. Two-thirds of the population lives in and around its capitol Whitehorse. The Alaska Highway, aka Alcan (Alaska-Canada) Highway or "The Oil Can Highway" built in 1942 is how mosyt people get into Yukon from Canada. Above the Arctic Circle (latitude 66° north), the Yukon is known as "the land of the midnight sun," because in the three months of summer, sunlight is almost continuous. In winter, however, darkness sets in, and the light of day is not seen for a quarter of the year.

STATISTICS/AVERAGES

Uncle Anthony: If at first you don't succeed, you're about average.

Uncle Anthony: If you are average that means you're as close to the bottom as you are to the top.

Aunt Mary Carlo: Statistics is fer baseball geeks – ya don't hitta ball er throw a coive wit statistics.

G. O. Ashley: Like other occult techniques of divination, the statistical method has a private jargon deliberately contrived to obscure its methods from non-practitioners.

Jean Baudrillard, French Postmodern Philosopher, Writer: Like dreams, statistics are a form of wish fulfillment.

Hilaire Belloc: It has long been recognized by public men of all kinds . . . that statistics come under the head of lying, and that no lie is so false or inconclusive as that which is based on statistics.

Hilaire Belloc: Statistics are the triumph of the quantitative method, and the quantitative method is the victory of sterility and death.

Bible: Apocrypha, Ecclesiasticus 1:2: The sand of the sea, the drops of rain, and the days of eternity – who can count them?

Bible: Genesis 13:16; Genesis 28:14: God speaking to Abraham: I will make thy seed as the dust of the earth: so that if a man can number the dust of the earth, then shall thy seed also be numbered.

Bible: Hosea 1:10: The number of the children of Israel shall be as the sand of the sea, which cannot be measured nor numbered.

Bible: Judges7:12; 1 Samuel 13:5; 2 Samuel 17:11: Their camels were without number, as the sand by the sea side for multitude.

Bible: Numbers 23:10: Who can count the dust of Jacob, and the number of the fourth part of Israel?

Bible: Psalms 23:5: My cup runneth over.

Bible: Psalms 40:12: They are more than the hairs of mine head.

Ambrose Bierce: DULLARD, n. A member of the reigning dynasty in letters and life. The Dullards came in with Adam, and being both numerous and sturdy have overrun the habitable world. The secret of their power is their insensibility to blows; tickle them with a bludgeon and they laugh with a platitude. The Dullards came originally from Boeotia, whence they were driven by stress of starvation, their dulness having blighted the crops. For some centuries they infested Philistia, and many of them are called Philistines to this day. In the turbulent times of the Crusades they withdrew thence and gradually overspread all Europe, occupying most of the high places in politics, art, literature, science and theology. Since a detachment of Dullards came over with the Pilgrims in the *Mayflower* and made a favorable report of the country, their increae by birth, immigration, and conversion has been rapid and steady. According to the most trustworthy statistics the number of adult Dullards in the United States is but little short of thirty millions, including the statisticians. The intellectual centre of the race is somewhere about Peoria, Illinois, but the New England Dullard is the most shockingly moral.

Ambrose Bierce: FINANCE, n. The art or science of managing revenues and resources for the best advantage of the manager. The pronunciation of this word with the i long and the accent on the first syllable is one of America's most precious discoveries and possessions.

Ambrose Bierce: GRAVITATION, n. The tendency of all bodies to approach one another with a strength proportioned to the quality of matter they contain – the quantity of matter they contain being ascertained by the strength of their tendency to approach one another. This is a lovely and edifying illustration of how science, having made A the proof of B, makes B the proof of A.

Hubert M. Blalock, Jr.: The manipulation of statistical formulas is no substitute for knowing what one is doing.

Logan E. Bleckley (Chief Justice of Georgia, 1827-1907): It is always probable that something improbable will happen. <u>Warren v. Purtell</u>, 63 Ga. 428, 430 (1979)

Louis Brandeis: I abhor averages. I like the individual case. A man may have six meals one day and none the next, making an average of three meals per day, but that is not a good way to live.

Lytton E.G. Bulwer: Fate laughs at probabilities.

George Canning: I can prove anything by statistics - except the truth.

Sir Winston Churchill: You cannot ask us to take sides against arithmetic.

Henry Clay (1777-1852, American Statesman, Orator): Statistics are no substitute for judgment.

William Cowper: A fool must now and then be right, by chance.

Benjamin Disraeli (1804-1881, British Statesman, Prime Minister) (also attributed to Mark Twain): There are three kinds of lies. Lies, damned lies, and statistics.

Havelock Ellis: Here, where we reach the sphere of mathematics, we are among processes which seem to some the most inhuman of all human activities and the most remote from poetry. Yet it is here that the artist has the fullest scope of his imagination.

Evan Esar: The definition of statistics: the science of producing unreliable facts from reliable figures.

Evan Esar: Statistician: a man who believes figures don't lie, but admits that under analysis some of them won't stand up either.

Euclid: There is no royal road to geometry.

Sam Walter Foss: The plain man is the basic clod / From which we grow the demigod; / And in the average man is curled / The hero stuff that rules the world.

Jerome Frank (New York, Judge, U.S. Circuit Court, 1889-1957): The improbable – by definition being not impossible – sometimes does occur. Old Colony Bondholders v. N.Y.N.H. & H. R. Co., 161 F.2d 413 (1947) (dissenting opinion)

Al Franken: You can lie with averages. Just look at the "average income" between yourself and Bill Gates. You average approximately $5 billion per year in average income.

Martin Friedman: Never try to walk across a river just because it has an average depth of 4 feet.

George Gallup (1901-1984, American Public Opinion Expert): I could prove God statistically.

W. I. Gates: Remember the story about the man who drowned crossing a stream with an "average depth" of 6 inches.

Maxim Gorky: One has to be able to count if only so that at fifty one doesn't marry a girl of twenty.

Francis Bret Harte: Give me a man that is capable of a devotion to anything, rather than a cold, calculating average of all the virtues!

Samuel Johnson 1709-1784, British Author: Round numbers are always false.

Fletcher Knebel: Smoking is one of the leading causes of statistics.

Andrew Lang, American Folk Singer: An unsophisticated forecaster uses statistics as a drunken man uses lampposts; for support rather than illumination.

Aaron Levenstein: Statistics are like a bikini. What they reveal is suggested, but what they conceal it is vital.

Walter Lippmann: You and I are forever at the mercy of the census taker and the census maker. That impertinent fellow who goes from house to house is one of the real masters of the statistical situation. The other is the man who organizes the results.

Father Larry Lorenzoni: The average person thinks he is not.

Lord William Murray Mansfield (Chief Justice, King's Bench, England, 1705-1793): An estimated value is a precarious measure of justice, compared with the specific thing. Fisher v. Prince, 3 Burr. 1363 (1762)

Bill Mauldin (1944 cartoon caption): I feel like a fugitive from the law of averages.

Pierre Mendes-France: Facts and figures illustrating (economic) progress fly across frontiers like guided missles directed at people's minds. And, of course, those who lag behind in such progress are the most exposed to this propaganda.

Moscow: Mathematicians who are only mathematicians have exact minds, provided all things are explained to them by means of definitions and axioms; otherwise they are inaccurate and insufferable, for they are only right when the principles are quite clear.

Adolphe Monod: There is no portion of our time that is our time, and the rest God's; there is no portion of money that is our money, and the rest God's money. It is all His; He made it all, gives it all, and He simply trusted it to us for His service. A servant has two purses, the master's and his own, but we have only one.

Michael A. Musmanno (Justice of Pa. Supreme Court, 1959): What is trivial is strictly a matter of comparison. Even an earthquake of sizable proportions is trivial against an atomic blast which lays waste half a continent.

Michael A. Musmanno (Justice of Pennsylvania Supreme Court, 1959): None of Our Other Patrons Were Injured: The Majority Opinion states that 1,297,802 "human bodies" had ridden the course "and absorbed the abruptness of this curve without injury." There was not a word or syllable in the testimony to support this statement; 1,297,802 persons did not testify that they had not been injured. This volunteered conclusion of the Majority is founded on the statement of the defendant's witness that there was no record of accident during the period in question. This is far from stating that no accident occurred or that no one had been injured. Many people could have sustained substantial jolts which did not seriously disable them. Others may have until later and then they did not connect them with the roller coaster ride. Others may have known they were injured by the roller coaster ride but preferred not to litigate. In addition, it does not matter how many rode without injury. The question is: Was there anything wrong with the Blue Streak on the day, hour and minute that the plaintiff was injured?... Moreover, before the fact of the multitudinous rides can be compared to the single ride involved in this case, there must be proof that the conditions in the million rides were exactly similar to the one's present in the instant case, as, for instance that there were three passengers in the front seat as in this case,... that the weight of the passengers in the front seat, in all the million rides was the same as that on the Wood ride, that the heights of the persons in the front seat in all the other rides tallied with the heights of the persons of this ride. There would have to be a determination also as to whether the passengers all the other rides were aware that they were coming to an abrupt bend. Also, did the passengers of the other rides brace themselves when they came to the bend or did they all slide over and crush the person on the outside seat, as happened in this case? There are innumerable variables which have to be considered before one can base a conclusion one multiplicity of events as against the one which is in focus. A million pedestrians may pass over a defect in the sidewalk and not been injured, but the 1,000,001st traveler may fall into the hole or trip over the defect and, if the facts reveal that the hole was caused by the negligence of the municipality, the injured person is entitled to a recovery, regardless of the army which had good luck to pass unscathed over the danger which reached up and pulled down that 1,000,001st traveler to his doom. If cases of this kind are to be decided on mere numbers instead of cause-and-effect, and logic and reason, there can be no need for a judicial inquiry. A computer will suffice, an IBM machine can dictate the verdict, a unifax can displace the jury and eventually the judge himself, all of which, of course, is absurd. (dissenting opinion, George Wood v. Conneaut Lake Park Inc., 417 Pa. 58).

Laurence Peter: Facts are stubborn things, but statistics are more pliable.

Sylvia Porter: The average family exists only on paper and its average budget is a fiction, invented by statisticians for the convenience of statisticians.

Ronald Reagan (40th President of the US): I will stand on, and continue to use, the figures I have used, because I believe they are correct. Now, I'm not going to deny that you don't now and then slip up on something; no one bats a thousand.

Robert A. Redfield (American lawyer): Good and bad come mingled always. The longtime winner is the man who is not unreasonably discouraged by persistent streaks of ill fortune nor at other times made reckless with the thought that he is fortunate. He keeps a cool head and trusts in the mathematics of probability, or as often said, the law of averages.

Robert Reich: Averages don't always reveal the most telling realities. You know, Shaquille O'Neal and I have an average height of 6 feet. (U.S. Labor Secretary Reich is 4' 10" tall; whereas US basketball star Shaquille O'Neal is 7'1" tall!)

Will Rogers: Now don't let them tell you it hasn't been hot here in California the past few weeks. Brother it's been roasting, and we haven't got the usual Alibi, "It's the humidity."

Will Rogers: In the early days of the Indian Territory, there were no such things as birth certificates. You being there was certificate enough.

Will Rogers: The nation is prosperous on the whole, but how much prosperity is there in a hole?

Andy Rooney: When 70% of the people who get arrested are black, in cities where 70% of the population is black, that is not racial profiling, it is the Law of Probability.

Theodore Roosevelt: I am only an average man but, by George, I work harder at it than the average man.

Bertrand Russell: Mathematics may be defined as the subject in which we never know what we are talking about, nor whether what we are saying is true.

Bertrand Russell: The true spirit of the life, the exultation, the sense of being more than Man, which is the touchstone of the highest excellence, is to be found in mathematics as surely as in poetry.

Carl Sandburg: Arithmetic is where the answer is right and everything is nice and you can look out the window and see the blue sky – or the answer is wrong and you have to start all over and try again and see how it comes out this time.

William Shakespeare (*Cymbeline*, Act III, ii): Learn'd indeed were that astronomer / That knew the stars as I his characters: / He'd lay the future open.

William Shakespeare (*II Henry VI*, Act IV, i): A cunning man did calculate my birth / And told me that by water I should die.

William Shakespeare (*Julius Caesar*, Act I, iii): Why old men fool and children calculate.
Herbert Spancer: A jury is a group of twelve people of average ignorance.
Joseph Stalin: A single death is a tragedy. A million deaths is a statistic.
Dr. Wilhelm Stekhel: Statistics is the art of lying by means of figures.
Rex Stout: There are two kinds of statistics, the kind you look up, and the kind you make up.
Lionel Strachey: Statistics are mendacious truths.
Mrs. Robert A. Taft: I always find that statistics are hard to follow and impossible to digest.The only one I can ever remember is that if all the people who go to sleep in church were laid end to end they would be a lot more comfortable.
Lewis Thomas: Statistically, the probability of any of us being here is so small that you'd think the mere fact of existing would keep us all in contented dazzlement of surprise.
Mark Twain (also attributed to Benjamin Disraeli): There are three kinds of lies. Lies, damned lies, and statistics.
UA: Often statistics are used as a drunken man uses lamp posts... for support rather than illumination.
Chris Watson (AC Press article "That's Not All, Folks! Lessons Learned From Cartoons Over Into Adult Situations"): Foghorn Leghorn, that pompous rooster-about-town, caught me how to spot vanity and pretentiousness. Because he had a valuable diploma from
Mae West: A man has one hundred dollars and you leave him with two dollars, that's subtraction.

STUDY (See TEACHING; THINKING)

STUPID/STUPIDITY (See CONSISTENCY; IGNORANCE; NEGLIGENCE)

SUBSTANTIAL CAUSE (SEE CAUSATION)

SUCCESS (See also FAILURE)

Uncle Anthony: T'be a success in life, all ya gotta do is t'be yerself
Uncle Anthony: Some people get to da top of da ladder only to find it's leanin' against the wrong wall!
Uncle Anthony: Yer judged by what ya finish, not what ya start.
Aunt Mary Carlo: A "success" ain't da person sittin' wit all da money, or da guy wit da biggest tombstone.
Cindy Adams: Success has made failures of many men.
Yogi Berra: Someone's got to win and someone's got to lose, and that was us.
Bible: Luke 12:48: Unto whomsoever much is given, of him shall be much required.
Bible: Luke 20:17; Mark 12:10; Matthew 21:42; Psalms 118:22: The stone which the builders rejected is become the head of the corner.
Bible: Mark 10:31; Matthew 19:30; Matthew 20:16: Many that are first shall be last; and the last first.
Bible: Psalms 37:29: The righteous shall inherit the land.
Ambrose Bierce: PERSEVERANCE, n. A lowly virtue whereby mediocrity achieves an inglorious success.
Ambrose Bierce: SAINT, n. A dead sinner revised and edited.
Ambrose Bierce: SUCCESS, n. The one unpardonable sin against one's fellows....
Josh Billings: One of the gretaest victories you can gain over someone is to beat him at politeness.
Jean de La Bruyere: The shortest and best way to make your fortune is to let people see clearly that is in their interests to promote yours.
David Charles Brink (South African businessman): A successful person is one who can lay a firm foundation with the bricks that others throw at him.
Charles Bukowski: You begin saving the world by saving one man at a time; all else is grandiose romanticism or politics.
George Burns: I'd rather be a failure at something I love than a success at something I hate.
James Cagney (1949 film *White Heat*, as he blows up in a ball of fire): Anyway, Ma, I made it ... Top of the world!
Anton Chekhov: Dividing people into successes and failures means looking upon human nature from the narrow, preconceived point of view.... Are you a failure or not? Am I? Napolean? Your servant Vasili?

Where is the criterion? One must be God to be able to distinguish successes from failures and not make mistakes.

Sir Winston Churchill: Success is the ability to go from one failure to another with no loss of enthusiasm.

Sir Winston Churchill: Success is not final, failure is not fatal: it is the courage to continue that counts.

Sir Winston Churchill: The price of greatness is responsibility.

Sir Winston Churchill: Everyone has his day and some days last longer than others.

Sir Winston Churchill: The problems of victory are more agreeable than those of defeat, but they are no less difficult

Sir Winston Churchill: Victory at all costs, victory in spite of all terror, victory however long and hard the road may be; for without victory there is no survival.

Count Galeazzo Ciano: As always, victory finds a hundred fathers, but defeat is an orphan.

James Bryant Conant: Behold the turtle: He only makes progress when he sticks his neck out.

Daniel Considine: To get the best out of a man go to what is best in him.

Sammy Davis, Jr.: Most of the trouble with most people in America who become successful is that they can really and truly get by on bullshit alone. They can survive on it.

Benjamin Disraeli: Every man has a right to be conceited until he is successful.

Mike Ditka: Success is not permanent, and failure is not fatal.

Amelia Earhart: In soloing – as in other activities – it is far easier to start something than it is to finish it.

Umberto Eco: The real hero is always a hero by mistake; he dreams of being an honest coward like everybody else.

Albert Einstein: A successful man is he who recieved a great deal more from his fellow-men, usually incomparably more than corresponds to his service to them.

Ralph Waldo Emerson: To laugh often and much; to win the respect of intelligent people and the affection of children; to earn the appreciation of honest critics and endure the betrayal of false friends; to appreciate beauty; to leave the world a bit better whether by a healthy child, a garden patch, or a redeemed social condition; to know even one life has ... breathed easier because you have lived, This is to have succeeded.

Michael J. Fox: I am careful not to confuse excellence with pefection. Excellence, I can reach for; perfection is God's business.

Thomas Fuller: All things are difficult before they are easy.

Paul Gallico (sportswriter and novelist): The single-mindedness necessary to fight one's way to the top, in no matter what spot, is something not shared by the majority of mortals.

Johann Wolfgang von Goethe: Divide and rule, a sound motto. Unite and lead, a better one.

Horace Greeley: After a Congressman told him, "I am a self-made man," Greeley replied, "that, sir, relieves the Almighty of a great responsibility."

Robert Heinlein: Progress isn't made by early risers. It's made by lazy men trying to find easier ways to do nothing.

Henry John Heinz (founder of H.J. Heinz Company in 1869, and the 1892 slogan "57 Varieties" of food products): The secret to success in marketing is to deo a common thing uncommonly well.

Lillian Hellman: Is it age, or was it always my nature, to take a bad time, block out the good times until any success became an accident and failure seemed the only truth?

Kenneth Hildebrand: Strong lives are motivated by dynamic purposes; lesser ones exist on wishes and inclinations. The most glowing successes are but reflections of an inner fire.

Conrad Hilton: I encourage boldness because the danger of our seniority and pension plans tempt a young man to settle in a rut named security rather than find his own rainbow.

Herbert Hoover: About the time we think we can make ends meet, somebody moves the ends.

Bob Hope: ON RECEIVING THE CONGRESSIONAL GOLD MEDAL: I feel very humble, but I think I have the strength of character to fight it.

Vernon Howard: You have succeeded in life when all you really want is only what you really need.

Elbert Hubbard: The line between failure in success is so fine that we scarcely know when we pass it; so fine that we are often on the line and do not know it.

Kin Hubbard: It's hard to tell which gets knocked the most, the success or the failure, but it's mighty close.

Kin Hubbard: Whoever wrote "to win success we must deserve it" must have been the same fellow who gave out the statement that two can live as cheaply as one.

Lee Iacocca: The trick is to make sure you don't die waiting for prosperity to come.

Italian Proverb: Success has many parents, but failure is an orphan.

Italian Proverb: We cannot direct the wind, but we can adjust the sails.

Thomas Jefferson: I have a great believer in luck, and I find the harder I work the more I have of it.

Dr. Samuel Johnson: The applause of a single human being is of great consequence.

Carl Jung: The psychotherapist learns little or nothing from his successes. They mainly confirm him in his mistakes, while his failures, on the other hand, are priceless experiences in that they not only open up the way to a deeper truth, but force him to change his views and methods.

Henry J. Kaiser: I make progress by having people around who are smarter than I—and listening to them. And I assume that everyone is smarter about something than I am.

Robert F. Kennedy: Only those who dare to fail greatly can ever achieve greatly.

Fritz Kreisler (American violinist): After finishing a concert he heard someone say "I give my life to play as you do." He said, "Madam, I did."

Christopher Lasch: Nothing succeeds like the appearance of success.

Ernest Lehman (1957 film title): Sweet smell of success.

Ernest Lehman (1956 film starring Paul Newman; based on life of 1947-48 World Middleweight Boxing Champion Rocky Graziano, whose autobiography had same title): Somebody Up There Likes Me.

Vince Lombardi: If you can accept losing, you can't win. If you can walk, you can run. No one is ever hurt. Hurt is in your mind.

Henry Wadsworth Longfellow: Most people would succeed in small things if they were not troubled with great ambitions.

Don Juan Manuel: He who praises you for what you lack wishes to take from you what you have.

Orison Swett Marden: It is just the little touches after the average man would quit that make the master's fame.

John McEnroe: Everybody loves success, but they hate successful people.

Margaret Mead: Never doubt that a small group of thoughtful, committed citizens can change the world. Indeed, it is the only thing that ever has.

Michel de Montaigne: There are some defeats more triumphant than victories.

Sir Isaac Newton: If I have seen further it is by standing on the shoulders of giants.

Jack Nicklaus: Achievement is largely the product of steadily raising one's levels of aspiration and expectation.

Sioux Chief "Old Lodge Skins" (after June 25-26, 1876 Battle of Little Big Horn): Yes, my son, is finished now... there is no permanent winning or losing when things move as they should in a circle. But the white men, who live in squares and straight lines do not believe as I do. To them it is everything or nothing.... Winning is all they care about. And if they can do that by scratching a pen across a paper or saying something into the wind, they are much happier.

General George Patton: Success is how high you bounce when you hit bottom.

Charles F. Richter (from the 1932 Richter Scale of measuring earthquakes): On a scale of one to ten ....

Preacher Roe (1940's Brooklyn Dodger "dipsy doo" pitcher): Some days you eat the bear. Some days the bear eats you. ... Yesterday, the bear ate us.

Will Rogers: We can't all be heroes, because somebody has to sit on the curb and clap as they go by.

Will Rogers: If you want to be successful, it's just this simple. Know what you are doing. Love what you are doing. And believe in what you are doing.

Will Rogers: We may elevate ourselves but we should never reach so high that we would every forget those who helped us get there.

Will Rogers: You've got to go out on a limb sometimes because that's where the fruit is.

Will Rogers: Do the best you can, and don't take life too serious.

Will Rogers: It's great to be great, but it's greater to be human

Will Rogers: The worst thing that happens to you may be the best thing for you if you don't let it get the best of you.

Will Rogers: The fellow that can only see a week ahead is always the popular fellow, for he is looking with the crowd. But the one that can see years ahead, he has a telescope but he can't make anybody believe that he has it.

Andy Rooney: I'd like to be lucky (successful) enough so I could throw the soap away after the letters are worn off.

Rudy Ruettiger (motivational speaker, Notre Dame football player, ND Class of 1973; his true story is in the movie *Rudy*): The only thing you can control is the effort, and you owe it to yourself to persevere and do whatever you decide to do with passion. Don't ask for permission to be successful. Go make it happen.

Bertrand Russell: No one gossips about other people's secret virtues.

Rosalind Russell: Success is a public affair. Failure is a private funeral.

Historian William W. Sears (about Civil War General George B. McClellan, commander of the Army of the Potomac): He was so fearful of losing, he would not risk winning.

Dr. Martin Seligman, et als (a scientific study shows): THE determinant ... THE critical determining element in life and business success is resilience in the face of adversity.

Thomas Sowell: Much of the history of the Western world over the past three decades has involved replacing what worked with what sounded good.

William Shakespeare (*II Henry IV*, Act IV, iii): I came, saw, and overcame.

William Shakespeare (*III Henry VI*, Act II, i): Didst thou never hear / That things ill got had ever bad success?

William Shakespeare (*III Henry VI*, Act II, v): To whom God will, there be the victory.

William Shakespeare (*III Henry VI*, Act V, iii): Thus far our fortune keeps an upward course, / And we are grac'd with wreaths of victory.

William Shakespeare (*Henry VIII*, Act I, i): To climb steep hills / Requires slow pace at first.

William Shakespeare (*Much Ado About Nothing*, Act I, i): A victory is twice itself when the achiever brings home full numbers.

William Shakespeare (*Richard III*, Act I, iii): They that stand high have many blasts to shake them; / And, if they fall, they dash themselves to pieces..

William Shakespeare (*Twelfth Night*, Act II, v): Some are born great, some achieve greatness, and some have greatness thrust upon 'em.

Herbert Bayard Swope: I cannot give you the formula for success, but I can give you the formula for failure, which is – try to please everybody.

Albert von Szent-Gyorgyi: Discovery consists of seeing what every body has seen and thinking what nobody has thought.

Albert von Szent-Gyorgi: Discovery is said to be an accident meeting a prepared mind.

Alfred Lord Tennyson: He makes no friend who never made a foe.

Mother Teresa: I do not pray for success, I ask for faithfulness.

Grant Tinker: Oddly enough, success over a period of time is more expensive than failure.

Mark Twain: Fame is a vapor, popularity an accident; the only earthly certainty is oblivion.

Mark Twain: All you need in this life is ignorance and confidence; then success is sure.

Mark Twain: Keep away from people who try to belittle your ambitions. Small people always do that, but the really great make you feel that you, too, can become great.

UA: A diamond is a piece of coal that stuck to the job.

UA: A man can fail many times, but he is not a failure until he begins to blame somebody else.

UA: The higher a monkey climbs up a tree, the more visible his ass.

UA (from awards to winners of games at fairgrounds): Give the man a (big) cigar!

U.S. Olympic Team (1980 Winter Olympics at Lake Placid): Go for the gold!

Dick Vitale (Special Commentary in Introduction of *Numbelievable! The Dramatic Stories Behind the Most Memorable Numbers in Sports History*): When an athelete is "in the zone" – totally focused, mentally and physically prepared – he or she can put up special performances.... Being in the zone leads to greatness ... truly remarkable stuff that you never expected to see.... This chapter is about atheletes that are awesome, baby, with a capital A!

Rudy Westmoreland (my friend and partner): Success is some ways is simply a matter of buying your experience cheap and selling it at a profit.

Rudy Westmoreland: He fails from **"ANALYSIS PARALYSIS"** – he overanalyzes, overthinks and overplans every problem or potential situation so that as a result the problem is never solved and/or the advantage (if any) is lost.

Billy Wilder, Charles Brackett, and D.M. Marshman, Jr. (1950 film *Sunset Boulevard*): Joe Gillis: "You used to be in pictures. You used to be big." Norma Desmond: "I am big. It's the pictures that got small."

George F. Will: Americans are overreachers; overreaching is the most admirable of the many American excesses.

Thomas Wolfe: There is nothing in the world that will take the chip off one's shoulder like a feeling of success.

Lin Yutang: Peace of mind is that mental condition in which you have accepted the worst.

SUFFERING (See EMOTIONAL DISTRESS; GRIEF & SORROW; PAIN)

SUITS (See LITIGATION)

SUPREME COURT (See APPEAL; and JUDGES)

SYMPATHY (See COMPASSION)

TAXATION/TAXES (See GOVERNMENT)

TEACHING

Uncle Anthony: Thomas, be an "osmotic" – absorb everything - as much knowledge as you can

Uncle Anthony: Thomas, if you can't explain your client's case to me and the rest of this family in the first 3 minutes, FURGGETTABOUDDIT!"

Aunt Mary Carlo: A college aptitude test? When I went to school they didn't even teach me what aptitude was.

Henry Adams: Nothing in education is so astonishing as the amount of ignorance it accumulates in the form of inert facts.

W. H. Auden: Political history is far too criminal a subject to be a fit thing to teach children.

Averroes: Knowledge is the conformity of the object and the intellect.

Francis Bacon: Knowledge itself is power.

Yogi Berra: He's learning me his experience.

William Beveridge: Ignorance is an evil weed, which dictators may cultivate among their dupes, but which no democracy can afford among its citizens.

Bible: Colossians 2:8: Beware lest any man spoil you through philosophy and vain deceit.

Bible: Ecclesiastes 12:12: Much study is a weariness of the flesh.

Bible: Exodus 18:20: Show them the way wherein they must walk, and the work that they must do.

Bible: Isaiah 28:10: Precept must be upon precept, precept upon precept; line upon line, line upon line; here a little, and there a little.

Bible: Isaiah 30:20: And though the Lord give you the bread of adversity, and the water of affliction, yet shall not thy teachers be removed into a corner any more, but thine eyes shall see thy teachers.

Bible: Isaiah 38:19: The father to the children shall make known the truth.

Bible: James 3:3: We put bits in the horses' mouths, that they may obey us.

Bible: 1 Kings 8:36: Teach them the good way wherein they should walk.

Bible: Luke 14:35; Matthew 13:9: He that hath ears to hear, let him hear.

Bible: Proverbs 4:13: Take fast hold of instruction; let her not go: keep her; for she is thy life.

Bible: Proverbs 13:24: He that spareth his rod hateth his son: but he that loveth him chasteneth him betimes.

Bible: Proverbs 22:6: Train up a child in the way he should go: and when he is old he will not depart from it.

Bible: Proverbs 29:15: A child left to himself bringeth his mother to shame.

Bible: Psalms 34:11: Come, ye children, hearken unto me: I will teach you the fear of the Lord.

Bible: Psalms 119:103: How sweet are Thy words unto my taste! Yea, sweeter than honey to my mouth!

Bible: Romans 2:21: Thou therefore which teachest another, teachest thou not thyself?

Bible: Titus 2:1: Speak thou the things which become sound doctrine.

Ambrose Bierce: ACADEME, n. An ancient school where morality and philosophy were taught.

Ambrose Bierce: ACADEMY, n. (from academe). A modern school where football is taught.

Ambrose Bierce: EDUCATION, n. That which discloses to the wise and disguises from the foolish their lack of understanding.

Ambrose Bierce: ERUDITION, n. Dust shaken out of a book into an empty skull.

Ambrose Bierce: LEARNING, n. The kind of ignorance distinguishing the studious.

Ambrose Bierce: LORE, n. Learning – particularly that sort which is not derived from a regular course of instruction but comes of the reading of occult books, or by nature. This latter is commonly designated as folk-lore and embraces popularly myths and superstitions.

Ambrose Bierce: TECHNICALITY, n. In an English court a man named Home was tried for slander in having accused a neighbor of murder. His exact words were: "Sir Thomas Holt hath taken a cleaver and stricken his cook upon the head, so that one side of the head fell upon one shoulder and the other side upon the other shoulder." The defendant was acquitted by instruction of the court, the learned judges holding that the words did not charge murder, for they did not affirm the death of the cook, that being only an inference.

Ambrose Bierce: SAW, n. A trite popular saying, or proverb. (Figurative and colloquial.) So called because it makes its way into a wooden head....

Ambrose Bierce: Example is better than following it.

Derek Bok: If you think education is expensive, try ignorance.

Lord Charles Bowen (English judge, 1835-1894, *Lecture on Education,* 1902): The system of competitive examinations is a sad necessity. Knowledge is wooed for her dowry, not her diviner charms.

Joseph P. Bradley (New Jersey lawyer, Assoc. Justice US Supreme Court, 1813-1892): The event is always a great teacher. *The Nevada*, 106 US 154, 27 L ed 149, 1 S Ct 234 (1882)

Henry Peter Brougham (writer, statesman, Lord Chancellor of Great Britain, 1778-1868, *Speech in House of Commons*, 1828): Let the soldier be abroad if he will, he can do nothing in this age. There is another personage, - a personage less imposing in the eyes of some, perhaps insignificant. The schoolmaster is abroad, and I trust him, armed with his primer, against the soldier in full military array.

Henry Peter Brougham: Education makes people it easy to lead, but difficult to drive; easy to govern, but impossible to enslave.

Bulgarian Proverb: A tree falls the way it leans.

Jakob Burckhardt: The greatest innovation in the world is the demand for education as a right of man; it is a disguised demand for comfort.

Edmund Burke: Education is the cheap defense of nations.

Jacob Chanowshi: It is important that students bring a certain ragamuffin, barefoot, irreverance to their studies; they are not here to worship what is known, but to question it.

Chinese Proverb: Give a man a fish, and he'll eat for a day. Teach him how to fish and he'll eat forever.

Chinese Proverb: Whatever you put into your head and stomach no one can take away from you.

Chinese Proverb: If you are planning for a year, sow rice; if you are planning for a decade, plant trees; if you are planning for a lifetime, educate people.

Sir Winston Churchill: Personally I am always ready to learn, although I do not always like being taught.

Agnes Cripps: Educate a man and you educate an individual—educate a woman and you educate a family.

Danish Proverb: He who is afraid of asking is ashamed of learning.

Dizzy Dean: Let the teachers teach English, and I will teach baseball. There is a lot of people in the United States who say isn't, and they ain't eating. A lot of folks that ain't saying ain't ain't eatin'

Diogenes: The foundation of every state is the education of its youth.

Benjamin Disraeli: Upon the education of the people of this country the fate of this country depends.

Henry L. Doherty: It is the studying that you do after your school days that really counts. Otherwise you know only that which everyone else knows.

Peter Drucker: The most important thing in communication is to hear what is not being said.
Will Durant: Education is the progressive discovery of our own ignorance.
Irwin Edman: Education is the process of casting false pearls before real swine.
Albert Einstein: Education is that which remains when one has forgotten everything learned in school.
Albert Einstein: We should take care not to make the intellect our god; it has, of course, powerful muscles, but no personality.
Albert Einstein: I believe that love is a better teacher than a sense of duty – at least for me.
Albert Einstein: If Euclid failed to kindle your youthful entusiasm, then you were not born to be a scientific thinker.
Albert Einstein: The mechanical learning there (in the Munich Gymnasium or High School he attended in 1888 at age 9 and left for "health reasons" when he was 16 in 1894) seemed very much akin to the methods of the Prussian Army; where a mechanical discipline was achieved by repeated repetition of meaningless orders.
Albert Einstein: The teachers at the elementary school (in Munich Germany) seemed to me like drill sergeants, and the teachers at the gymnasium (Munich High School) like lieutenants.
Albert Einstein (1908 upon becoming an apprentice professor): So, finally now I too am an official member of "The Guild of Whores." (i.e. professors)
Albert Einstein (1921 in Boston about Tom Edison's Test for new employees): The value of a college education is not the learning of many facts, but the training of the mind to think.
Albert Einstein: Schools need not preach political doctrine to defend democracy. If they shape men capable of critical thought and trained in social attitudes, that is all that is necessary.
Charles W. Eliot (President of Harvard University 1909): It is true that Harvard has become a storehouse of knowledge. But, I scarcely deserve credit for that. It is simply that the freshmen bring so much and the seniors take away so little.
Ralph Waldo Emerson: What school, college, or lecture bring to men depends on what men bring to carry it home in.
English Proverb: He who would climb the ladder must begin at the bottom
English Proverb (17th century): One father is more than a hundred schoolmasters.
Epictetus: Only the educated are free.
Anatole France: An education isn't how much you have committed to memory, or even how much you know. It's being able to differentiate between what you know and what you don't.
Benjamin Franklin: To America one schoolmaster is worth a dozen poets, and the invention of the machine or the improvement of an implement is of more importance than a masterpiece of Raphael.
Robert Frost: Education is the ability to listen to almost anything without losing your temper or your self-confidence.
Ibn Gabirol: In seeking knowledge, the first step is silence, the second listening, the third remembering, the fourth practicing, and the fifth—teaching others.
James A. Garfield: Next in importance to freedom and justice is popular education, without which neither freedom nor justice can be permanently maintained.
General Dynamics ad: One out of every five Americans is unable to read this sentence.
Geronimo (1905 speech to Carlisle Indian School students on his way to Teddy Roosevelt's Presidential Inaugural Parade in DC): You are here to study, to learn the ways of the white man. Do it well. Do as you are told all the time and you won't get hungry.
German Proverb: A teacher is better than two books.
Kahlil Gibran: I have learned silence from the talkative, toleration from the intolerant, and kindness from the unkind; yet strange, I am ungrateful to these teachers.
Gail Godwin: Good teaching is one fourth preparation and three fourths theater.
Johann Wolfgang von Goethe: Divide and rule, a sound motto. Unite and lead, a better one.
Harry Graham (*Ruthless Rhymes*, 1899): Father, chancing to chastise/ His daughter Sue, / Said: I hope you realize / That this hurts me more than you.
Rocky Graziano: I quit school in the fifth grade because of pneumonia. Not because I had it but because I couldn't spell it.

Greek Proverb (Euclid's reply to Ptolemy I, when asked if there was some easy way to master the science of geometry, c. 300 BC): There is no royal road to learning.

Philip G. Hamerton: have you ever observed that we pay much more attention to a wise passage when it is quoted then when we read it in the original author?

Susan Shown Harjo (American Indian): The schools I went to as a kid may be wary. It was clear to me that everything was a lie except math.

Helen Hayes: From your parents you learn love and laughter and how to put one foot in front of the other. But when books are opened you discover that you have wings.

Heinrich Heine: The Romans would never have had time to conquer the world if they had been obliged to learn Latin first of all.

Heinrich Heine: Experience is a good school. But the fees are high.

Robert Henri: If you want to know how to do a thing you must first have a complete desire to do that thing.

Oliver Wendell Holmes (*Oration before Harvard Law School Association*, 1886): The main part of intellectual education is not the acquisition of facts, but learning how to make the facts live.

Elbert Hubbard: This will never be a civilized country until we expend more money for books than we do for chewing gum.

Indian Proverb: The rain of tears is necessary to the harvest of learning.

Irish Proverb: Instinct is stronger than upbringing.

Irish Proverb: Necessity is the mother of invention.

Irish Proverb: Need teaches a plan.

Italian and Chinese Proverb: I hear and I forget. I see and I remember. I do and I understand.

Italian and Chinese Proverb: he who asks is a fool for five minutes, but he who does not ask remains a fool forever.

Japanese Proverb: To teach is to learn.

Thomas Jefferson: Enlighten the people generally, and tyranny and oppressions of both body and mind will vanish like evil spirits at the dawn of day.

Thomas Jefferson: The tax which will be paid for the purpose of education is not more than one-thousandth part of what will be paid to kings, priests and nobles who will rise up among us if we leave the people in ignorance.

Jewish Saying: First learn; then teach.

Jewish Saying: When a teacher fights with his wife, it's tough on his students.

Jewish Saying: Be very careful in teaching, for an error in teaching is tantamount to a willful transgression.

Jewish Saying: The ill-tempered cannot teach.

Lady Bird Johnson: Education is a loan to be repaid with a gift of self.

John F. Kennedy: It might be said that I have the best of both worlds: a Harvard education and a Yale degree.

John F. Kennedy: Liberty without learning is always in peril; learning without liberty is always in vain.

Henry Kissinger: University politics are so vicious precisely because the stakes are so small.

Nikolai Lenin: Whenever the cause of the people is entrusted to professors it is lost.

Maimonides: He who has not studied enough and teaches imperfect knowledge is to be treated as if he has sinned intentionally.

Al McGuire: I think the world is run by C students.

Herman Melville (*Moby Dick*, ch 24): A whale-ship was my Yale College and my Harvard.

Jules Michelet: What is the first part of politics? Education. The second? Education. And the third? Education.

Midrash: A pupil receives but a fifth of the reward that accrues to the teacher.

Wilson Mizner: A good listener is not only popular everywhere, but after a while he gets to know something.

Alberto Moravia: Nowadays, the illiterates can read and write.

Tom Mueller: Once upon a time, for a fotunate few, travel was the worldliest form of education and a vital part of life. From the late 17th century until the end of the 18th century, privileged young women and men made ready for adulthood by embarking on **the Grand Tour**, an extended journey through Western Europe that was a crucial rite of passage for the European and American elite.... // **The Grand**

Tour was an education in the root sense of the word, from the Latin *e + ducare*, "to lead forth" – to take people out of themselves, thereby widening their horizons, making them at once more resilient and worldlywise.

Friedrich Nietzsche: In large states public education will always be mediocre, for the same reason that in large kitchens the cooking is usually bad.

Friedrich Nietzsche: To scholars who become politicians a comic role is usually assigned: they have to be the good conscience of a state policy.

Louis Nizer: Defeat is education. It is a step to something better.

Roger North (English lawyer and writer, 1653-1734, *On the Study of Laws*): Sir Henry Finch used to say, study all the morning, and talk all the afternoon.

Eric Oliver: Remember – you and your audience were a READER long before you were a WRITER.

Jose Ortega y Gasset: Tell me to what you pay attention and I will tell you who you are.

M.P. "Pappy" Papadakis: "Even stupid questions may result in smart answers...listen."

Dorothy Parker: The cure for boredom is curiosity. There is no cure for curiosity.

Henry Peter: Education makes a people easy to lead, but difficult to drive; easy to govern but impossible to enslave.

Bum Phillips (former NFL head coach): The only discipline that lasts is self-discipline.

Plato: All learning has an emotional base.

Will Rogers: You should never try and teach a pig to read for two reasons. First, it's impossible; and secondly, it annoys the hell out of the pig!

Will Rogers: Successful colleges will start laying plans for a new stadium; unsuccessful ones will start hunting a new coach.

Will Rogers: There is only one thing that can kill the Movies, and that is education.

Will Rogers: A man only learns in two ways, one by reading, and the other by association with smarter people.

Will Rogers: America is becoming so educated that ignorance will be a novelty. I will belong to the select few.

Will Rogers: The schools ain't what they used to be and never was.

Will Rogers: When you give a lesson in meanness to a critter or a person, don't be surprised if they learn their lesson.

Will Rogers: Instead of giving money to found colleges to promote learning, why don't they pass a constitutional amendment prohibiting anybody from learning anything? If it works as good as the Prohibition one did, why, in five years we would have the smartest race of people on earth.

Will Rogers: Why don't they pass a constitutional amendment prohibiting anybody from learning anything? If it works as well as prohibition did, in five years Americans would be the smartest race of people on Earth.

Will Rogers: The more that learn to read the less learn how to make a living. That's one thing about a little education. It spoils you for actual work. The more you know the more you think somebody owes you a living.

Arthur Schopenhauer: Talent hits a target no one else can hit; genius hits a target no one else can see.

William Shakespeare (*All's Well That Ends Well*, Act II, ii): Highly fed and lowly taught.

William Shakespeare (*As You Like It*, Act II, vii): Then the whining school-boy, with his satchel, / And shining morning face, creeping like snail / Unwillingly to school.

William Shakespeare (*II Henry VI*, Act IV, ii): SMITH: He can write and read, and cast contempt. / JACK CADE: O monstrous! / SMITH: We took him setting of boy's copies. / JACK CADE: He's a villain.

William Shakespeare (*Henry VIII*, Act III, i): Woe upon ye / And all such false professors.

William Shakespeare (*Henry VIII*, Act III, ii): When I am forgotten,... say, I taught thee.

William Shakespeare (*Henry VIII*, Act IV, ii): He was a scholar, and a ripe and good one; / Exceeding wise, fair-spoken, and persuading; / Lofty and sour to them that lov'd him not; / But, to those men that sought him, sweet as summer.

William Shakespeare (*King Lear*, Act II, iv): We'll set thee to school to an ant, to teach thee there's no labouring in the winter.

William Shakespeare (*King Lear*, Act III, iv): I'll talk a word with this same learned Theban: / What is your study?

William Shakespeare (*Love's Labour's Lost*, Act I, i): Small have continual plodders ever won / Save base authority from others' books.

William Shakespeare (*Love's Labour's Lost*, Act I, i): So study evermore is overshot; / While it doth study to have what it would, / It doth forget to do the thing it should. / And when it hath the thing it hunteth most, / 'Tis won, as towns with fire; so won, so lost.

William Shakespeare (*Love's Labour's Lost*, Act I, i): Study is like the heaven's glorious sun, / That will not be deep-search'd with saucy looks; / Small have continual plodders ever won, / Save base authority from other's books.

William Shakespeare (*Love's Labour's Lost*, Act IV, iii): Learning is but an adjunct to ourself, / And where we are, our learning likewise is.

William Shakespeare (*Much Ado About Nothing*, Act III, iii): God hath blessed you with a good name: to be a well-favored man is the gift of fortune; but to write and read comes by nature.

William Shakespeare (*The Taming of the Shrew*, Act I, i): Schoolmasters will I keep within my house, / Fit to instruct her youth.

William Shakespeare (*The Taming of the Shrew*, Act I, ii): O this learning! What a thing it is.

William Shakespeare (*The Taming of the Shrew*, Act II, i): I do present you with a man of mine, / Cunning in music and the mathematics, / To instruct her fully in those sciences.

William Shakespeare (*Love's Labour's Lost*, Act II, i): To teach a teacher ill beseemeth me.

William Shakespeare (*Love's Labour's Lost*, Act IV, iii): Learning is but an adjunct to ourself, / And where we are our learning likewise.

George Bernard Shaw: He who can, does. He who cannot, teaches.

Ben Sirach: Hidden wisdom and concealed treasures—of what use is either?

B.F. Skinner: Education is what survives when what has been learned has been forgotten.

Joseph Solon: Education is a weapon, whose effects depend on who holds it in his hands and at whom it is aimed.

Spanish Proverb: Live with wolves, and you learn to howl.

Amos Alonzo Stagg (legendary University of Chicago football coach): No coach ever won a game by what he knows, it's what his players have learned.

Sir Richard Steele: Reading is to the mind what exercise is to the body.

Adlai Stevenson: Anti-intellectualism long been the anti-Semitism of the businessman.

Adlai Stevenson: If we value the pursuit of knowledge we must be free to follow wherever that search may lead us.

Talmud: Don't live in a city run by scholars.

Talmud: The real guardians of the state are the teachers.

Talmud: He who teaches a child is as if he had created it.

Talmud: The calf wants to suckle, but even more does the cow want to give suck. (The teacher may need to teach more than his pupils need to learn).

Talmud: God said: You must teach, as I taught, without a fee.

Talmud: In teaching, do not favor the children of the rich—and teach the children of the poor without compensation.

Talmud: The bad teacher's words fall on his pupils like harsh rain; the good teacher's, as gently as the dew.

Talmud: Blessed is the son who studies with his father, and blessed is the father who teaches his son.

Talmud: The man from whom people learn must be especially strict with himself.

Walter T. Tatara: Surely the shortest commencement address in history—and for me one of the most memorable – was that of Dr. Harold E. Hyde, president of New Hampshire's Plymouth State College. He reduced his message to the graduating class to these three ideals: "Know yourself—Socrates. Control yourself—Cicero. Give yourself—Christ."

Henry David Thoreau: What does education often do? It makes a straight-cut ditch of a free, meandering brook.

James Thurber: American college students are like American colleges—each has half-dulled faculties.

James Thurber: There are two kinds of light—the glow that illumines, and the glare that obscures.

George Trevelyan: Education... has produced a vast population able to read but unable to distinguish what is worth reading.

Mark Twain: Education consists mainly in what we have unlearned.

Mark Twain: Never learn to do anything. If you don't learn, you will always find someone else to do it for you.

Mark Twain: Soap and education are not as sudden as a massacre, but they are more deadly in the long run.

Mark Twain: It is noble to be good; it is still nobler to teach others to be good—and less trouble.

Mark Twain: I have never let my schooling interfere with my education.

Mark Twain: They spell it Vinci and pronounce it Vinchy; foreigners always spell better than they pronounce.

Mark Twain: Training is everything. The peach was once a bitter almond; cauliflower is nothing but cabbage with a college education.

Mark Twain: The Moral Sense teaches us what is right, and how to avoid it – when unpopular.

Mark Twain: A man can seldom – very, very, seldom – fight a winning fight against his training: the odds are too heavy.

UA: A proverb is a short sentence based on long experience.

Albert von Szent-Gyorgyi: Discovery consists of seeing what every body has seen and thinking what nobody has thought.

Daniel Webster: On the diffusion of education among the people rest the preservation and perpetuation of our free institutions.

Duke of Wellington: Educate men without religion and you make them but clever devils.

Alfred North Whitehead: Once learning solidifies, all is over with it.

Katherine Whitehorn: The easiest way for your chidren to learn about money is for you not to have any.

Oscar Wilde: Everybody who is incapable of learning has taken to teaching.

Woodrow Wilson: Power consists in one's capacity to link his will with the purpose of others, to lead by reason and a gift of cooperation.

W. B. Yeats: Education is not the filling of a pail, but the lighting of a fire.

Yiddish Proverb: A table is not blessed if it has fed no scholars.

THEORY/THEORIES (See OPINION; THINKING/THOUGHT)

THINKING/THOUGHT

Uncle Anthony: Your mind will never wear out, it can only rust from lack of use.

Uncle Anthony: If yer ashamed of tellin' me what yer thinkin' – then stop thinkin' that crap!

Aunt Mary Carlo: Didjaever stop to think and then forget to get started again?

Aunt Mary Carlo: Good thoughts don't pay the rent!

Franklin P. Adams: When the political columnists say "Every thinking man" they mean themselves, and when candidates appeal to "Every intelligent voter" they mean everybody who is going to vote for them.

Bahya Ibn Paquda: Words are the shell; meditation is the kernel.

Yogi Berra: Ninety percent of this game is half-mental.

Yogi Berra: Think?! How the hell are you gonna think and hit at the same time?

Bible: 1 Corinthians 13:11: When I was a child, I spake as a child, I understood as a child, I thought as a child: but when I became a man, I put away childish things.

Bible: Isaiah 55:8: My thoughts are not your thoughts, neither are your ways My ways, saith the Lord.

Bible: Jeremiah 4:14: How long shall thy vain thoughts lodge within thee?

Bible: 1 Peter 1:13: Gird up the loins of your mind.

Bible: Philippians 4:8: Whatsoeverthings are true, whatsoever things are honest, whatsoever things are just, whatsoever things are pure, whatsoever things are of good report; if there be any virtue, and if there be any praise, think on these things.

Bible: Proverbs 23:7: As a man thinketh in his heart, so is he.

Bible: Romans 7:22: I delight in the law of God after the inward man: But I see another law in my members, warring against the law of my mind, and bringing me into captivity to the law of sin.

Bible: Romans 12:3: Think soberly.

Bible: Romans 14:5: Let every man be fully persuaded in his own mind.

Bible: 2 Timothy 1:7: For God hath not given us the spirit of fear; but of power, and of love, and of a sound mind.

Ambrose Bierce: BRAIN, n. An apparatus with which we think that we think. That which distinguishes the man who is content to *be* something from the man who wishes to *do* something. A man of great wealth, or one who has been pitchforked into high station, has commonly such a headful of brain that his neighbors cannot keep their hats on. In our civilization, and under our republican form of government, brain is so highly honored that it is rewarded by exemption from the cares of office.

Ambrose Bierce: CUNNING, n. The faculty that distinguishes a weak animal or person from a strong one. It brings its possessor much mental satisfaction and great material adversity. An Italian proverb says: "The furrier gets the skins of more foxes than asses."

Ambrose Bierce: FAITH, n. Belief without evidence in what is told by one who speaks without knowledge, of things without parallel.

Ambrose Bierce: MAD, adj. Affected with a high degree of intellectual independence; not conforming to standards of thought, speech and action derived by the conformants from study of themselves; at odds with the majority; in sort, unusual. It is noteworthy that persons are pronounced mad by officials destitute of evidence that themselves are sane....

Ambrose Bierce: RECONSIDER, v. To seek a justification for a decision already made.

Ambrose Bierce: REFLECTION, n. An action of the mind whereby we obtain a clearer view of our relation to the things of yesterday and are able to avoid the perils that we shall not again encounter.

Ambrose Bierce: TEDIUM, n. Ennui, the state or condition of one that is bored. Many fanciful derivations of the word have been affirmed, but so high an authority as Father Jape says that it comes from a very obvious source – the first words of the ancient Latin hymn *Te Deum Laudamus*. In the apparently natural derivation there is something that saddens.

Ray Bradbury: Don't think! Thinking is the enemy of creativity. It's self-conscious, and anything self-conscious is lousy. You can't try to do things; you simply must do them.

John Cage: I can't understand why people are frightened of new ideas. I'm frightened of the old ones.

Lewis Carrol (*Alice's Adventures in Wonderland*, 1865): "I've got a right to think," said Alice ... "Just about as much right," said Duchess, "as pigs have to fly."

Sir Winston Churchill: The empires of the future are the empires of the mind.

Sir Winston Churchill: Let our advance worrying become advance thinking and planning.

Sir Winston Churchill: Half my lifetime I have earned my living by selling words, and I hope thoughts.

Greg Cusimano: Thought without action is just interesting; action without thought is a catastrophe.

Clarence Darrow: There is no such crime as a crime of thought; there are only crimes of action.

Clarence Darrow (in what some call "THE GREATEST COURTROOM SCENE IN ANGLO-AMERICAN HISTORY" = Darrow's Cross-examination of William Jennings Bryan, Monday July 20, 1925, during the "Scopes Monkey Trial" of math and science teacher John Scopes in Dayton, TENN: "Bryan: I do not think about the things I do not think about. Darrow: Do you think about the things you do think about? Bryan: Well, ... sometimes."

Leonardo da Vinci: The average human looks without seeing, listens without hearing, touches without feeling, eats without tasting, moves without physical awareness, inhales without awareness of odor or fragrance, and talks without thinking.

Rene Descartes: If you would be a real seeker of truth, it is necessary that at least once in your life you doubt, as far as possible, all things.

Rene Descartes: One cannot conceive (EDITOR: or opine) anything so strange and so implausible that it has not already been said by one philosopher or another.

John Dewey: Anyone who has begun to think places some portion of the world in jeopardy.

John Dewey: We can have facts without thinking, but we cannot have thinking without facts.

Benjamin Disraeli: Nurture your mind with great thoughts; to believe in the heroic makes heroes.

William J. Donnelly (*The Confetti Generation: How the New Communications Technology Is Fragmenting America*, 1986): There is little doubt about the revolutionary potential of the new electronic media in our society and culture.... at some very early point, nearly everyone between the ages of ten and forty-nine today will have at least two new electronic media in their homes: (1) a random acess information system (home computer, videotext, optical videodisc); and (2) a fickle access entertainment system (cable television, pay television, videocassette, video game)...The new media encompasses a quantum leap in the ability to store and retrieve information; a quantum leap in the availability of mimetic entertainment that is readily internalized; a quantum leap in services that provide controlled, individualized, remote transactions; and a quantum leap in speed, to the point of warping our sense of time...together, they will produce and define **THE CONFETTI GENERATION.**

William J. Donnelly (*The Confetti Generation: How the New Communications Technology Is Fragmenting America*, 1986): To appreciate the living experience of the Confetti Generation, we should ask ourselves a few simple questions. When ideas and experiences float down upon us like confetti – and just as cheaply – how do we expect to choose?....The electronification of our lives that began with television and the use of computers ... wil become pervasive and microspecific... That is our destination, but what is our destiny? ... In **THE CONFETTI GENERATION**, we will be living undirected lives and life-styles. We will think and act not only for ourselves, but by ourselves, isolated from the common experiences and judgments of others... we are about to think and choose and live differently than ever before in history.

John Dooley: Anyone who has begun to think places some portion of the world in jeopardy

David Dunham: Efficiency is intelligent laziness.

Thomas Alva Edison: There is nothing expedient to which a man will not go to avoid the real labor of thinking.

Albert Einstein (often used phrase): I will a little t'ink.

Albert Einstein: We should take care not to make the intellect our god; it has, of course, powerful muscles, but no personality.

Albert Einstein: If Euclid failed to kindle your youthful entusiasm, then you were not born to be a scientific thinker.

Albert Einstein (used this "BLIND BEETLE ANALOGY" to describe his great insight that Gravity was the curving of the fabric of Space-Time, when his youngest son Edward asked him why he was so famous?): When a blind beetle crawls over the surface of a curved branch, it doesn't notice that the track it has covered is indeed curved. I was lucky enough to notice what the beetle didn't notice.

Ralph Waldo Emerson: All ages of belief have been great; all of unbelief have been mean.

English Proverb (18th century): To talk without thinking is to shoot without aiming.

Bergen Evans: Freedom of speech and freedom of action are meaningless without freedom to think. And there is no freedom of thought without doubt.

William Faulkner: When they (ideas) come, I write them, when they don't come, I don't.

Paul Fix: The only reason some people get lost in thought is because it is unfamiliar territory.

Henry Ford: Thinking is the hardest work there is, which is the probable reason why so few engage in it.

Benjamin Franklin: Despair ruins some, Presumption many.

German Proverb: Think with the wise but walk with the vulgar.

Goethe: Daring ideas are like chessmen moved forward. They may be beaten, but they may start a winning game.

Alfred Whitney Griswold: Books won't stay banned. They won't burn. Ideas won't go to jail.

Sacha Guitry: What probably distorts everything in life is that one is convinced that one is speaking the truth because one says what one thinks.

Philip G. Hamerton: Have you ever observed that we pay much more attention to a wise passage when it is quoted then when we read it in the original author?

Learned Hand: We shall succeed only so far as we continue that most distasteful of all activity, the intolerable labor of thought.

John Heywood (*The Proverbs of John Heywood*, 1546): A penny for your thoughts.

Etty Hillesum: We are always in search of the redeeming formula, the crystalizing thought.

Adolph Hitler: What luck for rulers that men do not think.

Oliver Wendell Holmes, Jr.: Every idea is an incitement. It offers itself for belief and, if believed, it is acted on unless some other belief outweighs it, or some failure of energy stifles the movements at its birth.

Oliver Wendell Holmes, Jr.: If there is any principle of the Constitution that more imperatively calls for attachment than any other it is the principle of free thought—not free thought for those who agree with us but freedom for both thought we hate.

Oliver Wendell Holmes, Jr. (*Law And the Court*, 1913): Most men think dramatically, not quantitatively.

Oliver Wendell Holmes, Jr. (*Path of the Law*, 10 Harv. L. R. 457, 1896): Theory is the most important part of the dogma of the law, as the architect is the most important man who takes part in the building of a house.

Oliver Wendell Holmes, Jr. (*Profession of the Law, Speeches,* 1913): The secret isolated joy of the thinker, who knows that, a hundred years after he is dead and forgotten, men who never heard of him will be moving to the measure of his thought.

Victor Hugo: No army is as powerful as an idea whose time has come.

Virginia Hutchinson: An open mind, like an open window, should be screened to keep the bugs out.

William James: A great many people think they are thinking when they are merely rearranging their prejudices.

Lynden B. Johnson: If two men agree on everything, you may be sure that one of them is doing the thinking.

Carl Jung: Everything that irritates us about others can lead us to an understanding of ourselves.

Rudyard Kipling: I keep six honest serving men; They taught me all I knew. Their names are: What and Why and When, And How and Where and When.

Stanislaw Lec: Thoughts, like fleas, jump from man to man, but they don't bite everybody."

Walter Lippmann: Where all men think alike, no one thinks very much.

John Locke: The actions of men are the best interpreters of their thoughts.

Horace Mann: Never underestimate the human faculty for rejecting information.

Don Marquis: If you make people think they're thinking, they will love you; but if you really make them think, they will hate you.

P.B. Medawar (Biologist): The human mind treats a new idea the way the body treats a strange protein; it rejects it.

Mezeritzer Rabbi: Thought is nobler than words, because it guides them.

Olin Miller: You probably wouldn't worry about what people think of you if you could know how seldom they do.

Moses Ibn Ezra: Dive into the sea of thought, and find there pearls beyond price.

Moses Ibn Ezra: Thought serves as a mirror: it shows us the ugliness and the beauty within.

Nachman of Bratslav: Thinking is more precious than all five senses.

Thomas Paine: Credulity is not a crime.

Dorothy Parker: The cure for boredom is curiosity. There is no cure for curiosity.

Plutarch: The mind is not a vessel to be filled but a fire to be kindled.

Twiggy Rathbone: Reservations are the condoms in the birth of new ideas.

Carl Rogers: The very essence of the creative is its novelty, and hence we have no standard by which to judge it.

Will Rogers: I got no "Philosophy." I don't even know what the word means. The Fourth Reader, (McGuffy's) is as far as I ever got in schools. I am not bragging on it, I am thoroughly ashamed of it for I had every opportunity. Everything I have done has been by luck, no move was premeditated. I just stumbled from one thing to another. I may be making the wrong use of any little talent (if any) that I accidentally have. I don't know.

Will Rogers: People's minds are changed through observation and not through argument.

Bertrand Russell: Most people would sooner die than think; in fact, they do so.

Bertrand Russell: A stupid man's report of what a clever man says can never be accurate, because he unconsciously translates what he hears into something he can understand.

Russian Proverb: Take thy thoughts to bed with thee, for the morning is wiser than the evening.

Carl Sagan: Skeptical scrutiny is the means, in both science and religion, by which deep insight can be winnowed from deep nonsense.

George Santayana: Skepticism, like chastity, should not be relinquished too readily.

Arthur Schopenhauer: Talent hits a target no one else can hit; genius hits a target no one else can see.

William Shakespeare (*Antony and Cleopatra*, Act IV, ii): Drown consideration.

William Shakespeare (*Antony and Cleopatra*, Act V, ii): Make not your thoughts your prisons.

William Shakespeare (*Cymbeline*, Act III, iii): Their thoughts do hit The roofs of palaces.

William Shakespeare (*Hamlet*, Act I, iii): Give thy thoughts no tongue, / Nor any unproportion'd thought his act.

William Shakespeare (*Hamlet*, Act I, v): As swift / As meditation, or the thoughts of love.

William Shakespeare (*Hamlet*, Act II, ii): There is nothing either good or bad, but thinking makes it so.

William Shakespeare (*I Henry IV*, Act V, iv): But thought 's the slave of life, and life time's fool.

William Shakespeare (*II Henry IV*, Act IV, iv): The incessant care and labour of his mind / Hath wrought the mure, that should confine it in, / So thin, that life looks through, and will break out.

William Shakespeare (*Henry V*, Act V, *Prologue* 1.23): In the quick forge and working-house of thought.

William Shakespeare (*I Henry VI*, Act I, v): My thoughts are whirled like a potter's wheel.

William Shakespeare (*Julius Caesar*, Act I, ii): Yond Cassius has a lean and hungry look; / He thinks too much: such men are dangerous.

William Shakespeare (*King John*, Act V, i): Be great in act, as you have been in thought.

William Shakespeare (*Macbeth*, Act II, ii): You do unbend your noble strength, to think / So brainsickly of things.

William Shakespeare (*Macbeth*, Act III, ii): Why do you keep alone, / Of sorriest fancies your companions making? / Using those thoughts, which should indeed have died / With them they think on? Things without all remedy, / Should be without regard.

William Shakespeare (*Macbeth*, Act IV, i): The very firstlings of my heart shall be / The firstlings of my hand. And even now, / To crown my thoughts with acts, be it thought and done.

William Shakespeare (*Merchant of Venice*, Act III, ii): A maiden hath no tongue but thought.

William Shakespeare (*Midsummer Night's Dream*, Act II, ii): In maiden meditation, fancy-free.

William Shakespeare (*Othello*, Act III, iii): I pray thee, speak to me as to thy thinkings, / As thou dost ruminate, and give thy worst of thoughts / The worst of words.

William Shakespeare (*Richard III*, Act I, i): Dive, thoughts, down to my soul.

William Shakespeare (*Richard III*, Act III, vii): He is divinely bent to meditation; / And in no worldly suit would he be moved, / To draw him from his holy exercise.

William Shakespeare (*Sonnets*, 44.7): Nimble thought can jump both sea and land.

William Shakespeare (*The Tempest*, Act III, ii): Flout 'em and scout 'em, And Scout 'em and flout 'em; Thought is free.

William Shakespeare (*The Tempest*, Act IV, i): I do begin to have bloody thoughts.

William Shakespeare (*Twelfth Night*, Act I, iii): Thought is free.

James Thurber: All human beings should try to learn before they die what they are running from, and to, and why.

Mark Twain: Where prejudice exists it always discolors our thoughts.

Mark Twain: In religion and politics people's beliefs and convictions are in almost every case gotten at second-hand, and without examination.

Mark Twain: We have not the reverent feeling for the rainbow that a savage has, because we know how it is made. We have lost as much as we gained by prying into that matter.

Mark Twain: The slowness of one section of the world about adopting the valuable ideas of another section of it is a curious thing and unaccountable.

Marquis de Vauvenargues: When a thought is too weak to be expressed simply, it should be rejected.

Albert von Szent-Gyorgyi: Discovery consists of seeing what every body has seen and thinking what nobody has thought.

Bill Watterson: Sometimes I think the surest sign that intelligent life exists elsewhere in the universe is that none of it has tried to contact us.

West African Proverb: If I give you an egg, and you give me an egg, we will each have one egg. If I give you an idea, and you give me an idea, we will each have two ideas.

Oscar Wilde: Most people are other people. Their thoughts are someone else's opinions, their lives a mimicry, their passions a quotation.

Woodrow Wilson: One cool judgment is worth a thousand hasty councils. The thing to be supplied is light, not heat.

TOBACCO (See CIGARS)

TORTS (See NEGLIGENCE; WRONGDOING)

TORT REFORM

Uncle Anthony: The same guys who want to hang all the murderers and drug dealers, don't seem to want to punish (allow punitive damages against) the corporate big shots and drunk drivers who have assets and insurance.

Uncle Anthony: Hey! Howcome when these insurance companies say that they're losin' money, nobody that we elect ever asks to see their books? Howcome?

Aunt Mary Carlo: Ya can callit whaddever, but takin' my rights away an lettin' da insurance companies make more money, dat ain't a reform, dat's a reneging of my constitutional rights.

Aunt Mary Carlo: He's one of dem professional reformers dat takes da pie (money) otta the piety.

Brooks Adams: Law is merely the expression of the will of the strongest for the time being, and therefore laws have no fixity, but shift from generation to generation.

Aristotle: Even when laws have been written down, they ought not always to remain unaltered.

Ruth Benedict: It is no use to talk about Reform. Society will be very obedient when the myriad personalities that compose it have, and are aware that they have, an object in living.... The stench of atrophied personality.

Saint Bernard of Clairvaux: Were I to cry out against what is evil and say nothing about what is good, I would prove myself a mere backbiter and not a reformer, one who would rather carp at evil than remedy it.

Bible: 1 Corinthians 7:31: The fashion of this world passeth away.

Bible: 2 Corinthians 5:17: Old things are passed away; behold, all things are become new.

Bible: Galatians 1:23: He (Paul) which persecuted us in times past now preacheth the faith which once he destroyed.

Bible: Jeremiah 13:23: Can the Ethiopian change his skin, or the leopard his spots? Then may ye also do good, that are accustomed to do evil.

Bible: Luke 5:38; Mark 2:22; Matthew 9:17: New wine must be put into new bottles.

Bible: Proverbs 22:28: Remove not the ancient landmark, which the fathers (Editor:Founding Fathers) have set.

Ambrose Bierce: REDRESS, n. Reparation without satisfaction....

Ambrose Bierce: REFORM, n. A thing that mostly satisfies reformers opposed to reformation.

Henry Ward Beecher: Laws and institutions are constantly tending to gravitate. Like clocks, they must be occasionally cleansed, and wound up, and set to true time.

Benjamin Cardozo: The law, like the traveler, must be ready for the morrow. It must have the principle of growth.

Judge Cirillo: TORT REFORM: "Imagine if government took David's sling away and gave it to Goliath. Now you understand tort reform. The contingency, though much maligned and misunderstood, has been termed "the poor man's key to the courthouse." An automobile company may decide that it values profits over people and manufacture a car with an inexpensive but hazardous design. That car then blows up, leaving the driver nothing more than chard flash and his grieving family numb with shock and facing possible financial ruin. Could that poor family of Ford the per hour rate of the high-priced, Wall Street legal talent which the automobile company will employ to defend any suit they might bring? The answer is searingly obvious. A contingent B. agreement will enable that family to file suit and receive the compensation which they deserve. Any person whose heart stirs with the barest twinge of compassion must praise such a just result. Surely, large corporations and insurance companies will always be able to afford teams of high-priced attorneys. Pity the poor injured plaintiff who must finance such a contest from his own resources." Judge Cirillo, Romano v. Lubin, 530 A.2d 487 (Pa. Super. 1987).

Charles C. Colton: Law and equity are two things that God hath joined, but which man hath put asunder.

Ralph Waldo Emerson: Every reform was once a private opinion, and when it shall be private opinion again, it will solve the problem of the age.

Ralph Waldo Emerson: We are reformers in spring and summer; in autumn and winter we stand by the old – reformers in the morning, conservatives at night. Reform is affirmative, conservatism is negative; conservatism goes for comfort, reform for truth.

Grant Gilmore: The worse the society, the more laws there will be. In Hell there will be nothing but laws, and due process will be meticulously observed.

William T. Gossett (President, American Bar Association): The rule of law can be wiped out in one misguided, however well-intentioned, generation.

Edith Hamilton: When the freedom they wished for most was freedom from responsibility then Athens ceased to be free and was never free again.

Benjamin Harrison (23rd President of the United States): To the law we bow with reverence. It is the one king that commands our allegiance. We shall change our king when his rule is oppressive.

Oliver Wendell Holmes Jr.: It is perfectly proper to regard the study of law simply as a great anthropological document.

Oliver Wendell Holmes Jr.: It cannot be helped, it is as it should be, that the law is behind the times.

Oliver Wendell Holmes (1 *Holmes-Pollock Letters* 219, 1914): One thinks that an error exposed is dead, but exposure amounts to nothing when people want to believe. [EDITOR: This seems very appropriate for tort reform myths which, even when exposed as myths do not die but persist with many people who must, as Holmes says, "want to beliebe."]

Edgar Watson Howe: I think I am better than the people who are trying to reform me.

Victor Hugo: To reform a man, you must begin with his grandmother.

Molly Ivins: In the real world, there are only two ways to deal with corporate misbehavior: One is through government regulation and the other is by taking them to court. What has happened over 20 years of free-market proselytizing is that we have dangerously weakened both forms of restraint, first through the craze for "deregulation" and second through endless rounds of "tort reform," all of which have the effect of cutting off citizens' access to the courts. By legally bribing politicians with campaign contributions, the corporations have bought themselves immunity from lawsuits on many levels.

Michael Kinsley (American journalist): As tort law operates now, it is more like a lottery than like a rational system of justice.

Michel de Montaigne: Nothing is more subject to change than the laws.

Charles Louis de Montesquieu: Laws should not be changed without good reason.

Michael A. Musmanno (Justice of Pennsylvania Supreme Court, 1959): Doctors and Bus Drivers: I stand second to none in my boundless admiration for the medical profession. In my estimation, statesman, industrialists, inventors and philosophers are inconsequential, so far as contributing to human happiness is concerned, as against the doctor who is dedicated to health—the sweetest desideratum in life because without health one has not the strength to squeeze the orange of existence to obtain the elixir of the joy of living. But after having paid my sincere tribute to doctors, I would not place them on a marble pedestal of impeccability and infallibility. They are human and therefore subject to all the foibles and weaknesses of the flesh which occasionally manifest themselves through indifference or carelessness in a particular field which requires the maximum of competence, attention and care. And if one doctor is negligent, the rest of the medical world need not feel that this constitutes an adverse appraisement of their own skill and their own supreme dedication to the welfare of man. (dissenting, Demchuk v. Bralow, 404 Pa. 100).

Roscoe Pound: Law must be stable and yet it cannot stand still.

J. Danforth Quayle (44th Vice President of the United States): It is becoming increasingly clear that litigation is threatening our national economic viability. Sheer numbers tell the story. (Editor's note: these "sheer numbers" have been thoroughly discredited).

J. Danforth Quayle: Our system of civil justice is, at times, a self-inflicted competitive disadvantage.

Ronald Reagan (40th President of the United States): We have the means to change the laws we find unjust or onerous. We cannot, as citizens, pick and choose the laws we will or will not obey.

William H. Rehnquist: Somewhere "out there," beyond the walls of the courthouse, run currents and tides of public opinion which lap at the courtroom door.

Agnes Repplier: Reformatory measures are hailed as cure-alls by people who have a happy confidence in the perfectibility of human nature, and no discouraging acquaintance with history to dim it.

Will Rogers (speaking about special interest industries trying to exempt themselves from helping America out of the Great Depression): If we are really all in this together then we ought to act like it: Some industry can't come in and say, "Ours is special and unique business. You can't judge it by the others." Well no committee came into Jerusalem looking for Moses and saying "Ours is a special business." Moses just went up on the mountain with a letter of credit and some instructions from the Lord, and He just wrote 'em out, and they applied to the steel men, the oil men, the bankers, the farmers, and even the United States Chamber of Commerce. And he (Moses) said, "Here they are, Brothers, you can take 'em and live by 'em, or else.... (Instead) industries went to Washington and came back with "24 truckloads" worth of special interest exemptions.

Theodore Roosevelt: To submit tamely and meekly to theft or any other injury is to invite almost certain repetition of the offense.

Lord Leslie Scarman: Law reform is far too serious a matter to be left to the legal profession.

Linda Seebach (American journalist): A simple principle supports the medical litigation industry. Sue often enough, and eventually a sympathetic jury will return and outlandish verdict. (Editor's note: this "simple principle" has been shown to be unsupported speculation and thoroughly discredited).

William Shakespeare (*Antony and Cleopatra,* Act V, ii): My desolation does begin to make / A better life.

William Shakespeare (*Hamlet,* Act IV, vii): That we would do, / We should do when we would; for this *"would"* changes, / And hath abatements and delays as many, / As there are tongues, are hands, are accidents; / And then this *"should"* is like a spend-thrift's sigh, / That hurts by easing.

William Shakespeare (*I Henry IV,* Act I, ii): Like bright metal on a sullen ground, / My reformation, glittering o'er my fault, / Shall show more goodly, and attract more eyes, / Than that which hath no foil to set it off.

William Shakespeare (*I Henry IV,* Act IV, iii): Forsooth, takes on him to reform / Some certain edicts.

William Shakespeare (*Henry V,* Act I, i): Never came reformation in a flood / With such a heady currance.

William Shakespeare (*Henry VIII,* Act V, iii): Which are heresies, / And, not reform'd, may prove pernicious.

William Shakespeare (*King John,* Act IV, ii): Meantime but ask / What you would have reform'd that is not well.

William Shakespeare (*King John,* Act V, iv): When we were happy, we had other names.

William Shakespeare (*Taming of the Shrew,* Act III, i): I am not so nice, / To change true rules for odd inventions.

Ruth Shays: If you got the sayso you want to keep it, whether you are right or wrong. That's why they have to keep changing the laws—so they don't unbenefit any of these big white men.

Sidney Smith: When I hear any man talk of an unalterable law, the only effect it produces upon me is to convince me that he is an unalterable fool.

Stuart M. Speiser: "KICKING IN OF ROTTEN DOORS" The economist John Kenneth Galbraith observed that most revolutions resulting in human progress have come about through the kicking in of rotten doors. So it has gone in the saga of the underdog's progress in American tort cases, which some observers have described as a litigation revolution. Those of us who happen to be in the practice when the empowerment of the Equalizers (American trial lawyers in the beginnings of ATLA's history) took place in the last half of the 20th century would like to think of ourselves as the architects or master builders of a brand new legal system. But in truth we were more like a band of hikers wearing hobnail boots. Rather than erecting glittering new edifices, the real contribution of the Equalizers has been to use our hobnail boots to kick in the doors there were kept locked over the centuries to protect the powerful against the enforcement of the existing laws by the underdogs.

Gloria Steinem: Law and justice are not always the same. When they aren't, destroying the law may be the first step toward changing it.

James Todd (Executive Director of AMA, *Liability Week,* March 5, 1999): For all its ills, the tort system fault-based standard of care has promoted hospitals, medical societies, and most notably, physician-owned insurance companies to become very active in a variety of endeavors to reduce the risk of patient injury.

Kurt Vonnegut: Thanks to TV and for the convenience of TV, you can only be one of two kinds of human beings, either a liberal or a conservative.

Chester W. Weinberger (publisher of Forbes magazine): We have too many lawyers chasing too many dollars through too many endless lawsuits, and it is time to do something about it.

TRADITION (See PRECEDENT)

TRIAL (See also JURY; LAWYERS; LITIGATION)

Uncle Anthony: Trials are a SEARCH for the truth NOT A "HUNT" for a bad guy or a bad witch.

Uncle Anthony: Ya gotta get the case down to my level, soz me an the juryfolk can get our brains around what you been playin' with for a couple years. You know what's goin' on but the jury don't.

Aunt Mary Carlo: I tink da jurors are more scared den the participants in a trial– 'cause dey don't wanna make no mistakes wit somebody's case.

David Ball: Theater informs trial principally because each is: (1) a live human event; (2) a collaborative activity in which none of the individuality of the separate people is lost; (3) not about you, but about the person to whom you are talking, about the other person, not yourself.

Bible: Amos 5:24: Let judgment run down as waters, and righteousness as a mighty stream.

Bible: Deuteronomy 1:17: Ye shall hear the small as well as the great.

Bible: Exodus 23:7: Thou shalt not wrest the judgment of thy poor in his cause.

Bible: Ezekiel 7:8: I will judge thee according to thy ways, and will recompense thee for all thine abominations.

Bible: Job 31:6: Let me be weighed in an even balance, that God may know mine integrity.

Bible: Revelations 2:10: Behold, the devil shall cast some of you into prison, that ye may be tried.

Bible: Zechariah 7: 9: Execute true judgment, and show mercy and compassions every man to his brother.

Ambrose Bierce: PRECEDENT, n. In Law, a previous decision, rule or practice which, in the absence of a definite statute, has whatever force and authority a Judge may choose to give it, thereby greatly simplifying his task of doing as he pleases. As there are precedents for everything, he has only to ignore those that make against his interest and accentuate those in line of his desire. Invention of precedent elevates the trial-at-law from the low estate of a fortuitous ordeal to the noble attitude of a dirigible arbitrament [EDITOR: meaning the power to make "free floating" decisions that float like balloons with the winds of chance].

Ambrose Bierce: TRIAL, n. A formal inquiry designed to prove and put upon record the blameless characters of judges, advocates and jurors....

Roy Black (American lawyer): There are times when it's not the thrill of winning. It's the fear of losing.

Warren Burger: The trial of the case is a three-legged stool—a judge and two advocates.

Art Buchwald: Trials are a blood sport.

Tom C. Clark (Texas lawyer, US Attorney General, Assoc Justice US Supreme Court): The heightened public clamor resulting from radio and television coverage will inevitably result in prejudice. Trial by television is, therefore, foreign to our system.

Lewis Carroll (Alice's Adventures in Wonderland, 1865): "Let the jury consider their verdict," the King said, for about the twentieth time that day. / "No, no!" said the Queen. "Sentence first—verdict afterwards." / "Stuff and nonsense!" said Alice loudly. "The idea of having the sentence first!"

Greg Cusimano: A common mistake among lawyers is believing that trying cases makes one a Trial Lawyer— which is as faulty as believing that having a guitar makes one a guitarist.

Alan Dershowitz: All sides in the trial want to hide at least some of the truth.

Thomas Fuller: That trial is not fair where affection is judge.

Ned Good (American lawyer): Trial work requires a computer mind that is rapid in the challenge and response. It's like live TV with no rerun. Not everyone has a mental fastball and those who don't should not try cases.

Clifford Irving: A criminal trial is like a Russian novel: it starts with exasperating slowness as the characters are introduced to a jury, then there are complications in the form of minor witnesses, the protagonist finally appears and contradictions arise to produce drama, and finally as both jury and spectators grow weary and confused the pace quickens, reaching its climax in passionate final argument.

Arthur Lehman (American lawyer): Most of the great trial lawyers I know are very, very scared. Fear, for an actor, stirs you to a greater performance.

Robert Mark: The criminal trial today is... a kind of show jumping contest in which the rider for the prosecution must clear every obstacle to succeed.

H.L. Mencken: The penalty for laughing in the court room is six months in jail: if it were not for this penalty, the jury would never hear the evidence.

Michael A. Musmanno (Justice of Pa. Supreme Court, 1959): The trial of a lawsuit is not a game or gamble with either side gaining fortuitous advantages not based on legal principle or equitable consideration. The court room is not a gridiron where a fumble can be seized by the opposite side and, regardless of intrinsic merit, go on to score a victory with it.

Darlene Richter (American lawyer and legal journalist): OK, it's smoke and mirrors. So what? You'd be surprised how much of the legal process is exactly that. Just like in Hollywood, image is everything in the courtroom, dahhling.

William Shakespeare (*As You Like It*, Act II, i): Hath not custom made this life more sweet / Than that of painted pomp? Are not these woods / More free of peril than the envious court?

William Shakespeare (*Coriolanus*, Act II, i): You wear out a good wholesome forenoon in hearing a cause between an orange-wife and a fosset-seller; and then rejourn the controversy of threepence to a second day of audience.

William Shakespeare (*Othello*, Act V, ii): O, I were damn'd beyond all depth in hell, / But that I did proceed upon just grounds / To this extremity.

William Shakespeare (*Richard III*, Act I, iv): What lawful quest have given their verdict up / Unto the frowning judge?

Gerry Spence (American lawyer): I'm a hunter, a combatant in the courtroom. It's just like the forest: I walk through quietly but resolutely, ready to make a purposeful kill. You must have great love to kill, to combat, to advocate.

Right Honorable Sir Melford Stevenson (British Judge): Starting off a trial with a completely open mind is a terribly dangerous thing to do.

Lloyd Paul Stryker: Trying a case the second time is like eating yesterday morning's oatmeal.

Lloyd Paul Stryker: A trial is still an ordeal by battle. For the broadsword there is the weight of evidence; for the battle-axe the force of logic; for the sharp spear, the blazing gleam of truth; for the rapier, the quick and flashing knife of wit.

William Howard Taft (Ohio lawyer, US President, Chief Justice US Supreme Court, 1857-1930): I love judges, and I love courts. They are my ideals, that typify on earth what we shall meet hereafter in heaven under a just God.

Mark Twain: A joke, even if it be a lame one, is nowhere so keenly relished or quickly applauded as in a murder trial.

Mark Twain: Are you going to hang him *anyhow* – and try him afterwards?

Mark Twain (1873): There is no display of human ingenuity, wit, and power, so fascinating as that made by trained lawyers in the trial of an important case, nowhere else is exhibited such subtlety, acumen, address, eloquence.

John Waters: Trials are the most entertaining of all American spectacles, always better than the theater, and except for a few special cases, much more thrilling than movies.

Oscar Wilde: All TRIALS are TRIALS for one's life, just as all sentences are sentences of death.

TROUBLE (See also ISSUES/PROBLEMS)

Uncle Anthony: The best way out of trouble is to get yourself through it!

Uncle Anthony: He reminds me of that Al Capp character from 'Lil Abner – a cloud's always followin' him.

Aunt Mary Carlo: Joe E. Lewis used to say "A friend in need is a pest!"

Aunt Mary Carlo: Our mother always said to us: God only gives us enough trouble He knows we can handle.

American Proverb: You can't unscramble scrambled eggs.

American Proverb: Never trouble trouble till trouble troubles you.

Russell Baker: Usually, terrible things that are done with the excuse that progress requires them are not really progress at all, but just terrible things.

Bible: Apocrypha, Ecclesiasticus 11:25: In the day of prosperity, adversity is forgotten and in the day of adversity, prosperity is not remembered.

William Arnot: Men are born to trouble at first, and are exercised in it all their days. There is a cry at the beginning of life and a groan at the end of it.

Henry Ward Beecher: There are many troubles which you cannot cure by the Bible and the hymn book, but which you can cure by a good perspiration and a breath of fresh air.

Bible: Corinthians 10:32: Give none offence.

Bible: Deuteronomy 16:3: Thou shalt eat no leavened bread with it; seven days shalt thou eat unleavened bread therewith, even the bread of affliction; for thou camest forth out of the land of Egypt in haste: that thou mayest remember the day when thou camest forth out of the land of Egypt all the days of thy life.

Bible: Ecclesiastes: 7:14: In the day of prosperity be joyful, but in the day of adversity consider.

Bible: Isaiah 53:7: He was afflicted, yet he opened not his mouth: he is brought like a lamb to the slaughter, and as a sheep before his shearers is dumb, so he openeth not his mouth.

Bible: Job 5:6: Although affliction cometh not forth of the dust, neither doth trouble spring out of the ground; yet man is born unto trouble, as the sparks fly upward.

Bible: Job 5:7: Man is born unto trouble, as the sparks fly upward.

Bible: Job 14:1: Man that is born of a woman is of few days, and full of trouble.

Bible: John 14:1: Let not your heart be troubled: ye believe in God, believe also in me.

Bible: Proverbs 11:27: He that seeketh mischief, it shall come unto him.

Bible: Psalms 34:19: Many are the afflictions of the righteous: but the Lord delivereth him out of them all.

Bible: Psalms 50:15: Call upon me in the day of trouble: I will deliver thee, and thou shalt glorify me.

Bible: Psalms 119:67: Before I was afflicted I went astray; but now I have kept thy word.

Ambrose Bierce: CALAMITY, n. A more than commonly plain and unmistakable reminder that the affairs of this life are not of our own ordering. Calamities are of two kinds: misfortunes to ourselves, and good fortune to others.

Ambrose Bierce: CAT, n. A soft, indestructible automation provided by nature to be kicked when things go wrong in the domestic circle.

Ambrose Bierce: CLAIRVOYANT, n. A person, commonly a woman, who has the power of seeing that which is invisible to her patron – namely, that he is a blockhead.

Ambrose Bierce: DISTRESS, n. A disease incurred by exposure to the prosperity of a friend.

Ambrose Bierce: MISFORTUNE, n. The kind of fortune that never misses.

Ambrose Bierce: PRAY, n. To ask that the laws of the universe be annulled in behalf of a single petitioner confessedly unworthy.

Ambrose Bierce: PREDICAMENT, n. The wage of consistency.

Ambrose Bierce: WHANGDEPOOTENAWAH, n. In the Ojibwa tongue, disaster; an unexpected affliction that strikes hard.

The Birkenhead Drill (in 1852, the *HMS Birkenhead*, one of the first iron hulled ships, was taking 476 British soldiers to South Africa when she ran aground off Cape of Good Hope, the soldiers remained calm and let the twenty women and children on board use the lifeboats (only three out of eight lifeboats were useable; 445 lives were lost; the naval tradition of "The Birkenhead Drill" is also commonly called): Women and children first.

Robert Bramson, Ph.D. (book *Coping With Difficult People*): The Seven Categories or Groups of Difficult People:

1. Hostile/Aggressive Trio = Sherman Tanks, Snipers, and "Exploders"
2. Indecisives
3. Complainers
4. Negativists
5. Clams
6. Expert Know-It-Alls = Bulldozers & Hot Air Balloons
7. Super Agreeables

William Cullen Bryant: Difficulty, my brethren, is the nurse of greatness – a harsh nurse, who roughly rocks her foster-children into strength and athletic proportion.

William Cullen Bryant: They seemed / Like old companions in adversity.

G.K. Chesterton: I believe in getting into hot water; it keeps you clean.

Chinese Proverb: He who rouses a sleeping tiger exposes himself to danger.

Chinese Proverb: The pine stays green in winter...Wisdom in hardship.

Sir Winston Churchill (summer 1938, letter to his wife Clementine about FDR's willingness to help Britain with new U.S. Neutrality Laws and "Cash & Carry" and "Lend Lease"): Apparently you always have to have a disaster before anything sensible can be done which would prevent it.

Sir Winston Churchill: The British nation is unique in this respect. They are the only people who like to be told how bad things are, who like to be told the worst

Sir Winston Churchill: Kites rise highest against the wind, not with it.

Sir Winston Churchill: If you are going through hell, keep going.

Sir Winston Churchill: If this is a blessing, it is certainly very well disguised.

Sir Winston Churchill: Difficulties mastered are opportunities won.

Sir Winston Churchill: Still, if you will not fight for the right when you can easily win without bloodshed, if you will not fight when your victory will be sure and not so costly, you may come to the moment when you will have to fight with all the odds against you and only a precarious chance for survival. There may be a worse case. You may have to fight when there is no chance of victory, because it is better to perish than to live as slaves.

Sir Winston Churchill: When I look back on all these worries, I remember the story of the old man who said on his deathbed that he had had a lot of trouble in his life, most of which had never happened.

John Cleland (in his 1748 book *Memoirs of a Woman of Pleasure*): Fanny Hill: "...a dread of worse than death." (or as popularly used): **A fate worse than death.**

Dante (inscription over the Gate to Hell in *The Inferno*): "Abandon All Hope You Who Enter Here."

John W. DeForest: It is a matter of much satisfaction and gratitude with me to observe how heroically most of us endure the misfortunes of other people.

Duke Ellington: A problem is a chance for you to do your best.

Ralph Waldo Emerson: Bad times have a scientific value. These are occassions a good learner would not miss.

Ralph Waldo Emerson: Strong men greet war, tempest, hard times. They wish, as Pinder said, "to tread the floors of hell, with necessities as hard as iron."

Ralph Waldo Emerson: Some of your griefs you have cured, / And the sharpest you will have survived; / But what torments of pain you endured / From evils that never arrived!

English Proverb: He that seeks trouble always finds it.

English Proverb: The darkest hour is that before the dawn.

English Proverb: May as well be hanged for a sheep as a lamb.

Clare Francis (1977 book entitled): Come Hell or High Water.

Benjamin Franklin: The worst wheel of the cart makes the most noise.

Benjamin Franklin: If Man could Half his Wishes, he would double his Troubles.

Benjamin Franklin: For want of a Nail the Shoe is lost; for want of a Shoe, the Horse is lost; for want of a Horse the Rider is lost.

French Proverb: Nothing is as burdensome as a secret.

French Proverb: If you sit on a pile of thorns, you can never know which has pricked you.!

Joanne Greenberg ("Hannah Green" as title of 1964 novel, 1977 film): I never promised you a rose garden.

Oliver Hardy (exasperated saying to partner Stan Laurel, 1930): Here's another fine mess you've gotten me into!

John Heywood (*The Proverbs of John Heywood,* 1546): The fat is in the fire.

John Heywood (*The Proverbs of John Heywood,* 1546): Out of the frying pan into the fire.

Oliver Wendell Holmes, Jr.: Trouble creates a capacity to handle it.

Oliver Wendell Holmes, Jr. (1 *Holmes-Pollock Letters* 16, 1881): I sometimes even think that there is a certain advantage in difficulties, and that one sails better with the wind on the quarter than when it is directly astern.

Elbert Hubbard: If pleasures are greatest in anticipation, just remember that this is also true of trouble.

Elbert Hubbard: When trouble comes, wise men take to their work: weak men take to the woods.

Irish Proverb: Even a small thorn causes festering.

Italian Proverb: Trouble rides a fast horse.

Italian Proverb: It is often necessary to disguise a bad game with a good face.

Thomas Jefferson: How much pain have cost us the evils which have never happened.

Bert Lance (President Jimmy Carter's Director of the Office of Management and Budget, speaking on the subject of governmental reorganization, 1977): If it ain't broken, why fix it?

Henry Wadsworth Longfellow: Such was the wreck of the Hesperus, / In the midnight and the snow! / Christ save us from a death like this, / On the reef of a Norman's Woe!

Henry Wadsworth Longfellow: Oh, fear not in a world like this, / And thou shalt know erelong, / Know how sublime a thing it is / To suffer and be strong.

Henry Wadsworth Longfellow: And the night shall be filled with music, / And the cares, that infest the day, / Shall fold their tents, like the Arabs, / And as silently steal away.

Henry Wadsworth Longfellow: The nearer the dawn the darker the night.

James Lovell (See John L. Swigert,below; April 13, 1970): Houston, we have a problem.

James Russell Lowell: He saves me trouble, and that is a saving I would rather buy dear than any other. Beyond meat and drink, it is the only use I have ever discovered for money.

James Russell Lowell: Let us be of good cheer, however, remembering that the misfortunes hardest to bear are those which never come.

Joseph de Maistre: It is one of man's curious idiosyncracies to create difficulies for the pleasure of resolving them.

Don Marquis: There is always / a comforting thought / in time of trouble when / it is not our trouble.

Margaret Mitchell: Death and taxes and childbirth! There's never any convenient time for any of them!

Herbert Morrison (radio announcer from station WLS in Chicago; May 16, 1937, 7:25 PM, Lakehurst Naval Air Station, in New Jersey, made an eye witness account of "The Hindenberg Disaster" aka "The Titanic of the Sky"; the German zeppelin *Hindenberg,* the largest aircraft to ever fly, had made 11 successful trans-Atlantic flights, while attempting to land it burst into flames, 36 people died): It's crashing .... oh my, get out of the way, please! And the folks! Oh, it's terrible! This is one of the worst catastrophies in the world! **Oh, the humanity!** Oh, the passengers! All the people screaming here!

Persian Proverb: A drowning man is not troubled by rain.

Will Rogers: The best way out of a difficulty is through it.

Will Rogers: The worst thing that happens to you may be the best thing for you if you don't let it get the best of you.

Will Rogers: It isn't what we don't know that gives us trouble, it's what we know that ain't so.

Will Rogers: Last year we said, 'Things can't go on like this', and they didn't, they got worse.

Will Rogers: Things will get better despite our efforts to improve them.

Will Rogers: I hope we never live to see the day when a thing is as bad as some of our newspapers make it.

Franklin Delano Roosevelt: When you get to the end of your rope, tie a knot and hang on!

Arthur M. Schlesinger, Jr.: Troubles impending always seem worse than troubles surmounted, but this does not prove that they really are.

Dr. Martin Seligman, et als (a scientific study shows): "THE determinant ... THE critical determining element in life and business success is resilience in the face of adversity.

Seneca: It is not because things are difficult that we do not dare, it is because we do not dare that things are difficult.

William Shakespeare (*As You Like It*, Act II, i): Sweet are the uses of adversity, / Which, like the toad, ugly and venomous, / Wears yet a precious jewel in his head.

William Shakespeare (*Comedy of Errors,* Act II, i): They can be meek that have no other cause, / A wretched soul, bruis'd with adversity, / We bid be quiet, when we hear it cry.

William Shakespeare (*I Henry VI,* Act IV, iv): Bold adversity / Cries out for noble York and Somerset, / To beat assailing death from his weak legions, / And whiles the honourable captain there / Drops bloody sweat from his war wearied limbs.

William Shakespeare (*I Henry VI,* Act III, i): Cold news for me; / Thus are my blossoms blasted in the bud, / And caterpillars eat my leaves away.

William Shakespeare (*I Henry VI,* Act IV, ii): Is not this a lamentable thing, that of the skin of an innocent lamb should be made parchment? That parchment, being scribbled o'er, should undo a man?

William Shakespeare (*III Henry VI,* Act V, ii): Lo, now my glory smear'd in dust and blood! / My parks, my walks, my manors that I had, / Even now forsake me; and, of all my lands, / Is nothing left me, but my body's length! / Why, what is pomp, rule, reign, but earth and dust? / And, live we how we can, yet die we must.

William Shakespeare (*Henry VIII,* Act IV, ii): His overthrow heap'd happiness upon him; / For then, and not till then, he felt himself, / And found the blessedness of being little.

William Shakespeare (*Julius Caesar*, Act I, ii): The fault, dear Brutus, is not in our stars, / But in ourselves.

William Shakespeare (*King Lear*, Act IV, i): The worst is not / So long as we can say "This is the worst."

William Shakespeare (*King Lear,* Act IV, vi): Henceforth I'll bear / Affliction till it do cry out itself, / Enough, enough, and die.

William Shakespeare (*King Lear,* Act IV, vii): Thou art a soul in bliss; but I am bound / Upon a wheel of fire; that mine own tears / Do scald like molten lead.

William Shakespeare (*Macbeth*, Act I, vi): The love that follows us sometimes is our trouble.

William Shakespeare (*Macbeth*, Act IV, i): Double, double toil and trouble; Fire burn and cauldron bubble.

William Shakespeare (*Romeo and Juliet*, Act III, i): A plague o' both your houses.

William Shakespeare (*Romeo and Juliet,* Act III, iii): Affliction is enamour'd of thy parts, / And thou art wedded to calamity.

William Shakespeare (*Romeo and Juliet,* Act V, iii): O give me thy hand, / One writ with me in sour misfortune's book.

William Shakespeare (*Tempest*, Act II, ii): Misery acquaints a man with strange bedfellows.

William Shakespeare (*Tempest*, Act III, ii): If you trouble him ant more in's tale, by this hand, I will supplant some of your teeth.

William Shakespeare (*Tempest*, Act V, i): How camest thou in this pickle?

William Shakespeare (*Timon of Athens,* Act IV, ii): We have seen better days.

William Shakespeare (*Two Gentlemen of Verona,* Act IV, i): Then know, that I have little wealth to lose; / A man I am cross'd with adversity.

Socrates: Remember that there is nothing stable in human affairs; therefore, avoid undue elation in prosperity, or undue depression in adversity.

Spanish Proverb: Trouble will rain on those who are already wet.

Spiritual Song: Nobody knows the trouble I've seen, / Nobody knows but Jesus.

Gertrude Stein: Everybody knows if you are too careful you are so occupied in being careful that you are sure to stumble over something.

John Steinbeck: When a man is finally boxed and he has no choice, he begins to decorate his box.

George Sutherland (Assoc. Justice U.S. Supreme Court, 1862-1942): A nuisance may be merely a right thing in the wrong place – a pig in the parlor instead of the barnyard. Euclid v. Ambler Realty Co., 272 US 365, 71 L ed 303, 47 S Ct 114 (1926)

John L. Swigert (April 13, 1970, on the Apollo 13 space mission, he said): "OK, Houston, we've got a problem here." Commander James Lovell then added: "Oh, Houston, we've had a problem. We've had a Main B Bus Undervolt (indicating a fault in the electrical system)."

Mother Teresa: I know God will not give me anything I can't handle. I just wish that He didn't trust me so much.

Harry S. Truman (U.S. President, 1952): "If you can't stand the heat get out of the kitchen." Or, more probably: "If you can't stand the stink, get out of the shit-house."

Turkish Proverb: No rose without a thorn, or a love without a rival.

Mark Twain: All the modern inconveniences.

Mark Twain: I am an old man and have known a great many troubles, but most of them never happened.

Mark Twain: Life does not consist mainly—or even largely—of facts and happenings. It consists mainly of the storm of thoughts that is forever blowing through one's head.

Mark Twain: Well, then, says I, what's the use you learning to do right, when it's troublesome to do right and ain't no trouble to do wrong, and the wages is just the same?

UA (a phrase originally used by Chief Thunderthud on The Howdy Doody Show in the 1950's and re-popularized by the Teenage Mutant Ninja Turtles in 1990's): "KAWABONGA" or "kowa-bonga" or "COWABONGA!"

Tom Vesper: He/she/they/it was like "the last happy whistle of the canary before the mine shaft exploded!"

Ella Wheeler Wilcox: Laugh and the world laughs with you, / Weep and you weep alone; / For the sad old earth must borrow its mirth, / But has trouble enough of its own.

Meredith Wilson (*The Music Man*, 1957): Friend, either you are closing your eyes to a situation you do not wish to acknowledge, or you are not aware of the caliber of disaster indicated by the presence of a pool table in your community. Well, you got trouble, my firend! Right here! I say Trouble, right here in River City ....Ya got trouble, / Right here in River City, / With a capital T / And that rhymes with P / And that stands for Pool.

Yiddish Proverb: Bygone troubles are good to tell.

TRUTH/UNDERSTANDING (See also HONESTY)

Uncle Anthony: People don't care unless they share.

Uncle Anthony: You can never get lost on a straight road (that is, telling the truth).

Uncle Anthony: The best disinfectant is sunshine ... let the sun shine in!

Aunt Mary Carlo: Didja ever notice how many times ya hear the truth in yer uncle's jokes?

Aunt Mary Carlo: How you gonna "know and understand" 'da Universe, when you cantta even find yer way around Ebbetts Field or Little Italy (or Flatbush in Brooklyn, NY)

Aunt Mary Carlo: We don't see t'ings as they are, we see t'ings AS WE ARE!

Franklin P. Adams: When the political columnists say "Every thinking man" they mean themselves, and when candidates appeal to "Every intelligent voter" they mean everybody who is going to vote for them.

Henri-Frederic Amiel: The man who insists on seeing with perfect clearness before he decides, never decides.

Sherwood Anderson: Can we understand at all, ever, where we do not love?

Dr. Robert Anthony: You can only have two things in life, reasons or results. Reasons don't count.

Dr. Robert Anthony: There is no way to know before experiencing.

Aesop: Never trust the advice of a man in difficulties.

Arabic Proverb: Truth may walk through the world unarmed.

Aristotle: Generality is the refuge of a weak mind.

Armenian Proverb: He who speaks the truth must have one foot in the stirrup.

Louis Armstrong: There are some people that if they don't know, you can't tell 'em.

Isaac Asimov: Part of the inhumanity of the computer is that, once it is competently programmed and working smoothly, it is completely honest.

Richard Bach: What a student calls a tragedy, the master calls a butterfly.

Robert Baden-Powell (founder of the Boy Scouts of America, 1908): Scout's honor!

Pierre Agustin de Beaumarchais: It is not necessary to understand things in order to argue about them.

Irving Berlin: There's an element of truth in every idea that lasts long enough to be called corny.

Sir William Draper Best (British Chief Justice, 1820): Presumption means nothing more than, as stated by Lord Mansfield, the weighing of probabilities, and deciding, by the powers of common sense, on which side the truth is.

Bible: Apocrypha, 1 Esdras 4:22: Great is truth and strongest of all

Bible: Daniel 12:4: Many shall run to and fro, and knowledge shall be increased.

Bible: Ecclesiastes 9:16: The poor man's wisdom is despised, and his words are not heard.

Bible: Ephesians 4:25: Wherefore putting away lying, speal every man truth with his neighbor.

Bible: Job 8:9: We are but of yesterday, and know nothing, because our days upon the earth are a shadow.

Bible: Job 12:12: With the ancient is wisdom; and in length of days understanding.

Bible: Job 28:18: The price of wisdom is above rubies.

Bible: John, 8:32: Ye shall know the truth, and the truth shall make you free.

Bible: John 14:6: I am the way, the truth, and the life.

Bible: John 16:13: When he, the Spirit of truth, is come, he will guide you into all truth.

Bible: John 18:37: Every one that is of the truth heareth my voice.

Bible: Matthew 7:14: Straight is the gate, and narrow is the way, which leadeth unto life, and few there be that find it.

Bible: Proverbs 4:7: Wisdom is the principal thing; therefore get wisdom; and with all thy getting get understanding.

Bible: Proverbs 12:19: Truth stands the test of time; lies are soon exposed.

Bible: Proverbs 17:28: Even a fool, when he holdeth his peace, is counted wise: and he that shutteth his lips is esteemed a man of understanding.

Bible: Proverbs 23:23: Buy the truth, and sell it not.

Bible: Psalms 85:10: Mercy and truth are met together; righteousness and peace have kissed each other.

Bible: Psalms 111:10 and Proverbs 9:10: The fear of the Lord is the beginning of wisdom.

Ambrose Bierce: ADMIRATION, n. Our polite recognition of another's resemblance to ourselves.

Ambrose Bierce: CONSOLATION, n. The knowledge that a better man is more unfortunate than yourself.

Ambrose Bierce: ESOTERIC, adj. Very particularly abstruse and consummately occult. The ancient philosophies were of two kinds, - *exoteric*, those that the philosophers themselves could partly understand, and *esoteric*, those that nobody could understand. It is the latter that have most profoundly affected modern thought and found greatest acceptance in our time.

Ambrose Bierce: OPTIMISM, n. The doctrine or belief that everything is beautiful, including what is ugly, everything good, especially the bad, and everything right that is wrong.

Ambrose Bierce: TRUTH, n. An ingenious compound of desirability and appearance. Discovery of truth is the sole purpose of philosophy, which is the most ancient occupation of the human mind and has a fair prospect of existing with increasing activity to the end of time.

Ambrose Bierce: TRUTHFUL, adj. Dumb and illiterate.

Ambrose Bierce: UNDERSTANDING, n. A cerebral secretion that enables one having it to know a house from a horse by the roof on the house. Its nature and laws have been exhaustively expounded by Locke, who rode a house, and Kant, who lived in a horse.

Josh Billings: As scarce as truth is, the supply has always been in excess of the demand.

Josh Billings: Love looks through a telescope; envy through a microscope.

William Blake: A truth that's told with bad intent / Beats all the lies you can invent.

William Blake: When I tell the truth, it is not for the sake of convincing those who do not know it, but for the sake of defending those who do.

Franz Boas: The passion for seeking the truth only for truth's sake... can be kept alive only if we continue to seek the truth for truth's sake.

Niels Bohr: The opposite of a correct statement is a false statement. But the opposite of a profound truth may well be another profound truth.

Louis D. Brandeis (Assoc. Justice US Supreme Court): Sunlight is the best of disinfectants.

Louis D. Brandeis: The greatest dangers to liberty lurk in insidious encroachment by men of zeal, well-meaning but without understanding.

Georges Braque: Truth exists; only falsehood has to be invented.
Pearl Buck: Truth is always exciting. Speak it, then. Life is dull without it.
William F. Buckley, Jr.: Liberals claim to want to give a hearing to other views, but then are shocked and offended to discover that there are other views.
Charles Bukowski: Knowledge is knowing as little as possible.
George H. W. Bush: Don't confuse being "soft" with seeing the other guy's point of view.
Samuel Butler: Some men love truth so much that they seem to be in continual fear lest she should catch a cold on overexposure.
Albert Camus: I have never believed in the power of truth in itself. But it is at least worth knowing that when expressed forcefully truth wins out over falsehood.
Benjamin N. Cardozo (*Growth of the Law*, 1924): You think perhaps of philosophy as dwelling in the clouds. I hope you may see that she is able to descend to earth. You think that in stopping to pay court to her, when you should be hastening forward on your journey, you are loitering in bypaths and wasting precious hours.... Here you will find the key for the unlocking of bolts and combinations that shall never be pried open by clumsier or grosser tools. You think that there is nothing practical in a theory that is concerned with ultimate conceptions. That is true perhaps while you are doing the journeyman's work of your profession. You may find in the end, when you pass to higher problems, that instead of its being true that the study of the ultimate is profitless, there is little that is profitable in the study of anything else.
Willa Cather: Artistic growth is, more than it is anything else, a refining of the sense of truthfulness. The stupid believe that to be truthful is easy; only the artist, the great artist, knows how difficult it is.
George Carlin: Honesty may be the best policy, but it's important to remember that apparently, by elimination, dishonesty is the second best policy.
Lewis Cass: People may doubt what you say, but they will believe what you do.
Carlos Castaneda: Things don't change. You change your way of looking, that's all.
Charley Chaplin (to Albert Einstein at the 1930 premier of *"City Lights"* movie in Hollywood): They cheer me because they all understand me. They cheer you because no one understands you.
Anton Chekhov: When a man does not understand a thing, he feels discord within himself: he seeks causes for this dissonance not in himself, as he should, but outside himself, and the result is war with something he does not understand.
Chinese Proverb: The beginning of wisdom is to call things by their right names.
Chinese Proverb: Truth often hides in an ugly pool.
Chinese Proverb: The wise adapt themselves to circumstances, as water molds itself to the pitcher.
Sir Winston Churchill: Men occasionaly stumble over the truth from time to time, but most pick themselves up and hurry off as if nothing happened.
Sir Winston Churchill: The truth is incontrovertible. Panic may resent it; ignorance may deride it; makice may distort it, but there it is.
Sir Anthony Cleasby (English Judge, 1871): Truth and falsehood, it has been well said, are not always opposed to each other like black-and-white, but oftentimes, and by bizarre means, are made to resemble each other so as to be hardly distinguishable from each other, just as the counterfeit thing is counterfeit because it resembles the genuine thing.
Claud Cockburn: Never believe anything until it has been officially denied.
Irving Cohen: Truth is shorter than fiction.
Sir Edward Coke (*First Institute* 337b): The most learned doubteth most.
Confucius: I hear and I forget, I see and I remember, I do and I understand.
Jacques Cousteau: If we were illogical, the future would be bleak indeed. But we are more than logical. We are human beings, and we have faith, and we have hope, and we can work.
Marie Curie: Nothing in life is to be feared. It is only to be understood.
Greg Cusimano: It is not that the jury will believe it if they see it, instead it is if they believe it they will see it.
Greg Cusimano: I never know what I think about something, until I hear what I said about it.
Clarence Darrow: Chase after the truth like hell, and you'll free yourself, even though you never touch its coattails.

Clarence Darrow: I have suffered from being misunderstood, but I would have suffered a hell of a lot more if I had been understood.

Leonardo da Vinci's Motto: *Saper verdere* = Know how to see.

Leonardo da Vinci: You do ill if you praise, but worse if you censure, what you do not understand.

Charles Dickens: "It is," says Chadband, "the ray of rays, the sun of suns, the moon of moons, the star of stars. It is the light of truth."

Sir Arthur Conan Doyle: When you have eliminated the impossible, whatever remains, however improbable, must be the truth.

Peter Drucker: The most important thing in communication is to hear what is not being said.

David Dunham: Efficiency is intelligent laziness.

Will Durant: As we acquire knowledge, things do not become more comprehensible, but more mysterious.

Leo Durocher: Baseball is like church – lot's of people go, but not many understand.

Albert Einstein: Peace cannot be kept by force. It can only be won through understanding. Our longing for understanding is Eternal.

Albert Einstein: We should take care not to make the intellect our god; it has, of course, powerful muscles, but no personality.

Albert Einstein: Of course, *understanding* of our fellow-beings is important. But this understanding becomes fruitful only when it is sustained by sympathetic feeling in joy and sorrow.

Albert Einstein: Ethical axioms are found and tested not very differently from the axioms of science. Truth is what stands the test of experience.

Albert Einstein: A foolish faith in authority is the worst enemy of truth.

Albert Einstein (used this "BLIND BEETLE ANALOGY" to describe his great insight that Gravity was the curving of the fabric of Space-Time, when his youngest son Edward asked him why he was so famous?): When a blind beetle crawls over the surface of a curved branch, it doesn't notice that the track it has covered is indeed curved. I was lucky enough to notice what the beetle didn't notice.

Albert Einstein (1921 at Princeton cocktail party to someone who said his theory was disproved; later carved on mantle of fireplace of building that became home of the Institute of Advanced Studies): Subtle is the Lord, but malicious He is not!

Albert Einstein (June 1933 lecture at Oxford "On the Method of Theoretcal Physics"): To truly understand the methods and philosophies of physicists, don't listen to their words, fix your attention on their deeds.

Ralph Waldo Emerson: Truth is the summit of being; justice is the application of it to affairs.

Ralph Waldo Emerson: Truth is beautiful, without doubt; but so are lies.

Ralph Waldo Emerson: The more he talked of his honor the faster we counted our spoons.

Ralph Waldo Emerson: We do what we must, and call it by the best names.

Ralph Waldo Emerson: Every involuntary repulsion that arises in your mind give heed unto. It is the surface of a central truth.

English Proverb: Only the wearer knows where the shoe pinches

English Proverb: Time trieth truth.

Euripides: A man's most valuable trait is a judicious sense of what not to believe.

Greg Evans: Anger at lies lasts forever. Anger at truth cannot last.

F. Scott Fitzgerald: At eighteen our convictions are hills from which we look; at forty-five they are caves in which we hide.

Al Frankin: When you encounter seemingly good advice that contradicts other seemingly good advice, ignore them both.

Al Frankin (his book, *Lies, and the Lying Liars Who Tell Them*): " … they fight with lies. We can't do that. We have to fight them with the truth. Our added entertainment value will have to come from being funny, and attractive, and passionate, and idealistic, but also smart and not milk toasty. We've got to be willing to throw their lies in their face. F you... no F you! That's how were gonna win this thing. Truth to power!"

Felix Frankfurter: The mark of a truly civilized man is confidence in the strength and security derived from the inquiring mind.

Benjamin Franklin: Half the truth is often a whole lie.

Benjamin Franklin: Wise men don't need advice. Fools won't take it.
Erich Fromm: Understanding a person does not mean condoning; it only means that one does not accuse him as if one were God or a judge placed above him.
Robert Fulghum: All I ever needed to know I learned in kindergarten. Don't hit people. Clean up your own mess.
Margaret Fuller: Truth is the nursing mother of genius.
Galileo Galilei: I do not feel obliged to believe that the same God who has endowed us with sense, reason and intellect has intended us to forgo their use.
Galileo Galilei: All truths are easy to understand once they are discovered; the point is to discover them.
Galileo Galilei (1564-1642, born in Pisa): Reasoning (EDITOR: and jury verdicts?) is not the same as hauling; that is, the more horses you have means the more weight you can pull; but finding the truth does NOT depend on the number of horses you have, it depends on the fast steed. Nose counts do not equate with finding the truth
Jose Ortega y Gasset: Tell me to what you pay attention and I will tell you who you are.
German Proverb: Truth has a handsome countenance but torn garments.
Mahatma Gandhi: That which may appear as the truth to one person will often appear as untruth to another person. But that need not worry the seeker. Where there is honest effort, it will be realized that what appeared to be different truths are like the countless and apparently different leaves of the same tree."
Jean Giraudoux: No poet ever interpreted nature as freely as a lawyer interprets the truth.
Andre Gide: Believe those who are seeking the truth. Doubt those who find it.
Samuel Goldwyn: I don't want any yes man around me. I want everybody to tell me the truth even if it costs them their jobs.
Elizabeth Goudge: Most of the basic truths of life sound absurd at first hearing.
Greek Proverb: You cannot reason with a hungry belly; it has no ears.
Greek Proverb: Wonder is the beginning of wisdom.
Graham Greene: In human relations, kindness and lies are worth a thousand truths.
Martha Grimes: We don't know who we are until we see what we can do.
Albert Guinon: If everyone is against you, it means you are absolutely wrong—or absolutely right.
Sacha Guitry: What probably distorts everything in life is that one is convinced that one is speaking the truth because one says what one think.
Philip G. Hamerton: Have you ever observed that we pay much more attention to a wise passage when it is quoted then when we read it in the original author?
Harley Davidson Co.: If I have to explain, you wouldn't understand.
Sydney Harris: Any philosophy that can be put "in a nutshell" belongs there.
Georg W. Hegel: What ever is reasonable is true, and what ever is true is reasonable
Robert Heinlein: The truth of a proposition has nothing to do with its credibility. And vice versa.
Werner Heisenberg: What happens depends on our way of observing it or on the fact that we observe it.
Lillian Hellman: Cynicism is an unpleasant way of saying the truth
Heraclitus: Much knowledge does not teach wisdom.
Hindu Proverb: No one was ever ruined by speaking truth.
Mahlon Hoagland: It is often the scientist's experience that he senses the nearness of truth when... connections are envisioned. A connection is a step toward simplification, unification. Simplicity is indeed often the sign of truth and a criterion of beauty.
Ralph Hodgson: Things have to be believed to be seen.
Eric Hoffer: Absolute faith corrupts as absolutely as absolute power.
Oliver Wendell Holmes, Jr. (*Holmes-Cohen Correspondence*, 1948): As **a bettabilitarian** I bet the cosmos has in it a somewhat [Editor: or someone] that would strike us as pretty queer if we were capable of being struck by it with our present faculties. But I am swamped in the law.
Oliver Wendell Holmes, Jr. (2 *Holmes-Pollock Letters* 22, 1919): As to the universe my formula as **a bettabiliarian** (one who thinks you can bet about it but not know) is a spontaneity taking an irrational pleasure in a moment of rational sequence.
Oliver Wendell Holmes Jr.: The mind of the bigot is like the pupil of the eye. The more light you shine on it, the more it will contract.

Oliver Wendell Holmes Jr.: What is true is what I cannot help believing.

Oliver Wendell Holmes, Jr.: Certainty generally is an illusion, and repose is not the destiny of man.

Oliver Wendell Holmes, Jr.: A page of history is worth a volume of logic.

Oliver Wendell Holmes, Jr.: The ultimate good is better reached by free trade in ideas. The best test of truth is the power of the thought to get itself accepted in the competition of the market.

Oliver Wendell Holmes, Jr.: When I say that a thing is true, I mean that I cannot help believing it, I am stating an experience as to which there is no choice.

Oliver Wendell Holmes, Jr.: Pretty much all the honest truthtelling there is in the world is done by children.

Oliver Wendell Holmes, Sr.: I used to say, when I was young, that truth was the majority vote of the nation that could lick all others.

E.E. "Ed" Howe: A good scare is worth more to a man than good advice.

Judith Ward Howe (visiting a Union Army post near Washington, D.C. in 1861, she heard marching soldiers singing "John Brown's Body" and wrote a poem she sold to Atlantic Monthly for $4.00 which became the anthem of the North during the Civil War – The Battle Hymn of The Republic): "... and His Truth is marching on!."

Elbert Hubbard: Every man is a damn fool for at least five minutes every day; wisdom consists in not exceeding the limit.

Irish Proverb: The wearer best knows where the shoe pinches.

Irish Proverb: The well fed does not understand the lean.

Irish Proverb: Wine divulges truth.

Irish Proverb: Where the tongue slips, it speaks the truth.

Italian and Chinese Proverb: He who asks is a fool for five minutes, but he who does not ask remains a fool forever.

Italian Proverb: Not what you eat, but what you digest makes you healthy. Not what you earn, but what you save makes you wealthy. Not what you learn, but what you remember makes you wise.

William James: As a rule we disbelieve all the facts and theories for which we have no use.

Japanese Proverb: The reverse side also has a reverse side.

Thomas Jefferson: It is error alone which needs the support of government. Truth can stand by itself.

Thomas Jefferson: And, finally, that truth is great and will prevail if left to herself; that she is the proper and sufficient antagonist to error, and has nothing to fear from the conflict unless by human interposition disarmed of her natural weapons, free argument and debate; errors ceasing to be dangerous when it is permitted freely to contradict them.

Jewish Proverb: Truth is the safest lie.

Jewish Saying: Deep doubts, deep wisdom; small doubts, little wisdom.

Jewish Saying: Better the ugly truth than a beautiful lie.

Jewish Saying: A man is not honest because he has had no chance to steal.

Jewish Saying: If you walk straight, you won't fall.

Jewish Saying: The truth never dies—but it lives a wretched life.

Jewish Saying: When you tell the truth you don't have to remember what you said.

Jewish Saying: If you add to truth, you enter the domain of lies.

Jewish Saying: Truth is heavy, so few men carry it.

Jewish Saying: Nothing is more harmful to a new truth than an old error.

Jewish Saying: Ultimately, truth rises, like oil on water.

Jewish Saying: Many love truth, but not many speak it.

Jewish Saying: Half a truth is a whole lie.

Jewish Saying: Truth creeps; lies race.

Jewish Saying: A joke is a half-truth.

Jewish Saying: Truth can be the greatest deceiver.

Samuel Johnson: The use of travelling is to regulate imagination by reality, and instead of thinking how things may be, to see them as they are.

David Starr Jordan: Wisdom is knowing what to do next; virtue is doing it.

Carl Jung: Everything that irritates us about others can lead us to an understanding of ourselves.

John F. Kennedy: We must never forget that art is not a form of propaganda; it is a form of truth.

Rudyard Kipling: I reckon there's more things told than are true, / And more things true than are told!

Rudyard Kipling (1903 poem "Stellenbosch"): And it all goes into the laundry, / But it never comes out in the wash... Or as popularly stated: "It (the truth) will all come out in the wash."

Krishnamurti: Discipline does not mean suppression or control, nor is it adjustment to a pattern of ideology. It means a mind that sees "what is" and learns "what was."

Latin Proverb: Truth will be out.

Latin Proverb (familiar Latin expression *In vino veritas*): There is truth in wine.

Kurt Lewin: If you want to truly understand something, try to change it.

Walter Lippman: It requires wisdom to understand wisdom: the music is nothing if the audience is deaf.

John Locke: The actions of men are the best interpreters of their thoughts.

Henry Wadsworth Longfellow: Some falsehood mingles with all truth.

Maimonides: A truth, established by proof, does not again enforce the support of scholars; nor does it lose its certainty because of popular dissent.

Maimonides: A truth does not become greater by repetition.

Maimonides: No other purpose should be attached to truth than that you should know what is true.

Maimonides: Men cling to the opinions to which they are accustomed from youth; this prevents them from finding the truth, for they cleave to the opinions of habit.

Meritt Malloy: The truth isn't what we say, it's how we feel when we say it.

Dudley Malone (Clarence Darrow's co-counsel for the defense in "The Scopes Monkey Trial," Dayton, Tennessee, July 19, 1925; oral argument, outside the jury's presence, opposing the prosecution's motion to bar the testimony of Dr. Maynard Metcalf, and all scientific evidence on Darwinism as irrelevant): "TRUTH ALWAYS WINS! And we are not afraid of it. The Truth is no coward. The Truth does not need the Law. The Truth does not need the forces of government. The Truth does not need Mr. Bryan (Prosecutor William Jennings Bryan). The Truth is imperishable, eternal and immortal, and needs no human agency to support it. We are ready to tell the Truth as we understand it, and we do not fear all the Truth thatthey can present as fact. We are ready! We are ready! We feel that we stand with progress. We feel that we stand with science. We feel that we stand with intelligence. We feel that we stand with fundamental freedom in America. We are not afraid. Where is the fear? We meet it. Where is the fear? We defy it!"

Horace Mann: Never underestimate the human faculty for rejecting information.

Don Marquis: If you make people think they're thinking, they will love you; but if you really make them think, they will hate you.

Groucho Marx: Why, a four-year-old child could understand this report. Run out and find me a four-year-old child. I can't make heads or tails of it.

Groucho Marx: Truth goes out the door when rumor comes in.

Phyllis McGinley (American poet, 1905-1978, *Reflections at Dawn*): I wish I owned a Dior dress / Made to my order out of satin. / I wish I weighed a little less / And I could read Latin, / Had perfect pitch or matching pearls, / A better head for street directions, / And seven daughters, all with curls / And fair complexions. / I wish I'd tan instead of burn. / But most, on all the stars that glisten, / I wish at parties I could learn / To sit and listen. [EDITOR: THIS ADVICE ALSO APPLIES TO LAWYERS LISTENING TO THEIR CLIENTS]

P.B. Medawar: The human mind treats a new idea the same way the body treats a strange protein: it rejects it!

H.L. Mencken: The men the American public admire most extravagantly are the most daring liars; the men they detest most violently are those who try to tell them the truth.

H.L. Mencken: The most common of all follies is to believe passionately in the palpably not true. It is the chief occupation of mankind.

H.L. Mencken: There is always an easy solution to every human problem: it is neat, plausible, and wrong!

Bette Midler: I never know how much of what I say is true.

Wayne C. Minnick (American educator): There is an old story of blind men trying to describe an elephant. One felt the elephant's leg and declared that the creature was like a tree, another felt the enormous side and said the elephant was like a wall, while a third, feeling the tail, was positive the animal was like a rope. Each man had a notion of reality that was limited by the number and kind of attributes he had perceived.

George Moore: A man travels the world over in search of what he needs, and returns home to find it.

J. Pierpoint Morgan: A man generally has two reasons for doing anything. One that sounds good, and a real one.

Moses Ibn Ezra: At times even liars speak the truth.

Moses Mendelssohn: Hope and fear are not proper tests of truth.

Michael A. Musmanno (Justice, Sup. Ct. of Pennsylvania, 1959): Truth is a ripe fruit which must be timely plucked:

Sir Isaac Newton (1642-1727): 'Tis the temper of the hot and superstitious part of mankind in matters of religion ever to be fond of mysteries, and for that reason to like best what they understand least.

Sir Isaac Newton (Book III of his *Principis*): NATURE IS PLEASED WITH SIMPLICITY

Anais Nin: We do not see things as they are, we see things as we are.

Flannery O'Connor: The truth does not change according to our ability to stomach it.

Carol Orlock: When our knowledge coalesces with our humanity and our humor, it can add up to wisdom.

Lewis Orr: Science will never be able to reduce the value of a sunset to arithmetic. Nor can it reduce friendship to a formula. Laughter and love, pain and loneliness, the challenge of accomplishment in living, and the depth of insight into beauty and truth: these will always surpass the scientific mastery of nature.

George Orwell: Political language is designed to make it lies it sound truthful and murder respectable, and to give an appearance of solidity to pure wind.

George Orwell: The great enemy of clear language is insincerity. When there is a gap between ones real and ones declared aims, one turns as it were instinctively to long words and exhausted idioms, like a cuttle fish spurting out ink.

George Orwell: In a time of universal deceit, telling the truth is a revolutionary act.

Ovid: It is annoying to be honest to no purpose.

Dorothy Parker: Wit has truth in it; wisecracking is simply calisthenics with words.

Dorothy Parker: I don't care what is written about me so long as it is not true.

Blaise Pascal: We are generally the better persuaded by the reasons we discover ourselves than by those given to us by others.

William Penn: Truth often suffers more by the heat of its defenders, than from the arguments of its opposers.

Robert Persig: The only Zen you find on the top of mountains is the Zen you bring up there.

Pablo Picasso: Art is a lie that makes us realize the truth.

Lawrence J. Peter: You can always tell a real friend; when you've made a fool of yourself he doesn't feel you've done a permanent job.

Mary Pettibone Poole: To repeat what others have said, requires education; to challenge it, requires brains.

Alexander Pope: Some people will never learn anything because they understand everything too soon.

Antonio Porchia: Certainties are arrived at only on foot.

Elvis Presley: Truth is like the sun. You can shut out for a time, but it ain't goin' away.

Emerson Pugh: If the human mind was simple enough to understand, we'd be too simple to understand it.

Rashomon Effect: 1951 film RASHOMON set in 12th century Japan at the Rashomon Gate in Kyoto. A rape and murder was witnessed by a group of people. The "truth" is relative and depends upon who is telling the story.

Anthony Robbins: If you want to change our reality, change your focus. If you want to change our focus, change your questions.

Will Rogers: I have just enough white in me to make my honesty questionable.

Will Rogers: You know everybody is ignorant, only on different subjects.

Will Rogers: Nothing makes a man or body of men as mad as truth. If there is no truth in it they laugh if off.

Will Rogers: Rumor travels Faster, but it don't stay put as long as Truth.

Franklin D. Roosevelt: The truth is found when men are free to pursue it.

Franklin D. Roosevelt: Repetition does not transform a lie into the truth

Jean Rostand: We find it easy to believe that praise is sincere: Why should anyone lie in telling us the truth?

Bertrand Russell: A stupid man's report of what a clever man says can never be accurate, because he unconsciously translates what he hears into something he can understand.

Bertrand Russell: Our great democracies still tend to think a stupid man is more likely to be honest than a clever man.

Moslih Eddin Saadi: A traveler without observation is a bird without wings.

Carl Sagan: Skeptical scrutiny is the means, in both science and religion, by which deep insight can be winnowed from deep nonsense.

George Santayana: Those who cannot remember the past are condemned to repeat it

George Santayana: Children are on a different plane, belong to a generation and way of feeling properly their own; there is seldom complete understanding between them and their parents, so that affection here suffers from some strain and uncertainty, all the more painful the greater the affection is.

Arthur Schopenhauer: Talent hits a target no one else can hit; genius hits a target no one else can see.

Arthur Schopenhauer: All truth passes through three stages: First, it is ridiculed; Second, it is violently opposed; Third, it is accepted as being self-evident.

Arthur Schopenhauer: Every person takes the limits of their own field of vision for the limits of the world.

Albert Schweitzer: An optimist is a person who sees a green light everywhere. The pessimist sees only the red light. But the truly wise person is colorblind.

Albert Schweitzer: Truth has no special time of its own. Its hour is now—always.

Senegalese Saying: In the end we will conserve only what we love. We will love only what we understand. We will understand only what we are taught.

Charles Seymour: We seek the truth and will endure the consequences.

William Shakespeare (*All's Well That Ends Well*, Act III, v): No legacy is so rich as honesty.

William Shakespeare (*All's Well That Ends Well*, Act IV, ii): 'Tis not the many oaths that make the truth; / But the plain single vow, that is vow'd true.

William Shakespeare (*Antony and Cleopatra*, Act I, ii): Who tells me true, though in his tale lie death, / I hear him as he flatter'd.

William Shakespeare (*Antony and Cleopatra*, Act II, ii): That truth should be silent I had almost forgot.

William Shakespeare (*Cymbeline*, Act V, i): O, never say hereafter / But I am truest speaker.

William Shakespeare (*Hamlet*, Act I, iii): To thine own self be true; / And it must follow, as the night the day, / Thou canst not then be false to any man.

William Shakespeare (*Hamlet*, Act II, ii): If circumstances lead me, I will find / Where truth is hid, though it were hid indeed / Within the centre.

William Shakespeare (*I Henry IV*, Act II, iv): Is not the truth the truth?

William Shakespeare (*I Henry IV*, Act II, iv): Mark now, how plain a tale shall put you down

William Shakespeare (*I Henry IV*, Act III, i): O, while you live, tell truth and shame the devil!

William Shakespeare (*I Henry IV*, Act III, i): Tell the truth, and shame the devil. / If thou have power to raise him, bring him hither. / And I'll be sworn, I have power to shame him hence. / O, while you live, tell truth: and shame the devil.

William Shakespeare (*King Lear*, Act I, i): Truth's a dog must to kennel; he must be whipped out, when Lady the brach may stand by the fire and stink.

William Shakespeare (*Love's Labou'sr Lost*, Act I, i): As painfully to pore upon a book, / To seek the light of truth; while truth the while / Doth falsely blind the eyesight of his look.

William Shakespeare (*Macbeth*, Act I, iii): What, can the devil speak true?

William Shakespeare (*Macbeth*, Act I, iii): But 'tis strange: / And oftentimes, to win us to our harm, / The instruments of darkness tell us truths, / Win us with honest trifles, to betray 's / In deepest consequence.

William Shakespeare (*Macbeth*, Act V, v): I pull in resolution and begin / To doubt the equivocation of a fiend / That lies like truth.

William Shakespeare (*Measure for Measure*, Act V, i): Truth is truth / To th' end of reckoning.

William Shakespeare (*Merchant of Venice*, Act I, iii): The devil can site scripture for his own purpose! An evil soul producing holy witness is like a villain with a smiling cheek."

William Shakespeare (*The Merchant of Venice*, Act II, ii): Truth will come to light; murder cannot be hid for long.

William Shakespeare (*The Merchant of Venice*, Act V, i): We will answer all things faithfully.

William Shakespeare (*A Midsummer-Night's Dream*, Act V, i): Truth makes all things plain.
William Shakespeare (*Much Ado About Nothing*, Act I, iii): I cannot hide what I am: I must be sad when I have a cause, and smile at no man's jests; eat when I have stomach, and wait for no man's leisure; sleep when I am drowsy, and tend on no man's business; laugh when I am merry, and claw no man in his humour.
William Shakespeare (*Richard II*, Act I, iii): Truth hath a quiet breast.
William Shakespeare (*Richard II*, Act II, i): They breathe truth that breathe their words in pain.
William Shakespeare (*Richard III*, Act III, i): Methinks the truth should live from age to age, / As 'twere retail'd to all posterity, / Even to the general all-ending day.
William Shakespeare (*Sonnets*, 66): And simple truth miscall'd simplicity, / And captive good attending captain ill.
William Shakespeare (*Troilus and Cressida*, Act V, ii): O wither'd truth!
William Shakespeare (*Twelfth Night*, Act III, iv): If this were played upon a stage now, I could condemn it as an improbable fiction.
William Shakespeare (*The Winter's Tale*, Act IV, iv): Though I am not naturally honest, I am so sometimes by chance.
George Bernard Shaw: All great truths begin as blasphemies.
George Bernard Shaw: When a thing is funny, search it carefully for a hidden truth.
George Bernard Shaw: The power of accurate observation is commonly called cynicism by those who have not got it.
Upton Sinclair: It is difficult to get a man to understand something when his job depends on not understanding it.
Slovenian Proverb: Speak the truth, but leave immediately after.
H. Allen Smith: When there are two conflicting versions of a story, the wise course is to believe the one in which people appear at their worst.
Sophocles: One learns by doing the thing; for though you think you know it, you have no certainty until you try.
Thomas Sowell: There are only two ways of telling the complete truth – anonymously and posthumously
Spanish Proverb: He who knows nothing doubts nothing.
Spanish Proverb: Tell me who you live with and I will tell you who you are.
Spanish Proverb: Truth and oil always come to the surface.
Gerry Spence: I would rather have a mind opened by wonder than one closed by belief.
Stanislavski: Generality is the enemy of art (and Truth).
Dr. William Stekel: Candor is always a double-edged sword; it may heal or it may separate.
Casey Stengel: I can make a living telling the truth!
Adlai Stevenson: A lie is an abomination unto the Lord and a very pleasant help [Editor: meaning very handy and useful] in time of trouble.
Tom Stoppard: It is better to be quotable then to be honest.
Swiss Proverb: Sometimes you have to be silent to be heard.
Publilius Syrus (42 B.C.): Even false becomes true when the chief says so.
Publilius Syrus: In a heated argument we lose sight of the truth.
Talmud: When you add to the truth, you subtract from it.
J. Arthur Thomson: The most powerful factors in the world are clear ideas in the minds of energetic men of goodwill.
Henry David Thoreau: It takes two to speak the truth—one to speak and another to hear.
Henry David Thoreau: The lawyer's truth is not Truth, but consistency or a consistent.
Henry David Thoreau: Truth is always in harmony with herself, and is not concerned chiefly to reveal the justice that may consist with wrong doings.
Henry David Thoreau: All perception of truth is the detection of an analogy.
James Thurber: All human beings should try to learn before they die what they are running from, and to, and why.
James Thurber: There are two kinds of light—the glow that illumines, and the glare that obscures.
Henrik Tikkanen: Truly great madness cannot be achieved without significant intelligence.

Lily Tomlin: If truth is beauty, how come no one has their hair done in the library?
Harry S. Truman: I never did give anybody hell. I just told them the truth and they thought it was hell.
Mark Twain: When in doubt, tell the truth.
Mark Twain: Fiction is obliged to stick to possibilities. Truth is not.
Mark Twain: If you tell the truth you don't have to remember anything.
Mark Twain: Get your facts first, then you can distort them as you please.
Mark Twain: Truth is more of a stranger than fiction.
Mark Twain: Truth is mighty and will prevail. There is nothing the matter with this, except that it ain't so.
Mark Twain: There was things which he stretched, but mainly he told the truth.
Mark Twain: One learns peoples through the heart, not the eyes or the intellect.
Mark Twain: Most writers regard to truth as their most valuable possession, and therefore are most economical in its use.
Mark Twain: If you don't read the newspaper you are uninformed, if you do read the newspaper you are misinformed.
Mark Twain: Truth is the most valuable thing we have. Let us economize it.
Mark Twain: You cannot depend on your eyes when you're imagination is out of focus.
Mark Twain: When I was a boy of fourteen, my father was so ignorant I could hardly stand to have the old man around. But when I got to be twenty one I was astonished at how much the old man had learned in seven years.
Mark Twain: Tell the truth or trump – but get the trick.
Mark Twain: Truth *is* stranger than fiction, but it is because Fiction is obliged to stick to possibilities; Truth isn't.
Mark Twain: In religion and politics people's beliefs and convictions are in almost every case gotten at second-hand, and without examination.
Mark Twain: We have not the reverent feeling for the rainbow that a savage has, because we know how it is made. We have lost as much as we gained by prying into that matter.
Mark Twain: The history of our race, and each individual's experience, are sown thick with evidence that a truth is not hard to kill and a lie told well is immortal.
Mark Twain: Often the surest way to convey misinformation is to tell the strict truth.
Mark Twain: Wit is the sudden marriage of ideas which before their union were not percieved to have any relation.
Mark Twain: There ain't no way to find out why a snorer can't hear himself snore.
UA: The turth is the safest lie.
UA: Many a truth is spoke in jest.
UA: A proverb is a short sentence based on long experience.
UA: He doesn't want the truth. He wants something he can tell Congress.
UA: Truth is like iced water; it shocked two when it hits you, but no one has ever died from it.
UA: Longest journey you will make in your life is from your head to your heart. The journey is necessary to turn information into wisdom.
UA (1930's comic-strip, 1940's radio hero *Batman*): A never ending battle for truth, justice and the American way.
UA: I know you believe you understand what you think I said, but I'm not sure you realize, that what you heard, isn't what I meant.
Paul Valery: That which has always been accepted by everyone, everywhere, is almost certain to be false.
Abigail Van Buren: Wisdom doesn't automatically come with old age. Nothing does – except wrinkles. It's true, some wines improve with age. But only if the grapes were good in the first place.
Vincent Van Gogh: If one is master of one thing and understands one thing well, one has at the same time insight into and understanding of many things.
Albert Von Szent-Gyorgyi: discovery consists of seeing what every body has seen and thinking what I need nobody has thought.
George Washington: "The People must FEEL before they can SEE."
George Washington: "No nation (or man) is to trusted farther than it is bound by its (his) interests"
Daniel Webster: There is nothing so powerful as the truth, and often nothing so strange.

Welsh Proverb: A spoon does not know the taste of soup, nor a learned fool the taste of wisdom.
Edith Wharton: There are two ways to spread light: to be the candle or the mirror that reflects it.
William Allen White (News Editor of Emporia Gazette, 1944): If you present the facts fairly and honestly; truth will take care of itself.
Alfred North Whitehead: All truths are half truths.
Oscar Wilde: The cynic knows the price of everything and the value of nothing.
Oscar Wilde: Experience is the name everyone gives to their mistakes.
Billy Wilder: If you're going to tell people the truth, be funny or they'll kill you.
Tennessee Williams: Nobody sees anybody truly but only through the flaws of their own ego.
Woodrow Wilson: I would never read a book if it were possible for me to talk half an hour with a man who wrote it.
Henry Winkler: Assumptions are the termites of relationships.
Thomas Wolfe: Telling the truth is a pretty hard thing.
Anna Lloyd Wright (Frank L. Wright's mother Anna Lloyd Jones' family motto): TRUTH AGAINST THE WORLD.
Frank Lloyd Wright (His own family motto inscribed over the living room fireplace in his Oak Park, Illinois home): TRUTH IS LIFE.
Yiddish Proverb: A wise man hears one word and understands two.
Yiddish Proverb: How many will listen to the truth when you tell them?
Yiddish Proverb: The truth is not always what we want to hear.
Yugoslavian Proverb: Tell the truth and run
Lin Yutang: Peace of mind is that mental condition in which you have accepted the worst.
Emile Zola (Article "J'Accuse" in *Le Figaro*, 1898): Truth is on the march and nothing can stop it.

VALUE (See WORTH)

VICE (See EVIL)

WAR (See MILITARY)

WEALTH (See MONEY)

WIFE/WIVES (See MARRIAGE; WOMAN)

WISDOM (See ADVICE; CHARLEY CHAN; THINKING; TRUTH/ UNDERSTANDING)

WIT (See COMEDY)

WITNESS(ES) (See also EVIDENCE; LIES; HONESTY)

Uncle Anthony: I wish he had an answer, 'cause I'm gettin' tired of hearing him answer the same question.
Uncle Anthony: Y'now Thomas, I'd trust one good blue collar worker over a dozen starched shirt experts to help me decide if a person can do their job or not because of a physical disability.
Aunt Mary Carlo: Sometimes our eyes see what our imaginations tell us to see.
Aunt Mary Carlo: I believe more wit my eyes den wit my ears.
Ryunosuke Akutagawa (told a story about the Rashomon gate which inspired Akira Kurosawa's 1951 film, *Rashomon*): Built in 789, the Rashomon gate was the largest gate in Kyoto, the ancient capital of Japan. It fell into disrepair, cracking and crumbling in many places, and became a hide out for thieves and robbers as well as a dumping ground for unclaimed courses. In the 12th century a rape and murder was witnessed by a small group of individuals (a woodcutter, a priest, a police agent, a bandit, a wife and husband), all of the witnesses recollect the events in a different way. Despite each's best efforts, the "truth" remains elusive as various versions are told of the "truth." This phenomena of the relativity of "truth" which depends upon who is telling the story has come to be called the "Roshomon Effect.

Isaac Barrow: That justice should be administered between men, it is necessary that testimonies of fact be alleged; and that witnesses should apprehend themselves greatly obliged to discover the truth, according to their conscience, in dark and doubtful cases.

Yogi Berra: I really didn't say everything I said.

Yogi Berra: You can observe a lot by watching.

Yogi Berra: I wish I had an answer to that question because I'm getting tired of answering that question.

Bible: Apocrypha, Wisdom of Solomon 1:10: A jealous ear hears all things.

Bible: Deuteronomy 5:20; Exodus 20:16; Matthew 19:18: (9th Commandment) Thou shalt not bear false witness.

Bible: Deuteronomy 17:6: By the mouth of two or three witnesses shall he die that is to be slain. Let no man be put to death, when only one beareth witness against him.

Bible: Exodus 23:2: Nor shall you, when testifying in a lawsuit, side with the many in perverting justice. You shall not favor a poor man in his lawsuit.

Bible: Hebrews 12:1: A cloud of witnesses.

Bible: Isaiah xlii, 20: Seeing many things, but thou observest not; opening the ears, but he heareth not.

Bible: Luke, 16:10: He that is faithful in that which is least is faithful also in much; and he that is unjust in the least is unjust also in much.

Bible: Proverbs 14:5: A faithful witness will not lie but a deceitful witness uttereth a lie.

Ambrose Bierce: "PROOF, n. Evidence having a shade more of plausibility than of unlikelihood. The testimony of two credible witnesses as opposed to that of only one."

William Blake: A fool sees not the same tree that a wise man sees.

William Blake: The Eye altering alters all.

Sir Francis Buller (English judge 1745-1800): I have always told a jury that if a fact is fully proved by two witnesses, it is as good as if proved by a hundred.

Samuel Butler (English satirical poet 1612-1680): For witnesses, like watches, go / Just as they're set, too fast or slow.

Clarence Darrow (to Scopes in the Scopes Trial): If the jury would only mistake your perspiration for inspiration, I'd get you an acquittal.

Clarence Darrow (in Leopold and Loeb trial cross-examination of prosecution witness who contradicted himself): Witness: Sir, I am wedded to the truth." Darrow: "And how long have you been a widower?"

Charles Dickens: Lawyers hold that there are two kinds of particularly bad witnesses—a reluctant witness, and a too-willing witness.

Finley Peter Dunne: They cudden't get me into coort as a witness; no sir, not if 't was to hang me best friend. 'T is hard enough with newspapers an' cinsus officers an' th' mim'ry iv cab dhrivers to live down ye'er past without bein' foorced to dhrill it in a r-red coat an' with a brass band ahead befure th' eyes iv th' multitood. I did it wanst; I'll do it no more.

Ralph Waldo Emerson: Women see better than men, Men see lazily, if they do not expect to act. Women see quite [EDITOR: quite well! And, quite true, too! Just ask my two daughters] without any wish to act.

Ralph Waldo Emerson: The difference between landscape and landscape is small, but there is great difference in the beholders.

John Foxe: A prisoner in the Inquisition is never allowed to see the face of his accuser, or of the witnesses against him, but every method is taken by threats and tortures, to oblige him to accuse himself, and by that means corroborate their evidence.

Justice Frankfurter: In law also the right answer usually depends on putting the right question. *Rogers v. Commissioner,* 320US 410, 413, 88 L ed 134, 137, 64 S.Ct. 172 (1943)

Greek Proverb: One witness one liar; more witnesses, all liars"

Heraclitus of Ephesus: Eyes are more accurate witnesses than ears.

Hesiod (700 B.C.): When you deal with your brother, be pleasant, but get a witness.

Oliver Wendell Holmes, Jr.: A judge said: "I am not for sale." Mr. Justice Holmes replied: "Probably not, but you have been in the shop window a long time."

Aldous Huxley: Silence is as full of potential wisdom and wit as the unshown marble of great sculpture. The silent bear no witness against themselves.

Robert Green Ingersoll: But if the witnesses are inspired of God then there is no reason for their disagreeing on anything, and if they do disagree it is a demonstration that they were not inspired"

Jewish Proverb: He who shuts his eyes is hatching some scheme; He who tightens his lips is planning some mischief.

Franklin P. Jones: Nothing makes it easier to resist temptation than a proper bringing-up, a sound set of values and witnesses.

Abraham Lincoln: We better know there is a fire whence we see much smoke rising than we could know it by one or two witnesses swearing to it. The witnesses may commit perjury, but the smoke cannot.

Wayne C. Minnick (American educator): There is an old story of blind men trying to describe an elephant. One felt the elephant's leg and declared that the creature was like a tree, another felt the enormous side and said the elephant was like a wall, while a third, feeling the tail, was positive the animal was like a rope. Each man had a notion of reality that was limited by the number and kind of attributes he had perceived.

Richard Mounteney (Irish judge): Witnesses may lie, either be mistaken themselves, or wickedly intend to deceive others ... but ... circumstances cannot lie.

Muhammad: When you lend, have the borrower sign a paper before witnesses"

Michael A. Musmanno (Justice of the Sup. Ct. of Pennsylvania, 1959): Lawsuits are not decided by a mere counting of noses. One witness at home plate in the ballgame can be more depended on for accuracy than the shouts of 10 fans in the bleachers as to whether a runner was tagged out or not.

Michael A. Musmanno (Justice of the Sup. Ct. of Pennsylvania, 1959): Memory fades: Undue passage of time nearly always works adversely in the ascertainment of truth. Where there is controversy, truth is a ripe fruit which must be timely plucked. After maturity passes, disintegration sets in. Memory fades, and what is worse, it often enters into the shadowland of guesswork, loss of focus and even unconscious distortion. In addition, deaths, translocations and other mutations also make holes in the fabric intended to reproduce in testimony what has occurred in fact.

Michael A. Musmanno (Justice of the Sup. Ct. of Pennsylvania, 1959): Credibility in a trial is what a compass is to a ship, an altimeter to an airplane, a sight to a rifle, and a scale to a customer in a butcher shop. Without a standard for measuring direction, height, accuracy or weight, how does one know what is true or not true? How can we determine negligence unless we first decide that we can believe the person who is telling the story of alleged negligence or non-negligence? Without credibility to back up any story told from the witness stand, the witness's testimony is as meaningless as a sack of feathers thrown to the winds.

Michael A. Musmanno (Justice of the Sup. Ct. of Pennsylvania, 1959): Law is the distillation of common sense as drawn from the experience of mankind. And recorded experience through the centuries reveals that the person who fails to offer an explanation, when he is charged with misconduct, runs the risk of having the world believe he has no satisfactory explanation to produce. Thus, unless there exists a palpable reason for sealing one's lips, the world expects speech when the finger is lifted to accuse. We are not here considering the constitutional provision that no person is required to reply to any questions, the answer to which might subject him to criminal prosecution.

Michael A. Musmanno (Justice of Pa. Supreme Court, 1959): A Witness is Not a Tightrope Walker: It would be a mockery of fair trial procedure to deny a plaintiff, or any witness for that matter, an opportunity to change an answer he has made when he states he misunderstood the question or, for any reason, it becomes clear that his first answer did not accord with the truth as he now sees it. Any person on the witness stand is but a human being with all the frailties and imperfections which often go with human recollection. Nervousness, self-consciousness, timidity and inability to adjust to a strange environment may cause a witness to trip unintentionally. But a witness is not to be regarded as a tightrope walker crossing over Niagara Falls, when a misstep may plunge him into irreparable disaster.

Vladimir Nabokov: Resemblances are the shadows of differences. Different people see different similarities and similar differences.

Nietzsche: The man who sees little always sees less than there is to see; the man who hears badly always hears something more than there is to hear.

Robert Parry: For all plot hatched in hell, don't expect angels for witnesses.

Polybius (circa 200 B.C.): There is no witness so dreadful, no accuser so terrible as the conscience that dwells in the heart of every man.

Charles Peguy: One must always tell what one sees. Above all, which is more difficult, one must always see what one sees.

Quintilian: Witnesses appearing in away to a subpoena may be divided into two classes: those who desire to harm the accused, and those who do not.

Rashomon Effect: See Ryunosuke Akutagawa, *supra*.

Will Rogers: You never know how much a man can't remember until he is called as a witness.

Roman Legal Maxim: Testis unus testis nullus = one witness is no witness.

Russian Saying: He lied like an eyewitness.

Dwight Schultz: The Roswell incident, for instance, had over three hundred witnesses - some describing the bodies, some the craft, some the military procedures. Were they all perpetuating their own lives in a myth?

William Shakespeare (*All's Well That Ends Well*, Act II, iv): Many a man's tongue shakes out his master's undoing.

William Shakespeare (*Henry VIII*, Act I, iv): The red wine first must rise / In their cheeks: then we shall have them / Talk to us in silence.

William Shakespeare (*Julius Caesar*, Act II, i): Urged on the examination, proofs, confessions / Of divers witnesses.

William Shakespeare (*Merchant of Venice*, Act I, iii): The devil can site scripture for his own purpose! An evil soul producing holy witness is like a villain with a smiling cheek."

William Shakespeare (*Much Ado About Nothing*, Act III, i): One doth not know / How much an ill word way empoison liking.

William Shakespeare (*Richard III*, Act I, iii): Talkers are no good doers; be assur'd, / We go to use our hands, and not our tongues.

William Shakespeare (*Romeo and Juliet*, Act II, iv): A gentleman, nurse, that loves to hear himself talk; and will speak more in a minute, than he will stand to in a month.

William Shakespeare (*Tempest*, Act II, i): What a spendthrift is he of his tongue!

William Shakespeare (*Venus and Adonis*, Line 329): The heart hath treble wrong, / When it is barr'd the aidance of the tongue.

Sophocles: "There is no witness so terrible, no accuser so powerful as conscience which dwells within us.

Adlai Stevenson: I think that one of the most fundamental responsibilities... is to give testimony in a court of law, to give it honestly and willingly.

Mark Twain: I was gratified to be able to answer promptly, and I did. I said I didn't know.

UA: The worst informer is the face.

UA: The face will betray a secret.

UA: After you've heard two eyewitness accounts of an auto accident, you begin to wonder about history.

George Washington: No nation (EDITOR: or witness) is to be trusted farther than it is bound by its interests.

Eric Zagrans: Lies and liars come in all types of packages. At some point the difference between an honest witness in a dishonest one is attitude. Honest witnesses remember the facts the way they must have been; dishonest witnesses remember them the way they should have been.

WOE (See EMOTIONAL DISTRESS; GRIEF & SORROW)

WOMAN/WOMEN

Uncle Anthony: Be careful, Thomas, there are some four letter words that some brides get very upset about – like cook, iron, dust, wash.

Uncle Anthony: Some women work so hard to make good husbands that they never manage to make good wives.

Uncle Anthony: Some of dem strung-out-pot-smoking-broads who burnt their bras shoulda burnt all their clothes!

Aunt Mary Carlo: We are NOT DA WEAKER SEX! You guys may be stronger, but weez tougher!

Aunt Mary Carlo: What ya seez ain't what ya get wit a lotta women.

Susan B. Anthony: Modern invention has banished the spinning wheel and the same law of progress makes the woman of today a different woman from her grandmother.

Arabian Proverb: The whisper of a pretty girl can be heard further than the roar of a lion.

Nancy, Lady Astor: I married beneath me. All women do.

Jan Barrett: Veni, vidi, Visa (We came, we saw, we went shopping)

John Barrymore: So many beautiful women and so little time.

Bible: Genesis 2:18: It is not good that the man should be alone; I will make him an help mate for him.

Bible: Genesis 2:22: And the rib, which the Lord God had taken from man, made he a woman and brought her unto the man. And Adam said, This is now bone of my bones, and flesh of my flesh: she shall be called Woman, because she was taken out of Man.

Bible: Proverbs 11:22: As a jewel of gold in a swine's snout, so is a fair woman which is without discretion.

Bible: Proverbs 21:9: It is better to dwell in a corner of the house-top, than with a brawling woman in a wide house.

Bible: Proverbs 31:10: Who can find a virtuous woman? For her price is far above rubies.

Bible: Proverbs 31:11: A worthy woman is far more precious than jewels, strength and dignity are her clothing.

Ambrose Bierce: Here's to woman! Would that we could fall into her arms without falling into her hands.

Ambrose Bierce: ARTLESSNESS, n. A certain engaging quality to which women attain by long study and severe practice upon the admiring male, who is pleased to fancy it resembles the candid simplicity of his young.

Ambrose Bierce: BEAUTY, n. The power by which a woman charms a lover and terrifies a husband.

Ambrose Bierce: BELLADONNA, n. In Italian a beautiful lady; in English a deadly poison. A striking example of the essential identity of the two tongues.

Ambrose Bierce: CURIOSITY, n. An objectionable quality of the female mind. The desire to know whether or not a woman is cursed with curiosity is one of the most active and insatiable passions of the masculine soul.

Ambrose Bierce: FEMALE, n. One of the opposing, or unfair, sex....

Ambrose Bierce: HAG, n. An elderly lady whom you do not happen to like; sometimes called, also, a hen, or cat. Old witches, sorceresses, etc., were called hags from the belief that their heads were surrounded by a kind of baleful lumination or nimbus – hag being the popular name of that peculiar electrical light sometimes observed in the hair. At one time hag was not a word of reproach: Drayton speaks of a "beautiful hag, all smiles," much as Shakespeare said, "sweet wench." It would not now be proper to call your sweetheart a hag – that compliment is reserved for the use of her grandchildren.

Ambrose Bierce: HOSTILITY, n. A peculiarly sharp and specially applied sense of the earth's overpopulation. Hostility is classed as active and passive; as (respectively) the feeling of a woman for her female friends, and that which she entertains for all the rest of her sex.

Ambrose Bierce: MISS, n. A title with which we brand unmarried women to indicate that they are in the market. Miss, Missis (Mrs.) and Mister (Mr.) are the three most distinctly disagreeable words in the language, in sound and sense. Two are corruptions of Mistress, the other of Master. In the general abolition of social titles in this our country they miraculously escaped to plague us. If we must have them let us be consistent and give one to the unmarried man. I venture to suggest MUSH, abbreviated to Mh.

Ambrose Bierce: MOUTH, n. In man, the gateway to the soul; in woman, the outlet of the heart.

Ambrose Bierce: MUSTANG, n. An indocile horse of the western plains. In English society, the American wife of an English nobleman.

Ambrose Bierce: PRUDE, n. A bawd hiding behind the back of her demeanor.

Ambrose Bierce: UGLINESS, n. A gift of the gods to certain women, entailing virtue without humility.

Ambrose Bierce: WIDOW, n. A pathetic figure that the Christian world has agreed to take humorously, although Christ's tenderness towards widows was one of the most marked features of his character.

Ambrose Bierce: WITCH, n. (1) An ugly and repulsive old woman, in a wicked league with the devil. (2) A beautiful and attractive young woman, in wickedness a league beyond the devil.

Ambrose Bierce: WOMAN, n. An animal usually living in the vicinity of Man, and having a rudimentary susceptibility to domestication. It is credited by many of the elder zoologists with a certain vestigial docility acquired in a former state of seclusion, but naturalists of the postsusananthony period, having no knowledge of the seclusion, deny the virtue and declare that such as creation's dawn beheld, it roareth now. The species is the most widely distributed of all beasts of prey, infesting all habitable parts of the globe, from Greenland's spicy mountains to India's moral strand. The popular name (wolf-man) is incorrect, for the creature is of the cat kind. The woman is lithe and graceful in its movements, especially the American variety (*Felis pugnans*), is omnivorous and can be taught not to talk. - *Balthasar Pober.*

Ambrose Bierce: INDISCRETION, n. The guilt of woman.

Erma Bombeck: Women are never what they seem to be. There is the woamn you see and the woman who is hidden. Buy the gift for the woman who is hidden.

Erma Bombeck: The Rose Bowl is the only one I've seen that I didn't have to clean.

Kate Braverman: To be one woman, truly, is to be all women. Tend one garden and you will birth worlds.

General Benjamin F. "The Beast" Butler (a Union General also nicknamed "Spoons" for allegedly pocketing silverwear, named by President Lincoln as Military Governor of occupied New Orleans on May 1, 1862, after its capture during the Civil War, issued his infamous General Order #28 to the townsfolk as a result of his occupying Union soldiers being routinely insulted by New Orleans women, and after one woman in The French Quarter dumped her chamber pot onto Admiral David Glasgow Farragut): As the officers and soldiers of the United States have been subject to repeated insults from the women calling themselves ladies of New Orleans ... it is ordered that hereafter when any female shall by word, gesture or movement insult or show contempt for any officer or solder of the United States, she shall be regarded and held liable to be treated as a woman of the town plying her avocation.

Coco Chanel: I don't know why women want any of the things that men have when one of the things women have is men.

Chinese Proverb: A clever man will build a city, a clever woman will lay it low.

Sir Winston Churchill (to his Secretary of War, 1944): Who does not love beer, wine, women and song remains a fool his whole life..."

Joseph Conrad: Being a woman is a terribly difficult trade, since it consists principally of dealing with men.

William Congreve (*The Mourning Bride*): Hell hath no furry like a woman scourned.

Evelyn Cunningham: Women are the only oppressed group in our society that lives in intimate association with their oppressors.

Dumas: Woman inspires us to great things, and prevents us from achieving them.

Finley Peter Dunne: Woman's Rights? What does a woman want iv rights whin she has priv'leges?

George Eliot: The happiest women, like the happiest nations, have no history.

Ralph Waldo Emerson: Women see better than men, Men see lazily, if they do not expect to act. Women see quite [EDITOR: quite well! And, quite true, too! Just ask my two daughters] without any wish to act.

English Proverb: Six hours' sleep for a man, seven for a woman and eight for a fool.

Estonian Proverb: One woman never praises another.

W.C. Fields: Women are like elephants to me. I like to look at them but I wouldn't want to own one.

Benjamin Franklin: One good husband is worth two good wives; for the scarcer things are, the more they are valued.

Benjamin Franklin: Love well, whip well.

Benjamin Franklin: Dally not with other folks' women or money.

Sigmund Freud: The great question... which I have not been able to answer... is, "What does a woman want?

Diane Von Furstenberg: The more independent you want to be, the more generous you must be with yourself as a woman.

German Proverb: A woman has the form of an angel, the heart of a serpent, and the mind of an ass.

Guibert (French writer): Men make laws, women make manners.

Will Henry (American columnist, 1971): Nature gave women too much power, the law gave them too little.

Katharine Hepburn: Plain women know more about men than beautiful ones do.

Oliver Wendell Holmes, Jr.: It will need more than the Nineteenth Amendment to convince me that there are no differences between men and women.

Oliver Wendell Holmes, Sr.: The brain-women never interest us like the heart-women; white roses please less than red.

Italian Proverb: It is said that a good woman inspires a man, a brilliant woman interests him, a beautiful woman fascinates him, but a sympathetic woman gets him.

Italian Proverb: Choose neither a woman nor linen by candlelight.

Japanese Proverb: Women and sparrows twitter in company.

Japanese Proverb: Saying "No" a woman shakes her head lengthwise (that is: up and down, nodding assent as she says no).

Jewish Saying: An old man who marries a young wife grows younger—but she grows older.

Jewish Saying: It is better for a woman to have one husband, though he be useless, than wealthy children.

Jewish Saying: When a Man is too good for this world, it's too bad for his wife.

Jewish Saying: Men should take care not to make women weep, for God counts their tears.

Jewish Saying: Man's brains are his jewels; women's jewels are her brains.

Samuel Johnson: Nature has given women so much power that the law has very wisely given them little.

Carl Jung: The meeting of two personalities is like the contact of two chemical substances: if there is any reaction, both are transformed.

Rudyard Kipling (poem *The Female of the Species*): The female of the species is more deadly than the male.

Rudyard Kipling: When the Himalayan peasant meets the he-bear in his pride, / He shouts to scare the monster, who will often turn aside. / But the she-bear thus accosted rends the peasant tooth and nail. / For the female of the species is more deadly than the male.... But when hunter meets with husband, each confirms the other's tale – / The female of the species is more deadly than the male.

Hedy Lamarr: Any girl can be glamorous; all you have to do is stand still and look stupid.

Timothy Leary: Women who seek to be equal with men lack ambition.

Alan Jay Lerner & Frederick Loewe (in 1956 opening New York of their musical *My Fair Lady*, in the song *"A Hymn to Him,"* Professor Henry Higgins asks his friend Colonel Pickering why Eliza Doolittle has left): // Pickering, why can't a woman be more like a man? / Hm? Yes, **why can't a woman be more like a man?** // [See MAN for more of this song]

Gerald Lieberman: If you don't think women are explosive, drop one.

Lt. Gen James Longstreet (Confederate General during Civil War): Southern women like their men religious and a little mad. That's why they fall in love with preachers.

Anita Loos: It isn't that gentlemen prefer blondes, it's just that we look dumber.

Martin Luther: Who does not love **wine, women and song** / Remains a fool his whole life long. [EDITOR: Variations on this quote have been attributed to Martin Luther, but *Bartlett's Familiar Quotations* names Johann Heinrich Voss (1751-1826) as a more likely source].

Norman Mailer: You don't know anything about a woman until you meet her in court.

Steve Martin: I like a woman with a head on her shoulders. I hate necks.

Groucho Marx: Anyone who says he can see through women is missing a lot.

Menander: Of all the wild beasts of land or sea, the wildest is woman.

Larry Miller: Women are the most powerful magnet in the universe; all men are cheap metal.

Wilson Mizner: When a woman tells you her age it's all right to look surprised, but don't scowl.

John Mortimer (author of stories and TV plays *Rumpole of the Bailey*, referencing the wife of British barrister Horace Rumpole, commencing 1978): She who must be obeyed.

Maureen Murphy: The reason there are so few female politicians is that it is too much trouble to put makeup on two faces.

Ogden Nash (American poet, 1902-1971, *Allow Me, Madam, but It Won't Help*): .... Yes, if you desire *savoir-faire* that you could balance a cup on, / Consider the calmness of a woman trying to get her arm into the sleeve of a coat that she has sat down on too far up on. / Women are indeed the salt of the earth. / But I fail to see why they daily submit themselves voluntarily to an operation that a man only undergoes when he is trying to put on his trousers in an upper berth.

Friedrich Nietzsche: Woman was God's second mistake,

Aristotle Onassis: If women did not exist, all the money in the world would have no meaning.

Ovid: A woman is always buying something.

Dorothy Parker: the cure for boredom is curiosity. There is no cure for curiosity.

Mark Patinkin: Never date a woman you can hear ticking.

Will Rogers: The Nineteenth Amendment – I think that's the one that made Women humans by Act of Congress.

Will Rogers: Money and women are the most sought after and the least known about of any two things we have.

Will Rogers: I never expected to see the day when the girls would get sunburned in the places they do now.

Will Rogers: The whole thing about the women is, they lust to be misunderstood.

Will Rogers: Every time a woman leaves off something she looks better, but every time a man leaves off something he looks worse.

Will Rogers: There's two theories to arguing with a woman. Neither one works.

Will Rogers (1931): Say did you read in the papers about a bunch of Women up in British Columbia who sat as a protest against high taxes, sat out in the open naked, and they wouldent put their clothes on? The authorities finally turned a Sprayer that you use on trees, on 'em. That may lead into quite a thing. Woman comes into the tax office nude, saying I won't pay. Well they can't search her and get anything. It sounds great. How far is it to British Columbia?

Steve Rubenstein: Women speak two languages, one of which is verbal.

Russian Proverb: A dog is wiser than a woman; it does not bark at its master.

William Shakespeare (*Antony and Cleopatra*, Act III, vi): Age cannot wither her, nor custom stale / Her infinite variety.

William Shakespeare (*Antony and Cleopatra*, Act III, vi): Long ere she did appear: the trees by the way / Should have borne men; and expectation fainted.

William Shakespeare (*Antony and Cleopatra*, Act V, ii): A woman is a dish for the gods, if the devil dress her not.

William Shakespeare (*As You Like It*, Act I, iii): Beauty provoketh thieves sooner than gold.

William Shakespeare (*As You Like It*, Act II, vii): If ladies be but young, and fair, / They have the gift to know it.

William Shakespeare (*As You Like It*, Act III, ii): I thank God I am not a woman, to be touched with so many giddy offences as he hath generally taxed their whole sex withal.

William Shakespeare (*As You Like It*, Act III, ii): Run, run, Orlando: carve on every tree / The fair, the chaste, and unexpressive she.

William Shakespeare (*As You Like It*, Act III, ii): Do you not know I am a woman? When I think, I must speak.

William Shakespeare (*As You Like It*, Act IV, i): Make the door upon a woman's wit, and it will out to at the casement.

William Shakespeare (*Cymbeline*, Act II, iv): They are not constant, but are changing still.

William Shakespeare (*Cymbeline*, Act V, v): O most delicate fiend! / Who is it can read a woman?

William Shakespeare (*Hamlet*, Act I, ii): Frailty, thy name is woman!

William Shakespeare (*Hamlet*, Act V, i): One that was a woman, sir; but, rest her soul, she's dead.

William Shakespeare (*I Henry IV*, Act V, iii): She's beautiful; and therefore to be woo'd: / She is a woman; therefore to be won.

William Shakespeare (*III Henry VI*, Act I, iv): 'Tis beauty that doth oft make women proud;.... 'Tis virtue that doth make them most admir'd;.... 'Tis government that makes them seem divine.

William Shakespeare (*III Henry VI*, Act III, i): Her sighs will make a battery in his breast; / Her tears will pierce into a marble heart; / The tiger will be mild, while she doth mourn; / And Nero will be tainted with remorse, / To hear, and see, he plaints.

William Shakespeare (*Henry VIII*, Act I, iv): Two women placed together makes cold weather.

William Shakespeare (*Henry VIII*, Act III, ii): She is a gallant creature, and complete / In mind and fea of the ture.

William Shakespeare (*Julius Caesar,* Act II, i): I grant, I am a woman; but, withal, / A woman that lord Brutus took to wife: / I grant, I am a woman; but, withal, / A woman well-reputed Cato's daughter.

William Shakespeare (*Julius Caesar,* Act II, iv): Ay, me, how weak a thing / The heart of woman is!

William Shakespeare (*Julius Caesar,* Act II, iv): How hard it is for women to keep counsel!

William Shakespeare (*King John,* Act II, i): She in beauty, education, blood, / Holds hand with any princess of the world.

William Shakespeare (*King Lear,* Act III, ii): There was never yet fair woman but she made mouths in a glass.

William Shakespeare (*King Lear,* Act IV, vi): Down from the waist they are Centaurs, / Though women all above.

William Shakespeare (*Love's Labour's Lost,* Act I, i): A child of our grandmother Eve, a female; or, for thy more sweet understanding, a woman.

William Shakespeare (*Love's Labour's Lost,* Act V, ii): Fair ladies, mask'd, are roses in their bud: / Dismask'd, their damask sweet commixture shown, / Are angels vailing clouds, or roses blown.

William Shakespeare (*Measure for Measure,* Act II, iv): ANGELO: Nay, women are frail too. / ISABELLA: Ay, as the glasses where they view themselves: / Which are as easy broke as they make forms.

William Shakespeare (*Measure for Measure,* Act II, iv): Women! Help Heaven! man their creations mar / In profiting by them.

William Shakespeare (*Much Ado About Nothing,* Act II, i): She speaks poignards, and every word stabs: if her breath were as terrible as her terminations, there were no living near her; she would infect the north star.

William Shakespeare (*Much Ado About Nothing,* Act II, i): Would it not grieve a woman to be overmaster'd with a piece of valiant dust? To make an account of her life to a clod of wayward marl?

William Shakespeare (*Much Ado About Nothing,* Act III, i): I never yet saw man, / .... / But she would spell him backward; if fairfac'd / She would swear the gentleman should be her sister; / If black, why nature, drawing of an antic, / Made a foul blot.

William Shakespeare (*Much Ado About Nothing,* Act III, iii): One woman is fair; yet I am well: another is wise; yet I am well: another virtuous; yet I am well: But till all graces be in one woman, one woman shall not come in my grace.

William Shakespeare (*Much Ado About Nothing,* Act IV, i): O, she is fallen / Into a sea of ink., that the wide sea / Hath drops too few to wash her clean again.

William Shakespeare (*Much Ado About Nothing,* Act IV, i): Death is the fairest cover for her shame.

William Shakespeare (*Othello,* Act II, i): A maid / That paragons description, and wild fame; / One that excels the quirks of blazoning pens, / And in the essential vesture of creation, / Does bear all excellency.

William Shakespeare (*Othello*, Act II, i): You are pictures out of doors, / Bells in your parlours, wild-cats in your kitchens, / Saints in your injuries, devils being offended, / Players in your housewifery, and housewives in your beds.

William Shakespeare (*Othello,* Act V, ii): One that loved not wisely but too well, -

William Shakespeare (*The Passionate Pilgrim,* Line 335): The wiles and guiles that women work, / Dissembled with an outward show, / The tricks and toys that in them lurk, / The cock that treads them shall not know.

William Shakespeare (*The Passionate Pilgrim,* Pt. XIX): Have you not heard it said full oft, / A woman's nay doth stand for naught?

William Shakespeare (*The Rape of Lucrese*, 29): Beauty itself doth of itself persuade / The eyes of men without an orator.

William Shakespeare (*Richard III*, Act III, vii): Play the maid's part, still answer nay, and take it.

William Shakespeare (*Romeo and Juliet*, Act III, ii): Beautiful tyrant! fiend angelical!

William Shakespeare (*The Taming of the Shrew,* Act I, ii): Have I not in a pitched battle heard / Loud 'larums, neighing steeds, and trumpets clang? / And do you tell me of a woman's tongue?

William Shakespeare (*The Taming of the Shrew,* Act I, ii): I will board her, though she chide as loud / As thunder when the clouds in autumn crack.

William Shakespeare (*The Taming of the Shrew,* Act I, ii): Her only fault,, and that is faults enough, / Is that she is intolerable curst. / And shrewd and forward, so beyond all the measure / That, were my state far worser than it is, / I would not wed her for a mine of gold.

William Shakespeare (*The Taming of the Shrew,* Act II, i): Why, then thou canst not break her to the lute? / Why, no; for she hath brake the lute to me.

William Shakespeare (*The Taming of the Shrew,* Act II, i): Say, that she rail, why, then I'll tell her plain / She sings as sweetly as a nightingale; / Say, that she frown; I'll say, she looks as clear / As morning roses newly wash'd with dew; / Say, she be mute, and will not speak a word; / Then I'll commend her volubility, / And say she uttereth piercing eloquence.

William Shakespeare (*The Taming of the Shrew,* Act IV, ii): Kindness in women, not their beauteous looks, / Shall win my love.

William Shakespeare (*The Taming of the Shrew,* Act V, ii): Why are our bodies soft, and weak, and smooth, / Unapt to toil, and trouble in the world, / But that our soft conditions, and our hearts, / Should well agree with our external parts?

William Shakespeare (*The Taming of the Shrew,* Act V, ii): A woman moved is like a fountain troubled, / Muddy, ill-seeming, thick, bereft of beauty.

William Shakespeare (*The Taming of the Shrew,* Act V, ii): I am asham'd, that women are so simple / To offer war, where they should kneel for peace; / Or seek for rule, supremacy and sway, / When they are bound to serve, love, and obey.

William Shakespeare (*Troilus and Cressida,* Act II, ii): She is a pearl / Whose price has launch'd above a thousand ships, / And turn'd crown'd kings to merchants.

William Shakespeare (*Troilus and Cressida,* Act III, ii): As false / As air, as water, wind, or sandy earth, / As fox to lamb, as wolf to heifer's calf, / Pard to the hind, or stepdame to her son; / Yea, let them say, to stick the heart of falsehood, / As false as Cressid.

William Shakespeare (*Troilus and Cressida,* Act III, iii): A woman impudent and mannish grown / Is not more loath'd than an effeminate man.

William Shakespeare (*Troilus and Cressida,* Act IV, v): Fie, fie upon her! / There's language in her eye, her cheek, her lip, / Nay, her foot speaks; her wanton spirits look out / At every joint and motion of her body.

William Shakespeare (*Twelfth Night,* Act II, iv): For women are as roses, whose fair flower / Being once display'd, doth fall that very hour.

William Shakespeare (*The Two Gentlemen of Verona,* Act I, ii): I have no other but a woman's reason: I think him to so, because I think him so.

William Shakespeare (*The Two Gentlemen of Verona,* Act I, iii): Muse not that I thus suddenly proceed; / For what I will, I will, and there an end.

William Shakespeare (*The Two Gentleman of Verona,* Act III, i): Never give her o'er; / For scorn at first, makes after-love the more. / If she do frown, 'tis not in hate of you, / But rather to beget more love in you; / If she do chide, 'tis not to have you gone, / For why, the fools are mad if left alone.

William Shakespeare (*The Two Gentlemen of Verona*, Act III, i): To be slow in words is a woman's only virtue.

William Shakespeare (*The Two Gentlemen of Verona*, Act III, i): Take no repulse, whatever she doth say; / For, "get you gone," she doth not mean, "away."

William Shakespeare (*Winter's Tale,* Act V, i): If, one by one, you wedded all the world, / Or, from the all that are took something good, / To make a perfect woman, she, you kill'd, / Would be unparallel'd.

William Shakespeare (*Winter's Tale,* Act V, i): Women will love her, that she is a woman, / More worth than any man; men, that she is / The rarest of all women.

George Bernard Shaw: The fickleness of the women I love is only equalled by the infernal constancy of the women who love me.

Gloria Steinem: A liberated woman is one who has sex before marriage and a job after.

James Stephens: Women are wiser than men because they know less and understand more.

Talmud: It is easier to appease a male than a female—because the first man was created out of dust, which is soft, but the first woman was created out of bone, which is hard.

Talmud: Women want to be married more than men do.

Talmud: Females should be married before males, for the shame of a woman is greater than that of a man.

Alexis de Tocqueville: If I were asked to what the singular prosperity of the American people is to be mainly attributed, I should reply: to the superiority of their women.

Sophie Tucker: From birth to age 18, a girl needs good parents; from 18 to 35 she needs good looks; from 35 to 55 she needs a good personality; and from 55 on she needs cash.

Mark Twain: A thoroughly beautiful woman and a thoroughly homely woman are creations which I love to gaze upon, and which I cannot tire of gazing upon, for each is perfect in their own line.

Mark Twain: A woman springs a sudden reproach upon you which provokes a hot retort – and then she will presently ask you to apologize.

Mark Twain: If I were settled I would quit all nonsense & swindle some girl into marrying me. But I wouldn't expect to be *"worthy"* of her. I wouldn't *have* a girl that *I* was worthy of. *She* wouldn't do. She wouldn't be respectable enough.

Mark Twain (on women in the United States): They live in the midst of a country where there is no end to the laws and no beginning to the execution of them.

UA (1940's American radio program): Queen for a day.

John Webster (English dramatist, 1580-1625): When women go to Law, the Devil is full of Business.

Mae West: Women with pasts interest men because they hope history will repeat itself.

William Allen White: My advice to the women's clubs of America is raise more hell and fewer dahlias.

Charlotte Whitton: Whatever women do they must do twice as well as men to be thought half as good. Luckily, this is not difficult.

Wikipedia: The cliché **"WINE, WOMEN, AND SONG"** is a rhetorical figure of a triad or *hendiatris*. Similar tripartite mottoes have existed for a long time in many languages, for example:
Bengali/Hindi/Sanskrit - "Sur, Sura, Sundari" (music, wine and woman)
Czech - "Víno, ženy a zpěv" (wine, women and song)
Danish - "Vin, kvinder og sang" (wine, women and song); also "Øl, fisse og hornmusik" (beer, a slang word for female genitals, and horn music); also "Tjald og lal og lir" (slang words for cannabis, fooling around, and being sexually aroused)
German - "Wein, Weib und Gesang" (wine, women and song)
Greek - "Πύρ, γυνή και θάλαττα" (fire, women and the sea)
Hindi/Urdu - "Kabab, Sharab aur Shabab" (meat, wine and women/beauty)
Norwegian - "Kvinner, vin og sang" (women, wine and song)
Polish - "Wino, kobiety i śpiew"
Swedish - "Vin, kvinnor och sång" (wine, women and song)
Turkish - "At, Avrat, Silah" (horse, woman, weapon)
"Sex and Drugs and Rock and Roll" is a modern variation of it. The terms correspond to wine, women and song with edgier and updated vices. The term came to prominence in the sixties as rock and roll music, opulent and intensely public lifestyles, as well as liberal morals championed by hippies, came into the mainstream.
"Rum, bum, and concertina" is a British naval equivalent. Another British naval equivalent is "rum, sodomy and the lash."

Oscar Wilde: Women are a decorative sex; they never had anything to say, but they say it charmingly.

Virginia Woolf: Women are looking glasses possessing the magic and delicious power of reflecting the figure of man at twice its natural size.

WORDS (See also ADVERSARY; BOOKS)

Uncle Anthony: You got two eyes, two ears and only one mouth, that's 'cause God wanted you to watch out and listen up twice as much as you open your mouth to talk.

Uncle Anthony: The story of the creation of the world was told in 600 words. Try it sometime when you think you have big story to tell and you need lots of words.

Uncle Anthony: Sometimes it's a lot tougher to say somethin' than it is to do it.

Aunt Mary Carlo: Y'know 'dat one about "sticks an' stones can break yer bones, but woids can never hoit ya?" Well, when some people throw 'dem woids around, I'd rather get hit wit' some of 'dem stones.

Abigail Adams: We have too many high sounding words, and too few actions that correspond with them.

Henry Brooks Adams: No one means all he says, and yet few say all they mean. For words are slippery and thought is vicious.

Aeschylus: Words are the physicians of a mind diseased.

Aeschylus: Words provoke to senseless wrath.

Dr. Robert Anthony: What you can't communicate runs your life.

Dr. Robert Anthony: What you said is exactly what you intended to say.

Mary Jo Antone: There are people who complain about everything, they even complain about the noise when opportunity knocks."

Francis Bacon: Words are the tokens current and accepted for conceits, as monies are for values.

Francis Bacon: Words, as a Tartar's bow, do shoot back upon the understanding of the wisest, and mightily entangle and pervert the judgment.

Arthur J. Balfour (Prime Minister of England, 1848-1930, in retort in House of Commons to a lawyer who interrupted to remind him that "trade unions are not corporations"): I know that; I am talking English, not law.

Henry Ward Beecher: All words are pegs to hang ideas on.

Bible: Ecclesiastes 9:16: The poor man's wisdom is despised, and his words are not heard.

Bible: Job 6:25: How forcible are right words.

Bible: Proverbs 15:23: A word spoken in due season, how good it is!

Bible: Psalms 119:105: Thy word is a lamp unto my feet, and a light unto my path.

Bible: Acts, 26:25: Words of truth and soberness.

Bible: Ecclesiastes, 12:11: The words of the wise are as goads.

Bible: Joe, 6:25: How forcible are right words!

Bible: Matthew, 12:37: By thy words thou shalt be condemned.

Bible: Matthew, 24:35: Heaven and earth shall pass away, but my words shall not pass away.

Bible: Proverbs, 15:23: A word spoken in due season, how good it is!

Bible: Proverbs, 25:11: A word fitly spoken is like apples of gold in pictures of silver.

Ambrose Bierce: BLANK-VERSE, n. Unrhymed iambic pentameters – the most difficult kind of English verse to write acceptably; a kind, therefore, much affected by those who cannot acceptably write any kind.

Ambrose Bierce: CONVERSATION, n. A fair for the display of the minor mental commodities, each exhibitor being too intent upon the arrangement of his own wares to observe those of his neighbor.

Ambrose Bierce: GRAMMER, n. A system of pitfalls thoughtfully prepared for the feet of the self-made man, along the path by which he advances to distinction.

Ambrose Bierce: INSCRIPTION, n. Something written on another thing. Inscriptions are of many kinds, but mostly memorial, intended to commemorate the fame of some illustrious person and hand down to distant ages the record of his services and virtues. To this class of inscriptions belongs the name of John Smith, penciled on the Washington monument....

Ambrose Bierce: LEXICOGRAPHER, n. A persistent fellow who, under the pretense of recording some particular stage in the development of a language, does what he can to arrest its growth, stiffen its flexibility and mechanize its methods.

Ambrose Bierce: REPORTER, n. A writer who guesses his way to the truth and dispels it with a tempest of words.

Ambrose Beirce: SLANG, n. The grunt of the human hog (Pignoramus intolerabilis) with an audible memory.

Josh Billings: I don't care how much a man talks, if he only says it in a few words.

Colin Blackburn (Baron, English Judge): The meaning of words varies according to the circumstances of and concerning which they are used. *Allgood v. Blake*, L.R. 8 Ex. 160 (1873)

Louis Brandeis: In the case at bar, also, the logic of words should yield to the logic of realities.

Dr. Robert Burchfield (editor, Oxford English dictionary, 1986): The English language is rather like a monster accordion, stretchable at the whim of the editor, compressible ad-lib.

Lord Byron: I wish he would explain his explanation.

Lord Byron: A drop of ink may make a million think.

Benjamin Cardozo: We seek to find peace of mind in the word, the formula, the ritual. The hope is an illusion.

Benjamin Cardozo: Words after all are symbols, and the significance of the symbols varies with the knowledge and experience of the mind receiving them.

Benjamin Cardozo: The search is for the just word, the happy phrase, that will give expression to the thought, but somehow the thought itself is transfigured by the phrase when found.

Lewis Carroll (*Alice in Wonderland*, ch. 12): "If there's no meaning in it," said the King, "that saves a world of trouble, you know, as we needn't try to find any."

Chinese Proverb: If one word does not succeed, ten thousand are of no avail.

Chinese Proverb: If language is not used correctly, then what is said is not meant; if what is said is not meant, and what ought to be done remains undone; if this remains undone, morals and art will be corrupted; if morals and art are corrupted, Justice will go astray and the people will stand about in helpless confusion.

Chinese Proverb: If you wish to know the mind of a man, listen to his words.

Chinese Proverb: The tongue like a sharp knife...Kills without drawing blood.

Sir Winston Churchill: Short words are best and old words when short are best of all.

Sir Winston Churchill: Eating words has never given me indigestion.

Sir Winston Churchill: By swallowing evil words unsaid, no one has ever harmed his stomach.

Sir Winston Churchill: Official jargon can be used to destroy any kind of human contact, or even thought itself.

Sir Winston Churchill: From now on, ending a sentence with a preposition is something up with which I will not put.

Sir Winston Churchill: If we opened a quarrel between the past and the present, we shall find that we have lost the future.

Sir Winston Churchill: We are masters of the unsaid words, but slaves of those we let slip out.

Sir Winston Churchill: Please be good enough to put your conclusions and recommendations on one sheet of paper in the very beginning of your report, so I can even consider reading it.

Sir Winston Churchill: All the great things are simple, and many can be expressed in a single word: freedom, justice, honor, duty, mercy, hope.

Sir Winston Churchill: Everybody has a right to pronounce foreign names as he chooses.

Sir Winston Churchill: You see these dictators on their pedestals, surrounded by the bayonets of their soldiers and the truncheons of their police. Yet in their hearts there is unspoken – unspeakable! – fear. They are afraid of words and thoughts! Words spoken abroad, thoughts stirring at home, all the more powerful because they are forbidden. These terrify them. A little mouse – a little tiny mouse! – of thought appears in the room, and even the mightiest potentates are thrown into panic.

Sir Winston Churchill: Half my lifetime I have earned my living by selling words, and I hope thoughts.

Sir Winston Churchill: It cannot in the opinion of His Majesty's Government be classified as slavery in the extreme acceptance of the word without some risk of terminological inexactitude.

Charles Caleb Colton: Men are born with two eyes, but only one tongue, in order that they should see twice as much as they say.

Confucius: Without knowing the force of words, it is impossible to know men.

Confucius: For one word a man is often deemed to be wise, and for one word he is often deemed to be foolish. We should be careful indeed what we say.

Joseph Conrad: Words, as is well known, are great foes of reality.

Alistair Cooke: As always, the British especially shudder at the latest American vulgarity, and then they embrace it with enthusiasm two years later.

James Fenimore Cooper: The common faults of American language are an ambition of affect, a want of simplicity, and a turgid abuse of terms.

Frederick E. Crane, Chief Judge, New York Court of Appeals: Words, like men, grow an individuality; their character changes with years and with use. *Adler v. Deegan*, 251 N.Y. 467 (1929)

Charles Dickens: A word in earnest is as good as a speech.

Emily Dickinson: She dealt her pretty words like blades, / As glittering they shone, / And every one unbared a nerve / Or wantoned with a bone.

Benjamin Disraeli: With words we govern men.

Peter Drucker: the most important thing in communication is to hear what is not being said.

Elaine Goodale Eastman (a teacher at Fort Marion, Florida and Carlisle Indian Industrial School, biographer of General William Henry Pratt, the founder and first Superintendent of Carlisle, speaking about him): He felt he could change the current of a life by just a word.

Ralph Waldo Emerson: We infer the spirit of the nation in great measure from the language, which is a sort of monument to which each forcible individual in a course of many hundred years has contributed a stone.

Ralph Waldo Emerson: Every word was once a poem. Every new relation is a word.

Ralph Waldo Emerson: The poets made all the words, and therefore language is the archives of history, and, if we must say it, a sort of tomb of the muses. For though the origin of most of our words is forgotten, each word was at first a stroke of genius.

Ralph Waldo Emerson: Language is fossil poetry.

Ralph Waldo Emerson: There is no more welcome gift to men than a new symbol that satiates, transports, converts them. They assimilate themselves to it, deal with it in all ways, and it will last a hundred years. Then comes a new genius, and brings another.

F. Scott Fitzgerald: You can stroke people with words.

Felix Frankfurter: In law also the emphasis makes the song. Bethlehem Steel Co. v. New York State Labor Relations Board, 330 US 767, 91 L ed 1234, 67 S Ct 1026 (1947)

Felix Frankfurter: Words acquire scope and function from the history of events which they summarize.

Felix Frankfurter: But this is a case for applying the canon of construction of the wag who said, when the legislative history is doubtful, go to the statute. Greenwood v. US, 350 US 366, 100 L ed 412, 76 S Ct 410 (1956)

Felix Frankfurter: The notion that because the words of a statute are plain, its meaning is also plain, is merely pernicious oversimplification. US v. Monia, 317 US 424, 87 L ed 376, 63 S Ct 409 (1943)

Benjamin Franklin: Here comes the orator with his flood of words and his drop of reason.

Benjamin Franklin: Remember not only to say the right thing in the right place, but far more difficult still, to leave unsaid the wrong thing at the tempting moment.

Benjamin Franklin: *Saying* and *Doing*, have quarrel'd and parted.

Benjamin Franklin: As our alphabet now stands, the bad and spelling, or what is called so, is generally the best, as conforming to the sound of the letters and of the words.

French Proverb: Word by word the book is made.

Johann Wolfgang von Goethe: Divide and rule, a sound motto. Unite and lead, a better one.

German Proverb: A bad cause requires many words.

Carlo Goldoni (Italian dramatist): He who talks much cannot always talk well.

Graffiti: Don't say it—spray it.

Albert Guinon: When everyone is against you, it means that you are absolutely wrong—or absolutely right.

Learned Hand (*Sources of Tolerance*, 79 Univ. of Pa. L. Rev. 1, 1930): The words he [EDITOR: a judge] must construe are empty vessels into which he can pour nearly anything he will.

Learned Hand: The meaning of a sentence may be more than that of the separate words, as a melody is more than the notes, and no degree of particularity can ever obviate recourse to the setting in which all appear, and which all collectively create. *Helvering v. Gregory*, 62 F.2d 809 (1934)

Learned Hand: There is no surer way to misread any document than to read it literally.

Learned Hand: Words are chameleons, which reflect the color of their environment.

Learned Hand: Words are not the keys of persuasion, but the triggers of action.

Learned Hand: Words are not pebbles in alien juxtaposition.

Learned Hand: Law has always been unintelligible, and I might say that perhaps it ought to be. And I will tell you why, because I don't want to deal in paradoxes. It ought to be unintelligible because it ought to be in words – and words are utterly inadequate to deal with the fantastically multiform occassions which come up in human life ...

Sydney Harris: Any philosophy that can be put "in a nutshell" belongs there.

Thomas Hobbes: Words are wise men's counters, they do but reckon by them; but they are the money of fools.

Oliver Wendell Holmes, Jr.: A word generally has several meanings, even in the dictionary. You have to consider the sentence in which it stands to decide which of those meanings it bears in the particular case, and very likely will see that it there has a shade of significance more refined than any given in the word-book.

Oliver Wendell Holmes, Jr.: It is not the first use but the tiresome repetition of inadequate catch words which I am observing – phrases which originally were contributions, but which, by their very felicity, delay further analysis for fifty years.

Oliver Wendell Holmes Jr.: A word is not a crystal, transparent and unchanging, it is the skin of a living thought and may vary greatly in color and content according to the circumstances and time in which is used. Towne v. Eisner, 245 US 418, 62 L. ed. 372, 38 S Ct 158 (1917).

Oliver Wendell Holmes Jr.: Words express whatever meaning convention has attached to them. Trimble v. Seattle, 231 US 683, 58 L. ed. 435, 34 S Ct 218 (1914)

Oliver Wendell Holmes, Jr.: It is one of the misfortunes of the law that ideas become encysted in phrases and thereafter for a long time cease to provoke further analysis. Hyde v. United States, 225 US 347, 56 L. ed. 435, 34 S Ct 218 (1912)

Oliver Wendell Holmes, Jr. (2 *Holmes-Pollock Letters* 131): Profanity is vitriol, slang is vinegar, but reporters' English is rancid butter. I don't know that you have the thing to which I refer in England – an intrusion into the language of sentiment, as when they call a house a home.

Oliver Wendell Holmes Sr.: Life and language are alike sacred. Homicide and *verbicide* – that is, violent treatment of a word with fatal results to its legitimate meaning, which is its life – are alike forbidden.

Oliver Wendell Holmes, Sr.: We live by symbols, and what shall be symbolized by any image of the sight depends upon the mind of him who sees it.

Oliver Wendell Holmes Sr.: Every language is a temple, in which the soul of those who speak it is enshrined.

Oliver Wendell Holmes Sr.: Language! the blood of the soul, sir, into which our thoughts run, and out of which they grow.

Oliver Wendell Holmes Sr.: I would never use a long word were a short one would answer the purpose. I know there are professors in this country who "ligate" arteries. Other surgeons only tie them, and it stops the bleeding just as well.

Oliver Wendell Holmes, Sr.: (My writings are) Little fragments of my fleece that I have left upon the hedges of life.

Oliver Wendell Holmes, Sr. (*Theory of Legal Interpretation*, 12 Harv. L. Rev. 417, 1899): We do not inquire what the legislature meant; we ask only what the statute means.

Oliver Wendell Holmes, Sr.: The meaning of a sentence is to be felt rather than proved. US v. Johnson, 221 US 488, 55 L ed 823, 31 S Ct 627 (1911)

Homer: Then words came like a fall of winter snow.

Victor Hugo: Words are the mysterious messengers of the soul.

Aldous Huxley (*Brave New World*): HELMHOLTZ WATSON: "Words can be like x-rays if you use them properly. They'll go through anything. You read and you're pierced. That's one of the things I try to teach my students – how to write piercingly."

Irish Proverb: Mere words do not feed the friars.

Italian Proverb: Silence was never written down.

Italian Proverb: Words in haste do friendships waste.

Robert H. Jackson: The price of freedom of religion, or of speech, or of the press, is that we must put up with a good deal of rubbish.

Robert H. Jackson (Assoc Justice US Supreme Court): If ever we are justified in reading a statute, not narrowly as through a keyhole, but in the broad light of the evils it aimed at and the good it hoped for, it is here. US ex rel Marcus v. Hess, 317 US 537, 87 L ed 443, 63 S Ct 379 (1943)

Robert H. Jackson: I should concur in this result more readily if the Court could reach it by analysis of the statute instead of by psychoanalysis of Congress. US v. Public Utilities Com., 345 US 295, 97 L ed 1020, 73 S Ct 706 (1953)

Henry James: I'm glad you like adverbs—I adore them; they are the only qualifications I really much respect.

Japanese Proverb: The tongue is more to be feared than the sword.

Thomas Jefferson (on the French language): You will learn to speak better from women and children in three months, then from men in a year.

Thomas Jefferson (*Letter to William Johnson*, 1823): Laws are made for men of ordinary understanding, and should therefore, be construed by the ordinary rules of common sense. Their meaning is not to be sought for in metaphysical subtleties, which may make anything mean everything or nothing at pleasure.

Jewish Saying: Words are like medicine: measure them with care; an overdose can hurt.

Samuel Johnson: To make dictionaries is dull work.

Thomas a Kempis: To the intelligent man a word is enough.

Rudyard Kipling: Words are, of course, the most powerful drug use by mankind.

Lao-Tsze: He who lightly assents will seldom keep his word.

Abraham Lincoln: He can compress the most words into the smallest ideas of any man I ever met.

Abraham Lincoln: We all declare for liberty, but in using the same word we all do not mean the same thing.

Karl N. Llewellyn (American lawyer, philosopher, author, 1893-1962, commenting on the writings of Roscoe Pound, *A Realistic Jurisprudence*, 30 Col. L. Rev. 431, 435, 1930): At times the work purports to travel on the level of considered and buttressed scholarly discussion; at times on the level of bed-time stories for the tired bar.

Martin Luther: The Church was a "mouth-house" for speaking [oral preaching] and not a "pen-house" for writing.

English Chief Justice, Lord Manfield: Most disputes in the world arise from words.

Chief Justice John Marshall (1755-1835, Virginia statesman, Revolutionary War patriot, Chief Justice of the United States): Almost all compositions contain words, which, taken in their righteous sense, would convey a meaning different from that which is obviously intended. It is essential to just construction, that many words which import something excessive, should be understood in a more mitigated sense – in that sense which common usage justifies. The word "necessary" is of this description.... A thing may be necessary, very necessary, absolutely or indespensably necessary. *M'Culloch v. Maryland*, 4 Wheat 316, 4 L. ed. 579 (1819)

Chief Justice Marshall: Such is the character of human language, that no word conveys to the mind, in all situations, one single definite idea; and nothing is more common than to use words in a figurative sense. *M'Culloch v. Maryland*, 4 Wheat 316, 4 L. ed. 579 (1819)

Chief Justice Marshall: As men, whose intentions require no concealment, generally employ words which most directly and aptly express the ideas they intend to convey, and the people who adopted it, must be understood to have employed words in their natural sense, and to have intended what they have said. *Gibbons v. Ogden*, 9 Wheat 1, 6 L. ed. 23 (1824)

H.L. Mencken: To the man with any year for verbal delicacies – the man who searches painfully for the perfect word, and puts the way of saying nothing above the things said – there is in writing the constant joy of sudden discovery, of happy accident.

Michelle (WW II French Resistence agent, Nazi occupied France): Listen very carefully, I shall say this only once.

John Milton: Apt words have power to suage / The tumors of a troubled mind.

John Milton: To recount almighty works, / What words or tongue of seraph can suffice?

John Milton: Just deeds are the best answer to injurous words.

Montaigne: Saying is one thing, doing another.

Montaigne: Without doubt it is a delightful harmony when doing and saying go together.

Patrick O'Keefe (head of advertizing agency for the Society of American Florists, 1917): Say it with flowers.

Lawrence Olivier: We never converse, … we only confer.

Lawrence Olivier (about Lee Strazburg's "METHOD" of acting; EDITOR: METHOD ACTORS/TRIAL LAWYERS" talk about trial/acting, instead of practicing): DON'T OVER ANALYSE … JUST DO IT!!

P.J. O'Rourke: The U.S. Constitution is less than a quarter the length of the owner's manual for a 1998 Toyota Camry, and yet it has managed to keep 300 million of the world's most unruly, passionate and energetic people safe, prosperous and free.

Blaise Pascal: We are generally the better persuaded by the reasons we discover ourselves than by those given to us by others.

Mary Pettibone Poole: To repeat what others have said, requires education; to challenge it, requires brains.

Alexander Pope: Words are like leaves, and where they most abound, / Much fruit of sense beneath is rarely found.

Rabelais: To a man of understanding only a word is necessary.

Will Rogers: The way we got in the last war was through notes. We send so many that nations can't tell which one we mean. Our wars ought to be labeled, "Entered on account of too much penmanship."

Will Rogers: Syntax must be bad, having sin and tax in it.

Will Rogers: In Hollywood the woods are full of people that learned to write but evidently can't read. If they could read their stuff, they'd stop writing.

Will Rogers: The minute you read something and you can't understand it, you can be sure it was written by a lawyer. Then, if you give it to another lawyer to read and he don't know just what it means, then you can be sure it was drawn up by a lawyer. If its in a few words and is plain, and understandable only one way, it was written by a non-lawyer.

Will Rogers: Every time a lawyer writes something, he is not writing for posterity. He is writing so endless others of his craft can make a living out of trying to figure out what he said. 'Course perhaps he hadn't really said anything, that's what makes it hard to explain.

Franklin D. Roosevelt: During World War II, the Civil Defense Office of Far East had posters printed which read: "Illumination must be extinguished when premises are vacated." When he saw the signs, President Franklin Roosevelt exclaimed, "Damn, why can't they say "put out the lights when you leave"?"

Theodore Roosevelt: One of our defects as a nation is a tendency to use what have been called "weasel words." When a weasel sucks an egg, the meat is sucked out of the egg; and if you use a "weasel word" after another there is nothing left of the other.

Theodore Roosevelt: When, in 1906, Douglas MacArthur was the aid-de-camp to President Theodore Roosevelt, he asked him what he felt was the single factor that accounted for his popularity with the public. Roosevelt replied, "to put into words what is in their hearts and minds, but not in their mouths."

Theodore Roosevelt (1918): Every immigrant who comes here should be required within five years to learn English or leave the country.

Carl Sandburg: Look out how you use proud words. When you let proud words go, it is not easy to call them back. They wear long boots, hard boots.

John Selden: Syllables govern the world.

Seneca: Why should I spare words? They cost nothing.

Seneca: Words should be scattered like seed; no matter how small the seed may be, if it has once found favorable ground, it unfolds its strength.

William Shakespeare (*As You Like It*, Act I, iii): Celia: Not a word? Rosalind: Not one to throw at a dog.

William Shakespeare (*As You Like It*, Act III, ii): Answer me in one word.

William Shakespeare (*Comedy of Errors*, Act III, ii): Ill deeds are doubled with an evil word.

William Shakespeare (*Hamlet*, Act II, ii): POLONIUS: What do you read, my Lord? / HAMLET: words, words, words!

William Shakespeare (*Hamlet*, Act III, ii): Suit the action to the word, the word to the action.

William Shakespeare (*Hamlet*, Act III, iii): My words fly up, my thoughts remain below: / Words without thoughts, Never to heaven go.

William Shakespeare (*Henry V*, Act III, ii): Man of few words are the best man.

William Shakespeare (*Henry V*, Act IV, iii): Familiar in his mouth as household words.

William Shakespeare (*II Henry VI*, Act I, i): Let not his smoothing words Bewitch your hearts.

William Shakespeare (*Henry VIII*, Act III, ii): It is a kind of good deed to say well, / And yet words are no deeds.

William Shakespeare (*Julius Caesar*, Act V, i): Good words are better than bad strokes.

William Shakespeare (*King John*, Act II, ii): Zounds! I was never so bethump'd with words / Since I first called my brother's father dad..

William Shakespeare (*King Lear*, Act III, i): Few words, but to effect.

William Shakespeare (*Love's Labour's Lost*, Act V, i): He draweth out the thread of his verbosity finer than the staple of his argument.

William Shakespeare (*Love's Labour's Lost*, Act V, ii): The words of Mercury are harsh after the songs of Apollo.

William Shakespeare (*Macbeth*, Act IV, iii): I have words / That would be howl'd out in the desert air, / Where hearing should not latch them.

William Shakespeare (*Macbeth*, Act V, viii): I have no words: My voice is in my sword.

William Shakespeare (*The Merchant of Venice*, Act I, i): He speaks an infinite deal of nothing, more than any man of all Venice... his reasons are as two grains of wheat hid in two bushels of chaff; you shall seek all day ere you find them, and when you have them, they are not worth the search.

William Shakespeare (*The Merchant of Venice*, Act III, ii): Madam, you have bereft me of all words. / Only my blood speaks to you in my veins.

William Shakespeare (*The Merchant of Venice*, Act III, ii): Here are a few of the unpleasant'st words / That ever blotted paper!

William Shakespeare (*Much Ado About Nothing*, Act II, iii): His very words are a fantastical banquet, just so many strange dishes.

William Shakespeare (*Othello*, Act I, iii): But words are words; I never yet did hear / That the bruis'd heart was pierced through the ear.

William Shakespeare (*Othello*, Act III, iii): How long a time lies in one little word? / Four lagging winters, and Four wanton springs, / End in a word: Such is the breath of kings.

William Shakespeare (*Othello*, Act IV, ii): I understand a fury in your words, / But not the words.

William Shakespeare (*The Rape of Lucrece*, St. 146): Out, idle words, service to shallow fools! / Unprofitable sounds, weak arbitrators!

William Shakespeare (*Richard II*, Act I, iii): How long a time lies in one little word! Four lagging winters and four wanton springs / End in a word: such is the breath of kings.

William Shakespeare (*Richard II*, Act II, i): The tongues of dying men / Enforce attention, like deep harmony: / Where words are scarce, they are seldom spent in vain; / For they breathe truth, that breathe their words in pain.

William Shakespeare (*Richard III*, Act I, iii): Talkers are no good doers; be assured / We come to use our hands and not our tongues.

William Shakespeare (*Richard III*, Act III, i): I moralise two meanings in one word.

William Shakespeare (*Sonnets*, No. 76): So all my best is dressing old words new.

William Shakespeare (*The Tempest*, Act II, i): You cram these words into my ears against / The stomach of my sense.

William Shakespeare (*Titus Andronicus*, Act I, i): These words are razors to my wounded heart.

William Shakespeare (*Troilus and Cressida*, Act V, iii): Words pay no debts, give her deeds.

William Shakespeare (*Troilus and Cressida*, Act V, iii): Words, words, mere words, no matter from the heart.

William Shakespeare (*Twelfth Night*, Act III, i): Words are grown so false, I am loath to prove reason with them.

William Shakespeare (*Twelfth Night*, Act III, i): They that dally nicely with words may quickly make them wanton.

William Shakespeare (*The Two Gentlemen of Verona*, Act II, iv): A fine volley of words, gentlemen, and quickly shot off.

William Shakespeare (*The Two Gentlemen of Verona*, Act II, vii): His words are bonds, his oaths are oracles.

Isaac Bashevis Singer (Polish writer): Originality is not seen in single words or even sentences. Originality is the sum total of a man's thinking or his writing.

Socrates: Words are more plastic than wax.

Adlai Stevenson: Man does not live by words alone, despite the fact that sometimes he has to eat them.

Harlan F. Stone: Words, especially those of a constitution, are not to be read with such stultifying narrowness.

Jonathan Swift (*Gulliver's Travels: Houyhnhnms*, ch 5): A peculiar Cant and Jargon of their own, that no other Mortal can understand, and wherein all their laws are written.

Alfred Lord Tennyson: My words are only words, and moved / Upon the topmost froth of thought.

Alfred Lord Tennyson: Words, like Nature, half reveal / And half conceal the Soul within.

Terence: A word is enough for the wise.

Mother Teresa: Words which do not give the light of God increase the darkness.

James Bradley Thayer: That lawyer's Paradise is where all words have a fixed, precisely ascertained meaning.

J. Arthur Thomson: The most powerful factors in the world are clear ideas in the minds of energetic men of goodwill.

Henry David Thoreau: It is the man determines what is said, not the words.

James Thurber: There are two kinds of light—the glow that illumines, and the glare that obscures.

James Thurber: One of the favorite stories James Thurber told is of a conversation he had with a nurse while he was in a hospital. "What seven letter word has three u's in it?" He asked. The nurse thought for a while, and then replied, "I really don't know, but it must be unusual."

Mark Twain: One day, while shaving, Mark Twain cut himself. He recited his entire vocabulary of swear words. His wife, hoping to stun him, repeated all the swear words. Then, Twain turned to her and said, "you have the words, my dear, but you don't know the tune.

Mark Twain: A powerful agent is the right word. Whenever we come upon one of these intensely right words in a book or a newspaper the resulting effect is physical as well as spiritual, and electrically prompt.

Mark Twain: The difference between the right word and the almost-right word is the difference between the lightning and the lightning-bug.

Mark Twain: The right word may be effective, but no word was ever as effective as a rightly timed pause.

Mark Twain: They spell it Vinci and pronounce it Vinchy; foreigners always spell better than they pronounce.

Mark Twain: Words are only painted fire; a look is the fire itself.

Mark Twain: Some of his words were not Sunday-school words.... Some of those old American words do have a kind of a bully swing to them.

Mark Twain: Some of those old American words *do* have a kind of a bully swing to them; a man can *express* himself with 'em—a man can get what he wants to *say*, dontchuknow.

Mark Twain: As to the adjective, when in doubt strike it out.

Mark Twain: An average English word is four letters and a half. By hard, honest labor I've dug all the large words out of my vocabulary and shaved it down till the average is three and a half.... I never write "metropolis" for seven cents, because I can get the same money for "city." I never write "policeman," because I can get the same price for "cop." I never write "valetudinarian" at all, for not even hunger and wretchedness can humble me to the point where I will do a word like that for seven cents; I wouldn't do it for fifteen.

Mark Twain: Whenever the literary German dives into a sentence, that is the last you are going to see of him till he emerges on the other side of his Atlantic with his verb in his mouth.

UA: A proverb is a short sentence based on long experience

UA: Never engage in a war of wits with an unarmed person.

Virgil: He utters empty words, sound without thought.

Noah Webster (Connecticut lexicographer, 1758-1843): Language, as well as the faculty of speech, was the immediate gift of God.

Virginia Woolf: The word coining genius, as if thought plunged into a sea of words and came up dripping.

Voltaire: You who possess the talent of speaking much without saying anything.

WORDS OF WISDOM (See ADVICE; CHARLEY CHAN; MAXIMS)

WORK (See also PREPARATION)

Uncle Anthony: My grandfather told me "You find a job you love and you'll never work a day in your life."

Uncle Anthony: He works his gums talkin' himself into workin', then then he gums up the work!

Uncle Anthony: Yoh! Didja ever notice some people love to create an' cook, but dey don't like doin da clean up or dishes.

Aunt Mary Carlo: He/They are waitin' fer sometin' to turn up – he/they shoulda started a long time ago by rollin' up his/their sleeves.

Aunt Mary Carlo: She/he can't tell the difference 'tween woikin' uppa steam and makin' a fog.

Aunt Mary Carlo: Since he/she was hired – for dat short time – he/she has DISPLACED real genuine talent.

African Proverb: Every morning a lion wakes up and knows it must out run the slowest gazelle; every morning a gazelle wakes up and knows it must outrun the fastest lion. Whether you are a gazelle or a lion, when you wake up, you better start running!

Sir James Matthew Barrie: Nothing is really work unless you would rather be doing something else.

Billy Beane: My job (GM of Oakland Athletics baseball team) is like a soapbox derby – you build a car at the beginning of the year and after that you just push it down the hill and watch.

Henry Ward Beecher: Work is not the curse, but the drudgery is.

Simone de Beauvoir: A Darwinian nation of economic fitness abhors idleness, dependence, nonproductivity.

Max Beerbohm: No fine work can be done without concentration and self-sacrifice and toil and doubt.

Max Beerbohm: A man's work is rather the needful supplement to himself than the outcome of it.

St. Benedict of Nursia (480-543, motto of the Benedictine monks): To work is to pray.

Bhagavadgita: What is work? and what is not work? are questions that perplex the wisest of men.

Bible: Colossians 3:23: Whatsoever ye do, do it heartily, as to the Lord, and not unto men; Knowing that of the Lord ye shall receive the reward of the inheritance: for ye serve the Lord Christ.

Bible: I Corinthians, 3:13: Every man's work shall be made manifest.

Bible: Ecclesiastes 1:8: All things are full of labour; man cannot utter it: the eye is not satisfied with seeing, nor the ear Filled with hearing.

Bible: Ecclesiastes 2:10: My heart rejoiced in all my labour: and this was my portion of all my labour.

Bible: Ecclesiastes 3:13: Every man should eat and drink, and enjoy the good of all his labour, it is a gift of God.

Bible: Ecclesiasiastes 7:8: Better is the end of a thing than the beginning thereof.

Bible: Ecclesiastes 9:10: Whatsoever thy hand findeth to do, do it with thy might.

Bible: Exodus 20:8: Remember the sabbath day, to keep it holy. Six days shalt thou labour, and do all thy work: But the seventh day is the sabbath of the Lord thy God: in it thou shalt not do any work.

Bible: Exodus 34:21: Six days shalt thou work, but on the seventh day thou shalt rest.

Bible: Galatians 5:13: By love serve one another.

Bible: Galatians 6:9: Let us not be weary in well doing: for in due season we shall reap, if we faint not.

Bible: Genesis 2:3: God blessed the seventh day, and sanctified it: because that in it he had rested from all his work, which God created and made.

Bible: Genesis 3:16: In the sweat of thy face shalt thou eat bread, till thou return unto the ground; for out of it wast thou taken.

Bible: Genesis 3:19: In the sweat of thy face shalt thou eat bread.

Bible: Isaiah 6:8: Here am I; send me.

Bible: James 2:26: Faith without works is dead.

Bible: John 9:4: I must work the works of him that sent me, while it is day: the night cometh, when no man can work.

Bible: Luke 10:7: The labourer is worthy of his hire.

Bible: Luke 17:10: We are unprofitable servants: we have done that which was our duty to do.

Bible: Matthew 6:28: Consider the lilies of the field, how they grow; they toil not, neither do they spin: And yet I say unto you, That even Solomon in all his glory was not arrayed like one of these.
Bible: Matthew 7:20: By their fruits ye shall know them.
Bible: Philippians 2:16: I have not run in vain, neither laboured in vain.
Bible: Proverbs 6:6: Go to the ant, thou sluggard; consider her ways and be wise: / Which having no guide, overseer, or ruler, / Provideth her meat in the summer, and gathereth her food in the harvest.
Bible: Proverbs 14:23: In all labour there is profit.
Bible: Psalms, 104:23: Man goeth forth unto his work and to his labour until the evening.
Bible: Psalms 126:5: They that sow in tears shall reap in joy.
Bible: Romans 12:11: Not slothful in business; fervent in spirit; serving the Lord.
Bible: Romans 15:1: We then that are strong ought to bear the infirmities of the weak, and not to please ourselves.
Ambrose Bierce: APPETITE, n. An instinct thoughtfully implanted by Providence as a solution to the labor question.
Ambrose Bierce: LABOR, n. One of the processes by which A acquires property for B.
Ambrose Bierce: OVERWORK, n. A dangerous disorder affecting high public functionaries who want to go fishing.
Ambrose Bierce: SABBATH, n. A weekly festival having its origin in the fact that God made the world in six days and was arrested on the seventh.
Ambrose Bierce: What is worth doing is worth the trouble of asking somebody to do it.
Ambrose Bierce: A bad workman quarrels with the man who calls him that.
Jacob Bronowski: Whether our work is art or science or the daily work of society, it is only the form in which we explore our experience which is different.
John Mason Brown: Most people spend most of their days doing what they do not want to do in order to earn the right, at times, to do what they may desire.
Paul "Bear" Bryant: I don't hire anybody who's not brighter than I am. If they're not brighter than I am, I don't need them.
Georg Buchner: Everything under the son is work. Sweat, even in our sleep.
Samuel Butler: To do great work, a man must be very vital as well as very industrious.
Walter Camp (legendary Yale football coach): There is no substitute for hard work and effort beyond the call of mere duty. That is what strengthens the soul and ennobles one's character.
Albert Camus: There is dignity in work only when it is work freely accepted.
Thomas Carlyle: Blessed is the man that has found his work. One monster there is in the world, the idle man.
Thomas Carlyle: There is always hope in a man who actually and earnestly works. – In idleness alone is there perpetual despair.
Thomas Carlyle: He that will not work according to his faculty, let him perish according to his necessity: there is no law juster than that.
Thomas Carlyle: Every noble work is at first impossible.
Thomas Carlyle: He that can work is a born king of something.
Andrew Carnegie: Concentration is my motto – first honesty, then industry, then concentration.
Cervantes: Which I have earned with the sweat of my brows.
Alexander Chase: He who considers his work beneath him will be above doing it well.
Chinese Proverb: One generation plants the trees; another gets the shade.
Chinese Proverb: There are many paths to the top of the mountain, but the view is always the same.
Sir Winston Churchill (May 13, 1940): "Blood, toil, tears and sweat...."
Sir Winston Churchill: We shall not fail or falter; we shall not weaken or tire... **Give us the tools and we will finish the job.**
Sir Winston Churchill: Continuous effort - not strength or intelligence - is the key to unlocking our potential..
Sir Winston Churchill: To build may have to be the slow and laborious task of years. To destroy can be the thoughtless act of a single day.

Sir Winston Churchill: Every day you may make progress. Every step may be fruitful. Yet there will stretch out before you an ever-lengthening, ever-ascending, ever-improving path. You know you will never get to the end of the journey. But this, so far from discouraging, only adds to the joy and glory of the climb.

Arthur C. Clarke: The only way of discovering the limits of the possible is to venture a little way past them into the impossible.

Colette: We only do well the things we like doing.

Calvin Coolidge: No man ever listened himself out of a job.

Robert Copeland: To get something done, a committee should consist of no more than three men, two of whom are absent.

Richard Cumberland (English Bishop, 1718): It is better to wear out than to rust out.

Clarence Day: The ant is knowing and wise; but he doesn't know enough to take a vacation.

Joseph Conrad: A man is a worker. If he is not that he is nothing.

Leonardo da Vinci: The greatest geniuses accomplish more when they work less.

Thomas Dekker: Honest labor bears a lovely face.

Dostoevsky: To crush, to annihilate a man utterly, to inflict on him the most terrible of punishments so that the most ferocious murderer would shudder at it and dread it before hand, one need only give him work of an absolutely, completely useless and irrational character.

Dostoevsky: Originality and the feeling of one's own dignity are achieved only through work and struggle.

Finley Peter Dunne: Wurrk is wurruk if ye're paid to do it an' it's pleasure if ye pay to be allowed to do it.

Dutch Proverb: Roasted pigeons will not fly into one's mouth.

Thomas Alva Edison: As a cure for worrying, work is better than whiskey.

Thomas A. Edison: I never did anything worth doing by accident, nor did any of my inventions come by accident.

Thomas A. Edison: Results! Why, man, I have gotten a lot of results. I know several thousand things that won't work.

Havelock Ellis: Where there is most labor there is not always most life.

Ralph Waldo Emerson: We put our love where we have put our labor.

Ralph Waldo Emerson: The life of labor does not make men, but drudges.

Ralph Waldo Emerson: It is the privilege of any human work which is well done to invest the doer with a certain haughtiness.

Ralph Waldo Emerson: Every man's task is his life-preserver.

English Proverb: Practice makes perfect.

Estonian Proverb: The work will teach you how to do it.

Euphemisms (www.wikipedia.com): Euphemisms are popular in job titles. Many normal jobs have complicated titles that make the jobs sound more important, or skilled, than the common names imply. Many of these euphemisms may include words such as engineer, though in fact the people who do the job are not accredited in any form of engineering (in many jurisdictions it is technically illegal to use the term without a currently valid state certification, though widely unenforced). Extreme cases, such as sanitation engineer for janitor are cited humorously more often than they are used seriously. Less extreme cases, such as custodian for janitor, are considered terms of respect rather than euphemisms. These euphemisms can include, but are by no means limited to:

Binman - Waste Removal Officer (UK) or Sanitation Engineer (US)
Blacksmith - Equine Chiropodist
Bookkeeper – Office Manager
Cashier - Sales Assistant or Retail Representative
Cleaner - Domestic Assistant
Driver - Chauffeur
File clerk (in law office) – Legal Assistant
Insurance Company Defense Medical Examiner – Independent Medical Examiner
Investigator – Accident Reconstructionist
Lorry driver - Logistics Manager
Rubbish Collector - Garbiologist
Security guard - Loss Prevention Officer

Secretary - Administrative Assistant (particularly US)
Secretary (in law office) – Paralegal
Typist (in law office) – Legal Secretary (see Secretary)
Window washer - Vision Clearance Engineer

Euripides: Toil, says the proverb, is the sire of fame.

Frantz Fanon: If the building of a bridge does not enrich the awareness of those who work on it, then that bridge ought not to be built.

William Faulkner: One of the saddest things is that the only thing a man can do for eight hours a day, day after day, is work. You can't eat eight hours a day nor drink for eight hours a day nor make love for eight hours.

Berie Charles Forbes: Work is the meat of life, pleasure the dessert.

Malcolm Forbes: Diamonds are nothing more than chunks of coal that stuck to their jobs.

Henry Ford: He who would really benefit mankind must reach him through their work.

Benjamin Franklin: Industry need not wish, and he that lives upon hopes will die fasting. There are no gains without pains. He that hath a trade hath an estate, and he that hath a calling hath an office of profit and honor; but then the trade must be worked at, and the calling followed, or neither the estate nor the office will enable us to pay our taxes. If we are industrious, we shall never starve; for, at the workingman's house hunger looks in, but dares not enter. Nor will the bailiff or the constable enter, for industry pays debts, while idleness and neglect increase them.

French Proverb: Feather by feather the goose can be plucked.

French Proverb: One flower will not make a garland.

Eric Fromm: The danger of the past was that men became slaves. The danger of the future is that man may become robots.

Margaret Fuller: Men for the sake of getting a living forget to live.

John Kenneth Galbraith: Meetings are indispensible when you don't want to do anything.

Mohandas Karamchand Mahatma Gandhi: Whatever you do will be insignificant, but it is very important that you do it.

John Gardner: If one defines "dropout" to mean a person who has given up serious effort to meet his responsibilities, then every business office, government agency, golf club and university faculty would yield its quota.

José Ortega y Gasset: An unemployed existence is a worse negation of life than death itself. Because to live means to have something definite to do....

John Gay: Fortune may find a pot, but your own industry must make it boil.

Henry George: The man who gives me employment, which I must have or suffer, that man is my master, let me call him what I will.

George and Ira Gershwin (1937 song title): Nice Work If You Can Get It.

German Proverb: Who begins too much accomplishes little.

German Proverb: God gives the nuts, but he doesn't crack them.

Kahlil Gibran: All work is empty save when there is love.

Kahlil Gibran: Work is love made visible. And if you cannot work with love but only with distaste, it is better that you should leave your work and sit at the gate of the temple and take alms of those who work for joy.

Goethe: Most people work the greater part of their time for a mere living; and the little freedom which remains to them so troubles them that they use every means of getting rid of it.

Goethe: That hand that has the week-day broom to ply, / On Sunday gives the pleasantest caresses.

Oliver Goldsmith: Like the bee, we should make our industry our amusement.

Maxim Gorky: When work is a pleasure, life is a joy! When work is a duty, life is slavery.

David Grayson: Human happiness is the true odour of growth, the sweet exhaltation of work.

Michael Harrington: More and more university students are convinced that work in American society is morally empty, aesthetically ugly, and, under conditions of automation, economically unnecessary.

Hegel: Serious occupation is labor that has reference to some want.

Robert Heinlein: Progress isn't made by early risers. It's made by lazy men trying to find easier ways to do nothing.

Hericlitus (500 B.C.): It is weariness to keep toiling at the same things so that one becomes ruled by them.

John Heywood (*The Proverbs of John Heywood,* 1546): Rome was not built in a day.

John Heywood (*The Proverbs of John Heywood,* 1546): Two heads are better than one.

John Heywood (*The Proverbs of John Heywood,* 1546): Many hands make light work.

Oliver Wendell Holmes, Jr.: As I wrote many years ago, the mode in which the inevitable comes to pass is through effort. Consciously or unconsciously we all strive to make the kind of world we like.

Homer: To labor is a lot of man below;/ And when Jove gave us life, he gave us woe.

Edgar Watson Howe: There is only one thing for a man to do who is married to a woman who enjoys spending money and that is to enjoy earning it.

Elbert Hubbard: The best preparation for good work tomorrow is to do good work today.

Elbert Hubbard: Do your work with your whole heart and you will succeed—there is so little competition!

Elbert Hubbard: Folks who never do any more than they get paid for, never get paid for any more than they do.

Victor Hugo: A man is not idle because he is absorbed in thought. There is a visible labor and there is an invisible labor.

Albus Huxley: Work is prayer. Work is also stink. Therefore stink is prayer.

Indian Proverb (About laziness): It is better to sit down than to stand, it is better to lie down than to sit, but death is the best of all.

Irish Proverb: Two shorten the road.

Irish Proverb: Two thirds of the work is the semblance.

Irish Proverb: A trade not properly learned is an enemy.

Irish Proverb: The work praises the man.

Irish Proverb: It is the good horse that draws its own cart.

Irish Proverb: It takes time to build castles. Rome wan not built in a day.

Irish Proverb: Mere words do not feed the friars.

Italian Proverb: It is a poor art that maintains not the artisan.

Harold Janeen: I don't believe in just ordering people to do things, you have to sort of grab an oar and row with them.

Thomas Jefferson: I'm a great believer in luck, and I find the harder I work, the more I have of it.

Samuel Johnson: It very seldom happens to a man that his business is his pleasure.

Henry Kaiser: When your work speaks for itself, don't interrupt!

Helen Keller: The world is sown with good; but unless I turn my gland thoughts into practical living and till my own field, I cannot reap a kernel of the good.

Charles F. Kettering: Believe and act as if it were impossible to fail.

Jerome Kern (song *"Old Man River"* from musical *Showboat*): Here we all work on da Mississippi, here we all work 'till de Judgement Day ... tote dat barge, lift dat bale, ya get a little drunk, and ya lands in jail.

Charles Lamb: Who first invented work and bound the free / And holiday-rejoicing spirit down?

Doug Larson: Accomplishing the impossible means only that the boss will add it to your regular duties.

Leonardo da Vinci: Thou, O God, dost sell us all good things at the price of labor.

Abraham Lincoln (Second Inaugural Speech, March 4, 1865): ... With malice toward none; with charity for all; with firmness in the right as God gives us to see the right, let us strive on to finish the work we are in (Editor: Civil War); to bind up the nations wounds; to care for him who shall have bourne the battle, and for his widow and his orphan; to do all which may achieve and cherish a just and lasting peace among ourselves and with all nations.

John Locke: Where there is no desire, there will be no industry.

James Russell Lowell: No man is born into the world whose work / Is not born with him; there is always work, / And tools to work withal, for those who will.

Don Marquis: When a man tells you he got rich through hard work, ask him *whose*?

Karl Marx: Constant labor of one uniform kind destroys the intensity and flow of a man's animal spirits, which find recreation and delight in mere change of activity.

Ogden Nash (American poet): How Sunday into Monday melts!

Ogden Nash (American poet, 1902-1971, *Introspective Reflection*): I would live all my life in nonchalance and insouciance / Were it not for making a living, which is rather a nouciance.

Waslaw Nijinsky: God does not want men to overtax themselves. He wants men to be happy.

C. Northcote Parkinson (Parkinson's Law, 1962): Work expands to fill the time available for its completion.

Norman Vincent Peale: Think enthusiastically about everything; but especially about your job. If you do, you'll put a touch of glory in your life. If you love your job with enthusiasm, you'll shake it to pieces. You'll love it into greatness.

William Penn: Love labor; for if thou dost not want it for food, thou mayest for physict. It is wholesome for thy body and good for thy mind.

Persian Proverb: A broken hand works, but not a broken heart.

Charles Peters: Beaurocrats write memorandua both because they appear to be busy when they are writing, and because the memos, once written, immediately become proof that they were busy.

Pablo Picasso: Work is a necessity for man. Man invented the alarm clock.

Pablo Picasso: Inspiration does exist, but it must find you working.

Josiah Quincy: When you have a number of disagreeable duties to perform, always do the most disagreeable first.

Anna Quindlen: You cannot be really first-rate at your work if your work is all you are.

Ronald Reagan: It (unemployment insurance) provides prepaid vacations for a segment of our country which has made it a way of life.

Theodore Roethke: What we need is more people who specialize in the impossible.

Will Rogers: Plans get you into things but you got to work your way out.

Will Rogers: It's not what you pay a man, but what he costs you that counts.

Will Rogers: If all the time consumed in attending dinners and luncheons was consumed in some work, the production of this country would be doubled.

Theodore Roosevelt: Far and away the best prize that life offers is the chance to work hard at work worth doing.

Theodore Roosevelt: I don't pity any man who does hard work worth doing. I admire him. I pity the creature who doesn't work, at whichever end of the social scale he may regard himself as being.

Theodore Roosevelt: A man can be freed from the necessity of work only by the fact that he or his fathers before him have worked to a good purpose.

Leo Rosten: MITZVAH: (plural *mitzvot*): Hebrew: "commandment." (1) Commandment; divine commandment. (2) A meritorious act, a "good work," a truly virtuous, kind, ethical deed. *Mitzvah* is second only to *Torah* in the vocabulary of Judaism. *Mitzvot* are of various kinds: those of positive performance (e.g., caring for the widow and orphan), and those of negative resolve (e.g., not accepting a bribe); and those between man and God (fasting on *Yom Kippur*) and those between man and man (paying a servant promptly). Mitzvoth are regarded as profound obligations, but must be performed not from a sense of duty but with "a joyous heart." There are 613 separate *mitzvot* listed in the *Sefer Mitzvot Gadol*, of which 248 are positive and 365 negative. Maimonides listed all the *mitzvot* in his *Book of the Mitzvot*; he remarked that the man who performed only one of the 613 deserved salvation – *if* he did so not to win credit, but entirely for its own sake. The potential number of *mitzvot* is endless. Israel Zangwell called *mitzvot* the Jews' "sacred sociology."

John Ruskin: It is only by labor that thought can be made healthy, and only by thought that labor can be made happy, and the two cannot be separated with impunity.

John Ruskin: Labor without joy is base. Labor without sorrow is base. Sorrow without labor is base. Joy without labor is base.

Russian Proverb: Pray to God, but keep rowing to the shore.

Scottish Proverb: Better wear out shoes than sheets.

William Shakespeare (*Cymbeline*, Act II, iv): A piece of work / So bravely done, so rich, that it did strive / In workmanship and value.

William Shakespeare (*Cymbeline*, Act V, v): There's other work in hand.

William Shakespeare (*Hamlet*, Act I, i): Why such impress of shipwrights whose sore task / Does not divide the Sunday from the week.

William Shakespeare (*I Henry IV*, Act I, ii): Why, Hal, 'tis my vocation, Hal: 'tis no sin for a man to labour in his vocation.

William Shakespeare (*King Lear*, Act I, i): Nothing can come of nothing.

William Shakespeare (*Love's Labour's Lost*, Act IV, iii): Why, universal plodding prisons up / The nimble spirits in the arteries; / As motion, and long-during action, tires / The sinewy vigour of the traveller.

William Shakespeare (*Macbeth*, Act II, iii): The labour we delight in, physics pain.

William Shakespeare (*Midsummer Night's Dream*, Act V, ii): Now the hungry lion roars, / And the wolf behowls the moon; / Whilst the heavy ploughman snores, / All with weary tasks fore-done.

William Shakespeare (*Sonnets*, 111.6, 1609): My nature is subdued / To what it works in, like the dyer's hand.

William Shakespeare (*Timon of Athens*, Act III, ii): Policy sits above conscience.

William Shakespeare (*Troilus and Cressida*, Act I, i): I have had my labour for my travel.

William Shakespeare (*Twelfth Night*, Act I, v): Excellently done, if God did all.

William Shakespeare (*Venus and Adonis*, l. 419): The colt that's back'd and burden'd being young, / Loseth his pride and never waxeth strong.

George Bernard Shaw: A day's work is a day's work, neither more nor less, and the man who does it needs a day's sustenance, a night's repose, and due leisure, whether he be painter or ploughman.

Upton Sinclair: It is difficult to get a man to understand something when his job depends on not understanding it.

Samuel Smiles (Scottish writer, 1812-1904): If you have great talents, industry will improve them; if but moderate abilities, industry will supply their deficiencies.

Spanish Proverb: Tomorrow is often the busiest day of the week.

Alfred, Lord Tennyson: All things have rest: why should we toil alone, / We only toil, who are the first of things, / And make perpetual moan.

Mother Teresa: I am not sure exactly what heaven will be like, but I don't know that when we die and it comes time for God to judge us, he will NOT ask, How many good things have you done in your life?, rather he will ask, How much LOVE did you put into what you did?

Mother Teresa: We are all pencils in the hand of God.

Mother Teresa: I am a little pencil in the hand of a writing God who is sending a love letter to the world.

Mother Teresa: There is always the danger that we may just do the work for the sake of the work. This is where the respect and the love and the devotion come in - that we do it to God, ... and that's why we try to do it as beautifully as possible.

Mother Teresa: We, the unwilling,led by the unknowing,are doing the impossible for the ungrateful. We have done so much,for so long,with so little,we are now qualified to do anything with nothing.

Mother Teresa: It is not the magnitude of our actions but the amount of love that is put into them that matters.

Mother Teresa: Love begins at home, and it is not how much we do... but how much love we put in that action.

Mother Teresa: We ourselves feel that what we are doing is just a drop in the ocean. But the ocean would be less because of that missing drop.

Mother Teresa: The miracle is not that we do this work, but that we are happy to do it.

Henry David Thoreau: Lo! Men have become the tools of their tools.

Henry David Thoreau: Those who work much do not work hard.

Henry David Thoreau: Is not enough to be busy ...the question is: what are we busy about?

Henry David Thoreau: If you have built castles in the air, your work need not be lost; that is where they should be. Now put foundations under them.

Arnold Toynbee: The supreme accomplishment is to blur the line between work and play.

Mark Twain: Let us be grateful to Adam our benefactor. He cut us out of the "blessing" of idleness and won for us the "curse" of labor.

Mark Twain: The highest pleasure to be got out of freedom, and having nothing to do, is labor.

Mark Twain: I have often noticed that you shun exertion. There comes the difference between us. I court exertion. I love work. Why, sir, when I have a piece of work to perform, I go away to myself, sit down in the shade, and muse over the coming enjoyment.

Mark Twain: He (Tom Sawyer) had discovered a great law of human action, without knowing it—namely, that in order to make a man or a boy covet a thing, it is only necessary to make the thing difficult to attain. If he had been a great and wise philosopher, like the writer of this book, he would now have comprehended that Work consists of whatever anybody is *obliged* to do and that Play consists of whatever a body is not obliged to do.

John Updike: Any activity becomes creative when the doer cares about doing it right, or doing it better.

Voltaire: Work spares us from three great evils: boredom, vice, and need.

Kurt Vonnegut: Another flaw in human character is that everybody wants to build and nobody wants to do maintenance.

Booker T. Washington (Atlanta Exposition, Sept. 18, 1895): No race can prosper till it learns there is as much dignity in tilling a field as in writing a poem.

John Webster: The chiefest action for a man of spirit is never to be out of action; the soul was never put into the body to stand still.

Whately: A man who gives his children habits of industry provides for them better than by giving them a fortune.

Woodrow Wilson: No task, rightly done, is truly private. It is part of the world's work.

Zimmerman: Many are discontented with the name idler, who are nevertheless content to do worse than nothing.

WORK LIFE (See AGE/AGING; WORK)

WORTH (See also CHARACTER)

Uncle Anthony: Ya never know how much ya care for or love somebody 'till they go away.

Uncle Anthony: What your worth to your family ain't figured in salaries, bonuses and health benefits.

Uncle Anthony: Priceless don't mean worthless. Just 'cause ya can't find a price tag or a stock market quote for pain and suffering (or any intangible "non-economic" damages such as life's lost pleasures) don't mean their worthless.

Aunt Mary Carlo: Whatsa life woith (worth?) – it ain't a question fer some economist to figger.

William Alexander: A pilot's part in calms cannot be spy'd, / In dangerous times true worth is only try'd.

Amiel: It is not what he has, nor even what he does, which directly expresses the worth of the man, but what he is.

St. Augustine of Hippo (Latin Father of the Catholic Church, Bishop, religious writer, 354-430 AD): The sufficiency of my merit, is to know that my merit is not sufficient.

Francis Bacon: Merit is worthier than fame.

John Barth: *Nothing* is intrinsically valuable; the value of everything is attributed to it, assigned to it from outside the thing itself, by people.

Henry Ward Beecher: He is rich or poor according to what he *is*, not according to what he *has*.

Bible: Luke 6:43; Matthew 7:17: Every good tree bringeth forth good fruit; but a corrupt tree bringeth forth evil fruit

Bible: Luke 12:7; Matthew 10:31: Ye are of more value than many sparrows.

Bible: Luke 15:4; Matthew 18:12: If a man have an hundred sheep, and one of them be gone astray, doth he not leave the ninety and nine, and goeth into the mountains, and seeketh that which is gone astray?

Bible: Malachi 2:10: Have we not all one father? Hath not one God created us?

Bible: Matthew 5:13: Ye are the salt of the earth.

Bible: Matthew 7:6: Give not that which is holy unto dogs, neither cast ye your pearls before swine.

Bible: Proverbs 16:31: The hoary head is a crown of glory, if it be found in the way of righteousness.

Bible: Proverbs 25:27: For men to search their own glory is not glory.

Bible: Proverbs 27:2: Let another man praise thee, and not thine own mouth; a stranger, and not thine own lips.

Ambrose Bierce: VIRTUES, n. pl. Certain absentions.

Ambrose Bierce: MUGWUMP, n. In politics one afflicted with self-respect and addicted to the vice of independence. A term of contempt.

Samuel Butler: 'Tis virtue, wit, and worth, and all / That men divine and sacred call; / For what is worth, in anything, / But so much money as 't will bring?

R.O. Cambridge: What is the worth of anything / But for the happiness 't will bring?

Albert Camus: The rebel can never find peace. He knows what is good and, despite himself, does evil. The value which supports him is never given to him once and for all

Cato: What is not needed is dear at a farthing.

Charles Churchill: The little merit man can plead / In doing well, dependeth still / Upon his power of doing ill.

Sir Winston Churchill: It was the nation and the race dwelling all round the globe that had the lion's heart. I had the luck to be called upon to give the roar.

Sir Winston Churchill: Never in the field of human conflict was so much owed by so many to so few.

Sir Winston Churchill: Sure I am of this, that you have only to endure to conquer. You have only to persevere to save yourselves.

Sir Winston Churchill: We make a living by what we get, but we make a life by what we give.

Charles Caleb Colton: True friendship is like sound health; the value of it is seldom known until it be lost.

Thomas D'Ufrey: The worth of the thing is known by its want.

Albert Einstein: Try not to become a man of success, but rather try to become a man of value.

Ralph Waldo Emerson: A man passes for that he is worth. What he is engraves itself on his face in letters of light.

Ralph Waldo Emerson: Let him go where he will, he can only find so much beauty or worth as he carries.

Ralph Waldo Emerson: All great masters are chiefly distinguished by the power of adding a second, a third, and perhaps a fourth step in a continuous line. Many a man had taken the first step. With every additional step you enhance immensely the value of you first.

English Proverb: A bird in the hand is worth two in a bush.

English Proverb: They who love most are least valued.

Henry Fielding: Worth begets in base minds, envy; in great souls, emulation.

F. Scott Fitzgerald: The world is always curious, and people become valuable merely for their inaccessibility.

Sidonie Gabrielle: No temptation can ever be measured by the value of its object.

Greek Proverb: It's not good for all of our wishes to be fulfilled. Through sickness, we recognize the value of health; through evil, the value of good; through hunger, the value of food; through exertion, the value of rest.

Thomas Hobbes: The "value" or "worth" of the man, is, as of all other things, his price; that is to say, so much as would be given for the use of his power.

Thomas Hood: Give honest worth its honest praise.

Thomas Hood: Farewell! I did not know thy worth; / But thou art gone, and now 'tis priz'd; / So angels walk'd unknown on earth, / But when they flew were recogniz'd.

Horace: Hidden worth differs little from buried indolence.

Haaretz: Distinguish between baseness and merit, not by dissent, but by purity of life and hard.

William James: Where quality is the thing sought after, the thing of supreme quality is cheap, whaever the price one has to pay for it.

Samuel Johnson: Slow rises worth, by poverty depress'd: / But here more slow, where all are slaves to gold, / Where looks are merchandise, and smiles are sold.

LaRochefoucauld: There are people who disgust with merit, and others who please with faults.

LaRochefoucauld: Nature makes merit and fortune uses it.

LaRochefoucauld: Our merit wins the esteem of honest men, and our lucky star that of the public.

LaRochefoucauld: The world more often rewards the appearance of merit than merit itself.

LaRochefoucauld: Eminence is to merit what dress is to beauty.

LaRochefoucauld: There is merit without eminence, but there is no eminence without merit.

J. R. Lowell: Life is continually weighing us in very sensitive scales, and telling every one of us precisely what his real weight is to the last grain of dust.

Molière: Things are only worth what one makes them worth.

Oriental Proverb: If you wish your merit to be known, acknowledge that of other people.

Ovid: Not because you were worthy, but because I was indulgent.
Plautus: Worthy things happen to the worthy.
Alexander Pope: Worth makes the man, and want of it the fellow, / The rest is all but leather or prunella.
Alexander Pope: Beauties in vain their pretty eyes may roll; / Charms strike the sight, but merit wins the soul.
Francis Quales: The sufficiency of merit is to know that my merit is not sufficient.
Henry John Palmerston: What is merit? The opinion one man entertains of another.
Plautus: We should try to succeed by merit, not by favor.
Publilius Syrus: Everything is worth what its purchaser will pay for it.
Rabelais: So much is a man worth as he is themes himself.
Edwin Arlington Robinson: I never knew the worth of him / Until he died.
Will Rogers: It's not what you pay a man, but what he costs you that counts.
Richard Savage: Worth is thy worth in every rank admired.
Seneca: Great things cannot be bought for small sums.
Scottish Proverb: We'll never know the worth of water till the well go dry.
William Shakespeare (*Cymbeline*, Act V, v): They are worthy To inlay heaven with stars.
William Shakespeare (*I Henry IV*, Act I, ii): O, if men were to be saved by merit, what hole in hell were hot enough for him?
William Shakespeare (*Henry VIII*, Act I, i): The force of his own merit makes his way.
William Shakespeare (*King John*, Act II, i): I am not worth this coil that's made for me.
William Shakespeare (*King Lear*, Act IV, ii): Goneril: I have been worth the whistle. Albany: You are not worth the dust which the rude wind blows in your face.
William Shakespeare (*Measure for Measure*, Act I, i): Let there be some more test made of my metal, / Before so noble and so great a figure / Be stamped upon it.
William Shakespeare (*Merchant of Venice*, Act II, ix): O, that estates, degrees, and offices, / Were not deriv'd corruptly! And that clear honour / Were purchas'd by the merit of the wearer.
William Shakespeare (*Romeo and Juliet*, Act II, vi): They are but beggars that can count their worth.
William Shakespeare (*Sonnet XXXIX*): O, how thy worth with manners may I sing' / When thou art all the better part of me? / What can mine own praise to mine own self bring? / And what is 't but mine own when I praise thee?
William Shakespeare (*Troilus and Cressida*, Act II, ii): What is aught, but as 'tis valued?
Alfred Lord Tennyson: There is not one among my gentlewomen / Were fit to wear your slipper for a glove.
Henry David Thoreau: All good things are cheap: all bad are very dear.
Henry David Thoreau: There is no value in life except what you choose to place upon it and no happiness in any place except what you bring to it yourself.
Dale E. Turner: Why is it that, as we grow older, we are so reluctant to change? It is not so much that new ideas are painful, for they are not. It is that old ideas are seldom entirely false, but have truth, great truth in them. The justification for conservatism is the desire to preserve the truths and standards of the past; its dangers, of which we are seldom aware, is that in preserving those values, we may miss the infinitely greater riches that lie in the future.
Mark Twain: To do something, say something, see something, before *anybody* else—these are things that confer a pleasure compared with which other pleasures are tame and commonplace, other ecstasies cheap and trivial.
Edmund Waller: All human things / Of the dearest value hang on slender strings.
Charles Dudley Warner: There is no such thing as absolute value in this world. You can only estimate what a thing is worth to you.
Jeanette Winterson: What you risk reveals what you value.

WOUNDS (See PAIN)

WRITERS/WRITING (See BOOKS; WORDS)

WRONGDOING (See also EVIL)

Uncle Anthony: That was no "pure accident" that happened to your client. An "accident" is something nobody can do nuthin' about. But to me a wrong is something that can be prevented. It ain't no "Act of God," and to call something that can be avoided an "accident" is just to try to cover up what is wrong by making it look innocent.

Uncle Anthony: Y'know a whole lot of the damage (or "wrongs") done to some folks are self inflicted wounds.

Aunt Mary Carlo: Maybe dat guys not evil, but da stuff he does sure are evil.

Freda Adler: Stripped of ethical rationalizations and philosophical pretensions, a crime is anything that a group in power chooses to prohibit.

Freda Adler: (Rape) is the only crime in which the victim becomes the accused.

Aeschylus: The act of evil / breeds of others to follow, / young sins in its own likeness.

Aristotle: A bad man can do one million times more harm than a beast.

Aristotle: It makes no difference whether a good man has defrauded a bad men or a bad men defrauded a good man, or whether a good or bad men has committed adultery: the law can look only to the amount of damage done.

Aristotle: One may go wrong in many different ways, but right only in one, which is why it is easy to fail and difficult to succeed—easy to miss the target and difficult to hit it.

William Attwood (1960): *Payola* is this year's new word. It doesn't sound as ugly as *bribe*, but it means the same thing.

Stephen Vincent Benet: Some men wish evil and accomplish it / But most men, when they work in that machine / Just let it happen somewhere in the wheels. / The fault is no decisive villainous knife / But the dull saw that is the routine mind.

Bible: 1 Corinthians 15:33: Evil communications corrupt good manners.

Bible: Deuteronomy 32:5: They are a perverse and crooked generation.

Bible: Ecclesiastes 9:18: One sinner destroyeth much good.

Bible: Ecclesiastes 21:10: The way of sinners is made plain with stones but at the end thereof is the pit of hell.

Bible: Genesis 8:21: The imagination of man's heart is evil from his youth.

Bible: Isaiah 1:18: Though your sins be as scarlet, they shall be white as snow.

Bible: James 1:15: When lust hath conceived, it bringeth forth sin: and sin, when it is finished, bringeth forth death.

Bible: James 4:17: To him that knoweth to do good, and doeth it not, to him it is sin.

Bible: James 5:20: The error of his way.

Bible: 1 John 1:8: If we say that we have no sin, we deceive ourselves, and the truth is not in us.

Bible: 1 John 3:8: He that committeth sin is of the devil.

Bible: John, 3:20: Everyone that doeth evil hateth the light.

Bible: John 8:7: He that is without sin among you, let him first cast a stone.

Bible: Mark 6:11; Matthew 10:15: It shall be more tolerable for Sodom and Gomorrha in the day of judgment than for that city.

Bible: Matthew 6:34: Sufficient unto the day is the evil thereof.

Bible: Matthew 12:35: A good man out of the good treasure of the heart bringeth forth good things: and an evil man out of the evil treasure bringeth forth evil things.

Bible: Numbers 35:33: Ye shall not pollute the land which ye are.

Bible: Proverbs 4:14: Enter not into the path of the wicked, and go not in the way of evil men.

Bible: Proverbs 4:19: the way of the wicked is as darkness: they know not at what they stumble.

Bible: Proverbs 8:13: The fear of the Lord is to hate evil.

Bible: Proverbs 11:5: The wicked shall fall by his own wickedness.

Bible: Proverbs 11:21: The wicked shall not be unpunished.

Bible: Psalms 37:1: Fret not thyself because of evildoers, neither be thou envious against the workers of iniquity. For they shall soon be cut down like the grass, and wither as the green herb

Bible: Psalms 130:3: If thou, Lord, shouldest mark iniquities, O Lord, who shall stand?

Bible: Romans 5:12: Wherefore, as by one man sin entered into the world, and death by sin; and so death passed upon all men, for that all have sinned.
Bible: Romans 6:23: The wages of sin is death.
Bible: Romans 7:15: For that which I do I allow not: for what I would, that do I not: but what I hate, that do I ... For the good that I would I do not, but the evil which I would not, that I do.
Bible: Romans 12:17: Recompense to no man evil for evil.
Bible: Romans 14:14: There is nothing unclean of itself: but to him that esteemeth any thing to be unclean, to him it is unclean.
Bible: 1 Thessalonians 5:22: Abstain from all appearace of evil.
Ambrose Bierce: APOLOGIZE, v.i. To lay the foundation for a future offence.
Ambrose Bierce: FELON, n. A person of greater enterprise than discretion, who in embracing an opportunity has formed an unfortunate attachment.
Ambrose Bierce: KLEPTOMANIAC, n. A rich thief.
Ambrose Bierce: MISCREANT, n. A person of the highest degree of unworth. Etymologically, the word means unbeliever, and its present signification may be regarded as theology's noblest contribution to the development of our language.
Ambrose Bierce: MISDEMEANOR, n. An infraction of the law having less dignity than a felony and constituting no claim to admittance into the best criminal society....
Boileau: Often the fear of one evil leads one into a worse.
Marlon Brando: If we are not our brother's keeper, let us at least not be his executioner.
Van Wyck Brooks: If men were basically evil, who would bother to improve the world instead of giving it up as a bad job at the outset?
Robert Buchanan: But, dash my buttons, though you put it strong. / It's my opinion you're more right than wrong.
Edmund Burke: The councils of pusillanimity very rarely put off, whilst they are always sure to aggravate, the evils from which they would fly.
Hughie Cannon (song, 1902): Won't you come home, Bill Bailey, / Won't you come home?... I knows I've done you wrong.
Thomas Carlyle: Evil, once manfully fronted, ceases to be evil.
Thomas Carlyle: The deadliest sin were the consciousness of no sin.
Marcus Cato: I prefer to do right and get no thanks, rather than do wrong and get no punishment.
Cato the Younger: The authors of great evils know best how to remove them.
Charles Churchill: In full, fair tide let information flow; / That evil is half cured whose cause we know.
Sir Winston Churchill (May 13, 1940): What is our policy? ... to wage war against a monstrous tyranny, never surpassed in the dark, lamentable catalogue of human crime.
Sir Wnston Churchill: It is all right to rat, but you can't re-rat.
Sir Winston Churchill: I have been brought up and trained to have the utmost contempt for people who get drunk. [EDITOR: and anyone else who willfully or wantonly caused harm].
Cicero: Every evil in the bud is easily crushed; as it grows older, it becomes stronger.
Cicero: But it is the first function of the law to see that no one shall injure another unless provoked by some wrong.
Charles Waddell Chestnutt: Those who set in motion the forces of evil cannot always control them afterwards.
Charles Caleb Colton: Villainy that is vigilant will be an overmatch for virtue, if she slumber at her post.
Joseph Conrad: A transgression, a crime, entering a man's existence, eats it up like a malignant growth, consumes it like a fever.
The Dalai Lama: We live very close together. So, our prime purpose in this life is to help others. If you can't help them, at least don't hurt them.
Clarence Darrow: As long as the world shall last there will be wrongs, and if no man objected and no man rebelled, those wrongs would last forever .
Clarence Darrow (1902): In England there was a time when one hundred different offenses were punishable with death, and it made no difference. The English people strangely found out that so fast as they repealed the severe penalties and so fast as they did away with punishing men by death, crime decreased

instead of increased; that the smaller the penalty the fewer the crimes. Hanging men in our country jails does not prevent murder. It makes murderers.

John W. De Forrest: It is not the great temptations that ruin us; it is the little ones.

Daniel Deligman: Organized crime inevitably gravitates to cash.

W. E. B. Du Bois: The chief problem in any community cursed with crime is not the punishment of the criminals, but the preventing of the young from being trained to crime.

Jonathan Edwards: Some men spend their whole lives, from their infancy to their dying day, in going down the broad way to destruction.

Ralph Waldo Emerson: That which we call sin in others is experiment for us.

Ralph Waldo Emerson: You cannot do wrong without suffering wrong.

English Proverb: Set a thief to catch a thief.

Benjamin Franklin: Sin is not hurtful because it is forbidden, but it is forbidden because it is hurtful.

French Proverb: Whoever profits by the crime is guilty of it.

Joseph Gauld: The rod is only wrong in the wrong hands.

Henry George: For every social wrong there must be a remedy. But the remedy can be nothing less than the abolition of the wrong.

Oliver Goldsmith: Don't let us make imaginary evils, when you know we have so many real ones to encounter.

Oliver Goldsmith: Villainy, when detected, never gives up, but boldly adds impudence to imposture.

Thomas Hardy: The resolution to avoid an evil is seldom framed till the evil is so far advanced as to make avoidance impossible.

Thomas Whole: Evil is wrought by want of Thought / As well as want of Heart.

Horace: What does it avail you from many thorns to pluck out one?

Horace: All evils are equal when they are extreme.

Nathaniel Hawthorne: Not to be deficient in this particular, the author has provided himself with a moral—the truth, namely, that the wrongdoing of one generation lives into the successive ones.

William Hazlitt: We are not satisfied to be right, unless we can prove others to be wrong.

Lillian Hellman: Fashions in sin change.

Philip Henry: Sins are like circles in the water when a stone is thrown into it; one produces another.—When anger was in Cain's heart, murder was not far off.

William Ernest Hocking: Only the man who has enough good in him to feel the justice of a penalty can be punished; the others can only be hurt.

J.G. Holland: Wrong rules the land and waiting Justice sleeps.

Oliver Wendell Holmes, Jr.: Sin has many tools, but a lie is the handle which fits them all.

Oliver Wendell Holmes, Jr.: We have to choose, and for my part I think it a lesser evil that some criminals should escape than that the Government should play an ignoble part.

Oliver Wendell Holmes, Jr. [EDITOR: in his most notorious statement about contract law]: The duty to keep a contract at common law means a prediction that you must pay damages if you do not keep it,-and nothing else." [EDITOR: This has been interpreted to mean that a contracting party has a lawful option to perform or not. Holmes, however, was speaking of remedial limitations and did not espouse the belief that a contracting party had a right to breach. In other writings he equated a contractual breach with the commission of a tort and he labeled contract breaches as "wrongs." The misreading of Holmes has given comfort to theorists who espouse the notion of "efficient breach." Whatever the merits the theory of efficient breach may have as an economic model, it has none as a legal postulate. Moreover, theorists who espouse the efficient breach theory, have difficulty in explaining why the law regards interference with a contract as a tort. Holmes, was one of the prime architects of the modern law of **tortious interference**].

W.A. Howe: A whipping never hurts so mucjh as the thought that you are being whipped.

Elbert Hubbard: Every life is its own excuse for being, and to deny or refute the untrue things that are said of you is an error in judgment. All wrong recalls upon the doer, and the man who makes wrong statements about others is himself to be pitied, not the man he vilifies. It is better to be lied about them to lie. At the last no one can harm us but ourselves.

Elbert Hubbard: The only sure-enough sinner is the man who congratulates himself that he is without sin.

R. G. Ingersoll: Right and wrong exist in the nature of things. Things are not right because they are commanded, nor wrong because they are prohibited.
Bruce Jackson: America has the longest prison sentences in the West, yet the only condition long sentences demonstrably cure is heterosexuality.
Thomas Jefferson: Ignorance is preferable to error; and he is less remote from the truth who believes nothing, then he who believes what is wrong.
Rufus Jones: He who sins against men may fear discovery, but he who sins against God, is sure of it.
Junius: It is not that you do wrong by design, but that you never do right by mistake.
Florynce R. Kennedy: The biggest sin is sitting on your ass.
Peter Kirk: I hate this "crime doesn't pay" stuff. Crime in the United States is perhaps one of the biggest businesses in the world today.
Henry Kissinger: The illegal we do immediately. The unconstitutional takes a little longer.
La Fountaine: We believe no evil till the evil's done.
Walter Savage Landor: Wrong is but falsehood put in practice.
Robert Leighton: Sin is first pleasing, then it grows easy, then delightful, then frequent, then habitual, then confirmed; then the man is impenitent, then he is obstinate, then he is resolved never to repent, and then he is ruined.
Livy: The best-known evil is the most tolerable.
James Russell Lowell: Wrong ever builds on quicksands, but the Right / To the firm center lays its moveless base.
Martin Luther: The recognition of sin is the beginning of salvation.
Henry Miller: The study of crime begins with the knowledge of oneself.
Richard Miller: Some people try to use "Ecclesiastical Whiteout" – no one goes to church on prom night, only when they get caught making a big mistake or arrested for a crime, then all of a sudden they "find Jesus."
Jessica Mitford: When is conduct a crime, and when is a crime not a crime? When Somebody Up There – a monarch, a dictator, a Pope, a legislator – so decrees.
Montaigne: The oldest and best-known evil was ever more supportable than one that was new and untried.
Sir Thomas More: If evils come not, then our fears are vain; and if they do, fear but augments the pain.
Carry Nation (imprisoned 1901): You have put me in here a cub, but I will come out roaring like a lion, and I will make all hell howl!
Order of the Garter motto (originated by English King Edward III, 1349): Evil to him who thinks evil.
Pascal: Evil is easy and has infinite forms.
William Penn: If thou wouldst conquer thy weakness thou must never gratify it.—No man is compelled to evil; only his consent makes it his.—It is no sin to be tempted; it is to yield and be overcome.
Phaedrus: Submit to the present evil, lest a greater one befall you.
Plato: If I were sure God would pardon me, and men would not know my sin, yet I should be ashamed to sin, because of its essential baseness.
Alexander Pope: A man should never be ashamed to own he has been in the wrong, which is but saying in other words that he is wiser to-day than he was yesterday.
Plautus: Keep what you have got; the known evil is best.
Publilius Syrus: By bearing old wrongs you provoke new ones.
Publilius Syrus: He who is bent on doing evil can never want occasion.
Publilius Syrus: When evil is advantageous, he errs who does rightly.
Publilius Syrus: It is good to see in another's evil the things that we should flee from.
Publius Syrus: The remedy for wrongs is to forget them.
John Ray: Of evil grain no good seed can come.
Robert Rice: Crime is a logical extension of the sort of behavior that is often considered perfectly respectable in legitimate business.
Will Rogers: We don't seem to be able to check crime, so why not legalize it and then tax it out of business?
Will Rogers: It's one of the most progressive cities in the world. Shooting is only a sideline.
Theodore Roosevelt: No man is justified in doing evil on the ground of expediency.

Theodore Roosevelt: To submit tamely and meekly to theft or any other injury is to invite almost certain repetition of the offense.

Joseph Roux: Evil often triumphs, but never conquers.

George Santayana: For excess of evil, evil dies.

Schiller: The curse of an evil deed is that it must always continue to engender evil.

Carl Schurz (US Senator 1872): Our country, right or wrong. When right, to be kept right; when wrong, to be put right.

Seneca: No evil is great which is the last evil of all.

Seneca: There is no evil that does not offer inducement. Avarice promises money; luxury, a varied assortment of pleasures; ambition, a purple robe and applause. Vices tempt you by the rewards which they offer.

Seneca: No time is too brief for the wicked to accomplish evil

Seneca: Desperate evils generally make men column.

William Shakespeare (*Hamlet*, Act I, ii): Foul deeds will rise, / Though all the earth o'erwhelm them, to men's eyes.

William Shakespeare (*II Henry IV*, Act IV, v): Commit / The oldest sins the newest kind of ways?

William Shakespeare (*Henry V,* Act II, ii): If little faults, proceeding on distemper, / Shall not be wink'd at, how shall we stretch our eye / When capital crimes, chew'd, swallow'd, and digested, / Appear before us?

William Shakespeare (*I Henry VI,* Act IV, i): He hath done me wrong.

William Shakespeare (*Julius Caesar,* Act III, ii): The evil that men do lives after them; / The good is oft interred with their bones.

William Shakespeare (*King John,* Act III, scene iv): Evils that take leave, / On their departure most of all show evil.

William Shakespeare (*King John,* Act IV, iii): Beyond the infinite and boundless reach / Of mercy, if thou didst this deed of death, / Art thou damn'd, Hubert.

William Shakespeare (*King Lear,* Act III, ii): Tremble, thou wretch, / That hast within thee undivulged crimes, / Unwhipp'd of justice.

William Shakespeare (*Macbeth,* Act III, ii): There shall be done a deed of dreadful note.

William Shakespeare (*Macbeth,* Act III, iv): The times have been / That, when the brains were out, the man would die, / And there an end; but now they rise again, / With twenty mortal murders on their crowns, / And push us from our stools.

William Shakespeare (*Macbeth,* Act V, i): Unnatural deeds / Do breed unnatural troubles: Infected minds / To their deaf pillows will discharge their secrets.

William Shakespeare (*Measure for Measure,* Act III, i): O, dishonest wretch! / Wilt thou be made a man out of my vice?

William Shakespeare (*The Merchant of Venice,* Act III, i): The villainy you teach me, I will execute; / and it shall go hard but I will better the instruction.

William Shakespeare (*The Merchant of Venice,* Act III, ii): There is no vice so simple, but assumes / Some mark of virtue on his outward parts.

William Shakespeare (*The Merchant of Venice,* Act IV, i): To do a great right, do a little wrong.

William Shakespeare (*Othello,* Act V, ii): If you bethink yourself of any crime / Unreconcil'd as yet to heaven and grace, / Solicit for it straight.

William Shakespeare (*Pericles,* Act I, i): Few love to hear the sins they love to act.

William Shakespeare (*Pericles,* Act I, i): Vice repeated is like the wand'ring wind, / Blows dust in others' eyes, to spread itself.

William Shakespeare (*Richard II,* Act V, v): O, would the deed were good! / For now the devil, that told me – I did well. / Says, that this deed is chronicled in hell

William Shakespeare (*Richard III,* Act I, iii): The world is grown so bad / That wrens make prey where eagles dare not perch.

William Shakespeare (*Titus Andronicus,* Act V, i): For I must talk of murders, rapes, and massacres, / Acts of black night, abominable deeds.

William Shakespeare (*Titus Andronicus*, Act V, iii): Wrongs, unspeakable, past patience, / Or more than any living man could bear.

William Shakespeare (*Troilus and Cressida*, Act III, ii): Words pay no debts.

Shelley: All spirits are enslaved which serve things evil.

Robert South: Most sins begin at the eyes; by them commonly, Satan creeps into the heart: that man can never be in safety that hath not covenanted with his eyes.

Robert South: The wages that sin bargains for with the sinner, are life, pleasure, and profit; but the wages it pays him, are death, torment, and destruction. To understand the falsehood and deceit of sin, we must compare its promises and payments together.

Robert South: There is a vast difference between sins of infirmity and those of presumption, as vast as between inadvertency and deliberation.

Southey: Man creates the evil he endures.

Gloria Steinem: Evil is obvious only in retrospect.

Henry L. Stimson: The only deadly sin I know is cynicism.

George Sutherland (American judge): A nuisance may be merely a right thing in the wrong place, like a pig in the parlor instead of the barnyard.

Jonathan Swift: A man should never be ashamed to own he has been in the wrong, which is but saying, in other words, that he is wiser today than he was yesterday.

Thomas Talmage: Sin may open bright as the morning, but it will end dark as night.

Thomas Talmage: No man fully becomes fully evil at once; but suggestion bringeth on indulgence; indulgence, delight; delight, consent; consent, endeavor; endeavor, practice; practice, custom; custom, excuse; excuse, defense; defense, obstinacy; obstinacy, boasting; boasting, a seared conscience and a repprobate mind.

Henry David Thoreau: We cannot well do without our sins; they are the highway of our virtue.

Torriano: To who thinks evil, evil befalls him.

Henry David Thoreau: It is not a man's duty, as a matter of course, to devote himself to the eradication of any, even the most enormous wrong; he may still properly have other concerns to engage him; but it is his duty, at least, to wash his hands of it, and, if he gives it no thought longer, not to give it practically his support.

Richard Chenevix Trench: Evil, like a rolling stone upon a mountaintop, / A child may first impel, a giant cannot stop.

Mark Twain: I would throw out the old maxim, "My country, right or wrong," and instead I would say, "My country when she is right."

Mark Twain (deleted dedication of Mark Twain's book "Roughing It"): To the Late Cain, This Book is Dedicated, Not on account of respect for his memory, for it merits little respect; not on account of sympathy with him, for his bloody deed placed him without the pale of sympathy, strictly speaking; but out of a mere human commiseration for him in that it was his misfortune to live in a dark age that knew not the beneficent Insanity Plea.

Mark Twain: I asked Tom if countries always apologized when they had done wrong, and he says: "Yes; the little ones does."

Mark Twain: Talking of patriotism what humbug it is; it is a word which always commemorates a robbery. There isn't a foot of land in the world which doesn't represent the ousting and re-ousting of a long line of successive "owners," who each in turn, as "patriots," with proud swelling hearts defended it against the next gang of "robbers" who came to steal it and *did*—and became swelling-hearted patriots in *their* turn.

Rocco Vesper (bail bondsman): Thomas, there are 3 kinds of criminals or "bad guys" – 1st is "the Professionals." They keep their promises and pay their bills, and if they say you're dead, you are dead; 2nd is the "Screw Up" or "Sad Sack of Sh-t." They don't try or plan to hurt anybody, but they just screw up – like the gambler and the drunk driver or alchoholic; 3rd are "The Sickies." Stay far away from them, because they are mentally sick; they like to hurt people – like the serial killers, arsonists and rapists.

Tom Vesper: The 3 Acts of the Penitent (and perhaps modern-day tortfeasors?) (according to 1616 Council of Trent):

1. Contrition
2. Confession = Public Abduration
3. Satisfaction = prayer, fasting and Alms giving

Jo Wallach: Our system nurtures criminals with the same care the Air Force Academy uses to turn out second lieutenants.

Richard Wright: Men copied the realities of their hearts when they built prisons.

WRONGFUL DEATH (See DEATH)

YOUTH (See CHILDREN)

SELECTED BIBLIOGRAPHY & "CONCORDANCE"

Bob Abel & Michael Valenti, *Sports Quotes: The Insiders' View of the Sports World*, Facts On File Publications (1983)

Franklin Pierce Adams, *FPA's Book of Quotations*, Funk and Wagnalls, (1952)

Scott Adams, *Dogbert's Top secret Management Handbook, as told to Scott Adams author of "The Dilbert Principle."* Harper Business (1957)

Robert Andrews, *Famous Lines: A Columbia Dictionary of Familiar Quotations,* (1997)

William Andrews, *The Lawyer in History, Literature, and Humour,* Wm Andrews & Company (1896)

W. H. Auden and Louis Kronenberger, *The Viking Book of Aphorisms: A Personal Selection*, Viking Press (1966)

Hanan J. Ayalti, *Yiddish Proverbs*, Schocken Books Inc. (1949)

Joseph L. Baron, *A Treasury of Jewish Quotations*, A.S. Barnes and Company (1965)

John Bartlett, *A Complete Concordance or Verbal Index to Words, Phrases and Passages in the Dramatic Works of Shakespeare*, MacMillan Press (1972)

John Bartlett & Justin Kaplan, *Bartlett's Famous Quotations*, 6th Edition Little, Brown and Company (1882, 1992)

John Bartlett, Familiar Quotations: *A Collection of Passages, Phrases and Proverbs Traced to Their Sources in Ancient and Modern Literature*, Little, Brown & Co. (1948); 13th ed. (1955)

W. Gurney Benham, *Putnam's Complete Book of Quotations, Proverbs and Household Words*, G.P. Putnam's Sons (1927)

Noah benShea: *The Word: Jewish Wisdom Through Time* (1995)

Howard M. Berlin: *Charlie Chan's Words of Wisdom,* (2005)

Yogi Berra and Dave Kaplan, *What Time Is It? You Mean Now?,* Simon & Schuster (2002)

Ambrose Bierce, *The Devil's Dictionary*, Dover Publications (1993)

Arthur Bloch, *Murphy's Law and Other Reasons Why Things Go Wrong*, Price/Stern/Sloan Publishers, Inc. (1980)

John P. Bradley, Leo F. Daniels, Thomas C. Jones, *The International Dictionary of Thoughts*, J.G. Ferguson Publishing Company (1969)

Ed Brodow, *Negotiation Boot Camp: How To Resolve Conflict, Satisfy Customers and Make Better Deals,*

Herbert Broom, *A Selection of Legal Maxims*, T. & J.W. Johnson & Co. (1868)

Marshall Brown, *Wit & Humor of Bench and Bar*, T.M. Flood & Co. (1899)

Eugene E. Brussell, *Dictionary of Quotable Definitions*, Prentice Hall (1970)

Bureau of Business Practice, *Executive's Handbook of Humor for Speakers*, Bureau of Business Practice, Inc. (1971)

Robert Byrne, *The 2,548 Best Things Anybody Ever Said*, Simon & Schuster (1982)

Gorton Carruth and Eugene Ehrlich, *The Harper Book of American Quotations*, Harper & Row, Publishers (1988)

Ch'u Chai and Winberg Chai, ed. & trans., *The Sacred Books of Confucius*, University Books Inc. (1960)

J.M. Cohen and M.J. Cohen, *The Penguin Dictionary of Quotations,* Allen Lane/Viking Press (1977)

Robert and Mary Collision, *The Dictionary of Foreign Quotations*, Facts on File (1980)

Paul C. Cook, *A Treasury of Legal Quotations Selected by Paul C. Cook*, Vantage Press (1961)

Robert F. Cushman, *Leading Constitutional Decisions*, Prentice-Hall (1977)

Greg Cusimano & Roxanne Conlin, eds, *ATLA's Litigating Tort Cases*, West Group (2002)

Paul Dickson, *Baseball's Greatest Quotations*, Harper Collins Pub.(1991)

Stephen Donadio, Joan Smith, Susan Mesner, & Rebecca Davison, *The New York Public Library Book of 20th Century American Quotations*, The Stonesong Press, Inc. (1992)

Henry O. Dormann, *The Speaker's Book of Quotations*, Ballantine Books (1987)

Mike Edelhart and James Tinen, *America the Quotable*, New York: Facts on File (1983)

Erasmus, *Adagia(1539 translation by Richard Traverner)*

Bergen Evans, *Dictionary of Quotations*, Delacorte Press (1969)

Clifton Fadiman and Charles Van Doren, *The American Treasury, 1455-1955*, Harper and Brothers (1955)

Rosalind Fergusson, *The Facts On File Dictionary of Proverbs*, Facts on File (1983)

J. Kendall Few, *In Defense of Trial By Jury,* American Jury Trial Foundation (1993)

John Florio, *First Fruites (1578)* and *Second Fruites (1591)*

Monroe Freedman, *Understanding Lawyers' Ethics*, Matthew Bender (1990)

Edmund Fuller, *2500 Anecdotes For All Seasons,* Avenel Books, (1978)

Thomas Fuller, *Gnomologia*, (1732)

Eugene Gerhart, *Quote It? Memorable Legal Quotations*, Sage Hill Publishers (1969)

Michael J. Gelb, *How to Think Like Leonardo da Vinci: Seven Steps to Genius Every Day*, Bantam Dell, a Division of Random House (1998)

Jay Grenig & William Gleisner III, *eDiscovery & Digital Evidence,* West Group (2005)

Caroline Thomas Harnsberger, *Treasury of Presidential Quotations*, Follet Publishing Co. (1964)

Robert Debs Heinl, Jr., *Dictionary of Military and Naval Quotations* U.S. Naval Institute, Annapolis, MD (1966)

George Herbert, *Jacula Prudentum* (1640)

John Heywood, *Proverbs*

James Howell, *Proverbs* (1659)

Michael Jackman, *The Macmillan Book of Business & Economic Quotations*, (1984)

Marjorie Katz and Jean Arbeiter, *Pegs to Hang Ideas On*, M. Evans and Co. (1973)

Brian Kilmeade, *It's How You Play the Game: The Powerful Sports Moments That Taught Lasting Values to America's Finest*, Harper Collins Publishers (2007)

Howard J. Langer, *American Indian Quotations*, (1996)

Mark L. Levine & Eugene Rachlis, *The Complete Book of Bible Quotations*, Pocket Books, a division of Simon & Schuster (1986)

E. C. McKenzie, *14,000 Quips & Quotes For Writers & Speakers*, Greenwich House, 1984

M. Francis McNamara, *Ragbag of Legal Quotations Compiled by Francis McNamara*, Matthew Bender & Co. (1960)

M. Francis McNamara, *2,000 Famous Legal Quotations*, Matthew Bender & Co. (1960)

Leon Mead and F. Newell Gilbert, *Manual of Forensic Quotations*, J.F. Taylor & Co. (1903), reprinted by Gale Research Company (1968)

H. L. Mencken, ed., *A New Dictionary of Quotations on Historical Principles from Ancient and Modern Sources*, Alfred A. Knopf (1946)

Risa Mickenberg, *Taxi Driver Wisdom*, Chronicle Books (1996)

Wolfgang Mieder, Ed. In Chief, *A Dictionary of American Proverbs*, Oxford Univ. Press (1992)

F.C. Moncreiff, *Wit and Wisdom of the Bench and Bar*, Cassel, Peter, Golpin and Co. (1882)

Michael A. Musmanno, *That's My Opinion*, Michie Co. (1966)

Bruce Nash, Allan Zullo & Kathryn Zullo, *Lawyer's Wit and Wisdom*, Nash & Zullo Productions, Inc. (1995)

James William Norton-Kyshe, *The Dictionary of Legal Quotations*, Sweet and Maxwell (1904)

Oxford University Press, *The Concise Oxford Dictionary of Quotations, 2nd Ed.* (1981)

Elaine Partnow, ed., *The Quotable Woman, 1800-1975*, (1977)

Jim M. Perdue, *I Remember Atticus: Inspiring Stories Every Trial Lawyer Should Know*, State Bar of Texas (2004)

Jim M. Perdue, *Who Will Speak For The Victim? A practical Treatise on Plaintiff's Jury Argument*, State Bar of Texas (2002)

Peter Perlman, *Opening Statements*, ATLA Press/West Group (1994)

Leslie Pockell, *The 100 Best Poems of All Time*, Warner Books, Inc. (2001)

Bob Phillips, *Phillips' Book of Great Thoughts and Funny Sayings*, Tyndale House Publishers, Inc. (1993)

Suzy Platt, ed., *Respectfully Quoted, A Dictionary of Quotations from the Library of Congress, Congressional Quarterly, Inc.*, (1992)

John Ray, *English Proverbs* (1670)

Reader's Digest Press editors, *Reader's Digest Treasury of Modern Quotations*, Thomas Y. Crowell Co. (1975)

John Romano, *The Deposition Field Manual*, PESI Law Publications (2002)

Andy Rooney, *A Few Minutes With Andy Rooney*, Warner Books (1981)

Leo Rosten, *The Joys of Yiddish,* McGraw-Hill Co. (1970)

Leo Rosten, *Leo Rosten's Treasury of Jewish Quotations*, McGraw-Hill Co. (1972)

Louis Safian, *The Giant Book of Insults*, Citadel Press (1988)

Louis Safian, *2000 Insults For All Occasions,* Citadel Press (1965)

Louis Safian, *2000 More Insults*, Citadel Press (1967)

Jason A. Santamaria, Vincent Martino, and Eric K. Clemons, Ph.D., *The Marine Corps Way: Using Maneuver Warfare To Lead a Winning Organization*, McGraw-Hill (2004)

David Shrager and Elizabeth Frost, *The Quotable Lawyer*, New England Publishing Associates, Inc. (1986)

James B. Simpson, *Contemporary Quotations*, (1964)

A.F. Sisson, *Sissson's Word and Expression Locater*, Parker Publishing Co. (1981)

Stuart M. Speiser, *Lawyers and The American Dream*, M. Evans and Company (1993)

Gerry Spence, *With Justice For None*, Penguin Group (1989)

Leonard and Thelma Spinrad, Speaker's Lifetime Library, Parker Publishing Co. (1979)

Burton Stevenson, *The Home Book of Quotations, Classical and Modern,* Dodd, Mead & Co. (1935)

Burton Stevenson, *Home Book of Proverbs, Maxims & Familiar Phrases*, Macmillan Co. (1948)

Burton Stevenson, *The Macmillan Book of Proverbs, Maxims, and Famous Phrases*, (1965)

Dennis R. Siplee & Diana S. Donaldson, *The Deposition Handbook, 3rd Ed.*, Aspen Law & Business (1999)

Publius Syrus, *Sententiae* (Latin Proverbs)

Alfred Swaine Taylor, *A MANUAL OF MEDICAL JURISPRUDENCE* 10th Edition (1880)

Charles Taylor, *Sayings of the Jewish Fathers, Comprising Pirque Aboth in Hebrew and English*, KTAV, New York (1969)

Rhonda Thomas Tripp, *The International Thesaurus of Quotations,* Thomas Y Crowell, Publishers (1970)

George Seldes, ed., *The Great Quotations*, Citadel Press (1983)

James B. Simpson, *Contemporary Quotations: A Treasury of Notable Quotes Since 1950*, Thomas Y. Crowell (1964)

John Simpson, *The Concise Oxford Dictionary of Proverbs, 2nd Ed.*, Oxford Univ. Press (1992)

William S. Walsh, *International Encyclopedia of Prose and Poetical Quotations*, Holt, Rinehart and Winston (1951)

John Ware, *The Sayings of Confucius*, Mentor Books (1955)

Bartlett Jere Whiting and Helen Wescott Whiting, *Proverbs, Sentences, and Proverbial Phrases: From English Writings Mainly Before 1500*, Belknap Press, Harvard University Press (1968)

P.W. Wilson, *The Oxford Dictionary of English Proverbs, 3rd Ed.,* Oxford Univ. Press (1970)

Jess Winfield, *What Would Shakespeare Do?*, Ulysses Press(2000)

TABLE OF CONTENTS OF TOPICS

INDEX

[Finding Aid: This integrated Index consists of (1) all major topics, with the start page for each, and (2) all sources, with a list of topics in which they are quoted, without page numbers. To find, e.g., a Winston Churchill quote, go to Churchill, Winston in the Index, find an appropriate topic heading, and then go to the first page of the topic heading, using either headers on the odd-number pages in the text, or the topic heading in this Index; all sources within each topic are listed alphabetically by their last name or by the single name by which they are known—e.g., Aristotle.]

Advice
Age/Aging
Aggressive/Aggressiveness/Aggressor
Allegations
Ancestry
Appeal
Appearance(s)
Argument
Attitude
Bias
Books
Causation
Character
Charley Chan words of wisdom & proverbs
Cheap/Cheapness
Children
Choice
Cigars/Smoking (tobacco)
Civil rights
Comedy
Common sense
Compassion
Compromise
Computers
Consistency/Mistakes
Corporate thinking
Country-western expressions
Courage
Critics/Criticism
Damages
Death
Discovery
Divorce
Doctors/Medicine/Health
Economic loss
Emotional distress
Error
Ethics
Evidence
Evil/Crime/Sin
Excuses
Experience
Experts
Facts
Failure
Fees
Folly/Fool(s)
Foreseeable/Foreseeability
Fraud
Friendship/Friend
Games
Golf
Government/Politics
Grief & sorrow
Health
Honesty
Ignorance/Incompetence
Insults . . . with class
Insurance
Issues/Problems
Judges
Judgment
Jury
Justice
Knowledge/Reality
Law
Lawyers
Lies/Liars/Lying
Life
Litigation
Majority
Marriage
Maxims
Memory
Men
Military
Money
Motive/Inspiration
Neglect/Negligence
Negotiations
Nevada
New Jersey
New York
Norm/Normal
Opinions
Oratory/Succinctness/Speech
Pain
Parent
Police
Politics/Politicians
Precedent
Preparation
Principle/Hypocracy
Profanity
Reason/Logic
Risk
Science & technology
Sex
Statistics/Averages
Success
Teaching
Thinking/Thought
Tort reform
Trial
Trouble
Truth/Understanding
Uncle Ant'ny selected bibliography & "concordance"
Witness(es)
Woman/Women
Words
Work

U.S. NAV

C-LEVEL BUSINESS INTELLIGENCE · C-LEVEL BUSINESS INTELLIGENCE ·
ASPATORE
BOOKS